Sidney Davidson, Ph.D., CPA
Arthur Young Professor of Accounting
The University of Chicago

James S. Schindler, Ph.D., CPA
Professor of Accounting
State University of New York at Buffalo

Roman L. Weil, Ph.D., CPA, CMA
Mills B. Lane Professor of Industrial Management
Georgia Institute of Technology

FUNDAMENTALS OF ACCOUNTING

fifth edition

The Dryden Press
Hinsdale, Illinois

For Cherie
Freda
Jo

Copyright © 1942, 1947, 1953, 1959 by Holt, Rinehart and Winston, Inc.
Copyright © 1975 by The Dryden Press,
A Division of Holt, Rinehart and Winston, Inc.
All rights reserved
Library of Congress Catalog Card Number: 74–80399
ISBN: 0–03–082803–X
Printed in the United States of America
012 008 987654

Preface

This textbook is designed for use in the first course in accounting. It is relatively thorough in its exploration of the logic or theory that underlies accounting, and it is not intended for use where the major emphasis is upon procedural aspects of accounting. The major emphasis in this book is placed on developing the ability to analyze and report economic events as they relate to a business enterprise. An attempt has been made to present the problems of accounting in their modern setting as to record-keeping forms and procedures, terminology, and recent developments in professional standards, practices, and principles. One of the goals of this book is to free class time for additional discussion of concepts, theory, and controversy. We attempt to help the instructor achieve this goal by including in the text a reasonably full listing of account titles and descriptions as well as abundant journal entries.

As the careful reader will note from the frequent citations of generally accepted accounting principles promulgated within the past ten years, accounting is a dynamic discipline. By no means are all problems solved. Accounting presents many challenging opportunities, and we hope that the challenged student will consider making a career of accounting.

Since many of the readers of this book will choose careers other than accounting, stress is placed on the compilation and uses of accounting data by those who receive them in the form of reports. Chapter 7, perhaps the most important one in the book, presents the logic underlying net income determination. Emphasis upon accounting as a control device and a major tool of management is reflected in Chapter 8 on internal control, Chapter 19 on the statement of changes in financial position, Chapter 23 on the managerial uses of cost data, and Chapter 24 on capital budgeting decisions.

iii

The organization of material in this fifth edition is similar to that of the first four editions. Production situations are used frequently in the demonstrations and problems throughout the text. The principal changes in organization are reduced emphasis on record keeping and the addition of new chapters on:

1. compound interest and annuities (Chapter 13, placed just before the first chapter that uses compound interest calculations)
2. business combinations (Chapter 18, which eliminates material from the previous editions on branch accounting but includes a description of the cost and equity methods as well as pooling-of-interests accounting)
3. standard cost accounting (Chapter 22)
4. capital budgeting (Chapter 24).

Further, an extensive glossary is included in the back of the text. Not only are terms used in the book included, but also terms the student is likely to encounter in his or her other reading or class lectures.

Cost accounting and cost analysis are again given considerable attention. Chapters 20 through 24 (Part Four) constitute a comprehensive, but elementary, treatment of modern cost accounting, including the essential features of standard costs. These five chapters can be omitted in courses devoted to financial accounting. If so, the material in Chapter 23 on direct and absorption costing can be assigned at the time that either Chapter 7 on income determination or Chapter 12 on inventories is assigned.

There is little isolation of partnership and corporation accounting problems. The sole proprietorship, the partnership, and the corporation are used throughout the book. The impact of income taxes and tax regulations on accounting practices, such as for inventories, depreciation, and deferred taxes, is discussed at appropriate places.

Certain material that some instructors may think inappropriate for a first accounting course has been placed in appendices at the ends of chapters. Although the questions and problems cover the material included in the appendices, any appendix can be skipped without loss of continuity. The subjects of the appendices include:

1. a comprehensive example of detailed record-keeping procedures (Chapter 6)
2. work sheet preparation (Chapter 11)
3. lower-of-cost-or-market and dollar-value-LIFO inventory methods (Chapter 12)
4. compound interest and group depreciation methods (Chapter 14)
5. a comprehensive illustration of the statement of changes in financial position (Chapter 19)
6. the logically correct treatment of cost allocations to mutually (or reciprocally) interacting service departments (Chapter 20)
7. a comprehensive illustration of and a convenient tabular form for standard cost analysis (Chapter 22)
8. the shortcomings of the internal rate of return for choosing among investment projects (Chapter 24)
9. a simplified, but still thorough, treatment of primary and fully diluted earnings per share (Chapter 26).

Instructors who omit compound interest depreciation may want to cover Chapter 14 (depreciation) before Chapter 13 (compound interest) so that Chapter 13 serves as a pause between the study of assets (Chapters 12 and 14) and the study of liabilities (Chapter 15). The Instructor's Manual contains other suggested alternative omissions and reorderings for various kinds of courses.

Many instructors will not be content to wait for Chapter 19 in its ordinary sequence to take up the statement of changes in financial position. We have written that chapter so that its material through the first example can be assigned along with Chapter 5 or Chapter 11. (In fact, problems 25 and 26 of Chapter 4 require the derivation of a funds-like statement.) Our own preference is to delay discussion of that statement until after we treat deferred taxes (Chapter 15) and the equity method and consolidated statements (Chapter 18). At that point, the discussion of the various addbacks and subtractions for working capital produced by operations serves as a convenient review of virtually all financial accounting topics we teach.

At the end of each chapter is a set of questions and problems. The questions are designed for in-class use to facilitate discussion. The problems, varying in length and difficulty, are designed for homework exercises. Since we could not always decide where the questions end and the problems begin, we have included them in a single section. In general, the lower-numbered items are questions and the higher-numbered items are problems. We have included selected hints, key numbers, and partial answers to many of the questions and problems in Appendix B, which appears in the back of the text. The problems, or parts thereof, for which hints and answers appear are marked in the text with an asterisk.

The Prima, Primus, Secunda, Secundus, . . . , Quintus problems in the text have a "working-backwards" format—from one financial statement to another—in common. Many of these problems are adapted from problems by George H. Sorter, and we have found them useful in cementing understanding. We have adapted several ideas in the text and problems from writings by David O. Green —so many that we thank him here for his contribution. We gratefully acknowledge the many helpful comments we have received from our other colleagues, particularly Clyde P. Stickney, instructors who have used the earlier editions, as well as those who used and reviewed this text in its various drafts, including Gardner Jones and John W. Kennelly.

Thomas Horton and Daughters, Inc. has graciously given us permission to reproduce material from our *Accounting: The Language of Business*, published by them. The General Electric Company not only produces an outstanding annual report but also has given us permission to reproduce it here in Chapter 25. We thank them.

We thank the following people for their hard work in helping us to prepare the manuscript for, and contents of, this book: Mara Arndt, Celia-Frances, Ilene Haniotis, Frank Howrylak, Linda Huegel, James Karls, Vicky Longawa, Anthony Manno, James Miles, Jane Miller, Mitchell Piatek, K. Xenophon Rybowiak, Raymonde Rousselot, Katherine Schipper, Cherie B. Weil, Richard Wild, and David Yeung. We acknowledge our debt to Jonathan A. Cunitz of Xerox Corporation whose work on an earlier draft of some material in this edition was helpful.

Donna Conte supervised the production of the book. Not only did she do what appears to us to be an excellent job, she put up with an outrageous number of interruptions from the authors.

S. D.
J. S. S.
R. L. W.

Contents

PART FIVE   FINANCIAL STATEMENTS AND THEIR ANALYSIS   777

APPENDIX A   COMPOUND INTEREST, ANNUITY, AND BOND TABLES   873

PART

THE BASIC STRUCTURE OF ACCOUNTING

Chapter 1

Introduction

The much publicized acquisition of the Hartford Insurance Company by International Telephone and Telegraph was the largest merger in the history of American business. Obviously, the merger decision required an enormous amount of financial data. Many business transactions and decisions which the public never hears about also require large amounts of financial information. In today's interdependent economic world, the need for quantitative data, and especially financial information, for sound decision making is enormous. A good accounting system is essential to sound decision making because it provides a method of recording information which can be used to communicate meaningful data to interested parties. Accounting terminology is the language in which the day-to-day activity of business is expressed.

Definition of Accounting

Definitions often have limited meaning in the early stages of study of a subject. This simple statement is probably as meaningful a definition as can be offered: accounting is an information system designed to communicate significant financial facts. However, more formal definitions can contribute somewhat to an understanding of the area which a subject does or does not encompass, and the Committee on Terminology of the American Institute of Certified Public Accountants (AICPA) has stated the following general definition:

Accounting is the art of recording, classifying and summarizing in a significant manner, and in terms of money, transactions and events which are, in part at least, of a financial character and interpreting the results thereof.[1]

A few comments on the AICPA's definition may make it more useful. The first element of the definition states that accounting is concerned with the recording of transactions and events. Each event having financial significance must have its impact on the enterprise analyzed and then systematically recorded. The recorded data become more useful when they have been classified according to a predetermined plan.

Whatever its potential value, information that is not used is worthless. The information that has been recorded and classified must be summarized and presented in the form of reports (or "statements" or "schedules") so that decision makers can truly use information provided by the accounting system. The most common accounting reports reflect either the financial position of a company at a particular date or the results of operations, or flows, for a particular time period. The "balance sheet" reports the financial position of an entity at a given time. The "income statement" reports on operations for a period. The "statement of funds" or, more formally, the "statement of changes in financial position" reports the flows of cash and other working capital into and out of the firm during a period.

Analysis and interpretation of the reported data bring out relationships and trends which make that data more significant to the reader. Even though the accountant does not use the reports in making operating decisions, he must have a knowledge of the inherent problems in these areas if he is to provide the decision maker with useful data in a convenient format.

The AICPA's statement that accounting is concerned with "transactions and events which are, in part at least, of a financial character" and that it deals with them "in terms of money" affirms the quantitative nature of accounting. The only events included in formal accounting records are those that can be expressed in dollar terms with a reasonable degree of precision. The accountant tries to express the vast complex of business events so that the position and operations of a business may be compared with some desirable standard, with some other business, or with the same business at some earlier date.

Scope of Accounting

One approach to indicating the nature and scope of accounting is to list some of the information that accounting systems are designed to provide.

1. What are the results of operations?
a. Did the business enterprise operate profitably during the given

---

[1] *Accounting Terminology Bulletin*, No. 1 (New York: American Institute of Certified Public Accountants, 1953), p. 9.

period of time, such as a month, quarter, or year? The principal report that the accountant prepares to present such data is called the "income statement." Other titles frequently used for this report are "statement of earnings" and "statement of operations." The income statement shows the items which resulted in the net income or loss—the revenue (sales or services rendered) and various related expenses. This report is generally considered the most important one prepared by an accountant, because it is the most useful starting point for an overall analysis of the performance and earning potential of the enterprise.

b. What is the taxable income for the year? How much of the enterprise's income must be paid in taxes to state and federal governments? The required annual filing of federal and state income tax returns has probably been the most important influence in the installation of accounting systems and the development of adequate accounting records.

c. From what sources did the enterprise obtain working capital, that is, cash and other liquid assets, during the period, and for what purposes did it use this working capital? The accountant prepares a report called a "statement of changes in financial position" to present this information.

d. What were the costs of the operation of the factory and how were they related to the various items produced? These are the most common "cost accounting" problems.

e. What has it cost to sell or distribute the various products manufactured, the goods purchased for resale, or the services furnished to customers? This is another "cost accounting" problem, an area sometimes referred to as "distribution cost accounting."

f. How profitable and efficient are the various departments or divisions of a business enterprise? How much did it cost to operate them? The manager of a department store, for example, will want to know how profitable each department has been. An oil company operating ten service stations will want to know the cost and revenue characteristics as well as the profitability of each.

2. What is the overall financial position of the business? The report which supplies data to assist in the answer to this question is commonly known as the "balance sheet." Other titles frequently used for this report are the "statement of financial position" and the "statement of financial condition." The statement shows, for a given date, the resources or "assets" which the business owns, the debts or "liabilities" owed by the business to its creditors, and the ownership interests of the proprietor or the partners or the stockholders.

3. Are the results of operations and the financial position in accord with the plans that were made by management? To be efficiently managed, a complex enterprise must plan its operations by preparing a budget and must measure compliance with the budget during the operating period to determine whether deviations from the budget indicate that corrective action is needed. Accounting records are essential both in developing a budget and in reviewing and evaluating compliance with it.

4. Are payroll records properly maintained? One of the most expensive and time-consuming operations in accounting work is the keeping of payroll records. Not only is it necessary to calculate the amount earned by each employee and determine that his or her paycheck is prepared and distributed correctly, but numerous deductions must be computed and paid to the proper recipients. These deductions include such items as federal and state payroll taxes (for example, social security requirements and unemployment insurance), federal and state income taxes withheld, retirement- or pension-fund contributions, hospital insurance payments, and savings bond purchases. Federal and state tax authorities require that the firm report the amount each employee earned, the various amounts deducted from his wages, and the net amount he was paid for each payroll period as well as for the year.

5. Is information available for other reports to local, state, and federal governmental agencies? Many reports are required by various divisions of the government for statistical information and to meet statutory regulations. These include such items as city and county property tax returns, sales tax returns, census reports, compliance with employment regulations, reporting on foreign investments, reporting on imports and exports of goods, and the annual corporate reports.

Users of Accounting Data

Accounting information may be of interest to a wide variety of groups concerned with the activities of the enterprise. In the preceding section several questions were indicated. The answer to many of these questions have such varying degrees of significance for the various users that a satisfactory answer for one group of users would be quite inadequate for another. Some of the more easily identifiable groups are as follows:

> Management at all levels
> Present or potential stockholders or owners
> Present or potential creditors, short-term and long-term
> Vendors of materials and supplies, services, and utilities
> Employees
> Labor unions
> State and local tax agencies
> State utility regulation commissions
> Federal government agencies:
> > Treasury Department: Internal Revenue Service
> > Securities and Exchange Commission
> > Department of Defense
> > Department of Commerce: Bureau of the Census.

With so many groups having such potentially divergent interests, one may wonder whether one set of reports will suffice for all. Generally, they cannot. How, then, and to what extent are these divergent needs met?

General and Special Purpose Reports

An examination of the legal and economic positions of the various users will reveal that some are in a position to demand and to obtain data when desired. For example, the Internal Revenue Service may, and does, issue instructions or regulations for preparation of income tax returns in a specified format. Other governmental agencies are also in this position. Management of the enterprise clearly is likely to need special reports designed to deal with specific needs. Other users, such as investors holding a small percentage of shares in a corporation, do not have the legal or economic power to demand special reports and must rely on general purpose reports to stockholders or so-called outsiders. To protect this latter group, members of the public accounting profession, designated by the individual states as Certified Public Accountants, attach opinions, or "certificates," to financial statements prepared by management. Such opinions serve to assure readers that the statements meet certain accounting standards.

Internal and External Accounting

For certain purposes the users of accounting data are classified as either internal or external users.

Managerial decision making and control of operations are the goals of internal users. Internal accounting reports indicate, often in detail, the operations of the individual enterprise—the planning, control, and co-ordination carried out by management. Internal reporting frequently occurs at other than regular intervals. Rather than following somewhat standardized procedures and reporting practices, the special purpose reports are tailored to the needs of the management of the individual firm at a given time.

Evaluating overall enterprise performance and financial status are the goals of those classified as external users. Reporting for external users occurs at regular intervals following standardized procedures which are applied consistently from one accounting period to another.

The management of a particular firm would be classified as an internal user of accounting information. Labor unions would probably be classified as external users, but they find internal information useful as well. The other potential users of accounting information listed above are external users.

Financial and Managerial Accounting

The study of accounting is conveniently divided into "financial" and "managerial" accounting. Financial accounting is usually confined to the general purpose reports directed to external users, those who are deemed to have their primary interest in the review and evaluation of the operations and financial status of the business as a whole. It is generally agreed that to meet the needs of the diverse users of these reports there must be a degree of uniformity in the presentation of data. Out of this need for a degree of uniformity there has grown a body of "generally accepted accounting principles." Much of this text is devoted to the discussion of the underlying assumptions, measurements, and presentations that are within the realm of generally accepted accounting principles.

Managerial accounting is for internal users. At the present, managerial accountants are seeking to determine a body of concepts and procedures which are generally applicable to the area of internal reporting. Managerial accounting is less standardized than financial accounting, and many agree that there never will be a need for such uniformity as exists in financial accounting.

The breadth of managerial accounting is indicated by a definition developed by the Committee on Management Accounting of the American Accounting Association:

> Management accounting is the application of appropriate techniques and concepts in processing the historical and projected economic data of an entity to assist management in establishing a plan for reasonable economic objectives and in the making of rational decisions with a view toward achieving these objectives. It includes the methods, and concepts necessary for effective planning, for choosing among alternative business actions, and for control through the evaluation and interpretation of performance. Its study involves consideration of ways in which accounting information may be accumulated, synthesized, analyzed, and presented in relation to specific problems, decisions, and day-to-day tasks of business management.[2]

THE ROLE OF THE CPA

The public accountant offers his professional services to the public much the same as does the doctor or the lawyer. He has a unique relationship with his client, however, in that, as a "public accountant," he acts as an impartial reviewer of the financial statements of the client and comments favorably or unfavorably on them to third parties. The public accountant has a major responsibility to the investing and lending public. This role is quite different from that of a lawyer, an advocate, whose primary responsibility is to his client regardless of the merits of the case. The public accountant is in a special position of trust, and he must, therefore, maintain a completely independent attitude with respect to his client. Because of the public interest in the public accountant's work, all the states and territories have provided a licensing system for accountants engaged in public practice. A license to practice as a Certified Public Accountant, or CPA, is obtained by passing a comprehensive three-day examination covering the major areas of accounting and related subjects. All of the states now use the examination provided by the American Institute of Certified Public Accountants. In addition, almost all states also have education and

---

[2] "Report of Committee on Management Accounting," *Accounting Review*, 34 (April 1959), 210.

accounting experience requirements that must be met before the license to practice will be issued.

An individual certified public accountant may operate a public accounting office with the help of a few employees, but ordinarily two or more accountants organize an accounting "firm" as a partnership. Some of the larger CPA partnerships have branch offices in most of the important cities of the country and several have branches or correspondents in foreign countries.

One of the most important services offered by the CPA is the auditing or examination of the financial statements—income statement, balance sheet, statement of changes in financial position, and any related statements—of the client and the preparation of a report concerning them. The public accountant tests and checks the accounting records. The thoroughness of the test is determined formally by standards established by the public accounting profession. Further, the courts have found public accountants financially liable for their opinions. As we write this, many large CPA firms are defendants in legal suits involving millions of dollars. These suits center on whether the financial reports of the clients attested to by the CPA firm in fact fairly represented the position of the client.

The CPA's report may detail the work performed and may contain explanations of special items, but it is often quite short and is usually worded in the following standard short-form style:

> We have examined the balance sheet of X Company as of December 31, 19___, and the related statements of income and retained earnings and changes in financial position for the year then ended. Our examination was made in accordance with generally accepted auditing standards, and accordingly included such tests of the accounting records and such other auditing procedures as we considered necessary in the circumstances.
>
> In our opinion, the aforementioned financial statements present fairly the financial position of X Company at December 31, 19___, and the results of its operations and changes in financial position for the year then ended, in conformity with generally accepted accounting principles applied on a basis consistent with that of the preceding year.[3]

Such a report as this would be characterized as an "unqualified," or "clean," report. If the auditor were not permitted by the client to perform some desirable or standard procedure, or if for any reason the auditor was unsatisfied as to the validity of a significant item, the auditor would have to prepare a "qualified" report or would have to "disclaim" an opinion altogether and indicate why an unqualified opinion could not be given.

Note that the auditing work performed and the opinion issued do not represent a guarantee that there are no errors in the records. Rather, as the result of a carefully planned program of examination of the records and other evidence executed by a trained independent professional ac-

---

[3] *Statement on Auditing Standards No. 1,* American Institute of Certified Public Accountants, 1973, paragraph 511.04.

countant, the reader of these statements is given reasonable assurance that the accounts and records have been maintained accurately and in accordance with generally accepted accounting principles.

Other services commonly rendered by public accountants are the design and installation of accounting systems, preparation of tax returns, and special investigations. A public accountant's broad experience makes him useful as an advisor and consultant on many financial and business matters. Public accountants increasingly perform these "management services." The public accountant's primary function is the review of the records and the statements of the client and the expression of an opinion on them, but many accounting offices also do bookkeeping work for their clients, especially in connection with the more difficult and unusual types of business transactions.

Public accountants, like other professional groups, operate under a self-imposed set of professional ethics or rules of professional conduct. These rules are intended to bring about a high degree of independence on the part of the public accountant and the performance of his work with the highest degree of care and integrity.

Although CPA's play an important role in increasing public acceptance of and confidence in published financial statements to which they attest, they make up only a small portion of those engaged in accounting work. Many more accountants work in private business or industrial accounting than in public accounting.

ACCOUNTING TERMINOLOGY

The general purpose reports, commonly referred to as Annual Reports to Stockholders, reach a large, unidentified group of readers. The members of this group vary in their understanding of business and accounting. If accounting is to fulfill its potential contribution, it should address this broad group of readers rather than a select group of specialists. Thus there is a need for a terminology based as much as is feasible upon that of the general citizenry.

Some assumption must be made concerning the level of understanding of business and the related accounting if there is to be effective communication. While such a level has not been established, we suppose that a reasonable understanding of the material in this text would more than meet the minimum requirement.

By and large, accounting terminology follows that which is in common usage. Occasionally, however, commonly used words are given restricted technical meanings. For example, the word "reserve" in common usage indicates that something is earmarked or set aside, but in accounting terminology its meaning is altogether different. The term "surplus" may mean "too much" in commonly used terminology, but this is not its meaning when used in accounting. There are current efforts to prevent the possible confusion that can arise out of these and other similar altered usages of common terminology, so the student of accounting then can rely heavily on his vocabulary, which has been developed for general communication. But he will find it necessary to learn a rather limited vocabulary of new technical terms and to become aware of technical meanings assigned to a few common words such as *allowance, cost, credit, expense,* and *revenue*. A glossary of accounting terms and other terms with special meanings in accounting appears in the back of this book. A glossary is not a dictionary, and only the specialized meanings used in accounting and in this book are given there.

Financial Reporting Policies

The Annual Report to Stockholders of almost all large companies is attested to ("certified") by an independent certified public accountant. The CPA expresses his opinion on the fairness of the statements, resulting from his examination of them. The usual opinion states that the reports are "in conformity with generally accepted accounting principles." This may appear to imply that there is a neatly codified publication of accounting principles, practices, and procedures, which would indicate the accounting for each situation that might be encountered. In fact, there is no such codification, although there have been significant attempts in recent years to narrow the area of acceptable reporting standards and conventions.

There are some broad reporting policies, sometimes termed "doctrines" underlying financial statements. Among these are the following: full disclosure; objective evidence; consistency; and conservatism.

Full disclosure implies that all significant ("material") information is to be presented in the financial reports. The test of materiality of data is based upon a judgment of whether or not knowledge of specific information might influence the decision of the informed investor.

Objective evidence implies that formal quantification will not be given in the statements prior to the time that the magnitude of the events or changes can be measured objectively. Thus numbers shown in the statements are both free from bias and subject to verification by independent competent reporters or auditors. Objectivity is linked to the concept of "realization," which will be discussed in a subsequent paragraph.

Consistency implies that procedures, once adopted, should be followed from period to period by a business entity. The policy is not an inflexible one; it allows for changes in procedure, provided that adequate disclosure reflects the nature and impact of the change. "Consistency" is essential because analysis of financial data frequently is based upon observation of trends within an entity. Present attempts to refine the doctrine of "consistency" as well as to narrow the alternatives within the realm of generally accepted accounting principles are moving in the direction of providing for a greater comparability of data both within and among firms.

Conservatism is concerned with the uncertainty of the future and calls for careful consideration in reporting financial data in the present. In accordance with this view, it is better to present a cautious measurement of income and the ownership equity in uncertain circumstances. Even where there is no uncertainty about amounts, for example, about the total expenses to be recognized over several years, conservatism implies recognizing expenses early and revenue late.

In addition to the foregoing broad policies for accounting reporting, the Study Group on Objectives of Accounting has added that information presented in financial statements "should possess the qualitative characteristics of relevance and materiality, reliability, freedom from bias, comparability, consistency, understandability, and the recognition of substance over form."[4]

These qualitative characteristics are supplemented by a few major underlying concepts and assumptions: the business entity; continuity of operations; monetary measurement; and realization.

The *business entity* concept assumes that the financial reports relate to a specific economic unit which can be identified in terms of its objectives, resources, organization, and activities. The objective assumed for the business entity is that of carrying on its activities for a profit. Often the accountable entity may be a legal entity such as a corporation, which is separate and distinct from its stockholders. In the cases of the sole proprietorship and partnership forms of organization, the business entity is treated as being separate and distinct from the personal affairs of the sole proprietor or of the partners. The business entity may be defined as a subunit such as a department, a branch store, or an individual plant. The business entity may be defined as a group of centrally controlled companies each having its separate legal entity status, for example, a parent company and its subsidiary companies treated as an economic unit reporting together in "consolidated statements." Thus, to determine the accountable unit whose organization, resources, and activities are to be observed, analyzed, and reported requires precise delineation of the business entity.

The *continuity of operations* concept assumes that unless otherwise indicated, the business entity will continue its operations long enough for present plans to be completed. This concept recognizes that large, modern enterprises require long-range planning and long-term commitments in resources and financing. There may be changes in types and levels of operations over time. The general goals are, however, expected to continue as are the present plans for the long-lived assets and the firm's intention to meet its liabilities at their maturities. Assuming continuity of operations leads to the need for continuous and periodic reporting. The artificial splitting of continuous operations into periodic intervals requires estimates. Thus the periodic reports must be recognized and accepted as being provisional.

The *monetary measurement* concept assumes that money is the most suitable and adaptable unit of measurement in which to record and report on financial operations and status. The monetary measurements are assumed to reflect economic reality and are useful only to the extent that

[4] *Objectives of Financial Statements: Report of the Study Group on the Objectives of Accounting*, AICPA, 1973, p. 66.

they do. Since money has meaning only with respect to a stated level and structure of prices, it is possible that substantial changes may occur over time thereby affecting the comparability of reports based on monetary measurements. The potential limitations of the usefulness of financial reporting based upon the assumption of a stable level of prices will be discussed in subsequent chapters.

The *realization* concept assumes that changes in the value of assets and liabilities should not be recognized until such changes have become sufficiently definite and measurable to justify inclusion in the records and reports. For most merchandising and manufacturing enterprises, the time to recognize income is considered to be the time of sale (or exchange). Awaiting realization before recognizing income reflects the accountant's conservatism and preference for objectively verifiable evidence in reporting.

The foregoing concepts of the business entity, the continuity of operations, the monetary measurement, and realization are general guides upon which accounting recording and reporting standards are based. The implementation in practice of these broad concepts has led to the development of a body of generally accepted accounting principles.

ACCOUNTING AUTHORITIES AND LITERATURE

The ultimate authority for generally accepted accounting principles has been the financial community. The principles are not codified, and they are not promulgated by a single governmental, private, or professional authority. Rather they are to be found in the literature of the field including pronouncements of interested professional organizations and security exchanges, governmental regulations, articles, and textbooks.[5] Thus the accounting profession, the users of financial statements, and the governmental agencies contribute to the continued development of generally accepted principles of accounting. Some of the leading organizations and sources of accounting literature which influence the development of accounting principles are discussed below.

The *American Institute of Certified Public Accountants* (AICPA) is the national organization of certified public accountants. Its publications and committees are influential in the development of accounting principles and practices. It actively promulgates standards of ethics and reviews conduct within the profession. Among its influential publications are the following:

> *Journal of Accountancy.* A monthly periodical containing articles, pronouncements, announcements, and practical sections of direct interest to the practicing members of the profession.
>
> *Accounting Research Bulletins* Nos. 1–51 (1939–1959). A series of statements on accounting problems that contributed greatly to the narrowing of differences and inconsistencies in accounting practice

---

[5] A useful introduction to accounting literature is Stephen A. Zeff's "A First Guide to the Accounting Literature," in S. Zeff and T. Keller (eds.), *Financial Accounting Theory I: Issues and Controversies* (New York: McGraw-Hill, 1973), pp. 2–13.

and to the development and recognition of generally accepted accounting principles.

Opinions of the Accounting Principles Board Nos. 1–31 (1962–1973). A recently concluded series of statements on accounting problems and generally accepted accounting principles. These pronouncements will remain in effect until superseded by statements of the Financial Accounting Standards Board (see below).

Accounting Research Studies. A series of monographs on accounting problems to provide a basis for further development of generally accepted accounting principles in the particular area.

Statements on Auditing Standards. No. 1 (1973) of this series is a codification of all statements on auditing standards previously issued by the AICPA. Later numbers of the series deal with specific auditing standards. These publications form the basis of compliance with the first paragraph of the auditor's report (illustrated in this chapter) with respect to the scope of the examination.

Two publications of the American Institute of Certified Public Accountants are of special interest to students and scholars:

Accountants' Index. A series published each year in which the literature pertaining to the field for the period covered is indexed in detail.

Accounting Trends and Techniques. An annual publication presenting a survey of the accounting aspects of financial reports of some six hundred industrial and commercial corporations. It presents statistical tabulations on specific practices, terminology, and disclosures together with illustrations taken from individual annual reports.

In addition to the national organization, there are state societies of certified public accountants which contribute to maintaining high levels of professional performance and to developing procedures and practices.

Since 1973, the *Financial Accounting Standards Board* has been the highest authority on generally accepted accounting principles. The FASB issues *Statements* from time to time clarifying or establishing generally accepted accounting principles. The FASB is the successor to the Accounting Principles Board, but unlike the Accounting Principles Board, is independent of the AICPA.

The *American Accounting Association* is primarily an organization for accountants in academic work, but it is open to all who are interested in accounting. It participates in the development of generally accepted accounting principles and practice, and it promotes the academic phases of accounting theory, research, and instruction. Among its influential publications are the following:

The Accounting Review. A quarterly periodical containing articles and sections covering a broad span of subjects related to accounting practice, research, and instruction for purposes of both external and internal reporting.

Accounting and Reporting Standards for Corporate Financial Statements. A comprehensive presentation of accounting principles for external reporting purposes. The principles enumerated frequently indicate the direction toward which the association feels accounting reporting should be moving rather than necessarily a reflection of currently accepted accounting principles.

A *Statement of Basic Accounting Theory.* An integrated statement for educators, practitioners, and others interested in accounting. The statement seeks to identify the field of accounting, to establish standards by which accounting information can be judged, to point out possible improvements in accounting practice, and to present a useful framework for scholars who wish to extend the uses of accounting.

The *Securities and Exchange Commission* has a considerable responsibility assigned to it with respect to financial accounting under the Securities Act of 1933, the Securities Exchange Act of 1934, and the Public Utility Holding Company Act of 1935. Among its publications are the following:

Regulation S-X. A document pertaining to the form and content of financial statements required to be filed with the SEC.

Accounting Series Releases. A series of opinions on accounting principles which together with *Regulation S-X* are the primary statements on the form and content of financial statements filed with the Commission.

The *National Association of Accountants* is a national society generally open to all engaged in activities closely associated with managerial accounting. Among its publications are the following:

Management Accounting. A monthly periodical.

Research Series. A series of monographs on subjects of internal and external accounting.

Accounting Practice Reports. A series of summaries of surveys on current practice in a limited area of accounting.

The *Financial Executives Institute* is an organization of financial executives of large businesses, such as chief accountants, controllers, treasurers, and financial vice-presidents. Among its publications are the *Financial Executive*, a monthly periodical, and a number of studies on problems confronting accounting and financial management.

Income tax legislation and administration has had a substantial impact on adequate accounting record keeping and reporting. Although the income tax requirements in themselves do not establish principles and practices for general external reporting, their influence on choice of acceptable procedures is substantial. At the federal level, in addition to the *Internal Revenue Code* passed by the Congress, there are the *regulations* and *rulings* of the Internal Revenue Service, and the opinions of the United States Tax Court.

The *International Accounting Standards Committee* was organized in the early 1970s to promote the establishment of international accounting standards.

Concluding Comment

This chapter is an introduction to the subject area of accounting: its function, definition, scope, users, terminology, and principles. Now we turn to the study of accounting. We realize that most of the readers of this book will not choose careers in this field. Accordingly, emphasis is placed on the uses of financial data as well as its compilation and preparation for reports. We describe the methods of accumulating, classifying, recording, and reporting accounting data, the alternative procedures that are available, and the various concepts and methods of validation to assist the student in understanding the uses and limitations of financial data.

QUESTIONS AND PROBLEMS

*1. What is the function of accounting?

2. Why is accounting important in business affairs?

3. What groups would be interested in the accounting records of a particular business firm?

4. Accounting records are important to anyone who has to file an income tax return. Why?

5. Accounting records are highly useful to anyone who wants to obtain a loan at a bank. Why?

6. Contrast the partnership form of business organization with the sole proprietorship.

7. What are the essential features of a corporation?

8. Why has the corporation come to be the most important form of business organization?

9. Indicate whether the following statements are true or false:
   a. Accounting concerns itself primarily with transactions and events which can be expressed in monetary terms.
   b. Stockholders delegate control over the policies and administration of the corporation to the board of directors.
   c. The income statement indicates the financial position of the company.
   d. There are few legal barriers to the creation of a partnership.
   e. Most accounting principles used in accounting for private business cannot be applied to governmental bodies.
   f. Cost accounting is especially concerned with the study of the costs of manufacturing the various units of output of a firm.

* Hints, key numbers, or (partial) answers appear in the back of the book between the Appendix Tables and the Glossary.

g. State public utility regulatory commissions usually prescribe the accounting systems to be employed by the public utilities within the state.

h. Sole proprietorships are more significant in service enterprises than in manufacturing.

i. Each partner is usually fully responsible for all of the debts of the partnership.

j. The balance sheet shows the assets the firm owns.

k. The "certificate" issued by the independent auditor guarantees that there are no errors in the financial statements.

°10. How may a person in your state become a certified public accountant?

11. What have the economist and the accountant in common? The industrial engineer and the accountant?

12. Accounting is said to be largely historical in nature; that is, it presents a record of business transactions and events that have already taken place. How can you reconcile this statement with the fact that its greatest usefulness is in helping management in its plans for improving the operating efficiency and the profits of the enterprise in the future?

13. "Accounting would have no place in a completely socialist state." Do you agree? Discuss.

14. To what various uses could the financial records of an individual be put?

°15. Conservatism is an accepted accounting policy. Who, if anyone, might be hurt by conservatism in accounting and how?

°16. The public accountant is in an unusual professional position. Public accountants are hired and paid by one group (the corporations they audit) but are at least partly responsible to another (the general public). What problem do you think such an arrangement might cause? What solutions can you devise for this problem?

°17. Mr. Bulloch sells hot dogs at football games. He buys hot dogs for 30 cents each and sells them for 50 cents each. He must either buy 10,000 hot dogs or 20,000 hot dogs. He can sell 10,000 hot dogs if it rains or 20,000 hot dogs if the weather is clear. Of course, he can sell no more than he bought. Any hot dogs left over at the end of the day are given to the local orphanage. Ignore the income tax complication caused by the charitable deduction that occurs when Mr. Bulloch gives 10,000 hot dogs to the orphanage.

a. Construct a table with four cells that shows Mr. Bulloch's profit from buying either 10,000 or 20,000 hot dogs and when the weather is either clear or rainy.

b. Suppose that it rains for half the games and is dry for half the games. What is Mr. Bulloch's best strategy—to buy 10,000 or 20,000 hot dogs— and what is his expected profit?

c. Suppose that Mr. Bulloch knew before each game whether or not it would rain. What would he do then and what would his expected profit be?

d. Compare your answers in (b) and (c) to derive Mr. Bulloch's value of perfect information about the weather.

18. The value of information is defined as the payoff to the optimal action taken in the presence of information minus the payoff to the optimal action taken in the absence of information. To show that this definition has application outside economics and accounting, consider a medical context.

Suppose that a patient visits a doctor's office with a certain set of symptoms and that the doctor decides to take out the patient's appendix. Meanwhile, the doctor orders a white-cell blood count. The doctor says he is going to operate no matter what the blood count happens to be.

a. What is the value of the information about the blood count to the doctor?

b. Does your answer to (a) make sense?

c. Why might the doctor take the test anyway?

If a mother, with Rh negative blood bears a child whose father is Rh positive, then there may be complications (the medical name is *erythroblastosis foetalis*) in subsequent pregnancies unless a shot of Rhogam is given to the mother soon after the first child is born. Assume that 87 percent of all people have Rh positive blood, that 13 percent have Rh negative blood, and that matings occur randomly among blood types. Assume that the complication occurs in 5 percent of the matings where the mother is negative and the father is positive and that the cost of the complication is $12,000.

d. In what percentage of matings can the complication arise?

e. What is the expected cost per mating from the complication if the Rhogam shot is not given to any mothers?

f. What is the cost per mating if every mother is given the shot which costs $50?

g. Comparing your answers to (e) and (f), what is the optimal action in the absence of information about blood types and what is the expected cost per mating from following that action?

h. Suppose information on blood types is known. What is the expected cost per mating if the Rhogam shot is given only in matings with Rh negative mothers and Rh positive fathers?

i. Comparing your answers in (g) and (h), what is the value of perfect information about blood types?

j. How does your answer depend upon the (arbitrary) cost of $12,000 assigned to the discomfort and possible death that may result if the complication arises?

Chapter 2

The Accounting Equation

How does a man like Howard Hughes who owns many different kinds of businesses know which of his businesses is successful and which is not? One of the conventions of modern accounting helps him. Each business, according to accounting convention, is a separate entity and must have its own accounting system. Besides providing information about the performance of individual businesses, there is another practical reason for this convention. Different businesses have different needs for recording and reporting financial data. Thus, retail establishments, fast-service food franchises, and factories all have special needs that can be met best by individual accounting systems.

The owner's personal affairs, as well as his other business interests, should also be kept separate from the business. Corporations are, by law, separate entities and have their own accounting records. But this distinction holds true for proprietorships and partnerships as well. An individual might have an extremely successful business but be poor because of hospital bills or unsuccessful defense of a personal lawsuit. On the other hand, a man's business might be only moderately successful, but he may be very wealthy from personal investments. In either case, his personal financial condition should not be reflected in the accounting records of the business. The accounting entity is the focal point of accounting analysis. Every situation is considered from that point of view, and all transactions are analyzed in terms of their effect upon it; we will discuss the nature of that viewpoint and the analysis of transactions in this chapter.

EXPLANATION OF THE ACCOUNTING EQUATION

The logical basis of double-entry record keeping is a simple mathematical equation that describes the financial position of the accounting entity. There are several ways of presenting this equation.

Form of Invested Capital Equals Sources of Invested Capital

Any economic entity employs a certain amount of resources. These resources can be described in two different ways: first, they can be described according to the form in which items are purchased; they can be described in terms of the funds used to buy them. For example, if a business uses up $100,000 of its resources, an investigation will disclose the various properties or assets in which the $100,000 is invested—so much in land, buildings, machinery, unsold goods, unused supplies and materials, amounts due from customers, cash, and so on. An investor might ask where the $100,000 came from, or how it was provided. He would discover that part of the capital was supplied by the owner or the stockholders, part was furnished by the bank in the form of loans, part was furnished by employees who had worked for a time but had not yet been paid, and so on. Because a certain total of investment is merely being viewed in its two aspects, it follows that the totals of the two groups of items must be equal. Every cent of money that a business has invested in property must have been acquired from some source.

A meaningful way to describe this equality is to say: Resources = Sources. The items that make up the list of resources or the forms of invested capital are commonly referred to in accounting as *assets*. The sources of capital are the contributions or investments of creditors, described as *liabilities*, and the contributions of the owners, frequently shown under the heading of *proprietorship*. The equation is often expressed as: Assets = Liabilities + Proprietorship. An accurate expression of the equation for a corporation is: Assets = Liabilities + Stockholders' Equity.

The equation is sometimes shown as: Assets = Liabilities. The term *liabilities*, however, is not appropriate for the interest of the owner or stockholders, because there is no definite obligation to repay to them the amounts they have invested in the enterprise. This legal difference between the position of the creditors and that of the owners is a significant one, and it is a definite improvement to express the equation as Assets = Liabilities + Proprietorship.

Assets Equal Equities

The "Resources = Sources" formula is probably the most effective method of presenting the accounting equation, but it does have one deficiency. Consider, for example, a liability item like taxes payable, which arises out of a levy against the entity by a governmental authority. Ordinarily, we think of a source as being someone outside the firm providing something to the firm. In fact the governmental authority that is to receive the taxes is providing resources, because it does not insist on collecting the taxes at the instant the liability for taxes comes into being. Because the liability to pay the taxes arises from the activities of the firm, the fact that the government is the source of funds may not be immediately obvious.

To overcome this problem, a slightly different approach may be used. It starts with the proposition that any economic entity has in its possession certain assets which it owns, or in which it has a measurable interest, and that values can be assigned to each one of these assets. Against these assets there are claims or rights of others, such as note holders, wage earners for unpaid wages, the state and federal governments for unpaid taxes, and the stockholders or other owners. The term *equities* is sometimes used to describe all of these claims and rights. Because assets cannot exist without ownership claims or rights against them, it follows that the total of the asset values must be equal to the total of the claims against or equities in the assets. If there are $100,000 in assets, there must be $100,000 in equities. Therefore, Assets = Equities.

Assets Minus Liabilities Equal Proprietorship

Another method of demonstrating the inevitable arithmetic relationship involves a simple variation in the form of the equation. Again it begins with the proposition that any business owns or has an interest in certain assets and that it also owes certain amounts to its creditors. The difference between what it owns and what it owes, or between its assets and its liabilities, represents the owners' capital or proprietorship. If the assets amount to $100,000 and the liabilities to $60,000, the equation would be: Assets ($100,000) − Liabilities ($60,000) = Proprietorship ($40,000).

This form of the equation may be misinterpreted because it seems to imply that the proprietorship will always be determined to be the difference between whatever assets and liabilities are included in the lists. However, the amount of proprietorship is not determined by this residual process in double-entry record keeping. As we shall see when the record keeping process has been more fully developed, the proprietorship amount is determined just as directly and specifically as the amounts of the assets and liabilities.

Maintaining the Accounting Equation

The particular form in which the equation is expressed is unimportant. The three forms of the equation are merely different ways of stating the same relationship. The important thing to understand is that the equation, however stated, expresses a relationship upon which the techniques of double-entry record keeping are based. The principal *mechanical* task of the bookkeeper is to keep records so that the equality can periodically be demonstrated.

EQUATION TERMINOLOGY AND CONCEPTS

Nature of Assets

Intuitive notions about the nature of assets are generally satisfactory; assets are frequently equated with wealth, property, or resources. Probably the most satisfactory definition is offered in *Accounting and Reporting Standards for Corporate Financial Statements*:

> Assets are economic resources devoted to business purposes within a specific accounting entity; they are aggregates of service-potentials available for or beneficial to expected operations.[1]

Assets are "service potentials," or future benefits.

In a legal sense, assets are economic goods owned by a business or other economic unit. Complete legal ownership, however, is not necessary for an item to be included in the assets of a business. A machine may be purchased on the installment plan with the seller holding the title until the payments are completed, but the machine will still be considered an asset of the buyer. Conversely, the seller of merchandise on the installment plan does not consider the goods as his assets even though he may retain legal title until the payments are completed. Title to goods usually passes from the seller to the buyer when they have been delivered to a transportation agency such as a trucking firm, but it is common practice during an accounting period for the buyer to record goods as assets only when he has received them.

Physical possession of a resource is not necessary for a firm to recognize it as an asset. A common example of this situation is that of rented property. A contractor may rent a bulldozer from a firm that owns and rents such equipment. He may keep the bulldozer for many months, but it still appears as an asset on the records of its owner and is not shown as an asset on the records of the contractor.

Assets such as land, buildings, or merchandise have discernible physical existence, but other assets may lack physical being and exist only as legal rights or claims. Examples of intangible, or nonphysical, assets are amounts due from customers who have not yet paid their bills, government bonds, patent rights, and the right to use property when the rent has been paid for some time in advance.

Asset Titles

The asset titles in the following list are commonly used and will help in understanding the nature of assets as well as in selecting appropriate terms for problem solutions. The terms used here will be found suitable for many situations, but similar phrases are often used. Nor is the list ex-

---

[1] Committee on Concepts and Standards of the American Accounting Association, *Accounting and Reporting Standards for Corporate Financial Statements* (Columbus, Ohio: American Accounting Association, 1957), p. 3.

haustive; many business firms will have assets not included in it. Moreover, many firms will not possess all of the listed items.

Cash on Hand. Coins, currency, and items such as bank checks and money orders are included in Cash on Hand. The latter items are merely claims against individuals or institutions, but by custom they are called *Cash.*

Cash in Bank. Strictly speaking, Cash in Bank is merely a claim against the bank for the amount deposited. Cash in Bank consists of demand deposits, against which checks can be drawn, and time deposits, usually savings accounts and certificates of deposit. In published statements, the items cash on hand and cash in bank usually are combined under the title *Cash.*

Marketable Securities. Marketable Securities includes government bonds and corporate stocks and bonds. The word *marketable* implies that they can be bought and sold readily through some security exchange such as the New York Stock Exchange.

Accounts Receivable. Accounts Receivable includes amounts due from customers of a business for goods or services sold "on account." The collection of cash occurs some time after the sale. These accounts are also known as "charge accounts" or "open accounts." An alternative title is *Customers' Accounts.* The general term Accounts Receivable is used in financial statements to describe the figure representing the total amount receivable, but, of course, the firm keeps a separate record for each customer.

Notes Receivable. Amounts due from customers or from others to whom loans have been made or credit extended, when the claim has been put in writing in the form of a promissory note, are called *Notes Receivable.*

Interest Receivable. Interest on assets, such as promissory notes or bonds, which has accrued or come into existence through the passing of time is listed under *Interest Receivable.*

Merchandise. The Merchandise account includes goods on hand which have been purchased for resale, such as canned goods on the shelves of a grocery store or suits on the racks of a clothing store. It is frequently listed as *Merchandise Inventory.*

Finished Goods. Finished Goods is the name used for completed but unsold manufactured products.

Work in Process. Partially completed manufactured products are included under Work in Process.

Raw Material. Raw Material includes unused materials out of which manufactured products are made. Sometimes this account is combined with supplies under the title *Stores.*

Supplies. The Supplies account includes stationery, computer cards, pens and other office supplies; bags, twine, boxes, and other store supplies;

gasoline, oil, spare parts; and other delivery supplies. Several titles, such as *Office Supplies*, *Store Supplies*, and *Delivery Supplies* can be used for this account.

Factory Supplies. Lubricants, cleaning rags, abrasives, and other incidental materials used in manufacturing operations are listed under *Factory Supplies*.

Prepaid Insurance. The Prepaid Insurance account includes insurance premiums paid for future coverage. An alternative title is *Unexpired Insurance*.

Prepaid Rent. Rent paid for the future use of land, buildings, or equipment is included in Prepaid Rent.

Land. The Land account applies to land occupied by buildings held for other business purposes. The term "real estate" should not be used, since it includes both land and buildings.

Buildings. The Buildings account includes factory buildings, store buildings, garages, warehouses, and so forth.

Machinery and Equipment. Lathes, ovens, tools, boilers, computers, motors, bins, punches, cranes, conveyors, and so forth are included in the Machinery and Equipment account.

Furniture and Fixtures. Furniture and Fixtures includes desks, tables, chairs, counters, showcases, scales, and other such store and office equipment. Other titles such as *Office Furniture and Fixtures* and *Store Furniture and Fixtures* can be used.

Office Machines. The Office Machines account applies to typewriters, adding machines, bookkeeping machines, calculators, and so forth. It is sometimes combined with *Furniture and Fixtures*.

Automobiles. Delivery trucks, salesmen's cars, and so forth are listed in the Automobiles account.

Organization Costs. Costs incurred for legal fees, for incorporation fees, for printing the certificates for the shares of stock, and for accounting and any other costs incurred in organizing the business so it can begin to function are listed in the Organization Costs account. This asset is seen most commonly on the statements of a corporation.

Patents. A Patent is a right granted for seventeen years by the federal government for exclusive use of a certain process or device.

Goodwill. Goodwill is an amount paid that is greater than the sum of the values assignable to other assets in connection with the purchase of a business enterprise. It ordinarily reflects an estimate of higher-than-normal future earning power.

Asset Valuation

The assignment of values to asset items has been one of the most controversial issues in the field of accounting, and it is still unsettled. The prevailing accounting view, with few exceptions, is that the dollar amounts at which assets are shown should be based upon the acquisition cost at which the asset came into the business. Cash, of course, ordinarily involves no problem. Receivables, also, are relatively simple to value, usually being shown at the face amount of the obligation with adjustments for such factors as estimated uncollectible items and discounts to be taken. Inventories of merchandise, raw materials, work in process, and finished goods are shown at *acquisition cost*. There are several methods of arriving at an approximation of cost when different units of the same item have been purchased at different prices. Common, but questionable, practice shows the inventories at the lower of acquisition cost or present replacement cost (cost or market, whichever is lower). This issue is treated in Chapter 12. Land is commonly shown at its acquisition cost. Such assets as buildings and equipment are usually carried at acquisition cost less the amounts which have been deducted for "depreciation."

The cost of an asset may include more than its invoice price. Cost includes all expenditures or obligations incurred in order to put the asset into a usable condition. Transportation costs, costs of installation, handling charges, and any other necessary and reasonable costs incurred in connection with the asset up to the time it is put into service should be considered as parts of the total cost assigned to the asset. For example, the cost of an item of equipment might be calculated as follows:

Invoice price of equipment	$8,000
Less: 2% cash discount	160
Net invoice price	$7,840
Transportation cost	232
Installation costs	694
Total cost of equipment	$8,766

Nature of Liabilities

Liabilities are the debts of the accounting entity, that is, the claims of the creditors against the business for the resources they have furnished to it. Typically, they must be paid or liquidated at a definite time in the future according to the terms of the agreement with the creditors. Most liabilities result from legally enforceable contracts or voluntary agreements, while others, like taxes, are imposed by governmental authorities.

Usually there are no great problems in the valuation of liabilities, because the amounts are definitely indicated or can be computed. Sometimes, however, estimates must be used. The income tax liability, for example, is calculated on the results of twelve months' operations. If a statement is prepared at any time before the end of the twelve-month period, the income tax liability can only be estimated, because profits during the first part of the year may be offset by losses in the last part. Further, the rates to be applied often are not known until late in the year.

Most liabilities must be paid in cash, but there are exceptions. The principal one is the type of liability known as a "deferred credit," or unearned income. For instance, a customer sends an advance payment of $500 on goods he has ordered. The business has a liability recorded at $500 that will normally be discharged by the shipment of goods rather than the payment of cash.

Liability Titles

The liability titles in the following list will indicate some of the more common types of obligations. Just as for asset titles, the student should feel free to use different titles. The title used should be a good description of the particular obligation.

Accounts Payable. Accounts Payable are amounts owed for goods or services acquired under an informal credit agreement. They are usually payable within one or two months. The same items appear as *Accounts Receivable* on the creditor's books. When a certain office procedure, known as the voucher system, is employed, the title *Vouchers Payable* may be used. The term Accounts Payable covers the total amount due to all suppliers of goods and services, but the amount owed to each creditor is, of course, accounted for separately.

Notes Payable. The face amount of promissory notes given in connection with loans from the bank or the purchase of goods or services are recorded as *Notes Payable*. The same items appear as *Notes Receivable* on the creditor's books.

Payroll Taxes Payable. Amounts withheld from wages and salaries of employees for federal and state payroll taxes, and the required employer's contributions for this purpose, are classified under Payroll Taxes Payable. Individual titles—*Federal Insurance Contributions Act (FICA) Taxes Payable*, *State Unemployment Insurance Taxes Payable*, and *Federal Unemployment Insurance Taxes Payable*—can be used for each of the various kinds of taxes. Common practice lumps them all under the heading Payroll Taxes Payable.

Withheld Income Taxes. Withheld Income Taxes includes amounts withheld from wages and salaries of employees for income taxes. This is a tentative income tax on the earnings of employees; the employer merely acts as a tax collecting agent for the federal and state governments. A few cities also levy income taxes which the employer must withhold from wages.

Interest Payable. Interest on obligations that has accrued or accumulated with the passage of time is recorded under Interest Payable. The liability for interest is customarily shown separately from the face amount of the obligations.

Income Taxes Payable. Income Taxes Payable includes the estimated liability for income taxes, accumulated and unpaid, based upon the income of the business from the beginning of the taxable year to the date of the balance sheet. Since sole proprietorships and partnerships do not pay federal income taxes directly, this term will appear only on the books of a corporation or other taxable entity.

Unearned Rent. The Unearned Rent account is an example of the deferred-credit liability. The business owns a building which it rents to a tenant. The tenant has prepaid a certain amount of money to cover the rental charge for several months. The amount applicable to future months cannot be considered as earned until the time expires. In the meantime it represents a liability payable in service, that is, in the use of the building. On the records of the tenant the same amount would appear as an asset, Prepaid Rent. Other items of this sort would include deposits from customers for goods to be delivered later or subscription payments received by a publisher for newspapers or magazines to be furnished later.

Contracts Payable. Contracts Payable are debts that involve written installment contracts usually calling for payments each month until the debt is paid. Land, automobiles, and machinery are often acquired with the use of this type of contract.

Mortgage Payable. The Mortgage Payable account includes long-term promissory notes that have been given greater protection by the pledge of specific pieces of property as security for their payment. If the loan or interest is not paid according to the agreement, the creditor may have the property sold for his benefit.

Bonds Payable. Amounts borrowed by the business for a relatively long period of time under a formal written contract or indenture are classified under Bonds Payable. The loan is usually obtained from a number of creditors, each of whom gets one or more bond certificates as written evidence of his or her share of the loan.

Proprietary Equity

Whether the business is owned by one or many individuals, the proprietary equity, or proprietorship, represents the amount of the owners' interest. The titles used in the proprietary equity section of the financial statements indicate the form of business organization.

Sole Proprietorship. In a sole proprietorship the equity or interest of an owner in the business is the sum of his contributions of capital funds to the business plus the earnings from the operations of the business minus the losses and the owner's withdrawals of cash or other assets. This is usually presented under a title such as *J. R. Carson, Capital.*

Partnerships. Because each partner is a co-owner of the business that is a partnership, the interest of each of them must be shown separately. Each partner will, therefore, be represented by a "capital" account. The determination of the total proprietorship is made in the same way as in a sole proprietorship.

Corporations. A corporation obtains capital contributions from shareholders or stockholders. The corporation issues certificates representing a number of "shares" of its "capital stock" to a stockholder who makes a capital contribution to the corporation. If the shares of stock have been assigned a nominal, or par, value, this amount is shown under the title of *Capital Stock*. If there is more than one type of stock contract used, the amount is shown as *Preferred Stock, Common Stock*, or under other appropriate titles. If the shareholder has contributed more than the par value of his shares, the excess is shown under the titles *Additional Paid-in Capital* or *Premium on Capital Stock*. Two older and less satisfactory titles that are sometimes used to describe this excess are *Paid-in Surplus* and *Capital Surplus*. The longer, but more descriptive title, *Capital Contributed in Excess of Par Value*, has received authoritative support recently.[2] Stock issued at less than par value is called *discount* stock and is rarely issued, in part because the stockholder is contingently liable for the difference between par and issue price.

If the capital stock has not been assigned a par value but has been assigned a "stated" value, the entire amount contributed by the shareholders could logically be shown as *Capital Stock*, but the amount is frequently split between this account and *Additional Paid-in Capital*.

Just as in the other forms of business enterprise, the equity of the owners of the corporation, the stockholders, will increase if the operations of the business are successful or decrease if they are unsuccessful. This change in owners' equity is shown in the *Retained Earnings* account and is matched by a change in net assets. When dividends are declared, net assets are distributed and the amount in the Retained Earnings account is reduced. The term *net assets* means all assets minus all liabilities.)

Nonstock Corporations and Associations. Many organizations and institutions, such as schools, churches, fraternal organizations, and municipalities, own property and carry on business transactions. In most respects their accounting problems are similar to those of profit-seeking enterprises, but the ownership equity is unique in that it resides in no person or group of persons. Rather, the ownership equity belongs to the association itself as an impersonal entity. There are no distributions to owners because there are no profit-sharing owners. Such titles as *Contributed Capital* and *Retained Earnings* are used to indicate the capital contributed by the mem-

---

[2] The interested reader can consult *Accounting Trends and Techniques*, a publication of the AICPA described in Chapter 1, to ascertain current usage by corporations in this and other matters.

bers of the association and any accumulations resulting from dues, regular contributions, or gains from any source.

THE BALANCE SHEET

The accounting equation does not appear in public in mathematical form, but rather as an organized and classified list of assets, liabilities, and owners' capital known as a *balance sheet* or *statement of financial position*. Its only resemblance to an equation is that its traditional form presents two equal totals, one for the assets and the other for the sum of the liability and proprietorship items.

Nature of the Balance Sheet

Balance sheets are prepared at the close of regular intervals such as a quarter or year. Such a statement is only a picture of the financial position of a business at the close of a particular business day. Many of the items in it are changing continually.

A balance sheet is almost never a complete statement of the financial affairs of a firm. The backlog of unfilled orders, the future effect of contracts that have not yet resulted in the increase of any assets or liabilities, and the trend of the earnings of the business are examples of the many important financial matters that are not disclosed by a balance sheet. The skill and loyalty of the firm's working force and the public's recognition and acceptance of the firm's trade name or trademark are important resources. Their value is hard to quantify, and they are seldom found in a firm's statement of financial position.

The dollar figures that appear on a balance sheet are for the most part merely reflections of the transactions that have occurred in the past. Almost without exception, they are based upon acquisition costs rather than on current values. The amounts shown for most assets are merely those parts of acquisition costs that are to be charged to future operations. The asset total on the balance sheet does not indicate what the assets would yield if sold at a forced sale nor does it indicate what the cost would be to replace the assets at the date of the statement. As we shall see later, some of the figures necessarily are estimates rather than precise evaluations.

Balance Sheet Classification

A balance sheet should logically organize data so that they will emphasize the significant amounts and relationships between groups. There is no universal standard, but certain groupings are common.

Current Assets. Assets are usually divided into at least two categories—current and noncurrent, or fixed. Current assets include cash and other assets that will normally be converted into cash or consumed within a short period of time. A year is often arbitrarily taken as the dividing line between current and noncurrent, although a longer period may be used if the normal operating cycle of the business requires more than a year. Cash is received and spent almost continuously. Accounts and notes receivable are usually collected in from one to six months. Merchandise is bought and sold frequently so that the amount shown in the balance sheet normally "turns over" several times a year. Rent and insurance are usually prepaid for at most a year or two in advance and, hence, are largely "consumed" within a year. These, then, are common examples of current assets.

Current assets are usually presented on the balance sheet in the order of their relative currency or liquidity. Thus cash items are listed first and are followed by marketable securities. Notes and accounts receivable, along with interest receivable, are shown next. Inventories follow as a fourth category. In a retail business, inventories are merchandise and supplies; for a manufacturing firm inventories represent finished goods, work in process, raw materials, and supplies. Prepaid services such as insurance and rent make up the last class of current assets.

Noncurrent Assets. Noncurrent assets include those that are not consumed in operations, such as land or long-term investments, and those which can be used for a relatively long period of time, such as buildings, machinery, automobiles, patents, and natural resources.

The intention of the owner or the nature of the situation often determines whether a particular item is to be classified as current or noncurrent. A truck in the hands of an automobile dealer is one of his current assets (Merchandise Inventory), but one purchased by a store to be used as a delivery truck is a noncurrent asset of the store (Delivery Equipment). A desk on the floor of a furniture store is a current asset, Merchandise, but if the owner moves the same desk into his office it becomes a noncurrent asset, Office Furniture and Fixtures. Cash of any sort is normally a current asset, but if a special fund of cash has been set aside in a "sinking fund" for the retirement of the firm's debt, that fund would be reported as a noncurrent asset.

In practice, the grouping of the noncurrent assets is not completely uniform, nor is there unanimous agreement on their order of presentation. More than one grouping is frequently used. For example, one subgroup may be set up for plant and equipment, another for long-term investments, another for intangibles such as goodwill, patents, and organization costs, and so on. These variations will be presented and discussed later. Usually the plant and equipment items are presented first, in this order: land, buildings, equipment, and furniture and fixtures. Any other noncurrent assets, such as patents, copyrights, or goodwill, then follow.

Current Liabilities. Liabilities, also, are commonly divided into two groups—current and long-term. Current liabilities are those that are to be paid or otherwise discharged within a short period of time. The necessarily arbitrary dividing line should correspond with that used for the current assets and is normally one year. Some common examples of current liabilities are: Accounts Payable, Notes Payable, Deposits by Customers, Taxes Payable, and Withheld Income Taxes. Current liabilities, like current assets, turn over as a result of business operations, with new amounts replacing the ones paid.

The relationship between the current assets and current liabilities of a business is always observed with some interest. A generous excess of current assets over current liabilities—say a ratio of 1.5 to 1 or more— indicates a high probability that the current liabilities will be paid as they continue to come due. The difference between current assets and current liabilities is often called *working capital*; the quotient of these two numbers is called the *current ratio*.

SCHEDULE 2.1 PARTNERSHIP BALANCE SHEET

WILSON AND PALMER
Balance Sheet
June 30, 1975

Assets

Current Assets

Cash on Hand	$ 450	
Cash in Bank	1,247	
Accounts Receivable	4,722	
Merchandise	8,156	
Store Supplies	185	
Unexpired Insurance	300	
Total Current Assets		$15,060

Noncurrent Assets

Furniture and Fixtures		6,240
Total Assets		$21,300

Liabilities and Ownership Equity

Current Liabilities

Accounts Payable	$ 794	
Notes Payable	3,000	
Wages Payable	690	
Taxes Payable	398	
Total Current Liabilities		$ 4,882

Ownership Equity

M. G. Wilson, Capital	$8,209	
R. C. Palmer, Capital	8,209	
Total Ownership Equity		16,418
Total Liabilities and Ownership Equity		$21,300

The order of presentation of current liabilities is largely a matter of convention. It is customary to list the accounts and notes payable first, then the other payables such as wages payable and taxes payable, and finally the deferred credits, such as advances from customers.

Long-term Liabilities. Mortgages, bonds, and long-term contracts are examples of long-term liabilities. They are obligations that ordinarily do not have to be met within a year of the date of the balance sheet.

SCHEDULE 2.2 CORPORATE BALANCE SHEET

R. L. SMITH
BALANCE
DECEMBER

Assets

Current Assets

Cash:			
Undeposited Cash		$ 511	
Cash in Bank		6,558	$ 7,069
Marketable Securities (Market value $12,525)			10,500
Receivables:			
Accounts Receivable	$35,466		
Less: Allowance for Uncollectible Accounts	1,206	$34,260	
Notes Receivable		9,000	
Interest Receivable		90	43,350
Merchandise Inventory (at cost)			85,423
Store and Office Supplies			1,550
Prepaid Costs:			
Unexpired Insurance		$ 256	
Prepaid Rent		350	606
Total Current Assets			$148,498

Noncurrent Assets

Land (cost)		$10,000	
Buildings	$76,978		
Less: Accumulated Depreciation	22,556	54,422	
Furniture and Fixtures	$15,102		
Less: Accumulated Depreciation	6,064	9,038	
Delivery Equipment	$ 2,590		
Less: Accumulated Depreciation	1,554	1,036	
Organization Costs		500	
Goodwill		1,000	
Total Noncurrent Assets			75,996
Total Assets			$224,494

Balance Sheet Form (Schedule 2.1)

The partnership balance sheet for Wilson and Palmer will serve as a guide for the location of the various types of items. Notice the technical points, such as the systematic use of dollar signs, the double rulings of totals, and the heading, which should always give the name of the firm, the title of the statement, and the date.

The form of business organization has little effect upon the balance sheet except in the proprietorship section. If M. G. Wilson had been a sole proprietor, the balance sheet (Schedule 2.1) would conclude as follows:

STORES, INC.
SHEET
31, 1975

Liabilities and Stockholders' Equity

Current Liabilities

Vouchers Payable		$23,122
Notes Payable		8,000
Interest Payable		100
Wages Payable		655
Taxes Payable:		
Federal and State Income Taxes	$ 9,753	
Withheld Income Taxes	1,595	
Sales Taxes	2,533	
Payroll Taxes	555	14,436
Advances from Customers		1,000
Total Current Liabilities		$ 47,313

Noncurrent Liabilities

Contracts Payable (on fixtures)	$ 3,500	
Mortgage Payable (secured by land and buildings)	25,000	
Total Noncurrent Liabilities		28,500
Total Liabilities		$ 75,813

Stockholders' Equity

Preferred Stock—7% cumulative, authorized 1,000 shares, outstanding 500 shares, par value $100 per share		$50,000
Common Stock—no par, stated value $10 per share, authorized 10,000 shares, outstanding 7,500 shares	$75,000	
Capital Contributed in Excess of Stated Value of Shares	8,000	83,000
Retained Earnings		15,681
Total Stockholders' Equity		148,681
Total Liabilities and Stockholders' Equity		$224,494

Proprietorship

M. G. Wilson, Capital   16,418

    Total Liabilities and Proprietorship $21,300

If the firm had been incorporated and had capital stock of $12,500 and undistributed earnings of $3,918, the last section of the balance sheet (Schedule 2.1) would appear as follows:

Stockholders' Equity

Capital Stock $12,500

Retained Earnings   3,918

    Total Stockholders' Equity   16,418

    Total Liabilities and Stockholders' Equity $21,300

A Corporation Balance Sheet (Schedule 2.2)

The statement for R. L. Smith Stores, Inc. indicates the features of a well-organized balance sheet for a corporation. Certain items, such as the deduction of accumulated depreciation from the noncurrent assets, are shown for the sake of completeness even though we defer discussion of them and their meaning until later. Notice the extensive use of subtotals, the inclusion of significant details of the capital stock contracts, and the use of parenthetical information to supplement the figures taken directly from the books of account. Notice, too, the accounting convention for placing dollar signs in financial statements—next to the first number in any column of figures and next to any number below a horizontal line.

This statement follows the traditional horizontal arrangement with assets being shown at the left and liabilities and stockholders' equity at the right. The vertical form used in the Wilson and Palmer balance sheet is, however, entirely satisfactory when the number of items is not too great to permit such an arrangement on a single page. Other balance sheet forms will be considered later.

QUESTIONS AND PROBLEMS

1. From the standpoint of its position in the balance sheet, how does the equity of the bondholders differ from that of the stockholders? In what ways are they similar?

2. How can you determine from a balance sheet whether the enterprise is a corporation, partnership, or sole proprietorship?

3. "A balance sheet is always in part an expression of opinion, never entirely an expression of fact." Explain why this statement is true.

4. Is possession of an item sufficient to indicate it is an asset of the one possessing it? Give several examples to support your answer.

5. Refer to a recent edition of *Accounting Trends and Techniques,* published annually by the AICPA, to answer the following questions.
   a. What is the balance sheet called by the companies surveyed?
   b. What form of the accounting equation do the companies surveyed use for their balance sheets?
   c. What title do the companies surveyed use for the owners' equity portion of the balance sheet?

°**6.** Indicate which of the following items are assets according to our accounting definition:
   a. the cash which a customer advanced to the firm for services to be rendered in a future accounting period
   b. a contract signed by a customer to buy $1,000 of goods next year
   c. a favorable reputation
   d. a patent acquired on a new invention
   e. a good credit standing
   f. a degree in engineering from a university
   g. a favorable store location
   h. a delivery truck.

°**7.** Indicate which of the following are liabilities according to our accounting definition:
   a. unpaid wages of employees
   b. an obligation to maintain a rented office building in good repair
   c. the amount due for a newspaper advertisement which has appeared but for which payment is not due for thirty days
   d. an incompetent brother-in-law of one of the partners, employed in the business
   e. the reputation for not paying bills promptly
   f. the capital stock of a corporation
   g. merchandise due a customer next year on a signed contract, for which payment has been received
   h. an obligation to permit a tenant to use a building, the tenant having paid three months' rent in advance.

°**8.** Indicate whether or not each of the following situations gives rise to an asset at the time of the initial event. If an asset is involved, indicate the title and amount.
   a. An investment of $7,500 is made in a government bond that will be worth $10,000 in five years.
   b. An order for $800 worth of merchandise is received.
   c. Goods with a list price of $250 are purchased, payment being made in time to secure a 2-percent discount for prompt payment.
   d. Notice is received from a manufacturer that materials billed at $3,500, terms net thirty days, have been shipped by freight.

° Hints, key numbers, or (partial) answers appear in the back of the book between the Appendix Tables and the Glossary.

e. A contract is signed for the construction of a specially designed piece of machinery. The terms are $4,500 down upon the signing of the contract and the balance of $9,500 upon the delivery of the equipment. The downpayment is made. (Consider from the standpoint of the purchaser.)

*9. Indicate whether or not each of the following events gives rise to a liability at the time of the initial event. If a liability is involved, indicate the title and the amount. More than one liability account may be involved.

    a. A landscaper agrees to improve the land used by a company. The agreed price for the work is $375.

    b. Additional capital stock with a par value of $47,500 is issued for $50,000.

    c. A check for $10 for a two-year subscription is received by a magazine publisher.

    d. Consider item (e) of Question 8 from the standpoint of the manufacturer of the goods.

    e. During the last pay period, employees earned wages amounting to $10,000, which have not been paid as yet. The employer is also liable for payroll taxes of 8 percent of wages earned.

*10. A balance sheet of a business contains the following items. Indicate by the use of the appropriate number whether each is an (1) asset, (2) liability, or (3) stockholders' equity item:

    a. Wages Payable

    b. Accounts Receivable

    c. Retained Earnings

    d. Patent on Manufacturing Process

    e. Advances by Customers

    f. Land

    g. Mortgage Payable

    h. Advances to Employees

    i. Accounts Payable

    j. Raw Materials

    k. Interest Payable

    l. Capital Stock.

11. The assets of a business amount to $720,000 and its liabilities to $400,000. Present the proprietorship section of the balance sheet under each of the following assumptions.

    a. The business is a sole proprietorship owned by William Anderson.

    b. The business is a partnership. William Anderson has a 40-percent interest, John Hanson a 35-percent interest, and David Johnson a 25-percent interest.

    c. The business is incorporated. It has capital stock outstanding with a par value of $100,000. The remainder represents accumulated and undistributed earnings.

*12. Some assets of a firm correspond to liabilities on the balance sheet of the other party to the transaction. For example, an account receivable on a creditor's balance sheet corresponds to an account payable on the debtor's statement. For each of the following items, tell whether it is an asset or liability and give the corresponding title on the balance sheet of the other party to the transaction:

    a. Advances by Customers
    b. Bonds Payable
    c. Cash in Bank
    d. Interest Receivable
    e. Prepaid Insurance
    f. Rent Received in Advance.

13. Give an illustration, other than those in the text, of each of the following:
    a. a situation in which property is not shown as an asset of the one who has it in his possession
    b. a situation in which an item is shown as an asset of one who does not have complete legal ownership of it
    c. an asset that is intangible in nature
    d. a liability that is payable in goods or services rather than in cash (a "deferred credit").

14. A delivery truck with a list price of $2,900 is purchased. The dealer allows a discount of $300 from list for payment in cash. There is a 3-percent state sales tax on the net purchase. License fees for the remainder of the year are $80, and insurance for one year is $108. The cost of painting the firm's name and seal on the truck is $30. At what amount should the truck be shown on the balance sheet at the acquisition date?

15. The balance sheet of a business contains the following items. Indicate, by using the appropriate number for each item, whether it is an (1) asset, (2) liability, or (3) stockholders' equity item:
    a. Taxes Payable
    b. Delivery Equipment
    c. Notes Payable
    d. Prepaid Rent
    e. Organization Costs
    f. Work in Process
    g. Unexpired Insurance
    h. Withheld Income Taxes
    i. Buildings
    j. Capital Contributed in Excess of Par Value
    k. Investments.

16. Indicate whether or not each of the following events gives rise to an asset. If an asset is involved, indicate the title and the amount.
    a. A check for $600 is sent to the landlord for three months' rent in advance.
    b. A check for $800 is written to obtain an option to buy a tract of land, the price of which is $27,500.
    c. Raw materials with an invoice cost of $5,800, terms net thirty days, are received.
    d. Twenty-five year, 8-percent bonds with a face value of $100,000 are purchased at par. The interest coupons attached to the bonds and receivable at six-month intervals amount to $200,000.
    e. A purchase order is received for $4,750 of transistor radios to be delivered next month.

17. Indicate whether or not each of the following events gives rise to a liability. If a liability is involved, indicate the title and the amount.

a. Consider item (a) of Question 16 from the standpoint of the landlord.

b. A ninety-day, 8-percent loan for $5,000 is secured at the bank.

c. A newspaper receives $750 from an advertiser for an advertisement which ran last month.

d. Consider item (d) of Question 16 from the standpoint of the issuer of the bonds.

e. A firm signs a contract to purchase at least $10,000 worth of merchandise within the next three months.

*18. The financial records of the Bay City Manufacturing Company contain the following items on December 31, 1975:

Accounts Payable	$ 24,240
Finished Goods	41,010
Organization Costs	7,500
Capital Stock	400,000
Withheld Income Taxes	8,195
Land	13,880
Additional Paid-in Capital	40,520
Interest Receivable	360
Raw Materials on Hand	19,120
Accounts Receivable	47,870
Retained Earnings	219,200
Goods in Process	24,365
Property Taxes Payable	13,435
Notes Receivable	18,540
Buildings	254,360
Bonds Payable	150,000
Cash	12,015
Machinery and Equipment	427,500
Factory Supplies	8,920
Wages Payable	19,850

Prepare a balance sheet for the Bay City Manufacturing Company as of December 31, 1975.

*19. Alan Hanson and Frank Howard are equal partners in the operation of Tri-City Laundry. On September 30, 1975, they attempted to obtain a $10,000 loan from their local bank. Among other data, the bank requested a balance sheet for the partnership. Although complete accounting records had not been maintained, the following information regarding the partnership's financial position at September 30 was assembled:

(1) Undeposited cash amounts to $500.

(2) It is estimated that cleaning equipment in use, which cost $15,000 when new, has one half of its service life remaining.

(3) Amounts due from customers, $1,500.

(4) Amounts due suppliers, $500.

(5) Rent for the month of September, $200, has not been paid.

(6) Unpaid wages, $400.

(7) Payroll taxes withheld, $100.

(8) Other taxes payable, $150.

(9) Supplies on hand cost $500.

(10) Unpaid balance on equipment contract, payable at the rate of $300 per month, $3,300.

(11) The annual premium of $600 for an insurance policy for the year starting March 1, 1975, was paid in March.

(12) The bank statement at September 30 shows a balance in the bank of $750. According to the checkbook, though, three checks amounting to $200 and a deposit of $450 have not yet been recorded by the bank.

(13) The partnership owns a delivery truck which cost $4,000 when new. Since it is two years old, the partners have decided that $2,500 is an appropriate valuation for it.

Prepare a balance sheet as of September 30, 1975, for the Tri-City Laundry. Assume that the data relating to assets and liabilities are complete.

20. Yvonne M. Leone has been conducting her business as Yvonne M. Leone Company for a number of years using an incomplete or "single-entry" system of accounts. Since these records have proved to be unsatisfactory, she now wishes to install a set of "double-entry" books. The following information that has been assembled will enable you to set up a balance sheet as of December 31, 1975, and will form the basis of the double-entry system:

(1) The balances of customers' accounts total $8,500.

(2) The cash in the safe and cash register totals $380.

(3) Rent for January, $300, has been paid.

(4) The furniture and fixtures used in the store cost $6,000, but Ms. Leone estimates they have depreciated by $2,500.

(5) Unpaid bills from suppliers total $4,850.

(6) Ms. Leone conducted an inventory on December 31 and found that her stock of merchandise was $18,700 and supplies were $750.

(7) Ms. Leone received a note from a customer for $1,000. It is dated September 1, 1975, and is due April 30, 1976. It bears interest at 9 percent per annum, payable at maturity.

(8) Unpaid wages were $890.

(9) The bank statement for December 31, 1975, shows a balance on deposit in the checking account of $6,875, but a comparison of the returned checks with the checkbook shows two checks totaling $800 have not been cashed and returned.

(10) A fire insurance policy on the merchandise, supplies, and furniture and fixtures for $23,000 was paid in October. The annual premium is $300, and the policy is dated October 1, 1975, and expires October 1, 1976.

(11) Taxes payable amount to $1,100.

(12) Ms. Leone owes the bank $6,000 on an unsecured note, the proceeds of which were used to purchase merchandise. The note is dated August 1, 1975, and is due February 15, 1976. It bears interest at the rate of 8 percent per annum, payable at maturity.

Prepare the balance sheet at December 31, 1975.

21. The former office secretary at Cole Williams, Inc. carelessly let a burning cigarette damage the materials he was bringing to you to prepare the year-end balance sheet for 1975. Some of the amounts were scorched and could not be read, but all of the items to be included can still be ascertained. The available data are:

Unpaid taxes, $2,500
Cash on hand, $1,350
Cost of land (?)
Wages payable, $1,750
Notes payable (?)
Accounts payable, $12,500
Par value of capital stock, $100,000
Accounts receivable (?)
Interest payable on notes (three months at 8 percent), $140
Total current assets (?)
Building, $15,000
Equipment, $25,000
Balance in checking account, $5,300
Total noncurrent assets, $45,000
Merchandise inventory, $75,000
Store supplies inventory, $425
Total assets, $152,075
Total current liabilities, $23,890
Retained earnings (?)
Total stockholders' equity (?)
Total liabilities and stockholders' equity (?).

Prepare a balance sheet as of December 31, 1975. All of the accounts to be included are referred to in the data in the problem.

22. Most of the financial records of the Rowland Novelty Company were removed by an employee who, apparently, removed all the cash on hand from the store on October 31, 1975.

From the supplementary records the following information is obtained:

(1) Cash in bank, per bank statement, $5,730.
(2) Amounts due creditors, $4,720.
(3) Mr. Rowland's initial contribution to the business was $15,000. His total interest in the business at the time of the theft was $17,500.
(4) Cost of merchandise on hand, $11,380.
(5) A one-year fire insurance policy was purchased on September 1, 1975, for $900.
(6) Furniture and fixtures are rented from the Anderson Office Supply Company for $200 per month. The rental for October has not been paid.
(7) A note for $1,200 was given by a customer. Interest due at October 31, 1975, was $45.
(8) Amount due from other customers was $1,915.
(9) Mr. Rowland purchased a license from the city for $300 on July 1, 1975. The license permits him to operate for one year.

a. Determine the probable cash shortage.
b. Prepare a well-organized balance sheet presenting the financial position immediately preceding the theft.

Chapter 3

Balance Sheet Transactions and Accounts

The stock market "crash" in 1929 was not a planned event. The balance sheets of many companies that "went under" reported sound financial positions and led investors to predict rosy futures for these concerns. But their financial positions changed rapidly. This situation is true for all businesses, although it is usually less dramatic. The financial position of going businesses is almost always changing, and this is the limitation of the balance sheet: it reports the financial condition of an enterprise as of a specific time. Within this limitation, the accounting equation expressed in the balance sheet provides reliable financial reporting, since correct analysis of all transactions and events will always balance the equation.

TYPES OF TRANSACTIONS

Although many transactions may occur every day in a business, only *nine types* of transactions can occur. An equation will remain in balance if the same amount is added to both sides of the equation or if the same amount is subtracted from both sides of the equation. An equation will remain in balance if the same amount is added to and subtracted from items on one side of the equation. The accounting equation, Assets = Liabilities + Proprietorship, consists of three terms, so that the nine possible types of transactions are:

1. Increase in an asset; increase in a liability
2. Increase in an asset; increase in a proprietorship item
3. Increase in an asset; decrease in another asset
4. Decrease in a liability; decrease in an asset

5. Decrease in a liability; increase in another liability
6. Decrease in a liability; increase in a proprietorship item
7. Decrease in a proprietorship; decrease in an asset
8. Decrease in a proprietorship item; increase in a liability item
9. Decrease in a proprietorship item; increase in another proprietorship item.

The types of changes may be expressed algebraically as follows:

$$
\begin{array}{llll}
& A & = L & + \quad P \\
1. & +A & = +L & - \\
2. & +A & = - & +P \\
3. & +A -A & = - & - \\
4. & -A & = -L & - \\
5. & - & = -L +L & - \\
6. & - & = -L & +P \\
7. & -A & = - & -P \\
8. & - & = +L & -P \\
9. & - & = - & -P +P \\
\end{array}
$$

All possible transactions that in any way affect the balance sheet must fall into one of these types or be a combination of them.

Increase in an Asset; Increase in a Liability

This is a common type of transaction since it includes all purchases on account. For example, if $300 of merchandise were purchased on account from the Ace Supply Company, the effect would be:

Increase in the asset Merchandise, $300
Increase in the liability Accounts Payable—Ace Supply Co., $300

Another example of this type of change is the borrowing of $1,000 from the bank on a promissory note when the money is left on deposit in a checking account:

Increase in the asset Cash in Bank, $1,000
Increase in the liability Notes Payable, $1,000

Increase in an Asset; Increase in Proprietorship

The most common situation of this type is the investment of funds in a business by the stockholders, partners, or sole proprietor. If 1,000 shares of stock, with a par value of $100 per share, are issued at par for cash, the effect would be:

Increase in the asset Cash on Hand, $100,000
Increase in the proprietorship item Capital Stock, $100,000

If a partner, C. B. Warnock, turns over a parcel of land worth $20,000 to the partnership to be used as a site for a store building, the analysis is:

Increase in the asset Land, $20,000
Increase in the proprietorship item C. B. Warnock, Capital, $20,000

Increase in an Asset; Decrease in Another Asset

There are many transactions of this type. Collections of amounts owed by customers produce this type of change. If we collect $160 from William Raleigh, the effect would be:

> Increase in the asset Cash on Hand, $160
> Decrease in the asset Accounts Receivable—William Raleigh, $160

The deposit of funds in the bank account is a common example of this type of transaction involving an increase in one asset matched by a decrease in another asset. If $825 of cash received from various sources is deposited in the bank, the effect is:

> Increase in the asset Cash in Bank, $825
> Decrease in the asset Cash on Hand, $825

Another important transaction of this type occurs in the manufacturing process when lumber is made into furniture, pig iron into steel, steel into tools, and so on. If, for instance, lumber costing $1,200 is requisitioned from the yard and is put into production in the manufacture of furniture, the result is:

> Increase in the asset Work in Process, $1,200
> Decrease in the asset Lumber, $1,200

When the work is completed on an order of furniture on which the total accumulated costs are $2,515, a transfer is made from one asset to another:

> Increase in the asset Finished Goods, $2,515
> Decrease in the asset Work in Process, $2,515

All purchases of assets with cash are of this type, but such transactions are not common in modern practice where most business is carried on with the use of credit. In fact, purchases for cash are so rare in many firms that, when they do occur, the situation is handled as though it were two transactions—a purchase on credit followed by a payment of the resulting liability. This is done in order to avoid making exceptions to the usual record-keeping procedure.

Decrease in a Liability; Decrease in an Asset

All payments of liabilities fall into this type. For instance, a payment by check of $100 on the amount due the Ace Supply Company would be:

> Decrease in the liability Accounts Payable—Ace Supply Co., $100
> Decrease in the asset Cash in Bank, $100

If $50 of the merchandise is returned to the Ace Supply Company, the effect would be:

> Decrease in the liability Accounts Payable—Ace Supply Co., $50
> Decrease in the asset Merchandise, $50

Decrease in a Liability; Increase in Another Liability

This is a possible, but rare, type. Sometimes promissory notes are given to creditors who have extended credit on "open account." If the bill of the

Northern Service Corporation for $350 cannot be paid when it is due and a promissory note is given as a more formal evidence of indebtedness, the effect is:

> Decrease in the liability Accounts Payable—Northern Service Corporation, $350
> Increase in the liability Notes Payable—Northern Service Corporation, $350

Decrease in a Liability; Increase in Proprietorship

There are few examples of this type of transaction. Occasionally employees participate in stock purchase plans, with payment for stock being made by withholdings from their wages. If $1,000 of capital stock were issued in this way, the result would be:

> Decrease in the liability Wages Payable, $1,000
> Increase in the proprietorship item Capital Stock, $1,000

Some bonds contain a conversion privilege. This permits bondholders, at their option, to exchange bonds for stock. If $10,000 in bonds are exchanged for an equal amount of stock, the effect is:

> Decrease in the liability Convertible Bonds Payable, $10,000
> Increase in the proprietorship item Capital Stock, $10,000

Decrease in Proprietorship; Decrease in an Asset

All withdrawals of assets from the business by the owners fall in this category. If L. M. Wheeler, a sole proprietor, withdraws $400 in cash for his personal use, the recording would be:

> Decrease in the proprietorship item L. M. Wheeler, Capital, $400
> Decrease in the asset Cash on Hand, $400

Decrease in Proprietorship; Increase in a Liability

Proprietorship is decreased and a liability increased in a corporation when dividends are declared. Assume the board of directors votes to pay a dividend of $2 a share on the 10,000 shares of stock outstanding. From that time until the dividend is paid, the amount of the dividend is a liability of the corporation:

> Decrease in the proprietorship item Retained Earnings, $20,000
> Increase in a liability Dividends Payable, $20,000

When the dividend is paid, a transaction of the "decrease in a liability; decrease in an asset" type occurs. The transaction is shown as:

> Decrease in a liability Dividends Payable, $20,000
> Decrease in the asset Cash in Bank, $20,000

Decrease in Proprietorship; Increase in Proprietorship

A partner occasionally transfers part or all of his interest in the partnership to another partner. Suppose that C. B. Warnock sells $5,000 of his interest to F. W. Yardley; the effect would be:

> Decrease in the proprietorship item C. B. Warnock, Capital, $5,000
> Increase in the proprietorship item F. W. Yardley, Capital, $5,000

The money paid by Yardley to Warnock does not affect the firm's assets nor the total of its equities. It affects only the items within proprietary equity.

The balance sheet of a corporation shows only the amount of capital stock of each class outstanding without indicating the identity of the owner. Therefore, transfers of shares between individuals will not change the corporation's statement. Transactions involving an increase and decrease in proprietorship items of corporations do, however, sometimes occur. A corporation may transfer a portion of the stockholders' equity from Retained Earnings to the Capital Stock account, where it becomes part of the permanent investment of the stockholders and, in most states, is not available for cash dividends. This may be done by means of a "stock dividend." If 1,000 shares of stock, with a par value of $10 per share, are issued to stockholders without any payment on their part, the transaction is shown as:

> Decrease in the proprietorship item Retained Earnings, $10,000
> Increase in the proprietorship item Capital Stock, $10,000

Combinations of Types

Many transactions can be analyzed in terms of two items in the equation or balance sheet, as has been done in the last few pages. However, many other transactions do not fit into any one of the nine types but are, instead, combinations of two or more types. The method of analyzing the more complicated transactions is the same as with the more simple—determine which asset, liability, or proprietorship items are affected and whether they are increased or decreased. When the analysis is complete, make sure that the equation still balances. A few examples will indicate how these transactions are handled.

1. An automobile is purchased for $2,000. A check for $800 is given as a downpayment, and the balance is to be paid in monthly installments.

> Increase in the asset Automobile, $2,000
> Decrease in the asset Cash in Bank, $800
> Increase in the liability Contracts Payable, $1,200

Since the result is a net increase in assets of $1,200 (= $2,000 − $800) and an increase in liabilities of $1,200, the equation is maintained.

2. A tract of land that cost $2,200 is sold for $2,500 cash. Any gain or profit, such as the $300 in this case, increases the proprietary equity, because only proprietors share in the profits or losses of the business. If a single owner, A. R. Turner, is involved, the effect is:

> Increase in the asset Cash on Hand, $2,500
> Decrease in the asset Land, $2,200
> Increase in the proprietorship item A. R. Turner, Capital, $300

In this case, there is a net increase in assets of $300 and an increase in proprietorship of $300, so assets and equities are still equal.

3. Some complicated transactions may arise in connection with real estate. For example, a corporation acquires a tract of land for $25,000, and payment is made as follows:

The seller accepts as partial payment a tract of land that the corporation owns. The property cost the corporation $8,000, and there is a $5,000 mortgage on it. The seller agrees to assume the mortgage and to allow the corporation $4,000 for its equity. Preferred stock with a par value of $6,500 is issued to the seller, and he is given a check for $9,000. The balance of $5,500 is to be paid over an eight-year period under a land contract.

The analysis, step by step, would be:

Increase in the asset Land, $25,000
Decrease in the asset Land, $8,000
Decrease in the liability Mortgage Payable, $5,000
Increase in the proprietorship item Retained Earnings, $1,000
  [The equity in the land is $3,000 (= $8,000 − $5,000).
  There is a $1,000 gain because $4,000 is allowed.]
Increase in the proprietorship item Preferred Stock, $6,500
Decrease in the asset Cash in Bank, $9,000
Increase in the liability Land Contracts Payable, $5,500

The net increase in the Land account is $17,000, but the asset total increases by only $8,000 since there is also an asset decrease (in cash) of $9,000. Liabilities increase $500 (= $5,500 − $5,000) and proprietorship increases $7,500 (= $1,000 + $6,500). Thus there is an increase in total equities of $8,000, matching the increase in assets.

Events That Do Not Affect the Equation

Not every event that occurs in the conduct of the affairs of a business can be translated into accounting terms and recorded. Many events are important but do not lend themselves to expression in monetary terms. For example, the growth in the skill and loyalty of its work force benefits a firm, but there is as yet no practical way of recording the growing benefit in the accounting records.

Other transactions can be stated in monetary terms but are not accounting transactions. Businesses operate by making and carrying out agreements, and the changes produced by the execution of the agreements are recorded in the accounts. Agreements that are completely unexecuted do not produce measurable changes and, consequently, are not recorded as accounting transactions. For example, the signing of a contract for the purchase of raw material is an important event that eventually will bring about changes in assets, liabilities, and proprietorship. Ordinarily, though, the mere signing of such an agreement does not affect any of the balance sheet items, and no accounting record is made of it.

The receipt of an order from a customer is a desirable and significant event, and the total amount of unfilled orders on hand is an important indicator of the future trend of business. However, until an order is filled, or unless there is some advance of cash with an order, there is no change that can be recorded in the assets or equities. If a cash deposit accompanies an order, there is obviously an increase in the asset account Cash on Hand and there is also an increase in liabilities, since either goods must be shipped to the customer or his money must be refunded. An appropriate account in which to record this liability would be Advances by Customers or Unfilled Paid Orders.

ACCOUNTS

The Need for Accounts

Once a balance sheet has been prepared, the effect of any type of transaction can be shown either by erasing the old figures or by constructing an entirely new balance sheet. Neither method is efficient; moreover, neither approach will facilitate the compilation of operational data, which is, as we shall see, one of the most useful aspects of accounting. In practice, balance sheets are prepared periodically, rarely more often than once a month and in many businesses only once a year. To accumulate the changes that take place in each balance sheet item from one statement date to the next, we use a device known as an "account."

Requirement for an Account

The requirement for a satisfactory account is simple. Since a balance sheet item that changes can only increase or decrease, all an account need do is to provide for accumulating the increases and decreases that have taken place during the period of time. The balance carried forward from the previous statement is added to the total increases, the total decreases are deducted, and the result is the figure needed for the new balance sheet. Accounts usually have two sections (or sides): one for increases, the other for decreases.

Form of the Account

The account may take many possible forms, and several are commonly used in accounting practice. The skeleton account, sometimes called the *T-account*, is not used in actual practice, except, perhaps for memorandums or preliminary analyses. However, it satisfies all of the requirements of the account, and it is widely used in textbooks, problems, and examinations. As the name indicates, the T-account consists of a horizontal line bisected by a vertical line (see Figure 3.1). The name or title of the account is written on the horizontal line. One side of the space formed by the vertical line is used to record increases in the item and the other side to record the decreases. Each item listed in the balance sheet or used in the analysis of transactions is represented by a separate account. Dates and other information can, of course, be written in.

Account Title

Figure 3.1   T-account Form

The form that the account takes in actual records depends on the accounting system installed. In manual systems the accounts may be more elaborate than a T-account; in punched-card systems the account may take the form of a group of cards; in computer systems it may be a group of similarly coded items on a tape. Whatever its form, an account records an opening balance as well as the increases and decreases in the balance that result from the transactions of the period.

Placement of Increases and Decreases on the Account Form

Given the two-sided account, we must choose which side will be used to record increases and which side will be used for decreases. Up to this point the development of the bookkeeping technique has proceeded along logical lines, but now rules based on custom must be adopted.

Whenever the T-account form or any standard manual system form is used, it has long been the established custom to observe the following rules:

1. Increases in assets are entered on the left side; decreases, on the right.
2. Increases in liabilities are entered on the right side; decreases on the left.
3. Increases in proprietorship are entered on the right side; decreases, on the left.

This custom has an element of logic. A common form of balance sheet shows assets on the left and liabilities and proprietorship on the right. Following this example, asset balances should appear on the left side of accounts; equity balances on the right. But asset balances will appear on the left only if asset increases are recorded on the left side of the account. Similarly, right-hand equity balances can be produced only by recording equity increases on the right. When these rules are followed, negative numbers never appear in an account and any transaction results in equal entries on the left and right sides of the accounts.

Debit and Credit

Two terms may now be added to the bookkeeping vocabulary, *debit* (Dr.) and *credit* (Cr.). These terms have an interesting etymological history, but our concern is that they are convenient abbreviations or condensations. *Debit* is an abbreviation for "record an entry on the left side of the account" when used as a verb and is an abbreviation for "an entry on the left side of the account" when used as a noun or adjective. *Credit* is an abbreviation for "record an entry on the right side of the account" when used as a verb and for "an entry on the right side of the account" when used as a noun or adjective. These words have no other meaning in accounting. More convenient abbreviations than debit and credit certainly seem possible, but these have become part of accounting language through centuries of use and are not likely to be displaced. Often, however, the word *charge* is used instead of *debit*, both as a noun and as a verb. In terms of balance sheet categories:

Debit or *Charge* indicates

1. increase in an asset
2. decrease in a liability
3. decrease in a proprietorship item.

Credit indicates

1. decrease in an asset
2. increase in a liability
3. increase in a proprietorship item.

Any previous associations or meanings of the terms debit and credit should be disregarded in accounting. In popular parlance, to credit a person with something means to give him favorable recognition for some achievement and to debit him means to charge something unfavorable against him, but these terms have no such implications in accounting. Neither should any connection be assumed between the terms debit and credit and the terms debtor and creditor. The best procedure is simply to accept the terms *debit* and *credit* as technical symbols meaning *left* and *right*.

From now on, all transactions will be analyzed with the use of these terms. Analysis and reasoning must determine which accounts are affected and in what way, but the expressions can be condensed. Instead of "increase in the asset Cash in Bank," the expression will be merely "debit Cash in Bank"; instead of "increase in the liability Notes Payable," merely "credit Notes Payable."

Notice that the *equality of the two sides of the accounting equation can be maintained only by recording equal amounts of debits and of credits for each transaction.*

The conventional use of the account form and the terms debit and credit can be summarized graphically with the use of the skelton T-account form shown in Figure 3.2.

Any Asset Account

Opening Balance Increase + Dr. Closing Balance	Decrease − Cr.

Any Liability Account		**Any Proprietorship Account**	
Decrease − Dr.	Opening Balance Increase + Cr. Closing Balance	Decrease − Dr.	Opening Balance Increase + Cr. Closing Balance

Figure 3.2　Account Conventions

ILLUSTRATION

The following example illustrates the use of T-accounts to analyze transactions. Each transaction will first be analyzed in terms of increases and decrease in the appropriate accounts. Then the entries will be recorded in the T-accounts. Trace each entry carefully through the accounts. Notice that each entry results in equal debits and credits.

In order to emphasize the equality of debits and credits in each transaction, the descriptions of credit items are indented and the credit amounts are shown in a separate column to the right of debit amounts. This record-keeping procedure is commonly used in accounting practice.

All of the following transactions occur near the end of the month of July, 1975 and cover the organization of the firm of Irwin and Chadwick, which will open for business on August 1, 1975.

(1) Jane M. Irwin and Howard B. Chadwick form a partnership. Irwin contributes $8,000 in cash which is deposited in a checking account immediately. Chadwick contributes land worth $2,000, a building worth $14,000, and equipment worth $4,000.

Dr. (asset increase) Cash in Bank	8,000	
Cr. (proprietorship increase) Jane M. Irwin, Capital		8,000
Dr. (asset increase) Land	2,000	
Dr. (asset increase) Buildings	14,000	
Dr. (asset increase) Equipment	4,000	
Cr. (proprietorship increase) Howard B. Chadwick, Capital		20,000

(2) An automobile is purchased for $2,400 from the Central Auto Company. A check is drawn for $1,500, and the balance is covered by a contract payable in six monthly installments.

Dr. (asset increase) Automobile	2,400	
Cr. (asset decrease) Cash in Bank		1,500
Cr. (liability increase) Contracts Payable—Central Auto Company		900

(3) Materials and supplies are purchased on account from the Metropolitan Supply Company, $3,000.

```
Dr. (asset increase) Materials and Supplies ................  3,000
    Cr. (liability increase) Accounts Payable—
    Metropolitan Supply Company .......................        3,000
```

(4) Supplies are purchased by check, $400.

```
Dr. (asset increase) Materials and Supplies ................   400
    Cr. (asset decrease) Cash in Bank .....................         400
```

(5) A check for $200 is written to each partner for personal use.

```
Dr. (proprietorship decrease) Jane M. Irwin, Capital ..........   200
Dr. (proprietorship decrease) Howard B. Chadwick,
    Capital ...............................................   200
    Cr. (asset decrease) Cash in Bank .....................          400
```

(6) An employee earns $88; his time has been spent entirely on the installation of equipment. He is paid by check, after deductions of $10 for federal income tax and $5 for payroll taxes.

```
Dr. (asset increase) Equipment ...........................    88
    Cr. (asset decrease) Cash in Bank .....................          73
    Cr. (liability increase) Withheld Income Taxes ............       10
    Cr. (liability increase) Payroll Taxes Payable .............        5
```

(7) Supplies costing $64 are used in the installation of the equipment.

```
Dr. (asset increase) Equipment ...........................    64
    Cr. (asset decrease) Materials and Supplies ............          64
```

(8) A check for $2,000 and a six-month, 6-percent promissory note for $1,000 are given to the Metropolitan Supply Company. The note is dated August 1, 1975.

```
Dr. (liability decrease) Accounts Payable—Metropolitan
    Supply Company ......................................  3,000
    Cr. (asset decrease) Cash in Bank .....................        2,000
    Cr. (liability increase) Notes Payable—Metropolitan
    Supply Company ......................................        1,000
```

(9) Irwin buys out $4,000 of Chadwick's interest in the partnership.

```
Dr. (proprietorship decrease) Howard B. Chadwick,
    Capital ...............................................  4,000
    Cr. (proprietorship increase) Jane M. Irwin, Capital .......      4,000
```

(10) A payment of $150 is made by check on the automobile contract.

```
Dr. (liability decrease) Contracts Payable—Central
    Auto Company .........................................   150
    Cr. (asset decrease) Cash in Bank .....................         150
```

After the transactions are analyzed, they are entered in the T-account forms like the ones in Figure 3.3. In actual situations, accounts are usually arranged in statement order; that is, assets are first, followed by liabilities and proprietorship. In this illustration, however, as well as in most of the problems in this book, it is more convenient to arrange the accounts in the order they are encountered in the transactions. The terms Dr. and Cr. have been included in the account forms for illustrative purpose, but this is not customary. The numbers by the entries are keyed to the transaction numbers in the text. (Finding mistakes in worked problems is easier when all entries have been numbered.)

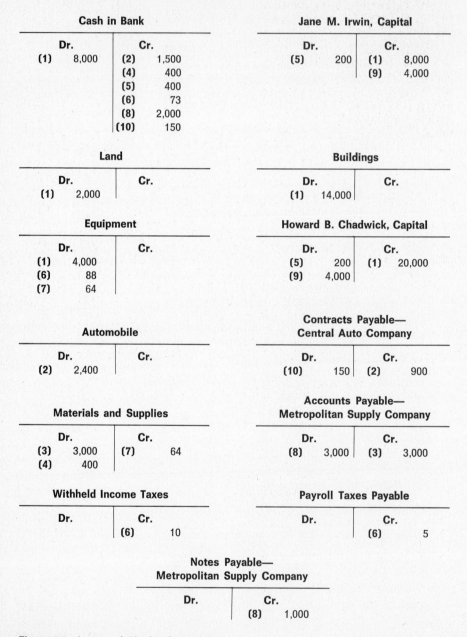

Figure 3.3   Irwin and Chadwick T-accounts

A balance sheet can be prepared by calculating the balance (the excess of total debits over total credits, or vice versa) of each account and arranging the results in conventional form. Note that, although it is necessary to record creditors' names in the accounts, it is not customary to show them in the balance sheet.

IRWIN AND CHADWICK
Balance Sheet
July 31, 1975

Assets

Current Assets

Cash in Bank	$ 3,477	
Materials and Supplies	3,336	
Total Current Assets		$ 6,813

Noncurrent Assets

Land	$ 2,000	
Buildings	14,000	
Equipment	4,152	
Automobile	2,400	
Total Noncurrent Assets		22,552
Total Assets		$29,365

Liabilities and Ownership Equity

Current Liabilities

Notes Payable	$ 1,000	
Contracts Payable	750	
Withheld Income Taxes	10	
Payroll Taxes Payable	5	
Total Current Liabilities		$ 1,765

Ownership Equity

Jane M. Irwin, Capital	$11,800	
Howard B. Chadwick, Capital	15,800	
Total Ownership Equity		27,600
Total Liabilities and Ownership Equity		$29,365

QUESTIONS AND PROBLEMS

1. Would a transaction that increased an asset account and decreased a liability account keep the accounting equation in balance? Explain your answer.
2. Which of the following transactions can be translated into accounting or monetary terms and recorded as an accounting transaction?

a. purchase of a used truck for cash
b. increased efficiency of management resulting from remodeling of the corporation's offices
c. receipt of a purchase order from a buyer for $5,000 of merchandise
d. receipt of merchandise ordered last month
e. deposit of $10,000 on a contract to purchase land.

3. What are the four basic kinds of information that any balance sheet account may show?

4. Would the essential features of double-entry bookkeeping be affected by the deletion of the terms *debit* and *credit* from the language?

5. Why are not increases in all balance sheet accounts recorded as debits and decreases in all balance sheet accounts as credits?

6. What difficulties, if any, would be caused by reversing the rules for the use of left and right sides of the accounts; that is, if the right side were used for debits and the left, for credits?

*7. a. Express the following transactions as increases or decreases in the balance sheet accounts of a corporation. Use this form:

Transaction No.	Increase or Decrease	Type of Account	Account Title	Amount
(1)	Increase	Asset	Cash on Hand	$35,000
	Increase	Stockholders' Equity	Capital Stock	35,000

(1) Shares of stock are issued to stockholders for cash, $35,000.
(2) Equipment is purchased on an installment contract for $12,000, terms $2,000 payable immediately and the balance in five quarterly installments.
(3) The remaining cash received in (1) is deposited in the bank.
(4) A check is issued to John Menken to reimburse him for costs incurred in organizing and promoting the corporation, $2,700.
(5) A check is issued for three-months' rent in advance for an office, $750.
(6) Office equipment is purchased for $625. A down payment of $125 is given the supplier with the balance to be paid in thirty days.
(7) A patent on a machine process is purchased for $10,000.
(8) For delivering the equipment purchased in (2), $375 is paid to Express Transfer Company.
(9) The first payment on the equipment installment contract is made.
(10) Supplies are purchased on account, $855.
b. Express the above transactions as debits and credits using the following form:

Transaction No.	Debit or Credit	Account Title	Amount
(1)	Debit	Cash on Hand	$35,000
	Credit	Capital Stock	35,000

* Hints, key numbers, or (partial) answers appear in the back of the book between the Appendix Tables and the Glossary.

8. a. Express each of the following transactions in a series of equations, each reflecting the result of the transaction and the preceding equation. Include account titles and amounts, for example:

Cash on Hand, $50,000 + Merchandise, $17,500
= Accounts Payable, $17,500 + Capital Stock, $50,000, after transaction (2).

(1) Five thousand shares of $10 par value capital stock are issued for cash.

(2) Merchandise is purchased on account from Robertson Bros. Supply Co., $17,500.

(3) The cash received in (1) is deposited in the bank.

(4) Store equipment is purchased for $3,200. A check is drawn for $700, and the balance is covered by an installment contract.

(5) Store supplies are purchased. Payment is made by check, $75.

(6) A check for $50 is cashed in order to establish a change fund.

(7) A sixty-day 8-percent promissory note is given to Robertson Bros. Supply Co. for the amount due them.

b. Record the transactions in skeleton accounts. Cross-number the entries.

*9. a. If an asset account should be debited in any of the following transactions, give the title of the account and the amount.

(1) Eight percent bonds of the Sommons Co. with a face value of $10,000 are purchased for $10,500.

(2) The Alfred Hansen Company signs a contract to buy 100 dozen of machine tool parts for each of two years at a price of $85 per dozen.

(3) Consider (2) from the standpoint of the supplier.

(4) Delivery of the first ten dozen parts is made in accord with the contract in (2). Consider from the standpoint of the Alfred Hansen Company.

(5) Consider (4) from the standpoint of the supplier. Payment has not yet been received.

b. If a liability account should be credited in any of the following transactions, give the title of the account and the amount.

(1) A check is received by a fire insurance company covering premiums on a policy two years in advance, $375.

(2) Coupon books are issued by a movie theater, redeemable in movie viewings, for cash, $25.

(3) A contract is signed for the construction of an apartment building. The total contract price is $135,000. The terms require $13,500 to be paid on the signing of the contract and the balance upon completion of the building. A check for $13,500 is received. Consider from the standpoint of the contractor.

(4) Consider (3) from the standpoint of the purchaser of the building.

(5) The Cardinal Construction Company issues 100 shares of $100 par 8-percent preferred stock for $10,250.

*10. The balances of the capital accounts of the partnership of Pearl and Allen at July 1, 1975, and June 30, 1976, are as follows:

Partner	July 1, 1975	June 30, 1976
Pearl	$31,550	$34,050
Allen	22,750	27,750

What was the profit or loss for the year and in what proportions was it distributed between the partners under each of the following assumptions?

a. If there were no additional investments and no withdrawals.

b. If Pearl withdrew $5,000, Allen withdrew $2,500, and there were no additional investments.

c. If Pearl invested an additional $1,500 and Allen an additional $3,500 and there were no withdrawals.

*11. On October 1, 1975, Robert Steiner organized a business and invested $67,500 in cash. On December 31, 1975, the accounts showed the following balances: Cash in Bank $1,350; Accounts Receivable $14,000; Accounts Payable $4,275; Equipment Contract Payable $13,600 (long-term obligation); Wages Payable $740; Raw Material $4,000; Land $17,500; Work in Process $8,250; Payroll Taxes Payable $300; Rent Due on Factory Building $450; Finished Goods $14,165; Equipment $49,000; Note Payable to Northeastern National Bank $13,500.

a. Prepare a balance sheet in good form.

b. Determine the net income for the year under each of the following assumptions:

(1) There were no new investments and no withdrawals during the year.

(2) New investments of $12,000; no withdrawals.

(3) Withdrawals of $3,000; no new investments.

(4) New investments of $8,000; withdrawals of $6,000.

12. **a.** Express the following transactions as increases or decreases in the appropriate balance sheet accounts of a corporation. Use the form shown for Problem 7(a).

(1) Ten thousand shares of $10 par value stock are issued for cash at par. The proceeds are deposited in the bank.

(2) Land and building are purchased for $60,000. Ten thousand dollars is paid by check and a twenty-year, 9-percent mortgage for the balance is assumed. The value of the land is $6,000 and the building $54,000.

(3) A used lathe is purchased for $2,850 in cash.

(4) Raw material is purchased from O'Hara Wholesalers on account, $6,200.

(5) Raw material is used in production, $3,200.

(6) Defective raw material is returned to O'Hara Wholesalers, $400.

(7) Finished goods which cost $4,350 are sold on account for $7,650.

(8) The bill of O'Hara Wholesalers (see (4) and (6)) is paid by check. A discount of 2 percent for prompt payment is taken.

(9) Collections from customers, $5,375.

(10) A check is drawn to pay a part-time employee whose time during the period has been used as follows: one-fourth in installing the lathe, the balance in installing new windows in the building. His total earnings were $400. Fifty dollars is withheld for employees' income tax and 6 percent is deducted for Federal Insurance Contribution Taxes.

(11) Fire insurance policies are taken out with coverage of $50,000. A bill is received from the Wm. Daly Agency for a one-year premium, $175, and is paid by check.

b. Express the above transactions as debits and credits. Use the form shown for Problem 7(b).

*13. Supply the missing figures in the following schedules:

	(1)	(2)	(3)	(4)
Stockholders' Equity, January 1, 1975	$?	$56,400	$21,400	$34,700
Stockholders' Equity, December 31, 1975	159,600	?	30,150	37,500
Stock Issued in 1975	18,600	15,000	—	2,500
Dividends in 1975	5,000	21,000	?	2,100
Net Income (Loss) in 1975	(7,200)	26,100	9,300	?

14. The records of the C. Norton Palmer Store show the following information on December 31, 1975:

Cash in Bank	$ 3,240	Land	$ 8,200
Notes Payable	5,050	Equipment	21,730
Accounts Receivable ...	16,015	Merchandise Inventory ..	10,050
Building	12,300	Accounts Payable	12,665
Taxes Payable	1,340	Wages Payable	4,270
Supplies on Hand	890	Cash on Hand	125

On January 1, 1975, there was an excess of assets over liabilities of $52,775. Early in the year Palmer turned over the business securities he personally owned valued at $7,500. These were sold and the proceeds were used in the business. During the year Palmer made regular withdrawals of $400 on the first of each month and withdrew an additional $5,000 in July.

a. Prepare a balance sheet in good form as of December 31, 1975.

b. Determine the net income or loss for the period. Show your computations.

15. Record the following transactions in skeleton accounts. Cross-number the entries.

   (1) The books of the Grover Corporation are opened with the issue of 500,000 shares of $1 par value stock for cash at par.

   (2) Two hundred and fifty thousand additional shares of stock are issued to a development corporation for a fully equipped factory building; of the total, $25,000 is assigned to the land, $135,000 to the equipment and the balance to the building.

   (3) The cash received in (1) is deposited in the bank.

   (4) Five thousand shares of stock are issued to J. M. Larken in payment for legal services rendered in obtaining the corporate charter.

   (5) Raw materials are purchased for $37,500. A check is issued.

   (6) Supplies are purchased on account for factory and office use from the Mead Supply Company. The cost of the factory supplies is $750; the cost of office supplies, $350.

   (7) A check for $1,200 is written to the Martin Insurance Agency for fire and general liability insurance for one year.

   (8) A check is issued to the Mead Supply Company (see (6)) in payment of its account. A discount of 2 percent is taken for prompt payment.

   (9) A special order for $125,000 of machine parts which the firm plans to produce is received from Knight Electronics Co. A deposit of 10 percent of the order is received and deposited in the bank.

   (10) A parcel of land which cost $7,500 is sold for $10,000. The proceeds are deposited in the bank.

16. Supply the missing figures in the following schedules:

	(1)	(2)	(3)	(4)
Proprietor's Capital, January 1, 1975	$25,050	$57,300	$65,870	$25,060
Proprietor's Capital, December 31, 1975	37,590	?	60,000	21,350
Added Investments During Year ..	7,000	22,000	?	—
Withdrawals During Year	1,600	2,500	—	?
Net Income (Loss) for Year	?	(17,890)	(9,830)	12,540

*17 **a.** If an asset should be debited in any of the following transactions, give the title of the account and the amount.

(1) A firm returns defective raw material to a supplier, $295 invoice cost.

(2) A new machine is purchased. Payment of $13,500, less 2-percent discount, is made.

(3) Labor costs of installing the machine purchased in (2) are $435; $38 is withheld for employees' income tax, $28 for payroll taxes, and $72 for employees' contribution to a retirement plan. The balance is paid by check.

(4) A firm receives a $10 cash refund from overpayment of a raw material invoice.

(5) Land which cost $3,000 is sold for $4,500 cash.

(6) A check for $700 is issued to a creditor.

b. If a liability account should be credited in any of the following transactions, give the title of the account and the amount.

(1) The directors order the president's salary to be increased from $5,000 a month to $6,000 a month, effective next month.

(2) Raw materials costing $900 are returned to a supplier (they were not previously paid).

(3) The Warren Company has taxable income for the month of $12,000. The applicable tax rate for the firm is 40 percent.

(4) A leasing agency receives a $300 monthly payment in advance for use of store building on a one-year contract.

(5) Earned but unpaid office salaries total $16,000.

(6) Consider (a) (3) from standpoint of the corporation.

18. Analyze the following transactions in terms of debits and credits. Use the form shown for Problem 7(b). The transactions do not apply to the same company.

(1) A check for $15,680 is drawn to the Director of Internal Revenue to pay income taxes which had previously been set up as a liability.

(2) Bonds payable of $40,000 are reacquired on the market for $41,250 and cancelled.

(3) A customer, Robert Singer, turns over a promissory note to apply on his account. He had received the note previously from a customer of his. The face of the note is $1,500 and $10 interest has accrued on it.

(4) An office building and site are purchased for $135,000. An appraisal indicates a value of $100,000 for the building and $35,000 for the land. The seller accepts as part payment a tract of land the company owns, placing a value of $65,000 on it. The company purchased the land three years ago for $50,000. In addition, the seller accepts

capital stock at par value of $20,000, and a ten-year, 10-percent mortgage for $25,000. The balance of the purchase price is paid by check.

(5) Record the data in (4) on the books of the seller. The office building is carried on his books at $90,000 and the land at $40,000.

19. Miles Standish and John Alden form a partnership to operate a laundry and cleaning business to be known as Priscilla Pilgrim's One Day Laundry and Cleaners. The following transactions occur late in June, 1975, prior to the grand opening on July 1, 1975.

(1) Standish contributes a $2,500 check and cleaning equipment, to be used in the business, valued at $3,500.

(2) Alden contributes cash in the amount of $1,500 and a delivery truck valued at $1,500.

(3) The check and cash are deposited in the bank.

(4) The July rent for the business premises of $250 is paid in advance by check.

(5) Cleaning supplies are purchased, on account, from the Wonder Chemical Company for $1,200. A discount of 2 percent is offered for payment within ten days.

(6) One hundred dollars is withdrawn from the bank to be used as a change fund for store operations.

(7) Insurance on the equipment and truck is purchased for a term of one year. The cost, $324, is paid by check.

(8) One thousand dollars is borrowed from the First National Bank. A 120-day, 8-percent note with interest payable at maturity is given, and the proceeds are deposited in the company account.

(9) The Wonder Chemical Company account is paid by check in time to secure the discount.

(10) A cash register is purchased from the American Cash Register Company for $900. Fifty dollars is paid by check and the balance is to be paid in ten equal monthly installments starting August 1.

a. Analyze the above transactions in terms of debits and credits. Use the following form:

Transaction No.	Debit or Credit	Cleaning Account Title	Amount
(1)	Debit	Cash on Hand	$2,500
	Debit	Equipment	3,500
	Credit	Miles Standish, Capital	6,000

b. Enter the transactions in skeleton accounts and prepare a balance sheet, the date of which is June 30, 1975. Cross-number the transactions as follows:

Cash on Hand	Equipment	Miles Standish, Capital
(1) 2,500	(1) 3,500	(1) 6,000

20. The following are transactions of Electronics Development Company during September, 1975, the month it is organized.

(1) The company issues 2,750 shares of $10 par value stock for cash at par.

(2) The cash is deposited in the University State Bank.

(3) A factory building is leased for three years, starting October 1, 1975. Monthly rental payments are $2,500. Two months' rent is paid in advance by check.

(4) Factory equipment is purchased from the Potter Equipment Company for $12,500. A check for $5,000 is given in part payment and the balance is to be paid to the supplier on a long-term contract.

(5) Costs of installing the new equipment are: labor, $250; supplies, $75. Checks are issued for the work.

(6) Raw materials are purchased, on account, from Stowman Electronic Supply Company, $3,700.

(7) A check for $700 is received from Arnold Hansen as a deposit on a special order of testing equipment which Electronics is scheduled to build for him. The contract price is $2,800. The cash is deposited in the bank.

(8) Office equipment is purchased. The list price is $275, but a discount of $12 is allowed. A check is issued.

(9) The company hires three employees. An advance of $100 is given to each of them by check. They will begin work on October 1, 1975.

(10) Harold Meyers, an attorney, performed legal services in obtaining the corporate charter. The bill for his services is $500. In order to conserve cash, fifty shares of capital stock are issued to Mr. Meyers.

(11) A $50,000 fire insurance policy is purchased with a one-year coverage. The premium of $250 is paid by check.

a. Analyze these transactions in terms of debits, and credits. Use the form illustrated in Problem 19.

b. Enter the transactions in skeleton accounts and prepare a balance sheet, the date of which is September 30, 1975. Cross-number the transactions as indicated in Problem 19.

21. Philip Gleason opened an appliance repair shop. During the period immediately prior to the opening of the shop, on September 1, 1975, the following transactions occur:

(1) Depositing $3,275 in the bank, Mr. Gleason opens an account for Gleason's Repair Shop. He also brings the tools and equipment he owns into the shop as a business asset. They are valued at $982.

(2) A stock of used appliances is purchased for $433. Payment is made by check.

(3) Mr. Gleason signs a lease for a store for three years at a rental rate of $100 a month. Four months' rent is paid in advance by check.

(4) Mr. Gleason purchases a secondhand automobile for use in the business. List price is $800. Sales tax is $24. A one-year auto license fee is purchased for $18. All payments are made by check.

(5) Robert Hennessey, Mr. Gleason's brother-in-law, agrees to lend $2,500 for use in the business. A one-year promissory note at 8-percent interest is given to Hennessey. The cash is deposited in the bank.

(6) New merchandise costing $873 is purchased by check.

(7) Additional testing equipment costing $790 is ordered. The supplying firm requires a 10-percent deposit with the order. The deposit is made, but delivery of the equipment is not received as of August 31, 1975.

(8) An advertisement in the local newspaper is ordered. The advertisement is to run twelve times after the opening date of the shop. A check for $36 is issued to the newspaper in payment for the first ad.

(9) A one-year insurance premium for the automobile is paid by check, $150.

(10) Mr. Gleason withdraws $500 from the bank account for his personal use.

(11) Decorating of the shop is done by Lloyd Hoff. A bill for $240 is received. (An appropriate asset title is Improvements to Leased Property.)

a. Analyze the transactions in terms of debits and credits. Use the form illustrated for Problem 19.

b. Enter the transactions in skeleton accounts and prepare a balance sheet. Cross-number the transactions as indicated in Problem 19.

22. The following transactions occur during June, 1975, for the Snyder Book Store.

(1) J. R. Snyder's capital contribution is $5,000 in cash, 200 shares of Western Corporation capital stock, and an inventory of books to be sold. The stock is quoted on the New York Stock Exchange at $13 per share, and it will be sold when additional cash is needed. The books are valued at $1,750.

(2) Three months' rent on a store building is paid in advance in cash. The bookstore will occupy the building on July 1. Rental is $200 per month.

(3) Store fixtures are purchased for $3,000, $500 of which is paid in cash and the balance is to be paid in ten equal monthly installments beginning August 1.

(4) The remaining balance of cash is deposited in the bank.

(5) Books costing $2,100 are purchased on account. Terms are 2/10, n/30 (payment is due within thirty days, but a 2-percent discount is offered for payment within ten days).

(6) A one-year insurance policy on the store's contents is purchased. The premium is $120. Payment is made by check.

(7) A check for $250 is issued to the Darwin Equipment Company for a cash register and other operating equipment.

(8) Merchandise costing $1,500 is ordered from a publisher. Delivery is scheduled for July 15.

(9) The merchandise purchased in (5) is paid for by check. Payment is made within the allowable discount period.

(10) One hundred shares of Western Corporation stock are sold, and the proceeds are deposited in the bank account. The amount received, after deducting fees and taxes, is $1,360.

(11) A one-year operating license is obtained from the city. The fee of $150 is paid by check.

a. Record the above transactions in skeleton accounts. Use account titles of your own choosing. Cross-number the entries for the transactions.

b. Prepare a balance sheet for the Snyder Book Store dated June 30, 1975.

Chapter 4

Measuring Business Income

The balance sheet, which we discussed in the previous chapter, reports the financial position of a business, its assets, liabilities, and proprietary equity, at a particular date. Income measurement is usually viewed as being of even greater concern to management, investors, and other agencies. Management and investors want to know whether or not a business is earning income and how much income it is earning. Stated simply, the goal of most businesses is to make money, and the primary source of information about the earning power of a business is the income statement. Its function is to summarize the transactions that produce business income. This chapter is primarily concerned with the accounting and reporting of those transactions.

THE ACCOUNTING PERIOD

The concept of an accounting period is particularly important in measuring business income. An accounting period may be defined as a segment of time for which an income statement (or other operating statement) is prepared and at the end of which a new balance sheet is presented.

At one time accounting periods were not all the same length of time; statements were prepared at some logical time, such as after the round-trip voyage of a ship from England to the colonies or at the completion of a construction project. To facilitate comparison and analysis, modern practice requires the use of a uniform accounting period. For reporting to management the period is frequently a month (or four weeks) or an even shorter period for some firms. Commonly used periods for reporting to stockholders (and others) are three, six, and twelve months. The shorter the period, the more difficult is the preparation of satisfactory statements.

Regardless of what the regular accounting period may be, annual reports must be prepared. Most corporate bylaws require an annual report to stockholders, and income tax laws require annual tax returns. Most firms prepare annual reports at the end of December, but the practice of using a "natural business year" is growing. The natural business year ends on a date that tends to mark the end of an operating cycle, such as a shopping season or when crops are harvested. In many cases this may also come at a time when there is a lull in business activities and inventories are at a relatively low level. For example, the fiscal year (the twelve-month operating period) for Sears, Roebuck and Company ends on January 31.

Types of Operations

The basic nature of business operations involves acquiring goods and services, combining these purchases to turn out a product, and furnishing this product to customers. Enterprises may be classified in terms of the nature of their output. For example, firms are described as engaging in mining, manufacturing, merchandising, finance, or services. Within each firm individual operations may be classified as falling within one of four functions: (1) acquiring resources, (2) fabricating a salable product, (3) selling, and (4) administration. Selling and administrative functions are reasonably similar for all classes of firms. Merchandisers and manufacturers—the two most important classes—can be distinguished by noting that merchandisers usually purchase their salable product in its final form, while manufacturers produce or fabricate their salable goods by combining raw materials, factory labor, and factory facilities.

ACCOUNTING FOR THE STAGES OF OPERATIONS

Assume that capital funds have been secured from owners, stockholders, or creditors and have been recorded. The next step is to record the operations of the enterprise. There are three stages or types of transactions in the accounting for business activities. The first is the acquisition of goods or services. The second is the production or manufacturing stage, in which materials and services are converted into a salable product. The third is the furnishing of goods and services to the public—customers, clients, or tenants of the enterprise. Administrative activities are typically considered to fall within the third stage.

Not all businesses have all three stages; typically only mining and manufacturing do. Retail and wholesale merchandisers carry on few, if any, activities other than buying and selling. The various financial and service enterprises such as banks, insurance companies, hotels, theaters, transportation companies, and professional firms also do not present more than a two-stage operating picture. The two operating stages of merchandising and service concerns will be considered in this chapter; the third stage of a manufacturing firm, production, is the subject of Chapter 5.

The Acquisition of Goods and Services

There are many examples of physical resources acquired for use in operations. For example:

Merchandise by a retailer to be sold to his customers
Raw materials and parts by a manufacturer to be made into his products
Office supplies such as pencils, stationery, ink, and paper clips
Store supplies such as wrapping paper, sacks, and twine
Factory supplies such as lubricants and fuel
Machinery
Tools
Office furniture and equipment
Store fixtures
Land and buildings
Mineral deposits.

Many kinds of services are required in business operations. For example:

Factory labor
Salesmen's services
Supervision and management
Labor used in maintenance and repairs
Legal service
Accounting service
Engineering service
Medical service
Insurance against various risks such as fire, burglary, tornado, injury to employees, damage to property of others, and embezzlement
Advertising services
Utilities—electricity, gas, telephone, and water
Governmental services, paid for either directly or indirectly in the form of taxes.

Accounting for the Acquisition
of Physical Resources

The procedures for acquiring resources such as merchandise, raw materials, and supplies vary from one business to another. A large enterprise will have a purchasing department headed by a purchasing agent and will use a number of specialized order forms. A smaller firm will have less red tape but will carry out the same essential steps. The following procedure is typical of the purchasing process of firms of medium or larger size.

1. *Notification or Request to Order.* Whenever an item is needed, the purchasing department is notified by means of a purchase request or purchase requisition. Since this form merely requests that certain goods be ordered, it does not generate an accounting entry.

2. *Placing of Order.* Next, the order is placed, usually by means of a purchase order. Ordinarily an accounting entry is not made in the accounts for the placing of an order. If a cash deposit is made, an entry is, of course, necessary. For example, if a check for $100 accompanies the order, an appropriate entry would be:

Dr. (asset increase) Advances on Orders 100
   Cr. (asset decrease) Cash in Bank 100

3. *Receipt of the Goods.* When the goods arrive they are unpacked, inspected, and compared with the purchase order or with a separate receiving report prepared for this purpose.

An accounting entry is not made, but the receiving records are carefully prepared and compared with the purchase invoice when it is received from the seller.

4. *Receipt of the Purchase Invoice.* The purchase invoice is a bill that lists the various items purchased together with the price of each item and the total amount of the bill. The seller would describe this document as a sales invoice.

When the invoice is received, the items on it are checked with the receiving records, the prices are checked for correctness, and all calculations are verified. An entry is then made on the books for the purchase. A typical entry, when a cash deposit is not sent with the order, would be:

Dr. (asset increase) Merchandise 200
   Cr. (liability increase) Accounts Payable, Grand
    River Furniture Company 200

Sometimes the invoice will be received before the goods arrive. Since the invoice must be checked with the receiving records before the amount of liability can be determined, no entry will normally be made until steps 3 and 4 are both complete.

5. *Payment of the Bill.* When payment is due, a check is drawn and sent to the creditor. The entry to record the payment of the bill would be:

Dr. (liability decrease) Accounts Payable, Grand
   River Furniture Company 200
   Cr. (asset decrease) Cash in Bank 200

Acquiring merchandise, materials, or other physical assets, then, involves nothing new in the way of accounting procedure. Any such transaction can be handled with the use of the balance sheet accounts already described, and the transactions usually fall into one of the common types, such as the exchange of assets or the increase of an asset accompanied by an increase in a liability. Using these purchased assets in the conduct of the business is a problem of the second (conversion) or third (selling) stage of operations.

Accounting for the Acquisition of Services

Most services are received and used in operations before any opportunity exists to record their acquisition. Labor service cannot be purchased and stored for future use; electricity is consumed as fast as the current flows through the meter. Even in these cases, the service acquisitions can be handled in the same way as the purchase of materials. The entry for acquiring service must be followed immediately by one for recognizing that all of the service had been used. Customarily, in such cases, the acquisition and use are combined in one transaction. Since the use of services is a problem of the conversion or of the selling stage of operations, the appropriate entries will be considered later.

When advance payments are made for services to be received in the future, the transaction is treated in the same manner as the purchase of materials. For instance, the payment of a fire insurance premium of $360 for one year in advance would be recorded as:

    Dr. (asset increase) Unexpired Insurance 360
        Cr. (asset decrease) Cash in Bank   360

Revenue

The major activity of a business enterprise is to provide goods and services to its customers. *Revenue* is the measure of the goods and services furnished to customers. A revenue transaction, like any other, leads to both debit and credit entries. The debit usually results in an increase in an asset such as cash, accounts receivable, or any other asset that the customer may give in exchange for the goods or services. Sometimes, there may be a decrease in liabilities instead of an increase in assets. For example, if a customer had sent cash in advance with his order, then the debit to record the shipping of goods would be to the liability account Advances by Customers.

The credit that results from the earning of revenue may be more complex. Most often, when revenue is earned, assets are used up. In practice there are a few instances in which the amount of consumed assets is so small that it is impractical to attempt to measure and record it. Interest earned on notes receivable is a common example, when the notes are held by a nonbanking enterprise such as a retailer. In terms of the balance sheet accounts, the earning of $60 interest which has not yet been collected would be shown (assuming a corporation) as:

    Dr. (asset increase) Interest Receivable 60
        Cr. (proprietorship increase) Retained Earnings   60

In most instances, there are some costs of consumed assets that can be identified with a revenue transaction. A complete analysis usually involves recording many asset expirations, such as the cost of goods furnished to the customers, supplies used, and a portion of the cost of fixed assets employed in handling and delivering the goods as well as recording an increase in certain liabilities such as wages or the commission earned by the salesman. When the revenue transaction is profitable, the debit recorded exceeds the credits. The excess, representing the profit, is an increase in, and therefore a credit to, a proprietorship account.

Suppose, for example, that a salesman in a store sells an electric refrigerator for $400; the buyer gives $100 in cash and a note for $300 as payment. Further, suppose that the refrigerator cost the store $245, that the salesman gets a commission of $40, and that it is possible to determine other costs as indicated in the analysis which follows:

Dr. (asset increase) Cash on Hand	$100	
Dr. (asset increase) Notes Receivable	300	
Total Revenue		$400
Cr. (asset decrease) Merchandise	$245	
Cr. (liability increase) Commissions Payable	40	
Cr. (liability increase) Wages Payable (to cover the services of other store employees, such as bookkeepers, delivery truck drivers, and janitors)	25	
Cr. (asset decrease) Supplies (to cover various office and store supplies used in connection with the transaction)	13	
Cr. (asset decrease) Store Building (for an "appropriate" amount of store building depreciation)	8	
Total assignable costs or "Expenses"		331
Cr. (proprietorship increase) Retained Earnings (for the profit from the transaction)		$ 69

Do not confuse revenue with cash receipts. Revenue is measured by the amount of goods and services rendered and not by the amount of cash received at the time of the transaction. In the example of the previous paragraph, revenue is $400 even though cash receipts are only $100.

Expenses

The deductions made from revenue in order to arrive at the increase in proprietorship or the "net income" are called *expenses*. All revenue transactions have some expenses. Even the recording of interest has some expense items that might be attached to it. Someone had to compute the amount of interest receivable and record it on the books. Thus, wages were earned and small amounts of paper, ink, heat, light, and shelter were used. Expenses are goods or services used or expired in the revenue-producing process. They are measured by the amount of assets used up or transferred to customers in revenue transactions. In brief, expenses can be described as "gone assets" or assets used up in the production of revenue. *Do not confuse expenses with expenditures.*

PERIODIC ACCUMULATION OF REVENUE AND EXPENSES

It is obviously impracticable to assign to each revenue transaction a share of all of the expenses of running a business, or to assign even as many as were shown above for the sale of the refrigerator. Some figures would be too small to justify their recording. In many cases, such as the depreciation on the store building, no allocation would be obvious, and any allocation would be arbitrary.

Even if such allocations could be made, the results would be unsatisfactory for management. There are thousands of transactions each period. In order to be able to comprehend or monitor the operations of the business and to watch the trend of revenues and expenses, the manager wants data that summarize operations for each accounting period. To meet this need, two new types of accounts, revenue accounts and expense accounts, are used. The causes of changes in proprietorship are classified and accumulated in revenue and expense accounts during the accounting period. These accounts are fundamentally a part of the system of proprietorship accounts, even though they do not appear on the balance sheet. We might say that revenue is a tentative increase in, or credit to, proprietorship, which will be offset by an appropriate amount of expenses before a correct balance sheet can be prepared.

Debit and Credit Rules

The rules for debit and credit in revenue and expense accounts are consistent with the nature of the accounts. Revenue accounts are credited for increases and debited for decreases, the same as other proprietorship accounts. Expense accounts are debited for increases and credited for decreases, since an increase in expense is, in effect, a decrease in proprietorship. Recall that a decrease in proprietorship is shown as a debit.

Any Expense Account			Any Revenue Account	
Dr.	Cr.		Dr.	Cr.
+	−		−	+

Revenue and Expense Entries

The total amount of each revenue transaction is credited to a revenue account. Since these accounts are used to accumulate information for a period of time, the expired costs assignable to the particular revenue transaction need not be determined immediately. The problem of matching revenue and expenses is shifted from the time of the individual transaction to the end of the accounting period. We try to calculate and assign to each accounting period all of the expenses relating to the operations of that period because we assume that these are the appropriate amounts to be charged against all the revenues earned during that period. An account is opened for each type of expense. The amount of expense is debited to the appropriate expense account and credited to the appropriate asset or liability account.

For an example of a revenue account, recall the sale of the refrigerator used earlier in this chapter. (A refrigerator selling for $400 was paid for by $100 cash and a $300 note.) This sale would be recorded as:

Dr. (asset increase) Cash on Hand	100
Dr. (asset increase) Notes Receivable	300
Cr. (revenue) Sales	400

Hereafter, all sales are recorded in revenue accounts. It is possible that expense entries would also be made at the time of the sale for the cost of the refrigerator and for the salesman's commission if these amounts were readily available.

Dr. (expense) Merchandise Cost of Goods Sold	245
Cr. (asset decrease) Merchandise	245
Dr. (expense) Commission Expense	40
Cr. (liability increase) Commissions Payable	40

Selling and Administrative Activities

The debit to Commission Expense in the preceding section records a portion of the selling activities. Recording other selling expenses and many types of administrative activity is illustrated in subsequent sections of this chapter.

In the example, the salesman's commission was charged directly to expense. It could have been recorded as an acquisition of an asset, followed immediately by an entry of the same amount crediting the asset and debiting commission expense. However, in this and most similar cases, an expense account is debited directly. We use this clerical shortcut because the service is acquired and used almost simultaneously. Salesmen's services, to be paid for in the form of commissions, are acquired and used at the same moment. The amount shown in the Commission Expense account simultaneously shows both the amount of resources acquired and the amount used.

Closing Revenue and Expense Accounts

At the end of the accounting period, schedules of revenue and expense items are prepared. Then the revenue and expense accounts are "closed" with resulting net income or net loss transferred to the proprietorship accounts. As a result, no revenue or expense account appears on the balance sheet, nor is any balance in them carried over to the next accounting period.

REVENUE AND EXPENSE ACCOUNT TITLES

The titles of revenue and expense accounts should indicate clearly their special nature. The following list contains some of the more common titles and types of accounts.

Revenue Accounts

Sales or Merchandise Sales. Sales is the most common revenue account. The principal source of revenue of all retailing, wholesaling, and manufacturing concerns is the selling of goods to customers.

Repair Service Revenue. Repair Service Revenue is used to record revenue from such services as automobile repairs by a garage. Revenue shown in such an account results from the performance of a service rather than from delivery of a product.

Revenue from Fees. Revenue from Fees is used by doctors, dentists, lawyers, and accountants to show billings for services rendered.

Rent Revenue. The revenues of apartment houses, office buildings, and so forth are recorded in a Rent Revenue account. It may also be used to record incidental revenue of firms not engaged in real estate activities.

Interest Earned. Alternative titles are: *Interest Revenue, Interest on Notes Receivable,* and *Interest on Investments.*

Expense Accounts

Cost of Sales. Alternative titles are *Merchandise Cost of Goods Sold* or *Manufacturing Cost of Goods Sold.* These titles are used to record the costs which were incurred in the purchasing or manufacturing goods that have been sold.

Selling and Delivery Expenses. Selling and delivery expenses are shown in accounts with titles such as:

> *Advertising* (newspaper, magazine, billboard, and so forth)
> *Salesmen's Salaries*
> *Salesmen's Commissions*
> *Salesmen's Traveling Expenses*
> *Printing* (catalogs, pamphlets, and so forth)
> *Postage* (as in direct mail advertising)
> *Delivery Wages*
> *Delivery Supplies*
> *Depreciation of Delivery Equipment*
> *Payroll Taxes* (for sales personnel).

General and Administrative Expenses. General and administrative expenses are shown in accounts with titles such as:

> *Salaries—Executives* (if there is a sales manager, his salary would be a selling expense)
> *Salaries—Office*
> *Janitors' Wages and Supplies*
> *Taxes—Property*
> *Taxes—Corporation*
> *Payroll Taxes* (for office personnel, janitors, and executives)

Office Supplies
Depreciation—Office Furniture and Fixtures
Telephone and Telegraph
Insurance (fire, theft, tornado, life, and so forth)
Rent.

These titles do not form a complete list of revenue and expense accounts but are, rather, suggestions of the various accounts which may be needed.

ILLUSTRATION: MERCHANDISING CONCERN

Richard Trumball operates a small candy store. He does all of the work himself and therefore has no payroll transactions. On March 31, 1975, the balances in asset and equity accounts used for the store are given in Schedule 4.1.

SCHEDULE 4.1

	Dr.	Cr.
Cash on Hand	$ 50	
Cash in Bank	417	
Merchandise	1,004	
Store Fixtures—Acquisition Cost	1,920	
Store Fixtures—Accumulated Depreciation		$ 320
Accounts Payable—Southern Candy Company		351
Richard Trumball, Capital		2,720
	$3,391	$3,391

A summary of the store's transactions for the month of April, 1975, is as follows:

(1) Purchases from the Southern Candy Company, all on account, $1,417

(2) Sales, all for cash, $1,985

(3) Deposits in bank, $1,940

(4) Store rent for month paid by check, $300

(5) Payment to Southern Candy Company by check, $1,502

(6) Store supplies purchased for cash and used, $37

(7) Depreciation of store fixtures, $20

(8) The merchandise cost of goods sold for the month, $1,053

Solution: Transactions Analyzed

Each transaction must, of course, be analyzed in terms of debits and credits.

(1) Recording merchandise purchases will be considered in detail later, but with the accounts employed so far, the purchase would be treated as an addition to the Merchandise account.

```
Dr. Merchandise ............................................. 1,417
    Cr. Accounts Payable—Southern Candy Co. ................        1,417
```

(2) This is a summary of the store's revenue transactions for the period.

```
Dr. Cash on Hand ..................................... 1,985
    Cr. Sales ..............................................        1,985
```

(3) Bank deposits merely result in a transfer from one asset account to another.

```
Dr. Cash in Bank ..................................... 1,940
    Cr. Cash on Hand ......................................        1,940
```

(4) The store building has been used for months, so Rent Expense is charged. This is an example of the "short-cut" procedure. A more complete recording would debit Rent Services and credit Cash in Bank; this would be followed by a debit to Rent Expense and a credit to Rent Services. The short-cut entry produces the same effect, of course.

```
Dr. Rent Expense ..................................... 300
    Cr. Cash in Bank ......................................        300
```

(5) This expenditure reduces a liability. It illustrates the fact that *expenditure* and *expense* are not synonymous.

```
Dr. Accounts Payable—Southern Candy Co. .................... 1,502
    Cr. Cash in Bank ......................................        1,502
```

(6) The store supplies have been used; hence, they are treated as an expense.

```
Dr. Store Supplies Expense ................................... 37
    Cr. Cash on Hand ......................................        37
```

(7) A portion of the service life of the store fixtures has been used, and a corresponding portion of the cost of the store fixtures is "charged off" as an expense.

```
Dr. Depreciation of Store Fixtures (an expense account) ........ 20
    Cr. Store Fixtures—Accumulated Depreciation .............        20
```

The credit could logically go to the Store Fixtures account. However, it is customary to record plant assets at acquisition cost and to record the periodic credits representing reduction of plant assets arising from depreciation in a separate account called Accumulated Depreciation. A separate Accumulated Depreciation account is usually opened for each asset or group of assets. The credit balance of $320 in the Store Fixtures— Accumulated Depreciation account is the total depreciation charged through March 31, 1975, on the fixtures. On the balance sheet, the Accumulated Depreciation account appears as a deduction from the asset to which it relates. It is known as a *contra* account, one which accumulates subtractions from another account.

(8) The cost of merchandise sold during the month was \$1,053. (The determination of merchandise cost of goods sold will be treated in the chapter on inventories.)

Dr. Merchandise Cost of Goods Sold 1,053
    Cr. Merchandise 1,053

Solution: Skeleton Accounts

The skeleton accounts are brought up to date at the end of April. The opening balances have been taken from the March 31, 1975, list shown in Schedule 4.1.

Cash on Hand

Bal.	50	(3)	1,940
(2)	1,985	(6)	37

Cash in Bank

Bal.	417	(4)	300
(3)	1,940	(5)	1,502

Merchandise

Bal.	1,004	(8)	1,053
(1)	1,417		

Store Fixtures—Acquisition Cost

Bal.	1,920

Store Fixtures—Accumulated Depreciation

		Bal.	320
		(7)	20

Accounts Payable—Southern Candy Co.

(5)	1,502	Bal.	351
		(1)	1,417

Richard Trumball, Capital

	Bal.	2,720

Sales

	(2)	1,985

Rent Expense

(4)	300

Store Supplies Expense

(6)	37

Depreciation of Store Fixtures

(7)	20

Merchandise Cost of Goods Sold

(8)	1,053

Figure 4.1

The Trial Balance

At the close of an accounting period, a list is usually prepared showing the title and balance of each account. The list is prepared on a sheet of paper that has two columns at the right side of the sheet. If an account has a debit balance, the amount is entered in the left-hand column; if it has a credit balance, the amount is entered in the right-hand column. When the list is complete, the two columns are added and the totals should be equal. Such a schedule is known as a *trial balance*. Data from the trial balance at March 31, 1975, are shown in Schedule 4.1. A trial balance for the Richard Trumball Store on April 30, 1975, is shown in Schedule 4.2.

SCHEDULE 4.2

RICHARD TRUMBALL STORE
Trial Balance
April 30, 1975

Cash on Hand	$ 58	
Cash in Bank	555	
Merchandise	1,368	
Store Fixtures—Acquisition Cost	1,920	
Store Fixtures—Accumulated Depreciation		$ 340
Accounts Payable—Southern Candy Company		266
Richard Trumball, Capital		2,720
Sales		1,985
Rent Expense	300	
Store Supplies Expense	37	
Depreciation of Store Fixtures	20	
Merchandise Cost of Goods Sold	1,053	
	$5,311	$5,311

The trial balance serves two important functions. First, it is a test of arithmetic. If equal debits and credits have been made in analyzing each transaction and no errors have been made in calculating the account balances, the two totals of the trial balance should be equal. A little experience will soon demonstrate, however, that it is possible to have a trial balance which is in balance even though errors have been made in the bookkeeping. For example, if an entry is completely omitted, or if the wrong account is debited or credited, the trial balance will still be in balance.

Second, the trial balance assists in the preparation of the balance sheet and the income statement. All of the accounts that have been used during the period and do not have zero balances are listed; then they can be reorganized into statement form. Since this trial balance is taken before the closing entries are made and before the financial statements are prepared, it is known as a *pre-closing trial balance.*

Although the trial balance is frequently useful in determining arithmetic accuracy and in facilitating statement preparations, it is not an essential part of the record-keeping process. If no recording errors have been made, the succeeding steps can be taken without first preparing a trial balance.

The Income Statement

Probably the most important statement prepared periodically from accounting records is the *income statement,* which summarizes the revenue and expense transactions. Some alternative titles are *statement of earnings* and *profit and loss statement.* It presents an analysis of the results of operations for the period. The form will vary somewhat with the type of enterprise and the complexity of the situation. The common practice is to present the revenue accounts first. They are followed by the expense accounts, the total of which is subtracted from the total revenue to obtain the *net income.*

The statement in Schedule 4.3 would be appropriate for the preceding illustration. Other variations of the statement will be presented later.

SCHEDULE 4.3

RICHARD TRUMBALL STORE
Income Statement
Month of April, 1975

Revenue		
Sales		$1,985
Expenses		
Merchandise Cost of Goods Sold	$1,053	
Rent Expense	300	
Store Supplies Expense	37	
Depreciation of Store Fixtures	20	
Total Expenses		1,410
Net Income		$ 575

The Balance Sheet

The balance sheet can be prepared next. All of the amounts needed except the owner's capital can be taken from the trial balance. Trumball's capital must be computed by adding the amount of net income for the period to the capital figure shown in the trial balance, which is Trumball's capital at the *beginning* of the period. The calculation of the new capital figure must be displayed in the statements to show the connection between the two statements. This is usually done in one of three places: in the proprietorship section of the balance sheet (as in this illustration), at the end of the income statement, or in a separate schedule of proprietorship or retained earnings. If the total of the asset accounts in the balance sheet equals the total in the equity accounts when the newly computed figure for owner's capital is used, the statements probably are arithmetically correct. This balancing, however, is not a proof of the correctness of the analysis of transactions that precedes the preparation of the statements. The balance sheet as of April 30, 1975, for the Richard Trumball Store is shown in Schedule 4.4.

SCHEDULE 4.4

RICHARD TRUMBALL STORE
Balance Sheet
April 30, 1975

Assets

Current Assets

Cash on Hand	$ 58	
Cash in Bank	555	
Merchandise	1,368	
Total Current Assets		$1,981

Noncurrent Assets

Store Fixtures	$1,920	
Less: Accumulated Depreciation	340	
Total Noncurrent Assets		1,580
Total Assets		$3,561

Liabilities and Proprietorship

Current Liabilities

Accounts Payable		$ 266

Proprietorship

Richard Trumball, Capital:

Balance, April 1, 1975	$2,720	
Net Income for April	575	
Balance, April 30, 1975		3,295
Total Liabilities and Proprietorship		$3,561

Closing Entries

The revenue and expense accounts were opened for the purpose of accumulating the details of operating results, or changes in proprietorship, for one accounting period. Now their balances must be eliminated so that the accounts will be prepared to record the data of the next accounting period. The basic process is simple: each revenue account must be debited with the amount of its current credit balance, and each expense account credited with its debit balance. The difference required to equate debits and credits is the net income or loss and is recorded in the proprietorship accounts.

(9) This is the simplest of several different procedures that are sometimes used to record closing entries. Others will be illustrated later.

Dr. Sales 1,985
    Cr. Merchandise Cost of Goods Sold 1,053
    Cr. Rent Expense 300
    Cr. Store Supplies Expense 37
    Cr. Depreciation of Store Fixtures 20
    Cr. Richard Trumball, Capital 575

The accounts, after the closing entry **(9)** is recorded and all closed accounts are ruled, are shown in Figure 4.2. Note that the revenue and expense accounts now have zero balances and are ready for recording the transactions of May.

Cash on Hand					**Cash in Bank**			
Bal.	50	**(3)**	1,940		**Bal.**	417	**(4)**	300
(2)	1,985	**(6)**	37		**(3)**	1,940	**(5)**	1,502

Merchandise					**Store Fixtures—Acquisition Cost**		
Bal.	1,004	**(8)**	1,053		**Bal.**	1,920	
(1)	1,417						

Store Fixtures— Accumulated Depreciation					**Accounts Payable— Southern Candy Company**			
		Bal.	320		**(5)**	1,502	**Bal.**	351
		(7)	20				**(1)**	1,417

Richard Trumball, Capital					**Sales**			
		Bal.	2,720		**(9)**	1,985	**(2)**	1,985
		(9)	575					

Rent Expense					**Store Supplies Expense**			
(4)	300	**(9)**	300		**(6)**	37	**(9)**	37

Depreciation of Store Fixtures					**Merchandise Cost of Goods Sold**			
(7)	20	**(9)**	20		**(8)**	1,053	**(9)**	1,053

Figure 4.2

As an added insurance that the accounts are ready for recording the transactions of the next period, a trial balance can be taken after the closing entries have been made. Such a trial balance is labeled a *post-closing trial balance* and contains the balances of only those accounts appearing in the balance sheet. The debit and credit column totals should, of course, be equal to one another, but they may exceed total assets and total equities because contra accounts, like Accumulated Depreciation, are shown as deductions from the accounts they are contra to on the balance sheet. Thus if store fixtures cost $1,920 and have $340 of accumulated depreciation, the balance sheet assets total includes only the net amount, $1,580.

Income Summary Account

Notice that in entry (9), all expense and revenue accounts are closed and the residual (credit, in this example) is closed to the owner's capital account. In working problems, using an Income Summary account will often be helpful at this stage. The Income Summary account merely serves as a surrogate for the income statement. All revenue accounts are closed to the Income Summary as credits, and all expense accounts are closed to the Income Summary as debits. The balance in the Income Summary, after these closing entries are made, is then closed to the appropriate ownership or proprietorship account. If an Income Summary account were being used for the Richard Trumball Store, entry (9) would have been replaced by the following series of entries.

Dr. Sales	1,985	
Cr. Income Summary		1,985
To close revenue account to Income Summary.		
Dr. Income Summary	1,053	
Cr. Merchandise Cost of Goods Sold		1,053
Dr. Income Summary	300	
Cr. Rent Expense		300
Dr. Income Summary	37	
Store Supplies Expense		37
Dr. Income Summary	20	
Cr. Depreciation of Store Fixtures		20
To close expense accounts to Income Summary.		

At this point, the Income Summary account has a credit balance of $575, and all revenue and expense accounts have been closed. The balance in the Income Summary account can then be closed to the owner's equity account with this entry:

Dr. Income Summary	575	
Cr. Richard Trumball, Capital		575

This sequence of steps has exactly the same effect as entry (9) illustrated earlier. When transactions are analyzed with T-accounts, an extra T-account for the income summary will often prove helpful in calculating the income for the period. The closing procedures both with and without an Income Summary account are discussed in more detail in Chapter 11.

SUMMARY AND CONCLUSIONS

Two new groups of accounts have been introduced in this chapter. Chapters 2 and 3 introduced the asset, liability, and proprietorship accounts, which appear on the balance sheet. This chapter introduces the expense and revenue accounts, which appear on the income statement. Revenue accounts show the amounts for goods and services furnished, and expense accounts accumulate the cost of the services expended in earning the revenue. The difference between revenue and expenses, called the net income (or net loss), measures the increase (or decrease) in proprietorship that has resulted from business operations.

In terms of the balance sheet, the revenue and expense accounts belong in the proprietorship group. Increases in expenses reduce proprietorship; increases in revenues increase it. The relationship and the rules for debit and credit can be expressed diagrammatically as shown in Figure 4.3.

Proprietorship

Dr.	Cr.
—	+

Expenses		**Revenue**	
Dr.	Cr.	Dr.	Cr.
+	—	—	+

Figure 4.3

At the end of an accounting period, the revenue and expense accounts provide the information needed to prepare the income statement. After the income statement is prepared, the revenue and expense accounts are closed, and the balance, which shows net income or net loss, is entered in the permanent proprietorship accounts—retained earnings for a corporation, or the owners' capital accounts for an unincorporated enterprise. Notice that the accounts to be closed are the ones that enter into the calculation of net income on the income statement.

QUESTIONS AND PROBLEMS

1. Why is it important to have a record of goods on order even though such information is not entered in the formal accounting records?

2. Prices and quantities are sometimes blocked out on the copies of the purchase order sent to the receiving department. What is the purpose of this?

3. "The concept of the accounting period is among the most important of accounting concepts." Why is it important?

4. Expense and revenue accounts are useful accounting devices, but they can be dispensed with. What is the alternative to their use?

5. Despite the earning of substantial amounts of revenue during a period, proprietorship may decrease instead of increase. How?

*6. Indicate the amount of revenue, if any, in each of the following transactions:

* Hints, key numbers, or (partial) answers appear in the back of the book between the Appendix Tables and the Glossary.

a. Goods that cost $700 are sold for $800 cash.

b. Goods that cost $700 are sold on account for $800.

c. Goods that cost $800 are sold on account for $800.

d. Goods that cost $850 are sold for $800 cash.

e. Cash of $800 is received from a customer to apply on his account.

f. A deposit of $800 is received on a $20,000 order for goods.

g. Bonds are issued for $20,000 cash.

h. Shares of stock are issued for $20,000 cash.

7. How much revenue is earned during the month of May in each of the following transactions?

a. Collection of cash from customers during May for merchandise sold and delivered in April, $5,200.

b. Sales of merchandise during May for cash, $3,600.

c. Sales of merchandise during May to customers to be collected in June, $5,400.

d. A store building is rented to a toy shop for $600 a month, effective May 1. A check for $1,200 for two months' rent is received on May 1.

e. Data of (d), except that no collection is received from the tenant in May.

8. Indicate the amount of expense for March, if any, in each of the following situations:

a. Three months' rent $1,800 was paid on March 1, for the period through May 31.

b. An advance on his April salary is paid to a salesman on March 28, $100.

c. Property taxes on the store building for the year of $1,200 were paid in January.

d. A salesman earned $800 in commissions during March, but he has not yet been paid.

e. Cost of equipment purchased on March 26 to be put into operation April 1, $5,000.

f. Eight hundred dollars of supplies were purchased during March. On March 1, supplies were on hand which cost $300. On March 31, supplies which cost $400 were still on hand.

g. Data of (f), except that $200 in supplies were on hand at March 1.

h. At March 1, the balance in the Unexpired Insurance account was $4,800. The insurance policy has 24 months to run at that time.

9. Give appropriate debits and credits for those transactions in the following list which require such formal analysis.

(1) The purchasing department receives a notice from the stockroom that the supply of ½-inch plywood has reached the minimum point.

(2) A purchase order is sent to the Central Lumber Company for $8,000 of this material.

(3) An acknowledgment of the order is received. It indicates that delivery will be made in fifteen days but that the price has been raised so that the material will be billed at $8,400.

(4) The shipment of plywood arrives and is checked by the receiving department. The correct quantity has been delivered.

(5) The purchase invoice arrives. The amount of $8,400 is subject to a 2-percent discount if paid within ten days. The bill is recorded at the net amount after deducting the discount available.

(6) On reinspection, goods with a gross invoice price of $100 are found to be defective and are returned to the vendor.

(7) The balance of the amount due the Central Lumber Company is paid in time to obtain the discount.

10. Give the debits which should be made upon the receipt of each of the following invoices by Sake's Department Store:

(1) The American Textile Mills, for a shipment of men's hosiery, $2,000.

(2) Smith's Garage, for repairs to delivery trucks, $140.

(3) The Hanna Furniture Company, for a desk to be used in the merchandise manager's office, $220.

(4) General Elevator Company, for repairs to elevators, $180.

(5) The *Daily News*, for newspaper advertising, $350.

(6) City Water Department, for water used during the month, $56.

(7) The *Marketing Journal*, subscription to a trade publication for a year in advance, $28.

(8) The Ace Maintenance Company, for building maintenance services, $300.

11. The following costs are incurred in connection with the purchase of a heavy piece of machinery: manufacturer's invoice price for the machine, $12,000; freight, $350; trucking from railroad depot to factory, $80; cost of constructing a special foundation, $420; special electric wiring, $50; installation, $300. What cost should be recorded for the machine? Why?

°12. Give the title of the account that would be debited and the amount of the debit in each of the following transactions:

(1) A firm of certified public accountants sends us a bill for $780 for the installation of a cost-accounting system.

(2) Marketable securities are purchased for $4,500 plus $90 for the broker's commission.

(3) A bill for $750 is received from Ronald and North, Attorneys at Law, for negotiating the purchase of a tract of land and checking title to it.

(4) A cashier leaves town with $3,000 of the firm's money. The loss is covered by insurance.

13. How would you allocate the cost of the following assets over their useful lives?

a. A building with an estimated useful life of thirty years.

b. A road leading to a timber tract. The road would normally last for fourteen years before extensive reconstruction would be necessary, but it is expected that the timber will all be cut in five years.

c. Rent prepaid for two years on a warehouse in Minneapolis.

d. A truck with an estimated service life of 90,000 miles.

e. Rent prepaid for a year on a shop used for boat repairs at a summer resort. The shop is open only from June 1 to September 15.

f. An ore deposit owned by a mining company.

°14. The trial balance of the Star Photographers at June 30, 1975, is on page 82.

a. Analyze the closing entries in terms of debits and credits. Use an Income Summary account. Profits and losses are divided equally between the partners.

STAR PHOTOGRAPHERS
Trial Balance
June 30, 1975

Accounts Payable		$ 1,800
Accounts Receivable	$ 3,900	
Advertising	1,500	
Roger P. Hinds, Capital		12,069
Cameras and Equipment	13,500	
Cash in Bank	2,451	
Depreciation—Cameras and Equipment	180	
Depreciation—Furniture and Fixtures	105	
Electricity	300	
Equipment Repairs	180	
FICA Tax Payable		486
Steve S. Jones, Capital		12,069
Furniture and Fixtures	9,600	
Insurance Expired	90	
Payroll Taxes	240	
Photographic Supplies on Hand	3,390	
Photographic Supplies Used	1,950	
Rent Expense	1,425	
Revenue—Commercial Photography		18,090
Revenue—Printing Service		4,680
Salaries	10,800	
Telephone Expense	120	
Undeposited Cash	543	
Unexpired Insurance	270	
Withheld Income Tax		1,350
	$50,544	$50,544

b. Set up in skeleton-account form the revenue, expense, Income Summary, and partners' capital accounts. Insert trial balance amounts and record the closing entries.

15. The trial balance on page 83 shows the condition of the accounts of the Sunset Court, an apartment house, after recording all of the transactions of January, 1975.

   a. Prepare a statement of income and retained earnings and a balance sheet.

   b. Analyze the closing entries in terms of debits and credits. Use an Income Summary account.

16. K. C. Peacock rents and operates a small cleaning shop. He does occasional tailoring and repair work and sends all of his cleaning work to a wholesale cleaner. The trial balance of the shop at September 30, 1975, is shown on the next page.

SUNSET COURT
Trial Balance
January 31, 1975

Accounts Payable		$ 8,400
Advances by Tenants		11,400
Building	$1,800,000	
Capital Stock		1,800,000
Cash in Bank	9,600	
Cash on Hand	1,200	
Depreciation of Building	6,000	
Depreciation of Equipment	1,800	
Equipment	240,000	
FICA Tax Payable		108
Insurance Expired	900	
Janitor Supplies on Hand	1,200	
Labor Costs	10,500	
Land	48,000	
Rent Receivable	8,400	
Rent Revenue		43,800
Repair Expense	2,700	
Retained Earnings		271,956
Supplies Used	1,200	
Taxes Expense	3,900	
Unexpired Insurance	900	
Withheld Income Tax		636
	$2,136,300	$2,136,300

Cash on Hand	$ 125	
Cash in Bank	1,200	
Supplies on Hand	1,450	
Accounts Payable, General Cleaners		$ 800
K. C. Peacock, Capital		1,975
	$2,775	$2,775

The following summarized transactions took place during October:

(1) Cash received for cleaning services, $4,900.

(2) Cash received for tailoring services, $1,450.

(3) Cash deposited in the bank, $5,500.

(4) Charge for cleaning services received from General Cleaners, $2,600.

(5) Payments by check to General Cleaners, $2,750.

(6) Supplies purchased and paid from cash, $700.

(7) October rent paid by check, $500.

(8) Other expenses paid from cash, $200.

(9) Supplies used, $900.

(10) Drawings by Peacock by check, $2,000.

Open skeleton accounts and insert the September 30 balances. Record the October transactions. Prepare an income statement for October and a balance sheet as of October 31, 1975.

17. Bill McCall operates a restaurant which he has rented fully equipped from its owner. The trial balance of the restaurant on November 1, 1975 is:

Cash on Hand	$ 675	
Cash in Bank	6,300	
Food on Hand	5,400	
Accounts Payable, Barry Meat Company		$ 1,350
Accounts Payable, Conell Wholesale Grocery		1,575
Payroll Tax Payable		621
Withheld Income Taxes		882
Bill McCall, Capital		7,947
	$12,375	$12,375

Open skeleton accounts and enter the above balances. Record the following selected transactions, which occurred during the month of November.

(1) Cash received from meals served, $26,550.

(2) Cash deposited in the bank, $26,100.

(3) Rent paid by check, $4,050.

(4) Food purchased on account from the Conell Wholesale Grocery, $7,650.

(5) Repairs to equipment paid with cash, $450.

(6) Food purchased on account from the Barry Meat Company, $4,725.

(7) Withheld income tax and payroll tax for October paid by check, $1,503.

(8) Payment to Barry Meat Company by check, $4,950.

(9) Payment to Conell Wholesale Grocery by check, $7,425.

(10) Salaries for the month, paid by check, $7,200, less $162 for payroll taxes and $765 for withheld income taxes.

(11) The employer's share of payroll taxes for the month is $378.

(12) Cost of food used, $11,925.

Take a trial balance to check the accuracy of your entries.

18. The balance sheet accounts of the Stylish Barber Shop at June 30, 1975, are as follows:

Cash on Hand	$ 200	
Cash in Bank	1,000	
Supplies on Hand	300	
Prepaid Magazine Subscriptions	60	
Furniture and Equipment	6,000	
Accounts Payable, Republic Supply Company		$ 400
Rent Payable		200
Equipment Contract Payable		2,000
Don Simson, Capital		2,480
Mark Evans, Capital		2,480
	$7,560	$7,560

A summary of the business for the month of July is as follows:

(1) Cash received from customers, $2,000.

(2) Cash deposited in the bank account, $1,950.

(3) Payment by check of an installment on the equipment contract, $400 plus interest for one month on the old balance at 8 percent per annum. (Debit Interest Charges for the amount of the interest.)

(4) Payment by check of rent for June and July, $400.

(5) Supplies purchased on account from the Republic Supply Company, $200.

(6) Payment for newspapers for the month, $8 from the cash drawer.

(7) Payments by check to the Republic Supply Company, $440.

(8) A bill is received from the Bright Laundry Service for laundry service for the month, $50.

(9) Supplies used, $340.

(10) Magazine subscription expirations applicable to the month of July, $10.

(11) Depreciation of furniture and equipment, $100.

(12) Each partner drew $400 for his personal use. Checks were written for this purpose.

Open skeleton accounts and insert the opening balances. Record the transactions for the month. Prepare a trial balance to check the accuracy of your work.

19. Give the debits to be made for each of the following bills which have been received by the Elite Appliance Company:

(1) From Western Electric Supply Company, $864 for repair parts.

(2) From Touch & Rose, certified public accountants, $200 for services in filing income tax returns.

(3) From the General Electric Company, $9,560, for refrigerators.

(4) From the White Stationery Company, $150, for office supplies.

(5) From the Showy Sign Company, $470, for a neon sign.

(6) From the Universal Lumber Company, $300; $250 of the lumber was used to construct display counters and $50 for repairs to the building.

(7) From Schutheis and Schutheis, attorneys, $750, for legal services in changing from the corporate to the partnership form of organization.

(8) From the Bell Telephone Company, $46, for the telephone service.

(9) From the Madison Avenue Garage, $52, for gasoline and oil used by the delivery truck.

(10) From the Municipal Electric Department, $126, for electricity used for lighting.

20. A corporation known as the Jackson Collection Agency is organized by Billy Jackson and Richard Henry. The business of the firm is to collect old accounts receivable of various clients on a commission basis. Open skeleton accounts and record the following selected transactions.

(1) Jackson, who has been in the same business before and has a number of clients who will patronize the new firm, contributes office supplies worth $2,000 and cash of $8,000. He is issued stock certificates for 500 shares with a par value of $30 a share, his goodwill contribution being valued at $5,000.

(2) Henry contributes $2,000 in cash and office equipment valued at $10,000. He is issued stock certificates for 400 shares.

(3) Cash, in the amount of $9,500, is deposited in the bank.

(4) The Jackson agency collected $800 on an account that was turned over to it by the Giggly Market. The commission earned is 50 percent of the amount collected.

(5) The cash collected in (4) is deposited in the bank.

(6) The stenographer's salary of $500 is paid by check. A deduction of $8 is made for payroll tax and $52 for income tax.

(7) A bill is received from Lyband and Linn, certified public accountants, for $300 to cover the cost of installing an accounting system.

(8) The amount due the Giggly Market [see (4)] is paid by check.

(9) An office is leased and the rent paid for three months in advance. A check is drawn for $1,200.

(10) An automobile is purchased for $3,500; $2,500 is paid by check, and an installment contract, payable to the Scotch Automobile Sales Company, is signed for the balance.

Prepare a trial balance. Indicate by a cross (X) accounts which are revenue or expense accounts.

21. The balance sheet accounts of Drake's Radio Shop at June 30, 1975, are as follows:

Cash on Hand	$ 50	
Cash in Bank	1,670	
Repair Parts on Hand	600	
Office Supplies on Hand	80	
Shop Equipment	1,200	
Office Equipment	600	
Accounts Payable		$2,200
Robert Drake, Capital		2,000
	$4,200	$4,200

A summary of the transactions for July is as follows:

(1) Performed repair services, for which $600 in cash was received immediately.

(2) Performed additional repair work, $200, and sent bills to customers for this amount.

(3) Paid creditors by check, $400.

(4) Took out insurance on equipment and issued a check to cover a year's premium of $72.

(5) Paid $40 out of cash on hand for a series of advertisements that appeared in the local newspaper during July.

(6) Issued check for $100 for rent of shop space for July.

(7) Paid telephone bill by check for the month, $20.

(8) Collected $80 of the amount charged to customers in item (2).

(9) Deposited $550 cash in the bank (from cash on hand).

(10) The insurance expired during July is calculated at $6.

(11) Cost of repair parts used during the month, $80.

(12) Cost of office supplies used during July, $20.

(13) Depreciation of shop equipment for the month is estimated at $10, and of office equipment, $4.

a. Open skeleton accounts and record the opening balances and the transactions for the month.

b. Prepare a trial balance at July 31, 1975.

c. Prepare an income statement and a balance sheet.

22. The trial balance of Speedy Cleaners and Dyers at February 28, 1975, is shown below. The books have not been closed since December 31, 1974.

Cash on Hand	$ 360	
Cash in Bank	3,200	
Accounts Receivable	15,200	
Supplies on Hand	4,800	
Unexpired Insurance	1,040	
Shop Equipment	44,000	
Trucks	7,200	
Office Furniture and Fixtures	3,200	
Accounts Payable		$ 4,800
Withheld Income Taxes		1,240
Payroll Taxes Payable		940
P. O. Frey, Capital		60,000
Sales		46,060
Wages—Shop Labor	20,800	
Wages and Commissions—Truck Drivers	3,400	
Office Salaries	2,400	
Outside Work	2,040	
Advertising	400	
Depreciation of Trucks	—	
Repairs, Insurance, Gas, etc.—Trucks	260	
Rent Expense	1,200	
Repairs and Maintenance—Shop	240	
Power, Gas and Water	780	
Telephone Expense	100	
Payroll Taxes	1,320	
Shop Supplies Used	—	
Office Supplies Used	—	
Depreciation—Shop Equipment	—	
Depreciation—Office Furniture & Fixtures	—	
Insurance Expense—Shop	—	
Miscellaneous Expense	1,100	
	$113,040	$113,040

A summary of the transactions for the month of March, 1975, is as follows:

(1) Sales: For cash, $14,000; on account, $5,800.

(2) Collections on account, $10,000.

(3) Cash deposited in the bank, $23,800.

(4) Purchases of outside work (cleaning done by wholesale cleaners), $800, on account.

(5) Purchases of supplies, on account, $2,800.

(6) Payments on account, by check, $4,000.

(7) Rent paid by check, $600.

(8) February payroll taxes and withheld income taxes were paid by check, $2,180.

(9) Supplies used (for the quarter): shop, $4,800; office, $540.

(10) Depreciation (for the quarter): shop equipment, $1,720; trucks, $600; office furniture and fixtures, $100.

(11) Wages, commissions, and salaries paid by check:

Shop labor	$10,000	
Truck drivers	1,600	
Office	1,200	
Total amount earned		$12,800
Less: Payroll taxes withheld	$ 288	
Income taxes withheld	1,392	
		1,680
Total amount paid		$11,120

(12) Employer's share of payroll taxes, $672.

(13) Bills received but not paid by the end of the month: advertising, $200; repairs to trucks, $60; power, gas, and water, $320; telephone, $60.

(14) Insurance expired (for the quarter): fire, theft, and damage to customers' clothing, $320; trucks, $80.

a. Open skeleton accounts and enter the trial balance figures.

b. Record the transactions for the month of March. Cross-number the entries.

c. Prepare a trial balance at March 31, 1975, an income statement for the three months ending March 31, 1975, and a balance sheet as of March 31, 1975.

d. Record the closing entries.

*23. (This problem and the next three are adapted from problems by George H. Sorter.) Prima Company presents the following incomplete trial balance as well as a statement of cash receipts and disbursements:

Debits

	1/1/75	12/31/75
Cash	$?	$?
Accounts Receivable	36,000	41,000
Merchandise Inventory	55,000	49,500
Accrued Interest Receivable	1,000	700
Prepaid Costs	4,000	5,200
Building, Machinery & Equipment	47,000	47,000
Total Debits	$?	$?

Credits

	1/1/75	12/31/75
Accounts Payable (Miscellaneous Services)	$ 2,000	$ 2,500
Accounts Payable (Merchandise)	34,000	41,000
Accrued Property Taxes Payable	1,000	1,500
Accumulated Depreciation	10,000	12,000
Mortgage Payable	35,000	30,000
Capital Stock	25,000	25,000
Retained Earnings	76,000	?
Total Credits	$183,000	$211,200

Cash Receipts	Year of 1975
1. Collection from Credit Customers	$144,000
2. Cash Sales	63,000
3. Collection of Interest	1,000
	$208,000

Less: Cash Disbursements	
4. Payment to Suppliers of Merchandise	$114,000
5. Repayment on Mortgage	5,000
6. Payment of Interest	500
7. Payment to Suppliers of Miscellaneous Services	57,500
8. Payment of Property Taxes	1,200
9. Payment of Dividends	2,000
	$180,200
Increase in Cash Balance for Year	$ 27,800

Prepare a statement of income and retained earnings for the year 1975.

24. Primus Company presents the following incomplete trial balance as well as a statement of cash receipts and disbursements:

Debits

	1/1/75	12/31/75
Cash	$?	$?
Accounts Receivable	41,000	50,000
Merchandise Inventory	49,500	52,000
Accrued Interest Receivable	700	500
Prepaid Costs	5,200	5,500
Building, Machinery & Equipment	47,000	47,000
Total Debits	$?	$?

Credits

	1/1/75	12/31/75
Accounts Payable (Miscellaneous Services)	$ 2,500	$ 3,000
Accounts Payable (Merchandise)	41,000	53,000
Accrued Property Taxes Payable	1,500	1,000
Accumulated Depreciation	12,000	14,000
Mortgage Payable	30,000	25,000
Capital Stock	25,000	25,000
Retained Earnings	?	?
Total Credits	$211,200	$?

Cash Receipts	Year of 1975
1. Collection from Credit Customers	$150,000
2. Cash Sales	66,000
3. Collection of Interest	1,000
	$217,000
Less: Cash Disbursements	
4. Payment to Suppliers of Merchandise	$120,000
5. Repayment on Mortgage	5,000
6. Payment of Interest	500
7. Payment to Suppliers of Miscellaneous Services	60,000
8. Payment of Property Taxes	1,200
9. Payment of Dividends	2,000
	$188,700
Increase in Cash Balance for year	$ 28,300

Prepare statement of income and retained earnings for the year of 1975.

*25. The Secunda Company presents the following post-closing trial balance at the beginning of 1975 and the pre-closing trial balance for the end of 1975.

Debits

	1/1/75	12/31/75
Cash	$ 20,000	$ 9,000
Accounts Receivable	36,000	51,000
Merchandise Inventory	45,000	60,000
Prepayments	2,000	1,000
Land, Buildings, and Equipment	40,000	40,000
Cost of Goods Sold	—	50,000
Interest Charges	—	3,000
Operating Expenses	—	29,000
Total Debits	$143,000	$243,000

Credits

Accumulated Depreciation	$ 16,000	$ 18,000
Interest Payable	1,000	2,000
Accounts Payable	30,000	40,000
Mortgage Payable	20,000	17,000
Capital Stock	50,000	50,000
Retained Earnings	26,000	16,000
Sales	—	100,000
Total Credits	$143,000	$243,000

All goods and services acquired during the year were bought "on account." Operating expenses include depreciation charges and expiration of prepayments.

Prepare a schedule showing all cash transactions for the year 1975.

26. The Secundus Company presents the following post-closing trial balance at the beginning of 1975 and the pre-closing trial balance for the end of 1975.

Debits

	1/1/75	12/31/75
Cash	$ 30,000	$ 25,000
Accounts Receivable	54,000	62,000
Merchandise Inventory	68,000	76,000
Prepayments	4,000	3,000
Land, Buildings, and Equipment	40,000	46,000
Cost of Goods Sold	—	87,000
Interest Charges	—	1,000
Operating Expenses	—	32,000
Total Debits	$196,000	$332,000

Credits

	1/1/75	12/31/75
Accumulated Depreciation	$ 24,000	$ 27,000
Interest Payable	1,000	—
Accounts Payable	45,000	51,000
Mortgage Payable	25,000	20,000
Capital Stock	80,000	80,000
Retained Earnings	21,000	19,000
Sales	—	135,000
Total Credits	$196,000	$332,000

All goods and services acquired during the year were bought "on account." Operating expenses include depreciation charges and expiration of prepayments.

Prepare a schedule showing all cash transactions for the year 1975.

Chapter 5

Measuring Business Income— the Manufacturing Firm

Our society is consumer oriented. The accounting procedures for retail and other businesses serving consumers were discussed in the previous chapter. Regardless of how consumer oriented our society becomes, we will always need manufacturers. Retail and service operations involve two basic processes: (1) acquisitions, and (2) sales of products or services. Manufacturing businesses, too, acquire goods and sell products, but they also convert raw materials into finished products. This conversion process introduces several new features that will be described by an illustration of the complete cycle of a manufacturing firm.

USING RESOURCES IN PRODUCTION

The Manufacturing Process

The manufacturing process consists of taking certain materials and converting them into various products. All costs of carrying out this conversion can be classified as one of two kinds: (1) direct factory costs, such as the cost of labor used for manufactured products, and (2) indirect factory costs, often known as overhead costs. Both direct and indirect factory costs are included in the cost of completed products.

Precise criteria for delimiting the costs to be included in overhead cannot be provided. A common, general rule is to count all costs, other than direct materials and direct labor, that are incurred in producing a product in the factory rather than purchasing it from others as overhead. Costs commonly included in overhead are the wages of truckers, sweepers, foremen, and night watchmen; factory supplies used; heat, light, power, insurance, taxes, and repairs; and part of the cost of long-lived assets being used in the manufacturing operations, that is, depreciation. An alternative treatment of certain overhead costs is described in the section on direct costing later in this chapter.

Accounting for Production

Entering production costs into accounts involves nothing new in principle. Using materials in production is merely a transfer or reclassification of assets; raw materials decrease and work in process increases. *Work in Process* is the title commonly used for the account that accumulates the cost of production until the product is completed. Just like the selling labor described in the previous chapter, factory labor service is ordinarily used as soon as, or even before, it is recorded. Thus the entry to record labor used directly in production can be handled as:

Dr. (asset increase) Work in Process
    Cr. (liability increase) Wages Payable
                or
    Cr. (asset decrease) Cash

Each of the indirect or overhead costs can logically be handled in the same way. A bill for electric power, for example, can be handled correctly as:

Dr. (asset increase) Work in Process
    Cr. (liability increase) Accounts Payable, Edison Power Company

Managers want, however, more detail about the costs of production. It is desirable, then, to introduce into the accounting system a set of accounts which may be characterized as *production cost* accounts. Their function is to accumulate the details of manufacturing costs for a specified period of time, usually the accounting period. At the end of this period, after schedules are prepared for further analysis and comparison, these temporary accounts are closed to the Work in Process account.

Even though they never appear on the balance sheet, these production cost accounts, strictly speaking, are asset accounts, because they show the details of the Work in Process account during the accounting period. Like balance sheet asset accounts, production cost accounts are debited for increases and credited for decreases.

The following list indicates some of the titles that may be used to record the costs of production operations in a manufacturing plant:

Raw Materials Used
Labor Costs
    Direct Labor (labor performed directly on the product)
    Factory Superintendent
    Foremen
    Machine Attendants

Sweepers and Truckers
Timekeepers
Cost Accountants
Power Plant Operators
Repair Service
Engineering
Night Watchman
Overhead or Indirect Costs
Electricity
Water
Gas
Depreciation—Factory Building
Rent of Factory Building
Depreciation—Machinery and Equipment
Depreciation—Tools
Amortization of Patents
Taxes—Property
Factory Supplies Used
Fire and Tornado Insurance
Workmen's Compensation Insurance
Repairs to Factory Building
Repairs to Machinery and Equipment

Some of the production cost titles such as Insurance and Taxes are like those used for expense accounts. Insurance on factory machinery, for example, is a production cost, but insurance on office equipment is an expense of the period. The cost of factory insurance has been converted into partially completed or finished goods, but office insurance costs have expired so that no asset remains. The distinction between production costs and expenses of the time period must be carefully maintained.

Production cost accounts are closed (or transferred) to Work in Process at the end of the accounting period. Then Work in Process must be analyzed to determine costs that remain in the inventory of unfinished goods and costs that should be transferred to the Finished Goods account. The Finished Goods account is comparable to the Merchandise account of a merchandising concern. In recording the final stage of operations, the cost of goods furnished to customers must be recognized by an entry debiting Manufacturing Cost of Goods Sold and crediting Finished Goods.

ILLUSTRATION: A MANUFACTURING CONCERN

Chapter 4 showed the accounting for a small retail store. To illustrate revenue and expense accounts for a firm engaged in manufacturing (or production) activities, the affairs of the Standard Products Company are now considered. The company rents a small factory where it produces engine parts. The trial balance of the company at March 31, 1975, is shown in Schedule 5.1.

SCHEDULE 5.1

STANDARD PRODUCTS COMPANY
Trial Balance
March 31, 1975

Undeposited Cash	$ 400	
Cash in Bank	4,500	
Accounts Receivable—Western Motors Company	4,000	
Accounts Receivable—All Other Customers	8,160	
Raw Materials	2,400	
Work in Process	1,800	
Finished Parts	700	
Factory Equipment	9,960	
Factory Equipment—Accumulated Depreciation		$ 2,420
Office Equipment and Furniture	1,020	
Office Equipment and Furniture—Accumulated Depreciation		340
Accounts Payable—Pine Company		3,400
Wages Payable		880
State Payroll Taxes Payable		270
Federal Payroll Taxes Payable		1,030
Withheld Income Tax		1,250
Capital Stock		22,000
Retained Earnings		1,350
	$32,940	$32,940

In this simplified example we ignore the liability for income taxes. The transactions for April, 1975, are summarized as follows:

1. Raw materials are purchased on account from the Pine Company, $8,000.
2. Sales on account to customers other than Western Motors Company are $26,000.
3. Western Motors Company pays $2,500 and gives a note for $1,500 to settle the amount due from them. The note is received on April 30.
4. Collections from various other customers are $24,800.
5. The receipts of **3.** and **4.** are deposited.
6. Wages earned during the month total $11,000. Of this amount, $9,600 represents earnings of factory workers and $1,400 earnings of office workers.
7. Factory rent for the month, $900, is paid by check.
8. Depreciation for the month: factory equipment $160 and office equipment and furniture $30.
9. The tax liabilities to the state and federal governments at March 31, 1975, are paid by check.
10. Wages of $10,400 less deductions of $624 for federal payroll taxes and $1,185 for withheld income taxes are paid by check.

11. Other factory costs (repairs, utility services, and so forth) were incurred in the amount of $4,900 and paid by check.

12. All selling activities are performed by Miller Company at a fee of $500 per month. The bill for April is paid by check.

13. The Pine Company is paid $9,500 by check.

14. The company's share of the payroll taxes is 2.7 percent for state unemployment insurance, .3 percent for federal unemployment insurance, and 6 percent for FICA benefits[1]—a total of 9 percent of wages earned. The company assigns an appropriate proportion of these payroll tax costs to production operations and the remainder as an additional office cost.

15. Raw materials in the amount of $8,400 were requisitioned from the storeroom and put into process.

16. The production cost accounts are closed to work in process.

17. Production records show that the cost of parts completed was $23,714.

18. The cost of finished parts shipped to customers was $23,604.

Solution: Transactions Analyzed

An analysis of the April, 1975, transactions into debit and credit elements and comments on certain entries follow:

(1)

Dr. Raw Materials	8,000	
Cr. Accounts Payable—Pine Company		8,000

(2) This is a summary of the firm's revenue transactions for the month. Most manufacturing firms customarily make most or all of their sales on account. To simplify the illustration, a single receivable account is used for all customers other than the major customer, Western Motors Company. The amount due from each customer would, of course, actually be recorded separately.

Dr. Accounts Receivable—All Other Customers	26,000	
Cr. Sales		26,000

(3) The account receivable from the Western Motors Company is reduced to zero, the cash on hand is increased by $2,500, and a new asset account is set up to show the receivable from the Western Motors Company in the form of a promissory note for $1,500. It is common practice to use one Notes Receivable account for all such receivables rather than a separate account for each maker. The notes themselves and other supporting memorandums provide an adequate record of the amounts due from each customer. There is little difference between an account receivable and a note receivable, but a note, the written acknowledgment

---

[1] Tax rates under the Federal Insurance Contributions Act are changed from time to time. In the demonstration and problems in this book 6-percent rates are used frequently. The rates currently in effect can be determined by reference to current tax materials, such as tax services or tax forms. Differences in tax rates will not affect the form of the entry but will, of course, alter the amounts.

of a debt, is somewhat better evidence of the claim's validity than is an account receivable. Moreover, a claim can more easily be transferred from one person to another when it is in the form of a promissory note.

```
Dr. Undeposited Cash .......................................     2,500
Dr. Notes Receivable ........................................     1,500
     Cr. Accounts Receivable—Western Motors Company ......              4,000
```

(4)

```
Dr. Undeposited Cash .......................................    24,800
     Cr. Accounts Receivable—All Other Customers ..........            24,800
```

(5)

```
Dr. Cash in Bank ...........................................    27,300
     Cr. Undeposited Cash ..................................            27,300
```

(6) Wages earned by factory workers are a cost of production and are therefore debited to the production cost account, Factory Labor. The cost of office labor, on the other hand, is treated as a charge against revenue in the period in which the labor services are received and is therefore debited to the expense account, Office Labor.

```
Dr. Factory Labor (production cost) .........................     9,600
Dr. Office Labor (expense) ..................................     1,400
     Cr. Wages Payable .....................................            11,000
```

(7) The entire building is used for factory operations, so the payment of rent for the present month is charged to the production cost account, Factory Rent.

```
Dr. Factory Rent ...........................................       900
     Cr. Cash in Bank ......................................              900
```

(8) Factory Equipment Depreciation is a production cost account; Depreciation of Office Equipment and Furniture is an expense account.

```
Dr. Depreciation of Factory Equipment ......................       160
Dr. Depreciation of Office Equipment and Furniture ..........        30
     Cr. Factory Equipment—Accumulated Depreciation .......              160
     Cr. Office Equipment and Furniture—
          Accumulated Depreciation ..........................               30
```

(9) Separate liability accounts are being used for payroll taxes payable to each governmental unit and for the withheld income tax. This is desirable since different reports have to be made to the state and federal governments when payments are made.

```
Dr. State Payroll Taxes Payable ............................       270
Dr. Federal Payroll Taxes Payable ..........................     1,030
Dr. Withheld Income Tax ....................................     1,250
     Cr. Cash in Bank ......................................             2,550
```

(10) The debits to Wages Payable this month do not correspond to the month's labor costs [see (6)] because the payroll period and the accounting period do not end on the same day. The customary deductions are made from the paychecks (state income taxes are ignored).

Dr. Wages Payable 10,400
   Cr. Cash in Bank 8,591
   Cr. Federal Payroll Taxes Payable 624
   Cr. Withheld Income Tax 1,185

(11) Separate accounts are usually used for each of the various types of other factory costs. To simplify the illustration, they are grouped under a single title here.

Dr. Other Factory Costs 4,900
   Cr. Cash in Bank 4,900

(12)

Dr. Selling Expense 500
   Cr. Cash in Bank 500

(13)

Dr. Accounts Payable—Pine Company 9,500
   Cr. Cash in Bank 9,500

(14) The payroll tax cost of the company is charged to a factory production cost account and an office expense account at the rate of 9 percent of earnings in each category. An alternative treatment that will be illustrated in other examples would view the payroll tax costs as additions to the labor cost in each area. The credit for the payroll tax liability is divided between the two liability accounts, and the amounts are determined by applying the stated percentages to the total wages earned during the month, $11,000.

Dr. Payroll Taxes—Factory 864
Dr. Payroll Taxes—Office 126
   Cr. State Payroll Taxes Payable 297
   Cr. Federal Payroll Taxes Payable 693

(15)

Dr. Raw Materials Used 8,400
   Cr. Raw Materials 8,400

After recording these entries, the T-accounts of the Standard Products Company would appear as in Figure 5.1.

At the end of the accounting period, all of the production costs of the period are summarized in the Work in Process account. This is accomplished by closing all of the production cost accounts into Work in Process, as explained in a later section. Before making this entry, however, it is desirable to take a trial balance and prepare a schedule of production operations. The preclosing trial balance for the illustration in this chapter is shown in Schedule 5.2.

The Statement of Production Operations

When the production cost accounts were first introduced, it was pointed out that the purpose of these accounts was to accumulate the details of

Figure 5.1

Undeposited Cash			
Bal.	400	**(5)**	27,300
(3)	2,500		
(4)	24,800		

Cash in Bank			
Bal.	4,500	**(7)**	900
(5)	27,300	**(9)**	2,550
		(10)	8,591
		(11)	4,900
		(12)	500
		(13)	9,500

Accounts Receivable—Western Motors Company			
Bal.	4,000	**(3)**	4,000

Accounts Receivable—All Other Customers			
Bal.	8,160	**(4)**	24,800
(2)	26,000		

Raw Materials			
Bal.	2,400	**(15)**	8,400
(1)	8,000		

Work in Process	
Bal.	1,800

Finished Parts	
Bal.	700

Factory Equipment	
Bal.	9,960

Factory Equipment— Accumulated Depreciation			
		Bal.	2,420
		(8)	160

Office Equipment and Furniture	
Bal.	1,020

Office Equipment and Furniture—Accumulated Depreciation			
		Bal.	340
		(8)	30

Accounts Payable— Pine Company			
(13)	9,500	**Bal.**	3,400
		(1)	8,000

Wages Payable			
(10)	10,400	**Bal.**	880
		(6)	11,000

State Payroll Taxes Payable			
(9)	270	**Bal.**	270
		(14)	297

Federal Payroll Taxes Payable			
(9)	1,030	**Bal.**	1,030
		(10)	624
		(14)	693

Withheld Income Tax			
(9)	1,250	**Bal.**	1,250
		(10)	1,185

Capital Stock			
		Bal.	22,000

Retained Earnings			
		Bal.	1,350

Sales			
		(2)	26,000

Notes Receivable	
(3)	1,500

Factory Labor	
(6)	9,600

Office Labor	
(6)	1,400

Factory Rent		Depreciation of Factory Equipment	
(7)	900	**(8)**	160

Depreciation of Office Equipment and Furniture		Other Factory Costs	
(8)	30	**(11)**	4,900

Selling Expense		Payroll Taxes—Factory	
(12)	500	**(14)**	864

Payroll Taxes—Office		Raw Materials Used	
(14)	126	**(15)**	8,400

SCHEDULE 5.2

STANDARD PRODUCTS COMPANY
Trial Balance
April 30, 1975

Undeposited Cash	$ 400	
Cash in Bank	4,859	
Accounts Receivable—All Other Customers	9,360	
Raw Materials	2,000	
Work in Process	1,800	
Finished Parts	700	
Factory Equipment	9,960	
Factory Equipment—Accumulated Depreciation		$ 2,580
Office Equipment and Furniture	1,020	
Office Equipment and Furniture—Accumulated Depreciation		370
Accounts Payable—Pine Company		1,900
Wages Payable		1,480
State Payroll Taxes Payable		297
Federal Payroll Taxes Payable		1,317
Withheld Income Tax		1,185
Capital Stock		22,000
Retained Earnings		1,350
Sales		26,000
Notes Receivable	1,500	
Factory Labor	9,600	
Office Labor	1,400	
Factory Rent	900	
Depreciation of Factory Equipment	160	
Depreciation of Office Equipment and Furniture	30	
Other Factory Costs	4,900	
Selling Expense	500	
Payroll Taxes—Factory	864	
Payroll Taxes—Office	126	
Raw Materials Used	8,400	
	$58,479	$58,479

production costs for limited periods of time. At the end of each period, a statement which summarizes the results of production operations for the period is prepared. This is called a *schedule of production operations* or a *schedule of cost of goods manufactured.* There is no standard form for such a statement, and its arrangement depends upon the nature and number of the items to be presented; however, it should emphasize significant figures and be constructed so that the important features can be comprehended easily. Calculations of unit cost are often made in order to make the statement more useful. The figures for the statement come from the trial balance shown in Schedule 5.2, except for the cost of parts completed in April. In this illustration, we have assumed that cost was determined to be $23,714. An appropriate schedule for the illustration is shown in Schedule 5.3.

SCHEDULE 5.3

STANDARD PRODUCTS COMPANY
Schedule of Production Operations
Month of April, 1975

Raw Materials Used		$ 8,400
Factory Labor		9,600
Factory Overhead Costs		
Factory Rent	$ 900	
Depreciation of Factory Equipment	160	
Payroll Taxes—Factory	864	
Other Factory Costs	4,900	6,824
Production Costs of April, 1975		$24,824
Work in Process, April 1, 1975		1,800
Total Production Costs		$26,624
Parts Completed in April		23,714
Work in Process, April 30, 1975		$ 2,910

Transfer or Closing Entries: Production Cost Accounts

Production cost accounts are opened in order to accumulate operating data for one accounting period. After they have served this purpose, their balances must be eliminated so that a new set of figures can be accumulated for the next period. This process involves a transfer of each production-cost total to the appropriate asset account. In the illustration, this asset account is Work in Process.

(16) The transfer or closing is carried out with debits and credits. A production cost account will always have a debit balance during the period. To close it, that is, to reduce its balance to zero, credit the production cost account and debit the Work in Process account. A simpler alternative is to make one debit to Work in Process for the sum of costs in production cost accounts. Entry (16) uses the simpler alternative.

Dr. Work in Process	24,824	
Cr. Raw Materials Used		8,400
Cr. Factory Labor		9,600
Cr. Factory Rent		900
Cr. Depreciation of Factory Equipment		160
Cr. Payroll Taxes—Factory		864
Cr. Other Factory Costs		4,900

(17) Determining the cost of goods completed presents a difficult problem, which will be considered in detail later. In the illustration, we assume that the figure, $23,714, is available from an analysis of the firm's production records.

Dr. Finished Parts	23,714	
Cr. Work in Process		23,714

(18) Determining the cost of goods sold poses a problem similar to that for determining costs of goods completed. Here, too, we assume that the figure is available from the company's records.

Dr. Manufacturing Cost of Goods Sold	23,604	
Cr. Finished Parts		23,604

The schedule of production operations shown in Schedule 5.3 could be converted into a schedule of production operations and of cost of goods sold by reversing the order of the last two lines and adding the information on finished parts. The last seven lines of such a schedule would be:

Total Production Costs	$26,624
Work in Process, April 30, 1975	2,910
Parts Completed in April	$23,714
Finished Parts, April 1, 1975	700
Total Finished Parts	$24,414
Finished Parts, April 30, 1975	810
Manufacturing Cost of Goods Sold	$23,604

After closing the production cost accounts and recording the cost of goods sold, a second trial balance could be taken. The balances will all be the same as those in the trial balance before entry (16), except that the Cost of Goods Sold account, with a balance of $23,604, will replace all of the production cost accounts closed in entry (16), and the balances of the Work in Process account and the Finished Parts account will be $2,910 and $810, respectively. That trial balance appears in Schedule 5.4.

SCHEDULE 5.4

STANDARD PRODUCTS COMPANY
Trial Balance
April 30, 1975

(After closing the production cost accounts and recording
the cost of goods sold.)

Undeposited Cash	$ 400	
Cash in Bank	4,859	
Accounts Receivable—All Other Customers	9,360	
Raw Materials	2,000	
Work in Process	2,910	
Finished Parts	810	
Factory Equipment	9,960	
Factory Equipment—Accumulated Depreciation		$ 2,580
Office Equipment and Furniture	1,020	
Office Equipment and Furniture—Accumulated Depreciation		370
Accounts Payable—Pine Company		1,900
Wages Payable		1,480
State Payroll Taxes Payable		297
Federal Payroll Taxes Payable		1,317
Withheld Income Tax		1,185
Capital Stock		22,000
Retained Earnings		1,350
Sales		26,000
Notes Receivable	1,500	
Factory Labor	—	
Office Labor	1,400	
Factory Rent	—	
Depreciation of Factory Equipment	—	
Depreciation of Office Equipment and Furniture	30	
Other Factory Costs	—	
Selling Expense	500	
Payroll Taxes—Factory	—	
Payroll Taxes—Office	126	
Raw Materials Used	—	
Manufacturing Cost of Goods Sold	23,604	
	$58,479	$58,479

Income Statement and Balance Sheet

Recall that income taxes are being ignored. An income statement similar
to the one in Schedule 5.5 may be prepared after entry (18).

As was indicated in Chapter 4, the calculation of the new Retained
Earnings balance from the old balance and the change for the period

SCHEDULE 5.5

STANDARD PRODUCTS COMPANY
Statement of Income and Retained Earnings
Month of April, 1975

Sales		$26,000
Expenses		
Manufacturing Cost of Goods Sold	$23,604	
Office Labor	1,400	
Depreciation of Office Equipment and Furniture	30	
Selling Expense	500	
Payroll Taxes—Office	126	
Total Expenses		25,660
Net Income		$ 340
Retained Earnings, April 1, 1975		1,350
Retained Earnings, April 30, 1975		$ 1,690

---

should be shown somewhere in the financial statements. In this example, the calculation is shown at the end of the income statement data in Schedule 5.5. When this method of presentation is used, the statement is frequently called a *statement of income and retained earnings* rather than an income statement. Instead, the calculation could have been shown in the proprietorship section of the balance sheet or in a separate schedule of retained earnings.

The balance sheet at the end of April is shown in Schedule 5.6.

SCHEDULE 5.6

STANDARD PRODUCTS COMPANY
Balance Sheet
April 30, 1975

Assets

Current Assets

Undeposited Cash	$ 400	
Cash in Bank	4,859	
Notes Receivable	1,500	
Accounts Receivable	9,360	
Raw Materials	2,000	
Work in Process	2,910	
Finished Parts	810	
Total Current Assets		$21,839

Noncurrent Assets

Factory Equipment	$9,960	
Less Accumulated Depreciation	2,580	$ 7,380
Office Equipment and Furniture	$1,020	
Less Accumulated Depreciation	370	650
Total Noncurrent Assets		8,030
Total Assets		$29,869

Liabilities and Stockholders' Equity

Current Liabilities

Accounts Payable	$ 1,900	
Wages Payable	1,480	
State Payroll Taxes Payable	297	
Federal Payroll Taxes Payable	1,317	
Withheld Income Tax	1,185	
Total Current Liabilities		$ 6,179

Stockholders' Equity

Capital Stock	$22,000	
Retained Earnings	1,690	
Total Stockholders' Equity		23,690
Total Liabilities and Stockholders' Equity		$29,869

Closing Entries: Revenue and Expense Accounts

To prepare the accounts for the next accounting period, the expense and revenue accounts must now be closed. The production cost accounts were closed in transactions (16). The closing-entry procedure for expense and revenue accounts was illustrated in Chapter 4. The same procedure is followed here. Net income is closed to the proprietorship account, Retained Earnings, for a corporation.

(19)

Dr. Sales	26,000	
Cr. Manufacturing Cost of Goods Sold		23,604
Cr. Office Labor		1,400
Cr. Depreciation of Office Furniture and Equipment		30
Cr. Selling Expense		500
Cr. Payroll Taxes—Office		126
Cr. Retained Earnings		340

Direct Costing

In the illustration just completed, all production cost accounts were closed into Work in Process. This procedure, called "absorption costing," is the one most commonly used in accounting practice. An alternative procedure known as "direct costing" (or more properly, "variable costing") has received substantial recognition in recent years. In direct costing, production costs are divided into variable manufacturing costs (those that tend to vary with output) and fixed manufacturing costs (those that tend to be relatively unaffected by the scale of operations). Fixed manufacturing costs are treated in the same way as selling and administrative expenses; that is, they are treated as costs assignable to the period rather than as costs assignable to the product produced. Fixed manufacturing costs are expenses of the period, and they are charged in their entirety against revenues in determining net income for the period. In direct costing, only variable manufacturing costs are product costs to be closed to Work in Process. Direct labor and direct materials are variable costs. Many overhead items, such as property taxes and depreciation of equipment, are fixed costs. There are some variable overhead costs such as factory payroll taxes and utility charges.

It would be possible to use the direct costing procedure in the Standard Products Company illustration if certain additional information were available. Assume, for example, that all raw materials used, factory labor, and factory payroll taxes are variable manufacturing costs but that factory rent and depreciation of factory equipment are fixed manufacturing costs. Other factory costs are half fixed and half variable. Assume also that the variable costs component of the beginning (April 1) inventory is $1,386 for work in process and $600 for finished parts. The variable cost of goods completed is $20,738, and the variable cost of goods sold is $20,652. With these facts the new schedule of production operations for the month of April, 1975, would appear as shown in Schedule 5.7.

SCHEDULE 5.7

STANDARD PRODUCTS COMPANY
Schedule of Production Operations
(Direct-Costing Method)
Month of April, 1975

Raw Materials Used		$ 8,400
Factory Labor		9,600
Variable Overhead Costs:		
Payroll Taxes—Factory	$ 864	
Other Variable Factory Costs	2,450	3,314
Variable Production Costs of April, 1975		$21,314
Work in Process, April 1, 1975		1,386
Total Variable Production Costs		$22,700
Work in Process, April 30, 1975		1,962
Variable Cost of Goods Completed		$20,738
Finished Parts, April 1, 1975		600
Total Finished Parts		$21,338
Variable Cost of Goods Sold		20,652
Finished Parts, April 30, 1975		$ 686

With the new schedule based on the direct-costing procedure, transactions (16) and (17) would be:

(16)

Dr. Work in Process	21,314	
Cr. Raw Materials Used		8,400
Cr. Factory Labor		9,600
Cr. Payroll Taxes—Factory		864
Cr. Other Factory Costs		2,450

(17)

Dr. Finished Parts	20,738	
Cr. Work in Process		20,738

A variety of income statement forms can be used for the direct-costing procedure. An appropriate form for this problem, assuming all nonmanufacturing expenses were fixed, is the one in Schedule 5.8.

SCHEDULE 5.8

STANDARD PRODUCTS COMPANY
Income Statement
Month of April, 1975

Sales		$26,000
Variable Cost of Goods Sold		20,652
Contribution Margin		$ 5,348
Fixed Expenses of Period:		
Factory Rent	$ 900	
Depreciation of Factory Equipment	160	
Other Factory Costs	2,450	
Office Labor	1,400	
Depreciation of Office Equipment and Furniture	30	
Selling Expense	500	
Payroll Taxes—Office	126	
Total Fixed Expenses		5,566
Net Loss		($218)

Transaction (18) would be:

(18)

Dr. Variable Cost of Goods Sold	20,652	
Cr. Finished Parts		20,652

Direct costing leads to a reported *loss* for April while absorption costing leads to a reported *profit*. Compare transactions (16) and (17) under absorption costing. The debit to Work in Process in transaction (16) exceeds the credit to Work in Process in transaction (17). That is, more costs were put into Work in Process through materials, labor, and factory overhead than were taken out in the form of finished parts. Compare, too, transaction (17) with transaction (18). The debit to Finished Parts in (17) is larger than the credit to Finished Parts in (18). That is, more costs were put into Finished Parts from Work in Process than were taken out in form of Manufacturing Cost of Goods Sold. Total inventories of Work in Process plus Finished Parts have grown during April. Thus, for example, part of the cost of factory depreciation for April remains in the inventories at the end of the month. Those depreciation costs will remain in a balance sheet inventory account until the parts worked on during April are sold. In contrast, under direct costing, the factory depreciation for April is considered an expense for the month and is charged against revenues for the month. Under direct costing, fixed factory costs are assumed to expire as time passes, while under absorption costing, fixed factory costs are assumed to expire only as the product flows out of the firm.

Because the recorded expenses for April are higher under direct costing than under absorption costing, the net income under direct costing is lower than under absorption costing. Absorption costing need not always lead to higher reported net income for a period than direct costing. After you have read the chapters on cost accounting you will be in a better position to understand the conditions under which direct costing will lead to a higher net income than absorption costing.

Direct costing is not accepted for formal financial statements, so the absorption costing procedures will be followed in all of the illustrations and problems of this book unless a specific statement to the contrary is made.

Flow of Costs Illustrated

The flow of production costs, as well as the disposition of other operating costs, is illustrated by the diagram in Figure 5.2. For a merchandising firm, the first stage would show a merchandise account in place of raw materials, factory labor, and other factory costs, and the second stage would be eliminated entirely.

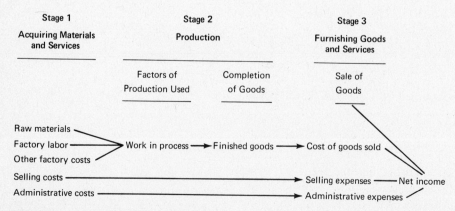

Figure 5.2 Diagram of Flow of Costs

Some costs, the most conspicuous of which is labor, represent the acquisition of nonstorable services, which must be transferred in their entirety from stage 1 to stage 2 or to stage 3 in the same period in which they are acquired. Other costs, most notably raw materials or merchandise, can be stored in their original form. They, therefore, move from stage 1 to stage 2 or stage 3 only as evidence of their use becomes available. Some items of factory overhead fall in the first category (for example, indirect labor and factory repairs), while other items such as factory supplies can be stored in their original form. Absorption costing assumes that fixed manufacturing costs are storable while direct costing assumes they are not.

Selling and administrative costs are shown flowing directly through stage 2. As was indicated earlier, this is merely a record-keeping shortcut. In a conceptual sense, these costs are used in stage 2 and charged to expense in stage 3. Since selling and administrative costs do not become part of the cost of work in process or of finished goods, their use and charge to expense always occur in the same period so that these costs can conveniently be shown as bypassing stage 2.

SUMMARY

Production cost accounts are clearly an integral part of an efficient manufacturing concern. They record the costs of production, provide information for the schedule of production operations, and, when they are closed to the appropriate balance sheet accounts, they show the cost of manufactured products. Even though production cost accounts do not appear on the balance sheet, they are asset accounts, and the asset debit and credit rules apply to them.

Once production costs have been recorded, the accounting process for manufacturing firms is the same as for merchandisers and retailers: services rendered to customers (revenue) and the assets consumed in the revenue-producing process (expenses) are reported in the income statement. The balance sheet shows all of the asset, liability, and proprietorship items with the production costs of unsold goods summarized in the Work in Process and Finished Goods accounts.

QUESTIONS AND PROBLEMS

*1. In those cases where formal entries are appropriate, give the debits and credits for the following events:

(1) The storeroom issues $360 of ¾-inch copper tubing for use in production activity.

(2) The storekeeper notes that the stock of this material is low and submits a purchase requisition for an additional 25,000 feet of it.

(3) A purchase order for $4,800 of the material is sent to the Consolidated Pipe Company.

* Hints, key numbers, or (partial) answers appear in the back of the book between the Appendix Tables and the Glossary.

    (4) The purchase invoice arrives. The amount is $4,800, subject to a 2-percent discount if paid within ten days.

    (5) The shipment arrives and the receiving report indicates that the goods are satisfactory.

    (6) The bill is paid in time to take the discount.

2. Indicate which of the following types of costs would be debited to (1) expense accounts, (2) production cost accounts, or (3) balance sheet asset accounts:

  a. Office supplies used
  b. Salary of factory foreman
  c. Purchase of a three-year fire insurance policy on the store building
  d. Expiration of one month's protection of the insurance in **c.**
  e. Property taxes on the factory building
  f. Wages of truck drivers used to deliver finished goods to customers
  g. Wages of factory workers installing a new machine
  h. Wages of mechanics used to repair factory machines
  i. Salary of the president of the company
  j. Depreciation of office equipment
  k. Construction of an addition to the factory building
  l. Factory supplies used.

3. "It is easy enough to see why material and labor costs become part of the cost of manufactured goods, but it is hard to see why indirect factory costs should be considered a part of production costs since they do not enter into the products." Comment.

4. What use can be made by the management of a business of a schedule of production operations?

5. After the books have been closed, what classes of accounts will not have balances? What classes of accounts will have balances?

6. Give the debits (account titles and amounts) to be made for each of the following bills that have been received by the Union Manufacturing Company. Put a check mark after the titles of the accounts that will be closed into Work in Process at the end of the period.

    (1) From the Acme Lumber Company, $1,460. The lumber is used as follows: $1,100 for constructing a warehouse, $300 for constructing an addition to the storeroom, and $60 for repairs to the factory building.

    (2) From the gas company, $655. The fuel is used as follows: $580 for producing power and $75 for heating the factory.

    (3) From the Rockon Insurance Agency, $500 for a three-year premium on a fire insurance policy.

    (4) From the Eternal Supply Company, $12,100 for raw materials.

    (5) From the Noman Equipment Company, $560; $450 is for new equipment and $110 is for repairs to equipment.

7. Why is proprietorship not affected by production operations?

8. At the end of the period the Factory Supplies account shows a balance of $5,600, representing a balance on hand at the start of the period of $600 plus purchases during the period of $5,000. An inventory is taken (a count of the supplies on hand) at the end of the period, and it shows $500 of supplies on hand. What entry should be made as a result of the inventory?

9. Analyze the following transactions into debits and credits. Use the following form:

Transaction no.	Debit or credit	Account title	Amount

(1) Raw materials are used in production, $25,600.

(2) The monthly bill for electricity is received from the power company. The total amount is $580, of which $504 is for power and $76 for lighting.

(3) Wages and salaries earned during the period are as follows: drying department, $2,600; mixing department, $6,000; packing department, $4,200; storeroom equipment construction, $467; supervision, $900.

(4) Payrolls aggregating $14,000 are paid by check during the period. See entry (3). Deductions of 6 percent from the gross amount are taken for Federal Insurance Contributions Act tax, $1,520 for withheld income tax, and $250 for hospital insurance.

(5) The employer's share of payroll taxes for the period is: $820 for Federal Insurance Contributions Act tax, $46 for federal unemployment insurance tax, and $325 for state unemployment tax.

(6) An invoice for $17,980 is received from the Smith Materials Company covering the following items: raw materials, $16,000; factory supplies, $1,000; supplies used in constructing a new factory building, $980. The goods have been received.

(7) A check is drawn to Carl Jones for $2,500 to cover architectural services in connection with the new building. No previous entry has been made for this bill.

(8) Fire insurance on building and equipment expired during the month, $79.

(9) A bill is received from the Wells Machine Works for repairs to machinery, $121.

(10) Depreciation for the month: building $50; equipment $150.

(11) Factory supplies are used, $600.

(12) Property taxes for the year have been paid in advance. The amount applicable to the present month is $110.

10. The following transactions are taken from the books of the Modern Foundry. Record the transactions in journal entry form like the journal entries (1)–(19) for the Standard Products Company illustrated in this chapter.

(1) Scrap metal is purchased on account from the Econo Salvage Company, $4,600.

(2) The Common Trucking Company is paid $432 by check for freight of the shipment of scrap metal.

(3) Raw material is purchased on account from the Star Steel Company, $15,500.

(4) An invoice is received from the Industrial Tool Company for new tools, $490.

(5) A bill is received from the Central Power Company for $256; $52 is for lighting and $204 is for power.

(6) The weekly payroll of $8,750 is paid by check less deductions of $241 for Federal Insurance Contributions Act tax (credit Payroll Taxes Payable), $1,120 for withheld income tax, and $120 for union dues. Wages earned are recorded once a month [see entry (9)].

(7) Raw materials, $13,100, and scrap metal, $4,100, are used in the production of castings.

(8) Supplies used: in the molding department, $170; in general foundry operations, $78; for the construction of new equipment, $60.

(9) Wages earned during the month: in the molding department, $9,021; in foundry operations, $34,200; in the construction of new equipment $456.

(10) The company's share of payroll taxes is $2,700.

(11) Machinery rental has been paid for a year in advance. The amount applicable to the present month is $312.

(12) Depreciation for the month of equipment owned by the company, $270.

11. Analyze the following selected transactions of the Genesee Company into debits and credits. Record the transactions in journal entry form like the journal entries (1)–(19) for the Standard Products Company illustrated in this chapter.

(1) An invoice is received from the National Metals Company for materials to be used in production, $36,500. The materials have been received and checked.

(2) Materials used in production, $13,612.

(3) Wages earned during the month: cutting department labor, $8,500; assembling department labor, $9,200; finishing department labor, $14,000; supervision, $12,000; miscellaneous plant labor, $5,600.

(4) A weekly payroll of $9,600 is paid by check. Deductions are made of 6 percent for payroll taxes and $980 for income tax.

(5) The expired premium on a workmen's compensation insurance policy amounts to $2 for each $100 of wages earned. See entry (3).

(6) The employer's share of payroll taxes is $1,806.

(7) Supplies used: for miscellaneous factory operations, $450; for construction of storage equipment, $270; for repairs to machinery, $90.

(8) A check is drawn to pay fire insurance premiums for two years in advance, $1,200.

(9) The expiration of fire insurance protection for the month is recognized. See entry (8).

(10) The gas bill received from the Cal Gas Company is for $271, of which $200 is applicable to the finishing department; the balance is for general factory heating.

(11) Depreciation on machinery amounts to $3,400; depreciation on the factory building is $520.

(12) An invoice covering rental of additional factory machinery for the month has been received from the Industrial Supply Company, $430.

(13) Property taxes accrued for the month amount to $540.

(14) All of the production cost accounts opened in entries (1) through (13) are closed to Work in Process.

*12. Indicate which of the following types of wages and salaries would be debited to (a) production cost accounts and (b) expense accounts:

1. Cutting machine operators
2. Delivery labor
3. Factory janitors
4. Factory payroll clerks
5. Factory superintendent
6. General office secretaries
7. Guards at factory gate
8. Inspectors in factory
9. Maintenance men used to service factory machinery
10. Night watchmen at the factory
11. Office clerks
12. Operator of a lift truck in the shipping room
13. President of the firm
14. Sales manager
15. Shipping room workers
16. Sweepers used to clean retail store
17. Traveling salesman.

13. What is the basic difference between production cost accounts and expense accounts?

14. Distinguish between a statement of production operations and an income statement as to content and purpose.

°15. The Central Packing Company is a manufacturing subsidiary of Hadly Foods, Inc. All Central Packing Company sales are made to Hadly Foods, Inc., at cost of production. The canning process is such that there is no work in process at the end of any day. The trial balance of the Central Packing Company at August 31, 1975, is as follows:

Accounts Payable		$ 54,300
Accounts Receivable—Hadly Foods, Inc.	$ 126,000	
Buildings	288,000	
Cash in Bank	30,000	
Capital Stock		900,000
Depreciation of Buildings and Equipment	8,400	
Electricity, Water and Gas	5,340	
Equipment	383,160	
Finished Product on Hand (Aug. 1)	108,000	
Insurance Expired	2,700	
Labor Costs	210,000	
Land	24,000	
Maintenance Costs	16,800	
Payroll Taxes	10,920	
Payroll Taxes Payable		15,900
Raw Materials on Hand	48,000	
Raw Materials Used	117,000	
Shipments of Finished Product to Hadly Foods, Inc.		381,240
Supervision	12,000	
Taxes—Property	2,700	
Unexpired Insurance	16,200	
Wages Payable		36,000
Withheld Income Tax		21,780
	$1,409,220	$1,409,220

Prepare a statement of production operations for the month of August and a balance sheet at August 31, 1975. Include a calculation of the new balance of the Finished Product on Hand account in the statement of production operations.

16. The following data relate to the manufacturing activities of the Graves Company during March 1975.

	March 1	March 31
Stocks of goods:		
Stock of raw materials	$32,400	$36,900
Stock of factory supplies	3,600	2,700
Stock of work in process	55,800	43,200

Acquisitions during month:
    Materials purchased, $65,700.
    Factory supplies purchased, $7,200
    Labor services received, $126,900
    Heat, light, and power, $1,260
    Factory rent, $3,600

Expirations of previous acquisitions:
    Depreciation of factory equipment, $1,800
    Prepaid insurance expired, $1,440

Prepare a statement of production operations for the month of March, 1975. Show the total of production costs for the period as a subtotal; add the opening stock of work in process to this to obtain total costs in process during the period and subtract the closing stock of work in process to determine cost of goods completed.

17. The Gordon Precision Company was formed in the fall of 1975. Its first production contract called for it to supply jet engine parts to the Accuton Engine Company. Work on the contract was begun on November 1, 1975. By November 30, 1975, a number of parts had been produced but none had been shipped or billed to the Accuton Engine Company. The trial balance at November 30 was:

Accounts Payable		$ 17,550
Advances by Accuton Engine Company		24,000
Building (Net)	$ 48,000	
Cash in Bank	2,550	
Cash on Hand	75	
Depreciation—Building, Machinery, and Equipment	1,350	
Employees' Income Tax Withheld		3,090
Peter Gordon, Capital		75,825
Heat, Light and Power	1,050	
Insurance	525	
Labor—Machining	19,050	
Labor—Assembling	8,625	
Land	9,000	
Machinery and Equipment (Net)	47,250	
Materials	8,250	
Materials Used	13,350	
Roman Gordon, Capital		45,465
Payroll Taxes	1,335	
Payroll Taxes Payable		1,905
Property Taxes	420	
Property Taxes Payable		2,100
Repairs and Maintenance	1,380	
Supervision	1,500	
Supplies on Hand	2,250	
Supplies Used	1,350	
Unexpired Insurance	2,625	
	$169,935	$169,935

a. Prepare a statement of production operations for the month of November 1975. The parts in process at November 30 had an accumulated cost of $15,750. Subtract this amount from the total production costs to arrive at the cost of finished parts produced.

b. Prepare a balance sheet as of November 30, 1975. The Parts in Process and the Finished Parts, as shown in the statement of production operations, appear in the balance sheet as assets.

°18. The Chapin Plastics Company was incorporated on September 16, 1975. By September 30, 1975, the firm was ready to begin operations. The trial balance at that date was as follows:

Cash in Bank	$387,200	
Raw Materials	19,200	
Factory Equipment	136,000	
Accounts Payable—National Materials Company		$ 22,400
Capital Stock		520,000
	$542,400	$542,400

The following data relate only to the manufacturing operations of the firm during October:

(1) Materials purchased from National Materials Company, on account, $141,600.

(2) Wages and salaries earned during the month, $128,000.

(3) Raw materials requisitioned and put into process during the month, $148,800.

(4) Equipment was acquired during the month at a cost of $112,000. A check for $40,000 was issued, and an equipment contract payable in nine equal monthly installments was signed in favor of the Miller Equipment Company.

(5) Additional payments by check:

National Materials Company	$120,000
Payrolls, $120,000 less $2,700 deducted for payroll taxes and $14,880 deducted for employee income taxes	102,420
Repairs to equipment	3,200
Factory building rent	6,000
Utilities	1,920
Insurance premiums (one year from October 1, 1975)	9,600
Miscellaneous factory costs	26,400
	$269,540

(6) Bills received but unpaid at October 31, 1975:

City Water Department	$ 120
Hoster Machine Supply Company, for additional equipment	2,400

(7) Employer's share of payroll taxes for the month, $6,720.

(8) Depreciation of equipment for the month, $1,200.

(9) One month's insurance expiration is recorded.

a. Open skeleton accounts and enter the items in the opening trial balance.

b. Record the transactions for the month. Open whatever accounts are needed.

c. Prepare a trial balance at October 31, 1975.

d. Prepare a statement of production operations for the month of October, 1975. The cost of parts finished in October was $291,760.

e. Close the production cost accounts and record the transfer to Finished Goods. Record the closing entries as transactions (10) and (11).

f. Prepare a balance sheet as of October 31, 1975, assuming no other transactions occurred during the month.

19. This problem is a continuation of Problem 18, Chapin Plastics Company. In addition to the manufacturing activities described in that problem, the following transactions relating to selling and administrative activities occurred during October 1975.

(12) Sales, on account, $320,600.

(13) Collections from customers, $280,000.

(14) Salaries earned during the month: Sales, $20,800; office, $21,200.

(15) Payments by check:

Sales salaries, $20,000, less $450 deducted for payroll taxes and $1,920 deducted for employee income taxes	$17,630
Office salaries, $20,000, less $450 deducted for payroll taxes and $2,000 deducted for employee income taxes	17,550
Advertising	7,200
Rent of office and office equipment for October	1,200
Office supplies	1,600
Miscellaneous office costs	1,400
Miscellaneous selling costs	2,800
	$49,380

(16) The employer's share of payroll taxes on sales and office personnel, $2,080.

(17) Office supplies used during the month, $1,400.

(18) The inventory of finished goods on October 31, 1975, is $49,000.

a. Employing the skeleton accounts of Problem 18 and whatever new accounts are needed, record the selling and administrative activities for the month.

b. Prepare a statement of income and retained earnings for the month.

c. Prepared a balance sheet as of October 31, 1975, to replace the one prepared in (**f**) of Problem 18.

d. Close the expense and revenue accounts.

20. The Potomac Foundry, which produces castings, was closed for four months. A contract for a large number of castings was then obtained, and the plant resumed operations on June 1, 1975. During the first month's operations, castings were produced, but no shipments were made. The trial balance on June 1, 1975, was as follows:

Cash on Hand	$ 700	
Cash in Bank	44,450	
Materials and Supplies	37,100	
Prepaid Insurance	2,100	
Land	14,000	
Buildings	121,100	
Equipment	280,000	
G. C. Potomac, Capital		$289,800
F. Q. Potomac, Capital		209,650
	$499,450	$499,450

During June the following transactions took place:

(1) Materials were purchased from the Simmons Metals Company, $18,900.

(2) The payroll for the month was as follows:

Cleaning labor	$ 2,100
Coremaking labor	16,800
Molding labor	8,750
Cupola (melting) labor	5,775
Indirect labor	2,975
	$36,400

(3) Checks drawn during June:

Payroll (first two weeks, $19,600 less $441 for payroll taxes and $2,142 for withheld income taxes)	$17,017
Repairs to equipment	609
Payments to Simmons Metals Company	13,580
Transportation on materials purchased	560
	$31,766

(4) Repairs to equipment paid from cash on hand, $84.

(5) Bills received but unpaid:

Ohio Gas and Electric Company (electricity, $420; gas $105) $525
Western Telephone Company 168
City Water Department 56
Penny's Supply Company for supplies 588

(6) Materials and supplies used, $26,950.
(7) Insurance expired, $525.
(8) Employer's share of payroll taxes for the month, $1,911.
(9) Depreciation of building for the month, $420.
(10) Depreciation of equipment for the month, $1,050.

a. Open skeleton accounts and enter the items in the opening trial balance.
b. Opening whatever additional accounts are needed, record the transactions for the month.
c. Prepare a trial balance at June 30, 1975.
d. Prepare a statement of production operations for the month of June.
e. Enter the transfer entries in the skeleton accounts [entry (11)].
f. Prepare a balance sheet as of June 30, 1975.

*21. On July 1, 1975, the accounts of the Flint Manufacturing Company showed the following balances:

Debit Balances		Credit Balances	
Cash on Hand	$ 10,000	Accounts Payable—	
Cash in Bank	100,000	Thomas Company	$ 40,000
Accounts Receivable	220,000	Wages Payable	24,000
Raw Materials	80,000	Payroll Taxes Payable	6,000
Work in Process	230,000	Withheld Income Tax	10,000
Finished Goods	170,000	Capital Stock	1,000,000
Factory Supplies	20,000	Retained Earnings	200,000
Manufacturing Equipment..	450,000		
	$1,280,000		$1,280,000

Transactions for the month of July are listed below in summary form:

(1) Sales, all on account, were $300,000.
(2) Labor services furnished by employees during the period amounted to $70,000. All labor is employed in the factory.
(3) Factory supplies were purchased for $7,500; payment was made by check.
(4) Raw materials purchased on account from Thomas Company, $90,000.
(5) Collections from customers, $325,000.
(6) Bank deposits, $322,000.
(7) The payroll tax and withheld income tax liabilities of July 1 were paid by check.
(8) Payment of $98,000 was made to Thomas Company by check.
(9) Payments to employees total $68,500 after deductions of $1,800 for payroll taxes and $9,700 for withheld income taxes were made from gross wages of $80,000.
(10) Rent on the factory for the month, $5,000, was paid by check.
(11) Depreciation of manufacturing equipment for the month, $10,000.
(12) The company's share of payroll taxes is $3,675.
(13) Other manufacturing service costs acquired and paid by check, $30,000.

(14) All selling and administrative services are furnished by Clark and Company for $8,000 per month. Their bill was paid by check.

(15) Raw materials used during month, $105,000.

(16) Factory supplies used during month, $9,000.

(17) Cost of goods completed during month, $248,000.

(18) Goods costing $251,500 were shipped to customers during the month.

a. Open skeleton accounts and record the trial balance figures. Opening new accounts as neeeded, record transactions (1) to (16).

b. Prepare a trial balance on July 31, 1975 before recording transaction (17). Use the first two columns of a sheet of four-column paper for this trial balance.

c. Prepare a statement of production operations, including the information on cost of goods completed of transaction (17).

d. Record the entries (17) and (18), closing the production cost accounts and recognizing the cost of goods completed and cost of goods sold.

e. After recording transactions (17) and (18), prepare a trial balance on July 31, 1975. Use the last two columns of the trial balance in (b).

f. Prepare a statement of income and retained earnings for July 1975.

g. Prepare a balance sheet at July 31, 1975.

h. Enter closing entries in the accounts and rule all closed accounts.

22. The trial balance of the Irwin Manufacturing Company on September 30, 1975, is as follows:

Cash on Hand	$ 3,500	
First National Bank	84,000	
Accounts Receivable	105,000	
Finished Goods	21,000	
Work in Process	105,000	
Materials and Supplies	94,500	
Prepaid Insurance	6,300	
Land	42,000	
Buildings	105,000	
Equipment	189,000	
Accounts Payable		$ 42,000
Wages Payable		6,300
Property Taxes Payable		1,575
Payroll Taxes Payable		14,700
Withheld Income Taxes		20,300
Capital Stock		630,000
Retained Earnings		40,425
	$755,300	$755,300

The transactions of the next quarter, in summary form, were as follows:

(1) Labor costs incurred: factory, $525,000; office $42,000; shipping, $21,000.

(2) Purchases of materials and supplies, all on account, $630,000.

(3) Sales, all on account, $1,470,000.

(4) Collections from customers, $1,491,000.

(5) Deposits in the bank, $1,484,000.

(6) Wages of employees total $574,000; after deducting $12,915 for payroll taxes and $63,700 for withheld income taxes, the balance is paid by checks to employees.

(7) The company's share of payroll taxes is $29,400. All taxes are viewed as operating expenses of the period.

(8) Tax payments by check: payroll, $41,650; withheld income taxes, $63,210.

(9) Additional property tax liability accrued during the quarter, $1,575. (Treat as an operating expense of the period.)

(10) Depreciation for the quarter: building, $2,100, equipment, $6,300. All of the building and equipment are used for factory operations.

(11) Rent of office facilities paid by check, $5,600.

(12) Unexpired insurance on December 31, 1975 is $5,250. All of the insurance is on factory facilities.

(13) Other costs incurred on account and used during the period: factory, $126,000; office, $5,250; shipping, $1,750.

(14) Payments of accounts payable by check, $735,000.

(15) Materials and supplies used, $651,000, of which $630,000 were used in factory operations. The remainder represents shipping supplies used.

(16) The cost of goods completed during the quarter was $1,253,000.

(17) The cost of goods delivered to customers was $1,267,000.

a. Open skeleton accounts and record the trial balance figures. Record transactions (1) to (15), and open new accounts as needed.

b. Prepare a trial balance on December 31, 1975, before transaction (16) is recorded. Use the first two columns of a sheet of four-column paper for this trial balance.

c. Prepare a statement of production operations. Include the information in transaction (16).

d. Record the entries (16) and (17); close the production cost accounts and recognize the cost of goods completed and the cost of goods sold.

e. After recording transactions (16) and (17), prepare a trial balance on December 31, 1975. Use the last two columns of the trial balance in (b).

f. Prepare a statement of income and retained earnings for the quarter.

g. Prepare a balance sheet as of December 31, 1975.

h. Enter closing entries in the accounts and rule all closed accounts.

23. The trial balance of the Reynolds Company at December 31, 1974, is as follows:

Debit Balances		**Credit Balances**	
Cash	$ 102,400	Accounts Payable	$ 140,000
Accounts Receivable	440,000	Wages Payable	12,000
Finished Goods	108,000	Utility Bills Payable	4,000
Work in Process	64,000	Payroll Taxes Payable	4,800
Raw Material	160,000	Withheld Income Taxes ...	8,000
Supplies	3,200	Capital Stock	940,000
Unexpired Insurance	8,600	Retained Earnings	155,200
Land	40,000		
Building	88,200		
Equipment	249,600		
	$1,264,000		$1,264,000

The following data are a summary of transactions during 1975.

(1) Suppliers:
Acquired raw materials, on account, $1,024,000.
Acquired supplies, on account, $19,200.
Payments to suppliers, $1,082,400.

(2) Utilities, see (11) for allocation:
Utility services used during the year, $36,000.
Payments to utility companies, $36,800.

(3) Employees and related taxes:
Employees earned $800,000 during the year.
Payments to employees amounted to $698,000, after $80,000 for
withheld income taxes and $16,000 for payroll taxes were deducted
from gross wages. Payroll taxes levied on the employer, $39,200.

(4) Tax payments:
Payment of payroll taxes, $54,800.
Payment of withheld income taxes, $79,200.

(5) Customers:
Sales to customers, on account, selling price, $2,132,000.
Collections from customers, $2,172,000.

(6) Raw material on hand, December 31, 1975, $144,000.

(7) Supplies on hand, December 31, 1975, $2,400.

(8) Insurance expired during the year, $5,000.

(9) Depreciation on building during the year, $4,200.

(10) Depreciation on equipment during the year, $41,600.

(11) When asked about the relative usage of various services, the management provided the following information:

	Sales	Adminis-trative	Factory
Raw Material	$ 0	$ 0	All
Supplies	2,000	2,000	Balance
Utilities	2,000	2,000	Balance
Depreciation of Building	100	100	Balance
Depreciation of Equipment	800	800	Balance
Insurance	100	100	Balance
Labor	100,000	48,000	Balance
Payroll Taxes	4,880	2,320	Balance

(12) When properly computed in accordance with the foregoing data,
the factory inventory of work in process on December 31, 1975, is
$80,000.

(13) The inventory of product ready for sale and delivery to customers
on December 31, 1975, is $120,000.

a. Open skeleton accounts and record the trial balance figures. Record
transactions (1) to (11), open new accounts as needed, and classify
sales and administrative expenses separately and in detail.

b. Before recording transaction (12), prepare a trial balance at December
31, 1975.

c. Prepare a schedule of production operations and include the information on cost of goods completed of transaction (12).

d. Record transactions (12) and (13) and include the closing of the production cost accounts.

e. Prepare a statement of income and retained earnings for 1975.

f. Prepare a balance sheet at December 31, 1975.

g. Enter closing entries in the accounts and rule all closed accounts.

°24. The following data relate to the Tertia Company:

(1) Post-closing trial balance at December 31, 1975:

Debits

Cash	$ 10,000
Marketable Securities	20,000
Accounts Receivable	25,000
Merchandise	30,000
Prepayments	3,000
Land, Buildings, and Equipment	40,000
Total Debits	$128,000

Credits

Accounts Payable (for merchandise)	$ 25,000
Interest Payable	300
Taxes Payable	4,000
Notes Payable (6%, long-term)	20,000
Accumulated Depreciation	16,000
Capital Stock	50,000
Retained Earnings	12,700
Total Credits	$128,000

(2) Income statement for 1975

Sales		$200,000
Less Expenses:		
Cost of Goods Sold	$130,000	
Depreciation Expense	3,000	
Taxes	8,000	
Other Operating Expenses	48,700	
Interest	1,200	
Total Expenses		190,900
Net Income		$ 9,100
Less: Dividends		5,000
Increase in Retained Earnings		$ 4,100

(3) Summary of cash receipts and disbursements in 1975:

Cash Receipts		
Cash Sales	$ 47,000	
Collection from Credit Customers	150,000	
Total Receipts		$197,000
Cash Disbursements		
Payment to Suppliers of Merchandise	$128,000	
Payment to Suppliers of Miscellaneous Services	49,000	
Payment of Taxes	7,500	
Payment of Interest	1,200	
Payment of Dividends	5,000	
Purchase of Marketable Securities	8,000	
Total Disbursements		198,700
Excess of Disbursements over Receipts		$ 1,700

(4) Purchases of merchandise during the period, all on account, were $127,000. All "Other Operating Expenses" were credited to Prepayments.

a. Prepare a balance sheet for January 1, 1975.

b. What is the interest payment date on the long-term notes?

25. The following data relate to the Tertius Company:

(1) Post-closing trial balance at December 31, 1975:

Debits

Cash	$ 40,000
Marketable Securities	100,000
Accounts Receivable	100,000
Merchandise	158,000
Prepayments	16,600
Land, Buildings, and Equipment	180,000
Total Debits	$594,600

Credits

Accounts Payable (for merchandise)	$110,000
Interest Payable	1,600
Taxes Payable	21,000
Notes Payable (6%, long-term)	80,000
Accumulated Depreciation	62,000
Capital Stock	270,000
Retained Earnings	50,000
Total Credits	$594,600

(2) Income statement for 1975:

Sales		$800,000
Less Expenses:		
Cost of Goods Sold	$520,000	
Depreciation Expense	10,000	
Taxes	20,000	
Other Operating Expenses	201,500	
Interest	4,800	
Total Expenses		756,300
Net Income		$ 43,700
Less: Dividends		20,000
Increase in Retained Earnings		$ 23,700

(3) Summary of cash receipts and disbursements in 1975:

Cash Receipts

Cash Sales	$178,000	
Collections from Credit Customers	580,000	
Total Receipts		$758,000

Cash Disbursements

Payment to Suppliers of Merchandise	$501,000	
Payment to Suppliers of Miscellaneous Services	185,000	
Payment of Taxes	30,000	
Payment of Interest	4,800	
Payment of Dividends	20,000	
Purchase of Marketable Securities	40,000	
Total Disbursements		780,800

Excess of Disbursements over Receipts $ 22,800

(4) Purchases of merchandise during the period, all on account, were $510,000. All "Other Operating Expenses" were credited to Prepayments.

a. Prepare a balance sheet at January 1, 1975.

b. What is the interest payment date on the long-term notes?

Chapter 6

Elements of the Accounting Data-Processing System

The local, corner grocery is involved in many transactions every day of every month and the owner usually believes his record keeping is complex; imagine the complexity of recording and reporting the number of daily transactions made by a large chain of stores. Similarly, if processing the accounting data of a small nuts and bolts manufacturer whose gross sales are $50,000 a month is complex, the problems of processing the accounting data for the thousands of daily transactions made by Bethlehem Steel, or Ford, or Texaco must, at first glance, seem insurmountable.

Although the preceding chapters of this book have presented a sound approach to recording the many transactions that a business will be involved in, and to processing accounting data, the complexity of handling this data should not be minimized. It is this very complexity that has led to the increased use of equipment—mechanical, electric (punch cards), and electronic (computers)—to facilitate handling of great amounts of data with greater speed and accuracy. Although the highly technical phases, the design of systems, and operation of data-processing equipment are beyond the limits of this book, this chapter will discuss the general elements of data-processing systems and illustrate some of the components and operations used in the accounting system.

THE DATA-PROCESSING SYSTEM

The literature of data-processing systems recognizes three basic elements in converting raw data into useful information: input, processing, and output. Input consists of the data introduced into the system. Processing is the reviewing, collating, and arranging of data to develop useful information. Output is information presented in the desired format for the intended use. This framework applies to all data-processing systems regardless of the complexity of the equipment that may be used.

Input data for accounting purposes consist of documents generated, externally and internally, by the firm's activities. The output, for purposes of this discussion, consists primarily of the financial statements, although other reports and documents may also be produced. Processing includes designing the various files for data storage that are maintained and updated, preparing the instructions that determine the operations to be performed on the data, and performing the necessary calculations.

The remainder of this chapter discusses a manual record-keeping process where the steps in the processing are separate and distinct. Data-processing equipment accomplishes the same result with, however, a different sequence of operations. The basic elements illustrated here have counterparts in nearly all systems, whatever the equipment used. Appendix 6.1 of this chapter illustrates the record-keeping process for a small firm for a short time period.

THE BOOKKEEPING PROCESS

The first step in the bookkeeping process is almost always the preparation or receipt of an *underlying document* depicting the transaction. Examples are a sales ticket made out by a department store clerk to signal a sale, a purchase invoice and receiving report for the acquisition of merchandise, a bank check to signal a payment, or a requisition to the storeroom to signal materials put in use. In a large enterprise there are few, if any, transactions that are not first represented by a systematic memorandum or underlying document of some sort. The underlying document may also accumulate or summarize certain types of activities. Cash sales, for example, are rarely recorded individually in the accounting records; rather, the total for an entire day is accumulated, usually by a cash register, and one entry made for the day's cash sales.

The second step, called *journalizing*, involves a written record on a form known as a *journal*. A journal is a chronological record of transactions, each analyzed into its debits and credits to show all accounts affected.

In the third step in the bookkeeping process, called *posting*, the transactions are recorded in the accounts. The set of accounts is known as a *ledger*. Posting is merely transferring dates and amounts from the journal onto the account forms in the ledger.

The fourth step in the bookkeeping process is the preparation of the output, the financial statements and supporting schedules, which are based upon the accumulated content of the accounts.

Business Documents

Preparing business documents and memorandums precedes the recording of data into the accounting records. The bookkeeper is responsible for accumulating the documents and memorandums that depict the transactions to be entered. The number of types of underlying documents varies from firm to firm.

Repetitive transactions, such as purchase of materials and supplies, acquisition of services, preparing payrolls, payments of accounts due, sales, and collection of cash, usually are organized into a routine format. Specialized documents, frequently with multiple copies, are designed, and a well-ordered document flow pattern is established. Infrequent or nonstandard transactions and end-of-period adjustments also require the preparation of evidence as a basis for recording. Some firms use a document known as a *journal voucher* which, when signed or initialed by the proper authority, serves as support for the nonroutine transactions.

Among the more widely used business documents and forms are the following:

Purchase Order	Mail Receipts Listing
Purchase Invoice	Bank Deposit Slip
Vendor's Statement	Bank Statement
Debit (Adjustment) Memo	Petty Cash Receipt
Voucher	Materials Requisition
Check	Time or Attendance Card
Sales Invoice	Payroll Summary
Customer's Statement	Payroll Distribution
Credit (Adjustment) Memo	Journal Voucher
Cash Register Tape	

The Journal

The *journal* presents a chronological record of transactions. *Journalizing* consists of analyzing the transactions into the proper debits and credits and recording the results of the analysis in a journal. The journal contains accounting information classified by transaction. Further, each transaction is analyzed and recorded completely before the next one is entered. The journal is the first place in which a complete formal record of the transaction is made. It is thus sometimes called *the book of original entry.* By recording all information relating to each transaction in one place, the journal provides a chronological history, or running record, of the various transactions. The number of transactions, even in a small business, is so large that errors are bound to occur. It would be almost impossible to locate errors if a record such as the journal were not kept. Each journal entry can be checked independently for equal debits and credits, and postings in the ledger accounts can be traced back to the journal to determine the origin, authorization, and analysis of each transaction.

The Two-Column Journal Form

The journal form most convenient to introduce the elements of the journalizing procedure is the two-column form presented. This two-column form

Date	Accounts and Explanation	Ref.	Debit	Credit

Figure 6.1   Two-Column Journal Form

is sometimes called a *general* journal. Essentials of the form are a pair of columns in which the debits and credits are recorded and a place to indicate the names of the accounts affected by the transaction. As posting is done, there will be entered in the reference (Ref.) column the number, or page, of the account to which the amount has been posted or, perhaps, a check mark to indicate that the posting has been done.

The Ledger

A group of accounts arranged in orderly fashion is known as a *ledger*. The account is the unit of classification within the ledger for accumulating information. There are few essential requirements for the form of a ledger account. Space should be provided for the following data: account title; date of transaction; debit and credit amounts; and a reference to trace the posting to its source in a journal. Space for other explanatory data may sometimes be useful. The standard ledger form presented in Figure 6.2 also provides space for an explanation of each entry. A separate column is sometimes added to show the balance of the account.

LEDGER FORM
Account Title

Account No._

Date	Explanation	Ref.	Dr.	Date	Explanation	Ref.	Cr.
1975				1975			
Feb. 5		J 6	10 00			J9	70 00
6		J 7	60 00				
14		J10	55 50				

Figure 6.2   Standard Ledger Form

Journalizing and Posting

The following transactions are journalized in Figure 6.3.

Sept. 1, 1975   Cash sales of $150 are made. Supplies costing $50 are purchased from the Western Paper Company on account;

Page 23

Date 1975		Accounts and Explanation	Ref.	Debit	Credit
Sept.	1	Cash on Hand		1 5 0 00	
		Sales			1 5 0 00
		Supplies		5 0 00	
		Accounts Payable—Western			
		Paper Co.			5 0 00
		Invoice of 8/31. Terms 2/10, n/30.			
	2	Cash in Bank		1 0 0 00	
		Cash on Hand			1 0 0 00
		Raw Materials Used		5 0 0 00	
		Raw Materials			5 0 0 00
		Requisition No. 819			

Figure 6.3   Entries in Journal Illustrated

        invoice of Aug. 31; terms: 2/10, n/30 (2-percent discount if paid in ten days; payment due, in any case, within thirty days).

Sept. 2, 1975   A deposit of $100 is made in the bank. Raw materials costing $500 are requisitioned from the storeroom on Requisition No. 819.

The entries in Figure 6.3 illustrate certain conventions that should be observed when a journal of this type is used.

1. The year is inserted at the top of the date column, and the month and day of the month are recorded as indicated in the entries.
2. The debited accounts and amounts are entered first in each transaction.
3. The titles of the accounts to be credited are indented.
4. An explanation should be inserted below the formal part of the entry, if the debits and credits themselves do not describe the transaction clearly and completely. A reference to underlying documents and memorandums may frequently be shown in the explanation space.
5. A blank line is left between transactions.

    Notice that each entry names the accounts to be debited and credited. The exact titles of the ledger accounts should be used in order to avoid difficulties in posting.

    The Cash on Hand account and the journal form reproduced in Figure 6.4 serve to indicate how the posting is made to the ledger accounts and how a cross reference is maintained between the journal and the ledger.

Proof of the Ledger and the Journal

The trial balance of account balances serves as a test of the arithmetic accuracy of the ledger. A similar technique called *proof of the journal* is

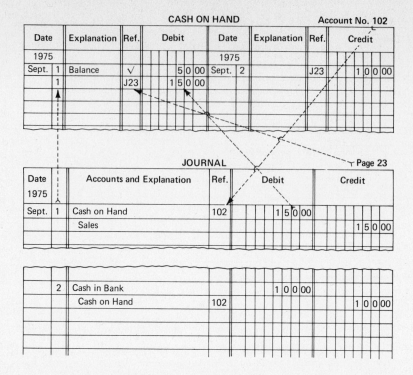

The arrows indicate steps in the posting procedure for the debit item of the first journal entry. The credit item of the September 2 journal entry has also been posted in the illustration. The "explanation" column in the ledger seldom is used except to indicate a balance in the account or to explain an unusual item.

Figure 6.4 Posting from the Journal to the Ledger

used as a test of the arithmetic accuracy of the journal. This operation consists of the addition of the debit amount column(s) and of the credit amount column(s) for a journal page or other group of journal entries. The totals are compared; the total debits must equal the total credits. If they do not, each transaction must be checked to insure that it has equal debits and credits.

SPECIALIZED-COLUMN JOURNALS

The process of posting, or transferring, figures from the journal to the ledger accounts is laborious and monotonous. When the two-column journal form is used, each journal debit and credit must be copied into the ledger individually. In practice this simple two-column form is usually replaced by a more elaborate journal or journals. One labor-saving device is to expand the journal into a multi-column record. The *specialized-column,* or *multi-column,* journal provides several debit and several credit columns to replace the two-column form. This subdivision permits separate columns to be reserved for the entering of debits or credits in accounts, such as Cash and Sales for a merchandising firm, that are used often. A simple multi-column journal form is shown in Figure 6.5.

		JOURNAL							Page 25
Date	Explana-tion	Cash		Mdse. Sales		Other Accounts			
		Debit	Credit	Debit	Credit	Debit	Credit	Ref.	Account Title

Figure 6.5   Multi-Column Journal Form

Construction of Specialized-Column Journals

Designing a specialized-column journal requires selecting the accounts to be allocated special columns. Specialized columns should be provided for the debits or credits, or both, of those accounts that are used most frequently. In practice it may not be easy to discover which will be used most often. If the business has been in operation for some time, the past transactions can be studied and a tabulation made of the number of entries to each side of each account. If there is no experience to use as a guide, an attempt is made to anticipate the types of transactions that will occur most frequently and a tentative set of column headings is selected. In any case, the column headings may have to be changed from time to time so the multi-column format may be efficiently used. When only one multi-column journal is used, two columns must always be reserved to record the debits and credits to the accounts for which specialized columns are not provided. The specialized column journal is composed of two segments: (1) specialized columns for frequent items and (2) an attached two-column journal form to provide for all other items.

Recording Entries in a Specialized-Column Journal

Recording transactions in a specialized-column journal is simpler than in a two-column journal. Frequently the transaction can be recorded on one line, but as many lines as necessary should be used in order to make the analysis of the transaction complete and clear. The explanation can be brief, but it must be sufficiently complete to provide adequate posting instructions.

Illustration

The Central Cleaner uses an eight-column journal. Through experience it has learned which accounts are most active and has provided specialized columns for them. Transactions for October 1, 2, and 31, 1975, appear in the specialized journal illustrated in Figure 6.6. The transactions were:

Oct. 1   Collections for cleaning service, $411.85.
           Cleaning supplies acquired for cash, $88.65.
Oct. 2   Collections for cleaning service, $424.90. Fire insurance premium for year paid by check No. 492 to Western Insurance Company, $128.00.
Oct. 31   Collections for cleaning service, $440.15. Bank deposit, $849.50. $4,000.00 is borrowed from the Merchants Bank on a sixty-day, 8-percent note.

Posting from a Specialized-Column Journal

There are two general rules for posting from specialized-column journals. (1) Post the individual items from the Other Accounts columns. (2) Post all column totals except those of the Other Accounts columns. Examples of posting from both types of columns are given in the illustrative multi-column journal. As that journal demonstrates, posting should be indicated by a notation of the account number in the reference column for items that have been posted individually; for items posted by total, the notation should appear below the column total. A check mark may be used to indicate posting if the accounts are not numbered, as when an alphabetical arrangement is used.

In summary, the procedure at the end of each month would include the following steps:

Total each amount column.
Prove equality of debit and credit column totals.
Post the specialized-columns totals.
Complete the posting of the Other Accounts column individual items.
Enter additional adjusting entries and closing entries at the end of the period in the Other Accounts columns (or the standard two-column journal).
Post transactions journalized in the preceding step.

Advantages of Specialized Columns

The principal advantage of using specialized columns is the savings in posting time. The posting of a column total takes the place of the posting of each of the individual items that appear in the column. Specialized columns also facilitate the process of journalizing, since most bookkeepers find it easier to analyze transactions when the commonly used accounts are spread across a columnar sheet. Each entry also takes less vertical space and more entries can, therefore, be made on a journal page.

Date	Explanation	Ck. No.	Cash in Bank Dr.	Cash in Bank Cr.	Cash on Hand Dr.	Cash on Hand Cr.	Cleaning Supplies Dr.	Cleaning Revenue Cr.	Other Accounts Dr.	Other Accounts Cr.	Ref.	Account Title
1975												
Oct. 1	Receipts for day											
1	Purchase of supplies	492										
2	Receipts for day				128 00						132	Unexpired Ins.
2	Western Insurance Co.											
31	Receipts for day		849 50									
31	Deposit			128 00	440 15	849 50	88 65	424 90		128 00	203	Notes Payable
31	8%, 60-day note, Merchants Bank											

Cash in Bank No. 102

Explanation	Ref.	Dr.	Date	Explanation	Ref.	Cr.
Balance	√ J16	567 23 11 468 42	1975 Oct. 31		J16	6 827 14
		4 000 00 11 468 42				

(102)   (102)

Cash on Hand No. 101

Explanation	Ref.	Dr.	Date	Explanation	Ref.	Cr.
Balance	√ J16	351 25 10 461 24	1975 Oct. 31		J16	6 827 14 10 518 97
		6 827 14				10 461 24

(101)   (101)

Cleaning Supplies No. 121

Explanation	Ref.	Dr.	Date	Explanation	Ref.	Cr.
		10 518 97	1975 Oct. 1	Balance	√ J16	1 921 60
		1 921 60				10 311 24

(121)   (401)

Unexpired Insurance No. 132

Explanation	Ref.	Dr.	Date	Explanation	Ref.	Cr.
		75 00 128 00				
		2 123 09 4 317 00				

Notes Payable No. 203

Explanation	Ref.	Dr.	Date	Explanation	Ref.	Cr.
			1975 Oct. 31	60-day, 8%	J16	4 000 00

Cleaning Revenue No. 401

Date	Explanation	Ref.	Dr.	Date	Explanation	Ref.	Cr.
				1975 Oct. 31		J16	10 311 24

Figure 6.6 Posting from Eight-Column Journal to Ledger

MULTIPLE JOURNALS

The advantages of specialization can be extended further by replacing the single multi-column journal by a group of specialized journals. To select the journals appropriate for a particular enterprise is a cost-benefit problem similar to that of selecting specialized columns for a multi-column journal. A study is made of actual or expected transactions in an attempt to discover which types of transactions occur most frequently. Specialized journals are provided for those types.

There is no standard set of journals suitable for all firms. However, in most concerns four specialized journals are likely to be cost effective: cash receipts; cash disbursements; revenue recognition (particularly sales); and acquisition of goods and services (particularly purchases of merchandise and raw materials). The size of the firm and the nature of its operations will, of course, affect the number and types of specialized journals employed.

A standard two-column, or general journal, form may be included to complete the system of journals. This journal would be used only for transactions that cannot be recorded in the specialized journals. Adjusting and closing entries at the end of the accounting period, in particular, are most likely to be recorded in a general journal. Posting from specialized journals follows the same principles outlined for the multi-column journal.

The only specialized journal illustrated in this chapter is the Voucher Register.

THE VOUCHER SYSTEM

The *voucher system* seeks to provide control over disbursements of cash by requiring written authorization or approval by a responsible official for each payment. The voucher becomes the underlying document for all transactions involving cash disbursements. A voucher, checked but not yet approved for payment, is shown in Figure 6.7. Additional control features of the system will be discussed in Chapter 8. There are many possible variations in the detailed forms and procedures of voucher systems, but the plan outlined below contains the essential features of an effective system.

The procedure is as follows:

1. A voucher is completed and payment approved after an invoice has been received and quantity, quality, and price have been checked.
2. The voucher is recorded in the voucher register, a specialized journal, in accordance with the distribution of accounts and amounts indicated thereon.
3. The vouchers are retained in an unpaid-voucher file pending date of payment.
4. The check for payment of the voucher is drawn, entered in the check register, and sent to the payee.
5. The voucher is transferred to the paid-voucher file.

VOUCHER FORM

SEYMOUR METAL PRODUCTS COMPANY 1731 Lake Ave. Chicago, Illinois 60612

Vou. No. 5785
Ck. No. _____

To MERCHANTS NATIONAL BANK 2-76   _____19___
Chicago, Illinois 60602

Pay to the order of Krebs Paper Company   _____ $ ____
_____Dollars

Seymour Metal Products Company

By _____
Treasurer

· ·

Seymour Metal Products Co.   Detach before depositing   Ck. No.

Our No.	Date of Invoice	Reference	Amount of Invoice	Deduc- tions	Dis- count	Balance
B5621	8/3/75		575.50			

VOUCHER DISTRIBUTION

Account No.		Explanation	Amount	Account No.		Explanation	Amount
Gen. Led.	Sub. Led.			Gen. Led.	Sub. Led.		
52	5213		575.50				

Ck'd By *ELD*   Entered By *RW*   Payment OK'd By _____

Figure 6.7   A Voucher

The Voucher Register

After the voucher is prepared and approved, it is entered in the Voucher Register such as the one in Figure 6.8. The payables column, when the voucher system is used, is usually headed Vouchers Payable rather than Accounts Payable.

A special procedure must be adopted when a bill is settled or cancelled by some means other than immediate payment, such as by issuing a promissory note or by returning the goods. One such procedure is illustrated in the voucher register by the notation in the Paid column for

VOUCHER REGISTER

Date	Voucher No.	Name	Paid		Vouchers Payable Cr.	Merchandise, Dr.				Operating Expense, Dr.			Other Accounts, Dr.			
			Date	Check No.		Gasoline	Kerosene	Oils	Accessories	Acct. No.	✓	Amount	Amount	Acct. No.	✓	Explanation
1975																
Aug. 1	2891	East Refining Co.	8/6	2560	220 62	220 62										
3	2892	Penn Oil Co.	8/3	2562	125 85			125 85								
3	2893	Central Auto Supply Co.	8/5	See GJ	174 93				174 93							
4	2894	East Refining Co.	8/3	2561	221 54	221 54										
5	2895	Murray Oil Co.	8/12	2563	205 75		205 75									
31	2942	Payroll	8/31	2603	1 654 00								1 900 00	213	✓	Wages Payable
													68 75	215-2	✓	Payroll Taxes Payable
													177 25	215-1	✓	Withheld Income Tax
31	2943	Ford Auto Sales			36 50					5206	✓	36 50				
					8 559 92	2 257 62	967 43	375 82	457 62			1 674 93	1 841 50			
					(211)	(113-G)	(113-K)	(113-O)	(113-A)			(50)				

Figure 6.8 Excerpt from a Voucher Register

voucher 2893. The notation refers to an entry made in the general journal on August 5 of a debit to Vouchers Payable and a credit to Notes Payable. When the time comes to pay the note, a new voucher must be prepared.

Another special problem arises when more than one check is issued to pay a single voucher. Provision must be made to indicate the partial payment of the voucher in the Paid column of the voucher register. If it is known in advance that an invoice will be paid in several installments, a separate voucher should be prepared for each installment. If one voucher has been entered for an invoice and it is later decided to pay the amount in a predetermined series of payments, the original voucher should be cancelled and new ones issued, one for each payment. The simplest way to record the new voucher is to debit Vouchers Payable (to cancel the old voucher) and credit Vouchers Payable (to set up the new vouchers) in the voucher register. The notation "Cancelled" should be made in the Paid column for the old voucher. When several vouchers are paid by one check, there need be no special procedure. The same check number and date are entered in the Paid column for each of the vouchers.

The handling of voucher 2942 indicates a procedure whereby both debits and credits are recorded in the same column. Since it can be assumed that only one voucher a month is prepared for the payroll, and since it is unlikely that there would be any other nonvoucher credits than those for salary deductions, an Other Accounts, Cr. column is not provided in the journal. Instead, the credits of $68.75 for Payroll Taxes Payable and $177.25 for Withheld Income Tax are circled (or shown in red) in the Other Accounts, Dr. column. In totaling the column, such items are subtracted from the noncircled debits appearing in the column.

CONTROLLING ACCOUNTS AND SUBSIDIARY LEDGERS

The Controlling-Account System

Up to this point, it has been assumed that all of the accounts are kept in a single ledger. In most firms, such a ledger would become bulky. To overcome this inconvenience, the ledger accounts are divided into several groups. Certain accounts which are sufficiently similar so that they can logically be grouped together are removed from the principal ledger, called the *general ledger*, and are replaced there by a single controlling account. The group of individual accounts, now kept together as a separate ledger, is known as a *subsidiary ledger*. Each controlling account exhibits summarized data relating to a group of accounts that are shown in detail in a subsidiary ledger. The general ledger will usually contain a number of controlling accounts as well as all of the other accounts which have not been organized into groups.

When a controlling-account system is in use, the journalizing and posting procedures must be so designed that, after completing the posting for a period such as a month, the balance of a controlling account in the general ledger will equal the sum of the balances of the individual accounts in the corresponding subsidiary ledger.

Controlling Accounts: Examples

The controlling-account system can be adapted to any group of similar accounts. Some common applications of this method are shown below. Notice that the subsidiary record is not always a group of ledger accounts on the standard ledger form. It may be a group of specially designed forms or merely be a file or memorandums.

General Ledger Controlling Account	Type of Subsidiary Record
Accounts Receivable	Individual customers' ledger accounts, or a file of uncollected sales invoices.
Accounts Payable	Individual ledger accounts, or a file of unpaid purchase invoices.
Expense Control	Individual expense accounts.
Capital Stock	A record of the stock certificates and number of shares held by each stockholder.
Notes Receivable	A file of uncollected notes receivable, or a "register" or book in which the notes are listed.
Raw Material on Hand	Separate record card for each item of material used in manufacturing.
Equipment	Separate record card for each item of equipment. This is often known as a plant ledger.
Land	Separate record cards showing description and cost of each parcel of land owned.

Accounts other than those listed above may serve as controlling accounts, and each would have an appropriate subsidiary record.

Operation of the Controlling-Account System

It has been indicated in the previous discussion that the balance of the controlling account must be equal to the sum of the balances of the individual subsidiary accounts, at least at the end of the accounting period. The bookkeeping procedure must, therefore, provide for some plan of posting so that the same data will be reflected in both the subsidiary record and the controlling account. For example, if a customer is invoiced for a sale of $10 on account, the amount must be reflected as a debit in the customer's account in the Accounts Receivable subsidiary record and also as a debit in the Accounts Receivable controlling account in the general ledger. Only one credit is reflected, however, in the Sales account. Although the debit amount is in both the customer's account and the Accounts Receivable account, the books will not be out of balance because the individual customer's account does not appear in the trial balance of the general ledger. Only the balance of the controlling account is listed.

    If the controlling-account system required every entry to be posted in duplicate, the use of controlling accounts could become an expensive and difficult process. Various methods are used to expedite the procedure. These methods provide for summarizing ("batching") of data for entry into a journal or the posting of a column total to the controlling account where feasible. It is not necessary that *individual* transaction amounts be posted to the controlling account, a summary account, although such detailed data are necessary in the subsidiary record.

Schedules of Subsidiary Ledgers

At the end of each posting period, the sum of the balances of the accounts in each subsidiary ledger should be reconciled with the balance of the corresponding controlling account. If they are found to be equal, it is reasonable to assume that posting to the subsidiary ledger and to the controlling account have been done properly. At the end of the accounting period, this comparison often takes the form of a schedule of the subsidiary ledger. The schedule lists the balances, account by account, of the subsidiary ledger and shows a total equal to that of the controlling account. An example schedule of Accounts Receivable is illustrated in Schedule 6.1.

SCHEDULE 6.1

Schedule of Accounts Receivable
May 31, 1975

Customer *A*	$110
Customer *B*	250
Customer *C*	375
Customer *D*	120
Accounts Receivable balance in the General Ledger	$855

CONTRA AND ADJUNCT ACCOUNTS

The controlling account technique was developed to relieve the general ledger of a large number of detailed accounts covering a similar area and to replace them with a single account. There are instances where the opposite effect is desired—namely, to expand the number of accounts to provide significant data in addition to that which would be sufficient for the major financial statements. The devices to provide the additional information are *contra* and *adjunct* accounts.

Prior illustrations have included a balance sheet contra-asset account, "Buildings—Accumulated Depreciation." When the balance in the Buildings—Accumulated Depreciation account is subtracted from the Buildings account, the undepreciated cost, or "book value," of the buildings is obtained. In this instance, both the original cost of the buildings and the accumulated depreciation are considered of such significance that it is desired that they be reflected in separate accounts. This is accomplished by establishing the pair of accounts, one of which is referred to as the primary account, the other as the *contra* account. A contra account merely accumulates subtractions from the primary account.

Accounts that accumulate additions to a primary account are called *adjunct accounts*. (No examples of adjunct accounts have been presented so far. One example, discussed in Chapter 15, is the Premium on Bonds Payable account, which shows proceeds of bond issues in excess of par, or face, value.) The contra and adjunct accounts are presented on the same financial statement as the primary account and are subtracted or added to the primary account. See the treatments of Accumulated Depreciation and the Allowance for Uncollectible Accounts in the balance sheet for R. L. Smith Stores, Inc. in Chapter 2. The contra and adjunct accounts are included in the general ledger and, accordingly, enter into the preparation of the trial balance.

THE CHART OF ACCOUNTS

Designing an accounting system requires determining the particular accounts that will contain the detailed information to appear on the financial statements. The list of required accounts is known as the *chart of accounts*. The chart shows the accounts in the order they appear in the ledger, which is usually determined by the order in which they appear in the financial statements. Each account is assigned a number, or other symbol, which appears on the corresponding ledger sheet. Care should be exercised in designing the numbering system. It should be flexible enough so that the number of accounts can be expanded substantially at any part of the classification. It should follow a definite pattern so that the classification of an account can readily be determined from its number and so that the numbers of the more frequently used accounts can easily be memorized by the bookkeeping staff. The chart of account's numbers are often substituted for the complete account title at various points in the accounting records.

The following chart of accounts is a simple illustration of such a list.

Chart of Accounts

1—Assets
    11—Current Assets
        111—Cash
            111–1—Cash on Hand
            111–2—Cash in Bank
        112—Receivables
            112–1—Accounts Receivable Control
                112–1C—Allowance for Uncollectible Accounts
            112–2—Notes Receivable
            112–3—Interest Receivable

113—Inventories
    113–1—Merchandise Inventory
    113–2—Store and Office Supplies Inventory
114—Prepayments
    114–1—Unexpired Insurance
    114–2—Advances to Employees
12—Noncurrent Assets
121—Land
122—Buildings
    122C—Accumulated Depreciation of Buildings
123—Furniture and Fixtures
    123C—Accumulated Depreciation of Furniture and Fixtures
124—Delivery Trucks
    124C—Accumulated Depreciation of Delivery Trucks

2—Liabilities
21—Current Liabilities
2101—Accounts Payable Control
2102—Notes Payable
2103—Wages and Salaries Payable
2104—Interest Payable
2105—Taxes Payable
    2105–1—Withheld Income Tax
    2105–2—Payroll Taxes Payable
    2105–3—Property Taxes Payable
    2105–4—Income Tax Payable
2106—Dividends Payable
2110—Advances by Customers
22—Indeterminate-term Liabilities
221—Deferred Income Taxes
23—Long-term Liabilities
231—Bonds Payable

3—Capital
31—Contributed Capital
311—Stock Outstanding
    311–1—Preferred Stock Outstanding
    311–2—Common Stock Outstanding
312—Premium on Capital Stock
32—Retained Earnings

4—Revenue
41—Sales
42—Interest Revenue
43—Dividend Revenue
49—Miscellaneous Revenue

5—Expenses
51—Cost of Goods Sold

52—Selling Expenses
    5201—Salesmen's Salaries
    5202—Advertising
    5203—Depreciation of Store Furniture and Fixtures
    5204—Depreciation of Delivery Trucks
    5205—Delivery Salaries
    5206—Repairs of Delivery Trucks
    5207—Payroll Taxes on Sales Force
    5208—Store Supplies Used
    5220—Miscellaneous Selling Expenses
53—General and Administrative Expenses
    5301—Officers' Salaries
    5302—Office Salaries
    5303—Office Supplies Used
    5304—Depreciation of Office Furniture and Fixtures
    5305—Janitors' Wages
    5306—Insurance Expense
    5307—Payroll Taxes on Office Force
    5308—Property and Corporation Taxes
    5309—Depreciation of Building
    5320—Miscellaneous General and Administrative Expenses
54—Interest Charges
55—Income Taxes

6—Income Distributions
    61—Dividends on Preferred Stock
    62—Dividends on Common Stock

Subsidiary ledgers may be included in the chart of accounts if the accounts lend themselves to such treatment. For instance, the classification title 52, Selling Expenses, could become a controlling-account title with numbers 5201 to 5220 being assigned to the individual accounts in the Selling Expense Subsidiary Ledger.

The account numbers are shown on the ledger sheets, and the accounts are usually kept in the same order in the ledgers as they appear on the chart. The account numbers are used in journals to indicate the accounts to which postings have been made.

SUMMARY OF THE BOOKKEEPING CYCLE

The essential steps in the bookkeeping cycle for a nonmanufacturing concern may be outlined as follows.

1. Journalize the transactions from day to day for a fixed period of time; a month usually is the most convenient period. Prove the journal by totaling the columns and then reconciling the debit and credit column totals.

2. Post the transactions to accounts in the ledger. All column total posting can usually be deferred until the end of a month. More frequent posting of the items in Other Accounts and controlling-account columns may be desirable.

3. Prepare a trial balance at the end of the month. The trial balance should consist of a list of the balances of the general ledger accounts, each controlling account being supported by a list of its subsidiary ledger accounts. The trial balance serves primarily as a check upon the clerical accuracy of the recording process.

4. If the end of the month is also the end of the accounting period, it is likely that additional adjusting entries will be required. These entries would be journalized, the journal proved, and the entries posted. Another trial balance might be taken at this point. This adjusted trial balance can serve as a convenient source of information for the construction of financial statements.

The following additional steps will be taken at the end of the accounting period.

5. Prepare the financial statements. The net income retained as shown on the income statement, when added to the retained earnings as shown on the trial balance, should provide a new retained-earnings amount that will enable the preparation of a balance sheet which is complete or in balance. A presentation of this calculation of the new balance of retained earnings should appear either in the balance sheet, at the close of the income statement, or in a special schedule.

6. Journalize the closing entries. All revenue and expense that have been provided to accumulate the details of operations for one accounting period should be closed and the net change in retained earnings (or other corresponding proprietary account if the enterprise is not incorporated) recorded in that account, so that only the balance sheet accounts contain balances to be carried into the following accounting period. Prove the journal.

7. Post the closing entries.

8. Rule all closed accounts.

9. Prepare a post-closing trial balance. The purpose of this step is to obtain a final check upon the work done on the accounts at the close of the period and to make certain that the accounts are in balance at the beginning of the following period. It is not necessary to prepare a formal schedule for this purpose. An adding machine tape which demonstrates the equality of balances will usually be sufficient.

Bookkeeping for a manufacturing concern follows the same pattern, except that a special statement of manufacturing operations will be prepared in addition to the financial statements and end-of-period entries will also include the transfer of the balances of the production-cost accounts to work in process.

Appendix 6.1 of this chapter illustrates a comprehensive example of the record-keeping process.

APPENDIX 6.1: ILLUSTRATION OF THE RECORD-KEEPING PROCESS

The Reliable Television Service Company was organized by J. A. Blair to acquire and continue the operation of a business formerly known as the Star Television Repair Shop. The following data relate to the acquisition of the business on December 20, 1975, and the operations for the remainder of the month.

Dec. 20   Mr. Blair assumed the following assets and liabilities upon payment of $15,000 to Mr. Star by personal check.

Assets

Repair Parts	$ 2,550
Supplies	260
Unexpired Insurance	600
Prepaid Rent	300
Prepaid Property Taxes	10
Office Equipment	1,980
Repair Equipment	5,700
Service Trucks	11,400
	$22,800

Liabilities

Accounts Payable, Eschen Supply Co.	$ 1,200
Accounts Payable, Roedel Supply Co.	600
Equipment Contracts Payable	6,000
	$ 7,800

Dec. 22   Receipts for December 22 activity: television service, $168; repair parts, $27. (All services and sales of parts are on a cash basis.)
A telephone was installed and a cash payment was made for one month's service, $45.

Dec. 23   Receipts of the day: television service, $335; repair parts, $55.
Purchase of parts, on account, Eschen Supply Company, $108.

Dec. 24   Deposit of receipts of December 23.
Receipts of the day: television service, $286; repair parts, $44.
Purchase of supplies, $36, cash.

Dec. 26   Deposit of receipts of December 24, less $36.
Receipts of the day: television service, $280; repair parts, $41.
Purchase of parts, on account, Roedel Supply Company, $96.
Purchase of gasoline and oil for trucks, $19, cash.

Dec. 27   Deposit of receipts of December 26, less $20.
Receipts of the day: television service, $265; repair parts, $42.
Payment on account, by check, to Eschen Supply Company, $300.

Dec. 29   Deposit of receipts of December 27.
Receipts of the day: television service, $282; repair parts, $44.
Purchase of parts, on account, Eschen Supply Company, $86.
Payment on account, by check, to Roedel Supply Company, $375.

Dec. 30   Deposit of receipts of December 29.
Receipts of the day: television service, $258; repair parts, $41.
Purchase of parts, on account, Roedel Supply Company, $110.

Gasoline, oil, and repairs for service trucks paid, by cash, $38.

Dec. 31   Deposit of receipts of December 30, less $38.

Invoice for advertising paid, by check, $41.

Receipts of the day: television service, $248; repair parts, $40.

Payment, by check, of office salary earned to date, $250.00, less withholding for payroll taxes, $15, and income tax, $35.

Payment, by check, of servicemen's wages earned to date, $800; less withholdings for payroll taxes, $48, and income tax, $122. A check was drawn to J. A. Blair for personal use, $150.

Additional data accumulated at the end of the year relative to the operations of December 22-31, 1975 (one third of a month) are as follows:

(1) Inventory of repair parts, December 31, $2,715.

(2) Inventory of supplies, December 31, $264.

(3) Estimated cost of electricity supplied by Union Electric Co., $21.

(4) Insurance premiums, per year, $648.

(5) Rent, per month, $450.

(6) Property taxes, per year, $360.

(7) Depreciation on office equipment, per year, $432.

(8) Depreciation on repair equipment, per year, $1,260.

(9) Depreciation on service trucks, per year, $2,592.

(10) Payroll taxes levied on employer, $95.

(11) Assign one third of a month's telephone service to the period.

This illustration will include the following detailed technical steps in the accounting cycle:

1. Journalizing of daily transactions
2. Proof of journal
3. Posting of daily transaction entries to the ledger
4. Preparation of an unadjusted trial balance
5. Journalizing of adjusting transactions
6. Proof of journal
7. Posting of adjusting transaction entries to the ledger
8. Preparation of an adjusted trial balance
9. Preparation of the income statement
10. Preparation of the balance sheet
11. Journalizing of closing transactions
12. Proof of journal
13. Posting of closing transactions entries to the ledger
14. Preparation of a post-closing trial balance
15. Ruling of closed accounts
16. Ruling and balancing of open accounts.

Journalizing Daily Transactions

The date of entry and the accounts and amounts to be debited and credited are entered for each transaction. Explanations are included only when essential to clarify the transaction. The posting reference column is to be completed at the time of posting. The journal is shown in Schedule 6.2.

JOURNAL

Page 1

Date 1975		Accounts and Explanation	Ref.		Dr.			Cr.	
Dec.	20	Repair Parts	131	2	550	00			
		Supplies	132		260	00			
		Unexpired Insurance	141		600	00			
		Prepaid Rent	142		300	00			
		Prepaid Property Taxes	143		10	00			
		Office Equipment	151	1	980	00			
		Repair Equipment	152	5	700	00			
		Service Trucks	153	11	400	00			
		Accounts Payable, Eschen Supply Co.	211				1	200	00
		Accounts Payable, Roedel Supply Co.	212					600	00
		Equipment Contracts Payable	214				6	000	00
		J. A. Blair, Capital	311				15	000	00
		Assumed assets and liabilities of Star Television Shop. Payment to Mr. Star, $15,000, by check.							
	22	Cash on Hand	111		195	00			
		Television Service Revenue	411					168	00
		Sales of Parts	412					27	00
	22	Prepaid Telephone Service	144		45	00			
		Cash on Hand	111					45	00
		Advance payment for one month							
	23	Cash on Hand	111		390	00			
		Television Service Revenue	411					335	00
		Sales of Parts	412					55	00
	23	Repair Parts	131		108	00			
		Accounts Payable, Eschen Supply Co.	211					108	00
	24	Cash in Bank	112		390	00			
		Cash on Hand	111					390	00
	24	Cash on Hand	111		330	00			
		Television Service Revenue	411					286	00
		Sales of Parts	412					44	00
	24	Supplies	132		36	00			
		Cash on Hand	111					36	00
	26	Cash in Bank	112		294	00			
		Cash on Hand	111					294	00

Date 1975		Accounts and Explanation	Ref.	Dr.			Cr.	
Dec	26	Cash on Hand	111	321	00			
		Television Service Revenue	411				280	00
		Sales of Parts	412				41	00
	26	Repair Parts	131	96	00			
		Accounts Payable, Roedel Supply Co.	212				96	00
	26	Truck Operations Expense	520	19	00			
		Cash on Hand	111				19	00
	27	Cash in Bank	112	301	00			
		Cash on Hand	111				301	00
	27	Cash on Hand	111	307	00			
		Television Service Revenue	411				265	00
		Sales of Parts	412				42	00
	27	Accounts Payable, Eschen Supply Co.	211	300	00			
		Cash in Bank	112				300	00
	29	Cash in Bank	112	307	00			
		Cash on Hand	111				307	00
	29	Cash on Hand	111	326	00			
		Television Service Revenue	411				282	00
		Sales of Parts	412				44	00
	29	Repair Parts	131	86	00			
		Accounts Payable, Eschen Supply Co.	211				86	00
	29	Accounts Payable, Roedel Supply Co.	212	375	00			
		Cash in Bank	112				375	00
	30	Cash in Bank	112	326	00			
		Cash on Hand	111				326	00
	30	Cash on Hand	111	299	00			
		Television Service Revenue	411				258	00
		Sales of Parts	412				41	00
	30	Repair Parts	131	110	00			
		Accounts Payable, Roedel Supply Co.	212				110	00

JOURNAL (Cont'd)

Date 1975		Accounts and Explanation	Ref.	Dr.			Cr.	
Dec.	30	Truck Operations Expense	520	38	00			
		Cash on Hand	111				38	00
	31	Cash in Bank	112	261	00			
		Cash on Hand	111				261	00
	31	Advertising Expense	524	41	00			
		Cash in Bank	112				41	00
	31	Cash on Hand	111	288	00			
		Television Service Revenue	411				248	00
		Sales of Parts	412				40	00
	31	Office Salary Expense	522	250	00			
		Payroll Taxes Payable	216				15	00
		Withheld Income Tax	215				35	00
		Cash in Bank	112				200	00
	31	Servicemen's Wages Expense	523	800	00			
		Payroll Taxes Payable	216				48	00
		Withheld Income Tax	215				122	00
		Cash in Bank	112				630	00
	31	J. A. Blair, Drawings	312	150	00			
		Cash in Bank	112				150	00
				29 589	00	29	589	00

Proof of the Journal

The totals of $29,589 in the debit and credit columns provide the proof of the journal to this point.

Posting of Daily Entries

Since this is a new firm, there are no opening balances in any of the ledger accounts. Account numbers have been inserted alongside the account titles in the ledger for posting reference purposes.

See the following ledger accounts and the reference column in the journal. Cross references are indicated by use of the corresponding ledger account numbers in the journal and the corresponding journal page numbers in the ledger. The ledger accounts are complete. They include not only the data posted from the daily transactions that have already been journalized, but also the adjusting and closing entries journalized later and the ruling and balancing operations.

LEDGER

Cash on Hand   (111)

Date	Explanation	Ref.	Dr.			Date	Explanation	Ref.	Cr.		
1975						1975					
Dec. 22		J1		195	00	Dec. 22		J1		45	00
23		J1		390	00	24		J1		390	00
24		J1		330	00	24		J1		36	00
26		J2		321	00	26		J1		294	00
27		J2		307	00	26		J2		19	00
29		J2		326	00	27		J2		301	00
30		J2		299	00	29		J2		307	00
31		J3		288	00	30		J2		326	00
						30		J3		38	00
						31		J3		261	00
						31	Balance	√		439	00
			2	456	00				2	456	00
1976											
Jan. 1	Balance	√		439	00						

Cash in Bank   (112)

Date	Explanation	Ref.	Dr.			Date	Explanation	Ref.	Cr.		
1975						1975					
Dec. 24		J1		390	00	Dec. 27		J2		300	00
26		J1		294	00	29		J2		375	00
27		J2		301	00	31		J3		41	00
29		J2		307	00	31		J3		200	00
30		J2		326	00	31		J3		630	00
31		J3		261	00	31		J3		150	00
						31	Balance	√		183	00
			1	879	00				1	879	00
1976											
Jan. 1	Balance	√		183	00						

Repair Parts   (131)

Date	Explanation	Ref.	Dr.			Date	Explanation	Ref.	Cr.		
1975						1975					
Dec. 20		J1	2	550	00	Dec. 31		J3		235	00
23		J1		108	00	31	Balance	√	2	715	00
26		J2		96	00						
29		J2		86	00						
30		J2		110	00						
			2	950	00				2	950	00
1976											
Jan. 1	Balance	√	2	715	00						

LEDGER (Cont'd)

Supplies (132)

Date	Explanation	Ref.	Dr.		Date	Explanation	Ref.	Cr.	
1975 Dec. 20		J1	260	00	1975 Dec. 31		J3	32	00
24		J1	36	00	31	Balance	✓	264	00
			296	00				296	00
1976 Jan. 1	Balance	✓	264	00					

Unexpired Insurance (141)

Date	Explanation	Ref.	Dr.		Date	Explanation	Ref.	Cr.	
1975 Dec. 20		J1	600	00	1975 Dec. 31		J3	18	00
					31	Balance	✓	582	00
			600	00				600	00
1976 Jan. 1	Balance	✓	582	00					

Prepaid Rent (142)

Date	Explanation	Ref.	Dr.		Date	Explanation	Ref.	Cr.	
1975 Dec. 20		J1	300	00	1975 Dec. 31		J4	150	00
					31	Balance	✓	150	00
			300	00				300	00
1976 Jan. 1	Balance	✓	150	00					

Prepaid Property Taxes (143)

Date	Explanation	Ref.	Dr.		Date	Explanation	Ref.	Cr.	
1975 Dec. 20		J1	10	00	1975 Dec. 31		J4	10	00

Prepaid Telephone Service (144)

Date	Explanation	Ref.	Dr.		Date	Explanation	Ref.	Cr.	
1975 Dec. 22		J1	45	00	1975 Dec. 31		J4	15	00
					31	Balance	✓	30	00
			45	00				45	00
1976 Jan. 1	Balance	✓	30	00					

Office Equipment   (151)

Date	Explanation	Ref.	Dr.		Date	Explanation	Ref.	Cr.	
1975 Dec. 20		J1	1 980	00	1975 Dec. 31 31	 Balance	J4 √	 1 968	12 00 00
			1 980	00				1 980	00
1976 Jan. 1	Balance	√	1 968	00					

Repair Equipment   (152)

Date	Explanation	Ref.	Dr.		Date	Explanation	Ref.	Cr.	
1975 Dec. 20		J1	5 700	00	1975 Dec. 31 31	 Balance	J4 √	 5 665	35 00 00
			5 700	00				5 700	00
1976 Jan. 1	Balance	√	5 665	00					

Service Trucks   (153)

Date	Explanation	Ref.	Dr.		Date	Explanation	Ref.	Cr.	
1975 Dec. 20		J1	11 400	00	1975 Dec. 31 31	 Balance	J4 √	 11 328	72 00 00
			11 400	00				11 400	00
1976 Jan. 1	Balance	√	11 328	00					

Accounts Payable—Eschen Supply Co.   (211)

Date	Explanation	Ref.	Dr.		Date	Explanation	Ref.	Cr.	
1975 Dec. 27 31	 Balance	J2 √	 1 094	300 00 00	1975 Dec. 20 23 29		J1 J1 J2	1 200 108 86	00 00 00
			1 394	00				1 394	00
					1976 Jan. 1	 Balance	 √	 1 094	 00

LEDGER (Cont'd)

Accounts Payable—Roedel Supply Co. (212)

Date	Explanation	Ref.	Dr.		Date	Explanation	Ref.	Cr.	
1975 Dec. 29		J2	375	00	1975 Dec. 20		J1	600	00
31	Balance	√	431	00	26		J2	96	00
					30		J2	110	00
			806	00				806	00
					1976 Jan. 1	Balance	√	431	00

Accounts Payable—Union Electric Co. (213)

					Date	Explanation	Ref.	Cr.	
					1975 Dec. 31		J3	21	00

Equipment Contracts Payable (214)

					Date	Explanation	Ref.	Cr.		
					1975 Dec. 20		J1	6	000	00

Withheld Income Tax (215)

Date	Explanation	Ref.	Dr.		Date	Explanation	Ref.	Cr.	
1975 Dec. 31	Balance	√	157	00	1975 Dec. 31		J3	35	00
					31		J3	122	00
			157	00				157	00
					1976 Jan. 1	Balance	√	157	00

Payroll Taxes Payable (216)

Date	Explanation	Ref.	Dr.		Date	Explanation	Ref.	Cr.	
1975 Dec. 31	Balance	√	158	00	1975 Dec. 31		J3	15	00
					31		J3	48	00
					31		J4	95	00
			158	00				158	00
					1976 Jan. 1	Balance	√	158	00

LEDGER (Cont'd)

J. A. Blair, Capital   (311)

Date	Explanation	Ref.		Dr.		Date	Explanation	Ref.		Cr.	
1975						1975					
Dec. 31		J4		150	00	Dec. 20		J1	15	000	00
31	Balance	√	15	463	00	31		J4		613	00
			15	613	00				15	613	00
						1976					
						Jan. 1	Balance	√	15	463	00

J. A. Blair, Drawings   (312)

1975						1975					
Dec. 31		J3		150	00	Dec. 31		J4		150	00

Television Service Revenue   (411)

1975						1975					
Dec. 31		J4	2	122	00	Dec. 22		J1		168	00
						23		J1		335	00
						24		J1		286	00
						26		J2		280	00
						27		J2		265	00
						29		J2		282	00
						30		J2		258	00
						31		J3		248	00
			2	122	00				2	122	00

Sales of Parts   (412)

1975						1975					
Dec. 31		J4		334	00	Dec. 22		J1		27	00
						23		J1		55	00
						24		J1		44	00
						26		J2		41	00
						27		J2		42	00
						29		J2		44	00
						30		J2		41	00
						31		J3		40	00
				334	00					334	00

Cost of Repair Parts Sold   (511)

1975						1975					
Dec. 31		J3		235	00	Dec. 31		J4		235	00

LEDGER (Cont'd)

Supplies Used

Date	Explanation	Ref.	Dr.		Date	Explanation	Ref.	Cr.	
1975 Dec. 31		J3	32	00	1975 Dec. 31		J4	32	00

Utilities Expense (513)

Date	Explanation	Ref.	Dr.		Date	Explanation	Ref.	Cr.	
1975 Dec. 31		J3	21	00	1975 Dec. 31		J4	36	00
31		J4	15	00					
			36	00				36	00

Expired Insurance (514)

Date	Explanation	Ref.	Dr.		Date	Explanation	Ref.	Cr.	
1975 Dec. 31		J3	18	00	1975 Dec. 31		J4	18	00

Rent Expense (515)

Date	Explanation	Ref.	Dr.		Date	Explanation	Ref.	Cr.	
1975 Dec. 31		J4	150	00	1975 Dec. 31		J4	150	00

Property Tax Expense (516)

Date	Explanation	Ref.	Dr.		Date	Explanation	Ref.	Cr.	
1975 Dec. 31		J4	10	00	1975 Dec. 31		J4	10	00

Depreciation of Office Equipment (517)

Date	Explanation	Ref.	Dr.		Date	Explanation	Ref.	Cr.	
1975 Dec. 31		J4	12	00	1975 Dec. 31		J4	12	00

Depreciation of Repair Equipment (518)

Date	Explanation	Ref.	Dr.		Date	Explanation	Ref.	Cr.	
1975 Dec. 31		J4	35	00	1975 Dec. 31		J4	35	00

LEDGER (Cont'd)

Depreciation of Service Trucks (519)

Date	Explanation	Ref.	Dr.		Date	Explanation	Ref.	Cr.	
1975 Dec. 31		J4	72	00	1975 Dec. 31		J4	72	00

Truck Operations Expense (520)

Date	Explanation	Ref.	Dr.		Date	Explanation	Ref.	Cr.	
1975 Dec. 26		J2	19	00	1975 Dec. 31		J4	57	00
30		J3	38	00					
			57	00				57	00

Payroll Taxes (521)

Date	Explanation	Ref.	Dr.		Date	Explanation	Ref.	Cr.	
1975 Dec. 31		J4	95	00	1975 Dec. 31		J4	95	00

Office Salary Expense (522)

Date	Explanation	Ref.	Dr.		Date	Explanation	Ref.	Cr.	
1975 Dec. 31		J3	250	00	1975 Dec. 31		J4	250	00

Servicemen's Wages Expense (523)

Date	Explanation	Ref.	Dr.		Date	Explanation	Ref.	Cr.	
1975 Dec. 31		J3	800	00	1975 Dec. 31		J4	800	00

Advertising Expense (524)

Date	Explanation	Ref.	Dr.		Date	Explanation	Ref.	Cr.	
1975 Dec. 31		J3	41	00	1975 Dec. 31		J4	41	00

Income Summary (611)

Date	Explanation	Ref.	Dr.			Date	Explanation	Ref.	Cr.		
1975 Dec. 31		J4	1	843	00	1975 Dec. 31		J4	2	456	00
31		J4		613	00						
			2	456	00				2	456	00

Preparation of Unadjusted Trial Balance

The following unadjusted trial balance is prepared after totaling the debits and credits in each account to this point and determining the net balance.

THE RELIABLE TELEVISION SERVICE CO.
Unadjusted Trial Balance
December 31, 1975

Accounts	Dr.	Cr.
Cash on Hand	$ 439	
Cash in Bank	183	
Repair Parts	2,950	
Supplies	296	
Unexpired Insurance	600	
Prepaid Rent	300	
Prepaid Property Taxes	10	
Prepaid Telephone Service	45	
Office Equipment	1,980	
Repair Equipment	5,700	
Service Trucks	11,400	
Accounts Payable, Eschen Supply Co.		$ 1,094
Accounts Payable, Roedel Supply Co.		431
Equipment Contracts Payable		6,000
Withheld Income Tax		157
Payroll Taxes Payable		63
J. A. Blair, Capital		15,000
J. A. Blair, Drawings	150	
Television Service Revenue		2,122
Sales of Parts		334
Truck Operations Expense	57	
Office Salary Expense	250	
Servicemen's Wages Expense	800	
Advertising Expense	41	
	$25,201	$25,201

Journalizing Adjusting Transactions

The following entries are necessary at the end of the period in order that the account balances will present information necessary for the preparation of statements.

SCHEDULE 6.2 (*continued*)

(Continuation of Page 3 of Journal)

			Adjusting Entries								
31	Cost of Repair Parts Sold	511	235	00		
	Repair Parts	131			235	00
31	Supplies Used	512	32	00		
	Supplies	132			32	00
31	Utilities Expense	513	21	00		
	Accounts Payable, Union Electric Co.	213			21	00
31	Expired Insurance	514	18	00		
	Unexpired Insurance	141			18	00

Page 4

Date 1975		Accounts and Explanation	Ref.	Dr.		Cr.	
Dec.	31	Rent Expense	515	150	00		
		Prepaid Rent	142			150	00
	31	Property Tax Expense	516	10	00		
		Prepaid Property Taxes	143			10	00
	31	Depreciation of Office Equipment	517	12	00		
		Office Equipment	151			12	00
	31	Depreciation of Repair Equipment	518	35	00		
		Repair Equipment	152			35	00
	31	Depreciation of Service Trucks	519	72	00		
		Service Trucks	153			72	00
	31	Payroll Taxes	521	95	00		
		Payroll Taxes Payable	216			95	00
	31	Utilities Expense	513	15	00		
		Prepaid Telephone Service	144			15	00
				695	00	695	00

Proof of the Journal. The totals of $695 in the debit and credit columns provide the proof of the journal for the adjusting entries.

Posting of Adjusting Entries. See ledger accounts and the reference column in the Journal.

Preparation of Adjusted Trial Balance

The following adjusted trial balance is prepared after totaling the debits and credits in each account to this point and determining the net balance.

THE RELIABLE TELEVISION SERVICE CO.
Adjusted Trial Balance
December 31, 1975

Accounts	Dr.	Cr.
Cash on Hand	$ 439	
Cash in Bank	183	
Repair Parts	2,715	
Supplies	264	
Unexpired Insurance	582	
Prepaid Rent	150	
Prepaid Telephone Service	30	
Office Equipment	1,968	
Repair Equipment	5,665	
Service Trucks	11,328	
Accounts Payable, Eschen Supply Co.		$ 1,094
Accounts Payable, Roedel Supply Co.		431
Accounts Payable, Union Electric Co.		21
Equipment Contracts Payable		6,000
Withheld Income Tax		157
Payroll Taxes Payable		158
J. A. Blair, Capital		15,000
J. A. Blair, Drawings	150	
Television Service Revenue		2,122
Sales of Parts		334
Cost of Repair Parts Sold	235	
Supplies Used	32	
Utilities Expense	36	
Expired Insurance	18	
Rent Expense	150	
Property Tax Expense	10	
Depreciation of Office Equipment	12	
Depreciation of Repair Equipment	35	
Depreciation of Service Trucks	72	
Truck Operations Expense	57	
Payroll Taxes	95	
Office Salary Expense	250	
Servicemen's Wages Expense	800	
Advertising Expense	41	
	$25,317	$25,317

Preparation of Income Statement

The adjusted trial balance or the ledger accounts provide the data for the following income statement.

THE RELIABLE TELEVISION SERVICE CO.
Income Statement
For the Period December 20–31, 1975

Television Service Revenue	$2,122	
Sales of Parts	334	
Total Revenue		$2,456
Operating Expenses:		
Cost of Repair Parts Sold	$ 235	
Supplies Used	32	
Utilities Expense	36	
Expired Insurance	18	
Rent Expense	150	
Property Tax Expense	10	
Depreciation of Office Equipment	12	
Depreciation of Repair Equipment	35	
Depreciation of Service Trucks	72	
Truck Operations Expense	57	
Payroll Taxes	95	
Office Salary Expense	250	
Servicemen's Wages Expense	800	
Advertising Expense	41	
Total Operating Expenses		1,843
Net Income of the Enterprise		$ 613

Preparation of Balance Sheet

The adjusted trial balance or the ledger accounts and the income statement provide the data for the balance sheet shown on the next page.

THE RELIABLE TELEVISION SERVICE CO.
Balance Sheet
December 31, 1975

Assets

Current Assets

Cash on Hand	$ 439	
Cash in Bank	183	
Repair Parts	2,715	
Supplies	264	
Unexpired Insurance	582	
Prepaid Rent	150	
Prepaid Telephone Service	30	
Total Current Assets		$ 4,363

Noncurrent Assets

Office Equipment	$ 1,968	
Repair Equipment	5,665	
Service Trucks	11,328	
Total Noncurrent Assets		18,961
Total Assets		$23,324

Liabilities and Proprietorship

Current Liabilities

Accounts Payable	$ 1,546	
Equipment Contracts Payable	6,000	
Withheld Income Tax	157	
Payroll Taxes Payable	158	
Total Current Liabilities		$ 7,861

Proprietorship

J. A. Blair, Investment, December 20, 1975		$15,000	
Net Income, 12/20-31/1975	$613		
Less: Personal Drawing	150	463	
J. A. Blair, Capital, December 31, 1975			15,463
Total Liabilities and Proprietorship			$23,324

Journalizing Closing Transactions

Additional entries at the end of the period are necessary in order to close the income accounts. The data for these entries are available from the adjusted trial balance, the income statement, or the ledger accounts.

Proof of the Journal. The totals of $5,062.00 in the debit and credit columns provide the proof of the journal for the closing entries.

Posting of Closing Entries. See the ledger accounts and the reference column in the journal.

Preparation of Post-Closing Trial Balance. The post-closing trial balance is prepared after totaling the debits and credits in each account and determining the net balance. Only the balance sheet accounts now contain balances, these balances being the same as on the balance sheet. It is assumed this trial balance consists of adding machine tapes, so it is not illustrated in the text.

Ruling of Closed Accounts. See the glossary (Ruling an Account) and Figure 11.1 in Chapter 11 for the mechanical steps and the ledger accounts in this illustration for examples.

Ruling and Balancing of Open Accounts. See the ledger accounts.

SCHEDULE 6.2 (*continued*)

(Continuation of Page 4 of the Journal)

	Closing Entries							
31	Television Service Revenue	411	2	122	00			
	Sales of Parts	412		334	00			
	Income Summary	611				2	456	00
31	Income Summary	611	1	843	00			
	Cost of Repair Parts Sold	511					235	00
	Supplies Used	512					32	00
	Utilities Expense	513					36	00
	Expired Insurance	514					18	00
	Rent Expense	515					150	00
	Property Tax Expense	516					10	00
	Depreciation of Office Equipment	517					12	00
	Depreciation of Repair Equipment	518					35	00
	Depreciation of Service Trucks	519					72	00
	Truck Operations Expense	520					57	00
	Payroll Taxes	521					95	00
	Office Salary Expense	522					250	00
	Servicemen's Wages Expense	523					800	00
	Advertising Expense	524					41	00
31	Income Summary	611		613	00			
	J. A. Blair, Capital	311					613	00
31	J. A. Blair Capital	311		150	00			
	J. A. Blair, Drawings	312					150	00
			5	062	00	5	062	00

Date 1975	Explanation	Cash on Hand		Cash in Bank		Repair Parts
		Dr.	Cr.	Dr.	Cr.	Dr.
Dec. 20	Assumption of assets and liabilities of Star Television Repair Shop. Check from Mr. Blair to Mr. Star.					
22	Day's receipts	195.00				
22	Installation of telephone		45.00			
23	Day's receipts	390.00				
23	Purchase of parts					108.00
24	Deposit		390.00	390.00		
24	Day's receipts	330.00				
24	Purchase of supplies		36.00			
26	Deposit		294.00	294.00		
26	Day's receipts	321.00				
26	Purchase of parts					96.00
26	Truck gasoline and oil		19.00			
28	Deposit		301.00	301.00		
28	Day's receipts	307.00				
28	Payment on account				300.00	
29	Deposit		307.00	307.00		
29	Day's receipts	326.00				
29	Purchase of parts					86.00
29	Payment on account				375.00	
30	Deposit		326.00	326.00		
30	Day's receipts	299.00				
30	Purchase of parts					110.00
30	Truck gasoline, oil, etc.		38.00			
31	Deposit		261.00	261.00		
31	Day's receipts	288.00				
31	Advertising invoice paid				41.00	
31	Payment of office salary				200.00	
31	Payment of servicemen				630.00	
31	Personal drawing, Mr. Blair				150.00	
		2,456.00	2,017.00	1,879.00	1,696.00	400.00
		(111)	(111)	(112)	(112)	(131)

Television Service Revenue	Sales of Parts	Other Accounts			
Cr.	Cr.	Dr.	Cr.	Ref.	Account
		The transaction of December 20 would be entered in the "Other Accounts" columns. The entry and posting are the same as in the two-column journal.			
		22,800.00	22,800.00	(Totals of the transaction.)	
168.00	27.00	45.00		144	Prepaid Telephone Service
335.00	55.00		108.00	211	Accounts Payable, Eschen Supply Co.
286.00	44.00	36.00		132	Supplies
280.00	41.00		96.00	212	Accounts Payable, Roedel Supply Co.
		19.00		520	Truck Operations Expense
265.00	42.00	300.00		211	Accounts Payable, Eschen Supply Co.
282.00	44.00		86.00	211	Accounts Payable, Eschen Supply Co.
		375.00		212	Accounts Payable, Roedel Supply Co.
258.00	41.00		110.00	212	Accounts Payable, Roedel Supply Co.
		38.00		520	Truck Operations Expense
248.00	40.00	41.00		524	Advertising Expense
		250.00		522	Office Salary Expense
			15.00	216	Payroll Taxes Payable
			35.00	215	Withheld Income Tax
		800.00		523	Servicemen's Wages Expense
			48.00	216	Payroll Taxes Payable
			122.00	215	Withheld Income Tax
		150.00		312	J. A. Blair, Drawings
2,122.00	334.00	24,854.00	23,420.00		
(411)	(412)				

Cash on Hand (111)

1975						1975						
Dec. 31		J1	2	456	00	Dec. 31		J1	2	017	00	
						31	Balance	∨		439	00	
			2	456	00				2	456	00	
1976												
Jan. 1	Balance	∨		439	00							

Cash in Bank (112)

1975						1975						
Dec. 31		J1	1	879	00	Dec. 31		J1	1	696	00	
1976						31	Balance	∨		183	00	
			1	879	00				1	879	00	
Jan. 1	Balance	∨		183	00							

Repair Parts (131)

1975						1975						
Dec. 20		J1	2	550	00	Dec. 31		J2		235	00	
31		J1		400	00	31	Balance	∨	2	715	00	
			2	950	00				2	950	00	
1976												
Jan. 1	Balance	∨	2	715	00							

Television Service Revenue (411)

1975						1975					
Dec. 31		J2	2	122	00	Dec. 31		J1	2	122	00

Sales of Parts (412)

1975						1975					
Dec. 31		J2		334	00	Dec. 31		J1		334	00

ALTERNATIVE ILLUSTRATION

The illustration of the record keeping for the Reliable Television Service Company will be altered by the substitution of a multi-column journal for the two-column journal form. Only the daily transactions will be presented; the adjusting and closing transactions would be in the Other Accounts columns where the journalizing and posting are the same as for the two-column form. (See the examples of adjusting and closing entries in the previous example in this appendix.)

The ledger accounts will contain the same postings except those accounts for which specialized columns have been provided in the multi-column journal. Compare the accounts presented in Schedule 6.3 with the corresponding accounts in use with the two-column journal form.

QUESTIONS AND PROBLEMS

1. Can double-entry bookkeeping be carried out without using a journal? Explain.

2. When should a journal entry be accompanied by a detailed explanation?

3. "The specialized-journal-column technique is a labor-saving device." Explain.

4. If an account receives only one or two entries a month, it should not appear as the heading of a specialized column in a journal. Explain.

5. Can the essential processes of double-entry bookkeeping—the recording of transactions and the preparing of financial statements—be carried on without a journal? Without a ledger?

6. When is it desirable to use controlling accounts and subsidiary ledgers?

7. "A controlling-account system adds more ledger accounts, but it is, nevertheless, a labor-saving device." Comment.

8. A controlling-account system may involve the double posting of certain items. Illustrate. Will this procedure result in an inequality of debits and credits in the trial balance? Explain.

9. Which of the following general ledger accounts are likely to be controlling accounts in the ledger of the Riley Wholesale Company? In each case where a controlling account is indicated, describe the nature of the information that will be found in the subsidiary ledger.
   a. Sales
   b. Interest Earned
   c. Capital Stock
   d. Accounts Receivable
   e. Prepaid Rent
   f. Notes Payable
   g. Cash on Hand
   h. Operating Expenses
   i. Goodwill
   j. Retained Earnings

10. Refer to the Chart of Accounts shown in this chapter. Indicate account numbers to be assigned to the following accounts, if they were to be added: Prepaid Rent; Telephone and Telegraph Expense; Mortgage Payable; Advertising Supplies Inventory; Maintenance of Office Equipment; Rent Payable; Prepaid Property Taxes; Contributions to Charities; Rent Receivable; Organization Costs; Maintenance of Store Equipment; Rent Revenue.

11. What are the major considerations in determining which specialized journals are to be included in an accounting installation? What are the major considerations in determining the column headings to be used in a specialized journal?

*12. "The posting period may be shorter than the accounting period, but it must not be longer." Explain.

*13. If an entry affecting a controlling account were recorded in the Other Accounts column of a journal, how would the entry be posted?

14 a. Indicate the major points of similarity and difference of a cash disbursements journal and a check register.
   b. Indicate major points of similarity and difference of the purchase journal, invoice register, and voucher register.

15. What document or memorandum probably would be used as the basis for the recording of the following transactions?
   a. A purchase on account by a retailer
   b. A deposit in a bank
   c. The recording of interest collected on a note receivable
   d. A sale on account by a manufacturing enterprise
   e. The transfer of material from the storeroom
   f. The recording of wages earned during the week
   g. The payment in cash for a parcel-post mailing
   h. The return of goods by a customer
   i. The return of goods to a vendor.

16. The documents and memorandums listed below serve as the basis for recording certain transactions. Indicate the accounts which should be debited and credited in the transaction based on each document.
   a. A cash register tape showing the total cash sales for the day
   b. An invoice for the acquisition of merchandise on account
   c. A duplicate bank-deposit slip
   d. Employees' timecards for production-line work
   e. A sales invoice
   f. A requisition for materials used in the factory
   g. A receipt for purchase of stamps at the post office
   h. A credit memorandum issued to a customer for defective merchandise returned by him.

* Hints, key numbers, or (partial) answers appear in the back of the book between the Appendix Tables and the Glossary.

*17. Assuming the accounting period is a calendar year, present entries in simple journal form for the following transactions during April and May 1975:

Apr. 1 Cash is received from a customer, J. A. Jones, to apply on his account, $5,200.

7 Finished product is sold on account for $5,000 to the Ringling Sales Company.

8 A bill for electricity consumed is received from the Union Electric Company, $70. The service was used as follows: factory, $55; office, $15.

10 A check for $889 is issued to the Internal Revenue Service to pay amounts previously withheld from employees' salaries and wages for income taxes.

11 Supplies are requisitioned for use in the general office, $44.

15 A $3,300 loan is secured from the bank on a two-month, 12-percent promissory note.

18 A check is issued to the Union Electric Company for the statement received on April 8.

23 Supplies are purchased on account from Central Supply Company, $200.

25 Supplies are requisitioned for use in factory operations, $120.

30 Insurance is expired, all applicable to factory operations, $75.

May 2 Shares of capital stock are issued for cash, $15,000.

2 Rent for the month is paid by check, $500.

5 Merchandise is purchased on account from the Missouri Dry Goods Company, $9,000.

9 A customer, R. S. Symington, gives a note to apply on his account, $600.

12 Fixtures are purchased for $1,500; a note is issued for $1,250 and the balance is paid by check.

13 Merchandise is sold for cash, $3,600.

14 Payment on account is made by check to the Missouri Dry Goods Company, $9,000.

19 A salary of $500 is paid by check subject to a withholding of $30 for payroll taxes and $100 for income tax.

18. Present entries in simple journal form for the following transactions during August, 1975.

Aug. 1 C and B agree to form a partnership. C invests $5,000 in cash, which is deposited immediately in the partnership bank account, and an automobile having a current value of $1,200. B invests real estate having a value of $16,000; the real estate consists of a building and building site, the latter having a value of $3,000; the building has a mortgage on it of $2,000, which is assumed by the partnership.

4 A telephone is installed. A bill for monthly service is paid by check, $30.

5 Fixtures are purchased from the Lammert Furniture Company for $2,000. A payment of $800 is made by check, and the balance is represented by an installment contract whereby monthly payments are to be made over the next twelve months.

6   A three-year fire insurance policy premium is paid by check to the Trout Insurance Agency, $150. The policy is effective as of August 1.

8   A stock of merchandise is purchased for $5,000 from the Brentwood Supply Company. A check is drawn for $2,000, and the balance is obtained on open account.

12   Merchandise is sold for cash, $400.

13   Cash is deposited in the bank, $350.

15   A customer, W. A. Burnham, purchases merchandise in the amount of $44 and is extended credit for the goods.

19. The Office Supply Company sells to a large number of customers. All sales are recorded as if made on account. Postings to the customers' ledger are made from supporting documents. All other subsidiary ledger postings are made from the journals.

The company uses the following journals:

An eight-column cash disbursements journal
A five-column cash receipts journal, including a column for deposits
A three-column purchases journal
A single-column sales journal
A two-column general journal.

*a. Identify the amount columns in each of the journals by account and debit-credit characteristics. (Review the transactions below to determine the columns; then check your answer in the back of the book before proceeding.)

b. Analyze each of the transactions below in two-column journal form. Indicate the journal in which the entry would be recorded and which journal columns would be used. Describe the posting from each of the columns used. The following is an example of the application of the instructions:

Transaction:

Salaries of $200, less $12 for payroll taxes and $52 for withheld income tax, are paid in cash.

Solution:

Salaries 200
    Cash on Hand 136
    Withheld Income Tax 52
    Payroll Taxes Payable 12
Recorded in cash disbursements journal. Columns used: Salaries, Dr.; Cash on Hand, Cr.; Withheld Income Tax, Cr.; and, Payroll Taxes Payable, Cr. All of these columns are to be posted in total.

Transactions to be recorded:
(1) Sales to 20 customers, $900.
(2) Purchases of merchandise from:

Alton Co. $300
A. H. Jones Co. 150
S. G. Gordon Co. 75

(3) Receipts from customers, $800, less $16 of sales discounts allowed.

(4) The invoice of a supplier, J. Grinden Co., for $500, is paid by check. The company deducts a discount of 2 percent for prompt payment. The invoice had been recorded previously.

(5) A new display case is purchased on account from the Store Supply Company, $225.

(6) The Jennings Company returns supplies for which a payment of $10 had been made. A refund is made from cash on hand.

(7) The cashier makes a deposit in the bank, $800.

(8) The owner, A. B. Dixon, invests additional capital, $1,000, in cash.

*20. Indicate whether each of the following statements is true or false.

   a. Posting is the process of recording entries in a journal.

   b. A general journal is not needed when specialized journals are used.

   c. The balances in the subsidiary ledger accounts are not included in the general ledger trial balance.

   d. A check register is a journal in which receipts of checks from customers are recorded.

   e. The debit and credit entries in the subsidiary ledger accounts are totaled, and the amounts are transferred to the controlling account.

   f. Specialized journals are selected on the basis of the frequency of various types of transactions.

   g. A controlling account represents a group of subsidiary ledger accounts that are kept in detail outside of the general ledger.

   h. The use of a voucher register facilitates the elimination of the detailed accounts payable ledger.

   i. A specialized journal must have an equal number of debit and credit columns.

   j. The use of specialized journals facilitates an effective division of labor among the clerical staff.

   k. The sales journal normally will not have an Other Accounts, Cr. column.

   l. The use of controlling accounts always saves posting time.

   m. A "general" journal is one designed to handle transactions that will be posted to the general ledger.

   n. The check register is eliminated whenever the voucher system is used.

   o. A journal must have at least one column for debits and at least another column for credits.

   p. Direct posting decreases the number of entries in the journal.

   q. A specialized column is provided for each controlling account in at least one journal.

   r. The use of a file of unpaid invoices in a controlling-account system instead of a formal subsidiary ledger reduces posting time.

   s. Double-entry bookkeeping can be carried on without a journal.

   t. The use of specialized columns in journals encourages an effective division of labor among the members of the clerical staff.

   u. The use of controlling accounts facilitates the taking of a trial balance.

   v. A "post-closing" trial balance is one taken just before journalizing the closing entries.

   w. Direct posting to the general ledger is used more often than direct posting to the subsidiary ledgers.

   x. When a controlling account is credited, one of the subsidiary ledger accounts is debited.

y. An invoice register and a voucher register would not normally be used in the same accounting system.

z. There is usually more detail in the journal than in the ledger.

°21. The D. Yeung Company proposes to adopt a twelve-column journal in its bookkeeping system.

The following types and number of transactions are expected to occur in January, 1975:

Sales for cash (daily totals): 26
Sales on account: 100
Collections on account: 90
Acquisition of merchandise on account: 20
Payments by check on merchandise accounts: 15
Deposits: 26
Payments by check of liabilities (other than accounts payable) accrued as of January 1: 4
Payments of various administrative and selling expenses during the month: by check, 10; by cash, 8
Accrual of liabilities at end of month (one debit and one credit each): 4
Recognition of depreciation at end of month: 2
Recognition of merchandise inventory at end of month: 1

a. Design a twelve-column journal.

b. Indicate the expected number of entries in each column.

c. Indicate the expected number of postings to the ledger.

d. Indicate the expected number of postings if a simple two-column journal were to be used.

°22. The trial balance of the general ledger of the Renuit Shop at July 1, 1975, is as follows:

Cash on Hand	$ 35	
Cash in Bank	665	
Handicraft Supply Co.		$ 625
Supplies on Hand	425	
Tools (cost less depreciation)	1,200	
W. A. Tincker, Capital		1,700
	$2,325	$2,325

The transactions for July are as follows:

(1) Cash received for repair work, $360.

(2) Cash deposited in the bank, $385.

(3) Supplies purchased on account from Handicraft Supply Company, $185.

(4) Cash received for repair work, $310.

(5) Cash deposited in the bank, $265.

(6) Cash payments: For supplies, $15; for electricity, $13.

(7) Payments by check: No. 555, Handicraft Supply Company, on account, $725; No. 556, Noonan Realty Service, for July rent, $150.

(8) Check No. 557 for $125 is written to "Cash," and the money is used by Tincker for personal purposes.

(9) Depreciation of tools, $55.

(10) Supplies used, $255.

   a. Open skeleton accounts and record the opening balances.

   b. Construct an eight-column journal containing the following money-column headings: Cash in Bank, Dr. and Cr.; Cash on Hand, Dr. and Cr.; Revenue from Repair Service, Cr.; Supplies, Dr.; Other Accounts, Dr. and Cr. Include Date, Explanation, Check No., Account Titles, and Ref. columns in the journal.

   c. Enter the transactions. (Use the Date column to record the transaction number.) Post to the skeleton accounts. (Indicate all postings from the journal by a check mark.) Open new accounts as needed.

   d. Take a trial balance.

23. The trial balance of Moe Landscape Gardeners at March 31, 1975, was as follows:

Cash on Hand	$ 500	
Cash in Bank	3,000	
Supplies	1,000	
Truck (cost less depreciation)	15,000	
Tools (cost less depreciation)	1,200	
Motor Sales Co.		$ 3,000
L. M. Moe, Capital		9,000
H. C. Moe, Capital		8,700
	$20,700	$20,700

The transactions for April are as follows:

Apr. 3 Cash collected for gardening service, $2,250.

      5 Cash withdrawn for personal use: L. M. Moe, $750; H. C. Moe, $500.

      7 Deposit in the bank, $600.

      8 Check No. 253 is drawn in favor of the Motor Sales Company, to apply on the balance of the automobile contract, $1,000.

   11 All of the cash collected for gardening service, $2,100 is deposited in the bank.

   14 Cash paid out for gasoline and oil for truck, $40.

   17 Cash collected for gardening service, $1,750.

   18 Deposit in the bank, $1,250.

   23 Check No. 254 is drawn in favor of the Human Hardware Company for new tools, $150.

   24 Cash collected for gardening service, $1,650.

   25 Deposit in the bank, $1,400.

   30 Depreciation for the month: truck, $400; tools, $60.

   30 Supplies used during the month, $300.

   30 A statement for $450 is received from the Lutz & Shields Garage for automobile repairs, gasoline, and so on. The statement indicates that $200 is for repairs to L. M. Moe's personal automobile and that the balance relates to the truck. By prior agreement the entire bill is to be paid from business cash and L. M. Moe's charges are to be debited to his capital account.

   a. Open skeleton accounts and record the amounts shown in the trial balance.

   b. Construct a nine-column journal containing the following money column headings: Cash in Bank, Dr. and Cr.; Cash on Hand, Dr. and Cr.;

L. M. Moe, Capital, Dr.; H. C. Moe, Capital, Dr.; Revenue from Gardening, Cr.; Other Accounts, Dr. and Cr. Include Date, Explanation, Check No., Account Titles, and Ref. columns in the journal form.

c. Enter the transactions for April, 1975.

d. Total the columns. Prove and rule the journal.

e. Post to the skeleton accounts, open new accounts as needed, and take a trial balance. Since account numbers or ledger pages are not given, indicate all postings by means of a check mark.

f. Prepare an income statement and a balance sheet. Prepare a schedule showing the changes in the balances of the partners' capital accounts including the distribution of the net income. Income and losses are shared equally by the partners.

g. Journalize the closing entries in the Other Accounts columns. Post closing entries. Rule all closed accounts.

24. Mr. A. J. Beal, assisted by one sales clerk, operates the Beal Antique Shop. A review of the operations of the business indicates that the most common transactions are as follows:

Sales for cash and on account
Payments for purchases of merchandise by cash and by check
Collections of cash from customers
Payments of operating expenses by cash and by check
Deposits in the bank.

Subsidiary ledgers are used for customers' accounts and operating expense accounts. A direct posting procedure is not to be used.

The following are the transactions for July 15-31:

July 15 Cash sales, $200.
   16 Sale, on account, L. C. Jones, $80; cash sales, $60.
   17 Mr. Beal invests an additional $500 in cash.
   18 Deposit in bank, $750.
   18 Cash sales, $250.
   20 Collection from a customer, A. C. Hines, $75.
   21 Sale, on account, A. O. Brown, $85.
   22 Store fixtures are purchased for $800 from the Office Supply Company. A check (No. 550) is issued, $200; the balance is covered by an installment contract.
   23 Merchandise is purchased for $650 from the East Antique Company. Check (No. 551) is issued in full payment.
   25 Cash sales, $200.
   25 Deposit in bank, $525.
   25 Collection from a customer, M. A. Cross, $90.
   27 A note payable is issued to the bank, $1,000. The proceeds are added by the bank to the firm's account.
   28 Sale, on account, W. I. Snow, $95; cash sales, $60.
   29 A telephone bill is received from the Bell Telephone Company. Check (No. 552) is issued, $12.
   30 Merchandise is acquired from the Specialty Furniture Company, $550. Check (No. 553) is issued in payment of the accompanying invoice.

31 The clerk is paid for the second half of the month. Check (No. 554) is issued for earnings of $300, less deductions of 6 percent for payroll taxes and $45 for income tax.

a. Prepare a four-column general journal (Subsidiary Ledgers, Dr. and Cr., and General Ledger, Dr. and Cr.) and enter the transaction data.

b. Prove the journal.

c. Present detailed instructions for posting the journal.

d. Design an eleven-column journal that would be efficient for Beal Antique Shop.

25. E. S. Brady and R. E. Brady operate Brady Business Services, providing mimeographing and public stenographic services. At September 30, 1975, the trial balance of the general ledger and the schedules of the subsidiary ledgers are as follows:

General Ledger

Cash on Hand	$ 500	
Cash in Bank	5,000	
Accounts Receivable	9,500	
Supplies on Hand	3,300	
Prepaid Insurance	960	
Office Equipment	12,300	
Accounts Payable		$ 4,900
Equipment Contract Payable		3,000
E. S. Brady, Capital		13,960
R. E. Brady, Capital		9,700
	$31,560	$31,560

Accounts Receivable

Baum & Co.	$ 1,220
Clark's Market	300
Davis Bros.	—
Forest Stores	1,800
H. B. Gross	590
Moll & Co.	750
Ohio Realty	—
Porter and Sons	290
A. B. Reck	1,450
Standard Service	3,100
	$ 9,500

Accounts Payable

Burton, Inc.	$ 250
City Supply Co.	2,360
Mears & Co.	450
P. A. Page, Inc.	1,080
Snell Bros.	760
	$ 4,900

The following transactions took place during the month of October:

October 1 Received $450 in cash for secretarial work completed and delivered today.

1 Completed mimeograph work for Moll & Company and invoiced them for $510.

2 Issued check (No. 100) for $600 to K. M. Bear for rent for the month of October. (Checks are issued in serial number order.)

3 Received check for $1,800 from Forest Stores in payment of their account balance.

3 Deposited $2,250 in the bank.

6 Issued checks in payment of September 30 balances to Burton, Inc., City Supply Company, P. A. Page, Inc., and Snell Brothers.

6 Received an invoice from City Supply Company for paper and other mimeograph supplies, $1,050.

7 Cash receipts for the day were $330 for stenographic service and $1,250 for mimeograph work.

7 Deposited $1,580 in the bank.

8 Received the following invoices: Mears & Company, $100, for repairs to office equipment; Burton, Inc., $480, for office supplies; P. A. Page, Inc., $250 for mimeograph supplies.

10 Received checks from the following customers for the September 30 balances: Baum & Company, Clark's Market, Moll & Company, Porter and Sons, and Standard Service.

10 Deposited $5,660 in the bank.

10 Issued check for $150 for advertising invoice received from the *Daily Register*.

13 Issued check for $1,500 to Hall Office Equipment, Inc., for monthly payment on the equipment purchase contract.

13 Completed the following mimeograph jobs and invoiced the customers: Ohio Realty, $460; Davis Brothers, $200; Standard Service, $930.

14 Receipts for the day for stenographic work, $620.

14 Deposited $620 in the bank.

15 Issued check for $90 to Blott Typewriter Services for repairs on machines.

16 Received a check for $550 from S. V. Smith for mimeograph work completed today.

17 Receipts for the day: stenographic services, $100; mimeograph work, $850.

17 Deposited $1,500 in the bank.

17 Issued checks to Mears & Company and P. A. Page, Inc. for invoices of October 8.

20 Issued checks to City Supply Company for invoice of October 6.

20 Received the following invoices for operating supplies: City Supply Company, $1,500; Snell Brothers, $950.

20 Issued check to a customer S. V. Smith as an adjustment reducing the amount he had paid for mimeograph work, $50 (adjustment due to error in calculating the charge on October 16).

21 Received a check from H. B. Gross for $590 in payment of September 30 balance.

21 Other cash receipts for the day: stenographic services, $440; mimeograph work, $460.

21 Deposited $1,490 in the bank.

23 Issued check for $450 to Mears & Company.

24 Billed the following customers for mimeograph work completed: Clark's Market, $210; Forest Stores, $445; Moll & Company, $1,070.

24 Issued a check for $500 to Devine Sports Shop for golf equipment for E. S. Brady (for his personal use).

27 Cash receipts for the day: stenographic services, $270; mimeograph work, $1,500.

27 Deposited $1,770 in the bank.

29 Issued a credit memo to Moll & Company for $100 as an adjustment on invoice of October 24 (incorrect rate used).

30 Issued check to Southwestern Telephone Company for telephone bill for the month, $120.

31 Paid $50 out of cash on hand for machinery repair.

31 Cash receipts for the day: mimeograph work, $435.

31 Issued checks as personal drawings: E. S. Brady, $2,750; R. E. Brady, $2,500.

31 Deposited $385 in the bank.

a. Open general ledger and subsidiary ledger accounts and insert the September 30 balances.

b. Record the October transactions in a thirteen-column journal. The amount-column headings in the journal are as follows: Cash on Hand, Dr. and Cr.; Cash in Bank, Dr. and Cr.; Accounts Receivable, Dr. and Cr.; Accounts Payable, Dr. and Cr.; Supplies on Hand, Dr.; Mimeographing Revenue, Cr.; Stenographic Revenue, Cr.; Other Accounts, Dr. and Cr. A direct-posting procedure is not used for either of the subsidiary ledgers.

c. Post to the general ledger and to the subsidiary ledgers.

*d. Prepare a trial balance of the general ledger and schedules of the subsidiary ledgers.

26. Refer to the data for Problem 25 above.

a. Open general ledger and subsidiary ledger accounts and insert the September 30 balances.

b. Record the October transactions in four-column journal form (Subsidiary Ledgers, Dr. and Cr.; General Ledger, Dr. and Cr.).

c. Post to the general ledger and to the subsidiary ledgers.

*d. Prepare a trial balance of the general ledger and schedules of the subsidiary ledgers.

27. This problem is a continuation of either Problems 25 or 26 above. Additional information as of October 31, 1975:

(1) Ending inventory of supplies amounts to $4,750.

(2) The insurance policy acquired on September 30, 1974 runs for three years.

(3) Office equipment was acquired on September 30, 1973, at a cost of $19,500. It was estimated that the salvage value of the equipment at the estimated retirement date, September 30, 1978, would be $1,500.

    a. Record the additional information in two-column or four-column journal form.

    b. Post entries from the journal.

    c. Prepare a trial balance of the general ledger (an adjusted trial balance).

    *d. Prepare an income statement. Add a section to include the division of income to partners who share equally in income.

    e. Prepare a balance sheet.

    f. Record the closing data in two-column or four-column journal form.

    g. Post entries from the journal.

    *h. Prepare a trial balance of the general ledger (a post-closing trial balance).

28. Referring to Problem 25, prepare the following journals:

    (1) Cash receipts and disbursements journal with the following columns: Date; Cash on Hand, Dr. and Cr.; Cash in Bank, Dr.; Accounts Receivable, Cr. (amount, reference, name of customer); Mimeographing Revenue, Cr.; Stenographic Revenue, Cr.; Other Accounts, Dr. (amount, reference, account title, explanation).

    (2) Revenue journal for use where credit is extended, with the following columns: Date; Name of customer; Reference; a single column for Accounts Receivable, Dr. and Mimeographing Revenue, Cr. (All stenographic work is paid for at the time the work is done.)

    (3) Invoice register with the following columns: Date; Name of Creditor; Accounts Payable, Cr. (amount and reference); Supplies on Hand, Dr.; Other Accounts, Dr. (amount, reference, account title, explanation).

    (4) Check register with the following columns: Date; Payee; Check Number; Cash in Bank, Cr.; Accounts Payable, Dr. (amount and reference); Other Accounts, Dr. (amount, reference, account title, explanation).

    a. Open general ledger and subsidiary ledger accounts and insert the September 30 balances.

    b. Record the October transactions in the journals.

    c. Post to the general ledger and the subsidiary ledgers.

    d. Prepare a trial balance of the general ledger and schedules of the subsidiary ledgers.

Two

MEASURING AND REPORTING INCOME

Chapter 7

Determining Net Income

A central problem in accounting is the determination of periodic net income. The economist measures income by the change in wealth and describes periodic net income as the net increase in wealth that could be distributed to the owners at the end of the period without reducing the "well offness" of the entity's prospects below those that prevailed at the start of the period. This concept requires well-defined rules for measuring a firm's prospects and wealth at the beginning and end of a period, and because these measurements are necessarily subjective, this concept cannot be implemented for accounting purposes.

A restricted version of this concept was widely accepted and used until the early 1900's. An entity's wealth was considered to be the total value of individual tangible assets rather than the worth of the firm as an operating unit. Thus, income was defined as the difference between total tangible assets at the beginning and the end of the period, after adjustments for changes in liabilities and owners' equity had been made.

At the turn of the century it became increasingly apparent that this approach was unworkable. It was becoming virtually impossible to value specialized long-term assets and inventories. Displacement of the view that income could be measured by changes in the values of assets was given even greater impetus by the graduated income tax, which was adopted in the United Kingdom in 1909 and in the United States in 1913. The new view emphasized the importance of the realized gains from sales in the market and was supported by the early tax decisions of the United States Supreme Court, which held that an enterprise did not earn income unless there had been a "severance" of property. In other words, income is generated by exchange of property in market transactions.

Emphasis has shifted further to evaluating the operating performance of the entity, and to a view of income that focuses on "matching" revenue and expenses. Matching revenue and expenses means associating revenue from a particular transaction or period with the costs that were used to generate that revenue. In practice, it is usually almost impossible to make a precise allocation of costs for individual transactions, so revenue and expenses are matched for accounting periods.

REVENUE CONCEPTS

The Nature of Revenue

Revenue is essentially a measurement or valuation of services rendered. When we ask, "What is the revenue for the year?" we want to know the market value of goods and services furnished to customers or clients during the year. Revenue is often measured by the inflow of new assets in connection with the rendering of goods and services. This description is usually satisfactory, but it is incomplete since a revenue transaction may result in the reduction of the liability, Advances from Customers, instead of an increase in an asset.

When revenue is recorded, the credit is usually made to a special revenue account, such as Sales, Revenue from Repair Services, or Rent Revenue. For example, if a theater sells tickets for $300, the entry would be:

```
Cash on Hand ............................................... 300
    Revenue from Admissions ...............................     300
```

In this form, the credit side of the revenue transaction can be described as a gross, or tentative, increase in owners' equity. Whether there will actually be an increase or decrease in owners' equity will depend upon the amount of the expenses associated with the revenue.

Revenue and Income Terminology

In the preceding paragraphs revenue transactions have been described in terms of the normal operating activities of the business. Revenue may also arise from other sources. A distinction is sometimes drawn between operating revenue and nonoperating revenue. Rent from the leasing of property not used in regular operations, interest and dividends earnings on investments, and gains from the sale of property other than stock in trade are examples of nonoperating revenues.

In its most significant sense, *income* is a "net" concept. In accounting, income refers to the excess of revenues over expense. The term income is sometimes used, especially when described as *gross income,* to indicate the charges to customers. Used in this way, it is synonymous with *revenue.*

This awkward use of the term income to describe gross revenue is on the decline in accounting practice; income is used only in the residual, or net, sense throughout this book.

The terms *profit, profits, net profit,* and *earnings* are frequently used interchangeably with *income* and *net income.* We read of the profit or gain on the sale of a piece of land, the profits for the year, the net profit for the month, and so on. In this text, the word *income* is used when we speak of the results of operations for a period; the term *gain* is used in describing the results of a specific transaction. The terms *profit* and *net profit* are restricted in this text to describing the effect of individual transactions, although they are used synonymously with *income* and *net income* in other references.

Loss Terminology

The term *loss* presents greater difficulty in usage. If the operations of the period result in expenses greater than revenues, the difference is called the *net loss* for the period. If an item of property is disposed of for less than its book value, the difference is described as a loss. If merchandise which cost $200 were sold for $190, the revenue would be $190, but there would be a loss on the transaction of $10 plus other related costs.

Occasionally, the net loss for the period is called the *deficit.* The term *deficit* should be used only to indicate a debit balance in the Retained Earnings account.

The Use of Revenue Accounts

Using separate, specifically labeled revenue accounts has become an established custom in accounting. Revenue accounts are almost invariably used for the regular sources of revenue, such as merchandise or product sales, professional fees, and admission charges. The accounts are seldom used for the more unusual transactions, such as the sale of securities held as a temporary investment or the sale of plant assets. A detailed presentation is not necessary for these unusual transactions, and only the net gain or loss arising from the transaction is recorded in a special account. For example, if securities (stocks or bonds) carried in the accounts at $25,600 are sold for $26,800, the entry would be:

Cash on Hand	26,800	
Marketable Securities		25,600
Gain on Sales of Securities		1,200

Presentation of Revenue on the Income Statement

Revenue from operations is normally the first item shown in the income statement. Sales might be used for manufacturing and merchandising enterprises, Admissions Revenue for a theater, Interest and Discount Earned for a bank, or Revenue from Repair Services for a television repair shop. Revenue from ancillary activities, like interest earned by a manufacturing firm or dividend income for a firm that holds securities only as investments, are then added to obtain a total revenue figure.

An alternative form of income statement divides revenues into two categories, operating and nonoperating. Operating revenue is shown first and operating expenses are deducted to obtain operating income. Then nonoperating revenue is shown, and nonoperating expenses are deducted from nonoperating revenue to arrive at the nonoperating income. The net income of the enterprise is the sum of operating and nonoperating income.

In recent years, evaluations of management have placed greater emphasis on *total-operations performance*. Such evaluations imply that management is responsible for making optimum use of the firm's resources and not merely for directing ordinary operations. For example, idle cash should be invested to earn a return and ancillary operations, which can grow out of the primary activity, should be developed.

Another reason for this emphasis on total operations is a practical one: in the actual performance of business activities, it becomes almost impossible to distinguish between operating and nonoperating revenue. Are popcorn and candy sales nonoperating revenues for a movie theater? Many theaters could not survive without such sales. The president of a large mail-order firm once stated that his firm made more money from interest and service charges on customers' credit accounts than from sales of merchandise. The total operations view of managerial activity questions the distinction between operating and nonoperating revenues and holds that all revenue should be shown in one place on the income statement.

RECOGNITION OF REVENUE

When has an enterprise actually earned income? This sounds like a simple question, but revenue recognition is one of the most difficult problems that the accountant must solve. Two criteria are usually employed to recognize revenue:

1. The revenue must be earned. That is, all or a substantial part of the service to be rendered must have been performed.
2. The revenues must be realized. That is, cash, receivables, or some other asset capable of objective measurement must have been received or a liability must have been satisfied.

The criteria can be ambiguous because difficult questions can arise: What constitutes "a substantial part of the service to be rendered"? Or, how precise need be the "objective measurement" of the asset received? These have been difficult questions to answer for land development companies, leasing companies, and franchisers, among others. Despite these problems of interpretation, both *earning* and *realization* are customarily required before revenue is recognized. The procedure is called the *completed-sales method of recognizing* revenues. In this method, recognition of revenue need not, and frequently does not, coincide with receipt of cash.

Cash Receipt before Revenue Recognition

Often a business receives cash before it furnishes goods or services. For example, a theater sells tickets weeks in advance of performances, a concert organization sells tickets for a season's program, an urban transportation company sells tokens to be used for rides at some later time, a customer orders goods and sends cash with his order, an insurance company receives a fire insurance premium for several years in advance, or a magazine publisher receives subscriptions for two or three years in advance. In such instances, even though cash is received in advance, rendering the service or delivering the goods is usually required before revenue is recognized.

When the cash is received, Cash on Hand is debited and a liability account, often called a customer's advance or an unearned income account, is credited. Such liabilities are discharged by rendering a service or delivering goods rather than by a cash payment. When the service is performed or the goods are delivered, the liability account is debited and a revenue account is credited. The entries are:

```
Cash on Hand ...............................................  5,000
      Advances from Customers ............................           5,000
Deposits on orders for future delivery.


Advances from Customers ..................................  3,000
      Sales ..................................................           3,000
Revenue recognized for orders filled and delivered which have
been paid for in advance.
```

Cash Receipt at Time of Revenue Recognition

The retail or service firm that does business on a cash basis has the simplest kind of revenue transaction to record. Furnishing the service and final settlement by the customer with cash payment occur almost simultaneously, so that the amount of cash received each day accurately measures the revenue to be recognized that day. The supermarket makes cash sales, the barber cuts the hair of his customer, the movie theater sells a ticket at 7:15 PM for a 7:30 PM performance, the bridge attendant collects a toll, or the bus driver collects a cash fare, and there is no question about recognizing revenue. A typical entry for a movie theater would be:

```
Cash on Hand ...............................................  3,160
      Revenue from Admissions .............................           3,160
Tickets sold for today's shows.
```

Cash Receipt Following Revenue Recognition

When a sale is made on credit, the service is rendered before collection. A large proportion of the business done in manufacturing and wholesaling involves a thirty- to ninety-day extension of credit. The increased use of charge accounts and credit cards means that retail and service firms will do a greater amount of business on this basis. If, for example, a department store sells $250 of merchandise to a customer who uses a charge account, the entry would be:

```
Accounts Receivable  .........................................  250
    Sales Revenue  .............................................         250
Sales on charge account.
```

The sale and delivery of goods is the usual basis for revenue recognition in trading and manufacturing concerns that purchase or fabricate goods and attempt to sell them at a profit. The sale usually involves exchanging the goods for cash or a promise to pay, but it may result, instead, in canceling a liability or acquiring assets other than cash or receivables. To determine when a sale has been consummated is not always easy, but the usual evidence is the legal transfer of title through delivery of the goods to a buyer or to a public transportation agency representing the buyer, such as a railroad or trucking company.

Revenue Recognized with Passage of Time

Although revenue may not be immediately collectible, it may be recorded when a claim has accumulated, or accrued, with the passage of time. Accruing revenue conforms to the view that revenue is earned when services are rendered. Interest accrues on notes receivable during the time when the borrower has the benefit of using the borrowed funds. Rent revenue is earned during the period when the tenant uses the property. Typical entries would be:

```
Interest Receivable  .........................................  190
    Interest Revenue  .........................................        190
Interest earnings for the month.


Advances from Tenants  ....................................  1,800
    Rent Revenue  .............................................      1,800
Rental earnings for the month.
```

Objections to Completed-Sales Method

Although the completed sale is normally used as the basis for revenue recognition, critics have argued that it is not applicable in certain special situations. There are two kinds of objections: some critics contend that the completed-sales method recognizes revenue too soon; others claim it does not recognize revenue soon enough. Those who argue that this method does not recognize revenue soon enough emphasize their objection to the criterion that all services must be rendered before revenue is recognized.

They argue that revenue should be recognized at the point of production, or perhaps, when orders are received. Those who contend that revenue is recognized too soon emphasize that revenue should be recognized only when cash is collected.

Revenue Recognition as Orders Are Received

One alternative to using completed sales as the basis for recognizing revenue is to use orders received. Certainly the receipt of orders is an important event for the firm. If the cost of filling an order could be predicted accurately and if order cancellations were rare or could be estimated accurately, this method would be attractive. But it is seldom used because it does not sufficiently meet either of the tests for revenue recognition. Nevertheless, in line with the customary conservatism of accounting, if it appears at the end of an accounting period that there will be a loss on an unfilled firm order, the loss is recognized in the period in which it becomes apparent that there will be a loss, rather than in the period when the goods are delivered.

The backlog of unfilled orders is an important indicator of the probable trend of future income. The backlog is sometimes reported in footnotes to the financial statements or in explanatory material accompanying them, even though it is almost never reported within financial statements. More general footnote reporting of backlogs would, in our view, increase the usefulness of financial statements.

Revenue Recognition at Time of Production

Production of goods that require future sales effort is rarely considered a justifiable point at which to recognize revenue. All production costs are viewed as part of the cost of goods being manufactured and ordinarily revenue is not recognized until the goods are sold.

An exception is sometimes made when the sales activity is incidental and merely requires the delivery of the goods to a well-established market. In these cases, the revenue is substantially earned as the good is produced because the market is virtually assured and the sales efforts required are minimal. Gold was once a good example. It was reasonable to assume that refined gold should be valued at the legally established market price, less a deduction for the cost of delivering it to the mint. Thus, the revenue from mining operations could be shown in the period of production, rather than in the period of sale, because the market price was certain and the demand was assured.

Production on special order presents a good case for income recognition on the basis of production because the sales contract is made prior to production. When the production period is short, there is no special problem, because delivery usually follows immediately upon completion.

Whether the point of sale or production is used as the basis of recognizing revenue makes little difference, especially when there are many orders each period. On the other hand, when the production period is long, as in the case of large construction projects, revenue is sometimes recognized in proportion to the degree of completion. This is known as the *percentage-of-completion* method of recognizing revenue. Under this method if a job is half done at the end of an accounting period, half of the total contract price is recognized as revenue for the period. The expenses of bringing the job to that stage of completion are matched with those revenues to determine net income for the period.

Accretion as Revenue

Accretion, the increase in value of assets caused by physical growth, is not usually considered recognizable revenue. For example, an orchard may take several years to develop before a significant crop can be picked. During that period, the orchard may increase in value by an amount considerably greater than the costs associated with its development. But the purpose of the orchard is to derive revenue from the sale of fruit, and there are risks of loss from frost and other natural and economic factors before the orchard matures, so it is reasonable to wait until fruit picking begins before recognizing any revenue. In these cases, the market price is not assured and a selling effort is required. The gain from any increase in the market value of the maturing orchard is recognized only if and when the orchard is sold.

Common practice, however, recognizes revenue from the natural increase in livestock operations. A value is assigned to all animals born during the accounting period, and this value is periodically changed to recognize increase or decrease in value.

When accretion is not recognized as revenue, all costs incurred in connection with the development and growth of the asset should be *capitalized*. That is, the costs should be accumulated in a work in process, or similar, account and carried forward as a production cost to be reported as an expense of the periods in which revenue is recognized.

Revenue Recognized as Collections Are Made

Where sales are made for cash, the completed-sales method and the cash collections method of recognizing revenue yield identical results. Most often, however, the receipt of cash follows the rendering of the service and the legal transfer of title. In most such cases, revenue is recognized at the time of sale, not at the time of collection. In some types of business, this method does not yield satisfactory results, because (1) extensive future services must still be rendered even though title has been transferred (revenue not earned) or (2) the uncertainty and delay of collections raise a question about the objective measurement of the current inflows to the firm (revenue not realized).

Many individuals or firms rendering professional services—doctors, lawyers, and accountants, for example—use the cash-collections method of recognizing revenue. Although receivables are not recognized in the formal accounting records when services are rendered, a memorandum record of charges to patients or clients must be made. Revenue is recognized only when payment is received. The entry would be:

```
Cash on Hand ...................................................   120
    Fees Collected (a revenue account) ........................          120
```

A similar approach is sometimes used by firms that sell goods on the installment plan. The payments extend over a long time, and sometimes, as with land development companies, with many future services yet to be rendered. The revenue from the sale is spread over the life of the installment contract in accordance with the cash collections. Although the procedure is the same as the cash collections method described in the previous paragraph, the method is frequently called the *installment* method of recognizing revenue.

The installment method is an acceptable method of recognizing revenue for income tax purposes if certain tests are met. As compared with the completed-sales method, it delays the recognition of revenue and thus delays the recognition of taxable income and the payment of income taxes. Many retailers selling on credit, for example, Sears Roebuck and J. C. Penney, use the installment method of recognizing revenue for tax purposes and the completed-sales method for their financial statements.

If the completed-sales method is used for financial reporting and there is a danger of uncollectibility of the accounts or future services must be rendered, an adjustment of the revenue (or an additional expense) for bad debts or future services must be made. Such adjustments are described in Chapters 9 and 10.

Summary of Revenue Recognition

This brief introduction to revenue recognition does not exhaust the possible problems that can arise. The problem is not simple. The answer in a particular case must depend upon factors such as the nature of the business as well as the importance of the various stages of production and selling.

The sale, which usually implies the delivery of goods or the rendering of services to the customer in exchange for cash or receivables, is the most commonly accepted criterion for revenue recognition. Other criteria are, and should be, used. Although the limitations of the completed-sales method of revenue recognition are apparent in some situations, it will be used almost exclusively in the discussion and illustrations that follow throughout this text.

EXPENSE CONCEPTS

The Nature of Expenses

An expense is an expired asset. A firm acquires assets to obtain the services or future benefits that the assets provide. All acquisitions are acquisitions of assets, that is, of future benefits. As the services are used up, as the future benefits disappear, assets become expenses. Expenses may thus be described as "gone assets," that is, as benefits or resources used up in the process of securing revenue. To decide when an asset (or its synonym, a cost) loses its power to provide future benefits and, hence, has become an expense is one of the most difficult problems in accounting.

Criteria of Expense Recognition

Several criteria are used to determine when expenses should be recognized. Some of these criteria produce results that do not satisfy our definition of expense, but they have evolved out of considerations of practicality and uncertainty about future events. There are five principal criteria used in determining the expenses for a period.

Direct Association with Revenue. An asset whose expiration can be directly associated with the revenue of the period is an expense of the period. The cost of the merchandise sold is an expense that can be directly associated with the sales revenue. Other items, less intimately connected with revenue transactions, still meet this test: examples are salaries or commissions earned by salesmen and delivery costs on goods sold.

Association with the Accounting Period. An item that can reasonably be associated with future revenue should continue to be shown as an asset. An item related to earning the revenue of the present period should be charged to operations of the period. For example, the month's rent for the offices of a wholesale enterprise is related primarily to the revenue recognized during the month and, hence, is an expense of the month.

Selling and administrative costs for a period become expenses for the period because they can be associated with revenue activities of the period. Operating costs arising in manufacturing become production costs, which are assets. *Production costs* are increases in the asset work in process, not immediate deductions from revenue. Depreciation of a *factory* machine or building, for example, is *not* an expense, but is, rather, a production cost, part of the building that is converted from that asset form into the asset work in process. Production costs become expenses only when the asset into which they have been converted is sold. Production costs that have become expenses are shown collectively under the Cost of Goods Sold title. Recall that costs are assets and sold means gone. Therefore, the cost of goods sold is a "gone asset" or an expense.

Inevitability. There are certain items that are treated as expenses although they seem to have little or no relationship to operations. Property taxes on store buildings and equipment, for instance, are levied by the government whether or not the business is operating. They do not vary with the fluctuations in business activity (they are beyond the control of the management), and it is almost impossible to observe any definite relationship between amounts paid and the benefits or services received. Such items are usually treated as incurred expenses because the business cannot continue to exist without paying its tax assessments and other such costs. Inevitable costs are reasonably assigned to each accounting period as expenses that help to generate revenues for the period.

Regularity. Asset expirations that occur frequently and more or less regularly are clearly expenses. For example, small, regularly occurring losses from shoplifting would be included with other operating expenses. Other asset expirations in unusual, probably nonrecurring transactions were treated in a variety of ways in the past.

An extended debate between those who felt that only regular, ordinary items should be charged as expenses with extraordinary items viewed as adjustments of retained earnings ("current operating performance" view of income) and those who felt that almost all items occurring this period should affect the determination of the period's net income ("all-inclusive" view of income) raged in the accounting literature. The debate was settled in the mid-1960's by an Opinion of the Accounting Principles Board which held, in effect, that extraordinary items must be deducted in determining net income, but that they could be segregated and shown in a category separate from the expenses.[1]

Later authoritative actions[2] have limited the extraordinary classification to material items that are both *unusual in nature* and *infrequent in occurrence*, as described in the section on extraordinary items later in this chapter. Thus, a large, noninsured loss by theft would be included among the expenses, rather than as an extraordinary item. It might be singled out for separate reporting among the expenses, but it would be included in the expense total.

Expediency and Materiality. Many items are charged to expense accounts merely because no other treatment is practicable. When detailed record keeping is costly or would delay the preparations of reports and when the amounts involved are so small that they would not materially affect the reported results of operations, items that might in theory continue to be assets are charged to expense accounts. For example, some office supplies are frequently charged to expense accounts as they are purchased because the amount involved is too small to justify the more detailed procedure of charging them to an asset account and then recording the amount issued from time to time. Small tools frequently are charged to production when issued from the storeroom. This procedure is especially likely to be adopted when there are many items of small unit cost.

Officers' salaries are often treated as current administrative expenses,

[1] Opinion No. 9, Accounting Principles Board, AICPA, issued December 1966.
[2] Opinion No. 30, Accounting Principles Board, AICPA, issued June 1973.

even though much of certain officers' efforts are devoted to manufacturing activities or to planning for future periods. Salaries paid for manufacturing and planning produce future benefits and, as such, should be classified as assets. But to allocate the president's time between assets and expenses is so difficult that the attempt is not often made. The entire salary is treated as an expense.

The salaries of buyers and other costs of the purchasing department are seldom allocated to the items purchased, again because of the practical difficulties and the likelihood that this refinement would have little effect on periodic income. Sales promotion is generally absorbed as an expense of the period in which it is incurred, even though the benefits presumably will continue for some time.

Interest as an Expense

Under the all-inclusive view of net income, interest is an expense, but in almost all cases it is shown as a separate item among the expenses. Interest is most clearly an expense in the case of a sole proprietorship when loans are made merely to finance current operations and are not carried for indefinite periods as a part of the permanent capital of the business. There seems to be a direct association with revenue-earning operations of the business; the owner "hires" the funds in much the same way that he hires a clerk or rents a building. If the business has a net loss instead of a net income, the owner continues to pay the interest just as he continues to pay his employees' wages.

At the other extreme is the corporation, such as a railroad or public utility, with an elaborate financial plan which includes a substantial proportion of long-term bonds. The bonds are seldom reduced in total amount; when one issue matures, a new one takes its place. The bondholders are sometimes represented on the board of directors and, while they may not take an active part in management as long as the operations are successful, they stand ready to take over the business if a default is made in the payment of interest or principal at any time. They often exercise an important indirect influence on managerial policies through the advisory relations of investment bankers to the business. The position of the bondholders and that of the preferred and common stockholders differ only in degree; each partakes in the functions and risks of ownership and investment. It is true that the bondholders have a prior fixed claim for periodic interest payments and that the corporation will maintain interest payments as long as possible, even though the result is to diminish the stockholders' equity in the business. With a large portion of the permanent equity represented by bonds, however, cash resources will not long permit the payment of interest during years of heavy losses, and bondholders will shortly be able to force a reorganization. In cases such as these, it may be desirable to present a subtotal on the income statement with the title "Income before Interest Charges" and then deduct interest charges to arrive at net income for the period. This is commonly done in public utility financial statements, but rarely elsewhere. Income before interest charges represents the earnings on all the capital invested in the business. Nevertheless, interest charges are usually shown on a separate line among the expenses.

Entries to Record Interest

A more complete discussion of the accounting analysis and treatment of interest transactions will be given later, but a few of the simpler entries can be demonstrated at this time.

If a $120,000, twenty-year bond issue, on which interest at the rate of 8 percent per annum is to be paid on each January 1 and July 1, is issued on January 1, 1975, and if we assume that the accounting period is one month, the entries during the first year would be as follows:

Jan. 1	Cash on Hand	120,000	
	Bonds Payable		120,000
	Issue of twenty-year, 8-percent bonds of par.		

Jan. 31	Interest Charges on Bonds	800	
	Interest Payable		800
	To accrue bond interest for January.		

The entry of January 31 is repeated at February 28 and at the end of each succeeding month. At July 1 and again at January 1, interest payments would be made:

July 1	Interest Payable	4,800	
	Cash in Bank		4,800
	Payment of semiannual interest.		

The interest entries of the first year would be repeated each year of the life of the bond.

The Interest Charges on Bonds account would have a zero balance at the start of each new accounting period, since it, like the other expense, revenues and production cost accounts, is opened to accumulate information for one accounting period only. All such accounts are closed at the end of each accounting period. The Interest Payable account will show a growing credit balance each month until the semiannual interest payment is made. The account shows a credit balance of $4,800 at the end of each year, which will appear in the balance sheet as a current liability and will be cancelled by the next interest payment on January 1.

When notes payable are issued, the interest is usually paid in its entirety with the face value of the note at the maturity date and, accordingly, payment of interest does not always coincide with the close of an accounting period. The following illustration demonstrates both of these features. A loan is obtained from a bank on June 1 upon the issuance of a note. The note has a face value of $1,000, is due in three months, and bears interest at the rate of 6 percent per year. The books are closed quarterly at March 31, June 30, and so on. The entries for this situation would be:

June 1   Cash in Bank   1,000
               Notes Payable   1,000
          Issue of a three-month, 6-percent note.

June 30   Interest Charges on Notes   5
               Interest Payable   5
          To accrue interest to date.

June 30   Income Summary   5
               Interest Charges on Notes   5
          To close.

Sept. 1   Notes Payable   1,000
          Interest Payable   5
          Interest Charges on Notes   10
               Cash in Bank   1,015
          Payment of note and interest.

Interest Charges on Notes			Interest Payable		
June 30	5	June 30 5	Sept. 1	5	June 30 5
Sept. 1	10				

No entries are made on July 31 and August 31, since the accounting period does not end until September 30, and nothing would be gained by making accrual entries at those intermediate dates. Interest is generally recognized only at the end of the accounting period (June 30 in the example) or when payment is made. On September 1, the liability, as it appears on the books, is cancelled by a debit of $1,000 to Notes Payable and a debit of $5 to Interest Payable, and the additional interest that has accrued this period (June 30 to September 1) is charged to the account that records the interest charges for the current period, Interest Charges on Notes. At September 30, this $10 item, together with any other amounts which may be in the account at that time related to other notes, will be closed as part of the regular closing-entry procedure.

Federal Income Taxes

The corporation is the only common form of business enterprise that has an accounting problem in connection with the payment of federal income taxes. Partnerships must file information returns indicating the amount of each partner's share of the earnings, and the accounting system must be designed to accumulate the information required on the report form. However, the tax is levied upon the partners as individuals, and they in turn file separate returns which include their share of partnership earnings in a report of earnings from all sources. The same thing is true of an individual; his tax return includes his income from all sources, including that of his business. No separate information return is required of a sole proprietorship, because the details of business income are included in the report filed by the owner.

From the managerial viewpoint, there is a reasonable basis for viewing income taxes as a distribution of income rather than a determinant of income. Income tax charges are beyond the control of management. Changes in income tax rates or methods of calculating taxable income can produce substantial changes in the income tax charge and distort net income comparisons if income taxes are viewed as an expense. The stockholders' view is usually dominant in financial reporting, so income taxes are treated as an expense in published financial statements and are so treated in all illustrations and problems in this text.

Accounting for Income Taxes

The details of the federal income tax on corporations are subject to change. The rates and schedules of payments used in the illustration that follows should not be taken as an indication of the exact procedure in force at any particular time, but rather as an indication of the type of accounting problem which is involved.[3] The accounting for state income taxes follows the same general pattern as that for federal income taxes, except for rates and dates of payment.

Federal income taxes formerly were payable by corporations in the year following the one in which the income was earned. The tax law has been changed several times, so corporations, like individuals, must pay estimated taxes during the year. This is frequently described as pay-as-you-go basis of taxation. For a corporation on a calendar year basis, and using 1975 as an example, 25 percent of the estimated tax for 1975 must be paid by April 15, 1975; 50 percent by June 15, 1975; 75 percent by September 15, 1975; and the entire estimated tax for 1975 must be paid by December 15, 1975.

The estimated income and, hence, estimated tax payment may change as the year passes. The corporation must report such changed estimates with each quarterly payment. The cumulative payment requirements take into account previous payments. Any tax due when the tax return is filed in 1976 must be paid, one-half by March 15, 1976, and one-half by June 15, 1976. The law provides for penalties if the amount estimated is substantially less than the actual tax liability.

The following illustration is appropriate if the books are closed annually. The X Company had paid $94,000 in estimated income taxes during 1974. At year end the actual income tax charge for 1974 was calculated to be $102,000.

Dec. 31, 1974	Income Taxes	8,000	
	Federal Income Taxes Payable		8,000
	To recognize balance of 1974 income taxes.		

Dec. 31, 1974	Income Summary	102,000	
	Income Taxes		102,000
	To close.		

[3] The discussion and demonstrations are based on the law and regulations in effect January 1, 1975. Throughout the remainder of the text, an income tax rate of 40 percent is used in almost all illustrations.

Payment of the tax is made by two payments in 1975.

```
Mar. 15, 1975  Federal Income Taxes Payable ............    4,000
                  Cash in Bank ........................             4,000
               Payment of one-half of remaining 1974 tax
               liability.
```

The second payment is made on June 15 and the March 15 entry is repeated. On April 15, 1975, it is estimated that 1975 income taxes will be $114,000. No entry is required for the estimate but a payment of $28,500 (25 percent of $114,000) is required.

```
Apr. 15, 1975  Income Taxes ............................    28,500
                  Cash in Bank ........................            28,500
               Payment of estimated tax.
```

Similar entries would be made at June 15, September 15, and December 15 assuming there was no change in estimates. At the end of the year, income taxes for 1975 are calculated to be $120,000. Recognition of an additional income tax charge of $6,000 is required on December 31.

```
Dec. 31, 1975  Income Taxes ............................     6,000
                  Federal Income Taxes Payable .........            6,000
               To recognize balance of 1975 income taxes.
```

```
Dec. 31, 1975  Income Summary .......................    120,000
                  Income Taxes ........................           120,000
               To close.
```

Payments of $3,000 (50 percent of $6,000) are made on March 15, 1976, and June 15, 1976, and are recorded with a debit to Federal Income Taxes Payable and a credit to Cash in Bank.

If income statements are prepared more often than quarterly or if the end of the reporting period does not coincide with the tax payment period, it is necessary to estimate the income tax at the close of that period so that a more nearly accurate statement can be made of the net income for the period. Monthly or other short-period estimates of the tax are likely to be far from dependable, because the tax rate is graduated (22 percent of the first $25,000 of taxable net income and 48 percent of the remainder), and early estimates of taxable income for the year are likely to be in error. All that can be done is to set up the best possible estimate of tax in the light of earnings of the year to date and the prospects for the remainder of the year.

Expense and Expenditure

As revenues are different from receipts, expenses are different from expenditures. Under modern conditions of expanding investment in plant and widespread credit dealings, the differences between costs expired (expense) and cash outlays for the period (expenditure) can be substantial. The differences arise principally from four types of events.

Changes in Current Assets and Current Liabilities. The disbursements for current costs such as merchandise, material, labor, utility service, and insurance are not usually equal to the costs used up in the production of revenue. When disbursements do not equal expired costs, the total of inventories and prepayments or the total of current liabilities, or both, will change from one period to the next.

Depreciation and Purchase of Plant Assets. Unless the amount disbursed for plant assets during the period equals the amount of depreciation included in expenses, another difference will arise. In periods of substantial plant expansion, expenditures for plant will be greater than depreciation expenses, while in other periods depreciation will exceed expenditures for plant.

Payments of Long-Term Liabilities. There may be occasional large expenditures to discharge mortgages, long-term notes, or bonds payable. These, of course, are not expenses because they reduce liabilities.

Withdrawals by Investors. Dividends to stockholders or drawings by sole proprietors or by partners usually require expenditures of cash, but they are income (or capital) distributions, not expenses.

These important differences between expense and expenditures, as well as the parallel differences between revenues and receipts, are brought out specifically in the statement of changes in financial position, described in Chapter 19. An expenditure may precede expense recognition as when plant assets are acquired. Expenditures and expense recognition may be virtually simultaneous as when electric power is used and paid for. An expenditure may follow expense recognition as when supplies are bought on credit and used before the bill is paid.

EXTRAORDINARY ITEMS AND PRIOR PERIOD ADJUSTMENTS

Extraordinary Items

As a preceding section indicated, the types of items that can be treated as extraordinary are severely restricted. They must be characterized by both their *unusual nature* and *infrequent occurrence*. The Accounting Principles Board affirmed its desire to limit the extraordinary category by italicizing its statement that ". . . an event or transaction should be presumed to be an ordinary and usual event of the reporting entity, the effects of which should be included in [ordinary] income from operations, unless the evidence clearly supports its classification as an extraordinary item."[4] The board went on to list several types of items that could *not* be viewed as extraordinary items. Included among those items are:

Write down or write off of receivables or inventories
Gains or losses on sale or abandonment of capital assets

[4] Opinion No. 30, Accounting Principles Board, AICPA, June, 1973.

Exchange gains or losses from fluctuations of foreign currencies
Gains or losses on the disposal of a segment of the business.

The board identified few items as specifically falling within the extraordinary category, but losses from an earthquake or from expropriation of property in a foreign country were included.

If extraordinary losses of $25,000 are recognized, the income statement presentation would be:

Revenues	$1,000,000
Expenses (shown in appropriate detail)	850,000
Income before Extraordinary Items	$ 150,000
Extraordinary Items	
(Less applicable income taxes; each	
item described separately.)	
Total Extraordinary Losses	25,000
Net Income	$ 125,000

Prior Period Adjustments

Adjustments excluded from the determination of net income and charged directly to retained earnings are called *prior period adjustments* and are extremely rare. A material refund or additional assessment of a prior period's income tax or receipt of a substantial sum in a legal proceeding for a patent infringement occurring in a prior period are examples of items that might be treated as prior period adjustments. Prior period adjustments should be shown in the financial statement that reconciles the opening and closing balances of Retained Earnings (or other proprietorship account). As indicated earlier, such a reconciliation may be done in the last section of a statement of income and retained earnings, in a separate statement of retained earnings, or in the ownership section of the balance sheet.

Occasionally it is necessary to record an entry that corrects the revenue or expenses recognized in a prior accounting period. For example, an invoice for a shipment to a customer in December may have been mislaid and will have to be entered in January. A bill for repair service may have been overlooked in one period and must be recorded in a subsequent period. In situations of this sort, the "correction" account is usually closed to an expense or revenue account (for the current period), especially if the amount is not large. If so, then the correction is not a prior period adjustment. Only in the rare cases when the correction account might be closed to Retained Earnings does the entry result in a prior period adjustment.

INCOME DISTRIBUTION

Dividends on Capital Stock

The net income of a corporation is an increase in the stockholders' equity, but it is not available to the stockholders until a formal dividend declaration has been made by the board of directors of the corporation. Declarations of dividends on preferred stock are usually made regularly as long as the corporation is financially able to pay the dividend; most preferred-stock dividends are paid quarterly. Dividends on common stock are declared with less regularity, but many corporations follow the policy of declaring regular quarterly dividends on common stock with extra dividends being added from time to time, particularly at the close of the fiscal year.

There are three significant dates in connection with dividend declarations: (1) the date of the declaration, when the amount of the dividend becomes a liability to stockholders as a group; (2) the date, sometimes called the *record* date, when the stock records will be closed and a list prepared of those entitled to the dividends; and (3) the date of payment. An illustration of the typical form for the announcement of a dividend declaration made, for example, on August 28, 1975, would be: "$1 per share payable on September 30, 1975, to stockholders of record at the close of business September 15, 1975."

Two entries are usually made in connection with dividends, one for the declaration and the other for the payment. In the usual case, when it is intended to make a distribution of current earnings, the entry would be (assuming a $50,000 dividend):

```
Dividends on Capital Stock ...............................   50,000
     Dividends Payable .......................................          50,000
```

The Dividends on Capital Stock account is an income distribution account and is closed at the end of the accounting period; unlike the expense accounts, however, it is closed directly to Retained Earnings. The entry for the declaration is sometimes recorded as a direct debit to Retained Earnings, especially when the intention is to indicate a distribution of earnings of previous periods. In that case, the entry would be:

```
Retained Earnings ........................................   50,000
     Dividends Payable .......................................          50,000
```

The entry for the payment of the dividend is made in the same manner as the entry for the payment of any liability. Its simplest form is:

```
Dividends Payable ........................................   50,000
     Cash in Bank ...........................................          50,000
```

Frequently, the total amount of the dividend is deposited in a special bank account, and a special series of dividend checks are used for the payment.

Proprietary Drawings

There are no legal limitations on the withdrawals of funds by sole proprietors or partners, although the partnership agreement may introduce a contractual limitation on partners' drawings. When an owner or partner draws funds from the firm, an entry would be:

```
R. L. Smith, Drawings ...........................................   200
     Cash in Bank ...............................................          200
Drawings by owner.
```

The Drawings account is usually considered to be an income distribution account rather than a deduction from accumulated capital, even though at the end of the accounting period it is usually closed to the owner's or partners' capital accounts rather than to the Income Summary account. If Mr. Smith's drawings during the period had totaled $5,000, the closing entry would be:

```
R. L. Smith, Capital .........................................   5,000
        R. L. Smith, Drawings ...................................           5,000
To close.
```

SUMMARY OF TYPES OF ACCOUNTS

The following types of accounts have been introduced and discussed to this point: (1) balance sheet assets, (2) liabilities, (3) ownership (proprietorship, partners' capital, or stockholders' equity), (4) production cost assets, (5) revenue, (6) expense, (7) extraordinary items, (8) income distribution, and (9) retained earnings adjustments. Types (5) through (9) have received special attention in this chapter.

The statement of income and retained earnings shown in Schedule 7.1 illustrates the recommended statement presentation of the types of accounts considered in this chapter. The numbers in parentheses to the left of the titles refer to the types of accounts listed in the previous paragraph.

SCHEDULE 7.1

MARIN MANUFACTURING COMPANY
Statement of Income and Retained Earnings
Year of 1975

(5) Revenues		
Sales	$835,000	
Interest Earned	2,000	
Total Revenues		$837,000
(6) Expenses		
Manufacturing Cost of Goods Sold (made up of		
type (4) items)	$715,000	
Selling Expenses (itemized)	33,000	
General and Administrative Expenses (itemized)	17,000	
Interest Charges	3,000	
Federal Income Taxes	24,000	
Total Expenses		792,000
Income before Extraordinary Item		$ 45,000
(7) Extraordinary Item: Loss from Earthquake		14,000
Net Income for Year		$ 31,000
(8) Dividends on Common Stock		14,000
Net Income Retained		$ 17,000
Retained Earnings, January 1, 1975	$ 84,000	
(9) Retained Earnings Adjustment		
Refund of 1972 Income Taxes	6,000	90,000
Retained Earnings, December 31, 1975		$107,000

QUESTIONS AND PROBLEMS

1. Can the concepts of revenue and expense exist without reference to an accounting period?

2. All revenue, expense, and income distribution accounts have zero balances at the start of an accounting period. Why is this so?

3. What is the essential difference between expense accounts and income distribution accounts?

4. Indicate the amount of revenue, if any, in each of the following transactions:
   a. Goods that cost $650 are sold for $750 cash.
   b. Goods that cost $650 are sold for $750, on account.
   c. The $750 of item (b) is collected one week later.
   d. A cash deposit of $50 is received by an appliance store on a color television set that will be delivered as soon as it is available.
   e. Goods that cost $650 are sold for $550, cash.
   f. $100,000 of twenty-year, 8½-percent bonds are issued for $98,600.

°5. Indicate which of the following transactions involve the immediate recognition of revenue or income:
   a. The delivery of an issue of a magazine to subscribers.
   b. The sale of an automobile by an automobile agency.
   c. A collection of cash from accounts receivable debtors.
   d. The borrowing of money at the bank.
   e. The sale of merchandise on account.
   f. A barber collects for a haircut.
   g. Dry-cleaning services are rendered on account.
   h. The issue of shares of preferred stock.
   i. Tickets for a concert to be given in two weeks are sold.
   j. An income tax refund is received.

6. Indicate whether the method of revenue recognition used by each of the following types of business is likely to be:
   (1) Recognition of revenue as production is carried on.
   (2) Recognition of revenue when goods are furnished or services rendered to customers.
   (3) Recognition of revenue only when payment is received from customers, if that time differs from (2).
   a. a drug store
   b. a manufacturer of umbrellas
   c. a bridge-building firm
   d. a real estate developer selling lots on long-term contracts
   e. a wholesale tobacco distributor
   f. a dentist
   g. a men's suit manufacturer
   h. a shipbuilding firm constructing an aircraft carrier
   i. a shoe store
   j. a supermarket.

° Hints, key numbers, or (partial) answers appear in the back of the book between the Appendix Tables and the Glossary.

7. Accounting Principles Board Opinion No. 30 specifies that an event must be characterized by *both* unusual nature and infrequent occurrence to be classified as an extraordinary item. Indicate which of the following events would qualify as extraordinary items.
   a. Loss on disposition of a building.
   °b. Loss from a typhoon.
   c. Gain on sale of stock held as an investment for ten years.
   d. A major write-off of receivables resulting from the bankruptcy of the company's largest customer.
   e. An income tax refund.
   f. Loss due to a prolonged strike at the company's largest plant.
   g. Loss resulting from the government's sudden prohibition of the continued sale of the company's major product.
   h. Gain on selling the only land owned by a steel fabricating company. The land was acquired ten years ago for future expansion, but shortly thereafter the company abandoned all plans for expansion and held the land for appreciation.
   i. Gain on the sale of land surrounding a warehouse. When the company buys property to establish a new warehouse, it usually buys more land than it expects to use, with expectation that the land will appreciate in value.
   j. Loss on sale of a block of common stock. The block of shares is the only security investment the company has ever owned.

8. Discuss the following statement from a decision of the United States Supreme Court: "Net earnings is what is left after paying current expenses and interest on debt and everything else the company is liable to pay."

9. Taxes are not costs related directly to the production of revenue of the period, but many types of taxes are classified as expenses. Why?

10. Give dated journal entries for 1975 for the following transactions. The accounting period is a semiannual one ending June 30 and December 31. Do not prepare closing entries.
    (1) On March 15, 1975, a tract of land shown on the books at its cost, $8,000, is exchanged for another lot with a fair market value of $9,000.
    (2) Semiannual interest payments are made on the outstanding $200,000, 6-percent bond issue on April 1 and October 1.
    (3) On August 15, the board of directors declared a dividend of $1 a share on the 120,000 shares of capital stock outstanding "payable on September 15 to stockholders of record August 30."
    (4) A $5,000 three-month, 8-percent loan was secured on May 1 and repaid with interest on August 1. A promissory note was given as evidence of indebtedness.

11. How would you recommend that the costs of operating an experimental laboratory be dealt with? Assume that this laboratory is considered to be necessary to maintain the company's position in the field, and assume further that many valuable formulas, devices, and economies result from its activities.

12. Indicate the account to be debited in each of the following transactions and indicate whether the account is (1) a balance sheet asset account,

(2) a production cost account, (3) an expense account, (4) an income distribution account, or (5) a capital or retained earnings deduction:

a. The income tax for the year is recorded.

b. Salaries of foremen in a factory are accrued.

c. Salaries of traveling salesmen of a manufacturing enterprise are accrued.

d. A partner withdraws merchandise for his own use.

e. The cost of goods sold is recorded.

f. Dividends are declared on preferred stock.

g. Depreciation of delivery trucks is recorded.

h. A donation is made to a church bazaar.

i. A payment is made for the cost of installing electric fixtures in a leased building. (The lease runs for eight years.)

j. A payment of a fire insurance premium for three years in advance is made.

k. Freight is paid on a new piece of store equipment.

l. An entry is made to record the accrued interest on notes payable.

13. During one pay period, the payroll of the Whipple Manufacturing Company showed men performing the following tasks, among others:

a. Salesmen: Sales calls on customers.

b. Laborers: Removing debris left in the factory yard by a hurricane.

c. Clerks: Factory cost accounting department.

d. Clerks: Customers' billing department.

e. Laborers: Working on the factory production line.

f. Laborers: Installing a new machine.

What type of account—expense, loss, balance sheet asset, or production cost—would be charged with the wages of each class of worker?

14. During 1975 the Simons Company has the following transactions with regard to promissory notes:

Feb. 15   A $2,000 loan from the First National Bank on a two-month, 6-percent note.

Mar. 1   An additional loan of $1,500 is obtained from the First National Bank on a three-month, 6-percent note.

Apr. 15   The February 15 note is paid with interest by check.

June 1   The March 1 note is extended for two months, but interest for the first three months is paid by check.

Aug. 1   The renewed note of March 1 is paid with interest by check.

Record the transactions (other than closing entries) in two-column journal form and date each entry under each of the following assumptions:

a. The company closes its books once a year on December 31.

b. The company closes its books quarterly on March 31, June 30, and so forth.

15. Prepare dated journal entries for 1975 for the following selected transactions of the Roberts Manufacturing Company. The company closes its books semiannually on June 30 and December 31.

(1) On June 20, 1975, the directors declared a dividend of $1 a share on the 15,000 shares of common stock outstanding. The dividend was payable July 25, 1975, to stockholders of record July 10, 1975. The dividend was paid on the payment date.

(2) The company has a $300,000, 6-percent bond issue outstanding. Semiannual interest payments were made on March 1, 1975, and September 1, 1975.

(3) The balance of the 1974 income tax liability was discharged by a payment of $157,000 on March 15, 1975, and an equal amount on June 15, 1975. At June 30, 1975, income tax on the profits of the first six months of 1975 was estimated to be $245,000. Payments of $116,000 were made on September 15, and December 15, 1975, on estimated 1975 income tax. At December 31, 1975, the total income tax liability for 1975 is calculated to be $580,000, with $348,000 remaining to be paid in 1976.

16. In which of the following situations should there be an immediate recognition of revenue or income?
   a. The shipment of goods paid for in advance.
   b. The collection on March 1 of the principal and interest of a note receivable. The books are closed monthly on the last day of the month.
   c. The receipt of an order for a carload of merchandise.
   d. The increase in the redemption value of government bonds.
   e. The issue of additional shares of stock for cash.
   f. The completion of production of a batch of shoes by a shoe factory.
   g. The deduction of union dues from an employee's pay check (from the standpoint of the employer).
   h. Transaction (g) from the standpoint of the union when the dues are received from the employer.
   i. The receipt of a refund from the Central Gas Company of overcharges of a previous year.
   j. The sale of a season ticket to a series of concerts.

17. A summary of the transactions relating to revenue and receivables of the Willow Dairy Company for March, 1975, is as follows:
   (1) Milk sold for cash, $9,200.
   (2) Coupons, good for future deliveries of milk, are sold to customers, $3,200.
   (3) Collections from charge customers, $7,200.
   (4) Coupons redeemed by delivery of milk, $2,560.
   (5) Deliveries of milk on account, $7,800.
   a. Record the transactions in two-column journal form.
   b. If the amount of coupons outstanding on March 31, 1975, was $580, what was the amount of coupons outstanding on March 1, 1975?

18. The Kennelly Company borrows $10,000 at the bank on a promissory note. The note is dated May 1, 1975, and is due on August 1, 1975. It bears interest at 6 percent per annum. The note and interest are paid at maturity. Give the dated journal entries (other than closing entries) which would be made in connection with this note and show the interest accounts (in skeleton account form and including closing entries) for each of the following conditions:
   a. Assume that the accounting period is the calendar year.
   b. Assume that a quarterly accounting period ending March 31, June 30, and so forth, is used.
   c. Assume that a monthly accounting period is used.

°19. Indicate whether the debit for each of the following transactions involves (1) an increase in expense, (2) a loss, or (3) an increase in an asset account.

a. Raw material is used in production.
b. Rent of the sales office is paid for the month.
c. Freight is paid on merchandise received.
d. Contributions to the Community Chest by a retail store.
e. Premiums for this period are paid on a fraud bond (insurance against embezzlement by employees).
f. The recording of a bill for installing a machine in the factory.
g. Depreciation of delivery equipment by a department store.
h. Uninsured loss by theft.
i. The monthly telephone bill is recorded.
j. The receipt of a bill for electric current by a department store.
k. The purchase of office supplies for cash.
l. Depreciation of machinery in a manufacturing plant.

20. In each of the following transactions, indicate whether the debit involves:
   (1) an increase in a balance sheet asset account
   (2) an increase in a production cost account
   (3) a decrease in a liability account
   (4) an increase in an expense account
   (5) a loss.
   a. Wages earned by laborers digging a foundation for a new building.
   b. The purchase of tools for cash.
   c. A fire insurance policy is carried by a shoe store. An entry is made to write off a month's portion of the year's premium.
   d. Depreciation of a factory building.
   e. A delivery truck is damaged in an accident. A full coverage insurance policy is carried.
   f. The show window of a department store is blown out by a wind storm. No insurance is carried to cover this type of risk.
   g. The return of store supplies, which have been found to be defective. Payment for them has not yet been made.
   h. The recording of a bill for gas used as fuel in a manufacturing plant.
   i. The recording of the water bill by a drug store.
   j. The payment of wages recognized previously.
   k. The recording of store rent for the month when a payment has previously been made for six months in advance.
   l. The purchase of store supplies on account.

21. In each of the following transactions, using the appropriate symbol, indicate whether the account which would be debited is:
   (A)   a balance sheet asset account
   (PC)   a production cost account
   (E)   an expense account
   (ID)   an income distribution account
   (RE)   a capital or retained earnings deduction
   (X)   Some other type of account
   The transactions do not all relate to the same set of books.
   a. A voucher is entered for four months' rent of a factory building in advance. The books are closed monthly.
   b. Factory supplies are used in production.
   c. A refund is made to an apartment house tenant of rent previously paid in advance.

d. The accrued liability for income taxes is recorded.

e. A voucher is prepared and entered for commissions due salesmen for the current month.

f. An entry is made to record the expiration of a fire insurance premium on a factory building.

g. Wages earned by a delivery truck driver, who has been working on an addition to the garage during the entire pay period, are recorded.

h. A dividend is declared on common stock as a distribution of current earnings.

i. Goods are returned by a customer. No entry had been made to record cost of goods sold.

j. A voucher is entered for a freight bill covering transportation charges on a new piece of factory equipment.

k. Depreciation of a truck used by a building contractor is recorded.

l. An uninsured tornado loss occurs.

m. A check is drawn to pay a voucher covering the purchase of office furniture. The voucher had previously been entered in the voucher register.

n. An entry is made to record the interest accrued on bonds payable.

o. The expiration of a fire insurance premium on a store building is recorded.

22. On May 16, 1975, M. C. Morgan entered into a contract to build an apartment house for the Ernst Realty Company. The contract price was $2,000,000 and Morgan estimated that the total cost of the project to him would be $1,900,000. The contract provided that Morgan was to receive payments on a percentage of completion basis; at the end of every month the architect was to estimate the percentage of completion, and Morgan was to receive that percentage of the contract price less 10 percent, which would be held back pending completion of the job.

Work began in July and at July 31 the architect estimated that the job was 7 percent complete. The Ernst Realty Company therefore paid Morgan $126,000 (7 percent of $2,000,000 minus 10 percent of that figure). The architect's estimates of percentage completion as rendered at the end of the following months were as follows:

August	15%
September	24%
October	33%
November	50%
December	70%

Appropriate payments were made by the Ernst Realty Company to Morgan on the third day of each month following the architect's estimates.

During 1975 the total expenditures on the project by Morgan were $1,320,000.

a. Assume that M. C. Morgan recognizes revenue on a "percentage-of-completion" (production) basis; record the transactions in two-column journal form and compute his net income for 1975.

b. Assume that M. C. Morgan recognizes revenue only when jobs are completed (sales basis); record the transactions in two-column journal form. What would be the balance sheet presentation of the accounts?

°**23.** The Humbolt Electric Company received a contract late in 1974 to build a large electricity generating unit. The contract price was $700,000, and it was estimated that total costs would be $600,000. Estimated construction time was fifteen months, and it was agreed that payments would be made by the purchaser as follows:

March 31, 1975	$ 70,000
June 30, 1975	105,000
Sept. 30, 1975	203,000
Dec. 31, 1975	161,000
March 31, 1976	161,000
	$700,000

Costs of construction incurred by the Humbolt Electric Company were as follows:

Jan. 1–March 31, 1975	$120,000
Apr. 1–June 30, 1975	120,000
July 1–Sept. 30, 1975	180,000
Oct. 1–Dec. 31, 1975	120,000
Jan. 1–March 31, 1976	60,000
	$600,000

The Humbolt Electric Company prepares financial statements quarterly at March 31, June 30, and so forth.

Prepare a four-column form with columns for period, revenue, expenses, and net income. Calculate the revenue, expense, and net income and fill in the form for each quarter for each of the following bases of revenue recognition:

a. production (percentage of completion) basis.

b. sales (completed contract) basis.

c. cash collection (installment) basis.

24. The following are selected transactions for the month of June 1975, on the books of the Bingham Coal and Ice Company.

(1) Coal sold for cash, $2,880.

(2) Coal sold on account, $4,400.

(3) Contracts for winter delivery of $37,200 of coal are received; checks for $1,860 accompany the contracts as advance payments.

(4) Ice sold for cash, $4,800.

(5) Coupon books, redeemable by ice deliveries, are issued to customers for cash, $2,100.

(6) Ice coupons redeemed by deliveries, $1,680.

(7) Ice sold on account, $6,900.

(8) Collections from account customers, $10,260.

(9) A delivery truck which was carried on the books at $2,160 is sold for $1,840.

Record the above transactions. Records of sales are maintained by commodities.

25. The books of the Ramada Apartments at October 1, 1975, showed rent receivable for September and earlier months of $2,700 and rent received in advance for October and later months of $4,080.

Collections from tenants during October were $28,800. At October 31 the books showed rent receivable of $3,000 and prepayments by tenants of $2,400.

During November, collections from tenants were $32,400. At November 30 the books showed rent receivable of $2,400 and prepayments by tenants of $3,600.

a. Record the October and November transactions with customers in two-column journal form.

b. What was the rent revenue for October? For November?

°26. The Pennsylvania Steel Company files its income tax returns on a calendar-year basis and issues financial statements quarterly as of March 31, June 30, and so on.

Assume the applicable income tax rates and rules for 1975 are:

(1) Effective tax rates are 22 percent of the first $25,000 of taxable income and 48 percent of all taxable income in excess of $25,000.

(2) Corporations must pay estimated taxes during the year. For a corporation on a calendar-year basis, by April 15, 1975, 25 percent of the estimated tax payment for the year 1975 must be paid; by June 15, 1975, 50 percent of the estimated tax payment for the year must have been paid; by September 15, 1975, 75 percent of the estimated tax payment for the year must have been paid; by December 15, all of the estimated tax payment for the year must have been paid.

(3) Any tax due when the tax return is filed in 1976 must be paid, one-half by March 15, 1976, and one-half by June 15, 1976.

The following data are applicable to the company's 1975 income tax.

1975

March 31   It is estimated that total taxable income for the year 1975 will be about $1.5 million. Income for the first quarter is $400,000.

April 15   The first payment on estimated taxes is made.

June 15   It is now estimated that total taxable income for the year will be about $1.7 million. The second payment on estimated taxes is made.

June 30   Income for the second quarter is $500,000.

Sept. 15   It is now estimated that total taxable income for the year will be about $1.6 million. The third payment on estimated taxes is made.

Sept. 30   Income for the third quarter is $300,000.

Dec. 15   It is now estimated that total taxable income for the year will be $1,750,000. The fourth payment on estimated taxes is made.

Dec. 31   Income for the year is $1,775,000.

1976

March 15   The first payment of the balance of 1975 taxes is made.

June 15   The second payment of 1975 tax balance is made.

a. Prepare schedules showing

   i. for tax returns: estimated taxes for year, cumulative payments due and payment made for April 15, June 15, September 15, and December 15 of 1975 as well as for March 15 and June 15 of 1976.

   ii. for financial statements: tax expenses for the quarterly reports and annual report.

    b. Record the tax-related transactions of 1975 in two-column journal form.

    c. Present the skeleton accounts for Cash, Prepaid Income Taxes, Income Tax Payable and Income Tax Expense.

27. Assume the applicable income tax rates and rules for the Pennsylvania Steel Company (Problem 26) are the same for 1976 as for 1975. The following data are applicable to the Company's 1976 income tax.

1976

March 31	Estimated taxable income for year 1976 is $1,800,000. Income for first quarter is $300,000.
April 15	The first payment on estimated taxes is made.
June 15	Estimated taxable income is $1,800,000. The second payment on estimated taxes is made.
June 30	Income for the second quarter is $400,000.
Sept. 15	Estimated taxable income is $1,800,000. The third payment is made.
Sept. 30	Income for the third quarter is $500,000.
Dec. 15	Estimated taxable income is $1,800,000. The fourth payment is made.
Dec. 31	Income for the year is $1,800,000.

Repeat steps (a) – (c) of Problem 26 for 1976.

Chapter 8

Internal Control and Cash

Everyone has lost change in a vending machine at least once. It is annoying, and because vending machine companies want to keep their customers' goodwill, they usually give their customers their lost change and promise to repair the faulty machine. Most businesses have petty cash funds for small refunds to customers, for change for delivery boys, or small purchases of paper clips and rubber bands. Besides petty cash, businesses handle larger amounts of money in the form of cash and checks every day. Cashiers in restaurants and retail stores handle money from sales, insurance agents collect premiums, loan officers accept and approve checks for loans, and purchasing agents and other corporate officials deal with large amounts of money as part of their jobs.

In the process of establishing itself, making money, and accumulating assets, a fledgling enterprise is faced with an important problem: How should cash and other assets be safeguarded? There are two aspects of this problem. First, most businesses need an internal control system to insure the honesty and accuracy of their accounting records. Second, most businesses use special accounts for change funds, petty cash, undeposited cash, and checking accounts. The ability to follow the flow of cash through these accounts and reconcile bank statements with the firm's records is important. This chapter provides discussion and illustration of both aspects of the problem of handling cash and checks.

INTERNAL CONTROL

Definition

Large enterprises require internal-control systems to insure that all business operations are carried out effectively and according to plan. The American Institute of Certified Public Accountants has described the control process as follows:

> *Administrative Control* includes, but is not limited to, the plan of organization and the procedures and records that are concerned with the decision processes leading to management's authorization of transactions. Such authorization is a management function directly associated with the responsibility for achieving the objectives of the organization and is the starting point for establishing accounting control of transactions.
>
> *Accounting control* comprises the plan of organization and the procedures and records that are concerned with the safeguarding of assets and the reliability of financial records and consequently are designed to provide reasonable assurance that:
>
> a. Transactions are executed in accordance with management's general or specific authorization.
> b. Transactions are recorded as necessary (1) to permit preparation of financial statements in conformity with generally accepted accounting principles or any other criteria applicable to such statements and (2) to maintain accountability for assets.
> c. Access to assets is permitted only in accordance with management's authorization.
> d. The recorded accountability for assets is compared with the existing assets at reasonable intervals and appropriate action is taken with respect to any differences.[1]

The discussion here treats the basic elements of a control system and the accounting functions related to safeguarding assets or to providing reliable data on business activities.

Basic Requirements

The first basic requirement for an effective system of internal control is an organizational structure that defines responsibility for the authorization and accomplishment of all the enterprise's activities. Such a plan requires that each employee be responsible to someone above him or her.

Second, an effective system of internal control divides responsibilities within the organizational structure. Three types of functions are to be distinguished—operations, physical custody, and records or reports. Although all departments must be organized to facilitate coordination and cooperation, a department must not be able to control the accounting records for its own operations. An accounting department which controls

---

[1] *Statement on Auditing Standards No. 1: Codification of Auditing Standards and Procedures,* American Institute of Certified Public Accountants, §320.27-28, 1973.

the records relating to the operating and custodial departments is able to present to management unbiased reports that provide assistance in controlling operations and safeguarding assets.

Third, an effective system of internal control divides duties so that no one person is in a position to control all steps of a transaction. An individual responsible for the custody of an asset should not have the accounting responsibility for it. The responsibility for the various operating activities in a particular transaction should, as far as practicable, be assigned among several departments and employees. To achieve further control within the operating activities, the responsibility for authorizing or initiating a transaction is separated from the responsibility for carrying it out. In addition to dividing responsibility and assigning duties to a variety of departments and individuals, dividing the duties within the accounting department may further contribute to an effective system of internal control.

A fourth basic requirement is a system for authorizing and recording procedures that provides accounting control. This requires the design of forms, the selection of equipment, and the establishment of a route or flow for the orderly processing of data, including a record of the approvals and actions taken by the individuals responsible for the various steps in the transaction.

Forms can help insure that prescribed procedures are followed by providing spaces for required supporting data and approvals. Multiple copies of a form often facilitate the use of common information for several different purposes. Serially numbered forms, together with a review of the use made of each form in sequence, provide a control over the completeness of data as well as over the authorized usage of a particular form.

Mechanical equipment may facilitate control in a number of ways. A cash register, for example, assists in preventing the failure to report cash sales. When a transaction occurs, the register shows the amount, records it, and prepares a receipt for the customer. Locked-in totals show up any difference between the recorded sales and the cash in the register. Machines that accumulate totals help to keep summaries and detailed records in agreement. The simultaneous preparation of several documents, or of copies of a form which contain common data, prevents some differences that might occur if preparation were separate.

Illustration

No one organizational structure, document design, and information flow uniquely provides adequate control. Each business must devise a system adapted to its particular needs. A detailed illustration of all phases of an internal-control system for any one company is beyond the scope of this textbook. An outline of the internal-control features of some of the major areas of accounting for a medium-sized manufacturing concern is presented below. It gives a general view of the operations of such a system.

Sales. Internal control over sales should insure the following objectives:

1. The sale is authorized and approved in detail
2. The sale is recorded on proper forms as evidence for the initiation of and subsequent steps in the transaction
3. Goods are released from stores only when authorized
4. The goods corresponding to those ordered are delivered
5. The billing agrees with the shipment and terms of the order
6. The transaction is entered properly in the formal accounting records.

A sale is initiated by an order received from a customer. An order invoice form is prepared and used for acknowledging the order, in obtaining credit approval, for releasing the goods from stores, in shipping the goods, in accounting procedures, and for billing the customer. The departments assumed to be concerned are sales order, credit, stores, shipping, and accounting (billing, accounts receivable, inventory, and general ledger divisions).

Upon receipt of an order from a customer, the sales order department prepares an order invoice form in multiple copies. A copy is sent to the credit department for approval. Upon approval for credit extension, copies are sent to the billing division. Copies are also sent to the stores department to authorize the release of goods to the shipping department, to expedite the shipping procedure, and to notify other departments of action taken. When the goods arrive from stores, accompanied by copies of the order invoice, the shipping department sends them to the customer, enclosing a copy as a packing slip. Shipping then returns the copy of the shipping order and other copies to the billing division. The billing division then sends copies of the invoice to the customer and to the accounting department for use by the accounts receivable (customer's accounts) and inventory (detailed inventory records) divisions; it sends a list or summary of invoices at designated intervals to the general ledger division of the accounting department. If periodic statements are sent to customers, further control is attained when an individual outside of the accounts receivable division, such as an internal auditor, compares the statements with the individual subsidiary ledger accounts and mails the statements.

Each department has received a written authorization for its action and, in turn, indicated its action on copies of the authorization being sent to other departments. Functions are segregated—each department performs only an operating, a custodial, or a record-keeping function. No one department or individual controls the entire transaction. Rather, the duties and responsibilities have been so divided that the activity of any one department or division is subject to a cross check or review by another.

Cash Receipts. Because cash is easy to conceal and transfer and because of its general exchangeability, cash is especially subject to mishandling. The system of control over cash receipts requires particular attention in order to insure that:

1. All cash is received only by authorized persons and adequate records are made immediately.
2. Cash on hand is subjected to adequate protection and safekeeping.

3. All cash received is deposited daily and intact.
4. The related transactions are entered properly in the formal accounting records.

Action is initiated by remittances received in the mail from customers. A detailed daily cash-receipts listing is prepared for the transfer of cash and for accounting purposes. A deposit slip is prepared to accompany the deposit of collections in the bank. The departments assumed to be affected are the mail room, treasury (cash receipts division), and accounting (accounts receivable and general ledger divisions).

When checks and currency arrive in the mail room, a detailed daily cash-receipts listing is prepared under the supervision of a representative of the treasurer, and a supporting form, such as a remittance advice sent by the customer, is completed as an individual record of receipt. A copy of the listing is sent to the cash receipts division together with the checks and currency, and a receipt for the transfer is obtained. There, a deposit slip is prepared, checks are endorsed, and the deposit is forwarded to the bank by a representative of the treasurer. A copy of the deposit slip is sent to the general ledger division. The mail room sends a copy of the daily cash-receipts listing together with individual remittance forms to the accounts receivable division. Individual collections are indicated in the subsidiary ledger accounts or file of uncollected invoices, and the detailed listing form is completed, indicating discounts taken and total credits to customers. The listing is transferred to the general ledger division where it is compared with the copy of the deposit slip, and the receipts for the day are journalized. Further control is attained when the bank account is reconciled by another person, who receives duplicate deposit slips and the bank statement directly from the bank. Reconciliation of bank statements is explained below.

Control over cash receipts arises from separating the custody and deposit of collections functions from the record-keeping function. The duties of various organizational units concerned are so divided that the activity of any one unit is subject to a cross-check or review by another. The amount of cash transferred to the treasurer's department is compared with the amount reported to the accounting department by a reconciliation of the daily listing and deposit slips in the general ledger division. If cash were withdrawn and not transferred or reported by the mail room, this discrepancy would be detected when a customer complained after a subsequent billing, since the maintaining of the customers' accounts has been separated from any control by mail room personnel.

Purchases. Control over purchases should insure that:

1. Details of the purchase are authorized and approved.
2. The purchase is recorded on proper forms for evidence of the initiation and subsequent steps in the transaction.
3. Items purchased are recorded when received and are under custody for use in the business.

4. Items received correspond to those ordered.
5. The vendor's invoice agrees with the prices and terms of the order.
6. The transaction is entered properly in the formal accounting records.

A purchase is initiated by a requisition form prepared by a production department. A purchase order form is prepared to be used for ordering from the vendor, for receiving and storing the goods, and for accounting purposes. A receiving report form is prepared to indicate the quantity and quality of individual items received and stored. It is assumed that, in addition to the requisitioning department and the purchasing department, the receiving, stores, and accounting (accounts payable, inventory, and general ledger divisions) are concerned.

Upon receiving the requisition, the purchasing department prepares the purchase order and acknowledges the requisition. Copies of the purchase order are sent to the vendor. When acknowledged by the vendor, copies are sent to the receiving, stores, and accounting (accounts payable and inventory divisions) departments.

When the goods are received and accepted, the receiving department prepares a receiving report. Copies are sent to the purchasing department and, along with the goods, to the stores department. The stores department forwards its copies to the accounting department (accounts payable and inventory divisions).

The invoice received from the vendor, frequently in multiple copies, is directed to the purchasing department where it is compared with the purchase order and receiving report. Then it is forwarded to the accounting department (accounts payable division). The purchase order, receiving report, and invoice are compared for terms and clerical accuracy. When they have been reconciled, a voucher is prepared. The approved voucher will be entered in the voucher register from which the general ledger division will post it to the accounts in the general ledger. The voucher, together with supporting documents, is held pending transfer to the treasurer's department in time for proper payment. The inventory division must see a copy of the invoice or the original invoice so that proper prices can be assigned to inventory items and the detailed inventory record will agree with the control account in the general ledger.

In the above illustration, the authorizing department does not have further responsibility for making the purchase. Each of the affected departments performs only an operating, custodial, or record-keeping function. The activities of each department are subject to cross-check or review by the activities of another. Each department acts only on the basis of a written authorization. Prior to approval of the voucher for payment the documents representing the responsibility for the purchasing, receiving, and storing steps have been reviewed and checked for authorized signatures as well as for the quantity, quality, price, and payment terms applicable to the goods received.

Cash Disbursements. Control over cash disbursements should insure that:

1. Disbursements are made only by authorized persons.
2. Adequate records support each disbursement. Such records attest that disbursement was for goods and services procured by proper authority and actually received by the business. The records attest that payment is made in accordance with the purchase contract.
3. The transaction is entered properly in the formal accounting records.

A disbursement is initiated by the submission of an approved voucher together with supporting documents, and payment is made by check. The departments assumed to be concerned are treasury (cash disbursements) and accounting (accounts payable and general ledger divisions).

Upon receiving the approved voucher and supporting documents from the accounts payable division, the treasurer's department will prepare a check. The data are reviewed, and the check is signed and mailed to the vendor. The voucher and supporting documents are canceled and forwarded to the accounts payable division which, in turn, indicates the payment in the voucher register. The checks issued are recorded in a check register which serves as a basis for posting to the general ledger by the general ledger division. Further control is attained when the bank statement and canceled checks are sent to and reconciled by a person who has not been a part of the payment transaction.

Payment is made only by checks issued by an authorized person. It is supported by an approved voucher with adequate evidence of acceptance of responsibility in the preceding steps of ordering, receiving, and storing of the goods. The voucher for payment must be prepared in accordance with the terms of the purchase contract. Responsibility for the custodial function is separated from the record-keeping function. As in the other procedures, the activity of each department is subject to a cross-check and review by another department.

CASH ON HAND

Change Funds

Wherever cash is received directly from customers, as in retail stores or theaters, or by delivery truck drivers, a supply of cash must be available for making change. While it would be possible to carry such funds as part of the undeposited cash or cash on hand, it is usually better to open special accounts for this purpose. The entries, for example, to establish a change fund of $500 would be:

Change Fund	500	
Cash in Bank		500

The check is drawn payable to Cash, the actual money is obtained by "cashing" the check at the bank or from other cash funds, and the money is made available to the cashiers. The total change fund might be divided into ten $50 funds, each one being assigned to a cash register or to a delivery truck driver. During a day's operations the change fund is merged with cash receipts, but at the close of the day the change fund is separated when the day's receipts are counted.

Once a change fund has been established, no further entries are made in the Change Fund account unless the amount of the fund is to be increased or decreased.

Petty Cash Funds

A petty cash, or *imprest*, fund provides for cash disbursements that are too small to deserve the more detailed treatment required for drawing a bank check. Such a fund is also convenient for making payments more promptly than is possible under the more formal system. Although the amounts involved are usually small, proper safeguards should be established to prevent minor defalcations, which easily evolve into major losses. The fund should be in charge of one person, and a signed receipt should be required for each payment from the fund.

Establishing a petty cash fund is similar to setting up a change fund. If a fund of $100 is to be provided, the entry is:

```
Petty Cash ...................................................... 100
     Cash in Bank ...............................................      100
```

The check is made payable to Cash, and it is converted into money that is placed in a special box, drawer, or cash register.

When a payment is made from the fund, a receipt indicating the nature of the payment is obtained so that the charge can eventually be made to the proper account.

Under some systems of handling petty cash, each payment is journalized separately in a petty cash journal, but accumulating receipts until the fund requires replenishment is a satisfactory alternative. At that time the payments made from the fund are analyzed, a check is drawn for the total amount spent, and the expenditures are charged to the appropriate accounts. The check is cashed, the money is placed in the fund, and the memorandums are filed for future reference and audit. For example, suppose that $94 has been spent out of the $100 fund and that an analysis of the receipts gives the following distribution of the expenditures:

Acct. No.	Account Title	Amount
114-2	Advances to Employees	$40.00
5202	Advertising	8.00
5220	Miscellaneous Selling Expenses	16.60
5303	Office Supplies Used	28.40
5320	Miscellaneous General and Administrative Expenses	1.00
		$94.00

The payments are charged to the proper accounts, replenishment of the fund is authorized, and a check is again cashed to restore the balance of the fund to $100. The entry would be:

Advances to Employees	40.00	
Advertising Expense	8.00	
Miscellaneous Selling Expenses	16.60	
Office Supplies Used	28.40	
Miscellaneous General and Administrative Expenses	1.00	
Cash in Bank		94.00

At the end of each accounting period, any previously unrecorded disbursements from the fund must be journalized. Usually the end of the accounting period is designated as a replenishment date regardless of how much is left in the fund, and the procedure for replenishment described previously is followed. In those cases in which the fund is not replenished at the end of the accounting period, the disbursements from the fund must be recorded before the financial statements are prepared. An adjusting entry debiting the appropriate accounts and crediting the fund is then necessary.

The Petty Cash Fund account usually does not receive any further entries once the fund has been established. Exceptions are made when the amount of the fund is to be altered or when an adjustment must be made at the end of the accounting period because a check has not been drawn to restore the fund to its original balance.

Undeposited Cash

The accounting for receipts and disbursements is discussed in Chapter 6. If the desirable plan of depositing all receipts is followed, there will be no disbursements except from checking accounts or from petty cash funds, and any balance in the Cash on Hand account will represent cash received since the last deposit, which usually will have been made on the previous business day. Sometimes the entry for the deposit of the previous day's receipts is dated "as of" the previous day. It is possible, in this way, to eliminate the necessity for a Cash on Hand account, because all receipts are then journalized as debits to Cash in Bank. The use of the Cash on Hand account, however, is recommended since any exceptions to the usual practice can then be handled without difficulty. Regardless of the policy established for cash receipts, disbursements, and deposits, a daily record of cash on hand is usually necessary. Similar reports may be received from various cashiers, drivers, and branches. The cash usually accompanies the report; it is counted, the report is audited, and a summary is prepared for the business as a whole.

Suppose that the daily cash report showed: cash on hand, morning: $120.00; cash sales: $347.65; collections on accounts receivable (separate list attached): $623.92; deposit in bank: $971.57; and cash on hand, night: $120.00.

The information in the daily cash report would result in the following analysis of transactions to be entered in the proper journals:

Cash on Hand	971.57	
Sales		347.65
Accounts Receivable		623.92
Cash in Bank	971.57	
Cash on Hand		971.57

Cash registers facilitate the accumulation of cash data. There are many types, but the usual cash register is a combination of cash drawer and a multiple adding machine. The transactions are recorded and accumulated by the register so that at the end of the day totals are available for each of several divisions of the day's business, such as the total cash sales (sometimes divided according to products or departments), total collections on account, total sales of each salesman, and total amounts paid out.

CASH IN BANK

Deposits

The deposit ticket provides the information for the entry to record the deposit of cash funds in the checking account. It should be prepared in duplicate, the original being kept by the bank and the duplicate by the firm. The duplicate is often initialed by the bank teller and used as a receipt for the funds. Checks are listed separately, and although banks sometimes request that the number of the drawee bank (to be found just after or below the name of the bank) be listed, the name of the drawer is usually the most important part of the description from the standpoint of the firm. With the development of high-speed and relatively inexpensive photographic equipment, many banks now require little descriptive information on the deposit slip. The total on the deposit slip is entered in a journal as a debit to Cash in Bank and a credit to Cash on Hand.

Issuing Checks

The information for the entry to record checks drawn in payment of bills comes from the approved voucher or from the check stub. The customary entry will be a debit to Accounts (or Vouchers) Payable and a credit to Cash in Bank.

THE BANK STATEMENT

At the end of each month (or other regular interval), the depositor receives a bank statement, the canceled checks that have been paid and deducted from the depositor's account, and memorandums of any other additions or deductions made by the bank.

The Bank Reconciliation

When the bank statement is received, it should be compared promptly with the record of deposits, checks drawn, and other bank items on the records of the firm. The balance shown on the bank statement will rarely correspond to the balance of the Cash in Bank account. The two basic causes of the difference are time lag and errors. In the normal flow of data, some items will have been recorded by either the bank or the firm without having reached the recording point on the other set of records. Causes of such differences are: checks outstanding (that is, checks recorded by the firm but not yet received by the bank on which they were drawn); deposits of the last few days of the month that do not appear on the bank statement because it may have been prepared before the deposits were made; and transactions (such as service charges, collections of notes or drafts, and the like) that have not yet been recorded on the firm's books. The other basic difference is caused by errors in record keeping by either

SCHEDULE 8.1

YOUNG SPRING COMPANY
Bank Reconciliation—First National Bank
March 1, 1975

Balance per bank statement, March 1, 1975		$2,327.36
Deposit of February 28, not yet credited by bank		642.53
Check of Young Wire Co. deducted in error		10.00
		$2,979.89

Outstanding Checks

#367	$ 2.65	
#459	1.10	
#466	55.67	
#470	142.53	
#471	75.59	
#472	131.44	
#473	65.92	
#474	243.55	
#475	305.52	
Total Outstanding Checks		1,023.97
Adjusted bank balance		$1,955.92
Balance per books, March 1, 1975		$1,457.55
Collection of sight draft on J. T. Munn unrecorded:		
Face of draft	$500.00	
Less collection charge	1.00	499.00
		$1,956.55
Check #467 for $168.81 was entered in the check register as $168.18. It was issued in February 1975, to pay a bill for office equipment		.63
Adjusted book balance		$1,955.92

the firm or the bank. The process of checking the bank statement with the books is known as *reconciling* the bank account, and the schedule that is prepared to demonstrate the results of the checking is called the *bank reconciliation*. A typical reconciliation statement is shown in Schedule 8.1.

In preparing a bank reconciliation, the following materials should be assembled: (1) the bank statement and the canceled checks and other memorandums that accompany it; (2) the previous reconciliation statement; (3) the check register for the past month; (4) the journal in which the deposits are entered; (5) the Cash in Bank account in the general ledger; and (6) any other journals that may have been used during the month for entries affecting the bank account. Then proceed as follows:

1. Compare the opening balance on the current bank statement with the closing balance on the previous statement, as indicated on the last reconciliation. They should be the same, but occasionally an error is made when the balance is carried forward.

2. Check the returned items with the bank statement to make sure that a canceled check or a "debit memo" has been received for each entry listed under "Checks" on the statement.

3. Sort the canceled checks in serial number order. Any unnumbered checks and other memorandums may be placed at the bottom of the pile.

4. Check the canceled checks first against the list of outstanding checks on the previous reconciliation and then against the entries in the Cash in Bank, Cr. column in the check register for the current month.

5. Check the unnumbered checks and memorandums against any corresponding entries in the journals. Lay aside any items that apparently had not been recorded in the firm's records.

6. Check the deposits on the bank statement first against any "deposits not credited" on the previous reconciliation and then against the journal entries of deposits for the month.

7. Inspect the Cash in Bank account for any other journal entries. These may offset some of the unchecked items in other parts of the bookkeeping system.

8. Prepare the reconciliation statement. (The following instructions assume that the bank statement ends not later than the last day of the month being checked. If, as occasionally happens, it includes a few days of the following month, certain obvious changes must be made in the procedure, since the statement might include deposits and checks recorded on the books in the next month.)

   a. Enter the balance as shown on the bank statement.

   b. Enter any deposits that have not been recorded on the bank statement. Such items usually occur because the bank has prepared the statement before the deposits for the last few days have been recorded. If there are any breaks in the list of deposits, the bank should be notified promptly.

   c. Enter any other adjustments of the bank's balance, such as errors in recording canceled checks or deposits, or the return of checks belonging to some other customer of the bank. Errors on bank statements are infrequent.

d. Obtain a total.

e. List the outstanding checks. A list should be prepared, beginning with the unchecked items on the previous reconciliation and continuing with the unchecked amounts in the check register.

f. Deduct the sum of the outstanding checks from the total obtained in step **d**. The balance is the adjusted bank balance—the balance that would be shown on the statement if all deposits had been entered, all checks written had been returned and no errors had been made; it is the final figure for this first section of the statement.

This will frequently conclude the reconciliation because this balance should correspond to the balance of the Cash in Bank account when there are no unrecorded transactions or errors. If these two amounts are not equal at this point, the following steps must be taken.

g. Enter the balance as shown on the books at the close of the month.

h. Add or deduct any errors or omissions that have been disclosed in the process of checking the items returned by the bank. These will include such items as errors in recording deposits or checks, unnumbered and counterchecks that have not been entered in the check register, and service charges and collection fees deducted by the bank.

i. The net result is the adjusted book balance, and it must correspond to the adjusted bank balance. If it does not, the search must be continued for other items that have been overlooked.

Adjusting Entries from Bank Reconciliation

The differences shown on the bank reconciliation fall within two distinct categories: (1) differences between the balance shown on the bank statement and the adjusted bank balance and (2) differences between the book balance and the adjusted book balance. Only the second type of difference requires entries on the firm's books. Any deposits not credited by the bank will presumably have been recorded by the time the reconciliation is prepared and, in any event, represent funds that the depositor may assume are in the bank subject to disbursement by check. If the business goes into a receivership or the owner dies, the outstanding checks then become general claims against the estate, and the full amount of the bank balance as shown on the bank's books appears as an asset; but in the normal going concern, it is convenient and appropriate to assume that the bank balance has been reduced as soon as the check is sent out and that there is no further liability on the transaction.

Entries must, however, be made for all of the differences between the book balance and the adjusted book balance, since they represent errors or omissions that must be corrected. The entries required by the reconciliation illustrated in Schedule 8.1 would be:

Cash in Bank 499.00
Collection Expense 1.00
    Accounts Receivable, J. T. Munn 500.00
Sight draft collected by bank.

Accounts Payable .... .63
    Cash in Bank .... .63
To correct entry of check No. 467.

The bank would, of course, correct any error on its books when the mistake is called to its attention. The entry on the bank's books to correct the error shown on the reconciliation is:

Deposits—Young Wire Co. 10.00
    Deposits—Young Spring Co. 10.00
To correct posting of check charged to Young Spring Co. account
  in error.

Special Bank Accounts

A business may have any number of regular checking accounts, and the accounting problems for each one are identical to those for a single account. Special accounts are often used, however, to serve particular types of payment needs. They involve some variations in accounting technique. For example, a special payroll bank account may be used. The usual procedure is as follows: when the payroll is made up, one check is drawn on the regular bank account for the total amount due the employees and is deposited in the payroll bank account.

Accrued Payroll 12,743
    Cash in Bank 12,743

Using a special series of numbers and specially designed checks, an employer can write checks against this special bank account for the amount owed to each employee. Instead of recording the checks in a check register, the employer usually lists check numbers on the payroll after the amount owed to each employee, so that the payroll serves as the check register for this purpose. The payroll bank account is reconciled by checking the returned checks against the payroll. Under the plan just outlined, the payroll bank account does not appear in the ledger. If a ledger account is used, it will always have a zero balance because the amount deposited is immediately paid out with checks to employees.

Sometimes a certain sum is kept on deposit in the payroll bank account over and above the amount required for payrolls in order to provide for advances or to avoid service charges. In this case an account must be provided for, and the extra deposit operates as a revolving fund much like a petty cash fund.

Special bank accounts are also used for dividend payments and, occasionally, for other purposes. The use of a special bank account (1) simplifies the accounting records for the regular checking accounts, (2) permits, for special purposes, the use of different signatures that are often printed by check-writing machines, and (3) facilitates the preparation of the bank reconciliation through the separation of large groups of transactions, each one of which can be verified by itself.

SUMMARY

Management is always concerned about getting the best and safest use of its resources, and an enterprise's most valuable resource, cash, is also its most vulnerable. An internal-control system is essential to the proper management of cash. One way to provide control is to maintain duplicate and independent records of cash flows, but this is not necessary if an enterprise uses the monthly bank statement as a duplicate record. Using the bank statement as an effective control device requires depositing receipts daily and making all disbursements by check or through petty cash funds. By this means the bank reconciliation serves as a control device because the bank record will reflect the cash inflows and outflows of the enterprise.

QUESTIONS AND PROBLEMS

1. What are the major objectives of a system of internal control?

2. Summarize the basic characteristics of an effective system of internal control.

3. Why is it difficult for a small business to have a rather complete "system of internal control"?

4. What evidence of the use of a "system of internal check" have you observed in a cafeteria? A department store? A theater? A gasoline service station?

5. A store is running short of change during a busy day, so the cashier takes some of the undeposited checks to the bank and exchanges them for small bills and coins. Is any journal entry necessary? Do you see anything objectionable in the practice?

*6. A petty cash fund is established in the amount of $50. An analysis of the petty cash receipts at the end of the first month reveals that the following disbursements have been made from the fund: postage, $12; express, $10; pencils and carbon paper for the office, $8. A check is drawn to replenish the fund. Present journal entries for the above transactions.

7. A fund of cash is to be established for making small disbursements. A check for $100 is issued to establish the fund. A memorandum is kept for each disbursement from the fund. At the end of the first month, an analysis of these memorandums gives the following information:

Postage	$ 26
Office Supplies	25
Telegrams	9
	$ 60

---

* Hints, key numbers, or (partial) answers appear in the back of the book between the Appendix Tables and the Glossary.

A check is issued to replenish the fund.

Present journal entries for the above transactions.

8. A petty cash fund is established in the amount of $200. An auditor reviews the petty cash box as of December 31, the last day of the accounting period, and finds the following data:

Receipts:
Postage	$ 30
Advances to employees	40
Office supplies	24
Bills and Coin	106
	$200

As of January 31 the petty cash box contains the following:

Receipts for January:
Postage	$ 32
Express charges on parts used in repairing machinery	10
Travel reimbursement	50
Receipts from before January 1	94
Bills and coin	14
	$200

A check is drawn on January 31 to replenish the petty cash and to increase the balance of the fund to $300.

Present journal entries for the above transactions.

*9. A driver's change fund is established in the amount of $40. At the end of the day, the driver's report shows the following information: collections on account, $60; cash sales, $105; payment for gasoline, $6; payments for merchandise being returned, $14; balance in purse, $185.

Present journal entries for the above transactions.

10. A special fund is set up for the use of the Chicago office of the Texas Sales Company. A check is drawn for $6,000. The new account will be called the Chicago Office Fund.

A report from the Chicago office indicates that the check was deposited in the Chicago National Bank and that checks have been drawn for the following items: two months' rent, $800; furniture and equipment, $1,200; office salaries, $900 less 6 percent for FICA tax and $108 for income tax withholdings; office supplies, $120; telephone and telegraph, $46; salesman's travel expense, $600. A check is drawn to replenish the fund.

Present journal entries for the above transactions.

11. The NCS Company has been making payments in cash from the cash register and by check. It has Cash on Hand and Cash in Bank accounts in its general ledger. Effective June 1, 1975, the company decided to adopt a system of disbursements based upon payment by checks and by coin and currency from a petty cash fund. A Petty Cash Fund account was added to the general ledger.

On June 1, 1975, a petty cash fund was set up in the amount of $200. On June 15, 1975, a check was drawn to replenish the fund. Expenditures since the establishment of the fund were as follows: postage, $24; office supplies, $36; COD merchandise received, $64; repairs to register, $20.

On June 30, 1975, the end of the company's accounting period, the petty cash fund cashier submitted a list of expenditures since June 15, 1975, as follows: office supplies, $20; COD merchandise received, $50; advance to employees, $30; postage, $40. A check was drawn to replenish the fund.

On July 15, 1975, a check was drawn to replenish the fund for expenditures since June 30, 1975. The expenditures were as follows: postage, $26; office supplies, $24; COD merchandise received, $32; telegrams, $18; railroad ticket for salesman, $60.

a. Present dated entries in two-column journal form from June 1, 1975, to July 15, 1975, inclusive.

b. Repeat (a). Assume that the voucher and check for the June 30, 1975, list of expenditures were drawn on July 1, 1975.

*12 a. Present journal entries for the following transactions.

(1) Check No. 508 is issued for $2,000 to establish a minimum balance in a payroll bank account.

(2) Check No. 598 is issued for the weekly office payroll of $6,000, less 6 percent for FICA tax and less $470 for withheld income tax.

(3) Payroll checks are drawn on the payroll bank account for the weekly payroll.

b. Indicate which journal in a set of specialized journals would be used for each entry.

13. A corporation wishes to use a special bank account for the payment of dividends. Outline the procedure to establish and operate such an account. Explain how such a bank account would be reconciled. What are the reasons for using a special account for this purpose?

14. Arrange the following data related to the Ayer Company in bank reconciliation form.

Adjusted bank balance	$6,453
Adjusted book balance	6,453
Balance per bank statement, October 31, 1975	7,532
Balance per books, October 31, 1975	5,873
Error in deposit of October 28; $457 deposit entered on books as $475	18
Outstanding checks	1,133
Payroll account check deducted from this account in error	54
Proceeds of sight draft on W. Y. Jones, taken by the bank for collection, less collection fee of $2	598

Present journal entries on the books of the Ayer Company to record the adjustments indicated in the bank reconciliation schedule.

*15. The bank statement received by the Kimball Company from the City National Bank contains the following information:

Balance, April 30, 1975	$ 7,440
Deposit for March 31, 1975 (reached the bank on April 1)	840
Deposits for April 1–30, including a credit memo for a sight draft of $450 collected for the company on April 15	32,140
Canceled checks (issued prior to April 1, 1975)	1,460
Canceled checks (issued during April, 1975)	27,970
Debit memo for interest on loan from bank	25
Debit memo for service charges	15

The Cash in Bank account of the company reflects the following:

Balance, April 1, 1975 .... $ 3,310
Deposits, April 1–30 33,120
Checks drawn, April 1–30 30,500

Neither the debit nor credit memos have been recorded on the books of the company. All checks issued prior to April 1, 1975, have now cleared the bank.

Prepare a bank reconciliation schedule at April 30, 1975.

16. The June bank statement of Nancy Company showed an ending balance of $118,400. During June the bank charged back NSF (nonsufficient funds) checks totaling $13,056 of which $11,856 has been redeposited by June 30. Deposits in transit on June 30 were $120,400. Outstanding checks on June 30 were $160,645, including a $110,000 check which the bank had certified on June 28. On June 14, the bank charged Nancy's account for a $12,300 item that should have been charged against the account of Nacy Company; the bank did not detect the error. Find the adjusted bank balance on June 30.

17. a. Prepare a bank reconciliation schedule at July 31, 1975, for the Home Appliance Company from the following information:

Balance per bank statement, July 29 .... $1,211
Balance per ledger, July 31 663
Deposit of July 30 not recorded by bank 180
Debit memo—service charges 6
Credit memo—sight draft collection (C. C. Wayne) 250

An analysis of the canceled checks returned with the bank statement reveals the following:

Check No. 901 for purchase of supplies was drawn for $58 but was recorded as $85.

The manager wrote a check for traveling expenses of $85 while he was out of town. The check was not recorded. The following checks are outstanding:

No. 650 .... $180
721 162
728 200
                                                          _____
                                                          $542

b. Journalize the adjusting entries required by the information revealed in the bank reconciliation schedule.

*18. On May 31, 1975, the books of the Locus Land Company show a debit balance in the Cash in Bank account of $3,977. The bank statement at that date shows a balance of $4,758. The deposit of May 31 of $302 is not included in the bank statement. Notice of collections made by the bank on mortgages of the company in the amount of $123, including interest of $8, and of bank service charges of $4 has not previously been received. Outstanding checks at May 31 total $964.

a. Prepare a bank reconciliation for the Locus Land Company at May 31, 1975.

b. Journalize the entries required upon preparation of the bank reconciliation schedule.

19. On July 31, 1975, the Cash in Bank account of the Barr Company has a balance of $3,503. The statement received from the County Bank at the end of the month shows a balance of $4,207. An analysis of the available information reveals the following: the deposit of July 30, $243, has not been recorded by the bank; a debit memo, $12, for service charges is discovered; a credit memo, $60, for collection by the bank of a check drawn on a bank in a foreign country is found; checks issued but not as yet clearing the bank amount to $899.

   a. Prepare a bank reconciliation for the Barr Company at July 31, 1975.
   b. Journalize the entries required to adjust the books of the firm.

20. The following items are taken from the April 30, 1975, bank reconciliation schedule of the Portor Company. Present a journal entry required on the books of the company for each item requiring an adjustment; indicate if an adjustment is not required. The company closes its books annually on June 30.

   (1) Outstanding checks total $1,650.
   (2) A check drawn as $196 for office supplies was recorded in the appropriate journal as $169.
   (3) Included among the checks returned by the bank was one for $150 drawn by the Porter Company and charged to this company in error.
   (4) The deposit of April 3 of $420 was not included on the bank statement.
   (5) A debit memorandum was included for service charges for April in the amount of $10.
   (6) The bank collected a note of $1,750, including $50 of interest, for the company.
   (7) Checks for traveling expenses of $250 had not been entered in the journal.
   (8) A check was written and recorded on April 29 for the regular monthly salary of an office employee who had resigned on March 31. The check has been voided, but an entry to record the voiding has not been made. The monthly salary was $600; deductions of 6 percent for FICA taxes and $50 for withheld income taxes were made.

*21. The bank reconciliation of the commercial account in the County Bank of the Smith Company at October 31, 1975, was as follows:

Balance per Bank Statement, October 28, 1975	$377,045
Unrecorded Deposits of October 28 and 31, 1975	35,554
	$412,599
Outstanding Checks	82,360
Adjusted Bank and Book Balance, October 31, 1975	$330,239

The records of the company indicate the following for November, 1975:

Balance at November 1, 1975	$330,239
Deposits for November	346,647
Checks drawn in November	342,634
Balance at November 30, 1975	334,252

No debit and credit memos had been received from the bank during the month.

The statement, returned checks, memos and so forth received from the bank at the end of November are reviewed and compared to company records with the following information thereby being made available:

Balance at October 28, 1975	$377,045
Deposits of October 28 and 31, 1975	35,554
Deposits of November 1–29, 1975	330,000
Canceled checks dated prior to November 1, 1975	80,330
Canceled checks dated during November, 1975	264,205
Debit memo for interest for the month of November on a promissory note	90
A debit memo for collection and service charges for November..	43
A credit memo for the collection of a check drawn on a bank in a foreign country which was held by the bank pending collection	187
Balance at November 30, 1975	398,118
The canceled checks included a check drawn by Smith Inc., dated November 15, 1975 charged by mistake to the account of Smith Company	56
A check issued in the amount of $185 on November 23, 1975, was recorded by the company as $158.	

a. Prepare a reconciliation statement at November 30, 1975.

b. Present the journal entries that must be made on the books of the Smith Company, as indicated by the reconciliation statement at November 30, 1975.

22. The bank reconciliation of the Clark Company at December 31, 1974, was as follows:

Balance per Bank Statement, December 31, 1974	$3,850
Unrecorded Deposit	475
	$4,325
Outstanding Checks	820
Adjusted Bank and Book Balance, December 31, 1974	$3,505

The bank statement, returned checks, and other documents received from the bank at the end of January provide the following information:

Balance, January 29, 1975	$ 3,685
Deposit of December 31, 1974	475
Deposits of January 1–29 including a credit memo for a collection of a note, $808	16,160
Canceled checks issued prior to January 1, 1975	600
Canceled checks issued during January, 1975	16,200

The Cash in Bank account of the Clark Company for the month of January shows deposits of $16,190 and checks drawn of $17,015. The credit memo has not as yet been recorded on the books of the company; it represents the collection of an $800 face value note on which $5 interest had been accrued as of December 31, 1974.

a. Prepare a bank reconciliation for the Clark Company at January 31, 1975.

b. Present in journal-entry form any adjustment of the company's books resulting from the information determined in the bank reconciliation.

*23. The bank reconciliation of the commercial account of the Wells Company at February 28, 1975, is as follows:

WELLS COMPANY
Midland Bank—Commercial Account
Bank Reconciliation
February 28, 1975

Balance per Bank Statement, February 28, 1975		$5,209
Unrecorded Deposit of February 28, 1975		636
Payroll Check No. 222 deducted from this account in error		49
		$5,894

Outstanding Checks

No. 109	$ 40	
214	700	
215	410	
216	60	
218	680	
220	399	
Total Outstanding Checks		2,289
Adjusted Bank Balance, February 28, 1975		$3,605

Balance per Books, February 28, 1975		$3,594
Error in Deposit of February 25; $573 entered as $537		36
		$3,630
Exchange and Collection Fees	$ 7	
Error in Check No. 209, $142 entered as $124	18	25
Adjusted Book Balance, February 28, 1975		$3,605

The check register during the month of March records the following checks:

No. 301	$ 2,020	No. 308	$ 1,330	No. 315	$ 72
302	154	309	626	316	1,432
303	235	310	424	317	456
304	1,010	311	367	318	1,185
305	222	312	1,000	319	500
306	446	313	234	320	125
307	77	314	660	321	320
					$12,895

The deposits journalized during the month of March are:

Mar.	1	$	552	Mar.	11	$	971	Mar.	23	$	613
	2		576		14		605		24		738
	3		615		15		546		25		984
	4		999		16		528		28		609
	7		513		17		679		29		541
	8		582		18		1,027		30		567
	9		563		21		592		31		585
	10		634		22		506				$15,125

The bank account in the ledger appears as follows:

Commercial Account—Cash in Bank

1975				1975			
March 1	Balance	√	3,605	March 15		GJ	55
31		CR	15,125	31		CR	12,895

General journal entries affecting the bank account and made during the month of March were:

```
March 15  Cash on Hand .....................................    55
              Cash in Bank ..................................          55
          Check of J. C. Thomas returned by bank subsequent to
          deposit—insufficient funds. To be redeposited.
```

Checks and other memorandums returned by the bank with the statement of March 31, 1975, after sorting in serial number order are:

No. 214	$	700	No. 304	$	1,010	No. 314	$	660
215		410	305		222	316		1,432
216		60	306		446	318		1,185
218		680	308		1,303	319		500
301		2,020	309		626	320		125
302		154	311		367			
303		235	312		1,000			

Debit memo—$55: check of J. C. Thomas returned because of insufficient funds.

Credit memo—$403: collection of note of $400 plus interest of $6 less fee of $3. (Interest of $5 was accrued as of February 28, 1975.)

Credit memo—$49: payroll check deducted in error in February. See February 28, 1975, bank reconciliation.

Deposits shown on bank statement for March:

$636	$634	$613
49 CM	971	403 CM
552	605	738
576	546	984
615	528	609
999	679	541
513	1,027	567
582	592	
563	506	

Balance shown on bank statement, March 31, 1975, $7,647.

a. Present journal entries that must be made on the books of the Wells Company following the preparation of the bank reconciliation at February 28, 1975.

b. Present the correcting entries that must be made on the books of the Midland Bank as indicated by the reconciliation.

c. Prepare a reconciliation statement at March 31, 1975. Assume that any error detected was made by the company rather than the bank.

d. Present the journal entries that must be made on the books of the Wells Company as indicated by the reconciliation statement of March 31, 1975.

24. On July 5, 1975, the Jennings Company received its monthly statement together with canceled checks and other documents from the Lindell Bank. The following information is available from the statement and accompanying documents:

(1) Balance, May 31, 1975, $13,256.

(2) Deposits: No. 106, $899; No. 107, $954; Nos. 108–127, $19,126.

(3) Credit Memo: deposit of May 23, 1975, previously erroneously added to the account of the Jenning Company, $203.

(4) Debit Memo: service charges for June, 1975, $23.

(5) Checks canceled during June, 1975:

No. 521	$1,039	No. 607	$ 910	No. 616	$ 604
524	910	608	1,063	617	747
525	1,020	609	454	619	713
526	325	610	378	620	394
601	807	611	676	621	960
602	836	612	801	622	654
603	860	613	1,020	623	678
604	889	614	667	723	329
606	870	615	472		

(6) Balance, June 30, 1975, $15,338.

A review of the records of the Jennings Company indicates the following information relative to the checking account in the Lindell Bank:

(1) Balance, May 31, 1975, $9,981.

(2) Deposits: Nos. 107–126, $19,070; No. 127, $1,009; No. 128, $930.

(3) Checks issued during June, 1975:

No. 601	$ 807	No. 610	$ 378	No. 619	$ 713
602	836	611	676	620	394
603	860	612	801	621	960
604	889	613	1,020	622	654
605	810	614	667	623	678
606	870	615	472	624	625
607	910	616	604	625	604
608	1,036	617	747	626	644
609	454	618	932	627	738

(4) Balance, June 30, 1975, $11,211.

(5) The reconciliation of May 31, 1975, indicated the following. Outstanding checks were as follows: No. 521, $1,039; No. 522, $423; No. 523, $660; No. 524, $910; No. 525, $1,020; No. 526, $325. Deposit in transit, No. 106, $899.

Deposit erroneously credited to Jenning Company, $203.

(6) Check No. 723 was issued by the Jenning Company, not by Jennings Company.

(7) Any other errors indicated by a difference between the bank records and the company records are found to be errors by the company.

a. Prepare a statement reconciling the difference between the balance on the bank statement and the balance in the ledger as of May 31, 1975.

b. Prepare a bank reconciliation statement as of June 30, 1975.

c. Present the journal entries that must be made on the books of the Jennings Company, as indicated in the reconciliation statement as of June 30, 1975.

Chapter 9

Sales and Purchases Analysis

General Motors introduces a new line of intermediate-sized cars at the outset of a new model year; Mobil Oil decides to reactivate an off-shore oil-drilling facility; although seed prices are high, a farmer in Nebraska decides to buy more seed when he hears about the prospects for continuing and increasing foreign demand for grain. In different ways, all of these events involve two considerations: sales and purchases.

Previous chapters introduced the accounting for the sale of merchandise and finished goods as well as the purchase of merchandise and raw materials. In each activity a single account was used: the Sales account to recognize sales revenue; the Merchandise and the Raw Materials accounts to recognize the acquisition of merchandise and raw materials, respectively. The gross sales amount may be adjusted in several ways before net sales revenue can be determined. Total acquisition costs of merchandise and raw materials may include various adjustments to the gross purchase cost. To provide additional information in the accounts about the adjustments of the gross amounts, a more complete analysis of the transactions related to selling and purchasing is required. This detail is provided by using contra and adjunct accounts. This chapter introduces and illustrates the additional accounts that are used to provide the detailed information for analysis of sales and purchases.

SALES ANALYSIS AND ACCOUNTS

The Sales Account

The short title Sales, instead of the more descriptive but cumbersome titles Merchandise Sales and Finished Product Sales, is generally used to record sales volume. Like any revenue account, the Sales account serves two important functions. It provides a measure of the volume of business during the accounting period, and it facilitates the postponement of a complete analysis of the sales transaction into expenses and net income until the close of the accounting period.

The total sales for a period is a significant figure for managerial purposes. A comparison of the volume of sales in the present period with that of past periods is a useful indication of the relative activity of the enterprise. The total sales figure can also be analyzed to compare the operations of different departments or branches or the effectiveness of the members of the sales force. The interpretation of sales figures must, of course, take into account the inherent weakness of any data expressed in monetary terms—sales in a period of high prices cannot be compared with sales in a period of low prices without making adjustments. Also generating net income rather than revenue is the goal of business activity, and equal sales for different departments or products do not necessarily produce equal net incomes. Nevertheless, sales amounts are watched closely as useful indexes of business activity. It is desirable to present the sales figure, even when it is possible to make a complete analysis of each sales transaction into its components, expense and net income, at the time of the sale.

The sales account is a technical necessity in most cases because an analysis of the cost of earning each item of revenue cannot be made at the time the sale is recorded. At best only a partial analysis can be made, so the usual procedure is to carry the gross amount of the sales "in suspense" in the sales account until the end of the accounting period. Then the expenses incurred in connection with the operations of the period as a whole can be analyzed. Sometimes certain expenses, such as the cost of goods sold and commissions on sales, can be determined and recorded for each sale; however, specific expenses are usually charged to appropriate expense accounts and the full amount of the sale is credited to the sales account.

Entries for Sales

Cash Sales. Sales for cash are common only in retail and service enterprises. The usual practice is to accumulate the cash sales for a day, often automatically on a cash register, and to make an entry in a journal for the amount of the day's sales.

Cash on Hand	1,370	
Sales		1,370

The occasional cash sale in a wholesale or manufacturing enterprise can be handled in the same manner or can be treated as a sale on account, followed immediately by a collection on account. The latter method is preferred because it provides a complete record of the business done with each customer in his ledger account. For example, a clothing manufacturer sells $3,000 worth of merchandise to A. L. Cohn, who is opening a small store and must pay cash for his purchases until his credit rating is better. A regular sales invoice is prepared, and the check received from Mr. Cohn is treated as a collection on account. The entry to record the sale would be as follows:

Accounts Receivable—A. L. Cohn	3,000	
Sales		3,000

The collection would be recorded immediately as follows:

Cash on Hand	3,000	
Accounts Receivable—A. L. Cohn		3,000

Sales on Account. Each sale on account may be journalized separately in a journal as:

Accounts Receivable—J. A. Smith	400	
Sales		400

Direct posting to customers' accounts from sales tickets or invoices is, however, commonly used, and under this plan one journal entry can be made for the total sales on account for a day.

Accounts Receivable	6,300	
Sales		6,300

Promissory notes, installment contracts, or almost any other type of asset might be received in exchange for merchandise, but the credit is always to the Sales account.

Prepaid Sales. In some cases, a payment may be received from the customer before the goods are delivered. Under such circumstances, the recording of a sale involves a cancellation of a liability instead of an increase in an asset. The most common examples are those where advances from customers have been received or coupon books redeemable in merchandise have been issued. For example, when advance payments are received, the entry is:

Cash on Hand	300	
Advances from Customers		300

When the goods are shipped to customers, the revenue entry is:

Advances from Customers	300	
Sales		300

If only a partial payment has been received in advance, the entry is:

Advances from Customers	300	
Accounts Receivable	500	
Sales		800

Use of Multiple Sales Accounts

In some situations multiple sales accounts may help to obtain a more effective analysis or distribution of revenue sources. An oil company, for example, might classify its sales according to products, and a typical entry for a day's cash sales would be:

Cash on Hand	4,900	
Sales—Gasoline		4,400
Sales—Oil		300
Sales—Accessories		200

A department store will usually have a separate sales account for each department. A distributor doing both a retail and wholesale business might well use Sales–Retail and Sales–Wholesale accounts.

Sales Adjustments

The amount credited to the sales account may have to be adjusted in order to determine the actual revenue for the period. While these adjustments may be recorded as direct debits to Sales, they are often accumulated in contra accounts that are shown on the income statement as deductions from the gross sales amount. The principal types of sales adjustments include sales discounts, sales returns, sales allowances, estimated uncollectible accounts, transportation charges paid for customers, sales taxes, and excise taxes. Although the latter three adjustments are discussed under the sales adjustment category, methods will be suggested for excluding them from the revenue total.

The discussion in the remainder of this chapter assumes that a single sales account is used. If total sales are distributed into classes, a corresponding set of adjustment accounts would have to be provided for each class of accounts.

Sales Discounts

The discount that frequently is allowed for prompt payment of accounts should be treated as a deduction from sales although it is often treated as a financial or "other" expense. There is nothing incongruous in the proposition that goods may have two prices, a cash price and a higher price if goods are sold on credit, because the cost of handling charge accounts can be substantial. Also, if bills are paid promptly, collection costs are reduced and a lower selling price is reasonable. A cash discount is offered, not only as an interest allowance on funds paid before the bill is due—the implied interest rate is unreasonably large—but also as an incentive for prompt payment so that additional bookkeeping and collection costs will not be incurred. To state it more realistically, goods are sold for a certain price if prompt payment is made, and a penalty is added in the form of a higher price if the payment is delayed. The bills rendered by many public utilities illustrate this more realistic approach. The amount of sales discount, then, should be considered as one of the adjustments in the determination of net sales revenue.

The need to prepare operating statements for relatively short periods leads to alternative possibilities for recording sales discounts and determining the amount of sales discounts applicable to a period. The theoretical issue is whether the amount of cash discount should be deducted from sales revenue at the time when revenue is recognized or at the time of collection. In determining the amount of sales discounts recognized for a period, the major alternatives are: (1) to recognize discounts when taken, without regard to the period of sale; (2) to estimate the amount of discounts which will be taken on sales made during the period; or (3) to record sales amounts reduced by all discounts available to customers and to recognize further revenues when a discount lapses. Different recording methods are appropriate for each of the alternatives.

Recording of Sales Discounts

Alternative No. 1. The simplest and most commonly used method of accounting for sales discounts is to record the sale at its gross price and then to record the discount taken at the time of collection from the customer. Assuming that a 2-percent discount is available, typical entries would be:

```
Accounts Receivable—Customer's Name .........................  100
    Sales .....................................................        100
To record sale.


Cash on Hand ..............................................   98
Sales Discounts ...........................................    2
    Accounts Receivable—Customer's Name ....................        100
To record collection and discount taken.
```

If all discounts were taken in the same period as the sale to which they relate, this method would be completely satisfactory.

The amount of sales discounts taken by customers in a particular period, however, is not an accurate adjustment of sales when the collection takes place in a period subsequent to that of the sale. If the discount is to be treated as a reduction in the selling price, it should be deducted in the period in which the goods are sold. Also, the balance of accounts receivable on a balance sheet is an inflated figure unless a deduction is made for sales discounts that will be taken by customers. To overcome these objections to the customary procedure, one or the other of two alternative procedures—the allowance for sales discounts method or the net price method—is sometimes used.

Alternative No. 2. To meet the problem of correctly treating discounts available at the end of the accounting period, it is necessary to estimate the amount of discounts that will be taken. Making a precisely accurate adjustment for discounts to be taken by customers is impossible, but estimating the amount usually gives satisfactory results. At the end of the accounting period, an estimate is made of the total discounts that will be taken on the sales made during the period. This estimate is based largely upon experience and can be expressed as a percentage of the sales on account. The amount of the estimated discounts is debited to the Sales

Discounts, an account contra to Sales, and credited to Allowance for Sales Discounts account, an account contra to Accounts Receivable. Discounts actually taken are debited to the Allowance for Sales Discounts account. The Sales Discounts account is shown as a deduction from Sales in the income statement, and the balance in the Allowance for Sales Discounts appears in the balance sheet as a deduction from Accounts Receivable.

The following illustration indicates how this method of handling sales discounts operates. A new firm is formed to take over the business of two previously separate companies, and a new set of books is opened. The firm's selling terms are 2/10, net/30 (2 percent discount from the billed, or invoiced, amount will be granted if payment is made within ten days and the full amount of the bill is due in thirty days). The experience of the predecessor companies indicates that three-fourths of the customers will take advantage of the discounts available to them, so it is estimated that 1.5 percent ($\frac{3}{4} \times 2$ percent) of the sales on account will be taken as cash discounts by customers. The Accounts Receivable account balance as of December 31, 1974, was $35,000; the balance of the Allowance for Sales Discounts account was $360.

The sales for January amount to $78,000.

Accounts Receivable	78,000	
Sales		78,000

During January, accounts amounting to $75,000 are collected on which discounts of $1,110 are taken.

Cash on Hand	73,890	
Allowance for Sales Discounts	1,110	
Accounts Receivable		75,000

At the end of January, an entry is made to record the estimated amount of discounts that will be taken on January sales, 1.5 percent of $78,000 or $1,170.

Sales Discounts	1,170	
Allowance for Sales Discounts		1,170

The balance in the Allowance for Sales Discounts account is now $420 (= $360 − $1,110 + $1,170) and is carried forward to the next period. It appears on the balance sheet as a deduction from the $38,000 balance of Accounts Receivable. The amount of sales discounts is shown on the income statement as a deduction from sales, and Sales Discounts, a revenue contra account, is closed with the expense and revenue accounts when the closing entries are recorded.

Once a year, the balance in the Allowance for Sales Discounts should be compared with the total amount of discounts available as determined by an inspection of each account. If the balance of the account seems to be too small (or too large), the estimation rate used for the following year should be adjusted.

Alternative No. 3. Under this method, sometimes called the net price method, all sales are recorded at the net sales price, and lapsed sales discounts are recognized only when the discounts are not taken. The entries under this method for a $100 sale, 2/10 net/30, paid within ten days would be:

```
Accounts Receivable—Customer's Name ..........................   98
    Sales ...................................................................        98
To record sale.


Cash on Hand ..................................................   98
    Accounts Receivable—Customer's Name ......................        98
To record payment.
```

If the bill is not paid within ten days, the following entry is required when the gross amount is received:

```
Cash on Hand ...................................................  100
    Accounts Receivable—Customer's Name .......................        98
    Sales Discounts Lapsed .......................................         2
```

The Sales Discounts Lapsed account is a revenue adjunct account and is shown on the income statement as an addition to the amount shown for Sales in the calculation of total revenue.

The net price method has its greatest justification when there is a strong likelihood that all, or almost all, sales discounts will be taken. Otherwise, the amount for Accounts Receivable on the balance sheet will be understated by the amount of lapsed discounts likely to be collected the next period on these accounts. Also, if the lapsed sales discounts are collected in a period subsequent to the one in which the sales took place, the upward adjustments of revenue will be recorded in the incorrect period.

Despite its logical appeal, the second alternative is seldom used because of its somewhat greater complexity and the relatively small amounts usually involved. The first alternative of recognizing discounts as they are taken is probably most common in practice, although there appears to be increasing use of the net price method of recording sales.

Trade Discounts

Businesses often quote list prices which are subject to *trade discounts*. If the list price is $500 subject to a trade discount of 25 percent, the invoice price is $375. Sometimes *chain discounts* are used, each percentage being applied to the remainder after deducting the preceding discount. For example, if the list price is $1,000, subject to discounts of 40 percent, 5 percent, and 2 percent, the invoice price is $558.60 (= $1,000 × .60 × .95 × .98).

Trade discounts do not pose special accounting problems. The sale price used is the price after all trade discounts are deducted. Trade discounts are useful when prices are quoted in catalogs because notifying customers of a change in the discount rate is simpler than revising prices throughout the catalog. Trade discounts are also convenient in quoting quantity prices and prices for different classes of customers.

Sales Returns

When a customer returns merchandise, the sale is canceled and an entry which reverses the recording of the sale is appropriate. In analyzing sales activities, management may be interested in the amount of goods returned. If this is the case, a Sales Returns account, contra to Sales, is used to accumulate the amount of returns for a particular period.

A cash refund, such as might be made in a retail store when a customer returns merchandise he purchased for cash, would be entered as:

```
Sales Returns ..................................................  23
    Cash on Hand ..............................................       23
```

Returns of goods by customers who buy "on account" usually involve the preparation of a credit memorandum which is, in effect, the reverse of a sales invoice. The credit memorandum lists the goods that have been returned and indicates the amount that is to be allowed the customer. The entry to record the issuance of the credit would normally be a debit to Sales Returns and a credit to Accounts Receivable.

Sale and Return in Different Periods. When goods are returned in a period after the sale, misleading sales figures may result. The sales and income amounts for the period of sale may be overstated because they reflect canceled transactions. Further, these amounts will be understated in the period of return. The same type of estimated allowance procedure for returns that was illustrated for discounts can be used, but because the amounts involved are usually relatively small and the procedure is complex, the estimated allowance procedure customarily is not used to report returns.

Another type of distortion that may occur is that the expenses incurred in making the sale, other than the cost of the goods, constitute a loss to the business and, strictly speaking, should not be charged against other completed sales. Occasionally a charge is made to the customer for delivery costs both ways on returned goods, or a deduction is made for loss in value of the goods from handling and shipment, but usually the privilege of return without penalty is granted as a part of the service of the merchant. It would be difficult, if not impossible, to isolate the costs relating to a particular returned sale, and it might be maintained that these costs are necessary to the continued conduct of the business and therefore can logically be absorbed as costs of making the sales which are not returned. There are techniques for meeting some of the foregoing considerations, but they are beyond the scope of this discussion.

Sales Allowances

A *sales allowance* is a reduction in price granted to a customer, usually after he has purchased the goods and has found them unsatisfactory or damaged. Again, as in the case of sales returns, the effect is a reduction in sales revenue, but it may be desirable to accumulate the amount of such adjustments as a part of the statistics of operation. A revenue contra account, Sales Allowances, may be used for this purpose, or a combined title, Sales Returns and Allowances, may be employed. The bookkeeping problems are similar to those caused by sales returns.

UNCOLLECTIBLE ACCOUNTS

Whenever credit is extended to customers, there will almost certainly be some losses from uncollectible accounts. The relative significance and regularity of these losses will vary among different types of enterprises. In recording uncollectible accounts, the practice is sometimes followed of waiting until a customer's account has clearly been demonstrated to be uncollectible and then recognizing the loss when the account is written off. This method is not appropriate when such losses involve significant amounts and occur frequently, as they do for retail stores. The better procedure is: (1) to estimate the amount of uncollectible amounts that will occur in connection with the sales of each period; (2) to make an adjusting entry to reduce the reported revenue of the period; and (3) to make a corresponding adjustment of the balance sheet figure for Accounts Receivable to the amount believed to be collectible. The entry involves a debit to Sales, Uncollectible Accounts Adjustment, a Sales contra account, and a credit to Allowance for Uncollectible Accounts, an account contra to Accounts Receivable. The credit must be made to a contra account rather than to Accounts Receivable because no specific, individual account is being written off by the entry. Because the Allowance for Uncollectible Accounts is contra to Accounts Receivable, its balance at the end of the period appears on the balance sheet as a deduction from Accounts Receivable. The Sales, Uncollectible Accounts Adjustment account, as a revenue contra, ought to be deducted from sales revenue on the income statement. In practice it is frequently presented in the administrative, or selling, expense section of the income statement and titled Bad Debt Expense. Whether the amount is treated as an adjustment of sales revenue or as a bad debt expense does not change reported income for the period.

Treatment of Uncollectible Accounts

If it is estimated that 2 percent of the sales made during the present period will not be collected, and sales on account are $35,000, then the entry would be:

```
Sales, Uncollectible Accounts Adjustment ........................  700
    Allowance for Uncollectible Accounts ........................      700
To record estimate of uncollectible accounts.
```

When a particular customer's account is judged uncollectible, it is charged off against the Allowance for Uncollectible Accounts. If, for example, it is decided that the balance of $135 due from Robert S. Thomley will not be collected, the entry to charge off the account is:

Allowance for Uncollectible Accounts 135
    Accounts Receivable—Robert S. Thomley   135
To write off Thomley's account.

By this procedure, the revenue for the period in which the sale takes place is charged for the amount of the estimated loss from uncollectible accounts rather than the period in which attempts at collection are finally abandoned, and the account is charged off.

Various methods are used for calculating the amount of the adjustment for uncollectible accounts. The best method in most cases is to apply an appropriate percentage to the total sales on account during the period; it seems reasonable to assume that uncollectible accounts losses will vary directly with the volume of credit business. The percentage to be used can be determined by a study of the experience of the business or by an inquiry into the experience of similar enterprises; the rates found in use will usually be within the range of 1/4 to 2 percent of credit sales. If cash sales occur in a relatively constant proportion to credit sales, the percentage, proportionately reduced, can be applied to the total sales for the period. The total sales figure may be more readily available than that for sales on account.

Another method of calculating the amount of the adjustment, often called *aging the accounts*, involves analyzing each customer's account. Accounts are classified by the length of time during which the accounts have been uncollected. Common intervals used for classifying items are less than thirty days, thirty to sixty days, sixty days to six months, and over six months. The presumption is that the balance in Allowance for Uncollectible Accounts should be large enough to cover all items due for more than six months and part of the more recent items. The total, of course, is a matter of estimate and judgment.

As an example of the adjustment to be made, assume that the present balance in the Accounts Receivable account is $45,000, and the balance in the Allowance for Uncollectible Accounts is $3,600. An analysis of the Accounts Receivable balances and estimated collectibility is shown in Schedule 9.1. The current adjustment made in Schedule 9.1 is to increase the

SCHEDULE 9.1

Classification of Accounts	Amount	Estimated Uncollectible Percentage	Estimated Uncollectible Amounts
Not due	$28,000	0.5%	$ 140
1–30 days past due	6,000	6.0	360
31–60 days past due	3,000	25.0	750
Over 60 days past due	8,000	50.0	4,000
	$45,000		$5,250

Allowance for Uncollectible Accounts balance to $5,250, an increase of $1,650. The adjusting entry is:

Sales, Uncollectible Accounts Adjustment 1,650
    Allowance for Uncollectible Accounts   1,650

Aging the accounts is useful in obtaining an occasional check upon the accuracy of the percentage used for the first method. If the balance in the Allowance for Uncollectible Accounts is apparently too large or too small, the percentage used can be raised or lowered so that the apparent error will work itself out through future adjustments.

Collections on Accounts Written Off

Another type of transaction occurs in connection with uncollectible accounts. When an account is written off, the ledger sheet is not destroyed. Collection efforts may continue for some time, and the customer may voluntarily pay part or all of his old account. The problem, then, is the treatment of collections on customers' accounts that have previously been charged off.

If Mr. Thomley pays $25 on his account, which originally had a balance of $135 and had been written off, the following entry could be made:

Cash on Hand 25
    Collections on Accounts Charged Off (a revenue account)   25

It may be felt, however, that this payment by Mr. Thomley is evidence that his account should not have been written off as uncollectible. Also, it is desirable to have a complete record of the payments in each customer's account. Therefore, the following entries might be considered preferable:

Accounts Receivable—Robert S. Thomley 135
    Allowance for Uncollectible Accounts   135
To reverse the entry made previously and to restore Thomley's account to active status.

Cash on Hand 25
    Accounts Receivable—Robert S. Thomley   25

OTHER SALES-RELATED ACCOUNTS

Transportation

When goods are sold FOB (free on board) the city in which the customer is located, the seller bears the cost of transporting them to his customer. It is sometimes suggested that these charges should be shown on the income statement as a deduction from Sales, but this does not seem reasonable. The selling price does not depend upon the amount of transportation charges. The transportation cost in this case is more like the general costs of selling, such as advertising, salesmen's commissions and salaries, and delivery costs, which, while they should be covered by the selling price, are not reductions in, nor adjustments of, the selling price.

When goods are sold FOB the point of sale, which means that the customer is responsible for the transportation costs, the seller may still pay the freight charges as a convenience to the customer and add them to the invoice. These postage or freight items are not part of the selling price nor of the revenue of the seller; they are more like loans that the customer repays when he pays for the goods. It is possible to record the sale without including the transportation costs in the credit to the Sales account. Suppose that a $120 bill of goods is shipped to a customer and that $2 is paid for transportation to be charged to the customer's account. The entry in a journal could be:

```
Transportation Charges Paid for Customers .......................   2
    Cash .........................................................        2
To record payment of transportation charges.

Accounts Receivable—Customer's Name .........................  122
    Sales ........................................................      120
    Transportation Charges Paid for Customers ..................        2
To record sale and amount owed by customer for transportation.
```

Under this method, the Transportation Charges Paid for Customers account is merely a "clearing" account whose balance is zero when both the transportation charges have been paid and the customer has been billed.

It may be more convenient, however, to credit Sales with the full amount debited to Accounts Receivable, in which case there would not be any credits to the Transportation Charges Paid for Customers during the period. The trial balance at the end of the period would show a debit balance in this account in the amount of payments made by the seller for these services during the period. This account would then be shown on the income statement as one of the adjustments in the determination of sales revenue.

Sales Taxes

In most jurisdictions, a sales tax must be collected on retail sales and periodically remitted by the merchant to the state or city treasurer. There is some difference of opinion among economists as to the incidence of this tax—that is, the extent to which the merchant can or cannot pass it on to the customer. It is commonly assumed that the retailer merely plays the role of tax collector, adding the tax to the real sales price. If this is the case, the tax should be deducted from the total charge to the customer in order to determine the true sales figure; the tax would not be considered an operating expense.

It is possible to handle the bookkeeping so that the sales tax does not appear in the income statement by crediting a liability account for the amount of the tax at the time the sale is recorded. For example, if a sale of $50 is made and the tax rate is 6 percent, the entry would be:

```
Cash or Accounts Receivable ......................................   53
    Sales .......................................................       50
    Sales Tax Payable ...........................................        3
```

The payment of the tax to the government would be recorded as a debit to Sales Tax Payable and a credit to Cash in Bank. This procedure is simple and effective, provided it is feasible to record the tax collected on each sale.

A somewhat easier plan, applicable only to those cases in which the tax is added to all sales, is to credit Sales with the full amount charged the customer.

Cash on Hand or Accounts Receivable	53	
Sales		53

At the end of the period the balance in the Sales account is divided by one plus the tax rate in order to arrive at the real sales figure ($53/1.06 = $50). The tax is the difference between the two sales figures, or it can be calculated by applying the tax rate to the computed sales. For example, if the Sales account shows a balance for the month of $21,730, the real sales would be:

$$\frac{\$21,730}{1.06} = \$20,500$$

The tax would be $21,730 — $20,500 (or 6 percent of $20,500), $1,230, and the entry would be:

Sales Tax	1,230	
Sales Tax Payable		1,230

The Sales Tax account, a revenue contra, is shown as a deduction from Sales on the income statement. Any difference between the amount paid to the government and the amount collected is automatically absorbed in the net sales figure.

Federal Excise Taxes

Federal excise taxes are levied upon certain retail sales, such as sales of cosmetics and jewelry, upon the sale of many items by manufacturers, and upon admissions. The accounting problems for these taxes are identical in principle with those connected with state and city sales taxes.

PURCHASES ANALYSIS AND ACCOUNTS

The Purchase Transaction

The procedure for recording purchases of merchandise, raw materials, and supplies varies a great deal from one business to another. Purchasing culminates, of course, when the goods are received and the purchase is entered in the records. From the legal point of view, purchases should be recorded in the formal accounting records when title to the goods passes from the seller to the buyer. The question of when title passes is often a highly technical matter, and the precise answer depends upon a consideration of all of the circumstances of the transaction. As a convenience, therefore, the accountant usually recognizes purchases only after both the invoice and the goods are received and checked. Exceptions may be made at the end of the accounting period in order to reflect the legal formalities.

In previous chapters, all purchase and purchase adjustment entries, as well as those to recognize cost of goods sold or raw materials used, were made with the use of one merchandise or raw materials account. Special accounts, however, are often used to give a more complete presentation of purchase transactions. In the description of purchases that follows, the examples and account titles are all given in terms of merchandise purchases. In almost all cases they would apply as well to purchases of raw materials.

Merchandise Purchases Account

During the accounting period acquisitions of merchandise are recorded in the Merchandise Purchases account. (The shorter title, Purchases, is used frequently in practice, but the full title will be used here to avoid ambiguity.) Although it is an asset account, since it shows the cost of assets acquired, Merchandise Purchases is closed at the end of each accounting period and does not appear in the balance sheet under its own title. The merchandise purchased during the period that is still on hand at the end of the period is included in the Merchandise Inventory account.

The entries for purchases of merchandise follow the same form as the purchase of any asset. A cash purchase is recorded as:

Merchandise Purchases	350	
Cash		350

A purchase of merchandise on account from the Western Supply Company is recorded as:

Merchandise Purchases	2,700	
Accounts Payable—Western Supply Co.		2,700

If a voucher system is used without a detailed creditors' ledger, the purchase is recorded as:

Merchandise Purchases	2,700	
Vouchers Payable		2,700

Other liability accounts, such as Notes Payable, may be involved in the purchase transaction, and assets other than cash may conceivably be given in exchange for merchandise.

Use of Multiple Purchases Accounts

The analysis of purchases should, if feasible, parallel the plan used for sales. For example, if sales are classified and accumulated by departments, a set of merchandise inventory and purchase accounts should be provided for each department. If sales are divided as to types of merchandise, such as Sales—Meat and Sales—Groceries, a similar division should be followed in the merchandise inventory and purchase accounts.

Merchandise Purchases Adjustments

The amounts debited to the Merchandise Purchases account when goods are purchased will seldom be the correct measure of the total acquisition cost. Additional costs may be incurred in transporting and handling the goods and deductions may be required for goods returned, allowances or adjustments of the price, or cash discounts. All of these adjustments could be handled through the one Merchandise Purchases account, but in common practice a number of contra and adjunct accounts are used for these purposes so that a more complete analysis of the cost of purchases will be available. Freight-in, Purchase Returns, Purchase Allowances, and Purchase Discounts (or Purchase Discounts Lost) are used to provide the needed detail. If purchases were to be accumulated by lines or departments, a corresponding distribution of adjustments must be made.

Cost Components of Merchandise

All costs incurred in connection with acquiring goods and preparing them for sale may appropriately enter into the valuation of the goods as assets. Such costs include buying, transportation, receiving, unpacking, and shelving costs as well as that portion of the bookkeeping and office cost that relates to the recording of purchases. Because some amounts involved are relatively small, and especially because it is extremely difficult to assign a definite dollar amount of many of these costs to specific purchases, the tendency in practice is to restrict the actual additions to a few significant items which can easily be identified with particular goods, such as transportation costs. The costs of operating a purchasing department, the salaries and expenses of buyers, the costs of the receiving and warehousing departments, and the costs of handling and shelving are usually treated as operating expenses of the period in which they are incurred, although they logically are part of the total cost of merchandise ready for sale.

A Freight-in or a Transportation on Purchases account, then, is one of the few accounts commonly found in use to record such additions. This account is charged with all freight and other transportation costs on purchases. The entry is:

Freight-in 470
    Accounts Payable—Trucking Company (or Cash) 470

In the schedule presenting the calculation of cost of goods sold, the balance in this adjunct account is shown as an addition to the Merchandise Purchases amount.

Merchandise Purchases Returns

When goods are returned, the usual procedure is to request a credit memorandum that can be applied against any unpaid bills or against future purchases. Unless the amount of the credit cannot be determined until the credit memorandum is received, the best procedure is to record the return as soon as the goods are shipped; otherwise, a memorandum record must be kept of the goods until notice is received of their arrival and of the amount of the credit allowed. The entry is:

Accounts Payable—Western Supply Co. 650
    Merchandise Purchase Returns 650

Merchandise Purchases Allowances

An adjustment of the purchase price may sometimes be obtained without the return of the goods. For example, a seller, rather than accept the return of faulty merchandise, may offer a reduced price in the form of an allowance to the buyer if he keeps it. The accounting is similar to that involved in handling purchase returns. A special account, Merchandise Purchase Allowances, may be used for the credit, but a combined account, Merchandise Purchase Returns and Allowances, frequently is employed for this purpose.

Merchandise Purchases Discounts

The largest adjustment of merchandise purchases is likely to be that for purchase discounts. The amount of discounts taken during a period is sometimes illogically shown as a special or "other" revenue item on the income statement. More appropriately, the discount is treated as an adjustment of the purchase price. Offering and accepting such discounts has become so common that a merchant should view the discounted price as representing the true price of the goods. If payment is delayed, an additional charge must be paid for the additional service that the seller is compelled to render. To view purchase discounts as revenue would indicate that services can be rendered simply by buying goods and paying for them within a specified time. The logical treatment defers showing the effect of the discount on net income until the goods have been sold.

As was the case with sales discounts, there are three major alternatives for treating discounts on merchandise purchases which are discussed: (1) recognize the amount of discounts on payments made during the period, without regard to the period of purchase (gross price method); (2) recognize this period's purchase discounts that have either been taken this period or are expected to be taken in the next period (adjusted gross price method); or (3) deduct all discounts available from gross purchase prices at the time of purchase (net price method).

Recording Discounts

Alternative No. 1: Gross Price Method. The conventional accounting for purchases records invoices at their gross price and accumulates the amount of discounts taken on payments made. Suppose that goods with a gross invoice price of $1,000 are purchased 2/10, net/30. The entries to record the purchase and the payment (a) under the assumption that the payment was made in time to take the discount, and (b) under the assumption that the payment was too late to take advantage of the discount, would be:

	(a) Discount Taken	(b) Discount Not Taken
Purchases	1,000	1,000
Accounts Payable	1,000	1,000
To record purchase.		
Accounts Payable	1,000	1,000
Cash	980	1,000
Purchase Discounts	20	—
To record payment.		

The Purchase Discounts balance is deducted from Purchases in the presentation of the calculation of cost of goods sold. Such a deduction approximates the results achieved by treating purchases discount as a reduction in purchase price. It is an approximation because the total adjustment includes only discounts taken this period, without regard to the period of purchase. An accurate adjustment would require the elimination of the discounts taken related to purchases of previous periods and include the amount of discounts available at the end of the accounting period that are expected to be taken in the following period. The adjusted gross price method introduces this refinement.

Alternative No. 2: Adjusted Gross Price Method. In some cases, the discount for goods purchased in one period will not be taken until the next period. The adjusted gross price method is used to attempt to match purchases and discounts by reporting them in the same period. After the amount of such discounts for the period is estimated, the entry is:

| Allowance for Purchase Discounts .... | 250 | |
| Purchase Discounts .... | | 250 |

The Allowance for Purchase Discounts account is a contra-liability account and is shown on the balance sheet as a deduction from Accounts, or Vouchers, Payable to indicate the probable amount of the liability. The total Purchase Discounts is deducted from the Purchases account, thereby reducing the cost of the merchandise purchased during the period to the actual amount paid or expected to be paid. In the following period, as these invoices are paid in time to take advantage of the discount, the credits are made to Allowance for Purchase Discounts rather than to Purchase Discounts. The refinement in the treatment of purchase discounts introduced by estimating an allowance for purchase discounts to be taken is seldom employed in practice.

Alternative No. 3: Net Price Method. The best way to handle purchase discounts is the net price method. As we pointed out in the discussion of sales discounts, the interest rate implied by sales discounts is much too high to be just a payment for receiving money sooner. From the point of view of the buyer, prompt payment to receive the benefit of discounts is so profitable that nearly all firms will want to take advantage of all purchase discounts. Management of such firms will want to know the amount of discounts lapsed, whatever the reason, and will assume that all discounts will be taken regardless of the amount. Under the net price method, the amount of the discounts lost rather than the amount taken is accumulated. The net price method also has an important recording advantage. Since purchases and liabilities are recorded on a cash basis at the outset, the need for adjustments as invoices are paid is eliminated, and the adjustments at the end of the accounting period are eliminated or simplified. This advantage is fully realized only if the business follows the policy, as all successful businesses must, of taking practically all purchase discounts.

When the transaction is recorded, the discount is deducted from the gross purchase price immediately upon the receipt of the invoice, and the net invoice price is used in the entries. The example used previously of a $1,000 invoice price for goods subject to a 2-percent cash discount would be recorded as follows under this method:

	(a) Discount Taken		(b) Discount Not Taken	
Purchases	980		980	
Accounts Payable		980		980
To record purchase.				
Accounts Payable	980		980	
Purchase Discounts Lost	—		20	
Cash		980		1,000
To record payment.				

At the end of the accounting period, the unpaid invoices should be inspected and the amount of expired discounts determined. An adjusting entry will then be made to correct the amount of the liability and to show the additional discounts lost during the period.

Purchase Discounts Lost	80	
Accounts Payable		80

However, this adjustment may not be completely accurate because still more discounts on goods already purchased may be neglected, but these amounts will not be ascertainable until the next accounting period.

Purchase Discounts Lost may be viewed as an additional cost of the merchandise purchased and, therefore, shown as an addition to Purchases in the presentation of the calculation of cost of goods sold. In almost all cases it will yield an amount for cost of goods sold that is identical to the amount provided by the adjusted gross price method. It is sometimes suggested, and with a good deal of logic, that discounts lost should be shown as a financial or general operating expense rather than as an addition to Purchases, because the cause of the failure to take discounts may be an inefficient office force or inadequate financing. In the illustrations, Purchase Discounts Lost will be treated as an addition to Purchases.

Inventory Valuation and Adjustments

The calculation of the cost of the inventory at the end of the period and the measure of the cost of goods sold should be consistent with the purchase adjustments. The cost should be the purchase price adjusted for transportation costs, purchase allowances, and purchase discounts. When it is difficult to make precisely accurate calculations for individual items, an approximate percentage adjustment is satisfactory.

SALES AND PURCHASES ACCOUNTS IN THE INCOME STATEMENT

The following partial income statement will serve as a summary of the Purchases and Sales accounts introduced in this chapter. The presence of Purchase Discounts Lost, an adjunct account, among the additions to Purchases indicates that the net price method of recording purchases is used. If either of the other two alternative methods of recording purchases had been adopted, the Purchases Discounts account balance would have been deducted from the Purchases amount.

The Gross Margin on Sales figure is frequently presented as indicated in Schedule 9.2, but its importance can easily be exaggerated. Net income is the excess of revenue over all expenses. Cost of Goods Sold is only one of the expenses to be deducted from revenue and, except for the point that it is usually the largest expense item, it merits no position of priority. Until all expenses are deducted, it may be misleading to present any figure with a title that connotes income. Even as an indication of trading margin, it is not an accurate figure, because common practice excludes from Purchases many of its costs such as buying, warehousing, and handling. The Gross Margin on Sales, or Gross Profit on Sales as it is more frequently but less properly called, does have value for internal comparative purposes if Purchase and Sale accounts are departmentalized; it may be useful in comparing results of different periods; and the merchant may often think of it as the margin out of which the other expenses must be met.

CLOSING THE SALES AND PURCHASES ACCOUNTS

All of the sales, sales adjustment, purchases, and purchase adjustment accounts are closed at the end of the accounting period. The Merchandise Inventory account is adjusted so that the amount of the final inventory of unsold goods is the balance in that account. As we suggested earlier, there are a number of possible variations in the closing entry procedure, but assuming that J. F. Crane, Inc., closes its books quarterly and uses an Income Summary account in the process, the set of entries in Schedule 9.3 would be appropriate for the accounts shown in the partial income statement, Schedule 9.2.

SCHEDULE 9.2 EXCERPT FROM INCOME STATEMENT

J. F. CRANE, INC.
Income Statement
For the three months ended June 30, 1975

Sales—Gross			$51,523
Less Sales Adjustments			
Sales Returns	$ 2,367		
Sales Allowances	1,126		
Uncollectible Accounts Adjustment	456		
Postage Paid for Customers	525		
Sales Discounts	857		
Sales Tax	3,091		
Total Adjustments		8,422	
Net Sales			$43,101
Cost of Goods Sold			
Merchandise Inventory—4/1/75		$24,562	
Purchases	$35,674		
Purchase Discounts Lost	33		
Freight-in	547		
	$36,254		
Less Purchase Returns and Allowances	1,891		
Net Purchases		34,363	
Goods Available for Sale During Quarter		$58,925	
Merchandise Inventory—6/30/75		26,654	
Cost of Goods Sold			32,271
Gross Margin on Sales			$10,830

(Continued)

The Cost of Goods Sold account frequently is not used, and the amount for the debit to Income Summary is reflected directly in the entry that closes the purchase accounts. The illustrative entry follows a formula that is traditional in accounting and is explained further in Chapter 12:

$$\text{Beginning Inventory} + \text{Net Purchases} - \text{Closing Inventory}$$
$$= \text{Cost of Goods Sold}$$

The Merchandise or Merchandise Inventory account rarely shows any entries during the accounting period when special purchase accounts are used. It shows the opening inventory carried forward from the previous period, and at the end of the period, it is adjusted so as to present the new inventory of unsold goods.

SCHEDULE 9.3 CLOSING SALES AND PURCHASES ACCOUNTS

Sales	51,523	
Sales Returns		2,367
Sales Allowances		1,126
Uncollectible Accounts Adjustment		456
Postage Paid for Customers		525
Sales Discounts		857
Sales Tax		3,091
Income Summary		43,101
To close the sales and sales adjustment accounts.		
Purchase Returns and Allowances	1,891	
Merchandise Inventory	26,654	
Cost of Goods Sold	32,271	
Merchandise Inventory		24,562
Purchases		35,674
Purchase Discounts Lost		33
Freight-in		547
To recognize the cost of goods sold.		
Income Summary	32,271	
Cost of Goods Sold		32,271
To close the Cost of Goods Sold account.		

QUESTIONS AND PROBLEMS

1. In some cases it would be possible and desirable to record sales without the use of a sales account; in other cases, the use of a sales account is virtually a technical necessity. Explain.

2. The accounts of the Brown Distributing Company, after recording the transactions of October, 1975, show the following balances among others: Sales (for the month of October, all on account), $30,000; Allowance for Sales Discounts, debit balance of $465; Sales Discounts, no entries.

   A cash discount of 3 percent for payment within fifteen days is offered all customers, but experience shows that discounts taken average 2½ percent of sales.

   a. A customer, C. D. Stanley, paid his account balance of $500 on October 13, in time to receive a discount. Give the entry.

   *b. How do you explain the debit balance in the Allowance for Sales Discounts, which is a contra-asset account?

   c. Give the entry to be made on October 31 for sales discounts.

3. The Johnson Shoe Company sells its shoes FOB at its factory, but on parcel-post shipments it pays the postage and adds it to the amount of the sales invoice. Give the entries required to record the sale of a $80 order on which $3 of postage was paid.

* Hints, key numbers, or (partial) answers appear in the back of the book between the Appendix Tables and the Glossary.

4. A manufacturer in Portland sells a $1,300 bill of goods to a merchant in Denver, terms 1/10, n/30.

    a. Assume that the shipment is to be FOB Portland but that the freight charges of $60 are paid by the seller and added to the invoice. The bill is paid during the discount period. Give the entries on the seller's books to record the sale and collection. The discount does not apply to the freight charges.

    b. Assume that the shipment is to be FOB Denver but that the manufacturer asks the Denver merchant to pay the freight and deduct the amount in making his remittance. Calculate the amount of the remittance and give entries for the sale and collection on the seller's books.

°5. The customary method of accounting for sales returns produces some distortion of the reported expense figures even if goods are returned in the same period in which they are sold; if the goods are returned in a period subsequent to that of the sale, distortion of the reported revenue figures also results. Explain how sales returns may produce each of the described effects.

°6. When sales taxes are levied as a percentage of monthly sales, it is often true that some merchants collect more taxes than they pay the government, while others collect less. What is the explanation?

7. The Mount Washington Company was formed on April 1, 1975. It decided to offer terms of 2/10, n/30 to all customers, to use the allowance for sales discounts method of recording sales discounts, and to close the books semiannually. During the first half year, the following transactions with customers took place:

    (1) Sales on account, $92,000.

    (2) Returns of goods by customers, $6,500.

    (3) Allowances granted to customers for damaged goods and late shipments, $2,000.

    (4) Collections from customers, $73,804, consisted of $58,604 from customers who took discounts and $15,200 from those who permitted their discounts to lapse.

    (5) The adjustment for sales discounts is based on the estimate that customers will take advantage of 80 percent of the discounts available to them.

    a. Record the transactions, including the adjustment for sales discounts, in two-column journal form.

    b. Present the sales section of the first income statement.

    c. How would the accounts with customers be shown on the September 30, 1975, balance sheet?

8. Prepare dated journal entries to record the following selected transactions of the Hudson Company. The company offers terms of 1/10, n/30 to all customers. It records sales at gross price:

    Aug. 1   A sale of $3,000 is made to the Graves Company.

    Aug. 6   A sale of $1,200 is made to the Feller Company. The Hudson Company pays freight charges of $18 on this shipment and adds them to the invoice.

    Aug. 10   The Feller Company informs the Hudson Company that some of the goods they received are defective. It is agreed that they will be granted a $100 allowance on their purchase.

Aug. 11 A check is received from the Graves Company to settle one half of their balance. They claim the proportionate discount, which is allowed.

Aug. 13 Goods with a gross price of $300 are returned by the Graves Company and accepted.

Aug. 15 The Feller Company pays its bill in full.

Aug. 31 As a result of a telephone conference, the Graves Company sends a sixty-day, 9-percent note to settle their account.

Record the above transactions in two-column form. If these were the only sales made during August, how would the revenue section of the income statement of the Hudson Company appear?

*9. Under what circumstances will the Allowance for Uncollectible Accounts and the Allowance for Sales Discounts have debit balances? The balance sheet figures for the Allowance for Uncollectible Accounts and Allowance for Sales Discounts will never show debit balances. Why?

10. The data in the following schedule pertain to the first eight years of the Gordon Company's credit sales and experiences with uncollectible accounts.

Year	Credit Sales	Uncollectible Accounts	Year	Credit Sales	Uncollectible Accounts
1	$100,000	$2,550	5	$250,000	$3,000
2	150,000	3,225	6	275,000	2,700
3	200,000	3,725	7	280,000	2,875
4	225,000	4,000	8	290,000	2,925

Gordon Company has not previously used an Allowance for Uncollectible Accounts but has merely charged accounts written off directly to Uncollectible Accounts Expense.

What percentage of credit sales for a year should Gordon Company charge to Sales, Uncollectible Accounts, Adjustment Account if it were to be set up now?

11. In auditing department store X, you find that cash discounts on purchases are regularly deducted from invoices when they are entered in the books, while in store Y the invoices are entered in full and the discounts are credited to a discount account as they are earned. Discuss the relative advantages and disadvantages of the two methods and state what variations, if any, would occur in the valuation of inventories under the two methods.

12. The following are selected transactions of the Wearever Shoe Store:

(1) A shipment of shoes is received from the Standard Shoe Company, $2,100. Terms: 2/30, n/60.

(2) Part of the shipment of (1) is returned. The gross price of the returned goods is $200, and a credit memorandum for this amount is received from the Standard Shoe Company.

(3) The invoice of the Standard Shoe Company is paid in time to take the discounts.

a. Assuming that the net price method is used, give entries on the books of the Wearever Shoe Store.

    b. Assuming that the gross price method is used, give entries on the books of the Wearever Shoe Store.

    c. Give entries on the books of the Standard Shoe Company, which uses an Allowance for Sales Discounts account.

13. A fire destroyed the entire stock of The Southern Emporium. From the books and records, the following information is obtained as to operations from the beginning of the fiscal year to the date of the fire. Compute the amount of merchandise at the date of the fire. The average gross margin on sales for the last three years has been 30 percent of net sales.

    Sales, $81,500; Sales Returns and Allowances, $950; Inventory of merchandise at the beginning of the period, $40,000; Merchandise Purchases, $54,200; Freight-in, $350.

14. The Western Eagle Company buys all of its merchandise from the White Corporation on terms of 2/10, n/30. Purchases during the first quarter of 1975 were as follows (amounts are gross invoice figures):

January 8	$4,200
February 3	2,800
February 27	2,600
March 16	1,900
March 26	2,000

Payments, including one in April, were as follows:

January 17	$4,116
February 12	2,744
March 25	1,862
March 27	2,600
April 4	1,960

    a. Using a four-column journal form with two columns for each method, journalize these items. Use (1) the gross price method and (2) the net price method. Assume that discounts available at the end of the period are recognized under the gross price method.

    b. How would Accounts Payable appear on the March 31, 1975, balance sheet under (1) the gross price method and (2) the net price method?

    c. Assuming that the merchandise inventory at December 31, 1974, was $3,420 and $4,160 at March 31, 1975, prepare a merchandise cost of goods sold schedule for the first quarter of 1975 under (1) the gross price method and (2) the net price method.

    d. Journalize the entry to recognize Cost of Goods Sold under each method.

15. Prepare a journal form with two pairs of columns, one headed net price method and the other headed gross price method. Using this journal form, show summary entries for the following events in the history of Evans and Foster, furniture manufacturers.

    (1) During the first year of operations, materials with a gross invoice price of $60,000 are purchased. All invoices are subject to a 2-percent cash discount if paid within ten days.

    (2) Payments to creditors during the year amount to $53,000, settling $54,000 of accounts payable at gross prices.

(3) Of the $6,000 (gross) in unpaid accounts at the end of the year, the discount time has expired on one invoice amounting to $400. It is expected that all other discounts will be taken. This expectation is reflected in the year-end adjustment.

(4) During the first few days of the next period, all invoices are paid in accordance with expectations.

16. The Harding Company was formed on July 1, 1975. It decided to use the net price method of recording purchases and to close the books semi-annually on June 30 and December 31. During the first six months of operations, merchandise with a gross invoice price of $57,000 was purchased. All suppliers offered terms of 2/10, n/30. It returned $3,000 (gross price) of goods as being unsatisfactory, and checks for $48,775 were sent to suppliers in settlement of bills with a gross amount of $49,700. Discounts are still available on all bills outstanding at December 31, 1975, except one for $400 (gross). The inventory of merchandise at December 31, 1975, is $9,210.

Journalize the foregoing on the books of the Harding Company, including entries to recognize Cost of Goods Sold.

17. The following account balances are found in the ledger of a retail store. Organize them in a typical income statement form so as to show Cost of Goods Sold and Gross Margin on Sales:

Merchandise Inventory, November 30	$10,660
Merchandise Purchases	16,280
Sales Returns and Allowances	780
Freight-in	320
Merchandise Inventory, November 1	9,820
Merchandise Purchase Discounts	220
Sales	20,620
Merchandise Purchase Returns and Allowances	240

What is the gross margin percentage on net sales?

18. Thieves broke into the warehouse of the Central Distributing Co. and stole most of the stock of merchandise. You are asked to compute the amount of merchandise on hand at the time of the theft. For the last three years, the average gross margin has been twenty-five percent of net sales. At the start of this year, the merchandise inventory was $16,000. The data for operations of the year to the date of the theft were as follows:

Freight-in	$ 450
Merchandise Purchases	51,000
Sales	72,000
Sales Returns	1,375
Merchandise Purchase Discounts	1,025
Sales Discounts	1,275

*19. Organize the following information of the Michaels Company to show the Cost of Goods Sold and the Gross Margin on Sales. What is the gross margin or mark-up percentage on cost? On net sales?

Merchandise Inventory, July 1	$26,250
Merchandise Inventory, July 31	24,000
Sales	30,150
Purchases	18,750
Sales Returns	750
Purchase Returns	375
Transportation Charges on Purchases	225
Sales Allowances	1,500
Purchase Allowances	900
Sales Discounts	525
Purchase Discounts	300

20. The Fama-Stex Company records merchandise purchases on a net price basis. The following data relating to their 1975 purchases are available.
   (1) Account balances as of 1/1/75: Accounts Payable, $12,000; Merchandise Inventory, $25,000.
   (2) Purchases during the year amounted to $200,000, invoice prices, subject to terms of 2/10, n/30.
   (3) Freight paid on purchases of the period amounted to $3,000.
   (4) Goods having an invoice price of $10,000 were returned to vendors.
   (5) Adjustments and allowances were granted on goods amounting to $3,000.
   (6) Payments to vendors during the year were as follows: all of the beginning of period balances, $12,020; purchases of the period, invoice prices, $170,000; discounts on $1,200 worth of invoice prices had expired.
   (7) An examination of the open account balances at the end of the year indicates that the discount period has lapsed on one bill for $800, invoice price.
   (8) The ending inventory properly computed is $26,750.
   a. Prepare journal entries to record the above data through entry (7).
   b. Present a cost of goods sold schedule for 1975.
   c. Recognizing the cost of goods sold, prepare a journal entry for (8).

*21. Indicate the position of each of the following accounts in the financial statements by the use of the following key. Not all the accounts will be found on one set of books. Place an X after the appropriate number if the account is a contra, that is, to be deducted on the financial statements.
   (1) Revenue section of the income statement
   (2) Cost of Goods Sold section of the income statement
   (3) Asset section of the balance sheet
   (4) Liability section of the balance sheet.

   a. Coupon Books Outstanding
   b. Purchase Discounts Lost
   c. Allowance for Sales Discounts
   d. Purchase Returns
   e. Sales Tax
   f. Freight-in
   g. Purchase Discounts
   h. Sales Allowances
   i. Federal Excise Tax Payable

j. Customers' Deposits

k. Allowance for Purchase Discounts

l. Merchandise Purchases

m. Merchandise Purchase Allowances

n. Sales Discounts Lapsed

o. Postage Paid for Customers.

22. The Wellington Company started in business on January 1, 1974. It makes all sales on account and offers terms of 2/10, n/30 to all customers. Data on dealings with customers in 1974, 1975, and 1976 are:

	1974	1975	1976
Sales at gross price	$100,000	$160,000	$190,000
Cash received from customers who took discounts*	73,700	123,400	147,400
Cash received from customers who did not take discounts	18,000	29,950	37,800

* With 2-percent discounts offered, collections from customers who take discounts are, of course, 98 percent of the gross amount of bills paid.

Carry calculations to the closest dollar.

a. Present the revenue section of the income statement for each of the three years under each of the following assumptions:

(1) Sales discounts are recognized only as they are taken.

(2) The net price method is used.

(3) An Allowance for Sales Discounts account is used. It is estimated that customers will take 80 percent of discounts available to them.

b. Present the receivable section of the balance sheet at the end of each year under each of the three assumptions of part **a**.

23. The Barnes Corporation makes all sales on account. It offers uniform terms of 2/10, n/30 to all customers, and it uses an Allowance for Sales Discounts account for recording sales discounts. Its balance sheet at December 31, 1974, showed Accounts Receivable of $36,930 and an Allowance for Sales Discounts of $624.

During 1975 the following transactions with customers took place:

(1) Sales $915,400.

(2) Collections from customers, $878,470; $789,880 was collected from customers who paid their bills within the discount period and $88,590 from customers who permitted their discounts to lapse.

(3) Sales returns, $8,400.

(4) Allowances granted to customers for goods damaged in shipment, $5,100.

(5) The company's experience over the past few years indicates that 90 percent of the amount of discounts available to customers are taken.

Round computations to the nearest dollar.

a. Record the 1975 transactions with customers, including the adjustment for sales discounts, in two-column journal form.

b. How would accounts with customers be shown on the December 31, 1975, balance sheet?

c. Present the sales section of the 1975 income statement.

24. The Sparks Manufacturing Company commenced operations on January 1, 1974. It makes all sales on account and offers terms of 2/10, n/30 to all customers. Data on transactions with customers for 1974, 1975, and 1976 are:

	1974	1975	1976
Sales at gross prices	$80,000	$120,000	$140,000
Sales returns at gross prices	800	1,400	1,700
Collections from customers:			
Cash received	74,210	113,680	133,210
Discounts taken	1,390	2,080	2,470

Round computations to the nearest dollar.

a. Present the revenue section of the income statement for each of the years under each of the following assumptions:

(1) Sales discounts are recognized only as they are taken.

(2) The net price method of recording sales is used.

(3) An Allowance for Sales Discounts account is used and an effort is made to allocate discounts to the same period as the sales to which they relate. It is estimated that customers will take 90 percent of the discounts available to them.

b. Present the receivables section of the balance sheet at the end of each year under each of the assumptions of part a.

*25. The balances of selected accounts from the December 31, 1974, balance sheet of the Chicago Products Company are:

Accounts Receivable $177,400
Allowance for Sales Discounts 3,240

The following transactions (in summary) affecting customers' balances occurred in 1975:

(1) Sales on account, $1,842,660.

(2) Cash collected from customers totaled $1,792,696. Terms of 2/10, n/30 are offered to all customers; $1,608,376 was collected from customers who paid their bills within the discount period and $184,320 from customers who permitted their discounts to lapse.

(3) Credit memorandums issued for returned sales and allowances, $18,940.

(4) The Company's experience over the past several years indicates that 90 percent of the discounts available to customers are taken.

Round computations to the nearest dollar.

a. Record the 1975 transactions with customers, including the adjustment for sales discounts, in two-column journal form.

b. How would accounts with customers be shown on the December 31, 1975, balance sheet?

c. Present the sales section of the 1975 income statement.

26. The Gilman Wholesale Grocery Company offers terms of 2/10, n/30 to all its customers. It uses the net price method of recording purchases in its voucher system and uses the allowance method of recording sales discounts. The following are its transactions for October, 1975:

(1) A bill is received from the Star Packing Company for $5,600. This covers "drop shipments" of canned goods sent directly from the canner to various customers of the Gilman Wholesale Grocery Company. Terms: 2/10, n/30.

(2) The shipments mentioned in (1) are billed to various customers, $6,600.

(3) Goods are shipped to the Parker Market, $160.

(4) Part of a shipment of goods is returned to the Dryden Company. The goods were billed at $400, less 3-percent cash discount, and it is estimated that $8 of freight was paid on this part of the shipment.

(5) A credit memo for $408 is received from the Dryden Company.

(6) A shipment is made to a customer, R. H. Yates, $310. For the convenience of the customer the goods are shipped prepaid and the amount of the freight, $10, is added to the invoice.

(7) The voucher due the Dryden Company is paid within the discount period. The original amount of the invoice was $2,000 less 3-percent cash discount. The credit memo [see entry (4)] is deducted, and a check is drawn for the balance.

(8) Collections from various customers [see entry (2)], $5,982, in payment of invoices of a gross amount of $6,100. One invoice for $500 is unpaid.

(9) A credit memo is issued to R. H. Yates [see entry (6)] for $10 to cover an adjustment on goods which arrived in an unsatisfactory condition.

(10) A shipment of soap and shortening is received from the Price and Green Company, $2,000. Terms: 1/10, n/30.

(11) Freight bills are received from the Central Trucking Company, $60 for incoming merchandise and $30 on shipments to customers. A voucher and check are drawn in payment.

(12) A check is received from R. H. Yates [see entries (6) and (9)] in full payment of his bill. It arrives in time to qualify for the discount.

(13) A credit memo for $100 (gross) is received from the Barth Fish Company to cover an adjustment on the price of goods that were unsatisfactory. A cash discount of 1 percent is still available on the unpaid voucher covering the original shipment.

(14) Due to delays in inspecting and checking a shipment from Beckwith Food Company, the purchase discount of 2 percent of their shipment of $800 (gross) is lost. Since the end of the accounting period has arrived, an appropriate entry should be made.

Journalize the above transactions in two-column form.

27. The Stewart-Kohn Company purchases merchandise from a large number of suppliers, all of whom offer terms of 2/10, n/30. At January 1, 1974, Accounts Payable to suppliers totaled $7,000, on which discounts of $130 were still available. It was anticipated that all of these discounts would be taken, because the company regularly seeks to take all discounts available to it.

Information about merchandise purchases and payments for 1974, 1975, and 1976 is as follows (all figures, including payments, are given in gross invoice prices):

	1974	1975	1976
Merchandise purchases	$100,000	$130,000	$150,000
Unpaid invoices at Dec. 31:			
On which discounts are available	7,800	8,900	9,300
On which discounts have lapsed	400	700	600
Payments during year:			
Current year's purchases:			
Invoices on which discounts were taken	90,000	117,200	136,500
Invoices on which discounts were not taken	1,800	3,200	3,600
Previous year's purchases:			
Invoices on which discounts were taken	6,500	7,800	8,700
Invoices on which discounts were not taken	500	400	900

All bills are paid in the period of purchase or in the following period.
a. Calculate the amount of net purchases to be shown in a schedule of cost of goods sold for each year under each of the following assumptions:
(1) The net price method is used.
(2) The adjusted gross price method is used.
(3) The gross price method is used and discounts are recognized in the period when bills are paid.
b. Show how accounts with suppliers would appear on the balance sheet at the end of each year under each of the assumptions of part a.

28. The Franklin Variety Store makes purchases from various suppliers, all of whom offer terms of 2/10, n/30. On January 1, 1975, the bills of creditors totaled $12,000 gross, and $220 in discounts were still available on these bills.

During 1975 purchases amounted to $240,000 in gross price terms, and payments by check to suppliers amounted to $237,945. Of this amount, $11,780 was payment for purchases made in 1974, $225,665 was payment for merchandise purchases (gross price, $230,100) made in 1975, and $500 was a deposit sent to Tucker Brothers with a $10,000 order.

Of the unpaid invoices at December 31, 1975, the discounts had lapsed on three purchases with a combined gross amount of $500. The goods ordered from Tucker Brothers had not been received at the end of the year.
a. Journalize the 1975 transactions in two-column journal form. Assume the net price method is used.
b. Journalize the 1975 transactions in two-column journal form. Assume the gross price method is used and discounts available at the end of the accounting period are not recognized.
c. Repeat part b, but recognize discounts available at the end of the period.
°d. How would accounts with suppliers be shown on the December 31, 1975, balance sheet under the assumption of a? Of b? Of c?

29. The Pittsfield Products Company makes all sales on account offering customers terms of 1/10, n/30. The company's experience indicates that 90 percent of all discounts available to customers are taken. All purchases are made on account and 2-percent discounts are offered by all suppliers for

payment within ten days. Some of the items in the trial balance at January 1, 1975, and in the trial balance at December 31, 1975, before adjustments, are:

	Jan. 1, 1975	Dec. 31, 1975
Accounts Receivable	$14,000 (Dr.)	$ 12,000 (Dr.)
Allowance for Sales Discounts	100 (Cr.)	2,580 (Dr.)
Sales	—	300,000 (Cr.)
Sales Discounts	—	—
Accounts Payable	18,000 (Cr.)	15,000 (Cr.)
Merchandise Purchases	—	208,000 (Dr.)
Allowance for Purchase Discounts	340 (Dr.)	—
Merchandise Purchase Discounts	—	4,040 (Cr.)

At December 31, 1975, discounts are available on all unpaid suppliers' invoices except one for $800.

a. Present a summary of the 1975 transactions with customers and suppliers in two-column journal form.

b. Present the skeleton accounts of the trial balance items as they would appear at December 31, 1975, after recording entries of part a.

c. Record the adjustments at December 31, 1975, with regard to these accounts.

d. Show how accounts with customers and with suppliers would appear on the December 31, 1975 balance sheet.

30. Lave Company commenced business on January 1 and plans to close its books semiannually. Since Lave Company had no prior experience that allowed it to judge the collectibility of its accounts receivable, it decided to charge 2 percent of credit sales to Sales, Uncollectible Accounts Adjustment until some experience had been obtained. The following events occurred during the first year.

February 5. Wrote off the account receivable of M. Ryan in the amount of $450.

March 3. Wrote off the account receivable of Swanson Company in the amount of $4,000.

April 1. A customer, Rutten Company, is declared bankrupt, and the receiver indicates that Rutten Company's assets are sufficient to pay $.15 per dollar of debt; Rutten owes Lave $2,000.

May 5. Received a payment of $75 from M. Ryan (see February 5) with a letter explaining that M. Ryan is going to attempt to pay all his bills. Lave Company estimates that half of Ryan's total debt will eventually be paid.

June 30. The credit sales for the first six months of operation totaled $400,000; 2 percent of sales (including amounts already written off) are assumed to be uncollectible.

July 1–
December 31. Credit sales of $500,000 are made; specific accounts receivable with balances of $7,000 are written off as uncollectible.

December 31. Books are closed.

December 31. Lave Company's accounts receivable show the following:

Age of Accounts	Balance Receivable
0–30 days	$150,000
31–60 days	50,000
61–120 days	25,000
more than 120 days	10,000

Lave Company's independent auditors suggest that the following percentages be used to compute the estimates of amounts that will eventually prove uncollectible; 0–30 days: ½ of 1 percent; 31–60 days: 1 percent; 61–120 days: 10 percent; more than 120 days: 60 percent. The suggestion is adopted and the books are adjusted.

Prepare journal entries in two-column form to record the transactions for the year that affect the Accounts Receivable, the Allowance for Uncollectible Accounts Receivable, and the Sales, Uncollectible Accounts Adjustment accounts.

Chapter 10

Periodic Procedures: Adjusting Entries

At the end of an accounting period, the accountant carries out several operations. After all day-to-day transactions have been journalized and posted, a trial balance is taken. The next step is to post and journalize adjusting entries. Every business engages in certain activities whose existence is recorded only at certain intervals. A manufacturer may lease a warehouse for twenty years, or he may be required to pay interest on a quarterly or semiannual basis on a note that he used to finance an equipment purchase. Although the rent and interest accrue every day, it is not feasible to record the accruals that often. When payments are made, that fact is recorded, but in addition it is almost always necessary to make adjusting entries at the end of the accounting period to bring the records up to date.

Unadjusted Trial Balance

At the end of the accounting period, after all the day-to-day transactions have been posted, a trial balance of the general ledger is taken. This is frequently referred to as an unadjusted trial balance. Likewise, the subsidiary ledgers' balances are determined and compared to the corresponding control accounts. These operations provide a useful test of clerical accuracy prior to proceeding into the final steps in the accounting cycle.

ADJUSTING ENTRIES

At the close of each accounting period, a number of transactions which, for one reason or another, have not been entered as a part of the regular data-processing routine during the period must be recorded. The entries are commonly known as *adjusting* entries, because they may be said to adjust, or correct, the account balances that emerge from the regular day-to-day record-keeping procedures. After the adjusting entries are journalized and posted, the financial statements may be prepared from the account balances with little or no additional information.

The method of analyzing the transactions does not differ from that applied to the ordinary recurring entries, but the nature of the situations and the gathering of the necessary information are sufficiently distinctive to justify treating these entries as a special phase of accounting procedure. Although only a few adjusting entries are made, they usually represent a crucial stage in the determination of periodic income.

Most adjusting entry data originate internally rather than externally; that is, a memorandum, whether given to or received from anyone outside of the enterprise, does not usually provide the basis for an adjusting entry. Some member of the accounting staff, or possibly an independent auditor, must assume the responsibility of reviewing the accounts and determining the necessary adjustments.

Since the adjusting entries are usually of a specialized, nonrepetitive nature and are likely to require detailed explanations, they are usually recorded in the general journal rather than in the specialized journals. Posting these entries to the ledger accounts is done in the usual manner.

TYPES OF ADJUSTING ENTRIES

Adjusting entries can be classified in many ways, but no classification scheme is likely to encompass all possible adjustments. The following list indicates the more common adjustments and serves as an outline of the discussion in this chapter.

1. Recognizing accrued revenue and receivables
2. Recognizing accrued expenses, costs, and payables
3. Allocating prepaid operating costs to periodic operations
4. Allocating unearned revenue to periodic operations
5. Recognizing depreciation, depletion, and amortization of noncurrent assets
6. Recognizing periodic adjustments in the valuation of receivables
7. Recognizing periodic adjustments of expenses and costs in the valuation of payables
8. Correcting errors
9. Recording omitted transactions.

Recognition of Accrued Revenue and Receivables

Revenue is earned as services are rendered. Rent is earned as a tenant uses or has the opportunity of using the property. Interest is earned as time passes on a loan. It is usually not convenient, however, to record these amounts as they accrue day by day. At the end of an accounting period, there are apt to be some situations in which revenue has been earned but for which the entry has not been made, either because the cash has not been received, or because the time has not arrived for a formal invoice to be sent to the customer. A claim has come into existence which, although it may not be immediately due and payable, should appear on the balance sheet as an asset and should be reflected in the revenue earned during the period. The purpose of the adjusting entry in this case, then, is to bring this accrued revenue into the records so that the income statement and the balance sheet will correctly present the condition of the accounts involved.

The entry for an accrual of revenue is to debit an asset account and to credit a revenue account. For example, if a note receivable for $1,500 is dated May 1 and bears interest at 8 percent per year, the accrued interest on June 30 would be $20 (two months' interest at 8 percent), and the adjusting entry, if June 30 were the end of the accounting period, would be:

Interest Receivable 20
    Interest Earned on Notes 20

Several other titles could, of course, be used. The asset account might be designated Accrued Interest Receivable or Interest Accrued on Notes Receivable. The revenue account might be designated Interest Revenue, Interest Earned, or Interest on Notes Receivable. The word *accrued*, if used at all for account titles for such entries, should be used only in asset titles. The revenue account credited is not a special one; it is the regular interest revenue account that may have previously been credited for interest earned and collected during the period.

Recognition of Accrued Expenses and Payables

As various services are received, their full cost should be recorded whether or not payment has been made or an invoice received. Here, also, it is frequently not convenient to record these amounts day by day, so there are almost always some adjustments of payables to be made at the end of the accounting period. The debit portion of the adjustment is necessary to present expenses properly in the income statement and to present assets, including the production costs in their new form, in the balance sheet. The credit recognizes the amount of the gradually increasing or accruing liability, which, although not immediately payable, represents an obligation for services received.

The entry for this type of adjustment is to debit an asset, production cost, or expense account, and to credit a liability account. Common adjustments of this type are those recording: (1) accrued rent of equipment, land or buildings; (2) accrued taxes—real estate taxes, personal property taxes, employer's share of payroll taxes, income taxes, and so forth, (3) accrued interest on notes or bonds; and (4) accrued wages, salaries, and commissions.

The treatment of accrued wages illustrates this type of adjustment. There will usually be an interval between the close of the last regular payroll period and the close of the accounting period, during which wages are earned but not recorded on the books. Assume that these "accrued" wages and salaries amount to $1,200 and that the distribution is as follows: Administrative Salaries Expense, $100; Sales Salaries Expense, $250; Direct Labor, $450; General Factory Operations, $300; and labor used in the construction of new equipment, $100. The entry would be:

Administrative Salaries Expense	100	
Sales Salaries Expense	250	
Direct Labor	450	
General Factory Wages (a production cost)	300	
Equipment (or Equipment under Construction)	100	
Salaries and Wages Payable		1,200

The liability account should clearly indicate the type of liability being recorded. The word *accrued* is unnecessary, but if it is used in this connection, it should be restricted to the liability title.

A special problem may arise in connection with utility services— electricity, gas, and water. Whenever these costs are important items, it may be desirable to record them on an accrual basis since the meter-reading and billing interval will seldom correspond to the accounting period. The company being served would read its own meters and make a calculation of the unbilled cost of service received during the period. For example, a business begins operations on September 1, 1975, reads its electric meter at September 30, and calculates the cost of electricity consumed during the month. Assuming an accounting period of one month, the adjusting entry would be:

Electricity—Factory	585	
Electricity—Office	112	
Utility Services Payable		697

Allocation of Prepaid Operating Costs

Another type of adjustment arises from the fact that some assets purchased for use in the operations of the business are not completely used during the accounting period in which they are acquired. Such items may be physical in nature, such as office supplies, or they may be services receivable in future periods, such as insurance bought with premiums paid in advance or the use of real estate bought with rent paid in advance. Merchandise is another example of such an asset, but because of its quantitative importance, it is usually singled out for special treatment. The cost of goods sold analysis, discussed in Chapter 9, is in reality a prepaid operating-cost adjusting entry.

At the end of each accounting period an appropriate amount of a prepaid item must be allocated to the operations of the present period, and the balance is carried forward, or deferred, to future periods. *Prepayment* in this context does not necessarily mean literal cash payment. Most of the entries involve, first, recording the invoice or the voucher as a debit to the appropriate prepayment account and a credit to accounts (or vouchers) payable and, then sometimes later, the payment in cash.

Recording this type of adjusting entry is complicated by the fact that there are two methods in common use for recording the acquisition of services and supplies, and the adjusting entry must be consistent with the previous entries that have been made. The two methods will first be considered under the simplifying assumption that there was a zero balance in the asset account at the start of the period. Under one method, the acquisition is debited to an asset account; the adjustment requires the calculation of the amount of the asset expired, or used, during the period. The adjusting entry is a debit to the production cost or expense account and a credit to the asset account. This is the most logical procedure. Sometimes, however, a second method is used in which the acquisition is charged directly to an expense or production cost account, and the adjustment requires the determination of the unused amount. The adjusting entry is to debit the asset account and to credit the expense (or production cost) account for the unused amount. The expense account is thus corrected. The adjusted result is the same under either method.

For example, a concern closes its books monthly, and it purchased store supplies during March for $300, and $220 of supplies were used. Store supplies worth $80 were still on hand at the end of March. The entries under the first method would be:

Mar. 1–31	Store Supplies on Hand	300	
	Vouchers Payable		300
31	Store Supplies Expense	220	
	Store Supplies on Hand		220
	Adjusting Entry.		

The two store supplies accounts would appear as follows:

Store Supplies on Hand				Store Supplies Expense		
3/1–31	300	3/31	220	3/31	220	

The same result would be achieved under the second method by these entries:

Mar. 1–31	Store Supplies Expense	300	
	Vouchers Payable		300
31	Store Supplies on Hand	80	
	Store Supplies Expense		80
	Adjusting Entry.		

Under this method, the store supplies accounts would appear as follows:

Store Supplies on Hand			Store Supplies Expense		
3/31	80		3/1–31	300	3/31	80

If the asset account has a balance at the beginning of the accounting period, the calculations are much the same. If in the previous example, there were an opening balance of $50 in the Store Supplies on Hand account and the closing inventory were, again, $80, the amount of supplies used would have been $270, rather than $220. Under the first method, the March 31 adjusting entry would be:

Mar. 31 Store Supplies Expense 270
          Store Supplies on Hand 270

The accounts would be as follows:

Store Supplies on Hand				Store Supplies Expense		
3/1	50	3/31	270	3/31	270	
3/1–31	300					

Under the second method, the adjustment would be only for the amount needed to correct the "on hand" balance at the end of the period. Since the asset balance was $50 at the start of the period, a $30 adjustment would be required to correct it.

Mar. 31 Store Supplies on Hand 30
          Store Supplies Expense 30

The accounts would show:

Store Supplies on Hand			Store Supplies Expense		
3/1	50		3/1–31	300	3/31	30
3/31	30				

If the store supplies on hand at the end of the period were $35, the adjusting entry under the second method would be:

Mar. 31 Store Supplies Expense 15
          Store Supplies on Hand 15

The form of the adjusting entry for allocating prepaid operating costs, then, will vary according to the method used for handling previous entries. It will either be a debit to the expense or production cost account and a credit to the asset account for the amount expired or used, or it will be a debit to the asset account and a credit to the expense or production cost account for the amount needed to correct the asset account balance.

Sometimes the regular recording of a charge to operations may, after exhausting the amount of the prepayment, create an accrued liability, and it is possible that a single account may be used first as an asset and then as a liability. Workmen's compensation insurance premiums, for example, are paid at the start of the year on the basis of an estimated payroll for the coming year, and the premium is then charged to operations in proportion to the payrolls of each month or quarter. If the total payrolls amount to more than the estimate, the periodic charges to operations will eventually exhaust the amount of the original premium and will create a liability that will form the basis of an additional premium due the insurance company. Suppose, for example, that the estimated payroll for a year is $65,000 and that the compensation insurance rate is 2 percent, or $2 per hundred. The entry for the advance premium would be:

Unexpired Compensation Insurance	1,300	
Vouchers Payable		1,300

If the payroll for the first month amounts to $6,000, the following adjusting entry would be made:

Compensation Insurance (an expense or production cost)	120	
Unexpired Compensation Insurance		120

If the credits to the Unexpired Compensation Insurance account eventually exceed the debits, the same entries could be continued, creating a temporary credit balance in the Unexpired Compensation Insurance account (now a liability account), which would be canceled by the next premium payment. Or, of course, a new liability account, such as Compensation Insurance Payable, could be opened for this interval.

Allocation of "Unearned Revenue"

There are many instances in which cash is received some time before the goods or services are furnished to the customer, in other words, some time before the revenue is earned. The entry to record this is to debit Cash and to credit an account such as Rent Received in Advance or Unearned Rent. Such credit balance accounts are usually described as "unearned revenue" accounts. (Technically, this is a contradiction in terms since revenue must be earned to be recognized, as is explained in Chapter 7. A designation for this group such as advance collection accounts might be more appropriate but is seldom used.) The problem is to allocate the revenue among the accounting periods. Until the goods or services are furnished, there is an obligation which may be discharged either by fulfilling the agreement or by refunding the money received. As the goods are delivered or the service furnished, a corresponding amount of revenue is earned and must be recognized.

Not all unearned revenue accounts require adjustment at the end of the period. Deposits by customers, for example, are frequently correctly eliminated by the sale entry when goods are delivered and require no further adjustment at the end of the period. Incidentally, such deposits may be carried as credit balances in customers' accounts during the accounting period rather than in special liability accounts.

The form of the adjusting entry for allocating these items will depend upon the method followed in recording the previous entries. If the payment by the customer has been credited to a liability account, then the adjustment involves a debit to cancel a portion of the liability and a credit to an earned revenue account. For example, if a tenant paid six months' rent, $2,400, in advance, the following entry would be made:

| Cash on Hand | 2,400 | |
| Unearned Rent | | 2,400 |

At the end of the first month, the required entry would be:

| Unearned Rent | 400 | |
| Rent Revenue | | 400 |

It is sometimes possible, however, to credit a revenue account with all such receipts, and in such a case, it is necessary to adjust the revenue account so that it will present only the revenue earned during the current accounting period. For example, a publisher may follow the practice of crediting all receipts on magazine subscriptions to Revenue from Subscriptions. At the end of each period, a calculation would be made of the amounts received for unpublished or undelivered numbers of the magazine and an entry made to adjust the unearned revenue account. If the amount of unearned subscriptions has increased by $7,500 since the beginning of the period, the entry would be:

| Revenue from Subscriptions | 7,500 | |
| Unearned Subscriptions | | 7,500 |

If the amount had declined, the accounts debited and credited would be reversed in the amount of the decrease.

Recognition of Depreciation, Depletion, and Amortization

When assets such as buildings, machinery, furniture, and trucks are purchased, their cost is charged to the appropriate asset accounts. Although these assets may provide services for a number of years, eventually they will have to be retired from service. Therefore the cost of each asset, less an estimate for probable scrap, or other value at retirement, is spread systematically over its estimated useful life. The charge made to current operations for the portion of the cost of such assets applicable to the current period is called *depreciation*. *Depletion* is a similar charge representing the cost of a "wasting" asset, or natural resource, consumed during the period, such as ore removed from a deposit in mining operations or oil pumped from an oil well. *Amortization* is a similar charge representing the periodic cost of an "intangible" asset such as a patent, trademark, copyright, or goodwill. These topics are discussed in Chapter 14. Their treatment involves nothing new in principle; it is identical with the prepaid operating-cost procedure previously presented. For example, the cost of a building may be considered as a prepayment for a series of future services and depreciation as the allocation of the cost of the services to the periods in which they are received.

The straight-line method of calculating periodic depreciation, which is widely used, divides the cost of an asset, less its estimated scrap or other value at retirement, by the number of periods during which it is expected the asset will be used. Or, what amounts to the same thing, a percentage rate is used such that if it is applied every period to cost less scrap value, then the cost will be reduced to scrap value at the end of the asset's estimated life. Scrap value is often assumed to be zero. Some common rates of depreciation are 10 percent a year for furniture and fixtures, 25 percent for automobiles, and 2 percent for brick or concrete buildings.

The calculations involved in the straight-line method can be illustrated as follows. A machine is purchased for $36,000. It has an estimated life of five years and an estimated scrap value of $1,000. The annual depreciation is:

$$\frac{\$36,000 - \$1,000}{5}, \text{ or } 20\% \text{ of } \$35,000 = \$7,000$$

If the scrap value is assumed to be zero, the calculation is:

$$\frac{\$36,000}{5}, \text{ or } 20\% \text{ of } \$36,000 = \$7,200$$

Depreciation entries are recorded as debits to production cost or expense accounts and credits to the contra-asset account, Accumulated Depreciation. This account shows the portion of the cost of the asset that has been charged off to date; it represents expired service life and service cost. Other titles frequently used are Allowance for Depreciation and Depreciation to Date. The account title Reserve for Depreciation was used extensively in the recent past, but its use is diminishing steadily. The inappropriateness of the title *Reserve* is discussed in Chapter 17.

The entry for a year's depreciation on the machine mentioned above would be:

Depreciation of Machinery (a production-cost account)   7,000
   Accumulated Depreciation of Machinery (a contra-asset
   account)   7,000

A separate Accumulated Depreciation account should be used for each type of depreciating asset, and it is also desirable to have more detailed underlying records, which distribute the depreciation among the individual units, represented by the balance sheet accounts. Accumulated Depreciation is shown on the balance sheet as a deduction from the asset account to which it refers. It is not usually canceled against the cost of the asset except in condensed statements.

The adjusting entries for depreciation, then, require the calculation of the depreciation for each noncurrent asset or group of assets that has a limited life and the recording of a series of entries similar to the one shown above.

Depletion is handled in a manner similar to that followed in connection with depreciation. The calculations in this case are based upon the amount of product removed. A unit cost is obtained by dividing the cost less estimated salvage value of the property at retirement by the estimated number of units of product that will be removed before the mine or well is abandoned. This unit cost is multiplied by the number of units removed during the period to determine the amount of depletion. The entry is usually made in the following form:

Depletion (a production cost account) 12,000
    Accumulated Depletion (a contra-asset account)   12,000

Allowance for Depletion or Depletion to Date are other acceptable credit titles.

Amortization of an intangible asset, like the depreciation and depletion procedures, should be based upon a systematic spreading of the cost of the asset over its estimated useful life. The estimation of the useful life of an intangible asset is frequently considerably more difficult than that for plant or wasting assets. Systematic procedures of amortization, as well as special considerations of partial or entire write-offs of intangible assets, are discussed in Chapter 14.

Valuation of Accounts Receivable

At the end of each accounting period, entries should be made that result in customers' accounts and sales revenue being stated correctly on the financial statements. The principal adjustment that must be made arises from the likely uncollectibility of some accounts. Other adjustments may include the provision for an allowance for outstanding sales discounts and sales returns, although these occur infrequently in practice.

The nature of the adjustment for uncollectible accounts is discussed in Chapter 9. It was noted that the practice is sometimes followed of waiting until a customer's account has clearly been demonstrated to be uncollectible and then writing it off as a loss. This method is not considered appropriate when such losses are significant in amount and frequent in occurrence, as in retail stores. The better procedure is to estimate the amount of bad debts that will occur in connection with the sales of each period, to make an adjusting entry to reduce the balance sheet figure for Accounts Receivable to the amount believed to be collectible, and to make a corresponding adjustment of the sales revenue for the period. The entry involves a debit to Sales, Uncollectible Accounts Adjustment and a credit to Allowance for Uncollectible Accounts. The Allowance for Uncollectible Accounts is a contra account to Accounts Receivable; its balance at the end of the period appears on the balance sheet as a deduction from Accounts Receivable. The Sales, Uncollectible Accounts Adjustment account, a revenue contra, is preferably presented as an adjustment of sales. There are various methods adopted in calculating the amount of the adjustment for uncollectible accounts as described in Chapter 9.

The adjusting entry for estimated uncollectibles is:

Sales, Uncollectible Accounts Adjustment 700
    Allowance for Uncollectible Accounts   700

Two other year-end adjustments of Accounts Receivable need only brief mention here. The amount of sales discounts available at the end of the period may be recognized by an entry debiting Sales Discounts and crediting Allowance for Sales Discounts, an Accounts Receivable contra account. The amount for Accounts Receivable shown on the balance sheet should equal the total of the accounts having debit balances in the customers' ledgers and credit balances in individual customers' accounts should be shown as liabilities. The balance in the control account will agree, of course, with the net balance in the subsidiary ledger. The segregation and reporting of the credit balances may be accomplished by reference to the schedule of the Accounts Receivable subsidiary ledger, or an adjusting entry may be made. If credit balances in Accounts Receivable totaled $3,500, the entry would be:

```
Accounts Receivable .........................................    3,500
      Deposits by Customers ...................................           3,500
```

Valuation of Accounts Payable

Two types of adjustments of the Accounts Payable balance may be made at the end of the period. First, if the firm records purchases at gross prices, more accurate results are achieved if an adjustment is made to record discounts available at the end of the period. The use of the allowance for purchase discounts accounts was discussed in Chapter 9. If purchases are recorded at net prices, it is necessary to record discounts lost on invoices unpaid at the end of the period. If $90 of such a discount were lost, the entry would be:

```
Purchase Discounts Lost ............................................     90
      Accounts Payable—Supplier's Name ...........................           90
```

Second, debit balances in Accounts Payable raise a question similar to that presented by credit balances in Accounts Receivable. Here, also, the asset balance may be segregated and reported by reference to the schedule of the subsidiary ledger, or by making an adjusting entry. If an adjusting entry were made at a time when debit balances in Accounts Payable totaled $1,200, the entry would be:

```
Advances to Suppliers .......................................    1,200
      Accounts Payable .......................................           1,200
```

Correction of Errors

Various types of errors may be discovered at the close of the accounting period when the general process of checking, reviewing, and auditing is carried out. Errors that come to light when the trial balance does not balance, such as mistakes in computing the balances of accounts, posting an incorrect amount, or posting to the wrong side of an account, do not require a journal entry to be corrected. Nor can they be corrected with any entry involving equal debits and credits. Instead, greater care and arithmetic accuracy are required. Errors in journalizing, such as recording an incorrect account or incorrect debit and credit amounts, can be corrected by an adjusting entry having equal debits and credits. The correction requires the determination of the entry that should have been made, a comparison of this entry with the one actually made, and then the designing of an entry that will correct the account balances. (Sometimes the incorrect entry made previously is "reversed"; that is, the original entry is duplicated with reversed debits and credits, and the entire correct entry, as it should have been made, is recorded.) The accounting procedures for the correction of an error involving the operations of a previous period are discussed in Chapters 7 and 14.

Recording Omitted Transactions

During the process of review at the close of a period, it is occasionally discovered that a regular transaction has, for some reason or other, not been recorded. An entry is made in the same form as though the entry were being made at the proper time, except that the general journal may be used if the appropriate specialized journal has been ruled and posted.

Holding the Books Open at the End of the Period

It is usually impossible to complete the recording of the transactions for a period on the last day of that period, or even on the day following. Many items may be in transit, and bills may not be received for several days. It is common practice, therefore, to hold the books open for a few days and to record as regular transactions these late items under the date of the last day of the period. Bills received will be entered as vouchers or accounts payable before the journals are ruled and posted. This practice tends to reduce the number of situations that must be treated as adjustments but must not be used to manipulate the reported results. For example, it would be objectionable to include the cash receipts of the first few days of the next period in order to avoid showing a bank overdraft on the balance sheet.

Adjusted Trial Balance

After the adjusting entries are journalized and posted, an adjusted trial balance of the ledger may be taken. In addition to serving as a partial test of clerical accuracy, it may serve as a convenient basis for the preparation of the financial statements. At this point, the account balances, with the exception of Retained Earnings, should be those that will appear on the statements. The objective of the adjusting-entry procedure is to provide those balances.

ILLUSTRATION OF ADJUSTING ENTRIES

The unadjusted trial balance of the Wright Merchandise Company as of June 30, 1975, is shown in Schedule 10.1. Additional information required for the preparation of the adjusting entries at the end of the month, is presented below. This illustration assumes that the accounting period is one month, so financial statements are prepared and closing entries made at the end of each month. It is finished in the next chapter where the financial statements and the end-of-the-period closing procedure are presented.

SCHEDULE 10.1

WRIGHT MERCHANDISE COMPANY
Unadjusted Trial Balance
June 30, 1975

Cash on Hand	$ 421	
Cash in Bank	4,867	
Change Fund	100	
Accounts Receivable Control	47,500	
Allowance for Uncollectible Accounts		$ 1,500
Allowance for Sales Discounts	200	
Notes Receivable	1,550	
Interest Receivable	2	
Merchandise	85,000	
Store Supplies	500	
Unexpired Insurance	600	
Land	5,450	
Building	30,000	
Accumulated Depreciation on Building		6,000
Furniture and Fixtures	10,000	
Accumulated Depreciation on Furniture and Fixtures		3,000
Vouchers Payable		25,035
Notes Payable		5,000
Interest Payable		105
Payroll Taxes Payable		780
Withheld Income Tax		675
Unfilled Paid Orders		1,500
Mortgage Payable		10,000
Capital Stock		80,000
Retained Earnings		4,558
Sales		56,645
Sales Allowances	1,000	
Sales Salaries	3,000	
Other Selling Expenses	1,258	
Office Salaries	2,500	
Property Taxes	350	
Other Office Expenses	500	
	$194,798	$194,798

Additional information:

1. A count of cash on hand shows a shortage of $1.
2. The bank statement shows a deduction for collection and exchange fees that have not yet been entered on the books, $5.
3. The change fund contains an IOU from the cashier for $10. This will be deducted from his next monthly salary.
4. An analysis of the customers' ledger accounts shows the following facts:
   a. The total of the balances of the individual accounts amounts to $47,475. A search reveals a credit for $25 in one of the accounts for a special allowance that was never journalized.
   b. The credit balances in customers' accounts, representing credit memos not yet used, amount to $500.
   c. The estimated cash discounts yet to be taken amount to $800. The company follows the allowance for sales discounts method.
5. The Notes Receivable consist of two notes, as follows: a $750 8-percent note dated June 1, 1975, and due August 1, 1975.
   An $800, 6-percent note dated May 15, 1975, and due November 1, 1975.
6. The merchandise inventory at June 30, 1975 is $45,000.
7. The balance in the store supplies account represents the inventory at June 1. All purchases of store supplies during the month have been charged to Other Selling Expenses. The inventory of store supplies at June 30 is $550.
8. The unexpired insurance at June 30 is $540.
9. The depreciation rate on furniture and fixtures is 1 percent of cost a month. No changes have taken place in the Furniture and Fixtures account during June.
10. The depreciation rate on the building is 2 percent of cost a year.
11. The mortgage is due on April 1, 1985. Interest at the rate of 6 percent per annum is payable on April 1 and October 1 of each year.
12. The Notes Payable item represents a sixty-day, 6-percent note payable at the bank, dated May 25, 1975.
13. Salaries earned but not paid at June 30: sales, $100; office, $50.
14. The employer's share of payroll taxes for the month of June is determined to be $510 (sales salaries, $280; office salaries, $230).
15. The estimated amount of uncollectible accounts to arise from sales in June is $250.
16. The state sales tax is 3 percent of sales. The company has credited Sales with the tax charged to customers.
17. Assume that the federal income tax rate is estimated to be 30 percent of taxable income, calculated on a twelve-month basis. During the first five months of 1975, the company had no taxable income nor loss.

The presentation and explanations of the required adjusting entries are as follows:

(1) Small cash shortages occur frequently where large numbers of cash transactions take place. It is common practice to provide an expense account to take up such items. The entry is:

```
Cash Short and Over (or Miscellaneous Financial Expense) ............  1
    Cash on Hand ...................................................       1
```

(2) The bank may make deductions for service charges, special services, and so forth, and insert a debit memo in the depositor's statement to inform him of the charge. This memorandum serves as the basis for the entry.

```
Collection and Exchange Expense (or Miscellaneous
    Financial Expense) ..............................................  5
    Cash in Bank ....................................................       5
```

(3) Since the IOU is not cash, it should be removed from the Change Fund account. The entry is:

```
Prepaid Salaries ...................................................  10
    Change Fund ....................................................      10
```

The debit could have been made to an account entitled Due from Employees, which would be treated as a receivable.

(4) (a) The $25 item is an omitted transaction and should be recorded in the same form as though it had been entered at the proper time:

```
Sales Allowances ...................................................  25
    Accounts Receivable Control ...................................      25
```

(b) An adjusting entry could be made setting up the liability in a special account as follows:

```
Accounts Receivable Control ......................................  500
    Customers' Credit Balances ..................................      500
```

An alternative procedure during the process of preparing the balance sheet would add the $500 amount to the Accounts Receivable Control balance as per books and record a liability, Advances by Customers or Credit Balances in Customers' Accounts, in the amount of $500 without making the formal adjusting entry.

(c) Since there is a $200 debit balance in the Allowance for Sales Discounts account, it will be necessary to credit it with $1,000 in order to create an $800 credit balance for the discounts estimated to be taken. The $1,000 also measures the estimated discounts applicable to the sales for the month. The entry is:

```
Sales Discounts ....................................................  1,000
    Allowance for Sales Discounts ..............................       1,000
```

(5) The interest accumulated on the two notes is calculated as follows:

```
8 percent of $750 for one month ........................................  $ 5
6 percent of $800 for one and one-half months ........................     6
                                                                         ───
Total interest accumulated .............................................  $11
                                                                         ═══
```

Since there is a $2 debit balance in the Interest Receivable account, it will be necessary to debit it for $9 in order to create the $11 debit balance representing the interest accumulated.

```
Interest Receivable  ...............................................   9
    Interest Earned on Notes  ......................................       9
```

(6) Since only one merchandise account has been used, the $85,000 represents the sum of the inventory on hand at June 1, plus the purchases during the month and plus or minus any adjustments of purchases for such items as transportation, returns, and allowances. If the inventory at June 30 is $45,000, the difference of $40,000 represents the cost of goods which presumably have been sold, so the appropriate entry is:

```
Cost of Goods Sold ......................................   40,000
    Merchandise  ..........................................       40,000
```

(7) An adjustment is required to increase the asset account to the amount of the ending inventory and to reduce the expense account which has been charged with the purchase of supplies.

```
Store Supplies  ....................................................   50
    Other Selling Expenses  ........................................       50
```

The effect is as though none of the supplies on hand June 1 had been used and $50 worth of the supplies purchased during the month were still on hand.

Another solution, identical in results but perhaps superior in its implications about physical flows, is to close the June 1 balance into the Other Selling Expenses account and then set up the new inventory of $550 as a debit to Store Supplies and a credit to Other Selling Expenses.

(8) The amount in the Unexpired Insurance account represents the balance carried forward from the previous month plus any premiums paid in June. If the amount unexpired at June 30 is $540, the insurance expense for the month of June must be $60.

```
Insurance Expense  ................................................   60
    Unexpired Insurance  ..........................................       60
```

(9) Since no changes have been made in the Furniture and Fixtures account during the month, the 1-percent rate can be applied to the balance of the account. If any decreases or increases had taken place, depreciation would be calculated for less than a month on the items retired or acquired.

```
Depreciation of Furniture and Fixtures ..........................   100
    Accumulated Depreciation on Furniture and Fixtures ..........       100
```

(10) Depreciation charges on the building for a year are $600. One month's charge would be $50.

```
Depreciation of Building ..........................................   50
    Accumulated Depreciation on Building ..........................       50
```

(11) The interest accrued on the mortgage from April 1, the last interest payment date, to June 1 has been recorded in the Interest Payable account. The adjustment required on June 30 is to record the interest accrued during June, $10,000 at 6 percent per annum for one month.

```
Interest on Mortgage Payable ......................................   50
    Interest Payable ..............................................       50
```

(12) The interest accrued on the note during the last six days of May was recorded in Interest Payable on May 31. The adjustment now required is to record the interest for June, thirty days at 6 percent per annum on $5,000.00.

Interest on Notes Payable	25	
Interest Payable		25

(13) Since no balance is shown in the Salaries Payable account, these accrued salaries must represent an addition to the June expenses.

Sales Salaries	100	
Office Salaries	50	
Salaries Payable		150

(14) The employer's share of payroll taxes for the month is computed on the sales and office salaries including the accruals, $3,100 and $2,550, respectively. The $510 amount includes the tax for state unemployment, for federal unemployment, and for Federal Old-Age Survivor and Disability Insurance benefits. The tax is payable on the basis of wages paid rather than accrued, but the cost to the employer should nevertheless be computed on an accrued-salaries basis. Special liability accounts could be used for each part of the tax, but it is assumed here that one account is considered sufficient and that underlying records will be kept to facilitate the accounting for the liability. The employees' share has been deducted at the time salaries were paid, and the accrued liability of the employer for these deductions is added to the Payroll Taxes Payable account.

Payroll Taxes—Sales	280	
Payroll Taxes—Office	230	
Payroll Taxes Payable		510

(15) The estimated uncollectible accounts adjustment for June represents that portion of the credit sales for the month which will probably be uncollectible.

Sales, Uncollectible Accounts Adjustment	250	
Allowance for Uncollectible Accounts		250

(16) No separate record has been kept of the amount of sales tax charged to customers. The amount charged has, however, been credited to the Sales account, and its balance is 103 percent of the basic sales figure. The apparent net sales of $55,620 (gross sales of $56,645 less allowances of $1,025) divided by 1.03 equals $54,000, which is taken as the real net sales of the period, and the sales tax is 3 percent of this amount, or $1,620 (which equals the difference between $55,620 and $54,000).

Sales Taxes	1,620	
Sales Tax Payable		1,620

(17) Before the liability for income taxes can be computed, a tentative calculation of income or loss must be made. In this illustration it is assumed that the taxable income is computed on the same basis as the

amounts in the ledger accounts. In this illustration in Schedule 10.2, taxable income for the month is $4,250, a figure that can be verified by closing all operating account balances to an income summary and computing the excess of credit entries over debit entries. The accrued liability for income taxes is 30 percent of this amount, or $1,275.

Federal Income Tax 1,275
        Federal Income Tax Payable 1,275

The adjusted trial balance of the general ledger prepared after posting of the foregoing adjusting entries follows. This adjusted trial balance is the basis of the financial statements to be presented in the following chapter.

SCHEDULE 10.2

WRIGHT MERCHANDISE COMPANY
Adjusted Trial Balance
June 30, 1975

Cash on Hand	$ 420	
Cash in Bank	4,862	
Change Fund	90	
Accounts Receivable Control	47,975	
Allowance for Uncollectible Accounts		$ 1,750
Allowance for Sales Discounts		800
Notes Receivable	1,550	
Interest Receivable	11	
Merchandise	45,000	
Store Supplies	550	
Unexpired Insurance	540	
Prepaid Salaries	10	
Land	5,450	
Building	30,000	
Accumulated Depreciation on Building		6,050
Furniture and Fixtures	10,000	
Accumulated Depreciation on Furniture and Fixtures		3,100
Vouchers Payable		25,035
Notes Payable		5,000
Interest Payable		180
Salaries Payable		150
Payroll Taxes Payable		1,290
Sales Tax Payable		1,620
Withheld Income Tax		675
Federal Income Tax Payable		1,275
Unfilled Paid Orders		1,500
Customers' Credit Balances		500
Mortgage Payable		10,000
Capital Stock		80,000
Retained Earnings		4,558
Sales		56,645

SCHEDULE 10.2 (*continued*)

Sales Allowances	1,025	
Sales Discounts	1,000	
Sales Taxes	1,620	
Sales, Uncollectible Accounts Adjustment	250	
Interest Earned on Notes		9
Cost of Goods Sold	40,000	
Sales Salaries	3,100	
Payroll Taxes—Sales	280	
Depreciation of Building	50	
Depreciation of Furniture and Fixtures	100	
Other Selling Expenses	1,208	
Office Salaries	2,550	
Payroll Taxes—Office	230	
Property Taxes	350	
Insurance Expense	60	
Collection and Exchange Expense	5	
Cash Short and Over	1	
Other Office Expenses	500	
Interest on Notes Payable	25	
Interest on Mortgage Payable	50	
Federal Income Tax	1,275	
	$200,137	$200,137

QUESTIONS AND PROBLEMS

1. When financial statements are prepared semiannually, is there any necessity to record adjustments at the close of each month? Discuss.

2. Indicate the distinctive features of adjusting entries.

3. Suggest a procedure designed to minimize the possibility of omitting a required adjusting entry.

4. Indicate various accounts which might appear as contra accounts in the following sections of the financial statements:
a. asset
b. liability
c. sales revenue
d. cost of goods sold.

5. A contra account is not a technical necessity for the recording of depreciation, but it is for the recording of the adjustment for uncollectible accounts. Explain.

6. Indicate the similarity of the accounting for plant assets and for supplies. In what respect is the accounting procedure usually different?

7. The Merchandise Supply Company received a $3,000, three-month, 12-percent promissory note, dated December 1, 1975, from Virdon Stores to apply on its account.
a. Present entries in two-column journal form for the Merchandise Supply Company from December 1, 1975, through collection at maturity. The books are closed quarterly. Include the closing entry.

b. Present entries in two-column journal form for Virdon Stores from December 1, 1975, through payment at maturity. The books are closed quarterly. Include the closing entry.

8. The Central Fuel Company rents a yard for coal storage from the Benson Realty Company for $600 a month, payable six months in advance. The company rents part of its office building to the Southside Realtors for $375 a month, payable at the end of each month.

   As of April 1, 1975, the rent on the storage yard had been paid in advance until June 1, 1975, and the rent on the office space for March was unpaid.

   On May 1, 1975, the Southside Realtors paid $750 rent to the Central Fuel Company.

   On July 1, 1975, the Central Fuel Company paid six months' rent to the Benson Realty Company.

   On July 1, 1975, the Southern Realtors paid $1,500 rent to the Central Fuel Company.

   Present dated entries in two-column journal form for the above transactions and for the adjustments from April 30 to September 30, inclusive, as they relate to the three companies:

   a. The Benson Realty Company closes its books quarterly (March 31, and so forth). The systems manual requires a credit to a liability account at the time of collection of rental cash.

   b. The Southside Realtors closes its books quarterly (March 31, and so forth). The systems manual requires a debit to an expense account upon the payment of rent.

   c. The Central Fuel Company closes its books monthly. The systems manual requires a debit to an asset account upon the payment for rent and a credit to a revenue account upon the collection of cash for rent.

   Each firm uses, when appropriate to do so, the following rent accounts: Rent Revenue, Rent Expense, Rent Payable, Rent Receivable, Prepaid Rent, and Unearned Rent.

9. The Missouri Realty Company rents office space to the Specialty Sales Company at the rate of $500 per month. Collection has been made for rental through January 31, 1975.

   The following transactions occurred on the dates indicated:

   (1) Feb. 2, 1975. Collection, $500.

   (2) Apr. 1, 1975. Collection, $1,000.

   (3) June 1, 1975. Collection, $1,500.

   Present dated entries in two-column journal form for the above transactions and for the adjustments from February 2 to June 30, inclusive, as they relate to the two companies.

   a. The Missouri Realty Company closes its books monthly.

   b. The Specialty Sales Company closes its books monthly.

10. The following data are selected transactions of the Covington Company. Present dated entries in two-column journal form for the transactions and for adjustments from January 15, 1975, through July 1, 1975. Assume that only the notes indicated were outstanding during this period. The accounting period is one month.

    (1) The company issued a $1,000, two-month, 12-percent promissory note on January 15, 1975, in lieu of payment on an account due that date to the White Wholesale Company.

    (2) The note and interest were paid at maturity.

    (3) The company issued a $2,000, three-month, 12-percent promissory note to the White Wholesale Company on the date of purchase of merchandise, April 1, 1975.

    (4) The note and interest were paid at maturity.

11. The following data represent a summary of all of the activity related to the notes payable of the Carnes Company for the accounting period from January 1, 1975, through March 31, 1975.

    (1) The balance in the Notes Payable account on January 1, 1975, was $10,000; in the Interest Payable account, $50.

    (2) Notes having a face value of $25,000 were issued at the time of purchase of merchandise.

    (3) Payments on notes and related interest amounted to $20,000 and $200, respectively.

    (4) The notes payable outstanding on March 31, 1975, were reviewed, and it was determined that a $5,000, six-month, 6-percent note, dated December 1, 1974, was outstanding and that interest accumulated on the other outstanding notes, all issued during the quarter, amounted to $90.

    Present entries in two-column journal form for the above transactions and for the adjustment on March 31, 1975, in accordance with each of the following sets of instructions which might be established in an accounting systems manual.

a. At the time of a payment on interest, an interest charge account is to be debited.

b. At the time of a payment on interest, a liability account is to be debited.

c. At the time of a payment on interest, an interest liability account is to be debited to the extent of the related amount previously recorded therein and an interest charge account is to be debited for the remainder.

12. The Landon Manufacturing Company paid rental on a machine for a six-month period ending August 31, 1975, by a check for $2,400, on March 2, 1975. No additional payments were made until October 1, 1975.

    Present dated entries in two-column journal form for the above transactions and for the adjustments from March 2, 1975, through September 30, 1975. Assume that:

a. The accounting period is one month.

b. The accounting period is the calendar quarter (March 31, and so on).

*13. On January 1, 1975, the Office Supplies account of the Drexel Company had a balance of $1,200. During the ensuing quarter, supplies were acquired, on account, in the amount of $6,000. On March 31, 1975, the inventory was taken and calculated to amount to $1,500.

    Present entries in two-column journal form to record the above acquisition and adjustment data in accordance with each of the following

---

* Hints, key numbers, or (partial) answers appear in the back of the book between the Appendix Tables and the Glossary.

sets of instructions which might be established in an accounting systems manual:

a. An expense account is to be debited at the time of acquisition of supplies.

b. An asset account is to be debited at the time of acquisition of supplies.

*14. Calculate the amounts of depreciation on the following assets of the A. C. Adams Company for the quarter ending March 31. Use the straight-line method.

Asset	Cost	Est. Life	Est. Residual Value
Building	$166,000	40 years	$6,000
Office Fixtures	1,200	10 years	160
Calculator	1,760	8 years	160
Typewriters	600	6 years	120
Delivery Truck	8,000	4 years	1,120

Present adjusting entry assuming the use of the following general ledger asset accounts: Building; Office Fixtures and Equipment; Delivery Truck. Use corresponding Accumulated Depreciation accounts.

15. Present entries in two-column journal form to record depreciation and depletion in the situations described below.

a. The Tanner Company purchased a machine on August 1, 1975, at an installed cost of $8,000. It is estimated that the machine will be used for six years when it will have a value of $800. The company closes its books annually on December 31. Record depreciation on this machine for 1975 and 1976.

b. A delivery truck was acquired by the Lever Sales Company on February 28, 1975, at a cost of $6,900. It is estimated that the truck will be operated 75,000 miles, after which it will be disposed of at an estimated price of $900. The mileage readings at March 31, April 30, and May 31, were 2,400 miles, 5,000 miles, and 7,500 miles, respectively. Record depreciation for March, April, and May.

c. The Pana Mining Company extracted 15,000 tons of ore from its mine during June 1975. The original cost of the ore deposit was $2,750,000. The original estimate of a deposit of 2,500,000 tons of ore has been continued. Record the depletion for June.

d. The Levy Company contracted for the construction of a building on January 2, 1975. The construction was undertaken immediately and the building was completed and placed into use on September 1, 1975. The contract price was $210,000. It is estimated that the building will be in use for fifty years, after which it will have a residual value of $12,000. Record the depreciation for 1975.

16. The sales, all on account, of the Nelson Company, in 1975, its first year of operation, were $500,000. Collections totaled $450,000. At December 31, 1975, it was estimated that 1½ percent of sales on account would likely be uncollectible. On that date, specific accounts in the amount of $2,500 were written off.

The company's trial balance before adjustment on December 31, 1976, included the following accounts and balances:

Accounts Receivable (Dr.) .... $ 60,000
Allowance for Uncollectible Accounts (Dr.)   3,000
Sales, Uncollectible Accounts Adjustment ....   —
Sales (Cr.) 600,000
Collection of Accounts Written Off (Cr.)   300

It was concluded that the estimated uncollectible account rate of 1½ percent of sales should be applied to 1976 operations.

Present summary entries in two-column journal form which portray the following:

a. Transactions and adjustments of 1975 related to sales and customers' accounts.

b. Transactions of 1976 resulting in the above trial balance amounts.

c. Adjustment for estimated uncollectibles for 1976.

17. The trial balance of the Wagner Company at the end of 1975, following the first year of operations, include $18,000 of outstanding customers' accounts. An analysis reveals that 90 percent of the total credit sales of the year had been collected and that no accounts had been charged off as uncollectible.

The auditor estimated that 1 percent of the total credit sales would be uncollectible.

On January 31, 1976, it was concluded that the account of H. J. Williams, who had owed a balance of $200 for six months, was uncollectible and should be written off at that time.

On July 1, 1976, the amount owed by H. J. Williams, previously written off, was collected in full.

Present dated entries in two-column journal form to record the following:

a. Adjustment for estimated uncollectible accounts on December 31, 1975.

b. Write-off of the H. J. Williams account on January 31, 1976.

c. Collection of the H. J. Williams account on July 1, 1976. Assume that it is felt that there is evidence that the account should not have been written off as uncollectible.

d. Collection of the H. J. Williams account on July 1, 1976. Assume that it is felt that there is evidence that the adjustment on December 31, 1975, was excessive. (Use special account.)

*18. In recording the adjusting entries of the Hammond Sales Company, Inc., at the end of 1975, the following adjustments were omitted:

(1) Depreciation on the delivery truck of $1,500.

(2) Insurance expired on the delivery truck of $300.

(3) Interest accrued on notes payable of $75.

(4) Interest accrued on notes receivable of $165.

Indicate the effect (exclusive of income tax implications) of these omissions on the following items in the financial statements prepared on December 31, 1975:

a. Current assets

b. Noncurrent assets

c. Current liabilities

d. Selling expenses

e. Net income

f. Retained earnings.

19. The following data relate to selected accounts of the Acme Packing Company during 1975. Present entries in two-column journal form. Assume that the books are closed monthly.

(1) The Office Supplies account on February 1 had a balance of $360. During the month acquisitions recorded totaled $180. On February 28, an inventory was taken and calculated to be $350. Record the February 28 adjustment.

(2) Referring to the data of (1) above, assume that the acquisitions had been debited to the Office Supplies Expense account. Record the February 28 adjustment.

(3) An invoice dated January 5 from the Handy Packing Material Company for shipping cartons amounting to $495 was discovered in the end-of-January audit and is to be recorded.

(4) Rental of a new canning machine is to be paid at the rate of 10 cents per case canned, with payments to be made quarterly. In July, 20,000 cases were canned; in August, 25,000 cases; in September, 10,000 cases. Payment for the quarter was made on October 1. Record related transactions and adjustments.

(5) The company reads its own electric meters in order to obtain a more accurate determination of its periodic costs. The calculation for the month of September is as follows: total current consumed, $600 of which $520 applies to the packing operations and $80 to the general offices. An invoice for the period from September 10 through October 12 is received on October 28 from the Central Power and Light Company for $630 and is paid immediately. Record the above data.

20. Present entries in two-column journal form for each of the following separate sets of data:

a. On January 15, 1975, a $2,000, two-month, 12-percent note was received by the company. Present adjusting entries at the end of each month and the entry for collection at maturity.

b. The company uses one Merchandise account to record the inventory, purchases, and purchases adjustments. The balance on December 31, 1975, was $480,000. The inventory of merchandise on hand at that time was $70,000. Present the adjusting entry.

c. The company rents out part of its building for office space at the rate of $500 a month, payable in advance for each calendar quarter of the year. The quarterly rental was received on February 5, 1975. Present adjusting and collection entries for the quarter. Assume the books are closed monthly.

d. The company leased branch office space at $1,000 a month. Payment is to be made the first of each six-month period. Payment of $6,000 was made on January 2, 1975. Present payment and adjusting entries through February 28, 1975. Assume that the books are closed monthly.

e. The balance of the Unexpired Insurance account on October 1, 1975, was $200. On December 1, 1975, the company renewed its insurance for another three years by payment of $3,960. Present renewal and adjusting entries through December 31, 1975. Assume the books are closed quarterly.

*f. The Office Supplies on Hand account had a balance of $300 on December 1, 1975. Purchases of supplies in the amount of $380 were recorded in the Office Supplies Expense account during the month. The inventory of office supplies on December 31, 1975, was $290. Present any necessary adjusting entry at December 31, 1975.

g. A building was constructed at a cost of $250,000. It was estimated that it would have a useful life of fifty years from the date of occupancy, October 31, 1975, and a residual value of $10,000. Present the adjusting entry for the depreciation of the building in 1975. Assume that the books are closed annually at December 31.

h. Experience indicates that 1 percent of the accounts arising from sales on account will not be collected. The Allowance for Uncollectible Accounts account had a debit balance of $200 on December 31, 1975. Sales on account during 1975 were $180,000. A list of uncollectible accounts totaling $400 as of December 31, 1975 was compiled. Present entries for the write off of the uncollectible accounts and the adjustment as of December 31, 1975. The books are closed annually.

*21. The following trial balance is taken from the books of the Burton Shoe Stores, Inc., at April 30, 1975. The books were closed on March 31, 1975.

Accounts Receivable	$ 30,000	
Accounts Payable		$ 9,000
Allowance for Uncollectible Accounts		3,000
Cash on Hand	600	
Cash in Bank	5,000	
Customers' Deposits		200
Capital Stock		90,000
Accumulated Depreciation		12,000
Expense Control	9,000	
Furniture and Fixtures	20,000	
Income Tax Expense	—	
Income Tax Payable		1,800
Interest Earned		10
Interest Charges on Notes	—	
Interest Payable		600
Interest Receivable	50	
Merchandise Cost of Goods Sold	—	
Merchandise Inventory	90,000	
Merchandise Purchases	73,000	
Notes Payable		20,000
Notes Receivable	5,000	
Payroll Taxes Payable		162
Prepaid Rent	200	
Rent Payable		—
Retained Earnings		10,803
Sales		88,000
Unexpired Insurance	3,550	
Withheld Income Tax		825
	$236,400	$236,400

Additional data:

(1) The Customers' Deposits account represents deposits that have been received from customers on orders not yet delivered. A review of the outstanding balance reveals that one such order in the

amount of $75 has been delivered and charged to the customer's account in the accounts receivable ledger. Also, it was determined that a deposit of $35 on April 10 was recorded as a sale, although the goods have not as yet been delivered.

(2) The $5,000 note receivable is dated February 1, 1975, and is due August 1, 1975. It bears interest at 6 percent per annum. A two-month, 6-percent note for $4,000 was collected with interest on April 15. The collection was recorded properly.

(3) The insurance premiums are $2,700 per annum.

(4) At April 1, 1975, rent had been prepaid to April 15, 1975. No rent payment was made during the month.

(5) Depreciation of 12 percent of cost per annum is to be charged on the furniture and fixtures.

(6) The $20,000 of notes payable represents a single note which bears interest at 9 percent per annum. The note is dated December 1, 1974, and is due June 1, 1976. Interest is to be paid on June 1 and December 1 of each year.

(7) It is estimated that 1½ percent of the charge sales of the month will prove to be uncollectible. Total charge sales, after giving effect to the correction of (1), were $70,400.

(8) The employer's share of payroll taxes for the month is $374.

(9) The merchandise inventory at April 30, 1975, is $88,500.

(10) Assume that taxable income is the same as net income reported on the financial statements. Use a tax rate of 40 percent.

Present adjusting entries in two-column journal form.

22. The following trial balance is taken from the books of the Knowland Clothing Company on July 31, 1975. The company closes its books monthly.

Accounts Payable		$ 11,000
Accounts Receivable	$ 18,000	
Accumulated Depreciation—Delivery Equipment		1,200
Accumulated Depreciation—Furniture and Fixtures		4,040
Advances by Customers		540
Allowance for Uncollectible Accounts		1,200
Allowance for Purchase Discounts	—	—
Cash in Bank	4,500	
Change Fund	100	
Capital Stock		40,000
Delivery Equipment	2,640	
Delivery Supplies and Repairs	145	
Depreciation of Delivery Equipment	—	—
Depreciation of Furniture and Fixtures—Office	—	—
Depreciation of Furniture and Fixtures—Sales	—	—
Dividends Declared	—	—
Dividends Payable	—	—
Furniture and Fixtures	12,000	
Income Tax Charge	—	—
Income Tax Payable		3,500
Insurance Expense—Office	—	—
Insurance Expense—Sales	—	—
Leasehold	10,800	
Merchandise Cost of Goods Sold	—	—
Merchandise Inventory	30,000	

Merchandise Purchases	19,500	
Miscellaneous General Expenses	100	
Office Stationery and Postage Expense	88	
Payroll Taxes—Office	—	—
Payroll Taxes—Sales	—	—
Payroll Taxes Payable		55
Purchase Discounts		360
Rent—Office	—	—
Rent—Sales	—	—
Retained Earnings		13,068
Salaries—Office	400	
Salaries and Commissions—Sales	2,020	
Salaries and Commissions Payable		500
Sales		25,000
Uncollectible Accounts Adjustment	—	—
Unexpired Insurance	450	
Withheld Income Tax		280
	$100,743	$100,743

Additional data:

(1) Depreciation on delivery equipment is to be calculated at 25 percent of cost per annum.

(2) Depreciation on furniture and fixtures is to be calculated at 10 percent of cost per annum. This depreciation is allocable 90 percent to sales and 10 percent to office activities.

(3) The leasehold represents long-term rent paid in advance by Knowland. The monthly amortization is $300. This rent is allocable 95 percent to sales and 5 percent to office activities.

(4) One invoice of $240 for the purchase of merchandise from the Peoria Company was recorded during the month as $204.

(5) Commissions unpaid at July 31, 1975, are $280. All salaries have been paid. The balance in the Salaries and Commissions Payable account represents the amount of commissions unpaid at July 1.

(6) Merchandise was recently delivered to a customer, J. V. Morgan, and charged to Accounts Receivable, although the customer had paid $150 in advance.

(7) The estimated uncollectible account rate is 1 percent of the charge sales of the month. Charge sales were 70 percent of the sales of the month.

(8) An analysis of outstanding customers' accounts indicates that two accounts totaling $140 should be considered as uncollectible.

(9) Discounts of 2 percent are available on $10,000 of suppliers' invoices.

(10) The employer's share of payroll taxes is 6 percent of the salaries and commissions earned during the month. [Note data in (5) above.]

(11) The balance in the Unexpired Insurance account relates to a three-year policy that went into effect on January 1, 1975. The insurance is allocable 80 percent to sales and 20 percent to office activities.

(12) A dividend of $1,000 was declared on July 31, 1975.

(13) The inventory of merchandise on July 31, 1975, was $29,500.

Present adjusting entries in two-column journal form at July 31, 1975.

23. The trial balance of The North Sales Company as of March 31, 1975, appears below. The accounting period covers three months of operations.

Accounts Receivable	$ 30,000	
Accumulated Depreciation		$ 10,000
Advances by Customers	—	—
Allowance for Uncollectible Accounts		400
Capital Stock		50,000
Cash in Bank	8,000	
Cash on Hand	725	
Cost of Goods Sold	—	—
Expense Control	15,295	
Furniture and Fixtures	20,000	
Income Tax Charge	—	—
Income Tax Payable	—	—
Interest Charges on Notes	40	
Interest Earned on Notes		50
Interest Payable		30
Interest Receivable	—	—
Merchandise	95,000	
Notes Payable		5,400
Notes Receivable	4,000	
Payroll Taxes Payable		72
Retained Earnings		13,160
Sales		82,600
Store Supplies on Hand	150	
Unexpired Insurance	480	
Vouchers Payable		11,528
Withheld Income Tax		450
	$173,690	$173,690

Additional data:

(1) A statement is received from the bank after the trial balance was taken. A comparison of the statement and accompanying documents with the accounting records indicates that:

A deposit of $150 on March 31 had not been journalized.

The bank has deducted $3 for collection and exchange fees that have not been entered on the books.

A check in the amount of $89 in payment of an advertising invoice of that amount had been recorded in the company records as $98.

(2) The furniture and fixtures are depreciated at the rate of 1 percent per month.

(3) The total of the estimated uncollectibles to arise from sales of the quarter is 1½ percent of the total sales.

(4) The inventory of merchandise on March 31 is $34,600.

(5) The insurance premiums are $960 a year.

(6) The employer's share of payroll taxes for the quarter is $500, of which $332 has been recognized previously at times of payment.

(7) The note receivable is a three-month, 12-percent note dated January 15, 1975.

(8) The notes payable consist of two notes as follows:

A $30,000, six-month 12-percent note dated December 1, 1974.

A $2,400, three-month, 10-percent note dated January 15, 1975.

(9) Inventory of store supplies on hand at March 31, 1975, is $190.

(10) A review of the Accounts Receivable Subsidiary Ledger reveals that one account with a $120 balance is deemed to be uncollectible. One account has a credit balance of $280.

(11) Federal income tax for the quarter is estimated to be $1,440.

a. Prepare adjusting entries in two-column journal form. Use only the accounts listed in the trial balance.

b. Make entries to an Expense Control account and indicate parenthetically the subsidiary ledger account affected.

24. R. E. Coleman operates the Capitol Barber Shop. A trial balance of the ledger at April 30, 1975, is as follows:

Accounts Payable		$ 280
Accumulated Depreciation		1,800
Barber Supplies on Hand	$ 893	
Barber Supplies Used	—	—
Cash in Bank	1,260	
Cash on Hand	200	
R. E. Coleman, Capital		4,947
Depreciation of Equipment and Furniture	—	—
Equipment and Furniture	9,500	
Insurance Expense	—	—
Interest on Notes Payable	—	—
Interest Payable		35
Linen Expense	80	
Miscellaneous Expense	317	
Notes Payable		3,000
Payroll Taxes	—	—
Payroll Taxes Payable		59
Prepaid Rent	300	
Rent Expense	—	—
Revenue from Barber Services		4,800
Salaries of Barbers	2,686	
Salaries Payable		132
Unexpired Insurance	180	
Withheld Income Tax		363
	$15,416	$15,416

Additional data:

(1) Salaries are paid at the end of each week. Salaries earned since the last pay day total $396. Payments to barbers during the period are charged to the Salaries of Barbers account, so the balance of Salaries Payable in the trial balance is the amount that was accrued as of March 31.

(2) The employer's share of payroll taxes is 6 percent of salaries earned during the month [see entry (1)].

(3) The bank imposes a monthly service charge of $3.

(4) Invoices are placed in an "unpaid invoices" file as received and transferred to a "paid invoices" file upon payment. During the period the payments are charged to the Barber Supplies on Hand, Equipment and Furniture, Linen Expense, Miscellaneous Expense, Prepaid

Rent, or Unexpired Insurance accounts. The unpaid invoices at March 31, 1975, related to the following: barber supplies, $150; linen expense, $20; miscellaneous expense, $110.

The unpaid invoices at April 30, 1975, relate to the following: barber supplies, $165; linen expense, $30; miscellaneous expense, $105.

(5) In reviewing the bank statement, it was determined that a check properly written to the Long Supply Company for a barber supplies invoice in the amount of $24 was recorded as a payment of $42.

(6) It was discovered that an invoice of April 1, for chairs, in the amount of $500 had been paid and charged to Barber Supplies on Hand instead of to Equipment and Furniture.

(7) Mr. Coleman had paid rent for March and April on March 16.

(8) There are two notes payable outstanding:

A two-month, 12-percent note payable to the bank for $2,000 dated March 16.

A six-month, 12-percent note payable to Barber Equipment Company, $1,000, dated January 16.

(9) The inventory of barber supplies on hand at April 30 is $150 [see entries (4), (5), and (6)].

(10) The depreciation rate on equipment and furniture is 1 percent per month [see entry (6)].

(11) Insurance expires at the rate of $15 per month.

Present adjusting entries in two-column journal form. Assume an accounting period of one month.

25. The following trial balance is taken from the ledger of the Rice Wholesale Dry Goods Company at December 31, 1975. The accounting period is the calendar year. The company operates in a rented building and subleases part of the ground floor to the Pickwick Hardware Company.

Accounts Receivable	$ 46,000	
Accumulated Depreciation		$ 13,400
Allowance for Uncollectible Accounts	2,250	
Capital Stock		250,000
Cash in Bank	6,600	
Cost of Goods Sold	—	—
Expense Control	1,133,935	
Furniture and Fixtures	75,000	
Income Tax Charge	—	—
Income Tax Payable	—	—
Interest Charges	1,075	
Interest Payable	—	—
Interest Receivable	—	
Interest Revenue		500
Merchandise	4,550,000	
Notes Payable		10,000
Notes Receivable	12,000	
Payroll Taxes Payable		1,080
Prepaid Rent	2,250	
Rent Receivable	—	—
Rent Revenue		2,250

Retained Earnings		51,040
Salaries Payable	—	—
Sales		5,500,000
Sales Discounts	—	—
Sales Returns and Allowances	27,400	
Supplies on Hand	—	—
Unearned Rent		500
Unexpired Insurance	5,200	
Vouchers Payable		27,800
Withheld Income Tax		5,140
	$5,861,710	$5,861,710

Additional data:

(1) An analysis of the accounts receivable ledger reveals the following: Individual accounts totaling $1,500 are uncollectible.

A collection of $500 on a customer's account that had been written off in 1974 has been credited to the customer's account. (Make the necessary correction. Use the Allowance for Uncollectible Accounts.)

A final balance in the Allowance for Uncollectible Accounts of $4,500 will adequately cover the probable amount of additional uncollectibles. Rice Wholesale treats charges for uncollectible accounts as Bad Debt Expense, a component of the Expense Control account.

(2) Interest has accrued on the notes receivable in the amount of $100.

(3) The inventory of supplies on hand at December 31, 1975, is $6,000.

(4) The expired insurance for the period is determined to be $2,700.

(5) The rental for the sublease is $250 a month. The balance in the Unearned Rent account is the result of an adjustment made at December 31, 1974. All collections of rent during the year have been credited to Rent Revenue.

(6) Depreciation on the furniture and fixtures is 8 percent per annum. There were no acquisitions nor dispositions during the year.

(7) The note payable of $10,000 bears interest at the rate of 10 percent per annum. The note is dated October 1, 1975.

(8) The inventory of merchandise on hand at December 31, 1975, is $275,000.

(9) On December 1, 1975 rent for the months of December, 1975 and January and February of 1976, $2,250, was paid in advance.

(10) A review of payroll data reveals the following:

(a) Salaries earned since the last salary payment date total $7,600.

(b) The present balance of the Payroll Taxes Payable account represents the FICA tax withheld from payments to employees during December 1975; the employer owes an equal amount. In addition, the employer will become liable for a tax on all of the $7,600 earned since the last pay period at the rate of 6 percent when salary payments to employees are made in Jannary 1976.

(11) The federal income tax applicable to the earnings of 1975 is calculated to be $18,160.

Present adjusting entries in two-column journal form as of December 31, 1975.

*26. The following trial balance was taken from the ledger of the Schnure Stores, Inc., at the close of business March 31, 1975. The company closes its books quarterly.

Accounts Receivable	$ 94,000	
Accumulated Depreciation		$ 17,000
Advances by Customers	—	—
Allowances for Uncollectible Accounts		1,400
Bonus to Manager	—	—
Bonus Payable	—	—
Capital Stock		160,000
Cash in Bank	8,270	—
Cost of Goods Sold	—	—
Expense Control	62,960	
Furniture and Fixtures	25,000	
Income Taxes	—	—
Income Taxes Payable	—	—
Interest Charges on Notes	620	
Interest Earned on Notes	—	—
Interest Payable		400
Interest Receivable	80	
Merchandise	376,000	
Notes Payable		24,000
Notes Receivable	9,600	
Payroll Taxes Payable		360
Prepaid Insurance	1,560	
Prepaid Rent	1,200	
Retained Earnings		13,860
Sales		326,000
Sales Returns and Allowances	6,000	
Sales Tax Payable		9,600
Supplies on Hand	1,200	
Undeposited Cash	500	
Vouchers Payable		32,400
Withheld Income Tax		1,970
	$586,990	$586,990

Additional Data:
(1) A deposit of $1,250 was made up, journalized, and posted on March 31 but actually was not deposited in the bank until April 1.
(2) The net total of balances in the customers' ledger is $94,025.
   The following facts were revealed when the accounts and entries were reviewed:
   Accounts having credit balances total $650.
   A $30 entry in the general journal representing a credit memo issued for a price adjustment was not posted to the customer's account.
   An error was discovered in computing the balance of a customer's account in the subsidiary ledger. The debit balance should be $325 instead of $320 as originally computed.
(3) The merchandise inventory at March 31 is $130,000.
(4) The insurance policies all expire on July 1, 1976. No payments on insurance policies were made this quarter.

(5) The rent is $1,200 per month and has been paid through May 31, 1975.

(6) The estimated uncollectibles to arise from the sales of the period are 1 percent of net sales.

(7) Depreciation on furniture and fixtures is 8 percent of cost per annum.

(8) All supplies purchased are charged to Supplies Used, a component of Expense Control. The inventory of supplies on hand at March 31 is $2,600.

(9) The employer's share of payroll taxes has been paid through March 1. The employer's share for March is calculated to be $1,680.

(10) The Notes Receivable account contains a 10-percent note for $9,600 dated December 1, 1974, and due June 1, 1975.

(11) The Notes Payable account contains a single 10-percent note for $24,000, dated January 15, 1975, and due July 15, 1975. All interest payable at March 31 is interest due on this note.

(12) The manager is to be paid a bonus of 10 percent of the pre-tax income of the enterprise exclusive of the bonus.

(13) The income tax for the quarter is estimated to be $2,160.

Prepare adjusting entries in two-column journal form as of March 31, 1975.

Chapter 11

Periodic Procedures: Preparing Financial Statements

The preceding chapter illustrated the types of adjusting entries that are made at the end of an accounting period. After adjusting entries have been made, the adjusted trial balance can be prepared to check the arithmetic and assemble data in a convenient place. The accountant can then begin to prepare financial statements, which is the subject of this chapter.

PRIMARY FINANCIAL STATEMENTS

The *income statement*, commonly called the earnings statement and, formerly the profit and loss statement, is generally viewed as the most important of the financial statements. It presents the results of operations for the period—the revenue earned and the expenses incurred—and indicates the participation in the earnings by the various investors in the capital of the enterprise. At best, however, it is not more than a reasonably accurate statement of the operating results of the accounting period just ended. The income statement alone indicates little or nothing about the future or what the results would have been under different conditions.

The *balance sheet* presents the balances of the accounts that will be carried forward into the next accounting period. The totals of the assets and equities, although often used in the calculation of certain ratios as explained in Chapter 26, are relatively unimportant. They do furnish a rough indication of the total resources employed by the firm, but they serve primarily as evidences of arithmetic completeness and accuracy, much the same as the totals of a trial balance. Certain individual items and groups of accounts, however, are of considerable significance. For example, a comparison of the total current liabilities with the total current assets provides an indication of short-term financial solvency. The financial plan or method of financing, the relative use of common stock, preferred stock, bonds, bank loans, and so forth, can be observed by inspecting the liabilities and stockholders' equity section of the statement; something about the nature of the business can be discovered from the types of assets which it holds.

To call a balance sheet a "statement of financial condition" or "statement of financial position," as is frequently done, is not objectionable, provided the significance and method of derivation of the amounts are understood and considered in subsequent analysis of the financial statements. It is important to keep four points in mind. First, the valuations on the balance sheet are not typically homogeneous; some amounts represent current costs and prices while others, especially noncurrent assets, may reflect costs and prices running back through the years when assets were acquired at quite different price levels. Second, the balance sheet amounts do not indicate what the business would realize on a sale, either of its individual assets piecemeal or in its entirety as a going concern. Third, the balance sheet amounts give little indication of the cost of reproducing or replacing either any particular asset or the group of assets as a whole. Fourth, some of the most important resources of the firm may not be shown at all or may be assigned only a nominal value. The skill and loyalty of its working force and management, the efficient technical processes and procedures which it has developed, its good credit standing, and the public's favorable attitude toward its products may be among the chief factors in explaining the value of a company, but they are not usually indicated on the balance sheet.

The balance sheet usually reflects the costs of previous investments or commitments and the techniques that have been applied in spreading these costs and commitments over the accounts and the accounting periods. The influence of past costs, of course, affects the income statement, particularly in connection with such items as depreciation, but, in general, the income statement is dominated by figures that have originated in the most recent accounting periods. It therefore tends to be more dynamic and to reflect current conditions to a greater extent than the balance sheet. The balance sheet is an important statement for the accountant and the business executive, but its meaning and significance have frequently been misunderstood and exaggerated.

Whereas formerly the income statement was considered primarily a connecting link in tying together two balance sheets, now the income statement is generally considered the dominant statement. The balance sheet is now considered a statement of "investment," that is, of uses of capital (assets) and its sources (equities), rather than of "value."

The statement of retained earnings is a connecting link between the income statement and the balance sheet. There should always be a positive demonstration that the retained income for the year, when added to the adjusted balance of retained earnings, will "balance" the balance sheet, that is, agree with the amount of retained earnings shown on the year-end statement. This demonstration may be made at the foot of the income statement or in the stockholders' equity section of the balance sheet, thus dispensing with a separate schedule. A separate statement of retained earnings may be useful if there are several transactions affecting retained earnings during the period, because all such events should be presented clearly in the set of financial statements. The statement of retained earnings, then, begins with the balance carried forward from the beginning of the period and indicates systematically all of the increases and decreases that have taken place during the period, including retained earnings (prior-period) adjustments, the net income earned, dividends declared, and retained earnings appropriations (explained in Chapter 17). Since prior-period adjustments and retained earnings appropriations are becoming increasingly rare, statements of retained earnings are tending to fall into disuse. In a sole proprietorship or partnership, a similar reconciliation of beginning and ending balances in the owner's or partners' capital accounts should be shown in some financial statement.

Another primary statement, the statement of changes in financial position, is designed to summarize the financing and investing activities of the firm during the period, with emphasis on the way funds have been generated from operations. The statement of changes in financial position is just as important as—some think more important than—the balance sheet. Generally accepted accounting principles require that such a statement be presented any time an income statement and balance sheet are presented. The method of preparing the statement and the kinds of transactions reported in it are sufficiently different from what has been presented to this point in the book that we consider that statement and its preparation only after the discussion of the many transactions that affect flows of funds. It is not less important than the other financial statements merely because we have not yet discussed it.

The income statement and balance sheet are frequently supported by subsidiary schedules, which provide detailed lists and calculations to support certain individual items in the financial statements. For example, the income statement may contain one item called Selling Expenses with the details of this group omitted and shown in a supporting schedule. The balance sheet may show property, plant, and equipment on one line with an accompanying footnote schedule showing the composition of the items in the group.

Statements prepared for stockholders and general publication are more condensed than those prepared for the management, because the details of operations would probably be of little interest to the general public and might serve to divert attention from the more significant amounts.

FORM OF THE INCOME STATEMENT

The income statement is not a highly standardized form. In published annual reports to stockholders two formats, the "single-step" form and the "multiple-step" are used. As indicated in Chapter 7, generally accepted accounting principles specify that the income statements distinguish between those items entering into ordinary income (income before extraordinary items) and the extraordinary items. The terms *single-step* and *multiple-step* refer to the presentation of the ordinary income section.

In the single-step form all revenue items are grouped together and totaled, and all expense items are grouped and totaled; the difference is the income before extraordinary items. A frequently adopted variation within the single-step form is one in which income before income taxes is presented as a subtotal, and then income taxes are deducted to arrive at income before extraordinary items. The single-step form is used in most illustrations throughout this textbook.

The multiple-step form contains several intermediate balances, with sections such as net sales, cost of goods sold, operating expenses, other revenues and expenses, income taxes, and other sections as desired. Over the years the use of the multiple-step form in published reports has declined steadily.

Model Income Statement: Wright Merchandise Company

The income statement of the Wright Merchandise Company in Schedule 11.1 is an example of a simplified income statement. Certain additional items are not included in the model but are introduced in other chapters as the phenomena on which they report are discussed. For example, the income statement presentation of extraordinary items is shown in Chapter 7. The statement in Schedule 11.1 is based upon the data, adjusting entries, and adjusted trial balance presented in Chapter 10.

Comments on Income Statement Form

The heading of the statement should always show the name under which the business is conducted, the title of the statement, and the period covered. Notice that the income statement is always prepared for a period of time— "for the year 1975," "for the three months ending March 31, 1975," and so forth—and not for a specific date.

The statement is presented in the single-step form. Accordingly, the ordinary income section is composed of two subsections, revenues and expenses. The revenue section includes the primary source of revenue with related adjustments and other revenues. This section includes other items such as gains on disposition of assets or settlement of liabilities, which are of a special nature but do not meet the criteria to be extraordinary items.

The expenses section presents several subclassifications that are useful in subsequent analysis of the financial statements. The cost of goods sold is presented as an individual item although the calculation of the amount can also be presented in the detail shown in Chapter 9. The single-step form does not show the "gross margin," illustrated in Chapter 9, even though it might be shown in the detailed statements prepared for management uses.

The distinction between "selling" and "administrative expenses" rarely is entirely precise. In condensed published reports they frequently are combined. Those expenses which are exclusively, or almost exclusively, associated with selling activities or for which the sales manager may be

SCHEDULE 11.1

WRIGHT MERCHANDISE COMPANY
Statement of Income and Retained Earnings
For the Month of June 1975

Revenues			
Sales		$56,645	
Less: Sales Allowances	$1,025		
Sales Discounts	1,000		
Sales Taxes	1,620		
Sales, Uncollectible Accounts Adjustment	250	3,895	
Net Sales		$52,750	
Interest Earned on Notes		9	
Total Revenues			$52,759
Expenses			
Cost of Goods Sold		$40,000	
Selling Expenses:			
Sales Salaries	$3,100		
Payroll Taxes	280		
Depreciation of Building	50		
Depreciation of Furniture & Fixtures	100		
Other Selling Expenses	1,208		
Total Selling Expenses		4,738	
Administrative Expenses			
Office Salaries	$2,550		
Payroll Taxes	230		
Property Taxes	350		
Insurance Expense	60		
Collection and Exchange	5		
Cash Short and Over	1		
Other Office Expenses	500		
Total Administrative Expenses		3,696	
Interest Charges			
On Notes Payable	$ 25		
On Mortgage Payable	50		
Total Interest Charges		75	
Federal Income Tax		1,275	
Total Expenses			49,784
Net Income			$ 2,975
Retained Earnings, June 1, 1975			4,558
Retained Earnings, June 30, 1975			$ 7,533
Earnings per Common Share (10,000 shares outstanding)	$.30		

said to be responsible are designated as "selling expenses." The "administrative expenses" relate to the overall administration of the business and those expenses which, while partly related to sales activity, cannot easily or accurately be divided among various activities. The division is made primarily to facilitate reading and comprehending the nature of the operating expenses. Consistency in the adopted classification is important when one period is compared with another.

Such items as depreciation and taxes may sometimes be analyzed in order to allocate an appropriate portion to each class of expenses. In a merchandising concern the depreciation may be included entirely among the selling expenses on the assumption that the assets are used primarily for selling activities. Tax expenses, other than payroll and income taxes, frequently are assigned to the general and administrative expense category.

Interest charges are presented as a separate category of expense. It is generally desirable to distinguish between interest on current and long-term obligations.

Income taxes are included among expenses. The taxes related to the ordinary income reported on the statement customarily are classified between those currently payable and those whose payment is deferred to a later date, as explained in Chapter 15. The model shown here omits that complication.

An "other" expense category often shown, but not included in the model, provides for the inclusion of certain unusual deductions such as a loss from foreign exchange fluctuations and the losses on disposition of assets or settlements of liabilities which do not meet the criteria to be extraordinary items; these are viewed as other expenses.

Current income statement presentation requires that any extraordinary items be shown separately from the elements of ordinary income. The income taxes attributable to the extraordinary items are presented in this section. The nature and criteria of extraordinary items are discussed in Chapter 7.

Combining the ordinary income section and the extraordinary items results in the *net income*. Note that this is the first and only reference in the income statement to net income. Further, the income is the total for all classes of stockholders, both preferred and common.

Current practice requires that earnings per share data be presented in the annual report to stockholders, preferably attached to the income statement, as in Schedule 11.1. The determination of the earnings per share amounts can be more complicated than shown here and is explained in Chapter 26.

THE STATEMENT OF RETAINED EARNINGS

A reconciliation of opening and closing balances of retained earnings should be made. In the Wright Merchandise Company example, the income statement is entitled statement of income and retained earnings. This follows the frequently adopted practice of combining the income and retained earnings statements. Such a combined statement is particularly appropriate when the net income for the period and dividends declared are the only changes in the Retained Earnings account. In the example, no dividends were declared in June of 1975.

A separate statement, which acts as a link between the income statement and the balance sheet, is sometimes prepared. It presents the changes that have taken place in retained earnings during the period and shows the calculation of the new balance at the close of the period. The form in Schedule 11.2 indicates the arrangement and content of a statement that includes several items affecting the retained earnings balance. Note that this illustration is not based upon the same data as the other statements in the chapter.

SCHEDULE 11.2

THE MARLEY PRODUCTS COMPANY
Statement of Retained Earnings
For the Year 1975

Retained earnings, January 1, 1975	
As previously reported	$5,800,000
Adjustment—Refund of 1971 income tax	100,000
As restated	$5,900,000
Net income to shareholders for 1975	1,500,000
Total retained earnings available for distribution	$7,400,000
Dividends:	
Cash dividends—	
Preferred stock	$ 120,000
Common stock	720,000
Stock dividend (5 percent)	360,000
Total dividends	$1,200,000
Retained earnings, December 31, 1975	$6,200,000

FORM OF THE BALANCE SHEET

The customary balance sheet form presents the items in two major groups: (1) assets and (2) liabilities and proprietorship or stockholders' equity. Within the two groups the current assets and current liabilities are shown first. Another form arranges the items so that the current position and the amount of shareholders' equity are emphasized. The items are presented in the following order: current assets minus current liabilities plus noncurrent assets minus long-term liabilities equals shareholders' equity. When this form is used, the statement is usually called a statement of financial position or condition. This form is illustrated in Chapter 25.

The customary balance sheet form is illustrated in Chapter 2. There the assets are divided into two classifications, current and noncurrent. The current group includes those assets expected to be realized in cash, sold, or consumed within a year, or within the firm's normal operating cycle if that is longer than one year. Although some prepayments, such as insurance, extend beyond a year, they are usually included in the current group.

The noncurrent assets are usually classified in three to five groups with some items being presented singly. Regulation S-X of the Securities and Exchange Commission requires the following classifications: current assets; investments; fixed assets; intangible assets; other assets and deferred charges. The classification title of "fixed assets," formerly used extensively, has been replaced most frequently by the designation property, plant, and equipment.

Following the basic accounting equation, Assets = Liabilities + Owners' Equity, the second major group on the balance sheet of a corporation generally recognizes the two components with a title such as "liabilities and stockholders' equity." The term "shareholders'" is frequently used in place of stockholders'; "investment" is frequently used for equity.

Current liabilities include those expected to be extinguished with current assets or replaced by other current liabilities, usually within a year.

The noncurrent liability grouping has many variations in the subgrouping in published reports. The category long-term debt is used to include long-term notes, loans, bonds, mortgages, and leases. Other noncurrent liabilities are frequently listed individually without further classification or under subgroupings such as the following: other liabilities, deferred credits, reserves, and minority interests in subsidiaries. Using the term *reserve* no longer has authoritative support and, as explained in Chapter 17, is deplorable.

The ownership section will vary in form according to the type of business organization. In the case of a sole proprietorship, a single title— John H. Butler, Capital—may be sufficient. In a partnership statement each partner's capital balance should be shown clearly. The corporate balance sheet should present the capital stock accounts for each class of shares, including parenthetically the significant features of each stock contract, the other accounts reflecting transactions with stockholders (frequently a single item entitled additional paid-in capital), and retained earnings. The stockholders' equity accounts are discussed in Chapters 16 and 17.

Model Balance Sheet Form and Comments

The balance sheet of the Blackstone Manufacturing Company shown in Schedule 11.3 presents a model balance sheet form. This format will be the basis of the balance sheets in the remainder of this text.

The heading of a balance sheet should give the name under which the business operates, the title of the statement, and the date. The date should indicate the last day of the accounting period.

The choice of a vertical or horizontal arrangement of the two major divisions is merely a matter of expediency. If the number of items is not large, a vertical arrangement may be convenient, but ordinarily, except in the case of condensed statements, a horizontal arrangement which uses two pages is more effective.

The current asset section of the model shows the items normally found in this section in the customary order. The noncurrent assets are classified into three subgroups: investments; property, plant, and equipment; intangibles.

Three groups of liabilities are set forth in the model statement form: current liabilities; long-term debt; indeterminate-term liabilities. The presentation of the current liabilities and long-term debt classifications as to detail and the total figure is in accord with present reporting practice. There is a wide variation in the presentation of the other noncurrent liability items in present reporting practice. These additional items are usually presented individually without further classification or in Deferred Credit or Reserves classifications. The total amount of liabilities is rarely presented even though the liability classification heading is prominently displayed. All items on the balance sheet should be classified as assets, liabilities, or owners' equity in accordance with the basic accounting equation. The classification "Indeterminate-term Liabilities" can be used to encompass those liabilities that do not meet the traditional criteria (discussed in Chapter 15). The two items included in the illustration, Deferred Income Taxes and Minority Interest in Consolidated Subsidiary, are included for completeness in the comprehensive model balance sheet form; they are discussed in Chapters 15 and 18, respectively.

The stockholders' equity section is further classified into contributed capital and retained earnings categories. To the extent information is available, the detail of contributed capital is reported by class of shares.

Balance Sheet: Wright Merchandise Company

The balance sheet of the Wright Merchandise Company shown in Schedule 11.4 is an adaptation of the model balance sheet form. The statement is based on the data, adjusting entries, and adjusted trial balance in the illustration in Chapter 10 and in Appendix 11.1 of this chapter. Additional information concerning the capital stock has been supplied, indicating that the shares have no par value and that 10,000 shares were authorized and issued. The current asset section presents four significant subgroupings in substantial detail. In the typical published report, the detail under the subgroup headings would not be presented; rather, the accounts would be summarized into the subgroup classifications or listed in a manner similar to that presented under the current liabilities heading.

The analysis of the Retained Earnings account could have been shown in the balance sheet in the following manner:

Stockholders' Equity

Capital Stock		$80,000
Retained Earnings:		
Balance, June 1, 1975	$4,558	
Net Income for June	2,975	
Balance, June 30, 1975		7,533
Total Stockholders' Equity		$87,533

BLACKSTONE MANU
Consolidated
December 31,

Assets

Current

Cash		$ 421,063
Marketable Securities		1,198,276
Notes Receivable		1,000,000
Accounts Receivable	$2,174,166	
Less: Allowance for Uncollectible Accounts	43,483	2,130,683
Raw Materials Inventory		615,786
Work in Process Inventory		460,000
Finished Goods Inventory		600,230
Unexpired Insurance		75,000
Prepaid Rent		289,469
Total Current Assets		$ 6,790,507

Investments

Investment in Bonds of A Co.	$ 184,000	
Investment in Common Stock of B Co.	500,411	
Total Investments		684,411

Property, Plant and Equipment

Land	$1,500,000	
Building	$ 8,000,000	
Less: Accumulated Depreciation	3,089,700	4,910,300
Machinery and Equipment	$10,500,000	
Less: Accumulated Depreciation	4,479,872	6,020,128
Total Property, Plant and Equipment		12,430,428

Intangibles

Goodwill	$ 200,000	
Patents	134,903	
Organization Costs	75,000	
Total Intangibles		409,903
Total Assets		$20,315,249

FACTURING COMPANY
Balance Sheet
1975

Liabilities and Stockholders' Equity

Current Liabilities

Notes Payable		$ 300,000
Accounts Payable		2,402,376
Wages Payable		728,149
Payroll Taxes Payable		71,851
Income Taxes Payable		741,081
Deferred Rent Revenue		86,284
Total Current Liabilities		$ 4,329,741

Long-term Debt

Mortgage Payable		$1,424,477	
Bonds Payable	$1,500,000		
Less: Discount on Bonds Payable	245,300	1,254,700	
Total Long-term Debt			2,679,177

Indeterminate-term Liabilities

Deferred Income Taxes		$ 593,938	
Minority Interest in Consolidated Subsidiary..		1,119,471	
Total Indeterminate-term Liabilities			1,713,409
Total Liabilities			$ 8,722,327

Stockholders' Equity

Preferred Stock ($100 par 6%, cumulative dividends): Par Value	$ 500,000		
Contributed in Excess of Par Value......	65,000	$ 565,000	
Common Stock ($1 par value, 1,500,000 shares authorized; 1,000,000 outstanding):			
Par Value	$1,000,000		
Contributed in Excess of Par Value	3,000,000	4,000,000	
Contributed Capital—Other		75,576	
Total		$4,640,576	
Retained Earnings		6,952,346	
Total Stockholders' Equity			11,592,922
Total Liabilities and Stockholders' Equity			$20,315,249

WRIGHT MERCHAN
Balance
June 30,

Assets

Currents Assets
Cash:

Cash on Hand	$ 420	
Cash in Bank	4,862	
Change Fund	90	
Total Cash		$ 5,372

Receivables:

Accounts Receivable		$47,975	
Less: Allowance for			
Uncollectible Accounts	$1,750		
Allowance for			
Sales Discounts	800		
		2,550	
		$45,425	
Notes Receivable	$1,550		
Interest Receivable	11		
		1,561	
Total Receivables			46,986

Inventories:

Merchandise		$45,000	
Store Supplies		550	
Total Inventories			45,550

Prepayments:

Unexpired Insurance		$ 540	
Prepaid Salaries		10	
Total Prepayments			550
Total Current Assets			$ 98,458

Property, Plant, and Equipment

Land			$ 5,450
Building		$30,000	
Less: Accumulated Depreciation		6,050	
			23,950
Furniture and Fixtures		$10,000	
Less: Accumulated Depreciation		3,100	
			6,900
Total Property, Plant, and Equipment			36,300
Total Assets			$134,758

DISE COMPANY
Sheet
1975

Liabilities and Stockholders' Equity

Current Liabilities

Vouchers Payable	$25,035	
Notes Payable	5,000	
Interest Payable	180	
Salaries Payable	150	
Payroll Taxes Payable	1,290	
Sales Tax Payable	1,620	
Withheld Income Tax	675	
Federal Income Tax Payable	1,275	
Unfilled Paid Orders	1,500	
Customers' Credit Balances	500	
Total Current Liabilities		$ 37,225

Noncurrent Liabilities

Mortgage Payable		10,000
Total Liabilities		$ 47,225

Stockholders' Equity

Capital Stock (no-par, authorized and issued 10,000 shares)	$80,000	
Retained Earnings (see Statement of Income and Retained Earnings)	7,533	
Total Stockholders' Equity		87,533
Total Liabilities and Stockholders' Equity		$134,758

CLOSING ENTRIES

After the statements for the period have been prepared, the bookkeeper must close the books. Those accounts that have been opened for the purpose of accumulating information for only one accounting period must be closed and prepared for recording the operations of the next period. This involves transferring their balances to accounts such as Work in Process for the production cost accounts or Retained Earnings for the revenue, expense, and income-distribution accounts. During the process of checking the records, making adjustments, and preparing the statements, several days or even weeks will usually have elapsed. Journal entries must be made for the events occurring during this period and postings must be made to accounts such as Accounts Receivable, but postings should not be made to accounts that must be closed. Closing entries, then, logically should be made before recording any entries for the new period, but in practice they are inserted "as of" the last day of the period just ended.

Closing entries are merely routine steps that should be carried out with a minimum of bookkeeping. They do not produce any significant change in the accounting equation, because they do no more than merge the temporary operating accounts with the permanent accounts for which they have provided a detailed analysis during one accounting period.

Closing Production Cost Accounts

Closing entries for production cost accounts were demonstrated in Chapter 5 and are included in Appendix 11.2 of this chapter.

Closing Income Statement Accounts

There are a number of possible alternative procedures for closing the income statement accounts, all of which can accomplish the basic objective, which is to prepare the temporary or periodic operating accounts for recording the activities during the next period. These variations in procedure center around whether accounts such as the Income Summary and Cost of Goods Sold are to be used and the degree of detail shown in these accounts.

Closing Procedure: Single-Step Method

Closing entries for many of the income statement accounts are illustrated in earlier chapters. In those illustrations, the income statement accounts are closed to an Income Summary account. This method is used primarily for ease of presentation. Although we illustrate the use of the Income Summary account in this chapter, we prefer the single-step method, illustrated below, which fully accomplishes the purpose of the closing procedure.

The single-step method consists of a single journal entry which (1) debits all accounts to be closed with any credit balance, and (2) credits all accounts to be closed with any debit balance, and then (3) balances ("plugs") the entry with a credit (if there is a net addition) or a debit (if there is a net deduction) to an owners' equity account. The single-step closing entry for Wright Merchandise Company for the month of June, 1975 would be:

Sales	56,645	
Interest Earned on Notes	9	
Sales Allowances		1,025
Sales Discounts		1,000
Sales Taxes		1,620
Sales, Uncollectible Accounts Adjustment		250
Cost of Goods Sold		40,000
Sales Salaries		3,100
Payroll Taxes—Sales		280
Depreciation of Building		50
Depreciation of Furniture and Fixtures		100
Other Selling Expenses		1,208
Office Salaries		2,550
Payroll Taxes—Office		230
Property Taxes		350
Insurance Expense		60
Collection and Exchange Expense		5
Cash Short and Over		1
Other Office Expenses		500
Interest on Notes Payable		25
Interest on Mortgage Payable		50
Federal Income Tax		1,275
Retained Earnings		2,975

Closing Procedure: Income Summary Account Method

To close the books using an Income Summary account, the balances of the accounts to be closed are transferred one at a time, or in groups, to the Income Summary account and its balance is transferred to an owners' equity account. An effective technique is to make a series of closing entries using information derived from the income statement with the entries corresponding to the groups of the items on the statement. The following entries close the books of the Wright Merchandise Company using an Income Summary.

Sales	56,645	
Sales Allowances		1,025
Sales Discounts		1,000
Sales Taxes		1,620
Sales, Uncollectible Accounts Adjustment		250
Income Summary		52,750
Interest Earned on Notes	9	
Income Summary		9
Income Summary	40,000	
Cost of Goods Sold		40,000

Income Summary	4,738	
Sales Salaries		3,100
Payroll Taxes—Sales		280
Depreciation of Building		50
Depreciation of Furniture and Fixtures		100
Other Selling Expenses		1,208

Income Summary	3,696	
Office Salaries		2,550
Payroll Taxes—Office		230
Property Taxes		350
Insurance Expense		60
Collection and Exchange Expense		5
Cash Short and Over		1
Other Office Expenses		500

Income Summary	75	
Interest on Notes Payable		25
Interest on Mortgage Payable		50

Income Summary	1,275	
Federal Income Tax		1,275

Income Summary	2,975	
Retained Earnings		2,975

The Income Summary account would appear as follows:

Income Summary

1975				1975			
June 30	Cost of Goods Sold	40,000		June 30	Sales	52,750	
30	Selling Expenses	4,738		30	Interest Earned	9	
30	Gen. & Adm. Expenses	3,696					
30	Interest Charges	75					
30	Federal Income Tax	1,275					
30	To Retained						
	Earnings	2,975					
		52,759				52,759	

Closing Entries for Merchandise Accounts

When an adjusting entry is not made to establish the Cost of Goods Sold account and several accounts are used to obtain an analysis of the merchandise inventory and purchases, the adjustment of the Merchandise Inventory account is made as a part of the closing entries. Assume that, in lieu of the single Merchandise account, having a balance of $85,000, the company had used detailed accounts for its purchasing activities as follows: Merchandise Inventory (beginning inventory), $35,000; Purchases, $55,000; Freight-in, $500; Purchase Returns, $4,000; Purchase Allowances, $800; and Purchase Discounts, $700. If the accounts were substituted for the Cost of Goods Sold account in the single closing entry illustrated above, the entry would appear as follows:

Sales	56,645	
Interest Earned on Notes	9	
Merchandise Inventory	45,000	
Purchase Returns	4,000	
Purchase Allowances	800	
Purchase Discounts	700	
Merchandise Inventory		35,000
Purchases		55,000
Freight-in		500
Sales Allowances		1,025
Sales Discounts		1,000
Sales Taxes		1,620
Sales, Uncollectible Accounts Adjustment		250
Sales Salaries		3,100
Payroll Taxes—Sales		280
Depreciation of Building		50
Depreciation of Furniture and Fixtures		100
Other Selling Expenses		1,208
Office Salaries		2,550
Payroll Taxes—Office		230
Property Taxes		350
Insurance Expense		60
Collection and Exchange Expense		5
Cash Short and Over		1
Other Office Expenses		500
Interest on Notes Payable		25
Interest on Mortgage Payable		50
Federal Income Tax		1,275
Retained Earnings		2,975

If a Cost of Goods Sold account were to be used, the following adjusting entry, similar in form and purpose to the one for J. F. Crane, Inc. explained at the end of Chapter 9, would be made to establish the Cost of Goods Sold account:

Cost of Goods Sold	40,000	
Merchandise Inventory	45,000	
Purchase Returns	4,000	
Purchase Allowances	800	
Purchase Discounts	700	
Merchandise Inventory		35,000
Purchases		55,000
Freight-in		500

The Cost of Goods Sold account would then be closed as illustrated previously.

Thus, there are many possible variations in the form of closing entries. The only essential requirements are that the procedure be systematic, easy to understand and check, and that it close all of the appropriate accounts and transfer the undistributed income to the retained earnings or proprietorship accounts.

Ruling and Balancing

When ordinary manual bookkeeping methods are used, all closed accounts should be ruled as indicated in the Income Summary account for the

Wright Merchandise Company. Accounts that are not closed are sometimes ruled and balanced as shown in Figure 11.1. The procedure is to: (1) calculate the account balance; (2) insert the balance on the opposite side so that the sums of debits and credits will be equal; (3) rule the account in the same manner as though it were closed; and (4) bring down the balance on the correct side of the account, dated as of the first day of the new period. Ruling and balancing an account does not change it in any fundamental way, and no journal entry is made for such a step. Formal ruling and balancing of accounts is seldom necessary, but it is a convenient procedure when the accumulated totals of the debits and credits become too large to comprehend easily.

An Open Account, Ruled and Balanced
(Steps indicated in parentheses correspond to text.)

1975					**1975**					
Jan.	13		VR	121.37	Sept.	15		J	.42	
Mar.	20		VR	56.42	Nov.	12		J	3.13	
June	5		J	138.09	Dec.	31	Balance	√	360.61	(1), (2)
Aug.	18		J	1.21						
Nov.	20		VR	38.43						
Dec.	7		VR	8.64						
(3)				364.16					364.16	(3)
	1976									
(4)	Jan.	1	Balance	√	360.16					

Figure 11.1

Post-closing Trial Balance

After the closing entries have been recorded and posted, a trial balance may be taken to make sure that the ledger is still in balance and ready for the postings of the next period. Such a trial balance is called a *post-closing trial balance* and contains only balance sheet accounts. It must be taken directly from the ledger in order to serve its purpose as a test of accuracy. One effective, informal method is to prepare an adding machine tape, first of the debit balances and then of the credit balances, to be filed for future reference.

REVERSING ENTRIES

Bookkeeping procedures should be routine and simple to execute. In the absence of the reversing entries described in this section, some procedures to be carried out in the first week, month, or quarter following the close of the preceding fiscal year would have to be different from the procedures ordinarily used. *Reversing*, or *reversal*, entries are designed so that the bookkeeper's tasks (or computer programs) can be identical in all accounting periods.

First, examine the problem that reversing entries are designed to solve. Suppose that salaries are paid every other Friday, with paychecks compensating employees for the two weeks just ended. Suppose, further, that total salaries accrue at the rate of $5,000 per five-day work week. The bookkeeper is accustomed to making the following entry every other Friday:

(1) Salary Expense 10,000
    Cash 10,000
    To record salary expense and salary payments.

Suppose that paychecks are delivered to employees on Friday, December 26, 1975. Then the adjusting entry made on December 31 (or, perhaps, later) to record accrued salaries for December 29, 30, and 31 would be:

(2) Salary Expense 3,000
    Salaries Payable 3,000
    To charge 1975 operations with all salaries accrued in 1975.

The Salary Expense account would be closed as part of the December 31 closing entries. On the next pay day, January 9, the salary entry would have to be:

(3) Salary Expense 7,000
    Salaries Payable 3,000
    Cash 10,000
    To record salaries split between 1976 expense and liability
    carried over from 1975.

To make this entry, the bookkeeper would have to look back into the records to see how much of the debit is to Salaries Payable accrued from the previous year so that total debits are properly split between this year's expense and the accrued liability from last year. Notice that this entry forces the bookkeeper not only to refer to balances in old accounts but also to make an entry different from the one customarily made, entry (1).

The reversing entry, made just after the books have been closed for the preceding year, makes the salary entry for January 9, 1976, the same as that made on all other Friday pay days. The entry, made on January 2, merely *reverses* the adjusting entry (2):

(4) Salaries Payable 3,000
    Salary Expense 3,000
    To reverse the adjusting entry.

This entry results in a zero balance in the Salaries Payable account and a *credit* balance in the Salary Expense account. If entry (4) is made on January 2, then the entry on January 9 will be the customary entry (1). Entries (4) and (1) together have exactly the same effect as entry (3). The bookkeeper need not be responsible for reversing entry (4), and his task is the same every pay period. The January 9 procedures are likely to be done more efficiently.

The following entries summarize the journal entries to record salaries, both with and without reversing entries.

		(a) Using Reversing Entries		(b) Not Using Reversing Entries	

1975

12/31	Salary Expense	3,000		3,000	
	Salaries Payable		3,000		3,000
	Adjusting entry to recognize accrued salaries.				
12/31	Income Summary	261,000		261,000	
	Salary Expense		261,000		261,000
	Closing Entry.				

1976

1/2	Salaries Payable	3,000		—	
	Salary Expense		3,000		—
	To reverse the adjusting entry of December 31, 1975.				
1/9	Salary Expense	10,000		7,000	
	Salaries Payable	—		3,000	
	Cash in Bank		10,000		10,000
	To record payment of salaries.				

The procedure followed when reversing entries are used can be outlined as follows:

1. The required adjustment is made at the end of an accounting period.
2. The closing entry is made as usual.
3. As of the first day of the following period, an entry is made reversing the adjusting entry.
4. When a payment is made, the entry is made as though no adjusting entry had been recorded.

Deciding whether or not to use reversing entries is another case where cost-benefit analysis is required in deciding on record-keeping procedures. The choice of whether or not to reverse has no effect, of course, on the financial statements.

APPENDIX 11.1: WORK SHEET PREPARATION AND ILLUSTRATIONS

To facilitate the procedures at the end of the accounting period, a form known as a *work sheet* is frequently used. The work sheet does not eliminate any of the previously indicated steps, although it does change their order to the following: take the unadjusted trial balance; prepare the work sheet; construct the financial statements and supporting schedules; journalize and post adjusting entries; journalize and post closing entries; rule accounts where appropriate; prepare a post-closing trial balance.

Purpose of the Work Sheet

The principal purpose of the work sheet in accounting practice is to facilitate the preparation of the income statement and the balance sheet. The preparation of these reports is an important goal of accounting activity, and they should be prepared as promptly as possible at the close of each accounting period. The adjustments can be calculated and recorded more quickly on a work sheet than they can on the actual books of accounts; the distribution of the items to the appropriate statement columns is a rapid process; and the preparation of the statements merely requires the arrangement of the items from each set of statement columns into a more readable form. The bookkeeping in connection with the adjusting and closing entries can be completed easily and quickly after the statements have been prepared.

Another useful purpose of the work sheet is that it makes possible the preparation of interim statements without going through the formalities of journalizing adjusting entries and closing the books each time statements are prepared. It is common practice to close the books formally only once a year but to prepare monthly or quarterly statements with the help of the work sheet. Only the adjustments made at the close of the year must be journalized; the others can be made on the work sheet.

Smaller enterprises may find the work sheet unnecessary. Larger enterprises and public accountants, who often determine part or all of the adjustments as they proceed with an audit of the financial statements, find the work sheet useful, if not indispensable.

Work Sheet Form

A work sheet is, in general, any columnar form used to analyze accounting or statistical data, but the form shown in Figure 11.2 is one which arranges the trial balance, the adjustments, and the information for the two major financial statements and closing procedures in parallel vertical columns. This type of work sheet usually has eight or ten columns with pairs of columns for:

1. the unadjusted trial balance
2. adjustments
3. the adjusted trial balance (not always used)
4. the income or income and retained-earnings statement and
5. the balance sheet.

Adjusted trial balance columns are useful when there are many complicated adjustments, because the numerical accuracy of the work can be checked before extending the figures to the statement columns. In most cases they can be omitted, and the result will be to speed up the process of the preparation of the work sheet.

The work sheet form illustrated in this appendix is designed for a nonmanufacturing enterprise. A work sheet better adapted to the handling of manufacturing accounts is presented in Appendix 11.2.

Preparation of the Standard Work Sheet

The work sheet should be prepared as follows:

1. Insert the unadjusted trial balance onto the work sheet directly from the ledger.

WORK SHEET FORM

Accounts	Trial Balance		Adjustments		Adjusted Trial Balance		Income Statement		Balance Sheet	
	Dr.	Cr.	Dr.	Cr.	Dr.	Cr.	Dr.	Cr.	Dr.	Cr.

Figure 11.2

2. Collect and use any additional information necessary to determine the adjustments. While determining the adjustments for entry onto the work sheet, prepare them so that their subsequent recording in the journal is made easier.

Additional accounts may be added below the initial trial balance accounts as they are needed. Cross-number the debits and credits of each adjusting entry to facilitate checking in case of error. All adjustments, except those that require a knowledge of the amount of net income or other intermediate summary amounts, should be made before extending the amounts to the statement columns.

3. When adjusted trial balance columns are used, each item should be extended to these columns. After all the extensions are made, add the two adjusted trial balance columns and make certain that the totals are equal before proceeding.

4. Extend each account balance to one of the statement columns. When adjusted trial balance columns are used, the amounts are taken directly from those columns. When the adjusted trial balance columns are omitted, the figure appearing in the trial balance is increased or decreased by any adjustments, and the net result is entered in one of the income statement or balance sheet columns. Take care to enter a debit balance in one of the statement debit columns and a credit balance in one of the statement credit columns. The account title, together with the nature of the balance, is usually sufficient to indicate in which statement the account appears.

5. Add the two income statement columns and determine the amount of the difference to this point.

6. Calculate and record any adjustments, such as income taxes and bonuses, based upon this difference.

7. Extend any items opened or modified by the adjustment in step 6.

8. If steps 6 and 7 were required, recompute the balance of the income statement columns. If the credits exceed the debits, enter the proper caption, such as Net Income to Stockholders or Balance of Net Income, and enter the balancing amount in the income statement debit column and the balance sheet credit column. If the debits exceed the credits, enter the caption as modified to indicate the loss, and enter the balancing amount in the income statement credit column and the balance sheet debit column.

9. Add the two balance sheet columns. If they are equal, there is a strong presumption that the work has been done correctly. There are certain types of errors, however, that will not be disclosed by this test. For example, if a debit balance of an asset account is entered in the income statement debit column, the net income figure will be wrong, but the two balance sheet columns will still be equal, and no error will be indicated. Also errors in analyzing the adjustments will not be disclosed. In other words, this test of accuracy is merely an arithmetic check similar to that obtained by taking a trial balance of a ledger.

Illustration: Standard Work Sheet Form (Merchandising Concern)

The work sheet illustrated in Schedule 11.5 is based on data presented in Chapter 10 for the Wright Merchandise Company. The corresponding financial statements and closing procedures are included in the body of this chapter.

Merchandise Accounts in the Work Sheet. Only one merchandise account is used in the illustration. An adjusting entry was made for the cost of goods sold, leaving the inventory of merchandise on hand in the Merchandise account. If a number of divisions of merchandise cost are used, so that there are special accounts for such items as Merchandise Inventory, Purchases, Freight-in, and Purchase Allowances, a variation in procedure must be introduced.

Assuming that it is desirable to include all of the detailed merchandise accounts in the income statement, the procedure would be:

1. Extend all merchandise accounts to the income statement columns.

2. Insert the amount of the final merchandise inventory in the income statement credit column and in the balance sheet debit column on the same line as that which records the beginning merchandise inventory.

In Schedule 11.6 the balances in the several merchandise accounts are shown in the trial balance columns in place of the $85,000 amount shown in the earlier work sheet illustration. Notice that the items in the income statement columns are equal to a net debit of $40,000, the same as the single figure recorded before for Cost of Goods Sold. Under this method, no adjusting entry is made for the new inventory and a Cost of Goods Sold account is not shown on the work sheet. The adjustment of the Merchandise Inventory account is made at the time closing entries are recorded.

SCHEDULE 11.5

WRIGHT MERCHANDISE COMPANY—WORK SHEET—Month of June 1975

Accounts	Trial Balance Dr.	Trial Balance Cr.	Adjustments Dr.	Adjustments Cr.	Income Statement Dr.	Income Statement Cr.	Balance Sheet Dr.	Balance Sheet Cr.
Cash on Hand	421.00			(1) 1.00			420.00	
Cash in Bank	4,867.00			(2) 5.00			4,862.00	
Change Fund	100.00			(3) 10.00			90.00	
Accounts Receivable Control	47,500.00		(4b) 500.00	(4a) 25.00			47,975.00	
Allowance for Uncollectible Accounts		1,500.00		(15) 250.00				1,750.00
Allowance for Sales Discounts	200.00			(4c) 1,000.00				800.00
Notes Receivable	1,550.00						1,550.00	
Interest Receivable	2.00		(5) 9.00				11.00	
Merchandise	85,000.00			(6) 40,000.00			45,000.00	
Store Supplies	500.00		(7) 50.00				550.00	
Unexpired Insurance	600.00			(8) 60.00			540.00	
Land	5,450.00						5,450.00	
Building	30,000.00						30,000.00	
Accumulated Depreciation on Building		6,000.00		(10) 50.00				6,050.00
Furniture and Fixtures	10,000.00						10,000.00	
Accumulated Depreciation on Furniture and Fixtures		3,000.00		(9) 100.00				3,100.00
Vouchers Payable		25,035.00						25,035.00
Notes Payable		5,000.00						5,000.00
Interest Payable		105.00		(11) 50.00 (12) 25.00				180.00
Payroll Taxes Payable		780.00		(14) 510.00				1,290.00
Withheld Income Tax		675.00						675.00
Unfilled Paid Orders		1,500.00						1,500.00
Mortgage Payable		10,000.00						10,000.00
Capital Stock		80,000.00						80,000.00
Retained Earnings		4,558.00						4,558.00

Account	Trial Balance Dr.	Trial Balance Cr.	Adjustments Dr.	Adjustments Cr.	Income Statement Dr.	Income Statement Cr.	Balance Sheet Dr.	Balance Sheet Cr.
Sales		56,645.00				56,645.00		
Sales Allowances	1,000.00		(4a) 25.00		1,025.00			
Sales Salaries	3,000.00		(13) 100.00		3,100.00			
Other Selling Expenses	1,258.00			(7) 50.00	1,208.00			
Office Salaries	2,500.00		(13) 50.00		2,550.00			
Property Taxes	350.00				350.00			
Other Office Expenses	500.00				500.00			
Cash Short and Over			(1) 1.00		1.00			
Collection and Exchange Expenses			(2) 5.00		5.00			
Prepaid Salaries			(3) 10.00				10.00	
Customers' Credit Balances			(4c) 1,000.00	(4b) 500.00				500.00
Sales Discounts					1,000.00			
Interest Earned on Notes				(5) 9.00		9.00		
Cost of Goods Sold			(6) 40,000.00		40,000.00			
Insurance Expense			(8) 60.00		60.00			
Depreciation of Furniture and Fixtures			(9) 100.00		100.00			
Depreciation of Building			(10) 50.00		50.00			
Interest on Mortgage Payable			(11) 50.00		50.00			
Interest on Notes Payable			(12) 25.00		25.00			
Salaries Payable				(13) 150.00				150.00
Payroll Taxes—Sales			(14) 280.00		280.00			
Payroll Taxes—Office			(14) 230.00		230.00			
Uncollectible Accounts Adjustment			(15) 250.00		250.00			
Sales Taxes			(16) 1,620.00		1,620.00			
Sales Tax Payable				(16) 1,620.00				1,620.00
Federal Income Tax			(17) 1,275.00		1,275.00			
Federal Income Tax Payable				(17) 1,275.00				1,275.00
	194,798.00	194,798.00	45,690.00	45,690.00	53,679.00	56,654.00	146,458.00	143,483.00
Net Income to Stockholders					2,975.00			2,975.00
					56,654.00	56,654.00	146,458.00	146,458.00

SCHEDULE 11.6

WORK SHEET

Account	Trial Balance		Adjustments		Income Statement		Balance Sheet	
	Dr.	Cr.	Dr.	Cr.	Dr.	Cr.	Dr.	Cr.
Merchandise Inventory ..	35,000				35,000	45,000	45,000	
Purchases	55,000				55,000			
Freight-in	500				500			
Purchase Returns		4,000				4,000		
Purchase Allowances ...		800				800		
Purchase Discounts		700				700		

Assuming that it were desired to include the detailed accounts in the ledger as well as the Cost of Goods Sold account, an adjusting entry would be made in the Adjustments columns reversing the debits and credits as included in the Income Statement columns in the illustration and adding a debit entry to the Cost of Goods Sold line in the amount of $40,000. Only the ending inventory amount, $45,000, and the Cost of Goods Sold amount, $40,000, then would be carried to the statement columns.

The Work Sheet and the End of the Period Cycle. As was stated before, the work sheet does not replace any of the necessary steps in the accounting period cycle; rather, it reorganizes the procedure to facilitate the preparation of the financial statements. In many cases, it may be useful, but it is never essential.

APPENDIX 11.2: WORK SHEET, CLOSING, AND STATEMENTS FOR MANUFACTURING CONCERN

This appendix presents the preparation of the work sheet, financial statements, and closing entries for a manufacturing enterprise. The production cost accounts, which are set up to accumulate the details of manufacturing operations, are introduced in Chapter 5, and from time to time problems and transactions involving the use of these accounts have been presented and discussed. The principal purpose of this illustration is to bring together in one complete demonstration the accounts required for manufacturing, selling, and administrative operations. The trial balance of Glenwood Products, Inc., at the close of operations for the year ending December 31, 1975, is shown in Schedule 11.7.

GLENWOOD PRODUCTS, INC.
Trial Balance for December 31, 1975

Petty Cash Fund	$ 1,000	
Undeposited Cash	34,000	
Cash in Bank	176,000	
Accounts Receivable	760,000	
Allowance for Uncollectible Accounts		$ 24,700
Raw Material	123,030	
Work in Process	364,460	
Finished Goods	475,890	
Supplies	84,750	
Unexpired Insurance	38,500	
Land	88,000	
Buildings	1,750,000	
Buildings—Accumulated Depreciation		981,400
Equipment	2,425,000	
Equipment—Accumulated Depreciation		769,700
Accounts Payable		81,200
Notes Payable		250,000
Wages and Salaries Payable		139,340
Payroll Taxes Payable		70,480
Withheld Income Tax		36,910
Capital Stock		2,500,000
Retained Earnings		950,200
Sales		6,970,000
Sales Returns and Allowances	48,450	
Sales Discounts	86,700	
Salaries and Commissions—Selling	126,500	
Advertising	26,700	
Payroll Taxes—Selling	11,380	
Other Selling Expenses	7,620	
Salaries—Administrative	109,000	
Payroll Taxes—Administrative	9,750	
Other General and Administrative Expenses	8,750	
Interest on Notes	17,500	
Dividends Declared	250,000	
Purchases—Raw Material	1,227,070	
Direct Labor	3,473,400	
Foremen's Salaries	102,130	
Other Indirect Labor	218,050	
Repairs to Buildings and Equipment	7,260	
Property Taxes	54,600	
Payroll Taxes—Manufacturing	331,210	
Heat, Light and Power	19,760	
Other Factory Costs	17,470	
Income Taxes	300,000	
	$12,773,930	$12,773,930

The following additional information is provided. Inventories at December 31, 1975:

> Raw material, $127,380
> Work in process, $420,170
> Finished goods, $438,800.

(1) Losses from uncollectible accounts are estimated to be .5 percent of gross sales.

(2) Uncollectible accounts amounting to $27,300 are written off.

(3) Inventory of supplies at December 31, 1975, $15,630. During the year, $4,640 of office supplies and $19,350 of shipping supplies were used. All other supplies used were for the factory.

(4) Unexpired insurance at December 31, 1975, is $23,050. Of the expired insurance, $1,550 is applicable to administrative operations and the balance to the factory.

(5) Depreciation of buildings is 2.5 percent of cost. Administrative operations should be charged $4,250, and the balance should be charged to factory operations.

(6) Depreciation of equipment is 8 percent of cost. Of the total, $12,160 is to be charged to equipment in the general office, and the balance to factory equipment.

(7) The notes payable have been at $250,000 throughout the year. The interest rate is 7 percent per year.

(8) Repair cost of $700 is to be charged to general office building and equipment, and the balance to the factory.

(9) Property taxes of $5,500 are to be charged to general administrative expenses; the balance to factory operations.

(10) It is estimated that $2,150 will cover the cost of heating and lighting the general office and that the balance of the Heat, Light, and Power account applies to factory operations.

(11) The federal income tax rate is 22 percent of the first $25,000 of taxable income and 48 percent of all taxable income in excess of the amount. The company has made income tax payments of $300,000 based upon estimates of taxable income for the year.

Comments on Work Sheet Procedures

The work sheet for Glenwood Products is shown in Schedule 11.8. The numbered entries correspond to the adjustment information above. The lettered entries correspond to the explanations below.

(a) The inventories of raw material, work in process, and finished goods appearing in the trial balance which represent balances carried over from the preceding year are extended to the appropriate statement columns as debits; the new inventory figures are inserted as credits in the operating statement sections and as debits in the balance sheet section. Because the raw-material and work in process inventories enter into the calculation of the cost of goods manufactured, they appear in the cost of goods manufactured section; the finished-goods inventory figures are entered in the income and retained earnings statement section because they will be used to calculate the cost of goods sold.

(b) A technique which has not previously been demonstrated is employed for the recording of expired insurance. The total amount expired, $15,450, is charged to a single operating account, Insurance Expired, in adjustment (4). The distribution of the total amount expired between administrative and factory operations is made as the item is spread across the work sheet. A debit of $13,900 is entered in the cost of goods manufactured section and a debit of $1,550 in the income and retained earnings statement section. In the closing-entry and statement-preparation procedures the Insurance Expired account will be treated as if there were two parts: Insurance Expired (Manufacturing) and Insurance Expired (General and Administrative). The technique is also used with respect to other cost expiration allocations including: Depreciation of Buildings; Depreciation of Equipment; Repairs to Buildings and Equipment; Property Taxes; and Heat, Light, and Power accounts.

(c) Before the calculation of the federal income tax can be made, several additional steps must be taken in the construction of the work sheet:

1. Each item in the trial balance, which has not already been extended, must be extended to the appropriate statement column. All production cost accounts are entered in the cost-of-goods-manufactured section. All revenue, expense, and income-distribution accounts are entered in the income and retained-earnings statement columns. All assets, liabilities, and stockholders' equity accounts, with the exception of Retained Earnings, are entered in the balance sheet columns. Since it is planned to prepare a combined income and retained earnings statement, the balance of the Retained Earnings account appearing in the trial balance is entered as a credit in the income and retained earnings statement section.

2. The difference in the totals of the cost-of-goods-manufactured debit and credit columns is obtained, $5,662,910, which is the cost of goods manufactured for the year. The caption is indicated on the work sheet; the amount is entered as a debit in the income and retained earnings statement section and as a credit in the cost-of-goods-manufactured section.

3. The difference in the totals of the income and retained earnings statement debit and credit columns is obtained, $1,132,700. This amount will usually require various adjustments before determining the amount of taxable income. It is assumed in this illustration that the data for taxable income can be obtained directly from the information used in the preparation of the work sheet. In order to obtain the taxable income from the work sheet data, items in the income and retained earnings statement columns not related to the determination of the taxable income must be eliminated. In this case the items are the opening balance of the Retained Earnings account and the dividends

Accounts	Trial Balance		Adjustments	
	Dr.	Cr.	Dr.	Cr.
Petty Cash Fund	1,000			
Undeposited Cash	34,000			
Cash in Bank	176,000			
Accounts Receivable	760,000			(2) 27,300
Allowance for Uncollectible Accounts		24,700	(2) 27,300	(1) 34,850
Raw Material	123,030			
Work in Process	364,460			
Finished Goods	475,890			
Supplies	84,750			(3) 69,120
Unexpired Insurance	38,500			(4) 15,450
Land	88,000			
Buildings	1,750,000			
Buildings—Accumulated Depreciation		981,400		(5) 43,750
Equipment	2,425,000			
Equipment—Accumulated Depreciation		769,700		(6) 194,000
Accounts Payable		81,200		
Notes Payable		250,000		
Wages and Salaries Payable		139,340		
Payroll Taxes Payable		70,480		
Withheld Income Tax		36,910		
Capital Stock		2,500,000		
Retained Earnings		950,200		
Sales		6,970,000		
Sales Returns and Allowances	48,450			
Sales Discounts	86,700			
Salaries and Commissions—Selling	126,500			
Advertising	26,700			
Payroll Taxes—Selling	11,380			
Other Selling Expenses	7,620			
Salaries—Administrative	109,000			
Payroll Taxes—Administrative	9,750			
Other General and Administrative Expenses	8,750			
Interest on Notes	17,500			
Dividends Declared	250,000			
Purchases—Raw Material	1,227,070			
Direct Labor	3,473,400			
Foremen's Salaries	102,130			
Other Indirect Labor	218,050			
Repairs to Building and Equipment	7,260			
Property Taxes	54,600			
Payroll Taxes—Manufacturing	331,210			
Heat, Light and Power	19,760			
Other Factory Costs	17,470			
Uncollectible Accounts Adjustment			(1) 34,850	
Factory Supplies Used			(3) 45,130	
Shipping Supplies Used			(3) 19,350	
Office Supplies Used			(3) 4,640	
Insurance Expired			(4) 15,450	
Depreciation of Buildings			(5) 43,750	
Depreciation of Equipment			(6) 194,000	
Income Taxes	300,000			
	12,773,930	12,773,930	384,470	384,470
Cost of Goods Manufactured				
Income Taxes (Additional)			(11) 45,100	
Income Taxes Payable				(11) 45,100
			429,570	429,570
Retained Earnings, December 31, 1975				

Cost of Goods Manufactured		Income and Retained Earnings Statement		Balance Sheet	
Dr.	Cr.	Dr.	Cr.	Dr.	Cr.
				1,000	
				34,000	
				176,000	
				732,700	
					32,250
(a) 123,030	(a) 127,380			(a) 127,380	
(a) 364,460	(a) 420,170			(a) 420,170	
		(a) 475,890	(a) 438,800	(a) 438,800	
				15,630	
				23,050	
				88,000	
				1,750,000	
					1,025,150
				2,425,000	
					963,700
					81,200
					250,000
					139,340
					70,480
					36,910
					2,500,000
			950,200		
			6,970,000		
		48,450			
		86,700			
		126,500			
		26,700			
		11,380			
		7,620			
		109,000			
		9,750			
		8,750			
		17,500			
		250,000			
1,227,070					
3,473,400					
102,130					
218,050					
(b) 6,560		(b) 700			
(b) 49,100		(b) 5,500			
331,210					
(b) 17,610		(b) 2,150			
17,470					
		34,850			
45,130					
		19,350			
		4,640			
(b) 13,900		(b) 1,550			
(b) 39,500		(b) 4,250			
(b) 181,840		(b) 12,160			
		300,000			
6,210,460	547,550	1,563,390	8,359,000	6,231,730	5,099,030
	(c) 5,662,910	(c) 5,662,910			
6,210,460	6,210,460				
		(c) 45,100			(c) 45,100
		7,271,400	8,359,000	6,231,730	5,144,130
		1,087,600			1,087,600
		8,359,000	8,359,000	6,231,730	6,231,730

declared during the period. We have included a detailed presentation of the calculations:

Total credits		$8,359,000
Total debits	$1,563,390	
Cost of goods manufactured	5,662,910	7,226,300
Balance of columns		$1,132,700
Deduct items included which do not enter into determination of taxable income:		
Retained Earnings, Jan. 1, 1975		950,200
		$ 182,500
Add items deducted which do not enter into determination of taxable income:		
Dividends declared	$ 250,000	
Payments on estimated income taxes	300,000	550,000
Taxable income		$ 732,500
Federal income tax (22% of $25,000 plus 48% of $707,500)		$ 345,100

The resulting entry on the work sheet for the federal income tax reflects the liability for the tax, $345,100, less the deposits made during the year on the basis of estimated income taxes, $300,000, or $45,100.

Preparation of Statements

The financial statements for Glenwood Products, shown in Schedules 11.9, 11.10, and 11.11, are prepared by organizing the amounts found in the three statement sections of the work sheet into conventional form.

SCHEDULE 11.9

GLENWOOD PRODUCTS, INC.
Statement of Cost of Goods Manufactured
Year 1975

Raw Materials Used:		
Inventory, Jan. 1, 1975	$ 123,030	
Purchases of Raw Materials	1,227,070	
	$1,350,100	
Inventory, Dec. 31, 1975	127,380	
Raw Materials Used		$1,222,720
Direct Labor		3,473,400
Factory Overhead:		
Foremen's Salaries	$ 102,130	
Other Indirect Labor	218,050	
Payroll Taxes	331,210	
Factory Supplies Used	45,130	
Property Taxes	49,100	
Insurance	13,900	

SCHEDULE 11.9 (continued)

Repairs to Buildings and Equipment	6,560	
Heat, Light and Power	17,610	
Depreciation—Buildings	39,500	
Depreciation—Equipment	181,840	
Other Factory Costs	17,470	
Total Factory Overhead		1,022,500
Total Manufacturing Costs Incurred		$5,718,620
Work in Process Inventory, Jan. 1, 1975		364,460
		$6,083,080
Work in Process Inventory, Dec. 31, 1975		420,170
Cost of Goods Manufactured		$5,662,910

SCHEDULE 11.10

GLENWOOD PRODUCTS, INC.
Income and Retained Earnings Statement
Year 1975

Revenue:			
Sales		$6,970,000	
Less: Sales Returns & Allowances	$ 48,450		
Sales Discounts	86,700		
Uncollectible Accounts Adjustment	34,850	170,000	
Total Sales Revenue			$6,800,000
Expenses:			
Cost of Goods Sold:			
Finished Goods Inventory, Jan. 1, 1975 ...	$ 475,890		
Cost of Goods Manufactured—			
Schedule 11.9	5,662,910		
Goods Available for Sale	$6,138,800		
Finished Goods Inventory, Dec. 31, 1975 ..	438,800	$5,700,000	
Selling Expenses:			
Salaries and Commissions	$ 126,500		
Payroll Taxes	11,380		
Advertising	26,700		
Shipping Supplies Used	19,350		
Other Selling Expenses	7,620		
Total Selling Expenses		191,550	
General and Administrative Expenses:			
Salaries	$ 109,000		
Payroll Taxes	9,750		
Office Supplies Used	4,640		
Property Taxes	5,500		
Insurance	1,550		
Repairs to Building and Equipment	700		
Depreciation—Buildings	4,250		

SCHEDULE 11.10 (*continued*)

Depreciation—Equipment	12,160	
Heat, Light and Power	2,150	
Other General and Administrative Expenses	8,750	
Total General and Administrative Expenses ...	158,450	
Interest on Notes	17,500	
Income Taxes	345,100	
Total Expenses		6,412,600
Net Income to Stockholders		$ 387,400
Dividends Declared		250,000
1975 Income Retained		$ 137,400
Retained Earnings, January 1, 1975		950,200
Retained Earnings, December 31, 1975		$1,087,600

SCHEDULE 11.11

GLENWOOD PRODUCTS, INC.
Balance Sheet
December 31, 1975

Assets

Current Assets

Cash:

Petty Cash Fund	$ 1,000		
Undeposited Cash	34,000		
Cash in Bank	176,000		
		$ 211,000	
Receivables:			
Accounts Receivable	$ 732,700		
Less: Allowance for Uncollectible Accounts	32,250		
		700,450	
Inventories:			
Raw Material	$ 127,380		
Work in Process	420,170		
Finished Goods	438,800		
Supplies	15,630		
		1,001,980	
Prepayments:			
Unexpired Insurance	23,050		
Total Current Assets		$1,936,480	

SCHEDULE 11.11 (*continued*)

Property, Plant and Equipment

Land		$ 88,000	
Buildings	$1,750,000		
Less: Accumulated Depreciation	1,025,150		
		724,850	
Equipment	$2,425,000		
Less: Accumulated Depreciation	963,700		
		1,461,300	
Total Property, Plant and Equipment			2,274,150
Total Assets			$4,210,630

Liabilities and Stockholders' Equity

Current Liabilities

Accounts Payable	$ 81,200	
Notes Payable	250,000	
Wages and Salaries Payable	139,340	
Payroll Taxes Payable	70,480	
Withheld Income Tax	36,910	
Income Taxes Payable	45,100	
Total Current Liabilities		$ 623,030

Stockholders' Equity

Capital Stock	$2,500,000	
Retained Earnings	1,087,600	
Total Stockholders' Equity		3,587,600
Total Liabilities and Stockholders' Equity..		$4,210,630

Closing Entries

There are a number of possible variations in the methods used to close the operating accounts. The simplest method is to reverse the debits and credits as shown in the cost-of-goods-manufactured and the income and retained earnings statement columns on the work sheet, with the exception of the beginning and ending balances of the Retained Earnings account. It is preferable to include the change in Retained Earnings in the entry, rather than the beginning and ending balances of that account in the work sheet. The amount would be the net income to stockholders for the period, $387,400, less the dividends declared, $250,000 or $137,400. A Cost of Goods Manufactured account can be used to break the closing entries into two parts to correspond to the two divisions of the work sheet. The entries would be:

Raw Material	127,380	
Work in Process	420,170	
Cost of Goods Manufactured	5,662,910	
Raw Material		123,030
Work in Process		364,460

```
Purchases—Raw Material ...............................        1,227,070
Direct Labor .........................................        3,473,400
Foremen's Salaries ...................................          102,130
Other Indirect Labor .................................          218,050
Repairs to Buildings and Equipment ..................            6,560
Property Taxes .......................................           49,100
Payroll Taxes—Manufacturing .........................          331,210
Heat, Light and Power ...............................           17,610
Other Factory Costs .................................           17,470
Factory Supplies Used ...............................           45,130
Insurance Expired ...................................           13,900
Depreciation of Buildings ...........................           39,500
Depreciation of Equipment ...........................          181,840
```
To close manufacturing operating accounts and to adjust the inventories of raw material and work in process.

```
Finished Goods .........................................    438,800
Sales ..................................................  6,970,000
    Finished Goods ....................................                  475,890
    Sales Returns and Allowances .....................                   48,450
    Sales Discounts ...................................                   86,700
    Salaries and Commissions—Selling .................                  126,500
    Advertising .......................................                   26,700
    Payroll Taxes—Selling .............................                   11,380
    Other Selling Expenses ............................                    7,620
    Salaries—Administrative ...........................                  109,000
    Payroll Taxes—Administrative ......................                    9,750
    Other General and Administrative Expenses ........                    8,750
    Interest on Notes .................................                   17,500
    Dividends Declared ................................                  250,000
    Repairs to Buildings and Equipment ...............                      700
    Property Taxes ....................................                    5,500
    Heat, Light and Power .............................                    2,150
    Uncollectible Accounts Adjustment ................                   34,850
    Shipping Supplies Used ............................                   19,350
    Office Supplies Used ..............................                    4,640
    Insurance Expired .................................                    1,550
    Depreciation of Buildings .........................                    4,250
    Depreciation of Equipment .........................                   12,160
    Cost of Goods Manufactured ........................                5,662,910
    Income Taxes ......................................                  345,100
    Retained Earnings .................................                  137,400
```
To close the expense and revenue accounts, to adjust the finished goods inventory, and to transfer the net income retained to Retained Earnings.

The Retained Earnings account, after posting the closing entries, will appear as follows:

Retained Earnings

12/31/75	Balance	1,087,600	1/1/75	Balance	950,200
			12/31/75	Net income for	
				1975 retained	137,400
		1,087,600			1,087,600
			1/1/76	Balance	1,087,600

QUESTIONS AND PROBLEMS

1. Why is it impossible to present an entirely accurate income statement?

2. Distinguish between a balance sheet and a post-closing trial balance.

3. Indicate the major sources of revenue for each of the following businesses as they are likely to be indicated on the income statement:
   a. an accounting firm
   b. an appliance store
   c. a bank
   d. a business college
   e. an employment agency
   f. a garage
   g. a laundry
   h. a magazine publisher
   i. a restaurant
   j. a wholesale grocer.

4. To what account are the production cost accounts closed? To what account(s) may the income statement accounts (revenue, expense, income distribution, and so on) be closed?

5. What types of items may appear in a statement of retained earnings?

6. What is the purpose of ruling accounts?

7. List several illustrations of adjusting entries that do not lend themselves to the technique of reversal entries.

°8. Indicate whether each of the following statements is true or false.
   a. The balance sheet presents a good indication of the current market value of a firm as a whole.
   b. The retained earnings amount on the balance sheet usually should be close to agreement with the cash on hand.
   c. The classification of an asset as current or noncurrent is, in general, determined by the length of the period before it is normally converted into cash or used in operations.
   d. A deficit on the balance sheet indicates that the stockholders' equity has been completely eliminated; in other words, liabilities exceed the assets.
   e. A balance sheet indicates the amount of assets and equities held during the period.
   f. The total of the expenses on the income statement is usually equal to the amount of expenditures during the period.
   g. The use of an Income Summary account is not essential in making closing entries.
   h. It is not necessary to use a Cost of Goods Sold account when adjusting the merchandise accounts and establishing the ending inventory.
   i. A work sheet is prepared as an internal accounting procedure and, hence, is not included in the financial statements sent to stockholders.

° Hints, key numbers, or (partial) answers appear in the back of the book between the Appendix Tables and the Glossary.

j. Reversal entries are not used in connection with depreciation adjustments.

9. Indicate the presentation of each of the following accounts in an income statement or a balance sheet or both. Assume that the statements have a reasonably complete classification and subdivision. The following illustrates the form of the solution which is desired: Unexpired Insurance—balance sheet; current assets; prepayment.
   a. Accumulated Depreciation of Buildings
   b. Advances to Employees
   c. Advances by Customers
   d. Allowance for Purchase Discounts
   e. Allowance for Uncollectible Accounts
   f. Bonds Payable
   g. Capital Stock
   h. Depreciation of Delivery Equipment
   i. Depreciation of Office Furniture and Fixtures
   j. Federal Income Tax
   k. Freight-in
   l. Goodwill
   m. Interest Charges on Bonds
   n. Interest Earned on Investments
   o. Interest Payable on Bonds
   p. Interest Receivable
   q. Marketable Securities
   r. Merchandise Inventory (at end of period)
   s. Mortgage Payable
   t. Notes Receivable
   u. Purchase Discounts
   v. Rent Received in Advance
   w. Sales Discounts
   x. Sales Returns and Allowances
   y. Undeposited Cash

10. Is the preparation of a work sheet an *essential* step in the procedures of the accounting cycle?

11. Answer the following questions relating to the entries made in the adjustments columns of the work sheet:
    a. Are they different than the adjusting entries considered in the preceding chapter?
    b. Why must they be journalized and posted to the ledger?

12. Why should the extension of account balances across the work sheet be deferred until the adjustments have been completed as far as possible?

13. Why should the formal financial statements be prepared when a work sheet containing all of the income statement and balance sheet data has been completed?

14. Is it preferable to prepare the financial statements upon completion of the work sheet, or should this step be deferred until after the journalizing and posting of the adjusting and closing entries? Why?

15. Describe a procedure whereby closing entries could be prepared directly from the work sheet without reference to the general ledger accounts.

16. The test of the accuracy in the preparation of the work sheet is said to take place when the balance sheet column totals are equated by inserting the amount previously required to equate the income statement columns, the equalizing amount being a debit in one pair of columns and a credit in the other. Does this proof establish completely that no errors have been made? Why?

17. In preparing a work sheet for Omaha Stores, the accountant erroneously extended the store supplies accounts. The Store Supplies on Hand account, $330, was extended to the income statement debit column; the Store Supplies Used account, $690, was extended to the balance sheet debit column.
    a. Would these errors be discovered in the routine completion of the work sheet?
    b. To what extent, if any, would the net income of the enterprise be overstated or understated as a result of these errors?
    c. To what extent would the net income of the enterprise be overstated or understated if both of the accounts had been extended to the income statement debit column?

18. Answer the following concerning the relationship of a trial balance and the work sheet:
    a. Indicate at what point in the accounting cycle a trial balance ordinarily is taken when a work sheet is to be prepared.
    b. Describe the appearance of a work sheet if the initial trial balance were not taken until after all of the activities affecting the period had been recorded.
    c. State the justification for omitting the adjusted trial balance columns from the work sheet.

19. The Steelman Company has a profit-sharing agreement with its employees which provides that they shall receive a bonus of 25 percent of the income to the enterprise as computed exclusive of the bonus and income taxes. Indicate a procedure for this item on the work sheet.

*20. Indicate which of the following errors related to the specified accounts would cause the work sheet to be "out of balance."
    a. Allowance for Uncollectible Accounts: a debit adjustment amount is treated as a credit in calculating the amount to be extended to the balance sheet credit column.
    b. Cash in Bank: a debit adjustment amount was entered on the line below, Accounts Receivable, in error.
    c. Interest Earned: balance extended into the balance sheet credit column.
    d. Interest Payable: interest was not accrued on a note outstanding at the end of the period.
    e. Land: balance in trial balance not extended.
    f. Purchase Discounts: balance extended into the income statement debit column.
    g. Rent Payable: balance extended into the income statement credit column.

h. Rent Revenue: balance extended into the income statement debit column.

i. Supplies Used: balance extended into the balance sheet debit column.

j. Unexpired Insurance: balance extended into the income statement debit column.

21. The Wages Payable account of the Howe Manufacturing Company for the month of July is as follows:

Wages Payable

				7/1	Balance	1,300
7/31	Check Register	21,700		7/31	General Journal	21,200

Ignore any tax withholdings in **a, b,** and **c.**

a. What was the amount of wages earned in June and paid in July?

b. What was the amount of wages earned in July and paid in July?

c. What was the amount of wages earned in July to be paid in August?

d. If the average income tax withholding rate was 20 percent and the payroll tax withholding rate was 6 percent, how much did the employees receive during July?

22. What are the similarities and differences between an inventory of work in process and an inventory of finished goods?

*23. The trial balance of Irving Stores, Inc. as of December 31 included the following items related to the merchandise inventory and acquisitions:

Freight-in	$ 1,500
Merchandise Inventory	75,000
Merchandise Purchases	120,000
Purchase Allowances	1,000
Purchase Discounts	1,200
Purchase Returns	5,000

The inventory of merchandise on hand at December 31, properly computed, amounts to $70,000.

a. Set up income statement and balance sheet columns of a work sheet and indicate how the above information would appear. Assume that no adjusting entries were to be made.

b. Set up adjustments, income statement, and balance sheet columns of a work sheet and indicate how the above information would appear. Assume that an adjusting entry to recognize the merchandise cost of goods sold must be made.

c. Assuming that only one account had been used for the merchandise inventory and acquisitions, indicate how the merchandise and merchandise cost of goods sold lines would appear on the work sheet.

24. The following account balances relating to merchandise appeared on the June 30 trial balance of the Witt Stores, Inc.: Merchandise Inventory, $70,000; Purchase Returns, $2,000; Merchandise Purchases, $80,000; Purchases Discounts Lost, $50; Transportation Charges on Purchases, $1,450. The merchandise on hand at June 30, properly computed, was determined to be $71,000.

Set up adjustments, income statement, and balance sheet columns of a work sheet and indicate how the work sheet would appear in accordance with each of the following:

a. Assume that no adjusting entry should be made.

b. Assume that an adjusting entry to recognize the merchandise cost of goods sold should be made.

c. Assume that only one Merchandise account had been used and adjusting entry to recognize the merchandise cost of goods sold should be made.

25. In each of the following cases, journalize the transactions in two-column journal form: **(a)** Assume reversing entries are not used, and **(b)** assume reversing entries are made on July 1.

Case 1:

(1) Received a two-month 12-percent note for $2,000, dated May 16, from J. P. Fisher to replace an existing account receivable from him.

(2) Present adjusting and closing entries on June 30, the end of the accounting period.

(3) The note and interest are collected at maturity.

Case 2:

(1) Salesmen's salaries paid during June, $6,400, from which 6 percent is withheld for payroll taxes and $1,500 for income tax. There was no liability as of May 31.

(2) Salaries for the last two days of June, amounting to $580, were not paid as of June 30.

(3) Closing entries are made.

(4) Salaries for the week ended July 3, $1,500, are paid, from which 6 percent is withheld for payroll taxes and $360 for income tax.

26. In each of the following cases **(a)** journalize the transactions without using reversing entries and **(b)** repeat the journalization and make the appropriate reversing entries on January 1 of each year. Include closing entries in each set of entries.

Case 1:

(1) Purchased supplies on account during 1975 amounting to $3,000 and charged the entire amount to the Supplies Used account. There were no supplies on hand on January 1, 1975.

(2) The inventory of supplies on hand at December 31, 1975, was $400.

(3) Purchased supplies on account during 1976 amounting to $2,800 and charged the entire amount to the Supplies Used account.

(4) The inventory of supplies on hand at December 31, 1976, was $500.

Case 2:

(1) Collections for magazine subscriptions during 1975, the first year of operations, were $55,000. The entire amount was credited to Subscriptions Revenue account.

(2) Subscriptions applicable to future issues as of December 31, 1975, were $25,000.

(3) Collections from subscribers in 1976 were $66,000. The entire amount was credited to Subscriptions Revenue account.

(4) Subscriptions applicable to future issues as of December 31, 1976, were $30,000.

27. Prepare a cost of goods manufactured statement for the Block Manufacturing Company from the following data:

Depreciation of factory building	$ 3,300
Depreciation of factory equipment	4,050
Direct labor	93,000
Factory supplies used	10,050
Indirect labor	18,750
Insurance expired—factory	1,125
Heat, light and power	1,800
Maintenance and repairs	7,650
Payroll taxes—factory	4,650
Purchases—raw material	136,800
Raw material inventory, Jan. 1, 1975	14,400
Raw material inventory, June 30, 1975	21,300
Work in process inventory, Jan. 1, 1975	15,750
Work in process inventory, June 30, 1975	11,850

*28. Prepare a work sheet for Problem 24 of Chapter 10. Leave three lines for Barber Supplies on Hand.

29. Prepare a work sheet for Chapter 10, Problem 25, for the Rice Wholesale Dry Goods Company. Leave two lines for Allowance for Uncollectible Accounts and six lines for Expense Control.

*30. Prepare a work sheet for Chapter 10, Problem 26, for the Schnure Stores, Inc. Leave four lines for Expense Control.

31. The adjusted trial balance of the Roe Stores, Inc., as of December 31, 1975, contains the following account balances:

Accounts Payable	$ 51,000
Accounts Receivable	33,000
Accumulated Depreciation on Store Building	10,000
Accumulated Depreciation on Office Equipment	1,580
Accumulated Depreciation on Store Equipment	3,500
Advertising Expense	5,800
Advertising Supplies Inventory	780
Allowance for Uncollectible Accounts	1,700
Capital Stock	75,000
Cash in Bank	30,600
Cash on Hand	800
Delivery Expense	4,250
Depreciation—Store Building	3,000
Depreciation—Office Equipment	820
Depreciation—Store Equipment	2,150
Dividend Charges	3,000
Freight on Merchandise Acquired	6,300
Income Taxes	5,300
Income Taxes Payable	5,300
Insurance Expense—Store Building	320
Insurance Expense—Store Merchandise and Equipment	300
Insurance Expense—Office Equipment	20
Interest Charges	2,000
Interest Payable	900
Interest Receivable	70
Interest Revenue	500

Land	12,000
Loss on Disposal of Equipment	1,000
Merchandise Inventory	60,000
Mortgage Payable	40,000
Miscellaneous Administrative Expenses	560
Miscellaneous Selling Expenses	280
Notes Receivable	4,200
Office Equipment	4,800
Office Salaries	18,000
Office Supplies Inventory	460
Office Supplies Used	2,100
Payroll Taxes—Office	840
Payroll Taxes—Sales	1,260
Payroll Taxes Payable	240
Postage Expense	500
Purchases	170,000
Purchase Discounts	2,400
Purchase Returns	1,200
Retained Earnings	56,260
Salaries Payable	980
Sales	282,000
Sales Discounts	3,000
Sales Returns and Allowances	2,800
Sales Salaries	30,000
Sales, Uncollectible Accounts Adjustment	950
Store Building	90,000
Store Equipment	24,100
Store Supplies Inventory	3,720
Store Supplies Used	2,960
Unexpired Insurance	1,000
Withheld Income Taxes	480

Additional data:

The merchandise inventory as of December 31, 1975, is $50,000.

The accounting period is the calendar year.

a. Prepare a cost of goods sold schedule.

b. Prepare a statement of income and retained earnings.

c. Prepare a balance sheet.

d. Prepare closing entries in two-column journal form, adding an Income Summary account and Merchandise Cost of Goods Sold account.

32. The following trial balance of The Cushing Store as of March 31, 1975, includes all adjustments except that for merchandise cost of sales and federal income taxes.

Additional data:

(1) Merchandise inventory on March 31, 1975, is $23,700.

(2) Income taxes for the quarter are $840.

(3) Employee earnings, payroll taxes, depreciation of furniture and fixtures, insurance, property taxes, and rent are assignable 75 percent to sales and 25 percent to general and administrative activities, respectively.

Accounts Receivable	$ 16,540	
Accumulated Depreciation on Delivery Trucks		$ 2,490
Accumulated Depreciation on Furniture and Fixtures		4,180

Advertising Expense	2,790	
Allowance for Uncollectible Accounts		570
Capital Stock		35,000
Cash in Bank	7,670	
Cash on Hand	480	
Commissions Payable		1,050
Compensation Insurance Deposit	220	
Delivery Trucks	4,900	
Depreciation of Delivery Trucks	245	
Depreciation of Furniture and Fixtures	200	
Dividends Declared	700	
Federal Excise Tax Payable		390
Furniture and Fixtures	8,500	
Income Taxes	—	—
Income Taxes Payable	—	—
Insurance Expense	240	
Interest Revenue		30
Interest on Notes	70	
Interest Payable		80
Interest Receivable	30	
Leasehold	6,000	
Merchandise Cost of Sales	—	—
Merchandise Inventory, January 1, 1975	23,445	
Miscellaneous Delivery Expenses	815	
Notes Payable		6,800
Notes Receivable	4,000	
Office Supplies on Hand	105	
Office Supplies Used	205	
Payroll Taxes	640	
Payroll Taxes Payable		450
Prepaid Advertising	560	
Prepaid Property Taxes	500	
Property Taxes	240	
Purchases	26,850	
Purchase Allowances		250
Purchase Discounts		2,440
Rent	2,400	
Rent Payable		100
Retained Earnings		4,360
Salaries and Commissions	12,360	
Sales		52,300
Sales Discounts	570	
Sales and Excise Taxes	2,100	
Sales Tax Payable		980
Sales, Uncollectible Accounts Adjustment	340	
Transportation on Purchases	2,410	
Unexpired Insurance	655	
Vouchers Payable		14,700
Withheld Income Taxes		610
	$126,780	$126,780

a. Prepare adjusting entries in two-column journal form to recognize the merchandise cost of sales and the income taxes for the period.

b. Prepare a statement of income and retained earnings.

c. Prepare a balance sheet.

d. Prepare closing entries in two-column journal form adding an Income Summary account.

33. The following adjusted trial balance is taken from the books of the Blair Laundry and Cleaners on March 31, 1975, the end of the accounting period of three months.

Accounts Receivable	$ 15,375	
Accumulated Depreciation—Office Furniture and Fixtures		$ 1,950
Accumulated Depreciation—Shop Equipment		11,100
Accumulated Depreciation—Trucks		3,150
Advertising	675	
Capital Stock		40,000
Cash in Bank	5,715	
Depreciation of Office Furniture and Fixtures	75	
Depreciation of Shop Equipment	1,300	
Depreciation of Trucks	650	
Dividend Declared	1,000	
Income Taxes	1,185	
Income Taxes Payable		1,185
Interest Charges on Notes	260	
Interest Payable		240
Miscellaneous Expenses	1,850	
Notes Payable (12%; dated 1/21/75, due 6/30/77)		8,000
Office Furniture and Fixtures	3,450	
Outside Work (subcontracting of laundry and cleaning)	3,195	
Payroll Taxes	1,980	
Payroll Taxes Payable		1,680
Power, Gas and Water	1,235	
Rent Expense	1,500	
Repairs and Maintenance	270	
Retained Earnings		18,365
Revenue—Cleaning		21,530
Revenue—Laundry		43,600
Shop Equipment	52,065	
Supplies on Hand	2,690	
Supplies Used	6,020	
Trucks	10,350	
Truck Operations	6,300	
Undeposited Cash	630	
Unexpired Insurance	720	
Vouchers Payable		2,370
Wages and Salaries	36,000	
Withheld Income Tax		1,320
	$154,490	$154,490

a. Prepare a statement of income and retained earnings.
b. Prepare a balance sheet.
c. Present closing journal entries using an Income Summary account.

*34. Murray Stores Company last closed its books on December 31, 1974. The trial balance as of December 31, 1975, of the general ledger of the Murray Stores Company is as follows:

Accounts Payable		$ 6,600
Accounts Receivable	$ 18,700	
Advertising Expense	5,360	
Allowance for Uncollectible Accounts		1,083
Allowance for Sales Discounts	3,680	
Accumulated Depreciation—Store Equipment		1,635
Accumulated Depreciation—Office Equipment		1,500
Capital Stock		25,000
Cash in Bank	6,000	
Deferred Property Taxes	—	
Delivery Expense	3,385	
Dividends Declared	—	—
Dividends Payable	—	—
Depreciation of Store Equipment	—	
Depreciation of Office Equipment	—	
Federal Excise Tax Payable		300
Federal Income Taxes	—	—
Heat, Light and Water	800	
Income Taxes Payable	—	—
Insurance Expense	—	—
Interest Charges on Notes	1,330	
Interest Earned		30
Interest Payable	—	
Interest Receivable	30	
Long-term Notes Payable		16,000
Marketable Securities	5,000	
Merchandise Inventory	45,000	
Merchandise Purchases	191,400	
Merchandise Sales		294,000
Miscellaneous Accrued Liabilities	—	—
Miscellaneous General Expenses	370	
Miscellaneous Selling Expenses	460	
Notes Payable		3,000
Notes Receivable	1,000	
Office Equipment	2,100	
Office Supplies on Hand	350	
Office Supplies Used	570	
Payroll Taxes—General and Administrative	542	
Payroll Taxes—Salesmen	1,160	
Payroll Taxes Payable		152
Prepaid Advertising	—	—
Prepaid Income Taxes	4,000	
Prepaid Insurance	1,725	
Prepaid Rent	2,520	
Property Tax Expense	760	
Purchase Returns and Allowances		640
Rent Expense	420	
Retained Earnings		6,807
Salaries—General and Administrative	16,350	
Salaries—Salesmen	25,350	
Salaries Payable	—	—
Sales Discounts	—	—
Sales Returns and Allowances	5,185	
Sales, Uncollectible Accounts Adjustment	—	—
Store Equipment	6,600	

Store Supplies on Hand	1,000	
Store Supplies Used	—	—
Telephone and Telegraph	1,080	
Transportation on Purchases	3,880	
Undeposited Cash	1,030	
Withheld Income Taxes		390
	$357,137	$357,137

Additional data:

(1) It is estimated that 0.75 percent of the gross sales of the year will prove to be uncollectible.

(2) Advertising supplies have been charged as an expense as acquired. Unused supplies amount to $80.

(3) A list of customers' accounts considered to be uncollectible totals $1,860.

(4) Depreciation data are as follows: store equipment—annual rate of 10 percent of cost (equipment costing $600 was added on October 1, 1975); office equipment—annual rate of 8⅓ percent of cost.

(5) Property taxes for a fiscal year beginning April 1, 1975, were paid on November 1, 1975, $600 and debited to Property Tax Expense.

(6) Salaries earned since the end of the last payroll period are as follows: sales, $1,500; office, $300.

(7) The insurance premiums paid beyond December 31, 1975, are determined to be $575.

(8) Payroll taxes levied on the employer unrecorded as of December 31, 1975, amount to $343: general and administrative, $83; salesmen, $260.

(9) Rent at the rate of $420 per month has been paid through January 31, 1976.

(10) Some of the utility service invoices are on a monthly basis which does not coincide with the calendar month. Estimated services received since date of last billings received are as follows: electricity, $72; water, $8; telephone, $80.

(11) The following inventories of supplies were determined as of December 31, 1975: office, $300; store, $400.

(12) In taking the merchandise inventory at the end of the period, it was found that merchandise in the amount of $400, which had been received on invoices, had not been recorded.

(13) A physical inventory of merchandise was taken as of December 31, 1975, and the cost of items on hand was properly computed to be $41,000.

(14) A review of the accounts receivable balances indicates that discounts totaling $120 probably will be taken by customers in 1976.

(15) A review of the bank statement received as of December 31, 1975, indicates the following previously unknown data: a customer's check (H. C. Johns) deposited on December 24, has been charged to the company account with a notation of "Not Sufficient Funds," $90; a service charge, $5, has been deducted from the account.

(16) There is one outstanding note receivable, bearing interest at 12 percent, dated October 31, 1975. This note is the only source of interest revenue for the year.

(17) The short-term notes payable were issued on December 1, 1975, at a 12-percent interest rate.

(18) The long-term notes payable were issued in 1973 at a 10-percent interest rate. Interest payments are to be made each March 31 and September 30.

(19) Federal income taxes expense for the year is $6,434; $4,000 has been paid in estimated quarterly payments.

(20) A dividend amounting to $2,000 was declared on December 31, 1975, by the board of directors.

a. Prepare journal entries for all adjustments and corrections indicated by the above information.

b. Prepare an eight-column work sheet for a statement of income and retained earnings and balance sheet.

c. For each balance sheet account shown in the work sheet indicate the proper balance sheet presentation. Use the following key.

Current Asset .... CA
Current Liability CL
Long-term Asset .... LA
Long-term Liability LL
Stockholders' Equity .... SE

In addition, use a third letter C to represent a contra account or A to represent an adjunct account.

For each statement of income and retained earnings account, use the following key to show proper presentation.

Revenue .... R
Expenses .... E
Income Distributions .... D

In addition, use a second letter C or A to indicate contra or adjunct accounts.

*35. The following trial balance is taken from the general ledger of the Brentwood Supply Company on December 31, 1975. The company closes its books each month, so that the revenue and expense accounts on the trial balance relate only to the month of December, and the accruals, prepayments, and so forth have been adjusted up to December 1.

Accounts Payable		$ 14,970
Accounts Receivable	$ 40,500	
Accumulated Depreciation—Building		22,500
Accumulated Depreciation—Equipment		17,500
Advances to Employees	—	—
Allowance for Uncollectible Accounts		2,625
Building	40,000	
Capital Stock		80,000
Cash in Bank	7,690	
Coupon Books Outstanding		1,000
Depreciation of Building	—	—
Depreciation of Equipment	—	—
Dividends Declared	—	—
Dividends Payable	—	—
Equipment	62,400	
Income Tax Charge	—	—

Income Tax Payable		6,600
Insurance Expense	—	—
Interest Charges	50	—
Interest Payable		30
Land	9,000	
Land Contract Payable		6,200
Merchandise—Inventory	27,000	
Notes Payable		3,000
Payroll Taxes Payable		380
Prepaid Rent on Equipment	100	
Purchases	21,500	
Purchase Discounts Lost	9	
Purchase Returns		650
Rent of Equipment	—	—
Rent Receivable	—	—
Rent Revenue	—	—
Repairs and Supplies Expense	625	
Retained Earnings		28,734
Sales		34,000
Sales Discounts	—	—
Sales, Uncollectible Accounts Adjustment	—	—
Transportation on Purchases	1,000	
Undeposited Cash	720	
Unexpired Insurance	1,685	
Unfilled Paid Orders	—	—
Wages and Salaries Expense	6,510	
Wages and Salaries Payable	—	—
Withheld Income Tax		600
	$218,789	$218,789

Additional data:

(1) A review of the bank statement indicates that a deposit of $575 on December 31, 1975, has not been journalized.

(2) A review of the bank statement indicates that a check in the amount of $25 was issued in payment of repairs but never recorded.

(3) The company issues coupon books redeemable in merchandise. Coupon Books Outstanding represents the amount of outstanding coupons. A review of the coupons redeemed and outstanding indicates that the last batch of coupons redeemed by customers, $525, has not been recorded.

(4) A customer sent in $50 with an order for merchandise. The receipt was treated as a cash sale, although the order has not as yet been filled.

(5) A review of customers' accounts indicates that two accounts totaling $200 are considered to be uncollectible.

(6) A list of balances in the customers' accounts shows a total that is $10 more than the balance of the controlling account. A debit of $10, not yet journalized, is discovered in a customer's account which represents a correction of an error in an invoice.

(7) It is estimated that 1 percent of the gross sales of the month never will be collected.

(8) The bank reconciliation indicates that a check for $816 of the Brentwell Company was charged against our account in error.

(9) On December 1, a part of the building was rented out to the Pyne Company for use as a warehouse. The rent for the month, $625, has not been received.

(10) Unexpired insurance as of December 31, 1975, is $1,310.

(11) On January 1, 1975, a year's rent, $1,200, was paid on equipment used by the business.

(12) The depreciation rate on the building is 6 percent per year.

(13) The depreciation rate on equipment is 10 percent per year.

(14) A review of unpaid accounts reveals that the discount period has lapsed on invoices billed at $900, with terms of 2/10, n/30. This lapsing has not been recognized in the accounts.

(15) Wages and salaries earned since the end of the last payroll period amount to $520.

(16) The employer's share of payroll taxes for December is $570. No entry has been made. These taxes are to be considered in this problem as a part of the wages and salaries expense.

(17) On December 28, a payment by check, $25, was made to an employee, deductible from his January, 1976, salary. The debit entry was made to Wages and Salaries Expense.

(18) The single outstanding note payable was issued on October 31, 1975, at a 12-percent interest rate. The interest on the Land Contract Payable has been paid through December 31, 1975.

(19) The merchandise inventory at December 31, 1975, properly computed, is $27,400.

(20) Income taxes arising from the December operations are estimated to amount to $925.

(21) A dividend was declared on December 31, 1975, $1,600.

a. Prepare adjusting journal entries. Assume a Merchandise Cost of Goods Sold account is not used.

b. Prepare an eight-column work sheet for a statement of income and retained earnings and a balance sheet.

c. Label account titles appearing in the work sheet. Use the key given in Problem 34.

°36. The following trial balance is taken from the books of Lee Stores, Inc., at June 30, 1975. The accounting period is a quarter of the calendar year.

Accounts Receivable	$ 21,500	
Accumulated Depreciation on Delivery Trucks		$ 2,310
Accumulated Depreciation on Furniture and Fixtures		4,000
Advertising Expense	4,400	
Allowance for Uncollectible Accounts		340
Capital Stock		30,000
Cash in Bank	8,000	
Cash on Hand	500	
Commissions Payable		—
Compensation Insurance Deposit	360	
Delivery Trucks	5,200	
Depreciation on Delivery Trucks	—	
Depreciation on Furniture and Fixtures	—	

Federal Excise Tax Payable	740	
Furniture and Fixtures	8,800	
Income Taxes	—	
Income Taxes Payable		350
Insurance Expense	—	
Interest Revenue		—
Interest Receivable	—	
Interest on Notes	—	
Interest Payable		50
Leasehold	7,800	
Merchandise Inventory	24,400	
Miscellaneous Delivery Expense	762	
Notes Payable		7,000
Notes Receivable	4,000	
Office Supplies on Hand	300	
Office Supplies Used	—	
Payroll Taxes—Office	143	
Payroll Taxes—Selling	352	
Payroll Taxes Payable		425
Prepaid Advertising	—	
Prepaid Property Taxes	810	
Property Taxes	—	
Purchases	20,500	
Purchase Allowances		330
Purchase Discounts Lost	28	
Rent Payable		—
Rent—Store Building	—	
Rent—Warehouse	200	
Retained Earnings		10,150
Salaries and Commissions—Selling	8,500	
Salaries—Office	4,000	
Sales		53,220
Sales and Excise Taxes	—	
Sales Tax Payable		—
Sales, Uncollectible Accounts Adjustment	—	
Transportation on Purchases	2,520	
Unexpired Insurance	870	
Vouchers Payable		16,010
Withheld Income Taxes		500
	$124,685	$124,685

The following data have not been entered in the accounts:

(1) Unrecorded commissions earned by salesmen amount to $1,100.

(2) The amount of the employer's share of payroll taxes for the quarter is $2,248 (selling, $1,528; office, $720).

(3) The rent for June on the warehouse, $500, has not been paid.

(4) The annual depreciation rate on furniture and fixtures is 10 percent.

(5) The annual depreciation rate on delivery trucks is 20 percent.

(6) The inventory of office supplies on hand at June 30 is $115.

(7) Advertising expenditures applicable to fall and Christmas trade amount to $1,250.

(8) Compensation insurance is $1 per $100 of salaries and commissions earned.

(9) Unexpired property insurance amounts to $745.

(10) Property taxes are paid once a year at January 2.

(11) On July 1, 1966, a ten-year lease was acquired on the store building for $62,400.

(12) During the quarter, a 10-percent federal "luxury" excise tax has been charged on sales invoices of $12,000 (that is, before taxes). The full amount charged the customer has been credited to Sales. The tax is payable monthly and the payments for April and May have been charged to the Federal Excise Tax Payable account.

(13) All sales include a charge of 6 percent for state sales tax. Sales tax is not charged on the excise tax. Establish the liability for sales tax. Sales taxes are paid to the taxing authority at the end of each quarter.

(14) It is estimated that 1 percent of the sales on account, $35,000, never will be collected.

(15) Two customer accounts in the amount of $280 are determined to be uncollectible.

(16) The bookkeeper follows the procedure of deducting available purchase discounts and entering all unpaid invoices at net invoice prices. An inspection of the unpaid vouchers discloses that due to a delay in checking a shipment the 2-percent cash discount period has lapsed on an invoice having a gross invoice price of $1,800.

(17) The Notes Receivable account contains a single note dated May 1, 1975, and bearing interest at 12 percent per annum.

(18) The Notes Payable account consists of two notes, each bearing interest at 12 percent per annum. One note has a face value of $5,000 and is dated March 1, 1975. The other note has a face value of $2,000 and is dated May 16, 1975.

(19) The merchandise inventory at June 30 amounts to $24,660.

(20) Estimated income taxes for the period are $540.

Follow instructions given for parts a, b, and c of Problem 35.

37. The trial balance of the Moon Manufacturing Company as of December 31, 1975, is as follows:

Accounts Payable		$ 5,000
Accounts Receivable	$ 40,000	
Accumulated Depreciation		25,000
Allowance for Uncollectible Accounts		1,000
Bonds Payable		55,000
Building, Machinery, and Equipment	132,000	
Capital Stock		125,000
Cash	18,000	
Direct Labor	65,000	
Dividends Declared	9,375	
Expense Control	33,550	
Finished Goods	12,500	
Income Tax Charge	—	—
Income Tax Payable	—	—
Interest Charges	2,750	
Land	25,000	
Material Purchases	55,000	
Overhead Control	32,000	
Prepaid Income Taxes	9,000	

Raw Material Inventory	6,400	
Retained Earnings		13,325
Sales		225,000
Unexpired Insurance	750	
Work in Process	8,000	
	$449,325	$449,325

Additional data:
  (1) Depreciation for the year: factory building, machinery, and equipment, $7,500; office equipment, $300.
  (2) Estimated income tax for the year, $13,220.
  (3) Inventories, December 31, 1975: raw materials, $10,000; work in process, $13,000; finished goods, $11,000.

Prepare a ten-column work sheet containing the following pairs of columns: Trial Balance; Adjustments; Cost of Goods Manufactured; Statement of Income and Retained Earnings; Balance Sheet.

Three

SPECIAL TOPICS IN FINANCIAL ACCOUNTING

Chapter 12

Inventories

INVENTORY TERMINOLOGY

The term *inventory* has several meanings. It can be used as a verb; to inventory stock means to prepare a list of items on hand at a specific date, to assign a unit price to each item, and to calculate the total cost of inventory. In law, an inventory is a complete list of assets, both current and noncurrent, that can be used by the executor of an estate or a trustee in bankruptcy.

In accounting in general and as it is used in this chapter, inventory means a stock of goods or other items on hand. Goods held for sale by a retail or wholesale business are called *merchandise* or *merchandise inventory*; goods held for sale by a manufacturer are called *finished goods*. The inventories of manufacturing concerns also include *work in process* (partially completed products) and *raw materials* (materials that will become a part of the goods to be produced). Various types of supplies used in administrative, selling, and manufacturing operations are also commonly included in inventories on the balance sheet.

Significance of Accounting for Inventories

A major objective of accounting is the determination of periodic income. The role of accounting for inventories in that process is to determine the proper assignment of costs to periods. The total cost of goods available for sale or use during a period must be allocated between the current period's usage (cost of items sold or used) and the amounts carried forward to future periods (the end-of-period inventory).

One equation, or identity, applies to all inventory situations and will facilitate our discussion of inventory problems:

Beginning Inventory + Additions — Withdrawals = Ending Inventory

If we start a period with 1,000 pounds of salt, if we purchase 1,200 pounds during the period, and if we use 1,300 pounds of salt during the period, there will be 900 pounds left at the end of the period.

If accounting were concerned merely with keeping track of physical quantities, there would be few inventory problems. But, of course, accounting reports dollar figures, not physical quantities. If all prices remained constant, inventory problems would be minor because any variation in values of inventories would be solely attributable to changes in quantities, but the major problems in inventory accounting arise from fluctuations over time in the acquisition costs of units of an item. To be specific, consider the inventory of goods for sale in a merchandising firm. The inventory equation is, then:

Beginning Inventory + Purchases — Cost of Goods Sold
= Ending Inventory

or, rearranging terms:

Beginning Inventory + Purchases — Ending Inventory
= Cost of Goods Sold

The valuation for ending inventory will appear on the balance sheet as the asset, Merchandise. The amount of Cost of Goods Sold will appear on the income statement as an expense of producing sales revenue.

To illustrate the process, suppose that the beginning inventory had been one toaster, which we will call toaster 1, which cost $25. Suppose further that two toasters were purchased during the period, toaster 2 for $29 and toaster 3 for $30 and that one toaster was sold during the period. The three toasters are alike in every respect except for their cost. The total cost of the three toasters is $84, and the average of the toasters is $28. There are at least four ways to apply the inventory equation to determine the cost of goods sold and the ending inventory.

Item Sold	Cost of Goods Sold	Ending Inventory
Toaster 1	$25	$59
"Average" Toaster	28	56
Toaster 2	29	55
Toaster 3	30	54

As the equation and the example both show, the higher the cost of goods sold, the lower is ending inventory. Furthermore, the lower the amount of ending inventory, the lower will be the future cost of goods sold.

The inventory valuation at any date is the cost of the goods on hand to be carried forward to future periods. The inventory valuation problem arises because there are *two* unknowns in the inventory equation. The values of beginning inventory and purchases are known but not the values of withdrawals nor ending inventory. The question is whether to value the ending inventory by using the most recent costs or the oldest costs or the average cost or some other alternative. Of course, the question could have been put in terms of valuing the withdrawals, because once we determine the value of one, the inventory equation automatically values the other. The relation between the two unknowns in the inventory equation is such that the higher the value given to one of them, the lower must be the value given to the other.

There are no historical-cost-based accounting methods for valuing inventories and, inversely, withdrawals that allow the accountant to show current values on both the income statement and the balance sheet. If current, higher costs are to be shown on the income statement, then older, lower costs must be shown on the balance sheet and vice versa. The accountant can present "current truth" in one place but not in both. Of course, combinations of current and out-of-date information can be shown in both places.

Problems of Inventory Accounting

Discussion of inventory accounting can be conveniently split into consideration of individual problems, treated more or less separately. The rest of this chapter discusses seven such problems:

1. Inventory methods
2. Valuation bases
3. Flow assumptions
4. Estimating inventory values
5. Inclusion problems and income tax regulations
6. Goods in transit
7. Goods out on consignment.

These problems are not equally difficult, nor are they equally important. The sections on valuation methods and flow assumptions merit particular attention.

The size of inventories can significantly influence the profitability of the firm. A firm whose inventory is too small may lose customers because of "stockouts" and one whose inventory is too large will incur the extra costs of holding unnecessary stock. The problems of managing inventory size are considered in management science and advanced managerial accounting courses.

INVENTORY METHODS

There are two principal methods of arriving at the quantity and amount of an inventory. One is known as the *periodic* inventory and the other, as the *perpetual* inventory.

Periodic Inventories

When *periodic inventories* are used, a record or entry is not made for the cost of goods sold or used until the end of the accounting period. Under these circumstances a physical count and an inventory valuation are made, and the cost of goods sold or the cost of material used is determined from the inventory equation. For example,

Merchandise Inventory, Jan. 1, 1975	$ 10,000
Merchandise Purchases during 1975	100,000
Goods Available for Sale during 1975	$110,000
Merchandise Inventory, Dec. 31, 1975	15,000
Cost of Goods Sold during 1975	$ 95,000

The principal disadvantage of the periodic inventory method is the assumption that all goods not accounted for by the inventory have been sold or used. Any "shrinkages" or losses from such causes as theft, evaporation, and waste are hidden in the cost of goods sold or the cost of materials used. Also, taking such an inventory is apt to interfere seriously with normal business operations for several days. Some firms using periodic inventories even close down and engage practically the entire staff on the physical count and measurement of the items on hand. To prepare operating statements more frequently than once a year is seldom possible when the inventory figures are obtained only from periodic inventories.

The periodic inventory method determines the ending inventory figure of units by physical count multiplied by cost per unit and uses the inventory equation to determine the withdrawals.

Perpetual Inventories

Under the *perpetual* (or *continuous*) inventory method, the system of records is designed so that the cost of merchandise sold or the cost of material used is recorded at the time these assets are sold or consumed. The perpetual method determines the withdrawals by physical observation and uses the inventory equation to determine (what should be in) the ending inventory.

Such entries as the following may be made from day to day.

Cost of Goods Sold	546	
Merchandise		546
To record the cost of goods sold.		

Raw Material Used	1,075	
Raw Material		1,075
To record the cost of material used in production.		

When postings for a period have been completed, the balance in the Merchandise account or in the Raw Material account is the cost of the goods still on hand. Operating statements can be prepared without a physical count.

Using perpetual inventories does not eliminate the need to take physical inventories. A physical count of the goods on hand must be taken from time to time to check on the accuracy of the book figures and to gauge the loss from shrinkages. Some businesses make a complete physical check at the end of the accounting period in the same way that the periodic inventory is taken. Frequently, however, a more effective procedure can be employed. Rather than taking the inventory of all items at one time, the count may be staggered throughout the period. An attempt may be made to check individual items when the supply on hand reaches a low point. All items should be counted at least once a year. Certain items may be checked more frequently, either because of their high value or because of a high probability of errors in recording their withdrawals.

Periodic and Perpetual Methods Compared

Controlling losses or shrinkages is difficult if they cannot be measured. The periodic method can be cheaper to administer than the perpetual method but does not provide data on losses. To gather data on losses from inventory requires both continuous tracking of withdrawals and periodic counts so that the actual amounts on hand can be compared to what the books say should be on hand. The perpetual method also helps maintain up to date information on quantities actually on hand. Thus its use is justified when being "out of stock" may produce costly results, such as the need to shut down production lines or strong customer dissatisfaction. As with other choices that have to be made in accounting, each method's costs must be compared with its benefits. Periodic methods are likely to be cost effective when being out of stock will not be extremely costly, when items are hard to steal, or when items have a low value-to-bulk ratio.

BASES OF INVENTORY VALUATION

The basis of valuation for inventories importantly affects periodic income. At least four bases of valuation are in current use. The two most common are: (1) original cost and (2) original cost or replacement cost, whichever is the lower. (This basis is commonly referred to as "lower of cost or market.") Two other bases, used less frequently, are (3) standard cost and (4) selling price.

Original Cost Basis

When the cost basis is used, items in inventory are carried at their cost until used or sold. Thus income or loss is not recorded until use or sale takes place. The figure shown in the balance sheet is, therefore, more or less out of date, depending upon how long the items have been on hand. "Cost" includes "the sum of the applicable expenditures and charges directly or indirectly incurred in bringing an article to its existing condition and location."[1] In other words, the term *cost* includes the invoice price of

[1] *Accounting Research Bulletin No. 43*, Committee on Accounting Procedure, American Institute of Certified Public Accountants, issued in 1953.

merchandise and supplies plus cost of transportation, less trade and cash discounts. Other costs such as purchasing, receiving, handling, and storage can be included. Such costs are usually charged, however, to the operations or expense of the period of their incurrence. If the business is a manufacturing enterprise, this definition of cost will apply to its raw materials and supplies; for its other inventories, cost includes all of the manufacturing costs that may have been incurred in producing the goods in process or the finished products.

When perpetual inventory records are kept, valuation by the *original* cost method is usually easiest, since original cost figures are commonly used in such records. For periodic inventories, replacement cost is often easier to determine since recent prices are usually more accessible than prices at various dates in the past.

If materials or goods have become damaged, shopworn, or obsolete, they should be written down to a figure below cost, such as "net realizable value." Original cost applies only to goods that are undamaged and can be used effectively in current operations.

Lower-of-Cost-or-Market Basis

The lower-of-cost-or-market (original cost or replacement cost, whichever is lower) valuation basis has received wide acceptance in principle, but there is reason to believe that its actual application has not been as extensive as the lip service it has received. The American Institute of Certified Public Accountants justified the need for the lower-of-cost-or-market valuation basis as follows:

> A departure from the cost basis of pricing the inventory is required when the utility of the goods is no longer as great as its cost. Where there is evidence that the utility of goods, in their disposal in the ordinary course of business, will be less than cost, whether due to physical deterioration, obsolescence, changes in price levels, or other causes, the difference should be recognized as a loss of the current period. This is generally accomplished by stating such goods at a lower level commonly designated as *market*.[2]

Use of the lower-of-cost-or-market basis involves the determination of both cost and market information for each item in the inventory.[3] The difficulty of gathering the necessary information for each of the hundreds or thousands of items on an inventory, to say nothing of the difficulty of calculating the cost of work in process and finished goods on the basis of present material prices, present labor rates, and present prices for each of the other costs of production operations, certainly lends much support to our opinion that the method has limited application. It is used frequently

---

[2] *Accounting Research Bulletin No. 43*, Committee on Accounting Procedure, American Institute of Certified Public Accountants, issued in 1953.

[3] Appendix 12.1 of this chapter spells out the steps necessary for applying the lower-of-cost-or-market rule.

for valuable raw materials and for other items where the change in price has been significant.

The lower-of-cost-or-market basis for inventory valuation is thought to be a "conservative" policy because (1) losses can be recognized before goods are sold, but income from increases in market value is never recorded before a sale takes place and (2) inventory figures on the balance sheet are never greater, but may be less, than original cost. An examination of the effects of using the lower of cost or market over a series of accounting periods shows why the "conservatism" argument is questionable. For any one unit of goods, there is only one income or loss figure—the difference between the original cost and the selling price—and the valuation rule merely determines how this figure of income or loss is to be spread over the accounting periods. When the lower-of-cost-or-market price is used, the net income of the present period may be lower than if the original cost basis were used, but the net income of the period when the unit is sold will then be higher.

Standard Costs

Manufacturing firms frequently use *standard cost* systems. They are discussed in Chapter 22. Standard cost is a predetermined estimate of what each item of manufactured inventory *should* cost, based upon studies of past cost data and planned production methods. Occasionally, units in inventory will be valued at standard cost, especially in the preparation of monthly or quarterly statements. If so, any difference between actual cost and standard cost is debited, if positive (credited if negative), to expenses of the period.

Selling Price

Selling price is occasionally used in inventory valuation. Agricultural products, for example, on hand at the close of an accounting period are often valued at selling price less costs of marketing, so that the income is recognized in the period of production rather than in the period of sale. By-products of manufacturing operations are usually valued on a similar basis. Net realizable values are appropriate for this purpose when cost figures are difficult to obtain and when an established market virtually eliminates the necessity for sales effort.

FLOW ASSUMPTIONS

If individual units can be identified, ascertaining original cost does not present a special problem. The cost can be marked on the unit or on its container or the item can be traced back to its purchase invoice or cost record. In most cases, however, new items are mixed with old on shelves, in bins, or in other ways, and physical identification is impossible or impractical. If more than one purchase of the same item at differing prices is made, then some assumption must be made as to the flow of costs in order to estimate the original cost applicable to the inventory. Three principal methods are used for this purpose: first-in, first-out; last-in, first-out; and weighted-average. The demonstrations of each of these methods which follow are based upon the data in Schedule 12.1.

SCHEDULE 12.1 DATA TO ILLUSTRATE FLOW ASSUMPTIONS

Date			Units	Unit Price	Total Cost
June 1	Inventory		100	$1.00	$100
7	Units received		300	1.10	330
12	" "		100	.90	90
			500		$520
June 5	Units issued		25		?
10	" "		10		?
15	" "		200		?
25	" "		150		?
			385		?
30	Inventory		115		?

First-In, First-Out

The first-in, first-out method, abbreviated FIFO, assigns the cost of the earliest items acquired to the withdrawals and the cost of the most recent acquisitions to inventory. The oldest materials and goods are assumed to be used first. This assumption conforms to good business practice, especially in the case of items that deteriorate or become obsolete.

When the periodic inventory method is used, the unit prices to be applied to quantities on hand are determined by working backward through the purchases until a sufficient quantity is obtained to cover the inventory at the end of the month. If a physical count reveals there are 115 units on hand at June 30, search the files for the latest invoices including this material. The first such is the invoice of June 12, which accounts for 100 units at a cost of $90.00. The search is continued until the invoice of June 7 is found, and the remaining 15 units are priced at the $1.10, which appears on that invoice, making the total value of the inventory $106.50.

```
100 units @ $ .90 ............................................... $ 90.00
 15 units @ $1.10 ...............................................   16.50
                                                                 $106.50
```

The first-in, first-out method has been appropriately characterized as the most-recent-invoice method when periodic inventories are used. The search for the proper invoices may be laborious unless the article involved is always purchased from the same source.

When FIFO is used with a perpetual inventory system, the balance carried forward after each receipt or issue must be analyzed to reflect all prices applicable to the unused items. The oldest prices are first applied to requisitions until the corresponding quantities are absorbed. The illustration in Schedule 12.2 indicates how the first-in, first-out method operates with the use of perpetual inventory records.

SCHEDULE 12.2 PERPETUAL INVENTORY: FIFO FLOW

Date	Received			Issued			Balance		
	Units	Price	Amount	Units	Price	Amount	Units	Price	Amount
6/1							100	1.00	100.00
6/5				25	1.00	25.00	75	1.00	75.00
6/7	300	1.10	330.00				75	1.00	75.00
							300	1.10	330.00
6/10				10	1.00	10.00	65	1.00	65.00
							300	1.10	330.00
6/12	100	.90	90.00				65	1.00	65.00
							300	1.10	330.00
							100	.90	90.00
6/15				65	1.00	65.00	165	1.10	181.50
				135	1.10	148.50	100	.90	90.00
6/25				150	1.10	165.00	15	1.10	16.50
							100	.90	90.00

The inventory at the end of the month is shown at a cost of $106.50.

15 units @ $1.10	....	$ 16.50
100 units @ $ .90	....	90.00
		$106.50

Last-In, First-Out

The last-in, first-out method, abbreviated LIFO, has attracted a good deal of attention since 1939, when it became acceptable for income tax determinations. In a period of rising prices it results in a lower reported income—and lower current income taxes—than either the first-in, first-out or average-cost methods.

The LIFO method assumes, physically, that the business carries a certain amount of reserve stock of materials or goods on hand and that current operations and sales are carried on with the use of items purchased most recently.[4] There are some situations where the physical conditions justify such an assumption, as where material is kept in a bin and new purchases are dumped in before the supply is completely exhausted. The quantity at the bottom of the bin may have been purchased many months or years ago. Most often, however, LIFO cannot be physically justified, but it is used because it produces a more up-to-date measure of income and reduces income taxes in a period of rising prices.

When the periodic inventory method is used, the procedure is to begin with the opening inventory and work forward through the purchase in-

[4] The LIFO method in the strict sense can be applied only to physically identical goods such as tons of ore or pounds of cotton. LIFO can be used for style good (for example, dresses and suits) or annual models of appliances by using a variant known as *dollar-value LIFO* or *retail method LIFO*. Dollar-value LIFO is explained in Appendix 12.2.

voices until sufficient units have been accumulated to cover the final
inventory. In the example, ending inventory is valued as follows:

```
100 @ $1.00 (from beginning inventory) ......................... $100.00
 15 @  1.10 (from first purchase, June 7) .......................   16.50
                                                                  ────────
                                                                  $116.50
                                                                  ════════
```

This type of calculation is realistic only when the quantity on hand has
never dropped below 100. This would not be known unless perpetual
inventory records were kept. The doubtful character of the necessary
assumption weakens the logic of LIFO when a periodic inventory system is
used. On the other hand, when a periodic inventory system is used, LIFO
usually requires less searching of the files than the other two do. Because
the quantity in the final inventory is apt to be somewhere near the quantity
in the beginning inventory, few invoices, if any, will have to be located
under the LIFO approach.

Under a LIFO perpetual-inventory system, the balance carried forward after each receipt or issue must be analyzed to reflect the prices
applicable to the unused items. LIFO, as opposed to FIFO, requires that
the most *recent* prices be applied to requisitions until the corresponding
quantities are absorbed and the balance on hand reflects the earliest
purchase prices. Schedule 12.3 illustrates the operation of LIFO with
perpetual inventories.

SCHEDULE 12.3 PERPETUAL INVENTORY: LIFO FLOW

Date	Received			Issued			Balance		
	Units	Price	Amount	Units	Price	Amount	Units	Price	Amount
6/1							100	1.00	100.00
6/5				25	1.00	25.00	75	1.00	75.00
6/7	300	1.10	330.00				75	1.00	75.00
							300	1.10	330.00
6/10				10	1.10	11.00	75	1.00	75.00
							290	1.10	319.00
6/12	100	.90	90.00				75	1.00	75.00
							290	1.10	319.00
							100	.90	90.00
6/15				100	.90	90.00	75	1.00	75.00
				100	1.10	110.00	190	1.10	209.00
6/25				150	1.10	165.00	75	1.00	75.00
							40	1.10	44.00

The inventory at June 30 is valued at $119.00.

```
75 units @ $1.00 ..............................................  $ 75.00
40 units @ $1.10 ..............................................    44.00
                                                                 ────────
                                                                 $119.00
                                                                 ════════
```

Weighted Average

To use a weighted-average periodic-inventory method, calculate a weighted
average of all the prices used during the month, including the price

applicable to the beginning inventory, and apply it to the units on hand at the end of the month.

6/1	100 @ $1.00	$100.00
6/7	300 @ $1.10	330.00
6/12	100 @ $ .90	90.00
	500 @ $1.04 (= $520/500)	$520.00
Inventory	115 @ $1.04	$119.60

This result is correct, strictly speaking, only if units were not used or sold until after the firm makes the last purchase that enters the computations of the weighted average. Seldom do all additions to inventory precede any withdrawals and, therefore, the logic of the method is considerably weakened. The method is physically appropriate, then, for liquids and not unreasonable for other types of products where distinguishing different lots is difficult.

With perpetual inventories, this method is often the easiest to apply, especially where the number of purchases is less than the number of requisitions. The technique requires the calculation of a new average unit cost after each purchase, but this unit cost figure is used to price all requisitions until the next purchase is made. Schedule 12.4 indicates how the weighted-average method operates with the use of perpetual inventory records.

SCHEDULE 12.4 PERPETUAL INVENTORY: WEIGHTED-AVERAGE FLOW

	Received			Issued			Balance		
Date	Units	Price	Amount	Units	Price	Amount	Units	Price	Amount
6/1							100	1.00	100.00
6/5				25	1.00	25.00	75	1.00	75.00
6/7	300	1.10	330.00				375	1.08	405.00
6/10				10	1.08	10.80	365	1.08	394.20
6/12	100	.90	90.00				465	1.0413	484.20
6/15				200	1.0413	208.26	265	1.0413	275.94
6/25				150	1.0413	156.20	115	1.0413	119.74

The inventory at the end of the month is valued at the last amount shown on the perpetual inventory form, $119.74. The unit price of $1.0413 is used only for determining subsequent withdrawals. The ending inventory of $119.74 is calculated as $275.94 less $156.20 (= 150 × $1.0413), not as 115 × $1.0413.

Comparison of Methods

FIFO results in balance sheet figures that are closest to current cost, because the latest purchases dominate the inventory valuation. The cost of goods sold, however, reflects earlier prices because it assumes earlier purchases are sold first. When prices fluctuate, FIFO leads to the highest reported net income of the three methods when prices are rising, and the smallest when prices are falling. When FIFO is used, both the perpetual and periodic inventory methods lead to the same figure for cost of goods sold and, hence, to the same figure for ending inventory.

LIFO leads to opposite results. LIFO produces balance sheet figures that may be far removed from present costs and a cost of goods sold figure close to current costs. The cost of goods sold under LIFO is the largest of the three when prices are rising, and the smallest when prices are falling. LIFO ordinarily results in the least fluctuation in reported income because selling prices tend to be changed as current prices of inventory items change. Under LIFO, the perpetual and periodic methods may lead to a different figure for cost of goods sold and, hence, for ending inventory.

The weighted-average method falls between the other two in its effect both upon the balance sheet and the income statement. Its inventory values are neither as close to present prices as FIFO nor as far removed as LIFO. The size of the fluctuation in net income is usually greater than when LIFO is used but not so great as with FIFO. Weighted averages reflect all of the prices during the period in proportion to the quantities purchased at those prices, as well as beginning inventory costs carried over from the previous period.

Both FIFO and the weighted-average method seem satisfactory, particularly if an attempt is made to select the one that corresponds more closely to the physical handling of the material. LIFO usually presents a cost of goods sold figure more closely related to current costs. It may also have the practical advantage of saving income taxes. LIFO may reduce income fluctuations and, thereby, please some stockholders. To say that LIFO's less variable income estimates are more accurate begs the question. The appearance of stability of income that LIFO tends to create may actually be misleading. The balance sheet figure for inventory that results from LIFO may become so far divorced from current values as to delude and confuse readers of statements. Finally, if matching physical flows with cost flows is considered important, then LIFO is unsatisfactory because it assumes an order of consumption that is usually poor and unrealistic business practice. Oldest materials are rarely used last.

ESTIMATING INVENTORY VALUES

The foregoing discussion of valuation bases has implied a calculation in terms of quantities of specified homogeneous items. Unit costs obtained from various invoices (or replacement-cost sources in the lower-of-cost-or-market method) are multiplied by the inventory quantities to determine the inventory amount. In some situations the calculation by such a procedure is unduly costly or time consuming. The accountant may wish to prepare interim statements without taking a physical inventory. Sometimes it is impossible to apply exact procedures, as when the inventory has been destroyed by fire. In these and other situations an estimated or statistical approach may be used to calculate inventory values. The next two sections discuss some of the more common methods used in *estimating* inventories.

The Retail Inventory Method

The retail method of estimating the amount of the merchandise inventory has become popular in department and chain stores. In particular, it has been used when there are many items of relatively small unit value. First, the goods available for sale are valued at selling price. Second, the ratio of cost to selling price is calculated for some selling unit such as a department or, conceivably, an entire store. Finally, the selling price of goods sold (or in ending inventory) is multiplied by the cost ratio to estimate a cost of goods sold (or ending inventory).

The percentage applied to the selling price is sometimes a standard percentage that is reviewed from time to time and compared to studies of actual costs and prices. The usual procedure, though, in making the inventory calculation is to determine the percentage on the basis of actual purchase cost and selling-price data.

Most often, the selling-price amount of the final inventory is calculated by deducting the sales of the period from the sum of the selling price of the beginning inventory and purchases, adjusted for changes in selling price during the period. The final inventory may, however, be taken by actual count and valued at selling price. This procedure ordinarily is not as difficult as a cost-valuation procedure because selling prices are more readily available.

The determination of the cost valuation of an ending inventory is illustrated below. The basic steps are:

1. pricing the beginning inventory at cost and selling price
2. pricing the purchases at cost and selling price
3. calculating the percentage of total cost to total selling price; called the *cost percentage*
4. deducting sales for the period from the sum of the beginning inventory and purchases at selling price to determine the ending inventory at selling price
5. multiplying the ending inventory at selling price by the percentage calculated in step 3 in order to determine the ending inventory at the cost valuation.

These steps are demonstrated as follows:

	Cost	Selling Price
1. Inventory, January 1, 1975	$ 60,000	$ 74,100
2. Purchases during January	90,000	113,400
Goods Available for Sale in January .... (including transportation and any other costs of acquiring merchandise)	$150,000	$187,500
3. Cost Percentage = 150,000/187,500 = 80%		
4a. Less: Sales during January		127,500
4b. Inventory at Selling Price, January 31, 1975		$ 60,000
5. Cost of Inventory, 80% of $60,000.....................	$ 48,000	

If the final inventory at selling price is determined by physical count, then the cost percentage is applied directly to that final inventory figure to get its cost.

Any change in selling price that takes place during the period complicates the retail method. Records must be kept of price changes applicable to the goods in stock at the time of the change. Increases in price above the original selling price are called *markups*. Decreases in price from the original selling price are called *markdowns*.

Many demonstrations of the retail method add net markups to the selling price of the beginning inventory and purchases but do not deduct net markdowns before making the cost-percentage calculation. This results in a lower cost percentage and, therefore, a lower inventory valuation than if both net markups and markdowns were recognized in the calculation. One justification for this procedure is the assumption that goods that were marked down during the period were undoubtedly sold and that they therefore should not enter into the cost-percentage calculation to be applied to the final inventory. If it can be assumed that the final inventory contains items that have been both marked up and marked down during the period, both the total markups and markdowns should be used in the calculation of the cost percentage.

Assume the data in the above illustration and that there also were net markups during January of $18,000 and net markdowns of $12,000. If the final inventory contains items marked down as well as items marked up, during the period, the inventory calculation schedule would be:

	Cost	Selling Price
Inventory, January 1, 1975	$ 60,000	$ 74,100
Purchases during January	90,000	113,400
Markups (net) during January		18,000
		$205,500
Markdowns (net) during January		(12,000)
Goods Available for Sale in January	$150,000	$193,500
Cost Percentage = 150,000/193,500 = 77.5%		
Less: Sales during January		127,500
Inventory at Selling Price, January 31, 1975		$ 66,000
Cost of Inventory, 77.5% of $66,000	$ 51,150	

Assuming the data in the preceding illustration and the common practice of recognizing only the net markups in the determination of the cost percentage, the calculation would be as follows:

Cost Percentage 150,000/205,500 = 73%
Cost of Inventory (73% of $66,000) $48,180

Gross-Margin Method

Another method for estimating inventory values is the gross-margin method. It, too, uses a cost percentage. The gross-margin percentage is 1 minus the cost percentage. This method may be used to prepare interim statements without taking an inventory. The method also is used in valuing an inventory that has been damaged or completely destroyed.

Assume the following data are available from the ledger for the month of January:

Inventory, January 1, 1975 (at cost)	$150,000
Purchases	210,600
Transportation-in	2,400
Purchase Returns and Allowances	3,000
Sales	300,000
Sales Returns and Allowances	12,000

Assume further that previous income statements indicate an average gross margin of 25 percent of net sales and that this relationship was valid for January. The inventory at the end of the month could be calculated as follows:

Inventory, January 1, 1975		$150,000
Net Purchases:		
Purchases	$210,600	
Transportation-in	2,400	
	$213,000	
Less: Returns and Allowances	3,000	210,000
Total of Goods Available for Sale		$360,000
Estimated Cost of Goods Sold:		
Sales	$300,000	
Less: Returns and Allowances	12,000	
Net Sales	$288,000	
Less: Estimated Gross Margin (25% of $288,000)	72,000	216,000
Estimated Inventory, January 31, 1975		$144,000

INCLUSION PROBLEMS AND INCOME TAX REGULATIONS

What manufacturing costs are to be included in inventories? In Chapter 5, the difference between an *absorption cost* and a *direct cost* answer to this question was illustrated in the Standard Products Company example. Of course, manufacturing costs not included in inventory become an expense of the period. When the firm uses absorption costing, it will have higher inventory amounts and lower cumulative expense totals. When the firm uses direct costing, it will have lower inventory amounts and higher cumulative expense totals. Insofar as the firm must choose between absorption costing and direct costing, the choice made will affect the trade-off between inventory costs and period expenses. For tax purposes, most firms would choose to accelerate expense recognition in order to defer recognition of taxable income; thus they would prefer direct costing.

In practice, firms are not allowed much choice. Generally accepted accounting principles and the Internal Revenue Service both require absorption costing. We think direct costing superior to absorption costing, but until the Internal Revenue Service and accounting authorities change their regulations, there is little any firm can do except report results assuming absorption costing. The issue of direct versus absorption costing is discussed further in Chapter 23. Briefly, our conclusions are that variable costs should be product costs but that fixed costs should be period costs.

There is only one major area in accounting where the Internal Revenue Service requires firms to use identical methods for tax returns and reports to stockholders: When the LIFO flow assumption is elected for tax returns, it must also be used for reports to stockholders. Furthermore, all firms must request permission from the Internal Revenue Service to use the LIFO flow assumption. Once a firm has chosen to adopt the LIFO flow assumption, it must request permission to change back to FIFO and may incur a tax liability if it does so. In recent years, many firms that earlier adopted LIFO so that income taxes would be lower (at the cost of reporting lower net income in the financial statements) have switched back to FIFO so that reported net income would be higher (at the cost of paying larger current income taxes).

Finally, the Internal Revenue Service requires that if the lower-of-cost-or-market valuation basis is used, it may not be coupled with a LIFO flow assumption. Consider the effect of allowing LIFO and lower of cost or market. When prices are rising, the LIFO flow assumption results in a lower closing inventory amount and the lower reported income than does FIFO. When prices are falling, the lower-of-cost-or-market basis with LIFO leads to a closing inventory amount equal to that of FIFO coupled with lower of cost or market. The IRS is unwilling to allow a flow assumption that results in lower taxable income when prices are rising and no higher taxable income when prices are falling. LIFO coupled with lower of cost or market, were it allowed, would result in a guarantee of no worse position (falling prices) and the hope of a better position (rising prices) as compared with FIFO plus lower of cost or market.

GOODS IN TRANSIT

Legal title to property usually passes to the purchaser when the seller places the goods in the hands of a trucking firm or other public transportation agency. Strictly speaking, therefore, all goods in transit should be shown as assets of the purchaser and should be offset by a corresponding liability to the seller. Common practice, however, ignores this legalistic situation and includes in the inventory only those goods received at the close of the accounting period. Care must be exercised to make sure that the last few days' receipts of goods are properly included in accounts payable as well as in the inventory.

If, on the other hand, the purchaser decides to recognize the legal transfer of title, the following entry would be made for merchandise in transit:

Merchandise in Transit	4,000	
Accounts Payable		4,000

This entry would normally be reversed at the beginning of the following period. The Merchandise in Transit account balance would be added to the inventory of goods on hand, the entire amount being included in the Merchandise Inventory account on the balance sheet.

GOODS OUT ON CONSIGNMENT

When goods are "sold" on consignment, the agent or consignee gets possession of the goods, but the seller or consignor retains legal title. The agent disposes of the goods for the owner and settles with him according to the terms of their agreement.

The consignment relationship is legally one of agency, with the consignee actually selling the goods for the consignor and receiving a commission for his services. Thus, the goods sent out on consignment must be carried as an inventory asset by the consignor and valued by him at cost plus any expenditures for items such as transportation and insurance. When a sales report is received from the agent, the consignor adjusts or closes out the merchandise account (usually called Goods Out on Consignment) and records the revenue and expense of the transaction.

Sometimes, however, the consignment sale arrangement is used merely as a means of credit protection. Both the buyer and the seller look upon the transaction as a completed sale with the consignment agreement being used merely to safeguard the position of the seller, who can then recover the goods in case the buyer does not pay for them. For accounting purposes such a transaction is handled as a sale on account and the goods are not included in the inventory of the seller.

SUMMARY

Inventory measurements affect both the cost of goods sold expense on the income statement for the period and the amount shown for the asset inventory on the balance sheet at the end of the period. The sum of the two must be equal to the beginning inventory plus the cost of purchases, at least in double-entry record keeping as we know it. The allocation between expense and asset depends on three factors: (1) the valuation basis used, (2) the flow assumption, and (3) the types of manufacturing costs included in inventory. The first factor involves a choice between the cost basis and the lower-of-cost-or-market basis. The second concerns whether a FIFO, a LIFO, or a weighted-average flow assumption should be made. The third factor requires a choice between absorption and direct costing.

APPENDIX 12.1: APPLYING LOWER-OF-COST-OR-MARKET INVENTORY BASIS

Implementing the lower-of-cost-or-market rule of inventory valuation is more complicated than the name implies. Original cost and replacement cost (market) for each item must, of course, be determined. Valuation at the lower of these two amounts is subject to two constraints on market value. First, the market value of an item used in the computation cannot exceed its *net realizable value*—an amount equal to selling price less reasonable costs to complete production and to sell the item. Second, the market value of an item used in the computation cannot be *less* than the *net realizable value minus the normal profit* ordinarily realized on disposition of completed items of this type. The lower-of-cost or market valuation is chosen at the lower of original *cost* or replacement cost (*market*) subject to the upper and lower bounds on replacement cost established in the first two steps.

Many accountants find the method for valuing by lower of cost or market easier to remember and use when the method is translated into symbols as follows. Let OC represent original cost, RC represent replacement cost, NRV represent net realizable value, and $PROF$ represent the normal profit. Then the lower-of-cost-or-market valuation is:

$$\text{minimum } [OC, NRV, \text{maximum } (RC, NRV - PROF)].$$

In other words, find the maximum of replacement cost and net realizable value minus normal profit. Call that quantity MAX. Then choose the smallest of original cost, net realizable value, and MAX. (The minimum of NRV and MAX is the "market" figure used in the computation.)

Schedule 12.5 illustrates the application of the rule for lower of cost or market when the normal profit margin is nine cents ($.09) per unit.

SCHEDULE 12.5 LOWER OF COST OR MARKET ILLUSTRATED

	Item			
	1	2	3	4
(a) Original Cost	$.90	$.97	$.96	$.90
(b) Net Realizable Value	.95	.95	.95	.95
(c) Net Realizable Value Less Normal Profit Margin	.86	.86	.86	.86
(d) Replacement Cost	.92	.96	.92	.85
(e) Maximum [(d), (c)] = MAX	.92	.96	.92	.86
(f) Lower of Cost or Market = Minimum [(a), (b), (e)]	.90	.95	.92	.86

Notice that each of the four possible valuations is used once to determine lower of cost or market. Item 1 uses original cost; item 2 uses net realizable value; item 3 uses replacement cost; and item 4 uses net realizable value less normal profit.

Another complication in lower cost or market is that the valuation can be applied to individual items, to classes of items, or to the entire inventory. If the valuations differ, the lowest inventory valuation will result from applying the rule item-by-item, and the highest from applying the rule to the entire inventory. The income tax regulations require that if lower of cost or market is used, then it must be applied on an item-by-item basis. Schedule 12.6 illustrates how the valuations can differ.

SCHEDULE 12.6

| Item | Per Unit | | | For All Units | | Lower of Cost or Market Applied | | |
	Quantity	Cost	Market	Cost	Market	Item by Item	To Inventory Classes	To Total Inventory
Class I								
A	20	$ 20	$ 18	$ 400	$ 360	$ 360		
B	25	100	110	2,500	2,750	2,500		
Class Total				$2,900	$3,110		$2,900	
Class II								
C	80	$ 6	$ 5	$ 480	$ 400	400		
D	60	12	10	720	600	600		
Class Total				$1,200	$1,000		1,000	
Grand Total				$4,100	$4,110	$3,860	$3,900	
Ending Inventory at Lower of Cost or Market						$3,860	$3,900	$4,100

APPENDIX 12.2: DOLLAR-VALUE LIFO METHOD

The LIFO method as described earlier was applied to *items* and unit costs of the items to determine cost flow and to identify ending inventory "layers." Where there are many different items, the task of calculation is quite formidable. Where the items continually change, such as style goods or annual models of appliances, the method cannot be readily applied. To surmount these problems, those seeking to use LIFO can use the *dollar-value LIFO method*. The specific calculations in using the two methods are somewhat different. The dollar-value LIFO method identifies layers of inventory costs by using aggregates rather than individual items. To indicate the underlying characteristics of the methods, a simplified illustration of the dollar-value LIFO method is presented in Schedule 12.7.

Under dollar-value LIFO methods, dollars of cost rather than units, are counted. Since prices change with time, any method that adds together prices of items bought at different times must take those changes into account if it is to present meaningful data. In the schedule, assume that at the end of 1970, the inventory was valued in end-of-1970 replacement prices at $100,000. A base year must be chosen. The convenient year to choose for the base is the earliest year from which records show the firm still holds inventory. The base year for the illustration is 1970. The price index for 1970 is assumed to be 1.00. If the price index for the base year were not 1.00, we would divide all price indexes by the index for the base year so that we could have a price series with base year price index equal to 1.00.

At the end of any year (called here, the *calculation* year) for which the method is to be applied, we are given a price index and the value of inventory at current (or replacement) cost. These data are shown in lines A and B of the schedule. First, calculate the value of calculation

SCHEDULE 12.7 ILLUSTRATION OF DOLLAR VALUE LIFO INVENTORY VALUATION

Price Index for 12/31/70 = 1.00
Inventory Value at 12/31/70 at 12/31/70 Prices = $100,000

	Year(*t*)				
	1971	1972	1973	1974	1975
A. End-of-year inventory at end-of-year (or replacement) prices	$120,000	$90,000	$110,000	$100,000	$120,000
B. Replacement price index for end of year, p_t	1.10	1.20	1.15	1.25	1.20
1. End-of-year inventory at 1970 prices [= $(A)/(B)$]	$109,091	$75,000	$ 95,652	$ 80,000	$100,000
LIFO Inventory layers at base-year (1970) prices					
2. From 1970 stock	100,000	75,000	75,000	75,000	75,000
3. From 1971 stock	9,091	0	0	0	0
4. From 1972 stock	—	0	0	0	0
5. From 1973 stock	—	—	20,652	5,000	5,000
6. From 1974 stock	—	—	—	0	0
7. From 1975 stock	—	—	—	—	20,000
[Sum of lines (2) through (7) = lines (1)].					
LIFO Inventory layers at cost in year of acquisition					
8. From 1970 stock = (2) × p_{1970}/p_{1970} = (2) × 1.00..	100,000	75,000	75,000	75,000	75,000
9. From 1971 stock = (3) × p_{1971}/p_{1970} = (3) × 1.10..	10,000	0	0	0	0
10. From 1972 stock = (4) × p_{1972}/p_{1970} = (4) × 1.20..	—	0	0	0	0
11. From 1973 stock = (5) × p_{1973}/p_{1970} = (5) × 1.15..	—	—	23,750	5,750	5,750
12. From 1974 stock = (6) × p_{1974}/p_{1970} = (6) × 1.25..	—	—	—	0	0
13. From 1975 stock = (7) × p_{1975}/p_{1970} = (7) × 1.20..	—	—	—	—	24,000
14. End-of-year LIFO Inventory at original costs = sum of lines (8) through (13)	$110,000	$75,000	$ 98,750	$ 80,750	$104,750

year-end inventories at base year prices. This is shown on line (1).
For example, at December 31, 1973, the replacement cost of inventories
is $110,000 and the price index is 1.15. The December 31, 1973, inventory
shown on line (1) would have cost $95,652 in base year (or 1970) prices.

Second, in lines (2) through (7), the LIFO layers, which add to the
amount shown in line (1), are calculated. Here, we use the fact that

last-in, first-out implies first-in, still-here (LIFO = FISH). To construct the calculation year's layers, start from the oldest stock on hand (from the previous year) and build up layers until the calculation year's inventory shown in line (1) is accounted for. For example, on December 31, 1974, $80,000 of base-year-priced inventory is to be accounted for. A total of $75,000 comes from the 1970 stock and the rest from the 1973 stock.

Third, the LIFO layers in base year prices just found on lines (2) through (7) are converted to original cost in the year the layer was acquired. These calculations are shown on lines (8) through (13).

Finally, the calculation-year ending inventory is shown on line (14) as the sum of the layers shown on lines (8) through (13).

The method is easier to use than to explain.

QUESTIONS AND PROBLEMS

*1. Goods which cost $800 are sold for $1,000 cash. Present the journal entries to record the sale (a) when a periodic inventory system is used and (b) when a perpetual inventory system is used.

2. Two television dealers may have identical stocks of goods on hand, but their inventories as stated in their respective balance sheets may be different in amount. Explain how this might occur.

3. "Original cost for inventory valuation is reasonable from the standpoint of the income statement but misleading for balance sheet purposes." Comment on this statement.

4. Under what circumstances would the perpetual and periodic inventory systems yield the same inventory amount if the last-in, first-out method were used? If the weighted-average method were used? If the first-in, first-out method were used? Which of the two methods, periodic or perpetual, would you expect to find used in each of the following situations?
   a. The greeting card department of a retail store
   b. The fur coat department of a retail store
   c. Supplies storeroom for an automated production line
   d. Grocery store
   e. College bookstore
   f. Diamond ring department of a jewelry store
   g. Ballpoint pen department of a jewelry store.

5. Which of the three methods of approximating original cost comes closest to presenting current costs in statements of operations? In the balance sheet?

6. Compare the inventory amounts in the balance sheets during periods of rising prices using (a) the first-in, first-out, (b) the weighted-average, and (c) the last-in, first-out methods of arriving at original cost. Assume no changes in physical quantities.

7. Refer to the preceding question. Assuming periods of declining prices, present the comparison.

* Hints, key numbers, or (partial) answers appear in the back of the book between the Appendix Tables and the Glossary.

8. Compare the merchandise cost of goods sold amounts in the income statements during periods of rising prices under (a) the first-in, first-out, (b) the weighted-average, and (c) the last-in, first-out methods of arriving at original cost. Assume that there are no changes in physical inventory quantities.

9. Refer to the preceding question. Assuming periods of declining prices, present the comparison.

10. An invoice for merchandise in the amount of $900 was received and entered in the voucher register on January 20, 1975. The goods were received on December 29, 1974, and were included in the inventory taken on December 31, 1974, at a cost of $900. The purchase should have been recorded in 1974.
   a. What was the effect on reported net income for 1974?
   b. What entry is required to correct the error if it is discovered after the invoice has been recorded?
   c. What entry would be required if the error were discovered when the invoice was received?

°11. On December 30, 1974, merchandise amounting to $750 was received and was included in the December 31 inventory. The invoice was not received until January 4, at which time the acquisition was recorded. Indicate the effect (overstatement, understatement, none) on each of the following amounts: (1) Inventory, 12/31/74; (2) Inventory, 12/31/75; (3) Cost of Sales, 1974; (4) Cost of Sales, 1975; (5) Net Income, 1974; (6) Net Income, 1975; (7) Accounts Payable, 12/31/74; (8) Accounts Payable, 12/31/75; (9) Retained Earnings, 12/31/74; (10) Retained Earnings, 12/31/75. Assume the error was not discovered by the firm when the invoice was received.

12. The inventory at September 1 and the purchases during September of a certain item of raw material were as follows:

9/1	Inventory	1,000 lbs.		$ 4,000
9/5	Purchased	3,000 lbs.		13,500
9/14	Purchased	3,500 lbs.		17,500
9/27	Purchased	3,000 lbs.		16,500
9/29	Purchased	1,000 lbs.		6,000

The inventory at September 30 is 1,800 pounds.
   Compute the cost of the inventory under (a) the first-in, first-out method, (b) the weighted-average method, and (c) the last-in, first-out method.

°13. The following information concerning an item of raw material is available:

Nov. 2	Inventory	4,000 lbs. @ $5
9	Issued	3,000 lbs.
16	Purchased	7,000 lbs. @ $6
23	Issued	3,000 lbs.
30	Issued	3,000 lbs.

   a. Compute the value of the inventory at November 30 and the cost of withdrawals during the month. Assume that the company uses perpetual inventory records under (1) the first-in, first-out method, (2) the weighted-average method, and (3) the last-in, first-out method. Carry unit cost calculations to the nearest tenth of a cent.

    b. Repeat (a) assuming that the periodic inventory method is used. Carry unit cost calculations to the nearest tenth of a cent.

14. The following data relate to one of the items in the inventory of the Morton Manufacturing Company:

October 1	Inventory	....	4,000 units @ $10
October 15	Purchased	....	4,000 units @ 9
October 27	Purchased	....	3,500 units @ 8

A physical inventory at October 31 indicated 4,500 units on hand.

    a. Calculate the cost of the units on hand and of the units withdrawn by (1) the first-in first-out method, (2) the weighted-average method, and (3) the last-in, first-out method. Carry unit costs to the nearest tenth of a cent.

    b. Repeat (a) assuming that a perpetual inventory system was in use and that issues were as follows:

October 14	....	2,000 units
October 25	....	2,500 units
October 31	....	2,500 units

Carry costs to the nearest tenth of a cent.

15. The following data relate to an item of raw material of the Grace Company:

March 1	Inventory	....	200 units @ $ 8
3	Issued	....	100 units
10	Purchased	....	600 units @ 9
17	Issued	....	400 units
20	Purchased	....	300 units @ 10
26	Issued	....	400 units
31	Purchased	....	100 units @ 11

    Calculate the inventory on March 31 and the cost of withdrawals during the month by (a) the first-in, first-out, (b) the weighted-average, and (c) the last-in, first-out methods of inventory valuation. Assume that perpetual inventory records are not used. Carry unit cost calculations to the nearest tenth of a cent.

16. Refer to the data in the preceding problem. Assume that perpetual inventory records are used. Calculate the inventory on March 31 and cost of withdrawals during the month by (a) the first-in, first-out, (b) the weighted-average, and (c) the last-in, first-out methods of inventory valuation. Carry unit cost calculations to the nearest tenth of a cent.

°17. The Central Supply Company has in its inventory on May 1 three units of item *K*, all purchased on the same date at a price of $60 per unit. Information relative to item *K* is as follows:

Date	Explanation	Units	Unit Cost	Tag Number
May 1	Inventory	3	$60	K—515, 516, 517
3	Purchase	2	65	K—518, 519
12	Sale	3		K—515, 518, 519
19	Purchase	2	70	K—520, 521
25	Sale	1		K—516

Compute the cost of units sold in accordance with the following:

a. Specific identification of units sold

b. First-in, first-out method (perpetual inventory records used)

c. First-in, first-out method (perpetual inventory records not used)

d. Last-in, first-out method (perpetual inventory records used)

e. Last-in, first-out method (perpetual inventory records not used)

f. Weighted-average method (perpetual inventory records used)

g. Weighted-average method (perpetual inventory records not used).

18. The Wilson Company sells chemical compounds made from expensium and cheap, inert chemicals. The company has used a LIFO inventory-flow assumption for many years. The inventory of expensium on January 1, 1970 consisted of 2,000 pounds from the LIFO inventory layer bought in 1966 for $30 a pound. The following schedule shows purchases and physical ending inventories of expensium for the years 1970 through 1975.

Year	Purchase Price per Pound for Year	Cost of Units Purchased	End-of-Year Inventory in Pounds
1970	$48	$240,000	2,000
1971	46	296,000	2,200
1972	48	368,000	3,000
1973	50	384,000	3,600
1974	50	352,000	2,600
1975	52	448,000	4,000

Because of temporary scarcities, expensium is expected to cost $62 per pound during 1976 but to fall back to $52 per pound in 1977. Sales for 1976 are expected to require 7,000 pounds of expensium. The purchasing agent suggests that the inventory of expensium be allowed to decrease from 4,000 to 600 pounds by the end of 1976 and be replenished to the desired level of 4,000 pounds early in 1977.

The controller argues that such a policy would be foolish. If inventories are allowed to decrease to 600 pounds, then the cost of goods sold will be extraordinarily low (because the older LIFO layers will be consumed), and income taxes will be extraordinarily high. Furthermore, he points out that the economic disadvantage of making smaller orders during 1976, as required by the purchasing agent's plan, would lead to about $1,000 of extra costs through lost quantity discounts. He suggests that 1976 purchases should be planned to maintain an end-of-year inventory of 4,000 pounds.

Assume that sales for 1976 do require 7,000 pounds of expensium, that the prices for 1976 and 1977 are as forecast, and that the income tax rate for Wilson Company is 40 percent.

Calculate the cost of goods sold and end-of-year LIFO inventory:

a. for each of the years 1970 through 1975

b. for 1976 assuming the controller's advice is followed so that inventory at the end of 1976 is 4,000 pounds

c. for 1976 assuming the purchasing agent's advice is followed and inventory at the end of 1976 is 600 pounds.

Assuming that the controller's, rather than the purchasing agent's, advice is followed, calculate:

d. The tax savings for 1976.

e. The extra cash costs for inventory.

f. Using the results derived so far, what should Wilson Company do?

g. Would your advice be different if Wilson Company used a FIFO inventory-flow assumption?

19. Use the same data for **Problem 18** except the 1976 price is expected to be, and is, $58 a pound. Repeat steps (b) through (e) of 18.

°20. The Wagner Company uses the "retail" method of inventory valuation. On July 1, 1975, its inventory of merchandise amounted to $60,000 at cost and $88,000 at selling prices. During July, purchases at cost amounted to $79,000, and it was estimated they would sell for $120,000. Freight on the purchases amounted to $1,000. During the month, certain items were increased in price by $3,000, and others were decreased by $1,000. Sales during the month totaled $114,000. Compute the cost of the inventory at July 31.

21. The following information has been compiled during the month of June for Department A of the Western Department Store:

	Cost	Selling Price
Inventory, June 1, 1975	$ 50,000	$ 80,000
Purchases during June	112,400	150,000
Markups		5,000
Markdowns		3,000
Sales		182,000

Compute the cost of the inventory on June 30 and the cost of sales for the month by the "retail" method.

22. The following information is available from the records for a department of the Noble Department Store:

	Cost	Selling Price
Merchandise, Inventory, 1/1/75	$26,600	$45,000
Purchases in January	29,000	48,700
Freight-in on Purchases	620	
Sales in January		70,500

Calculate the cost of the inventory at January 31, 1975. Use the retail inventory method.

°23. The merchandise inventory of the Park Sales Store was destroyed by fire on July 4, 1975. The books and records were saved and provided the following information:

Merchandise Inventory, January 1, 1975	$ 46,000
Merchandise Purchases, January 1 to July 4, 1975	98,000
Sales, January 1 to July 4, 1975	120,000

The average markup during 1974 was 50 percent of the cost. Compute the estimated cost of the inventory of merchandise on hand at the time of the fire.

24. The merchandise inventory of the Young Clothing Company was destroyed by fire on October 18, 1975. The books and financial statements were in a fireproof vault and are available for inspection. The insurance company asks for an estimate of the cost of the goods on hand at the time of the fire. Compute the amount from the following information:

Merchandise Inventory, 1/1/75	$ 68,000
Purchases, 1/1/75 to 10/18/75	332,000
Sales, 1/1/75 to 10/18/75	500,000
Sales, 1970 through 1974	3,452,700
Cost of Sales, 1970 through 1974	2,416,890

25. The inventory of merchandise of the Penny's Company at November 1, 1975, amounted to $19,500. On November 21, a fire destroyed the entire stock of merchandise. The purchases and sales during November to this date were $30,500 and $65,000, respectively. The average gross margin rate in recent months had been 40 percent. Calculate an amount for the inventory on hand at the time of the fire.

*26. The Venture Corporation is determining the value of its inventory at year end. The normal profit margin on inventory is 50 percent of original cost. Using the lower-of-cost-or-market rule, state the unit value which would be employed for inventory-pricing purposes for each of the items listed below:

Item	Original Cost	Replacement Cost	Selling Price	Estimated Cost to Complete and Sell
1	$36	$26	$ 60	$15
2	48	53	95	20
3	18	15	30	5
4	48	46	100	35
5	50	56	80	20
6	56	52	70	20
7	22	21	30	10
8	64	60	84	23

27. Calculate the inventory of Department K at the lower of cost or market from the following data, applying the method on an item-by-item basis:

Item	Quantity	Original Unit Cost	Present Unit Cost
P	50	$15	$14
Q	70	18	20
R	20	25	25
S	100	27	28

28. From the following information, calculate the value of the inventory of Department Q (a) at original cost, (b) at present cost, and (c) at lower of original or present cost (cost or market, whichever is lower) on an item-by-item basis.

		Unit Costs	
Item No.	Quantity	Original	Present
2310	500	$20	$21
2316	400	33	32
2320	800	10	11
2330	1,000	15	16
2340	600	40	40
2350	300	55	54
2355	150	95	90

°29. Present income statement data through the gross margin on sales for the years 1974 and 1975 under (a) the original cost and (b) the lower of cost or market as the basis of inventory valuation.

	1974	1975
Merchandise Inventory:		
1/1/74—cost	$ 100,000	
1/1/74—market	112,000	
12/31/74—cost	124,000	
12/31/74—market	110,000	
12/31/75—cost		$ 150,000
12/31/75—market		140,000
Merchandise Purchases	1,000,000	1,124,000
Merchandise Sales	1,500,000	1,560,000

°30. The following information relative to the activity of one of the raw materials used by the Watson Manufacturing Company is available at the close of business on June 30.

	Quantity	Unit Price	Amount
Inventory, June 1:			
Purchased: May 20	200	$5	$1,000
May 27	300	6	1,800
	500		$2,800
Purchases: June 10	300	$5	$1,500
June 20	400	7	2,800
June 27	400	6	2,400
	1,100		$6,700
Total Available	1,600		$9,500
Withdrawals: June 5	300		
June 13	400		
June 24	300		
	1,000		
Inventory, June 30	600		

a. Calculate the cost of the raw material used during the month and the cost of the month-end inventory, assuming that perpetual inventory records are not used, under (1) the first-in, first-out, (2) the last-in, first-out, and (3) the weighted-average methods. Carry unit-cost figures to two decimal points.

b. Repeat (a) assuming that perpetual inventory records are used. Carry unit-cost figures to three decimal points.

31. The following information is available from the records of the Jensen Clothing Shop for the first quarter of 1975:

	Cost	Selling Price
Merchandise Inventory, 1/1/75	$ 95,000	$125,000
Merchandise Purchases	425,000	575,000
Purchase Returns	5,000	5,500
Freight-in	10,000	
Markdowns		9,000
Markups		5,500
Sales		698,000
Sales Returns		12,000

a. Calculate the ending inventory at selling price and at cost in accordance with the retail inventory method. Assume that the marked-down merchandise has been sold as of March 31, 1975, the end of the quarterly fiscal period.

b. Calculate the cost of merchandise sold during the period.

32. The Edison Company regularly prices its merchandise at 50 percent above gross price on the supplier's invoice and then takes successive markdowns and occasional markups until the goods are sold. On March 26, 1975, a fire destroyed all of the merchandise of the Edison Company. The records of the company were kept in a fireproof safe, and they were not damaged. The following information from the records is available:

   (1) A physical inventory was taken on December 31, 1974. The cost of merchandise on hand at that date was $60,000. It was estimated that the selling price of the goods was only 45 percent above cost due to markdowns and other factors.

   (2) The gross invoice price of purchases made from January 1 to March 26, 1975, was $126,000. Freight-in on these purchases was $5,800 and discounts taken amounted to $1,400.

   (3) Merchandise markdowns from January 1 to March 26, 1975, totaled $4,980 and markups during that same period were $980.

   (4) Sales from January 1 to March 26, 1975, were $97,500.

   Estimate the cost of the merchandise destroyed. Assume that these goods were representative of those available during the period.

33. The Santo Company started to manufacture a new product in May. During May, the following purchases and requisitions from the storeroom of a material used in the new product occurred.

Date	Purchases	Requisitions
May 2	7,000 @ $30	
3		5,500
6	3,000 @ $31	
9		4,000
12	10,000 @ $32	
16		6,000
23		4,000
27	9,000 @ $33	
31		5,500

a. Calculate the cost of the material used during the month and the cost of the month-end inventory. Assume that perpetual inventory records are not used, under (1) the first-in, first-out, (2) the last-in, first-out, and (3) the weighted-average methods. Carry unit cost figures to four decimal places and round inventory costs to the nearest dollar.

b. Repeat (a) assuming that perpetual inventory records are used.

34. The merchandise inventory of the King Record Shop was destroyed by fire on May 4, 1974. The books and records were saved and provided the following information.

Merchandise Inventory, January 1, 1974	$ 56,715
Merchandise Purchases, January 1 to May 4, 1974	103,285
Sales, January 1 to May 4, 1974	188,500

The average markup during 1974 was 45 percent of cost.

Compute the estimated inventory of merchandise on hand at the time of the fire.

35. The Manson Company is determining its inventory cost on December 31, 1975. State, for each of the items listed below, the unit value which would be used for inventory-pricing purposes under the lower-of-cost-or-market rule.

Item	Original Cost	Replacement Cost	Selling Price	Estimated Cost to Complete and Sell	Normal Profit Margin
A	$ 42	$ 40	$ 44	$ 5	$ 2
B	406	400	450	33	18
C	95	85	95	5	4
D	17	18	22	3	1
E	218	210	220	12	8
F	150	120	200	100	50
G	12	14	20	10	5
H	200	170	280	100	70
I	25	12	36	10	9
J	180	150	400	100	100

36. The Salem Company began business on January 1, 1974. The information concerning merchandise inventories, purchases, and sales for the first three years of operations is as follows:

	1974	1975	1976
Sales	$300,000	$330,000	$450,000
Purchases	280,000	260,000	350,000
Inventories, December 31:			
At cost	80,000	95,000	95,000
At market	75,000	80,000	100,000

a. Compute the gross margin on sales for each year (1) under the lower-of-cost-or-market basis in valuing inventories and (2) under the cost basis.

b. Indicate your conclusion whether the lower-of-cost-or-market basis of valuing inventories is "conservative" in all situations for which it is applied.

37. At November 1 there were 2,500 gallons of chemicals in the warehouse of the Settlage Chemical Company acquired at a cost of $5 per gallon. During the month of November, purchases were made as follows:

November	5	4,500 gallons @ $5
	13	7,000 gallons @ $6
	25	4,000 gallons @ $7

Requisitions during the month were:

November	3	1,000 gallons
	9	3,000 gallons
	16	5,400 gallons
	23	2,600 gallons
	26	1,000 gallons
	29	2,000 gallons

a. Calculate the cost of the chemical used during the month and the cost of the month-end inventory, assuming that perpetual-inventory records are not used, under (1) the first-in, first-out, (2) the last-in, first-out, and (3) the weighted-average methods. Carry unit-cost figures to three decimal places and inventory costs to the nearest dollar.

b. Repeat (a) assuming that perpetual-inventory records are used.

*38. The following data show ending inventories at end-of-year prices of the Smith Company and a replacement-cost price level index.

	1971	1972	1973	1974	1975
A. End-of-year inventory at end-of-year (or replacement) price	$150,000	$180,000	$210,000	$200,000	$250,000
B. Price index at end of year, P_t	100	115	120	130	125

Prepare a schedule following the outline of the illustration in Schedule 12.7 and compute the ending inventory at LIFO cost for the four years 1972–1975 in accordance with the dollar-value LIFO method.

39. The Clapper Company uses the dollar-value LIFO method of pricing the ending inventory. The following data represent inventories valued at end-of-year replacement prices and a replacement-cost price index for the succeeding five years.

Year	Inventory at End-of-Year Replacement Prices	Price Index at End of Year
1970	$ 72,000	100
1971	100,000	125
1972	150,000	150
1973	105,600	120
1974	100,000	100
1975	81,400	110

Prepare a schedule showing the calculation of the ending inventory at LIFO cost for the five years 1971–1975.

40. The Montango Corporation uses the dollar-value LIFO method of inventory valuation. Given the following data on inventory valued at end-of-year replacement prices and an index of prices, compute the ending inventory at LIFO cost for each of the four years 1972–1975.

Year	Inventory at End-of-Year Replacement Prices	Price Index at End of Year
1971	$150,000	100
1972	220,000	120
1973	390,000	130
1974	250,000	125
1975	200,000	120

41. The Burch Corporation began a merchandising business on January 1, 1975. It acquired merchandise costing $100,000 in 1975, $125,000 in 1976, and $135,000 in 1977. Information about Burch Corporation's inventory, as it would appear on the balance sheet under different inventory valuation methods and flow assumptions, is shown below:

**INVENTORY VALUATIONS FOR BALANCE SHEET
UNDER VARIOUS ASSUMPTIONS**

Date	LIFO Cost	FIFO Cost	Lower of (FIFO) Cost or Market
12/31/75	$40,800	$40,000	$37,000
12/31/76	36,400	36,000	34,000
12/31/77	41,200	44,000	44,000

In answering each of the following questions, indicate how the answer is deduced. Keep in mind for parts **c-f** the form of the equation relating gross profits and inventories that says, for comparing any inventory Method A against any other Method B:

$$\text{Income}_{\text{Method A}} - \text{Income}_{\text{Method B}} = \text{Increase in Inventory}_{\text{Method A}}$$
$$- \text{Increase in Inventory}_{\text{Method B}}$$

   a. Did prices go up or down in 1975?
   b. Did prices go up or down in 1977?
   c. Which inventory basis would show the highest income for 1975?
   d. Which inventory basis would show the highest income for 1976?
   e. Which inventory basis would show the lowest income for all three years combined?
   f. For 1977, how much higher or lower would income be on the FIFO cost basis than it would be on the lower-of-cost-or-market basis?
   g. The notes to the financial statements in a recent annual report of the Westinghouse Electric Corporation contain the following statement. "The excess of current cost [of inventories] . . . over the cost of inventories valued on the LIFO basis was $230 million at [year end] and $163 million at [the beginning of the year]." How much higher or lower would Westinghouse's pre-tax reported income have been if its inventories had been valued at current costs, rather than with a LIFO cost flow assumption? Westinghouse reported $28 million net income for the year and tax expense equal to 48 percent of pre-tax income. By what percentage would Westinghouse's net income increase if a FIFO flow assumption had been used?

Chapter 13

Compound Interest and Annuities

Money is a scarce resource and its owner can use it to command other resources. Like owners of other scarce resources, owners of money can permit others (borrowers) to rent the use of their money for a period of time. Payment for the use of money differs little from other rental payments, such as those made to a landlord for the use of his property or to a car rental agency for the use of its car. Payment for the use of money is called *interest*. Accounting is concerned with interest because it must record transactions where the use of money is bought and sold.

Accountants are concerned with interest calculations for another, equally important, reason. Expenditures for an asset most often do not occur at the same time as the receipts for services produced by that asset. Money received sooner is more valuable than money received later. The difference in timing can affect whether or not acquiring an asset is profitable. Amounts of money received at different times are different commodities. *Money at one time is incommensurate with money at another time.* Accountants use interest calculations to make amounts of money to be paid or received at different times comparable. For example, an analyst compares two amounts to be received at two different times by using interest calculations to find the equivalent value of one amount at the time the other is due. Money contracts involving a series of money payments over time, such as bonds, mortgages, notes and leases, are evaluated by finding the *present value* of the stream of payments. The present value of a stream of payments is a single amount of money due at one time that is the economic equivalent of the entire stream.

Interest calculations inherently involve mathematics, mostly the tools of algebra. The treatment of interest presented in this chapter and the use of interest calculations later in the textbook is as unmathematical as we can reasonably make it. One can understand interest calculations without understanding mathematics. One can perform interest calculations without mathematics by using tables such as the ones in the Appendix in the back of this book.

The presentation of interest calculations in this chapter is divided into treatments of a single payment and of series of payments. For both single payments and series of payments study can further be divided into examining future values and present values. This "double dichotomy"—either a single payment or a series and either a present or a future value—can be represented as follows where the numbers show the order of presentation in this chapter.

| | | **Time** | |
		Now	Later
Number of Payments	One	(2) Present Value of Single Payment	(1) Future Value of Single Payment
	Many	(4) Present Value of Series of Payments	(3) Future Value of Series of Payment

The student, rather than trying to memorize the steps of the different kinds of calculations, should understand the simple principles involved so that with a set of interest tables he or she can derive the steps to be followed for a given problem.

COMPOUND INTEREST

The quotation of interest "cost" is typically specified as a percentage of the amount borrowed per unit of time. Examples are 6 percent per year, 1 percent per month, and, for discounts on purchases, 2/10, net/30 which is equivalent to 2 percent for twenty days because if the discount is not taken, the money can be used for an extra twenty days. The amount borrowed or loaned is called the *principal*. To *compound* interest means either to pay to the lender at the end of the period the interest earned during the period or, at the end of the period, to add the interest in with the principal so that the principal for the next interest period is larger. These two ways of defining compounding are equivalent. The lender who is paid interest in cash usually has the option of depositing the cash, thereby increasing the principal. The lender whose interest is automatically added in with the principal frequently has the option of withdrawing some of it in cash. The period between interest calculations, during which the principal earns interest, is called the *compounding* period. A technical term sometimes used for the interest-earning period is the *conversion* period. The use of the word conversion arises from the definition of compound interest that says the interest earned is *converted* (added) to principal at the end of the interest-earning period.

If you deposit $1,000 in a savings account that pays compound interest at the rate of 6 percent per year, you will be credited with $60 at the end of a year. (The bank's credit is your debit.) Thus, $1,060 will be earning interest during the second year. During the second year your principal of $1,060 will earn $63.60 interest, $60 on the initial deposit of $1,000 and $3.60 on the $60 earned the previous year.

The "force," or effect, of compound interest is more substantial than many people realize. For example, compounded annually at 6 percent, money "doubles itself" in less than 12 years. Put another way, if you put $49.70 in a savings account that pays 6 percent compounded annually, you will have $100 in twelve years. If the Indians who sold Manhattan Island for $24 in May, 1626, had been able to invest that principal at 8 percent compounded annually, the principal would have grown to almost $12 trillion by May, 1976, 350 years later. The rate of interest affects the amount of accumulation more than you might expect. If the Indians invested at 6 percent rather than 8 percent, the $24 would have grown to "only" $16 billion in 350 years.

When only the original principal earns interest during the entire life of the loan, the interest due at the time the loan is repaid is called *simple* interest. At simple interest of 6 percent per year, the Indians' $24 would have grown to only $528 in 350 years, $24 of principal and $504 of simple interest. Nearly all economic calculations involve compound interest. Simple interest is computed as the principal multiplied by the rate, multiplied by the time, or $24 \times .06 \times 350 = $504, for the Indians' investment.

Problems involving compound interest fall into two groups with respect to time: first, there are the problems for which we want to know the *future value* of money invested or loaned today; second, there are the problems for which we want to know the *present value*, or today's value, of money to be received later.

Future Value

When one dollar invested today at 6 percent is compounded annually, it will grow to $1.0600 at the end of the year, $1.1236 at the end of two years, $1.1910 at the end of three years, and so on according to the following formula:

$$F_n = P(1 + r)^n$$

where

P represents the initial investment today
F_n represents the accumulation or future value
n is the number of periods from today, and
r is the interest rate per period.

The amount F_n is the future value of the present payment, P, compounded at r percent per period for n periods. Appendix Table 1 shows the future values of $P = \$1$ for various numbers of periods and for various interest rates. Extracts from that table, rounded to four decimal places, are shown in Table 13.1.

TABLE 13.1 (Appendix Table 1) FUTURE VALUE OF $1 AT 6% AND 8% PER PERIOD
$$F_n = (1 + r)^n$$

Number of Periods = n	Rate = r 6%	8%
1	1.0600	1.0800
2	1.1236	1.1664
3	1.1910	1.2597
10	1.7908	2.1589
20	3.2071	4.6610

Sample problems involving future value

1. How much will $1,000 deposited today at 6 percent compounded annually be worth 10 years from now?

One dollar deposited today at 6 percent will grow to $1.7908; therefore $1,000 will grow to $1,000(1.06)^{10} = \$1,000 \times 1.7908 = \$1,790.80$.

2. How much will $500 deposited today at 8 percent compounded annually be worth 23 years from today?

The tables do not show values for 23 periods. Interpolation between the numbers shown in tables is imprecise; rather, notice that $F_{23} = P(1.08)^{23} = P(1.08)^{20}(1.08)^3$. Calculate the future value for 23 years in two steps: first, determine the amount that $1 will grow to in 20 years at 8 percent or $4.6610. Then let $4.6610 be the principal that grows for three (more) years. One dollar invested for 3 years at 8 percent grows to $1.2597. Therefore $4.6610 invested for 3 years grows to $4.6610 \times 1.2597 = \$5.8715$. (Note that factors for any two periods that sum to 23 can be used and produce the same answer. For example: $(1.08)^{11} \times (1.08)^{12} = (1.08)^{23} = 2.33164 \times 2.51817 = 5.8715$.) So $1 invested for 23 years at 8 percent has future value of $5.8715, and $500 invested for 23 years at 8 percent grows to $500 \times 5.8715 = \$2,935.75$.

3. How long does it take for an initial investment to quadruple at 8 percent compounded annually?

Turn to Appendix Table 1. Scan down the 8 percent column until you find 1 quadrupled, or 4. The number 4 does not appear in the column, but we see 3.9960 in the row corresponding to 18 periods. Thus $1 will grow to $4 in just over 18 years when invested at 8 percent compounded annually. To get the exact answer requires using logarithms to solve for n in the equation $\$4 = \$(1.08)^n$. The answer is

18.013 periods, but such calculations are beyond the accuracy that the accountant ordinarily requires.

A rule of thumb worth remembering for rough calculations is the *Rule of 72*. For interest rates between 3 percent and 12 percent per period, the number of periods required for an amount to double in value when invested at r percent per period is $72/r$. The Rule of 72 says, for example, that money invested at 4 percent per period doubles in $72/4 = 18$ periods; the exact answer is slightly more than 17.67 periods. At 10 percent, the Rule of 72 suggests that money doubles in 7.2 periods which is reasonably close to the correct answer, approximately 7.27 periods.[1]

Present Value

The preceding section developed the tools for computing the future value, F_n, of a sum of money, P, deposited or invested today. P is known; F_n is calculated. This section deals with the problems of calculating how much P has to be invested today in order to have a specified amount, F_n, n periods in the future. F_n is known; P is calculated. In order to have \$1 one year from today when interest is earned at 6 percent, P of \$.9434 must be invested today. That is, $F_1 = P(1.06)^1$ or \$1 = \$.9434 $\times$ 1.06. Since $F_n = P(1 + r)^n$, dividing both sides of the equation by $(1 + r)^n$ yields:

$$\frac{F_n}{(1 + r)^n} = P,$$

or

$$P = \frac{F_n}{(1 + r)^n} = F_n (1 + r)^{-n}.$$

To have $F_2 = \$1$, two years from today the amount P that must be invested at 6 percent is $P = \$1/(1.06)^2$. The value of $(1.06)^2$ can be read from Table 13.1 (2-period row, under the $r = 6\%$ column) as 1.1236. The quotient is $1/1.1236 = .8900$. In order to accumulate \$1 at the end of two periods, \$.89 must be invested when the interest rate is 6 percent.

The number $(1 + r)^{-n}$ is the present value of \$1 received after n periods when interest is earned at r percent per period. The term *discount* is used in this context as follows: the *discounted* present value of \$1 received n periods in the future is $(1 + r)^{-n}$ when the *discount* rate is r percent per period for n periods. The number r is the discount *rate* and the number $(1 + r)^{-n}$ is the discount *factor* for n periods. A discount factor $(1 + r)^{-n}$ is merely the reciprocal, or inverse, of a number, $(1 + r)^n$, in Table 13.1.

---

[1] An even better rule, one that works for interest rates between ¼ percent and 100 percent is the Rule of 69: compounded at r percent per period, money doubles in $69/r + .35$ periods. See John P. Gould and Roman L. Weil, "The Rule of 69," *Journal of Business*, 47 (July 1974).

Therefore, tables of discount factors are not necessary for present value calculations if tables of future values are at hand. But present value calculations are so frequently needed, and division is so onerous that tables of discount factors are as widely available as tables of future values. Portions of Appendix Table 2, which shows discount factors or, equivalently, present values of $1 for various interest (or discount) rates for various numbers of periods are shown in Table 13.2.

TABLE 13.2 (Appendix Table 2)   PRESENT VALUE OF $1 AT 6% AND 8% PER PERIOD
$$P = F_n (1 + r)^{-n}$$

Number of Periods = n	Rate = r 6%	8%
1	.9434	.9259
2	.8900	.8573
3	.8396	.7938
10	.5584	.4632
20	.3118	.2145

Sample problems involving present values

1. What is the present value of $1 due 3 years from now if the interest (equivalently, the discount) rate r is 8 percent?

From Table 13.2 (8% column, 3-period row), the present value of $1 received 3 periods later at 8 percent is $.7938.

2. You are promised $800 ten years from today. How much is that promise worth today if your discount rate is 8 percent per period?

One dollar received 10 years later discounted at 8 percent has a present value of $.4632. Thus the promise is worth $800 × .4632 = $370.56.

3. (Review problem) How much will you have in 10 years if you invest $370.56 today at 8 percent compounded annually?

From Table 13.1, $1 invested at 8 percent is worth $2.1589 ten years from now; thus $370.56 invested today will be worth $370.56 × 2.1589 = $800 after ten years.

4. What is the present value of $5,000 to be received 23 years hence, when the discount rate is 6 percent per year?

The tables do not show values for 23 periods. Interpolation is not precise; rather, note that $P = F_{23}(1.06)^{-23} = F_{23}(1.06)^{-20}(1.06)^{-3}$. Calculate the present value in two steps: first, find the present value of $1 received 20 years later discounted at 6 percent, $.3118. Then let $.3118 represent the amount to be received 3 years later. The present value of $1 received 3 years later discounted at 6 percent is $.8396. Therefore the present value of $.3118 to be received 3 years later is $.3118 × .8396 = $.2618. [Factors for any two periods that sum to

23 could be used: for example, $(1.06)^{-23} = (1.06)^{-11} \times (1.06)^{-12} =$ .52679 $\times$ .49697 $=$ .2618.] So $1 received 23 years from now is currently worth $.2618, and $5,000 received 23 years from now is worth $5,000 $\times$ .2618 $=$ $1,309 today when the discount rate is 6 percent per year.

Changing the Compounding Period: Nominal and Effective Rates

"Six percent, compounded annually" is the price for a loan; this means that interest is added to or *converted* into principal once a year at the rate of 6 percent. Often, however, the price for a loan states that compounding is to take place more than once a year. A savings bank may advertise that it pays 6 percent, compounded quarterly. This means that at the end of each quarter the bank credits savings accounts with interest calculated at the rate 1.5 percent ($=$ 6 percent/4). Corporate bonds usually pay interest twice a year. In this section the effect of changing the compounding period is examined.

If $1,000 is invested today at 12 percent compounded annually, its future value one year later is $1,120. If the rate of interest is stated as 12 percent compounded semiannually, then 6-percent interest is added to the principal every six months. At the end of the first six months, $1,000 will have grown to $1,060. At the end of the second six months, interest at 6 percent is computed on a principal of $1,060 so that the accumulation will be $1,060 $\times$ 1.06 $=$ $1,123.60 by the end of the year. Notice that 12 percent compounded *semiannually* is equivalent to 12.36 percent compounded *annually*.

Suppose the price is quoted as 12 percent, compounded quarterly. Then an additional 3 percent of the principal will be added to, or converted into, principal every three months. By the end of the year $1,000 will grow to $1,000 $\times$ $(1.03)^4$ $=$ $1,000 $\times$ 1.1255 $=$ $1,125.50. Twelve percent compounded quarterly is equivalent to 12.55 percent compounded annually. If 12 percent is compounded monthly, then $1 will grow to $1 $\times$ $(1.01)^{12}$ $=$ $1.1268. Thus, 12 percent compounded monthly is equivalent to 12.68 percent compounded annually.

For a given *nominal* rate, such as the 12 percent in the examples above, the more often interest is compounded or converted into principal the higher the *effective* rate of interest paid. If a nominal rate, r, is compounded m times per year, then the effective rate is $(1 + r/m)^m - 1$. When a nominal rate of 12 percent is compounded semiannually, the effective rate is $(1 + .12/2)^2 - 1$ or 12.36 percent.

Some savings banks advertise that they compound interest daily or even continuously. The mathematics of calculus provides a mechanism for finding the effective rate when interest is compounded continuously. We will not go into details but merely state that if interest is compounded continuously at nominal rate r per year, then the effective annual rate is $e^r - 1$ where e is the base of the natural logarithms. Tables of values of e^r

are widely available.[2] Six percent per year compounded continuously is equivalent to 6.1837 percent compounded annually; 12 percent per year compounded continuously is equivalent to 12.75 percent compounded annually. Do not confuse the compounding period with the payment period. Some banks, for example, compound interest daily but pay interest quarterly. You can be sure that such banks do not employ clerks or even computers to calculate interest every day. They merely use tables to derive an equivalent effective rate to apply at the end of each quarter.

In practice, to solve problems that require computation of interest quoted at a nominal rate of r percent per period compounded m times per period for n periods, merely use the tables for rate r/m and $m \times n$ periods. For example, 8 percent compounded quarterly for 7 years is equivalent to the rate found in the interest tables for $r = 8/4 = 2$ percent for $m \times n = 4 \times 7 = 28$ periods.

Sample problems in changing the compounding period

1. What is the future value five years hence of $600 invested at 8 percent compounded quarterly?

   Eight percent compounded four times per year for 5 years is equivalent to 2 percent per period compounded for 20 periods. Appendix Table 1 shows the value of $F_{20} = (1.02)^{20}$ to be 1.48595. Six hundred dollars then, would grow to $600 \times 1.48595 = $891.57.

2. How much money must be invested today at 6 percent compounded semiannually in order to have $1,000 four years from today?

   Six percent compounded two times a year for 4 years is equivalent to 3 percent per period compounded for 8 periods. The *present* value, Appendix Table 2, of $1 received 8 periods hence at 3 percent per period is $.7894, so that to have $1,000 in 4 years, $1,000 \times .7894 = $789.40 must be invested today.

ANNUITIES

An *annuity* is a series of equal payments made at the beginning or end of equal periods of time. Examples of annuities include monthly rental payments, semiannual corporate bond coupon (or interest) payments, and annual payments to a retired employee under a pension plan. Armed with an understanding of the tables for future and present values, you can solve any annuity problem. Annuities arise so often, however, and their solution is so tedious without special tables that annuity problems warrant special study and the use of special tables.

Terminology

The terminology used for annuities can be confusing because not all writers use the same terms. Definitions of the terms used in this text follow.

[2] See, for example, Sidney Davidson, *Handbook of Modern Accounting* (New York: McGraw-Hill, 1970), Chapter 8, p. 6.

An annuity whose payments occur at the *end* of each period is called an *ordinary annuity* or an *annuity in arrears*. Corporate bond coupon payments are usually paid in arrears or, equivalently, the first payment does not occur until after the bond has been outstanding for six months.

An annuity whose payments occur at the *beginning* of each period is called an *annuity due* or an *annuity in advance*. Rent is usually paid in advance so that a series of rental payments is an annuity due.

A *deferred* annuity is one whose first payment is at some time later than the end of the first period.

Annuities can be paid forever. Such annuities are called *perpetuities*. Bonds that promise payments forever are called *consols*. The British and Canadian governments have, from time to time, issued consols. A perpetuity can be in arrears or in advance. The only difference between the two is the timing of the first payment.

Annuities can be confusing. Their study is made easier with a time line such as the one shown below.

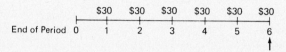

A time line marks the end of each period, numbers the periods, shows the payments to be received or paid, and shows the time at which the annuity is valued. The time line just pictured represents an ordinary annuity (in arrears) for 6 periods of $30 to be valued at the end of period 6. The end of period 0 is "now." The first payment is to be received one period from now.

Annuities in Arrears (Ordinary Annuities)

The future values of ordinary annuities are shown in Appendix Table 3, portions of which are reproduced in Table 13.3.

TABLE 13.3 (Appendix Table 3) FUTURE VALUE OF AN ANNUITY OF $1 IN ARREARS AT 6% AND 8% PER PERIOD

Number of Periods = n	Rate = r	
	6%	8%
1	1.0000	1.0000
2	2.0600	2.0800
3	3.1836	3.2464
5	5.6371	5.8666
10	13.1808	14.4866
20	36.7856	45.7620

Consider an ordinary annuity for 3 periods at 6 percent. The time line for the future value of such an annuity is:

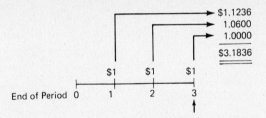

The $1 received at the end of the first period earns interest for 2 periods, so it is worth $1.1236 at the end of period 3. The $1 received at the end of the second period grows to $1.06 by the end of period 3, and the $1 received at the end of period 3 is, of course, worth $1 at the end of period 3. The entire annuity is worth $3.1836 at the end of period 3. The mathematical expression for the future value, F, of an annuity of A per period compounded at r percent per period for n periods is:

$$F = \frac{A[(1+r)^n - 1]}{r}.$$

The present values of ordinary annuities are shown in Appendix Table 4, portions of which are reproduced in Table 13.4.

TABLE 13.4 (Appendix Table 4) PRESENT VALUE OF AN ANNUITY OF $1 IN ARREARS AT 6% AND 8% PER PERIOD

Number of Periods = n	Rate = r	
	6%	8%
1	0.9434	0.9259
2	1.8334	1.7833
3	2.6730	2.5771
5	4.2124	3.9927
10	7.3601	6.7101
20	11.4699	9.8182

The time line for the present value of an ordinary annuity of $1 per period for 3 periods, discounted at 6 percent, is:

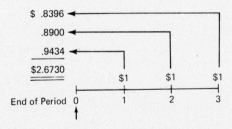

The $1 to be received at the end of period 1 has present value $.9434, the $1 to be received at the end of period 2 has present value $.8900, and the dollar to be received at the end of the third period has present value $.8396. Each of these numbers comes from Table 13.2. The present value of the annuity is the sum of these individual present values, $2.6730, shown in Table 13.4.

The present value of an ordinary annuity for n periods is the sum of the present values of $1 received 1 period from now plus $1 received two periods from now, . . . , plus $1 received n periods from now. The mathematical expression for the present value, P_A, of an annuity of A per period, for n periods, compounded at r percent per period is:

$$P_A = \frac{A[1 - (1 + r)^{-n}]}{r.}$$

Sample problems involving ordinary annuities

1. What is the present value of an annuity in arrears of $30 every six months to be received for 10 years at 6 percent compounded semiannually?

Six percent compounded semiannually for 10 years is equivalent to 3 percent per period compounded for 20 periods. From Appendix Table 4, 3-percent column and 20-payment row, $1 received at the end of each period has present value $14.8775. So the $30 semiannual annuity has present value $30 × 14.8775 = $446.3250.

2. What is the future value of $1 invested per year compounded at 6 percent for 23 years if the first dollar is invested one year from now (an ordinary annuity for 23 periods)?

The time line is:

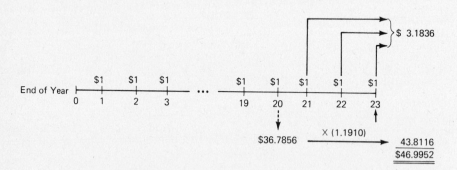

The tables do not show future values for 23 years. At the end of year 20, the annuity will have grown to $36.7856 (Table 13.3). That accumulation will grow for 3 more years at 6 percent, so (from Table 13.1 future value of $1 compounded at 6 percent for 3 periods) it will grow to $36.7856 × 1.1910 = $43.8116. In addition, as of the end of year 20, the payments from the ends of years 21, 22, and 23 are an ordinary annuity for 3 years with future value $3.1836. The entire annuity has future value $43.8116 + $3.1836 = $46.9952.

3. What is the present value of an ordinary annuity of $1 per year for 23 years at 6 percent?

The time line for this problem is:

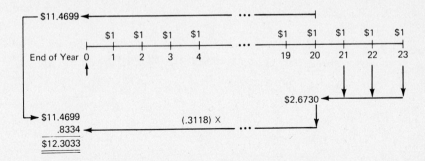

The first 20 payments have present value $11.4699, as shown in Table 13.4. As of the end of year 20, the final three payments have present value of $2.6730. One dollar received in 20 years is worth $.3118 at the start of year zero, so $2.6730 is worth $2.6730 × .3118 = $.8334 at the start of year zero. The entire annuity is worth $11.4699 + $.8334 = $12.3033.

Annuities in Advance (Annuities Due)

The time line for the future value of a 3-period annuity in advance is:

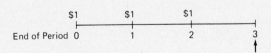

Notice that the future value is defined for the *end* of the period at the start of which the last payment is made. When tables of ordinary annuities are available, tables for annuities due are unnecessary.

Compare the time line for the future value of an annuity in advance for 3 periods *with the time axis relabeled to show start of period* and the time line for the future value of an ordinary annuity (in arrears) for 4 periods.

Annuity in Advance

Start of Period

Annuity in Arrears

End of Period

A $1 annuity in advance for n periods has future value equal to the future value of a $1 annuity in arrears for $n + 1$ periods *minus $1*. The $1 circled in the time line for the annuity in arrears is the $1 that must be subtracted to calculate the future value of an annuity in advance. The "note" at the foot of Appendix Table 3 says: "To convert this table [of future values of ordinary annuities] to values of an annuity in advance, take one more period and subtract 1.0000."

The time line for the present value of an annuity in advance for 3 periods is

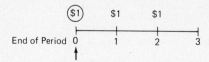

Notice that except for the first, circled, payment it looks just like the present value of an ordinary annuity for 2 periods. A $1 annuity in advance for n periods has present value equal to the present value of a $1 annuity in arrears for $n - 1$ periods *plus* $1. The "note" at the foot of Appendix Table 4 says: "To convert this table to values of an annuity in advance, take one less period and add 1.0000."

Sample problems involving annuities due

1. What is the present value of rents of $350 to be paid monthly, in advance, for 1 year when the discount rate is 1 percent per month?

The present value of $1 per period *in arrears* for 11 periods is $10.3676; the present value of $1 per period in advance for 12 periods is $10.3676 + $1.00 = $11.3676 and the present value of this year's rent is $350 × 11.3676 = $3,978.66.

2. Mr. Mason is sixty-two years old today. He wishes to invest an amount today and equal amounts on his sixty-third, sixty-fourth and sixty-fifth birthdays so that starting on his sixty-sixth birthday he can withdraw $5,000 on each birthday for eleven years. His investments will earn 8 percent per year. How much should be invested on the sixty-second through sixty-fifth birthdays?

The time line for this problem is:

$$\begin{array}{cccccccccc}
 & X & X & X & X & -\$5,000 & -\$5,000 & \cdots & -\$5,000 & -\$5,000 \\
\text{End of Year} & 62 & 63 & 64 & 65 & 66 & 67 & \cdots & 75 & 76
\end{array}$$

For each $1 that Mr. Mason invests on his sixty-second, sixty-third, sixty-fourth, and sixty-fifth birthdays, he will have $4.8666 = $5.8666 − $1 (Table 13.3) on his sixty-sixth birthday. On his sixty-sixth birthday Mr. Mason needs to have accumulated an amount large enough to fund an 11-year, $5,000 annuity in advance. An 11-year, $1 annuity in advance has present value of $7.7101 = $6.7101 + $1 (Table 4). Mr. Mason then needs on his sixty-sixth birthday an accumulation of $5,000 × 7.7101 = $38,550.50. Since each $1 deposited on the sixty-second through sixty-fifth birthdays grows to $4.8666, Mr. Mason must deposit $38,550.50/4.8666 = $7,921.44 on each of the sixty-second through sixty-fifth birthdays to accumulate $38,550.50.

Deferred Annuities

When the first payment of an annuity occurs some time after the end of the first period, the annuity is *deferred*. The time line for an ordinary annuity of $1 per period for 4 periods deferred for 2 periods is:

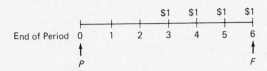

The arrow marked "*P*" shows the time for which the present value is calculated; the arrow marked "*F*" shows when the future value is calculated. The *future* value is not affected by the deferral and equals the future value of an ordinary annuity for four periods.

Notice that the time line for the present value looks like one for an ordinary annuity for 6 periods *minus* an ordinary annuity for 2 periods:

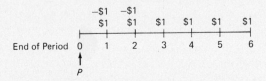

Calculate the present value of an annuity of *n* payments deferred for *d* periods by subtracting the present value of an annuity for *d* periods from the present value of an annuity for *n* + *d* periods.

An example of a deferred annuity

1. What is the present value of Mr. Mason's *withdrawals*? Recall that Mr. Mason is sixty-two years old, and will receive $5,000 on his sixty-sixth through seventy-sixth birthdays, and his investment earns 8 percent.

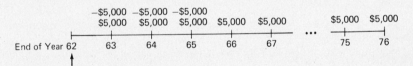

The present value at 8 percent of $5,000 received for 14 years, starting one year hence is $5,000 × 8.2442 = $41,221 (Table 4). The present value at age sixty-two of the $5,000 he will *not* receive on birthdays sixty-three through sixty-five is —$5,000 × 2.5771 = —$12,885.50. The present value of the actual payments to Mr. Mason is $41,221.00 — $12,885.50 = $28,335.50.

Perpetuities

A periodic payment to be received forever is called a *perpetuity*. Future values of perpetuities are undefined. If $1 is to be received at the end of every period and the discount rate is r percent, then the present value of the perpetuity is $1/r. This expression can be derived with algebra or by observing what happens in the expression for the present value of an ordinary annuity of $A per payment as n, the number of payments, approaches infinity:

$$P_A = \frac{A[1 - (1 + r)^{-n}]}{r}.$$

As n approaches infinity $(1 + r)^{-n}$ approaches zero, so that P_A approaches $A(1/r)$.

If the first payment of the perpetuity occurs now, the present value is $A[1 + 1/r]$.

Examples of perpetuities

1. The Canadian government offers to pay $30 every six months forever. What is that promise worth if the discount rate is 8 percent compounded semiannually?

    Eight percent compounded semiannually is equivalent to 4 percent per six-month period. If the first payment occurs six months from now, the present value is $30/.04 = $750. If the first payment occurs today, the present value is $30 + $750 = $780.

2. Every two years, Mr. Lane gives $6,000 to the University to provide a scholarship for an entering student in a two-year business administration course. If the University earns 6 percent per year on its investments, how much must Mr. Lane give to the University to provide such a scholarship every two years forever, starting two years hence?

    A perpetuity in arrears assumes one payment at the end of each period. Here, the period is two years; 6 percent compounded once a year over two years is equivalent to a rate of $(1.06)^2 - 1 = .1236$ or 12.36 percent compounded once per two-year period. Consequently, the present value of the perpetuity paid in arrears every two years is $6,000/.1236 = $48,544. A gift of $48,544 will be sufficient to provide a $6,000 scholarship forever. A gift of $54,544 is required if the first scholarship is to be awarded now.

Combinations of Cash Flows

Financial instruments may combine annuities and single payments. Bonds typically pay a specified sum every six months and a single, lump sum payment along with the final periodic payment. Bonds are treated in more detail in Chapter 15, but here is a simple example: the U.S. government promises to pay $30 every six months, the first payment to occur six months from now, for ten years and an additional $1,000, ten years from now. If payments are discounted at 6 percent, compounded semiannually, then the $1,000 single payment has present value $1,000 $\times$ .5537 = $553.70 and the present value of the annuity is $30 $\times$ 14.8775 = $446.33. The sum of the two components is approximately $1,000. (This is a $1,000 par value, ten-year bond with 6-percent semiannual coupons issued to yield 6 percent compounded semiannually.)

Life-Contingent Annuities

The annuities discussed above all last for a certain or specified number of payments. Such annuities are sometimes called *certain annuities* to distinguish them from *contingent annuities*, for which the number of payments depends on an event to occur at an uncertain date. For example, businesses often want to know the cost of an annuity (pension) that will be paid only so long as the annuitant (retired employee) lives. Such annuities are called *life-contingent* or *life annuities*. Some texts show an incorrect calculation for the cost of a life annuity. The details of life-annuity calculations are beyond the scope of this text but an unrealistic, hypothetical example is shown below so that our readers will be properly warned about the subtleties of life annuities.

Mr. Caplan is sixty-five years old today, and he has an unusual disease. He will die either 1½ years from today or 10½ years from today. Mr. Caplan has no family, and his employer wishes to purchase an ordinary life annuity for Mr. Caplan that will pay him $10,000 on his sixty-sixth birthday and $10,000 on every birthday thereafter on which Mr. Caplan is still alive. Funds invested in the annuity will earn 10 percent per year. How much should Mr. Caplan's life annuity cost?

The Wrong Calculation. Mr. Caplan's life expectancy is 6 years: one-half chance of his living 1½ years plus one-half chance of his living 10½ years. The employer expects that six payments will be made to Mr. Caplan. The present value of an ordinary annuity of $1 for 6 years at 10 percent is $4.3553 (Table 4). Therefore the annuity will cost $43,553.

The Right Calculation. Mr. Caplan will receive one payment for certain. The present value of that payment of $10,000 at 10 percent is $9,091 (Table

2). Mr. Caplan will receive nine further payments if he survives the critical second year. Those nine payments have present value $52,355; which is equal to the present value of a nine-year ordinary annuity that is deferred for one year, $61,446 — $9,091 (Table 4). The probability is one-half that Mr. Caplan will survive to receive those nine payments. Thus, their *expected* present value is $26,178 (= .5 $\times$ $52,355), and the *expected* present value of the entire life annuity is $9,091 + $26,178 = $35,269.

Mr. Caplan's life annuity, correctly calculated, costs only 81 percent as much as is found by the incorrect calculation. Actuaries for insurance companies use mortality tables to estimate probabilities of an annuitant's receiving each payment and, from those data, calculate the expected cost of a life annuity. Different mortality tables are used for men and women because of the well-documented difference in life expectancies.

SUMMARY

Accountants typically use one of four kinds of compound interest calculations: the present or future value of a single payment or a series of payments. These four calculations are pictured in the following diagram.[3]

Present Values	Amounts or Future Values
Single Payment	
$P = F_n/(1 + r)^n$	$F_n = P(1 + r)^n$
(Table 2)	(Table 1)

Backward Looking	Forward Looking
Series of Payments	
$P_A = (1 - P)/r$	$F_A = P[(1 + r)^n - 1]/r$
(Table 4)	(Table 3)

The table numbers shown correspond to the table numbers in the Appendix which gives the appropriate factors. As is apparent from a study of the formulas, all the compound interest factors in Tables 2, 3, and 4 can be derived from numbers in Table 1. Nevertheless, the other tables are given because the calculations are done relatively often and having all the tables makes for fewer odious calculations.

In working annuity problems, you will find drawing a time line helpful in deciding which particular kind of annuity is involved. The following time lines summarize the various kinds of annuities that accountants must understand. In each case, except for the perpetuity, an annuity for four periods is illustrated.

[3] David O. Green of the University of Chicago was the first to present this diagram.

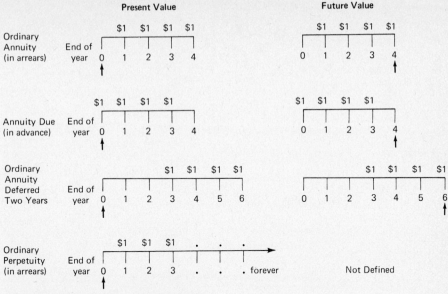

QUESTIONS AND PROBLEMS

(In the absence of instructions to the contrary, round all present value factors to three places after the decimal point.)

1. Does the present value of a given amount to be paid in ten years increase or decrease as the interest rate increases? Suppose the amount were due in five years? Twenty years?

2. Does the present value of an annuity to be paid for ten years increase or decrease as the discount rate decreases? Suppose the annuity were for five years? Twenty years?

3. Rather than pay you $100 a month for the next twenty years, the man who injured you with his car is willing to pay a single amount now to settle your claim for injuries. Would you rather he used an interest rate of 6 percent or 12 percent in computing the present value of the lump sum settlement?

4. "Nearly all economic calculations involve compound interest." Can you think of any economic calculations that involve simple interest?

5. State the rate per period and the number of periods, in each of the following:
   *a. 12 percent per annum, for 5 years, compounded annually.
   b. 12 percent per annum, for 5 years, compounded semiannually.
   c. 12 percent per annum, for 5 years, compounded quarterly.
   d. 12 percent per annum, for 5 years, compounded monthly.

6. Compute the future value of:
   *a. $100 invested for 5 years at 4 percent compounded annually.
   b. $500 invested for 15 periods at 2 percent compounded once per period.
   c. $200 invested for 8 years at 3 percent compounded semiannually.

* Hints, key numbers, or (partial) answers appear in the back of the book between the Appendix Tables and the Glossary.

   d. $2,500 invested for 14 years at 8 percent compounded quarterly.

   e. $600 invested for 3 years at 12 percent compounded monthly.

7. Compute the present value of:
   - *a. $100 due in 33 years at 4 percent compounded annually.
   - **b.** $50 due in 27 years at 6 percent compounded semiannually.
   - **c.** $250 due in 8 years at 8 percent compounded quarterly.
   - **d.** $1,000 due in 2 years at 12 percent compounded monthly.

8. Compute the amount (future value) of an ordina. annuity (an annuity in arrears) of:
   - *a. 13 rents of $100 at 1½ percent per period.
   - **b.** 8 rents of $850 at 6 percent per period.
   - **c.** 27 rents of $375 at 4 percent per period.
   - **d.** 35 rents of $1,400 at 3 percent per period.

9. What is the amount (future value) of an annuity due (in advance) of:
   - *a. 13 rents of $200 each at 6 percent per period.
   - **b.** 9 rents of $75 each at 4 percent per period.
   - **c.** 24 rents of $100 each at 2 percent per period.

10. Compute the present value of an ordinary annuity (an annuity in arrears) of:
    - *a. $1,000 for 29 years at 4 percent per year.
    - **b.** $1,500 for 31 years at 6 percent per year.
    - **c.** $400 for 41 years at 8 percent per year.
    - **d.** $750 for 75 years at 10 percent per year.

11. What is the present value of an annuity due (in advance) of:
    - *a. 28 rents of $50 at 12 percent per period.
    - **b.** 32 rents of $45 at 10 percent per period.

12. Mr. Adams has $500 to invest. He wishes to know how much it will amount to if he invests it at:
    - *a. 6 percent per year for 21 years.
    - **b.** 8 percent per year for 33 years.

13. Mr. Black wishes to have $15,000 at the end of 8 years. How much must he invest today to accomplish this purpose if the interest rate is:
    - *a. 6 percent per year.
    - **b.** 8 percent per year.

14. Mr. Case plans to set aside $4,000 each year, the first payment to be made on January 1, 1975, and the last on January 1, 1980. How much will he have accumulated by January 1, 1980, if the interest rate is:
    - *a. 6 percent per year.
    - **b.** 8 percent per year.

15. Ms. David wants to have $450,000 on her sixty-fifth birthday. She asks you to tell her how much she must deposit on each birthday from her fifty-eighth to sixty-fifth, inclusive, in order to receive this amount. Assume an interest rate of:
    - *a. 4 percent per year.
    - **b.** 6 percent per year.

16. If Mr. Edwards invests $900 on June 1 of each year from 1975 to 1985, inclusive, how much will he have accumulated on June 1, 1986, if the interest rate is:
    °a. 5 percent per year.
    b. 10 percent per year.

17. How much must Mr. Frank invest on July 1 of each of the years 1975 to 1982, inclusive, to have $300,000 on July 1, 1983? Assume an interest rate of:
    °a. 8 percent per year.
    b. 10 percent per year.

18. Mr. Grady has $145,000 with which he purchases an annuity on February 1, 1975. The annuity consists of six annual payments, the first to be made on February 1, 1976. How much will he receive in each payment? Assume an interest rate of:
    °a. 4 percent per year.
    b. 6 percent per year.

19. Ms. Howe wishes to provide her two sons with an income of $7,500 each for five years. How much must she invest on January 1, 1975, to provide for five such payments, the first to be made on January 1, 1978? Assume interest rates of:
    °a. 6 percent per year.
    b. 10 percent per year.

20. Mr. Irons borrowed money from a friend, and he agreed to repay $8,000 on March 1, 1975. On that date he was unable to pay his friend, so he made the following arrangement with the Regional Loan Company: the loan company paid the friend the $8,000 on March 1, 1975, and Mr. Irons agreed to repay the loan in a series of five equal annual payments. Assume an interest rate of 8 percent per year. How much must Mr. Irons pay each year if he makes the first payment on March 1:
    °a. 1975?
    b. 1976?
    c. 1977?

°21. Mr. Jones bought a car for $4,500, and agreed to pay for it in twelve equal monthly installments with interest at 12 percent per year, the first payment to be made immediately. What is the monthly payment?

22. Mr. Karls agrees to lease a certain property for ten years, at the following annual rentals, payable in advance:

> Years 1 and 2—$1,000 per year.
> Years 3 to 6 —$2,000 per year.
> Years 7 to 10—$2,500 per year.

What single immediate sum will pay all of these rents if they are discounted at:
    °a. 6 percent per year?
    b. 8 percent per year?
    c. 10 percent per year?

23. In order to establish a fund that will provide a scholarship of $3,000 a year indefinitely, with the first award to occur now, how much must be deposited if the fund earns:

*a. 6 percent per period?
b. 8 percent per period?

24. Consider the scholarship fund in Problem 23. Suppose that the first scholarship is not to be awarded until one year from now. How much should be deposited if the fund earns:
   *a. 6 percent per period.
   b. 8 percent per period.
   Suppose that the first scholarship is not to be awarded until five years from now. How much should be deposited if the fund earns:
   c. 6 percent per year?
   d. 8 percent per year?

25. The state helps a rural county maintain an old bridge and has agreed to pay $6,000 every two years toward the expenses. The state wishes to discharge its obligation by paying a single sum to the county now in lieu of the payment due and all future payments. How much should the state pay the county if the discount rate is
   *a. 4 percent per year?
   b. 6 percent per year?

26. Mr. and Mrs. Clark want to establish a fund that will pay a $25,000 prize to an outstanding academic accountant. The first prize is to be awarded five years from now, and the prize is to be awarded every ten years thereafter. How much should be deposited if the fund earns:
   *a. 8 percent per year?
   b. 10 percent per year?

27. An oil-drilling company figures that $300 must be spent for an initial supply of drill bits and that $100 must be spent every month to replace the worn out bits. What is the present value of the cost of the bits if the company plans to be in business indefinitely and discounts payments at 1 percent per month?

28. If you promise to leave $25,000 on deposit at the Quarter Savings Bank for four years, the bank will give you a new car now and your $25,000 back at the end of four years. How much are you, in effect, paying today for the car if the bank pays 8 percent interest compounded quarterly?

29. When Mr. Shafer died, his estate after taxes amounted to $300,000. His will provided that Widow Shafer would receive $24,000 per year starting immediately from the principal of the estate and that the balance of the principal would pass to the Shafer's son on Widow Shafer's death. The state law governing this estate provided for a *dower* option. If Widow Shafer elects the dower option, she renounces the will and can have one-third of the estate in cash now. The remainder will then immediately pass to their son. Widow Shafer wants to maximize the present value of her bequest. Should she take the annuity or elect the dower option if she will receive five payments and discounts payments at
   a. 8 percent per year?
   b. 12 percent per year?

30. Mrs. Heileman occasionally drinks beer. She consumes one case in twenty weeks. She can buy beer in disposable bottles for $6.60 per case or for $6.00 a case of returnable bottles if a $1.50 refundable deposit is paid at

the time of purchase. If her discount rate is 1 percent per week, how much in present-value dollars does she save by buying the returnables and losing the use of the $1.50 deposit for twenty weeks?

31. When the General Electric Company first introduced the Lucalox ceramic, screw-in light bulb, the bulb cost 3½ times as much as an ordinary bulb but lasted 5 times as long. An ordinary bulb cost $.50 and lasted about 8 months. If a firm has a discount rate of 12 percent compounded three times a year, how much would it save in present-value dollars by using one Lucalox bulb?

32. The Roberts Dairy Company switched from delivery trucks with regular gasoline engines to ones with diesel engines. The diesel trucks cost $2,000 more than the ordinary gasoline trucks but $600 per year less to operate. Assume that the operating costs are saved at the end of each month. If Roberts Dairy uses a discount rate of 1 percent per month, how long, at a minimum, must the diesel trucks remain in service for the switch to save money?

33. In the mid-1950s, International Business Machines Corporation (IBM) entered into a consent judgment with the U.S. Justice Department by agreeing to offer its business machines for sale. Prior to that time IBM would only rent its machines.

   a. Assume that the type 402 accounting machine had been renting for $5,220 per year, paid in advance, and the selling price of $27,950 was set so that it was equal to the present value of seven rental payments. What annual discount rate did IBM use in determining the selling price?

   °b. If a type 82 card sorter had been rented for $55 a month paid in advance and the purchase price had been set at $3,400, what number of rental payments is equivalent to the purchase price. Assume that the rental payments were discounted at ½ percent per month. (Although the Appendix Tables do not show columns for ½ percent, you can solve this problem with the 1 percent column if you are careful.)

   c. If a type 24 key-punch machine had been rented for $40 a month, paid in advance, and if IBM wanted to set a purchase price so that the price would be equal to the discounted present value of 48 months' rent discounted at ½ percent per month, what should the purchase price be?

34. When Warner & Swasey Company first decided to allow its customers to rent as well as buy its machine tools, it offered the following rental plans:

Under	Customer Pays This Percent of the Purchase Price as Rent in Advance	Each Year for This Many Years
Plan *A*	36%	2
Plan *B*	24%	3
Plan *C*	18%	4

In addition, rent payments were due for a total of seven years in amounts such that the total rent paid was equal to 114 percent of the purchase price. Assume that the rents required for each of the remaining years were constant under a given plan. For example, under Plan C, rents for each of the last three years would be 14 percent per year.

Should a customer buy outright or lease under one of the plans? If leasing is preferred, which plan should be elected? Assume that the machine tool costs $1,000 if purchased and a discount rate of:

a. 5 percent per year.

b. 10 percent per year.

c. 12 percent per year.

Certain preferred customers who decide to rent under Plan C are also given a purchase option. At the end of the second, third, and fourth years, such customers can purchase the machine for 105 percent of the original purchase price plus 5 percent for each year during which the machine was rented less the sum of the rent payments already made. That is, for example, at the end of year three, the price would be 1.20 times original price less three years of rental payments.

What strategy has lowest present value of cost for a preferred customer? Assume the machine tool costs $1,000 if purchased and a discount rate of:

d. 5 percent per year.

e. 10 percent per year.

f. 12 percent per year.

°35. (This problem is the basis of the major illustration of Chapter 24.) The Garden Winery Company invests $10,000 at the end of year 0 so that it may receive the following stream of payments (initial investment also shown):

End of Year	Cash Payment
0	−$10,000
1	4,000
2	3,400
3	3,100
4	2,800

What is the present value at the end of year zero of that stream of payments if the discount rate is:

a. 0 percent per year?

b. 2 percent per year?

c. 6 percent per year?

d. 10 percent per year?

e. 14 percent per year?

f. Construct a graph which shows the discount rate on the horizontal axis and the net present value for the Garden Winery payment on the vertical axis. Plot the points derived in (a)–(e).

g. Is the line connecting the plotted points a straight line?

36. On January 1, 1974, Outergarments, Inc. opened a new textile plant for the production of synthetic fabrics. The plant is on leased land; twenty years remain on the nonrenewable lease.

The cost of the plant was $2 million. Net cash flows to be derived from the project is expected to be $300,000 per year. The company does not normally invest in such projects unless the anticipated yield on cash flows is at least 12 percent.

On December 31, 1974, the company finds cash flows from the plant to be $280,000 for the year. On the same day, farm experts predict cotton production to be unusually low for the next two years. Outergarments estimates the resulting increase in demand for synthetic fabrics to boost cash flows to $350,000 for each of the next two years. Subsequent years' estimates remain unchanged. Ignore tax considerations.

a. Calculate the present value of the future expected cash flows from the plant when it was opened.

b. What is the present value of the plant on January 1, 1975, after the reestimation of future incomes?

c. On January 1, 1975, the day following the cotton production news release, Overalls Company announces plans to build a synthetic fabrics plant to be opened in three years. Outergarments, Inc. keeps its 1975–77 estimates but reduces the estimated annual cash flows for subsequent years to $200,000. What is the value of the Outergarments plant on January 1, 1975, after the new projections?

d. On January 2, 1975, an investor contacts Outergarments about purchasing a 20-percent share of the plant. If the investor expects to earn at least a 12-percent return on each of his investments, what is the maximum amount that he should be willing to pay? Assume that the investor and Outergarments, Inc. use the same estimates of annual cash flows.

37. A group of investors has decided to purchase a large herd of beef cattle and to sell it after six years. They have also agreed that no investment of the syndicate should return less than 10 percent annually.

They purchase the cattle on January 1, 1974, for a price of $1,200,000, and they expect to sell the herd on December 31, 1979 for the same price. The projected cash flows from sale of beef during the six years is $200,000 per year.

On December 31, 1974, the syndicate finds that its cash flows from the herd is $210,000. But during December, the herd was stricken with a disease and 20 percent of the cattle died. The syndicate wants to rebuild the herd, and they decide to sell only enough beef to cover expenses until the herd grows to its original size. They anticipate that this process will result in zero cash flows for 1975 and $200,000 for each of the remaining four years.

Ignore tax considerations in your calculations.

a. Calculate the present value of the herd to the syndicate at time of purchase.

b. If there had been no disease, what would have been the value of the herd on January 1, 1975? Use only future cash flows for this and subsequent computations.

c. What was the value of the herd on January 1, 1975, after the disease and the decision to rebuild?

d. What was the cost to the syndicate of the disease on their herd?

e. On January 1, 1975, Mr. Bovine, who has a 25-percent interest in the herd, decides to sell his share. What is the least amount that he should be willing to accept for his share? Assume he is looking at alternative investments which would yield 10 percent per year.

Chapter 14

Long-lived Assets: Amortization, Depreciation, and Depletion

When the man of the street uses the term *asset*, he means something good, something that is beneficial and will provide some kind of benefit in the future. With one important refinement, this definition of asset is applicable to businesses. There are two kinds of assets: short-lived and long-lived assets. A business acquires a short-lived asset, such as cash, in one period and can use up its benefits in the same period. A long-lived asset is different: to enjoy all its benefits, the owner must use it for many years. In these cases, the accountant must apportion, or allocate, the cost of the asset over several accounting periods. This procedure is called *amortization*. Amortization of *plant assets*, which include the fixtures, machinery, equipment, and physical structures of a business, is called *depreciation*.

In addition to its plant assets, a company such as Gulf Oil has other long-lived assets. Oil companies own natural gas and oil wells. These natural resources are called *wasting assets*. Oil wells, coal mines, uranium deposits, and other natural resources are eventually used up, and amortization of the cost of these wasting assets is called *depletion*.

Businesses may also acquire nonphysical assets. These are *intangible assets* and, while there are many examples of them, some of the best ones are probably close at hand. A local operator may pay several thousand dollars to acquire a McDonald's or Chicken Delight franchise. Such franchises are not viewed as having perpetual life, and the accountant must also amortize their costs.

Most of this chapter is devoted to depreciation because plant assets are the most common long-lived assets, but most amortization problems have counterparts in problems of depreciation.

PLANT ASSETS AND DEPRECIATION

Plant Assets

The terms *plant assets* and *fixed assets* are often used interchangeably. They refer to long-lived assets used in the operations of trading and service enterprises and manufacturing concerns.

The cost of a plant asset includes all charges necessary to prepare it for rendering services, and it is often recorded in a series of transactions. Thus the cost of a piece of equipment will be the sum of the entries to recognize the invoice price (less any discounts), transportation costs, installation charges, and any other necessary costs before the equipment is ready for use. When a firm constructs or fabricates its own buildings or equipment, many entries to record the labor, material, and overhead costs will normally be required before the total cost is recorded on the books.

Repair and maintenance *expenses* will almost certainly occur during the life of the asset. These expenses are required to maintain the service level provided by the asset. Once an asset is in service, certain costs are incurred to *improve* the asset and should be "capitalized" or added to cost. Improvements are defined as those costs that extend the life of the asset, increase the asset's output, or reduce the asset's operating cost. It is often difficult to decide whether a particular expenditure is a repair expense or a cost of improvement. The line between maintaining service and improving or extending it is not a distinct one. Some expenditures seem to meet the criteria for both a repair expense and an improvement cost. There is frequent disagreement between Internal Revenue Service agents and taxpayers as well as among accountants over this question.

An important characteristic of plant assets is that, while they can be kept intact and in usable operating condition for some time, eventually they must be retired from service. The central purpose of the depreciation accounting process is to allocate the cost of these assets to the periods of their use in a reasonable and orderly fashion.

Depreciation

Through a process of evolution in accounting terminology, the term depreciation has come to be restricted to the expiration of the cost or appraised value of plant assets. Although in popular speech *depreciation* is often associated with a decline in value of any kind of property, special terms have been developed in accounting usage for the decline in value of assets other than plant assets. As was suggested earlier, depletion refers to the using up of wasting assets, and amortization refers to the periodic reduction of long-term investments or intangibles. Merchandise and materials may become shop-worn or obsolete, but the recognition of this fact is described as an inventory adjustment rather than as depreciation.

It is useful to think of the cost of an asset with a finite life as the price paid for a series of future services—a purchase of so many hours or other units of service. When deciding to purchase a building or machine, the purchaser need not make elaborate calculations (such as those described in Chapter 24) to arrive at the present value of a series of precisely appraised future benefits, but the purchaser must at least roughly approximate those procedures. One machine is preferred over another because its cost of operation per hour or unit of product will be less. It would be irrational to purchase an asset if the discounted value of the services expected to be received from it were known to be less than the required investment.

The investment in a depreciating asset is the price paid for a series of future services. The asset account may well be considered as a prepayment, similar in many respects to prepaid rent or insurance—a payment in advance for services to be received. As the asset is used in each accounting period, an appropriate portion of the investment in the asset is treated as the cost of the service received and is charged to the operations of the period or to goods produced during the period.

The Causes of Depreciation

The causes of depreciation are the causes of decline in service and of ultimate retirement because unless the asset must eventually be retired from its planned use, there is no depreciation. Land is not retired from service nor, hence, depreciated. Many factors lead to the retirement of assets from service, but they can be classified as either *physical* or *functional* causes of depreciation. The physical factors include such things as ordinary wear and tear from use, chemical action such as rust or electrolysis, and the effects of wind and rain. The most important functional or nonphysical cause is obsolescence. Inventions, for example, may result in new equipment, the use of which reduces the unit cost of production to the point where continued operation of the old asset is uneconomical, even though it may be relatively unimpaired physically. Retail stores often replace display cases and store fronts long before they are worn out in order to keep the appearance of the store as attractive as their competitors'. Changed economic conditions may also become functional causes of depreciation as when old airports must be rebuilt to meet the requirements of heavier traffic, or a reduction in demand for a product results in a reduced scale of operations.

Identifying the specific causes of depreciation is insignificant when considering the fundamental problem of its measurement. It is enough to know that almost any physical asset will eventually have to be retired from service and that in some cases the retirement will become necessary at a time when physical deterioration is negligible. The specific causes become important only when the attempt is made to predict the useful life of an asset.

Depreciation as a Decline in Value

Depreciation is frequently characterized as a decline in the value of assets. Such an interpretation is fundamentally sound when applied to the entire service life—there certainly is a decline in the value of an asset from the time it is acquired until it is retired from service. However, a decline in asset values is a somewhat unsatisfactory description of the charge made to the operations of each accounting period. One incorrect inference from such a description is that if, in a given period of time, there has been an increase in the value of an asset, such as an increase arising from changing price levels, then there has been no depreciation during that period. Rather there have been two partially offsetting processes: (1) a holding gain on the asset (usually not recognized in historical-cost-based accounting) and (2) depreciation of the asset's historical cost.

Further, the word *value* has so many uses and connotations that it is not a serviceable term for a definition. If depreciation is defined as a decline in value and the undepreciated balance of an asset account as a "present" value, it is usually necessary to explain that it is value to the going concern based on historical cost, not exchange value, secondhand value, or reproduction cost. The word value is not entirely inappropriate to define depreciation, but it is not helpful in isolating its essence.

Summary of Depreciation Concepts

A depreciation problem will exist whenever (1) capital is invested in services to be rendered by a plant asset, and (2) at some reasonably predictable date in the future the asset will have to be retired from service with a residual value less than its cost. The problem is to interpret and account satisfactorily for this diminution of capital investment.

Note especially that replacing the asset is *not* essential to the existence of depreciation. Depreciation is the expiration or disappearance of capital investment from the time the plant asset is put into use until the time it is retired from service. Whether or not the asset is replaced has nothing to do with the amount or treatment of its depreciation.

DEPRECIATION ACCOUNTING PROBLEMS

There are three principal accounting problems in regard to depreciation:

1. calculating and recording the depreciation charge which is made to operations of each accounting period for its share of the total cost of the asset
2. revising the depreciation charge during the life of the asset because of changes in either the estimated useful life of the asset or its value in use
3. handling the retirement of the asset from service.

Calculating the Periodic Charge

Determining the amount of the periodic charge for depreciation is not an exact process. The cost of the plant asset is a *joint cost* of the several benefited periods. There is usually no logically correct way to allocate a joint cost. (Joint cost allocations are discussed in Chapter 21.) The depreciation process seeks to assign reasonable and logical periodic charges that reflect a careful and systematic method of calculation.

Whenever it is feasible to do so, depreciation should be computed for individual items such as a single building, machine, or truck. Where many similar items are in use and each one has a relatively small cost, individual calculations may be impractical and the depreciation charge is usually calculated for the group as a whole. Furniture and fixtures, tools, and telephone poles are examples of depreciating assets that are usually handled as groups. Group depreciation techniques are discussed in Appendix 14.2 of this chapter.

The calculation of the periodic depreciation charge is based upon (1) the cost of the depreciating asset, (2) the estimate of its net residual value, (3) the estimate of its useful service life, and (4) the pattern of expiration of its services.

The Cost of a Depreciating Asset. As was pointed out earlier, the cost of a depreciating asset is calculated just like any other asset. It includes all reasonable and necessary costs incurred in acquiring the asset, getting it to its place of use, and installing it. Cash discounts should be recorded, just like purchases of inventory, as a reduction in the asset's cost. When a firm acquires a new asset in exchange for an old one, such as in a trade-in transaction or in a bartered transaction, the fair market value of the assets given up plus any cash involved should be used as the cost of the new asset. Trade-in transactions are discussed later in this chapter.

Estimating Residual Value. The total depreciation of an asset over its life is the difference between its cost and the amount which can be received for the asset when it is retired from service, either in a cash sale or as a trade-in allowance. This amount is described as the asset's *residual value*, and it is necessary to estimate it in making the depreciation calculation.

For buildings, common practice assumes a zero salvage value based upon the view that the cost of tearing down the building will approximate the sale value of the scrap materials recovered. For other assets, however, the salvage or trade-in value may be substantial and should be estimated and taken into account in making the periodic depreciation charge. This is particularly true where it is planned to retire an asset when it will be of considerable value to another user. For example, a car rental firm will replace its automobiles at a time when they can be used for several years more by other owners and it will be able to realize a substantial part of original cost from the sale of used cars. Past experience usually forms the best basis for estimates of salvage, or other residual, value.

Estimates of salvage value are necessarily subjective. Disputes over salvage value have led to many disagreements between Internal Revenue Service agents and taxpayers. Partly to reduce such controversy, the Internal Revenue Code was amended to provide, in effect, that starting in 1962 salvage value of up to 10 percent of an asset's cost may be ignored in depreciation calculations for tax purposes. The same rule is frequently followed in making calculations for the financial records but should not be used in working problems in this text.

Estimating Service Life. The third factor in the depreciation calculation is the estimated economic service life of the asset. In making the estimate, both the physical and the functional causes of depreciation must be taken into account. Experience with similar assets, corrected for differences in the planned intensity of use or alterations in maintenance policy, is usually the best guide for this estimate.

In July 1962, the Internal Revenue Service published guidelines of suggested useful lives. The guidelines show estimated useful lives based on categories of assets by broad classes. Example guideline lives are:

Warehouses	60 years
Factory Buildings	45 years
Land Improvements	20 years
Office Furniture, Fixtures, Machines, and Equipment	10 years
Heavy Trucks	6 years
Light Trucks	4 years
Automobiles	3 years

In 1971, the Internal Revenue Service ruled that the guideline lives need not be strictly followed. Rather, the IRS said that taxpayers may use a life anywhere in the range from 80 percent to 120 percent of the guideline life. Such ranges are called *Asset Depreciation Ranges.*

Despite the abundance of data from experience, estimation of service lives is the most difficult task in the entire depreciation calculation. Making proper allowances for obsolescence is an especially uncertain part of the process, because it depends for the most part on forces external to the firm. Unless the estimator possesses prophetic powers, it is likely that he will make significant errors. For this reason, it is wise to reconsider the estimates of useful service life of important assets or groups of assets every few years.

Pattern of Charges. Once the cost, salvage value, and service life have been determined, the total of depreciation charges to the whole life of the asset has been determined. To determine the pattern for allocating the total charge to specific years remains. There are only five basic patterns in use, labeled *A*, *S*, *D*, *E*, and *N* in Figure 14.1. If salvage value is assumed to be zero, then, of course, the salvage value line coincides with the horizontal axis and the entire cost will be depreciated.

The patterns are discussed in more detail in the next section. A repre-

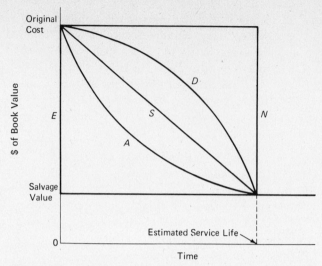

Figure 14.1   Patterns of Depreciation: Book Value over Life
of Asset

sents *accelerated* depreciation; S *uniform* or *straight-line* depreciation; D, *decelerated* depreciation. A and S are much more common than D. (Understanding the terms "accelerated" and "decelerated" is easier if you think of the pattern of cumulative depreciation charges—not of the period charges.) The pattern E, of course, represents immediate expensing of the asset. All costs are charged to the period when the expenditures occur. This pattern is discussed further in the section on intangibles. The pattern N represents the situation, such as for land, where there are no periodic amortization charges. The asset is shown on the books at cost until it is sold or otherwise disposed of.

DEPRECIATION METHODS

All depreciation methods should aim to allocate, reasonably and systematically, the cost of the asset minus its estimated salvage value, to the periods in which it is used. The methods discussed here are:

1. straight-line method
2. production or use method
3. declining-balance method
4. sum-of-the-years'-digits method
5. compound interest methods

When a depreciable asset is acquired or retired during an accounting period, depreciation should be calculated only for that portion of the period during which the asset is used.

The Straight-Line Method

The allocation method that is probably used most commonly is known as the straight-line method, represented by pattern S in the figure. It was used almost exclusively until 1954, when the income tax laws were revised to specifically recognize other depreciation methods. Under the straight-line method, the cost of the asset, less any estimated salvage or trade-in value, is divided by the number of years of its expected life in order to arrive at the annual depreciation:

$$\text{Annual depreciation} = \frac{\text{Cost less salvage value}}{\text{Estimated life in years}}.$$

For example, if a machine costs $12,000, has an estimated salvage value of $1,000, and has an expected useful life of five years, the annual depreciation would be $2,200 = ($12,000 − $1,000)/5. Occasionally, instead of a salvage value, there is a cost of removal which should be added to the cost of the asset in making the calculation. Thus, if a building is constructed for $37,000, and it is estimated that it will cost $5,000 to remove it so that a new one can be built at the end of 25 years, the annual depreciation would be $1,680 = ($37,000 + $5,000)/25.

A common practice, especially when the salvage value is assumed to be zero, is to apply an appropriate percentage, known as the depreciation rate, to the cost figure in order to calculate the annual charge. This rate, of course, will charge the entire cost off over the estimated life. A rate of 10 percent will write off the cost of an asset in ten years, a rate of 25 percent in four years, and so on.

Production or Use Method

Although the straight-line method is widely used, it is justifiable only because it frequently corresponds roughly to the amount of use which is made of the asset and because it requires only simple arithmetic. Many assets are not used uniformly. Manufacturing plants often have seasonal variations in operation so that certain machines may be used twenty-four hours a day at one time and eight hours or less a day at another time of year. Trucks are not apt to receive the same amount of use in each month or year of their lives. The straight-line method of depreciation may, then, result in an illogical depreciation charge for such assets.

When usage varies from period to period and when the total usage of an asset over its life can be reliably estimated, the depreciation charge should be based on actual usage during the period. For example, depreciation of a truck for a period should be based upon the ratio of miles driven during the period to total miles expected to be used over the truck's life. The depreciation cost per unit (mile) of use is:

$$\text{Depreciation cost per unit} = \frac{\text{Cost less salvage value}}{\text{Estimated number of units}}.$$

The arithmetic of the calculation is simple, but it is necessary to keep a special record of the units of operation of each unit or of the number of units produced. If it is estimated that a truck which cost $9,000, with an estimated trade-in value of $600, will be driven 100,000 miles before it is retired from service, the depreciation per mile would be $.084 = ($9,000 − $600)/100,000. Then, if the truck is operated 1,000 miles in a given month, the depreciation charge for the month is 1,000 × $.084 = $84.

Declining-Balance Method

The efficiency and earning power of many plant assets decline as the assets grow older. Cutting tools lose some of their precision; printing presses are shut down more frequently for repairs; rentals in an old office building are lower than those in its gleaming new neighbor. These examples show the tendency of some assets to provide more and better services in the early years of their lives and to require increasing amounts of maintenance as they grow older. Where this is the case, methods that recognize progressively smaller depreciation charges in successive periods may be justified. Such methods are referred to as *accelerated depreciation* methods because the depreciation charges in the early years of the asset's life are larger than in later years. Accelerated depreciation leads to a pattern like *A* in Figure 14.1.

The *declining-balance method* is one accelerated depreciation method. In this method, the depreciation charge is calculated by multiplying the *net book value* of the asset (cost less accumulated depreciation) at the start of each period times a fixed rate. The estimated scrap value is not subtracted from the cost in making the calculation. Since the net book value declines from period to period, the result is a declining periodic charge for depreciation throughout the life of the asset.

In this method, the fixed depreciation rate used is one that will charge the cost less salvage value of the asset over its service life. The formula for computing the rate is:

$$\text{Depreciation rate} = 1 - \sqrt[n]{s/c} = 1 - (s/c)^{1/n}.$$

In this formula n = estimated periods of service life, s = estimated salvage value, and c = cost.

Estimates of salvage value have a profound effect upon the rate. Unless a positive salvage value is assumed, the rate is 100 percent—that is, all depreciation is charged in the first period. For an asset costing $10,000, with an estimated life of five years, the depreciation rate is 40 percent per period if estimated salvage value is $778, but it is 60 percent if estimated salvage value is $102.

The effect of small changes in estimated salvage value on the rate and the seeming mathematical complexity of the formula have resulted in widespread use of approximations or rules of thumb instead of the formula. The most common rate used is the maximum one permitted for income tax purposes, which is twice the straight-line rate. When this rate is used, the method is called the *double-declining-balance method*. Thus, for example, an asset with an estimated ten-year life would be depreciated at a rate of 20 percent (=1/10 × 2) per year of the book value at the start of the year. To take another example, if a machine costing $5,000 is purchased on January 1, 1975, and it is estimated to have a five-year life, a 40-percent $(= 1/5 \times 2)$ rate would probably be used. The depreciation charges would be calculated as shown in Schedule 14.1.

SCHEDULE 14.1   DOUBLE-DECLINING-BALANCE DEPRECIATION

Year	Original Cost (1)	Accumulated Depreciation As of Jan. 1 (2)	Net Book Value As of Jan. 1 (1)–(2) (3)	Depreciation Rate (4)	Depreciation Charge for the Year = (3) × (4) (5)
1975	$5,000	$ 0	$5,000	.40	$2,000
1976	5,000	2,000	3,000	.40	1,200
1977	5,000	3,200	1,800	.40	720
1978	5,000	3,920	1,080	.40	432
1979	5,000	4,352	648	.40	259

The undepreciated cost as of December 31, 1979 ($389 = $648 — $259) is not likely to equal the salvage value at that time. This problem is usually anticipated and solved by adjusting the depreciation charge in one or more of the later years. Under income tax rules, the asset cannot be depreciated below salvage value if that value is large; if the salvage value is small, the undepreciated cost minus scrap value can be written off in straight-line fashion over the last years of life. In the previous example, if the asset had an estimated salvage value of $200, the depreciation charges in 1978 and 1979 could be $440 a year (net book value at January 1, 1978, of $1,080 less the estimated salvage value of $200 divided by two years of remaining life). In general, the switch to straight-line charge-off over the remaining life is made when the switch will produce a greater depreciation charge than the one resulting from continued application of the double-declining-balance method. For assets with zero scrap value, this ordinarily occurs just after the midpoint of the service life.

Sum-of-the-Years'-Digits Method

The other accelerated depreciation method mentioned in the tax code is the *sum-of-the-years'-digits method.* Under this method, the depreciation charge is determined by applying a fraction, which diminishes from year to year, to the cost less estimated salvage value of the asset. The numerator of the fraction is the number of periods of remaining life at the beginning of the year for which the depreciation calculation is being made. The denominator is the sum of all such numbers, one for each year of estimated service life: if the service life is n years, the denominator for the sum-of-the-years'-digits method is: $1 + 2 + \cdots + n = n(n+1)/2$.

The method is illustrated by again considering an asset costing $5,000 purchased January 1, 1975, which has an estimated service life of five years and an estimated salvage value of $200. The sum of the years' digits is 15 or $(1 + 2 + 3 + 4 + 5) = (5 \times 6)/2$. The depreciation charges are shown in Schedule 14.2.

For assets with lives of eight or more years, the present value of depreciation charges for most firms will be higher if the sum-of-the-years'-digits, rather than the double-declining-balance, method is used.[1]

Compound Interest Method

The compound interest method is not widely used in financial accounting, but it is theoretically sound for certain management decisions. For plant assets producing equal annual net cash inflows, compound interest depreciation leads to a pattern like D in Figure 14.1. The method is described in Appendix 14.1 of this chapter.

The Entry for Periodic Depreciation

The debit made in the entry to record periodic depreciation is usually to a production cost account or an expense account such as Depreciation of Building, Depreciation of Machinery, or Depreciation of Automobiles. The classification of these accounts depends upon the nature of the operations. In a manufacturing concern the depreciation of factory buildings and equipment is a production cost, a part of the work in process and finished product. Depreciation on sales equipment is a selling expense. The matching credit for periodic depreciation could logically be made directly to the asset account affected, such as buildings or equipment. While such an entry is sometimes made, it is customary to credit a special contra-asset account so that the acquisition cost of the asset will be left undisturbed and so that the total amount written off as estimated depreciation can readily be observed. The effect, however, is precisely the same as a direct

SCHEDULE 14.2   SUM-OF-THE-YEARS'-DIGITS DEPRECIATION

Year	Cost Less Estimated Salvage Value (1)	Remaining Life in Years (2)	Fraction = (2)/15 (3)	Depreciation Charge for the Year = (3) × (1) (4)
1975	$4,800	5	5/15	$1,600
1976	4,800	4	4/15	1,280
1977	4,800	3	3/15	960
1978	4,800	2	2/15	640
1979	4,800	1	1/15	320
				$4,800

[1] See Sidney Davidson and David F. Drake, "The 'Best' Tax Depreciation Method—1964," *Journal of Business*, 37 (July 1964), 258–60.

credit to the asset account. We have used Accumulated Depreciation (of Buildings, Equipment, and so on) as the title of the account to be credited. The entry, then, to record periodic depreciation on buildings is:

```
Depreciation of Buildings ....................................  1,500
      Accumulated Depreciation of Buildings ....................       1,500
```

The Depreciation of Buildings account is closed at the end of the accounting period as a part of the regular closing-entry procedure. (For convenience, accelerated charges for a given year are allocated on a straight-line basis to periods less than a year in length.) The Accumulated Depreciation account remains open and is shown on the balance sheet as a deduction from the asset account to which it refers. The balance in the Accumulated Depreciation account usually represents the total charges to past operations for the depreciation on assets now in use. The difference between the balance of the asset account and the balance of its accumulated depreciation account (with possibly an adjustment for salvage value) represents the amount that will presumably be charged to future operations. This difference is often called the *book value* of the asset.

Retirement of Assets

When an asset is retired from service, the cost of the asset and the related amount of accumulated depreciation must be removed from the books. As part of this entry, the amount received from the sale or trade-in and the difference between that amount and book value must be recorded. The difference between the proceeds received on retirement and book value is a gain (if positive) or a loss (if negative). Before making the entry to write off the asset and its accumulated depreciation, an entry should be made to bring the depreciation up to date; that is, the depreciation that has occurred between the start of the present accounting period and the date of disposition must be recorded.

To illustrate the retirement of an asset, assume that a machine costs $5,000, is expected to last four years, has an estimated salvage value of $200, and is depreciated on a straight-line basis. The machine is sold two years and seven months after it was acquired. Assume that date of sale is three months after the start of the current accounting period. First, record the depreciation from the start of the accounting period to the date of sale:

```
Depreciation of Machinery ......................................  300
      Accumulated Depreciation of Machinery ......................       300
```

The book value of the asset is now its cost less thirty-one months of straight-line depreciation of $100 per month or $5,000 − $3,100 = $1,900.

1. Suppose that the machine was sold for $1,900 cash. The entry to record the sale would be:

```
Cash ........................................................  1,900
Accumulated Depreciation of Machinery ......................  3,100
      Machinery ..............................................       5,000
```

2. Suppose that the machine was sold for $2,500 cash. The entry to record the sale would be:

Cash	2,500	
Accumulated Depreciation of Machinery	3,100	
Machinery		5,000
Gain on Retirement of Machinery		600

3. Suppose that the machine was sold for $1,500. The entry to record the sale would be:

Cash	1,500	
Accumulated Depreciation of Machinery	3,100	
Loss on Retirement of Machinery	400	
Machinery		5,000

Group Depreciation

The methods discussed thus far were assumed to be used for each individual plant asset owned by the firm. If a firm records depreciation for each asset owned, it may have a difficult record-keeping task. Firms are allowed, both by generally accepted accounting principles and by tax regulations, to account for groups of assets using the technique of *group* or *composite* depreciation. The method is called *group* depreciation when similar, or homogeneous, assets are considered together, and it is called *composite* depreciation when dissimilar assets are considered together. The mechanics of group depreciation are described in Appendix 14.2 of this chapter.

Changes in Periodic Depreciation

There are two reasons why the depreciation charge for a particular asset may need to be changed. The previous estimate of useful life (and possibly the scrap value as well) may have been incorrect, or the asset may be appraised and assigned a new value that will increase or decrease the amount to be charged to future operations. The accounting for appraisals and the corresponding revision of depreciation is an unusual problem, too involved to be included in this discussion, but to change the depreciation plan because of errors in previous estimates is common and desirable.

Errors in the estimates of the remaining useful life of an asset may become apparent at any time during its life. It is usually possible to improve the degree of accuracy of the estimates as the time of retirement approaches. If it appears that the error of the estimate will be relatively minor, an adjustment usually is not made. If the error appears to be substantial, corrective action must be taken if the effect of the previous estimation error is to be kept at a minimum. The generally accepted procedure for handling this problem is to make no adjustment for the past error, but to spread the undepreciated balance less the revised estimate of scrap value over the new estimate of remaining service life of the asset. A second, more logical, possibility is to make an adjustment for the error of the past periods, and use the corrected rate of depreciation for the remaining portion of the life of the asset.

The following illustration will be used in the discussion of these two methods. A machine is purchased on January 1, 1970, for $9,200. It is estimated that it will be operated for twenty years with a scrap value of $200. On December 31, 1975, before the books are closed for the year, it is decided that, in view of the evidence then available, a total useful life of thirty years with the same scrap value of $200 would be a more accurate estimate.

The depreciation charge for each of the years from 1970 through 1974 under the straight-line method would initially have been $450[= ($9,200 − $200)/20]. If the revised estimate of service life were ignored, the original annual depreciation charge of $450 would be continued through 1989. The years 1990 to 1999 would receive no charge to operations for the use of the machine. The Accumulated Depreciation account would remain undisturbed for those years until the machine was retired from service. Thus, during the last ten years that the machine was in service, a charge for depreciation would not be made.

The accepted procedure for recognizing this substantial increase in service life is to revise the future depreciation so that the correct total will presumably be accumulated in the Accumulated Depreciation account at the end of the revised service life. In our example, the total amount yet to be covered by depreciation charges before the 1975 adjustments is $6,750 (= $9,000 − $2,250). The new estimate of the *remaining* life is twenty-five years, so the new annual depreciation charge is $6,750/25, or $270. The only change in the accounting procedure is to substitute, for the annual depreciation of $450, the new amount of $270. The depreciation entry on December 31, 1975, and each year thereafter would be:

Depreciation Expense 270
    Accumulated Depreciation 270

This adjustment method is used because it avoids adjusting retained earnings for the past error. As Chapter 7 states about prior-period adjustments, the generally accepted accounting principle is that retained earnings are readjusted only under exceptional circumstances. One prerequisite is that the occurrence that causes the adjustment be caused by some force outside the firm.[2] The generally accepted method can only be defended, however, as an expedient procedure, for it merely offsets errors made in past operating charges by creating errors in the other direction for future operating charges.

An attempt to correct the past errors through an adjustment to Retained Earnings and to apply a correct depreciation rate to the remaining life of the asset is the only theoretically correct approach. In this illustration, $2,250 has been charged off for depreciation through the year 1974 under the straight-line method. The correct annual depreciation of $300 would

[2] APB Opinion No. 9, *AICPA* (December 1966).

only have amounted to $1,500, so an error of $750 has been made during this five-year period. The entry to correct the error, ignoring income tax effects, would be:

Accumulated Depreciation	750	
Retained Earnings		750

Then, beginning with December 31, 1975, the correct annual depreciation of $300 would be recorded each year.

Trade-In Transactions

Instead of selling the asset when it is retired from service, it may be traded in on a new unit. This is a particularly common practice for automobiles. The trade-in transaction can best be viewed as the sale of an old asset at the trade-in value, followed by a purchase of a new asset. The accounting analysis is similiar to that followed in the sale or retirement of an asset; in addition to the entries recognizing the disposition of the old asset, an entry is added to record the purchase of the new one.

For example, a truck that cost $4,300 on January 1, 1972, and which was estimated to have a five-year service life and a resale value of $300, is traded in on a new truck on December 31, 1975, before end-of-year adjusting entries are made. The price of the new truck is $5,000, with a trade-in allowance of $900 granted for the old truck. The entries to record the sale of the old truck and purchase of the new one, assuming straight-line depreciation, are:

Depreciation of Truck	800	
Accumulated Depreciation		800
To record depreciation for the year.		

Cash	900	
Accumulated Depreciation	3,200	
Loss on the Exchange of Truck	200	
Truck (old)		4,300
To record exchange of old truck.		

Truck (new)	5,000	
Cash		5,000
To record purchase.		

The transaction could have been recorded in a combined entry:

Truck (new)	5,000	
Accumulated Depreciation	2,400	
Depreciation of Truck	800	
Loss on the Exchange of Truck	200	
Truck (old)		4,300
Cash		4,100

Sometimes, the list price of plant assets is inflated with the expectation that trade-in allowance in excess of current market values for used assets will reduce the actual purchase cost to a realistic level. For example, the dealer who sells the new truck is indifferent between the $5,000 list price with $900 trade-in and a cash price of $4,400 with a $300 trade-in because he receives $4,100 cash and the old truck under either set of terms.

In new automobile transactions, an artificially high trade-in allowance is often offered along with an inflated purchase price. In instances of this type, the value of the asset traded in, as determined by established second-hand markets, is the proper amount to use for the trade-in allowance. The invoice price of the new asset will then be adjusted by the amount of the discount included in the trade-in allowance. If, in the previous example, the cash value of the old truck was actually $400 and not the $900 allowance offered, then the true cash price of the new truck must be $4,500 (= $400 + $4,100) and the combined entries would be:

Truck (new)	4,500	
Accumulated Depreciation	2,400	
Depreciation of Truck	800	
Loss on the Exchange of Truck	700	
Truck (old)		4,300
Cash		4,100

The solution just presented for the handling of a trade-in is the preferable one. Federal income tax regulations, however, require a different treatment which must be followed in the preparation of a tax return but is seldom desirable for any other purpose. The tax treatment does not permit the recognition of a gain or loss on the trade-in of an old asset in acquiring a new, but similar, asset. Instead, the cost of the new asset is considered to be the book value of the old plant asset plus any cash or other assets (called "boot") given in payment or any liabilities incurred. Under this interpretation, the entries for the trade-in would be:

Truck (new)	5,200	
Accumulated Depreciation	2,400	
Depreciation of Truck	800	
Truck (old)		4,300
Cash		4,100

There may be some virtue in viewing list prices and trade-in values with skepticism, because they often are inflated. There does not seem to be any good reason, however, for deliberately understating or overstating asset values, thus causing corresponding misstatements of the depreciation charges on that asset.

The Accounting Principles Board in Opinion No. 29 (1973) requires a slightly different treatment of trade-ins. The APB requires that if a *gain* would otherwise be recognized on a trade-in transaction involving *similar* assets, then the income tax method of deferring recognition of the gain must also be used for financial accounting. (This aspect of APB Opinion No. 29 seems questionable to us.) Losses on trade-ins of assets, whether similar or dissimilar, should be recognized currently. If the asset traded-in is of a different kind from the new one acquired, then APB Opinion No. 29 requires that the fair-market value of the old asset be used in determining the cost of the new asset and either gain or loss is to be recognized currently.

The problem of handling trade-ins may be summarized with the following entry based on the example used in this section.

Truck (new)	A	
Accumulated Depreciation	2,400	
Depreciation of Truck	800	
Adjustment on Exchange of Truck	B	
Truck (old)		4,300
Cash		4,100
Generic entry for trade-in transaction.		

Loss B is book value minus market value of trade-in. The list-price method, illustrated first, enters the list price for A and plugs for B. (If B is a credit it is, of course, shown as a gain.) The second method uses the market-determined trade-in value to solve for B and then plugs for A. The federal tax method requires B to be zero so that A is the plug required for equal debits and credits.

Depreciation and Repairs

Depreciation is not the only cost of using a depreciating asset. There will almost always be some repair and maintenance costs during the life of the asset. The repair policy adopted by the business will often affect the rate of depreciation. If, for example, machinery, trucks, and so forth are checked frequently and repaired as soon as any difficulty develops, such assets will have a longer useful life and, therefore, a lower depreciation rate than otherwise. The more commonly used depreciation rates assume that reasonable repairs will be made during the life of an asset.

Although some major parts of an asset may have shorter lives than the asset as a whole, it is frequently impracticable to account for them by means of a depreciation accounting technique. Thus the cost of replacing a set of tires is usually charged to repairs, although it would be possible to treat the tires as a separate asset subject to depreciation. The size of the depreciating unit can often be reduced to good advantage, however. For example, using single machines instead of a group of machines, or dealing with motors in aircraft separately from the rest of the asset may be a practical procedure.

Repairs must be distinguished from improvements and from rehabilitation. *Repairs* are the small adjustments and replacements of parts, whose effect does not extend materially beyond a year or two. *Improvements* involve adding a part or installing a new part that is substantially better than the old one. The benefit from the improvement will be received for a significant time over the future, but the total useful life of the asset will not ordinarily be extended. *Rehabilitation* involves extensive reconstruction or remodeling so that the life of the asset is extended considerably beyond the original estimated date of retirement.

For example, the replacement of shingles which have blown off a roof would be treated as a repair. The replacement of a shingled roof with a metal roof, or the building of an addition to the building, would be an improvement. The reconstruction of the interior, the construction of a new front, or the reinforcement of the foundation would, in most cases, come under the definition of rehabilitation.

Repairs are expensed as expenditures are incurred. Improvements are customarily debited to the asset account and the depreciation for the remaining life of the asset is increased accordingly. Rehabilitation may be viewed as a replacement of the asset and entries may be made just as though the old asset were retired from service and a new one acquired. A short-cut technique, employed especially where the rehabilitation is only partial, is to debit the accumulated depreciation account for the cost of rehabilitation. For example, if $1,700 is spent for a new motor and tires for a truck that has been used for several years, the entry could be:

Accumulated Depreciation of Trucks 1,700
    Cash   1,700

A new estimate must then be made of the remaining life and the scrap value in order to revise the depreciation charge.

WASTING ASSETS AND DEPLETION

The costs of finding natural resources and preparing to extract them from the earth should be capitalized and amortized. Amortization of wasting assets, or natural resources, is called *depletion*. The depletion method most often used is the "units of production" method. For example, if $750,000 is spent to discover and to prepare pumping equipment for an oil well that contains an estimated 1.5 million barrels of oil, then the costs of $750,000 would be amortized at the rate of $.50 (= $750,000/1,500,000) for each barrel of oil removed from the well.

The major accounting problems of extractive industries stem from the high degree of uncertainty attached to exploratory efforts and special tax laws that permit computation of depletion for measuring taxable income by methods that are not generally acceptable for financial accounting. These problems are too complex for an introductory accounting text.

The "percentage depletion allowances" that are the bane of tax reformers have little to do with amortization of costs of developing wasting assets. The "percentage depletion allowances" are merely a device instituted by the U.S. Congress to make searching for extractive resources more attractive than it would otherwise be. The effect of "percentage depletion" is to allow firms to deduct as expenses amounts equal to or larger than the expenditures incurred.

INTANGIBLE ASSETS AND AMORTIZATION

Nonphysical assets can provide future benefits equally as well as physical assets. Examples are research costs, advertising costs, patents, trademarks, and copyrights. The first problem with such intangible assets is to decide whether the expenditures have future benefits and should be "capitalized" and amortized over a period of time or whether they have no future benefits and thus are expenses of the period. In this latter case, the immediate expensing of the assets' cost is represented by pattern *E* in Figure 14.1.

The second problem to solve is how to amortize the costs if they have been capitalized. Amortization of capitalized intangibles can be done with straight-line, accelerated, or decelerated methods, whichever seems most appropriate. The next four sections discuss some common intangibles and the issues involved in deciding whether to expense or to capitalize their costs.

Research and Development

Some of the more common intangible costs are for research and development (R and D). This type of cost is incurred for various reasons. One reason might be to seek to develop a technological or marketing advance in order to have an edge on competition. Another might be to explore possible applications of already existing technology to design a new product or improve an old one. Other research is undertaken in response to government contract, in preparing for bids on potential contracts, or in pursuit of "discoveries," with no specific product in mind. Whatever the reason, practically all research costs will yield their benefits, if any, in future periods. Herein lies the accounting issue: to expense research and development costs immediately when they are incurred (pattern E in Figure 14.1), or to capitalize and amortize them over future periods.

Generally accepted accounting principles require immediate expensing of research and development costs because the future benefits from most R and D efforts are too uncertain to warrant capitalization. Nevertheless, we think that there must be future benefits in many cases or else research would not be pursued. Theoretically, then, research costs should be matched with their benefits through the capitalization procedure with amortization over the benefited periods.

Some difficulties arise if R and D costs are to be capitalized. The first is to determine and analyze R and D costs. Direct costs for each research project should be segregated for management control purposes. General R and D overhead costs may be either expensed in total, or spread to specific projects and treated just as the rest of the specific project costs are treated. The second problem is deciding which projects should be capitalized. Where it is obvious that no foreseeable benefits are forthcoming from a certain line of research, its costs should be expensed. Costs of projects that result in future benefits should be capitalized. A third accounting problem is to determine over what period capitalized R and D costs should be amortized. Usually, the life span of benefits is highly uncertain, and the benefits are unevenly distributed over the years. As a consequence, firms would then select an arbitrary time period which they feel is reasonable, such as five years, over which to amortize the costs.

Advertising

The case for capitalizing and then amortizing advertising costs is not so strong as that for R and D. Advertising expenditures are normally designed to increase sales of the period in which they are made, but there is an obvious lag between the occurrence of these costs and their impact. Often the primary impact of advertising will extend into the next period and a secondary impact will extend much longer.

Common practice expenses all advertising and sales promotion costs, regardless of the timing of their impact. Those supporting this practice argue that: (1) it is more conservative to do so; (2) it is almost impossible to quantify the future effects and timing of benefits derived from these costs; and (3) when these costs remain stable from year to year, they produce no distorting effect on income after the first few years.

Nevertheless, there is still some support for capitalization treatment. Doing so will better match costs and resulting benefits. Also, advertising expenditures are at management's discretion, just as are R and D expenditures. Capitalization on a consistent basis reduces the temptation to manipulate annual income by changing these expenditures.

Goodwill

Goodwill is an intangible asset that will be briefly mentioned here. A more detailed discussion follows in Chapter 18. Goodwill arises from the purchase of one company by another and is the difference between the amount paid for the acquired company's individual assets and their current value. Thus, goodwill will appear in the accounts of the company making the acquisition. Under present practice, the amount of goodwill is recognized only when it is acquired in the purchase of another business and then is amortized over a time period not longer than forty years.

Patents

A patent is an exclusive right obtained from the federal government to the benefits from an invention. The legal life of patent protection is seventeen years, although the economic life of the patent may be considerably less. Patent costs depend upon whether the patent was purchased from another party or acquired by development. If the former, the purchase price is capitalized. If the latter, the total cost of product development and patent application is capitalized. Patent costs are usually amortized over the shorter of: (1) seventeen years—the legal patent life, or (2) its estimated economic life. If for some reason the patent becomes worthless, the remaining capitalized cost is immediately charged to the expenses of the period.

SUMMARY

Although there are three major classes of long-lived assets, plant assets, wasting assets (natural resources), and intangibles, the major accounting problems for each class are the same: (1) determine the cost of the asset; (2) estimate the total period of benefit or the amount of expected benefits; and (3) assign the cost among the benefited periods or units of benefit in a systematic and reasonable fashion.

We have focused our attention on plant assets and their depreciation. For these assets, the cost figure to be charged off is frequently reduced by estimated salvage value. The period (or number of units) of benefit is determined by judgment based upon experience or by relying on guidelines set down by the Internal Revenue Service. The pattern of depreciation charges over the asset's life is usually based on some conventional method; the most common in practice are straight-line, double-declining-balance, and sum-of-the-years'-digits.

If the asset is retired or traded-in before the end of the estimated service life or for an amount different from estimated salvage value, the loss, if any, must be recognized. Gain may or may not be recognized currently, depending upon the situation.

APPENDIX 14.1: COMPOUND INTEREST DEPRECIATION

The straight-line and accelerated depreciation methods described in this chapter are conceptually simple and easy to use. They do, however, have one flaw which will be explained shortly. The *compound interest* method of depreciation is designed to correct this flaw. As the name implies, the method is based upon the use of compound interest calculations, as introduced in Chapter 13.

To illustrate both the compound interest method and the flaws in the other methods, consider the five-year asset described earlier that cost $5,000 and that has a salvage value of $200 at the end of the fifth year. Assume further that acquisition of this asset increases cash flow (increases revenues or decreases other operating expenses, not counting depreciation charges) as follows:

Year	Increase in Cash Flow
1975	$2,450
1976	1,980
1977	1,460
1978	980
1979	460

Management is often evaluated on the rate of return on investment it produces. The rate of return on investment is defined to be net income for the period divided by book value of assets for the period. Ordinarily (see Chapter 26), some average of the entire year's assets is used in the denominator. To keep this example simple, the book value of assets at the beginning of the year is used for the denominator. Schedule 14.3 shows the rate-of-return calculation for the asset when depreciation is calculated with the straight-line, the sum-of-the-years'-digits and the compound interest methods.

Note that when the straight-line method is used, the rates of return range from 29.8 percent in 1975 to —43.1 percent in 1979. The fluctuations

SCHEDULE 14.3 ILLUSTRATION OF RATE OF RETURN CALCULATION FOR 5-YEAR ASSET COSTING $5,000 WITH SALVAGE VALUE $200

Year (1)	Book Value at Start of Year = Cost − Accumulated Depreciation (2)	For Year			
		Net Cash Flow (Given) (3)	Depreciation Charge (Calculated) (4)	Income = (3) − (4) (5)	Rate of Return = (5)/(2) (6)
		Straight-Line Method			
1975	$5,000	$2,450	$ 960	$1,490	.298
1976	4,040	1,980	960	1,020	.252
1977	3,080	1,460	960	500	.162
1978	2,120	980	960	20	.009
1979	1,160	460	960	(500)	−.431
1980	200 = Salvage Value				
		Sum-of-Years'-Digits Method			
1975	$5,000	$2,450	$1,600	$ 850	.170
1976	3,400	1,980	1,280	700	.206
1977	2,120	1,460	960	500	.236
1978	1,160	980	640	340	.293
1979	520	460	320	140	.269
1980	200 = Salvage Value				
		Compound Interest Method (Rate of Return = 20 Percent)			
1975	$5,000	$2,450	$1,450	$1,000	.200
1976	3,550	1,980	1,270	710	.200
1977	2,280	1,460	1,004	456	.200
1978	1,276	980	725	255	.200
1979	551	460	350	110	.200
1980	201 = Salvage Value (Rounding error, should be $200)				

in the rate of return implied by the sum-of-the-years'-digits methods are less severe but nevertheless troublesome. The flaw in these methods is that using them distorts the calculated rate of return on investment. The asset is, after all, a single investment. The measured rate of return from holding a given investment per unit of time ought to be the same no matter what period of time is used to measure the return.

The compound interest method is designed to produce depreciation charges that will hold constant the reported rate of return on the investment for an asset. The subtleties and details of calculations for the compound interest method are beyond the scope of introductory accounting and are, hence, omitted from this book.

Briefly, the steps in using the compound interest method are:

1. Find the rate of interest such that the present value of the cash
inflows, including eventual salvage value, from an asset are exactly
equal to the present value of the cash outflows to purchase and use
the asset. That rate is called the *internal rate of return* and, in the
example, is 20 percent per year. This step is the only tedious one.
The internal rate of return can be found with the following trial-and-
error procedure.

   a. Make a reasonable approximation or guess at the internal rate of
   return.

   b. Calculate the present value of the cash inflows using the current
   approximation of the internal rate of return.

   c. Compare the amount found in (b) with the present value of the
   cash outflows required to acquire the asset.

   d. If the amount found in (b) is less than the present value of the
   outflows, then lower the internal rate of return approximation and
   return to step (a).

   e. If the amount found in (b) exceeds the present value of the outflows, raise the internal rate of return approximation and return
   to step (a).

   f. When the amounts are equal, then the current approximation is the
   internal rate of return.

2. Find for each year the income required so that the implied rate of
return (income for year divided by book value at start of year) is
exactly equal to the rate found in step 1. In the example, column (5)
is calculated as 20 percent of column (2).

3. Find depreciation charge for the year by subtracting the income just
found in step 2 from the cash flow for the year. In the example, column
(4) is calculated as the difference, column (3) minus column (5).

Some writers use examples that have equal annual cash flows to
illustrate the compound interest method. These writers use the name
annuity method for this technique which insures constant implied rates
of return on investment. (When the annual cash flows are level, annuity
tables can be used in step 1, making that step easier.) When the cash
flows are level, the depreciation charge will increase over time. Some
accountants reject the compound interest method because it can lead to
increasing depreciation charges. Since cash flows from an asset seldom
remain level over the life of the asset, the phenomenon of increasing
depreciation charges in artificially constructed examples should not be a
justification for rejecting the method.

The argument just given on the rate of return on the asset is used in
the literature to justify the compound-interest method. Another argument,
which may be more convincing, runs as follows.

An asset is acquired because of its future benefits. Amortization tracks
the reduction in the asset's book value as the future benefits are used up.
Suppose that we wanted the depreciation method to write off the asset's
cost for a period in direct proportion to the present value dollars of benefit

from the asset that have occurred during the period. We would then have the compound-interest method of depreciation.

In the example of this appendix, the present value of the cash flow benefits from the asset at the time it is acquired is $5,000. At the end of the first year, the present value of the cash flow benefits yet to be received is $3,550 (= $1,980 × .83333 + $1,460 × .69444 + $980 × .57870 + $660 × .48225). Thus $1,450 (= $5,000 − $3,550) of the benefits, in present value terms, to be received from the asset were received in the first year and the asset should be written down by that amount. A little experimentation should convince you that compound-interest depreciation writes off an asset's cost in exact "straight-line" proportion to the number of present value dollars of benefit that have been generated by the asset during the period.

To use the compound interest method requires estimates of cash flows for each year of the asset's life. Accurate estimates are hard to make, but management can use the same estimates for calculating depreciation that were used to make the decision to acquire the assets in the first place.

APPENDIX 14.2: GROUP DEPRECIATION

When group depreciation is used, items can be grouped by expected life or by function. For example, a firm might put all assets with five-year expected lives into one group, all assets with ten-year expected lives into another, and so on. Or the firm might put all trucks into one group, all furniture into another, all machines into still another, and so on. Further, for example, there can be a group for trucks purchased in 1975, another for trucks purchased in 1976, and so on.

The straight-line, the declining-balance, and the compound interest methods can be used to determine the yearly charge for the group depreciation method. Sum-of-the-years'-digits method does not lend itself to group depreciation because the assets in the group need not all be the same age and the numerator of the fraction for calculating the depreciation charge can be indeterminate. If the double-declining-balance method is used, tax rules require that all items in a group be purchased in the same year.

The year's depreciation charge is calculated as either (a) some fraction of the cost of the assets in the group (if the straight-line method is used), or (b) some fraction of the book value of the assets in the group (if declining-balance methods are used). The depreciation charge can never be larger than the current book value of the assets in the group.

The major difference between group depreciation and item-by-item methods is the treatment of asset retirements. The group method assumes, in effect, that although items have the same expected service life, there will be individual items that will be retired earlier than average and others that will remain in use longer than average. Items retired from a group are assumed to be sold, or otherwise disposed of, *at book value*. Consequently gain or loss is not recognized on retiring assets from a group until either (1) the last item in the group has been retired, (2) the group has book value zero, or (3) accumulated depreciation after acquisition date becomes zero, whichever of these three comes first. There is not uniform agreement on criterion (3) for recognizing loss. Some would debit the Accumulated Depreciation account with the cost less proceeds of disposition, thereby creating a debit balance in the Accumulated Depreciation account. Following this procedure, recognition of loss would be deferred until one of the first two criteria was met. In the following examples, we use criterion (3) for loss recognition.

Since groups of assets (other than those grouped by year of acquisition) may be replenished with purchases subsequent to the initial ones, the recognition of gain or loss may be indefinitely postponed. If a machine that cost $5,000 and was expected to last for five years with no salvage value is retired from a group at the end of two years for $1,000, then the entry would be:

Cash	1,000	
Accumulated Depreciation on Machinery Group	4,000	
Machinery Group		5,000

The amount of the debit to Accumulated Depreciation is merely the "plug" necessary to yield equal debits and credits.

If, instead, the firm were required to pay $100 to a scavenger to remove the machine, receiving no proceeds, then the entry to record its retirement from a group would be:

Accumulated Depreciation on Machinery Group	5,100	
Cash		100
Machinery Group		5,000

Flow Assumption

In the entries just illustrated, the amount of the credit to Machinery Group is $5,000. How is this amount determined? In theory, the amount should be the cost of the particular machine retired. The very nature of group depreciation, however, implies that the items in a group are so sufficiently alike that the time-saving method of group depreciation is warranted. Therefore, the burdensome task of determining which particular assets have been retired and their original cost is not necessary. Rather, a flow assumption can be made, much the same as the flow assumption made in valuing inventories.

The easiest flow assumption to implement in group depreciation, and the one most consistent with the theory of group depreciation, is the weighted-average flow assumption. Thus, for example, assume a group consists of 1,000 telephone poles which were purchased at many different times and together originally cost $80,000. If 150 poles are retired (through replacement) during a period, the weighted-average flow assumption would imply that $12,000 (= 150/1,000 × $80,000) of acquisition costs are retired.

When the group consists of relatively unlike items, such as a group of all office furniture and equipment, then a FIFO flow assumption is easier to implement. For example, as typewriters are retired, we assume that the first typewriter purchased is the first retired, and so on.

In some cases, units retired are specifically identified, and the acquisition cost of the specific units retired forms the basis for the retirement entry. Thus, the group method can use the weighted-average or FIFO flow assumptions or specific identification of units retired.

Group Depreciation Illustrated

Schedule 14.5 illustrates the use of the group depreciation method assuming first, straight-line and then, double-declining-balance depreciation. Also shown for comparison are the results of item-by-item, straight-line depreciation. For the illustration assume that trucks with an expected life of four years are grouped, that ten trucks were bought at the beginning of the first year for $12,000 each, and that three more trucks were bought at the end of the second year for $15,000 each. The history of purchases and retirements of trucks in the group is shown in Schedule 14.4. Trucks retired can be specifically identified.

SCHEDULE 14.4 ASSET ACQUISITION AND RETIREMENTS FOR GROUP DEPRECIATION ILLUSTRATION

End of Year	Retirements [a] Number from First Purchase	Retirements [a] Number from Second Purchase	Proceeds from Disposition	Purchases [a] Number	Purchases [a] Cost
0	—	—	—	10	$120,000
1	—	—	—	—	—
2	4	—	$6,000	3	45,000
3	3	—	5,000	—	—
4	2	1	3,000	—	—
5	1	1	2,000	—	—
6	—	1	1,000	—	—

a All retirements take place on the last day of the year, just before purchases are made.

The straight-line method is illustrated using the weighted-average and FIFO flow assumptions as well as specific identification for retirements. Since the group consists only of trucks, the weighted-average flow assumption is easiest to implement. Under the double-declining-balance method, the tax regulations require separate groups for purchases in different years and the illustration shows the required separation into two groups.

In the illustration, the group is allowed to lapse so that the gain or loss on retirement can be shown. Note that under the straight-line group method, the accumulated depreciation becomes zero before the end of

SCHEDULE 14.5 GROUP AND INDIVIDUAL ITEM DEPRECIATION METHODS ILLUSTRATED

			Start of Year Trucks in Use			Depreciation Charges for Year (5)
		Year (1)	No. (2)	Cost (3)	Book Value (4) a	
Group Depreciation: Straight-Line at a Rate of ¼ of Cost Per Year: (5) = ¼ × (3)	FIFO Flow Assumption	1	10	$120,000	$120,000	$ 30,000
		2	10	120,000	90,000	30,000
		3	9	117,000	99,000	29,250
		4	6	81,000	64,750	20,250
		5	3	45,000	41,500	11,250
		6	1	15,000	15,000	3,750
						$124,500 e
	Weighted-Average Flow Assumption	3	9	117,000	99,000	$ 29,250
		4	6	78,000	64,750	19,500
		5	3	39,000	39,000	9,750
		6	1	13,000	13,000	3,250
			Six-year Totals			$121,750 e
	Specific Identification of Retirements	4	6	81,000	64,750	$ 20,250
		5	3	42,000	41,500	10,500
		6	1	15,000	15,000	3,750
			Six-year Totals			$123,750 e
Group Depreciation: Double-Declining Balance at a Rate of ½ of Book Value: (5) = ½ × (4)		1	10	120,000	120,000	$ 60,000
		2	10	120,000	60,000	30,000
	(1st Group)	3	6	72,000	24,000	12,000
	(2nd Group)	3	3	45,000	45,000	22,500
	(1st Group)	4	3	36,000	7,000	3,500
	(2nd Group)	4	3	45,000	22,500	11,250
	(1st Group)	5	1	12,000	1,500	750
	(2nd Group)	5	2	30,000	10,250	5,125
	(2nd Group)	6	1	15,000	4,125	2,063
						$147,188 e
Individual or Item-by-Item Depreciation: Straight-Line at a Rate of ¼ of Original Cost Per Year Until Original Cost is Fully Depreciated.		1	10	120,000	120,000	$ 30,000
		2	10	120,000	90,000	30,000
		3	9	117,000	81,000	29,250
		4	6	81,000	42,750	20,250
		5	3	42,000	15,000	7,500 f
		6	1	15,000	3,750	3,750
						$120,750 e

a Book value = cost shown in (3) less accumulated depreciation shown in (11) for end of previous year.

b (9) = (7) — (8) — (10) always; for group methods, (9) = (7) — (8) except when gain or loss is recognized.

c (11) = accumulated depreciation in (11) from previous year + (5) — (9).

d The group lapses when accumulated depreciation becomes zero; loss or gain can be recognized.

End of Year

Retirements

No. (6)	Credit to Cost (7)	Debit for Proceeds of Disposition (8)	Debit to Depreciation Accumulated (9)[b]	Loss, Dr. or (Gain), Cr. (10)	Accumulated Depreciation on Books (11)[c]
0	0	0	0	—	$30,000
4	$ 48,000	$ 6,000	$ 42,000	—	18,000
3	36,000	5,000	31,000	—	16,250
3	36,000	3,000	33,000	—	3,500
2	30,000	2,000	14,750	$13,250 [d]	0
1	15,000	1,000	3,750	10,250 [g]	0
	$165,000 [e]	$17,000 [e]	$124,500	$23,500 [e]	
3	$ 39,000	$ 5,000	$ 34,000	—	13,250
3	39,000	3,000	32,750	$ 3,250 [d]	0
2	26,000	2,000	9,750	14,250	0
1	13,000	1,000	3,250	8,750 [g]	0
	$165,000 [e]	$17,000 [e]	$121,750	$26,250 [e]	
3	$ 39,000	$ 3,000	$ 36,000	—	500
2	27,000	2,000	11,000	$14,000 [d]	0
1	15,000	1,000	3,750	10,250 [g]	0
	$165,000 [e]	$17,000 [e]	$123,750	$24,250 [e]	
0	0	0	0	—	60,000
4	$ 48,000	$ 6,000	$ 42,000	—	48,000
3	36,000	5,000	31,000	—	29,000
0	0	0	0	—	22,500
2	24,000	2,000	22,000	—	10,500
1	15,000	1,000	14,000	—	19,750
1	12,000	1,000	11,250	$ (250) [g]	0
1	15,000	1,000	14,000	—	10,875
1	15,000	1,000	12,938	1,062	0
	$165,000 [e]	$17,000 [e]	$147,188	$ 812 [e]	
0	0	0	0	—	30,000
4	$ 48,000	$ 6,000	$ 24,000	$18,000	36,000
3	36,000	5,000	27,000	4,000	38,250
3	39,000	3,000	31,500	4,500	27,000
2	27,000	2,000	23,250	1,750	11,250
1	15,000	1,000	15,000	(1,000)	0
	$165,000 [e]	$17,000 [e]	$120,750	$27,250 [e]	

[e] For totals: cost of trucks = $165,000 = (5) + (8) + (10) = sum of debits for depreciation expenses plus proceeds from disposition plus losses (or minus gains) from disposition.
[f] Trucks from first purchase have been fully depreciated so the depreciation charge is ¼ the cost of the two trucks remaining from the second purchase.
[g] The last item in the group has been retired.

the sixth year. Under criterion (3) above, loss on retirement can be recognized in the fifth year even though there are still trucks in use.

Under the double-declining-balance group method, there must be two groups—one for each set of purchases. Each group lapses at the time the last truck is retired from the group. Under item-by-item depreciation, gain or loss is recognized for each retirement.

Note that expenses (depreciation charges plus loss on retirement) under all methods total $148,000. Only the timing of expenses differs among the methods. This expense total plus the $17,000 of proceeds on disposition equals the $165,000 acquisition cost of the trucks.

QUESTIONS AND PROBLEMS

For the following questions and problems, round all answers to the nearest whole dollar.

1. "Accounting for depreciating assets would be greatly simplified if accounting periods were only long enough or the life of the assets short enough." What is the point of the quotation?

2. "The major purpose of depreciation accounting is to provide funds for the replacement of assets as they wear out." Do you agree? Explain.

°3. On April 30, 1975, the Tico Company bought a new machine for $14,000. The seller agreed to accept the company's old machine, $7,000 in cash, and a 12-percent one year note for $4,000 in payment.

The old machine was purchased on January 1, 1970, for $10,000. It was estimated that it would be useful for eight years after which it would have a salvage value of $400. Due to technological improvements, it is estimated that the new machine will have a service life of ten years and a salvage value of $800.

Assuming that the Tico Company uses the straight-line method of depreciation and closes its books annually on December 31, give the entries that were made in 1975.

4. On July 1, 1952, a building and site were purchased for $96,000. Of this amount, $40,000 was allocated to the land and the remainder to the building. The building is depreciated on a straight-line basis.

On July 1, 1974 (no additions or retirements having been recorded in the meanwhile), the net book value of the building was $25,200. On March 30, 1975, the building and site were sold for $60,000. The fair market value of the land was $50,000 at this date.

The firm closes its books annually at June 30. Give the entries required on March 30, 1975.

5. Give the journal entries for the following selected transactions of the Eagle Manufacturing Company. The company uses the straight-line method of calculating depreciation and closes its books annually on December 31.

(1) A machine is purchased on November 1, 1975, for $15,000. It is

_____

° Hints, key numbers, or (partial) answers appear in the back of the book between the Appendix Tables and the Glossary.

estimated that it will be used for ten years and that it will have a scrap value of $300 at the end of that time. Give the entry for the depreciation at December 31, 1975.

(2) Record the depreciation for the year ending December 31, 1976.

(3) In August, 1981, it is decided that the machine will probably be used for a total of twelve years and that its scrap value will be $200. Make a correction of prior years' earnings and record the depreciation for the year ending December 31, 1981.

(4) What procedure should have been followed for the information in (3) according to generally accepted accounting principles?

(5) The machine is sold for $500 on March 31, 1986. Record the entries of that date, assuming depreciation is recorded as indicated in (3).

6. On March 1, 1975, one of the buildings owned by the Metropolitan Products Company was destroyed by fire. The cost of the building was $100,000; the balance in the Accumulated Depreciation account at January 1, 1975, was $38,125. A service life of forty years with a zero salvage value had been estimated for the building. The company uses the straight-line method. The building was not insured.

a. Give the journal entries made at March 1.

b. If there have been no alterations in the service life estimate, when was the building acquired?

°7. Journalize the following transactions:

(1) A piece of equipment is purchased for $850 cash.

(2) Depreciation for one year of $85 is recorded.

(3) The equipment is sold for $400. At the time of the sale, the Accumulated Depreciation account shows a balance of $425. Depreciation of $85 for the year of the sale has not yet been recorded.

°8. A building which cost $150,000 is on the books at a depreciated amount of $75,000 after having been in use for twenty years. The building is depreciated on a straight-line basis. The assumption is that removal costs will equal salvage value. In the twenty-first year it is decided that the building will probably last fifty years in all.

Calculate the amount of the depreciation charge (1) in the twenty-first and (2) in the forty-second years of use:

a. if depreciation charges continue to be based on the original estimates

b. if the undepreciated cost after twenty years is to be spread over the estimated remaining life

c. if a correction of prior periods' earnings is made and depreciation charges thereafter are based on the new estimates.

9. Give correcting entries for the following situations. In each case, the firm uses the straight-line method of depreciation and closes its books annually on December 31. Recognize all gains and losses currently.

a. A cash register was purchased for $300 on January 1, 1970. It was depreciated at a 10-percent rate. On June 30, 1975, it was traded in on a new cash register costing $500. An allowance of $200 was given on the old register, and $300 was paid by check. The bookkeeper made the following entry to record the trade-in transaction:

| Store Equipment | 300 | |
| Cash in Bank | | 300 |

b. A used truck was purchased in May, 1975, for $4,000. Its cost when new was $6,000, and the bookkeeper made the following entry to record the purchase:

Truck	6,000	
Accumulated Depreciation		2,000
Cash		4,000

c. A testing mechanism was purchased on April 1, 1973, for $600. It was depreciated at a 10-percent annual rate. On June 30, 1975, it was stolen and the bookkeeper made the following entry:

Theft Loss	600	
Testing Mechanism		600

°**10.** Give the journal entries for the following transactions:
   (1) A building is constructed at a cost of $36,000. It is estimated that it will be usable for forty-five years when it will have a scrap value of $2,250. It was put into operation on September 1, 1941. Give the entry for depreciation for the last four months of 1941. The straight-line method of depreciation is used.
   (2) Record the depreciation for the year 1942.
   (3) In 1975 it is decided that the total life of the building will be only forty years, and its salvage value will be $3,000. Make a retained earnings adjustment to correct for 1941-74 although such adjustments are not sanctioned by generally accepted accounting principles. Record the depreciation for the year of 1975.
   (4) The building is abandoned for operational purposes on March 1, 1977. It is sold to wreckers for $2,000. Record the entries at March 1, 1977.

11. The Grogan Manufacturing Company started business on January 1, 1975. At that time it purchased Machine A for $20,000, payment being made by check.

   Due to an expansion in the volume of business, Machine B, costing $25,000, was purchased on September 30, 1976. A check for $15,000 was issued with the balance to be paid in annual installments of $2,000 plus interest at the rate of 6 percent on the unpaid balance. The first installment is due on September 30, 1977.

   On June 30, 1977, Machine A was traded in on a larger model, Machine C, which cost $30,000. An allowance of $13,000 was given for the trade-in of Machine A, and the balance was paid by check.

   All installments are paid on time.

   All machines have an estimated life of ten years with an estimated salvage value equal to 10 percent of original cost. The company closes its books on December 31. The straight-line method is used.

   Prepare dated journal entries to record all transactions through December 31, 1977, including year-end adjustments but excluding closing entries.

12. Calculate the depreciation charge for the first and second years of the asset's life in the following cases. Where the declining-balance method is used, the rate is twice the straight-line rate.

Asset	Cost	Salvage	Life (Years)	Depreciation Method
*a. Blast Furnace	$800,000	$25,000	20	Declining-Balance
*b. Hotel	500,000	50,000	45	Straight-Line
*c. Typewriter	400	40	8	Sum-of-the-Years'-Digits
d. Tractor	6,000	500	10	Declining-Balance
e. Ferris Wheel	7,600	400	12	Straight-Line
f. Delivery Truck	5,500	1,300	6	Sum-of-the-Years'-Digits

13. The Thomas Cookie Company purchases a new automobile for the use of one of its salesmen on May 17, 1975. The car costs $4,000. It is estimated that it will be driven for 100,000 miles before being traded in and that its trade-in value will be $400.

Odometer readings are as follows:

December 31, 1975	12,420
December 31, 1976	40,357
December 31, 1977	61,987
March 16, 1978	97,354

On March 16, 1978, the automobile is traded in for a new one with a list price of $4,500. The used automobile has a fair market value of $200, but the dealer allows $500 on it toward the list price of a new car. The balance of the purchase price is paid by check.

a. Record the depreciation charges for each year through 1977.

b. Record the entries for March 16, 1978.

14. On January 1, 1975, the Central Production Company purchased a new turret lathe for $36,000. It was estimated to have a useful life of four years and no salvage value. The company closes its books annually on December 31.

Indicate the amount of the depreciation charge for each of the four years under:

a. the straight-line method

*b. the declining-balance method at twice the straight-line rate

c. the sum-of-the-years'-digits method.

15. Give the annual or unit depreciation charge in the following cases. The firm uses the straight-line method or the units-of-production method.

Asset	Cost	Estimated Salvage	Estimated Life
a. Adding Machine	$ 400	$ 40	12 years
b. Taxicab	5,000	100	100,000 miles
c. Building	37,000	1,000	18 years
d. Desk	280	30	20 years
e. Aircraft Engine	25,000	500	2,000 flying hours
f. Bakery Oven	6,800	350	16 years
g. Display Counter	2,000	400	12 years

16. A machine is purchased for $8,900. It is expected to last eight years and to be operated for 25,000 hours during that time. It is estimated that its salvage value will be $1,700 at the end of that time.

    Calculate the depreciation charge for each of the first three years using:

a. The straight-line method.

b. The sum-of-the-years'-digits method.

c. The declining-balance method at twice the straight-line rate.

d. The units-of-production method. Operating times are as follows: first year, 3,500 hours; second year, 2,325 hours; third year, 4,895 hours.

17. A machine is purchased for $15,000. It is expected to last for nine years and have a scrap value of $600. It is estimated that the machine will operate 20,000 hours before being retired.

    Calculate the depreciation for each of the first three years using:

a. The straight-line method.

b. The declining-balance method, with a rate twice the straight-line rate.

c. The sum-of-the-years'-digits method.

d. The units-of-production method. The machine is operated 2,130 hours the first year, 1,675 hours the second year, and 2,576 hours the third year.

18. The Slowpoke Shipping Company buys a new truck for $10,000 on January 1, 1975. It is estimated that it will last six years and have a salvage value of $1,000. Early in 1977, it is determined that the truck will last only an additional two years. The company closes its books on December 31.

a. Present a table showing the depreciation charges for each year from 1975 to 1978 and give the adjusting entry made in 1977. Assume that the company desires to follow the theoretically correct method of correcting the past errors in depreciation so that the future depreciation charges will not also be in error. Follow the instructions for each of the following methods:

    (1) The straight-line method.

    (2) The sum-of-the-years'-digits method.

    (3) The declining-balance method with depreciation at twice the straight-line rate. The remaining undepreciated cost less salvage value is to be written off in the last year.

b. Present a table showing the depreciation charges for each year from 1975 to 1978 under each of the methods in part (a). Assume that the company follows the policy of charging off the undepreciated cost less salvage over the remaining life when service life estimates are revised.

19. The Linder Manufacturing Company buys a new machine for $7,200 on July 1, 1975. It is estimated that it will have a service life of six years and then have a salvage value of $900. The company closes its books annually on June 30.

a. Prepare computations of the depreciation charges for each year of the asset's life assuming the use of:

    (1) The straight-line method.

    (2) The sum-of-the-years'-digits method.

    (3) The declining-balance method, with a rate twice the straight-line rate.

b. If the machine were sold for $700 on October 30, 1980, give the entries that would be made on that date under each of the methods in part (a).

20. The Black Manufacturing Company buys a new machine for $4,500. It is estimated that it will have a service life of six years and a salvage value of $300. The machine was purchased on July 1, 1975; the company closes its books on June 30.
    a. Prepare a table showing the depreciation charges for each year of the asset's life assuming the use of:
    (1) The straight-line method.
    (2) The sum-of-the-years'-digits method.
    (3) The declining-balance method at twice the straight-line rate. Switch to straight-line depreciation for the last year of the asset's life.
    b. If the machine were sold for $250 on October 31, 1980, prepare the journal entries that would be required on that date for each of the methods under part (a).
    c. Assume the machine originally had been estimated to have a salvage value of $250 and to produce cash flows of $1,000 at the end of each year, for six years. Verify that the internal rate of return on the machine is about 10 percent and compute a depreciation schedule for the compound interest method using a 10-percent internal rate of return.

21. Prepare journal entries for the transactions below.
    7/1/75   The Acme Tool Rental Shop purchases ten electric typewriters for cash at a cost of $400 each. It is estimated that they will have a life of ten years.
    12/31/75 The books are closed for the year. Record the depreciation from July 1 to December 31, 1975. The straight-line method is used with a 10-percent rate applied to original cost.
    4/1/76   A sticking key causes one machine to short circuit, which causes damage and reduces the machine to scrap. A claim is filed with the insurance company for its book value, $350.
    5/1/76   A manual typewriter is purchased for cash to replace the destroyed machine. The cost of the unit is $200, and the life is ten years. Salvage value is estimated to be zero. Do not change the depreciation rate.
    5/15/76   The insurance company sends a check for $300 to settle the claim, which Acme accepts.
    12/31/76 The books are closed. Record the depreciation on the machines for the year.
    12/31/77 Before closing the books for the year, the remaining life of the electric typewriters is determined to be only four more years. The life estimate for the manual unit is to remain unchanged. In the light of these new facts, compute depreciation for the year. (Make no adjustment of prior years' depreciation charges.)
    7/1/78   It is decided to turn in the manual typewriter for an electrical unit. The dealer allows $100 for the manual typewriter on the cost of the new electric unit. The price of the new machine is $500. The balance is paid in cash. The new machine has an estimated life of ten years and $50 salvage value.
    12/31/78 The books are closed. Record the depreciation for the year.

*22. The Chisholm Manufacturing Company purchased a plot of land for $50,000 as a plant site. There was a small office building on the plot, conservatively appraised at $8,000, which the company will continue to use. The company had plans drawn for a factory and received bids for its construction. It rejected all bids and decided to construct the plant itself. Below are the items which management feels should be included in capital accounts.

(1) Cement block, bricks, and tile	$ 77,345
(2) Cement, sand, and gravel	39,864
(3) Lumber, sash, and plumbing	84,392
(4) Other materials and supplies	47,204
(5) Cellar excavation	12,000
(6) Labor on construction	138,639
(7) Cost of remodeling old building into office building	9,473
(8) Interest on money borrowed by Chisholm	4,592
(9) Interest on Chisholm's own money used	11,394
(10) Cash discounts on materials used	6,439
(11) Supervision by management	9,500
(12) Compensation insurance premiums	8,000
(13) Payment of claim for injuries not covered by insurance	2,500
(14) Clerical and other expenses of construction	7,943
(15) Paving of streets and sidewalks	4,879
(16) Architect's plans and specifications	3,000
(17) Legal expense of conveying land	1,300
(18) Legal expense of injury claim	900
(19) Profits credited to profit and loss account, being the difference between the foregoing cost and the lowest contractor's bid	12,345

Show in detail the items to be included in the following accounts: Land, Factory Building, Office Building, and Site Improvements.

23. A machine with a life of five years is purchased for $10,652. The cash flows which will occur due to the ownership of this asset are as follows:

January 1, 1975	$—10,652
December 31, 1975	+ 1,000
December 31, 1976	+ 2,000
December 31, 1977	+ 3,000
December 31, 1978	+ 4,000
December 31, 1979	+ 5,000

Compute the annual depreciation charges for this asset using the compound interest method. The internal rate of return is between 8 percent and 15 percent.

24. An asset is purchased for $5,000 on January 1, 1975, and is expected to have no salvage value at the end of its five-year life.

Taking into account all costs and revenues produced by the ownership of this asset, the net cash flows are as follows:

January 1, 1975	$—5,000
December 31, 1975	+1,000
December 31, 1976	+1,100
December 31, 1977	+1,200
December 31, 1978	+1,300
December 31, 1979	+1,392

Compute the annual depreciation charges for this asset using the compound interest method. The internal rate of return is between 5 percent and 8 percent.

25. Work Problem 13 on compound-interest depreciation at the end of Chapter 24.

26. Jonathan Corporation uses the group method of depreciation on its fleet of delivery trucks. All trucks are placed in a single group where such treatment is allowed by the tax regulations and are assumed to have zero salvage value.

The group was first established in 1973. For simplicity, it is assumed that truck purchases and retirements take place on January 1 of each year. The following data are available:

	Purchases		Retirements		
Year	Number of Trucks	Cost per Truck	Number of Trucks	Cost per Truck	Proceeds per Truck
1973	10	$3,000	—	—	—
1974	8	3,100	1	$3,000	$1,000
1975	4	3,200	2	3,000	800

Compute the depreciation charges for each of the three years above on the group method using:
a. the straight-line method and a 20-percent annual rate
°b. the double-declining-balance method and a rate of 40 percent.

27. The Acme Rental Company rents heavy-duty rug shampooing machines on a week-to-week basis. The expected life of a machine is ten years. Below is a summary of purchases and disposals of machines for the first five years of the firm's existence:

End of Year	Acquisitions	Total Cost	Retirements	Proceeds
0	10	$10,000	0	0
1	2	2,100	1	$300
2	0	0	1	250
3	0	0	1	200
4	3	3,500	1	100
5	0	0	0	0

The company adopted the group method of depreciation for its rug shampooing machines. All machines are placed in a single group when tax regulations permit such treatment. Compute depreciation for the first five years assuming a FIFO flow for retirements, zero salvage value and the use of:
a. the straight-line method.
b. the declining-balance method at twice the straight-line rate.

*28. Dr. Kadlac buys a new car every year with list price $6,000. He trades in a one-year-old car and pays $2,500 cash. Operating the car is a legitimate business expense. Dr. Kadlac depreciates the car using a three-year life. After fifteen years of following this practice, Dr. Kadlac discovered that the book value of the new car for tax purposes was identical every year. What is that book value if Dr. Kadlac uses

   a. straight-line depreciation?
   b. double-declining-balance depreciation?
   c. sum-of-the-years'-digits depreciation?

*29. The Internal Revenue Service allows automobiles used for business purposes to be depreciated by assuming no salvage value either on a straight-line basis with a depreciable life of 2½ years or on an accelerated basis (double-declining-balance or sum-of-the-years'-digits) with a depreciable life of three years. Which of the three depreciation methods leads to the largest present value of depreciation expenses for an automobile costing $6,000? Assume a discount rate per year of:

   a. 10 percent.
   b. 20 percent.
   c. What about discount rates between 10 and 20 percent per year? (Round present value factors to three digits and calculations to the nearest dollar.)

Chapter 15

Liabilities

This chapter and the next two examine the accounting problems of the right-hand side of the balance sheet, which shows the sources of a firm's capital. Business capital comes from two sources: owners and nonowners. Ownership equity is examined in the following two chapters. This chapter discusses capital provided to a business by nonowners. Banks or creditors providing debt on a long-term basis are aware of their role as providers of capital, but suppliers, employees, and customers usually do not think of themselves as contributing to a firm's capital, even though they do. The obligation that a business incurs to these nonowning contributors of capital is called a liability.

A definition of a liability, as the term is used by accountants, is a definite legal obligation to make a payment of a definite (or reasonably certain) amount at a definite (or reasonably certain) time in return for a current benefit. There are usually four operable constraints on an obligation before it is recognized as a liability: legal obligation, certainty of amount, certainty of due date, and the receipt of a current benefit. Most of the liabilities discussed in this chapter meet all four criteria. Any item designated as a liability that does not meet all four criteria is noted in the discussion of that item.

CURRENT LIABILITIES

Current liabilities are normally those due within one year. They include accounts payable to creditors, payroll accruals, taxes payable, short-term notes payable, and a few others. Current liabilities are continually discharged and replaced with new ones in the course of business operations.

Accounts Payable to Creditors

Companies seldom pay for goods and services on receipt. Payment is usually deferred until a bill is received from the supplier. Even then, the bill might not be paid immediately, but instead, accumulated with other bills until a specified time of the month when all bills are paid. Since interest is not paid on these accounts, management tries to obtain as much capital as possible from its creditors. Nevertheless, failure to pay creditors according to schedule can lead to poor credit ratings and restrictions of future credit.

As an incentive for prompt payment of bills, some suppliers offer a discount for payment within a short period, such as ten days. Although this "cash discount" is usually only 1 or 2 percent, ignoring it can be expensive. For example, assume that a 2-percent discount is offered on an invoice of $1,000 for payment within ten days and that the payment is due within thirty days. If the firm refuses the discount of $20 offered for payment in ten days, it may use $980 for an extra twenty days. The $20 charge for 20 days' use of $980 is equivalent to interest on borrowed money. A nominal rate of 2.04 percent ($= 20/980$) compounded every twenty days is equivalent to an effective rate of more than 44 percent per year. It is sensible to take advantage of most discounts.

Payroll Accruals

Deductions are taken from an employee's gross pay to cover federal income taxes, payroll (FICA[1] or social security) taxes, medical plans, pension plans, insurance plans, and other items. The accounting for these deductions is relatively simple, although time consuming. Instead of showing the gross pay as entirely payable to his employees, the employer shows the net pay, and deductions are shown as payable to the relevant recipients. For example, gross wages of $2,000 might be shown as:

Labor Expense	2,000	
Wages Payable		1,500
Federal Withholding Taxes Payable		240
State Withholding Taxes Payable		80
Payroll Taxes Payable		120
Medical Plan Payable		20
Pension Plan Payable		30
Insurance Plan Payable		10

In addition, the employer is required to match the FICA contributions of his workers. Assuming that in this example, the labor contract requires the employer also to match the medical and pension plan contributions of the workers, and those contributions are judged to be a component of labor expense, the additional journal entries would be:

[1] FICA is the Federal Insurance Contribution Act. The actual deduction depends on several factors and has steadily increased over time. For the purpose of illustrations and problems in this book, it will be assumed that the tax is calculated at 6 percent of the first $12,000 of gross income for each employee.

```
Labor Expense ................................................. 170
    Payroll Taxes Payable ........................................     120
    Medical Plan Payable .........................................      20
    Pension Plan Payable .........................................      30
```

Short-term Notes and Interest Payable

Businesses get interim financing for less than a year from banks or other creditors in return for a short-term note called a *note payable*. Such notes are called promissory notes and have a specified interest cost and a repayment date. The Interest Payable account shows interest owed but not yet paid. (The holder of the note owns a short-term asset. The holder treats the note and interest receivable in a way exactly the reverse of the treatments described here for the borrower, or maker.)

All promissory notes are payable at some determinable time, but the maturity date can be expressed in various ways. Some common examples are:

> On demand I promise to pay . . . [Although the date on which the note comes due is not stated definitely, it can be determined, since the holder can demand payment whenever he chooses.]
>
> Sixty days after date . . . [In this case the actual number of days in a month is used in calculating the maturity date. If, for example, a note is due sixty days after February 16, 1975, the due date is April 17—twelve days in February, thirty-one in March, and seventeen in April. The first day is not counted; the last day is.]
>
> Two months after date . . . [The due date usually would be the same day of the month in the second month following the date of origin. If a two-month note were written on February 16, 1975, it would be due on April 16, 1975. A two-month note dated on July 31, however, would be due on September 30, this being the last day of that month.]

For the sake of uniformity and simplicity, we shall use the following rules in connection with the calculation of interest throughout the text and problems:

1. When the terms are given in months, consider one month to be one-twelfth of a year; three months, one-fourth of a year; six months, one-half of a year, and so on, regardless of the actual number of days in the period. This is equivalent to regarding any one-month period as being 30 days in a 360-day year.
2. When the terms are given in days, use the 360-day year. Consider 30 days to be one-twelfth of a year, 60 days to be one-sixth of a year, 17 days to be 17/360 of a year, and so on. Determine maturity dates by using the actual number of days.

Issuing a Note and Payment at Maturity

Promissory notes usually are given by a customer in connection with a purchase or with the settlement of an open account or account payable. For example, if on July 1, 1975, the Suren Company were to issue a sixty-day, 8-percent note for $3,000, dated July 1, 1975, to the Mullen Company to apply to accounts payable to Mullen, Suren's entry would be:

```
July 1  Accounts Payable—Mullen Company ..................  3,000
            Notes Payable ...................................         3,000
```

Assuming that the accounting period for the Suren Company is the calendar year, the entry upon payment at maturity would be:

```
Aug. 30  Notes Payable ...................................  3,000
             Interest Expense ...............................     40
             Cash ...........................................         3,040
```

If the accounting period of the Suren Company were one month, the interest adjustment ($20 = $3,000 × .08 × 30/360) at the end of the period, July 31, would be:

```
July 31  Interest Expense .........................................  20
             Interest Payable ......................................         20
```

The entry upon payment at maturity would then be:

```
Aug. 30  Notes Payable ...................................  3,000
             Interest Payable ..............................     20
             Interest Expense ..............................     20
             Cash ...........................................         3,040
```

Alternatives to Payment at Maturity

At the maturity date, the note may be: (1) paid, as above, (2) renewed, (3) partially paid with the balance renewed, or (4) dishonored by the maker.

Often the holder may extend the time of payment by accepting a new note for a maturing one. If interest is paid, the face value of the new note would be the same as the old. If the Suren Company renewed its note, paid accrued interest, and kept its books on a calendar-year basis, the entry at maturity of the original note would be:

```
Aug. 30  Interest Expense ...............................     40
             Notes Payable ...............................  3,000
             Cash ...........................................         40
             Notes Payable ...............................         3,000
```

Even though it has no effect on the notes payable balance, the debit and credit to Notes Payable should be recorded so that the records will show that the note was renewed.

If the interest of $40 and a partial payment on principal of $1,000 had been paid and if there had been a partial renewal of the note, the entry at maturity would be:

```
Aug. 30  Interest Expense ...............................     40
             Notes Payable ...............................  3,000
             Cash ...........................................         1,040
             Notes Payable ...............................         2,000
```

If, at maturity, Suren dishonors the note and that action is not legally contested, then it must be because Suren is insolvent or approaching bankruptcy. Thus the normal accounting for going concerns is no longer appropriate. Accounting for insolvent firms is beyond the scope of this book.

Noninterest-bearing Notes

A noninterest-bearing note has a face amount equal to the total amount due at maturity. The basic elements of such a note might read "Sixty days after date (July 1, 1976), the Suren Company promises to pay to the order of the Mullen Company the amount of $3,000." No explicit rate of interest is given. Of course the value of the note prior to maturity will be less than the maturity value of $3,000. The difference between the face value and value at time of issue is called the *discount* on the note and represents the implicit interest cost.

For *short*-term notes, both holder and issuer have two options. First, either may record the note at face value, disregarding implicit interest. Second, either may recognize the implicit interest by recording the note at its face value and recording in an account, Discount on Notes Payable (or Receivable), the difference between face value and market value. The accounting treatment of Discounts on Notes is similar to the treatment of Discounts on Bonds Payable (or Receivable), which is discussed later in this chapter. Generally accepted accounting principles require the recognition of discount on *long*-term notes; recognition is permitted but not required for short-term obligations.[2]

Deferred Performance Liabilities

Another current liability arises from advance payments by customers for goods or services. This liability, unlike the preceding ones, is discharged by delivering goods or services, rather than by paying cash. This liability represents "unearned revenue"; that is, cash was received before the goods or services were furnished to the customer.

An example of this type of liability is the advance sale of theatre tickets, say for $200. Upon the sale, the following entry would be made:

```
Cash ......................................................  200
    Liability for Advance Sales ..................................      200
```

Note that in these cases, the certainty of due date criterion for liabilities may not be met. After the theatre performance represented by these tickets, revenue would be recognized and the liability would be removed:

```
Liability for Advance Sales .....................................  200
    Performance Revenue .........................................      200
```

Other examples of deferred performance liabilities are magazine subscriptions, transportation tickets, and service contracts.

[2] Opinion No. 21, Accounting Principles Board, AICPA, August, 1971.

A related type of deferred performance liability arises when a firm provides a warranty for free service or repairs for some period after the sale. At the time of sale, the firm can only estimate the likely amount of warranty liability. If during the accounting period sales of $28,000 were made and the firm estimated that 4 percent of the receipts from the sale would eventually be used to satisfy warranty claims, the entry would be:

Accounts Receivable	28,000	
Warranty Expense	1,120	
Sales		28,000
Deferred Warranty Liability		1,120

Note that this entry recognizes the warranty expense in the period when revenue is recognized, even though the repairs may be made in a later period. In this case, two criteria for liabilities, the certainty of the amount and the due date, are not met, but the need to recognize the related expense in the same period as the revenue is considered to be of overriding importance. Because the expense is recognized, the deferred liability is created.

When expenditures of, say, $675 are made for repairs under the warranty, the entry would be:

Deferred Warranty Liability	675	
Cash (or other assets consumed for repairs)		675

With experience, the firm will adjust the percentage of sales it charges to Warranty Expense so that the credit balance in the Deferred Warranty Liability account stays within a reasonable range. This treatment of warranty costs is much like the "allowance method" introduced in Chapter 9 for the treatment of uncollectible accounts.

Contingent Liabilities—Potential Obligations

One of the criteria for an item to be classified by the accountant as a liability is that there be a legal obligation. The world of business and law is full of uncertainties. At any given time the firm may find itself potentially liable for events that have occurred in the past. A *contingent liability* is not currently a legal obligation but a potential future obligation. It arises from an event that has occurred in the past but whose outcome is not now known. Whether or not the item becomes an obligation, and how large an obligation it will become, is to be determined by a future event, such as the outcome of a lawsuit.

Suppose the company is sued for damages in a formal court proceeding for an accident involving a customer who was visiting the company. The suit is not scheduled for trial until after the close of the accounting period. If the company's lawyers and auditors agree that the outcome is likely to be favorable for the company or that, if unfavorable, the amount of the damage settlement will not be large, then no obligation or liability will be recognized in the accounts. The footnotes to the financial statements must disclose, however, significant contingent liabilities.

If either the company's lawyers or auditors think the outcome will be unfavorable and the amount of damages awarded by the court will be significant, then the item would not be a contingent liability but an estimated liability and would be disclosed in the accounts. At the end of the period, the following adjusting entry should be made to recognize the estimated amount of the court's award of damages.

```
Loss on Damage Claim .....................................   50,000
    Estimated Liability for Damages ..........................          50,000
To recognize estimated damage arising from lawsuit.
```

The debit in the above entry is to a loss account (presented among other expenses on the income statement), and the credit is to an estimated liability which should be treated as a current liability, similar to the Deferred Warranty Liability, on the balance sheet. In practice, firms try to avoid making such entries because it is a partial admission of guilt that might actually affect the outcome of the trial.

The term *contingent liability* is used only when the item is not recognized in the accounts but, rather, in the footnotes. A recent annual report of the General Motors Corporation illustrates the disclosure of contingent liabilities as follows.

> *Note 15.   Contingent Liabilities*
> There are various claims and pending actions against the Corporation and its subsidiaries in respect of taxes, product liability, alleged patent infringements, warranties, alleged air pollution and other matters arising out of the conduct of the business. Certain of these actions purport to be class actions, seeking damages in very large amounts. The amounts of liability on these claims and actions at . . . [year end] were not determinable but, in the opinion of management, the ultimate liability resulting will not materially affect the consolidated financial position or results of operations of the Corporation and its consolidated subsidiaries.

LONG-TERM LIABILITIES

The principal long-term liabilities are mortgages and bonds. The significant differences between long-term and short-term, or current, liabilities are that: (1) interest on long-term liabilities is ordinarily paid at regular intervals during the life of a long-term obligation while interest on short-term debt is usually paid in a lump sum at maturity; (2.a) the principal of long-term obligations is often paid back in installments, or (2.b) special funds are accumulated by the borrower for retiring the liability.

Mortgages

A *mortgage* is a contract in which the lender is given legal title to certain property of the borrower, with the provision that the title reverts to the borrower when the loan is repaid in full. (In a few states the lender merely acquires a lien on the borrower's property rather than legal title to it.)

The mortgaged property is security for the loan. The customary terminology designates the lender as the *mortgagee* and the borrower as the *mortgagor*.

As long as the mortgagor meets his obligations under the mortgage agreement, the mortgagee does not get the ordinary rights of an owner to possess and use the property. If the mortgagor defaults on either the principal or interest payments, the mortgagee can *foreclose* the mortgage or arrange to have the property sold for his benefit. The mortgagee has first right to the proceeds from the foreclosure sale for satisfying his claim. If there is an excess, it is paid to the mortgagor. If the proceeds are insufficient to pay the remaining loan, the lender becomes an unsecured creditor for the unpaid balance.

There may be more than one mortgage on a piece of property. The mortgages would then be known as the first mortgage, the second mortgage, and so on. If there were two mortgages, the first mortgagee would have the first claim to the proceeds from a foreclosure, the second mortgagee would have the next claim, and the borrower would receive anything that is left or be liable for any deficiencies.

In some states the *trust deed* is more commonly used than the mortgage. The general effect is the same, but the legal relations are different. Under a trust deed, title to the property is transferred to a third party, such as a bank or trust company, known as the *trustee*. The trustee holds title to the property during the loan's life and transfers title to the borrower if the loan is repaid. If the borrower fails to fulfill his agreement, the trustee sells the property and uses the proceeds to pay the debt.

Two common types of situations give rise to mortgage or trust-deed contracts. First, property already owned may be mortgaged to raise funds. Second, property may be purchased and financed with the proceeds of a *purchase-money* mortgage. A purchase-money mortgage may be a new agreement between buyer and seller, or the buyer may agree to assume a mortgage that already exists on the property.

Accounting for Mortgages

Some of the more common problems in accounting for mortgages are presented in the following illustration.

On October 1, 1974, the Midwestern Products Company borrows $30,000 for five years from the Home Savings and Finance Company to obtain funds for additional working capital. As security, it gives a mortgage on several parcels of land that it owns and that are on its books at a cost of $50,000. The interest rate is 8 percent per year, with payments due on April 1 and October 1. Midwestern agrees to make ten equal payments over the five years of the mortgage that are just large enough so that when the last payment is made on October 1, 1979, the loan and all interest will have been paid. The Midwestern Products Company closes its books annually on December 31.

First, find the payment that Midwestern must make each six months to discharge its obligation in five years. At the time the loan is made, it has present value of $30,000. Since payments are to be made every six months, we must find the ordinary annuity payment that has present value of $30,000 when the number of payments is 10 and the interest rate is 4 percent per period. Table 4 in the Appendix to this book indicates that the present value of an ordinary annuity of $1 per period for 10 periods discounted at 4 percent per period is $8.1109. The annuity payments must be large enough so that their present value is $30,000. Therefore each payment must be $30,000/8.1109 = $3,698.73. Assume that Midwestern Products agrees to pay $3,700 for each of the first nine payments and a final payment somewhat smaller than $3,700 but large enough to discharge the debt. (One of the chapter-end questions asks you to find the size of that final payment to discharge the debt.)

The entries from the time the mortgage is given through December 31, 1975, would be:

10/1/74	Cash	30,000	
	Mortgage Payable		30,000
	Loan made with Home Savings and Finance Company for five years at 8 percent compounded semi-annually.		
12/31/74	Interest Expense	600	
	Interest Payable		600
	Interest accrued on mortgage from 10/1/74 to 12/31/74 (.08 × $30,000 × 3/12).		
4/1/75	Interest Expense	600	
	Interest Payable	600	
	Mortgage Payable	2,500	
	Cash		3,700
	Interest accrued on mortgage from 1/1/75 to 4/1/75, payment of six months' interest, and reduction of loan by the difference $3,700 − $1,200 = $2,500.		
10/1/75	Interest Expense	1,100	
	Mortgage Payable	2,600	
	Cash		3,700
	Payment of interest from 4/1/75 to 10/1/75 [.08 × ($30,000 − $2,500) × 1/2].		
12/31/75	Interest Expense	498	
	Interest Payable		498
	Interest accrued from 10/1/75 to 12/31/75 [.08 × ($30,000 − $2,500 − $2,600) × 3/12].		

Midwestern Products Company experienced a major, uninsured loss in February, 1976, and is unable to make the required $3,700 payment on April 1, 1976. The Home Savings and Finance Company forecloses, the mortgaged property is sold at auction by the sheriff, and $40,000 is realized from the sale after deducting legal fees and other costs. The mortgagee receives a payment equal to the sum of the remaining principal, $24,900, and the interest due on April 1, 1976, $996. The remaining $14,104 is

turned over to Midwestern. Since the mortgaged land was carried on the
books at $50,000, a $10,000 loss must be recognized. The entry to record the
foreclosure would be:

```
4/1/76  Cash  ............................................  14,104
        Mortgage Payable  ...............................  24,900
        Interest Expense  .................................    498
        Interest Payable  .................................            498
        Loss on Foreclosure of Mortgage  ..................  10,000
            Land  ........................................          50,000
```

Bonds

Mortgages or notes are used whenever the funds being borrowed can be
obtained from a small number of sources. When large amounts are needed,
the firm may have to borrow from the general investing public through
the use of a bond issue. Bonds are used primarily by corporations and
governmental units. The distinctive features of a bond issue are:

1. A *bond indenture*, or agreement, is drawn up which shows in
detail the terms of the loan and the rights and duties of the borrower and
other parties to the contract.

2. *Bond certificates* are used. Engraved certificates are prepared,
each one representing a portion of the total loan. The usual minimum
denomination in business practice is $1,000, although $500 and even $100
bonds are sometimes used. Government bonds are issued in denominations
as small as $25.

3. A *trustee* is named to hold title to any property serving as security
for the loan and to act as the technical representative of the bondholders.
The trustee is usually a bank or trust company.

4. An agent is appointed, usually a bank or trust company, to act as
registrar and *disbursing agent*. The borrower deposits interest and principal
payments with the disbursing agent, which distributes the funds to the
bondholders.

5. Most bonds are *coupon bonds*. Coupons are attached to the bond
certificate covering the interest payments throughout the life of the bond.
When a coupon comes due, the bondholder cuts it off and deposits it with
his bank. The bank sends the coupon through the clearing system to the
disbursing agent.

6. Bonds are commonly *registered as to principal*, which means that
the holder's name appears on the bond certificate and on the records of
the registrar. Sometimes both the principal and interest of bonds are
registered, in which case the interest payments are mailed directly to the
bondholder and coupons are not used. Registered bonds are easily replaced
if lost, but the transfer from one holder to another is cumbersome. Un-
registered bonds may be transferred merely by delivery, while registered
bonds have to be assigned formally from one holder to another.

7. The entire bond issue is usually sold by the borrower to an investment banking firm, or to a group of investment bankers known as a *syndicate*, which takes over the responsibility of reselling the bonds to the investing public.

Types of Bonds

Real estate bonds, sometimes called *mortgage bonds*, carry a mortgage on real estate as security for the repayment of the loan. *Collateral trust bonds* are usually secured by stocks and bonds of other corporations. The most common type of corporate bond, except in the railroad and public utility industries, is the *debenture bond*. This type carries no specific security or collateral; instead, it is issued on the general credit of the business. To give added protection to the bondholders, provisions are usually included in the bond indenture that limit the amount of subsequent long-term debt that can be incurred. *Convertible bonds* are debentures that the holder can exchange, possibly after some specified period of time has elapsed, for a specific number of shares of stock.

Almost all bonds provide for the payment of interest at regular intervals, usually semiannually. The amount of interest is usually expressed as a percentage of the principal. For example, an 8-percent, ten-year, semiannual coupon bond with face or principal amount of $1,000 would promise to pay $40 every six months starting six months after issue until a total of twenty payments were made. At the time of the final $40 coupon payment, the $1,000 principal is also due to be paid. The *par value* of a bond is its face or principal amount. A bond can sell below par, at par, or above par.

Income bonds, a rare type used principally in financial reorganizations, contain a provision that interest will be paid in a period only if the corporation earns a specified amount for the period.

Proceeds of a Bond Issue

The amount received by the borrower may be more or less than the par value of the bonds issued. The difference arises primarily because there is a difference between the coupon rate printed on the bond certificates and the interest rate the market thinks the firm should pay to borrow under the circumstances. If the coupon rate is less than the rate the market, in aggregate, thinks the firm should pay, then the bonds will sell for less than par and the difference between par and selling price is called the *discount* on the bond. If the coupon rate is larger than the rate the market thinks appropriate, then the bonds will sell above par and the difference between selling price and par is called the *premium* on the bond.

The market interest rate, called the *yield* or *effective rate*, is seldom a "round" number but is more likely to be a fraction such as $7\frac{7}{8}$ or 8.05 percent. Because it is inconvenient to express coupon rates in cumbersome fractions, coupon rates are more likely to be different from market rates than they are to be the same. Another factor that makes the proceeds to the firm from a bond issue different from the selling price is the charge made by the investment banker for handling the loan—investigations, printing of certificates, commissions, and so on. Do not confuse the coupon rate with the effective rate.

The presence of a discount or premium indicates nothing about the credit standing of the borrower. A firm with a credit standing that would enable it to borrow funds at 6¼ percent might issue 6-percent bonds that would sell at a discount, while another firm with a lower credit standing that would require it to pay 7¾ percent on loans might issue bonds at 8 percent which would sell at a premium.

The following illustrations cover the calculations of the proceeds of a bond issue when the effective interest rate is equal to, more than, and less than the coupon rate.

The Macaulay Corporation issues $100,000 face value of 8 percent semiannual coupon debenture bonds. The bonds are dated July 1, 1975, and are due July 1, 1985. Coupons are dated on July 1 and January 1. The coupon payments promised at each interest payment date total $4,000. Assuming that the issue was taken by L. Fisher and Company, investment bankers, on July 1, 1975, at a rate to yield 8 percent compounded semiannually, the calculation of the proceeds to Macaulay would be as follows:

(a) Present value of $100,000 to be paid at the end of ten years .... $ 45,639
(Appendix Table 2 shows the present value of $1 at 4 percent per period for 20 periods to be .45639.)
(b) Present value of $4,000 to be paid each six months for ten years.. 54,361
(Appendix Table 4 shows the present value of an ordinary annuity of $1 per period for 20 periods discounted at 4 percent to be $13.59033. $4,000 × 13.59033 = $54,361.)

Total Proceeds $100,000

The issue price would be stated as 100 (that is, 100 percent of par), which implies that the market rate was 8 percent compounded semiannually, the same as the coupon rate.

Assuming that the bonds were issued at a price to yield 9 percent compounded semiannually, the calculation of the proceeds would be:

(a) Present value of $100,000 to be paid at the end of ten years .... $ 41,464
(Present value of $1 received in 20 periods at 4½ percent per period = $0.41464.)
(b) Present value of $4,000 to be paid each six months for ten years.. 52,032
(Present value of an ordinary annuity of $1 per period for twenty periods, discounted at 4½ percent per period = $13.00794; $4,000 × 13.00794 = $52,032.)

Total Proceeds .... $ 93,496

If the issue price were stated on a conventional pricing basis in the market at 93.50 (93.50 percent of par), the issuing price would be $93,500. This amount implies a market yield of slightly less than 9 percent compounded semiannually.

Assuming that the bonds were issued at a price to yield 7 percent compounded semiannually, the calculation of the proceeds would be:

(a) Present value of $100,000 to be paid at the end of ten years .... $ 50,257
(Present value of $1 received in 20 periods at 3½ percent per period = $0.50257.)

(b) Present value of $4,000 to be paid each six months for ten years..   56,850
(Present value of an ordinary annuity at $1 per period for twenty periods, discounted at 3½ percent per period = $14.2124; $4,000 × 14.2124 = $56,850.)

Total Proceeds $107,107

If the issue price were stated on a conventional pricing basis in the market at 107.11 (107.11 percent of par), the issuing price would be $107,110. This price would imply a market yield of slightly less than 7 percent compounded semiannually.

Bond Tables

Fortunately, a firm does not have to make these tedious calculations every time it wants to issue a bond. Special bond tables have been prepared to show the results of calculations like those just described. Examples of such tables are included in the Appendix. Appendix Table 5 shows for 6-percent, semiannual coupon bonds the price as a percent of par for various effective interest rates (yields) and years to maturity. Appendix Table 6 shows effective rates and implied prices for 8 percent, semiannual coupon bonds.

The percentages of par shown in these tables represent the present value of the bond indicated. Since the factors are expressed as a percent of par, they have to be multiplied by 10 to find the price of a $1,000 bond. If you have never used bond tables before now, turn to Appendix Table 6 and find in the 10-year column the three different prices for the three different effective yields used in the preceding example. Notice further that a bond will sell at par if and only if it has an effective yield equal to its coupon rate.

Such tables are useful whether a bond is being issued by a corporation or resold later by an investor. The approach to determining the market price will be the same in either case, although the years to maturity will be less than the original term of the bond when it is resold. The following generalizations can be made regarding bond prices:

1. When the effective yield equals the coupon rate, the market price will equal par.
2. When the effective yield is greater than the coupon rate, the market price will be less than par.
3. When the effective interest rate is less than the coupon rate, the market price will be greater than par.

Accounting for Bonds Issued at Par

The following illustration covers the more common problems associated with bonds issued at par.

Assume that the data presented in the previous section for the Macaulay Corporation where the bonds were issued at par and that the accounting period is the calendar quarter. The entry at time of issue would be:

```
7/1/75   Cash ...........................................   100,000
            Debenture Bonds Payable ...................            100,000
         $100,000 of 8 percent, ten-year bonds issued at par.
```

The entries for interest would occur at the end of the accounting period and on the interest payment dates. Entries through January 2, 1976, would be:

```
9/30/75   Interest on Bonds ...............................   2,000
             Interest Payable .............................            2,000
          To record accrual of interest for three months.

12/31/75  Interest on Bonds ...............................   2,000
             Interest Payable .............................            2,000
          To record accrual of interest for three months.

1/2/76    Interest Payable .................................   4,000
             Cash .........................................            4,000
          To record payment of six months' interest.
```

Accounting for Bonds Issued at a Discount

The following illustration covers the more common problems associated with bonds issued at a discount.

Assume the data presented for the Macaulay Corporation where the bonds were issued for $93,500 and that the accounting period is the calendar quarter. The entry at the time of issue would be:

```
7/1/75   Cash ...........................................   93,500
         Discount on Debenture Bonds Payable ............   6,500
            Debenture Bonds Payable .....................            100,000
         $100,000 of 8-percent, ten-year bonds issued at a dis-
         count.
```

The discount is primarily an indication that 8 percent is not a sufficiently high rate of interest for the bonds to bring their face value in the open market. Because the market wants to charge approximately 9 percent compounded semiannually, Macaulay actually acquires the use of only $93,500. Macaulay agrees to pay to bondholders the face value of $100,000 when the bond matures as well as the twenty semiannual payments of $4,000. The difference between the par value and the amount of proceeds, $6,500, represents additional interest which will be paid as a part of the face value at maturity. Thus the total interest that must be charged to the periods during which the loan is outstanding is $86,500 (periodic payments totaling $80,000 plus the $6,500 included in the principal payment at maturity).

The periodic interest expense includes the coupon payment *plus* an expense representing amortization of an appropriate part of the discount. The simplest approach to discount amortization involves the straight-line allocation of discount over the life of the bond. It is illustrated in this section. Although the straight-line method is acceptable under generally accepted accounting principles, the more technically correct and preferred approach involves compound-interest calculations and is known as the *effective-interest method.*[3] It is illustrated in the next section.

Under the straight-line method, the amount of discount to be amortized each quarter is the total discount to be amortized over the life of the bond divided by the number of quarters of the bond's life. In this illustration, the quarterly straight-line amortization of bond discount is $6,500/40 = $162.50 per quarter until the discount is fully amortized at the maturity date.

The entries to record the interest expense through January 2, 1976, would be:

9/30/75	Interest on Bonds	2,162.50	
	Interest Payable		2,000.00
	Discount on Debenture Bonds Payable		162.50
	To record the accrual of interest and amortization of discount for three months.		
12/31/75	Interest on Bonds	2,162.50	
	Interest Payable		2,000.00
	Discount on Debenture Bonds Payable		162.50
	To record the accrual of interest and amortization of discount for three months.		
1/2/76	Interest Payable	4,000.00	
	Cash in Bank		4,000.00
	To record payment of six months' interest.		

The bond and interest accounts would appear as follows:

Debenture Bonds Payable		Discount on Debenture Bonds Payable	
	7/1/75 100,000.00	7/1/75 6,500.00	9/30/75 162.50
			12/31/75 162.50

Interest on Bonds		Interest Payable	
	(Closing Entries)		
9/30/75 2,162.50	9/30/75 2,162.50	1/2/76 4,000.00	9/30/75 2,000.00
12/31/75 2,162.50	12/31/75 2,162.50		12/31/75 2,000.00

This series of entries will continue until July 1, 1985, when the bond discount will be completely amortized and the face value of the bonds will be paid.

[3] Opinion No. 21, Accounting Principles Board, AICPA, August, 1971.

The Discount on Debenture Bonds Payable account is a contra-liability account. Since the discount represents additional interest that will be paid as part of the face value at maturity, it is an adjustment of the amount of the obligation. The Discount on Debenture Bonds Payable should be shown on the balance sheet as a deduction from the liability account, Debenture Bonds Payable. The balance sheet for December 31, 1975 would show:

Debenture Bonds Payable $100,000
Less: Discount on Debenture Bonds Payable 6,175 $93,825

Amortization of Discount by the Effective-Interest Method

The amortization of discount by the straight-line method results in periodic interest expenses that are constant over the life of the loan. Since the effective liability, par value less unamortized discount, is changing, straight-line amortization results in a changing *rate* of interest each period. To calculate an interest charge each period that results in a constant interest *rate*, as implied by the present value calculations of the proceeds from issue, the *effective-interest* method of amortization is used. The total interest charges over the life of the bonds will be the same as when the straight-line method is used, but the charge per period will increase for bonds issued at a discount.

Assume the data presented for the Macaulay Corporation where the bonds were issued for $93,500 to yield approximately 9 percent compounded semiannually and the accounting period is the calendar quarter. An amortization schedule, like the one in Schedule 15.1 which assumes an effective yield of 9 percent, would be prepared.

SCHEDULE 15.1 AMORTIZATION SCHEDULE FOR BONDS ISSUED AT A DISCOUNT

Period (6-month intervals) (1)	Liability at Start of Period (2)	Effective Interest 4½% per Period a (3)	Coupon Rate: 4% of Par (4)	Discount Amortization b (5)	End of Period Unamortized Discount c (6)	Net Liability d (7)
0					6,500.00	93,500.00
1	93,500.00	4,207.50	4,000.00	207.50	6,292.50	93,707.50
2	93,707.50	4,216.84	4,000.00	216.84	6,075.66	93,924.34
3	93,924.34	4,226.60	4,000.00	226.60	5,849.06	94,150.94
4	94,150.94	4,236.79	4,000.00	236.79	5,612,27	94,387.73

(Calculations continued for 20 periods)

| 20 | 99,521.53 | 4,478.47 | 4,000.00 | 478.47 | 0 | 100,000.00 |
| Total .... | | 86,500.00 | 80,000.00 | 6,500.00 | | |

a .045 × (2)
b (3) — (4)
c (6), previous period, minus (5), current period
d 100,000 — (6) = (2) + (5)

The effective interest for a period, shown in column 3, is determined by multiplying the net liability at the start of the period (column 2) by the effective yield rate on the bond issue *at the time of issue*. Since the effective yield at issue is 9 percent compounded semiannually, the effective rate for the six-month period is 4½ percent. The net liability is increased at the end of each period by the amount of discount amortization for the period.

For convenience, interest charges within a six-month period are usually allocated on a straight-line basis. The interest-related entries through March 31, 1976, would be as follows:

9/30/75	Interest on Bonds	2,103.75	
	Discount on Debenture Bonds Payable		103.75
	Interest Payable		2,000.00
	To record accrual of interest and amortization of discount for three months of the first period (3/6 × 207.50).		
12/31/75	Interest on Bonds	2,103.75	
	Discount on Debenture Bonds Payable		103.75
	Interest Payable		2,000.00
	To record accrual of interest and amortization of discount for three months of the first period (3/6 × 207.50).		
1/2/76	Interest Payable	4,000.00	
	Cash		4,000.00
	To record payment of interest for six months.		
3/31/76	Interest on Bonds	2,108.42	
	Discount on Debenture Bonds Payable		108.42
	Interest Payable		2,000.00
	To record accrual of interest and amortization of discount for three months of the second period (3/6 × 216.84).		

The series of entries will continue with an increasing amortization each period until the entire discount will have been amortized at the maturity date, July 1, 1985.

Accounting for Bonds Issued at a Premium

The following illustration covers the more common problems associated with bonds issued at a premium.

Assume the data presented for the Macaulay Corporation where the bonds are issued to yield approximately 7 percent for $107,100 and that the accounting period is the calendar quarter. The entry at time of issue would be:

7/1/75	Cash	107,100.00	
	Debenture Bonds Payable		100,000.00
	Premium on Debenture Bonds Payable		7,100.00
	$100,000 of 8 percent, ten-year bonds issued at a premium.		

The Premium on Debenture Bonds, like discount on bonds, represents an adjustment of the cost of borrowing. The account itself is a liability adjunct. When the premium is amortized, either at an interest-payment date or at the end of an accounting period, the effect of amortization will be to *reduce* the interest expense below the cash actually paid for coupons. The true interest expense on the loan each period will be the difference between the amount paid or payable to bondholders and the amortization of premium. The total interest that must be charged to the periods during which the loan is outstanding is $72,900 (periodic payments totaling $80,000 less the premium of $7,100). As in the case of amortization of discount, the premium can be amortized by the straight-line or effective-interest method.

The amount of premium amortization each quarter using the straight-line method is the total premium divided by the number of quarters of the loan. In this illustration, the premium to be amortized is $7,100/40 = $177.50 per quarter until the bonds mature and the premium is fully amortized.

The entries to record the interest expense and premium amortization through January 2, 1976, would be:

9/30/75	Interest on Bonds	1,822.50	
	Premium on Debenture Bonds Payable	177.50	
	Interest Payable		2,000.00
	To record the accrual of interest and amortization of premium for three months.		
12/31/75	Interest on Bonds	1,822.50	
	Premium on Debenture Bonds Payable	177.50	
	Interest Payable		2,000.00
	To record the accrual of interest and amortization of premium for three months.		
1/2/76	Interest Payable	4,000.00	
	Cash		4,000.00
	To record payment of six months' interest.		

The series of entries will continue until July 1, 1985, when the bond premium will be completely amortized and the face value of the bonds will be paid.

The Premium on Debenture Bonds Payable is an adjunct to a liability account. It should be shown on the balance sheet as an addition to the liability account Debenture Bonds Payable.

Amortization of premium under the effective-interest method would follow the same principles used in discount amortization. A partial *premium* amortization schedule for the Macaulay Corporation's 8-percent, semiannual coupon bonds assumed to have been issued for $107,100 to yield approximately 7 percent compounded semiannually is shown in Schedule 15.2.

Provisions for Bond Retirement

If the issuing firm is required to make a special provision for retiring the bond issue, the details of that requirement will be spelled out in the bond

SCHEDULE 15.2 AMORTIZATION SCHEDULE FOR BONDS ISSUED AT PREMIUM

| | | | | | End of Period | | |
Period (6-month intervals) (1)	Liability at Start of Period (2)	Effective Interest 3½% per Period [a] (3)	Coupon Rate: 4% of Par (4)	Premium Amorti- zation [b] (5)	Unam- ortized Premium [c] (6)	Net Liability [d] (7)
0					7,100.00	107,100.00
1	107,100.00	3,748.50	4,000.00	251.50	6,848.50	106,848.50
2	106,848.50	3,739.70	4,000.00	260.30	6,588.20	106,588.20
3	106,588.20	3,730.59	4,000.00	269.41	6,318.79	106,318.79
4	106,318.79	3,721.16	4,000.00	278.84	6,039.95	106,039.95

(Calculations continued for 20 periods)

20	100,483.09	3,516.91	4,000.00	483.09	0	100,000.00
Total		72,900.00	80,000.00	7,100.00		

[a] .035 × (2)
[b] (4) — (3)
[c] (6), previous period minus (5), current period
[d] 100,000 + (6) = (2) — (5)

indenture. There are two major types of retirement requirements. One provides that certain portions of the principal amount will come due on a succession of maturity dates; the bonds of such issues are known as *serial bonds*. The other major type of retirement provision stipulates that the firm must accumulate a fund of cash or other assets that will be used to pay the bonds when the maturity date arrives or to reacquire and retire portions of the bond issue from time to time. Funds of this type are commonly known as *sinking funds* although *bond-retirement funds* would be a more descriptive term. The sinking fund is usually held by the trustee of the bond issue.

Some bond issues make no provision for installment repayment or for accumulating funds for the payment of the bonds when they come due. Such bonds are usually well protected with property held by the trustee as security or by an exceptionally high credit standing of the issuer. Under these circumstances the entire bond liability may be paid at maturity out of cash in the bank at that time. Quite commonly, however, this procedure is not followed. Instead the bond issue is *refunded*—a new set of bonds is issued to pay or replace the old ones when they come due.

A common provision gives the issuing company the right to retire portions of the bond issue if it so desires, but does not require it to do so. In order to facilitate such reacquisition and retirement of a part of the bond issue, the bond indenture usually provides that the bonds shall be *callable*. That is, the issuing company will have the right to reacquire its bonds at specified prices, usually by lot after public notice. The *call price* is usually set a few percentage points above the par value and declines as the maturity date approaches.

A firm might wish to call the bonds because the current market rate of interest is less than the coupon rate on the bonds. If, for example, the firm had issued 8-percent semiannual coupon bonds at par, but market interest rates and the firm's credit standing would allow it to borrow at 6 percent, the firm would be paying more to borrow the face value than it need pay. If an 8-percent coupon bond did not have a call provision, if the market rate of interest were 6 percent, and if the bonds had five years until maturity, the bonds would sell in the market for 108.53 percent of par. If the bonds have a call price less than 108.53, the market price of the bonds will not be as high as 108.53 because the market will anticipate the possible call. If $10,000 par value bonds issued at par are called for 105, the entry, in addition to the one to record the accrued interest expense, would be:

Bonds Payable	10,000	
Loss on Retirement of Bonds	500	
Cash		10,500

If called bonds were originally issued at a discount (or premium), on retiring the bonds, the appropriate portion of the unamortized discount (or premium) must be retired as well. Suppose $100,000 par value bonds were issued at a premium several years ago and that the unamortized premium is now $3,500. If $10,000 par value bonds are called, the entry to record the retirement would be:

Bonds Payable	10,000	
Premium on Bonds Payable	350	
Loss on Retirement of Bonds	150	
Cash		10,500

The market rate of interest a firm must pay depends upon two factors: the general level of interest rates and its own credit worthiness. If the market rate of interest has risen since bonds were issued (or the firm's credit rating has declined), the bonds will sell in the market at less than issue price. A firm that wanted to retire such bonds would not *call* them because the call price is typically greater than issue price. Instead the firm would purchase its bonds in the open market and realize a gain on the retirement of bonds.

Serial Bonds

In a *serial bond* issue, separate certificates are provided for each of a series of maturity dates. Bonds maturing on one date are really a separate issue from bonds maturing on another date, but they are all grouped together under one bond indenture, and the proceeds for the entire group are received in a single sum from the investment banker. When the bonds are sold to the public, each series will ordinarily have its own price. The following example illustrates the problems of serial bond issues.

The Gould Realty Company issues $100,000 of par value mortgage bonds on January 1, 1975. It receives $97,000 as the proceeds of the issue.

Interest at the rate of 8 percent per annum is payable on January 1 and July 1 of each year. The maturity of the bonds is as follows:

January 1, 1980	$ 10,000
January 1, 1981	10,000
January 1, 1982	10,000
January 1, 1983	20,000
January 1, 1984	20,000
January 1, 1985	30,000
	$100,000

The entry for the issue of the bonds involves no new problem:

Cash on Hand	97,000	
Discount on Mortgage Bonds Payable	3,000	
Mortgage Bonds Payable		100,000

To amortize the discount using the straight-line method requires a special calculation. To charge the same amount to a period in which $100,000 of the loan was outstanding as to a period in which only $90,000, or some other amount, was being used by the borrower makes little sense. The simplest procedure is to distribute the discount over the life of the bonds in proportion to the amount outstanding during each period. Schedule 15.3 shows the calculation and amount of amortization for each year.

SCHEDULE 15.3 SERIAL BOND DISCOUNT AMORTIZATION

	During Year		
Year	Bonds Outstanding	Amortization of Discount	
1975	$100,000	$ 365.85 ⎫	
1976	100,000	365.85 ⎪	
1977	100,000	365.85 ⎬ = (3,000 × 100,000/820,000)	
1978	100,000	365.85 ⎪	
1979	100,000	365.85 ⎭	
1980	90,000	329.27	= (3,000 × 90,000/820,000)
1981	80,000	292.68	= (3,000 × 80,000/820,000)
1982	70,000	256.10	= (3,000 × 70,000/820,000)
1983	50,000	182.93	= (3,000 × 50,000/820,000)
1984	30,000	109.77	= (3,000 × 30,000/820,000)
	$820,000	$3,000.00	

When entries are made to accrue or to pay interest, the amortization of the discount is determined by referring to a schedule like Schedule 15.3. For example, if the firm closes its books on December 31 of each year, the entries relating to interest for 1975 would be:

7/1/75	Interest on Bonds	4,182.93	
	Cash in Bank		4,000.00
	Discount on Mortgage Bonds Payable		182.93
	Payment of interest and amortization of discount		
	on mortgage bonds from 1/1/75 to 7/1/75.		

```
12/31/75  Interest on Bonds .........................  4,182.92
          Interest Payable .........................              4,000.00
          Discount on Mortgage Bonds Payable ......               182.92
          Accrual of interest and amortization of discount
          on mortgage bonds from 7/1/75 to 12/31/75.
```

The corresponding entries in 1984 would be:

```
7/1/84    Interest on Bonds .........................  1,254.89
          Cash .....................................              1,200.00
          Discount on Mortgage Bonds Payable ......                54.89

12/31/84  Interest on Bonds .........................  1,254.88
          Interest Payable .........................              1,200.00
          Discount on Mortgage Bonds Payable ......                54.88
```

Sinking Funds

Any *sinking fund* accumulates a fund of cash or other assets to facilitate the retirement of bonds, but there are many variations in the terms of such bond-retirement-fund agreements. The accounting for the sinking fund, of course, seeks to reflect the terms of the agreement. Entries to reflect growth of the fund are relatively standard. For each period in which a deposit to the fund is made, the entry (assuming a $100,000 deposit) is:

```
Sinking Fund .............................................  100,000
  Cash in Bank .........................................              100,000
```

The fund is in the hands of the trustee and after the first period, there will be interest and dividend earnings on the investments made by the trustee. When the trustee reports those earnings, say $10,000, the entry would be:

```
Sinking Fund .............................................  10,000
  Interest and Dividends Earned on Sinking Fund ..........           10,000
```

The Interest and Dividends Earned on Sinking Fund account, like all other interest and dividends earned accounts, is closed to Income Summary in the closing entries at the end of the period. Entries are not usually made on the borrower's books to reflect the investments made by the sinking-fund trustee. The single Sinking Fund account stands in place of the detailed listing of securities held by the trustee. The only exception to this comes if the trustee buys, and thus effectively retires, the bonds to which the sinking fund relates. Then the customary entry for bond retirement is made. For example, if the trustee acquires bonds originally issued at par for $40,000 on the market for $38,000, the entry would be:

```
Bonds Payable .............................................  40,000
  Sinking Fund ..........................................              38,000
  Gain on Bond Retirement ...............................               2,000
```

The sinking fund is sometimes shown on the balance sheet as a deduction from the bond liability because for all practical purposes a portion of the loan has been paid when the sinking-fund deposit is made. Legally, however, the sinking fund is merely an asset of the borrower, and actual payment is necessary before the obligation is discharged.

Contracts and Long-term Notes

Real estate is often purchased on a *land contract*. Equipment is frequently acquired on the installment plan, and the liability is called an *equipment contract*. Payments on such contracts are usually made monthly. Sometimes an explicit interest rate is provided in the contract, while in other cases so-called *carrying charges* are added to the purchase price, and the total is divided over a certain number of months without any specific charge being made for interest. A common arrangement, particularly in the case of real estate, is to have a regular monthly payment which is applied first to interest accrued since the last payment, with the balance of the payment reducing the principal.

When there is no explicit mention of interest on such a long-term contract or note, generally accepted accounting principles require that the liability be shown at its present value.[4] The difference between the present value and the face value of the liability is a discount that must be treated much the same as the discount on bonds payable. The discount must be amortized over the life of the liability and periodic interest expenses must be shown.

There are two acceptable ways to determine the present value of the liability. The first is to use the market value of the assets acquired. For example, if equipment, which has a list price of $12,000 but can be bought for $10,500 cash, is purchased in return for a note with face amount $13,500 payable in three years, the entry would be:

```
Equipment  ...............................................    10,500
Discount on Long-term Note Payable  ......................     3,000
      Long-term Note Payable  ...............................             13,500
```

If undeveloped land had been purchased with the same three-year note, the firm might not be able to establish the current market value of the asset acquired. The firm would then use the interest rate it would have to pay for a similar loan in the open market to find the present value of the note. This is the second acceptable method for quantifying the amount of the liability. Suppose the market rate for notes such as the one above is 8 percent compounded annually. The present value at 8 percent per year of $1 paid three years hence is $.7938 (Appendix Table 2). Therefore, the present value of the note is $13,500 $\times$ .7938 or $10,716. The entry to record the purchase of land and payment with the note would be:

```
Land  .....................................................    10,716
Discount on Long-term Note Payable  ......................     2,784
      Long-term Note Payable  ...............................             13,500
```

A note that is the long-term liability of the borrower is a long-term asset of the lender. Generally accepted accounting principles require the

[4] Opinion No. 21, Accounting Principles Board, AICPA, August, 1971.

lender to show the asset in the Long-term Note Receivable Account at its present value. The rate at which the lender discounts the note should in theory be the same as that used by the borrower, but in practice the two rates may differ.

Pension Plans

Most firms have pension plans that, in one form or another, provide for payments to its retired ex-employees. The actuarial and accounting details of pension liabilities are beyond the scope of introductory accounting, so we will merely introduce some of the terminology and accounting problems here. Many of the calculations for pension liability involve tools, such as compound interest, that have already been discussed.

There are almost as many different kinds of pension plans as there are employers who have them. The basic variables of a pension plan are its requirements for contributions by employees and treatments of vesting, funding, past service costs, and prior service costs. Each of these variables will be discussed in turn.

Under a *noncontributory plan*, the employee makes no explicit contribution to his pension, only the employer contributes. Under a *contributory plan* both the employee and the employer contribute, but they do not necessarily contribute equal amounts. The employee retains a claim to his explicit contributions under virtually all plans. His rights to the employer's contributions are determined by the vesting provisions.

Pension benefits may be *fully vested*, *partially vested*, or *nonvested*. If benefits are fully vested, the employee's rights to pension benefits purchased with the employer's contributions cannot be taken away from the employee. If the rights are *nonvested*, the employee loses rights to the employer's contributions if his or her employment ceases before retirement. Under some *partially vested plans,* rights vest gradually so that, for example, an employee in the fifth year of work has no vested rights but by the time he or she has been employed for 15 years, all rights will be vested. Federal law requires that all pension benefits be vested by the time the employer has been employed for 15 years. The choice of vesting provisions will, of course, influence the expected present value of the pension liabilities generated during an accounting period. The expected present value of future liabilities under a partially vested plan might be as little as one-half that under a fully vested plan.

A pension plan may be *fully funded* or *partially funded*. Under a fully funded plan, the employer sets aside cash, or pays cash to an outside trustee such as an insurance company, equal to the present value of all expected pension liabilities. Partially funded plans do not have cash available in an amount equal to the present value of all pension obligations.

Generally accepted accounting principles[5] now require the employer

---

[5] Opinion No. 8, Accounting Principles Board, AICPA, November, 1966.

to show as an expense of the period the present value of the pension liabilities generated during the period. For example, if actuarial calculations showed the expected present value of pension obligations arising during the year to be $45,000, the entry, independent of funding provisions, would be:

Pension Expense 45,000
    Deferred Pension Liability   45,000

The Deferred Pension Liability does not meet the certainty-of-amount and due-date criteria for liabilities. Both the amount and date can be estimated with sufficient accuracy by actuarial computations, however, so that these departures are not considered major ones.

When a pension plan is adopted, current employees will usually receive retroactive benefits for service prior to the plan's adoption. The expected present value of the liability to employees at the time the plan is adopted is called the *past service cost*. From time to time, the pension plan may be made more generous; that is, the benefits to employees may be "sweetened." At the time the plan is made more generous, there will usually be retroactive, extra benefits that are given to employees. Consequently at any given time, the total expected present value of unfunded benefits arising from employees' service before that time can be substantial. That total is called *prior service cost*. Past service cost is part of prior service cost. The obligation for prior service costs is not recognized as a liability in the accounting records, but its unfunded amount must be disclosed in the notes to the financial statements. Prior service costs may be gradually funded. Whatever the provision for funding those costs, at a minimum the employer must count as expenses of the period at least the interest on the expected present value of unfunded prior service costs. The employer may amortize (straight-line method) the prior service cost obligation by regular charges to operations, but the maximum charge in any one year is 10 percent of the original prior service cost. For example, if the prior service cost on January 1, 1974, were $10,000, and prior service cost was increased by $2,000 on January 1, 1976, because of an amendment to the plan, the maximum amortization charge in 1974 and 1975 would be $1,000 (= .10 × $10,000) but in 1976 would be $1,200 [= .10 × ($10,000 + $2,000)].

Generally accepted accounting principles tolerate a wide range of treatments of pension accounting problems. Certain minimum disclosures should be made: the notes to the balance sheet should disclose the unamortized prior service costs, if there are any, and the time over which they are being amortized. The notes should explain the actuarial methods used and the impact of vesting provisions on the expected present value of future liabilities. The funding and vesting provisions are, of course, matters negotiated between employers and employees, subject to laws passed by the Congress. The annual report of the General Electric Company, reproduced in the last section of Chapter 25, illustrates the disclosure of pension-related matters. See pages 34 and 35 of the report, under the heading "Employee's compensation."

Leases

Recall that a liability is a legal obligation to pay a definite amount at a definite time in return for a current benefit. There is one business obligation that meets all these criteria but is still not treated as a liability. That obligation is a long-term, noncancelable lease accounted for as an ordinary short-term lease. Many firms are currently acquiring rights to use assets through long-term noncancelable leases. A company might, for example, agree to lease an airplane for fifteen years, or a building for forty years, agreeing to pay a fixed periodic fee for the duration of the lease. Agreeing to make an irrevocable series of lease payments commits the firm just as a bond indenture or mortgage does, but generally accepted accounting principles allow the firm to treat the obligation more favorably than either bonds or mortgages. Perhaps the more favorable accounting for these leases helps to explain why so many firms choose to acquire the services of assets with leases.

Let us examine the accounting for noncancelable leases, how it may differ from the usual accounting treatment for similar commitments, and the effects on the financial statements of both treatments. Suppose the Myers Company wants to acquire a computer that has a three-year life and costs $30,000, and suppose that Myers Company can borrow money for three years at 8 percent per year. The computer manufacturer is willing to sell the computer for $30,000 or to lease it for three years on a noncancelable basis. That is, Myers Company must make payments for three years no matter what. Myers Company is responsible for maintenance and repairs of the computer under either the purchase or leasing plans.

Assume that the lease is signed on January 1, 1975, and that payments on the lease are due on December 31, 1975, 1976, and 1977. In practice, lease payments are usually made in advance, but the example computations are simpler if we assume payments at the end of the year. Compound interest computations show that each lease payment must be $11,641. (The present value of $1 paid at the end of this year and each of the next two years is $2.5771 when the interest rate is 8 percent per year. Since the lease payments must have present value of $30,000, each payment must be $30,000/2.5771 = $11,641.)

Operating Lease Treatment. Under an *operating lease*, the owner or lessor maintains the asset and merely sells the rights to use the property to the lessee for specified periods of time. The telephone company leases telephones by the month, and car rental companies lease cars by the day or week on an operating basis. If the Myers Company lease was accounted for as an operating lease, then no entry would be made on January 1, 1975, when the lease is signed, and the following entry is made on each of the dates December 31, 1975, 1976, and 1977.

```
Rental Expense .............................................  11,641
    Cash ...................................................          11,641
To recognize expense of leasing computer.
```

Under currently accepted principles, the Myers Company would probably account for its lease in just this way.

Financing Lease Treatment. If this lease were judged to be a form of borrowing to purchase the computer, then it would be accounted for as a *financing lease*. This treatment recognizes the signing of the lease as the simultaneous acquisition of a long-term asset, called a *leasehold*, and the incurring of a long-term liability for lease payments. At the time the lease is signed, both the leasehold and the liability are brought on to the books at their present value, $30,000 in the example.

The entry made at the time Myers Company signs its three-year noncancelable lease would be:

```
Asset—Computer Leasehold ...............................  30,000
    Liability—Present Value of Lease Obligations ............          30,000
To recognize acquisition of asset and liability.
```

At the end of each year, two separate entries must be made. The leasehold is an asset and like any asset it must be amortized over its useful life. The first entry made at the end of each year recognizes the amortization of the leasehold asset. Assuming Myers Company uses straight-line amortization of its leasehold, the entry made at the end of 1975, 1976, and 1977 would be:

```
Amortization of Asset—Computer Leasehold ................  10,000
    Asset—Computer Leasehold ...........................          10,000
```

(An alternative treatment would be to credit an asset contra, Accumulated Amortization of Computer Leasehold.) The second entry made at the end of each year recognizes the lease payment, which is part payment of interest on the liability and part reduction in the liability itself. The entries made at the ends of the three years would be:

```
December 31, 1975
Interest Expense .........................................  2,400
Liability—Present Value of Lease Obligations ...............  9,241
    Cash ...................................................          11,641
To recognize lease payment, interest on liability for year (.08 ×
$30,000 = $2,400) and the plug for reduction in liability. The
present value of the liability is $20,759 = $30,000 − $9,241 after
this entry.

December 31, 1976
Interest Expense .........................................  1,661
Liability—Present Value of Lease Obligations ...............  9,980
    Cash ...................................................          11,641
To recognize lease payment, interest on liability for year (.08 ×
$20,759 = $1,661) and the plug for reduction in liability. The
present value of the liability is $10,779 = $20,759 − $9,980 after
this entry.
```

December 31, 1977

Interest Expense	862	
Liability—Present Value of Lease Obligation	10,779	
Cash		11,641

To recognize lease payment, interest on liability for year (.08 × $10,779 = $862) and the plug for reduction in liability. The present value of the liability is zero (= $10,779 − $10,779) after this entry.

Notice that in this treatment, the total expenses over the three years is $34,923, consisting of $30,000 (= $10,000 + $10,000 + $10,000) for amortization expenses and $4,923 (= $2,400 + $1,661 + $862) for interest charges. This is exactly the same as the total cash outflows from the firm, three lease payments of $11,641, and the total expense recognized under the operating method described above. The difference in the two treatments occurs in the *timing* of the expense recognition and the entries in balance sheet accounts. (The operating method is often described as "off-balance sheet financing" because it recognizes neither asset nor liability.) The financing lease treatment recognizes expenses sooner than does the operating lease treatment as summarized in the schedule below.

	Expenses Recognized Each Year under	
Year	Operating Method	Financing Method
1975	$11,641	$12,400
1976	11,641	11,661
1977	11,641	10,862
Total	$34,923	$34,923

In this simple example, the financing method's expenses are only slightly larger than the operating method's expenses in the first year. In more realistic cases, where the lease extends over twenty years, the expense in the first year is more than twice as large under the financing method.

Most firms prefer to use the operating method wherever they can, because the reported income is higher in the earlier years of the lease than it would be under the financing method. Starting in 1974, however, the Securities and Exchange Commission requires that if the operating method is used when the SEC thinks the financial method is more appropriate, the footnotes to the financial statements must disclose how much lower net income would have been if the financial method were used. A recent annual report of the J. C. Penney Company, Inc. illustrates this supplementary disclosure. A footnote to the financial statements says, in part,

If financing leases had been capitalized and the resultant property rights amortized on a straight-line basis over the primary terms of these leases, net income [of $186 million] would have been reduced $8.1 million [or about four and one-half percent] . . .

We see no good reason for generally accepted accounting principles[6] to allow liabilities such as financing leases—which have the same inherent commitments as bonds or mortgages—to be accounted for as operating leases with its attendant off-balance sheet financing.

DEFERRED INCOME TAX LIABILITY

As we have indicated at various points in this book, there are some areas where there are alternative generally accepted accounting principles. The tax laws and regulations similarly allow a choice of alternative treatments for the same event. One example is in the calculation of depreciation charges. Both generally accepted accounting principles and the tax law allow the firm to choose from among straight-line, sum-of-the-years'-digits and double-declining-balance depreciation methods.

In selecting among alternative methods for tax purposes, management appropriately tries to minimize the present value of the firm's tax liabilities for a given set of operating results. (The principles of income tax management are summarized conveniently by the expression "Pay the least amount of tax, as late as possible, within the law." This is sometimes known as the *least and latest* rule.) It is difficult to generalize about which of alternative accounting principles management selects, or should select, for financial reporting. Some have suggested that management would probably use the method that maximizes current income.

Suppose that for whatever reasons it deems appropriate, management decides to use straight-line depreciation for a given plant asset for financial reporting. Suppose, further, that management has calculated that the present value of taxes paid will be smallest if the sum-of-the-years'-digits method is used for tax purposes. The firm is allowed to use straight-line for financial reporting and sum-of-the-years'-digits for taxes. The firm will thereby show a higher pre-tax income in its financial reports than in its tax return. This is permissible, but the firm must show in its income statement as a *deferred income tax expense* the difference between the tax payment that results from using the accelerated method and the tax payment that *would have* resulted had it used the straight-line method for tax reporting.[7] Since the expense is recognized but payment is deferred, a liability is created.

The problems of deferred income tax liabilities can perhaps be best understood by examining an example. Assume that Drake Incorporated pays income taxes at the rate of 40 percent of taxable income. Suppose that Drake purchased a plant asset for $170,000 that has a five-year life and an estimated salvage value of $20,000. Suppose further that this asset produces net cash flows of $44,000 a year. That is, after paying for the cash costs of running and maintaining the asset, the firm enjoys a $44,000 per year excess of receipts over expenditures from it. Drake uses straight-line depreciation for financial reporting and the sum-of-the-years'-digits method for calculating its taxes. Thus in the first year the new plant asset

[6] APB Opinions No. 5 (September, 1964) and No. 31 (July, 1973).
[7] Opinion No. 11, Accounting Principles Board, AICPA, December, 1967.

is used, depreciation on the financial records will be $30,000 (= $150,000/5) and on the tax return will be $50,000 (= $150,000 × 5/15). Suppose that in addition to the $44,000 of net cash flow from the plant asset, other pre-tax income for the year is $80,000. Schedule 15.4 summarizes the computation of taxes.

SCHEDULE 15.4 DRAKE INCORPORATED TAX COMPUTATIONS

First Year	Financial Reports	Tax Return
Other pre-tax income	$80,000	$80,000
Cash flow from plant asset	44,000	44,000
Depreciation	(30,000)	(50,000)
Income before taxes	$94,000	$74,000
Income tax expense (at 40 percent)	37,600	
Income tax currently payable (at 40 percent)		29,600

By using the accelerated method for tax purposes, Drake is able to pay $8,000 less in taxes than the financial records will show as the tax expense for the year. The entry to record the tax transaction would be:

Income Tax Expense	37,600	
Income Tax Payable		29,600
Deferred Income Tax Liability		8,000

If only one asset is considered, the $8,000 difference does not represent taxes forgiven but merely taxes delayed. Later, in the fourth and fifth years of this example, the financial records will show larger depreciation and smaller income than the tax return will show. Consequently, the income tax expense will be lower than the income taxes payable in those years and Drake will debit the Deferred Income Tax Liability. Schedule 15.5 summarizes the tax computations for the fifth year of Drake's plant asset assuming nothing has changed except for the passage of time.

SCHEDULE 15.5 DRAKE INCORPORATED TAX COMPUTATIONS

Fifth Year	Financial Reports	Tax Return
Other pre-tax income	$80,000	$ 80,000
Cash flow from plant asset	44,000	44,000
Depreciation	(30,000)	(10,000)
Income before taxes	$94,000	$114,000
Income tax expense (at 40 percent)	37,600	
Income tax currently payable (at 40 percent)		45,600

The entry to record the fifth year's tax transaction would be:

Income Tax Expense	37,600	
Deferred Income Tax Liability	8,000	
Income Tax Payable		45,600

Schedule 15.6 shows a summary of the entries in Drake's Deferred Income Tax Liability account for the five years during which its uses the plant asset. Notice that the total taxes paid over the asset's life are the same under both depreciation methods, but that the accelerated method defers payment and thus leads to a lower present value of taxes paid.

In general, the deferred income tax liability arises from differences in timing between financial reporting of revenues and expenses and tax reporting of these items. The following list shows some of the ways in which the timing differences can arise.

1. Depreciation for tax purposes is larger than shown in the financial records either because different asset lives or different depreciation patterns, or both, are used for the two purposes.
2. Revenues from installment sales are entered in the financial records on the date of sale but are entered in the tax returns for periods when payments are collected.
3. Revenues from long-term construction projects are recognized in financial records on the percentage-of-completion basis but on tax returns under the completed-contract basis.
4. Advertising costs are capitalized, then amortized, for financial records but treated as expenses of the period for tax returns.

As the Drake example shows, the deferred tax liability arising from any one asset will eventually be paid. In reality, a growing firm may be able to defer payment indefinitely or at least have increasingly larger credit balances in the Deferred Income Tax Liability account as time passes. If Drake, or any other company, adds to plant assets each year as much as, or more than, it had added in the preceding year, then the Deferred Tax Liability account will never have any debit entries.

SCHEDULE 15.6 SUMMARY OF DEFERRED INCOME TAX LIABILITY ACCOUNT FOR DRAKE INCORPORATED

			Tax Return			Deferred Income Tax Liability		
Year (1)	Income Before Depreciation Expense (2)	Financial Records Tax Expense (3)[a]	Depreciation Deduction (4)[b]	Pre-Tax Income (5)[c]	Taxes Payable (6)[d]	Dr. (7)	Cr. (8)	Credit Balance At Year End (9)
1	124,000	37,600	50,000	74,000	29,600		8,000	8,000
2	124,000	37,600	40,000	84,000	33,600		4,000	12,000
3	124,000	37,600	30,000	94,000	37,600	—	—	12,000
4	124,000	37,600	20,000	104,000	41,600	4,000		8,000
5	124,000	37,600 188,000	10,000	114,000	45,600 188,000	8,000		0

a $(124{,}000 - 30{,}000) \times .40$.
b $(170{,}000 - 20{,}000) \times t/15$ where $t = 5, 4, 3, 2, 1$ for the years, in order.
c $(124{,}000 - (4))$.
d $(5) \times .40$.

The deferred income tax liability clearly does not meet the four criteria suggested for liabilities. It fails three of the tests: contractual obligation, certainty of amount, and certainty of due date. Nevertheless, generally accepted accounting principles wish to match the reported income tax expense with the reported pre-tax income of a period and, thus, require the firm to recognize the deferred income tax expense in the usual case. The account credited when the deferred income tax expense is recognized has a special nature which Accounting Principles Board Opinion No. 11 says is a "deferred credit" and not a liability.[8] Since we feel that the right-hand side of the balance sheet logically contains only liabilities and proprietorship, we include the deferred income tax liability in the indeterminate-term liability section of the model balance sheet shown in Chapter 11.

SUMMARY

A liability is generally a legal obligation of a definite amount due at a definite time incurred in return for a current benefit. Some obligations of the firm do not meet all the criteria to be liabilities but are, nevertheless, treated as such. Examples of such liabilities are those for deferred warranties, deferred pension liabilities, and deferred income taxes. We suggest that the last one be viewed as a liability of indeterminate term.

Accounting for long-term liabilities is accomplished by recording these obligations at their present value at the date the obligation is incurred and then showing the change in that present value as the maturity date of the obligation approaches. Retirement of long-term liabilities can be brought about in a variety of ways, but in each case, the procedure is the same. The net obligation is offset against what is given in return, usually cash, with gain or loss on retirement recognized as appropriate.

QUESTIONS AND PROBLEMS

1. What factors determine the amount of money a firm actually receives when it offers a bond issue to the market?

2. Why do noninterest-bearing notes have a smaller value at time of issue than at time of maturity?

3. What are the relative advantages and disadvantages of the straight-line versus the effective-interest method of bond discount (or premium) amortization?

4. What are the four major methods used to retire bonds?

5. A call premium is the difference between the call price of a bond and par value. What is the purpose of such a premium?

6. Under what circumstances may a deferred tax liability arise? If a firm is growing, what does this imply about when the liability is likely to be paid?

[8] Opinion No. 11, Accounting Principles Board, AICPA, December, 1967.

*7. On May 20, 1975, the McGraw Company received a note from S. McQueen to be applied on his account. The note is dated April 20, 1975, and is due October 20, 1975. The face value is $600, and it bears interest at 8 percent per year. The maker is R. O'Neill. McQueen is given credit for the face value plus one month accrued interest. O'Neill pays the note at maturity.

    a. Present entries for the note for the McGraw Campany, which closes its books annually on June 30.

    b. Present entries on the books of O'Neill for the note. O'Neill issued the note to McQueen on account. O'Neill closes his books quarterly on March 31, June 30, and so on.

    c. Present entries on the books of S. McQueen for the note. McQueen closes his books annually on December 31.

    Round all answers to the nearest cent.

*8. On December 1, 1974, the Percival Company obtained a ninety-day loan for $12,600 from the Twin City State Bank at an annual interest rate of 10 percent. On the maturity date the note was renewed for another thirty days, with a check being issued to the bank for the accrued interest. The Percival Company closes its books annually at December 31. Present entries on the books of the Percival Company to record the issue of the note, the year-end adjustment, the renewal of the note, and the payment at maturity of the renewed note.

9. Refer to the data in Problem 8. Present entries at maturity date of the original note for the following variations in the settlement of the note of the Percival Company.

    a. The original note is paid at maturity.

    b. The note is renewed under the same terms except that the new note bears interest at 12 percent per annum.

    c. The note is renewed for ninety days under the same terms as in Problem 8 except that the bank has raised its interest rate from 10 percent to 12 percent, and the accrued interest is added to the face value of the new note.

10. For each of the following items indicate:

    (1) Does the item meet the accountant's definition of a liability?

    (2) If the answer to (1) is no, is it nevertheless shown on the balance sheet as a liability? Why?

    (3) If the item is recognized as a liability, how is the amount of the liability determined?

    a. Interest accrued but not paid on a note.

    b. Advances from customers for goods and services to be delivered later.

    c. Firm orders from customers for goods and services to be delivered later.

    d. Mortgages payable.

    e. Bonds payable.

    f. Product warranties.

    g. Pension plan obligations arising from employee service before institution of the pension plan.

* Hints, key numbers, or (partial) answers appear in the back of the book between the Appendix Tables and the Glossary.

h. Pension plan obligations arising from current employee service.

i. Fifteen-year cancelable lease on an office building.

j. Twenty-year noncancelable lease on a factory building.

k. Deferred taxes.

l. Damages the company must pay if a pending legal case is lost.

m. Cost of restoring strip mining sites after mining operations are completed.

11. Present journal entries for the following transactions on the books of the Franklin Company (round answers to the nearest cent):

   (1) Receipt of a note from a customer, C. Murray, to apply on his account, on December 1, 1974. The 120-day, 9-percent note for $5,000 was issued to Murray by G. J. Simpson on November 11, 1974. The note is accepted at face value plus accrued interest.

   (2) Accrual of interest to December 31, 1974.

   (3) Accrual of interest to January 31, 1975.

   (4) Discounting of the note at the Crestwood Bank on February 9, 1975, at 9 percent per annum.

   (5) Payment to the bank by C. Murray on the due date.

12. On March 1, 1975, Melville Products Company sells merchandise to the Royal Stores Company for $8,000, terms 2/10, n/30. On March 10, 1975, Royal Stores Company issues a check to the Melville Products Company for $1,000 and a sixty-day, 10-percent note for the balance due after allowance of the full discount.

   On April 10, 1975, the Melville Products Company discounts the note at the Ohio Bank. The bank uses a 10-percent discount rate. The note is paid at maturity.

   a. Present dated entries on the books of the Melville Products Company which closes its books quarterly on March 31, June 30, and so on.

   b. Present dated entries on the books of the Royal Stores Company which closes its books monthly.

13. The trial balance of the Johnson Supplies Company on December 31, 1975, before adjusting entries, contained the following account balances, among others:

Discount on Notes Payable	$ 270.00	
Discount on Notes Receivable		$ 209.71
Interest Earned on Notes		103.00
Interest Receivable	—	
Loss on Discounting Notes Receivable	1.76	
Notes Payable		18,000.00
Notes Receivable	41,400.00	
Notes Receivable Discounted		25,200.00

The company follows the procedure of recording interest upon collection or payment and at the end of the accounting period. The company closes its books annually on December 31.

The following additional data are available.

   (1) On September 16, 1975, a 120-day, 12-percent note for $9,000 was received from a customer, P. R. Harding, in a sales transaction.

   (2) On October 15, 1975, the Company issued a ninety-day, noninterest-bearing note for $18,000. The proceeds were $17,730.

(3) On November 1, 1975, a ninety-day noninterest-bearing note for $7,200 was received from a customer, B. Anderson, to apply on his account. He was granted credit for the discounted value of the note; the company used a 12-percent annual rate in determining the value of the note.

(4) On November 16, 1975, a ninety-day, 12-percent note for $14,400 dated November 1, 1975, was received from a customer, J. Shelby, to apply on his account. It was accepted at face value plus accrued interest. On the same day the note was discounted at the bank at a 12-percent rate.

(5) On December 1, 1975, a sixty-day, 12-percent note for $10,800 was received from a customer, A. R. Beining, to apply on his account. The note was discounted at the bank, at a 12-percent rate, on December 21, 1975.

(6) The balance in Interest Earned on Notes includes collections on notes which came due during the period.

a. Present the journal entries which were made by the Johnson Supplies Company on September 16, October 15, November 1, November 16, December 1, and December 21, 1975.

b. Present necessary adjusting entries with regard to these accounts on December 31, 1975.

Round all answers to the nearest cent.

14. On September 1, 1975, Howell Stores, Inc., issues twenty-year, first mortgage bonds with a face value of $1,000,000. The proceeds of the issue are $1,060,000. The bonds bear interest at the rate of 8 percent per annum, payable semiannually at March 1 and September 1. Howell Stores, Inc. closes its books annually at December 31. Present dated entries in two-column journal form related to the bonds from September 1, 1975 through September 1, 1976, inclusive. Assume that Howell Stores, Inc. uses the straight-line method to amortize the bond premium.

15. Refer to the data in Problem 14. Repeat instructions. Assume that the company uses an effective-interest method. The effective-interest rate to be used is 7.4 percent.

16. The Huston Products Company issued $160,000 of 10-percent notes on July 1, 1975. The proceeds of the issue were $156,432. Of the principal of the notes, $40,000 is due each July 1 from 1976 through 1979. Annual interest payments are made on July 1 on the amount of principal outstanding during the year. The company closes its books annually on December 31. Present journal entries from July 1, 1975, through July 1, 1979, inclusive. Assume that Huston Products Company uses the straight-line method to amortize the bond discount.

*17. Refer to the data in Problem 16. Repeat instructions assuming that the Huston Products Company uses an effective-interest method. The effective-interest rate to be used is 11 percent. (Note: Since the exact effective-interest rate is slightly higher than 11 percent, charge the balance of unamortized discount at the end of the third year to the last year.)

18. The Hannifin Machinery Company purchases several pieces of new equipment on July 1, 1975, and issues $1,500,000 of serial notes secured by

the equipment. The notes carry 8-percent interest coupons, payable semi-annually at January 1 and July 1. The proceeds of the issue are $1,474,500. The serial maturities specified in the note contract are as follows:

July 1, 1978	$150,000
July 1, 1980	150,000
July 1, 1981	300,000
July 1, 1982	300,000
July 1, 1983	300,000
July 1, 1984	300,000

The company closes its books annually on December 31.

a. Prepare a schedule to show the amortization of discount on the notes. Assume that the distribution is in proportion to the notes outstanding during each period.

b. Give journal entries for the following transactions:

(1) The issue of the notes on July 1, 1975.

(2) The adjusting entry on December 31, 1975, when the annual closing of the books takes place.

(3) The payment of interest coupons is made on January 1, 1976, and on July 1, 1976.

(4) The payment of interest and principal on July 1, 1978.

(5) The adjusting entry on December 31, 1978.

(6) The payment of interest and principal on July 1, 1984.

*19. At the time of issue, a firm purchases $1 million (face value) of 8-percent, thirty-year, semiannual coupon bonds at a price to yield 8.6 percent. Ten years later, the firm sells $250,000 (face value) of these bonds for $242,500. Use the effective-interest method of bond discount (premium) amortization.

a. What is the firm's total interest income on these bonds during the first year of ownership?

b. What is the gain or loss on sale after ten years?

c. What is the total interest income for the eleventh year of ownership?

*20. In late 1970, the Hornbier Company arranged to issue $1 million of 8-percent *annual* coupon bonds to mature on December 31, 1980. The bonds were issued on January 2, 1971. Late in 1975, when interest rates had dropped so that Hornbier Company could borrow for 6 percent, management decided to call the bond issue for 106 percent of par. On January 2, 1976, $1 million was borrowed from the Equity Insurance Company for 6-percent interest, payable annually, with the principal due on December 31, 1980. Ignore income taxes and round present value factors to four significant digits. What is the net present value of the future cash savings from reduced interest payments less the initial cash outlay (to retire the bond issue) if the discount rate is 6 percent per year and the bonds had originally been issued for:

a. 96 percent of par.

b. 99 percent of par.

c. 101 percent of par.

21. John Bergman bought for $1,075 a twenty-year, 8-percent $1,000 par value bond issued by the Holt Company. Attached to the bond was a warrant entitling the owner to purchase twelve shares of Holt Company stock at a price of $42 per share at any time during the next ten years.

At the time of purchase, Holt stock was selling at $33 per share. The market yield on bonds similar to those issued by the Holt Company was 8.4 percent at that time.

a. How much of the $1,075 purchase price of the bond was actually payment for the warrant?

b. If Mr. Bergman expects a 20-percent return before taxes on his investments in stock and if he exercises the warrant five years after purchasing the bond, what is the lowest market price of the common stock at that time that would justify the price he paid for the warrant? Assume semiannual compounding.

*22. The Howell Sales Company sells a building lot to Ruth Sanders on September 1, 1975, for $27,000. The down payment is $3,000, and minimum payments of $266.64 a month are to be made on the contract. Interest at the rate of 12 percent per annum on the unpaid balance is deducted from each payment, and the balance is applied on the principal. Payments are made as follows: October 1, $266.64; November 1, $266.64; December 1, $600; January 2, $266.64. Prepare a table showing payments, interest and principal, and remaining liability at each of these dates.

23. Mary Blake secures a mortgage loan of $27,000 from the Oakley National Bank. The terms of the mortgage require monthly payments of $413.10. The interest rate to be applied to the unpaid balance is 9 percent per annum. Calculate the distribution of payments for the first four months between principal and interest and present the new balance figures. Follow the form used for Problem 22.

24. Balcrest Enterprises borrows $300,000 for six years from the Snavely Bank on July 1, 1974. The loan bears interest at the rate of 10 percent per annum, payable quarterly on January 1, April 1, July 1, and October 1 of each year. As security Balcrest Enterprises grants the bank a mortgage on some of its land holdings.

Interest payments are made regularly until July 1, 1977, when the company is unable to make the required payment. The principal of the loan becomes due immediately under terms of the mortgage and the bank forecloses.

On August 15, 1977, the mortgaged property is sold at auction in accordance with a court order and the proceeds, after deducting costs, are $340,000. The principal and unpaid interest to date are turned over to the Snavely Bank, and the balance is remitted to Balcrest Enterprises.

Present journal entries of Balcrest Enterprises during 1977. The company closes its books annually on December 31. The property sold at auction was carried on the books at $380,000.

*25. On April 1, 1975, the Oliver Company acquired $1,000,000 par value of bonds of the Bret Company for $1,350,000. Costs of acquisition amounted to an additional $50,000. The bonds bear interest at 9 percent payable on March 31 and September 30 and mature on March 31, 1985. Use straight-line amortization of premium. Present entries on the books of the Oliver Company from April 1, 1975, through March 31, 1976, inclusive. Assume the books are closed annually on December 31.

*26. Refer to the data in Problem 25. Present the entry (or entries) for the sale of the bonds on July 1, 1978, at 103.5 plus accrued interest.

27. Refer to the data for the Midwestern Products mortgage example in the chapter. Compute the amount of the last payment in this example.

28. On June 1, 1975, the Southern Oil Company purchases a warehouse from F. S. Brandon for $60,000, of which $10,000 is assigned to the land and $50,000 to the building. There is a mortgage on the property payable to the Dixie National Bank, which, together with the accrued interest, will be assumed by the purchaser. The balance due on the mortgage is $24,000. The mortgage provides that interest at the rate of 10 percent per annum on the unpaid balance, and $2,000 on the principal will be paid on April 1 and October 1 of each year. A ten-year second mortgage for $15,000 is issued to F. S. Brandon; it bears interest at the rate of 12 percent per annum, payable on June 1 and December 1. A check is drawn to complete the purchase. Prepare entries for the Southern Oil Company for June 1, October 1, and December 1, 1975.

*29. The Hardin Manufacturing Company issues $5 million of 10-percent debenture bonds at par on June 1, 1975. The bonds are dated June 1, 1975, and provide for interest payments on December 1 and June 1 of each year. The bond indenture provides that sinking fund deposits, as well as deposits of funds for interest payments, will be made with the trustee according to the following schedule:

Date	Annual Deposit	Total Deposits
June 1, 1976–1980	$100,000	$ 500,000
June 1, 1981–1985	200,000	1,000,000
June 1, 1986–1990	300,000	1,500,000
June 1, 1991–1995	400,000	2,000,000
		$5,000,000

The indenture also provides that the trustee may call bonds by lot at June 1 of any year at the following schedule of call prices:

1976–1980	103
1981–1985	102
1986–1990	101

The company is to make additional payments to the trustee in the amount of the call premium on bonds acquired. The company closes its books annually on August 31.

a. Present entries for 1975.

b. Present entries for 1976. Assume bonds with a face value of $90,000 were called on June 1, 1976.

c. Assuming that the trustee has called all bonds for which he has had funds and that the practice is continued in 1989, present all the entries to be made in the year 1989.

*30. The Rollins Company has authorized a $6 million bond issue. The bonds are dated July 1, 1975, and are due on July 1, 1995. The accounting period of the Rollins Company is the year ending June 30.

On July 1, 1990, the board of directors decide to establish a sinking fund which will be sufficient to retire the bonds at the maturity date. Equal semiannual contributions are to be made on December 31 and June 30, the first payment to be made on December 31, 1990. The fund is expected to earn interest at the rate of 10 percent per annum.

a. Determine the amount of the payment to be made into the sinking fund for each six months.

b. Present dated journal entries for the recognition of contributions and earnings of the sinking fund. Assume that earnings are as expected, from December 31, 1990 to June 30, 1992, inclusive.

°31. In 1973, the Central Power Company issued $2 million of bonds in two series, A and B. Each series had face amount of $1 million and effective yield of 7 percent. Issue A contained semiannual 6-percent coupons. Issue B contained 8-percent semiannual coupons. In 1975, Central Power issued series C, with face amount of $1,000,000. This issue contained 8-percent semiannual coupons; the effective yield was 8.6 percent. Issues A, B, and C all mature thirty years from issue date.

Answer the following questions for each issue A, B, and C:

a. What is the selling price of the issue?

b. Make the journal entry for the day of bond issue.

c. Using the effective-interest method, show the journal entries made on the first semiannual interest payment date.

d. Repeat (c) for the second and third payment dates.

e. Show the semiannual entry if straight-line amortization of discount (or premium) is used.

32. On January 1, 1975, Kayco Company instituted a pension plan. The past service cost—the present value of the retroactive benefits awarded to current employees—is $1,200,000. The present value of the benefits earned by employees during both 1975 and 1976 is $700,000 at the end of each of those years. Kayco Company designates the Retirement Insurance Company as the trustee of the pension plan and deposits all funding payments with the insurance company at the end of each year. Interest on unfunded liabilities is accrued at a rate of 8 percent per year. Kayco Company plans to fund an amount each year equal to the pension expense recognized for the year.

Show the journal entries that Kayco Company would make on December 31, 1975 and 1976, for its pension plan and related expenses under the following assumptions, each of which is generally acceptable.

a. Past service cost is amortized over ten years.

b. Past service cost is amortized over forty years.

c. Past service cost is not amortized.

d. What is the present value on January 1, 1975, of the cash outlays related to past service costs under each of the three assumptions, above, if the outlays are discounted at 8 percent per year?

33. Refer to the pension plan data for Kayco Company in Problem 32. Assume that the present value at the end of each year of the pension benefits earned during the year continues to be $700,000. Show the entries related to the pension plan for the three assumptions about past service cost amortization on

a. December 31, 1984.

b. December 31, 2014.

c. December 31, 2015.

°34. The Myrtle Lunch sells coupon books that patrons may later use to purchase meals. Each coupon book sells for $17 and can be used to purchase meals with menu prices of $20. On July 1, redeemable unused coupons with face value of $1,500 were outstanding. During July, 250 coupon books were sold; during August, 100; during September, 100. Cash receipts exclusive of coupons were $1,200 in July, $1,300 in August, and $1,250 in September. Coupons with a face value of $2,700 were received during the three months.

   a. If the Myrtle Lunch had a net profit of $500 for the quarter ending September 30, how large were expenses?

   b. What effect, if any, do the July, August, and September coupon sales and redemption have on the right-hand side of the September 30 balance sheet?

35. The Jones Company sells service contracts to repair copiers at $300 per year. When the contract is signed, the $300 fee is collected and Deferred Contract Revenues is credited. Revenues on contracts are recognized on a quarterly basis during the year in which the coverage is in effect. On January 1, 1975, 1,000 service contracts were outstanding. Of these, 500 expired at the end of the first quarter, 300 at the end of the second quarter, 150 at the end of the third quarter, and 50 at the end of the fourth quarter. Sales and service during 1975 came to these amounts (assume all sales occurred at the beginning of the quarter):

	Sales of Contracts	Service Expenses
First quarter	$120,000 (400 contracts)	$50,000
Second quarter	240,000 (800 contracts)	60,000
Third quarter	90,000 (300 contracts)	45,000
Fourth quarter	60,000 (200 contracts)	55,000

   a. Prepare the first three quarterly entries for 1975 for the Jones Company. Assume that quarterly reports are prepared on March 31, June 30, and September 30.

   b. What is the balance in the Deferred Contract Revenues account on December 31, 1975?

36. The following events are recorded on the books of the K. Schipper Company during 1975:

   (1) Machinery costing $100,000 is purchased. Estimated service life is five years with no salvage value.

   (2) Installment sales of $800,000 are made; cost of goods sold is $600,000. During 1975, $500,000 of this amount is collected.

   (3) The estimated future warranty liability on sales is charged to warranty expense for the year and amounts to $100,000. Of this amount, $25,000 is actually incurred during 1975. Tax regulations require that deductions from revenues for warranty expense cannot exceed actual expenditures for that purpose.

   (4) Outlays for research and development are $50,000. Management estimates that benefits of this R and D outlay will accrue to the company over a five-year period.

Recall the "least and latest rule," make the unrealistic assumption that only these four events occurred during 1975. Compute the income before taxes, tax liabilities, and income after taxes for the K. Schipper Company.

If there is a difference between tax expense and tax currently payable, indicate how this difference is recorded. Assume a tax rate of 40 percent. Use straight-line depreciation for financial reports and sum-of-the-years'-digits depreciation for tax purposes.

°37. In the years 1975 and 1976, the Golden Que Company undertook rapid expansion. The firm purchased $300,000 of plant assets at the start of 1975 and $460,000 at the start of 1976. These assets were purchased with the proceeds of an $800,000 bond issue that pays semiannual coupons of 8 percent for fifteen years. The issue sold for $760,000 on January 1, 1975. The assets are expected to last ten years, with no salvage value. Assume that the management of the Golden Que follows the "least and latest rule."

   a. Compute the net income to stockholders assuming a 40-percent tax rate, and present journal entries to account for the accrual of the income tax liability for 1975. Income before depreciation and interest was $800,000 in both 1975 and 1976. Use straight-line depreciation for plant assets in financial reports and sum-of-the-years'-digits depreciation in tax returns. Use the effective-interest method of bond discount amortization in financial reports and the straight-line method in tax returns.

   b. Repeat (a) for 1976.

   c. Compute the difference in the tax payment for 1975 and 1976 if double-declining-balance depreciation had been used for plant assets, rather than sum-of-the-years'-digits depreciation, in tax returns. Round off all answers to the nearest dollar.

38. Equilibrium Company adopted a program of purchasing a new grinding machine each year under the income tax provision which permits the use of the sum-of-the-years'-digits method of depreciation. Each machine costs $15,000 installed. The estimated service life is five years with no expected salvage value. Calculate:

   a. Depreciation for each of the first seven years in accordance with the sum-of-the-years'-digits method of depreciation.

   b. Depreciation for each year in accordance with the straight-line method of depreciation.

   c. Annual difference in depreciation calculated in (a) and (b) above.

   d. Annual increase or decrease in Deferred Income Tax Liability account. Assume a 40-percent tax rate and straight-line depreciation in financial reports.

   e. Year-end balances of Deferred Income Tax Liability account.

   f. If Equilibrium Company continues to follow its policy of buying a new machine every year, what will happen to the deferred tax liability?

39. The Carom Company is going to acquire, as of January 1, 1976, a computerized cash register system that costs $100,000 and that has a five-year life and no salvage value. The company is considering two plans for acquiring the system.

   (1) Outright purchase. To finance the purchase, $100,000 of par value 10-percent semiannual coupon bonds will be issued January 1, 1976, at par.

   (2) Lease. The lease requires five annual payments to be made on December 31, 1976, 1977, 1978, 1979, and 1980. The lease payments are such that they have present value of $100,000 on January 1, 1976, when discounted at 10 percent per year.

Straight-line amortization methods will be used for all amortization computations.

a. Verify that the amount of each lease payment is $26,380.

b. What balance sheet accounts will be affected by the choice of plan and the accounting for the lease if Plan (2) is selected?

c. What will be the total depreciation and interest expenses for the five years under Plan (1)?

d. What will be the total expenses for the five years under Plan (2) if the lease is accounted for as an operating lease? As a financing lease?

e. Why are the answers in (d) the same? Why are the answers in (d) different from the answer in (c)?

f. What will be the total expenses for the first year, 1976, under Plan (1)? Under Plan (2) accounted for as an operating lease? Under Plan (2) accounted for as a financing lease?

g. Repeat part (f) for the fifth year, 1980.

Chapter 16

Owners' Equity: Capital Contributions

Many large corporations began as "mom and pop" enterprises. About twenty years ago, one man began a restaurant business with a small investment; his specialty was chicken. When the business earned money, he reinvested part of his profits in the restaurant and invested the rest in successful real estate ventures, the profits from which were ultimately reinvested in his business. Members of his family also contributed their money and talent; a relative suggested that he expand through franchising. Today, this is one of the largest chicken franchises in the country. The way that ownership equity was handled and grew was an important part of that success.

Although the legal difference between a corporation and a partnership or a sole proprietorship requires different record-keeping procedures, the same principles govern the accounting for the owners' equity of all of the major forms of business organization. The owners' equity of any business firm consists of two elements: capital contributed by the owners or stockholders, and earnings retained in the business.

This chapter describes the accounting for capital contributions to partnerships and corporations separately, and the next chapter concerns the accounting problems involved in the administration of net income and the recording of earnings reinvested in a business.

CAPITAL CONTRIBUTIONS: PARTNERSHIPS

The amount and the form of the capital contribution of each partner are determined by the partnership agreement. The property contributed may be in the form of cash or other property, or it may be in the form of goodwill—above-normal earnings expected to be derived from the reputation or experience of a particular partner. A separate capital account is opened for each partner. This account is credited with the amount of each partner's original investment and with any additional amounts subsequently contributed to the business.

The capital balances may be increased by the investment of additional funds or by the retention of earnings, and they may be decreased by partners' withdrawals or by losses. The privilege of making additional investments or withdrawing funds should be covered by the partnership agreement. The partners may, for example, agree to keep the ratios of capital accounts constant, which implies that withdrawals by partners must be in proportion to one another.

The amount appearing in each partner's capital account is significant for a number of purposes. Its proportion to the total partners' capital indicates his *interest in the capital of the business*. For example, if the total capital is $40,000 and one partner's capital account has a balance of $10,000, then that partner has a one-quarter, or 25-percent interest, in the partnership at that time. The capital balances are often a factor in the distribution of net income, as when an "interest" allowance is made on capital balances or when profits are distributed in proportion to capital balances. In case of dissolution, the balance in each partner's account indicates his share in the net assets (assets less liabilities). Any profits or losses incurred in the disposition of the assets would, of course, change the capital account balances.

The legal features of partnerships may require a partner to make additional contributions in order to meet the liabilities of the firm. Partners usually are "jointly and severally" liable for partnership obligations, so that one partner may not only lose his entire investment in the enterprise but also may have to pay the debts of the business. Such a partner would then try to collect from the other partners their proportionate shares of the debts.

Formation of a Partnership

Accounting for the formation of a partnership is demonstrated in the following illustration.

John A. Stone and Lois L. Baker start business as partners. Each is to contribute $20,000 of capital. Stone's contribution consists of $8,000 cash, office equipment valued at $5,000, an automobile valued at $3,600, and his promissory 8-percent demand note for $3,400. Baker, who has been in business before, contributes some installment notes receivable from her customers with a face value of $7,000 but worth $6,000, office equipment worth $3,000, cash of $1,000, and her uncompleted contracts and customer contacts valued at $10,000 as goodwill. In transactions of this sort, it is necessary for the partners to agree on the valuation that is to be assigned to each asset; this is especially true in the case of goodwill. The entries would be:

Cash on Hand	8,000	
Office Equipment	5,000	
Automobile	3,600	
Notes Receivable—Partners	3,400	
J. A. Stone, Capital		20,000

Installment Notes Receivable	7,000	
Office Equipment	3,000	
Cash on Hand	1,000	
Goodwill	10,000	
Allowance for Uncollectible Notes		1,000
L. L. Baker, Capital		20,000

The opening balance sheet of the partnership would appear as shown in Schedule 16.1.

Admission of a New Partner

From time to time new partners may be admitted to the firm. Legally, the admission of a partner creates a new partnership, but customarily the accounting records of the old firm are used, and the new firm is treated merely as a continuation of the old one for accounting (and almost all other) purposes. The revised partnership agreement should be given careful attention. The incoming partner may, for instance, bring benefits of experience or contacts that justify an arrangement giving him an interest in the firm larger than the amount of cash or other tangible assets contributed. On the other hand, the new partner may benefit from the business's having

SCHEDULE 16.1

BAKER & STONE
Balance Sheet
(Date)

Assets			Liabilities and Capital	
Cash on Hand		$ 9,000	L. L. Baker, Capital	$20,000
Installment Notes			J. A. Stone, Capital	20,000
Receivable	$7,000			
Less: Allow. for				
Uncollectible				
Notes	1,000	6,000		
Notes Receivable—Partners		3,400		
Office Equipment		8,000		
Automobile		3,600		
Goodwill		10,000	Total Liabilities	
Total Assets		$40,000	and Capital	$40,000

passed its organizational stage and, we shall assume, being profitable. He may be asked to accept an interest that is smaller than the percentage his contributed capital represents of the old partners' capital accounts.

The new partner may acquire an interest in the firm in either of two ways: (1) he may buy the interest (or a part of it) from an old partner by making payment to the old partner but contributing no assets to the firm, or (2) he may contribute assets to the business. Each of these alternatives is considered below.

New Partner Buys Interest from Old Partner

When a new partner buys the interest of an existing partner, the arrangements between them are treated as a personal matter. The financial facts of the transaction may not even be known to the other partners, although they usually must give their approval to the admission of a new partner. The only entry to be made is to close or reduce one partner's capital account and to open a new capital account for the incoming partner. For example, if in the preceding illustration Baker sells one half of her interest to S. J. Newland, the entry, regardless of the amount Newland pays Baker, ordinarily would be:

L. L. Baker, Capital	10,000	
S. J. Newland, Capital		10,000

It is sometimes suggested that if the new partner pays more or less than the book value of the interest he acquires from the old partner, this should be accepted as evidence that the assets of the partnership are undervalued or overvalued, or that the goodwill valuation would be altered. This involves a number of complications and is a matter on which the partners must come to an agreement. Further consideration of this problem will be left for more advanced accounting courses.

New Partner Contributes Assets to Business

When a new partner contributes assets to the business, the amount of his contribution may be:

1. equal to the book value of the interest he acquires
2. more than the book value of the interest he acquires
3. less than the book value of the interest he acquires.

To demonstrate each of these alternatives, we shall assume an existing partnership with the following condensed balance sheet on the date a new partner is admitted:

Assets		$40,000	Liabilities		$10,000
			X, Capital	$20,000	
			Y, Capital	10,000	30,000
		$40,000			$40,000

Contribution Equal to Book Value of Interest Acquired. When a new
partner contributes assets that are equal in value to the business interest
which he acquires, the accounting is simple. The new partner's capital
account is merely credited with the amount of his contribution to the
firm. In the example, if Z contributes $10,000 for a 25-percent interest
in the firm, total capital would be $40,000 ($30,000 plus the new contribution of $10,000), and his 25-percent share of this would be $10,000,
so he has made a contribution equal to the book value of the interest he
has acquired. The entry on the partnership books would be:

Cash (or Other Assets) 10,000
    Z, Capital   10,000

Contribution Greater than Book Value of Interest Acquired. Sometimes the incoming partner contributes tangible assets to which values
are assigned that are greater than the book value of the interest acquired.
The explanation of this situation usually is that the partnership has been
so successful that the new partner is willing to pay a premium or bonus
in order to become a part-owner. To put it another way, the partnership
assets shown on the books are either undervalued, or there is an unrecog-
nized asset, goodwill, which is taken into account in the negotiations
between the old and new partners.

Assume, for example, that Z contributes $12,000 in cash for a 25-percent
interest in the business. The accounting analysis and entries will depend
upon the interpretation placed upon the arrangement by the partners. If
they agree that the assets will be changed only to recognize Z's tangible
asset contribution, then an adjustment is made among the partners' capital
accounts to arrive at the results of the agreement. Under this approach,
known as the *bonus method*, the total partners' capital is now $42,000, the
original $30,000 plus the contribution of Z of $12,000. Z will be credited
with 25 percent of this amount, or $10,500, and the difference between
the credit to his account and the amount of his contribution, $1,500
(= $12,000 −$10,500), will be credited to X and Y. The allocation will be
made according to the terms of the partnership agreement, but it will
ordinarily follow the original profit and loss sharing ratio. Assume that the
original agreement between X and Y provided that they would share profits
and losses equally. The entry would be:

Cash (or Other Assets) 12,000
    X, Capital   750
    Y, Capital   750
    Z, Capital   10,500
To record Z's capital contribution and the related capital adjustment for X and Y.

The partners may, instead, decide to recognize the goodwill implied
by the agreement. This approach is frequently described as the *goodwill
method*. Under it, the amount of goodwill would be calculated as follows:

1. If Z is willing to contribute $12,000 for 25 percent of the total capital,
total capital must be $12,000/.25, or $48,000.

2. X's and Y's 75-percent share of total capital should be shown at
.75 × $48,000, or $36,000.

3. X's and Y's capital are now shown at $30,000, so $6,000 of goodwill
should be recognized.

The division of the $6,000 of goodwill between X and Y will, again,
depend upon the partnership agreement, but as a form of gain, it would
ordinarily be divided according to the old profit- and loss-sharing ratio.
The entries to record the adjustment and the admission of Z as a partner
would be:

Goodwill	6,000	
X, Capital		3,000
Y, Capital		3,000

To recognize goodwill of partnership prior to admission of Z
as partner.

Cash (or Other Assets)	12,000	
Z, Capital		12,000

Z's capital contribution.

Contribution Less than Book Value of Interest Acquired. In some
cases the incoming partner contributes tangible assets that have a
value lower than the book value of the interest he acquires. This possibility
can be explained on several grounds: the partnership assets are overvalued
on the books; the past earnings do not justify a larger payment by the incoming partner; the business has had difficulty in obtaining funds by
borrowing; or the new partner brings with him a reputation or special
ability which justifies the arrangement. To put this last point another way,
the new partner brings goodwill into the business in addition to contributing
tangible assets.

To deal with specific data, assume in the original example that Z
contributes $9,000 in tangible assets and receives a 25-percent interest
in the firm. As in the previous illustration, the accounting analysis and
entries will depend upon the interpretation of the situation made by the
partners. One approach does not recognize any goodwill that may be
involved but adjusts the partners' capital accounts to reflect the terms of
the agreement. The total capital will now appear as $39,000, the original
$30,000 plus Z's $9,000 contribution. Z will be credited with 25 percent
of the total or $9,750. The $750 difference between his contribution and
the credit to his account will be deducted from the capital accounts of
X and Y, usually in proportion to their profit- and loss-sharing ratios.
The entry would be:

Cash (or Other Assets)	9,000	
X, Capital	375	
Y, Capital	375	
Z, Capital		9,750

If the interpretation is made that Z contributes goodwill as well as
cash to the business and that this should be recognized in the accounts,
the calculation of the amount of goodwill would be as follows:

1. Since Z is to have a 25-percent interest, X and Y's capital of $30,000 must represent 75 percent of total capital.

2. If $30,000 is 75 percent of total capital, total capital must be $30,000/.75, or $40,000. Z's 25-percent interest will be 25 percent of $40,000 or $10,000.

3. Z has contributed tangible assets worth only $9,000, so he must also have contributed goodwill of $1,000.

The entry would be:

Cash (or Other Assets)	9,000	
Goodwill	1,000	
Z, Capital		10,000

To recognize Z's cash contribution and the goodwill resulting from his entry into the firm.

Partnership Growth by Merger

Partnerships are sometimes formed, or enlarged, by the merger of two or more going concerns. The following demonstration illustrates the creation of a three-person partnership by the merger of a two-person partnership with a sole proprietorship. It also illustrates the fact that when a merger takes place, or a new partner is admitted, the tangible assets or liabilities of the existing firm or firms may need to be adjusted to reflect present financial conditions more realistically.

    R. A. Blott and S. P. Norton are partners in a civil engineering practice. T. R. Stanger is in practice by himself, and it is now planned to merge the two businesses under the name of Blott, Norton & Stanger. The trial balances of the two firms at the date of the merger are shown in Schedule 16.2.

SCHEDULE 16.2 TRIAL BALANCE FOR MERGING PARTNERSHIPS

Blott & Norton			T. R. Stanger		
Cash in Bank	$ 1,000		Cash in Bank	$ 400	
Receivables	6,000		Receivables	2,200	
Furniture and			Furniture and		
Equipment	12,000		Equipment	5,000	
Accumulated			Accumulated		
Depreciation		$ 2,000	Depreciation ..		$1,000
Rent Payable		800	Accounts Payable.		600
Accounts Payable ..		200	T. R. Stanger,		
R. A. Blott, Capital..		12,000	Capital		6,000
S. P. Norton, Capital		4,000			
	$19,000	$19,000		$7,600	$7,600

The books of Blott & Norton will be continued in use to record the transactions of the new firm. Stanger will turn over his furniture and equipment at a valuation of $3,400. He will retain his cash and receivables as personal assets and will retain his accounts payable as a personal liability. It is agreed that the goodwill of Blott & Norton is to be valued at $24,000 and that of Stanger at $16,600. Blott & Norton have shared profits and losses in proportion to their capital balances.

Before merging the two businesses, entries should be made on each set of books to record the adjustments indicated in the agreement. The following entries would be made to adjust Stanger's accounts:

T. R. Stanger, Capital	600	
Accumulated Depreciation		600
To reduce the book value of the furniture and fixtures from $4,000 (= $5,000 — $1,000) to $3,400.		

Goodwill	16,600	
T. R. Stanger, Capital		16,600
To set up goodwill account in connection with merger with Blott & Norton.		

The entry on Stanger's books to show the transfer of his assets to the partnership would be:

Investment in Blott, Norton & Stanger	20,000	
Accumulated Depreciation	1,600	
Furniture and Equipment		5,000
Goodwill		16,600
To transfer furniture, equipment, and goodwill to Blott, Norton & Stanger.		

The entry to adjust the books of Blott & Norton would be as follows:

Goodwill	24,000	
R. A. Blott, Capital		18,000
S. P. Norton, Capital		6,000
To set up goodwill in connection with merger with T. R. Stanger and to apportion it between partners in their profit and loss sharing ratio, which is 75 percent for Blott and 25 percent for Norton.		

The entry to convert the books of Blott & Norton to Blott, Norton & Stanger would be:

Goodwill	16,600	
Furniture and Equipment	5,000	
Accumulated Depreciation		1,600
T. R. Stanger, Capital		20,000
To record investment of T. R. Stanger.		

The opening trial balance of the firm of Blott, Norton & Stanger, showing the results of the merger, would be:

Cash in Bank	$ 1,000	
Receivables	6,000	
Furniture and Equipment	17,000	
Accumulated Depreciation		$ 3,600
Goodwill	40,600	
Rent Payable		800
Accounts Payable		200
R. A. Blott, Capital		30,000
S. P. Norton, Capital		10,000
T. R. Stanger, Capital		20,000
	$64,600	$64,600

CAPITAL CONTRIBUTIONS: CORPORATIONS

A corporation has no exact counterpart to the sole owner of a business or to a partner in a partnership. The corporation has a separate legal existence, and capital contributions are made by individuals under a contract between themselves and the corporation. Because those who contribute residual capital funds are usually issued certificates for shares of stock, they are known as stockholders or shareholders. The rights and obligations of a stockholder are determined by:

1. The corporation laws of the state in which incorporation takes place. Some of the legal provisions cannot be waived or changed while others apply only in the absence of statements to the contrary in the articles of incorporation, bylaws, or stock contract.
2. The articles of incorporation or *charter*. This is the agreement with the state in which the business is incorporated. The enterprise is granted the privilege of operating as a corporation for certain stated purposes and of obtaining its capital through the issue of shares of stock.
3. The bylaws of the corporation. They are adopted by the board of directors and act as the rules and regulations under which the internal affairs of the corporation are conducted.
4. The stock contract. Each type of capital stock has its own provisions as to such matters as voting power, share in earnings, distribution of earnings, and share in assets in case of dissolution.

Some corporations have a small number of stockholders and operate much the same as a partnership. The few people involved agree to the amount of capital to be contributed, elect each other to be members of the board of directors and officials of the firm, and agree upon a policy of dividends and salaries. They may restrict the transfer of shares to outsiders and may even become liable for debts of the corporation by endorsing its notes and bonds.

In the case of large, widely owned corporations, the effect of the legal entity becomes more pronounced. Officials and even some directors may not be stockholders or, at least, not substantial stockholders. Actual control is likely to be in the hands of a few individuals who own or control enough shares to elect a majority of the board of directors. Most "minority" stockholders think of their stock holdings merely as investments and take little direct interest in the conduct of the affairs of the corporation. The stockholders assume no obligation for the debts of the business. Shares of stock change hands at the will of the stockholder, and the records of the corporation may not show the change for some time after it has occurred.

Issue of Shares of Stock

The accounting for the initial issue of shares of stock is normally a routine matter. In the usual case where the shares are issued for cash, the entry is:

Cash on Hand	1,250,000	
Capital Stock		1,250,000

In addition to exchanges for cash, stock certificates are sometimes issued in exchange for property, for personal services rendered, or in settlement of a liability. The form of the entry in these cases is the same as the one illustrated above, but the debit will be made to the property or services received or the liability settled.

Classes of Stock

Corporations are often authorized to issue more than one class of stock, each representing ownership in the business. Most stock issued is either *common* or *preferred*. Occasionally, there may be several classes of common or preferred stock. Each share of common stock has the same rights and privileges as every other share of common of the same class. Likewise, each share of preferred has the same rights as every other share of preferred of the same class.

Common stock has the claim to earnings of the corporation after commitments to preferred stockholders have been satisfied. Frequently, common stock is the only voting stock of the company. In the event of corporate dissolution, all of the proceeds of asset disposition, after settling the claims of creditors and required distributions to preferred stockholders, go to the common stockholders.

Preferred stock is granted special privileges. While these features vary considerably from issue to issue, preferred stock usually entitles its holder to dividends at a certain rate which must be paid before dividends can be declared and paid to common stockholders. Sometimes, though, these dividends may be postponed or omitted, according to the provisions of the issue. If the preferred dividends are *cumulative*, then all current and previously postponed dividends must be paid before common-stock dividends can be distributed.

Most preferred stock issued in recent years by corporations has been *callable*. Callable preferred may be reacquired by the corporation at a specified price, which may vary according to a predetermined time schedule. Callability is provided primarily for the benefit of the corporation. If sufficient financing is otherwise available, especially if that alternative financing is available at a lower cost than the rate previously fixed for the preferred stock, a corporation may wish to lessen the relatively fixed commitment of preferred dividends (as compared to common). All else equal, investors prefer noncallable to callable stock.

Increasingly, preferred stock is *convertible*. Convertible preferred stock may be converted into a specified amount of common stock at specified times by its owner. The conversion privilege may appear advantageous to both the individual stockholder and the corporation. The stockholder enjoys the security of a relatively assured dividend as long as he holds the stock. He also has the opportunity to realize capital appreciation by converting his shares into common stock when the market price of the common has risen sufficiently. Because of the convertible feature, the market price of preferred stock will often parallel a rise in the market price of the same common stock and will produce an unrealized capital gain on the preferred stock, even though it is not converted. The firm may benefit from the conversion option. By including it in the issue, the company usually is able to specify a lower dividend rate on the preferred than otherwise would have been required to issue the stock for a given price.

A major consideration in the issue of preferred stock is that preferred stock dividends are not deductible in calculating taxable income. However, bond interest is deductible, thereby reducing the after-tax cost of borrowing as compared to issuing preferred stock.

Separate accounts are used for each class of stock. On the balance sheet, each class of stock is shown separately, many times with a short description of the major features of the stock. Customarily, preferred stock is listed before common stock on the balance sheet.

Par Value and No-Par Stock

Shares of capital stock often have a *par*, or nominal, value per share specified in the articles of incorporation and printed on the face of the stock certificates. The par value of common stock has legal significance but little accounting significance. Stock assigned a certain par value will almost always sell on the stock market at a price different from par. Also, the book value of a share of common stock—the total common-stock equity divided by the number of shares outstanding—is almost always greater than the par value of the stock, in part because retained earnings are usually positive. The par value, then, rarely denotes the worth of the stock. The par value of common stock is used primarily to record shares of stock outstanding in the capital stock account. It is the amount which the creditors can usually rely upon as the minimum investment that has been made by the shareholders in the corporation. Par value of preferred stock is more meaningful. The dividend rate specified in the preferred-stock contracts is almost always based upon par value. Any preference as to assets in liquidation that preferred stockholders may have is usually related to the par value of the preferred shares.

Although preferred stock usually has a par value, no-par value common stock is widely issued. When no-par-value shares are issued, there need be no problem of assigning a nominal value to the shares issued, because the amount actually contributed can be credited directly to the capital stock account. However, common practice assigns a *stated* value to the no-par shares, which has much the same effect as assigning the shares a par value. Some state corporation laws require the directors to assign a stated value to no-par shares. The stated value can usually be changed from time to time at the discretion of the directors, but par value is usually fixed by the articles of incorporation and can be altered only by a formal legal process.

Contributions in Excess of Par or Stated Value

One awkward convention in accounting is that the capital stock account is usually credited with the par or stated value of the shares issued. Shares issued after the corporation's organization are frequently issued for amounts greater than par. Stockholders who come into the corporation some time after it is organized should pay a higher price per share to compensate current owners for the additional capital that has been accumulated by the retention of earnings in the business. Such an excess over par or stated value is credited to an account called Additional Paid-in Capital or Premium on Capital Stock. (The titles Paid-in Surplus and Capital Surplus have been used for this account, but the terms are not properly descriptive of the capital contribution which has taken place.) The title Capital Contributed in Excess of Par (Stated) Value is probably the most appropriate one, but it is considered by many to be too cumbersome to be used extensively.

The entries to record additional paid-in capital involve nothing new. If par-value shares are used, the credit to the Additional Paid-in Capital account is always the difference between the amount paid in and the par value of the shares issued to the stockholders. For no-par-value shares, the additional paid-in capital is the excess of the amount paid in over the stated value. Thus the entry to record issuing 100 shares of no-par-value stock, with a stated value of $1 per share, for $10,000, would be the same as the entry to record the issuance of a like number of $1 par-value shares with the same proceeds:

Cash on Hand	10,000	
Capital Stock—Stated Value		100
Additional Paid-in Capital		9,900

Since stock has no maturity date, the Additional Paid-in Capital, or Premium on Capital Stock, account remains on the books indefinitely as a partial measure of contributions by stockholders. This account differs from Premium on Bonds, considered in Chapter 15, in two important respects. Premium on Capital Stock appears in the stockholders' equity section of the balance sheet, while Premium on Bonds is shown in the long-term liability section; Premium on Capital Stock is not amortized, while Premium on Bonds is amortized over the life of the bonds to which it relates.

Contributions of Less than Par Value

It is rare to find shares of stock issued for assets with market value less than par value. Such shares are sometimes called *watered* stock. Many states prohibit such issues. Others make the shareholder liable to the creditors of the corporation, in case it encounters financial difficulties, for the difference between the par value and the fair market value of his original contribution. When such a stock issue does occur, the difference is recorded and carried as a debit balance in a contra-equity account called

Discount on Capital stock. To show a discount on no-par-value stock is never necessary because the stated value per share can be changed.

Subscriptions to Capital Stock

The previous illustrations have assumed that the offer to purchase the shares, collection for them, and issuance of the stock certificates take place at the same time. This may well be true for small corporations, but in large corporations the issue of shares of stock sometimes involves three steps rather than the one illustrated previously: (1) recognition of subscription contracts, (2) collection of subscriptions, and (3) issuance of stock certificates.

Subscriptions. The prospective stockholder signs an agreement to acquire a certain number of shares at a specified price and to pay for them either upon demand or according to the other terms of the agreement. In some cases the subscription may merely be an offer to acquire shares, but once the offer has been accepted by the corporation through its officials or other representatives, it becomes an enforceable contract which the corporation can treat as an asset, a receivable from the subscriber.

If subscriptions are received for 1,000 shares of capital stock at par or stated value of $50 a share, the entry would be:

```
Stock Subscriptions Receivable ...........................  50,000
    Capital Stock Subscribed ..............................         50,000
```

The Stock Subscriptions Receivable account is an asset control account that summarizes the detail of the individual subscription agreements. The Capital Stock Subscribed account is a temporary capital stock account. It is treated in the same way as the permanent capital stock account which will supersede it. Common Stock Subscribed and Preferred Stock Subscribed are titles that would be used if there were two classes of stock outstanding.

Collection of Subscriptions. Depending upon the terms of the subscription agreement, the collection of the subscriptions may be made in one sum, in regular installments, or upon the call of the corporation.

If $20,000 of cash is collected on stock subscriptions, the entry would be:

```
Cash ....................................................  20,000
    Stock Subscriptions Receivable ........................         20,000
```

Issuance of Certificates. Stock certificates are usually issued only after the full amount of a subscription has been collected. The entry to record the issue merely involves a transfer from the temporary capital stock account to the permanent one. When full payment has been received for the 1,000 shares in the illustration, the entry would be:

```
Capital Stock Subscribed ..................................  50,000
    Capital Stock—Par (or Stated) Value ...................         50,000
```

The three-step method of recording the issue of stock should be used whenever significant intervals of time separate the three stages. If they all occur on the same day or within a short period of time, the single entry of a debit to cash and a credit to the capital stock accounts is sufficient.

Treasury Stock

Shares of stock reacquired by the issuing corporation are called *treasury stock* or *treasury shares*. The firm's motivation for reacquiring its own shares may be to obtain shares for later distribution under stock options or as stock dividends. The firm may also see treasury stock as a worthwhile use for idle cash funds. Treasury stock is shown in the stockholders' equity section of the balance sheet in an account contra to stockholders' equity. Generally accepted accounting principles do not permit a company to show in the income statement a gain or loss on its dealings in treasury stock.

When treasury shares are acquired, the Treasury Stock—Common account is debited with the total amount paid to reacquire the shares.

```
Treasury Stock—Common ................................  11,000
   Cash ...............................................           11,000
$11,000 paid to reacquire 1,000 shares of $2 par value common
stock.
```

If the treasury shares are reissued by the corporation, cash or other assets will be debited and treasury stock credited. It is unlikely, of course, that the reissue price will precisely equal the amount paid to acquire the treasury shares. If the reissue price is greater, the Additional Paid-in Capital (Premium on Capital Stock) account is credited to make the entry balance. Assuming that the 1,000 shares reacquired in the entry illustrated above were reissued for $14,000, the entry would be:

```
Cash ....................................................  14,000
   Treasury Stock—Common ............................           11,000
   Additional Paid-in Capital .............................            3,000
Reissue of 1,000 shares of treasury stock.
```

If reissue price is less than the amount paid, the debit to make the entry balance is also to Additional Paid-in Capital, as long as there is a sufficient credit balance in that account. If there is not, the additional balancing debit is made to Retained Earnings.

Treasury stock is shown on the balance sheet as a deduction from the total of the other stockholders' equity accounts. A recent balance sheet of the Firestone Tire and Rubber Company illustrates this method:

```
Stockholders' Equity
   Preferred Stock (Cumulative), Par Value $100 per share,
      Authorized 150,000 shares, none issued
   Common Stock, Authorized 36,000,000 shares, 29,522,465
      issued without par value ............................  $   61,505,135
   Additional [Paid-in] Capital .............................      177,540,817
   Retained Earnings ......................................      783,269,451
                                                              ─────────────
      Total ...............................................   $1,022,315,403
   Less: Treasury Stock (217,617 shares) at Cost ...........       11,836,071
                                                              ─────────────
   Total Stockholders' Equity .............................   $1,010,479,332
                                                              ═════════════
```

The footnotes on page 40 of the General Electric Company's annual report reproduced at the end of Chapter 25 illustrate the treatment of "gain" on the reissue of treasury shares.

Conversion of Partnership to Corporation

Many corporations arise from existing partnerships or sole proprietorships. The owners turn over their interests in the existing business as their capital contributions and receive stock certificates in return. If the new business is merely a continuation of the old, a new set of books is not necessary. The next illustration shows how the conversion can be made using the original partnership records.

The following statement is a condensed balance sheet of the Midtown Druggists, a partnership. Profits and losses have been divided equally by the two partners.

Assets		Liabilities and Capital	
Cash	$ 2,000	Accounts Payable	$10,000
Receivables (Net)	12,000	H. J. Holmes, Capital	50,000
Inventory	60,000	R. A. Reeves, Capital	34,000
Furniture and Fixtures (Net)	20,000		
	$94,000		$94,000

Holmes and Reeves decide to incorporate and to issue stock to A. L. Soule. Before carrying out the reorganization, the partners agree to recognize $10,000 of goodwill on their books, and to recognize an allowance for uncollectible accounts of $2,000, as requested by Soule. The entries would be:

Goodwill	10,000	
H. J. Holmes, Capital		5,000
R. A. Reeves, Capital		5,000

To set up goodwill in connection with incorporation.

H. J. Holmes, Capital	1,000	
R. A. Reeves, Capital	1,000	
Allowance for Uncollectible Accounts		2,000

To set up allowance for uncollectible accounts in connection with incorporation.

The corporation is organized under the name of Midtown Druggists, Inc., and 20,000 shares of stock with a par value of $10 per share are authorized. No entry is required for this step, although an accurate record of the number of shares authorized and issued must be maintained, because shares issued over the number authorized by the articles of incorporation have no legal standing. The partners receive shares of stock in exchange for their equities. The entry merely substitutes a stockholders' equity account for the partners' capital accounts.

H. J. Holmes, Capital	54,000	
R. A. Reeves, Capital	38,000	
Capital Stock		92,000

To record the receipt by H. J. Holmes of 5,400 shares and by R. A. Reeves of 3,800 shares in Midtown Druggists, Inc., in connection with incorporation of the business.

At this time a subsidiary record, the stockholders' ledger, is opened in which are recorded the number of shares and the serial numbers of the certificates held by each stockholder.

A. L. Soule is now issued a certificate for 1,000 shares for which he contributes $10,000 in cash.

```
Cash .....................................................    10,000
    Capital Stock ........................................           10,000
Certificate for 1,000 shares of stock issued to A. L. Soule.
```

The opening condensed balance sheet of the corporation appears as shown in Schedule 16.3.

New Books Opened

The following changes would be made in the solution to the preceding illustration if new books were opened for the corporation. After recording the goodwill and setting up the allowance for uncollectible accounts, the partnership books would be closed with these entries:

```
Stock of Midtown Druggists, Inc. ..........................    92,000
Accounts Payable .........................................    10,000
Allowance for Uncollectible Accounts .....................     2,000
    Cash .................................................            2,000
    Receivables ..........................................           12,000
    Inventory ............................................           60,000
    Furniture and Fixtures (net) .........................           20,000
    Goodwill .............................................           10,000
To record transfer of assets and liabilities of partnership to
corporation in exchange for shares of stock.

H. J. Holmes, Capital ....................................    54,000
R. A. Reeves, Capital ....................................    38,000
    Stock of Midtown Druggists, Inc. .....................           92,000
To close partnership books. 5,400 shares of stock taken by
Holmes and 3,800 shares by Reeves.
```

The new books of the corporation would open with an entry to take over the assets and liabilities from the partnership.

```
Cash .....................................................     2,000
Receivables ..............................................    12,000
Inventory ................................................    60,000
Furniture and Fixtures (net) .............................    20,000
Goodwill .................................................    10,000
    Allowance for Uncollectible Accounts .................            2,000
    Accounts Payable .....................................           10,000
    Capital Stock ........................................           92,000
To take over assets and liabilities of Midtown Druggists, part-
nership, and to record issue of stock certificates for 5,400
shares to Holmes and 3,800 shares to Reeves.
```

The entry to record the issue of shares of stock to A. L. Soule would appear next:

```
Cash .....................................................    10,000
    Capital Stock ........................................           10,000
Certificate for 1,000 shares of stock issued to A. L. Soule.
```

SCHEDULE 16.3

MIDTOWN DRUGGISTS, INC.
Balance Sheet
(at incorporation date)

Assets			Liabilities and Stockholders' Equity		
Cash		$ 12,000	Accounts Payable		$ 10,000
Receivables	$12,000		Capital Stock		102,000
Less: Allow. for					
Uncollectible					
Accounts	2,000	10,000			
Inventory		60,000			
Furniture and Fixtures (net).		20,000			
Goodwill		10,000			
		$112,000			$112,000

The opening balance sheet of the corporation using this approach would, of course, be the same as the one shown in Schedule 16.3.

QUESTIONS AND PROBLEMS

1. Under what circumstances would you expect par-value stock to be issued at a price in excess of par? What is the entry to record such an issue?

2. A construction corporation is attempting to borrow money on a note secured by some of its property. A bank agrees to accept the note, provided that the president of the corporation will personally endorse it. What is the point of this requirement? Would the bank be likely to require a similar endorsement if the firm were a partnership?

3. "Par value of preferred stock is frequently a significant figure, but par value of common stock possesses little significance." How may par value of preferred stock be significant? In what way is the par value of common stock with a par value different from the stated value of no-par common stock?

4. Give journal entries for the following sequence of transactions:
   (1) Subscriptions are received for 2,000 shares of $50 par value common stock at par.
   (2) Cash of $50,000 is received on the subscriptions.
   (3) Subscriptions for 400 shares were fully paid in (2) and the stock certificates are issued.
   (4) The remainder of the subscriptions is collected.
   (5) The remaining stock certificates are issued.

*5. Using the data of Problem 4, except that the subscription amount is $60 per share, prepare journal entries for the transactions.

---

* Hints, key numbers, or (partial) answers appear in the back of the book between the Appendix Tables and the Glossary.

6. Smith and Jones are partners, sharing profits and losses and related adjustments in proportion to their capital balances. Smith has a capital of $40,000 and Jones has a capital of $20,000. Kenson is to be admitted as a partner. It is agreed that the partnership possesses unrecorded goodwill in the amount of $9,000. In order to acquire one-fourth interest, Kenson contributes $23,000 in cash to the partnership. Give journal entries on the books of the partnership: (a) assume that goodwill is to be set up on the books and (b) assume that goodwill is not to be set up on the books.

7. What is treasury stock? How is it reported on the balance sheet?

*8. The condensed balance sheet of K. S. Robin on March 31, 1975, shows the following:

Assets	$100,000	Liabilities	$ 15,000
		K. S. Robin, Capital	85,000
	$100,000		$100,000

P. T. Vincent buys a one-half interest in the enterprise on March 31, 1975. Give the journal entries and the resulting balance sheets for each of the following cases:
   (1) Vincent contributes $77,500 to the assets of the business; goodwill is not recognized.
   (2) Vincent contributes $100,000 to the assets of the business; goodwill is recognized.
   (3) Data of (2), except goodwill is not recognized.
   (4) Vincent pays Robin $45,000 personally.
   (5) Vincent pays Robin $40,000 personally.

9. Journalize the following transactions of the Bell Candy Company:
   (1) Subscriptions at par are received for 2,000 shares of $40 par value common stock.
   (2) The subscriptions are paid by turning over the assets and liabilities of the Peter's Candy, a partnership. Assets: accounts receivable (face amount, $5,500) valued at $5,000; materials and supplies, $14,000; land, $29,000; building (cost $27,000) at depreciated book value of $22,000; machinery and equipment (cost $23,000) at depreciated book value of $18,000. Liabilities assumed: accounts payable $6,500; taxes payable, $1,500.
   (3) The stock certificates are issued.

10. The balance sheet of Norton & Blott shows assets of $180,000, liabilities of $50,000, and capital of $130,000 divided between Norton, whose capital balance is $70,000, and Blott, whose capital balance is $60,000. The firm incorporates and 1,300 shares with a par value of $100 each are issued to the partners.
   a. Give the entry on the corporation's books under the assumption that a new set of books will be opened for the corporation.
   b. Give the entry for the conversion to a corporation under the assumption that the partnership books will be continued in use by the corporation.

11. The Larry Company is formed with an authorization of 25,000 shares of no-par capital stock. The directors place a stated value of $100 per share on the stock. Journalize the following transactions:

(1) Cash is received for 2,000 shares issued at $105 per share.

(2) Subscriptions are received for 2,000 shares at $108 per share. A down payment of 30 percent is received with each subscription.

(3) The company takes an option on a tract of land to be used as a building site. The purchase price of the land is $100,000 and the company pays $3,000 for the option. If the option is exercised within sixty days, it will be applied toward the purchase price.

(4) An additional 30-percent payment on the subscriptions is received.

*(5) The land option is exercised. The owner of the land accepts 500 shares of stock and an additional $40,000 in cash in full payment for the land.

(6) The remainder of the subscription price is collected and the certificates are issued.

12. On March 1, 1975, William A. Strover, Larry J. Martin, and Robert R. Dawson form a partnership to conduct a retail business. The partnership agreement provides for the following contributions by the partners:

(1) William A. Strover, who has been conducting a retail business as a sole proprietor, is to turn over all the assets of his business except the cash to the partnership and the partnership is to assume all its liabilities. The store's condensed balance sheet at February 28, 1975, showed the following assets and liabilities:

Assets:
Cash, $8,000;
Accounts Receivable, $7,600;
Merchandise, $30,200;
Store Furniture and Fixtures (net), $7,800.

Liabilities:
Accounts Payable, $3,800.

The partners agree that an allowance for uncollectible accounts of $1,000 should be set up for the receivables and that the store furniture and fixtures should be valued at $7,000.

(2) Larry J. Martin is to contribute a delivery truck valued at $3,000, his six-month, 8-percent note for $10,000, and cash of $7,000.

(3) Robert R. Dawson is to contribute $16,000 in cash and office equipment valued at $4,000.

All capital contributions are made as set forth in the partnership agreement.

a. Make the entries on Strover's books to show his investment in the partnership.

b. Record the partners' contributions on the new set of books that is opened for the partnership.

*c. Present a balance sheet of the partnership on March 1, 1975, after the contributions have been made.

13. Give journal entries for the following transactions:

(1) Subscriptions are received for 1,000 units of stock at $250 per unit. Each unit consists of two shares of $100 par-value preferred stock and two shares of no-par common stock.

(2) Cash of $125,000 is collected on the subscriptions.

(3) Subscriptions for 280 units were fully paid in (2) and the stock certificates are issued.

(4) One subscription for fifty units by L. P. Rowy is forfeited after an initial collection of $1,000. The law in the state of incorporation requires that the shares be offered for issuance again and any balance of the issue proceeds over the balance due on the subscription be refunded to the subscriber. Set up an account, Subscription Forfeiture Suspense, to record the $1,000 credit required in this transaction.

(5) The shares mentioned in (4) are issued for cash at $242 a unit. The certificates are issued. Debit Subscription Forfeiture Suspense as required.

(6) The refund is made to Rowy. Debit Subscription Forfeiture Suspense to close that account.

(7) The remaining subscriptions are collected in full and the certificates issued.

14. Journalize the following transactions:

(1) Subscriptions are received for 2,000 shares of preferred stock, par value $100 per share, at $103 per share.

(2) Cash is collected on the subscriptions of $140,000.

(3) Subscriptions for 400 shares were fully collected in (2) and stock certificates are issued.

(4) One subscription for forty shares is forfeited after an initial collection of $400. The collection made is forfeited and credited to additional paid-in capital. [The collection was recorded in (2).]

(5) The remaining subscriptions are collected.

(6) Stock certificates are issued for the fully collected subscriptions.

15. The condensed balance sheet of the Campbell Estate Company at April 30, 1975, is as follows:

Assets		Liabilities & Stockholders' Equity	
Cash in Bank	$ 6,000	Accounts Payable	$ 2,200
Marketable Securities	30,000	Mortgage Payable	10,000
Contracts Receivable	48,000	Capital Stock	90,000
Unsold Lots	20,000	Retained Earnings	4,400
Office Equipment (net)	2,600		
	$106,600		$106,600

The shares of stock are held as follows: John A. Campbell, 200 shares; Susan N. Campbell, 5 shares; Harold W. Cass, 205 shares; Louis R. Sundwall, 40 shares; total, 450 shares.

It is decided to dissolve the corporation at May 1, 1975, and continue business as a partnership. A new set of books is not to be opened.

Give journal entries for the following transactions relating to the termination of the corporation and the conversion to the partnership. Assume the books are closed as of April 30, 1975 and ignore income tax effects except in transaction (4).

*(1) Marketable securities that cost $6,000 are sold for $6,300. The proceeds are deposited in the bank.

(2) Mr. Sundwall is to retire from the firm and he is to receive $225 a share for his stock. He surrenders his stock certificates and receives a check in payment.

(3) A bill is received from Robert K. Sloan for $700 to cover fees and legal services in connection with the change in the form of business organization. The bill is paid by check.

(4) A federal income tax return is filed for the portion of the year that the corporation was in existence. The tax of $1,750 is paid by check. No accrual for income taxes has been recorded.

(5) Mrs. Campbell assigns her shares to Mr. Campbell. Messrs. Campbell and Cass surrender their certificates and become partners in the new firm. Profits and losses are to be shared as follows: Campbell, 60 percent; Cass, 40 percent.

(6) A bill is received from Quality Printing Company for $115 for cards announcing the organization of the new firm.

(7) Mr. Campbell gives the firm a typewriter that he previously used at his home. The partners agree upon a value of $75.

*16. The balance sheet of Stone and Baker on January 1, 1975, shows assets of $117,000, liabilities of $12,000, and capital for Stone of $35,000 and for Baker of $70,000. The partnership agreement provides that they will share all profits and losses equally.

It is decided that the business needs additional funds for expansion purposes, so Gould is invited to invest sufficient cash to acquire a one-fourth interest in the firm. Stone states that an investment of $35,000 should be required, Baker states that $40,000 is more appropriate, and Gould states that a $30,000 investment would be fair.

a. Journalize the entry to record the admission of Gould as a partner with a one-fourth interest in capital. Assume the appropriate amount of goodwill is recognized, under the terms of: (1) Stone, (2) Baker, and (3) Gould.

b. Repeat the entries of the three parts of (a). Assume that no goodwill is to be recorded in the accounts.

17. Journalize the following transactions relating to Jones and Munsey, Inc. The corporation is organized with an authorization of 20,000 shares of capital stock of $100 par value per share.

(1) T. C. Jones contributes the following assets:
inventories, $42,000
land, $20,000
building, $56,000
equipment, $28,000.
The corporation agrees to assume a mortgage of $32,000 on the land and building and to pay trade creditors $10,000 due them. A certificate is issued to Jones for the appropriate number of shares.

(2) S. M. Munsey issues a check for $60,000 for 600 shares.

(3) P. R. Rowe subscribes for 1,000 shares at par and makes a down payment of 30 percent on the subscription price.

(4) A bill for $7,000 is received from Gatzer and Montang, attorneys, for services relating to the formation of the corporation.

(5) Gatzer and Montang agree to accept seventy shares of stock in payment of their bill.

(6) It is discovered that there was an error in Jones' accounts. One bill for $600 which was included in the payables had been paid previously. An additional certificate is issued to Jones for six shares.

(7) Rowe pays the balance due on his subscription, and a certificate for 1,000 shares is issued to him.

18. Remington and Doyle are partners in the Doton Company. At June 30, 1975, Remington's capital balance is $40,000 and Doyle's is $60,000. The partners share equally in all income and additional capital contributions credited to them.

　　At that date, Morgan acquires a one-third interest in the capital of the firm. Each alternative listed below is independent of the others.

*a. If Morgan contributes $40,000 in cash and the appropriate goodwill is recognized, what will be the balance in Morgan's capital account? In Remington's?

*b. If Morgan contributes $53,600 in cash and no other change in assets is recognized, what will be the balance in Morgan's capital account? In Doyle's?

c. If Morgan pays Doyle $40,000 to acquire the one-third interest, what will be the balance in Morgan's capital account? In Doyle's?

d. If it is agreed that an allowance for uncollectible accounts of $4,000 is to be set up, the Accumulated Depreciation account balance is to be increased by $8,000 and Morgan is to contribute $52,000 in cash, give the entries to record the admission of Morgan on the assumption that the appropriate goodwill is recognized.

e. Record the data of (d), without recording goodwill in the accounts.

19. The condensed balance sheet of Anderson and Johnson at December 31, 1975, is as follows:

Assets		Liabilities & Capital	
Cash in Bank	$12,000	Accounts Payable	$ 7,600
Accounts Receivable	38,000	Taxes Payable	3,200
Merchandise	22,000	Anderson, Capital	40,000
Equipment (net)	2,800	Johnson, Capital	24,000
	$74,800		$74,800

At that date, the firm decides to incorporate. An allowance for uncollectible accounts of $3,200 is established and 2,500 shares of stock with a par value of $20 per share are issued to the partners.

a. Give the entry for the conversion to a corporation under the assumption that the partnership books will be continued in use by the corporation.

b. Give the entry on the corporation's books under the assumption that a new set of books will be opened for the corporation.

20. Peterson and Munice are equal partners, each having a capital balance of $100,000. Haldman is admitted as a new partner, and it is agreed that each partner will have a one-third interest in the firm. Journalize the entries to record Haldman's admission into the firm under each of the following alternatives:

*a. Haldman contributes $112,000 in cash to the business and no goodwill is recognized.

b. Journalize the data of (a) recognizing goodwill.

c. Haldman contributes $82,000 in cash to the firm and no goodwill is recognized.

d. Journalize the data of (c), recognizing goodwill.

*e. Haldman pays $36,000 directly to both Peterson and Munice.

f. Haldman pays $96,000 into the business, and it is decided that an allowance for uncollectible accounts of $2,600 should be established. No goodwill is to be recognized.

21. Wood and Laughlin, partners, have capital balances of $64,000 and $32,000, respectively, and share profits and losses in the ratio of 60 percent to Wood and 40 percent to Laughlin. Record in two-column journal form the admission of Cox as a partner under each of the following alternatives:

a. Cox contributes $44,000 for a one-fourth interest and goodwill is to be recognized.

b. Record the data of (a) without recognizing goodwill.

c. Record the data of (a). Assume that Cox contributes $28,000 in cash.

d. Cox acquires a one-fourth interest in the firm by paying $20,000 to Wood for one-fourth of his interest and $12,000 to Laughlin for one-fourth of his interest.

e. Cox contributes equipment worth $24,000 and a check for $14,000 for a one-fourth interest in the firm. It is agreed that an allowance for uncollectibles of 5 percent of the $20,000 balance of receivables of the firm should be established and an appropriate amount of goodwill recognized.

f. Record the data of (e) without recognizing goodwill.

22. S. Walter, R. Ron, and K. Kelvin are partners engaged in a retail business under the name of Prosperity Company. Their partnership agreement provides that net income or loss is to be shared in the following manner:

(1) Interest at the rate of 8 percent per annum is to be allowed on the partners' average capital balances during the year.

(2) The following salary allowances are to be provided: Ron $17,000 and Kelvin $14,400. Walter is no longer active in the business and receives no salary allowance.

(3) Any remaining income or loss is to be divided 40 percent to Walter, 35 percent to Ron, and 25 percent to Kelvin.

The partners' capital accounts during 1975 show the following data:

S. Walter, Capital					R. Ron, Capital				
3/31/75	2,000	1/1/75	80,000		6/30/75	2,000	1/1/75	36,000
6/30/75	2,000				8/31/75	4,000	4/30/75	14,000
9/30/75	2,000				10/31/75	6,000		

K. Kelvin, Capital			
1/31/75	6,000	1/1/75	24,000
10/31/75	3,000	9/30/75	4,000

The net income from operations for 1975, before deducting any allowances, was $54,960.

a. Show the calculation of the partners' average capital balances.

b. Prepare a schedule showing the distribution of net income to the partners for 1975.

*c. Prepare a schedule of partners' capital accounts for 1975.

23. The following data are selected from the records of capital stock and retained earnings of the Wheellock Company.

(1) July 5, 1975. Articles of incorporation are filed with the secretary of state. The authorized capital stock consists of 1,000 shares of 6-percent preferred stock with a par value of $100 per share and 10,000 shares of no-par common stock.

(2) July 8, 1975. The company issues 3,000 shares of common stock for cash at $50 per share.

(3) July 9, 1975. The company issues 6,000 shares of common stock for the goodwill and other assets of the partnership of Wheellock and Wheellock. Their tangible assets are valued as follows: accounts receivable, $30,000; inventories, $60,000; land, $12,000; buildings, $90,000; and equipment, $100,000.

(4) July 13, 1975. Subscripitons are received for 750 shares of preferred stock at par.

(5) July 17, 1975. Subscriptions are collected in full for 500 shares of preferred stock.

(6) July 19, 1975. A subscription for 10 shares of preferred stock is cancelled.

(7) July 19, 1975. Certificates for the 500 shares of preferred stock, collected in full on July 17, are issued.

(8) July 22, 1975. The company collects 40 percent of the subscription price from the remaining preferred stock subscribers (240 shares).

(9) December 31, 1975. The balance in the Income Summary account after closing all expense, revenue, and income distribution accounts is $200,000. That account is to be closed to the Retained Earnings account.

(10) January 4, 1976. The regular semiannual dividend on the preferred stock (500 shares) and a dividend of $2 per share on the common stock are declared. The dividends are payable on February 1.

(11) January 6, 1976. A certificate for fifty shares of common stock, originally issued to J. C. Perry, is received from its present owner, P. H. Homes, and a new certificate is issued to him.

(12) January 12, 1976. The remainder of the subscription price of the 240 shares of preferred stock is collected from the subscribers.

(13) January 16, 1976. Certificates for the 240 shares of preferred stock, collected in full on January 12, are issued.

(14) February 1, 1976. The dividends declared on January 4 are paid.

(15) July 2, 1976. The regular semiannual dividend on the preferred stock (740 shares) is declared. The dividend is payable on August 1.

(16) August 1, 1976. The dividend declared on July 2 is paid.

Give journal entries as required for the above transactions.

24. The trial balance of the general ledger of Keswick Brothers at July 1, 1976, appears as follows:

Debits			**Credits**		
Cash on Hand	$	1,200	Accumulated Depreciation ..	$	5,300
Cash in Bank		7,000	Accounts Payable		6,000
Accounts Receivable		25,000	Rent Payable		2,100
Notes Receivable		5,000	Taxes Payable		500
Merchandise Inventory		90,000	Notes Payable		8,500
Prepayments		1,200	A. K. Keswick, Capital		75,000
Furniture and Fixtures		18,000	S. R. Keswick, Capital		50,000
		$147,400			$147,400

Net income and losses are apportioned 60 percent to A. K. Keswick and 40 percent to S. R. Keswick.

J. H. Jarman, who owns the building in which Keswick Brothers' store is located, is to be admitted as a one-third partner. The new firm will be known as Keswick and Company.

Keswick and Company will continue to use the books of Keswick Brothers, but an auditor is called in and he recommends the following adjustments, which are agreed to by the Keswick brothers and Jarman.

(1) The inventory should be written down to $86,000.

(2) Analysis of the customers' accounts indicates that accounts totaling $400 should be written off as uncollectible and that a further adjustment of $800 should be made to allow for estimated uncollectibles.

(3) The note receivable is dated April 1, 1976, and bears interest at the rate of 8 percent per annum.

(4) A study of the depreciation rates on furniture and fixtures indicates they have been too high and that the balance in the Accumulated Depreciation account should be reduced by 10 percent.

(5) The note payable is dated March 1, 1976, and accrued interest since that time is $222.

It is agreed by the partners that Jarman's contribution will be made as follows:

(1) The building in which the store is located, which cost $60,000, will be turned over to the partnership at its depreciated value of $42,000.

(2) Land valued at $10,000 will be turned over to the partnership.

(3) Jarman has connections which, it is agreed, will entitle him to a capital credit of $4,000 as a recorded goodwill contribution.

(4) The unpaid rent will be applied toward his capital contribution.

(5) The balance required to give him a one-third interest will be contributed in cash and will be deposited in the bank.

a. Journalize the necessary adjustments on the books of Keswick Brothers.

*b. Calculate the total contribution Jarman must make.

c. Journalize the entries to record Jarman's admission as a partner.

*d. Prepare a balance sheet for Keswick and Company after the adjustments and Jarman's contribution.

25. Wright, Bond, and Lee are partners in the Quarry Company. The following table presents data about their capital accounts and their partnership agreement.

	Capital Jan. 1, 1976	Percent of Residual Profit	Annual Salary Allowance
Wright	$200,000	40%	$20,000
Bond	175,000	35%	18,000
Lee	125,000	25%	18,000
	$500,000	100%	$56,000

The partnership agreement also provides that each partner will be allowed 8 percent on his capital balance at the start of the year and that all drawings during the year will be charged interest at the rate of 8 percent per annum. Drawings during 1976 were as follows:

	Wright	Bond	Lee
March 1	$10,000		
July 1		$10,000	$12,000
October 1	8,000		
December 31	4,000	4,000	4,000
	$22,000	$14,000	$16,000

Income in 1976 before deducting any allowances was $110,000.

a. Prepare a schedule showing the distribution of net income for 1976.

b. Prepare an entry closing the Income Summary account.

c. Prepare a schedule showing the changes in partners' capital accounts for 1976.

26. The condensed balance sheet of The Ozer Drug Supply Company on December 31, 1976, is as follows:

THE OZER DRUG SUPPLY COMPANY
Balance Sheet as of December 31, 1976

Assets

Cash		$ 2,000
Accounts Receivable	$20,000	
Less: Allowance for Uncollectible Accounts	3,000	17,000
Merchandise Inventory		61,000
Land		6,000
Buildings	$30,000	
Less: Accumulated Depreciation	10,000	20,000
Furniture and Fixtures	$50,000	
Less: Accumulated Depreciation	16,000	34,000
Total Assets		$140,000

Liabilities and Capital

Accounts Payable	$ 10,000
Wages and Taxes Payable	2,000
Mortgage Payable	8,000
M. T. Ozer, Capital	80,000
B. N. Stein, Capital	40,000
Total Liabilities and Capital	$140,000

Profits and losses are divided equally.

The General Drug Company acquires the business of The Ozer Drug Supply Company as of January 1, 1977, on the following terms: cash—retained by the partnership; accounts receivable—$7,000 (face value) and the allowance for uncollectibles retained by the partnership and the balance transferred to the corporation at face (and estimated) value; merchandise inventory—taken at a value of $50,000; land and buildings—retained by the partnership; furniture and fixtures—taken at book value; accounts payable, wages and taxes payable, and mortgage payable—to be settled by the partnership. Payment is made by the issue of $100,000 (par value) of the debenture bonds and 1,000 shares of the no-par Class A stock with stated value of $20 per share of The General Drug Company. The partners agree to value the bonds at face value and the stock at $20 per share.

The balance sheet of The General Drug Company at December 31, 1976, just prior to the purchase of The Ozer Drug Supply Company, was as follows:

THE GENERAL DRUG COMPANY
Balance Sheet as of December 31, 1976

Assets

Cash		$ 6,800
Accounts Receivable	$200,000	
Less Allowance for Uncollectibles	22,000	178,000
Inventories		334,000
Land		80,000
Buildings	$360,000	
Less Accumulated Depreciation	120,000	240,000
Equipment	$350,000	
Less Accumulated Depreciation	150,000	200,000
Total Assets		$1,038,800

Liabilities and Stockholders' Equity

Accounts Payable	$ 95,000
Notes Payable	30,000
Wages and Taxes Payable	20,400
Debenture Bonds Payable	200,000
Capital Stock—Class A ($20 stated value, 24,820 shares outstanding) ...	496,400
Capital Stock—Class B ($10 stated value, 10,600 shares outstanding) ...	106,000
Retained Earnings	91,000
Total Liabilities and Stockholders' Equity	$1,038,800

The General Drug Company values the goodwill acquired at $23,000.

a. Give journal entries for the transfers and adjustments on the books of The Ozer Drug Supply Company.

°b. Prepare a balance sheet for The Ozer Drug Supply Company after the receipt of The General Drug Company stock and bonds.

c. Record the purchase of The Ozer Drug Supply Company business on the books of The General Drug Company.

°d. Prepare a balance sheet of The General Drug Company after the purchase.

27. The following events relate to stockholders' equity transactions of the Richardson Copper Company during its first year of its existence.

(1) Jan. 2, 1975. Articles of incorporation are filed with the State Corporation Commission. The authorized capital stock consists of 5,000 shares of $100 par value, preferred stock which offers a 5-percent annual dividend, and 50,000 shares of no-par common stock. The original incorporators are issued 100 shares of common stock at $20 per share; cash is collected for the shares. A stated value of $20 per share is assigned to the common stock.

(2) Jan. 6, 1975. Fifteen thousand shares of common stock are issued for cash at $20 per share.

(3) Jan. 8, 1975. Subscriptions are received for 2,800 shares of preferred stock at par. Subscriptions are collected in full for 500 shares and a 20-percent down payment is collected on the other subscriptions.

(4) Jan. 9, 1975. Certificates for the fully paid shares of preferred stock are issued.

(5) Jan. 9, 1975. The tangible assets and goodwill of Richardson Copper Works, a partnership, are acquired in exchange for 600 shares of preferred stock and 10,000 shares of common stock. The tangible assets acquired are valued as follows: inventories, $40,000; land, $25,000; buildings, $80,000; and equipment $95,000.

(6) July 3, 1975. The semiannual dividend on the preferred stock outstanding is declared, payable July 25, to stockholders of record of July 12.

(7) July 5, 1975. Operations for the first six months have been profitable and it is decided to expand. The company issues 20,000 shares of common stock for cash at $23 per share.

(8) July 16, 1975. The remainder of the subscription price of 2,240 shares of preferred stock is collected from subscribers.

(9) July 16, 1975. A subscription for sixty shares of preferred stock is canceled and the collection thereon is forfeited.

(10) July 17, 1975. Certificates for the fully collected shares of preferred stock are issued.

(11) July 25, 1975. The preferred stock dividend declared July 3 is paid.

(12) Oct. 2, 1975. The directors declare a dividend of $1 per share on the common stock, payable October 25, to stockholders of record of October 12.

(13) Oct. 25, 1975. The common stock dividend declared October 2 is paid.

Record the above transactions in two-column journal form.

Chapter 17

Owners' Equity: Retention of Earnings

After a new business has established itself and is profitable, it usually generates additional equity from undistributed earnings. These undistributed earnings come from the net income that remains after dividends have been paid to corporate stockholders or the owners of an unincorporated business have made their proprietary withdrawals. Retention of earnings increases owners' or stockholders' equity and, as in the case of the man mentioned in the introduction to Chapter 16 who began his food-franchising business, often provides the main source of capital for expansion. This chapter discusses the accounting for retained earnings.

Net Income and Cash Position

One misconception about net income is that it represents a fund of cash available for distribution or spending. Earnings from operations usually go through the cash account—goods are sold to customers, the cash is collected, more goods are purchased, bills are paid, more sales are made, and so on—but earnings do not remain in cash. Only under completely static conditions, with net plant and equipment, inventories, receivables, and liabilities remaining at constant figures, would it be reasonable to suppose that the earning of net income resulted in a corresponding increase in cash at the end of the period. Indeed, an interesting paradox is that for many businesses an increased net income is frequently associated with decreased cash, while contraction of net income may be accompanied by an increase in cash. In the first stages of a business decline, cash may start to build up from the liquidation of inventories and receivables that have not been replaced, as well as from postponing replacement, or expansion of plant. When conditions improve, inventories and receivables are expanded, new plant acquired, and a cash shortage may develop.

The statement of changes in financial position explained in Chapter 19 shows how cash and other working capital produced by income have been used in the business.

A well-managed firm keeps its cash at a reasonable minimum. If cash starts to accumulate, the firm may pay off some obligations, increase its stock of goods, buy more equipment, declare dividends, or use the funds in some other way. This process of cash management goes on continuously. Thus, there is no way of predicting how the retention of earnings will be reflected in the individual asset and liability accounts. The only certain statement that can be made about the effect of retaining earnings is that it results in increased *net* assets (that is, an increase in the excess of all assets over all liabilities).

RETAINED EARNINGS: PARTNERSHIPS

In a partnership, the increase in ownership equity shown in each partner's capital account is determined in two steps: (1) allocating net income of the period among the partners and (2) deducting partners' drawings during the period.

Allocation of Partnership Net Income

At the end of each accounting period, the net income of the period is allocated among the partners. The partnership agreement determines the fraction to which each partner is entitled. If the partnership agreement does not specify the sharing arrangements, the Uniform Partnership Act provides that profits and losses are to be shared equally.

There are many variations in the arrangements that may be specified by the partnership agreement. The more common types of arrangements for the allocation of profits and losses are: (1) a fixed percentage allocation, (2) allocation in proportion to capital balances, and (3) allocation on a combination of bases to reflect various aspects of the partners' contribution of services and capital to the business.

The entry to record this allocation is usually the final closing entry. In it, each of the partners' capital accounts is credited, and the Income Summary account is debited with an amount which reduces its balance to zero. If there is a loss for the period, the debits and credits of the previous sentence are, of course, reversed.

The simplest form of net income or loss distribution is the allocation to each partner of a fixed fraction or percentage of the total net income or net loss. For example, if there are three partners, A, B, and C, each may be entitled to one third, or some other proportion may be used. If the net income for the year is $75,000, and the profits and losses are to be distributed 40 percent to A and 30 percent each to B and C, the closing entry would be:

Income Summary	75,000	
A, Capital		30,000
B, Capital		22,500
C, Capital		22,500

Allocation Proportional to Capital Account Balances

The partners sometimes agree to allocate profits and losses in proportion to capital account balances. The simplest variation of this method is to make the allocation in proportion to the balances at the beginning or end of the accounting period. If the balance of a partner's capital account changes during the period because of withdrawals or additional investments of capital, the use of opening or closing capital balances could be inequitable. Therefore, a fairly common practice provides that profits or losses shall be divided in proportion to the average capital balances.

More elaborate methods of allocating partnership net income or loss are sometimes used. The distribution may attempt to make allowances for differences in the position of the partners with regard to such matters as capital investment or time contributed to the partnership.

Such an agreement might assign "salary allowances" of varying amounts to some or all of the partners. It might then provide for a credit to each partner for "interest" on his average capital balance for the year at some interest rate. Any remaining balance, debit or credit, would then be divided among the partners in equal, or other specified, percentages.

Partners' Withdrawals

In a partnership there are no legal barriers to the adoption of any desired policy with regard to the retention or distribution of net income. The withdrawal of assets by the partners is guided only by the wishes of the partners and the provisions of the partnership agreement. These withdrawals seldom present accounting complications and do not merit extended discussion.

Partners' Capital Accounts

One capital account for each partner will often be sufficient. It will be credited with his share of the net income as well as with his capital contributions and debited with his share of any losses and the amount of any withdrawals. The balance of such an account may be withdrawn at any time except for restrictions imposed by the partners themselves in their partnership agreement.

Although a single capital account for each partner is usually sufficient, a second account, known as a *drawing* account (other titles frequently used are *current* account or *personal* account) is often used. The drawing account records each partner's withdrawals for personal use and other current charges against him. At the end of the period, each partner's share of net income is transferred to his drawing account. The balance in the drawing account at the end of the period, either a debit or credit balance depending on whether the partner's withdrawals exceed his share of net income, is then closed into the capital account.

RETAINED EARNINGS: CORPORATIONS

The stockholders of a corporation do not directly control distribution of corporate net income. The corporation bylaws almost always delegate the authority to declare dividends to the board of directors. The directors, in considering whether or not to declare dividends, must conclude both (1) that the declaration of a dividend is legal and (2) that it would be financially expedient. The legal restrictions upon dividend declaration can be statutory or contractual.

Statutory Restrictions upon Dividends

The limitations in state corporation laws impose certain restrictions upon the directors' freedom to declare dividends. These restrictions are designed primarily to protect creditors, who otherwise might be in a precarious position because neither stockholders nor directors are liable for debts of the corporation.

Generally, the laws provide that dividends may not be paid "out of capital" but can only be paid "out of earnings." The rule's interpretation varies among jurisdictions. "Capital" is frequently defined to be equal to the total amount paid in by stockholders. In some jurisdictions, however, "capital" is defined to be the amount shown in the Capital Stock account so that the amount in the Additional Paid-in Capital account may be used for dividend declarations. In other states, the corporation must indicate a certain amount of stated capital below which stockholders' equity may not be reduced through dividend payments. This stated capital amount may be less than the total paid-in capital. In some jurisdictions dividends may be declared out of the earnings of the current period even though there is an accumulated deficit from previous periods. There are other specialized features and variations among the state statutes.

These legal restrictions have little influence upon the accounting for stockholders' equity, net income, and dividends. A balance sheet does not purport to spell out all the legal niceties of amounts available for dividends, but it should seek to provide information necessary for the user to apply the legal rules of the state in which the business is incorporated. For example, if stated capital is an important figure, its amount should be indicated either by showing the total of its components or by a parenthetical notation. The state statute may provide that "treasury stock may be acquired only with retained earnings." If so and if shares of stock are reacquired by the issuing corporation, the amount of this restriction should be indicated by a footnote to the balance sheet. It would be possible to show this restriction in more formal fashion by setting up a special account and making the following entry:

Retained Earnings	450,000	
Retained Earnings Restricted by Acquisition of Treasury Stock		450,000

Formal entries restricting retained earnings for treasury stock acquisitions were once common but are now rarely found. Whatever the method of noting the restriction, it is of course necessary to record the acquisition of the treasury shares by the entry:

Treasury Stock	450,000	
Cash		450,000

Contractual Limitations upon Dividends

Contracts with bondholders or preferred stockholders often place restrictions upon dividend payments and thereby compel the retention of earnings. For example, a recent balance sheet of the Caterpillar Tractor Company contains the following footnote:

> There are varying restrictions on the payment of cash dividends under the indentures relating to the long-term debt . . . . Under the terms of the most restrictive indenture, approximately $300 million of profit employed in the business was not available for the payment of dividends.

Another example can be found in a recent balance sheet of the Champion Spark Plug Company. A footnote reads:

> The [bond] indenture restricts the amount of retained earnings available for the distribution of cash dividends. The unrestricted portion of consolidated retained earnings which can be distributed as dividends amounted to $127,000,000 [at year end].

The restrictions which may be imposed by preferred-stock contracts are illustrated by the following note from a statement of the National Gypsum Company.

> The terms of outstanding promissory notes and the $4.50 Cumulative Preferred Stock limit the payment of dividends (other than stock dividends) and the purchase or redemption of the company's issued capital stock. Under the most restrictive provisions, retained earnings of $39,628,000 were available for either the payment of dividends or the acquisition of capital stock. An additional $15,384,000 was available only for the acquisition of capital stock.

Bond contracts often provide that the retirement of the obligation, either by means of a sinking fund or by serial payments, shall be made "out of earnings." Such a provision involves curtailing dividends so that the necessary deposits or payments can be made without disturbing the normal cash requirements of the business. The policy does not in any sense use up earnings. The result is merely to force the stockholders to increase their investment in the business by restricting their dividends.

For example, assume that the indenture of a bond issue of $1,000,000 requires the issuing corporation to accumulate a sinking fund at the rate of $100,000 a year. Each year an entry must be made to record the deposit in the fund:

Bond Sinking Fund	100,000	
Cash in Bank		100,000

If, in addition, the indenture requires that the sinking fund payments be made "out of earnings," the following annual entry might also be made:

Retained Earnings	100,000	
Retained Earnings Appropriated for Bond Sinking Fund		100,000

(Another title sometimes used for the appropriated retained earnings account is Reserve for Sinking Fund. We think that it would be better if the word *reserve* never appeared in a balance sheet account title. If it is used at all *reserve* should be restricted to accounts indicating appropriated retained earnings, as above.) The entry does not reduce the amount of total retained earnings; the Retained Earnings Appropriated for Bond Sinking Fund account is a part of the total retained earnings of the firm and it appears in the retained earnings section of the balance sheet.

When the bonds come due, they are paid out of the sinking fund or the proceeds of the sale of the assets in which the fund may have been invested. The entry would be:

Bonds Payable	1,000,000	
Bond Sinking Fund		1,000,000

Then it is necessary to dispose of the Retained Earnings Appropriated for Bond Sinking Fund account, which has not been affected by the payment of the bonds. Since the terms of the bond contract have been met, the amount could be transferred back to the Retained Earnings account. However, the amount of cash available for dividend distribution has not been increased, and it might be misleading to show a sharp rise in unrestricted retained earnings under such circumstances. This portion of retained earnings could be transferred to a permanent or "stated" capital category by the declaration of a *stock dividend,* explained below. The accountant, however, must wait for some decision on the part of the directors or management before making any disposition of the Retained Earnings Appropriated for Bond Sinking Fund account. The question is not primarily one of accounting analysis.

Financial Restrictions on Dividends

Dividends are seldom declared up to the limit of the amount legally available for distribution. The principal reasons why the directors may decide to allow the retained earnings to increase as a matter of financial policy are:

1. The earnings may not be reflected in a corresponding increase of available cash.

2. A restriction of dividends in prosperous years may permit the payment of dividends in poor years.
3. Funds may be needed for expansion of plant and equipment.
4. It may be considered desirable to reduce the amount of indebtedness rather than declare all or most of the net income in dividends.
5. It may be desirable to put the corporation into better financial position so that it will be less vulnerable to unexpected losses and contingencies.

Earnings Are Not Cash

Earlier in the chapter it was emphasized that net income does not represent a fund of available cash. It is quite possible, then, that the directors might decide that although there were ample earnings, either current or accumulated, cash could not be spared for dividends equal to the net income of the period. Such factors as maturing bank loans, a rise in the price of merchandise which would increase the investment in the inventory, or the need for new machinery could easily consume all available cash in spite of substantial profits. The statement of changes in financial position, discussed in Chapter 19, helps the reader understand how earnings, and other sources of funds, have been used during the year.

Equalization of Dividends

Many stockholders of corporations prefer to receive a regular minimum cash return. In order to accommodate such stockholders and in order to create a general impression of stability of the corporation, directors commonly attempt to declare a regular dividend which they try to maintain through good years and bad. When earnings and finances permit, they may declare "extra" dividends.

The legal requirements for declaring regular dividends can be met by retaining part of income over several periods to build up a balance in retained earnings. Such a policy, however, does not mean that a fund of cash will always be available for the regular dividends. Managing cash is a specialized problem of corporate finance; cash for dividends must be anticipated just as well as cash for the purchase of equipment, the retirement of debts, and so on. For example, borrowing from the bank to pay the regular dividend is unobjectionable provided the corporation's financial condition justifies an increase in liabilities.

Equalizing dividends does not lead to special accounting problems. The usual entries for the declaration and payment of dividends are made. Studying the accounts will not usually indicate whether or not the board of directors plans to distribute dividends regularly.

Financing Expansion

Many corporations have financed substantial increases in their plant and equipment without issuing bonds or additional shares of stock. Funds that are not paid out as dividends may be used to acquire additional plant facilities. Increased retained earnings cannot be associated with any particular item or group of items in the balance sheet, but it can be appropriate to say that expansion has been financed "out of" or through the retention of earnings.

From the corporation's standpoint, the overall financial result is the same as when a substantial amount of cash has been distributed as dividends and an equal amount of cash has been obtained through issuing additional shares of stock. It has, however, saved the trouble and cost of obtaining subscriptions and issuing the additional stock certificates. Stockholders who want to maintain their proportion of ownership in a growing firm will prefer a policy that restricts dividends in order to finance expansion, because if larger dividends are issued they will use them to buy an equivalent amount of the new shares issued to finance the expansion. Such stockholders will be saved one set of income taxes because if the corporation pays dividends, the stockholder must pay income taxes on his receipts before he can reinvest them. If the funds are reinvested directly by the corporation, there is a saving in personal income taxes.

Other stockholders want a steady flow of cash and are unable, for contractual or psychological reasons, to sell a portion of their shares to raise the wanted cash if regular dividends are not declared. Such stockholders will resent being forced to reinvest in the corporation when expansion is financed out of retained earnings. They may seek to force the board of directors to adopt a more liberal dividend policy. The degree to which expansion should be financed out of earnings is basically a problem of managerial finance, not accounting. Recent research in finance suggests that, within wide limits, what a firm does makes little difference so long as it tends to follow the same policy over time. Stockholders who want earnings reinvested can buy shares of firms that finance expansion with earnings, while others who want a steady flow of cash can buy shares of firms that pay out earnings in dividends.

Financing expansion out of earnings does not require special accounting entries. Since dividends have not been declared in the full amount of net income, the balance in the Retained Earnings account has been growing. Acquisition of new assets is recorded in the usual manner. Building up resources available for expansion may be accomplished by depositing cash in a special *expansion*, or *replacement*, *fund* to make sure funds will be available when needed. Corresponding portions of the Retained Earnings account might be transferred to a special account to show more clearly the policy being followed by the board of directors. An appropriate title for such an account, if used, would be Retained Earnings Appropriated for Expansion, but the misleading title Reserve for Expansion has been used for this purpose. (A reserve is never a fund of cash or other assets, but in this context, merely represents appropriated retained earnings.)

Suppose, for example, that the directors of a corporation decide to provide for a $1,000,000 plant addition at the end of a five-year period and pass a resolution to "set up an expansion fund out of profits at the

rate of $200,000 a year for five years beginning December 31, 1975."
This resolution requires at least two steps each year. First, $200,000
a year must be deposited in a special fund, which is either kept in the
form of a separate bank account or invested in marketable securities. Second, if the fund is indeed to be "out of profits," the balance of the Retained
Earnings account must be allowed to increase by at least $200,000 a year.
(Thus, dividends declared during a year cannot be larger than earnings
in excess of $200,000.) A third step would be optional: $200,000 of the
annual increase in retained earnings could be transferred to a Retained
Earnings Appropriated for Expansion account. The last step is rarely taken.

Voluntary Reduction of Indebtedness

Contractual arrangements for reducing long-term debt may impose legal
restrictions on the directors' dividend-paying powers. Even though there
is no contractual obligation to do so, the directors may decide to reduce
the amount of the liabilities and to obtain funds for this purpose by
refraining from paying dividends. No new accounting problems are involved.
No special entries or accounts are required, since the balance of the Retained Earnings account is allowed to increase by the required amount.
A special account, under a title such as Retained Earnings Appropriated
for Reduction of Debt, can be used if it is felt that it will contribute to an
understanding of the policy being followed.

Appropriations for Contingencies

Up to this point we have described several accounts with titles of the
form "Retained Earnings Appropriated for . . ." and their purpose. The
earmarking or appropriation of retained earnings is illogical unless all
retained earnings are marked with their purpose—a policy which is neither
practical nor desirable. Earmarking retained earnings has no purpose that
cannot be accomplished in an alternative manner. For example, the following entry reflects an actual transaction of financial significance.

Bond Sinking Fund	100,000	
Cash		100,000

The following entry, which may accompany it, accomplishes nothing:

Retained Earnings	100,000	
Retained Earnings Appropriated for Sinking Fund		100,000

Bond indentures can restrict dividends without requiring an appropriation
of retained earnings. In our opinion, appropriation of retained earnings is
without merit. Nevertheless some firms persist in appropriating earnings,
and the reader should understand the accounting process involved as well
as its lack of meaning.

Retained earnings appropriations that are not accompanied by a
corresponding earmarking of cash are especially questionable. A firm may
restrict its dividends because management thinks that a provision should be

made for contingencies or for unexpected or unpredictable catastrophic losses. This procedure may be formalized by creating a balance in a Retained Earnings Appropriated for Contingencies account (sometimes misleadingly called Reserve for Contingencies) by transfer entries from the Retained Earnings account. The entry is:

```
Retained Earnings ........................................  75,000
    Retained Earnings Appropriated for Contingencies ........    75,000
```

This entry does not imply that a fund of assets has been set aside. The balance of such an account is a part of the total retained earnings of the corporation.

Such a step by itself cannot help the corporation finance losses when they occur. A *contingency fund* is the only way in which adequate protection can be provided. Appropriated retained earnings may be invested in plant assets just as unappropriated retained earnings. Funds may have to be borrowed to pay for losses and damages even in the presence of a large appropriation for contingencies. It is true that, if a portion of net income is retained, net assets will be larger than if all of the net income had been declared as dividends, and that, therefore, the corporation will be in a better position to borrow funds. Not paying dividends, rather than appropriating retained earnings, accomplishes this purpose.

When an unexpected loss occurs, the entry should be made as though no special account had been created. For example, if the firm suffers a flood loss amounting to $75,000, the entry should be:

```
Loss from Flood Damage ...................................  75,000
    Building (Net) .........................................    50,000
    Equipment (Net) .......................................    25,000
    To record loss of assets by flood.
```

When the Loss account is closed to income at the end of the period, Retained Earnings will be reduced by $75,000 (ignoring income tax effects). If it is felt that this is the type of loss for which the Retained Earnings Appropriated for Contingencies account had been created, $75,000 can be transferred from that account back to the Retained Earnings account so that the amount presumed to be available for dividends will not be affected by the loss which has been suffered.

```
Retained Earnings Appropriated for Contingencies ............  75,000
    Retained Earnings .....................................    75,000
```

Notice that the loss is no less harmful because retained earnings had been appropriated.

In general, creating special contingency accounts as described in the preceding paragraphs may confuse the average person inspecting a balance sheet. He is not apt to be aware of the significance of the account Retained Earnings Appropriated for Contingencies (or, Reserve for Contingencies) and may easily draw unwarranted conclusions from such a presentation. As we stated before, refraining from declaring the entire net income as dividends accomplishes the desired purpose. Special retained earnings accounts are not needed in order to do so.

Balance Sheet Presentation
of Retained Earnings Appropriations

The following illustrative retained earnings section of a balance sheet demonstrates one proper presentation of the restrictions and appropriations of retained earnings considered in this chapter. When such appropriations are made, the Retained Earnings account could well be called Unappropriated Retained Earnings.

Retained Earnings:
Unappropriated Retained Earnings (Note 1) $329,434
Appropriations of Retained Earnings:
Appropriated for Bond Sinking Fund ..... $ 80,000
Appropriated for Expansion 40,000
Appropriated for Contingencies 150,000

Total Retained Earnings Appropriations 270,000

Total Retained Earnings $599,434
Note 1.   The retained earnings are legally restricted as to declaration of dividends by the amount of $16,000, representing the cost of 200 shares of common stock reacquired and held in the treasury.

This balance sheet presentation illustrates our criticism of the policy of appropriating retained earnings. Readers of the balance sheet may wonder why, if appropriations have been made for such a variety of purposes, a balance in *unappropriated* retained earnings has been permitted to accumulate. Unless all, or nearly all, of the retained earnings balance is appropriated, appropriations will not help clarify the corporation's dividend and other financial policies. Any effort to appropriate all of the retained earnings balance is likely to produce such a multitude of accounts as to be confusing.

The criticism of appropriations of retained earnings is even more forceful when the appropriations are disguised under misleading "reserve" titles and when they are shown in a catch-all reserve section of the balance sheet between liabilities and stockholders' equity. One of the most objectionable features of many published balance sheets has been the inclusion of a group of retained earnings appropriations and estimated liabilities (such as Reserve for Employees' Benefits) in a separate reserve section. All that these accounts have in common is the objectionable use of the term *reserve* in their titles. Both the use of the *reserve* title and the inclusion of a reserve section in the balance sheet have been declining in recent years. *Reserve* is always the name for an account with a normal credit balance—an asset contra, an estimated liability, or appropriated retained earnings. Reserves are never assets.

Stock Dividends

The previous sections have indicated that through the retention of earnings there may be substantial increases in the amount of stockholders' equity that is more or less permanently committed to the business. To indicate such a permanent commitment of reinvested earnings, a *stock dividend* may be issued. When a stock dividend is issued, stockholders receive additional shares of stock in proportion to their existing holdings without making any additional contributions. If a 20-percent stock dividend is issued, each stockholder receives one additional share for every five shares he held before the dividend. In the accounts, a stock dividend requires a transfer from retained earnings to capital stock accounts. Generally accepted accounting principles require that the transfer from retained earnings be charged at the market value of the shares issued. For example, the directors of a corporation decide to issue a stock dividend of 5,000 additional shares of common stock with a par value of $10 per share at a time when the market price of a share is $130. The entry would be:

Retained Earnings	650,000	
Common Stock—Par		50,000
Additional Paid-in Capital		600,000

The most significant internal effect of the stock dividend is to convert a portion of the stockholders' equity which had been legally available for dividend declarations to a more permanent form of capital. A stock dividend logically shows that the funds, represented by past earnings, have been invested in plant expansion, have been used to replace assets at higher price levels, have been used to retire bonds or other debt and are therefore unavailable for cash dividend declarations.

A stockholder should not feel particularly gratified upon receiving a stock dividend. If the shares are of the same type that he held before, his proportionate interest in the capital of the corporation and his proportionate voting power have not changed. The book value per share (total capital divided by number of shares outstanding) will have decreased, but the total book value of his holdings will remain unchanged since he now holds a proportionately larger number of shares. The market value per share will decline, but, all else equal, the total market value of the stockholder's holdings will not change. The stockholder cannot dispose of the additional shares without affecting his proportionate interest in the corporation, and he could have achieved that result by selling a portion of his original holdings. To describe such a distribution of shares as a "dividend" is, therefore, misleading but is, nevertheless, common practice.

If the stockholder receives shares of a different type from those he held before, the situation may be slightly different. For example, if a corporation has preferred stock outstanding and issues preferred shares to common stockholders as a stock dividend, it alters the position of the common stockholders in relation to the preferred stockholders. Similarly, issuing common shares to preferred stockholders alters the relative position of the two classes of stockholders.

If a corporation issues shares of stock in another unrelated corporation to its stockholders as a dividend, such a distribution is not a stock dividend.

It is described as a *dividend in kind* or a *property dividend.* Another example of a dividend in kind would be a distribution of a corporation's products to its shareholders as a dividend.

Stock Splits

A stock split (or, more technically, *split-up*) is similar to a stock dividend. Additional shares of stock are issued to shareholders in proportion to existing holdings. No additional capital is raised and assets are unaffected. In a stock split the par or stated value of all the stock in the issued class is reduced in proportion to the additional shares issued. A corporation may, for example, have 1,000 shares of $100 par-value stock outstanding, and by a stock split exchange those shares for 2,000 shares of $50 par-value stock (a two-for-one split), or 4,000 shares of $25 par-value stock (a four-for-one split), or any number of shares of no-par stock. If the stock outstanding has no par nor stated value, the shareholders are merely issued additional stock certificates.

A stock split does not require a journal entry. The retained earnings are not reduced. The amount shown in the capital stock account is merely represented by a larger number of shares. Of course, it is necessary to record the additional number of shares held by each stockholder in the subsidiary capital stock ledger.

It is customary to limit stock dividends to 20 percent (that is, one share for every five shares held) or less. Distributions in a greater ratio are usually accounted for as stock splits.

A stock split or a stock dividend usually reduces the market value per share, all other factors remaining constant, in inverse proportion to the split or dividend. Thus a two-for-one split could be expected to result in a 50-percent reduction in the market price per share. Stock splits and stock dividends have, therefore, usually been used to prevent the market price per share from rising to a price level unacceptable to management. For example, if management feels that a market price of $30 to $40 is an effective trading range for its stock (this is purely a subjective estimate, and is almost never supported by firm evidence) and its stock has risen to $60 in the market, it may declare a two-for-one split. Stock splits and stock dividends are seldom, if ever, used by corporations whose stocks are not traded on a stock exchange or in an over-the-counter market.

Stock Options

Stock options are often a part of employee compensation plans. Under such plans, employees are granted an option to purchase, at some time within a specified number of years in the future, shares in their company at a specified price, usually the market price of the stock on the day the option is granted. Frequently, shares acquired through exercise of stock options must be held for a certain length of time before they can be sold.

Stock option plans are *qualified* if they meet requirements that make the options nontaxable at time of exercise to the recipient-employee. Stock options present two kinds of accounting problems: (1) recording the granting of the option and (2) recording its exercise or lapse.[1]

Granting the Option. The generally accepted accounting treatment[2] of options usually results in no entry being made at the time the options are issued. If the exercise price is equal to the market price at the date the option is granted, the prevailing view is that the grant of the option does not result in compensation to the employee or expense to the employer. A better treatment, but one not generally acceptable, would be to record the granting of an option as the compensation expense that it is. Although pricing such options is difficult, recently created public options markets may give some clues about appropriate valuations. In any case, valuation at zero is inappropriate. If, at the time an option was granted, the market value of that option were quantified at $7,500, the entry would be:

Salary Expense	7,500	
Capital Contributed in Excess of Par (or Stated) Value		7,500

Generally accepted accounting principles require that the terms of options granted, outstanding, and exercised during a period be disclosed in text or notes accompanying the financial statements. The notes of the financial statements issued by the General Electric Company shown at the end of Chapter 25 (page 41 of the report) provide an illustration of such disclosure. Notice the commendable inclusion of the average exercise price. Many published statements omit this useful information.

Exercise or Lapse. When the option is exercised, the conventional entry is made to treat the transaction simply as an issue of stock at the option price. The credit will be to Capital Stock and, usually, to Capital Contributed in Excess of Par Value. If the option lapses or expires without being exercised, there would be no entry.

Stock options are designed to attract and retain qualified employees. Salary increases for well-paid executives can be largely absorbed by personal income taxes. Stock options may provide an opportunity for management personnel to obtain long-term capital gains that are taxed at lower rates than ordinary income. Stockholders, though, may have mixed feelings about stock option plans. Options can result in higher reported corporate income if they are granted in lieu of salary increments for employees, because no explicit salary expense is recorded. Moreover, options may provide special motivation to executives who hold them. Yet when options are exercised, the equity of existing stockholders is reduced, or diluted,

---

[1] Do not confuse stock options with the put-and-call options traded in various public exchanges. Such put-and-call options do not require any accounting entries by the company whose stock is involved.

[2] Opinion No. 25, Accounting Principles Board, AICPA, issued in October, 1972.

because the price at exercise date is less than the current market price. (If the exercise price were not lower than current market price, the options would not be exercised.)

Stock Rights and Warrants

In addition to stock options, opportunities to buy shares can be granted through stock rights and warrants. While both are similar to options, some distinctions exist. Stock options are limited to employees, are nontransferable, and are a form of compensation. In contrast, both stock rights and warrants are usually transferable and thus can be traded in public markets. Both rights and warrants are associated with attempts to raise new capital for the firm.

Stock warrants entitle the owner to purchase shares of the company stock at a specified price. Warrants are generally exercisable for a limited period, but occasionally are good indefinitely. A *stock right* entitles its holder to subscribe to some portion of a capital stock issued by a corporation, often at a price less than market value of the issue. Stock rights must be exercised within a specified time, generally less than three months. Stock rights, unlike warrants, have short exercise periods and are restricted to new issues.

Journal entries are usually not necessary when stock rights or warrants are granted. In the rare case where the issuing corporation sells the warrants or rights, the entry would be:

Cash	15,000	
Capital Contributed in Excess of Par (or Stated) Value		15,000

When rights or warrants are exercised, the entry is like the one to record the issue of new shares at whatever price is paid. The amounts and terms of outstanding rights and warrants should be disclosed in the notes of the financial statements.

QUESTIONS AND PROBLEMS

1. There are no legal restrictions upon the amount of proprietary withdrawals of a partnership, but all state corporation laws place limitations upon the power of the directors of a corporation to declare dividends. How do you explain this difference in legal treatment?

2. A partner had a balance in his capital account of $15,000 on January 1. During the year, he made withdrawals of $500 on March 1, $1,000 on May 1, and $500 on October 15. He invested an additional $1,500 on August 1. What was his average invested capital during the year?

*3. The partnership agreement of Durance and Sinn provides for the following sharing of profits and losses each year:

* Hints, key numbers, or (partial) answers appear in the back of the book between the Appendix Tables and the Glossary.

(1) Each partner will be credited with a salary allowance of $10,000.

(2) The balance of net income will be distributed in proportion to the average capital balance of each partner.

The partners' capital accounts for 1975 appear as follows:

B. Y. Durance, Capital				O. T. Sinn, Capital			
3/31/75	1,000	1/1/75	20,000	6/1/75	400	1/1/75	10,000
		8/1/75	600			11/30/75	2,800
		11/1/75	3,000				

The net income for 1975 amounted to $32,000. Calculate the amount that will be credited to each partner's capital account.

4. The net income of the firm of Donald, Marvin and Patron for the year 1975 is $54,000. The partnership agreement provides that the net profits shall be divided in the following manner:

   (1) Interest at 8 percent per annum on the average investment of each partner during the year shall be computed and credited to their respective capital accounts.

   (2) The partners' capital accounts shall be credited with a special salary allowance as follows: Donald, $30,000; Marvin, $20,000; Patron, $10,000.

   (3) The balance of the net income or loss shall be divided equally among the partners' capital accounts.

The capital accounts of the partners show the following data:

	Donald	Marvin	Patron
Balance, January 1, 1975	$20,000	$10,000	$10,000
Withdrawals, June 30, 1975	(10,000)	(4,000)	(6,000)
Invested, September 30, 1975		4,000	4,000
Balance December 31, 1975 before distributing income for 1975	$10,000	$10,000	$ 8,000

Calculate and present in a schedule the division of the net income among the three partners. Neither partners' salaries nor interest on capital contributions are treated as expenses in the determination of net income.

5. A certain corporation retained almost all of its earnings, only rarely paying a cash dividend. When some of the stockholders objected, the reply of the chairman of the board of directors was: "Why do you want cash dividends? You would just have to go to the trouble of reinvesting them and where can you find a better investment than our own company?" Comment.

6. "So confident were G. E.'s new chairman and president . . . last week, that they boldly confronted the one big licking G. E. may have to take. . . . This is on the $56,200,000 worth of G. E. property abroad, of which $29,100,000 worth is outside the Western Hemisphere. G. E.'s reserves, they said, not counting its $124,310,000 earned surplus, are big enough to permit a write-off of the whole extrahemispheric investment." (From comments on General Electric in *Time*, August 5, 1940.)

   Explain carefully how the presence of large surplus reserves or a large balance of earned surplus (retained earnings) eases the blow of having to write off investments in foreign properties. Or does it?

7. Compare the position of a stockholder who receives a cash dividend with one who receives a stock dividend.

8. Explain whether each of the following increases, decreases, has no effect on (1) the Retained Earnings account and (2) the total retained earnings of a corporation:
   a. a cash dividend
   b. a stock dividend
   c. an investment of $30,000 in government bonds
   d. the deposit of $4,000 with a sinking fund trustee
   e. the setting up of a sinking fund reserve
   f. the payment of a bond issue for which a sinking fund had been set up, and for which a sinking fund reserve had been created
   g. the payment of a bond issue for which no sinking fund had been set up, but for which a sinking fund reserve had been created
   h. an uninsured fire loss
   i. the issuance of stock above par value
   j. the sale of a bond issue below face value
   k. the creation of an expansion fund with an equal amount being transferred to a Reserve for Expansion
   l. the retirement of a bond issue at more than its book value.

9. The Taleb Corporation shows a Retained Earnings Appropriated for Expansion account with a balance of $750,000 on its books, but the directors state that the corporation is unable to buy a plant costing that amount with the cash resources on hand. Is this a reasonable possibility? Explain.

10. At the 1976 stockholders' meeting, the president of the Santa Cris Corporation made the following statement: "The net income for the year, after taxes, was $1,096,000. The directors have decided that the corporation can only afford to distribute $500,000 as a cash dividend." Are the two sentences of this statement compatible?

*11. Gordon and Ginn are partners with capital balances of $90,000 and $120,000, respectively, on January 1, 1975. Their partnership agreement provides:
   (1) Salaries are to be allowed to Gordon, $15,000 per year; to Ginn, $14,000 per year.
   (2) Each partner is to be credited with an interest allowance at the rate of 8 percent per annum on his capital balance at the beginning of the year.
   (3) The balance of profits or losses is to be distributed 60 percent to Gordon and 40 percent to Ginn.
   During 1975, both partners drew their full salary allowances. What would the balances in the partners' capital accounts be at December 31, 1975, under the following alternative conditions? Assume that net income figures are calculated before salary and interest allowances are deducted.
   a. net income during 1975 was $30,000
   b. net income during 1975 was $70,000
   c. net income during 1975 was $120,000.

*12. The partnership agreement of partners Graff, Morton and Soudon provided that income and losses are to be shared as follows: Each partner is to be credited with 8 percent of his average capital balance during the year;

Graff is to be credited with a salary allowance of $14,000 per annum; the residual income and losses are to be shared equally. During 1975, the average balances in the capital accounts of Graff, Morton and Soudon were $20,000, $30,000 and $50,000, respectively. Graff's salary is not treated as an expense in the determination of net income. Assume that net income figures are calculated before salary and interest allowances are deducted.

a. If net income for 1975 was $40,000, what was Soudon's share of residual profits?

b. If net income for 1975 was $40,000, what was Graff's total share?

c. If net income for 1975 was $15,000, what was Soudon's total share?

d. If net income for 1975 was $15,000, what was Graff's total share?

e. If net income for 1975 was $9,500, what was Morton's total share?

f. What was the partnership net income for 1975 if Soudon's total share was $9,500?

g. What was the partnership net income for 1975 if Graff's total share was $13,000?

13. Indicate whether each of the following statements is true or false.

a. Cash dividends reduce the book value per share of capital stock.

b. If a corporation has set up a reserve for contingencies, it can absorb losses with less difficulty than if the same amount is carried in the Retained Earnings account.

c. The allocation of partnership income is governed by the terms of the partnership agreement.

d. A stock dividend does not affect the Retained Earnings account.

e. The "investment of 50 percent of the profits in government bonds" has no effect upon the amount legally available for dividends.

f. The act of retiring bonds does not in itself change the amount in the "reserve for bond retirement."

g. If a partnership is regarded as a separate legal business entity, partners' salaries are treated as expenses.

h. A corporation can replace property destroyed by fire out of an "insurance reserve."

i. There is usually a depreciation fund to match the depreciation reserve.

j. Most of the statutory limitations on the right of directors to declare dividends are designed for the protection of corporate creditors.

14. At a meeting of a board of directors, the financing of a proposed plant expansion is being discussed. One director suggests that a bond issue should be used. A second director points out that the last balance sheet showed a contingency reserve, a depreciation reserve, a reserve for expansion, an investment in marketable securities, and a balance in retained earnings, any one of which would provide for the necessary expenditure without borrowing any money. Comment on the remarks of the second director.

15. Journalize the following transactions:

(1) A cash dividend of $2 a share is declared on the outstanding preferred stock. There are 5,000 shares authorized, 3,000 shares issued, 1,000 shares subscribed but not fully paid or issued, and 100 shares reacquired and held in the treasury.

(2) A cash dividend of $1 a share is declared on the no-par common stock of which there are 10,000 shares authorized, 7,000 shares issued, and 1,000 shares reacquired and held in the treasury.

(3) The dividend on the preferred stock is paid.

(4) The dividend on the common stock is paid.

16. Indicate whether each of the following statements is true or false:

   a. The building up of a sinking fund does not in itself affect the balance of Retained Earnings.

   b. Restrictions of retained earnings resulting from acquisition of treasury stock are often shown in a note to the balance sheet.

   c. Stock dividends reduce the book value per share of capital stock.

   d. The declaration of a cash dividend does not reduce the amount of the stockholders' equity.

   e. The distribution of a stock dividend tends to reduce the market value per share of capital stock.

   f. A stock split does not affect the Retained Earnings account.

   g. A reduction of indebtedness "out of profits" reduces the amount of the the stockholders' equity.

   h. A stock-dividend declaration is usually accompanied by a reduction in par or stated value per share.

   i. Declaration and payment of a stock dividend does not affect the amount of stockholders' equity.

   j. The increase in the balance of the Accumulated Depreciation account has the same effect upon available funds as a growth in the balance of the Reserve for Contingencies account.

17. Indicate the effect of each of the following transactions upon (1) the balance in the Retained Earnings account, (2) the total of retained earnings, and (3) the total stockholders' equity.

   a. Bonds are issued at a discount.

   b. A check is written to the Internal Revenue Service for additional income taxes levied on past years' income (no previous entry).

   c. A stock split is voted by the directors. The par value per share is reduced from $200 to $50 and each shareholder is given four new shares in exchange for each old share.

   d. The manager is voted a bonus of $3,500 by the directors.

   e. Notes payable in the face amount of $50,000 are paid by check.

   f. An addition is made to the reserve for expansion.

   g. A dividend in preferred stock is issued to common stockholders (no previous entry).

   h. Securities held as an investment are sold at book value.

   i. A building site is donated to the company by the local chamber of commerce.

   j. A building is sold for less than its book value.

   k. An uninsured fire loss occurs and is charged against the reserve for contingencies.

   l. New machinery costing $280,000 is purchased out of an expansion fund accumulated for such a purpose. A corresponding reserve for expansion is transferred to retained earnings.

18. At a meeting of the board of directors of the Norris Corporation, the question of handling the sinking-fund requirements of a bond issue is being

discussed. The controller of the company offers a resolution whereby the required semiannual sinking-fund deposit is to be made with the Saving and Trust Company and an appropriation of retained earnings is to be built up in an amount equal to the sinking fund. The following objections are raised to the plan. Discuss each one, and indicate your agreement or disagreement.

a. The setting up of both the sinking fund and the appropriation of retained earnings will create a double charge against the net income of the company.

b. The plan will result in an incorrect showing of net income.

c. The use of a retained earnings appropriation will reduce the balance of retained earnings available for dividends.

d. The use of a retained earnings appropriation will reduce the stockholders' equity and thereby injure the firm's credit position.

e. Making the appropriation of retained earnings is a useless bit of procedure having no effect on the company's actions.

19. Give journal entries for the following transactions. Retained earnings appropriations are made whenever funds are required to be built up "out of earnings."

   *(1) Outstanding shares of stock are acquired by the issuing corporation at a cost of $500,000. Under the laws of the state involved, treasury stock can only be acquired "out of earnings."

   (2) The reserve for contingencies is increased by $200,000.

   (3) A deposit of $100,000 is made in a bond-retirement fund. Under the provisions of the bond indenture, this fund is to be set up "out of earnings."

   (4) Dividends are declared on preferred stock, $120,000.

   (5) A dividend is paid to common stockholders consisting of shares of preferred stock in the same corporation with a par value of $200,000.

   (6) A dividend is paid to common stockholders consisting of shares of no-par common stock in the same corporation. The amount assigned to these shares of stock is $600,000.

   (7) A building is purchased out of an expansion fund accumulated for such a purpose. A corresponding "reserve for expansion" is transferred to retained earnings. The amount involved in each case is $350,000.

   (8) The building is mortgaged for $100,000, and this amount is distributed to the common stockholders as a cash dividend.

20. Give journal entries, if required, for the following transactions which are unrelated unless otherwise specified:

   *(1) The regular quarterly dividend is declared on the 5-percent, $100 par-value preferred stock. There are 10,000 shares authorized, 8,000 shares issued, and 1,600 shares reacquired and held in the treasury.

   (2) The dividend on the preferred stock [see (1)] is paid.

   (3) A customer, who was injured in a fall on the company's property, is awarded $20,000 in his suit against the company. The directors vote to charge the payment to the reserve for contingencies.

   (4) A deposit of $200,000 is made in a sinking fund for bond repayment. The bond indenture provides that "the fund is to be set up out of earnings."

(5) A stock dividend of $250,000 of common stock is issued to common stockholders.

(6) A building replacement fund of $125,000 is created. The fund is to be used to purchase a new building when the present one becomes inadequate.

(7) Bonds of $500,000 are retired out of the sinking fund created for that purpose.

(8) The shares of no-par stock of the corporation are selling on the market at $300 a share. In order to bring the market value down to a more popular figure and thereby increase the distribution of its stock-holdings, the board of directors votes to issue four extra shares to stockholders for each share already held by them. The shares are issued.

21. The following transactions all relate to the same set of records. Use the straight-line method for amortizing bond discount and premium.

   *(1) The company issues 23,000 shares of common stock (par value, $100 per share) for cash at $105 per share.

   *(2) A twenty-year, 8-percent bond issue for $500,000 is issued for $492,000.

   *(3) Interest expense on the bond is recognized at the time the first semi-annual interest payment is made.

   (4) The bond indenture requires a sinking fund to be built up to pay the principal of the bonds at maturity. The company deposits $18,600 with the sinking-fund trustee.

   (5) A sinking-fund reserve, equal in amount to the sinking fund, is created.

   (6) A cash dividend of $2 per share of common stock is declared.

   (7) A reserve for contingencies of $100,000 is created.

   (8) The company's warehouse is flooded, and a loss of $19,000 results from damage to merchandise stored there. This is the type of situation that was envisaged when the reserve for contingencies was established. The company does not have flood insurance.

   *(9) At the end of the twentieth year of the life of the bonds, the final semiannual interest payment is made and the bonds are retired. There are sufficient funds in the sinking fund to accomplish the retirement.

 (10) A stock dividend is issued to dispose of the sinking-fund reserve, the balance of which is $500,000. The company issues 5,000 shares.

 (11) A fund of $50,000 is created for future expansion.

   *(12) An additional 7,000 shares of common stock are issued for cash at $110 a share.

Journalize the above transactions.

*22. The comparative balance sheet of the Forty-Misty Company shows the following data:

	Dec. 31, 1975	Dec. 31, 1976
Common Stock	$1,200,000	$1,320,000
Retained Earnings	460,000	400,000

During 1976, common stockholders received $50,000 in cash dividends and $120,000 stock dividends. A refund on 1974 taxes of $30,000 was received on March 1, 1976, and was credited to Retained Earnings. A loss on retirement of plant assets of $5,600 occurred during the year and was incorrectly charged to Retained Earnings.

What was the net income reported to stockholders for 1976? Show your calculations.

23. On April 15, 1974, the Easton Corporation issued 50,000 shares of no-par, convertible preferred stock at an issue price of $110. All shares were paid for in cash. Each share of these preferred stocks offers $7 per year in dividends and can be converted into 5 shares of common stock (par value, $10 a share). After two extremely profitable years, all shares of preferred were converted into common shares at the end of the fourth quarter of 1976. Other data are as follows.

Market prices for	April 15, 1974	December 31, 1976
Easton common stock	$ 22	$ 44
Easton $7 preferred stock	110	220
Book value for Easton common share		
(before conversion of preferred)	30	35

*a. Prepare journal entries to record the issuance and conversion of the preferred stock.

b. Explain briefly the effect of the conversion on book values and earnings per common share. Assume one millon shares of common outstanding and earnings of $3 per share before conversion; that is, net income for 1976 was $3 million.

c. What was the effect of the conversion of the preferred shares into common stock on the common shareholder's equity? Explain briefly.

24. The following transactions do not all relate to the same set of records.
   (1) The shares of no-par stock of a corporation are selling on the market at $200 a share. In order to bring the market value down to a more popular figure and thereby increase the distribution of its stock holdings, the board of directors votes to issue five shares to stockholders in exchange for each share already held by them. The shares are issued.
   (2) The treasurer of the corporation reports that cash on hand exceeds normal requirements by $200,000. Pending a decision by the board of directors on the final disposition of the funds, investments in marketable securities in the amount of $198,640 are made.
   (3) The net income for the year is $150,000. The directors vote to issue 500 shares of 6-percent, $15 par value preferred stock as a stock dividend on the 2,500 shares of no-par common stock outstanding. The preferred's market price is $20 a share. The common's market price is $5 a share.
   (4) A corporation is planning to retire its preferred stock in 1981. At December 31, 1975, the directors decide to begin the accumulation of a fund for this purpose "out of earnings." They decide to invest $70,000 in government bonds and make an appropriation of retained earnings of the same amount. Both steps are taken.
   (5) Notice is received on June 12, 1976, that the Internal Revenue Service has reviewed the corporation's income tax return and that $17,593 of additional taxes must be paid. The corporation had anticipated this

action and at December 31, 1975, had set up a liability account, called Estimated Income Taxes Payable, of $18,000. A check is drawn on June 15, 1976, in payment of the additional assessment.

(6) On January 2, 1976, a corporation issued $400,000 of 8-percent bonds at 98. The bonds mature in twenty years. Interest is payable on January 1 and July 1 of each year. The bond indenture requires the corporation to deposit $20,000 annually on December 31 with the trustee for the redemption of the bonds at maturity. The indenture provides that the deposits are to be made "out of profits" and a reserve for bond redemption is to be established. (January 2 transaction only.)

(7) The bond interest payment is made on July 1, 1976 [see (6)]. Straight-line amortization is used.

(8) The interest accrued on the bond issue at December 31, 1976 [see (6)] is recognized.

(9) The transactions required under the bond indenture [see (6)] are carried out and recorded on December 31, 1976.

(10) After the books are closed, it is discovered that an error was made in calculating depreciation on equipment for the preceding period. The depreciation charged was $900 too high.

Give the journal entries for each of the above transactions.

25. The following accounts all have the word "reserve" in their titles, but they fall into three different categories of accounts—asset contras, estimated liabilities, and appropriations of retained earnings.

(1) Reserve for Sinking Fund
(2) Reserve for Anticipated Inventory Losses
(3) Reserve for Depreciation
(4) Reserve for Extraordinary Losses
(5) Debt Retirement Reserve
(6) Reserve for Income Taxes
(7) Reserve for Treasury Stock
(8) Reserve for Bad Debts
(9) Reserve for Contingencies
(10) Reserve for Expansion.

a. Indicate in which of the three categories each of the accounts belongs.

b. Present in two-column journal form the most common type of entry in which the account is credited and the most common type of entry in which it is debited.

26. The comparative balance sheet of the Royal Corporation shows the following information:

	Dec. 31, 1975	Dec. 31, 1976
Preferred Stock, 6 percent	$ 750,000	$ 600,000
Common Stock	1,400,000	1,540,000
Retained Earnings	324,000	372,000

During 1976 stock dividends of $140,000 were issued to common stockholders. In addition, common stockholders received $70,000 in cash dividends; the preferred stockholders received $40,500 in cash dividends. On July 1, 1976, preferred stock with a par value of $150,000 was called at 104, that is, $156,000 was paid to retire the shares. What was the net income reported to stockholders for 1976?

*27. The Racer Corporation was a growth-oriented company, and in October, 1973, it approached the Security Trust Company to borrow $5,000,000 for expansion. However, Security followed a policy of not lending money at interest rates in excess of 8 percent, and it indicated to Racer that because of the risk involved, it could not approve a loan to Racer at 8 percent or less.

Racer then persuaded Security Trust to make the loan by offering Security Trust warrants containing the option to purchase 50,000 shares of Racer common stock at $30 per share. The warrants were to be valid for three years from the date of the loan.

The 8-percent loan was granted to Racer in October, 1973. Racer's common stock was then selling at $25 a share. In September, 1976, when Racer's stock was selling at $50 a share, Security Trust exercised the warrants and purchased the 50,000 shares.

a. Indicate what information should be included in a footnote to the Racer Corporation's 1973 financial statements. Why would such a disclosure be desirable? What harmful consequence to investors would occur if Racer failed to disclose this information?

b. Did the exercise of the warrants in 1976 constitute dilution of the equity? How did this affect the Racer Corporation's liabilities and shareholders' equity?

c. How might the cost of the warrants be measured? Did they add to the cost of the loan?

*28. The Norton Manufacturing Company was organized with an authorized capital of 5,000 shares of 6-percent cumulative, convertible preferred stock with a par value of $200 per share and 100,000 shares of no-par common stock. The preferred-stock contract provides that each share of preferred may be exchanged for ten shares of common at any time within the first five years of the corporation's life at the option of the stockholders. The following transactions occur during the first two years of the corporation's existence:

(1) The stock is offered for sale in units of one share of preferred and four shares of common for $264 a unit. Subscriptions are received for 3,000 units. The directors determine that $200 of the price of the unit is applicable to the preferred stock. The directors decide to place a stated value of $16 per share on the no-par shares.

(2) At the same time that the subscriptions are received, 2,500 shares of common stock are issued to the promoters to cover the organization and promotion costs.

(3) At this same time, a building and its site, owned by one of the incorporators, is turned over to the corporation in exchange for 500 shares of preferred stock and 5,000 shares of common stock. A value of $30,000 is placed on the site.

(4) All of the stock subscriptions are collected with the exception of one subscription for twenty units. This subscriber gives the corporation his six-month, 5-percent note for the amount of his subscription with the understanding that his subscription right will continue and that his stock will be issued when the note is paid.

   (5) The certificates of stock, for which the subscriptions have been collected, are issued.

   (6) The regular semiannual dividend on preferred stock is declared. According to the bylaws, only stock outstanding at the declaration date is entitled to the dividend.

   (7) The preferred-stock dividend is paid.

   (8) The balance of the preferred stock is offered for sale at $210 per share. Subscriptions are received for 620 shares.

   (9) Stock rights are issued to present common stockholders which allow them to subscribe for one share of common stock for each share that they hold, on a basis of $18 per share. Subscriptions are received from holders of rights for 12,500 shares.

 (10) The rights expire. The unsubscribed shares of (9) are offered for sale at $20 per share. The entire amount is subscribed.

 (11) The note mentioned in (4) is collected with six months' interest and the stock certificates are issued.

 (12) The subscriptions to the preferred stock are all collected except one subscription for twenty shares. The fully paid shares are issued.

 (13) The subscriptions to the common stock are all collected except a subscription for ten shares at $20 per share. This subscription is uncollectible and is canceled.

 (14) The certificates of stock, for which the subscriptions have been collected, are issued.

 (15) A holder of fifteen shares of preferred stock exchanges them for common stock. Ten shares had been issued in the original unit form and five shares had been issued at $210. (The converted shares cannot be reissued.)

a. Journalize the transactions.

b. Compute the balance of each of the stockholders' equity accounts except Retained Earnings in terms of both the number of shares and the amount, and show how these accounts would appear on a balance sheet; indicate the number of unissued shares.

Investments in Corporate Securities, Consolidated Statements, and Business Combinations

For a variety of reasons corporations often acquire the stock of other corporations. First, a corporation may find that the excess cash it holds can be used for any of several purposes—to retire some of its debt, buy government securities, open a savings account, or make an investment in the capital stock of another corporation. A corporation may purchase the stock of another corporation if its management feels that the investment is the most profitable use they can make of these excess funds. Second, a corporation may acquire another's stock to gain control over the acquired company's operations or to make easier the integration of separate operations. Occasionally, a corporation may purchase stock of another corporation merely as a long-term investment without seeking to affect its operations.

This chapter discusses the problems of (1) recording such acquisitions, (2) recognizing income subsequent to acquisition, and (3) reporting the nature and effect of the relationship between the corporation acquiring the stock and the one whose stock is acquired. Recording the acquisition of shares, including their price and other acquisition costs, is usually quite straightforward. The only major problem arises when one corporation acquires all (or almost all) of the stock of another in a single transaction. Under some circumstances, such a transaction is accounted for as a *pooling of interests*; in others, as a *purchase*. The purchase method is discussed in most of the chapter. The rationale of the pooling of interests method and a comparison of the results of using it, rather than the purchase method, are presented in the last section of this chapter.

The procedures discussed in the chapter concentrate on two important concerns: recognition of income by the acquiring company and its valuation and reporting of its interest in the acquired company. Three different treatments are currently in use for differing fractions of ownership. If the acquiring company owns less than 20 percent of the stock of the acquired company, it accounts for its investment by the *cost method*. If it owns from 20 percent to 50 percent of the acquired company, it must use the *equity method*. If the acquiring company owns more than 50 percent of the stock of the acquired company, the *consolidation method* is usually employed, but the equity method may be used in this case under special circumstances. The three methods are discussed in the following sections.

Throughout this chapter, we consider the accounting required when one corporation buys shares in another. We call the acquiring corporation P for *purchaser* or for *parent*, depending on the context. S stands for *seller* or for *subsidiary*.

COST METHOD

When a corporation, P, holds less than 20 percent of the stock of another corporation, S, P will use the cost method to account for its investment under current generally accepted accounting principles. Suppose that P buys 1,000 shares of S for $40,000. The entry to record the purchase would be:

Investment in S	40,000	
Cash		40,000

If the purpose of the purchase were merely a short-term investment to use idle cash, the debit might be to Marketable Securities.

If, while P holds this stock, S declares an ordinary dividend of $2 per share, P would make the following entry:

Dividends Receivable	2,000	
Dividend Revenue		2,000

When the dividend is collected, P will debit Cash and credit Dividends Receivable.

If P sells all its stock of S, P will debit cash and credit the Investment in S account to reduce the balance in that account to zero and then will credit Gain on Sale of Stock (or debit Loss on Sale of Stock) to complete the entry. If P sells its 1,000 shares of S for $40,500 the entry would be:

Cash	40,500	
Investment in S		40,000
Gain on Sale of Stock		500

If, under these same conditions, P sells half its investment in stock, the entry would be:

Cash	20,250	
Investment in S		20,000
Gain on Sale of Stock		250

On the balance sheet an investment in corporate securities where less than 20 percent of the other corporation's shares are held is shown either as a marketable security among current assets or as an investment in the noncurrent category. Relatively small holdings which are not held to influence the policy of the corporation whose stock is acquired and which are readily marketable will probably be reported as marketable securities in the current asset section. However classified, such holdings are valued at acquisition cost (or at lower of cost or market) under current generally accepted accounting principles.

There is perhaps no other generally accepted accounting principle more at odds with economic reality than the principle of showing marketable securities at cost rather than at current market value. Since at least 1939, accounting theorists have argued convincingly that marketable securities should be shown at market value. Their very marketability makes valuation on a current basis objective. Showing marketable securities at cost fails to recognize the objective, easily measurable changes in a firm's economic position and gives management an opportunity to manipulate reported income for a period. All management need do to raise income for a period is to sell securities that are recorded at cost but have appreciated in value since acquisition in an earlier period. To lower income, sell securities that have declined from book value. In current practice, many firms show the current market value of their marketable securities *parenthetically* on the balance sheet or in notes to the financial statements. Others use lower of cost or market, which recognizes the effects of price fluctuations below acquisition price, but not those above acquisition price. Permitting or requiring departures from the cost basis for marketable securities was considered several times by the Accounting Principles Board but no final action was taken. The case for departure from the cost basis here is so strong that this is likely to be the first area where upward revaluations of acquisition cost with recognition of current income, but without an exchange transaction, will become acceptable.[1]

EQUITY METHOD

Notice that under the cost method P in the earlier example makes entries only when it buys stock, receives a dividend, or sells stock. Suppose that S follows a policy of financing its own growing operations through retention of earnings so that S consistently pays dividends less than net income. The market price of a share of S's stock may appreciate. P's records will continue to show the investment in S at original cost. Further, if P holds a substantial fraction of the shares of S, P may be able to influence the financial policy of S. Under these conditions, the cost method may not reasonably reflect reality. The equity method is designed to provide a more realistic picture of investments in securities where there are substantial holdings.

[1] The history of the theory and other related matters about showing marketable securities is discussed by Robert R. Sterling, "Accounting Research, Education, and Practice," *The Journal of Accountancy* (September 1973), pp. 44–52.

When a corporation, *P*, owns 20 percent or more of the common stock of another corporation, *S*, but not more than 50 percent of it, generally accepted accounting principles require that the investment by *P* in *S* be accounted for on the *equity method*.[2] The equity method may also be used under special circumstances when there is more than 50 percent ownership; these circumstances will be considered later. Under the equity method, the purchase and sale of stock is recorded just as under the cost method; however, *P* treats as income (or revenue) its proportionate share of the earnings since acquisition of shares, not merely the dividends, of *S*. Dividends paid by *S* to *P* are treated by *P* as a reduction in its Investment in *S*.

Suppose that *P* buys 30 percent of the outstanding shares of *S* for $600,000. The entry to record the purchase would be:

    (1) Investment in *S* 600,000
          Cash 600,000

Between the time of the acquisition and the end of *P*'s next accounting period, *S* earns income of $80,000. *P*, using the equity method, would record:

    (2) Investment in *S* 24,000
          Revenue from Investments 24,000
        To record 30 percent of income earned by investee accounted for on the equity method.

If *S* declares a dividend of $30,000 to holders of common stock, *P* would be entitled to receive $9,000 and would record:

    (3) Dividends Receivable 9,000
          Investment in *S* 9,000
        To record dividends receivable from investee accounted for on the equity method and the resulting reduction in investment.

Notice that the credit is to the Investment in *S* account. *P* records income earned by *S* as an *increase* in investment so that the dividend becomes an income distribution which is a return of capital or a *decrease* in investment. Note that this method produces the same result, revenues of $24,000, as treating the dividends ($9,000) as investment income and recognizing *P*'s share of *S*'s *undistributed* earnings for the year [30 percent of ($80,000 — $30,000) or $15,000] as additional income.

Suppose that *S* subsequently reports earnings of $100,000 and simultaneously declares dividends of $30,000. *P*'s entries would be:

    (4) Investment in *S* 30,000
          Revenue from Investments 30,000
    (5) Dividends Receivable 9,000
          Investment in *S* 9,000
        To record revenue and dividends from investee accounted for on equity method.

[2] Opinion No. 18, Accounting Principles Board, AICPA, issued in March, 1971.

P's account Investment in *S* now has a balance of $636,000 as follows:

Investment in S

(1)	600,000	9,000	(3)
(2)	24,000	9,000	(5)
(4)	30,000		

Suppose that *P* now sells one-quarter of its shares for $152,500, reducing its holdings. *P*'s entry to record the sale would be:

Cash	152,500	
Loss on Partial Liquidation of Investment in *S*	6,500	
Investment in *S*		159,000

The equity method as described so far is simple enough to use. To make financial reports using the equity method more realistic, generally accepted accounting principles require some modification of the entries under certain circumstances.[3]

Even though *S* does not pay all its earnings in dividends, *P* reports its proportionate share of *S*'s earnings as income. But this income to *P* is not currently taxable. Consequently, there will often be an entry in the deferred tax accounts. Determination of the amount of the deferred tax charge presents issues too complex for this introductory text.

An additional complication in the equity method arises from the accounting for goodwill—the excess of the shares' cost over their book value as shown in *S*'s records. This is also a problem in the consolidation method and is considered in the discussion on that topic.

On the balance sheet, an investment accounted for on the equity method is shown in the noncurrent assets section. The amount shown is the balance in the Investment in *S* account. It will generally be equal to the acquisition cost of the shares plus *P*'s share of *S*'s undistributed earnings since the date the shares were acquired. On the income statement, *P* shows its share of *S*'s income as revenues each period.

CONSOLIDATED STATEMENTS

If one corporation owns more than 50 percent of the stock of another corporation, that relationship is usually reported by using the consolidation method; that is, consolidated statements are prepared for the two corporations. Consolidated statements are designed to report the financial position and operations of two or more legally distinct entities as if they were a single, centrally controlled economic entity. Since each legal entity must have a set of records of its own, consolidated statements bring together and summarize the data from several sets of records. In a legal sense, consolidated statements merely supplement, and do not replace, the separate statements of the individual corporations, although it is common practice to present only the consolidated statements in published annual reports.

[3] Opinion No. 18, Accounting Principles Board, AICPA, issued in March, 1971.

Rationale for Consolidated Statements

Control of one corporation (S) by another (P) is assured when P owns more than 50 percent of S's voting stock. When the stock is widely distributed, however, a block of considerably less than 50 percent is likely sufficient to control a stockholders' meeting. When control is not assured but is likely, the equity method is used. Generally accepted accounting principles have concluded, perhaps arbitrarily, that in almost all cases the owning corporation should use the equity method when it owns between 20 and 50 percent of voting shares. Consolidated statements are generally preferred when there is more than 50 percent ownership, but they are not required if the nature of the subsidiary's operations differs substantially enough from that of the parent, or if institutional arrangements make complete control of S difficult, as when it is located in a foreign country where withdrawal of profits is limited by exchange controls. If consolidated statements are not prepared in these cases, then the equity method must be used.

The corporation exercising control through stock ownership is known as the *parent*, and the one subject to control of the parent is known as the *subsidiary*. The term *holding company* is sometimes used to denote a parent whose principal assets are stocks of other corporations. A holding company is different from an *investment trust* or a *mutual fund*, both of which hold securities of other corporations for investment purposes rather than for control.

Using several corporations, instead of one, serves several purposes. From the standpoint of the parent, the more important reasons for the existence of subsidiary companies are:

1. To reduce the financial risk. Separate corporations may be used for mining raw materials, transporting them to a manufacturing plant, producing the product, and selling the finished product to the public. If any one part of the total process proves to be unprofitable or inefficient, the corporation performing the particular step can be dissolved and the required goods or services can be purchased from other sources without seriously interfering with the operations of other corporations in the group. Losses from insolvency will fall only on the owners and creditors of the one subsidiary corporation.

2. To meet more effectively the requirements of state corporation and tax legislation. If an organization does business in a number of states, it is often faced with overlapping and inconsistent taxation, regulations, and requirements. It may be more economical to organize separate corporations to conduct the operations in the various states.

3. To expand with a minimum of capital investment. A firm may absorb another company by acquiring a controlling interest in its voting stock. The result may be accomplished with a substantially smaller capital investment, as well as with less difficulty and inconvenience, than if a new plant had been constructed or a complete merger were arranged.

4. To vary the distribution of income and loss among the individuals interested in the total activities of the business. A separate corporation may be organized to own such assets as real estate or patents and to lease them to the operating parent company. The distribution of stock ownership of this subsidiary corporation may not be the same as that of the parent company. The distribution of total income or loss of the entire organization may therefore be substantially different than if only one corporation were used.

Significance of Consolidated Statements

If a parent, engaged in manufacturing, accounted for its investment in a subsidiary selling company using the equity method, the parent's balance sheet would present an incomplete analysis because the two corporations operate as a single economic unit. A more realistic picture of the position of the single economic entity is provided by combining all of the individual asset and liability items of the two independent legal entities in a consolidated balance sheet.

The income statement of the parent company may, by itself, be unsatisfactory. A statement of the total sales to outside interests, the cost of goods sold, and other expenses of the combined companies offers a more meaningful picture of the operations of the economic unit.

Consolidated statements, then, present the results of operations and the financial condition substantially as they would appear if the entire business had been conducted as one corporation. The figures do not correspond to those found on any one set of books but are combined from the records of the separate legal entities involved.

CONSOLIDATED STATEMENTS: PROCEDURES

Many complicated problems, beyond the scope of this discussion, are encountered when constructing consolidated statements. This presentation illustrates the characteristic steps of the procedure and may help to clarify the significance of consolidated statements. The items on a consolidated balance sheet are little more than the sum of the balance sheet items of the corporations being consolidated. There are, however, adjustments to eliminate double counting and intercompany transactions. For example, the parent's balance sheet will show an asset item for Investment in Subsidiary. The subsidiary's balance sheet will show its assets. If the two balance sheets were merely added together, the sum would show both the parent's investment in the subsidiary's assets and the assets themselves. The parent's balance sheet item, Investment in Subsidiary, must be eliminated from the sum of the balance sheets, and since balance sheets must maintain the accounting equation, corresponding eliminations must be made from the right-hand side as well. The balance is maintained by eliminating the stockholders' equity items of the subsidiary.

A parent may lend money to its subsidiary. If the separate balance sheets were merely added together, those funds would be counted twice: once as the notes receivable on the parent's books and again as the cash or other assets on the subsidiary's books. Consolidated balance sheets eliminate intercompany transactions that would not be reported for a single, integrated enterprise.

The parent may not own 100 percent of the subsidiary. If the parent owns less than 100 percent, there are, of course, minority stockholders in the subsidiary. They continue to have a proportionate interest in the stockholders' equity of the subsidiary as shown on its separate corporate records. Consolidated balance sheets show the stockholders' equity of minority stockholders as the *minority interest*. We show this item in our model balance sheet (Chapter 11) as an indeterminate-term liability. Because minority interest is not part of the majority stockholders' equity, it must be a liability; because it is not an obligation to pay at a definite time, its term is indeterminate.

A consolidated income statement is little more than the sum of the operating income statements of the parent and the subsidiaries. Intercompany transactions, for example sales and purchases, are eliminated so that a more realistic picture is presented. For example, if a manufacturing parent sells to a subsidiary which, in turn, sells to the public, the sum of individual income statements would double-count sales and purchases. Suppose that the parent sells to the subsidiary but that the subsidiary has not yet sold the items to the public: the parent will have recorded profits on the sale, but from the standpoint of the overall entity, no profits for stockholders have actually been realized because the items are still in the inventory of the overall entity. Consequently, profits from parent's sales to subsidiaries that have not been realized by subsequent sale to outsiders are eliminated from (not shown in) consolidated income statements.

Some of these problems will be treated next. Readers who study these sections should be able to understand published consolidated statements but should be wary of trying to construct them.

Analysis of Acquisition

There are essentially two ways in which Company *P* can acquire controlling interest in Company *S*. They are discussed below.

(1) Company *P* can organize Company *S*. Rather than start a new division, Company *P* may find it convenient to set up a separate legal entity. For example, many large corporations will set up separate subsidiaries whose function is to finance customer purchases or to do business in a different locale. The majority of companies consolidated in financial statements are companies that have been organized by the parent. Accounting for the acquisition in these cases is straightforward. If $900,000 is spent to acquire 100 percent of the stock of a new subsidiary, the entry is:

Investment in Subsidiary	900,000	
Cash		900,000
To record purchase of 100 percent of the stock of Company S.		

(2) The second way Company *P* can make an acquisition is by buying the shares of an existing company. In this case, analysis of the acquisition

may be slightly more complex because there may be goodwill arising from the purchase. *Goodwill* is the excess of the cost of the acquisition over the (perhaps revalued) book value of the assets acquired. For example, assume that at the time the stock in the acquired company is purchased, its books show Capital Stock plus Additional Paid-in Capital of $600,000 and Retained Earnings of $200,000. The book value of the acquired company is, therefore, $800,000. If the parent paid $800,000 for its 100 percent interest, there would be no further problem. When the parent pays precisely book value, there is no goodwill to be recognized and the entry is like the one shown above except that the amounts are $800,000.

If the parent paid $900,000 for its 100 percent interest, the excess of cost over book value acquired is $100,000. This excess could arise for several reasons. For example, the assets of the acquired company might be undervalued on its books, having a larger current value than the historical cost less accumulated depreciation. In addition, perhaps the acquired company has built up good relations with its employees, customers, and suppliers so that as a going concern the whole is worth more than the mere sum of the parts. The assets of the acquired company must be revalued to current appraised values at the date of the acquisition. If cost exceeds book value acquired after all tangible assets of the acquired company are reasonably shown at current values, the excess is called *goodwill* and is formally recognized in the consolidated statements. The entry in Company *P*'s books at the time of acquisition is just the entry shown in (1). The goodwill acquired will be reported only in consolidated financial statements, as described in the next section of this chapter.

The goodwill arising from a purchase is a long-lived asset and generally accepted accounting principles require that this asset be amortized over a period of no more than forty years.[4] Some theorists disagree with this treatment and argue that goodwill ought never be recognized. Others disagree in the opposite direction; they contend that the future benefits can have an indefinite life, and therefore, amortization is not appropriate in all cases. (Goodwill arising from the purchase of an interest in another company accounted for on the equity method must similarly be amortized over a period not to exceed forty years although the goodwill is not formally recognized as an asset separate from the Investment in S account.[5])

If less than 100 percent of the subsidiary's stock were acquired, the goodwill recognized would be calculated as the acquisition price minus the fraction of the stock acquired times book value (after any asset revaluations). Thus in the preceding example where the book value of S is $800,000, if a 60-percent interest were acquired for $600,000, goodwill plus asset revaluations would be $120,000 (= $600,000 − .60($800,000)).

The parent could conceivably pay less than $800,000 for its 100 percent interest in the subsidiary. This suggests that the asset amounts shown on the subsidiary's books are overvalued or the liabilities are undervalued

---

[4] Opinion No. 17, Accounting Principles Board, AICPA, issued in August, 1970.
[5] Opinion No. 18, Accounting Principles Board, AICPA, issued in March, 1971.

or both. If the parent paid only $700,000 for its 100 percent interest, then the excess of cost over book value acquired would be negative. The amounts shown for unrealistically valued assets and liabilities must be changed so that book value (assets less liabilities) is equal to $700,000.

Illustration of Consolidated Balance Sheet Preparation

Company P purchased 90 percent of the outstanding shares of Company S on January 1, 1971, for $600,000. At that date the capital accounts of Company S had the following balances: Capital Stock—$500,000, Premium on Capital Stock—$10,000, and Retained Earnings—$140,000, or a total of $650,000. The appraised values of S's assets and liabilities on January 1, 1971, were equal to their book values so that the goodwill at acquisition was $15,000 (= $600,000 − .90($650,000)). P decided to amortize that goodwill over thirty years on a straight-line basis in its consolidated statements.

The condensed balance sheets of Company P and Company S at December 31, 1975, are shown in Schedule 18.1. P accounts on its own books for its investment in S by using the cost method. (P need not use the equity method on its own books because consolidated statements are to be issued to P's stockholders.)

SCHEDULE 18.1

CONDENSED BALANCE SHEETS AS OF DECEMBER 31, 1975

Assets

	Company P	Company S
Cash	$ 60,000	$ 20,000
Accounts Receivable	200,000	25,000
Investment in Stock of Company S (at cost)	600,000	
Other Investments	200,000	
Other Assets	1,912,500	960,000
	$2,972,500	$1,005,000

Liabilities and Stockholders' Equity

	Company P	Company S
Accounts Payable	$ 75,000	$ 15,000
Bonds Payable (8%)		250,000
Other Liabilities	70,000	30,000
Capital Stock	500,000	500,000
Premium on Capital Stock	2,000,000	10,000
Retained Earnings	327,500	200,000
	$2,972,500	$1,005,000

Of Company P's accounts receivable, $12,500 represents amounts payable to P by S; $50,000 of Company P's Other Investments are bonds of Company S acquired at par value. In preparing a balance sheet for Company P consolidated with Company S, the following steps, characteristic of the consolidation procedure, will be illustrated:

1. adjustment of parent company's Investment account
2. recognizing goodwill and its accumulated amortization
3. elimination of parent company's Investment account
4. elimination of intercompany receivables and payables
5. determination of minority interest.

The entries resulting from the adjustments and eliminations are numbered consecutively and they correspond to the numbers shown in the adjustment and eliminations column on the work sheet in Schedule 18.2. Note that the entries are recorded on the work sheet only—not in the journal and ledger. Such a work sheet is usually necessary to prepare consolidated statements. The first two columns show the single company statements and the last column shows the consolidated statement. Its items are the horizontal sum of the single-company items plus or minus any adjustments and eliminations.

Adjustment of the Parent Company's Investment Account. Since P Company maintains its Investment in Stock of Company S account on a cost basis, the investment account should be adjusted for P's share of the undistributed income or losses of the subsidiary arising since the date of acquisition in order to show the amount of the Investment in S as it would be were the equity method used.

The procedure may be outlined as follows. Assume that no change has taken place in the number of outstanding shares of stock of the subsidiary since the parent company acquired its holdings.

1. Determine the retained earnings of the subsidiary pertaining to the type of stock held by the parent company. In most cases this will be the balance in the Retained Earnings account, but it will also include any appropriations of retained earnings.
2. Compute the difference between the figure found in (1) and the corresponding retained earnings total at the date the stock was acquired by the parent company. The difference represents the increase (if positive, decrease if negative) in the subsidiary's retained earnings since acquisition.
3. Multiply the increase (or decrease) of retained earnings found in (2) by the percentage of subsidiary stock outstanding held by the parent company.
4. Debit the Investment in Stock of Company S and credit the Retained Earnings accounts of the parent company with the amount found in (3).

In the illustration, the increase in retained earnings for Company S for the five years is $60,000 ($= $200,000 − $140,000$). Company P's share is 90 percent of $60,000, or $54,000. The entry to record the adjustment would be:

(1) Investment in Stock of Company S 54,000
　　　Retained Earnings (Company P) 54,000

Such an entry would not ordinarily be made on the books of Company P, since the consolidating procedure does not affect the accounting records of the separate legal entities. The entry would, however, be made in the adjustments and eliminations column of a work sheet like the one shown in Schedule 18.2. A record of the calculation and the entry should be kept on file to facilitate the preparation of the next consolidated balance sheet.

Once this adjustment is made, the balance in the Investment in Stock of Company S account on P's books is the same as it would have been if P had used the equity method, rather than the cost method, on the books. If P had used the equity method, then the consolidation procedure would start here.

Recognizing Goodwill and Its Accumulated Amortization. Goodwill acquired at the time Company S was purchased amounted to $15,000, as calculated earlier. This goodwill must be recognized on the consolidated balance sheet as must its amortization since acquisition. We show the recognition and past amortization of goodwill in two separate steps for the sake of clarity.

Debit Goodwill and credit the Investment in Stock of Company S account in the amount of originally acquired goodwill.

In the illustration, the entry will be:

(2) Goodwill 15,000
　　　Investment in Stock of Company S 15,000
　　To recognize a portion of the acquisition cost as goodwill.

Debit Retained Earnings (Company P) and credit Goodwill with the amortization of goodwill to date.

In the illustration, goodwill amortization for the first five years of ownership is $2,500 since P decided to amortize the goodwill over thirty years ($5/30 \times \$15,000 = \$2,500$). Because the amortization reduces the consolidated retained earnings, the entry would be:

(3) Retained Earnings (Company P) 2,500
　　　Goodwill 2,500
　　To show amortization of goodwill for five years.

When the equity method, rather than the consolidation method, is used, generally accepted accounting principles require a similar amortization of goodwill, that is, of the excess of the purchase price of the shares over the underlying book value acquired. That amortization charge increases the amount of P's expenses.

Elimination of Parent Company's Investment Account. If the stock of the subsidiary company were acquired at its book value, the investment account, after making the adjustment for accumulated undistributed income or loss, will equal the parent company's share of the subsidiary's capital stock and retained earnings. Before adding the single-company balance sheet items to obtain consolidated totals, the parent's Investment in Stock of Company S account must be eliminated so that assets are not counted twice.

To eliminate the investment account, debit the subsidiary's contributed capital and retained earnings accounts for the proportion applicable to the parent company's interest and credit the investment account with its adjusted balance [after entry (2) above]. This amount will equal the cost of shares at date of acquisition plus parent company's share of subsidiary's undistributed earnings since acquisition less original goodwill.

The entry in the illustration to effect the cancelation of the Investment in Stock of Company S account would be:

(4) Capital Stock (Company S) 450,000
    Premium on Capital Stock (Company S) 9,000
    Retained Earnings (Company S) 180,000
        Investment in Stock of Company S 639,000
    To cancel the adjusted Investment in Stock of Company S account ($600,000 + $54,000 − $15,000) against 90% of the capital stock and retained earnings of Company S.

This entry does not affect the records of Company P or Company S. It is recorded only on the work sheet.

Elimination of Intercompany Receivables and Payables. A parent company may sell goods to or buy goods from a subsidiary company and treat the resulting obligation as an account receivable or account payable. A parent company often makes loans to subsidiaries, which appear as Notes Receivable and Notes Payable or under the titles of Advances to Subsidiaries and Advances from Parent Company. One company may have invested in bonds issued by another company within the group. These transactions are similar to transactions between divisions of a single company and must be eliminated from a consolidated statement.

In the illustration the following entry would be necessary to eliminate the intercompany receivables and payables:

(5) Accounts Payable 12,500
    Bonds Payable (8%) 50,000
        Accounts Receivable 12,500
        Other Investments 50,000
    To eliminate intercompany receivables and payables.

Determination of Minority Interest. Ten percent of the stock of Company S is owned outside the parent company. When a minority interest exists, the proprietorship consists of two elements, the majority interest and the minority interest. The minority interest consists of the minority's proportional share of S's stockholders' equity. At this stage of the computations, the minority interest is equal to the uneliminated portion of the contributed capital and retained earnings accounts of the subsidiary company.

No adjustment nor elimination entry is required to set up the minority interest. The balances remaining in the subsidiary's contributed capital and retained earnings accounts on the work sheet can merely be carried over to the final column and assembled in the consolidated balance sheet when it is prepared from the data on the work sheet. An entry may be made, however, to transfer these balances to a new position under a clearer title. We suggest that the Minority Interest account be shown on the consolidated balance sheet as an indeterminate-term liability, since from the viewpoint of the majority stockholders, the minority interest is not ownership equity but an obligation to others.

In the illustration, an entry is made to set forth the minority interest of Company S:

(6) Capital Stock (Co. S)	50,000	
Premium on Capital Stock (Co. S)	1,000	
Retained Earnings (Co. S)	20,000	
Minority Interest in Co. S		71,000
To show minority interest as 10 percent of Company S's stockholders' equity.		

The work sheet in Schedule 18.2 illustrates all six of the adjustment and elimination entries which have been made. The last column of the work sheet is simply the sum of the preceding four columns. It furnishes the data for the preparation of the consolidated balance sheet. Some of the special problems relating to the form of consolidated balance sheets are considered in Chapter 25.

Consolidated Income Statement

A procedure similar to the one for the consolidated balance sheet is used to prepare the consolidated income statement. Intercompany transactions, such as sales and purchases, are eliminated. An attempt is made to present sales, expenses, and net income figures that show the results of operations of the group of companies as though they were a single corporation. The final consolidated income is allocated to show the portions applicable to the parent company interest and to the minority interest.

Limitations of Consolidated Statements

The consolidated statements do not replace those of individual corporations; rather, they supplement those statements and aid in their interpretation. Creditors must rely upon the resources of one corporation and may be misled if forced to rely entirely upon a consolidated statement that combines the data of a company in good financial condition with those of one verging on insolvency. Dividends can legally be declared only from the retained earnings of one corporation. Where the parent company does not own all of the stock of the subsidiary, the outside or minority

SCHEDULE 18.2 WORK SHEET TO DERIVE CONSOLIDATED BALANCE SHEET

COMPANIES P AND S
as of December 31, 1975

Debits	Company P	Company S	Adjustments and Eliminations Dr.	Cr.	Consolidated Balance Sheet
Cash	60,000	20,000			80,000
Accounts Receivable ...	200,000	25,000		(5) 12,500	212,500
Investment in Stock				(2) 15,000	
of Company S	600,000	—	(1) 54,000	(4) 639,000	—
Other Investments	200,000	—		(5) 50,000	150,000
Goodwill	—	—	(2) 15,000	(3) 2,500	12,500
Other Assets	1,912,500	960,000			2,872,500
	2,972,500	1,005,000	69,000	719,000	3,327,500
Credits					
Accounts Payable	75,000	15,000	(5) 12,500		77,500
Bonds Payable (8%) ...	—	250,000	(5) 50,000		200,000
Other Liabilities	70,000	30,000			100,000
Minority Interest					
in Co. S	—	—		(6) 71,000	71,000
Capital Stock	500,000	500,000	(4) 450,000		500,000
			(6) 50,000		
Premium on Capital					
Stock	2,000,000	10,000	(4) 9,000		2,000,000
			(6) 1,000		
Retained Earnings					
(Co. P)	327,500	—	(3) 2,500	(1) 54,000	379,000
Retained Earnings					
(Co. S)	—	200,000	(4) 180,000		
			(6) 20,000		
	2,972,500	1,005,000	775,000	125,000	3,327,500
			844,000	844,000	

(1) To record as increase in consolidated retained earnings P's share of S's undistributed earnings since acquisition. This is equivalent to changing P's recording of S from the cost basis to the equity basis.
(2) To recognize goodwill arising from the original purchase.
(3) To account for amortization of goodwill since purchase.
(4) To eliminate P's adjusted investment account against S's capital accounts.
(5) To eliminate intercompany receivables and payables.
(6) To recognize the remainder (10 percent of original amounts) of S's capital accounts as minority interest.

stockholders can judge the dividend possibilities, both legal and financial, only by an inspection of the subsidiary's statements.

In the best of all possible worlds, parent corporations would report on their own and their subsidiaries' operations in both single-company and consolidated reports. Generally accepted accounting principles do not require the publication of both single-company and consolidated reports. Only the consolidated report need be published and, in fact, we know of no major United States corporation that publishes both.

POOLING OF INTERESTS

The previous sections assume that P accounts for its acquisition of S as a purchase and shows the construction of a consolidated balance sheet for a purchased acquisition. Under certain restricted conditions described later, the acquisition of S would be accounted for as a pooling of interests rather than as a purchase.

To understand the rationale for a pooling of interests, reconsider some of the effects on consolidated financial reports from an acquisition treated as a purchase. Suppose that P purchases 100 percent of S after S has been in operation for several years. Under most conditions of favorable operations, the current value of S's assets minus liabilities, as appraised by the market price of S's stock or by fair valuations of its assets and liabilities, will be greater than the book value of the stockholders' equity in S. That is, P is likely to have to pay more for S's stock than S's book value which equals S's assets less S's liabilities. When the cost to P exceeds the book value it acquires, P must either increase the value of S's assets shown on the consolidated statements or set up goodwill, or both. No matter how P recognizes the excess of cost over book value acquired, the consolidated assets will be larger than the sum of the assets shown on the books of the two companies before the acquisition. This increased amount of assets (except for land) must be amortized in calculating periodic income in the future. Increased assets imply increased amortization expenses; increased expenses, in turn, imply smaller income when revenues do not change.

It is possible, of course, that the combination of corporations will produce larger revenues than the sum of the individual revenues before the acquisition, or it may produce smaller total expenses. However, there is no necessary reason for combination to produce this happy result, and most of the empirical evidence suggests that combination does not augment revenues or reduce expenses in spite of the results anticipated from combining.

The rules of accounting for a purchase pose a problem for corporations considering a merger. The consolidated enterprise resulting from a purchase may be a sound business undertaking, but the reported income of the new enterprise may be smaller than the sum of the incomes before consolidation. This problem arises from the historical-cost basis of accounting. The current values of both P's and S's assets are likely to be larger than their book values. In unconsolidated operations, the increases in book values of an individual company's assets need not be recognized so that there is no later increased amortization with resulting larger expenses and lower income. As soon as a purchase occurs, S's assets will be revalued and reported expenses will rise. The purchase and consolidation change nothing except the book value of the assets of the acquired company. Since management is often evaluated by the reported income of the enterprise, management has sought ways of bringing about a combination in such a way that purchase accounting, with its effects of reducing combined reported income, is not required.

Pooling of interests accounting seeks to reflect a continuity of ownership interests in the combined companies by the stockholders of P and S. The rationale for the use of this method is that there is not a purchase by P nor a sale by S but, rather, a pooling or combining or merging of the interests of both ownership groups. It also makes it possible for P to acquire S without increasing the reported value of S's assets in the consolidated reports.

Generally accepted accounting principles[6] allow pooling of interests only under a set of restrictive conditions all of which must be met. One of the conditions requires that P must issue voting common stock for S rather than purchasing S for cash. The acquisition by stock issue must occur in a single transaction rather than being spread over a period of time. Another restriction requires that P acquire at least 90 percent of S's stock. Under pooling of interests accounting, no assets are revalued so that no extra amortization expenses are required. The balance sheet resulting from a pooling of interests is even more like a summation of the single-company balance sheets than is the balance sheet resulting from purchase accounting.

POOLING OF INTERESTS AND PURCHASE COMPARED

This section illustrates the consolidated statements resulting from a pooling of interests and compares them to those where the acquisition is treated as a purchase.[7] P and S decide to combine operations in order to save $50,000 a year, after taxes, in expenses of running their combined businesses. Columns 1 and 2 in Schedule 18.3 show abbreviated single-company financial statements for P and S before combination. S has 20,000 shares of stock outstanding that sell for $84 per share in the market. The market value of S as a going concern is, then, $1,680,000. As shown in column 3, S's stockholders have $1,230,000 of equity not recorded on the books. Of this $1,230,000, $400,000 is attributable to undervalued noncurrent assets and $830,000 is assigned to goodwill. P has 100,000 shares outstanding which sell for $42 each in the market. The illustration ignores income taxes.

Purchase

Assume that P purchases S to combine their operations. P issues (sells) 40,000 additional shares on the market for $1,680,000 and uses the pro-

---

[6] Opinion No. 16, Accounting Principles Board, AICPA, issued in August, 1970.
[7] The illustration is adapted from one by H. Nurnberg and C. Grube, "Alternative Methods of Accounting for Business Combinations," *The Accounting Review*, 45 (October 1970), pp. 783–89.

ceeds to purchase all shares of S for $84 each. (Each share of S is, in effect, "sold" for two shares of P.) P has acquired 100 percent of the shares of S and now owns S.

P's acquisition of S satisfies the conditions for purchase accounting. P decides to amortize the increased asset costs and goodwill over ten years. The resulting combination, accounted for as a purchase, will issue consolidated financial reports similiar to those shown in column 4. The consolidated balance sheet is the sum of columns 1 and 3 except for the stockholders' equity section. Since P issued 40,000 new shares for $42 each, the Common Stock account shows 140,000 shares at $5 per value. The Premium on Common Stock account shows P's former Premium on Common Stock plus the additional premium arising from the new stock issue: $200,000 + [40,000 × ($42 − $5)] = $1,680,000. The retained earnings of the consolidated enterprise are equal to P's retained earnings.

The consolidated income statement, when the acquisition is treated as a purchase, starts with the combined incomes before consolidation. To that amount is added the cost savings of $50,000 resulting from the more efficient operations of the combination. Then both the additional depreciation expense arising from the asset revaluations and the goodwill amortization expense are subtracted. The resulting net income is $387,000.

Pooling of Interests

Examine the accounting, shown in column 5, if the acquisition qualifies for treatment as a pooling of interests. Assume that P issued the 40,000 shares of stock directly to the owners of S in return for their shares, which are then retired. The balance sheet items, except for the individual stockholders' equity accounts, are merely the sum of the single-company amounts shown in columns 1 and 2. The stockholders' equity after pooling must then equal total stockholders' equity before pooling.

The capital stock of the pooled enterprise must, of course, equal the par value of the shares outstanding after pooling. After pooling there are 140,000 shares outstanding with a par value of $700,000. The general rule is that the pooled retained earnings balance is the sum of the retained earnings before pooling. The example illustrates the general rule. The total paid-in capital (par value plus capital contributed in excess of par or premium) after pooling will generally equal the sum of the paid-in capital accounts of the firms before pooling. Thus the premium of the pooled firm is, ordinarily, the plug to equate the pooled paid-in capital with the sum of the paid-in capital accounts before pooling.

The income statement resulting from a pooling of interests shows the same revenues and cost savings as those following a purchase. There are, however, no extra depreciation and amortization expenses resulting from increased asset valuations. Consequently, the pooled enterprise reports net income of $510,000 and stockholders' equity of $2,350,000 (rate of return of 22 percent), whereas the identical enterprise accounted for as

SCHEDULE 18.3 PURCHASE AND POOLING COMPARED

Pro Forma Consolidated Statements Comparing Purchase and Pooling of Interests Methods

	Historical Cost		S Shown at Current Values	P & S Consolidated	
	P	S		Purchase	Pooling of Interests
	(1)	(2)	(3)	(4)	(5)

Balance Sheet

Assets					
Current Assets	$1,500,000	$450,000	$ 450,000	$1,950,000	$1,950,000
Long-term Assets Less					
Accumulated Depreciation	1,700,000	450,000	850,000	2,550,000	2,150,000
Goodwill	—	—	830,000	830,000	—
Total Assets	$3,200,000	$900,000	$2,130,000	$5,330,000	$4,100,000
Equities					
Liabilities	$1,300,000	$450,000	$ 450,000	$1,750,000	$1,750,000
Stockholders' Equity:					
Common Stock ($5 par)	500,000	100,000	100,000	700,000 [a]	700,000 [a]
Premium on Common Stock	200,000	150,000	150,000	1,680,000 [b]	250,000 [e]
Retained Earnings	1,200,000	200,000	200,000	1,200,000 [c]	1,400,000 [d]
Unrecorded Equity at					
Current Valuation	—	—	1,230,000	—	—
Total Liabilities and					
Stockholders' Equity	$3,200,000	$900,000	$2,130,000	$5,330,000	$4,100,000

Income Statement

Pre-combination Income	$ 300,000	$160,000		$ 460,000	$ 460,000
From Combination:					
Cost Savings	—	—		50,000	50,000
Extra Depreciation Expense	—	—		(40,000)	—
Amortization of Goodwill	—	—		(83,000)	—
Net Income	$ 300,000	$160,000		$ 387,000	$ 510,000
Number of Common Shares					
Outstanding	100,000	20,000		140,000	140,000
Earnings Per Share	$3.00	$8.00		$2.76	$3.64

[a] P's 100,000 original shares plus 40,000 new shares at $5 par.
[b] P's $200,000 original premium plus 40,000 $\times$ ($42 — $5).
[c] P's retained earnings.
[d] Sum of P's and S's retained earnings.
[e] Plug to equate pooled stockholders' equity to total stockholders' equity before acquisition.

a purchase reports smaller income, $387,000, and larger stockholders' equity of $3,580,000 (return of 11 percent). Notice that the earnings per share figure—one often scrutinized by the stock market—from the pooling-of-interests method is 32 percent larger than for the purchase method.

In summary, if the acquisition qualifies as a purchase, then the reported income of the combined enterprise may be reduced by additional depreciation and amortization expenses. The extra depreciation and amortization expenses result from recognizing increased asset valuations and, perhaps, goodwill. If the acquisition qualifies as a pooling of interests, reported income for the consolidated enterprise will ordinarily be larger than for the same consolidated enterprise accounted for as a purchase. In our opinion, every business combination is, in reality, a purchase of some sort. There is no logical reason, we think, for the pooling-of-interests method of accounting.

SUMMARY

Businesses acquire stock in other businesses for a variety of reasons and in a variety of ways. Accounting for the acquisition and subsequent events depend both on the amount of stock involved and the manner of acquisition. Under the cost method, income is recognized only when dividends are declared by the investee. Consolidated statements and the equity method both have the same effect on the income statement: the acquiring firm shows as income its proportional share of the acquired firm's periodic income after acquisition.

Recording an acquisition as a pooling of interest rather than as a purchase produces different results in the income statement and balance sheet. Under pooling, assets and equities will be shown at lower values on the balance sheet, and the income statement will report a higher net income.

QUESTIONS AND PROBLEMS

1. What is the significance of a "consolidated" balance sheet? What items are usually eliminated in its preparation?

2. The following item appears on a consolidated balance sheet: Minority Interest in Subsidiary Companies. What does it represent?

3. A consolidated balance sheet does not include an item of "goodwill." What are the possible explanations? Consider stock acquired when subsidiary was formed and stock acquired on the market after the subsidiary had been in existence for several years.

4. Why is it impossible to determine from a consolidated balance sheet the amount of retained earnings legally available for dividends, either for the parent company or for the minority interest?

5. Indicate some of the types of eliminations which may be necessary in the preparation of a consolidated income statement.

*6. Why is the equity method sometimes called a *one-line consolidation*?

7. Company *P* buys 100 percent of the stock of Company *S* at a time when *S* has negative retained earnings, that is, a deficit. *P* pays more for *S* than the book value of *S*'s owners' equity. How can this happen?

8. In consolidated statements that are based on the purchase method, the assets of the acquired firm are revalued to current costs. In consolidated statements that account for a pooling of interests, no assets are revalued.
   a. What would be the effect on consolidated statements if the assets of both acquiring and aquired firms were revalued?
   b. What would be the logic to consolidations based on revalued assets for both firms?

9. Buyer Corporation purchased machinery for $20,000, its fair market value, from its wholly owned subsidiary. The machinery had been carried on the books of the subsidiary at a cost of $30,000 and had accumulated depreciation of $15,000. What cost for this machinery would be shown on:
   a. Buyer Corporation's single-company books?
   b. Consolidated balance sheet for Buyer and its subsidiary?
   c. What adjustments would have to be made on the consolidated income statement because of this intercompany transaction?

10. The Roe Company purchased 80 percent of the stock of the Danver Company on January 2, 1975, at its book value, $480,000. The total capital stock of the Danver Company at that date was $450,000 and the retained earnings balance was $150,000. During 1975 the "net income to stockholders" of the Danver Company was $90,000; dividends declared were $36,000. Present adjustment and elimination entries which would be necessary in the preparation of the December 31, 1975 consolidated balance sheet.

11. The Hart Company acquired control of the Keller Company on January 2, 1975, by purchase of 80 percent of its outstanding stock for $700,000. The entire excess of cost over book value acquired is attributed to goodwill which is amortized over forty years. The stockholders' equity accounts of the Keller Company appeared as follows on January 2, 1975, and December 31, 1975.

	Jan. 2, 1975	Dec. 31, 1975
Capital Stock	$600,000	$600,000
Retained Earnings	200,000	420,000

The accounts receivable of the Hart Company at December 31, 1975, contain $4,500 which are amounts due it from the Keller Company. Present entries, in two-column journal form, for the following adjustments and eliminations in the December 31, 1975, working papers for the preparation of the consolidated balance sheet:
   a. the adjustment of the investment in Keller Company at December 31, 1975
   b. the elimination of the investment in Keller Company
   c. the amortization of goodwill

* Hints, key numbers, or (partial) answers appear in the back of the book between the Appendix Tables and the Glossary.

d. the elimination of intercompany obligations

e. the determination of the minority interest.

*12. On January 1, Buyer Company bought common stock of X Company. At the time, the book value of X Company's stockholders' equity was $100,000. During the year, X Company earned $25,000 and declared dividends of $20,000. How much income can Buyer Company report from its investment under the assumption that Buyer Company:

 a. paid $10,000 for 10 percent of the common stock and uses the cost method to account for X Company?

 b. paid $30,000 for 30 percent of the common stock and uses the equity method to account for X Company?

 c. paid $40,000 for 30 percent of the common stock and uses the equity method to account for X Company? Give the *maximum* income that buyer can report from the investment.

13. Company P owns 70 percent of a consolidated subsidiary, Company S. During the year, Company P's sales to Company S amounted to $50,000. The cost of those sales was $35,000. The following data are taken from the two companies' income statements:

	Company P	Company S
Sales	$120,000	$250,000
Cost of Goods Sold	70,000	150,000

Compute consolidated sales and consolidated cost of goods sold for the year assuming

 a. Company S sold all the goods purchased from Company P.

 b. one-third of the goods remains in Company S's inventory at the end of the year.

14. Miller Company and Gordon Company merge in a pooling of interests. Miller Company issues 12,500 shares with market value of $150,000 for 100 percent of Gordon's shares, which have book value of $125,000. Data for the two companies before the merger are shown below.

	Miller Company	Gordon Company
Common Stock (at Par)	$100,000	$ 20,000
Capital Contributed in Excess of Par	50,000	30,000
Retained Earnings	200,000	75,000
Stockholders' Equity	$350,000	$125,000

 a. Over what range of par values for Miller's stock will the pooled retained earnings be equal to the sum of the retained earnings accounts before pooling?

   Construct the pooled stockholders' equity accounts. Assume that Miller Company's stock has a par value per share of:

 *b. $4

 c. $6

 d. $10

 *e. $12

15. The condensed balance sheets of the Ely Company and the Hill Company at December 31, 1975, are as follows:

	Ely Company	Hill Company
Assets		
Cash	$ 60,000	$ 5,000
Receivables	120,000	15,000
Investment in Hill Company Stock	80,000	—
Other Assets	540,000	100,000
	$800,000	$120,000
Liabilities and Stockholders' Equity		
Current Liabilities	$250,000	$ 30,000
Capital Stock	400,000	50,000
Retained Earnings	150,000	40,000
	$800,000	$120,000

The receivables of the Ely Company and the liabilities of the Hill Company contain an advance from the Ely Company to the Hill Company of $5,500.

The Ely Company acquired 85 percent of the capital stock of the Hill Company on the market at January 2, 1975, for $80,000. At that date the balance in the Retained Earnings account of the Hill Company was $30,000. Amortize goodwill over forty years.

Prepare entries, in two-column journal form, for the adjustments and eliminations on the December 31, 1975, consolidated working papers to:
a. adjust the investment in the Hill Company
b. eliminate the investment in the Hill Company
c. amortize goodwill
d. eliminate intercompany obligations
e. determine the minority interest.

16. Refer to the data in Problem 15. Prepare a work sheet for the consolidated balance sheet.

17. a. The Little Company is a subsidiary of the Butler Company. Present entries, in two-column journal form, for the following selected transactions. Record in one group the entries on the books of the Little Company, and in another, the entries on the books of the Butler Company.

   (1) On January 2, 1975, the Butler Company acquired on the market, for cash, 80 percent of all the capital stock of the Little Company. The outlay was $325,000. The total par value of the stock outstanding was $300,000; the retained earnings balance was $80,000. The excess of cost over book value acquired is all attributed to goodwill.
   (2) The Little Company purchased materials from the Butler Company at the latter's cost, $23,000.
   (3) The Little Company obtained an advance of $9,000 from the Butler Company. The funds were deposited in the bank.

(4) The Little Company paid $19,000 on the purchases in (2) above.

(5) The Little Company repaid $7,500 of the loan received from the Butler Company in (3) above.

(6) The Little Company declared and paid a dividend of $24,000 during the year.

(7) The "net income to stockholders" of the Little Company for the year was $40,000. Present only the entry to close the Income Summary account.

b. Prepare adjustment and elimination entries, in two-column journal form, which would be necessary in the preparation of the December 31, 1975 consolidated balance sheet, recognizing the effects of only the above transactions. Amortize goodwill over forty years.

18. Marmee Company and Small Enterprises agree to merge at a time when the balance sheets of the two companies are as shown below.

	Marmee Company	Small Enterprises
Assets	$700,000	$312,000
Liabilities	$150,000	$100,000
Common Stock ($1 Par)	160,000	64,000
Premium on Common Stock	120,000	34,000
Retained Earnings	270,000	114,000
Total Equities	$700,000	$312,000

Marmee issues 50,000 shares with market value $400,000 to the owners of Small in return for their 64,000 shares representing equity of $212,000. The excess of Marmee's cost over the book value of Small's assets acquired results from Small's book value of assets being $148,000 less than their current value and from $40,000 of goodwill.

Prepare consolidated balance sheets as of the merger date assuming the merger is treated as a:
a. purchase
b. pooling of interests.

19. The income statements for Marmee Company and Small Enterprises (see Problem 18) are shown below for the first year after the merger.

	Marmee Company	Small Enterprises
Sales	$2,000,000	$1,500,000
Other Revenues	50,000	10,000
Total Revenues	$2,050,000	$1,510,000
Cost of Goods Sold	1,700,000	1,300,000
Pre-tax Income	$ 350,000	$ 210,000

Make the following assumptions:

(1) The income tax rate for the consolidated firm is 40 percent.

(2) Where necessary, the extra asset costs that must be recognized in the consolidated statement are amortized over five years, and the goodwill is amortized over forty years.

(3) Amortization of extra asset costs and goodwill are not deductible from taxable income in calculations for tax returns.

Prepare consolidated income statements and consolidated earnings per share for the first year following the merger. Assume that the merger is treated as a:

a. purchase

b. pooling of interests.

20. (Adapted from a problem by Clyde P. Stickney.) The following balance sheets show current data for Quarta Company alone and for Quarta Company consolidated with its subsidiary:

	Quarta	Quarta Consolidated
Assets		
Current Assets	$213,000	$358,000
Plant	79,000	147,000
Investment in Subsidiary	159,000	—
Goodwill	—	7,000
	$451,000	$512,000
Equities		
Current Liabilities	$ 78,000	$145,000
Minority Interest	—	29,200
Capital Stock and Premium	320,000	320,000
Retained Earnings	53,000	17,800
	$451,000	$512,000

Quarta purchased 80 percent of the subsidiary several years ago and accounts for the investment using the cost method. The subsidiary issued $100,000 of capital stock at the time of its incorporation and has not changed that amount over the years. Assume there are no intercompany transactions and that goodwill is not being amortized. That is, the excess of cost over book value originally acquired was $7,000.

a. What would be the current balance in Quarta's Investment account had it accounted for the subsidiary using the equity, rather than the cost, method? (You should be able to answer this question without the calculations called for below. If you cannot, then do the other parts and come back to this one.)

*b. Reconstruct the subsidiary's current balance sheet.

c. What was the balance in the subsidiary's retained earnings account at the time it was purchased by Quarta?

d. What is the current stockholders' equity in the subsidiary?

*21. The condensed balance sheets of Companies R and S on December 31, 1975, are as follows:

	Company R	Company S

Assets

	Company R	Company S
Cash	$ 18,000	$ 13,000
Accounts and Notes Receivable	90,000	25,000
Dividends Receivable	—	—
Inventories	220,000	125,000
Investment in Stock of Company S	300,000	—
Plant Assets	300,000	212,000
Total Assets	$928,000	$375,000

Liabilities and Stockholders' Equity

	Company R	Company S
Accounts and Notes Payable	$ 55,000	$ 17,000
Dividends Payable	—	12,500
Other Liabilities	143,000	11,000
Capital Stock	600,000	250,000
Capital Contributed in Excess of Stated Value	—	50,000
Retained Earnings	130,000	34,500
Total Liabilities and Stockholders' Equity	$928,000	$375,000

Additional information:

Company R owns 90 percent of the capital stock of Company S. The stock of Company S was acquired on January 1, 1974, when Company S's retained earnings amounted to $20,000.

Company R has not recorded its share of the dividend declared by Company S.

Company R holds a note issued by Company S in the amount of $8,200.

Excess of cost over book value acquired is all attributable to goodwill, to be amortized over forty years.

a. Present adjustment and elimination entries in journal entry form.

b. Prepare a work sheet for a consolidated balance sheet.

22. The condensed balance sheets of Companies A, Y, and Z on December 31, 1975, are as follows.

	Company A	Company Y	Company Z

Assets

	Company A	Company Y	Company Z
Cash	$ 4,820	$ 3,610	$ 3,230
Accounts Receivable	48,030	14,880	24,220
Notes and Interest Receivable	8,040	—	4,820
Other Assets	509,060	138,880	249,890
Investment in Stock of Company Y	80,500	—	—
Investment in Stock of Company Z	180,000	—	—
Total Assets	$830,450	$157,370	$282,160

Liabilities and Stockholders' Equity

Vouchers Payable	$ 90,050	$ 13,890	$ 24,070
Notes and Interest Payable	—	10,030	—
Other Liabilities	157,710	25,250	32,090
Capital Stock (Par)	500,000	90,000	200,000
Retained Earnings	82,690	18,200	26,000
Total Liabilities and Stock-holders' Equity	$830,450	$157,370	$282,160

Additional information:

Company Z owes Company A, $7,450 on account.

Company A holds a note issued by Company Y, $6,000 plus accrued interest of $25.

Company A owns 75 percent of Company Y. The stock was acquired on January 1, 1970, when Company Y's retained earnings amounted to $12,000. The entire excess of cost over book value acquired was attributable to goodwill to be amortized over forty years.

Company A owns 90 percent of the stock of Company Z. The stock was acquired at par value when Company Z was organized.

a. Present adjustment and elimination entries in journal entry form.

b. Prepare a work sheet for a consolidated balance sheet.

23. The condensed balance sheets of Companies X and Y on December 31, 1975, are as follows:

	Company X	Company Y
Assets		
Investment in Company Y (cost)	$180,000	—
Other Assets	320,000	$290,000
Total Assets	$500,000	$290,000
Liabilities and Stockholders' Equity		
Current Liabilities	$100,000	$ 50,000
Capital Stock	320,000	160,000
Retained Earnings	80,000	80,000
Total Liabilities and Stockholders' Equity	$500,000	$290,000

Additional information:

Company X owns 80 percent of the capital stock of Company Y. The stock of Company Y was purchased on January 1, 1973. There had been no changes in the outstanding shares of Company Y since December 31, 1970. An analysis of the retained earnings account of Company Y is as follows:

Retained Earnings, January 1, 1973		$ 60,000
Net Income:		
1/1/73—12/31/73	$22,000	
1/1/74—12/31/74	11,000	
1/1/75—12/31/75	23,000	56,000
		$116,000

Dividends:

1/1/73—12/31/73	$12,000	
1/1/74—12/31/74	12,000	
1/1/75—12/31/75	12,000	36,000
Retained Earnings, December 31, 1975		$ 80,000

a. Present journal entry to record purchase of stock of Company Y on January 1, 1973.

b. Calculate, as of January 1, 1973, the amount of goodwill arising in connection with the acquisition of the stock of Company Y.

c. Present the entries that would be made on the working papers of December 31, 1973, for each of the following:

(1) adjustment of parent company's investment account
(2) elimination of parent company's investment account
(3) amortization of goodwill over forty years
(4) determination of minority interest.

d. Repeat (**c**) for working papers of December 31, 1974.

e. Repeat (**c**) for working papers of December 31, 1975.

24. The condensed balance sheets of Companies X and Z on December 31, 1975, are as follows:

	Company X	Company Z
Assets		
Investment in Company Z (cost)	$210,000	—
Other Assets	340,000	$335,000
Total Assets	$550,000	$335,000
Liabilities and Stockholders' Equity		
Current Liabilities	$120,000	$ 60,000
Capital Stock	330,000	250,000
Retained Earnings	100,000	25,000
Total Liabilities and Stockholders' Equity	$550,000	$335,000

Additional information:

Company X owns 90 percent of the capital stock of Company Z. The stock of Company Z was purchased on July 1, 1973. There have been no changes in the outstanding shares of Company Z since December 31, 1972. An analysis of the retained earnings account of Company Z is as follows:

Retained Earnings (deficit) January 1, 1973		($24,000)
Net Income: 1/1/73— 6/30/73	$ 4,000	
7/1/73—12/31/73	9,000	
1/1/74—12/31/74	26,000	
1/1/75—12/31/75	30,000	69,000
		$45,000

Dividends:	1/1/73— 6/30/73	$ —	
	7/1/73—12/31/73	5,000	
	1/1/74—12/31/74	7,500	
	1/1/75—12/31/75	7,500	20,000
Retained Earnings, December 31, 1975			$25,000

Instructions:

    a. Present journal entry to record purchase of stock of Company Z on July 1, 1973.

    b. Calculate, as of July 1, 1973, the amount of goodwill arising in connection with the purchase of the stock of Company Z.

    c. Present the entries that would be made on the working papers at December 31, 1973 for each of the following:

        (1) adjustment of parent company's investment account
        (2) elimination of parent company's investment account
        (3) amortization of goodwill over forty years
        (4) determination of minority interest.

    d. Repeat (c) for working papers of December 31, 1974.

    e. Repeat (c) for working papers of December 31, 1975.

*25. General Products (G.P.) Company manufactures heavy-duty industrial equipment and consumer durable goods. In order to enable its customers to make convenient credit arrangements, G. P. Company organized General Products Credit Corporation on January 1, 1970. The G. P. Credit Corporation was organized to finance customer purchases from G. P. Products. G. P. Credit Corporation is 100 percent owned by G. P. Company which invested $55 million cash in the credit company on January 1, 1970. On occasion, G. P. Company advances funds to G. P. Credit Corporation. G. P. Company accounts for its investment in G. P. Credit Corporation using the equity method and shows the investment on its books at equity plus advances. From 1970 through 1973, G. P. Credit Corporation paid dividends of $12 million. Simplified, comparative balance sheets and income statements for 1974, 1975, and 1976 are shown at the end of this problem. G. P. owns stock in many companies and consolidates several of them in its statements.

    a. What was the balance of advances from G. P. Company to G. P. Credit Corporation at the end of each of the three years, 1974, 1975, and 1976?

    b. Given that G. P. Company accounted for its investment in G. P. Credit Corporation on the equity method, identify for each of the three years:

      (i) The components of G. P. Company's income that are attributable to the Credit Corporation's dividends and undistributed earnings.

      (ii) The items on G. P. Company's balance sheet that would be different had there been no investment in the Credit Corporation. That is, show the accounts and balances on G. P. Company's books on the assumption that there had been no investment in the Credit Corporation and that all customers had made the same purchases but merely financed them elsewhere.

    c. For each of the three years, assume that G. P. Company had accounted for its investment in the Credit Corporation using the *cost method.*

      (i) Show the components of G. P. Company's income from the Credit

GENERAL PRODUCTS COMPANY AND CONSOLIDATED AFFILIATES

Financial Position	**(In Millions of $)** December 31		
	1976	1975	1974
Current Assets	$ 3,979.3	$3,639.0	$3,334.8
Investments a	754.9	714.3	630.9
Other Assets	2,667.6	2,534.5	2,232.8
Total Assets	$ 7,401.8	$6,887.8	$6,198.5
Total Current and Long-term Liabilities	$ 4,273.8	$4,043.6	$3,603.6
Minority Interest in Equity of Affiliates	$ 43.4	$ 42.4	$ 41.3
Common Stock	$ 463.1	$ 462.3	$ 460.9
Capital Contributed in Excess of Par Value	396.6	368.8	330.0
Retained Earnings	2,371.4	2,096.2	1,874.1
Less: Common Stock Held in Treasury	(146.5)	(125.5)	(111.4)
Stockholders' Equity	$ 3,084.6	$2,801.8	$2,553.6
Total Equities	$ 7,401.8	$6,887.8	$6,198.5

Current and Retained Earnings	**For the Year**		
	1976	1975	1974
Sales	$10,239.5	$9,425.3	$8,726.7
Net Earnings of Credit Corporation	41.1	30.9	19.9
Other Revenues	148.1	121.1	86.9
Total Revenues	$10,428.7	$9,577.3	$8,833.5
Less:			
Expenses	($9,895.6)	($9,102.3)	($8,499.8)
Minority Interest in Earnings of Affiliates	(3.1)	(3.2)	(5.2)
Net Earnings	$ 530.0	$ 471.8	$ 328.5
Less: Dividends	254.8	249.7	235.4
Earnings Retained for year	$ 275.2	$ 222.1	$ 93.1
Retained Earnings at January 1	2,096.2	1,874.1	1,781.0
Retained Earnings at December 31	$ 2,371.4	$2,096.2	$1,874.1

a Investments in G. P. Credit Corporation
are carried on the books at equity plus
advances in the following amounts .... $ 275.8 $ 232.7 $ 200.7

Corporation and compute how much larger or smaller G. P. Company's income would have been.

(ii) Identify any G. P. Company balance sheet accounts that would have different balances and calculate the differences from what is shown in the actual statements and what would be shown had the alternative treatment been used.

d. For each of the three years, assume that G. P. Company had accounted for its investment in the Credit Corporation by *consolidating* it. Perform the same computations as required in (i) and (ii) of part (c) above.

GENERAL PRODUCTS CREDIT CORPORATION

Financial Position	(In Millions of $) December 31		
	1976	1975	1974
Cash and Marketable Securities	$ 120.9	$ 80.0	$ 73.2
Receivables (Net)	2,648.3	2,262.0	2,068.9
Other Assets	20.3	16.7	14.9
Total Assets	$2,789.5	$2,358.7	$2,157.0
Total Liabilities	$2,529.5	$2,126.8	$1,967.0
Capital Stock	$ 110.0	$ 90.0	$ 55.0
Retained Earnings	150.0	141.9	135.0
Stockholders' Equity	$ 260.0	$ 231.9	$ 190.0
Total Equities	$2,789.5	$2,358.7	$2,157.0

Current and Retained Earnings	For the Year		
	1976	1975	1974
Revenues	$ 319.8	$ 280.0	$ 247.5
Less: Expenses	278.7	249.1	227.6
Net Income	$ 41.1	$ 30.9	$ 19.9
Less: Dividends	33.0	24.0	15.0
Earnings Retained for Year	$ 8.1	$ 6.9	$ 4.9
Retained Earnings at January 1	141.9	135.0	130.1
Retained Earnings at December 31	$ 150.0	$ 141.9	$ 135.0

Chapter 19

Statement of Changes in Financial Position

The three major accounting statements considered so far—the balance sheet, the income statement, and the statement of retained earnings— are comprehensive statements. Virtually every kind of transaction is reflected, one way or another, in those statements. Yet there are certain kinds of transactions that do not appear in those three statements in a way commensurate with their importance to the firm. Financing transactions are often treated within the three statements in ways that make it difficult to appreciate their significance. To remedy this situation, a statement of changes in financial position, such as the one shown in Schedule 19.4, is now required in all annual reports. The statement of changes in financial position was formerly known as a *funds statement* and is still frequently referred to by that name. It provides "information concerning the financing and investing activities of a business enterprise and the changes in its financial position for a period [that] is essential for financial statement users, particularly owners and creditors, in making economic decisions."[1]

RATIONALE FOR THE STATEMENT OF CHANGES IN FINANCIAL POSITION

In describing the relationship of the statement of changes in financial position to the other financial statements, the Accounting Principles Board said that it

[1] Opinion No. 19, Accounting Principles Board, AICPA, issued in March, 1971.

is related to both the income statement and the balance sheet and provides information that can be obtained only partially, or at most in piecemeal form, by interpreting them. . . . The [statement of changes in financial position] cannot supplant either the income statement or the balance sheet but is intended to provide information that the other statements either do not provide or provide only indirectly about the flow of funds and changes in financial position during the period.[2]

For example, a transaction such as the acquisition of land, building, or equipment is not described specifically in the balance sheet or income statement. Such a transaction would be recognizable, if at all, only as a change in one balance sheet item. Although comparing balance sheets might indicate that there had been such a transaction, the single-period statement would give no indication.

Acquiring and financing additional plant is only one of a large number of transactions of this kind. Acquiring or disposing of investments, refunding or retiring debt, and issuing or repurchasing corporate securities are other examples. Some of these transactions appear in the income statement if they include an element of gain or loss. Only a portion of the transaction is reported in the income statement, however. The other parts of the transaction—the amounts received from the sale of investments or plant, the amounts expended to reduce debt, and so on—are not reflected in the income statement and appear in the balance sheet only as they are reflected as elements of the net changes in specific items.

Furthermore, a number of partially offsetting nonincome transactions can occur in a way that obscures the picture. Only the net effect is reported in the balance sheet. For instance, if depreciated old machines were replaced with new ones of the same cost, the balance sheet would not show a change in the asset item machinery. (The contra-asset account showing accumulated depreciation would, of course, change.) If the new machines cost more than the ones they replaced, only the increment in cost would be discernible as a balance sheet change.

Perhaps the most important factor not reported by the balance sheet and income statement alone is how the operations of the period have affected the liquidity of the enterprise. It is easy to assume that increased profits should imply increased holdings of cash (or other liquid assets). But inventories may have increased, new plants may have been acquired, debt may have been paid, and many similar events may have occurred. Some find it hard to understand how a company can report large profits on the income statement and still be pressed for cash. On the other hand, as is pointed out in Chapter 17, increased liquidity can accompany reduced income.

The statement of changes in financial position attempts to explain these apparent paradoxes. Whereas the income statement shows the relation between revenues and expenses, the statement of changes in financial position shows the relation between inflows and outflows of cash and other

[2] Opinion No. 19.

current assets. Rather than analyze the changes in cash alone, the statement of changes in financial position analyzes the changes in *working capital*: the pool of current resources provided by long-term investors, which may be calculated as the excess of current assets over current liabilities.

Until 1971, statements of changes in financial position, or other statements with the same purposes but different names, were issued at the discretion of the firm. The Accounting Principles Board had suggested the use of such statements as early as 1963[3] but did not require them until 1971.[4]

The statement of changes in financial position is based upon the same underlying data used to construct the income statement, the balance sheet, and the statement of retained earnings. It is designed to help answer questions such as:

1. How was net income used?
2. How were purchases of noncurrent assets financed?
3. Why did working capital decrease although income was positive?
4. What uses were made of the proceeds of a security issue?
5. Why must more funds be borrowed for expansion?

The statement of changes in financial position provides useful information otherwise unavailable to the reader of financial statements.

FUNDS: ALTERNATE DEFINITIONS

The statement of changes in financial position is designed to show the flow of current funds through the firm. The first problem is to decide what measure of funds is most useful for showing changes in financial position. There are at least five useful definitions of funds:

1. Cash.
2. Quick assets = cash plus marketable securities plus receivables.
3. Current assets.
4. Net quick assets = quick assets minus current liabilities.
5. Working capital or net current assets (= current assets minus current liabilities).

Clearly, cash is the most restrictive definition of funds, but monitoring cash flows will not ordinarily provide the clearest picture of financial activity. Preparing cash budgets and summaries of cash flows are important for the firm, but owners and creditors are better served by a statement based upon a broader measure of liquidity.

The first three possible definitions of funds are all unsatisfactory because none takes into account any change, particularly increases in current liabilities. If, for whatever reason, a firm wanted to show an increase in funds for the end of a period and one of the first three definitions were used,

---

[3] Opinion No. 3, Accounting Principles Board, AICPA, issued in October, 1963.
[4] Opinion No. 19, Accounting Principles Board, AICPA, issued in March, 1971.

it need only borrow cash for one or two days. A definition of funds based on *net* position is more useful. Net quick assets is probably the best measure of solvency, but working capital (net quick assets plus inventories and current prepayments) is the generally accepted definition of funds. The flows of working capital are explained by the statement of changes in financial position.

The statement of changes in financial position is basically derived from a comparison of balance sheet items during the period being reported on. Transactions involving both working capital (current) accounts and other (noncurrent) balance sheet accounts produce or use funds as follows:

A Transaction Is a

Source of Funds	Use of Funds
If It Results in	**If It Results in**
Decrease in Noncurrent Asset accounts	Increase in Noncurrent Asset accounts
Increase in Noncurrent Liability accounts	Decrease in Noncurrent Liability accounts
Increase in Owners' Equity accounts	Decrease in Owners' Equity accounts

In general, working capital is produced by transactions that increase normal credit balances or decrease normal debit balances in noncurrent item accounts.

PREPARING THE STATEMENT OF CHANGES IN FINANCIAL POSITION

The statement of changes in financial position for a period shows the sources of working capital, its uses, and the change in working capital, both its total and separate components, during the period. One need not know how to construct a statement of changes in financial position in order to effectively use it. Nevertheless, as with other accounting reports, learning how to construct the statement is a good way to understand it. In the next section a step-by-step procedure for preparing the statement of changes in financial position is presented along with a simple illustration. Then, a more complicated illustration is presented. Appendix 19.1 to this chapter presents a comprehensive list of the items included in a statement of changes in financial position, and an explanation of how many of the items are derived.

The Procedure and First Illustration

Step 1. First prepare balance sheets for the beginning and end of the period for which the statement of changes in financial position is to report. In the illustration, the statement is to be prepared for the Stickney Trucking Company for the year of 1975.

Step 2. In two columns to the right of the comparative balance sheets, compute the change in each balance sheet item for the year. In one column show all net debit changes and in the other, all net credit changes. The sum of the debit changes should equal the sum of the credit changes. The comparative balance sheets and calculated changes in balance sheet items for the Stickney Trucking Company are shown in Schedule 19.1.

Step 3. Gather any additional information supplied in the problem statement, in the income statement, or in notes to the balance sheets. Stickney Trucking Company earned income of $92,000 in 1975 and declared and paid $73,000 in dividends.

Step 4. Prepare an analysis of changes in working capital for the period. Such a schedule shows the net change in working capital for the period. Recall that working capital consists of current assets minus current liabilities. You may find it useful to draw lines in the balance sheets to separate the current assets from the noncurrent assets and to separate the current liabilities from the noncurrent liabilities and owners' equity. The analysis of changes in working capital for Stickney Trucking Company is shown as the last section in its statement of changes in financial position in Schedule 19.4. Notice in this example that current liabilities decreased for the year so that the increase in working capital, $7,000, is larger than the increase in its current asset components alone, $6,000. There are no special or technical problems involved in constructing the analysis of changes in working capital other than properly classifying balance sheet items as current or noncurrent. The difficulties in practice are denoting negative changes differently from positive ones and making clear that the net change in current liabilities is subtracted from the net change in current assets to arrive at the net change in working capital. That change may, of course, be negative.

Step 5. Prepare "double-T-accounts" on a separate work sheet, as follows. A "double-T-account" is an ordinary T-account with an extra horizontal line such as the following:

Trucks

42,000	

The only purpose of the extra section in the double-T-account is to show the net change for the period in the item represented by that account. Prepare one such double-T-account for each balance sheet item that is *not* a component of working capital. Enter into the top section of each account the net debit or credit change in that item for the period. (The change in each working capital account has been already accounted for in the analysis of changes in working capital.) In addition, prepare one master double-T-account titled Sources and Uses of Working Capital. This account, when properly completed, will contain all of the information needed to prepare the remainder of the statement of changes in financial position. Care in labeling all entries into this account will facilitate preparing the actual statement. In the top portion of the master double-T-account, enter the change in working capital to be explained for the year, a $7,000 debit change (in-

SCHEDULE 19.1

STICKNEY TRUCKING COMPANY
Comparative Balance Sheets for
December 31, 1974 and 1975

			Net Change for Year	
	Dec. 31, 1975	Dec. 31, 1974	Debit	Credit
Assets				
Cash	$ 10,000	$ 8,000	$ 2,000	
Accounts Receivable	80,000	76,000	4,000	
Trucks (Cost)	160,000	118,000	42,000	
Less Accumulated Depreciation	(58,000)	(38,000)		$20,000
Total Assets	$192,000	$164,000		
Equities				
Accounts Payable	$ 43,000	$ 46,000	3,000	
Notes Payable	2,000	—		2,000
Capital Stock	60,000	50,000		10,000
Retained Earnings	87,000	68,000		19,000
Total Equities	$192,000	$164,000		
Total Changes			$51,000	$51,000

---

crease) in the illustration. Working capital is essentially an asset notion so increases in working capital are debits and decreases are credits. The explanatory material shown in the body of the master double-T-account for Stickney Trucking Company need not be shown. Our purpose in showing it is to make the explanation as clear as we can.

The complete set of double-T-accounts as prepared for Stickney Trucking Company is shown in Schedule 19.2. There are double-T-accounts for each noncurrent balance sheet account and one master account to accumulate sources and uses of working capital. Each double-T-account contains a debit or credit change which is to be explained. At this stage, the sum of the debit changes indicated in the top portion of the accounts should equal the sum of the credit changes. In Schedule 19.2 the debit changes total $49,000, as do the credit changes.

Step 6. Each change in a balance sheet double-T-account is to be explained and will be explained when entries have been made in it that yield a debit (or credit) balance equal to the debit (or credit) change shown. The purpose of these entries is to reconstruct the entries originally recorded in the accounts during the year. The process of making the entries to explain the charges is usually easiest if the supplementary information, gathered in Step 3, is accounted for first. For Stickney Trucking Company,

SCHEDULE 19.2 DOUBLE-T-ACCOUNT WORK SHEET FOR STICKNEY TRUCKING COMPANY

Sources and Uses of Working Capital	
7,000	

From Operations	
Income and Additions	Subtractions

Other Sources	Other Uses

Trucks (Cost)	
42,000	

Accumulated Depreciation	
	20,000

Retained Earnings	
	19,000

Capital Stock	
	10,000

we are told that income was $92,000. The analytical entry to record this information into the double-T-accounts is

(1) Sources and Uses of Working Capital (Income) 92,000
        Retained Earnings 92,000

The information is recorded in the double-T accounts; the "journal entry" above need not be written down. This entry and others, to follow, are entered and numbered in the double-T-accounts shown in Schedule 19.3, but are not entered in the journal and ledger.

Stickney Trucking Company declared and paid $73,000 in dividends. The entry to enter this information into the double-T-accounts is:

(2) Retained Earnings 73,000
        Sources and Uses of Working Capital (Use) 73,000

Each entry into the master account, Sources and Uses of Working Capital, is placed, not just by order of entry, but rather in the appropriate section with a descriptive label. Notice that entries (1) and (2) exactly account for the change to be explained in the Retained Earnings double-T-account.

Next, take any other noncurrent balance sheet account with a change to be explained and reconstruct an appropriate entry or entries. There is a

$42,000 debit change (asset increase) for the account Trucks(Cost). In the absence of information to the contrary, we deduce that new trucks, costing $42,000, were purchased during the year. Consequently the entry would be:

(3) Trucks (Cost) 42,000
        Sources and Uses of Working Capital (Use) 42,000

The next unexplained change is in the account for Accumulated Depreciation. Accumulated Depreciation increased $20,000 (contra-asset credit increase) during the year. Depreciation charges of $20,000 must have been deducted from revenues for the year. These charges, while reducing income, did not require the use of working capital, because they are merely a reduction in a noncurrent asset. To account correctly for the working capital produced by operations, the amount of the depreciation charges must be added to working capital produced by income with the following entry:

(4) Sources and Uses of Working Capital (Addition) 20,000
        Accumulated Depreciation 20,000

The only remaining unexplained change is the balance sheet account Capital Stock. Capital Stock increased (credit increase) by $10,000 during the year. We must assume that $10,000 of additional capital stock was issued. The entry to record the issue and the working capital produced thereby would be:

(5) Sources and Uses of Working Capital (Source) 10,000
        Capital Stock 10,000

All double-T-account changes have been explained. If the work has been done correctly, the change in working capital has also been explained. That is, the sum of the debit entries less the sum of the credit entries in the master account should yield a debit or credit balance exactly equal to the change (debit or credit) in working capital shown at the top of the master account. In the example, the total of the debits is $122,000 and the total of the credits is $115,000. The difference, a debit balance of $7,000, equals the change in working capital to be explained.

Step 7. The Statement of Changes in Financial Position is compiled from information in the double-T-account Sources and Uses of Working Capital. The statement for Stickney Trucking Company is shown in Schedule 19.4.

Extension of Illustration

This illustration for Stickney Trucking Company, now complete, is simpler than the typical problem in at least two respects: First there are not many balance sheet changes to be explained. Second, several types of difficult transactions that affect the sources from operations are not involved and each transaction recorded in Step 6 involves only one debit and one credit.

Before going on to a full-scale, more complicated illustration, recon-

SCHEDULE 19.3 DOUBLE-T-ACCOUNT WORK SHEET FOR STICKNEY TRUCKING COMPANY

Sources and Uses of Working Capital			Trucks (Cost)		
7,000			42,000		
		(3)	42,000		

From Operations

Income plus Additions	Subtractions
Income (1) 92,000 Depreciation Expense (4) 20,000	

Accumulated Depreciation		
	20,000	
	20,000	(4)

Other Sources	Other Uses
Capital Stock Issue (5) 10,000	73,000 (2) Dividends Declared 42,000 (3) Purchase of Trucks

Retained Earnings			
		19,000	
(2)	73,000	92,000	(1)

Capital Stock		
	10,000	
	10,000	(5)

sider Stickney Trucking Company with the following additional information given at Step 3. Stickney Trucking Company sold some trucks during 1975. These trucks cost $10,000 and were sold for $3,000 at a time when accumulated depreciation on the trucks sold was $6,000 resulting in a loss of $1,000. The entry made to record the sale of trucks in the journal at the time of sale was:

Cash	3,000	
Accumulated Depreciation	6,000	
Loss on Sale of Trucks	1,000	
Trucks (Cost)		10,000

SCHEDULE 19.4 STATEMENT OF CHANGES IN FINANCIAL POSITION

STICKNEY TRUCKING COMPANY
Year of 1975

Sources of Working Capital

From Operations:		
Net Income	$92,000	
Addback Excess of Expenses over Working Capital Used for		
Those Expenses:		
Depreciation	20,000	
Total Sources from Operations		$112,000
Proceeds from Capital Stock Issue		10,000
Total Sources of Working Capital		$122,000

Uses of Working Capital

Dividends	$ 73,000
Purchase of Trucks	42,000
Total Uses of Working Capital	$115,000
Increase in Working Capital for the Year (Sources Minus Uses)	$ 7,000

Analysis of Changes in Working Capital

Current Asset Item Increases:		
Cash	$ 2,000	
Accounts Receivable	4,000	
Net Increase (Decrease) in Current Asset Items		$ 6,000
Current Liability Item Increases:		
Accounts Payable	$(3,000)	
Notes Payable	2,000	
Net Increase (Decrease) in Current Liability Items		(1,000)
Increase in Working Capital for the Year (Current Asset Increases Minus Liability Increases)		$ 7,000

Assume that the comparative balance sheets as shown in Schedule 19.1 are correct and that the net change in working capital for 1975 is still $7,000. The statement of changes in financial position would differ accordingly.

Had we been given this supplementary information in Step 3, an additional entry in Step 6 to reflect the new supplementary information would have been necessary:

(1a) Sources and Uses of Working Capital (Sources)	3,000	
Sources and Uses of Working Capital (Additions)	1,000	
Accumulated Depreciation	6,000	
Trucks (Cost)		10,000

The debit to Sources and Uses of Working Capital (Sources) shows the proceeds of the sale. The debit to Sources and Uses of Working Capital (Additions) adjusts the working capital produced from operations to recognize that the Loss on Sale of Truck is a loss that does not require the use of working capital although it reduced income. As a result of this entry, double-T-accounts for Trucks (Cost) and Accumulated Depreciation would then be:

Trucks (Cost)		Accumulated Depreciation	
42,000			20,000
	10,000 (1a)	(1a) 6,000	

Then later, in Step 6, when the time comes to explain the change in the account Trucks(Cost), there is a $42,000 net debit change (asset increase) and an entry (1a) of $10,000 to recognize the disposal of trucks. The increase in Trucks(Cost) can only be accounted for, given the decrease already entered, by assuming that $52,000 of new trucks had been purchased during the period. Then the entry to explain the Trucks(Cost) double-T-account in Step 6 would be:

| (3a) Trucks (Cost) .... | 52,000 | |
| Sources and Uses of Working Capital (Use) .... | | 52,000 |

When the double-T-account for Accumulated Depreciation is explained, there is a credit change of $20,000 and a debit decrease of $6,000 shown as a result of entry (1a). Thus the depreciation expense for 1975 must have been $26,000 and the entry to explain the Accumulated Depreciation would be:

| (4a) Sources and Uses of Working Capital (Addition) .... | 26,000 | |
| Accumulated Depreciation .... | | 26,000 |

The entries for transactions (1), (2), and (5) would be just as before, and the completed master account would appear as shown in Schedule 19.5.

Second Illustration: Western Machine Products Company

Western Machine Products Company purchased 100 percent of the stock of Green Machine Tools Incorporated in 1970. The goodwill arising from the purchase is being amortized at the rate of $10,000 per year. A consolidated statement of changes in financial position is to be constructed for the consolidated enterprise for the year 1975.

Step 1. Western Machine Products Company's consolidated balance sheets for December 31, 1974, and December 31, 1975, are shown in Schedule 19.6.

SCHEDULE 19.5

STICKNEY TRUCKING COMPANY
(Revised to Include Loss on Sale of Trucks)
Sources and Uses of Working Capital

		7,000	

From Operations

Income plus Additions				Subtractions
Income	(1)	92,000		
Loss Not Requiring				
Working Capital	(1a)	1,000		
Depreciation Expense	(4a)	26,000		

Other

Sources					Uses
Capital Stock Issue	(5)	10,000	73,000	(2)	Dividends Declared
Sale of Trucks	(1a)	3,000	52,000	(3a)	Purchase of Trucks

Step 2. The changes for the year in the balance sheet items are calculated and shown in the comparative balance sheets. Notice the separate subtotals for working capital items.

Step 3. The supplementary information supplied includes the consolidated statement of income and retained earnings for 1975, shown in Schedule 19.6, and the following additional items:

   a. Cost of goods sold for the year includes $15,675 of depreciation charges for buildings, machinery, equipment, and tools.

   b. Patent amortization expenses were $600 for the year.

   c. Land costing $5,000 was sold for $5,500.

Step 4. The analysis of changes in working capital is prepared and shown in Schedule 19.8 in the statement of changes in financial position. Working capital increased by $8,567 during 1975. (The sum of the debit changes in working capital items minus the sum of credit changes in working capital items shown in Step 2 is $8,567.)

Step 5. The master double-T-account and accounts for each of the noncurrent balance sheet items that show changes for the year are constructed and the net change for the year is entered in the top portion. The master account, Sources and Uses of Working Capital, shows a net debit change (increase) of $8,567 to be explained. Fourteen noncurrent balance sheet accounts show changes. Double-T-accounts for these fourteen accounts and the master account are shown in Schedule 19.7.

Step 6. The supplementary information is recorded in the double-T-accounts.

   (1) Income for the year, shown in the income statement, is $38,591.

(1) Sources and Uses of Working Capital (Income) 38,591
    Retained Earnings 38,591

(2) Information given in Step 3 indicates depreciation charges for the year, which reduced reported income without using working capital, are $15,675.

SCHEDULE 19.6 WESTERN MACHINE PRODUCTS COMPANY

Comparative Consolidated Balance Sheets
for December 31, 1974 and 1975

	Dec. 31 1975	Dec. 31 1974	Net Change for Year Debit	Credit
Assets				
Current Assets				
Cash	$ 40,275	$ 32,208	$ 8,067	
Receivables	97,100	176,470		$ 79,370
Inventories	225,150	137,260	87,890	
Current Prepayments	10,325	8,345	1,980	
Total Current Assets	$372,850	$354,283	$ 97,937	$ 79,370
Noncurrent Assets				
Buildings (Cost)	$150,000	$150,000		
Machinery and Equipment (Cost)	330,000	304,000	$ 26,000	
Tools (Cost)	1,500	1,500		
Less: Accumulated Depreciation	(195,275)	(179,600)		$ 15,675
Land (Cost)	12,500	10,000	2,500	
Patents	4,000	3,500	500	
Bond Sinking Fund	50,082	45,065	5,017	
Goodwill	140,000	150,000		10,000
Total Noncurrent Assets	$492,807	$484,465	$ 34,017	$ 25,675
Total Assets	$865,657	$838,748	$131,954	$105,045
Liabilities and Stockholders' Equity				
Current Liabilities				
Accounts Payable	$ 40,500	$ 43,500	$ 3,000	
Notes Payable (Due in One Year)	21,000	8,000		$ 13,000
Total Current Liabilities	$ 61,500	$ 51,500	$ 3,000	$ 13,000
Noncurrent Liabilities				
Deferred Taxes	$ 11,000	$ 10,000		$ 1,000
Notes Payable (Due 1980)	6,000	12,000	$ 6,000	
Bonds Payable (9%)	100,000	100,000		
Less: Discount on Bonds Payable	(7,176)	(7,794)		618
Total Noncurrent Liabilities	$109,824	$114,206	$ 6,000	$ 1,618

SCHEDULE 19.6 (*continued*)

Stockholders' Equity

Preferred Stock	$210,000	$200,000		$ 10,000
Premium on Preferred Stock	10,500	10,000		500
Common Stock	50,000	45,000		5,000
Premium on Common Stock	384,565	375,065		9,500
Retained Earnings	39,268	42,977	$ 3,709	
Total Stockholders' Equity	$694,333	$673,042	$ 3,709	$ 25,000
Total Liabilities and				
Stockholders' Equity	$865,657	$838,748		
Total Changes			$144,663	$144,663

**Consolidated Statement of Income and
Retained Earnings, Year of 1975**

Revenues and Gains

Sales		$810,730
Interest on Investments in Sinking Fund		4,250
Gain on Sale of Land		500
Total Revenues and Gains		$815,480
Expenses		
Cost of Goods Sold	$560,050	
Selling Expenses	106,103	
Administrative Expenses	50,000	
Interest Charges	10,236	
Amortization of Goodwill	10,000	
Income Taxes:		
Currently Payable	$39,500	
Deferred Taxes	1,000	
Income Tax Expense	40,500	
Total Expenses		776,889
Net Income		$ 38,591
Retained Earnings, January 1, 1975		42,977
Cash Dividends on Preferred Stock	$12,300	
Cash Dividends on Common Stock	30,000	
Income Distributions		(42,300)
Retained Earnings, December 31, 1975		$ 39,268

---

(2) Sources and Uses of Working Capital (Addition)	15,675	
Accumulated Depreciation		15,675

(**3**) Patent amortization expense for the year, which reduced reported income without using working capital, is $600, given in Step 3. No balance sheet account is shown for the accumulated amortization on patents so we assume that the balance sheet item shown for Patents is net of accumulated amortization.

(3) Sources and Uses of Working Capital (Addition) 600
    Patents 600

(**4**) Land, costing $5,000 was sold for $5,500 producing working capital of $5,500. The resulting gain of $500 produced no additional working capital although it increased reported income. Consequently, working capital from operations must be *reduced* by the amount of the gain.

(4) Sources and Uses of Working Capital (Source) 5,500
    Land 5,000
    Sources and Uses of Working Capital (Subtraction) ... 500

This is the first example of a subtraction from working capital produced by operations. Since the entire proceeds of the land sale, $5,500, are shown as a source, the amount of the gain, $500, must be subtracted so that the working capital produced by this transaction is not counted twice.

The obvious supplementary information has been recognized. (Dividends, as shown in the statement of retained earnings, might be recognized at this point. We do not account for them now, but we shall get a signal later that they need recognition.) Next remains the task of explaining the changes shown for each of the noncurrent balance sheet accounts remaining. These are treated in the order of appearance on the balance sheet.

(**5**) To account for the increase in the Machinery and Equipment account, we must assume that such items costing $26,000 were purchased during the year.

SCHEDULE 19.7 WESTERN MACHINE PRODUCTS COMPANY (Consolidated)

Sources and Uses of Working Capital

		8,567			

From Operations					
Income and Additions				Subtractions	
Income	(1)	38,591	500	(4)	Gain on Sale of Land
Depreciation	(2)	15,675			
Patent Amortization	(3)	600			
Goodwill Amortization	(9)	10,000			
Current Income Tax Liability Less than Income Tax Expense	(10)	1,000			
Bond Discount Amortization	(12)	618			

Other					
Other Sources				Other Uses	
Sale of Land	(4)	5,500	26,000	(5)	Purchase Machines
Preferred Stock Issue	(13)	10,500	7,500	(6)	Purchase Land
Common Stock Issue	(14)	14,500	1,100	(7)	Purchase Patents
			5,017	(8)	Addition to Bond Sinking Fund
			6,000	(11)	Retire Notes Payable
			12,300	(15)	Dividends on Preferred Stock
			30,000	(16)	Dividends on Common Stock

SCHEDULE 19.7 (*continued*)

Machinery and Equipment		Goodwill		Premium on Preferred Stock	
26,000			10,000		500
(5) 26,000			10,000 (9)		500 (13)

Accumulated Depreciation		Deferred Taxes		Common Stock	
	15,675		1,000		5,000
	15,675 (2)		1,000 (10)		5,000 (14)

Land		Notes Payable (Due 1980)		Premium on Common Stock	
2,500		6,000			9,500
(6) 7,500	5,000 (4)	(11) 6,000			9,500 (14)

Patents		Discount on Bonds Payable		Retained Earnings	
500			618		3,709
(7) 1,100	600 (3)		618 (12)	(15) 12,300	38,591 (1)
				(16) 30,000	

Bond Sinking Fund		Preferred Stock	
5,017			10,000
(8) 5,017			10,000 (13)

| (5) Machinery and Equipment .... | 26,000 | |
| Sources and Uses of Working Capital (Use) .... | | 26,000 |

The change in the Accumulated Depreciation account has been explained with entry (2).

(6) The Land account shows a net increase of $2,500 for the year. As a result of entry (4), there was a decrease of $5,000 during the year. We deduce that land costing $7,500 must have been purchased during the year.

| (6) Land .... | 7,500 | |
| Sources and Uses of Working Capital (Use) .... | | 7,500 |

(7) Patents show a net increase for the year of $500. However, entry (3) recognized a decrease of $600. Hence, patents costing $1,100 must have been purchased during the year.

| (7) Patents .... | 1,100 | |
| Sources and Uses of Working Capital (Use) .... | | 1,100 |

(8) The Bond Sinking Fund account shows a net increase of $5,017 for the year. (Income on Sinking Fund investments shown in the Income Statement is part of this amount.) Additional funds ($767 = $5,017 − $4,250) must have been deposited with the trustee. The total use of working capital (investment income plus new deposit) is classified here as an acquisition of a long-term asset although it might reasonably be shown as an "other" use of working capital.

(8) Bond Sinking Fund	5,017	
Sources and Uses of Working Capital (Use)		5,017

(9) Goodwill decreased, net, by $10,000 which can be explained by the amortization of the goodwill arising from the purchase of Green Machine Tools Incorporated in 1970. Such amortization is an expense that does not use working capital.

(9) Sources and Uses of Working Capital (Addition)	10,000	
Goodwill		10,000

(10) The Deferred Taxes account shows a net increase (credit) of $1,000 for the year. That information is consistent with the income statement, which shows current taxes payable to be $1,000 less than tax expense for the year. Hence the amount of working capital used for tax payments is smaller by $1,000 than the tax expense deducted from revenues, so $1,000 must be added to working capital produced by operations.

(10) Sources and Uses of Working Capital (Addition)	1,000	
Deferred Taxes		1,000

(11) Notes Payable (Due 1980) shows a debit change (decrease) of $6,000, which must have been the amount of notes retired during the year.

(11) Notes Payable (Due 1980)	6,000	
Sources and Uses of Working Capital (Use)		6,000

(In principle, when long-term notes become current and are reclassified as a current liability, working capital is decreased, and an entry similar to (11) would also be made.)

(12) The net credit change (decrease) in Discount on Bonds Payable of $618 can be explained by deducing that interest expense for the year included amortization of bond discount. That amortization used no working capital but reduced reported income.

(12) Sources and Uses of Working Capital (Addition)	618	
Discount on Bonds Payable		618

(13) The net increases in Preferred Stock and Premium on Preferred Stock accounts can be explained by deducing that the proceeds of a preferred stock issue during the year were $10,500. In the statement of changes in financial position, the distinction between par value and premium is ignored because the primary concern is the effect on working capital.

(13) Sources and Uses of Working Capital (Source) 10,500
      Preferred Stock   10,000
      Premium on Preferred Stock   500

(**14**) The net changes in Common Stock and Premium on Common Stock accounts are similarly explained by deducing an issue of stock during the year.

(14) Sources and Uses of Working Capital (Source) 14,500
      Common Stock   5,000
      Premium on Common Stock   9,500

(**15**) and (**16**) The Retained Earnings account shows a net decrease of $3,709 to be explained. Entry (1) shows an additional increase of $38,591. Thus a $42,300 total decrease in retained earnings must be explained. The Retained Earnings account is decreased by dividends. An examination of the statement of retained earnings shows that $42,300 of dividends ($12,300 of preferred and $30,000 of common) were declared during the year. Had this fact been noticed during Step 3, the following entries could have been made then.

(15) Retained Earnings 12,300
      Sources and Uses of Working Capital (Use)   12,300
(16) Retained Earnings 30,000
      Sources and Uses of Working Capital (Use)   30,000

After entry (16) all balance sheet double-T-account changes have been explained. The sum of debits minus the sum of credits in the Sources and Uses of Working Capital account yields a debit balance of $8,567, which is exactly equal to the change in working capital which was to be explained.

Step 7. The consolidated statement of changes in financial position is constructed from the information shown in the master account, Sources and Uses of Working Capital. The statement is shown in Schedule 19.8.

SUMMARY

The statement of changes in financial position shows the sources and uses of working capital for the entity. The content of this statement can be summarized by comparing it to one form of the basic accounting equation.
    Assume the following abbreviations:

CA = Current Assets
NCA = Noncurrent Assets
CL = Current Liabilities
NCL = Noncurrent Liabilities
SE = Stockholders' Equity.

The accounting equation states that

$$CA + NCA = CL + NCL + SE.$$

SCHEDULE 19.8

WESTERN MACHINE
Consolidated Statement
Financial Position,

Sources of Working Capital

A. From Operations

Net Income		$38,591
Expense and Revenue Adjustments		
Add Back Excess of Expenses over		
Working Capital Used for Those Expenses:		
Depreciation	$15,675	
Amortization of Patents	600	
Amortization of Goodwill	10,000	
Amortization of Bond Discount	618	
Taxes Currently Payable Less Than		
Tax Expense	1,000	
Total Addition to Working Capital		
from Expense and Revenue Adjustments ...	27,893	
Less Excess of Gain over Working Capital		
Produced by That Gain	(500)	
Total Sources from Operations		$65,984

B. Proceeds from Securities Issues:

Preferred Stock Issue	$10,500	
Common Stock Issue	14,500	
Total Sources from Security Issues		25,000

C. Proceeds from Sale of Land .... | | 5,500

Total Sources of Working Capital		$96,484

Furthermore, this equation is true for both the start-of-period and end-of-period balance sheets. Let the symbol "$\triangle$" represent the change in an item so that, for example, $\triangle CA$ denotes the change in Current Assets during a period. Then the accounting equation can be rewritten as

$$\triangle CA + \triangle NCA = \triangle CL + \triangle NCL + \triangle SE.$$

Rearranging terms in the above equation,

$$\triangle CA - \triangle CL = \triangle NCL + \triangle SE - \triangle NCA.$$

The quantity $CA - CL$ is working capital so that the left-hand side of the last equation denotes the net change in working capital. Therefore, the right-hand side is also equal to the net change in working capital. The details of the left-hand side are shown in the last portion of the statement of changes in financial position under the subtitle Analysis of Changes in Working Capital. The right-hand side of the equation is reflected in the

PRODUCTS COMPANY
of Changes in
Year of 1975

Uses of Working Capital

A. Income Distributions
    Dividends on Preferred Stock $12,300
    Dividends on Common Stock 30,000
    Total Income Distributions $42,300
B. Retirement of Notes Payable (Due 1980) 6,000
C. Acquisition of Noncurrent Assets
    Machinery $26,000
    Land 7,500
    Patents 1,100
    Addition to Bond Sinking Fund 5,017
    Total Acquisitions of Noncurrent Assets 39,617
    Total Uses of Working Capital $87,917

Net Increase in Working Capital for Year
    (Sources Minus Uses) .... $ 8,567

Analysis of Changes in Working Capital

Current Asset Item Increases (Decreases)
    Cash .... $ 8,067
    Receivables .... (79,370)
    Inventories 87,890
    Current Prepayments 1,980
Net Increase in Current Asset Items $18,567
Current Liability Item Increases (Decreases)
    Accounts Payable .... $(3,000)
    Notes Payable (Due in One Year) 13,000
Net Increase in Current Liability Items 10,000
Net Increase in Working Capital for Year
    (Current Asset Increases Minus Current Liability Increases)... $ 8,567

---

sources and uses of working capital shown in the Sources and Uses sections. Transactions involving working capital accounts that also increase long-term liabilities or stockholders' equity must increase working capital while transactions involving working capital accounts that increase long-term assets must decrease working capital.

The statement of changes in financial position, as the above equations show, is merely the information from two balance sheets shown in a different format. Since the balance sheet balances and every properly analyzed transaction maintains the balance, so must every transaction, properly analyzed, maintain the equality of working capital changes shown in the statement of changes in financial position. Examine any conceivable transaction in Figure 19.1.

Assets	Liabilities and Stockholders' Equity
Current Assets (1)	Current Liabilities (2)
Noncurrent Assets (3)	Noncurrent Liabilities and Stockholders' Equity (4)

(dashed line marked —Current Line separates quadrants 1,2 from 3,4)

Figure 19.1 Schematic Balance Sheet

Any transaction for which all debits and credits are above the current line, in quadrants 1 and 2, will affect only the analysis of changes in working capital. For example, the collection of a receivable, the discharge of a payable, and the sale of marketable securities for cash all affect accounts above the current line and affect only the analysis of changes in working capital. Any other transaction, with two exceptions, will affect the statement of changes in financial position. The exceptions, stock splits and the issue of stock dividends, affect only retained earnings and contributed capital. They have no effect on working capital and will not appear in the statement of changes in financial position.

APPENDIX 19.1: COMPONENTS OF A COMPREHENSIVE STATEMENT OF CHANGES IN FINANCIAL POSITION

This appendix gives a detailed example of a statement of changes in financial position, and an explanation of how some of the items are derived. Schedule 19.9 shows a detailed statement of changes in financial position for the Cole-Vatter Corporation. Each entry in the example statement is numbered for reference in later explanation. No published statement we know of contains all the items shown here, but we show this much detail to illustrate the various items that may appear in the statement.

The statement of changes in financial position for a period shows the sources and uses of working capital and an analysis of the changes in specific working capital components during the period. The statement of changes in financial position shown here maintains a balance between its two, dual portions: the sources and uses of working capital on the one hand (lines 1-45) and the analysis of changes in working capital on the other (lines 46-54). Generally accepted accounting principles allow a variety of formats for this statement and, because the analysis of changes in working capital shown in lines 46-54 is so easy to derive from comparative balance sheets, accounting principles do not require that it be shown as part of the statement itself, but allow it to appear in footnotes. Showing the analysis of changes in working capital in footnotes obscures the elegance and balance of the statement of changes in financial position. The following sections explain the components of the statement in the order of their appearance.

Working Capital from Operations (Lines 1–21)

The section of the statement of changes in financial position that shows the sources of working capital resulting from operations presents the information about fund flows that many users of the statement believe to be the most important. The difficulties in preparing this section arise not so much from the inherent complexity of any one adjustment as from there being so many possible adjustments.

The first entry (line 1) in the statement of changes in financial position is the income before extraordinary items taken from the income statement. (The effects of extraordinary items and the adjustments thereto are, by accepted convention, shown separately from other items.) Not all revenues produce working capital nor do all expenses use working capital. Consequently, the remainder of the first section (lines 2–15) is devoted to adjustments to ordinary income (line 1) for income-related transactions that do not affect working capital.

The first set of adjustments to working capital produced by operations are "addbacks," items that reduced reported income without reducing working capital (lines 2–9).

The most common addback is one for depreciation. Depreciation is an expense that does not use working capital. *Depreciation is not a source of working capital.* Rather, depreciation reduces income without using working capital, because it diminishes a noncurrent asset, plant. The most flagrant error made by users of the statement of changes in financial position is to consider depreciation to be a source of funds or working capital. It is a common error abetted by many published statements of changes in financial position. For example, a recent statement of changes in financial position of the General Electric Company, whose accounting reports we think generally superior to others we have seen, reads in part as follows:

Sources of funds	(In millions)
From Operations:	
Net Earnings	$585.1
Depreciation	334.0

Depreciation is not a source of funds.

Nor is amortization of patents or other intangibles a source of funds. Such amortization is an expense that is not a use of working capital, because it reduces a noncurrent asset. It is an addback (line 3) in the determination of working capital produced by income from operations. (See the statement of changes in financial position of the Zenith Radio Corporation,

SCHEDULE 19.9

Sources of Working Capital			($ in 000's)
A. From Operations			
(1) a	Income Before Extraordinary Items		$48,278
	Expense and Revenue Adjustments		
	Additions for Excess of Expenses and Losses Over Working Capital Used for Those Items:		
(2)	Depreciation of Plant	$30,082	
(3)	Amortization of Patents	2,027	
(4)	Losses from Company S1 Accounted for on Equity Method	3,632	
(5)	Loss on Sale of Land or Plant or on Bond Retirement	1,288	
	Income Tax Timing Differences b		
(6)	(Tax Expense greater than Tax Payable)	1,450	
	Bonds Payable Discount Amortization		
(7)	(Interest Expense greater than Interest Payable)	605	
	Minority Shareholders' Equity in Income		
(8)	Retained by Consolidated Subsidiaries	398	
	Total Additions to Working Capital from		
(9)	Expense and Loss Adjustments	$39,482	
	Subtractions for Excess of Working Capital Used for Expenses Over Those Expenses; Subtractions for Excess of Revenues or Gains Over Working Capital Produced by Those Revenues or Gains:		
	Income Tax Timing Differences b		
(10)	(Taxes Payable greater than Tax Expense)	—	
	Bonds Payable Premium Amortization		
(11)	(Interest Payable greater than Interest Expense)	$ 205	
	Share of Earnings Retained by Company S2		
(12)	Accounted for on Equity Method	795	
(13)	Gain on Sale of Land or Plant or on Bond Retirement	214	
	Total Subtractions from Working Capital from		
(14)	Expense and Gain Adjustments	$ 1,214	
(15)	Total Expense, Loss, and Gain Adjustments		38,268
	Extraordinary Items and Adjustments:		
(16)	Income from Extraordinary Items (from Income Statement)	$ 1,284	
	Plus Charges for Extraordinary Items Not Using Working Capital:		
(17)	Loss from Expropriation of Plant in Country X	100	
(18)	Minority Shareholders' Equity in Extraordinary Items	59	
		$ 1,443	
(19)	Less Extraordinary Income Not Producing Working Capital	73	
(20)	Working Capital from Extraordinary Items as Adjusted		1,370
(21)	Working Capital Produced by Operations and Extraordinary Items, as Adjusted		$ 87,916
	B. Proceeds from Security and Debt Issues		
(22)	Bond Issue (7%, maturing in 1995)	$20,250	
(23)	Mortgage (to Acquire Land)	1,500	
(24)	Common Stock Issued for Options Exercised by Employees	13	
(25)	Common Stock Issued for Expansion	500	
(26)	Proceeds from Securities and Debt Issues		22,263
	C. Proceeds from Long-term Asset Dispositions		
(27)	Sale of Land	$ 730	
(28)	Sale of Plant	6,356	
(29)	Proceeds from Long-term Asset Dispositions		7,086
	D. Other Sources		
(30)	Partial Refund of Income Taxes from 1973		214
(31)	Total Working Capital Produced by All Sources		$117,479

IN FINANCIAL POSITION
Corporation
of 1975

	Uses of Working Capital	($ in 000's)	
	A. For Income Distributions		
(32) a	Cash Dividends on Common Stock ($.50 per share)	$ 7,000	
(33)	Cash Dividends on Preferred Stock	100	
(34)	Uses for Income Distributions		$ 7,100
	B. Expenditures for Security and Debt Retirements		
(35)	Bonds (8%, maturing in 1990)	$10,125	
(36)	Preferred Stock (6%)	32,781	
(37)	Acquisitions of Common Stock for Treasury	5,128	
(38)	Uses for Security and Debt Retirements		48,034
	C. Expenditures for Long-term Asset Purchases		
(39)	Land	$10,000	
(40)	Plant	3,023	
(41)	Stock of Company S3 for Investment Purposes	27,743	
(42)	Uses for Purchases of Long-term Assets		40,766
	D. For Other Uses		
(43)	Additional Payment for 1972 Income Taxes		217
(44)	Total Working Capital Used		$96,117
	Increase (Decrease) in Working Capital for Year:		
	Sources (line 31) of Working Capital Minus		
(45)	Uses (line 44) of Working Capital		$21,362

Analysis of Changes in Working Capital

	Current Asset Item Changes		
(46)	Cash	$ 1,357	
(47)	Marketable Securities	15,483	
(48)	Receivables	2,129	
(49)	Inventories	4,077	
(50)	Increase (Decrease) in Current Asset Items		$23,046
	Current Liability Item Changes		
(51)	Payables	$ 529	
(52)	Notes	1,155	
(53)	Increase (Decrease) in Current Liability Items		1,684
	Increase (Decrease) in Working Capital for Year:		
	Current Asset Changes (line 50) Minus		
(54)	Current Liability Changes (line 53)		$21,362

a Line numbers are shown for easy reference.
b Only one of these two items will appear for any one year.

reproduced in Chapter 25, for a good way to disclose the nature of addbacks for amortization.)

In Chapter 18, the equity method of accounting for subsidiaries is explained. When a corporation accounts for its investments in a subsidiary on the equity method, the corporation will show as revenue its proportionate share of income earned and retained by the subsidiary. Such income produces no working capital for the owning corporation but, instead, affects the investments account, a noncurrent asset. To adjust for revenue not producing working capital requires a subtraction, such as shown on line 12. If the subsidiary reports a loss for the period, the owning corporation will show its share of that loss. But such losses do not use the owner's working capital and must be added back (line 4) to determine the owner's working capital from operations.

The disposition of a long-term asset introduces a subtle problem in the preparation of a statement of changes in financial position. Suppose that plant costing $1,000,000 with $850,000 of accumulated depreciation is sold for $140,000. The entry to record that transaction in the journal would be:

Cash	140,000	
Accumulated Depreciation	850,000	
Loss on Sale of Plant	10,000	
Plant		1,000,000

Working capital is produced by the disposition of long-term assets with the proceeds, $140,000, being shown on line 28. The Loss on Sale of Plant does not use working capital because it was matched by a reduction of a noncurrent asset, plant. The working capital resulting from operations must be adjusted to reflect that fact. Consequently, the amount of loss that did not use working capital is added back on line 5 to the amount for working capital resulting from operations. *Losses do not produce working capital.* Rather, they are a reduction in income that did not use working capital. The net change in working capital resulting from disposition for a gain will always be larger than the working capital resulting from disposition of the same asset at a loss. Consider the same plant disposition but assume that the proceeds were $160,000. The entry to record that transaction in the journal would be:

Cash	160,000	
Accumulated Depreciation	850,000	
Plant		1,000,000
Gain on Sale of Plant		10,000

The statement of changes in financial position would show the $160,000 proceeds from the sale of plant as a source of working capital (line 28). Notice that the Gain on Sale of Plant is part of income before extraordinary items (line 1). In the absence of adjustments to account for this problem, the gain from sale of the long-term asset, Plant, would be counted twice as a source of working capital: once in income (line 1) and again as part of the proceeds from the disposition (line 28). To correct for this, the gain on sale of plant is treated as revenue not producing working capital, and the working capital produced by operations is adjusted to reflect that fact. This adjustment is shown on line 13. (Equally logically, the adjustment could be made on the line showing the proceeds of disposition. Rather than show the entire $160,000 as proceeds, the proceeds producing working capital equal to the book value of $150,000 could be shown on line 28.

If this second method were adopted, then the title of subsection C would have to be changed in order to accurately describe the amount shown there. The accepted accounting convention, however, is to show the entire proceeds of a disposition as such and to make adjustments only in the section reporting working capital produced by operations. That convention confines possible confusion to the one top section instead of spreading it over the entire statement.)

In Chapter 15, deferred income taxes are explained. Income tax expense need not, and usually will not, be exactly equal to income taxes paid or payable for the period. This difference, if positive as is usual, is an expense that does not use working capital and must be added back (line 6) to derive working capital produced from operations. As was explained in Chapter 15, income tax expense can be smaller than the amount paid or payable for the period. Then, the difference (expense minus paid or payable) will be negative and more working capital will be used for income taxes than the income statement shows. In that case, the adjustment to working capital produced by operations is a deduction (line 10).

The nature of the Discount on Bonds Payable account and amortization of the discount are explained in Chapter 15. When bonds are issued at a discount, interest expense (effective rate times outstanding loan) is larger than interest paid or payable (via coupons) for the period. Since the expense shown on the income statement is larger than the amount of working capital used for that expense, the part of expense that did not require working capital, namely the amortized discount, must be added back (line 7) to determine working capital produced by operations.

On the other hand, bonds may be issued at a premium. When the premium is amortized, interest expense shown on the income statement will be smaller than working capital paid, or payable, to bondholders through redemption of coupons. The portion of working capital paid, or payable, to bondholders that was not an expense, namely the amortized premium, does not appear on the income statement and must be subtracted (line 11) to determine working capital produced by operations. Examine the entry the Macaulay Corporation (Chapter 15) would make to record interest expense for the first six months of a $100,000 8-percent semiannual coupon bond issue sold for $107,100, to yield 7 percent.

Interest Expense ($107,100 × .07/2)	3,749	
Amortization of Premium on Bonds Payable	251	
Interest Payable ($100,000 × .04)		4,000

This transaction consumed $4,000 of working capital, but only $3,749 was charged as interest expense on the income statement. The other $251 paid reduced the long-term liability, Premium on Bonds Payable, and must be subtracted (line 11) to determine working capital produced from operations.

The last addback to ordinary income (line 8) in the determination of working capital from operations results from the treatment of the minority interest in less-than-wholely-owned subsidiaries. Refer to the consolidated income statement shown in Chapter 25, Schedule 25.3, for W. R. Grace &

Company. Notice, there, that "Income applicable to minority stockholders" is subtracted *before* the consolidated income figure is derived. Such subtractions will appear on consolidated income statements reporting on operations of subsidiaries that are not wholly owned. Such charges are quite proper in determining the income to the shareholders of the parent, but they do not use any working capital of the consolidated enterprise. Consequently, charges against consolidated income to recognize the minority interest must be added back (line 8) to income to determine working capital produced by operations. The existence of a minority interest in the income of consolidated subsidiaries does not reduce working capital. Aside from the effect of dividends, whether or not a consolidated subsidiary is wholly owned does not affect the working capital of the consolidated enterprise.

The subtractions from working capital shown in lines 10-14 arise from transactions similar to those requiring addbacks. Subtractions are required either when less working capital is produced than is recorded as revenues and gains, or when more working capital is used than is recorded as expenses or losses.

Finally, the effect of extraordinary items on working capital must be taken into account (lines 16-20). Such items introduce nothing new in principle. Their separate treatment reflects the generally accepted accounting principle that segregation of the unusual and infrequent extraordinary items from ordinary items presents a fairer picture of activities. The section of the income statement reporting extraordinary items is itself a miniature income statement. Thus, the adjustments to determine the effects of extraordinary items on working capital are similar to the ones for ordinary income. They require no additional description.

Sources of Working Capital Other than from Operations (Lines 22-31)

Working capital can be provided from the issue of securities or debt and from the disposition of long-term assets. (Disposition of current assets, such as marketable securities (line 47) for cash (line 46), is merely an exchange of one form of working capital for another. Such exchanges will affect only the analysis of changes in working capital.) Recording the issue of securities in the statement of changes in financial position is straightforward. If common stock is issued for cash, then the proceeds will appear in the statement of changes in financial position as a source (line 25) and as an increase in the working capital item, cash (line 46).

Uses of Working Capital (Lines 32-45)

Working capital is "used" in many ways. A majority of the uses of working capital are for operations affecting income and, hence, are reflected in line 1 of the statement of changes in financial position. The three other important uses of working capital can be classified as distributions of income to owners (lines 32-34), retirements of securities (lines 35-38), and purchases of long-term assets (lines 39-42). Other uses of working capital (lines 43-44), such as the payment of extra taxes to settle prior years' claims of the government, are infrequent.

Accounting for these explicit uses of working capital does not present special recording problems. Consider the transaction that results from the retirement of bonds at a loss. Suppose that the journal entry to record the retirement of bonds was:

Bonds Payable	10,000	
Loss on Retirement of Bonds	500	
Cash		9,500
Discount on Bonds Payable		1,000

The loss of $500 is reflected in the income statement and, hence, in line 1 of the statement of changes in financial position. The expenditure of $9,500 to reacquire the bonds is shown on line 46. To avoid double counting, the $500 loss must be shown as an addback on line 5. Had the bonds been retired for $8,500 cash, producing a $500 gain, a subtraction to be shown on line 13 would be necessary.

Suppose that preferred stock were retired for less than par value. Since no gain nor loss is recognized on capital stock transactions, a typical journal entry might be:

Preferred Stock	10,000	
Cash		9,500
Capital Contributed in Excess of Par		500
To recognize additional paid-in capital resulting from retirement of preferred stock at less than par.		

Both the Preferred Stock and Capital Contributed in Excess of Par accounts are owners' equity accounts. The net reduction in owners' equity is $9,500. Hence the statement of changes in financial position would show a use of $9,500 of working capital to retire securities (line 36) and a $9,500 decrease in cash (line 46).

Notice that all acquisitions of long-term assets are shown in the statement of changes in financial position, no matter how the acquisition was financed. If the firm acquired land for cash, the transaction would result in an increase in a long-term asset (line 39) and a decrease in cash (line 46). If the firm acquired land in exchange for a mortgage, the acquisition would nevertheless be shown as a use of working capital (line 39), and the proceeds of the mortgage would be shown as a source of working capital (line 23). In effect, the acquisition of land in exchange for a mortgage is treated in the statement of changes in financial position as two transactions: (1) the issue of a mortgage for cash and (2) the purchase of land for cash. The total amount of working capital is unchanged by such transactions.

Similarly, if stock were issued for the acquisition of a plant, the transaction would be recorded both as a source (line 25) and a use of working capital (line 40) although none was explicitly produced nor used. The fiction that cash is raised by a stock issue and then used for plant acquisition is consistent with the requirement in APB Opinion No. 19 that the statement of changes in financial position discloses all financing transactions.

Analysis of Changes in Working Capital (Lines 46-54)

The final section of the statement of changes in financial position shows the change in each of the components of working capital for the period. This section may have one of several titles or may appear in footnotes. The rest of the statement of changes in financial position explains how the changes reported here came about. (In fact, one of the earliest mentions of a similar statement was called, simply "Where Got" for the sources and "Where Gone" for the uses.[5]) The many transactions with either debit or credit entries in noncurrent asset, liability noncurrent, and stockholders' equity accounts bring about the actual changes in the working capital items.

QUESTIONS AND PROBLEMS

1. What is the objective of a statement of changes in financial position?

2. Can the statement of changes in financial position substitute for the balance sheet? The income statement?

3. Indicate the presentation, if any, of each of the following in a statement of changes in financial position:
   a. increase in allowance for uncollectible accounts
   b. increase in accumulated depreciation
   c. gain on sale of machinery
   d. issue of bonds at a premium
   e. amortization of bond premium
   f. issue of shares of common stock as a dividend to common stockholders
   g. declaration of a cash dividend on common stock. The dividend has not been paid at the close of the fiscal year.
   h. increase in retained earnings appropriated for contingencies.

4. Indicate the presentation, if any, of each of the following in a statement of changes in financial position:
   a. issue of preferred stock at more than par value
   b. issue of common stock at less than par value
   c. gain on sale of investments
   d. purchase discounts
   e. reacquisition and retirement of bonds at more than book value
   f. refund of income taxes for payment made three years ago
   g. issue of bonds at less than par value.

5. Indicate the treatment of the following items in the preparation of a statement of changes in financial position:
   a. amortization of patent charged to production activities

---

[5] William Morse Cole, *Accounts: Their Concept and Interpretation* (New York: Houghton-Mifflin, 1908).

    b. amortization of patent charged to royalty revenues

    ***c.** acquisition of a factory site by donation from a city

    d. issuance of stock to founders for promotional services which are treated as expenses of the period

    ***e.** uninsured fire loss of a warehouse

    ***f.** uninsured fire loss of merchandise stored in the warehouse

    g. loss on sale of sinking fund investments

    h. issuance of bonds at less than par value

    i. issue of common stock in conversion of bonds.

6. Indicate the presentation, if any, of the following in a statement of changes in financial position:

    a. collection of accounts receivable

    b. retirement of preferred stock at less than par value

    c. issue of bonds at less than par value

    d. an addition to retained earnings appropriated for plant expansion

    e. transfer from retained earnings appropriated for plant expansion to retained earnings

    f. sale of equipment at less than book value

    g. amortization of discount on investment in bonds of another company.

7. A statement of changes in financial position contains an item entitled "decrease in deferred charges" as a source of working capital. What is the nature of this item?

8. One writer stated that "Depreciation was the chief source of funds for growth in some industries." A reader criticized this statement replying: "the fact remains that if the companies listed . . . had elected, in any year, to charge off ten million more depreciation than they did charge off, they would not thereby have added one dime to the total of their funds available for plant expansion or for increasing inventories or receivables. Therefore, to speak of depreciation as a source of funds . . . has no significance in a discussion of fundamentals."

    Comment on these statements, ignoring income tax effects.

***9.** The comparative balance sheet of the Johns Company showed a balance in the Buildings and Equipment account at December 31, 1975, of $24,645,000; at December 31, 1974, the balance was $24,150,000. The Accumulated Depreciation account showed a balance of $8,670,000 at December 31, 1975, and $7,655,000 at December 31, 1974. The president's report states that expenditures for buildings and equipment for the year totaled $1,325,000. The income statement indicates a depreciation charge of $1,205,000 for the year and a gain of $52,750 from the disposition of buildings and equipment in the determination of the periodic income.

    a. Determine the original cost and accumulated depreciation of the buildings and equipment retired during the year and the proceeds from their disposition.

    b. Indicate the presentation of all of the above data on the statement of changes in financial position.

---

* Hints, key numbers, or (partial) answers appear in the back of the book between the Appendix Tables and the Glossary.

10. The income statement of the Weller Company reports an excess of sales over cost of goods sold of $55,360,500 for 1975. $7,835,000 of depreciation is included in the items making up the cost of goods sold. Included among the other items in the determination of income are the following:

Dividend revenue, including $100,000 not yet received ...... $ 450,000
Gain on sale of depreciable assets 80,000
Uninsured fire loss 70,000
Interest charges, including $7,500 of
    bond-discount amortization 125,250
Income taxes (expense = payable) 17,600,000

Determine the amount of working capital made available from regular operations during the year. Show your calculations.

11. The comparative balance sheets of the Rocker Company showed the following items:

	12/31/74	12/31/75
Plant, Property, and Equipment	$12,437,000	$13,648,000
Accumulated Depreciation	6,055,000	6,215,000

The income statement of 1975 included an item of $10,700 as a gain on sale of plant, property, and equipment and a depreciation charge of $527,000 for the year. The president's comments indicate that $1,691,000 was expended on new plant, property and equipment during the year.
a. Determine the original cost and accumulated depreciation of the plant, property, and equipment retired during the year.
b. Determine the proceeds of the sale of plant, property, and equipment.
c. Indicate the presentation of all of the above data on the statement of changes in financial position.

12. The Cole-Vatter Corporation owns 90 percent of a finance company and accounts for it using the equity method. The finance company earned $50,000 for the year and paid $20,000 in dividends. What lines of its statement of changes in financial position (Appendix 19.1) will be affected and by how much?

13. The Cole-Vatter Corporation sells equipment with accumulated depreciation of $20,000 at a loss of $10,000 for $40,000. What lines of its statement of changes in financial position (Appendix 19.1) will be affected and by how much?

14. The following lines appear in the Beaver Company's statement of changes in financial position:

Sources of Working Capital

Income Before Extraordinary Items $60,000
    Plus Addbacks
        Depreciation $20,000
        Amortization on Bonds 170

a. The depreciation was for a two-year-old (at start of year) asset with a service life of 4 years. If the asset is being depreciated on the sum-of-the-years'-digit method, what is the depreciable cost of the asset?

b. Beaver Company issued $100,000 of 8-percent annual coupon bonds at a price to yield 8.6 percent several years ago and amortizes discount and premium using the effective-interest method. What was the amount of the discount or premium at the start of the year?

*15. Condensed financial statement data for the Lee Company for the year ending December 31, 1975, are presented below:

LEE COMPANY
Post-Closing Trial Balance
Comparative Data

	12/31/75	12/31/74
Debits		
Cash	$ 46,960	$ 53,870
Accounts Receivable	183,710	156,180
Plant and Equipment	1,859,340	1,703,650
	$2,090,010	$1,913,700
Credits		
Accounts Payable	$ 64,180	$ 61,370
Accumulated Depreciation	560,210	491,650
Long-term Debt	279,810	223,480
Capital Stock	645,750	611,350
Retained Earnings	540,060	525,850
	$2,090,010	$1,913,700

Income and Retained Earnings Statement Data

Sales	$1,037,150
Cost of Goods Sold	690,930
Selling and Administrative Expenses	124,990
Depreciation	109,760
Other Expenses	1,270
Federal Income Taxes	37,840
Interest Charges	10,410
Loss on Disposal of Plant and Equipment	7,780
Dividends Declared—Paid in Cash	5,560
Dividends—Payable in Capital Stock	34,400

Expenditures on plant and equipment for the year amounted to $219,740.

Prepare a statement of changes in financial position including an analysis of working capital for the Lee Company for the year 1975.

16. Condensed financial statement data of the Alberta Company for the years ending December 31, 1975, and December 31, 1974, are presented below:

ALBERTA COMPANY
Post-Closing Trial Balance
Comparative Data

	12/31/75	12/31/74	12/31/73
Debits			
Current Assets	$ 326,800	$ 316,190	$ 290,160
Noncurrent Assets	1,874,630	1,679,220	1,616,390
	$2,201,430	$1,995,410	$1,906,550
Credits			
Current Liabilities	$ 83,450	$ 79,860	$ 81,530
Accumulated Depreciation	746,770	720,970	697,390
Long-term Debt	135,070	90,110	105,760
Capital Stock	513,720	423,220	376,670
Retained Earnings	722,420	681,250	645,200
	$2,201,430	$1,995,410	$1,906,550

Income and Retained Earnings Statement Data

	1975	1974
Sales	$ 970,260	$ 909,690
Cost of Goods Sold	413,810	370,170
Selling and Administrative Expense	301,120	319,920
Depreciation	97,800	87,140
Interest and Other Revenue	7,220	4,740
Federal Income Taxes	72,350	66,370
Gain (Loss) on Disposal of Plant and Equipment	(4,680)	5,320
Dividends Declared	46,550	40,100

Expenditures on noncurrent assets amounted to $317,930 during 1975. Prepare a statement of changes in financial position for the year 1975.

17. Refer to the data of Problem 16. Prepare a statement of changes in financial position for 1974. Book value of noncurrent assets sold during 1974 was $43,950.

18. Condensed financial statements for the Edward Construction Company for the end of years 1973, 1974, and 1975 are presented below:

EDWARD CONSTRUCTION COMPANY
Comparative Balance Sheets

	12/31/75	12/31/74	12/31/73
Assets			
Current Assets	$302,060	$262,230	$245,040
Noncurrent Assets (Cost)	511,470	483,550	439,470
Less: Accumulated Depreciation	(185,710)	(167,230)	(146,790)
Total Assets	$627,820	$578,550	$537,720
Liabilities			
Current Liabilities	$103,690	$ 87,810	$ 96,720
Bonds Payable	84,390	97,610	63,410
Total Liabilities	$188,080	$185,420	$160,130
Stockholders' Equity			
Common Stock	$150,000	$150,000	$150,000
Additional Paid-in Capital	7,430	6,870	6,870
Retained Earnings	282,310	247,020	220,720
Less: Treasury Stock	—	(10,760)	—
Total Stockholders' Equity	$439,740	$393,130	$377,590
Total Liabilities and Stockholders' Equity	$627,820	$578,550	$537,720

Additional Information:
(1) In 1975, noncurrent assets originally costing $50,040 were sold for their book value of $6,150.
(2) In 1975, net income to stockholders was $106,570, and dividends on common stock were $71,280.
(3) Additional Paid-in Capital increased as a result of reissue of treasury stock.

From the above information, prepare a statement of changes in financial position for the year 1975.

19. Refer to the financial statement data for the Edward Construction Company in Problem 18 and to the additional information below:
(1) Net income to stockholders in 1974 was $97,410 and included a loss of $5,120 on disposition of noncurrent assets.
(2) Depreciation expense in 1974 amounted to $57,880 and acquisitions of noncurrent assets totaled $146,230.
(3) Dividends declared in 1974 were $71,110.
Prepare a statement of changes in financial position for the year 1974.

20. Financial statement data for the Perkerson Supply Company for the years ending December 31, 1974, and December 31, 1975, are shown on page 606:

PERKERSON SUPPLY COMPANY
Comparative Balance Sheets

	12/31/75	12/31/74

Assets

Current Assets	($ in 000's)	
Cash	$ 240	$ 267
Accounts Receivable	325	223
Inventory	633	482
Current Prepayments	38	39
Total Current Assets	$1,236	$1,011

Noncurrent Assets		
Land	$ 153	$ 142
Buildings	2,133	2,052
Accumulated Depreciation Buildings	(446)	(367)
Machinery	1,423	1,312
Accumulated Depreciation Machinery	(595)	(490)
Total Noncurrent Assets	$2,668	$2,649

Total Assets	$3,904	$3,660

Liabilities and Stockholders' Equity

Current Liabilities		
Accounts Payable	$ 231	$ 138
Taxes Payable	104	117
Other Short-term Payables	392	301
Total Current Liabilities	$ 727	$ 556

Noncurrent Liabilities		
Bonds Payable	$ 938	$ 970
Deferred Taxes	33	25
Minority Interest in Affiliated Companies	44	37
Total Noncurrent Liabilities	$1,015	$1,032

Stockholders' Equity		
Preferred Stock	$ 240	$ 240
Common Stock	587	567
Retained Earnings	1,335	1,265
Total Stockholders' Equity	$2,162	$2,072
Total Liabilities and Stockholders' Equity	$3,904	$3,660

Additional Information:

(1) Depreciation expense for the year was $79,000 for buildings and $131,000 for machinery.

(2) Machinery originally costing $53,000 with accumulated depreciation $26,000 was sold for $30,000.

(3) Net income for the year was $152,000 and dividends were $20,000 for preferred stock and $62,000 for common stock.

Prepare a statement of changes in financial position and an analysis of changes in working capital for the Perkerson Supply Company for 1975.

21. Financial statement data for the Ellwood Corporation are presented below:

ELLWOOD CORPORATION
Comparative Balance Sheets

($ in '000)

	12/31/75	12/31/74	12/31/73	12/31/72
Assets				
Current Assets				
Cash	$ 3,338	$ 3,157	$ 2,844	$ 3,425
Accounts Receivable	19,010	18,968	15,735	12,426
Inventory	16,523	13,347	9,327	8,369
Current Prepayments	348	325	156	282
Other Current Assets	4,048	3,600	8,068	6,976
Total Current Assets	$43,267	$39,397	$36,130	$31,478
Noncurrent Assets				
Land	$ 1,120	$ 1,103	$ 978	$ 924
Plant and Equipment	10,470	10,253	8,997	7,999
Accumulated Depreciation	(4,088)	(3,917)	(3,812)	(3,630)
Investment in Ellwood Credit Corporation	5,363	3,659	1,068	916
Total Noncurrent Assets	$12,865	$11,098	$ 7,231	$ 6,209
Total Assets	$56,132	$50,495	$43,361	$37,687

Liabilities and Stockholders' Equity

	12/31/75	12/31/74	12/31/73	12/31/72
Current Liabilities				
Accounts Payable	$ 3,586	$ 2,417	$ 2,078	$ 1,833
Income Taxes Payable	4,101	5,129	3,707	2,938
Notes Payable Due Within One Year	1,073	750	677	651
Dividends Payable	974	821	733	289
Total Current Liabilities	$ 9,734	$ 9,117	$ 7,195	$ 5,711

Noncurrent Liabilities

Notes Payable	$ 3,099	$ 3,636	$ 4,203	$ 5,087
Bonds Payable (5%)	3,750	2,500	2,500	2,500
Discount on Bonds	(151)	(159)	(167)	(175)
Deferred Taxes	875	734	701	672
Total Noncurrent Liabilities	$ 7,573	$ 6,711	$ 7,237	$ 8,084
Total Liabilities	$17,307	$15,828	$14,432	$13,795

Stockholders' Equity

Common Stock	$12,590	$10,645	$ 9,870	$ 8,925
Preferred Stock	6,340	6,991	6,991	5,785
Premium on Preferred Stock	307	307	307	201
Retained Earnings	19,588	16,724	11,761	8,981
Total Stockholders' Equity	$38,825	$34,667	$28,929	$23,892
Total Liabilities and Stockholders' Equity	$56,132	$50,495	$43,361	$37,687

Additional Information (dollar amounts in thousands):

(1) Net income to stockholders was $7,376 in 1975. During the year dividends of $379 on preferred stock, and $4,133 on common stock were declared.

(2) During 1975, plant and equipment originally costing $498 on which there was accumulated depreciation of $346 was sold for $93.

(3) During 1975, $1,250 of 5-percent, ten-year bonds were issued at par.

(4) Investment in the Ellwood Credit Corporation is accounted for on the equity method.

Prepare a statement of changes in financial position and an analysis of changes in working capital for the year 1975.

22. Refer to the comparative balance sheet data of Problem 21 for the Ellwood Corporation and to the additional information below.

Additional Information (dollar amounts in thousands):

(1) Net income to stockholders was $5,814 in 1974. During the year, dividends of $402 on preferred stock and $449 on common stock were declared.

(2) During 1974, plant and equipment originally costing $207 was sold at $100 for a gain of $22.

(3) Investment in the Ellwood Credit Corporation is accounted for on the equity method.

Prepare a statement of changes in financial position and an analysis of changes in working capital for the year 1974.

23. Refer to the comparative balance sheet data of Problem 21 for the Ellwood Corporation and to the additional information below.

Additional Information (dollar amounts in thousands):

(1) Net income to stockholders was $5,056 during 1973. During the year, dividends of $365 on preferred stock and $1,911 on common stock were declared.

(2) During 1973, plant and equipment on which there was accumulated depreciation of $107 was sold for a loss of $23 at $201.

(3) Investment in the Ellwood Credit Corporation is accounted for on the equity method.

Prepare a statement of changes in financial position and an analysis of changes in working capital for the year 1973.

24. The Quinta Company presents the following post-closing trial balance and statement of changes in financial position for the year 1975.

Post-Closing Trial Balance, December 31, 1975

Debit Balances

Working Capital	$200,000
Land	40,000
Building and Equipment	500,000
Investments	100,000
	$840,000

Credit Balances

Accumulated Depreciation	$200,000
Bonds Payable	100,000
Common Stock	200,000
Retained Earnings	340,000
	$840,000

Statement of Changes in Financial Position for the Year 1975
Sources of Working Capital

($ in 000's)

A. From Operations		$200
Additions for Expenses and Losses Not Using Working Capital:		
Depreciation	$ 60	
Loss on Sale of Investments	10	
Total Additions	$ 70	
Subtractions for Gains not Producing Working Capital:		
Gain on Sale of Buildings and Equipment	5	
Total Expense and Revenue Adjustments		65
B. Proceeds of Issues of Securities and Debt		
Capital Stock Issue	$50	
Bond Issue	50	
Total Proceeds		100
C. Proceeds of Disposition of Long-term Assets		
Sale of Investments	$40	
Sale of Buildings and Equipment	15	
Sale of Land	10	
Total Proceeds		65
Total Sources of Working Capital		$430

Uses of Working Capital

A. Dividends $200
B. Acquisition of Buildings and Equipment 130

Total Uses of Working Capital $330

Increase in Working Capital for Year
(Sources Minus Uses) $100

Net Increase in Working Capital Items
(Current Asset Increases Minus Current Liability Increases) $100

The accumulated depreciation of the equipment sold was $20,000. Current liabilities were $75,000 at the start of the year and $125,000 at the end of the year.

Prepare a balance sheet for the beginning of the year, January 1, 1975.

25. A balance sheet, statement of changes in financial position, and analysis of changes in working capital are presented for the Quintus Company below:

QUINTUS COMPANY
Balance Sheet
for January 1, 1975

Assets

Current Assets
Cash .... $ 12,974
Receivables 27,045
Inventories 49,206

Total Current Assets .... $ 89,225

Noncurrent Assets
Land .... $ 4,563
Plant and Equipment 157,594
Less Accumulated Depreciation .... (59,899)
Investment in Quintus Credit Corporation 1,230
Patents 332
Goodwill 11,500

Total Noncurrent Assets $115,320

Total Assets $204,545

Liabilities and Stockholders' Equity

Current Liabilities
Accounts Payable .... $ 45,331
Income Taxes Payable 9,752

Total Current Liabilities .... $ 55,083

Noncurrent Liabilities

Bonds Payable	$ 51,550
Premium on Bonds Payable	146
Deferred Taxes	7,194
Total Noncurrent Liabilities	$ 58,890

Stockholders' Equity

Preferred Stock	$ 5,007
Common Stock	12,764
Premium on Common Stock	3,960
Retained Earnings	68,841
Total Stockholders' Equity	$ 90,572
Total Liabilities and Stockholders' Equity	$204,545

QUINTUS COMPANY
Statement of Changes in Financial Position
Year of 1975

Sources of Working Capital

From Operations

Net Income		$ 13,238
Expense and Revenue Adjustments Plus Excess of Expenses and Losses over Working Capital Used for Those Items:		
Depreciation	$ 11,085	
Amortization of Patents	27	
Amortization of Goodwill	2,300	
Loss on Sale of Plant and Equipment	472	
Income Tax Timing Differences	2,588	
Total Addition to Working Capital from Expense and Loss Adjustments		16,472
Less Excess of Working Capital Used for Expenses; Less Excess of Gain over Working Capital Produced by That Gain:		
Bond Premium Amortization	$ 39	
Gain on Sale of Land	107	
Share of Year's Earnings Retained by Quintus Credit Corporation Accounted for on Equity Method	208	
Total Subtractions		(354)
Total Sources from Operations		$ 29,356
From Issue of Common Stock		9,863
From Disposition of Long-term Assets		
Sale of Plant and Equipment	$ 1,056	
Sale of Land	314	
Proceeds from Disposition of Long-term Assets		1,370
Total Sources of Working Capital		$ 40,589

Uses of Working Capital

Income Distributions
 Dividends on Preferred Stock .... $ 4,719
 Dividends on Common Stock 5,094

Total Income Distributions	$ 9,813
Retirement of Preferred Stock	522
Purchases of Plant and Equipment	13,983
Total Uses of Working Capital	$ 24,318
Increase in Working Capital for Year	$ 16,271

Analysis of Changes in Working Capital

Current Asset Item Changes
 Cash .... $ (1,598)
 Receivables 4,010
 Inventories .... (2,714)

Decrease in Current Asset Items	$ (302)
Current Liability Item Changes	

 Accounts Payable .... $(13,718)
 Income Tax Payable .... (2,855)

Decrease in Current Liability Items	(16,573)
Increase in Working Capital for Year	$ 16,271

The stockholders' equity account, Premium on Common Stock, was $5,784 on December 31, 1975. Plant and equipment sold had originally cost $12,974.

Prepare a balance sheet for the Quintus Company for December 31, 1975.

26. A statement of changes in financial position including an analysis of changes in working capital for the Quintus Company for the year 1974 are presented below:

QUINTUS COMPANY
Statement of Changes in Financial Position
Year of 1974

Sources of Working Capital

From Operations
 Net Income .... $ 10,808
 Expense and Revenue Adjustments Plus Excess of Expenses
  and Losses over Working Capital Used for Those Items:
   Depreciation .... $ 11,987
   Amortization of Patents 25
   Amortization of Goodwill 2,300

Losses from Quintus Credit Corp. Accounted for on Equity Method 148
Income Tax Timing Differences 2,283

Total Addition to Working Capital from Expense and Loss Adjustments 16,473
Less Excess of Working Capital Used for Expenses over Those Expenses; Less Excess of Gain over Working Capital Produced by That Gain
Bond Premium Amortization .... $ 22
Gain on Sale of Plant and Equipment 87

Total Subtractions .... (109)

Total Sources from Operations .... $ 27,442
From Issue of Securities and Debt
Bond Issue (Par Value $28,000) .... $ 28,073
Common Stock Issued 3,231

Proceeds from Securities and Debt Issues 31,304
From Disposition of Plant and Equipment 326

Total Sources of Working Capital .... $ 59,072

Uses of Working Capital

Income Distributions
Dividends on Preferred Stock .... $ 5,037
Dividends on Common Stock 1,792

Total Income Distributions .... $ 6,829
Retirement of Preferred Stock 617
For Acquisitions of Long-term Assets
Land .... $ 467
Plant and Equipment 39,149
Patents 58

Total Used for Acquisition of Long-term Assets 39,674

Total Uses of Working Capital .... $ 47,120

Increase in Working Capital for Year .... $ 11,952

Analysis of Changes in Working Capital

Current Asset Item Changes
Cash .... $ 4,769
Receivables 8,924
Inventories 9,184

Increase in Current Asset Items .... $ 22,877
Current Liability Item Changes
Accounts Payable .... $ 8,768
Income Tax Payable 2,157

Increase in Current Liability Items 10,925

Increase in Working Capital for Year .... $ 11,952

Common Stock outstanding on January 1, 1974, had a face value of $10,392. Accumulated depreciation on the plant and equipment sold was $807.

Prepare a balance sheet for January 1, 1974 from the statement of changes in financial position and the analysis of changes in working capital above and the balance sheet for January 1, 1975, given in Problem 25.

27. Financial statement data for the Claire Corporation for the years ending December 31, 1974, and December 31, 1975, are presented below:

CLAIRE CORPORATION
Comparative Balance Sheet

	12/31/75	12/31/74
Assets		
Current Assets		
Cash	$ 400,690	$ 423,600
Accounts Receivable	687,590	517,230
Inventory	2,434,020	2,370,370
Total Current Assets	$ 3,522,300	$3,311,200
Noncurrent Assets		
Investments	$ 350,000	$ 300,000
Land	1,050,000	1,140,000
Buildings	3,900,000	2,250,000
Accumulated Depreciation, Buildings	(430,000)	(475,000)
Equipment	2,800,000	2,400,000
Accumulated Depreciation, Equipment	(1,375,000)	(1,289,000)
Delivery Equipment	37,500	29,500
Accumulated Depreciation, Delivery Equipment	(16,500)	(13,000)
Leasehold Improvements	69,000	72,000
Bond Sinking Fund	300,000	250,000
Goodwill	50,000	60,000
Total Noncurrent Assets	$ 6,735,000	$4,724,500
Total Assets	$10,257,300	$8,035,700
Liabilities and Stockholders' Equity		
Current Liabilities		
Accounts Payable	$ 373,140	$ 291,080
Short-term Notes Payable	815,090	730,520
Total Current Liabilities	$ 1,188,230	$1,021,600
Long-term Liabilities		
Bonds Payable	$ 1,900,000	$1,000,000
Discount on Bonds	(202,461)	(104,651)
Total Long-term Liabilities	$ 1,697,539	$ 895,349
Total Liabilities	$ 2,885,769	$1,916,949

Stockholders' Equity

Preferred Stock	$ 937,000	$ 302,000
Premium on Preferred Stock	18,570	—
Common Stock	2,000,000	2,000,000
Retained Earnings	4,415,961	3,816,751
Total Stockholders' Equity	$ 7,371,531	$6,118,751
Total Liabilities and Stockholders' Equity	$10,257,300	$8,035,700

Additional Information:

(1) Net income to stockholders for the year was $818,300. Dividends declared during the year were $97,900 for preferred stock and $121,190 for common stock.

(2) Land valued at $90,000 was sold during the year for $105,000.

(3) Buildings originally costing $414,000 were sold for $110,000. Depreciation expense for buildings for the year was $197,000.

(4) Equipment with a book value of $42,000 was sold for $39,000. Depreciation expense for equipment for the year was $214,000.

(5) The bonds outstanding on January 1, 1975, pay annual coupons at the rate of 4 percent and had been issued several years ago at a price to yield 5 percent per year. Discount is amortized with the effective-interest method. The bond indenture requires an annual payment of $50,000 to a sinking fund. On December 31, 1975, $900,000 5-percent bonds were issued at a price to yield 6 percent.

(6) No delivery equipment was sold during the year.

Prepare a statement of changes in financial position and an analysis of changes in working capital for Claire Corporation for the year 1975.

28. The Johns and White Company, incorporated in 1965, manufactures a line of small electrical appliances for sale to local discount houses. At the time of incorporation, Johns and White each contributed $150,000, and $250,000 was supplied by a venture capital firm. Business was good and profits grew steadily with only a slight decrease in the rate of growth of profits during the years 1969 and 1970. By 1972, Johns and White had bought out the venture capital firm's interest and were in sole command of the company.

In 1973, feeling that the only constraint on their profitability was their limited manufacturing capacity, Johns and White began buying and rehabilitating old factories and equipping them to manufacture the Johns and White line of products. By 1977, Johns and White hoped to have quadrupled their 1973 manufacturing capacity. They financed the expansion through retained earning and a series of ninety-day revolving notes with a local bank. During the years 1973, 1974, and 1975, Johns and White's profits continued to grow.

In late January, 1976, Johns and White were informed simultaneously by their largest supplier and the bank that they had insufficient funds to cover their outstanding bills with the supplier. Johns and White were mystified. During the years, they had kept a careful watch on their profitability to ensure that they maintained their steady rate of growth of profits. Their profits for 1975 had been their highest ever. During the years, however, they had paid little attention to their solvency or working capital.

In consultation with the bank it was brought out that Johns and White would need a large sum of money in the near future to finance inventories and continue normal operations. However, the bank stated that Johns and White had already borrowed beyond prudent levels and that the bank could not extend further loans to Johns and White under the existing terms. The terms imposed by the bank for a new loan would be such that not only would profitability be decreased due to the high interest rate on the additional loan and further expansion plans curtailed for the foreseeable future, but that Johns and White felt they would no longer be in full control of the company.

Explain what happened to Johns and White Company through the use of statements of changes in financial position. Comparative balance sheets and income statements are presented for the relevant periods below.

JOHNS AND WHITE COMPANY
Comparative Balance Sheets

	12/31/75	12/31/74	12/31/73	12/31/72
Assets				
		($ in 000's)		
Current Assets				
Cash	$ 17	$ 23	$ 38	$ 35
Accounts Receivable	101	89	79	71
Inventory	118	119	116	112
Total Current Assets	$236	$231	$233	$218
Long-term Assets				
Land	$ 39	$ 32	$ 22	$ 10
Plant and Equipment	400	279	193	143
Accumulated Depreciation	(85)	(67)	(51)	(42)
Total Long-term Assets	$354	$244	$164	$111
Total Assets	$590	$475	$397	$329
Liabilities and Stockholders' Equity				
Current Liabilities				
Accounts Payable	$ 96	$ 81	$ 73	$ 61
Income Taxes Payable	9	7	6	6
Total Current Liabilities	$105	$ 88	$ 79	$ 67
Long-term Liabilities				
Notes Payable	$199	$142	$104	$ 70
Mortgage Payable	27	17	8	—
Total Long-term Liabilities	$226	$159	$112	$ 70

Stockholders' Equity

Common Stock	$ 55	$ 55	$ 55	$ 55
Retained Earnings	204	173	151	137
Total Stockholders' Equity	$259	$228	$206	$192
Total Liabilities and Stockholders' Equity	$590	$475	$397	$329

JOHNS AND WHITE COMPANY
Comparative Income Statement
Years Ended December 31

	($ in 000's)		
	1975	**1974**	**1973**
Sales	$387	$339	$298
Cost of Goods Sold			
Wages	$143	$137	$133
Materials	117	113	109
Total Cost of Goods Sold	$260	$250	$242
Depreciation	$ 18	$ 16	$ 9
Other Expenses	$ 27	$ 19	$ 16
Earnings before Interest and Taxes	$ 82	$ 54	$ 31
Less: Interest Expense	30	18	8
Earnings before Taxes	$ 52	$ 36	$ 23
Less: Income Taxes	21	14	9
Net Income	$ 31	$ 22	$ 14

Four

SPECIAL TOPICS IN MANAGERIAL ACCOUNTING

Chapter 20

Cost Accounting: Accumulation of Costs

The Need for Cost Accounting

Chapters 5 and 11 summarize the procedure for treating manufacturing costs in the general accounting system. Although the methods of the general accounting system serve the basic financial needs of the firm, they are inadequate for effective managerial control and planning. This is the role that cost accounting fills. Robert McNamara's tenure at Ford is probably one of the best illustrations of the importance of cost accounting to large manufacturers. When McNamara and the other "Whiz Kids" went to Detroit in the late forties, Ford was in serious financial difficulty due, in part, to outmoded and inefficient operations. One of the reasons for Ford's resurgence in the fifties was the system of cost analysis that McNamara instituted. His efforts produced, among other things, the Falcon, the biggest moneymaker Ford had had since the Model A.

Financial accounting reports are insufficient for internal control for several reasons. The calculation of the cost of goods manufactured requires that a figure be available for the inventory of work in process at the close of the year. In the absence of detailed records, this figure reflects crude estimates and is usually one of the weakest and least reliable points in the entire accounting structure. The product in process should be valued at the cost of raw material used, the amount of labor performed directly upon it, and an appropriate amount of the factory "overhead." Even if only one simple product is involved, it is difficult to tell what these costs should be since different batches of product are likely to be at different stages of completion. When, as is usual, the plant makes a variety of products, the calculations become even more difficult and the results less reliable. Test runs must be made, estimates based upon original specifications must be available, and opinions of experienced factory employees must be solicited.

The computation of the cost of goods sold and its companion figure, the inventory of finished goods, likewise involves the use of gross estimates. A physical count can be made of the items of finished product on hand, but the unit cost to be used in the valuation of the inventory is again a matter of conjecture. This means that any losses are probably concealed in the cost of goods sold figure. If the amount of work in process inventory is not too large, the total cost of producing the finished product can be determined with a fair degree of arithmetic accuracy, but when several products are manufactured, there is no systematic way of breaking down the total costs among the individual products.

It is obvious, in view of the difficulties connected with taking and pricing the inventories, that frequent preparation of operating statements is difficult, if not impossible. When periodic rather than perpetual inventories are used, statements are typically prepared only once a year.

One of the most serious deficiencies of the methods demonstrated earlier is the lack of detailed analysis of factory operations. In order to obtain adequate control over the efficiency of production activities, the plant must be divided into significant processes or departments, each one having its set of operating accounts. It must be possible to make detailed comparisons between budgeted and actual results, between specifications and actual quantities of labor and material used, between the costs of different batches of product, and so on.

Cost accounting attempts to remedy these inadequacies of ordinary accounting procedures. This chapter and the next four outline the essential features of cost accounting and managerial control. They will serve as an introduction to these special phases of accounting. More extensive and detailed treatment will be left for specialized courses. In cost accounting there are few generally accepted principles because the procedures used by a firm are designed to facilitate decision making within that firm. Of the many possible ways to solve a particular problem in cost accounting, the right way for a given firm is the way that is most useful to its managers. More often than not, the most useful way to solve a problem can be discovered by reference to concepts of economics, behavioral science, and mathematics as well as accounting.

Features of Cost Accounting

The distinctive features of cost accounting are indicated in the following list of some of its methods and objectives:

1. Records are kept in such a way that a unit cost of each product manufactured can be determined. These cost figures are available for the partly completed products as well as for the goods completed during the period. To compute product costs, it is necessary to assign the costs of raw materials used, direct labor, and factory overhead to individual departments or jobs and then to products.

The cost of materials and supplies used is determined directly at the time they are used and is charged immediately to the individual product or process. This means that perpetual inventory records are indispensable for good cost accounting systems. Records are also kept of the specific purposes for which direct labor is used, so that these costs can be allocated to the appropriate products or processes.

The assignment of factory overhead costs, however, cannot usually be so precise. It frequently reflects some arbitrary cost allocations or is the result of more or less expedient and convenient cost distributions. The salary of a factory superintendent or of a night watchman, for instance, is a cost of production but there is no one correct method of allocating such a cost to the various departments or products.

2. The cost of products completed and the cost of finished products sold can be determined directly from the accounts. As a result, financial statements can be prepared frequently and promptly so that price and production policies can be evaluated effectively.

3. The production costs are analyzed or broken down by departments of the plant, types of products, or special jobs. This analysis facilitates control over costs, which is the most valuable contribution of cost accounting to efficient business management. This control is most effective where costs can be determined with considerable accuracy and with a minimum of indirect allocation. The amount of material used for a given number of units of product can be compared with the results of other periods or with the original plans and specifications. The number of pieces handled or turned out per hour by a workman can be compared with the past performance of the same person, with the performance of other employees, or with the planned production schedule. The costs of operating a particular division or department of the plant can be compared with the operating statistics of past periods and with the budget for the present period. Effective cost accounting requires the use of perpetual inventory records at many points and these records provide control over materials, supplies, and products. Such records isolate the amount of losses and waste that do occur and thereby permit management to take steps to keep them at a reasonable minimum. In general, then, production cost accounting, by providing detailed statistics of production operations, promotes a higher degree of efficiency in plant operation than would be possible without such assistance.

The Relation of Cost Accounting to Financial Accounting

Cost accounting should not be considered separate from financial or general accounting. It is more accurate to say that cost accounting procedures are superimposed upon the general accounting system to provide a greater degree of cost classification and to effect a closer control over costs. The requirements of cost analysis dictate many of the features of the system of underlying memoranda, such as the material requisitions and the payroll records. The ledger accounts used to record the results of daily operations must furnish most of the figures needed for cost calculations. The results of the cost computations are reflected in the computation of cost of goods sold on the income statement and in the inventory figures on the balance sheet. Cost accounts are an important part of a coordinated accounting system.

COST BEHAVIOR

Distinguishing several kinds of cost behavior helps in understanding the fundamental nature of cost accounting data. The response of costs to levels of activity can be described in one of four basic ways. These are illustrated in Figure 20.1.

1. *Variable costs* change as the volume of production changes and are zero when production is zero. Raw materials and direct labor are typical variable costs. In accounting, variable costs are usually assumed to be linear, such as shown by the line *OA* in Figure 20.1. Strictly speaking, variable costs can be nonlinear such as in lines *OB* and *OC*, but nonlinear cost curves are seldom used by accountants. Thus, for convenience, *variable cost*, in accounting, typically means a cost that is constant per unit of output or one that is strictly proportional to output. For example, if raw materials costs are variable and ten units of final product require $50 of raw material, then twenty units of final product will require $100 of raw material and, in general, X units of final product will require $5X$ of raw material.

2. *Fixed costs* remain constant during an accounting period within a reasonable range of activity. Costs quoted as a price per unit of time, such as rent per month, insurance premiums per year, and supervisors' salaries per week, are typical examples of fixed costs. Fixed costs are represented in Figure 20.1 by line *DE*. Such costs are not fixed forever, merely for the accounting period. Many fixed costs will change if the plant is expanded or an extra production shift is added.

3. *Semivariable costs,* by convention, refer to costs that have fixed and variable components such as represented by lines *FG*, *FH*, and *FJ* in Figure 20.1. Repair and maintenance costs or utility costs exemplify semivariable cost behavior. There is a fixed cost (*OF*) to provide a repair service within the plant, such as for depreciation of equipment used for repairs and regular salaries of repair personnel, but as repairs are actually performed, costs increase as materials are used and overtime wages are paid. Utility companies typically charge a fixed minimum per month (*OF*) for providing service and an extra charge for uses of the service above some minimum amount. If the charge per unit of, say, electricity decreases at certain stages as consumption increases, then the cost curve would look like line

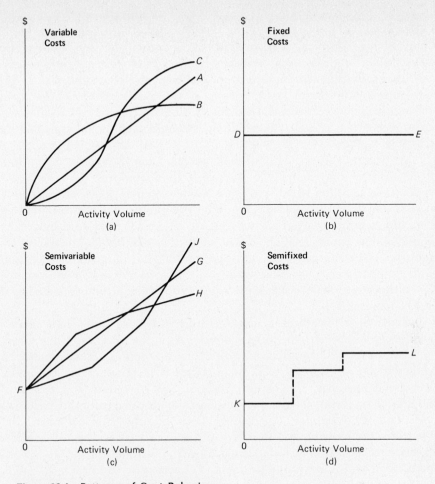

Figure 20.1 Patterns of Cost Behavior

FH. If the per-unit charge increases as usage increases, then the costs would look like line *FJ*.

4. *Semifixed costs,* by convention, refer to costs that increase in steps, such as shown by the broken line *KL*. If a quality control inspector can examine 1,000 units per day, then inspection costs will be semifixed with a break for every 1,000 units per day examined. Neither the vertical nor horizontal breaks, or steps, need be of equal size. Semifixed costs are sometimes described as *step* costs.

ACCUMULATION OF MANUFACTURING COSTS BY DEPARTMENTS

The first job of cost accounting is to record the accumulation of costs by departments. The second job, assigning accumulated costs to products, is discussed in the next two chapters.

Types of Departments

In all but small businesses, operations are organized by major divisions or departments. Manufacturing costs are usually accumulated by departments, and each departmental supervisor is held responsible for the costs of his department. To control the efficiency of operations and to check upon the results achieved in each department, departmental costs are in many cases compared with a budgeted or standard figure, as explained in Chapters 22 and 23.

A department suitable for cost accumulation purposes may differ from a department suitable for administrative purposes. To avoid confusion, the unit for which costs are accumulated is frequently called a *cost center* or a *production center*. A cost or production center should be characterized by relatively homogeneous equipment and functions. One consideration in designating a cost center should be its suitability for purposes of cost classification and cost control. For example, a single drop forge might constitute a reasonable cost center, while in another instance an entire floor of similar automatic machine tools might be designated as a production center.

Some departments of a manufacturing plant are *production departments* in which work is performed directly upon the products, while others are *service departments* that contribute to the general operation of the plant but do not directly work on products. The power plant, the maintenance department, the factory hospital, the personnel and employee services department, the stock room, and the cost accounting department are examples of service departments. Often, the costs of furnishing the service of the building and the "general factory costs" are treated as additional service departments. Occasionally a department will be both a production and a service department. For example, the firm may use a computer to render service to its own production departments and also sell idle capacity or unused time to others.

Direct and Indirect Material Costs

Material required for production is obtained from the storeroom by making out a material requisition form. The design of requisition forms varies a good deal from one situation to another, but the form must contain space for showing the type, quantity, and cost of the materials requisitioned as well as the department that will use them.

The data from the requisitions serve as basis of the record keeping in the raw materials subsidiary ledger, or stores ledger as it is frequently called, as well as in the manufacturing cost accounts. At the end of each accounting period, a total is obtained of the direct material requisitions issued during the period to each department and an entry made to record the material put in process. A typical entry would be:

Material in Process—Dept. *A*	25,000	
Material in Process—Dept. *B*	17,500	
Material in Process—Dept. *C*	40,000	
Raw Material		82,500

Materials requisitioned for service departments are similarly recorded and later allocated to production departments, as explained below.

Direct and Indirect Labor Costs

Direct labor is usually defined as labor which is performed physically, or specifically, on the product being manufactured. Indirect labor, on the other hand, can be described as facilitating or auxiliary factory labor— labor which contributes to an orderly and efficient flow of production but is not performed directly on the product. It includes nondirect labor in the production departments as well as all labor in the service departments and any other general factory labor costs recognized under specific titles, such as Superintendence or Night Watchmen. Indirect labor costs become part of production-overhead costs.

At the end of each period, or sometimes more frequently, labor costs during the period are analyzed and an entry is made charging appropriate direct labor, indirect labor, and expense accounts. Employee time cards, wage schedules, and salary schedules provide the basis for this entry. The direct labor costs are usually charged to accounts titled "labor in process." This title is not sufficiently restrictive since it does not indicate that only direct labor is included in the category; "direct labor in process" might be a better title.

An illustrative entry for labor costs would be:

Labor in Process—Dept. *A*	25,903	
Labor in Process—Dept. *B*	14,194	
Labor in Process—Dept. *C*	9,512	
Maintenance Dept. Labor	2,072	
Factory Storeroom Labor	6,999	
Foreman's Salary—Dept. *A*	2,100	
Foreman's Salary—Dept. *B*	1,950	
Foreman's Salary—Dept. *C*	1,500	
Factory Night Watchman	500	
Selling Dept. Labor	2,430	
General and Administrative Labor	1,860	
Wages and Salaries Payable		69,020

An entry such as this covering all of the employees' earnings for the period may be made once a period, even though weekly or other frequent payroll payments have been made during the period.

Production Overhead

Direct material and direct labor may constitute a substantial portion of the total of manufacturing costs, but there is always a third element of factory cost, *production overhead*. Other titles sometimes used are "manufacturing overhead," "burden," "other factory costs," and "manufacturing expense." The last title is an unfortunate one since the items included in this element are production costs, which can remain in inventories, rather than expenses.

The term *production overhead* embraces those indirect costs of production which are not, or cannot conveniently be, associated directly with final units of output. The various types of indirect labor, depreciation of buildings and equipment, insurance, taxes, heat, light, power, and supplies used in factory operations are examples of costs included in the production overhead category. All factory costs other than raw materials going into the final output and labor costs of workers engaged directly in the fabrication process conventionally are included in the production-overhead total.

Some overhead costs, such as the wages and salaries of machine attendants and departmental foremen, are accumulated directly by departments in their original bookkeeping entries. Other costs, such as general superintendence, fire insurance, and property taxes, can more conveniently be charged to specific production cost accounts, sometimes known as *clearing accounts*, and later distributed to the various productive and service departments by means of an overhead-distribution schedule.

Recording Overhead Costs

Recording overhead costs as they are incurred is largely routine and does not involve new accounting problems. Some typical entries to record overhead costs would be (these are not related to entries shown elsewhere in this chapter):

Factory Power	400	
Factory Light	50	
Utility Bills Payable		450
Depreciation of Factory Building and Equipment	3,780	
Accumulated Depreciation—Building		1,050
Accumulated Depreciation—Equipment		2,730
Factory Supplies Used	2,250	
Janitors' Supplies Used	800	
Supplies on Hand		3,050

Summary of requisitions of supplies for the period.

Records of supplies issued to individual departments might have been maintained, in which case the last entry would be recorded as follows:

Factory Supplies Used—Dept. *A*	600	
Factory Supplies Used—Dept. *B*	900	
Factory Supplies Used—Dept. *C*	300	
Factory Supplies Used—Maintenance Dept.	450	
Janitors' Supplies Used	800	
Supplies on Hand		3,050

Sometimes materials and supplies are combined in a single account. In those cases, the entry to record factory supplies used is usually combined with the one to record the usage of direct materials.

The entry to record the indirect labor costs is illustrated above in the section "Direct and Indirect Labor Costs."

ALLOCATION OF PRODUCTION OVERHEAD TO DEPARTMENTS

As the previous discussion indicated, some items of overhead cost can be accumulated directly by departments while other "general" overhead cost components must be distributed to the various production and service departments on some allocation basis. Some of the general overhead can be distributed on a relatively sound and logical basis; for example, fire insurance premiums can be spread in proportion to the value of the insurable assets in each department. Other types of cost may have to be allocated on an expedient or arbitrary basis; for instance, the factory superintendent's salary and the night watchman's wages are often assigned on such bases as the area of the department or the amount of departmental labor, or are distributed equally over the various divisions of the plant.

In order to assign all of the overhead costs to products, the cost of operating the service departments must be allocated to the production departments. After the total cost of operating the service departments is accumulated, these amounts are assigned to production departments on as reasonable a basis as possible. Building costs, for example, are usually distributed in proportion to the floor space occupied by each department, and power department costs in proportion to the capacity or requirements of the machinery in each department.

Illustration of Overhead Allocation

The following illustration will serve to indicate the types of problems involved in departmental overhead distribution and to demonstrate the construction of an overhead distribution schedule. Such a schedule can be used as a part of the operating statements. It should show a complete list of the overhead accounts. The details of the interdepartmental distributions need not be reproduced in the ledger accounts.

The overhead accounts of the Berdan Products Company for the month ending March 31, 1975, are as follows. (Those accounts marked with asterisks are explained below.)

```
* Foreman's Salary—Dept. A ......................................  $ 2,100
* Foreman's Salary—Dept. B ......................................    1,950
* Foreman's Salary—Dept. C ......................................    1,500
* Foreman's Salary—Dept. M (Maintenance) ......................    2,100
* Maintenance Labor—Dept. M ....................................    6,000
* Storeroom Labor—Dept. S ......................................    2,400
  Night Watchman's Salary ......................................      500
* Supplies Used—Dept. A ........................................      600
```

* Supplies Used—Dept. *B*	900
* Supplies Used—Dept. *C*	300
* Supplies Used—Dept. *S*	800
* Supplies Used—Dept. *M*	450
Property Taxes	1,200
Fire Insurance	300
Workmen's Compensation Insurance	800
Payroll Taxes	5,000
* Depreciation of Equipment—Dept. *A*	1,200
* Depreciation of Equipment—Dept. *B*	900
* Depreciation of Equipment—Dept. *C*	330
* Depreciation of Equipment—Dept. *S*	180
* Depreciation of Equipment—Dept. *M*	120
Rent—Factory Building	720
Electricity, Gas, and Water	600
Miscellaneous Factory Costs	750
Total	$31,700

Departments *A*, *B*, and *C* are production departments and Departments *M* and *S* are service departments.

The first step in the construction of an overhead-distribution schedule is to enter the account balances on a columnar sheet (see Schedule 20.1), assigning them as far as possible to the various departments. Each of the items marked with an asterisk (*) in the above list can be assigned directly to a department.

Each of the items that has not been assigned to a specific department must now be allocated to the various departments on some reasonable basis. Notice the types of additional information which must be available in order to make these distributions.

(1) The night watchman's salary, $500, is distributed in proportion to the number of visits made to each department during a typical night.

Dept.	No. Visits	Percent	Distribution
A	8	20	$100
B	8	20	100
C	8	20	100
S	16	40	200
M	0	—	—
Totals	40	100	$500

(2) Property taxes and fire insurance are distributed in proportion to the value of the equipment and inventories in each department. (See data at the top of page 631.)

(3) Workmen's compensation insurance and payroll taxes are distributed in proportion to departmental labor costs. In the following schedule the amounts shown for direct labor indicate the amount of earnings by production-line workers in each production department. The indirect labor in the production departments is the foreman's salary plus the allocated night watchman's salary in step (1). In the service departments the indirect-

Dept.	Value of Assets	Percent	Distribution of Property Taxes	Distribution of Fire Insurance
A	$100,000	50	$ 600	$150
B	60,000	30	360	90
C	10,000	5	60	15
S	26,000	13	156	39
M	4,000	2	24	6
Totals	$200,000	100	$1,200	$300

labor total is made up of department labor plus foreman's salary for Department M plus allocated night watchman's salary for Department S.

Dept.	Direct Labor	Indirect Labor	Total Labor	Percent
A	$17,100	$ 2,200	$ 19,300	19.3
B	37,950	2,050	40,000	40.0
C	28,400	1,600	30,000	30.0
S	—	2,600	2,600	2.6
M	—	8,100	8,100	8.1
Totals	$83,450	$16,550	$100,000	100.0

Dept.	Percent	Distribution of Work. Comp. Ins.	Distribution of Payroll Taxes
A	19.3	$154	$ 965
B	40.0	320	2,000
C	30.0	240	1,500
S	2.6	21	130
M	8.1	65	405
Totals	100.0	$800	$5,000

(4) The rent of the factory building is distributed in proportion to the floor space occupied by each department.

Dept.	Square Feet of Floor Space	Percent	Distribution
A	15,000	37.50	$270
B	15,000	37.50	270
C	8,500	21.25	153
S	1,000	2.50	18
M	500	1.25	9
Totals	40,000	100.00	$720

(5) Electricity, gas, and water are distributed according to the capacity and needs of the equipment in each department. The schedule at the top of page 632 is the result of a study of the departmental requirements.

(6) Miscellaneous factory costs are distributed equally over the five production and service departments.

Dept.	Utility Services (Percent)	Distribution
A	50	$300
B	30	180
C	15	90
S	3	18
M	2	12
Totals	100	$600

The results of these allocations of overhead costs are shown on the overhead distribution schedule in Schedule 20.1.

(7) When the distribution of the overhead accounts to the various departments has been completed, it is then necessary to redistribute the totals of the service departments. The completely logical method, where

SCHEDULE 20.1 ALLOCATION OF OVERHEAD BY APPROXIMATE, STEP-DOWN PROCEDURE

BERDAN PRODUCTS COMPANY
Overhead-Distribution Schedule
Month ending March 31, 1975

	Total	Dept. A	Dept. B	Dept. C	Dept. S Storeroom	Dept. M Maintenance	
Foremen's Salaries	$ 7,650	$ 2,100	$ 1,950	$1,500	$ —	$2,100	*
Maintenance Labor	6,000	—	—	—	—	6,000	*
Storeroom Labor	2,400	—	—	—	2,400	—	*
Night Watchman's Salary	500	100	100	100	200	—	(1)
Supplies Used	3,050	600	900	300	800	450	*
Property Taxes	1,200	600	360	60	156	24	(2)
Fire Insurance	300	150	90	15	39	6	(2)
Workmen's Compensation Insurance	800	154	320	240	21	65	(3)
Payroll Taxes	5,000	965	2,000	1,500	130	405	(3)
Depreciation of Equipment ..	2,730	1,200	900	330	180	120	*
Rent—Factory Building	720	270	270	153	18	9	(4)
Electricity, Gas, and Water ..	600	300	180	90	18	12	(5)
Miscellaneous Factory Costs .	750	150	150	150	150	150	(6)
Totals	$31,700	$ 6,589	$ 7,220	$4,438	$4,112	$9,341	
Redistribution—Dept. M	—	3,736	1,868	2,989	748	(9,341)	(7)
	$31,700	$10,325	$ 9,088	$7,427	$4,860		
Redistribution—Dept. S	—	1,620	1,620	1,620	(4,860)		(8)
Total Production Department Costs	$31,700	$11,945	$10,708	$9,047			(9)

two or more service departments serve each other as well as the production departments, requires an algebraic solution. This method is illustrated in Appendix 20.1 of this chapter. A less exact, but simpler solution, is: (a) Distribute the total costs of that service department which receives the smallest dollar amount of service from the other service departments over the other service and production departments; (b) then in the same manner distribute the total costs of another service department, and so on, until all service department costs have been charged to the production departments. This is sometimes called a *step-down* allocation procedure.

In the illustration it is assumed that the Maintenance Department receives little or no service from the Storeroom Department, so the redistribution begins by allocating the total costs of Department M in proportion to the time spent doing work specifically for certain departments.

Dept.	Chargeable Hours	Percent	Distribution
A	400	40	$3,736
B	200	20	1,868
C	320	32	2,989
S	80	8	748
Totals	1,000	100	$9,341

(8) It is difficult to find a logical, and at the same time practicable, basis for the spreading of storeroom costs. They should bear some relationship to the quantity of supplies and materials that have been issued and in part they may be interpreted as a cost of the materials and supplies on hand. If the inventories at the end of the period are small compared to the quantities used during the period, storeroom costs might be allocated on the basis of a physical measure or dollar value of materials issued. If, in the example, materials and supplies are requisitioned in about equal quantities by Departments A, B, and C, the costs of Department S might be apportioned about equally between those departments, as is done here.

The completed overhead-distribution schedule appears in Schedule 20.1. It supplements the regular operating statements.

Overhead-Distribution Entries

The entry to reflect the data on the overhead-distribution schedule is shown in Schedule 20.2.

DISTRIBUTION COST ACCOUNTING

Techniques similar to those employed in manufacturing cost analysis are often applied to selling and administrative expenses. A department store, for example, wishes to have its operating expenses allocated, as far as possible, by departments; a wholesaler wishes to have information as to the

SCHEDULE 20.2 OVERHEAD DISTRIBUTION ENTRY

Overhead in Process—Dept. *A*	11,945	
Overhead in Process—Dept. *B*	10,708	
Overhead in Process—Dept. *C*	9,047	
Foreman's Salary—Dept. *A*		2,100
Foreman's Salary—Dept. *B*		1,950
Foreman's Salary—Dept. *C*		1,500
Foreman's Salary—Dept. *M* (Maintenance)		2,100
Maintenance Labor—Dept. *M*		6,000
Storeroom Labor—Dept. *S*		2,400
Night Watchman's Salary		500
Supplies Used—Dept. *A*		600
Supplies Used—Dept. *B*		900
Supplies Used—Dept. *C*		300
Supplies Used—Dept. *S*		800
Supplies Used—Dept. *M*		450
Property Taxes		1,200
Fire Insurance		300
Workmen's Compensation Insurance		800
Payroll Taxes		5,000
Depreciation of Equipment—Dept. *A*		1,200
Depreciation of Equipment—Dept. *B*		900
Depreciation of Equipment—Dept. *C*		330
Depreciation of Equipment—Dept. *S*		180
Depreciation of Equipment—Dept. *M*		120
Rent—Factory Building		720
Electricity, Gas, and Water		600
Miscellaneous Factory Costs		750

profitability of different territories and types of customers; or a manufacturer is interested in the cost of handling and selling his products.

Department-Store Cost Analysis

The calculation of departmental operating costs in a department store is much the same as the allocation of departmental overhead in a manufacturing plant. Some items, such as salaries and commissions of salesmen, are accumulated by departments as they are recorded. Others, such as rent, insurance, and supervision, have to be allocated after a preliminary accumulation in clearing accounts. Appropriate bases for the distribution of such costs are adopted, as is done for manufacturing overhead costs. For example, floor space is used as the basis for the spreading of building-service costs, but usually on a weighted basis. The different weights applied to the area occupied by different departments makes allowance for the greater value of certain sections of the store. For example, first-floor space of a given size would be weighted more heavily than the same amount of space on an upper floor.

The complete allocation of all operating costs in a department store is not so necessary as for a manufacturing plant. Except where direct costing is used, all manufacturing costs must be completely distributed so that they can be absorbed in the products produced and unit costs for inventories can be derived. In the department store, the results of allocations are used only for judging the relative profitability of each department and for comparing the results of the present period with the budget and with past periods. There is good reason for the opinion that such purposes will be served better if the distribution of expenses is limited to those that can be assigned on some reasonably logical basis without attempting to distribute the general expenses, such as office salaries and expenses, executives' salaries, general store advertising, and warehouse expenses, which can only be allocated to departments on an arbitrary basis. Although each department should contribute toward this general overhead, it is often impossible to determine how much it should absorb with any useful degree of reliability.

Special Cost Studies

Such calculations as the cost of serving different types of customers or territories, or the profitability of various products, are usually made as special studies apart from the accounting records proper. This is possible, again, because such cost distributions can be made as supplementary calculations and analyses without regard to any inventory figures. It is often difficult to find a reasonable basis for distributing certain costs, and the approach indicated above in connection with department stores is useful here. Unreasonable and illogical distributions have little value. Whenever the cost is a true joint cost, that is, when producing several products or services requires a single cost, it is usually impossible to determine the individual cost of the separate products; any attempt to distribute costs must then be based upon an arbitrary and, possibly, misleading basis.

Bases of Cost Distribution

The following list indicates some of the bases of distribution that have been suggested for the selling and administrative costs. One striking aspect of the problem of such cost analysis is that extensive statistical data must be accumulated in addition to the regular accounting information. Some of the statistics can be accumulated regularly; other items, because of the cost of obtaining the information, will be made the subject of occasional studies in order to establish or to correct normal or standard costs of the operation.

For Distribution of	Basis
1. Insurance	Average value of finished goods
2. Storage and building costs	Floor space
3. Cost of sending monthly statements, credit investigations, etc.	Number of outlets (dealers or jobbers)
4. Various joint costs such as advertising and supervision of selling activities	Sales, classified by dealers, territories, or products

5. Credit investigation, postage,   Number of orders received
   stationery, and other such ex-
   penses
6. Handling costs   Tonnage handled
7. Salesmen's expenses   Number of salesmen's calls
8. Order writing and filing   Number of items on an order
9. Stenographic expense   Number of letters written
10. Automobile operation, delivery   Number of miles operated
    expense, etc.

APPENDIX 20.1: MATRIX ALLOCATION OF SERVICE DEPARTMENT COSTS

As mentioned in the text of the chapter, a completely logical method for allocating service departments costs to production departments requires algebra. The presentation and derivation of this method are easiest with the algebra of matrices. We use matrix algebra in this appendix. Readers who are not prepared to deal with matrix algebra should skip this appendix without fear of losing continuity with the rest of this book.[1]

The problem is to logically allocate to production departments the costs of service departments that serve each other as well as the production departments. The data necessary to perform the logical allocation are shown for Berdan Products Company in Schedule 20.3. The maintenance and storeroom service departments both provide service to each other as well as to production Departments A, B, and C.

SCHEDULE 20.3 FRACTIONS OF SERVICE DEPARTMENTS' OUTPUTS USED BY SERVICE AND PRODUCTION DEPARTMENTS, BERDAN PRODUCTS FOR MARCH, 1975

| | | Services Performed Here | |
		Maintenance (M)	Storeroom (R)
	Service Departments		
Services	Maintenance	0	.148	Matrix S
	Storeroom	.08	.262	
Used	Production Departments		
	A	.40	.197	Matrix P
Here	B	.20	.295	
	C	.32	.098	
		1.00	1.000	
Costs to be Allocated		$9,341	$4,112	

[1] Readers who are comfortable with matrix algebra and who wish to pursue this problem further should refer to Robert S. Kaplan, "Variable and Self-Service Costs in Reciprocal Allocation Models," *The Accounting Review,* 48 (October, 1973), 738–48.

The costs of the service departments to be allocated are $9,341 in maintenance and $4,112 in the storeroom. In the simplified procedure explained in Schedule 20.1, it was assumed that the storeroom's costs were allocable equally to the three production departments. A more realistic treatment assumes that the costs should be allocated in proportion to the cost of factory supplies issued by the storeroom for use by each of the departments. The total of factory supplies used is $3,050. Note that maintenance consumed $450 or 14.8 percent of that total. Consequently, in the schedule that shows the fractions of storeroom services consumed by the five departments, the storeroom column contains the figure .148 to indicate the maintenance department's consumption. The other entries in the storeroom column (including the self-service in the storeroom $800/$3,050 = .262) are derived by dividing the factory supplies used in that department by the total factory supplies used, $3,050. The basis for distributing Maintenance Department costs is the same as that used in the step-down procedure explained in computation (7) on page 633.

Notice that each column in the schedule adds exactly to one. Exactly 100 percent of a service department's output is used somewhere. The top portion of the schedule shows the service department use of service department outputs. That section of the schedule is denoted by matrix S where s_{ij} represents the fraction of service department j's output used by service department i. For example, $s_{MR} = .148$, or 14.8 percent of the storeroom's (R) output is used by the maintenance department (M). (The abbreviation for the storeroom is R so that it will not be confused with "S," which stands for the entire service department matrix.) The bottom portion of the schedule shows the production department usage. That section of the schedule is denoted by matrix P where p_{ij} represents the fraction of service department j's output used by production department i. To allocate the service department costs to production departments we need an allocation matrix such as the one shown in Schedule 20.4. In matrix A, a_{ij} represents the fraction of service department j's cost that is allocable to production department i after taking account of mutual use of service department output by service departments.

The matrix A is calculated by the matrix equation $A = P(I - S)^{-1}$ where I is the identity matrix and $(I - S)^{-1}$ means the inverse of the

SCHEDULE 20.4 ALLOCATION MATRIX FOR BERDAN PRODUCTS COMPANY MARCH, 1975

		Services Performed Here	
	Production Departments	Maintenance (M)	Storeroom (R)
Service Costs Allocated Here	A	.428	.353
	B	.236	.447
	C	.336	.200
		1.000	1.000

Matrix A

matrix $(I - S)$. The derivation of the equation for A is not difficult. For example, a_{CM} represents the fraction of the maintenance department's (M) output allocable to production Department C. That fraction is

$$a_{CM} = p_{CM} + a_{CM}s_{MM} + a_{CR}s_{RM}$$
$$= .32 + a_{CM} \times 0 + a_{CR} \times .08$$

or the direct use of maintenance by Department C (p_{CM}) plus the fraction of maintenance costs used by maintenance that is allocable to Department $C (a_{CM}s_{MM})$ plus the fraction of maintenance costs used by the storeroom, that is, allocable to Department C $(a_{CR}s_{RM})$. Notice that a_{CM} is defined in terms of itself and other a_{ij} so that a system of simultaneous equations for the a_{ij} results.

Consider another example, a_{BR}:

$$a_{BR} = p_{BR} + a_{BM}s_{MR} + a_{BR}s_{RR}$$
$$= .295 + a_{BM} \times .148 + a_{BR} \times .262$$

The fraction of storeroom costs allocable to Department B is the sum of the direct use of the storeroom by Department B (p_{BR}) plus the fraction of storeroom costs used by maintenance that is allocable to Department B $(a_{BM}s_{MR})$ plus the fraction of storeroom costs used by the storeroom that is allocable to Department B $(a_{BR}s_{RR})$.

Writing out a similar equation for each a_{ij}, where i represents production Departments A, B, or C, and j represents service Departments M or R, the entire system can be represented by the matrix equation

$$a_{ij} = p_{ij} + \sum_{k=M,R} a_{ik}s_{kj}$$

or

$$A = P + AS$$

Rearranging terms yields:

$$A - AS = P$$

or

$$A(I - S) = P$$

Postmultiply both sides by $(I - S)^{-1}$ to get [2]

$$A = P(I - S)^{-1}.$$

Once the matrix A is calculated, the allocation of service department costs to production departments is straightforward. The allocation is shown in Schedule 20.5 along with the allocation provided by the easier, but approximate, step-down procedure demonstrated earlier.

---

[2] If the inverse of $(I - S)$ does not exist, then a subset of the service departments completely uses the entire output of themselves without providing any service to the other service departments or to production departments. If the subset of service departments that mutually consume the output of each other is eliminated from the problem, then the procedure can be carried out.

SCHEDULE 20.5 ALLOCATION OF SERVICE DEPARTMENT COSTS TO PRODUCTION DEPARTMENTS BERDAN PRODUCTS COMPANY, MARCH, 1975

Production Departments	Service Departments			Step-down Approximation Method
	Matrix Method			
	Maintenance	Storeroom	Total	
A	$3,998	$1,452	$ 5,450	$ 5,356
B	2,204	1,838	4,042	3,488
C	3,139	822	3,961	4,609
	$9,341	$4,112	$13,453	$13,453

Observe that the matrix method gives different answers from the approximation. The matrix method is cumbersome to carry out by hand. The solution to the set of simultaneous equations (or the matrix inversion) is tedious and, except for small problems, should be done on a computer. Only when all entries in the S matrix are zero, that is when all service department outputs are used directly by production departments, will the matrix procedure and the approximate step-down procedure give the same answer.

QUESTIONS AND PROBLEMS

*1. a. What factor differentiates between production overhead that is accumulated directly by production departments and production overhead that is first accumulated in clearing accounts and then allocated to production departments?

 b. What principle forms the basis of methods used to allocate general overhead costs to production departments? In what circumstances does this principle fail?

2. When service costs are allocated to production departments, why are these costs first accumulated rather than assigned directly to production departments?

3. What distinguishes a production department from a service department?

*4. Why are the generally accepted accounting principles that form the basis of financial accounting so little emphasized in cost accounting?

5. What is the reasoning behind the opinion that in merchandising (as opposed to manufacturing) enterprises, only those costs that can be assigned on some obviously logical basis should be allocated?

6. Comment on this statement: the purpose of cost accounting is to determine the cost of producing a unit of product, so that this production cost can be used to determine a sales price that yields the desired gross profit margin.

---

* Hints, key numbers, or (partial) answers appear in the back of the book between the Appendix Tables and the Glossary.

7. How can the use of perpetual inventory records (as opposed to periodic inventory counts) aid in maintaining the optimal level of inventories and reduce losses from theft?

8. **a.** Why should service department costs be allocated to production departments?
   b. When should the step-down method of allocating service department costs be used instead of the matrix method?

9. Are the following costs usually fixed, variable, semifixed, or semivariable? Why?
   a. electricity for heat and light in the factory and for running machinery
   b. advertising
   c. office supplies
   d. general manager's salary
   e. license fees
   f. direct labor
   g. maintenance of company cars

10. Sketch a graph to describe the behavior of each of the following four costs.
    a. Raw materials cost $20 per unit of product.
    b. A legal research service is retained at $25 per hour. The contract stipulates that the service is guaranteed at least $500 per month in payments. Show hours of legal service on the horizontal axis.
    c. Supervisors are hired as production expands.
    d. A salesman's compensation is earned by commissions only.
    e. Royalty payments per period are $.07 per unit on the first 100,000 units and zero per unit thereafter.

*11. **a.** Give journal entries for the following transactions.
    (1) Factory supplies costing $1,500 are purchased on account.
    (2) Raw materials costing $15,000 are purchased on account.
    (3) Previously recorded wages and salaries of $22,000 are paid for factory labor. The firm withholds from employee paychecks 6 percent of gross wages for FICA tax and 13 percent of gross wages for income tax.
    (4) Costs for indirect labor are as follows:
    superintendence: $20,000
    maintenance: $12,000
    nightwatchmen: $2,000.
    (5) The employer's share of payroll taxes on factory labor is:
    $1,200 for federal unemployment insurance
    $1,000 for state unemployment insurance
    $1,300 for FICA tax.
    (6) Depreciation on the machinery is $6,000 and on the factory building is $5,500.
    (7) Raw materials costing $1,400 are used in Department 271.
    b. Which accounts are overhead accounts?

12. Give journal entries to account for the following transactions of the Hermann Company.
    (1) An invoice for raw materials purchased from the Harris Company is entered, $7,500.

(2) Monthly wages are paid to employees for October. The gross payroll amounts to $52,500, and a liability for that amount has been recorded. Deductions include 6 percent for FICA, $6,825 for federal income tax, and $700 for advances previously made to employees.

(3) A bill from Winter and Sons, covering machinery repairs costing $110, is entered.

(4) Depreciation on factory machinery for the month is $900.

(5) The following materials and supplies are used during the month:
raw materials used in production: $60,000
factory supplies used in operations: $550
factory supplies used for building repairs: $800.

(6) The distribution of wages and salaries earned during November is:
direct labor: $70,000
supervision in factory: $7,100
other indirect factory labor: $11,000
construction of equipment: $900
office salaries: $6,500
sales salaries: $9,500.

13. The Hayseed Manufacturing Company carries on all of its operations in a single department. Separate general ledger accounts are employed for each type of factory overhead cost. The following are the summarized transactions relating to factory operations for the month of March, 1975.

(1) Cash in the amount of $42,910 was paid for payrolls of the period. This is the net amount after making deductions of $1,500 for payroll taxes and $6,000 for withheld income taxes.

(2) The gross wages earned during the period were distributed as follows:

Direct labor	$39,000
Indirect labor	4,200
Factory supervision	3,000
Factory equipment repairs	210
Office salaries	1,800
Salesmen's salaries	2,200

(3) The employer's contribution to payroll taxes is 6 percent of payroll. The taxes on factory labor are treated as a separate factory overhead item.

(4) An invoice is received from the Logan Iron Works for repairs to factory machinery, $1,280.

(5) An invoice for factory supplies is received from Myrtle and Johnson, $5,000.

(6) An invoice is received from Lewis and Michaelson for raw material in the amount of $36,000.

(7) Factory supplies used: $2,800.

(8) Raw materials charged to jobs during the month as shown by material requisitions: $36,000.

(9) Depreciation on the factory building for the month is $380; on machinery and equipment used in the factory, $1,600.

(10) Insurance expired on the factory and machinery used in the factory: $220.

(11) Miscellaneous factory overhead costs incurred during the month were $5,720.

(12) The factory overhead accounts are closed to Work in Process.

(13) The cost of work completed during the month is $84,900.

(14) All of the completed jobs are delivered to customers. The total selling price is $117,800.

Present journal entries for the above transactions.

°**14.** The Norton Company sells to wholesalers and retailers. The following data are available for 1975 operations:

NORTON COMPANY

	Wholesale	Retail	Total
Sales	$1,000,000	$1,500,000	$2,500,000
Cost of Goods Sold	640,000	1,000,000	$1,640,000
Salesmen's Salaries			270,000
Advertising			90,000
Office Costs			140,000
Storage Costs			70,000
Total Costs for Year			$3,210,000
Data for Allocation:			
Number of Salesmen's Calls	90	810	900
Number of Invoice Lines	305	1,830	2,135

Cost	Allocation Basis
Salesmen's Salaries	Number of Calls
Office Costs	Number of Invoice Lines
Advertising	Gross Sales
Storage Costs	Gross Sales

a. Prepare a three-column income statement with columns for wholesale, retail, and total.

b. Which channel of trade has the higher ratio of operating income to sales?

°**15.** The Apco Company applies manufacturing overhead to all departments by means of allocation ratios. The four departments are: (1) Melting; (2) Molding; (3) Coring; (4) Cleaning. From the data shown on page 643, prepare an overhead distribution sheet showing in detail the manufacturing overhead chargeable to each department.

°**16.** The Kellermeyer Specialty Shop has three departments: Clothing, Accessories, and Shoes. The operating expenses for the year ending December 31, 1975, are shown on page 644.

a. Prepare a four-column statement of operating expenses with columns headed as follows: Clothing; Accessories; Shoes; Total. Begin with

APCO COMPANY

Manufacturing Overhead Costs per Month

Indirect labor
Melting .... $ 6,000
Molding 1,800
Coring 600
Cleaning 1,800
Supplies used
Melting 300
Molding 300
Coring 1,200
Cleaning 600
Taxes (Machinery and Equipment, $72; Building, $144) 216
Compensation Insurance 390
Power 300
Heat and Light 480
Depreciation—Building 384
Depreciation—Machinery and Equipment 360

Total $14,730

APCO COMPANY: OTHER OPERATING DATA

Department	Floor Space (Sq. Ft.)	Cost of Machinery and Equipment	Direct Labor per Month	Compen-sation Insurance [a]	Horse-power Rating
Melting 1,000		$20,000	—	$6.00	60
Molding 4,000		5,000	$ 4,800	3.00	—
Coring 1,000		15,000	2,000	3.00	60
Cleaning 2,000		20,000	5,200	4.50	180
Total 8,000		$60,000	$12,000		300

[a] Rate per $100 of payroll.

direct departmental expenses and show a subtotal. Then continue with the allocated expenses; assigning each item to the various departments. Round all values to the nearest dollar. Carry ratios to three decimal places.

b. Prepare a condensed income statement with the following columnar headings: Clothing; Accessories; Shoes; Total. Show the total of operating expenses, calculated in part (a) above, as a single deduction from gross margin.

*17. The allocation matrices (A) for the Twin City Manufacturing Company for April, May, and June of 1975 were derived and are shown on page 645.

KELLERMEYER SPECIALTY SHOP

	Clothing	Acces-sories	Shoes	Un-assigned	Total
Salaries—Clerks	$78,240	$69,360	$50,400	—	$198,000
Salaries—Others	—	—	—	$48,000	48,000
Supplies Used	3,800	3,200	2,600	1,400	11,000
Depreciation of Equipment	1,600	3,560	2,000	—	7,160
Advertising	4,000	7,000	1,960	5,200	18,160
Building Rent	—	—	—	19,000	19,000
Payroll Taxes	—	—	—	12,300	12,300
Workmen's Compen-sation Insurance ...	—	—	—	2,080	2,080
Fire Insurance	—	—	—	1,000	1,000
Delivery Expense	—	—	—	1,800	1,800
Miscellaneous Expenses	1,000	800	480	900	3,180

Additional data for the period are:

KELLERMEYER SPECIALTY SHOP

	Clothing	Accessories	Shoes	Total
Sales	$600,000	$400,000	$200,000	$1,200,000
Cost of Goods Sold	440,000	236,000	124,000	800,000
Equipment	10,080	24,960	12,960	48,000
Inventory (average) ...	100,800	81,600	57,600	240,000
Floor Space (sq. ft.) ...	2,400	2,400	1,200	6,000
Number of Employees ..	8	12	5	25

KELLERMEYER SPECIALTY SHOP

Expense	Basis of Allocation
Salaries—Other	Gross margin
Supplies Used	Sales
Advertising	Sales
Building Rent	Floor space
Payroll Taxes	Salaries (including both direct and allocated other salaries)
Workmen's Compensation Insurance	Salaries (including both direct and allocated other salaries)
Fire Insurance	Cost of equipment and inventory
Delivery Expense	Sales
Miscellaneous Expenses	Number of employees

ALLOCATION MATRICES FOR TWIN CITY MANUFACTURING COMPANY

		Services Performed Here	
		Repairs (R)	Administration (A)
	April		
	Production Departments		
Services	Cleaning (C)	.435	.343
Used	Mixing (M)	.215	.358
Here	Pouring (P)	.350	.299
		1.000	1.000
	Costs to be allocated	$50,000	$60,000

		Services Performed Here	
		Repairs (R)	Administration (A)
	May		
	Production Departments		
Services	Cleaning (C)	.40	.30
Used	Mixing (M)	.40	.20
Here	Pouring (P)	.20	.50
		1.00	1.00
	Costs to be allocated	$52,000	$58,000

		Services Performed Here	
		Repairs (R)	Administration (A)
	June		
	Production Departments		
Services	Cleaning (C)	.45	.35
Used	Mixing (M)	.25	.40
Here	Pouring (P)	.30	.25
		1.00	1.00
	Costs to be allocated	$55,000	$64,000

Use the allocation matrices to determine how much each production department should be charged for service costs for the month of

a. April
b. May
c. June.

18. The following data describe services produced and consumed by the four departments of the Oak Bank, during October, 1975. Using these data, write the system of simultaneous equations describing the proper allocation

FRACTIONS OF SERVICE DEPARTMENTS' OUTPUT USED BY SERVICE AND
PRODUCTION DEPARTMENT, OAK BANK FOR OCTOBER, 1975

| | | Services Performed Here | |
		Personnel (P)	Administration (A)
Services Used Here	Service Departments		
	Personnel (P)	—	.30
	Administration (A)	.10	—
	Production Departments		
	Services (S)	.60	.20
	Loans (L)	.30	.50
	Costs to be allocated	$40,000	$60,000

of service department costs to the production departments. Let a_{ij} represent the fraction of service department j's cost that is allocable to production department i, after accounting for service department use of service department output. Let p_{ij} be the direct use of department j by department i. Let s_{ij} be the use of department j by department i, when i and j are both service departments. Solve for the final allocation of costs with simultaneous equations or the matrix method explained in Appendix 20.1.

*19. The Schneider Spaghetti Company has three production departments: Tubing, Slicing, and Packing. There are also three service departments: Quality Control, Administration, and Maintenance. In June, 1975, the Quality Control department provided 2,000 hours of service: 500 hours each to Tubing and Slicing, 250 hours to Maintenance, and 750 hours to Packing. In the same month, Administration provided 5,000 hours of service, 1,000 to each of the other five departments. Also in June, Maintenance provided 1,200 hours of service to Tubing, 1,500 hours to Slicing, 1,800 hours to Packing, 300 hours to Quality Control, and 200 hours to Administration. Costs for Quality Control were $20,000, costs for Administration were $60,000, and costs for Maintenance were $75,000.

     a. Using the step-down procedure that allocates service costs sequentially, beginning with the service department that receives the least benefit from other service departments, allocate the service costs of the Schneider Spaghetti Company to its three production departments. Start with Administration, then allocate Maintenance and, finally, Quality Control. Check your solution by making sure $155,000 is allocated to the three production departments.

     b. Following the method outlined in Appendix 20.1, set up the full matrices of services output, S, and usage, P, based on the above data.

     c. Express algebraically the fraction of the Maintenance department's output allocable to Tubing. Use the notation described in Appendix 20.1 for the Berdan Products example.

     d. Express algebraically the fraction of the Quality Control department's output allocable to Slicing. Use the notation described in the appendix for the Berdan Products example.

     e. Use matrices S and P to solve for matrix A, the allocation matrix.

     f. Use the results of matrix A to allocate the service department costs.

*20. The Horton Hose Factory is engaged in the manufacture and sale of garden hoses. The firm's three production departments are Extruding, Slicing, and Nozzles. These departments are served by the Computer Department, Personnel, and Administration. In January, 1975, the Extruding department consumed the following services: 500 hours from Personnel, 300 from Computer, and 200 from Administration. Slicing used 250 hours from Personnel, 200 from Computer, and 100 from Administration. Nozzles consumed 450 hours from Personnel, 100 from Computer, and 300 from Administration. In addition, Personnel supplied 150 hours each to Computer and Administration and consumed 100 hours from Computer and 200 from Administration. Computer supplied Administration with 600 hours of service and consumed 300 hours from Administration. Costs for Computer were $100,000; for Personnel, $60,000; for Administration, $50,000.

   a. Allocate all service costs; use the step-down procedure described in Problem (19a). Treat service departments in the following order: Personnel, Computer, Administration. Round answers to the nearest dollar.

   b. Set up matrices S and P as described in Appendix 20.1. Round entries to two decimal places but make sure all columns sum to 1 by allocating any rounding error to self-service.

   c. Using the notation explained in Appendix 20.1 for the Berdan Products example, express algebraically the following fractions:

     (1) fraction of Computer output allocable to Slicing

     (2) fraction of Personnel output allocable to Nozzles; to Slicing

     (3) fraction of Administration output allocable to Extruding.

   d. Use matrices S and P to solve for matrix A, the allocation matrix.

   e. Use the results of matrix A to allocate the service department costs. What problems does the rounding of answers to two decimal places cause?

*21. (Adapted from a problem by David O. Green.) The Quality Cotton Mill located a plant in the South. At the time of construction there were no utility companies equipped to provide this plant with water, power, or fuel. Therefore included in the original facilities were: (1) a water plant which pumped water from a nearby lake and filtered it; (2) a coal-fired boiler room which produced steam used in part for the manufacturing process and the balance for producing electricity; and (3) an electric plant.

    An analysis of these activities revealed that water is used 70 percent for the production of steam and 30 percent in manufacturing. Steam produced is used 40 percent for the production of electric power and 60 percent for manufacturing. Ten percent of the electric power is used by the water plant and 90 percent goes to manufacturing.

    For the year 1975 the costs charged to these departments were:

QUALITY COTTON MILL

	Variable	Fixed	Total
Water Plant	$ 5,000	$10,000	$15,000
Steam Room	20,000	18,000	38,000
Electric Plant	10,000	7,000	17,000

A new power company has offered to sell electricity to Quality for 3.5 cents a kilowatt hour. In 1975, the electric plant generated 500,000 kilowatt hours. The manager of the electric plant has advised that the offer be rejected since (he says) "our variable costs were only two cents per kilowatt hour in 1975." Was this the right answer? (Support with computations.)

Cost Accounting: Assignment of Costs to Output for Job Order and Process Costing Systems

The accumulation of manufacturing costs by departments was considered in the preceding chapter. This chapter and the next are concerned with the assignment of departmental cost to units of product and the determination of their total cost from the sum of their costs in the several production departments.

Cost Accounting Methods

Many different methods can be used to assign departmental production costs to output. Two principal methods of assigning *actual* costs to product can be distinguished. They are commonly known as the *job order* method and the *process* method. Job order costing is useful for firms whose manufacturing operations are designed for specific jobs or orders such as in a print shop, custom furniture manufacturing, and construction. In job order costing, actual costs are accumulated for each specific batch or project. Process costing may be used where the manufactured product is relatively uniform or where it flows through a series of standardized processes. Process costing would be used by oil refineries, producers of chemicals, and automobile manufacturers. In process costing, costs are collected by departments and then assigned to units of output at the end of the accounting period. The *standard cost method*, discussed in Chapter 22, assigns a predetermined or estimated cost to each unit of output of a department; at appropriate intervals the difference or variance between actual costs and the predetermined costs assigned to product must be isolated for analysis and disposition. The method used in a given situation will depend on the nature of the manufacturing operations and the sophistication of the accounting system employed.

THE JOB ORDER METHOD

When the job order method is used, costs are accumulated for each project or batch of work as it progresses through the production process from one department to the next. This method is the only one that can be used where the products of a firm differ markedly from one another or where standardized production techniques are not used. A construction firm, for example, may have several dissimilar buildings under construction at the same time and a record must be kept of the costs of each one. A shop that turns out patterns or machines on special order also calls for the use of the job order method. On the other hand, the job order method would not be used where the product is uniform or where it flows through a series of standardized processes.

The Cost Sheet

A specialized ledger form known as a *cost sheet* is the customary recording device of the job order system. A cost sheet is opened for each job or production order for which a separate cost record is to be kept. As the job or order is worked on, the details of its cost are accumulated on the form. The cost sheets as a group constitute the subsidiary ledger for the departmental Materials in Process, Labor in Process, and Overhead in Process accounts in the general ledger. Frequently a single Work in Process account is substituted for these accounts, and it then serves as the controlling account for the subsidiary ledger made up of the cost sheets.

There is no standardized form for a cost sheet, since it should be designed to handle the special requirements of each job and business, but the form shown in Figure 21.1 will serve to indicate its usual features.

When a job is completed, the details are summarized, the total cost and the unit cost are computed, and the cost sheet is transferred from the active or work in process file to a file of completed jobs. The Selling Price and Profit and Loss items in the Summary section of the form used as an illustration are sometimes omitted and, in any case, do not form the basis for any accounting entries. Sometimes a similar memorandum is inserted for an estimated portion of the selling and administrative expenses.

Direct Material and Direct Labor Costs

Accounting for the departmental accumulation of direct material and direct labor costs was described in Chapter 20. If the job order method is used, the material requisitions must show the appropriate job order number as well as the department to which the materials are issued. The requisitions then serve as the basis of entries in the Material section of the cost sheets.

JOB ORDER COST SHEET

Date _____   Order No. _____

  Name _____

  Description _____

  _____

Promised ____(Date)____   Finished ___(Date)___

Estimated Cost _____   Price _____

Material			Labor			Overhead			
Date	Req. No.	Amount	Date	Ticket No.	Amount	Date	Hours	Rate	Amount
						Summary			
						Material Labor Overhead			
						Total			
						Units Unit Cost Selling Price Profit or Loss			

Figure 21.1 Job Order Cost Sheet

This recording may be done by direct posting from the requisitions, or from a columnar analysis sheet on which a group of requisitions for a day or week are distributed to the various job orders.

Direct labor under the job order method is labor that can be assigned specifically to an individual job order. As an employee works on particular jobs, a record is kept of the amount of time spent (or pieces made if a piece-rate method of compensation is used) on each one. Usually a separate time ticket is prepared for each job on which an employee works during the day. The time tickets then serve as the basis of entries in the Labor section of the cost sheets. The entries in the cost sheets are either made directly from the time tickets or from an intermediate columnar analysis sheet.

Allocation of Overhead to Jobs

The allocation of direct material and direct labor costs to specific jobs is relatively simple, and these costs can usually be assigned quite accurately. The allocation of production overhead, however, poses a more difficult problem.

There are two basic methods of handling this problem of overhead allocation. One procedure is to wait until the actual overhead has been accumulated for an accounting period, allocate it to the appropriate departments, and then distribute it over the jobs in production during that period. Entries are made on each cost sheet for the amount assigned to that job and a closing entry is made to close the individual overhead accounts to Overhead in Process or Work in Process. The entry to record the closing was given in the illustration of overhead allocation of the Berdan Products Company summarized in Schedule 20.1 of Chapter 20.

This method has certain unsatisfactory features. For one thing, it is impossible to determine the cost of the jobs or orders as they are completed. Therefore comparison of the estimated costs for each job with the amounts actually incurred is not possible until the end of the period, when overhead is allocated; thus, the checking of inefficiencies is delayed. The method is also defective in that overhead costs incurred for a given accounting period may not have a reasonable relationship with the volume of work handled during that time. Many overhead items are fixed in that they do not vary with the volume of production, so that an unreasonably high amount of overhead may be charged to jobs performed in periods of low production, while jobs performed during periods of exceptionally high output may receive exceptionally low overhead charges.

The second method seeks to overcome these objections by using a predetermined rate for applying overhead to individual jobs. The rates are usually set as a percentage of direct labor cost or as an hourly rate to be applied to the number of direct labor hours or machine hours required by each job. The question of setting of rates is considered in detail in the next section, but it is appropriate here to say that rates are set which either (1) attempt to distribute an estimate of actual overhead or (2) are based upon some conception of a normal or standard overhead cost that will give a reasonable overhead charge even in periods of abnormal production.

When predetermined rates are used, overhead is entered on the individual cost sheet. The total of the charges to the individual job sheets is accumulated and an entry such as the following is made at the end of the period:

Work in Process	320,000	
Overhead Absorbed		320,000

Overhead Applied is another title frequently used for the credit.

The credit to Overhead Absorbed is made in place of crediting the entire group of individual overhead accounts, but it will almost never be precisely equal to the amount of overhead actually incurred. When closing entries are made for the period, the Overhead Absorbed account is closed, together with the individual overhead accounts, and the difference between them, representing the excess of overhead absorbed over actual overhead, or vice versa, is credited to Overabsorbed Overhead or debited to Underabsorbed Overhead. The entry is:

Overhead Absorbed	320,000	
Indirect Labor		82,500
Factory Supplies Used		47,800
Janitors' Supplies Used		9,600
Factory Power		7,000
Factory Light		3,100
Depreciation of Factory Building and Equipment		135,000
Other Overhead Accounts (details omitted)		15,000
Overabsorbed Overhead		20,000

To close the production overhead accounts and record the amount of overabsorbed overhead for the period.

If Overhead Absorbed were $300,000, there would be no entry for overabsorbed overhead. If Overhead Absorbed were less than $300,000, the difference would be debited to Underabsorbed Overhead. The disposition of over- and underabsorbed overhead is discussed later in this chapter.

Bases of Overhead Allocation

Regardless of whether or not predetermined rates are used, a basis must be selected for charging overhead to the various jobs in process during the periods. The bases most frequently used are: (1) a percentage of direct labor cost; (2) a dollar and cents rate per direct labor hour worked on the job, called a labor-hour rate; (3) a machine-hour rate; and (4) a percentage of *prime cost*, the total of direct material and direct labor costs. The following discussion will first consider this problem when predetermined rates are used.

Percentage of Direct Labor Cost. At the beginning of the period (usually a year), estimates are made of the total amount of direct-labor cost and the total amount of production-overhead cost expected to be incurred during the coming period. The overhead-distribution rate is calculated by dividing the total estimated overhead by the total estimated direct labor and expressing the result as a percentage. For example:

Estimated production overhead	$300,000
Estimated direct labor	$150,000
Overhead allocation rate (applied to direct labor)	200%

When a job is completed, the rate is applied to the amount of direct labor shown on the cost sheet for the job. For example, if the cost sheet for job No. 310 shows direct labor charges totaling $600, and the overhead allocation rate is 200 percent, $1,200 will be entered in the overhead section of the cost sheet for that job. At the end of the period, overhead is added to all jobs still in process at that time, if overhead has not yet been added to the individual cost sheets.

The amount of overhead thus absorbed may be larger or smaller than the amount of overhead costs actually incurred, and the difference is the over- or underabsorption for the period. For example:

Total actual direct labor $160,000

Overhead absorbed—200% of direct labor $320,000
Total actual overhead 310,000

Overabsorbed overhead .... $ 10,000

This method is convenient because the amount of direct labor is shown on each cost sheet and no further statistics are required. It is often defective, however, in that a job using labor paid a high hourly rate will be assigned more overhead than one using labor paid a lower hourly rate, even though in each case the same use may be made of the general plant facilities.

Labor-Hour Rate. To meet the objection just made to the method of assigning overhead as a percentage of direct labor cost, overhead can be applied on the basis of the number of direct labor hours charged to each job worked on during the period.

At the beginning of the period, the following estimates are made:

Estimated factory overhead $300,000
Estimated direct labor hours .... 100,000 hrs.
Overhead allocation rate .... $3/hr.

This rate is applied to the direct labor hours accumulated on each cost sheet. If the cost sheet for job No. 316 shows 390 direct labor hours worked, $1,170 would be entered in the overhead section of the form.

The results for the period may show, for this method also, an underabsorption or overabsorption of overhead.

Actual direct labor hours .... 104,000 hrs.

Overhead absorbed at $3.00 per hr. $312,000
Total actual overhead 310,000

Overabsorbed overhead .... $ 2,000

This method necessitates keeping records of the number of direct labor hours charged to each job processed during the period, as well as its direct labor cost.

Machine-Hour Rate. In some plants or departments, machine maintenance and depreciation are the major items of overhead, and in these cases the number of hours that machines operate may be a more appropriate basis for overhead allocation. This method requires that a record be kept on each cost sheet of the number of hours that each job spends in production. The procedure is similar to that followed under the direct-labor-hours method.

Estimated factory overhead $300,000
Estimated machine hours .... 400,000 hrs.
Overhead allocation rate .... 75¢/hr.

Actual machine hours .... 410,000 hrs.

Overhead absorbed at 75¢ per hour $307,500
Total actual overhead 310,000

Underabsorbed overhead .... $ 2,500

Percentage of Prime Cost. This method has been widely used in cost accounting practice. The sum of direct labor and direct material on each job is obtained and then a percentage is added for overhead. It is not, however, a justifiable method in most cases, since there is usually little or no logical relationship between the cost of labor plus material for a job and the use made of plant facilities by that job.

Predetermined Rates Not Used

Even if predetermined rates are not used, an allocation basis must still be chosen. Estimates will not be required, however, and there will never be overabsorbed or underabsorbed overhead. The total of actual overhead costs will be divided by the number of actual direct labor hours (or whatever other basis is used), and the resulting rate will be used to apply all of the actual overhead to the jobs of the period. The allocation must, of course, be done at the end of the period.

Completion of Order

When a job order has been finished, the costs are summarized on the cost sheet and the unit cost, if relevant, is calculated. An entry is made either at this time to record the transfer of the cost of this order from work in process to finished goods, or the amount is recorded on a summary sheet and an entry is made at the end of the period for the total cost of jobs completed during the period. In either case, the typical entry would be:

Finished Goods	774,000	
Work in Process		774,000

Disposition of Underabsorbed or Overabsorbed Overhead

How to dispose of underabsorbed or overabsorbed overhead is one of the thornier questions in cost accounting and only a brief description of the possible alternatives will be offered here. The following three methods are found in practice, each one reflecting a different interpretation of the cause of the difference between the actual and the absorbed overhead for the period.

1. Carry the amount of the underabsorption or overabsorption forward as a deferred charge or deferred credit to future operations. It is expected that differences in one direction will be offset later by differences in the opposite direction. This method is usually employed only for monthly balances. At the end of the fiscal year, the balance must be disposed of by one of the other methods.
2. Transfer the amount of the overabsorbed or underabsorbed overhead to the Cost of Goods Sold account. This assumes that the difference is an error in measuring overhead assignable to each job and provides

a rough correction. A more refined variation would correct the inventories of Work in Process and Finished Goods as well.

3. Close the balance of overabsorbed or underabsorbed overhead to the Income Summary account as a special adjustment. It is assumed that the calculated overhead-distribution rates represent normal production conditions and that unit costs of production should not be affected by abnormal conditions as far as overhead costs are concerned. This method leads to the same reported income as method 2, above, but shows additional information that may be useful to management.

Diagram of Job Order Method

The diagram in Figure 21.2 summarizes the preceding discussion of the job order method. It carries the procedure one step further to include the recording of the cost of goods sold.

Production Report: Job Order Method

The production report for the job order method summarizes the information shown on the cost sheets. For each period it shows total material used, total direct labor, total overhead applied, the cost of product finished, and the cost of work still in process. It should contain data on production

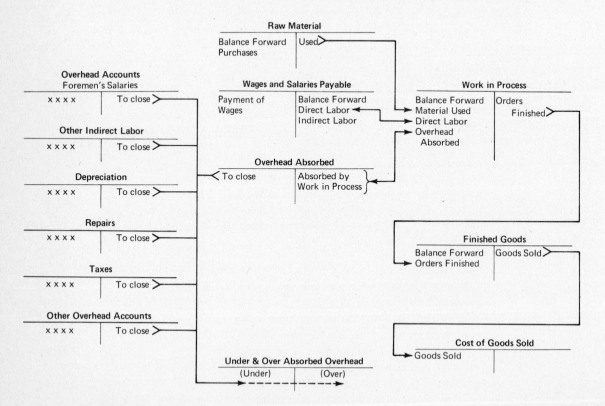

Figure 21.2   Job Order Method: Diagram of Cost Flows

overhead absorbed, as does the one illustrated below. The schedule will frequently contain two additional lines—one to show overhead absorbed and the other to show the amount of underabsorbed or overabsorbed overhead in each department. The latter figure will be, of course, the difference between actual overhead and overhead absorbed in each department.

Schedule 21.1 indicates a possible arrangement of the production report.

THE PROCESS METHOD

Features of the Process Method

The process method is most suitable for continuous production of standardized products. It should be used where the product flows or moves through a succession of steps or stages of the total productive process. Many mass-production plants, where the assembly-line manufacturing is employed, use this method of cost accounting. The critical assumption of process costing is that all units of output flowing through a process-costing center are economically indistinguishable. The essential characteristics of the accounting for the process method are:

1. Each process or stage of production becomes a center for cost accumulation. For example, a product may go through the following steps or processes: (a) cutting, (b) assembling, (c) finishing, (d) painting, and (e) inspection. Under the process method, the cost of carrying out each of the five processes is determined separately.
2. Costs are accumulated for uniform periods of time, such as a month.
3. The number of units produced in each process must also be determined, and the unit cost for the process is calculated by dividing the total costs for the period by the total number of units produced. If

SCHEDULE 21.1 PRODUCTION REPORT FOR A JOB ORDER COSTING SYSTEM

CENTER MANUFACTURING COMPANY
Production Report
November 1975

Order No.	Work in Process Nov. 1	Direct Material	Direct Labor	Overhead Absorbed	Total Cost	Work in Process Nov. 30	Finished Orders
1617	$1,820	$ 200	$ 1,540	$ 2,310	$ 5,870	$ —	$ 5,870
1618	3,270	—	720	1,080	5,070	—	5,070
1619	1,780	400	275	412	2,867	—	2,867
1620	—	1,220	910	1,365	3,495	—	3,495
1629	—	1,640	1,180	1,770	4,590	—	4,590
1630	—	890	620	930	2,440	2,440	—
1631	—	1,210	210	315	1,735	1,735	—
1632	—	470	50	75	595	595	—
	$6,870	$18,410	$12,265	$18,397	$55,942	$4,770	$51,172

some units are only partially complete, the work done is translated
into an *equivalent number* of completed units.

4. The determination of the final or total unit cost of the product is
essentially one of adding together the unit costs of each process through
which the product goes.

Simplified Illustration of Process Costing

The schedule of production costs shown in Schedule 21.2 indicates the way
in which process costs are accumulated and the method of computing unit

SCHEDULE 21.2 PROCESS COSTING ILLUSTRATION

LESTER METAL PRODUCTS COMPANY
Production Costs
Month of July 1975

	Units	Amount	Unit Costs	
Process A				
Raw material used		$10,800	$ .40	
Direct labor		35,100	1.30	
Other costs (details omitted)		5,400	.20	
Total cost of units completed during July	27,000	$51,300		$1.90
Units on hand 7/1/75 at $2.024	5,000	10,120		
	32,000	$61,420		
Units on hand 7/31/75 at $1.90	1,000	1,900		$1.90
Transferred to Process *B*	31,000	$59,520		
Process B				
Transferred from Process *A*	31,000	$59,520		$1.92
Direct labor		9,920	$ .32	
Other costs (details omitted)		3,410	.11	.43
Total cost of units completed during July		$72,850		$2.35
Units on hand 7/1/75 at $2.563	1,500	3,845		
	32,500	$76,695		
Units on hand 7/31/75 at $2.35	500	1,175		
Transferred to Process *C*	32,000	$75,520		
Process C				
Transferred from Process *B*	32,000	$75,520		$2.36
Parts used		1,600	$ .05	
Direct labor		4,800	.15	
Other costs (details omitted)		1,280	.04	.24
Total cost of units completed during July		$83,200		$2.60

costs for the Lester Metal Products Company. The significant features of the situation are:

1. The plant produces a single product, which passes through three successive processes.
2. The nature of the production technique is such that at the end of the month all products have just completed one or more of the processes. (This assumption precludes ending inventories of work only partially complete for a process and the resulting difficulties in accounting for the equivalent units of work done. This assumption is the one that makes this illustration "simplified.")
3. Units that have completed Process A and Process B are held at those points until needed in the next process. Those that have completed Process C are immediately transferred to the warehouse, where they are held until sold.
4. The first-in, first-out technique is used in valuing inventories in all processes.

Comments on Illustration

In Process A, the unit costs are determined by dividing the various cost items by the number of units of product made from the material used during the month, 27,000. In Processes B and C, the unit costs are calculated by dividing the various cost items by the number of units transferred from the preceding processes, 31,000 for Process B and 32,000 for Process C.

"Other costs" include all of the costs of production except the direct material and labor which are chargeable to the three processes. Indirect labor, depreciation, maintenance, insurance, taxes, supplies, light, heat, and power are common examples. (The sum of direct labor costs and these "other costs" is often called *conversion cost*.) The problem of distributing the "other" overhead costs to various processes is discussed and demonstrated in Chapter 20.

The unit-cost figures used at July 1 in pricing the inventories of units not yet transferred to the next process—for example, the $2.024 used in Process A—are obtained from the production-cost schedule for the month of June.

Since the first-in, first-out inventory technique is used, the work in process inventories at July 31 are priced at the unit cost of July operations—for example, the $1.90 used in Process A. The unit cost shown for the items transferred to the next process can be calculated in one of two equivalent ways. First, the basic inventory equation, introduced in Chapter 12, can be used to derive the total number of units and total costs transferred. For example, to cost the units transferred from Process A to Process B during July, use the following form of the inventory equation, which is illustrated in Schedule 21.3.

Beginning Inventory + Additions − Ending Inventory = Withdrawals.

Second, the unit cost shown can be calculated as the weighted average of

SCHEDULE 21.3   FIFO COSTING OF UNITS TRANSFERRED FROM PROCESS *A* TO PROCESS *B*

	Units	Amount	Unit Costs
Units on hand 7/1/75 (Beginning Inventory)	5,000	$10,120	$2.024 (June, Process *A*)
Produced during July (Additions)	27,000	51,300	$1.90 (July, Process *A)*
Units on hand 7/31/75 (Ending Inventory)	(1,000)	(1,900)	$1.90 (July, Process *A)*
Total transferred to Process *B* during July (Withdrawals) ..	31,000	$59,520	$1.92 (= $59,520/31,000)

the amount carried over from June and the amount transferred from production during July. The unit cost transferred from Process *A* to Process *B* could be calculated directly in the following manner:

$$\frac{\$10,120 + (26,000 \times \$1.90)}{5,000 + 26,000} = \$1.92$$

Accounting under Process Method

Recording the ordinary daily transactions under the process method involves nothing new in the way of bookkeeping procedure. Costs are assigned directly to individual processes whenever it is feasible to do so. The indirect overhead costs are charged to general overhead cost accounts that are later allocated to the productive processes.

The following selected transactions indicate the typical requirements of accounting analysis under this method. It is assumed that controlling accounts are used for each group of process accounts and for the general production-overhead accounts. Appropriate detail accounts are, of course, maintained in each case. (These transactions involve operations of the Lester Metal Company for the month of July, 1975.)

(1) Material is purchased from the Northwest Steel Company. The invoice totals $15,725.

Raw Material	15,725	
Accounts Payable		15,725

(2) When materials, parts, or supplies are needed for production, they are requisitioned from the stockroom. A summary of the requisitions issued during the month is as follows:

Raw Material, Process *A*	$10,800
Parts, Process *C*	1,600
Supplies, Process *A*	150
Supplies, Process *B*	475
Supplies, Process *C*	50
Janitors' Supplies	25

The entry, omitting detail accounts, would be:

Process *A* Control	10,950	
Process *B* Control	475	
Process *C* Control	1,650	
Production Overhead Control	25	
Raw Material		10,800
Parts		1,600
Supplies		700

(3) The payroll distribution for the month provides the following information:

Direct Labor, Process *A*	$35,100
Direct Labor, Process *B*	9,920
Direct Labor, Process *C*	4,800
Superintendence	550
Maintenance Labor	600
Janitors' Wages	500
Nightwatchman's Wages	200

The entry, omitting detail accounts, is:

Process *A* Control	35,100	
Process *B* Control	9,920	
Process *C* Control	4,800	
Production Overhead Control	1,850	
Wages and Salaries Payable		51,670

(4) Depreciation for the month is as follows:

Machinery and Equipment, Process *A*	$ 675
Machinery and Equipment, Process *B*	1,125
Machinery and Equipment, Process *C*	125
Building	100

The entry would be:

Process *A* Control	675	
Process *B* Control	1,125	
Process *C* Control	125	
Production Overhead Control	100	
Accumulated Depreciation of Machinery and Equipment		1,925
Accumulated Depreciation of Building		100

At the close of the month, the production overhead accounts are allocated to the various processes (as explained in Chapter 20) and a statement of production costs is prepared (such as the one in Schedule 21.2). If the total costs shown in that statement are to appear in the process control accounts, the entry to close the Production Overhead Control account is:

Process *A* Control	4,575	
Process *B* Control	1,810	
Process *C* Control	1,105	
Production Overhead Control		7,490

(Other overhead costs than those shown in entries (2) to (4) will, of course, have been entered if the balance in Production Overhead Control is $7,490.)

The cost of the units transferred from one process to another is recorded, the transfer from Process *C* being made to the Finished Goods account.

Process *B* Control (Transfers from Process *A*) 59,520
    Process *A* Control (Transfers to Process *B*)   59,520
Units completed in Process *A* transferred to Process *B*.

Process *C* Control (Transfers from Process *B*) 75,520
    Process *B* Control (Transfers to Process *C*)   75,520
Units completed in Process *B* transferred to Process *C*.

Finished Goods 83,200
    Process *C* Control (Transfers to Finished Goods)   83,200
Units completed in Process *C*.

The T-accounts shown in Schedule 21.4 summarize the illustration for the Lester Metal Company.

Diagram of Process Costing Method

The diagram in Figure 21.3 indicates how costs of production flow through the accounts and finally emerge in the Cost of Goods Sold account when goods are sold to customers. It is stated in general terms rather than corresponding to any illustration.

Other Process Cost Problems

The preceding discussion is confined to the simpler aspects of process costing. Several problems can occur, but the presentation of their detailed solution will be left for a more comprehensive discussion of cost accounting.

Partially Completed Product. The handling of partially completed products within a process is one of these more complicated problems. Where, for example, production is carried on as a continuous process as in oil refining, the manufacture of steel, or on an assembly line, there are always certain amounts of partly processed products at each stage of production. (In the preceding illustration for Lester Metal Products Company, this complication was avoided by assuming that the work in process had completed one or more of the various processes.) Partly processed units should each be charged with a portion of the costs of the process in which they are found at the close of the period.

The procedure commonly used involves computing an *effective* or *equivalent* number of completed units to be used in place of the actual number of partially completed units in spreading the process costs. For example, assume that Department *Y* had 1,000 units in process at the start of the period and 2,000 units in process at the end of the period. Department *Y* is a continuous assembly line so that, on average, each of

SCHEDULE 21.4 CONTROLLING ACCOUNTS FOR THE LESTER METAL PRODUCTS COMPANY FOR JULY, 1975

Process A Control

7/1/75	Balance, 5,000 at $2.024	10,120	July	Transferred to Process B	59,520
July	Raw material	10,800	7/31/75	Balance, 1,000 at $1.90	1,900
	Supplies	150			
	Direct labor	35,100			
	Depreciation	675			
	Other production overhead	4,575			
		61,420			61,420
8/1/75	Balance, 1,000 at $1.90..	1,900			

Process B Control

7/1/75	Balance, 1,500 at $2.563	3,845	July	Transferred to Process C	75,520
July	Supplies	475	7/31/75	Balance, 500 at $2.35..	1,175
	Direct labor	9,920			
	Depreciation	1,125			
	Other production overhead	1,810			
	Transferred from Process A	59,520			
		76,695			76,695
8/1/75	Balance, 500 at $2.35 ..	1,175			

Process C Control

July	Parts and supplies	1,650	July	Transferred to Finished Goods	83,200
	Direct labor	4,800			
	Depreciation	125			
	Other production overhead	1,105			
	Transferred from Process B	75,520			
		83,200			83,200

the units in process is half complete. During the period 8,500 units were completed and transferred to Department Z. The equivalent units of completed work done during the period is 9,000 units, calculated from the inventory equation rearranged to show

Additions = Ending Inventory + Withdrawals — Beginning Inventory:

Equivalent Units of Completed Work

Ending inventory (½ of 2,000)	1,000
Units transferred to Department Z (withdrawals)	8,500
Beginning inventory (½ of 1,000)	(500)
During period (additions)	9,000

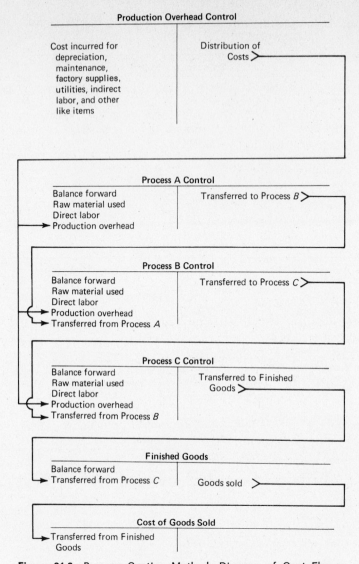

Figure 21.3 Process Costing Method: Diagram of Cost Flows

If the total costs of operating Department Y during the period were $18,900, the cost of production per completed unit or equivalent in the department for the period would be $2.10 ($ = \$18,900/9,000$ units). The 2,000 partially completed units at the end of the period would carry a cost of $2,100 ($ = 1,000$ equivalent completed units $\times \$2.10$ per unit).

The calculation of equivalent production where operations are not continuous follows the same principle. For example, assume that Process M had 1,500 units in process at the start of the period which were, on average, one-third complete. At the end of the period, the inventory in Process M showed 1,600 units on hand which were, on average, one-fourth complete. During the period 14,000 units were completed and transferred to Process *N*. The equivalent production for the period is 13,900 units, calculated as follows:

Equivalent Units of Completed Work

Ending inventory (¼ of 1,600)	400
Units transferred to Process *N* (withdrawals)	14,000
Beginning inventory (⅓ of 1,500)	(500)
During period (additions)	13,900

Shrinkage in Volume. Another problem is that of shrinkage in volume from such causes as evaporation. Ordinarily this is handled by subtracting the amount of the shrinkage in terms of units and spreading the total process costs over the smaller number of remaining units. If, for example, 20,000 units enter a process, but only 18,000 units emerge due to shrinkage in volume, the accumulated costs through the process are divided by 18,000 to get a unit cost which absorbs the decline in volume.

Spoilage and Breakage. Measurement problems similar to shrinkage also arise from spoilage and breakage. If the spoilage or breakage is considered to be normal in amount, it is absorbed automatically in the cost of the good units in the same manner as the shrinkage from evaporation. If it is considered to be abnormal or preventable, the full accumulated cost of the spoiled or broken goods is charged to a special loss account, and none of it is charged to the good product. Thus normal spoilage is included in product costs, while abnormal spoilage is a period expense.

Suppose, in Process *P*, that total costs for the period were $15,000, that 30,000 good units were completed, and that 1,000 equivalent units were spoiled. If all of the spoilage is considered normal, the unit cost for inventories or cost of units transferred is:

$$\frac{\text{total costs}}{\text{good units}} = \frac{\$15,000}{30,000} = \$.50 \text{ per unit}$$

If all of the spoilage is abnormal, then the unit cost is:

$$\frac{\text{total costs}}{\text{good units} + \text{spoiled units}} = \frac{\$15,000}{31,000} = \$.48387 \text{ per unit}$$

The loss for the period from abnormal spoilage is $484 (= $.48387 × 1,000 equivalent units abnormally spoiled). If, as is more likely a certain portion, say 1 percent of good units, is expected to be spoiled, then the unit cost is:

$$\frac{\text{total costs}}{\text{good units} + \text{abnormal spoilage}} = \frac{\$15,000}{30,000 + [1,000 - .01 \times 30,000]}$$

$$= \frac{\$15,000}{30,000 + 700} = \frac{\$15,000}{30,700} = \$.4886 \text{ per unit}$$

The charge for the period from abnormal spoilage is $342 (= $.4886 × 700 equivalent units abnormally spoiled). The good units would carry costs of $14,658 (= $.4886 × 30,000 good units) so that the total costs of $15,000 (= $342 + $14,658) are accounted for.

BY-PRODUCTS AND JOINT PRODUCTS

A cost allocation problem arises when more than one product emerges from a single production process. The numerous products of meat-packing plants, the variety of metals often found and extracted together in mining operations, the inevitable production of various grades of finished lumber in the operation of a lumber mill, and the several products made from the original material in the dairy and petroleum industries, are common examples of jointly produced goods.

The problems of joint production are not limited to manufacturing and mining. For instance, in real estate a similar problem exists in the development of a subdivision. The total cost of developing the tract represents a joint cost of all of the lots which are to be sold, and some reasonable method of allocating this total figure must be found, so that a cost and profit can be calculated for each lot sold and a cost assigned to the unsold lots.

In accounting for jointly produced products, it is customary to distinguish between by-products and joint products. A by-product is produced as the inevitable result of the production of a main product and is of relatively small value. For example, steel shavings in a machine shop, scraps of lumber in a furniture factory, and buttermilk in a dairy are typical instances of by-products. A joint product is one that is treated as equally significant with other products which emerge from a process. The different grades of lumber in a lumber mill, milk and butter in dairy operations, and subdivision lots are examples of joint products. The difference between by-products and joint products, then, is one of degree; the dividing line is not distinct. A power plant, for instance, that produces both electricity and steam may consider one or the other as a by-product or may treat them both as joint products.

By-Product Accounting

The distinctive feature of by-product accounting is that no processing cost is assigned to the by-product until it is separated from the joint process. The normal procedure is to deduct its net realizable or sales value from the total accumulated cost, and the remaining costs become the cost of the main product, or products. The *net realizable sales value* of the by-product, or by-products, is its estimated selling price less any costs yet to be incurred for further processing or handling. If the job order method is used, this deduction of the value of the by-product can sometimes be made on the cost sheet. If this is not feasible, the value of the by-product can be treated as a reduction of the general manufacturing overhead. When the process-cost method is used, a similar choice exists: the value of the by-product can either be deducted from the accumulated costs in the process where it is separated from the main product, or it can be treated as an adjustment of the general overhead.

For example, a machine shop collects and sells the steel shavings that result from the production of its orders. During the month of March the accumulated steel shavings are valued at $5,000. It is not considered practicable to assign the value of this by-product to the job orders, so it is handled as a blanket reduction in shop overhead. The entry would be:

Steel Shavings on Hand 5,000
    Steel Shavings Produced 5,000
Steel shavings produced during the month of March.

The Steel Shavings Produced account would appear on the overhead-distribution schedule or on the statement of production operations as a deduction from the total shop overhead. When the shavings are sold, there will be a profit or loss only if the selling price turns out to be different from that used in assigning a value to the shavings. The entry for the sale of accumulated shavings with book value of $15,000 for $16,500 would normally be:

Cash on Hand 16,500
    Steel Shavings on Hand 15,000
    Gain on Disposal of Shavings (or Overhead) 1,500

By-products are assigned a cost so that the expected gain or loss on the sale of the by-products is zero. The cost assigned to the by-products reduces the cost of the main product or products.

Joint-Product Accounting

Strictly speaking, it is impossible to compute the cost of each product produced under a joint process. Total cost can usually be determined with a satisfactory degree of accuracy, but there is no theoretically correct or logical method of spreading the total cost over the various joint products. The methods used can best be described as feasible, reasonable, or expedient. In spite of this apparently insurmountable barrier, attempts are nevertheless made to allocate joint costs, primarily in order to provide figures which can be used for inventory purposes.[1]

[1] If demand curves, or schedules, are available for the various joint products, then the mathematics of Kuhn-Tucker theory and Lagrangian multipliers provides a logical technique for deriving costs to be allocated to the joint products. The technique provides sensible answers, because using them, rather than answers from some other method, will induce management to make decisions that maximize the profits to the firm. For example, beef sold as meat and hides sold for making shoes are both derived from a single cow. So long as the firm must merely cost the hides or beef left over at the end of the period, the economic returns to the firm, as opposed to the accounting profits reported, will be unaffected by a decision to treat the hides as by-products or as joint products with some arbitrary allocation of the cost of the cow. But if management is given the opportunity to purchase hides alone from a separate supplier, it will need to know the economic cost of the hides produced jointly with beef in order to decide whether buying from the outside supplier offers a profitable return. The mathematical technique provides the information management needs to make the correct decision if, to repeat, the demand curves for beef and hides are known. The method is given by Roman L. Weil, "Allocating Joint Costs," *American Economic Review*, (December 1968) and is explained in a cost accounting framework in Chapter 14 of Nicholas Dopuch, Jacob G. Birnberg, and Joel Demski. *Cost Accounting*, Harcourt Brace Jovanovich, 2nd ed., 1974.

Joint costs are usually allocated with one of two methods: the relative-sales-value method or the physical-units method. Both are described in an illustration from real estate development. Sorter Homes Development Company purchases a two-acre tract of land adjoining a lake for $35,000 and spends $5,000 in legal fees to have the land subdivided into five lots. Houses are built on each of the lots. Various cost and price data are shown in Schedule 21.5.

SCHEDULE 21.5 SORTER HOMES DEVELOPMENT COMPANY

		Data for Joint-Cost Allocations			
Lot Number (1)	Size (in acres) (2)	Resale Price After Subdivision (3)	Selling Price for House and Lot (4)	Cost to Build House (5)	Approximate Sales Value of Land at Split-off (6)
1	½	$16,000	$ 75,000	$ 50,000	$ 25,000
2	½	25,000	80,000	50,000	30,000
3	½	25,000	80,000	50,000	30,000
4	¼	4,000	35,000	30,000	5,000
5	¼	10,000	40,000	30,000	10,000
	2	$80,000	$310,000	$210,000	$100,000

(3) market prices given
(6) = (4) — (5)

The differing prices for lots of equal size result from differing proximity to the lake. The joint-cost problem in this context is to allocate the $40,000 cost of the land to each of the five lots so that financial reports can be constructed if not all lots and houses are sold in the same accounting period.

Relative-Sales-Value Method. First suppose that once the land is legally subdivided, there is a ready market for the lots without houses and that the market prices for the five lots are as shown in column (3). If such information is available, then a sensible method of allocating the $40,000 of joint cost is to allocate that cost to the lots in proportion to their current market values. Since the cost is 50 percent of the sum of the current market values ($40,000/$80,000), each lot would be assigned a cost of 50 percent of its current market value. The cost of Lot 1, for example, would be $8,000.

To alter the illustration, suppose that the legal agreement allowing subdivision prohibits Sorter Homes from reselling the lots without houses or that for some other reason the information shown in column (3) is not available. The diagram in Figure 21.4 may help in understanding the nature of the problem. Such a diagram will usually be helpful in analyzing joint-cost allocation problems. The split-off point here is the point after which all costs are directly allocable to individual products. Then to use the relative-sales-value method, approximations to the relative sales values must be derived, as shown in column (6). The approximate sales value of a lot (joint product) is defined to be the selling price of the lot-house

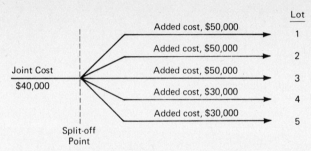

Figure 21.4 The Split-off Point in Allocating Joint Costs

combination (final product) less the cost to complete the lot-house combination. Here, the cost to complete is the cost of building the house. The approximate sales value of Lot 1 is $25,000, or the price of the house-lot combination, $75,000, less the cost of the house, $50,000. Since the cost of the land is 40 percent of the sum of the approximate sales values, each lot would be assigned a cost of 40 percent ($= \$40,000/\$100,000$) of its approximate sales value. Lot 1, for example, would be allocated $10,000 ($= .4 \times \$25,000$).

Physical-Units Method. The physical-units method is not based upon dollar costs but upon some obvious physical measure. Here, the obvious measure is area in acres. In other contexts the obvious physical measure might be weight or volume. Since Lots 1, 2, and 3 each contain ½ acre out of 2 acres, each would be allocated (½)/2 $\times$ $40,000 or $10,000. Each ¼-acre lot would be allocated (¼)/2 $\times$ $40,000 or $5,000.

The physical-units method is usually easy to apply, but its results may not make good sense. For example, if the physical-units method using pounds of salable product is used to allocate the cost of a beef cattle to cuts of meat, tenderloin will carry the same cost per pound as will sweetbreads. Then the sales of tenderloin will appear extraordinarily profitable while sweetbreads will usually be sold at a loss. The relative-sales value method will allocate more of the joint costs of beef cattle to a pound of tenderloin than to a pound of sweetbreads.

By-Products with Joint Products. The problems of costing by-products and joint products can occur together. Suppose that at the time Sorter Homes arranged for legal subdivision of the land purchase, it also sold to the municipality the rights for the public to use the lake for $2,000. The rights to the lake probably should be viewed as a by-product in this case, so they would be treated as a reduction in the cost of the land. The entry would be:

Cash	2,000	
Land (two-acre lot)		2,000

Then the joint cost of the land to be allocated to the five lots would be only $38,000. Schedule 21.6 summarizes the joint cost allocation under the various scenarios discussed above.

SCHEDULE 21.6 SORTER HOMES DEVELOPMENT COMPANY: JOINT COST ALLOCATION UNDER VARIOUS METHODS WITH AND WITHOUT BY-PRODUCT

Lot Number	Joint-Product Cost = $40,000			By-Product Cost = $2,000 Joint-Product Cost = $38,000		
	Basis of Allocation			Basis of Allocation		
	Relative Sales Values (1) a	Approximate Relative Sales Values (2) b	Physical Units (3) c	Relative Sales Values (4) d	Approximate Relative Sales Values (5) e	Physical Units (6) f
1	$ 8,000	$10,000	$10,000	$ 7,600	$ 9,500	$ 9,500
2	12,500	12,000	10,000	11,875	11,400	9,500
3	12,500	12,000	10,000	11,875	11,400	9,500
4	2,000	2,000	5,000	1,900	1,900	4,750
5	5,000	4,000	5,000	4,750	3,800	4,750
Total	$40,000	$40,000	$40,000	$38,000	$38,000	$38,000

a (1) = Column (3) of Schedule 21.5 × 40/80.
b (2) = Column (6) of Schedule 21.5 × 40/100.
c (3) = $40,000 × [Column (2) of Schedule 21.5]/2.
d (4) = (1) × 38/40 = Column (3) of Schedule 21.5 × 38/80.
e (5) = (2) × 38/40 = Column (3) of Schedule 21.5 × 38/100.
f (6) = (3) × 38/40.

QUESTIONS AND PROBLEMS

1. What are the essential differences between the process method and job order method of cost accounting?

2. Manufacturing overhead is sometimes assigned to job orders in proportion to material cost. Do you think this is likely to be a satisfactory procedure?

3. Assuming that other factors work out as planned, what is the effect upon the absorption of overhead of:
   a. an excess of actual direct labor cost over estimated direct labor cost, when overhead is allocated as a percentage of direct labor cost
   b. a decrease in the pace of operations so that estimated machine hours exceed actual machine hours, when a machine hour rate of allocating overhead is used
   c. an excess of the actual amount of overhead incurred over the estimated overhead for the period.

4. a. What differentiates a joint product from a by-product?
   b. What is the accounting significance of this difference?
   c. What are two accounting methods of assigning joint costs to joint products?

5. The Johnson Products Company uses a job order cost accounting system. In May, 1975, total overhead was $80,000 and the number of direct labor hours worked was 20,000.

   a. What overhead rate might be used?
 °b. Job No. 247 is a special order for 100 special design tables. The cost
     sheet shows raw material costs of $4,600, direct labor costs of $7,600,
     and 1,200 direct labor hours charged to the job. What is the total cost
     of job No. 247? What is the unit cost of each table on that job?

 6. What is the significance of the split-off point in accounting for joint products?

 7. The Facon Manufacturing Company distributes its factory overhead over
    its job orders as a percentage of direct labor cost. The rate set for the
    third quarter of 1975 was 150 percent, based upon an estimated total
    overhead of $75,000 and an estimated total direct labor cost of $50,000.
        Indicate the amount of overabsorbed or underabsorbed overhead for
    the quarter under each of the following assumptions:
    a. actual overhead, $70,000; actual direct labor, $48,000
    b. actual overhead, $79,000; actual direct labor, $52,000
    c. actual overhead, $80,000; actual direct labor, $50,000
    d. actual overhead, $84,000; actual direct labor, $56,000
    e. actual overhead, $68,000; actual direct labor, $44,000
    f. actual overhead, $76,000; actual direct labor, $49,000.

 8. What are two methods of accounting for by-products?

 9. A noted transportation economist once said, "God Almighty does not know
    the cost of carrying a hundred pounds of freight from Boston to New
    York." What are the difficulties of determining the cost of railroad service
    rendered?

10. A summary of the production of the Brealey Machine Company for the
    month of September is shown below:

	#540	#545	#547	Total
Work in Process, Sept. 1	$2,530	$ 9,620		$12,150
Raw Material Used	550		$ 5,930	6,480
Direct Labor	2,240	6,750	10,300	19,290
Overhead Absorbed	1,120	3,375	5,150	9,645
Total Cost	$6,440	$19,745	$21,380	$47,565
Work in Process, Sept. 30	—	—	21,380	21,380
Cost of Jobs Completed	$6,440	$19,745	$ 0	$26,185

    a. What are the method and rate of overhead allocation to the job orders
       that appear to be used?
    b. Give the journal entry to record the allocation of factory overhead to
       the job orders.
    c. Give the journal entry to record the completion of the jobs.
    d. If the balance in the Factory Overhead Control account at September 30
       was $9,875, give the closing entry for the overhead accounts.

°11. The Speed Way Boat Company uses a job order cost accounting system.
     Factory overhead is allocated to jobs on a direct labor-hours basis at the

---

° Hints, key numbers, or (partial) answers appear in the back of the book between the
Appendix Tables and the Glossary.

rate of $3 per hour. Overabsorbed or underabsorbed overhead is closed directly to Income Summary at the end of each year.

a. Job No. 745 required $8,400 of materials and 1,000 hours of direct labor at an average rate of $4 per hour. What was the total cost shown for job No. 745?

b. Job No. 305 required $6,300 of materials and 3,000 hours of direct labor at an average rate of $4 per hour. Job No. 305 sold for $30,000. What was the "gross margin" on this sale?

c. During the entire year total raw material used was $220,000, 70,000 direct labor hours were worked at an average rate of $5 per hour, and total overhead was $230,000. (Jobs No. 745 and No. 305 are included in these figures.) What was the total of debits to Work in Process during the year?

12. The Robinson Machine Company uses a job order cost accounting system and closes its books annually at December 31. Manufacturing overhead is applied to jobs on a direct-labor-cost basis at a rate of 50 percent of direct labor cost. A Manufacturing Overhead Control account is used to accumulate actual overhead costs during the month. At the end of the month, that account and the Overhead Absorbed account are closed and an entry made to the Overabsorbed or Underabsorbed Overhead account. The overabsorbed or underabsorbed overhead is carried forward from month to month and closed to the Income Summary account at the end of the year.

At August 1, 1975, the balances of selected general ledger accounts were as follows:

Work in Process	$34,524 (Dr.)
Overabsorbed or Underabsorbed Overhead	57 (Cr.)
Manufacturing Overhead Control	—
Overhead Absorbed	—

The following jobs were in process at August 1, 1975:

Job No.	Materials	Direct Labor	Overhead	Total
478	$ 5,100	$ 9,620	$4,810	$19,530
479	3,470	3,960	1,980	9,410
480	4,120	976	488	5,584
	$12,690	$14,556	$7,278	$34,524

Selected transactions for the month of August are as follows:

(1) Materials issued: Job 480, $449; Job 481, $3,570; Job 482, $2,100; general factory use, $390; total, $6,509.

(2) Labor costs are assigned as follows: Job 478, $334; Job 479, $2,650; Job 480, $7,800; Job 481, $5,890; Job 482, $1,726; general factory, $853; total, $19,253.

(3) The employer's share of payroll taxes is 8 percent of wages earned. All factory payroll taxes are treated as manufacturing overhead costs.

(4) Depreciation of factory equipment for the month is $3,200.

(5) Building depreciation for the month is $1,200. It is allocated 90 percent to factory costs and 10 percent to selling costs.

(6) Other manufacturing costs vouchered in the month include: power, $730; repairs, $520; and utility services $450.

(7) Expirations of prepayments: fire insurance $183 and property taxes $317. These costs are allocated in the same way as building depreciation.

(8) Manufacturing overhead for the month is applied to jobs.

(9) Jobs 478 and 479 are completed and transferred to the finished goods warehouse.

a. Journalize the selected transactions and closing entries for August.

b. What are the balances at August 31, 1975, in the following accounts: Work in Process, Over- or Underabsorbed Overhead, Manufacturing Overhead Control, and Overhead Absorbed?

c. Present a schedule showing the cost of all jobs included in Finished Goods and Work in Process at August 31, 1975.

13. Two of the lines of the May 31, 1975, trial balance of the McKinley Machine Company, before recording the factory overhead absorbed and the work completed during May, are:

Work in Process $16,842
Factory Overhead Control   3,100

The cost sheets show the following data:

	Job No. 576	Job No. 577	Job No. 578	Job No. 579	Job No. 580
Work in Process, May 1					
Material	$ 953	$ 824			
Direct Labor	1,250	1,507			
Factory Overhead ...	1,075	945			
	$3,278	$3,276			
Costs Incurred in May					
Material	$ 170	$ 520	$1,240	$ 950	$1,312
Direct Labor	1,260	842	2,500	1,302	192
Factory Overhead ...	630	421	1,250		
May Costs	$2,060	$1,783	$4,990	$2,252	$1,504
Total Costs to Date ...	$5,338	$5,059	$4,990	$2,252	$1,504

Jobs 576, 577, and 578 were completed during May. Overhead was added on the cost sheets of the completed jobs at the predetermined rate of 50 percent of direct labor cost in order to complete the cost sheets and calculate the cost of the jobs; no entry was made in the general ledger, however, to record these overhead allocations or the job completions. Jobs 579 and 580 are still in process at May 31, 1975.

a. Prepare a production report for the month of May, 1975.

b. Give journal entries for:

(1) the absorption of factory overhead for the month

(2) the completion of Jobs 576, 577, and 578 (one entry)

(3) the closing of the Factory Overhead Control account and the recording of the underabsorbed or overabsorbed overhead.

14. The Matron Products Company uses the direct labor hours basis of allocating overhead to jobs. It was estimated on January 1, 1975, that

total overhead for the coming year would be $400,000 and 100,000 direct labor hours would be worked.

The actual overhead and direct labor hours for the first five months of 1975 were as follows:

	Actual Overhead	Actual Direct Labor Hours
January	$ 51,000	12,500
February	40,000	9,600
March	61,000	15,500
April	58,500	14,200
May	50,000	13,000
	$260,500	64,800

a. What was the overabsorbed or underabsorbed overhead for each month?
b. If the overabsorbed or underabsorbed overhead were treated as a deferred charge or a deferred credit until the end of the year, what would be the balance of the Overabsorbed or Underabsorbed Overhead account at May 31, 1975?

15. The Hamilton Company has two producing departments and a maintenance department. In addition, the upkeep costs for the entire plant are kept in a separate account. The estimated cost data for 1976 are:

Cost	Producing Dept. #1	Producing Dept. #2	Maintenance	General Plant
Direct labor	$50,000	$30,000	—	—
Indirect labor	28,000	14,000	$22,500	$20,000
Indirect materials	9,000	7,000	900	8,000
Miscellaneous	3,000	5,000	1,600	5,000
	$90,000	$56,000	$25,000	$33,000
Maintenance	7,000 hrs.	13,000 hrs.	—	—

Assume that General Plant benefits the other three departments in proportions 50 (Dept. 1): 30 (Dept. 2): 20 (Maintenance). Compute the overhead allocation rates for Departments 1 and 2, including the allocation of estimated service department costs. Assume that direct labor cost is the best estimate of activity and allocate maintenance costs based on maintenance hours.

16. What are the equivalent units of production for the period in each case below?
a. In Department Y there were 3,000 units in process at the beginning of the period that were, on the average, one quarter complete. At the close of the period, there were 5,000 units in process that were, on the average, three quarters complete. During the period 20,000 units were completed and transferred to Department X.
b. In Department A there were 8,000 units in process at the start of the period. They were, on the average, one-half complete. During the period 55,000 units were transferred from Department B into Department A. At the end of the period there were 9,000 units in process in Department A. They were, on the average, one-third complete.

*17. In Department *K*, 8,000 units of product are produced at a total cost of $38,000. Upon inspection it is discovered that 500 units are defective and can only be sold as scrap material at $1 each.

    a. Compute the unit cost of production if (1) the spoilage is to be absorbed in the cost of the good units, and (2) if the spoilage is to be isolated.

    b. If the spoilage loss is to be isolated, what is the amount of the loss?

18. The Homes Metals Company uses a process cost accounting system. Process *E* is the fifth in their series of seven processes. Material is added proportionately throughout processing. The following data relate to the operations of that process during March, 1975:

> Work in process, March 1, none.
> Costs incurred during the month:
> Materials and supplies $139,000
> Direct labor 157,000
> Other factory costs 82,000
> Units transferred from Process *D*, 75,000 at a cost of $12 per unit.
> Work in process, March 31, 20,000 units, 40 percent completed.

    a. What was the effective production for the month?

    b. What was the unit cost of operations in Process *E*?

    c. What was the entry to transfer the completed units to Process *F*, the next process?

    d. What was the valuation of the inventory of Work in Process of Process *E* at March 31?

19. Describe briefly the cost accounting treatment you would recommend for the following items or situations. Consider such points as: the absorption of spoilage in the cost of the good product or the isolation of the spoilage loss; the handling of the value of waste, scrap, or spoiled work; the treatment of isolated spoilage loss. Justify your recommendations.

    a. Defective gallon drums resulting from normal inaccuracies in automatic machine process.

    b. Spoiled leather soles due to carelessness of workmen.

    c. Scrap wool remaining after cutting garments from a bolt of cloth.

    d. Shavings which accumulate from operating a metal lathe.

20. At the conclusion of Process 4, the total cost of processing 25,000 gallons of chemical product *K* is $362,000. At this point, 5,000 gallons of by-product *Y* emerge and the remaining 20,000 gallons of *K* are transferred to Process 5 for further work. The *Y* material will require further processing at an estimated cost of $1 per gallon and then it can be sold for $3 per gallon.

    a. Give the entries for the emergence of *Y* and the transfer to Process 5 of Product *K*. Process control accounts are used.

    b. What is the cost per gallon of chemical Product *K* transferred to Process 5?

21. Up to the point of separation of joint Products *X*, *Y*, and *Z*, total production costs amount to $51,500. The following quantities are produced:

> Product *X* 3,000 units at an estimated sales value of $3 per unit.
> Product *Y* 4,500 units at an estimated sales value of $4 per unit.
> Product *Z* 9,700 units at an estimated sales value of $5 per unit.

a. Prepare a schedule showing the allocation of production costs to the three joint products and the unit cost of each product.

b. Repeat (a) assuming that Product X is treated as a by-product.

°22. The following estimates for 1975 were made by the accountants of the Roberts Specialty Company:

	Cutting Department	Assembling Department	Painting Department
Estimated overhead	$36,000	$50,000	$56,000
Estimated direct labor cost ..	$60,000	$50,000	$70,000
Estimated direct labor time ..	12,000 hrs.	12,500 hrs.	14,000 hrs.

a. Compute the departmental overhead distribution rates using (1) direct labor cost and (2) direct labor hours as a basis.

b. Apply the results obtained in (a) to the data given below for job No. 407. Show the total cost of the job for each assumption.

	Cutting Department	Assembling Department	Painting Department
Direct material	$ 600	—	$ 80
Direct labor cost	$1,500	$2,000	$200
Direct labor time	250 hrs.	400 hrs.	38 hrs.

23. Journalize the following transactions. Control accounts are used for each process and for factory overhead. All overhead costs are first charged to Factory Overhead Control and corresponding subsidiary accounts and then allocated to the various processes. There was no work in process in Process 6 at the beginning or end of the period. There were no finished goods on hand at the start of the period.

(1) A total cost of $18,700 for 6,700 units are transferred from Process 5 to Process 6.

(2) Costs of Process 6 during the period: labor, $2,600; overhead, $2,400.

(3) From Process 6 there emerge 700 units of by-product C, having an estimated net sales value of $1 per unit.

(4) The following finished goods, which are treated as joint products, also emerge from Process 6: Product X, 2,000 units with an estimated sales value of $4 per unit; Product Y, 4,000 units with an estimated sales value of $5 per unit.

(5) Sales during the period: Product X, 1,200 units at $4 per unit; Product Y, 2,900 units at $5 per unit. Record the sales and the cost of goods sold.

24. The General Manufacturing Company uses a process cost accounting system. Process C is the third in their series of five processes. The following data relate to the operations of that process during August, 1975. There were no goods in process at August 1, 1975.

Cost incurred during August:
Materials and supplies	$67,500
Direct labor	91,000
Other manufacturing costs	41,500

Units transferred from Process B: 65,000 at a cost of $9 per unit. Work in process at August 31: 25,000 units which are on the average 40 percent complete as to the work of Process C. Materials are added continuously throughout the process.

a. What are the equivalent units of production for the month?

b. What is the unit cost of operations in Process C?

c. What is the entry to transfer the completed units to Process D?

d. What is the valuation of the inventory of Work in Process of Process C at August 31, assuming material is added continuously throughout processing?

25. The Baby-Joy Toy Company makes wooden blocks in a continuous process. On November 1, 1975, 20,000 blocks were in process and were 60 percent complete. None of these blocks was eventually found to be defective. By the end of the month, 40,000 blocks had been sent to the warehouse for shipping. Another 1,200 had been rejected as defective at final inspection. On November 30, 12,000 blocks were in process. These blocks were 40 percent complete. However, it is discovered that 2,000 of these partially completed blocks were nicked and had to be discarded.

Costs for the period were: $50,000 for raw materials and $70,000 for labor and overhead.

a. Assume that all spoilage is normal. Compute the ending work in process inventory in equivalent units of completed work. The FIFO inventory method is used.

b. What is the unit cost per block, if all spoilage is considered normal? What is the spoilage expense for November?

What are the unit cost and loss from spoilage assuming:

c. that all spoilage is considered abnormal?

d. 2 percent of good work done is the normal spoilage rate?

*26. The factory cost accounts of the Cummings Products Company for the month of March, 1975, are as follows:

Direct Process Costs	Process X	Process Y
Raw Materials Used	$ 43,156	$ 32,810
Direct Labor	154,000	286,000
Repairs and Maintenance	1,360	925
Compensation Insurance	750	1,042
Supplies Used	4,514	3,403
Depreciation	840	1,200
Total	$204,620	$325,380

Indirect Costs	
General Supervision	$13,020
Factory Office Salaries	8,700
Compensation Insurance—Misc. Factory	1,200
Factory Office Supplies Used	950
Power	1,530
Insurance—Factory Contents	400
Factory Building Rent	4,750
Miscellaneous Factory Costs	5,280
Total	$35,830

General Supervision, Factory Office Salaries, and Compensation Insurance—Misc. Factory are allocated to processes on the basis of process direct labor costs. Power and Insurance on Factory Contents are assigned to processes in proportion to the amount of machinery used in each process; the ratio is 40 percent for Process X and 60 percent for Process Y. All other indirect costs are distributed to processes in proportion to total direct process costs. Materials are added continuously throughout the process.

The physical production figures for the month are as follows:

Process X	Units
Work in Process, March 1	
(one-half through process)	80,000
Put into Process	500,000
Work in Process, March 31	580,000
(one-half through process)	80,000
Transferred to Process Y	500,000

Process Y	
Work in Process, March 1	
(three-fourths through process)	100,000
	600,000
Work in Process, March 31	
(one-fourth through process)	60,000
Transferred to warehouse	540,000

a. Prepare a process-cost distribution schedule for the month of March.

b. Compute the unit cost of production in Process X and in Process Y for the month of March. Carry your computations to three decimal places.

27. The Burns Company uses a job order system of cost accounting. The data presented below relate to operations in its plant during January, 1975.

There are two production departments and one service department. The factory overhead costs accumulated during the month are $4,000. At the end of the period the overhead costs are allocated as follows: Department A, $2,100; Department B, $1,600; Department C, $300. The service department (Department C) overhead is redistributed as follows: ⅔ to Department A; ⅓ to Department B. Overabsorbed or underabsorbed overhead is closed to Income Summary at the end of the month when the books are closed.

Factory overhead is applied to job orders at the following predetermined rates: 60 percent of direct labor costs in Department A; 80 percent in Department B. The jobs are delivered upon completion. Job orders completed in January are Nos. 789, 790, and 791.

a. Prepare a table similar to the Job Order Production Record shown and fill in all of the blanks.

b. Prepare skeleton account forms for the following accounts: Direct Material; Direct Labor; Factory Overhead Costs; Department A—Overhead; Department B—Overhead; Department C—Overhead; Department A—Overhead Absorbed; Department B—Overhead Absorbed; Department A—Overabsorbed or Underabsorbed Overhead; Department B—Overabsorbed or Underabsorbed Overhead; Jobs in Process; Completed and Delivered Jobs; and Income Summary. Enter

JOB ORDER PRODUCTION RECORD

Job Order No.	Jobs in Process 1/1/75	Direct Labor		Direct Matl.		Overhead		Total Costs	Jobs in Process 1/31/75	Completed Jobs
		Dept. A	Dept. B	Dept. A	Dept. B	Dept. A	Dept. B			
788	$1,200	$ 300	$ 150	$ 250	$ 150	$	$	$	$	$
789	850	600	300	450	300					
790		800	450	550	350					
791		1,000	600	600	450					
792		1,200	650	900	400					
Totals	$2,050	$3,900	$2,150	$2,750	$1,650					

the opening balances and record the transactions, including closing entries, of January, 1975. Use key numbers for all transactions. Since not all of the accounts of the general ledger are presented, equal debits and credits will not be shown for all transactions.

°28. The Tru-Life Mannequin Company manufactures female, male, and infant mannequins. The process consists of melting, molding, shaping, sanding, assembling, and painting.

In October of 1975 the following types of costs were incurred and assigned to the classes of products as follows:

Unassigned process costs (other than related to wigs and painted hair): 250,000 pounds of plaster, costing $0.10 per pound; labor costs, $90,000; other costs, $35,000.

Assigned processing costs (other than related to wigs and painted hair): female, $8 each; male, $9 each; infant, $2 each.

Wigs for female mannequins: material, $1 each; labor, $10,000; overhead, $7,500.

Painted-hair for male and infant mannequins: material, males, $0.15 each; material, infants, $0.05 each; labor, $18,000; other, $12,000.

Production for October (with no ending work-in-process inventory) was 50,000 females, 60,000 males, and 30,000 infants. Female mannequins sell for $15 each; males, for $11 each, and infants, for $8 each.
a. Allocate the joint costs using the relative-sales-value method.
b. Allocate the joint costs using the physical units method.

°29. The Roving Eye Cosmetics Company buys bulk flowers and processes them into perfumes. Their highest-grade perfume, Seduction, and a residue that is processed into Romance and Longingly come from a certain mix of petals. In July, 1975, the company used 25,000 pounds of petals. Costs involved in Process A, reducing the petals to Seduction and the residue were:

$200,000 direct materials
110,000 direct labor
90,000 overhead and other costs.

The additional costs of producing Romance and Longingly in Process *B* were:

$ 25,000 direct materials
50,000 direct labor
40,000 overhead and other costs.

At the end of the month, total production was 5,000 ounces of Seduction, 10,000 ounces of Romance, and 18,000 ounces of Longingly. In addition, 10,000 ounces of Romance and 15,000 ounces of Longingly were still in Process *B* (a continuous process), so that these units were, on average, one-half complete.

Packaging costs for each product were: Seduction, $40,000; Romance, $60,000; Longingly, $100,000. The sales price of Seduction is $90 an ounce; of Romance, $50 an ounce; and of Longingly, $20 an ounce.

a. Allocate the joint costs using the relative-sales-value method.

b. Allocate the joint costs using the physical units method.

c. Is there any inconsistency in using the physical units method in this case?

d. Assume that Roving Eye can sell squeezed petals to greenhouses for use as fertilizer. In July, there were 12,000 pounds of squeezed petals left over and sold for 8⅓¢ per pound. With this new information, answer parts (a) and (b). Assume that the squeezed petals are a by-product of Process B.

Chapter 22

Standard Cost Accounting

The preceding two chapters outline the procedures designed to determine costs for cost centers and for specific jobs or processes. *Actual* costs of operations, specifically incurred during the accounting period, are accumulated and allocated. Whereas job order and processing cost accounting allocate actual production costs to units of output, *standard cost accounting* assigns predetermined, estimated costs to units of output. Any difference between actual and standard costs is closed at the end of the period, usually to current income. Standard costs are used in more sophisticated cost accounting systems.

There are several ways to define standard costs, but the most useful way is to consider standard cost as the cost that should or will be incurred under normal operating conditions. Standard material, labor, and overhead cost figures are determined from detailed studies, and the estimated cost figures become the basis of the production cost entries. The actual costs incurred are also recorded and are compared periodically with the standard costs. The standard costs are assumed to be the best guess of "correct" costs. The differences between actual costs and allocated standard costs are called *variances* and are sometimes considered presumptive evidence of inefficiency (if positive) or of extraordinary efficiency (if negative).

Actual cost systems for operations involving many products or stages of production, or both, require substantial record keeping and are, therefore, expensive. Such systems are not effective in indicating areas where increased management control is needed. The major purposes of standard cost accounting are:

1. to provide information for more effective managerial control of operations
2. to increase the cost effectiveness of the accounting system, that is, to decrease costs or increase benefits of recording factory operations or both.

Using standard cost accounting involves certain complexities. The work required to estimate normal or standard costs is expensive and must be done regularly so that the standards reflect current reality. It requires consideration of changing technology, worker morale, likely supply conditions and a host of other factors.

TYPES OF STANDARDS

Standard costs may be conceived of in several ways. Here we describe three kinds of standards although a greater variety of concepts exists in practice.

Basic Standard Costs. Standard costs that are established only once and remain fixed over the years are called *basic standard costs.* The virtue of basic standard costs is that comparisons over time of actual performance can be made against a single, permanent base. Such comparisons make the estimation of trends easier than is otherwise possible. As prices and labor skills change over time, however, the standard costs become increasingly obsolete so that comparing the efficiency of actual performance with effective performance is difficult. Further, as methods of production and products change, the basic standard costs must change so that the virtue of comparisons over time is often more apparent than real. Basic standard costs are rarely used.

Ideal or Maximum Efficiency Standard Costs. The levels of costs that would be incurred under the most efficient operating conditions for existing specifications and equipment are called *ideal standard costs.* Rarely, if ever, will costs incurred be so small as the ideal. Ideal standard costs are used where management thinks that such costs provide the best incentive to good performance. Generally, however, empirical research tends to show that standards do not provide an incentive to perform well unless the employee, whose performance is measured against the standard, perceives the standard to be reasonable and attainable. Ideal standards can be criticized, then, since workers may become discouraged from seeking to achieve objectives that can seldom be attained and lose initiative for seeking more efficient production.

Normal or Currently Attainable Standard Costs. Costs which can be attained under efficient operating conditions are called *normal standard costs.* Such standards include provision for normal spoilage, rest periods, and other time that is reasonably lost because of, for example, machine breakdowns. Normal costs are, by definition, those that management could reasonably expect but are stringent enough so that workers who achieve them have reason to be satisfied with their own performance.

The terminology used to describe standard cost systems varies across industries. Generally, firms use some combination of ideal or normal standards, although they may refer to such systems by other names. For the remainder of this discussion, we use normal cost standards in describing typical standard cost systems.

DEVELOPING STANDARDS

Standard cost systems are based on physical measures. Materials usage standards are measured in, for example, pounds, units, or gallons. Labor standards are grounded in some appropriate measure of time, perhaps man-minutes or man-hours of a given skill level. Physical standards should be prepared wherever possible from sound engineering studies. For accounting purposes, the physical standards are converted into dollars so that the various inputs to a process or product are measured in comparable units. For example, a standard amount of three pounds of material, at $1.50 per pound, may be required to manufacture one unit of product. The standard material costs per unit of product would be $4.50. The conversion of raw material into finished product is expected to take five hours per unit. If the usual employee doing the work earns $6 per hour, the standard labor cost per unit of product would be $30 ($= 6×5 hours).

Physical measures are the basis of materials standards and labor standards. Standards for indirect, or overhead, costs are calculated somewhat differently. The complications of setting and applying overhead standards are discussed later.

From management's viewpoint, standard costs should be set with the cooperation of employees who are to be held responsible for attaining the standards. Without participation, employees may lack the commitment to attain the standard and may logically justify an unwillingness to achieve an unreasonably set standard. In establishing and revising standards, the physical standards are developed by engineers and are converted into dollar-based standards by accountants. Nothing about the standard-setting process precludes the participation of operating employees, either in the development stage or in the review or acceptance of the standards.

MECHANICS OF STANDARD COSTS

As described so far, standard cost systems seem to require more work than actual cost systems, whereas we started this chapter by commenting that standard cost systems are used, in part, because they are cost-effective means of record keeping. The time saving in standard cost systems occurs in tracing the flow of goods and services through the firm. Rather than trace the actual cost of each economic service that flows, the standard cost of the item is credited to its source and debited to its destination. Thus, the entry made when material is requisitioned does not require a search of invoices to determine actual costs, because the cost credited to raw material inventory, and debited to work in process, is the standard price per unit of the material requisitioned.

As you might imagine, record keeping is simple when the unit amounts for all entries are predetermined. Under the typical standard cost system, material, labor, and overhead standard costs are all charged to the Work in Process account. Treatment of these costs, once they are assigned to work in process, is similar to the procedures under an actual cost system. As goods are completed, their standard costs are transferred to the Finished Goods Inventory. As the units are sold, their costs are removed from Finished Goods at standard cost and transferred to the Cost of Goods Sold account for the accounting period. Since products are not necessarily sold in the same period of their production, the standard costs may not immediately find their way into the income statement.

But, of course, actual prices will deviate from standard prices, and actual material usages will deviate from standard usages. The difference between an actual cost and a standard cost is called a *variance*. If the difference is positive, the variance is unfavorable and if negative, the variance is favorable. (This definition of a variance is an arbitrary convention. A variance might be defined as standard cost minus actual cost, but it is not.)

The variances incurred under a standard cost system must be closed at the end of the accounting period. In practice, the variances are usually closed to the Cost of Goods Sold account and, thus, ultimately to income of the period. Strict adherence to actual, historical cost concepts might imply an allocation of variances between work in process, finished goods and cost of goods sold in proportion to the amounts of a period's production that remain in each class of inventory or have been sold. If realistic and up-to-date standards are being used, substantial unfavorable variances are likely to result from major inefficiencies or from the volume of output falling far below normal expectations. Under these circumstances, charging all of the unfavorable variances to income of the period would be justified; inventory valuations should not be increased to reflect inefficiencies. Closing favorable variances to Cost of Goods Sold, and thus to income, results in inventory being shown at an amount in excess of "actual historical" cost and recognizes income before goods are sold. Believers in a conservative approach are inclined to allocate the excess of standard costs over actual costs to inventories as well as to Cost of Goods Sold. Favorable variances are more likely to be small, however, and thus there is a willingness to close them to Cost of Goods Sold in their entirety since doing so is not likely to have a material effect on the financial statements.

Variance accounts may thus be viewed as expense adjunct accounts (or expense contras, if the variance is favorable), adjusting the amount of cost of goods sold initially stated at standard cost. Hence, unfavorable variances imply debit balances, and favorable variances imply credit balances, in the variance accounts.

The relationship between actual costs, standard costs applied to product, and variances is:

Actual Costs = Standard Costs Applied + Variances, or

Variances = Actual Costs − Standard Costs Applied.

Unfavorable variances are positive and favorable variances are negative. The following example illustrates the calculation and treatment of variances in a simple standard cost system. (As will be made clearer below, the treatment of the overhead variance is particularly simple.)

The Baltimore Manufacturing Company manufactures a single uniform product and the following unit standard costs have been established after investigation:

10 pounds of material at $.40	$ 4
3 hours of direct labor at $3	9
Factory overhead	7
Unit standard cost	$20

There were no beginning inventories of material or work in process. During the period, 11,000 pounds of material were purchased at an average price of $.41 per pound ($4,510), 2,940 hours of direct labor were worked at an average rate of $3.10 per hour ($9,114), and actual overhead costs were $7,150. To manufacture 1,000 units, 10,300 pounds of material were used. There was no work in process at the end of the period.

The entries to record this information in a standard cost system would be:

(1) Material 4,400
    Material Price Variance 110
        Accounts Payable   4,510
    To record the acquisition of 11,000 pounds of material at standard ($.40) and record the excess over standard price paid for material as an unfavorable price variance.

(2) Direct Labor 8,820
    Direct Labor Rate Variance 294
        Wages Payable   9,114
    To charge direct labor with 2,940 hours at standard ($3) and record the excess over standard rate paid for direct labor as an unfavorable rate variance.

(3) Factory Overhead 7,150
        Factory Supplies, Wages Payable, Vouchers Payable,
            Accumulated Depreciation, etc   7,150
    To record the actual overhead costs of the period.

(4) Work in Process 4,000
    Material Quantity Variance 120
        Material   4,120
    To credit material with actual quantity at standard price (10,300 × $.40) and charge production with standard quantity at standard price, the difference being the unfavorable material quantity variance.

(5) Work in Process 9,000
    Direct Labor   8,820
    Direct Labor Quantity Variance   180
    To close the Direct Labor account and to charge production
    with standard time at standard rates, the difference being
    the favorable direct labor quantity variance.

(6) Work in Process 7,000
    Overhead Variance 150
    Factory Overhead   7,150
    To close the Factory Overhead account and to charge pro-
    duction with a standard amount of overhead, the difference
    representing an unfavorable overhead variance.

(7) Finished Goods 20,000
    Work in Process   20,000
    1,000 units completed at a unit standard cost of $20.

(8) Income Summary 494
    Direct Labor Quantity Variance 180
    Material Price Variance   110
    Direct Labor Rate Variance   294
    Material Quantity Variance   120
    Overhead Variance   150
    To close the variance accounts. The debit to Income Sum-
    mary is the amount required for equal debits and credits.

By this method of allocating all costs to production on a standard cost basis, the discrepancies between planned and actual performance are brought to light in the variance accounts. The causes of variances are analyzed in Chapter 23. For the moment, observe that both rate and quantity variances are calculated. The labor rate variance and the labor quantity variance are of opposite signs in the example. Labor more expensive than standard was used in smaller than standard quantities. Variances will be offsetting when a higher (or lower) quality of input is used in smaller (or larger) quantities than is standard.

Direct Material Standard Costs and Variances

Standard costs are calculated from a combination of physical standards and unit prices. Actual costs can vary from standard costs either because of variations in physical quantities used or because of variations in prices paid or both. Direct material standard costs and variances depend upon material prices and quantities of materials used.

Material price standards are established in consultation with the purchasing department. The prevailing or expected future price is established as the standard. Standards should assume normal buying conditions and reflect purchase discounts or charges, such as for transportation, that ordinarily occur.

Material quantity standards are typically derived from engineering or production department studies on the amount of material needed, including normal waste, to manufacture one unit of product. If engineering studies are too expensive, then standards might be derived from an analysis of past production usages. However derived, the full description of all material quantity standards required for one unit of finished product is presented in a *standard bill of materials.*

Goods purchased by the firm are added to the Raw Materials Inventory account at standard cost, determined by multiplying the actual number of units received by their standard price per unit. In the Baltimore Manufacturing Company example, the first debit in transaction (1) shows the additions to Raw Materials Inventory at standard prices. The difference between the amount paid for the raw material and the standard costs is the material price variance, $110 unfavorable in the example. The materials price variance can always be calculated by using this formula:

$$\begin{bmatrix} \text{Materials Price} \\ \text{Variance} \end{bmatrix} = \begin{bmatrix} \text{Quantity of} \\ \text{Units Purchased} \end{bmatrix} \times \begin{bmatrix} \text{Actual Price} & \text{Standard Price} \\ \text{Per Unit} & - \quad \text{Per Unit} \end{bmatrix}$$

Materials requisitioned for production are charged to work in process in *standard* quantities at standard costs as in entry (4) in the example. Such entries are the ones that make standard cost systems economical in practice. The Raw Materials Inventory is credited with an amount equal to the *actual* quantity issued at standard prices. The difference between the credit for actual quantities used and the debit for standard quantities used is the materials quantity variance. This variance arises only when goods are transferred from raw materials inventory to production in other than standard amounts. The materials quantity variance can always be calculated from

$$\begin{bmatrix} \text{Materials Quantity} \\ \text{Variance} \end{bmatrix} = \begin{bmatrix} \text{Quantity of} & \text{Standard} \\ \text{Units Issued} & - \quad \text{Quantity} \end{bmatrix} \times \begin{bmatrix} \text{Standard} \\ \text{Price} \end{bmatrix}$$

This variance will be positive, or unfavorable, when more materials are used than standard.

When higher-than-normal quality materials are purchased, the price variance will usually be unfavorable, since high-quality materials usually cost more than standard-quality materials. But if high-quality materials are available, then less-than-standard amounts will probably be used. When the standard price is realistic, price and quantity variances will tend to be offsetting. Of course, if prices have generally risen since the standards were set, price variances will be unfavorable without implying that quantity variances should be favorable. In the Baltimore Manufacturing Company example, the unfavorable materials price variance is not offset with a favorable quantity variance.

The relation between price and quantity variances can be studied in the following graphical analysis. In Figure 22.1 the horizontal axis shows the quantity in pounds of raw material used for a unit of product and the vertical axis shows the price per pound of raw material. The standard quantity of raw material for one unit of product is shown to be ten pounds and the standard cost of a unit of raw material is shown to be $.40 per pound. The standard materials cost of a unit of finished product is $4

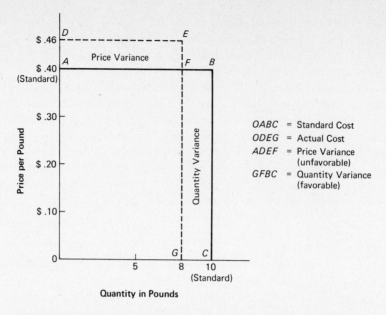

Figure 22.1 Illustration of Partially Offsetting Price and Quantity Variances

(= 10 × $.40). Suppose high-quality raw material is purchased for $.46 per pound and only eight pounds are used to make a unit of product for $3.68. The unfavorable materials price variance is:

$.48 = 8 units purchased × ($.46 actual price − $.40 standard price)

The favorable quantity variance is:

− $.80 = (8 pounds used − 10 pounds standard) × $.40 standard price

The difference between actual costs of $3.68 and standard costs of $4.00 is −$.32 which is exactly equal to the sum of the price and quantity variances. The overall favorable materials variance is the result of an unfavorable price variance and a more-than-offsetting favorable quantity variance. (The standards should probably be changed to reflect the more efficient combination of material input that appears possible.)

When materials price and quantity variances are both in the same direction, say unfavorable, the picture is not so neat. Consider Figure 22.2 which shows purchases for $.43 per pound and use of 12 pounds, both amounts larger than standard. The rectangle *ADEB* ($.30) represents the "pure" price variance, that is, the variance in price ($.43 − $.40) times the standard quantity. The rectangle *CBGH* ($.80) represents the "pure" quantity variance, that is the variance in quantity (12 − 10) times the standard price. The rectangle *BEFG* ($.06) results from the interaction of the two pure variances. If one or the other of the other two variances were zero, there would be no such rectangle and no extra variance. This

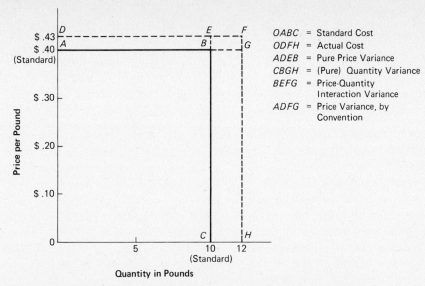

Figure 22.2 Illustration of Unfavorable Price and Quantity Variances

variance is attributable to both price and quantity variations and cannot be logically assigned either to price or to quantity variance. Nevertheless, by long-established convention, the interaction between price and quantity variances is arbitrarily assigned to the price variance. Thus the price variance in the situation shown in Figure 22.2 would be the rectangle *ADFG* ($.36). Notice that the equations shown earlier in this section to define the price and quantity variance have implicitly used the convention that any interaction between variances is assigned to the price variance. The convention is based on the presumption that purchase of materials precedes use and a sometimes-warranted assumption that prices of materials are less controllable by the firm than are amounts used.

Although the interaction-variance problem was not mentioned in connection with the situation shown in Figure 22.1, the problem is there just the same. The amount shown in Figure 22.1 as the quantity variance is a "pure" quantity variance: variance in quantity times standard price. The amount shown there as the price variance is not the "pure" price variance (variance in price times standard quantity) but is variance in price times *actual* quantity.[1] The accounting conventions used to report variances can

---

[1] Algebraically, the interaction-variance problem can be demonstrated as follows. Let P_s represent standard price, and let Q_s represent standard quantity. Let ΔP represent the deviation in price from the standard and let ΔQ represent the deviation in quantity from the actual quantity. Then

$$\text{Actual Cost} = (P_s + \Delta P)(Q_s + \Delta Q)$$

$$= \underset{\substack{\text{Standard} \\ \text{Cost}}}{P_s Q_s} + \underset{\substack{\text{"Pure"} \\ \text{Quantity} \\ \text{Variance}}}{P_s \Delta Q} + \underset{\substack{\text{"Pure"} \\ \text{Price} \\ \text{Variance}}}{\Delta P Q_s} + \underset{\substack{\text{Price-Quantity} \\ \text{Interaction} \\ \text{Variance}}}{\Delta P \Delta Q}$$

be summarized by noting that

materials quantity variance = "pure" quantity variance
materials price variance = "pure" price variance
+ price-quantity interaction variance

Direct Labor Standard Costs and Variances

Direct labor standard costs and variances are almost analogous to direct materials standard costs and variances. The major difference is that while materials are purchased, inventoried, and then used, labor is purchased and used simultaneously. The physical measure for labor has a time dimension, usually man-hours, and the price is expressed as the wage rate per unit of time, usually wage rate per hour. Labor cost standards, just as materials cost standards, reflect both quantity and price dimensions.

Labor rate standards are fairly easy to determine. The standard is set as the wage rate of the employee with the skill needed to perform the required operation for minimum total costs. Labor rate standards are usually increased as wage rates increase.

Labor quantity standards, sometimes called *labor efficiency standards*, are usually set through industrial engineering studies. The standards are expressed in time per finished unit of product such as, for example, man-hours per case of finished goods. Setting labor quantity standards so as to optimize their psychological impact on the work force is one of the most difficult problems in industrial engineering and behavioral science.

In a standard cost system, direct labor costs are charged to production at standard rates times standard quantities. The variance caused by a difference between the standard rate and the actual wage rate, analogous to the materials price variance, is called the *labor rate variance*. The rate-quantity interaction is, again by convention, arbitrarily allocated to the rate variance. The labor rate variance can always be calculated from

$$\begin{bmatrix} \text{Labor Rate} \\ \text{Variance} \end{bmatrix} = \begin{bmatrix} \text{Quantity of} \\ \text{Labor Used} \end{bmatrix} \times \begin{bmatrix} \text{Actual} & \text{Standard} \\ \text{Wage Rate} & - & \text{Wage Rate} \end{bmatrix}$$

The labor quantity variance is exactly analogous to the materials quantity variance and can always be calculated from

$$\begin{bmatrix} \text{Labor Quantity} \\ \text{Variance} \end{bmatrix} = \begin{bmatrix} \text{Quantity of} & \text{Standard} \\ \text{Labor Used} & - & \text{Labor Quantity} \end{bmatrix} \times \begin{bmatrix} \text{Standard} \\ \text{Wage Rate} \end{bmatrix}$$

The labor rate variance will be unfavorable when the wage rate paid is greater than the standard wage. The labor quantity variance will be unfavorable when the amount of time used is greater than the standard amount. If labor is paid a higher-than-standard wage because of higher-than-standard skills, then one would expect an unfavorable rate variance to be at least partially offset by a favorable quantity variance. One would not expect the favorable quantity variance to be greater than the unfavorable rate variance incurred through the use of unusually skilled labor because if there were a persisting overall favorable labor variance, then the standards were inappropriate in the first place. The job should have been standardized assuming labor of greater skill being paid a higher rate. Indeed, a pattern of consistently offsetting, but favorable overall, rate and quantity variances signals that standards should be revised.

The labor quantity variance is sometimes called a *labor efficiency* variance. We prefer not to use the word *efficiency* because of the pejorative interpretation of an unfavorable variance caused by using more than standard amounts of labor. The unfavorable quantity variance might arise from using a less-skilled employee as well as from using an employee who has standard skills but had an off day. Whatever term is used for this variance, quantity or efficiency, the same term should be used for both the materials and labor variances. The term *quantity variance* is always appropriate, whereas the term *efficiency variance* may not be.

OVERHEAD STANDARD COSTS AND VARIANCES

Although the techniques may seem complicated on first exposure, developing and using standard costs for direct materials and direct labor do not present conceptual problems. Standards for indirect variable costs present no conceptual problems but are more difficult to determine in practice than are direct materials and direct labor cost standards. Indirect variable costs are one component of overhead costs; fixed costs are the other. Setting standards for fixed costs presents a conceptual problem. The problem arises, in our opinion, because generally accepted accounting principles do not allow the theoretically correct treatment of fixed costs in published accounting statements and because the need for inventory data for published statements influences internal accounting systems. The issue is the difference between direct and absorption costing first introduced in Chapter 5, mentioned again in Chapter 12, and treated in more detail in Chapter 23. In this section we treat the practical problems of separating overhead cost into its variable and fixed components, the accounting for indirect variable costs, and the accepted accounting technique (absorption costing) of including fixed costs in standard cost systems. Chapter 23 discusses standard cost systems based upon the direct costing concept as well as the merits of direct costing.

The overhead variance calculated for the Baltimore Manufacturing Company is called a *one-way* analysis of overhead variance. The difference between actual and standard overhead costs applied is a single overhead variance. Typically, management prefers a more detailed breakdown of overhead variances. The discussion below splits overhead variances as follows:

for variable overhead: price and quantity
for fixed overhead: price, capacity, and quantity

Identifying Variable and Fixed Overhead Cost Components

Overhead costs will almost always have a portion that remains fixed over relatively long time periods (several months or more) for the relevant range of production quantities and usually another portion that varies directly with material cost or labor cost or both. Therefore, standard cost systems require a splitting of fixed and variable overhead expenses and separate treatment for each.

Determining the fixed and variable components of overhead costs could conceivably be done with engineering studies but is more likely to be accomplished in practice with statistical cost estimation or with some other approximate method for estimating costs. The fixed component is expressed as an amount of dollars per accounting period, such as $7,000 per month. The variable portion is expressed as a rate per unit of *base activity* such as $3 per direct labor hour, $1 per direct labor dollar, $.50 per direct materials dollar, or $6 per machine-hour. The base used for the variable portion should be the relevant measure of factory activity. In principle, the variable portion might include several bases, but only the most sophisticated standard cost systems use more than one base for variable overhead costs. In the following discussion we shall assume that variable overhead costs are calculated on the basis of direct labor hours so that total overhead costs per month can be expressed as:

$$\begin{matrix} \text{Total Overhead} \\ \text{Costs per} \\ \text{Month} \end{matrix} = \begin{matrix} \text{Fixed} \\ \text{Costs} \end{matrix} + \begin{matrix} \text{(Variable Cost Rate Per Direct Labor Hour)} \\ \times \text{(Direct Labor Hours for Month)} \end{matrix}$$

The problem is to estimate the fixed portion and the rate to be charged for each direct labor hour used.

To determine the fixed and variable components of overhead costs with statistical methods, a schedule of total overhead costs per period for past periods is compiled. The data should cover as much of the past as is thought to be an accurate representation of the future. Suppose the Chicago Manufacturing Company is seeking to determine in July, 1975, the components of fixed and variable costs per month and has available the data in Schedule 22.1, which shows total overhead costs for the previous twelve months.

These data in Schedule 22.1 would be plotted on a graph such as the one shown in Figure 22.3, which shows the total overhead costs for the month on the vertical axis and the number of direct labor hours used during the month on the horizontal axis. A line would be fit to the twelve data points. Statistical cost analysis would use techniques of linear regression to fit the line. The line can also be visually fit to the data by drawing a line that appears to fit well.

The line shown in the figure was visually fit and represents the equation

$$\begin{matrix} \text{Total Overhead Costs} \\ \text{Per Month} \end{matrix} = \$1,000 + \$.75 \times \begin{matrix} \text{(Direct Labor Hours} \\ \text{Used for Month)} \end{matrix}$$

SCHEDULE 22.1 CHICAGO MANUFACTURING COMPANY

Month	Direct Labor Usage in Hours	Overhead Cost (Total)
June	2,000	$ 3,080
May	2,500	2,455
April	3,000	2,830
March	4,000	3,580
February	5,500	4,330
January	6,000	5,580
December	7,500	6,930
November	7,000	5,580
October	6,500	6,580
September	5,000	5,330
August	4,500	4,455
July	3,500	4,080
	57,000	$54,810

(A least-squares regression analysis of these data shows fixed monthly costs of $1,002 and variable overhead costs of $.751 per direct labor hour.) The point where the line intercepts the vertical axis is the estimate of the

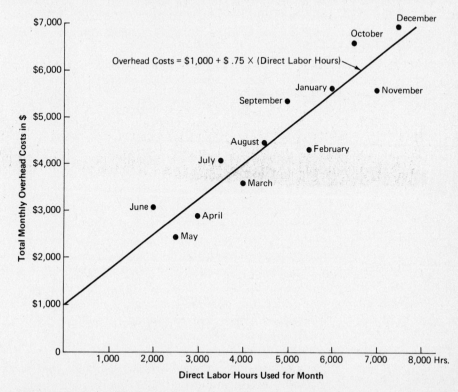

Figure 22.3 Graphical Illustration of the Relation between Total Overhead Costs and Direct Labor Hours, Chicago Manufacturing Company

monthly fixed costs and the slope of the line is the estimate of the incremental or variable costs that are incurred for each extra direct labor hour used for the month. The Chicago Manufacturing Company would prepare its standards for overhead assuming fixed costs of $1,000 per month and indirect variable costs of $.75 per direct labor hour used for the month.

Most standard cost systems implicitly assume that the overhead cost function is linear. That is, the total costs are assumed to be the sum of a fixed cost plus some rate times the base activity, such as direct labor hours. Overhead costs need not be a linear function, nor need they depend upon only a single activity base. (For example, separate linear functions might be fit to individual components of overhead costs.) Nevertheless, we think it likely that a great majority of manufacturing firms use overhead cost analyses that are no more sophisticated than the one illustrated here. Techniques of statistical cost estimation are taught in advanced cost accounting courses or as applications in statistics and econometrics courses.

A less sophisticated method for separating fixed and variable components of overhead for the Chicago Manufacturing Company· might proceed as follows. If fixed costs for the past year were estimated to have been $15,000, then $39,810 of overhead costs (= $54,810 — $15,000) were variable. Since 57,000 hours of direct labor were used during the year, the variable overhead cost per direct labor hour would be estimated as $.70 (= $39,810/57,000) per hour. This less sophisticated technique will work well if the fixed costs can be accurately estimated. If, for example, fixed costs for the year were estimated to be $12,000, then the estimate of variable costs would be $.75 per direct labor hour, exactly the same as was found by visually fitting a straight line to the monthly data. The method is sometimes known as the "account classification" method for separating fixed and variable components of overhead costs.

Variable Overhead Standard Costs and Variances

The variable overhead standard cost is always expressed as a rate per unit of base activity. The discussion here continues to assume that the rate is based upon direct labor hours worked during the period although, in practice, other bases are sometimes used. The actual amount of overhead costs incurred during the accounting period is accumulated in a variable overhead control account. At the conclusion of the accounting period, an amount is transferred from the control account to an overhead applied account. The amount transferred is equal to the standard overhead rate times the standard measure of base activity. When the base measure is direct labor hours per month, then the amount transferred is the variable overhead rate per direct labor hour times the standard number of direct labor hours that should have been used for production that period. The costs remaining in Variable Overhead Control account are either *variable overhead price variance* or *variable overhead quantity variance*. The costs in the Overhead Applied account are closed to Work in Process or to Finished Goods and thus become product costs.

The variable overhead price variance is analogous to both the materials price variance and the labor rate variance. If the variable overhead is based upon the number of direct labor hours used during the period, then the variable overhead price variance would be calculated by this formula:

$$\begin{bmatrix} \text{Variable Over-} \\ \text{head Price} \\ \text{Variance} \end{bmatrix} = \begin{bmatrix} \text{Actual Number of} \\ \text{Direct Labor} \\ \text{Hours Used} \end{bmatrix}$$

$$\times \begin{bmatrix} \text{Actual} & & \text{Standard} \\ \text{Variable} & - & \text{Variable} \\ \text{Overhead Rate} & & \text{Overhead Rate} \end{bmatrix}$$

Under this method, the actual variable overhead rate equals actual variable overhead costs divided by the actual number of units of base activity, such as direct labor hours, performed during the period. Alternatively, the Variable Overhead Price Variance might be calculated directly by the following:

$$\begin{bmatrix} \text{Variable Overhead} \\ \text{Price Variance} \end{bmatrix} = \begin{bmatrix} \text{Actual Variable} \\ \text{Overhead Costs} \end{bmatrix}$$

$$- \begin{bmatrix} \text{Actual Number} \\ \text{of Direct Labor} \\ \text{Hours Used} \end{bmatrix} \times \begin{bmatrix} \text{Standard} \\ \text{Variable} \\ \text{Overhead Rate} \end{bmatrix}$$

The variable overhead quantity variance is analogous to both the materials quantity variance and the labor quantity variance. If variable overhead is based upon the number of direct labor hours used during the period, then the variable overhead quantity variance would be calculated by the following formula:

$$\begin{bmatrix} \text{Variable Overhead} \\ \text{Quantity Variance} \end{bmatrix} = \begin{bmatrix} \text{Actual Number of} & & \text{Standard Number} \\ \text{Direct Labor} & - & \text{of Direct Labor} \\ \text{Hours Used} & & \text{Hours Used} \end{bmatrix}$$

$$\times \begin{bmatrix} \text{Standard} \\ \text{Variable} \\ \text{Overhead Rate} \end{bmatrix}$$

The variable overhead *price* variance is often called the variable overhead *spending* variance. In our opinion, the number of terms ought to be kept to a minimum, so we prefer to use the word *price* rather than introduce new terminology. The term *spending* is really more accurate, though, because insurance expenses, for example, can increase either because of increased rates (price dimension) or increased coverage (quantity dimension) or both.

Calculation of variable overhead variances and journal entries can be illustrated by taking the Chicago Manufacturing Company example further. Suppose that as a result of the cost analysis done in the month of July, standard costs are set. Variable overhead costs are charged to the product at the rate of $.75 per direct labor hour used for the month. In August,

1975, a total of 5,000 direct labor hours were used to manufacture products that would require 5,500 direct labor hours at standard quantities. Actual variable overhead costs for August were $4,000.

The actual variable overhead rate can be calculated as:

$$\frac{\$4,000 \text{ actual variable costs}}{5,000 \text{ actual hours of direct labor}} = \begin{bmatrix} \$.80 \text{ Actual Variable Overhead} \\ \text{Cost Per Actual Direct} \\ \text{Labor Hour Used} \end{bmatrix}$$

With this information, both variable overhead price and quantity variances can be calculated:

$$\begin{array}{l} \text{Variable Overhead} \\ \text{Price Variance} \end{array} = 5,000 \text{ actual hrs.} \times \begin{array}{l} (\$.80 \text{ actual rate} - \$.75 \\ \text{standard rate}) \end{array}$$

$$= \$250 \text{ (unfavorable)}$$

$$\begin{array}{l} \text{Variable Overhead} \\ \text{Quantity Variance} \end{array} = (5,000 \text{ actual hrs.} - 5,500 \text{ standard hrs.}) \times \$.75$$

$$= - \$375 \text{ (favorable)}$$

Since

Actual Costs = Standard Costs Applied + Variances

we have:

$$\$4,000 = 5,500 \text{ hrs.} \times \$.75/\text{hr.} + \$250 - \$375$$
$$= \$4,125 + \$250 - \$375$$

The entries to record variable overhead actual costs, standard costs, and variances would be:

(1) Variable Overhead Control 4,000
      Accounts Payable, Wages Payable, etc. 4,000
    To record variable overhead costs for August.
(2) Overhead Applied ($.75 × 5,500 standard hours) 4,125
      Variable Overhead Control 4,125
    To apply standard variable overhead costs.
(3) Variable Overhead Price Variance (unfavorable) 250
      Variable Overhead Control 250
    To recognize the price variance.
(4) Variable Overhead Control 375
      Variable Overhead Quantity Variance (favorable) 375
    To recognize the quantity variance.

At this point, the Variable Overhead Control account has a zero balance. All variable overhead costs have been accounted for. The following entries would be made to close the Overhead Applied and variance accounts:

(5) Work in Process (at standard costs) 4,125
      Overhead Applied 4,125
    To apply standard variable overhead costs to product.
(6) Variable Overhead Quantity Variance 375
      Variable Overhead Price Variance 250
      Income Summary 125
    To close variance accounts to income for period. Total variable overhead variance was favorable.

The reader is now in a position to see why the Baltimore Manufacturing Company example shown earlier in this chapter is simplified. The overhead variances were not split between price and quantity nor was attention paid to splitting the overhead costs into fixed and variable components. The next section discusses fixed overhead costs. Appendix 22.1 of this chapter brings together the entire standard cost system and calculation of the several variances into a single paradigm that should make understanding the entire process easier.

Fixed Overhead Standard Costs and Variances

In a standard cost system using absorption costing, a fixed cost rate per unit of some base activity, such as direct labor hours, is charged to work in process for each unit of the base activity that is actually done during the period. To allocate fixed costs to product in a standard cost system requires the following steps:

1. Select an activity base that reasonably measures the capacity of the plant or factory. Suppose, again, that direct labor hours is selected as the base. (The activity base might also be in terms of machine hours or raw materials processing capacity.)
2. Calculate the capacity for the year in terms of the base selected in step 1. Suppose, for example, that the capacity of the Chicago Manufacturing Company is determined to be 60,000 direct labor hours per year.
3. Estimate or budget the fixed costs for the year. The Chicago Manufacturing Company's fixed costs were estimated to be $1,000 per month, or $12,000 per year.
4. Calculate the fixed overhead rate to be applied to product as the base activity is carried out. The costs estimated in step 3 are divided by the capacity estimated in step 2. Chicago Manufacturing Company would calculate a fixed cost rate of $.20 ($= $12,000/60,000$) to be applied to product for each standard direct labor hour worked.
5. Apply (debit) to Work in Process (or to Overhead Applied), and credit to Overhead Cost Control, fixed costs at the rate derived in step 4 for each standard unit of base activity performed during the accounting period.

For fixed costs, *three* kinds of variances can emerge. First, analogous to the price and rate variances for labor, materials, and variable overhead, prices can deviate from those expected or budgeted for. For example, rent and insurance premiums, which are fixed costs, may be larger than expected. For fixed costs, this variance is often called a *spending* or *budget variance* but, to maintain consistency in the terminology, we call it the fixed overhead *price* variance. The fixed overhead price variance can always be calculated in the following manner:

$$\begin{bmatrix} \text{Fixed Overhead} \\ \text{Price Variance} \end{bmatrix} = \begin{bmatrix} \text{Actual Fixed} \\ \text{Costs} \end{bmatrix} - \begin{bmatrix} \text{Budget or Estimated} \\ \text{Fixed Costs} \end{bmatrix}$$

Second, analogous to the quantity variances, fixed costs applied to product can deviate from amounts expected to be applied because of a deviation in the amounts of base activity from standard amounts for the given production level. The fixed overhead quantity variance can always be calculated by this formula:

$$
\begin{bmatrix} \text{Fixed Overhead} \\ \text{Quantity Variance} \end{bmatrix} = \begin{bmatrix} \text{Actual Units of} & \text{Standard Units} \\ \text{Base Activity} & - \text{ of Base Activity} \\ \text{Performed} & \text{Applied} \end{bmatrix}
$$

$$
\times \begin{bmatrix} \text{Standard Fixed} \\ \text{Overhead Rate} \\ \text{Per Unit of Base} \\ \text{Activity} \end{bmatrix}
$$

Third, fixed costs applied to product can deviate from amounts expected to be applied because the amount of base activity performed during the period may deviate from the expected capacity derived in step **2**. For example, suppose that Chicago Manufacturing Company determines capacity to be 60,000 direct labor hours for the year and that fixed charges applied at a rate of $.20 per direct labor hour will account for budgeted fixed costs of $12,000. If during the year only 56,000 hours of direct labor were charged with fixed overhead, then $4,000 \times \$.20 = \$800$ of fixed costs would not be accounted for. This underapplied fixed overhead is called an unfavorable fixed overhead *capacity* variance. If on the other hand, 63,000 direct labor hours were charged with fixed overhead, then $3,000 \times \$.20 = \$600$ of fixed costs would be applied to product in excess of budgeted fixed costs, which results in a favorable fixed overhead capacity variance.

The fixed overhead capacity variance can be studied graphically in Figure 22.4. The horizontal axis shows the direct labor hours charged with fixed overhead for the year. The vertical axis shows the fixed overhead costs charged to product when $.20 is applied to product for each hour of direct labor used. If 60,000 hours of direct labor is used for the year, then the fixed costs charged will be exactly equal to $12,000, the budgeted amount. If only 56,000 hours of direct labor are charged with fixed overhead costs, then only $11,200 of fixed costs will be accounted for, resulting in the unfavorable fixed overhead capacity variance. This variance results merely from plant being used for the year at less than planned capacity. Had management anticipated that only 56,000 direct labor hours would be used during the year, then the fixed cost rate applied to product for the year would have been computed in step 4 to be $12,000/56,000 = \$.2143$, and fixed costs would have been entirely accounted for.

The fixed overhead capacity variance can always be calculated by this formula:

$$\begin{bmatrix} \text{Fixed Overhead} \\ \text{Capacity Variance} \end{bmatrix} = \begin{bmatrix} \text{Units of Base} \\ \text{Activity Planned} \end{bmatrix} - \begin{bmatrix} \text{Actual Units of} \\ \text{Base Activity} \\ \text{Performed} \end{bmatrix}$$

$$\times \begin{bmatrix} \text{Standard Fixed} \\ \text{Overhead Rate} \\ \text{Per Unit of Base} \\ \text{Activity} \end{bmatrix}$$

Notice that the capacity variance is computed from the *actual* number of units of base activity performed, whether or not that actual number differs from the standard amount that should have been used during the period for that amount of output.

To illustrate the fixed overhead variance calculations, assume that the Chicago Manufacturing Company estimated 60,000 direct labor hours would be used to make 15,000 units of product (4 hours of direct labor for each unit of product) and that fixed costs were budgeted at $12,000 for the year. Fixed costs are to be applied to product at a rate of $.20 per standard direct labor hour; that is, $.80 of fixed costs would be applied to each unit of product. Suppose that 16,000 units of product were actually produced, that 65,000 hours of direct labor were actually used, and that fixed costs were actually $14,000 for the year.

The fixed overhead price variance would be:

$14,000 actual — $12,000 expected or budgeted = $2,000 (unfavorable)

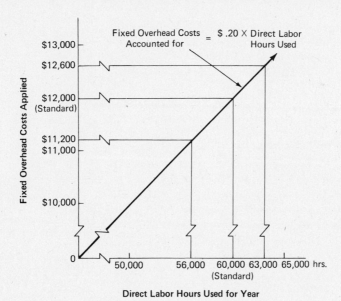

Figure 22.4 Illustration of Fixed Overhead Applied at Varying Levels of Base Activity, Chicago Manufacturing Company

The fixed overhead capacity variance would be:

(60,000 budgeted hrs. — 65,000 hrs. used) × $.20
= — $1,000 (favorable)

The fixed overhead quantity variance would be:

(65,000 actual hrs. — 64,000 standard hrs.) × $.20
= $200 (unfavorable)

Since

Actual Costs = Standard Costs Applied + Variances

we have:

$14,000 = 64,000 hrs. × $.20/hr. + $2,000 — $1,000 + $200
= $12,800 + $2,000 — $1,000 + $200

The journal entries to record the information on fixed overhead costs for the Chicago Manufacturing Company would be:

(1) Fixed Overhead Control 14,000
        Accounts Payable, Wages Payable, etc.   14,000
    To record actual fixed costs for year.

(2) Overhead Applied (at standard = 64,000 × $.20) 12,800
        Fixed Overhead Control   12,800
    To apply fixed overhead at standard rates.

(3) Fixed Overhead Price Variance (unfavorable) 2,000
    Fixed Overhead Quantity Variance (unfavorable)   200
        Fixed Overhead Capacity Variance (favorable)   1,000
        Fixed Overhead Control   1,200
    To recognize variances; the credit to Fixed Overhead Control is the plug calculated to give equal debits and credits.

The closing entries would be:

(4) Work in Process 12,800
        Overhead Applied   12,800
    To apply fixed overhead costs to product.

(5) Fixed Overhead Capacity Variance 1,000
    Income Summary (Variances) 1,200
        Fixed Overhead Price Variance   2,000
        Fixed Overhead Quantity Variance   200
    To close variance accounts to Income Summary; the debit to income summary is the plug calculated to give equal debits and credits.

The treatment of standard fixed overhead costs is, then, only slightly more complicated than the treatment of standard materials, labor, and variable overhead costs. The complication results from having to allocate to an unknown (at the beginning of the period) quantity of product an amount of fixed overhead that will be incurred, by its very nature, no matter what production turns out to be. These fixed costs are just the ones that would be allocated to period, not product, costs in a direct costing system. This issue is discussed at greater length in the next chapter.

SUMMARY

The old saying about computers is equally applicable to cost accounting systems: the information you receive is only as good as the information put into it. The difficulties in implementing standard cost accounting arise from the difficulty of developing reasonable standards and accounting for the differences between estimated and actual costs. Accounting for these differences is done by means of the nine variances, two each for direct materials, labor, and variable overhead costs, and three for fixed overhead costs. This information can be grouped according to three conceptually different variances: the price or rate variance, the quantity variance, and the capacity variance. In spite of the difficulty and expense of developing a standard cost system, the entries made to charge work in process with standard amounts and rates for materials, labor, and overhead can simplify record keeping and facilitate effective control. The appendix to this chapter presents a comprehensive example and a tabular schedule for keeping track of all the variances.

APPENDIX 22.1: A PARADIGM FOR STANDARD COSTS AND COMPREHENSIVE EXAMPLE

Calculating and keeping track of the nine variances, two each for direct materials, direct labor, and variable overhead, plus three for fixed overhead, are easier than may appear on first exposure. The Standard Cost Tableau, introduced in this section, displays the calculations' uniformity.[2] To use the Standard Cost Tableau and to review the operation of a standard cost system, consider the following data for the Buffalo Manufacturing Company for the month of September, 1975.

The Buffalo Manufacturing Company produces a single product. The standard cost system data are:

Standard direct labor cost per hour .... $6 per hour
Standard materials costs per pound .... $1.50 per pound
Standard quantity of materials per finished unit of product ... 3 pounds
Standard direct labor hours per finished unit of product ..... 5 hours
Variable overhead rate applied per standard direct labor hour.. $1.35 per hour
Budgeted fixed costs for September $9,375
Budgeted capacity for September in units of finished product.. 2,500 units

Overhead is applied to product on the basis of direct labor hours. The information on actual events for the month of September is:

[2] The Standard Cost Tableau used here is adapted from one devised by David O. Green.

Raw materials purchased (10,000 lbs. @ $1.60 per lb.) $16,000
Raw materials used in pounds ....   5,400 pounds
Direct labor costs incurred (11,000 hrs. @ $5.70 per hr.) $62,700
Variable overhead costs incurred $14,300
Fixed overhead costs incurred .... $ 9,525
Equivalent number of finished units produced in September ..   2,000 units

The Standard Cost Tableau for the Buffalo Manufacturing Company's operations during the month of September, 1975, is shown in Table 22.1. The numbers in the top left-hand corner of each cell correspond to the numbers in the paragraphs below, which show how costs and variances are calculated in the tableau. In general, actual costs are shown in column A. Column E shows the actual inputs to production at standard, or budgeted, costs. Column H shows the standard costs applied to product. Columns B, F, and G show the nine variances that will become period costs; F is used only for fixed overhead, the only cost component with a capacity variance. Columns C and D are used only for the direct materials calculations. Recall that the materials price variance is computed for all units purchased whereas the materials quantity variance is computed only for units of raw material used. Column C records raw materials received at standard prices and column D records raw materials used in production at standard prices. The order of the computations shown in Table 22.1 could be somewhat different.

Materials

(1) Record in column A the actual purchase price for 10,000 pounds of raw materials bought for $16,000 or $1.60 per pound.

(2) Record in column C the raw materials received into inventory at standard costs. The entry is 10,000 pounds times $1.50 per pound.

(3) Calculate the raw materials price variance for column B. 10,000 × ($1.60 − $1.50) = $1,000 (unfavorable). That variance could be determined as the difference between columns A and C, but the independent calculation is 10,000 pounds purchased × ($1.60 per pound paid − $1.50 per pound standard). In the Standard Cost Tableau all unfavorable variances are positive and marked (U). All favorable variances are negative and are marked (F). The journal entry that records the above tableau entries would be:

Raw Materials Inventory 15,000
Materials Price Variance (unfavorable) 1,000
    Miscellaneous Accounts Payable   16,000

(4) Record the issue of raw materials into the production process. During the month 5,400 pounds were used at a standard cost of $1.50 per pound. The amounts in columns D and E are always identical and equal the standard cost of raw materials used: 5,400 × $1.50 = $8,100.

(5) Calculate and record in column H the standard costs of raw materials applied in manufacturing the finished product. Two thousand units were produced and require, at standard, 3 pounds of material with

standard cost $1.50 per pound: 2,000 units $\times$ 3 pounds $\times$ $1.50 per pound = $9,000.

(6) Calculate and record in column G the materials quantity variance. That variance could be determined as the difference between the amounts in columns E and H, but the independent calculation is:

(5,400 pounds used — 6,000 pounds standard) $\times$ $1.50 standard cost = — $900 (favorable)

The journal entry that records tableau entries (4), (5), and (6) would be:

```
Work in Process (standard usage at standard cost) ............    9,000
    Materials Quantity Variance (favorable) ...................              900
    Raw Materials Inventory (actual usage at standard cost) ....            8,100
```

Direct Labor

(7) Record in column A the actual direct labor costs of $62,700.

(8) Record in column E the direct labor costs that would be charged at standard rates for actual direct labor usage:

11,000 hours $\times$ $6 per hour standard = $66,000

(9) Calculate the labor rate variance. That variance could be determined as the difference between columns A and E, but the independent calculation is:

11,000 hours used $\times$ ($5.70 rate paid — $6.00 standard rate) = — $3,300 (favorable)

(10) Record in column H the standard direct labor costs applied in manufacturing the finished product. Two thousand units were produced and each requires, at the standard performance level, 5 hours with standard rate $6 per hour. Two thousand units $\times$ 5 hours $\times$ $6 per hour = $60,000 of direct labor costs applied at standard rates.

(11) Calculate and record in column G the direct labor quantity variance. That variance could be determined as the difference between the amounts in columns E and H, but the independent calculation is:

(11,000 actual hours — 10,000 standard hours) $\times$ $6 per hour = $6,000 (unfavorable)

The journal entries to record the direct labor information in tableau entries (7) through (11) would be

```
Work in Process (standard usage at standard cost) ..........   60,000
Direct Labor Quantity Variance (unfavorable) ...............    6,000
    Wages Payable (actual costs) .........................            62,700
    Direct Labor Price Variance (favorable) ................             3,300
```

Variable Overhead

The problem data indicate that variable overhead is applied using direct labor hours as the activity base at a rate of $1.35 per standard direct labor

TABLE 22.1 BUFFALO MANUFACTURING COMPANY

Standard Cost Tableau for the Month of September, 1975

$$A = H + B + F + G + [C - D]$$

Actual Costs = Costs Applied + Variances

+ [Net Change in Raw Materials Inventory at Standard Cost]

		A	*B*	*C*	*D*
		Actual Cost Incurred	**Price and Rate Variances** [a]	**Raw Materials Inventories at Standard Cost**	
				Purchased	**Used**
1.	Direct Material	(1) $10,000 \times \$1.60$ $16,000	(3) $10,000 \times$ ($1.60 - $1.50) $1,000 (*U*)	(2) $10,000 \times \$1.50$ $15,000	(4) $5,400 \times \$1.50$ $8,100
2.	Direct Labor	(7) $11,000 \times \$5.70$ $62,700	(9) $11,000 \times$ ($5.70 - $6.00) −$3,300 (*F*)		
3.	Variable Overhead	(12) $1.30 = $14,300/11,000 $14,300	(14) $11,000 \times$ ($1.30 - $1.35) −$550 (*F*)		
4.	Fixed Overhead	(17) $9,525	(19) $9,525 - $9,375 $150 (*U*)		
Column Totals		$102,525	−$2,700 (*F*)	$15,000	$8,100

[a] For all variances: Positive numbers marked (*U*) are unfavorable. Negative numbers marked (*F*) are favorable.

hour charged to production. The actual variable overhead costs were $14,300 and 11,000 direct labor hours were actually used. Therefore the actual variable overhead cost per actual direct labor hour used is $14,300/11,000 = $1.30.

(12) Record in column *A* the actual variable overhead costs of $14,300.

(13) Record in column *E* the variable overhead costs that would be charged at standard rates for direct labor hours actually used:

	E	F	G	H
	Actual Input at Standard Prices (Standard Cost Control)	**Capacity Variance** a **(at Standard Cost)**	**Quantity Variances** a **(at Standard Cost)**	**Actual Output at Standard Prices (Standard Cost Applied)**
=	(4) $1.50 × 5,400		(6) $1.50 × [5,400 — (2,000 × 3)]	(5) $1.50 × (2,000 × 3)
	$8,100		—$900 (F)	$9,000
	(8) $6.00 × 11,000		(11) $6.00 × [11,000 — (2,000 × 5)]	(10) $6.00 × (2,000 × 5)
	$66,000		$6,000 (U)	$60,000
	(13) $1.35 × 11,000		(16) $1.35 × (11,000 — 10,000)	(15) $1.35 × (2,000 × 5)
	$14,850		$1,350 (U)	$13,500
	(18) Budgeted Fixed Costs $9,375/12,500 = $.75	(21) $.75 × (12,500 — 11,000)	(22) $.75 × (11,000 — 10,000)	(20) $.75 × (2,000 × 5)
	$9,375	$1,125 (U)	$750 (U)	$7,500
	$98,325	$1,125 (U)	$7,200 (U)	$90,000

11,000 hrs. × $1.35 per hour = $14,850

(14) Calculate the variable overhead price variance. That variance could be determined as the difference between columns A and E, but the independent calculation is:

11,000 direct labor hours used × ($1.30 actual rate — $1.35 standard rate) = — $550 (favorable)

(15) Record in column H the standard variable overhead costs applied in manufacturing the finished product. Two thousand units were

produced and each requires, at the standard level of performance, 5 hours of direct labor each of which is charged with $1.35 of standard variable overhead costs:

2,000 units $\times$ 5 direct labor hours $\times$ $1.35 standard charge per hour = $13,500.

(16) Calculate and record in column *G* the Variable Overhead Quantity Variance. That variance could be determined as the difference between the amounts in columns *E* and *H*, but the independent calculation is:

(11,000 actual direct labor hours — 10,000 standard hours) $\times$ $1.35 per hour = $1,350 (unfavorable).

The journal entries to record the variable overhead cost information in tableau entries (12) through (16) would be:

Variable Overhead Control	14,300	
Miscellaneous Accounts Payable		14,300
To record variable overhead costs.		
Overhead Applied (at standard)	13,500	
Variable Overhead Quantity Variance (unfavorable)	1,350	
Variable Overhead Price Variance (favorable)		550
Variable Overhead Control		14,300
To apply variable overhead and to record variable overhead variances.		

Fixed Overhead

The problem data indicate that the budgeted fixed costs for the month are $9,375 and that the activity base is direct labor hours. The capacity for September is given as 2,500 finished units. The fixed overhead variances could be calculated using finished units for the activity base, but since direct labor hours are specified as the activity base for overhead, we use direct labor hours as the activity base for fixed costs. Since 5 direct labor hours at standard are required for one unit of finished product, the capacity for September in direct labor hours is 5 $\times$ 2,500 = 12,500 direct labor hours. The fixed cost rate to be applied to product is, then, $9,375/12,500 = $.75 per hour. (If units of finished product were used as the activity base, the fixed costs would be applied to units of finished product at $9,375/2,500 = $3.75 per unit.)

(17) Record in column *A* the actual fixed overhead costs of $9,525.

(18) Record in column *E* the budgeted fixed overhead costs of $9,375. For fixed overhead costs, the "Actual Inputs at Standard Prices" (column heading for *E*) are the budgeted fixed costs for the period.

(19) Calculate the fixed overhead price variance as the difference between columns *A* and *E*. Ordinarily there is no independent calculation.

(20) Record in column *H* the standard fixed overhead costs applied to the product. The activity base is direct labor hours:

2,000 units of product $\times$ 5 hours per unit $\times$ $.75 per direct labor hour = $7,500

(Alternatively, if the activity base is units of finished product, 2,000 $\times$ $3.75 = $7,500.)

(21) Calculate and record in column F the Fixed Overhead Capacity Variance. That variance must be calculated as follows:

(12,500 hours budgeted capacity — 11,000 hours used) $\times$ $.75 per hour = $1,125 (unfavorable)

(22) Calculate and record in column G the fixed overhead quantity variance. That variance could be determined as column E minus columns F and H, but the independent calculation is:

(11,000 actual hours — 10,000 standard hours) $\times$ $.75 per hour = $750 (unfavorable).

The journal entries to record the fixed overhead cost information in tableau entries (17) through (22) would be:

Fixed Overhead Control	9,525	
Miscellaneous Accounts Payable		9,525
To record fixed overhead costs.		

Overhead Applied (at standard)	7,500	
Fixed Overhead Price Variance (unfavorable)	150	
Fixed Overhead Quantity Variance (unfavorable)	750	
Fixed Overhead Capacity Variance (unfavorable)	1,125	
Fixed Overhead Control		9,525
To apply fixed overhead and to record fixed overhead variances.		

One of the chapter-end questions asks you to compute the fixed overhead variances using finished units as the activity base. The variances, so calculated, are different from those shown here. This should not be surprising, since 80 percent (2,000/2,500) of capacity was used in September if finished product is the activity base, while 88 percent (11,000/12,500) was used if direct labor hours is the capacity base. When the activity base is measured in units of *output*, rather than units of input, the quantity variance will always be zero because there is, by definition, no deviation between actual output and "standard output" for that actual output. The resulting variance analysis is sometimes called a "four-way" analysis of overhead variances because only four—two for variable and two for fixed overhead —variances are computed.

Tableau Relations

The order in which columns E, F, G, and H are shown in the tableau derives from the order of appearance of the various measures of the activity base used in the multipliers for the fixed overhead calculations. The major time-saving device of the Standard Cost Tableau is the information in column E. The numbers shown there after the first row are not part of any standard-cost journal entry, but they are, nevertheless, used or usable for all of the variance calculations but one (capacity). Notice in the top portion of the tableau cells that there is a helpful pattern of repeating uses of the same number as a multiplier for the various multiplications that must be performed. For standard cost problems, you will probably find remembering the row and column headings useful as well as remembering the following relations that hold within the tableau.

For row 1 (direct materials):
$$A = B + C \qquad D = E \qquad E = G + H$$

For rows 2 and 3 (direct labor and variable overhead):

$$A = B + E \qquad\qquad E = G + H$$

For row 4 (fixed overhead):

$$A = B + E \qquad\qquad E = F + G + H$$

For all rows:

$$A = H + B + F + G + (C - D)$$

The last equation says that actual costs (A) equal the sum of standard costs applied (H), plus all variances (B, F, and G), plus the net change in raw materials inventory ($C - D$). Work in process is debited with the amounts in column H, while the variances from columns B, F, and G are charges (if positive) or credits (if negative) to income for the period.

QUESTIONS AND PROBLEMS

1. What conditions may be responsible for a material quantity variance? For a direct labor quantity variance?

2. What change can cause fixed overhead variances computed in one period to be inconsistent with and not reasonably comparable to fixed overhead variances computed in a later period? Why?

3. What are standard costs? Why are they used instead of comparisons of actual data with past data? Comment on the following statement: "A standard cost accounting system involves more work than cost accounting based on actual amounts and prices, but the standard system may produce data which are worth the added effort."

4. What is a one-way analysis of overhead variance? Why is it not typically used?

5. Under what circumstances will the price and quantity variances for labor and materials be offsetting, that is, of opposite signs?

*6. Refer to the data given for the Buffalo Manufacturing Company in Appendix 22.1. Assume that the base activity is units of final product and that the normal volume is 2,500 units per month.

* Hints, key numbers, or (partial) answers appear in the back of the book between the Appendix Tables and the Glossary.

    a. Compute the fixed overhead price, capacity, and quantity variances for the month of September.

    b. Why is the quantity variance equal to zero? Is this a coincidence?

7. The engineers of the American Family Hi-Fi Systems Company have determined the number of hours required to assemble a finished loudspeaker system for labor of varying skills. The labor negotiator has reported an estimate of wages per hour for the next year by skill level. The information is as follows:

Skill Level	Wage Rate per Hour	Hours to Complete One Unit
A	$2	11.0
B	3	7.2
C	4	5.2
D	5	4.1
E	6	3.5

    a. What labor standards should be set for a loudspeaker system?

    b. Suppose that, in spite of the analysis in (a), standards are set based upon skill level B and that 10,000 systems are built during the year. How much higher are standard labor costs than they should have been?

    c. Suppose that to produce 10,000 systems with standards based upon skill level B, 72,000 hours are used at a cost of $216,000. What labor variances would be reported for the year?

    d. Reconcile the answers to (b) and (c).

8. Uncured tubing can be purchased for $.25 a pound. During trimming, 10 percent by weight of the tubing is recovered as scrap that can be sold for $.02 a pound. During the curing process following trimming, the tubing shrinks to 80 percent of its weight after trimming. If a final batch of tubing weighs twenty pounds, what is the standard net materials cost per pound of finished tubing? (Round answers to the nearest cent.)

9. The Pelhall Company uses a standard cost accounting system in which storage costs are allocated among four sales areas according to sales. The budget data on which the standards for 1975 are based and data for October, 1975, transactions are as follows:

PELHALL COMPANY

	Area 1	2	3	4	Total
Cubic feet of product to be sold during the year ...	501,000	200,400	721,440	581,160	2,004,000
Cost for storage to be incurred during the year..					$12,375
Cubic feet of product sold during October	39,600	18,150	54,450	52,800	165,000
Cost of storage incurred during October					$990

a. Prepare general journal entries to account for actual and standard storage costs in October. Assume that each area records its own liability for storage costs and that all such liabilities are carried at standard cost.

b. Prepare the journal entry to account for overall storage costs. Close any variance to Income Summary.

10. The Rubber Duckie Company produces bath toys. Recently established standard costs are as follows:

> Materials: 5 pieces per unit at $.20 per piece
> Labor: .50 hour per unit at $4.50 per hour

In November, 1975, production of finished goods was 5,000 units. Twenty-seven thousand pieces of material were used which cost $5,130. Labor costs were $12,015 for 2,700 hours worked.

Assuming that there were no opening and closing inventories, compute the labor and materials variances for November, 1975.

*11. The Tidy Box Company's budget contains these standards for materials and direct labor for a unit of 10 boxes:

> Material — 2 pounds @ $.50 . . . . $1.00
> Direct Labor — 1 hour @ $4.50 . . . . . . 4.50

Although 100,000 units were budgeted for September, 1975, only 97,810 were produced. Two hundred thousand pounds of materials were purchased for $105,500. Materials weighing 193,880 pounds were issued to production. Direct labor costs were $396,800 for 99,200 hours.

a. Calculate the labor and materials variances.

b. Provide the journal entries necessary to record the above data.

12. The standard fixed overhead cost per unit of product Z is $4.80, calculated as three machine hours at $1.60 per hour. The fixed overhead budget for the first quarter of 1975 is $144,000, based on an estimate of 90,000 hours of machine use during the period. During the first quarter of 1975, 28,000 units were produced and 89,500 machine hours were worked. Actual fixed overhead costs were $137,000.

Calculate the three fixed overhead variances and their total.

*13. You are given the following variance data for the month

	Material A	Material B	Material C
Material price variance	−$42,000F	−$25,000F	$21,000U
Material quantity variance	40,000U	30,000U	48,000U
Net material variance	−$ 2,000F	$ 5,000U	$69,000U
Units produced	100,000	110,000	125,000

Two pounds of each kind of material are required for each unit of output. For Material A, the average price paid was $.20 per pound less than standard; for Material B, $.10 greater; for Material C, $.07 greater. There are no opening or closing inventories of any kind of material.

For each of the three materials, calculate the following:
a. number of pounds of material purchased
b. standard cost per pound of material
c. total standard material cost for each kind of material.

14. You are given the following data for October, 1975:

	Standards per Batch	Actual
Materials	2 pounds at $5 per pound	195,000 pounds
Labor	3 hours at $6 per hour	280,000 hours
Units		96,000 batches

During the month, 100,000 pounds of materials were purchased for $505,500. Wages earned were $1,708,000.
a. Compute all labor and material variances.
b. Provide the journal entries to record these data.

°15. The following data are available concerning the overhead costs incurred in the tubing department of the Smith Company:

Standard Overhead Rates

Variable	$1.50 per direct labor hour
Fixed	$2.20 per direct labor hour

April, 1975	May, 1975
7,000 units of work produced	7,300 units of work produced
22,000 direct labor hours worked	21,500 direct labor hours worked
Variable costs $33,800	Variable costs $31,900
Fixed costs $47,900	Fixed costs $48,000

Normal volume is 23,000 direct labor hours. Three direct labor hours are required for one unit at standard.
a. Calculate the overhead variances for April and May, 1975.
b. What are the expected fixed costs for April and May, 1975?

16. The following data on actual performance and standards for overhead are taken from the production records of the Hirschhorn Company for October, 1975, and November, 1975.

Standard Costs (Overhead)

Variable	$2.00 per unit (1 machine hour at $2.00)
Fixed	1.00 per unit (1 machine hour at $1.00)

Actual Costs (Overhead)

	October	November
Variable	$86,000	$89,150
Fixed	44,980	43,960

Normal capacity volume is 45,000 machine hours. Actual machine hours were 43,200 and actual production was 43,000 units in October. In November, actual machine hours were 43,950 and actual production was 44,000 units.
a. Calculate all overhead variances for October.
b. Calculate all overhead variances for November.

17. The following table shows the unit standard cost of Product *K*:

Material — 2 pounds @ $3.00	$ 6.00
Labor — 1 hour @ $5.00	5.00
Overhead	4.00
	$15.00

During October, 1975, 10,000 units of Product *K* were started and completed. This output required 20,250 pounds of material, and 10,080 direct labor hours. Overhead costs were $39,800. Wages amounted to $49,896. On September 30, 25,000 pounds of raw materials were purchased at a cost of $74,750. The firm uses LIFO for inventory valuation.

Compute the following variances:

a. materials price
b. materials quantity
c. labor price
d. labor quantity
e. total overhead variance.

18. The unit standard cost of Product *A* of the Acme Company is $12.50, composed of the following items:

Material — 6 pounds @ $.75	$4.50
Labor — 1 hour @ $5.00	5.00
Overhead	3.00

During January 1975, 30,000 pounds of material were purchased at an average cost of $.76 a pound and 29,000 pounds were used; 5,000 direct labor hours were worked at an average rate of $5.05 per hour; and actual overhead costs were $15,500. There were 5,000 units started and completed during the month.

Compute the amount of each of the following variances.

a. material price variance
b. material quantity variance
c. labor price (rate) variance
d. labor quantity variance
e. overhead variance.

19. Henry Alger has formed a company to manufacture salad bowls. He and the students in his sixth grade class make two types of bowls, *A* and *B*. Because they use the school's facilities, they pay no fixed overhead. The following are the standards and production data for November, 1975:

STANDARD COSTS

	Bowl *A*	Bowl *B*
Raw Materials..	$ .25 (.05 lb. @ $5.00)	$ .50 (.10 lb. @ $5.00)
Labor	$ .40 (6 min. @ $4.00)	$ .45 (6 min. @ $4.50)
Overhead	$1.60 per direct labor hour	$1.50 per direct labor hour

PRODUCTION DATA FOR NOVEMBER, 1975

	Bowl A	Bowl B
Units	5,000	3,000
Pounds of Raw Materials Used	250	305
Direct Labor Hours Used	500	299
Labor Costs Incurred	$2,060.00	$1,330.55

Total overhead was $1,236. This is to be allocated proportionately to the two products on the basis of standard direct labor hours. One thousand pounds of raw materials were purchased for $5,020. The labor quantity variance for Bowl A was zero.

a. Compute all variances for Bowl A production in November, 1975.

b. Compute all variances for Bowl B production in November, 1975.

°**20.** The Sheldon Company manufactures plastic squirt guns. Since the cycle is so short for this product, work in process inventory is negligible. A job order cost system is in use in the factory. A general overhead rate is established every three months on the basis of expected production volume for the next three months.

At the end of September, the fiscal year ends. Because so few squirt guns are sold in the winter months, there is normally no finished goods inventory on September 30.

The following data are available:

ESTIMATED OVERHEAD COSTS

Production per Quarter	Overhead Costs
1,000,000 units	$500,000
1,100,000 units	550,000
1,200,000 units	600,000
1,300,000 units	650,000
1,400,000 units	700,000

Quarter	Estimated Production	Actual Production	Actual Overhead Costs	Units in Finished Goods Inventory	Sales in Units
1	1,100,000	1,060,000	$742,000	159,000	901,000
2	1,300,000	1,350,000	$850,500	?	109,000

The company uses the FIFO basis for inventory valuation, assuming all overhead is variable.

a. Compute the amount of the overhead price variance for each quarter.

b. Indicate for each quarter the amount of manufacturing overhead costs that would be carried to cost of goods sold and the amount that would remain in the end-of-quarter inventories if: (1) overhead variances are closed out to cost of goods sold at the end of the quarter; (2) if the variances are allocated between the inventories and cost of goods sold in the same proportions as the quarter's production appears in inventories and cost of goods sold.

21. Under the flexible budget of the Ceramic Tile Company, budgeted variable overhead is $60,000 when 60,000 direct labor hours are worked, while budgeted direct labor costs are $300,000.

The following are some of the variances for February, 1975:

Variable Overhead Price Variance	$12,000U
Variable Overhead Quantity Variance	10,000U
Materials Price Variance	15,000F
Materials Usage Variance	8,000U
Fixed Overhead Quantity (usage) Variance	2,000U

$325,500 of direct labor costs and $70,000 of fixed overhead costs were incurred in February, 1975. According to the standards, one pound of material should cost $2.00. One pound of material is the standard for each unit of product. One hundred thousand units were produced in February, 1975. The unit materials price variance was $.20 per pound, while the average wage rate exceeded the standard average rate by $.25.

Compute the following for February; assume that there are no opening or closing inventories:

a. pounds of materials purchased
b. pounds of material usage over standard
c. standard hourly wage rate
d. standard direct labor hours for the total February production
e. fixed overhead standard rate.

*22. The production of widules requires raw materials and labor. They are processed through production departments P_1 and P_2, both of which use services from two service departments, S_1 and S_2. For the production of 5,000 units in October, 1975, these costs were incurred:

Costs	Where Used	
	P_1	P_2
Direct Material	$ 5,500	$ 8,500
Direct Labor	50,000	60,000
Variable Overhead	2,200	1,800
Fixed Overhead	8,000	6,000

Service Department Data	Labor Hours Required	Labor Rate	Fixed Costs
S_1	2,500	$6/hr.	$12,000
S_2	3,500	$5/hr.	$ 9,000

Allocation matrix A (See Appendix 20.1 of Chapter 20)

Costs Incurred Here	Are Allocated Here	
	P_1	P_2
S_1	.55	.45
S_2	.60	.40

a. Develop standard costs for one widule; assume that 5,000 units per month is normal and that costs incurred in October, 1975, are normal.
b. Assume that in November, 1975, 5,000 units are produced and all costs incurred equal standard costs. Set up all necessary T-accounts and make entries to trace the flow of goods and services as the 5,000 units are produced.

23. The Old Style Company mass-produces pseudo-antique roll-top desks. The standard costs per unit are:

Wood:	25 pounds @ $3.20	$ 80
Trim:	8 pounds @ $5.00	40
Direct labor:	5 hours @ $6.00	30
Variable overhead:	5 hours @ $3.00	15
Fixed overhead:	5 hours @ $2.00	10
Total cost per desk		$175

Note that the variable overhead rate is $3.00 per direct labor hour, while the fixed overhead rate is $2.00 per direct labor hour.

One-half of the wood and trim is added at the start of the process, while the other half is added at the 50-percent completion stage. Labor and overhead are added evenly throughout the process.

Transactions during February, 1975, were as follows:

(1) Eighty tons of wood were purchased at $3.25 per pound; 155,000 pounds were issued to production.

(2) Twenty-five tons of trim were purchased at $4.80 per pound. 48,500 pounds were issued to production.

(3) The direct labor payroll was 31,000 hours at $5.75.

(4) Variable overhead costs were $89,000.
Fixed overhead costs were $62,000.

(5) Planned production for the month was 6,200 equivalent units.

(6) Four thousand desks, 40 percent completed at the beginning of the period, were finished, while 6,000 desks were put into process. Six thousand desks were transferred to finished goods, while another 4,000 remained in process, 40 percent complete.

Compute a summary analysis of all variances, *or* prepare a standard cost tableau for the month of February. Compute separate materials variances for wood and trim.

*24. The Seasonal Company manufactures Christmas cards and other greeting cards. Fixed overhead is budgeted at $6,000 per month. The normal capacity is 10,000 direct labor hours per month. Variable overhead is budgeted at $9,500 when 10,000 direct labor hours are worked per month.

The following data are available for April, 1975:

Capacity Variance	$1,500U
Materials Purchased	20,000 units
Direct Labor Costs Incurred	$36,000
Total of Direct Labor Rate and Quantity Variances	—$500F
Average Actual Wage Rate ($.20 less than the standard wage rate)	$4.80
Variable Overhead Costs Incurred	$9,000
Total Overhead Costs Incurred	$13,875
Materials Price Variance	—$200F
Materials Quantity Variance	—$610F
Price of Purchased Materials	$.60 per unit
Materials Used	15,000 units
Planned Operating Capacity	10,000 direct labor hours

Using the above data, identify and present computations for all variances. Present a schedule of variances and the actual costs incurred. *Or* prepare a standard cost tableau.

25. The Pittsburgh Manufacturing Company uses a standard cost system that records raw materials at actual cost and records materials price variance at the time that raw materials are issued to work in process. All variances are prorated between inventories and costs of goods sold at year end. Direct materials variances are prorated to finished goods inventory and to cost of goods sold based on the standard direct materials in the finished goods inventory and the cost of goods sold accounts. Direct labor and overhead variances are prorated based on the standard direct labor costs in the

finished goods inventory and the cost of goods sold accounts. There were no beginning inventories and no ending work-in-process inventory. Manufacturing overhead is applied at 80 percent of standard direct labor costs. The following information is available for the Pittsburgh Manufacturing Company for the year ended December 31, 1975.

Raw Materials Inventory at December 31, 1975	$ 130,000
Finished Goods Inventory at December 31, 1975:	
Direct Material	174,000
Direct Labor	261,000
Applied Manufacturing Overhead	208,800
Cost of Goods Sold for the Year Ended	
December 31, 1975:	
Direct Material	696,000
Direct Labor	1,479,000
Applied manufacturing Overhead	1,183,200
Direct-material Price Variance	20,000 (U)
Direct-material Quantity Variance	−30,000 (F)
Direct-labor Rate Variance	40,000 (U)
Direct-labor Quantity Variance	−10,000 (F)
Manufacturing Overhead Incurred	1,380,000

For year end, December 31, 1975, calculate:

a. the amount of direct-material price variance to be prorated to finished goods inventory

b. the total costs of direct material in finished goods inventory after all variances have been prorated

c. the total costs of direct labor in the finished goods inventory after all variances have been prorated

d. the total costs of goods sold after all variances have been prorated.

*26. The Doppler Company manufactures exotic whistles and chains, which are sold separately. The firm uses a standard cost system for direct labor and direct materials cost. Overhead costs are accumulated in special accounts and kept separate from other product costs. The whistles and chains are formed in the W department. In the C department, they are sanded, finished, and then packed for shipping.

Materials inventories are carried at standard cost. Each department has a work in process account for Materials and one for Labor. Materials received from inventory are charged to the Materials in Process account at standard cost. When partially completed products are transferred to Department C, the standard labor and materials costs accrued in Department W are charged to Materials in Process of Department C at standard cost.

The following transactions took place during October, 1975:

	Actual Cost	Standard Cost
(1) Raw materials purchased	$25,625	$24,375
(2) Materials issued to Dept. W		46,300
Materials issued to Dept. C		15,800
(3) Direct labor costs, Dept. W	43,500	43,400
Direct labor costs, Dept. C	41,750	42,250
(4) Whistles transferred to Dept. C: 5,000		
Whistles transferred to Finished Goods: 6,000		

Chains transferred to Dept. *C*: 2,000

Chains transferred to Finished Goods: 2,500

(5) Work in Process, October 1

Dept. *W*: 500 whistles, complete through Operation *B*

Dept. *C*: 1,500 chains, complete through Operation *G*; that is, no work has been done in Dept. *C*

(6) Work in Process, October 31

Dept. *W*: none   Dept. *C*: none

The following data are available:

STANDARD COST PER UNIT OF WHISTLE

Operation	Department	Labor Cost	Materials	Cumulative Cost
A	W	$4.00	$2.00	$ 6.00
B	W	5.00	6.00	17.00
C	C	2.00	.75	19.75
D	C	.50	—	20.25
E	C	1.50	.25	22.00

STANDARD COST PER UNIT OF CHAIN

Operation	Department	Labor Cost	Materials	Cumulative Cost
F	W	$2.50	$5.00	$ 7.50
G	W	1.00	.50	9.00
H	C	4.50	.25	13.75
I	C	3.25	—	17.00

a. Prepare the journal entries to record the month's transactions.

b. Compute all variances for labor and materials costs; indicate whether each is favorable or unfavorable.

*27. The Junior Dog Manufacturing Company produces electrical equipment for animal hospitals. The following information is provided in the standard cost records for the production of green and yellow machines for the month of November, during which 5,000 green and 4,000 yellow machines were produced. Each machine type is made from separate raw materials and is manufactured in separate plants so that overhead costs for each are independent of the other. Overhead is charged to units of product on the basis of direct labor hours.

Actual Costs Incurred for Month	Green Machines	Yellow Machines
Direct Materials Purchased (in pounds)	7,000	8,000
Direct Materials Costs (per pound)	$1.50	$1.25
Direct Materials Used for Month (in pounds)..	9,000	9,000
Direct Labor Hours Worked during Month	21,000	?
Direct Labor Wage Paid (per hour)	$4.80	$4.80
Variable Overhead Costs Incurred	$26,250	$5,025
Fixed Overhead Costs Incurred	$8,500	$10,000

Variances Recorded for the Month

Direct Materials Price Variance	$3,500 (F)	$2,000 (U)
Direct Materials Quantity Variance	$7,000 (F)	$1,000 (U)
Direct Labor Rate Variance	$4,200 (F)	$9,000 (U)
Direct Labor Quantity Variance	?	—$3,000 (F)
Variable Overhead Rate Variance	$5,250 (U)	—$600 (F)
Variable Overhead Quantity Variance	?	—$375 (F)
Fixed Overhead Price Variance	—$500 (F)	$2,000 (U)
Fixed Overhead Capacity Variance	—$1,500 (F)	—$1,000 (F)
Fixed Overhead Quantity Variance	$500 (U)	—$600 (F)

From this information, calculate separately for each type of machine:

a. the numbers omitted in the schedule above for which "?" is shown

b. the standard costs for direct materials per pound, direct labor per hour, the variable overhead charge per direct labor hour, and the fixed overhead charge per direct labor hour

c. standard quantities of materials and direct labor per finished machine

d. the standard cost of a finished machine

e. budgeted fixed costs for the month and the normal capacity in direct labor hours

f. the net decrease in raw materials inventory for the month at standard prices

g. the standard costs applied for the month for direct materials, direct labor, variable overhead, and fixed overhead.

As an alternative to (a) through (g) above,

h. Construct and fill in a standard cost tableau for each machine type for the month.

Chapter 23

Managerial Control: Using Cost Data

Christmas is the big season for toy manufacturers, but most of them operate throughout the year. Many of them manufacture other seasonal products, such as sports equipment. Although different products have different specifications, the same machinery, with minor adjustments, can be used to make them. When management must make a decision about shifting its production or introducing a new product, it uses cost data to help make the decision. This chapter will discuss some of the ways that management uses cost data to plan and control operations.

Limitations of Cost Data

The primary service of cost accounting to management is not, paradoxically, the calculation of unit costs for products. The nature and amount of joint and common costs, both in production and selling operations, make computing the "actual" cost of any single unit in any absolute sense impossible. Most modern plants produce more than one product with the same buildings, equipment, and labor force. One salesman may sell a hundred or more items and not be able to account for the time spent on each one. The whole process of distributing the cost of overhead among departments, the redistribution of service department costs, and the allocation of overhead to particular jobs or products is characterized by the use of arbitrary and approximate bases. The attempted calculation of full unit costs of production is a necessary part of the cost accounting but not its most useful contribution to business management.

The production costs obtained from the accounting records are, at best, incomplete. The costs of administration, such as executives' salaries and office costs, are rarely assigned to production operations. Imputed costs, such as interest on investment, are usually ignored in regular accounting procedures.

Another factor that weakens the significance of cost accounting figures is the presence of fixed costs, those which do not vary much with the fluctuations in production over a given time period. The salaries of a factory superintendent and of other supervisors, property taxes, rent, fire insurance, and a number of other costs do not tend to vary except with changes in the size of the plant. As a result, if actual costs incurred are allocated to the goods actually produced, unit costs will rise when operations contract and fall when production expands. The fixed cost per unit varies inversely with the level of output.

Remember also that managerial decisions are based only in part on cost data. Questions of employee morale, government regulation, customer relations, and similar matters must be considered in the decision-making process. For example, a department in a store may consistently operate at a loss according to the cost calculations but still be continued as "good business practice." Virtually all stores have, according to cost accounting calculations, unprofitable departments or unprofitable months. Many businesses have unprofitable seasons. Asked "Why not close down the unprofitable department or during the unprofitable season?", the businessman answers, "That would be bad business practice"; he is implicitly saying that the cost accounting, which signals unprofitable operations, is faulty.

Uses of Cost Data

In spite of their limitations, data from cost analyses serve significantly useful purposes. Cost accounting contributes to the process of evaluating the efficiency of various operations. The direct costs of a job order, a process, or a service department operation, before arbitrary allocations, have considerable significance. Any such calculations consistently made from period to period will help to indicate trends or variations from expected results. The performance of both personnel and equipment can be studied and checked by accumulation of detailed cost data. If a standard cost system is used, the variances from standard offer an excellent starting point for reviewing ineffective performance and for seeking remedies.

Production cost records are necessary to obtain unit costs that can be used for calculating the cost of goods sold as well as the value of inventories of work in process and finished goods. Although never more than approximately correct, production cost records provide a systematic mechanism for accounting for the flow of costs through the plant and then, to customers. Production cost records, coupled with perpetual-inventory records, permit frequent preparation of financial statements.

The cost records help budgeting or planning business activity. Not only are the historical-cost data useful in preparing the forecast cost figures for the budget, but frequent statements can be prepared to help correlate sales and production with budget plans and otherwise to review the progress of the budget. The budgetary system assigns responsibility for certain costs to specific departments or individuals, so deviations from planned activity can be pinpointed.

There is undoubtedly some connection between cost data and selling prices, but the relationship is complicated and easily misunderstood. In the competitive situations typical of most business environments, selling prices are dictated by market conditions and are not apt to be specifically related to the costs of a particular producer. Even under conditions of monopoly, computed cost may have little relation to the price that is charged. In some instances the out-of-pocket variable, or incremental, costs which will have to be specifically incurred in order to take on a certain order, may be those which have the most influence on the price charged. Costs and prices are related, but the relationship is complex with many factors involved.

Some of the most important decisions in business require cost data that cannot be obtained directly from financial statements or even from the accounts. If a choice is to be made between methods of production, products to be produced, departments to be discontinued or added, or other such alternatives, the cost data that emerge from the accounting records may not be relevant. If a choice concerning increased mechanization must be made, the depreciation and maintenance of a machine purchased years ago, when prices and technology may have been considerably different should not be used in the comparison, because only current marginal or incremental costs of alternatives should influence the choice. Such factors as the rate of return on the required investment in machines, and the comparative risks involved—data not obtainable from the cost records—must be considered. The cost accounting system helps to solve problems, however, by providing a framework of cost elements that must be taken into account, some without adjustment and others with changes made necessary by factors that are not reflected in the book figures. Special studies, based largely on cost accounting data, usually offer the most effective method of providing the cost data for important decisions.

Each of these major uses of cost accounting data by management is considered in the subsequent sections of this chapter.

Costs Attached to Products: Absorption vs. Direct Costing

Two different product costing systems allocate different costs to inventories of work in process and finished goods. Under both absorption and direct costing systems, variable costs, such as for materials, direct labor, and variable overhead, are applied to products as they are produced. Under *absorption* or *full* costing, fixed overhead costs are allocated to products as well. Under *direct* or *variable* costing, fixed manufacturing costs are charged to period expenses. As was demonstrated in Chapters 5 and 12, absorption and direct costing systems will provide the same income estimates whenever beginning and ending inventories are zero. The differences between the two income estimates arise when, as is typical, ending inventory amounts differ from beginning inventory amounts.

Generally accepted accounting principles do not yet permit inventory valuations based upon direct costs for published financial reports nor has the Internal Revenue Service allowed direct costing for inventory valuation in computing taxable income. Consequently, absorption costing is currently used more often than is direct costing even for internal accounting purposes. Advocates of absorption costing argue that full costs better represent the long-run costs of production. They argue that inventories should carry a fair portion of fixed costs required for production and that separation of variable and fixed costs, as required by direct costing, is not usually feasible in practice.

Advocates of direct costing argue that fixed costs are required for remaining in business but are not related to specific units produced. Under absorption costing, the unit costs of identical units of a product can vary depending upon the volume of production for the period. Direct costing provides cost classifications more useful than does absorption costing for short-run pricing decisions and for the kinds of special studies described later in this chapter. Under direct costing systems, there are no fixed overhead cost standards for units of product and, hence, none of the puzzling fixed overhead variances to be calculated and explained. As to the difficulty in separating fixed and variable costs, we argue that here and elsewhere it is better to be vaguely right than precisely wrong.

Fortunately, firms need not use only one or the other of the two systems. Direct costing can be used for internal purposes, and absorption costing for financial reports and tax returns. To see how easy it is to provide both direct costing and absorption costing reports, consider the following data for The D. C. Company for the year 1975. For simplicity, beginning inventories are assumed to be zero, but the existence of beginning inventory does not change the principle.

The D. C. Company, Year of 1975

Variable cost per unit of product	$5 per unit
Fixed costs for year	$45,000
Production for year in units	15,000 units
Sales for year in units at $10 each	10,000 units

The journal entries in the direct costing system used by The D. C. Company, in simplified form, would be:

(1)	Finished Goods Inventory	75,000	
	Assets, Wages Payable, and Work in Process		75,000
	To record variable costs of production as the cost of finished goods.		
(2)	Fixed Costs Control	45,000	
	Assets, Accounts Payable and Accumulated Depreciation		45,000
	To record fixed costs.		

(3) Accounts Receivable 100,000
           Sales (10,000 units at $10)   100,000
      To record sales for year.

(4) Cost of Goods Sold (10,000 units at $5) 50,000
           Finished Goods Inventory   50,000
      To record cost of sales as reduction in inventory.

The various accounts now appear as follows:

Finished Goods Inventory		Other Assets and Liabilities		Sales	
(1) 75,000	50,000 (4)	(3) 100,000	75,000 (1)		100,000 (3)
			45,000 (2)		

Cost of Goods Sold		Fixed Costs Control	
(4) 50,000		(2) 45,000	

If direct costing were being used for internal purposes, Sales, Cost of Goods Sold, and Fixed Costs Control would be closed to the Income Summary with entries such as:

(5) Sales 100,000
           Income Summary   100,000

(6) Income Summary 50,000
           Cost of Goods Sold   50,000

(7) Income Summary 45,000
           Fixed Costs Control   45,000
      To close operating accounts assuming direct costing.

As a result of these entries, the Income Summary has a credit balance of $5,000, the income for the year under direct costing. Assuming entries (5)–(7) were made on the books for internal purposes and financial reports require absorption costing, the following adjusting entry will accomplish the conversion from direct costing to absorption costing:

(8) Finished Goods Inventory 15,000
     Cost of Goods Sold 30,000
           Income Summary   45,000
      To allocate fixed costs for the year to sales ($2/3$) and to
      ending inventory ($1/3$), in effect removing $15,000 from
      expenses of the period.

The Cost of Goods Sold account is, of course, closed back into the Income Summary. The net effect of entry (8) is to remove $15,000 from expenses of the period and to allocate that $15,000 to Finished Goods Inventory. Under absorption costing, income for the year would be $20,000. The difference between absorption and direct costing income for the year, $15,000, is exactly the difference between absorption and direct costing ending inventory costs, $15,000, since beginning inventory is assumed to be zero.

Controllability

Costs are *controllable* if they can be influenced at some level within the firm. Employees should be held responsible only for those costs that they can control. The assignment of responsibility is easier said than done because many costs are partially controllable at different management levels within the firm. For example, labor costs are partially controlled by the individual employee, who decides how hard and efficiently to work, by foremen, who decide which employees to use and where, by superintendents, who schedule work, by labor negotiators, who bargain about wage rates, and by management, who may order overtime production that incurs extra costs.

Do not commit the common error of supposing that all variable costs are controllable while fixed costs are not. Direct materials costs, though variable with the amount used in production, are beyond the control of anyone to the degree that prices generally increase in competitive markets. A fixed cost, such as rent, though not controllable at low levels within the firm, is controlled by someone in top management.

ANALYSIS OF STANDARD COST VARIANCES

Where the job order or process cost methods of allocating actual costs are used, deviations from expected results may be found by comparing current cost figures with those of earlier periods, corrected for changed conditions. In standard cost systems, variations from expected performance are indicated directly in the several variance accounts. The calculation of variances is illustrated in Chapter 22.

Analysis of variances provides effective, yet economical, managerial cost control. Management can direct attention to those areas where substantial variance balances signal that something unusual has happened. Large unfavorable variances indicate that something may have gone wrong and that remedial action may be necessary. Investigation may reveal that the standards themselves are in error, but if they are not, then managerial effort will usually be devoted to solving the problem. Large favorable variances, not offset with unfavorable ones, may indicate that employees or supervisors, or both, have discovered new work methods that should be standardized and communicated to other operating departments. The notion of directing managerial activity to those areas where deviations from standard have occurred is frequently described as *management by exception*.

A well-designed standard cost system can be used to assign responsibility for costs incurred so that variances can be traced to individuals. Each particular variance may have a variety of causes, some beyond control within the firm. An effective system diagnoses the cause of each variance, suggests methods for preventing variances, and prescribes remedies for continuing variances.

Detailed cost accounting and analysis of variances are costly and, in general, only as much should be undertaken as is likely to produce greater operating savings than is added to record-keeping costs. Determining the optimal level of record keeping is, of course, more difficult than stating the principle that benefits and costs ought to be considered together. Many sophisticated standard cost systems use the techniques of *statistical quality control*, a subject of advanced cost accounting, for deciding when to investigate variances and when to leave them alone.

Materials Variances

Materials price variances are usually analyzed by individual types of material; materials quantity variances can be isolated by jobs, processes, or departments depending upon the amount of detailed record keeping that is to be done.

Materials price variances are usually the responsibility of the purchasing department. Frequently such variances result from changing market prices, but they may be caused by using an improper grade of materials, ordering in uneconomically small quantities, failing to take discounts, or paying unnecessarily high freight charges. Materials price variances may be caused, however, by late notification of material requirements by a production department. The immediate need for materials may require orders that do not allow sufficient time to acquire the material by the methods contemplated when the standard price was established. A classic case[1] is cited by one accountant in which the standard cost of a part was $.32 per hundred; the actual cost was $.49 per hundred. Investigation revealed that faulty shipping instructions had caused deliveries in small quantities at the higher price. The shipping orders were changed and the standards were met.

Materials quantity variances are more likely to be the responsibility of the operating departments than are materials price variances. They may reflect wasteful use of materials, excessive spoilage, or occasionally the purchasing department's ordering of materials of improper specifications. In the same firm cited in the preceding paragraph, a large material quantity variance led to the discovery that sheets of steel were being ordered that were more than ample to secure three washing-machine covers, but too short by three inches to obtain four washing-machine covers. Alteration in the size of the sheets ordered virtually eliminated the quantity variance.

Direct Labor Variances

Direct labor rate variances result from changes in wage rates not yet reflected in standards or from the assignment of workers of a different wage-skill class than that specified in the standard. There is little that can usually be done about the former cause, but the latter may frequently be

[1] Paul C. Taylor, "Functioning of Standards in Cost Control," *National Association of Cost Accountants Bulletin* (March 1951), pp. 796–99.

corrected by closer control. The direct labor quantity variance is, of course, generally considered to be controllable and major managerial attention is usually focused on it. This variance may also be analyzed by jobs, processes, or departments depending upon the amount of detailed record keeping and other effort that is thought to be worthwhile.

Offsetting Variances

A price or rate variance ought not to be looked at separately from the corresponding quantity variance. As suggested in Chapter 22, material of higher than standard quality or labor costing higher than standard rates may have been substituted for standard qualities. If so, then the rate and quantity variances may be offsetting—unfavorable rate and favorable quantity variances when higher quality input is used, favorable rate and unfavorable quantity variances when lower quality input is used. Clearly, to reward the purchasing department for a favorable price variance and to penalize the foreman for an unfavorable quantity variance would be faulty variance analysis when the cause is merely the purchase of sub-standard materials. If the sum of the two variances is favorable, then standards should be revised to reflect the more economical combination of factor inputs.

Overhead Variances

In Chapter 22, the so-called *one-way* analysis of overhead variances is shown for the Baltimore Manufacturing Company and the more typical *five-way* analysis of overhead variances is shown for the Chicago and Buffalo Manufacturing Companies. As mentioned in Chapter 22, a *four-way* analysis of overhead variances results from using a measure of output, rather than input, as the activity base. To determine the level of analysis used in practice, one must weigh the benefits against the costs of more detail.

Overhead variances are more difficult to control than either material or labor variances. Overhead costs consist of a mingling of items, and "variable" overhead costs are often semivariable. Responsibility for overhead costs is difficult to assign. Some attempts can nevertheless be made to prevent overhead variances and to minimize costs in the first place.

The variable overhead price variance, for example, might reflect price increases in supplies, wage increases for maintenance workers, or utility rate increases. An unfavorable variable overhead price variance could result from the increased costs caused by time lost when shipping or receiving clerks and maintenance jobs take longer than planned.

Variable overhead costs normally will increase proportionately to the direct labor hours, direct labor dollars, or machine hours used. When higher-than-standard amounts of the activity base are used per unit of output, an unfavorable variable overhead quantity variance will result. This unfavorable quantity variance results from the same causes that produced higher-than-standard amounts of the activity base used, and responsibility for it is, therefore, the same as for labor quantity variances.

Of the fixed overhead variances, only the fixed overhead price variance contains many items that are at all directly controllable. Such a variance results from spending either more or less than planned for fixed overhead during an accounting period. Supervisory salary increases, rent increases, added depreciation charges, and hikes in other fixed costs all will create unfavorable fixed overhead price variances. Such variances will result in many cases from managerial decisions. The fixed overhead quantity variance, like the labor and variable overhead quantity variances, is caused by those factors that result in nonstandard usage of the activity base. As discussed earlier, the fixed overhead capacity variance is a direct result of failing to operate at the budgeted level of activity. The inability to control the capacity variance, except through more accurate forecasts of actual activity, is one symptom that the capacity variance has no place in rational decision making and, hence, that absorption costing, which requires it, is illogical.

BUDGETS

Any accounting report that can be compiled at the end of a period from actual data can be matched by a similar statement compiled at the beginning of the period from hypothetical, or projected, data. A *budget*, simply put, is a financial report prepared in advance, a proforma report usually at the beginning of a period, from data that are expected to reflect operations of the period. It is a plan of operations expressed in financial terms. All businesses do some planning or forecasting, but in many firms, the process is informal. Budgets state the future plans in a more formal and precise way. They forecast the results of all transactions that are anticipated during the period so that projected financial statements for the period can be evaluated. Budgets make possible a comparison of results with plans and, thereby, facilitate control.

Budget Preparation

The starting point in budget preparation is the selection of the primary limiting factor in operations. Normally this will be the volume of sales that can be made, but shortages of materials, labor, or plant capacity may in some cases set the limits on activity. The physical and dollar volume of sales of products (or other limiting factor) must be estimated for the budget period, usually a year. In addition to annual plans of sales, forecasts by months or other interim periods are frequently made.

From these sales estimates, budgets in physical and dollar terms are usually prepared for each of the production and service departments. In addition, budgets for the selling and administrative functions are usually prepared. All of the operating costs of the period are assigned to some department or activity in a complete budgetary system.

Standard cost systems facilitate the preparation of budgets for the production departments. Standard costs have not been widely used for service departments, clerical activities, and sales functions, however, and determining budgets in these areas can be more difficult.

For the budget to function effectively as a control device, budgeted costs ought to be classified in accordance with organizational responsibilities. The classification of accounts in the cost accounting and general accounting system should be based upon an organizational structure that assigns definite responsibilities. The process of analyzing costs for preparing a budget sometimes indicates that the existing organizational plan does not provide for a clear-cut assignment of responsibilities. Accordingly, the organizational plan requires review and, possibly, revision. An incidental benefit of a budgetary procedure is the periodic scrutiny of the firm's organizational plan.

In preparing budgets for cost centers, the assistance of the foremen and other employees responsible for the activities of the operation unit is sometimes sought. Employees can furnish valuable information because of their intimate knowledge of the operations of the department and they may be more highly motivated to reach budgeted goals if they have helped to establish these goals.

Budgetary Control

The primary reasons for the budgetary process are planning and control—the check to determine whether the formulated plans are being realized. Control requires a comparison of actual costs with the budgeted figures at regular and frequent intervals. If both the budget and the account classifications fully reflect the existing organization, the comparative data will be readily available from the accounts. A sample budget, or performance report, is shown in Schedule 23.1.

From this report, a manager can see how the department's performance compares with expectations. Comments or explanations of the differences between planned and actual costs can be included in the report before it is forwarded on to the next higher level of management. Heads of operating divisions will receive copies of the budget reports for each of the departments under their control; major executives will usually receive summaries of budget reports by operating divisions. Thus, every executive, from the department foreman to the president, will have the performance of the area under his or her control compared with the goals that were established previously. Unfavorable deviations will furnish a guide to the problems that merit management attention.

Flexible Budgets

The preceding discussion and budget report have been based on a *static* or *fixed* budget. A *static budget* projects expectations for the period based on a single level of sales and production. A *flexible,* or *variable, budget*

SCHEDULE 23.1 BUDGET REPORT

THE ABBOTT COMPANY
Budget Report
Month Ending April 30, 1975

Department J

	This Month			Year to Date		
	Budget	**Actual**	**Over or (Under)**	**Budget**	**Actual**	**Over or (Under)**
Physical Measures:						
Production, in units	16,000	15,240	(760)	59,800	58,420	(1,380)
Direct labor hours	9,600	9,725	125	35,880	36,200	320
Machine hours	28,800	28,640	(160)	107,640	106,100	(1,540)
Operating Costs:						
Direct material	$ 9,600	$ 9,640	$ 40	$ 35,700	$ 34,950	$ (750)
Direct labor	38,800	38,950	150	144,100	146,720	2,620
Power	1,400	1,380	(20)	5,200	5,110	(90)
Supplies	980	940	(40)	3,690	3,820	130
Maintenance	470	520	50	1,900	2,140	240
Other Costs	2,120	2,190	70	8,460	8,590	130
Total	$53,370	$53,620	$250	$199,050	$201,330	$2,280
Cost per unit:	$3.3356	$3.5184	$.1828	$3.3286	$3.4463	$.1177

Explanation and comment:

---

presents plans for several possible levels of activity. All costs, except fixed costs, have amounts budgeted for them that depend upon the varying levels of output. A different budget total is shown for each level of output. Usually budget columns are prepared for a relatively small number of output levels, and budget amounts for intermediate levels are calculated by interpolation or from the same formula used to construct the components of the flexible budget.

The preparation of a flexible budget is similar to the preparation of a static budget, except that figures must be developed for a range of output levels. It is thus more costly and time consuming. Costs, such as direct materials or direct labor, which vary directly (linearly) or almost directly with production present no problem. The same is, of course, true of costs that are entirely fixed; property taxes and building depreciation are examples of this type. Special attention must be given to costs that vary, but not proportionally, with changes in production. Detailed study of these items will be necessary for determining the cost function.

Semivariable costs can be classified into fixed-cost and variable-cost components, and then a formula for any level of output can be obtained. Multiplying the budgeted variable cost per unit by the number of units yields total budgeted variable cost. The budget for any level (L) of activity can then be shown as:

Budget at (L) level of activity = Budgeted fixed cost plus budgeted variable cost per unit times (L) units.

In preparing manufacturing-cost flexible budgets, attention is usually centered on overhead costs. Direct labor and direct material costs are likely to be entirely variable, and can usually be estimated more easily than overhead.

A condensed flexible manufacturing-cost budget for the Baltimore Manufacturing Company is shown in Schedule 23.2.

Budgets' Impact on People

Earlier we suggested that participation by employees in setting budgets is a good idea. The empirical research, done by psychologists and others, does not yield such unambiguous conclusions. Participation by employees in setting budgets can affect employee morale, but participation has been found to lead to increased output in some settings and decreased output in others.[2] Argyris found more than twenty years ago—and no research we know of since that time has overturned his findings—that supervisors distrust the whole budgetary process and that insofar as budgets are set on unrealistic standards, the budgets are ignored.[3] In cost centers or

SCHEDULE 23.2 BALTIMORE MANUFACTURING COMPANY

		Flexible Budget March, 1975		
	Variable Cost Per	Costs at Various Output Levels in Units		
Cost Element	Unit	900	1,000	1,100
Direct Materials	$ 4	$ 3,600	$ 4,000	$ 4,400
Direct Labor	9	8,100	9,000	9,900
Variable Overhead ..	4	3,600	4,000	4,400
Fixed Overhead	—	3,060	3,060	3,060
Total	$17	$18,360	$20,060	$21,760

[2] Selwyn Becker and David Green, Jr., "Budgeting and Employee Behavior," *Journal of Business*, 35 (October 1962), p. 401.

[3] Chris Argyris, *The Impact of Budgets on People* (New York: Controllership Foundation, 1952).

organizations where there is no good measure of output for the period, such as in service departments or nonprofit institutions, research results tend to show that components of budgets are merely projected at some constant rate from the previous period for all departments and that supervisors act to insure that all appropriated funds are spent so that budgets will not be cut for the next period.

In conclusion then, budgets are easy to prepare and use in an accounting sense, but as yet poorly understood devices for directing behavior.

COST-VOLUME-PROFIT RELATIONSHIPS

The flexible-budget procedure seeks to indicate the effect of changes in the volume of production on total operating costs. If information on selling prices and volume of sales is considered along with these cost data, the effect of changes in volume on income can be seen. In the sections that follow, the Baltimore Manufacturing Company illustration will be continued. In that illustration, it is assumed that there are no changes in inventories of finished goods or work in process; that is, units produced equals units sold. Under those circumstances, all manufacturing costs become expenses during the period. Since this is so and since much of the literature in the field traditionally is worded in terms of costs, our use of *costs* and *expenses* is synonymous in this illustration and its discussion. Assume that the selling price of the Baltimore Manufacturing Company's product is $30 per unit. Schedule 23.3 summarizes the information concerning manufacturing costs, presented previously, and additional data on selling as well as general and administrative costs. In this schedule and in the examples that follow, we assume that all costs can be divided into fixed and (linearly) variable elements. For many items of cost, this assumption is hard to justify but is usually a reasonable approximation.

Profit Charts

The revenue-cost graph, shown in Figure 23.1, presents the relationship of changes in volume to the amount of profit, or income. On such a graph,

SCHEDULE 23.3 BALTIMORE MANUFACTURING COMPANY

Cost Classification	Variable Cost (per unit)	Fixed Cost (per month)
Manufacturing costs:		
Direct material	$ 4	—
Direct labor	9	—
Overhead	4	$3,060
Total manufacturing costs	$17	$3,060
Selling, general, and administrative costs	5	1,740
Total costs	$22	$4,800

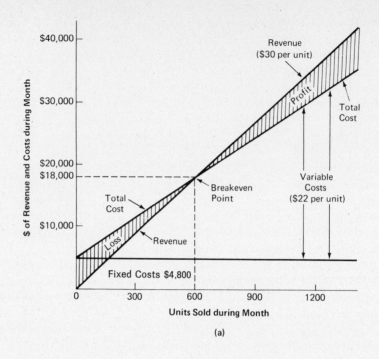

(a)

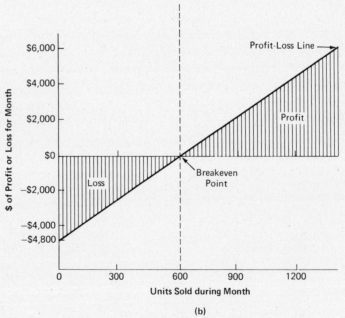

(b)

Figure 23.1 Cost-Volume-Profit Graphs for the Baltimore Manufacturing Company

total revenue and total costs for each volume level are indicated, and profit or loss at any volume can be read directly from the chart. The profit-volume graph, also shown in Figure 23.1 does not show revenues and costs but more readily indicates profit (or loss) at various output levels.

Two caveats should be kept in mind about these graphs. Although the curve depicting variable cost and total cost is shown as being a straight line for its entire length, it is likely that at very low or very high levels of output variable cost would probably be different from $22 per unit. The variable-cost figure was probably established by studies of operations at some broad central area of production. For very low (or very high) levels of activity, the chart may not be applicable. For this reason, the total cost and profit-loss curves are sometimes shown as dotted lines at lower volume levels. Second, this chart is vastly simplified by assuming a single-product firm. For a multi-product firm, the horizonal axis would have to be stated in dollars rather than in physical units of output. Profit charts for multi-product firms necessarily assume that constant proportions of the several products are sold and changes in this mixture as well as in costs or selling prices would invalidate the chart. Multi-product cost-volume-profit analyses are most conveniently done with linear programming.

Special attention is frequently focused on the *breakeven point*, the level of sales at which there is neither profit nor loss. In fact, the graphs are frequently called *breakeven charts*. In this illustration, it can be seen that the break-even point occurs at sales of 600 units or $18,000. The break-even point is frequently expressed as a percentage of capacity. If 1,200 units represent practical capacity, it can be seen that the Baltimore Manufacturing Company breaks even if it operates at 50 percent (600/1,200) of capacity.

The Contribution Concept

The relationship between volume changes and net income may be expressed arithmetically by using the contribution concept. This concept states that each unit sold makes a contribution towards fixed costs and the earning of income. The *contribution margin* is the excess of unit selling price over unit variable cost. In the Baltimore Manufacturing Company illustration, the contribution margin would be calculated as follows:

$$\text{Contribution margin (per unit)} = \text{Unit selling price} - \text{Unit variable costs}$$
$$= \$30 - \$22 = \$8$$

Income at any level of operations can be predicted by this formula:

$$\text{Income} = (\text{Contribution margin per unit} \times \text{Units sold}) - \text{Fixed costs}$$

In the illustration, income would be equal to $8 per unit times the number of units sold less the $4,800 of fixed costs. The breakeven point in units can always be calculated as follows:

$$\text{Breakeven Point in Units} = \frac{\text{Fixed Costs}}{\text{Contribution Margin (per Unit)}}$$

In the illustration the breakeven point in units is $4,800/$8 = 600 units.

Contribution may be expressed as a percentage of sales price or revenue as well as an amount per unit. In the illustration, the contribution percentage is $8/$30 or 26⅔ percent. In more general terms, the contribution percentage is calculated as follows:

$$\text{Contribution Percentage} = \frac{\text{Unit Selling Price} - \text{Unit Variable Cost}}{\text{Unit Selling Price}}$$

or

$$\text{Contribution Percentage} = \frac{\text{Total Revenue} - \text{Total Variable Cost}}{\text{Total Revenue}}$$

The breakeven point in revenues can always be calculated from

$$\text{Breakeven Point in Revenue} = \frac{\text{Fixed Costs}}{\text{Contribution Margin (per Unit)}} \times \text{Revenue per Unit}$$

$$= \frac{\text{Fixed Costs}}{\text{Contribution Percentage}}$$

In the illustration, the breakeven point in revenue is

$$\text{Breakeven Revenue} = \frac{\$4,800}{\$8} \times \$30 = 600 \times \$30 = \$18,000, \text{ or}$$

$$= \$4,800/26⅔\% = \$18,000.$$

INCREMENTAL COSTS AND DECISION MAKING

The distinction between fixed and variable costs is the core of the cost-volume-profit and contribution concepts. The same distinction is frequently of central importance for other business decisions. The fixed-variable cost distinction drawn previously was made in terms of costs which varied with changes in the overall volume of activity. Similarly, it is possible to classify costs into those that would be changed if a specific activity were added or discontinued and those that would be unaffected by such a change. The terms *incremental* or *differential* costs refer to the total costs that would be added (or removed) if a specific activity were started (or discontinued).

For example, the decision whether or not to abandon a seemingly unprofitable product (department or territory) of a firm having several products (departments or territories) hinges on this distinction. If the revenue produced by a department is greater than the incremental costs required to produce the revenue, the department contributes to profits even though it shows a loss when allocated its share of fixed or common costs. Many fixed or common costs, such as building depreciation, heat, power, and executive salaries, would not be affected by the abandonment of a single department. If a department more than covers its incremental costs and makes the most profitable use of the fixed facilities, the department should be retained.

Consider, for example, the data in Schedule 23.4 on these product lines for a single company.

SCHEDULE 23.4 DATA FOR ABANDONMENT DECISION

	Product R	Product S	Product T	Total
Sales	$10,000	$80,000	$50,000	$140,000
Less variable costs	8,500	51,000	31,500	91,000
Contribution margin	$ 1,500	$29,000	$18,500	$ 49,000
Less fixed costs (allocated) a ...	2,000	16,000	10,000	28,000
Income (loss)	($ 500)	$13,000	$ 8,500	$ 21,000

a Allocations of the $28,000 of fixed costs made in proportion to sales: 20 percent ($28,000/$140,000) of sales dollars charged to each product as fixed costs.

Product R shows a loss of $500 for the period and unsophisticated management might want to drop the product line. If R is dropped total profits will be $1,500 less, since the incremental revenues from R are $1,500 larger than the incremental costs. Still, the firm will want to investigate other uses for the resources used in producing R for it is clearly the weakest part of the line. Notice that if direct costing is used, rather than absorption costing, management will not get a signal that R is unprofitable. Under direct costing, no attempt to allocate fixed costs is made.

Acceptance of Special Orders

Sometimes, a firm has unused capacity and is confronted by an opportunity to sell a special order of goods at a price lower than average total cost. Should such an order be accepted? As the previous discussion suggests, if the price offered is greater than the incremental cost of producing the order, the firm would increase its income by accepting the order. Here again, the incremental or differential cost concept must be considered in its proper operating environment. In this case, the incremental cost would be the change in total costs associated with accepting this order.

In such cases, the effect of a special order on sales of the primary product must also be considered. To accept the lower price offer at the expense of losing equal sales at a higher unit price clearly would not be profitable. Only if the two markets are separate, or can be separated, is such an arrangement worthwhile. Similarly, there must be idle capacity so that the new order will be produced with facilities that would otherwise be idle. In general, correct short-run decisions result from undertaking projects where incremental revenues exceed incremental costs.

SPECIAL STUDIES

The cost analysis procedures considered in the previous section are important in many business decisions concerned with longer-run planning: decisions such as what size of plant to build, whether to replace equipment, whether facilities should be purchased or leased, and whether certain parts should be made in the plant or bought from outsiders. The cost data regularly accumulated for the continuing objective of income determination and cost control are not likely to be directly helpful for these special problems. The accounting aspects of these questions are, instead, usually considered in special costs studies. The tendency for recorded costs to become out of date and the need for including return on investment among the costs in planning for these projects are among the reasons for relying on special studies. Some of the problems associated with choosing projects are discussed in the next chapter.

Changing Prices and Accounting Data

Almost all accounting records are historical costs. As time passes, the historical cost of building and equipment—and the depreciation charges based on them—may no longer indicate the economic significance of these assets. If prices change relatively frequently, the same is true of the cost of materials. (Some of the efforts to deal with this problem in general terms are considered in Chapter 26.) In making plans for the future, it is not even present costs, much less those related to past, historical costs, that are needed; estimates of costs in the future must be made. In deciding whether operating savings of the next ten years will justify purchase of new equipment, the anticipated prices for that ten-year span should be used.

Interest on Investment

Customarily, interest is recorded in the accounts only when specific contractual arrangements call for interest payments. In long-range planning, interest or return on capital must be considered if proper decisions are to be reached. If a firm is considering buying new equipment for $10,000, it must recognize that the $10,000 will not be available for investment elsewhere. The interest or return foregone on alternative investment opportunities is an implicit cost of new equipment.

Determination of the precise interest or return rate to be used, whether it should be applied to the amount initially invested or the average investment over the life of the asset, and similar questions, are troublesome problems that must be settled in preparing the special studies. Such problems of *capital budgeting* are discussed in Chapter 24.

Special Studies and Accounting Data

The preceding paragraphs have considered the data drawn from outside the accounting records that must be considered in the special studies for long-run planning. Although much of the data needed for long-range planning do not come from accounting records, the cost accounting records provide the framework of cost elements to be considered and furnish much cost data that can be used without adjustment, as well as providing a starting point for the items that must be adjusted.

SUMMARY

Chapters 20, 21, and 22 considered the accumulation of costs by departments and the allocation to various jobs, processes, and products. This chapter outlines the use of cost data and related figures by management. Cost figures, standard cost variances, budgets, and performance reports are powerful tools for management in its efforts to plan and to control costs. The classification of costs into fixed and variable components and the presentation of this concept by means of profit graphs or contribution analysis serve in planning of operations, in decisions on product, department, or territorial abandonment, and in consideration of special offers. Cost records aid longer-range planning for investment decisions and similar problems.

QUESTIONS AND PROBLEMS

1. What effect could the following changes, occurring independently, have on the (1) breakeven point, (2) contribution margin, and (3) expected income?
   a. An increase in fixed costs
   b. A decrease in wage rates applicable to direct, strictly variable labor
   c. An increase in the selling price of the product
   d. An increase in production volume
   e. An increase in insurance rates.

2. Assume two years of constant production quantities and rising inventory quantities. In year two, fixed costs are substantially higher than in year one. Compare the difference between absorption and direct costing income in years one and two.

3. Under what circumstances would the shift from absorption costing to direct costing have little effect on the financial statements?

4. What is the underlying reason for the difference in net income under direct costing and absorption costing?

5. Who, among management personnel, is most likely to be able to control each of the following:
   a. raw materials used (quantity)
   b. electricity for machinery
   c. charge for floor space
   d. machinery depreciation
   e. unit price of materials
   f. insurance on machinery
   g. direct labor (quantity)

h. cost of annual overhead of machines (rate determined by management)

i. electricity used for lighting

j. actual wage cost

k. standard wage rate.

*6. An analysis of the operations of the Homes Company shows the fixed costs to be $100,000 and the variable costs to be $4 per unit. Selling price is $8 per unit.

    a. What is the breakeven point expressed in units?

    b. What is the breakeven point expressed in dollars of revenue?

    c. How many units would have to be sold to earn a profit of $140,000?

    d. What would income be if revenue from sales were $1,000,000?

7. An excerpt from the income statement of the Wooster and Valley Company is shown below.

DATA FOR PROBLEMS 7 AND 8

WOOSTER AND VALLEY COMPANY
Income Statement
Year Ended December 31, 1975

Sales		$2,000,000
Operating Expenses:		
Cost of Goods Sold	$950,000	
Selling Expenses	300,000	
Administrative Expenses	150,000	
Total Operating Expenses		1,400,000
Operating Income		$ 600,000

It was estimated that fixed costs in 1975 were $440,000.

    a. What percentage of sales revenue is variable cost?

    b. What is the breakeven point for Wooster and Valley Company?

    c. Prepare a profit-volume graph for Wooster and Valley Company.

8. Use the data of Problem 7.

    *a. If sales revenue falls to $1,800,000, what will be the amount of operating income?

    b. What volume of sales would be required to produce an operating income of $1,120,000?

9. The Dodd Manufacturing Company produces machinery of which part No. 301 is a subassembly. Part No. 301 is presently being produced by the Dodd Manufacturing Company in its own shops, but the West Products Company offers to supply it at a cost of $200 per five hundred units. An

---

* Hints, key numbers, or (partial) answers appear in the back of the book between the Appendix Tables and the Glossary.

analysis of the costs of producing part No. 301 by the Dodd Manufacturing Company reveals the following information:

	Cost per 500 Units
Direct Material	$ 65
Direct Labor	90
Variable Overhead	22
Fixed Overhead a	110
Total	$287

a Fixed overhead consists largely of depreciation on general purpose equipment and factory buildings.

a. Should the offer by the West Products Company be accepted, if the plant is operating well below capacity?
b. Should the offer be accepted if the price is reduced to $165 per five hundred?
c. If other profitable uses can be found for the facilities now used in turning out part No. 301, what is the maximum purchase price that should be accepted?

10. The operating data of the Snavely Company for April, 1975, are as follows:

	Fixed	**Variable**	**Total**
Sales			$2,200,000
Operating Expenses:			
Cost of Goods Sold	$550,000	$610,000	$1,160,000
Administrative Expenses	110,000	30,000	140,000
Selling Expenses	185,000	42,000	227,000
Total Expenses	$845,000	$682,000	$1,527,000
Operating Income			$ 673,000

There were 110,000 units sold in April, 1975.
a. What is the breakeven point in terms of units of product? In dollars of sales?
b. If sales can be increased to 200,000 units, what will operating income be?
c. At a revenue of $1,800,000, what will operating income be?

*11. The Exton Company is considering making a bid on a contract to supply the Defense Department with 500,000 gallons of chemicals. The capacity of their plant is 10,000,000 gallons a year, and they are currently producing at the rate of 8,500,000 gallons a year. The fixed costs of the plant aggregate $5,400,000 per year. The variable cost of chemicals of this type is approximately $2 per gallon. The sales manager says that a bid of no more than $1,200,000 would probably enable the company to get the contract.
a. Would such a bid be profitable? Explain.
b. If the present production is being sold at an average price of $3 per gallon and average variable costs equal $2 per gallon, present income statements as they would appear (1) if the government contract were

not obtained and (2) if the government contract were obtained at a bid of $1,200,000.

12. The Mark Machine Company manufactures heavy industrial machinery. Many of the parts which go into the machines can either be manufactured in the Mark Machine Company's plant or purchased from outside suppliers. The company regularly reconsiders its decisions to make or buy specific parts.

The standard direct labor cost in the plant is $5 per hour. Overhead is allocated on a direct-labor-hours basis at the rate of $3 per direct labor hour. At the level of operations used to set the overhead rate, overhead costs are 40 percent variable and 60 percent fixed. Manufacturing cost statements indicate that the standards have been adhered to closely in the recent past.

The company is presently considering whether or not to make the following parts, which they now purchase.

	Part No. 414	Part No. 416	Part No. 947
Raw Material Cost per Hundred Units	$15	$ 38	$21
Standard Direct Labor Time, per Hundred Units	5 hours	9 hours	5 hours
Suppliers Price per Hundred Units	$50	$113	$60

a. If the company has idle capacity, which of the parts should be manufactured in its own plant?

b. If the company is operating at capacity, which of the parts should be considered first for manufacture in its own plant?

13. The estimate of operating costs of the Tarmin Company for 1975 is that fixed costs will total $300,000 and that variable costs will be $2 per unit.

a. At a selling price of $3 per unit, at what level of revenue will the Tarmin Company break even?

b. At a selling price of $4 per unit, at what level of revenue will the Tarmin Company break even?

c. In order to earn $150,000 of net income, how many units will have to be sold at a price of $5 per unit?

*14. The Milky Way Company produces a precision part for use in rockets, missiles, and a variety of other purposes. In the first half of 1975, it operated at 80 percent of capacity and produced 160,000 units. Manufacturing costs in that period were as follows:

Raw material	$430,000
Direct labor	770,000
Variable overhead	150,000
Fixed overhead	450,000

The parts were all sold at a price of $14 per unit.

The AMF Aircraft Company offers to buy as many units of the part as the Milky Way Company can supply at a price of $10 per unit. It is estimated that to increase operations to a capacity level would increase office and administrative costs by $50,000 for a six-month period. Management feels that sales to AMF at this price will not affect their ability to reach the previous level of sales at the regular price.

   a. Would it be worthwhile to accept the AMF offer? Show your calculations.

   b. Would it be worthwhile to build an additional plant to increase sales to AMF? Why?

15. In 1975, the sales of the Woodward Company were $1,200,000, fixed costs were $400,000, and variable costs were $600,000.

   a. At what sales volume would the company break even?

   b. If sales volume increased by 15 percent but prices are unchanged, by how much will income increase? By what percentage?

   c. If fixed costs were reduced by 10 percent, by how much would income increase? By what percentage?

   d. If variable costs were reduced by 10 percent, by how much would income increase? By what percentage?

   e. If the changes of (b), (c), and (d) all occur, by how much will income increase? By what percentage?

16. The Norwood Printing Company operates a medium-sized printing shop. On May, 1975, it received an inquiry from a prospective customer about its prices for furnishing an advertising booklet in quantities of 2,000 copies, 8,000 copies, and 15,000 copies. After analyzing the job, the estimating staff furnished the following estimates of cost:

Set up costs for job	$500
Material cost per 100 booklets	50
Direct labor cost per 100 booklets	45

In the company's cost accounting records, overhead and administrative costs are allocated to jobs on a direct-labor-cost basis, at a rate of 80 percent of direct labor costs. This rate was set assuming operations at 100 percent of capacity; capacity operations require about $200,000 of direct labor costs. That is, it was estimated that *total* overhead and administrative costs would be $160,000 when total direct labor costs were $200,000. *Variable* overhead and administrative costs vary proportionally with direct labor costs, and are equal to 60 percent of direct labor costs at all levels of output.

The company seeks to make a profit of 10 percent of the bid price on each order. During 1975 the printing shop was operating at about 75 percent of capacity.

   a. Assuming that the bid was to be based on average total cost and a 10-percent profit margin, what price should be quoted for each quantity?

   b. By how much would income of the firm increase if the price quoted in part (a) for 8,000 copies were accepted? What percent of selling price would this represent?

   c. Repeat part (b) for 15,000 copies.

   d. What is the minimum bid that could be accepted for 2,000 copies without decreasing net income? For 8,000 copies? (Show computations for all parts of the question.)

 *17. The Monmouth Company is preparing its budget for the year of 1975. If the same selling policies that were in effect in 1974 are continued in 1975, the budget officer estimates that the income statement will appear as shown below.

All variable expenses vary with the number of units sold. The company could increase its output to 1 million units per year without increasing its fixed manufacturing and administrative costs. In order to increase its income, the company is seeking to utilize the presently unused capacity. Two plans have been suggested to improve the profit picture.

Plan A. It is estimated that unit sales could be increased by 25 percent, if (a) selling price per unit is reduced by 5 percent, and (b) an additional advertising campaign is instituted which would increase fixed selling expenses by $15,000.

Plan B. The company has an opportunity to obtain a government contract for an additional 200,000 units, if it quotes a low enough price. If the government contract were obtained it would have no effect on the regular sales of 800,000 units.

a. Assuming *Plan A* were adopted and it works out as anticipated, present the income statement for 1975.

b. If it is anticipated that *Plan A* will work out as planned, what is the lowest price the company should bid on the government contract? (Show your computations.)

c. If it is decided that *Plan A* is not feasible, what is the lowest price the company should bid on the government contract? (Show your computations.)

PROBLEM 17

THE MONMOUTH COMPANY
Projected Income Statement
Year of 1975

Sales (800,000 units at $2 per unit)			$1,600,000
Operating Expenses:			
Cost of Goods Sold:			
Variable	$600,000		
Fixed	300,000		
Total Cost of Goods Sold		$900,000	
Administrative Expenses:			
Variable	$ 20,000		
Fixed	100,000		
Total Administrative Expenses		120,000	
Selling Expenses:			
Variable	$ 30,000		
Fixed	120,000		
Total Selling Expenses		150,000	
Total Operating Expenses			1,170,000
Operating Income			$ 430,000

18. The Norwood Corporation has patented a new household product and is now marketing it actively. Its income statement for the first quarter of 1975 is shown below.

The $7 per unit manufacturing cost is presently made up of material cost, $2; direct labor cost, $4; and overhead costs, $1. The productive capacity of the present plant, working one eight-hour shift per day, is 50,000 units per quarter. The sales manager is certain that additional units could be sold if they were available. Top management is reluctant to increase the size of the plant and, instead, decides to consider the advisability of adding a second, and perhaps a third, shift.

The production manager estimates that each additional shift would increase output by 50,000 units per quarter. He also estimates that if a second shift were added, labor costs per unit on the output of that shift would be 10 percent higher and total overhead cost would be increased 25 percent. If a third shift were added, labor cost per unit for the output of that shift would be 25 percent higher than for one-shift operations and total overhead would be 75 percent higher than for one-shift operations. With three-shift operations, it is estimated that material costs of all units could be reduced 4 percent due to larger quantity purchases.

The sales manager estimates that 100,000 units a quarter could be sold at the current price, but that to sell 150,000 units a quarter unit price would have to be reduced by 5 percent. He estimates that selling expenses for 100,000 units will be 50 percent higher and for 150,000 units 90 percent higher than for 50,000 units. Administrative costs are expected to increase by 20 percent and by 40 percent from the 50,000 unit figure for sales of 100,000 units and 150,000 units, respectively.

Prepare projected second-quarter income statements assuming:
a. two-shift operation
b. three-shift operation.

*19. The Able Bakery now purchases frozen pre-cut cookie dough at a cost of $.03 per cookie. Management is considering purchasing either an automatic

PROBLEM 18

THE NORWOOD CORPORATION
Income Statement
January 1 to March 31, 1975

Sales (50,000 units at $10 per unit)		$500,000
Operating Expenses:		
Cost of Goods Sold ($7 per unit)	$350,000	
Selling Expenses	45,000	
Administrative Expenses	30,000	
Total Expenses		425,000
Operating Income		$ 75,000

or semi-automatic cookie cutter. If the automatic machine is purchased, the annual fixed costs will be $8,000. In addition, there will be a $.010 variable cost per cookie cut. Use of the semi-automatic machine will lead to $4,500 in fixed costs per year, plus $.015 of variable costs per cookie cut.

a. At what volume of operations will the total annual costs incurred by using the semi-automatic machine equal outside purchase costs?

b. At what volume of operations will the total annual costs incurred by using the automatic machine equal outside purchase costs?

c. Which of the three alternatives is least costly if annual production volume is 600,000 cookies?

d. Which of the three alternatives is least costly if annual production volume is 800,000 cookies?

e. At which level of production volume are the costs incurred by using the two machines equal?

20. The management of the Glide-Rite Company, which manufactures no-stick spray starch, plans to increase sales by cutting the sales price in 1976. You are given the following data for 1975 and estimates for 1976:

	500,000 Cans (1975 Sales)	750,000 Cans (Projected 1976 Sales)
Sales Price per Can	$.890	$.790
Cost per Can	.675	.600

Compute the incremental cost, the incremental revenue, and the incremental profit if the price cut takes place.

21. The Brunson Grain Company has four large milling machines of approximately equal capacity. Each was run at close to its full capacity during 1975. Each machine is depreciated separately using an accelerated method. Data for each machine are:

	No. 1	No. 2	No. 3	No. 4
Date Acquired	1/1/69	1/1/70	1/1/73	1/1/74
Cost	$50,000	$60,000	$75,000	$80,000
Operating Costs: 1975				
Labor	$20,000	$18,000	$22,000	$21,500
Maintenance	5,000	6,000	4,500	3,000
Repairs	1,000	1,000	700	550
Depreciation	3,363	5,454	10,910	13,091
Total	$29,363	$30,454	$38,110	$38,141

Activity in 1976 is expected to be less than in 1975 so that one machine is to be dropped from service. It has been proposed that No. 4 should be that machine on the grounds that it has the highest operating cost. Do you agree with this proposal? Why or why not?

22. The Brozen Manufacturing Company maintains a fleet of 300 automobiles for use by its employees. It has determined that buying the cars is cheaper than leasing them. The automobiles cost $5,000 each and are depreciated using the double-declining-balance method over three years. Various cost data are given in the schedule below. Cars are driven about 10,000 miles a year. At the beginning of the fifth year, the cars can be sold for

$1,575. The Brozen Manufacturing Company had to choose a replacement policy: Should it sell cars and buy new ones every year, every two years, every three years, or every four years? It carried out the analysis and chose the policy that implied the lowest annual cash outlay per year. The age-structure of the fleet is constant. That is, under a two-year replacement policy, 150 cars would be sold and replaced every year, under a three-year replacement policy 100 cars would be sold and replaced every year, or under a four-year policy, 75 cars would be sold and replaced every year. All gains realized on sale of used cars are taxed at 40 percent as is all other income. There is sufficient other income that all depreciation and operating expenses reduce taxable income for the year of the expense.

PROBLEM 22: ASSUMED COST DATA FOR EACH YEAR OF LIFE

	Year			
	1	**2**	**3**	**4**
Market Value at Beginning of Year	$5,000	$3,750	$2,800	$2,100
Depreciation Expense for Year	$3,333	$1,111	$ 556	—
Gas and Oil Costs	2,000	2,200	2,400	$2,600
Maintenance Costs	75	75	75	75
Repair Costs	25	100	200	300
Tire Costs	0	100	150	175
Insurance	160	140	110	80
	$5,593	$3,726	$3,491	$3,230

a. What is the replacement policy that leads to lowest annual costs, taking taxes and the time value of money into account?

b. Why do you not need to know Brozen's discount rate for a present value calculation to answer the question above?

°23. The Eastern States Railroad (ESRR) has four locomotives, each of approximately equal capability. Each was run full time during 1975. Each locomotive is depreciated separately using an accelerated method. Data for each locomotive are as follows:

	A	**B**	**C**	**D**
Year Acquired	1969	1973	1974	1975
Operating Costs, 1975:				
Labor	$15,500	$15,800	$15,900	$15,900
Maintenance and Repairs	5,000	3,500	3,500	4,200
Depreciation	13,250	15,750	15,000	20,500
Total	$33,750	$35,050	$34,400	$40,600

Locomotive A originally cost $220,000; Locomotives D and C were purchased for $240,000 each; and Locomotive B cost $250,000.

Rail traffic is expected to decrease in 1976 so that one locomotive will be put on a standby basis. The vice-president in charge of operations has suggested that Locomotive D be put on standby because it has highest operating costs. Do you agree? If not, which one should be put on standby and why?

24. The Jamie Company bought a machine ten years ago for $42,000 and has been depreciating it on a straight-line basis. The book value of the machine is $12,000, and it can be sold today for $7,000. The Jamie Company must decide whether to keep the machine, whether to sell it and purchase a new machine, or whether to trade it in on a new machine. The income tax rate paid by the Jamie Company is 40 percent.

   If the Jamie Company sells the machine today, the loss on disposal can be used to offset other income.

   a. What is the relevant opportunity cost of keeping the machine rather than selling it?

   b. Suppose that the new machine can be bought for $50,000 cash or for $40,000 cash and the old machine (traded-in). What is the opportunity cost of the new machine?

25. The Horwell Company is considering accepting an order for a product not in its present product line. The machinery and labor needed to fill the order are available, but there is some question of incremental materials and labor costs. The data available to management are summarized below.

   (1) The order requires 5,000 units of Halcyon. Although Halcyon is not used in Horwell's regular manufacturing processes, some 20,000 units are presently on hand. These units were acquired for $100,000 as part of a special purchase. Replacement costs would amount to $220,000, but the best offer Horwell has received for the 20,000 units of Halcyon is $80,000.

   (2) The order requires 7,000 units of Miserly. Because Horwell uses Miserly regularly, there is a large inventory on hand. Although the average price per unit of Miserly in inventory is $3, the price has recently risen to $3.80. If 7,000 units are used to fill a special order the purchasing department will have to reorder two months earlier than planned, incurring an expected cost per unit of $2.90. The drop in price is due to seasonal factors, which should drive the price of Miserly down to $2.50 about six weeks or two months after the price falls to $2.90.

   (3) One thousand units of Sludge, a by-product of a present Horwell manufacturing process, are needed. Generally it costs Horwell $.02 per unit to dispose of Sludge.

   (4) The order will require fifteen hours of supervisory time at $12 per hour. At present, the ten workers who would be involved in filling the order are working thirty-seven hours per week at $6 and being paid $4 per hour stand-by wages for three hours per week. The order should require ninety hours of worker time and must be filled within two weeks. Overtime rates are 150 percent of the regular wage rate.

   a. What is the relevant cost of (1) Halcyon, (2) Miserly, and (3) Sludge required for the special order? Why?

   b. What is the relevant labor cost? Why?

°26. The salesmen of the Piney Paper Company have secured two orders, either of which, in addition to regular orders, will keep the plant operating at capacity through the slack season. One order is for 200,000 printed place-mats and the other is for 300,000 sheets of engraved office stationery. The proposed prices are $.0070 per mat for the placemats and $.0062 per sheet for the stationery. Cost estimates are as follows:

	Mats Cost per 100 Mats	Stationery Cost per 100 Sheets
Labor: variable costs..............	$.1100	$.0993
Labor: fixed costs................	.0300	.0089
Manufacturing overhead:		
Variable	.0430	.0330
Fixed	.0370	.0523
Raw materials	.3550	.2775
Selling expense		
(to procure order)	.0900	.0912
Administrative expense		
(to procure order)	.0950	.0878
Total cost per 100 items	$.7600	$.6500
Selling price per 100 items	$.7000	$.6200

Based on the above data, what decision should the management of Piney Paper Company make? Why?

°27. (This problem and the next three are adapted from problems by David O. Green.) Reporting on Chrysler Corporation's performance for 1969, the *Wall Street Journal* pointed out that Chrysler had boosted its market share from 10 percent in 1962 to 18 percent in 1968. In 1969, however, counter-measures by Ford and General Motors coupled with a 10-percent decline, or 1 million cars, in industry sales created problems for Chrysler. Chrysler cut prices and increased advertising so that the contribution per car was $100 less in 1969 than in 1968. Fixed costs were reduced 20 percent in 1969 from what they had been in 1968. Nevertheless, Chrysler's 1969 profits were only $80 million on sales of 1.4 million autos whereas 1968 profits had been $300 million. From this information calculate industry sales (in autos) for 1968 and 1969, Chrysler's total fixed costs for 1968 and 1969, and Chrysler's contribution per car in 1968 and 1969.

28. During 1963 Studebaker sold 90,000 cars for $250 million and realized a loss for the year of $24 million. The breakeven point was 120,000 cars. For 1963 calculate the contribution per car, total fixed costs, and earnings for 1963 had sales been twice as large.

29. When Britain's auto business slumped in 1921, William R. Morris (the "Henry Ford of Britain") gambled on cost saving from his new assembly lines and cut prices to a point where his expected loss per car in 1922 would be $240 if sales were the same as in 1921, 1,500 cars. However, sales in 1922 rose to 60,000 cars and profits for the year were $810,000. For 1922 calculate the contribution per car, total fixed costs, and break-even point in cars.

30. In 1967, reported *Time* magazine, the future of the American Motor Company seemed so shaky that its creditors, a consortium of banks headed by Chase Manhattan, examined the books every ten days. The new man-

agement trimmed fixed costs by $20 million to cut the breakeven point from 350,000 cars in 1967 to 250,000 cars in 1968.

From this information calculate the contribution per car (assumed constant for 1967 and 1968), fixed costs for 1967 and 1968, 1967 losses assuming sales of 300,000 cars, and 1968 profits assuming sales of 400,000 cars.

31. Some indirect variable costs in the Sand Casting Department of the Rhino Heavy Duty Machinery Company are budgeted as follows:

	Standard Cost per Direct Labor Hour	Flexible Budget Based upon 70,000 Direct Labor Hours Worked
Repairs to machinery	$.80	$56,000
Rework of marred castings	.60	42,000
Sand sweeping	.50	35,000

During October, 1975, actual costs incurred included $58,000 for repairs, $40,000 for reworking, and $34,000 for sweeping. At standard, 66,000 direct labor hours should have been allowed for the finished output of the Sand Casting Department.

a. Given the information in the budget, what are the apparent variances for October's production? Why is this information possibly misleading?

b. How can the budget be improved?

c. Compute a variance for repairs, reworking, and sweeping using the improved budget.

'32. The Cord Department of the Flat Iron Company produces cords for steam irons. Because of machine breakdowns and worker absenteeism, this department encounters some fluctuations in activity levels from month to month. The following table presents cost estimates of obtainable efficiency, given a normal level of activity of 100,000 units of production per month:

	Budgeted Cost at "Normal" Production of 100,000 Units
Direct Labor	$ 90,000
Raw Materials	60,000
Power Used in Machinery	7,500
Repairs to Machinery	2,500
Other Variable Overhead	5,000
Depreciation on Machinery	10,000
Insurance	2,000
Other Fixed Overhead	13,000
	$190,000

a. Prepare a flexible budget that shows expected costs for production of 90,000 units, 95,000 units, and 105,000 units.

b. Derive a formula to express the budget for various levels of activity.

c. Sketch a graph showing how budgeted costs change in the production range between 90,000 units and 105,000 units.

33. The following data pertain to operations in 1975 and 1977:

	1975	1977
Opening Inventory in Units	6,000	0
Units Produced	48,000	50,000
Units Sold	50,000	48,000
Fixed Overhead Production Costs	$12,000	$12,000
Variable Overhead Production Costs	14,000	12,000
Fixed Administrative Costs	10,000	10,000
Direct Labor	40,000	36,000
Direct Materials	50,000	48,000

There are no work in process inventories or variances and a FIFO inventory flow assumption is used.

a. Compute the dollar value of ending finished-goods inventory in 1975 under direct and absorption costing.

b. Compute the dollar value of ending finished-goods inventory in 1977 under direct and absorption costing.

c. Which method implies higher reported income in 1975? In 1977?

34. The plant of the Merridew Company, manufacturers of table lamps, has a maximum capacity of 35,000 units per month. The normal operating level is 25,000 units per month. The following data are available:

Sales Price per Unit	$ 35
Standard Unit Labor Cost	10
Standard Unit Materials Cost	7
Standard Unit Variable Overhead	3
Variable Selling Costs per Unit Sold	5
Fixed Factory Overhead per Year	180,000
Fixed Selling Costs per Year	96,000

In October, 1975, sales were 22,000 units. Production was 24,000 units and the beginning inventory was 2,000 units. The only variance was a $1,000 unfavorable variance in the variable overhead account. This variance is to be included in the cost of goods sold account, as is any under- or over-applied overhead.

a. Prepare income statements for October, 1975, under direct and absorption costing.

b. Explain the source of the difference in net income as computed under the two methods.

35. The following data relate to the cost and revenue structure of AC/DC Company.

Budgeted costs:		
Variable costs (per unit):	Material	$ .90
	Labor	1.20
	Overhead	.90
	Total	$3.00

Fixed costs:
Estimated per period: $15,000
Capacity level for costing: 15,000 units
Fixed cost charged per unit of production 1.00

Total standard cost per unit $4.00

Assume the following data with respect to sales and production levels (units):

Period	Sales	Production
1	15,000	15,000
2	15,000	16,000
3	15,000	14,000
4	14,000	14,000
5	14,000	15,000
6	14,000	16,000
7	16,000	16,000
8	16,000	15,000
9	16,000	14,000

Sales are effected at a selling price of $6.00 per unit.

a. Calculate for each period the following, assuming an absorption costing method is adopted and the standard costs indicated above: Sales; Cost of Goods Sold; Gross Margin; Over- or Under-Absorbed Overhead; Contribution to Profit.

b. Calculate for each period the following under the assumption that a direct costing method is adopted and the standard costs indicated above: Sales; Cost of Goods Sold; Contribution Margin; Fixed Costs; Contribution to Profit.

c. How does the relationship among capacity, sales, and production affect net income for the period, when absorption costing is used? When direct costing is used?

Chapter 24

Capital Budgeting: The Investment Decision

Management must often decide whether to add a product to the line, whether to buy a new piece of machinery, or in general, whether to make investments of capital today in return for benefits that will accrue later. Chapter 23 discusses decision making when there is excess capacity. These decisions are based on incremental analysis of cash expenditures and receipts. This chapter discusses the theory and the mechanism for making investment decisions when outlays are required for new capacity. The tools and concepts needed for making the capital investment decision are, by now, familiar: the compound interest techniques treated in Chapter 13, the depreciation techniques treated in Chapter 14, the distinction between funds flows and income treated in Chapter 19, and the accumulation of cost data treated in the preceding four chapters.

No decisions are more important for the success of the firm than deciding which investment projects to undertake. For instance, should AT&T keep its basic commercial model telephone and make only minor improvements, such as push-button dialing? Or should it make major research and development expenditures to mass produce picture telephones? The proper mode of analyzing investment decisions is one of the most controversial topics in accounting. In addition to presenting what we and other theorists consider to be the preferred method for making the investment decision, we discuss some alternative methods used and their shortcomings.

INDEPENDENCE OF INVESTMENT AND
FINANCING DECISIONS

A firm faced with the choice of adding a new product line or buying plant assets must decide both whether to undertake the new project and how to raise the capital required by the new activity. Once a project has been accepted by the firm, the necessary funds can be raised in several different ways or in a combination of ways. Funds can be raised through borrowing, by retaining earnings in the firm, or from issuing capital stock.

One of the most significant contributions to the theory of finance in recent years is the discovery that an investment decision should be made independently of the financing decision. That is, the investment decision should be made first, and only after a project gets the go-ahead, should management begin to consider how to finance it. Recall the discussion of appropriated retained earnings in Chapter 17; there we argue that unless all capital in the firm is earmarked with its use within the firm, then none should be. All of the assets of the firm are financed by all of its capital. The same logic underlies the conclusion that the investment decision is independent of the financing decision for new undertakings. A new project will involve investing capital, but once the project is added to the firm's portfolio of activities, it too is financed by all of the firm's capital.

Raising capital and managing cash are important problems, but they need not concern us here. Financing decisions and cash management are properly dealt with in finance courses. This chapter discusses the investment decision.

CASH FLOWS VERSUS INCOME FLOWS

Rational investment decisions require analysis of cash or fund flows, not income flows. To illustrate why, and to introduce the investment decision, a typical project is examined next. Consider the decision facing the Garden Winery Company, which is contemplating acquiring a machine that will allow it to bring to market a new variety of wine. The machine costs $10,000 and is expected to last four years. Schedule 24.1 shows information about the new machine, the cash outlays (required for labor, grapes, and bottles), as well as the revenues expected from the sales of the new variety of wine. The decreasing pattern of revenues over the four years of the machine results in part from the machine's becoming less productive over time and in part by the expected reaction of other wine sellers, who will copy the new wine variety and force down the selling price in the market. For simplicity, assume that Garden Winery Company uses straight-line depreciation, that the machine has no scrap value, and that income taxes are payable at the rate of 40 percent of taxable income.

At the end of year zero, that is to say, at the start of the project, the machine is purchased for $10,000, as shown in column (9). In each of the next four years, revenues are received as shown in column (2), and current cash outlays for materials (grapes, bottles, and so on) and labor are incurred as shown in column (3). Inflows of funds or cash, as forecast, are shown in column (4). Depreciation charges of $2,500 per year are shown in column (5) and pre-tax income [columns (2) — (3) — (5)] is shown in column (6). Income taxes, shown in column (7), are 40 percent of pre-tax income. Net income [= (6) — (7)] is shown in column (8). Column (9) shows the cash or funds flows for each of the years and can be derived from either of two computations:

1. cash inflows, (2), less cash outflows [= (3) + (7)]
2. net income, (8), plus expenses (depreciation) not using cash, (5).

Note that the only effective use of the depreciation amounts is in the computation of the income taxes payable for a year.

The sum-of-the-years' net income, $3,300, from the project exactly equals the sum-of-the-years' net cash flows. Only the timing of numbers in the two series differs. The accounting income figures shown in column (8) for the project being considered by Garden Winery Company implicitly assume that the capital asset being purchased requires $2,500 each year while, in fact, it requires a cash outlay of $10,000 at the beginning of the first year. Making investment decisions on the basis of accounting income figures, such as those in column (8), ignores the time value of money. The cash flows shown in column (9) accurately depict the time dimension of the economic costs and benefits to the firm. (One of the alternative methods for evaluating investment decisions, the accounting rate of return, is based upon net income figures, such as those shown in column (8) and is discussed later in the chapter. By the time we treat that method, the reader should be better able to understand its shortcomings.)

Once the data on projected cash flows for a project have been compiled (not necessarily an easy task), the capital budgeting problem is to evaluate those data and to decide whether or not to undertake the project.

SCHEDULE 24.1 GARDEN WINERY COMPANY

Revenues, Expenses, Income and Cash Flows from New Wine Project

End of Year (1)	Revenues (2)	Other Cash Outlays (3)	Pre-Tax Cash Flows (4)	Depreciation Charge (5)	Pre-Tax Income (6)	Income Tax (7)	Net Income (8)	Net Cash Flows (9)
0	—	—	—	—	—	—	—	($10,000)
1	$ 6,000	$1,000	$ 5,000	$ 2,500	$2,500	$1,000	$1,500	4,000
2	5,000	1,000	4,000	2,500	1,500	600	900	3,400
3	4,500	1,000	3,500	2,500	1,000	400	600	3,100
4	4,000	1,000	3,000	2,500	500	200	300	2,800
	$19,500	$4,000	$15,500	$10,000	$5,500	$2,200	$3,300	$ 3,300

(2), (3): Given
(4) = (2) — (3)
(5) = $10,000/4

(6) = (4) — (5)
(7) = .40 × (6)
(8) = (6) — (7)

(9) = (4) — (7)
    = (8) + (5)

The Net Present Value Graph

Given the cash flow data for a project, a convenient way to assess the desirability of a project is to construct a Net Present Value Graph, such as the one shown in Figure 24.1 for the Garden Winery Company project. The horizontal axis shows the discount rate, and the vertical axis shows the net present value of the cash flows computed for each discount rate. The *net present value* of a series of cash flows is the sum of the discounted present values of each individual cash flow.[1] For example, if the discount rate is zero, then the net present value of the project is the sum of the net cash flows, or $3,300. Thus, the net present value curve shown in Figure 24.1 intersects the vertical axis at $3,300. To see how the net present value curve is constructed for positive discount rates, consider a discount rate of 10 percent per year and the calculations in Schedule 24.2.

For each cash flow, for example the $3,400 that flows in at the end of the second year, the present value (at the start of year 1) of that flow is computed ($3,400 $\times$ .82645 = $2,810) from the present value of $1

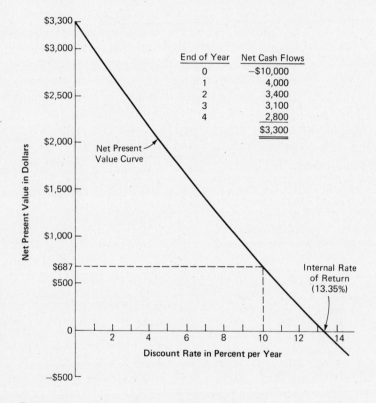

Figure 24.1 Garden Winery Company—Net Present Value Graph

---

[1] In Chapter 13, nearly all cash flows series considered are annuities in which the payment each year, except perhaps in the first or last year, is the same as the payment in all other years. The numbers shown in Appendix Table 4 are *net present values* of annuities.

SCHEDULE 24.2 GARDEN WINERY COMPANY PROJECT EVALUATION

End of Year	Net Cash Flows	Present Value Discounted at 10 Percent of $1	of Cash Flows from Project
0	($10,000)	× 1.00000 =	($10,000)
1	4,000	× .90909 =	3,636
2	3,400	× .82645 =	2,810
3	3,100	× .75131 =	2,329
4	2,800	× .68301 =	1,912
Totals	$ 3,300		$ 687

numbers shown in Appendix Table 2. The present value of the initial outlay is, of course, −$10,000. The present values of each of the years' cash flows are computed and the sum of those numbers is found. That sum, $687, is the net present value of the cash flows from the project when the discount rate is 10 percent per year. For any other discount rate, a net present value is similarly computed and a point on the curve can be plotted. (The net present value curve shown in Figure 24.1 was drawn through the net present value amounts calculated on a computer for discounts rates $r = 0, 1, 2, \ldots, 15$ percent. It is *not* a straight line.)

The discount rate, 13.35 percent in the example, where the net present value curve crosses the horizontal axis is called the *internal rate of return*. The internal rate of return of a series of payments is the discount rate that equates the net present value of those payments to zero. One of the alternative methods for evaluating investment projects, discussed below, is based upon the internal rate of return.

The net present value graph shows, then, for various discount rates, the net present value of the cash flows from a project. The investment decision rule can now be simply stated: if, for the appropriate discount rate, the net present value of the cash flows from a project is positive, then that project should be undertaken. That rule is simple enough once "the appropriate discount rate" is selected. Determining that discount rate is discussed next.

THE COST OF CAPITAL

The appropriate discount rate to use in evaluating investment projects is the firm's *cost of capital*. The cost of capital is easy to define but, in practice, is difficult to measure. Several definitions of the cost of capital are given below. These definitions do not necessarily appear to be saying the same thing, but the modern theory of finance can demonstrate their equivalence. The *cost of capital* can be defined by any of the following:

1. the average rate that the firm must pay for funds invested in the firm
2. the average rate the firm would earn if it repurchased its own securities

and paid off its liabilities in the proportions those equities are out-standing
3. the rate of return for new investment projects such that, if all projects undertaken by the firm yield that rate, then the market value of the firm's stock will remain unchanged
4. the stock market's expectation of the rate of return on investment in the company's common stock.

The easiest of these definitions to consider is the first. The equities side of the balance sheet (liabilities and stockholders' equity) shows the sources of capital to the firm. Each of the components of capital provided to the firm has a price. Current liabilities, such as accounts payable, provide capital to the firm at no explicit cost. Notes and bonds payable have an explicit, or contractual, interest cost. Preferred stock usually carries a specified dividend rate which, for these purposes, may be considered to be its cost. Whereas the after-tax cost to the firm for interest on notes and bonds is less than the quoted interest rate, the effective price to the firm for preferred stock is the actual dividend rate, since preferred stock dividends are not expenses but earnings distributions. The price for capital in the form of common stockholders' equity (common stock, additional paid-in capital, and retained earnings) is the rate of discount that equates the present value of the total dividend stream the market expects the firm to distribute over its life to the current market price of the firm's stock. The rate of return on the common stock accounts is, of course, the hardest to compute in practice.

Another way to think of the cost of capital is to ask, "What can the firm do with new funds without changing the basic nature of the firm?" The firm can purchase marketable securities or additional inventories and can retire some of its debt. The earnings rate from the average investment (with risk and return equal to that from the average project in the firm), regardless of the actual financing method, is the cost of capital.

A firm should undertake an investment project if the net present value of the cash flows is positive when the cash flows are discounted at the cost of capital.

Sensitivity of Profits to Estimates

Among the alternatives for evaluating investment projects, there are essentially two kinds: those that take into account the time value of money and those that do not. Those that do are the preferred alternatives, and they all require an estimate of the cost of capital or, as it is called in other contexts, the "cutoff" or "minimum acceptable" rate of return. Estimated rates of 10 to 15 percent, after taxes, are commonly used. The subtleties of computing the cost of capital rate are properly the subject of finance courses. Here, the emphasis is on using that rate.

When the net present value of a project is computed by using an estimate of the cost of capital, the signal will usually be unequivocal: the new project clearly is or is not worthwhile. Only when the net present value is close to zero, would there be concern about the accuracy of the estimate of the cost of capital being used. But when the net present value is nearly zero, then the firm is nearly indifferent to accepting or rejecting the project. Consequently, the firm will make "nearly correct" decisions by using approximations to the cost of capital. The firm's loss from errors caused by an incorrect estimate of the cost of capital is relatively small and almost surely will be smaller than the cost of errors made in estimating cash flows.

The decision rule for evaluating investment projects is to accept a project that has a positive net present value when its cash flows are discounted at the cost of capital and to reject it otherwise. In the Garden Winery Company example, the net present value of the cash flows is positive for all discount rates less than 13.35 percent. Consequently, if management felt that its cost of capital was about 10 percent, then the project is worthwhile. At a cost of capital of 10 percent, the net present value of flows from the project is $687. The net present value of $687 is not to be interpreted as the amount of return on investment in the project but the *excess amount* over what the firm normally expects to earn on its investment. If the cost of capital for Garden Winery Company is less than 13.35 percent, the stockholders will be better off if the project is accepted than if it is rejected.

What loss does the firm suffer if it incorrectly calculates its cost of capital? Suppose Garden Winery's cost of capital is 15 percent, while management acts as though it is 10 percent. Management miscalculates the cost of capital by 50 percent $[= (.15 - .10)/.10]$. That large error still has a small effect on the firm. Management believes the firm will be $687 better off by accepting the project. When the project is accepted and the cost of capital is 15 percent, the firm will actually be $312 worse off, because the net present value at 15 percent is —$312. The total error in present-value dollars is $999 (= $687 + $312), which is about 10 percent of the initial investment, $10,000. Thus a 50-percent error in the calculation of the cost of capital used to make the decision implies only a 10 percent error in terms of the amount of the initial investment. In general, if a project is marginally profitable for a given cost of capital, it will ordinarily not be grossly unprofitable for slightly higher rates. Conversely, projects that are clearly worthwhile when the cost of capital is 10 percent are likely to be worthwhile when the cost of capital is 15 percent.

INCOME TAX CONSIDERATIONS

Income taxes are a major expense of doing business. Income tax regulations affect both the *amounts* of cash flows and the *timing* of cash flows, and, consequently, must be considered in making investment decisions. The most obvious effect of tax laws on investment decisions arises from the accelerated depreciation charges that the tax laws permit. Accelerating depreciation charges on the tax returns shifts taxable income to later years from earlier years. Although it does not change the total tax liability generated by a project, it does influence the profitability, measured in present-value terms, of a project because of timing differences.

Suppose, for example, that the Garden Winery Company decides to use the double-declining-balance method to depreciate the machine required by the new wine variety. Then the net cash flows for the project would be as shown in Schedule 24.3.

SCHEDULE 24.3 GARDEN WINERY COMPANY
(Double-Declining-Balance Depreciation)

End of Year	Revenues Less Cash Expenses	Depreciation Charge	Pre-Tax Income	Income Tax	Net Cash Flows
0	—	—	—	—	($10,000)
1	$ 5,000	$ 5,000	$ 0	$ 0	5,000
2	4,000	2,500	1,500	600	3,400
3	3,500	1,250	2,250	900	2,600
4	3,000	1,250	1,750	700	2,300
	$15,500	$10,000	$5,500	$2,200	$ 3,300

Compare Schedule 24.3 with Schedule 24.1. Note that the net cash flows total $3,300 and the income taxes payable total $2,200 for both depreciation methods, but the accelerated method effectively shifts $1,000 of tax liability from the first year to the third year ($500) and to the fourth ($500). Schedule 24.4 compares the net present values from the project at various discount rates.

SCHEDULE 24.4 NET PRESENT VALUES FOR GARDEN WINERY PROJECT COMPARED FOR DIFFERENT DEPRECIATION METHODS

Discount Rate in Percent Per Year	Depreciation Method	
	Straight-Line	Double-Declining-Balance
10	$687	$880
11	474	680
12	268	487
13	68	300
14	(125)	119
15	(312)	(57)

With straight-line depreciation, the project is marginally acceptable at 13 percent and unacceptable at 14 percent, but with accelerated depreciation, it is clearly acceptable for costs of capital almost as high as 15 percent. Nothing has changed except the depreciation method used for tax purposes.

Accelerated depreciation is merely one of the tax-delaying and tax-saving aspects of the income tax regulations. Others include the treatment of long- and short-term capital gains, effects of offsetting losses from one project against gains from another, and the off-again, on-again tax-saving device variously known as the "investment tax credit" and the "job development credit" used as an instrument of fiscal policy during the 1960s and 1970s.

CHOOSING BETWEEN PROJECTS

Mutually Exclusive Projects

Two different kinds of problems arise in the context of choosing between projects. First are the problems of choosing one from several, mutually exclusive projects. Alternative projects that use the same plant site would be mutually exclusive as would be projects that called for using a single, nonduplicatable asset such as a given stock of managerial talent. The decision rule for choosing between mutually exclusive projects is to accept the project with the largest net present value and reject the others.

Capital Rationing

The second problem arises in the context of capital rationing. Suppose a manager is faced with a set of investment alternatives, each of which requires cash outlays now and has positive net present values but altogether require more funds this year than are available. For example, assume that a manager has $20,000 to invest in projects, is told to use a 12-percent cost of capital, and may choose from the set of four projects shown in Schedule 24.5.

SCHEDULE 24.5   DATA FOR CAPITAL RATIONING ILLUSTRATION

| | | At Cost of Capital of 12 Percent | | |
Project Name (1)	Initial Cash Outlay Required (2)	Present Value of Cash Inflows (3)	Net Present Value of Cash Flows (4)	Excess Present Value Index (5)
A	$12,000	$17,000	$5,000	1.42
B	11,000	15,000	4,000	1.36
C	7,000	10,000	3,000	1.43
D	3,000	5,500	2,500	1.83

(4) = (3) − (2)   (5) = (3)/(2)

The *Excess Present Value Index* shown in column (5) of Schedule 24.5 is one of the alternative measures often used in making investment decisions. It shows for each dollar of initial cash outlay the present value of the cash inflows. For example, Project A returns $1.42 (= $17,000/$12,000) in present value of cash inflows for every $1 invested in the project.

All four projects represent worthwhile investments but the manager,

SCHEDULE 24.6 DILEMMA CAUSED BY CAPITAL RATIONING

Project Combinations	Initial Cash Outlays	Sum of Present Value of Cash Inflows	Net Present Values	Excess Present Value Index
A, C	$19,000	$27,000	$8,000	1.42
A, D	15,000	22,500	7,500	1.50
B, C	18,000	25,000	7,000	1.39
B, D	14,000	20,500	6,500	1.46
C, D	10,000	15,500	5,500	1.55

given a $20,000 constraint on first-year cash outlays, may not undertake them all. Juggling the possibilities, we can see from Schedule 24.6 that the manager must choose one of several combinations of projects.

What is the manager to do? In order to maximize the net present values of the cash flows to the firm, he must choose the combination of Projects A and C and leave the others alone. (Any funds not invested in these four projects must be used elsewhere in the firm and will, presumably, return the cost of capital.) The most profitable project per dollar of investment, Project D, apparently must be rejected if the manager is to act rationally within his constraints.

The problem is the inherent contradiction in telling a manager to use a cost of capital of, say, 12 percent while simultaneously limiting his capital budget. A limited capital budget implies a high, if not infinite, cost of capital. With a budget constraint, the firm is implicitly telling the manager that the cost of capital for funds in excess of $20,000 per year is so large that extra capital expenditures should not be contemplated. But since all capital finances all projects, then the larger cost of capital is the rate the manager (and the firm) should use for evaluating all potential investment projects. For these purposes, the cost of capital is not a number that increases as more capital is used. Using the cost of capital to calculate net present values of cash flows contains the only needed budgeting device: managers will not invest funds in projects returning less than the cost of capital because the net present values of such projects will be negative. Capital rationing has no place in a profit-seeking firm that chooses between investment alternatives by taking the time value of money into account.

ALTERNATIVE METHODS FOR EVALUATING PROJECTS

Many methods are used for evaluating projects, but most are conceptually inferior to using the net present value method with a discount rate equal to the cost of capital. Some are better than others: some alternatives that take the time value of money into account often give the same decision results as the net present value rule and, in practice, prove to be satisfactory. The alternative methods that do not take the time value of money into account are easy to use, because they do not involve present-value computations, but easiness is their chief virtue.

Excess Present Value Index

The excess present value index was defined earlier as the number of present value dollars of cash inflows per dollar of initial outlay. The excess present value index rule calculates the excess present value index for each project and ranks projects according to their score, or index. Projects which result in less than $1 of present value cash inflows per $1 of initial outlay are rejected. The excess present value index rule will give the same results as the net present value rule so long as projects are not mutually exclusive. Consider Projects A, B, C, and D shown in Schedule 24.5 when the cost of capital is 12 percent. If only one of these projects can be chosen, then Project A is the preferred alternative under the net present value rule and the one that will help the firm the most. Project D is the most desirable according to the excess present value index rule but is the least attractive according to the net present value rule. The excess present value index rule pays no attention to the *amount* of capital that can be invested in a project. This so-called *scale effect* is discussed in Appendix 24.1.

The Internal Rate of Return

The *internal rate of return*, sometimes called the *time-adjusted rate of return*, of a stream of cash flows is defined as the discount rate that makes the net present value of that stream equal to zero. (Appendix 24.1 of this chapter and Appendix 14.1 of Chapter 14 show ways to compute the internal rate of return.) As was illustrated earlier, the internal rate of return is the point on the net present value graph where the net present value line crosses the horizontal axis. The decision rule for using the internal rate of return specifies a cutoff rate and states that projects should be accepted when the internal rate of return on the project is greater than or equal to the cutoff rate and should be rejected otherwise.

Advocates of the internal rate of return argue that the method does not require knowing the firm's cost of capital. However, for the internal rate of return rule to give the correct answers, the "cutoff" rate must be the cost of capital. Otherwise, some projects that will increase the value of the firm to its owners will either be rejected when they should be accepted or vice versa.

Another shortcoming of the internal rate of return rule is that a project can have more than one internal rate of return. This surprising mathematical phenomenon can occur when the pattern of yearly net cash flows contains an intermixing of cash inflows and outflows. For example, if at the end of a project's life, expenses will be incurred to return the plant site to its original condition, then individual cash flows can be negative both at the beginning and at the end of a project's life, but positive in between. Projects with intermixing of cash inflows and outflows are likely to have multiple internal rates of return. (Solving for the internal rate of return involves finding the roots of a polynomial. Descartes' Rule of Signs tells how to determine the limit to the number of roots of such a polynomial. See the Glossary for an explanation of this rule.)

The internal rate of return rule ranks projects in the same order as the net present value rule:

a. if the cutoff rate used for the internal rate of return rule is equal to the cost of capital,

b. if projects are not mutually exclusive,

c. if projects have the same life, and

d. if there is only one internal rate of return.

Otherwise, the internal rate of return may lead to a wrong decision. The illustrations in Appendix 24.1 show how the internal rate of return can lead to incorrect project rankings.

Payback Period

The *payback period* is the length of time that elapses before total cumulative cash inflows from the project equal or exceed the initial cash outlay for the project. The Garden Winery Company project, for example, has a payback period of about three years for both methods of depreciation, although if the cash flows occur uniformly over the years, then the payback period is shorter for the accelerated depreciation method than for straight line. The payback-period decision rule states that projects be accepted when the payback period is as short as some cutoff number, such as two years, and rejected otherwise.

The weakness in the payback-period rule, of course, is that both the time value of money and all cash flows subsequent to the payback date are ignored. One project could have a shorter payback period than another but much smaller net present value. The payback-period rule is designed to emphasize concern with the firm's liquidity and to facilitate calculations when many small, similar projects are considered. The net present value rule, however, provides for liquidity because the cost of capital used for discounting cash flows, by definition, accurately measures the costs of securing additional funds should that become necessary.

If the net cash inflows per year from a project are constant and occur for a number of years at least twice as long as the payback period, then the reciprocal of the payback period is approximately equal to the internal rate of return on the project. (This phenomenon occurs when the discount rate is reasonably large, say 10 percent per year or more.) Thus the payback period will rank projects in the same way that the internal rate of return analyses would if the two stated conditions are met.

Discounted Payback Period

Given the widespread use[2] of the payback-period rule and its inability to yield good decisions, some accountants have suggested that firms who want a payback rule should use the discounted payback period. The *discounted payback period* is similar to the ordinary payback period, but it is defined as the length of time that elapses before the *present value* of the cumulative cash inflows is at least as large as the initial cash outlay. The discount rate used in this calculation is most often the cost of capital. The discounted payback period does give some recognition to the time value of funds that flow before payback is accomplished. The ordinary payback periods of Projects *J* and *K* in Schedule 24.7 are the same, three years, but the discounted payback criteria will properly rank *K* as better than *J*.

Either payback rule would improperly prefer both *J* and *K* to Project *L*. Analysts sometimes recommend the discounted payback rule to firms that are wary of applying the net present value rule to projects like Project *L*. The manager who made the original forecast of $50,000 for year 5 may not be around to be held accountable by the time it is learned the forecast was too optimistic.

Bailout and Discounted Bailout Periods

The payback period procedures discussed above ignore the recovery value from a project cut short before the end of its normal or expected life. The *bailout*, or *discounted bailout*, period is the time span over which the initial capital outlay can be recovered from cash flows, or discounted cash flows, taking into account the recoverable value at the end of each year from the assets purchased for the project.

Bailout is much superior to payback because bailout takes into account, at least to some degree, the flows subsequent to the termination date being considered. The recoverable value at any given date incorporates an estimate of the present value of the project's cash flows after the termination date.

SCHEDULE 24.7 ILLUSTRATIVE DATA FOR PAYBACK RULES

Project Name	Cash Flow at End of Year					
	0	1	2	3	4	5
J	($10,000)	$2,000	$3,000	$5,000	$2,000	—
K	(10,000)	5,000	3,000	2,000	2,000	—
L	(10,000)	—	—	—	—	$50,000

[2] See the results of the survey reported by Thomas Klammer, "Empirical Evidence of the Adoption of Sophisticated Capital Budgeting Techniques," *Journal of Business*, 45 (July 1972), p. 393.

Accounting Rate of Return

The *accounting rate of return*, sometimes called the *rate of return on book value*, is defined for a project as:

average yearly income from the project
average investment in the project

In the Garden Winery Company example, the total income from the project is $3,300 over four years or an average of $825 per year. The average investment in the project, assuming straight-line depreciation and beginning-of-year book values of the machine, is $6,250 [= ($10,000 + $7,500 + $5,000 + $2,500)/4]. Hence, the accounting rate of return would be $825/$6,250 = 13.2 percent. The accounting rate of return pays no attention to the time value of money because it uses income, rather than cash flow, data.

We can think of little good to say about the accounting rate of return except that it is easy to compute. (Sometimes, as in the Garden Winery example, it gives a result similar to the internal rate of return, but this is coincidence.) Many companies use the accounting rate of return. As recently as 1970, a survey showed that for about 25 percent of the firms in the sample, the accounting rate of return was the most sophisticated capital budgeting tool used. Other firms used more sophisticated techniques. In 1959, 35 percent of firms in the sample used the accounting rate of return.[3] We approve of the trend's direction.

Summary of Evaluation Rules

The methods that do not take the time value of money into account should not be used for obvious reasons. All the methods that take the time value of money into account require using a cutoff rate or discount rate that must be set equal to the cost of capital if optimal economic decisions are to result. If the cost of capital rate is to be used at all, then the net present value rule is no more complex than the others, and using it will lead to decisions that will make present value of the firm's wealth at least as large as using any of the other rules.

LEASES

Armed with present value tables and the net present value rule, one should be able to make capital investment decisions that will yield maximum economic benefits to the firm. Evaluating leases, however, poses such a subtle problem that we think special treatment of that topic is warranted. Increasingly, firms have the option to lease machinery from the manufacturer, rather than purchase the machinery outright. If the manufacturer is unwilling to lease, perhaps a leasing firm can be found which is willing

[3] *Ibid.*

to buy the machine from the manufacturer and, in turn, lease it to the firm who wants to use it.

Leases are either *noncancelable* or *cancelable*. Under a noncancelable lease, the firm commits itself to payments over the term of the lease whether or not the leased asset continues to be used. A noncancelable lease may be accounted for by the lessee as a financing or as an operating lease, depending on the circumstances. Refer to the discussion of leases in Chapter 15. Cancelable leases, such as for the use of telephones and rented cars, present no new problems. The cash flows for lease payments are treated as any other cash expenses are treated.

The problem arises for noncancelable leases. We pointed out above that in capital budgeting decisions, the investment decision should be kept separate from the financing decision. Noncancelable leases are a form of financing in which money is borrowed from the manufacturer (or leasing firm).

Paradigm for Evaluating Noncancelable Leases

Since a noncancelable lease is a commitment to make a series of payments, the payments themselves are a form of debt, much like a bond. In order to evaluate a leasing alternative, the firm should determine the interest rate it would have to pay in order to secure a loan with a pattern of repayments like those called for in the lease contract. Then it should use that rate to find the present value of the lease payments. That present value is the *lease-equivalent purchase price*. The lease-equivalent purchase price is the initial cash outlay that makes the firm economically indifferent between leasing and buying. Once the lease-equivalent purchase price is known, that price is compared to the actual purchase price, and the lower of the two prices is used as the initial outlay required to acquire the asset in the analysis of cash flows.

Evaluating noncancelable leases involves two separate steps:

1. first, determining whether leasing is cheaper than buying outright,
2. second, determining whether or not the asset should be acquired.

Once the lease-equivalent purchase price is derived and the firm knows which of the buying and leasing alternatives is less costly, the analysis proceeds just as for any other investment evaluation.[4]

---

[4] The payments under a lease contract need not be level. A leasing contract may call for lease payments that are much larger in early years than in later ones. The patterns of deductions from pre-tax income implied by such a lease contract can conceivably be so large that no comparable pattern of deductions on an owned asset, from depreciation expenses and interest payments to borrow money, can be arranged. If so, then the analysis is slightly more complicated. The entire analysis is given in Chapter 6 of *Cost Accounting* by N. Dopuch, J. Birnberg, and J. Demski (Harcourt Brace Jovanovich, 1974). In competitive markets, the manufacturer will offer the same lending terms as would some other lender of funds so that the lease-equivalent purchase price would seldom be much different from the outright purchase price. For a summary of the controversy involving the proper evaluation of leases see Katherine Schipper, John R. Twombly, and Roman L. Weil, "Evaluating Leases Under Uncertainty," *The Accounting Review*, 49 (October, 1974).

Example of Noncancelable Leases

Assume that the manufacturer of the machinery that the Garden Winery Company may acquire states that the equipment can be leased for $2,850 a year for four years, with the first payment due immediately. Assume, further, that Garden Winery determines that it could borrow $10,000 at 8 percent per year from a bank, repaying in equal yearly installments at the beginning of each year. The lease-equivalent purchase price is, then, the present value, discounted at 8 percent, of four payments of $2,850 commencing now and continuing for three more years. Such a stream is, of course, an annuity in advance of four payments. The present value, discounted at 8 percent, of an annuity in advance of $1 per payment for four payments can be calculated from Appendix Table 4. That value is 3.57710 (for an annuity in advance, take the value of an ordinary annuity for one less period, 2.57710, and add 1.0). The lease-equivalent purchase price is, then, 3.57710 × $2,850 = $10,195. Because that price is larger than the available purchase price of $10,000, the Garden Winery Company would choose to buy outright rather than to lease.

All this seems simple enough, but the unwary analyst is likely to forget that a noncancelable lease is merely a form of financing and to evaluate the lease as shown in Schedule 24.8. That schedule applies the net present value rule, assuming the same revenue and cost data as given earlier, a tax rate of 40 percent, and a cost of capital of 10 percent. The net cash flow shown for the end of year zero assumes that the first-year loss on this project can be offset against other income so that the net cash outflow during year zero is the after-tax cost of the lease payment or 60 percent of the actual lease payment.

The incorrect analysis shows that the net present value of the lease alternative, when the cost of capital is 10 percent, is about $1,555, considerably more than the $687 net present value of the purchase alternative. The faulty analysis seems to indicate that leasing is preferred to purchasing outright. The error, of course, results from discounting the lease payments at the cost of capital rather than at the actual interest rate the firm would have to pay to borrow. However, if the manufacturer offered the machine on a cancelable lease, then the analysis shown in Schedule 24.8 would be valid and leasing would be preferable to buying outright.

SUMMARY

The capital budgeting problem consists of two decisions that should be kept separate: should a project be undertaken and how should it be financed? This chapter treats the first of these questions and leaves the second to finance courses. The time value of money should be taken into account in evaluating investment proposals so that cash flows, not accounting income figures, are the basic data to be analyzed. The appropriate discount rate for evaluating investment projects is the firm's cost of capital.

SCHEDULE 24.8 GARDEN WINERY COMPANY

Incorrect Net Present Value Analysis of Noncancelable Lease Alternative
Cost of Capital = 10 Percent

End of Year (1)	Reve- nues (2)	Lease Pay- ments (3)	Other Cash Expenses (4)	Pre-Tax Income (5)	Income Tax (6)	Net Cash Flows (7)	Present Value Factors at 10% (8)	Present Value of Net Cash Flows (9)
0	—	$2,850	—	($2,850)	($1,140)	($1,710)	1.00000	($1,710)
1	$6,000	2,850	$1,000	2,150	860	1,290	.90909	1,173
2	5,000	2,850	1,000	1,150	460	690	.82645	570
3	4,500	2,850	1,000	650	260	390	.75131	293
4	4,000	—	1,000	3,000	1,200	1,800	.68301	1,229
								$1,555

(2), (3), (4): Given
(5) = (2) — (3) — (4)
(6) = .4 × (5)

(7) = .6 × (5) = (5) — (6)
(8): Appendix Table 2
(9) = (7) × (8)

The decision rule that will maximize the expected wealth of the firms' owners is to accept a project if and only if the net present value of its cash flows is positive. From mutually exclusive projects, select the one with the largest net present value.

The internal rate of return and payback methods of evaluating investment proposals may lead to incorrect decisions and are, hence, inferior to the net present value rule. The methods for evaluating proposals that do not take into account the time value of money, such as the payback period and accounting rate of return rules, are clearly inappropriate.

APPENDIX 24.1: SHORTCOMINGS OF THE INTERNAL RATE OF RETURN CRITERION FOR CHOOSING AMONG INVESTMENT PROJECTS

Under certain conditions, the rule of accepting investment projects whose internal rate of return is larger than the cost of capital rate will give the same results as using the net present value rule. However, the internal rate of return criterion may lead to incorrect decisions, as explained in the examples described in this appendix.

Mutually Exclusive Projects

Assume that the after-tax cost of capital is 10 percent per year and that only one of the two Projects, E or F, as shown in Schedule 24.9, can be chosen.

SCHEDULE 24.9   PROJECTS *E* AND *F*

Project Name	Cash Flows by End of Year		Internal Rate of Return	Net Present Value at 10 Percent
	0	1		
E	($100)	$120	.20	$ 9.09
F	(300)	345	.15	13.63

Project *E* provides a simple illustration for calculating the internal rate of return. The internal rate of return on Project *E* is the rate *r* such that

$$-\$100 + \frac{\$120}{1+r} = 0$$

solving for *r* gives *r* = .20. The internal rate of return in Project *F* is similarly easy to calculate. The internal rate of return rule would rank Project *E* as better than *F* while the net present value rule prefers Project *F*. To see that Project *F* is better for the firm, consider what the firm must do with the "idle" $200 it will have to invest if Project *E* is chosen. That $200 must be invested, by definition, at the cost of capital of 10 percent and will provide $220 at the end of the first year. So the total flows available at the end of the first year from Project *E* and from the investment of the idle funds at 10 percent will be $120 + $220 = $340, which is less than the $345 available from Project *F*. The firm will prefer the results from choosing Project *F* as the net present value rule signals.

Figure 24.2 shows the net present value graphs for Projects *E* and *F*. Note that *E* crosses the horizontal axis farther to the right than does *F*, but at 10 percent, the firm's cost of capital, the net present value of *F* is larger than that of *E*.

The net present value graph makes the rankings of the two projects clear. The two net present value curves cross at 12.5 percent, which is the rate *r* that satisfies the equation

$$-\$100 + \frac{\$120}{1+r} = -\$300 + \frac{\$345}{1+r}$$

For costs of capital less than 12.5 percent, Project *F* is preferred to *E* and for costs of capital greater than 12.5 percent, Project *E* is preferred to *F*.

Perhaps you can better understand this point if you decide whether you would rather invest $.10 today to get $2 a year from now or invest $1,000 today to get $2,500 a year from now. You may not do both. We presume that you would prefer the second alternative even though the internal rate of return on the first is eight times as large as for the second. The internal rate of return rule, applied to mutually exclusive projects, ignores the *amount* of funds that can be invested at that rate. This shortcoming, sometimes called the scale effect, applies to the Excess Present Value Index rule as well.

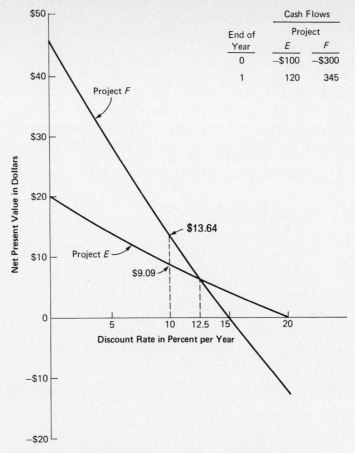

	Cash Flows	
End of Year	Project E	Project F
0	−$100	−$300
1	120	345

Figure 24.2   Net Present Value Graphs for Projects *E* and *F*

Projects with Different Lifetimes

Consider Projects *G* and *H*.

Project Name	Cash Flows by Year End of Year			Internal Rate of Return	Net Present Value at 10 Percent
	0	1	2		
G	−$100	$125	—	.25	$13.64
H	− 100	50	$84	.20	14.87

The internal rate of return on project *H* is the rate *r* that satisfies the equation

$$- \$100 + \frac{\$50}{(1 + r)} + \frac{\$84}{(1 + r)^2} = 0$$

You can verify that the internal rate of return is 20 percent by using Appendix Table 2, 20-percent column. The internal rate of return rule ranks Project *G* as better than *H*, while the net present value rule ranks Project *H* better than G. To see why Project H is better for the firm, consider what the firm must do during year 2. If Project G were accepted, $125 must be invested at the cost of capital, 10 percent, so that at the end of the year 2, the firm will have $125 \times 1.10 = $137.50. If Project H is accepted, the $50 cash outflow from the end of the first year will be invested at 10 percent and will grow to $50 \times 1.10 = $55 by the end of the year 2. Thus, the total funds available at the end of the second year are $55 + $84 = $139, which is larger than the $137.50 if Project G were accepted. The internal rate of return rule ignores the fact that idle funds must be invested at the cost of capital. One of the chapter-end questions requires the construction of a net present value graph for Projects G and H.

QUESTIONS AND PROBLEMS

In the absence of instruction to the contrary, round all discount factors to three digits after the decimal point.

1. Chapter 19 says, "Depreciation is not a source of funds." This chapter says that accelerated depreciation methods provide larger cash flows than do straight-line depreciation. Reconcile these two truths.

2. The internal rate of return rule and the net present value rule both take the time value of money into account and usually give the same decision. When may they give different decisions?

3. Financing decisions should be kept separate from investment decisions. Bonds are a form of financing yet bond refunding is a capital budgeting decision. Reconcile these truths.

4. What are the weaknesses of using the payback period as a device for capital budgeting decisions?

5. Define the internal rate of return of a series of cash flows.

*6. Work Problem 20 of Chapter 15 on bond refunding. Take into account the effect of income taxes. Assume that an income tax rate of 40 percent applies to all years and that bond premium (or discount) is amortized with the straight-line method for tax purposes.

7. There is no contractual obligation to pay anything to common stockholders. How can the capital they provide be said to have a cost other than zero?

*8. "But Mr. Miller, you have said that one conceptual measure of the cost of capital is the rate of return on the marginal investment project available to the firm. So long as the firm has debt outstanding, one opportunity for idle funds will be to retire debt. Therefore, the cost of capital cannot be higher than the debt rate for any firm with debt outstanding." How should Mr. Miller reply?

9. What is the internal rate of return on the following projects each of which requires a $10,000 cash outlay now and returns the cash flows indicated?

* Hints, key numbers, or (partial) answers appear in the back of the book between the Appendix Tables and the Glossary.

See Appendix 14.1 for a systematic method for finding the internal rate of return.

  a. $5,530.67 at the end of years 1 and 2

 *b. $1,627.45 at the end of years 1 through 10

  c. $1,556.66 at the end of years 1 through 13

  d. $2,053.39 at the end of years 1 through 20

  e. $2,921.46 at the end of years 3 through 7

  f. $2,101.77 at the end of years 2 through 10

  g. $24,883.20 at the end of year 5 only.

*10. What is the payback period of the projects in Problem 9 (a) through (g)?

11. Compare the internal rate of return on the projects in Problem 9 (a) through (d) with the *reciprocal* of the payback period for those projects computed in Problem 10. Notice that the internal rate of return on (d) is exactly equal to the reciprocal of its payback period, but this relation does not hold for the other projects. Explain.

*12. What is the payback period of the projects in Problem 9 (a) through (g), assuming cash flows occur uniformly throughout the year?

*13. Compute a depreciation schedule by using the compound interest method of depreciation for projects (a), (b), (e), (f), and (g) of Problem 9.

14. Construct net present value graphs for Projects G and H, with cash flows as shown below, by calculating the net present values for both projects using discount rates of 0, .04, .08, .12, .16, .20, and .24. Then connect the plotted points with a smooth line. At what discount rate do the two projects have equal net present values? State the decision rule for choosing between Projects G and H as a function of the firm's cost of capital.

End of Year	Project Name G	H	Present Value Factors Not Given in Appendix $r = .16$	$r = .24$
0	−$100	−$100	1.000	1.000
1	125	50	.862	.806
2	—	84	.743	.650

15. For mutually exclusive projects, the project with the lowest net present value of cash inflow per dollar of initial cash outlay can be the best alternative for the firm. How can this be?

16. The Larson Company must choose between two mutually exclusive projects. The cost of capital is 12 percent. Given the data below, which project should Larson choose and why?

Project Label	After Tax Cash Flows End of Year 0	1	2	3
M	($500,000)	$175,000	$287,500	$400,000
N	(450,000)	477,000	195,000	60,000

17. The Wisher Washer Company purchased a made-to-order machine tool for grinding washing machine parts. The machine cost $100,000 and was installed yesterday. A salesman offers to sell the company a machine tool

that will do exactly the same work but costs only $50,000. Assume that the cost of capital is 12 percent, that both machines will last for five years, that both machines would be depreciated on a straight-line basis with no salvage value, that the income tax rate is and will continue to be 40 percent, and that Wisher Washer Company earns sufficient income that any loss from disposing of or depreciating the "old" machine can be used to offset other taxable income.

How much, at a minimum, must the "old" machine fetch on resale at this time to make purchasing the new machine worthwhile?

18. The Jamie Company must decide whether or not to continue selling a line of children's shoes manufactured on a machine that can be used for no other purpose by the company. The machine is capable of producing 6,500 pairs of shoes a year. The machine has a current book value of $12,000 and can be sold today for $7,000. The machine is being depreciated on a straight-line basis assuming no salvage value and could continue in use for four more years. If the machine is kept in use, it can be disposed of at the end of four years for $600, although this will not affect the depreciation charge for the next four years. The variable costs of producing a pair of shoes on the machine are $5, and the shoes are sold to customers for $7. To produce and sell the children's shoes requires cash outlays of $10,000 per year for administrative and overhead expenditures as well. The tax rate paid by Jamie Company is 40 percent. The rate applies to any gain or loss on disposal of the machine as well as to other income. From its other activities, Jamie Company earns more income than any losses from the line of children's shoes or from disposal of the machine.

  a. Prepare a schedule showing all the flows that Jamie Company needs to consider to decide whether to keep the machine.

     Should Jamie Company keep the machine if its cost of capital is

  b. 10 percent?

  c. 12 percent?

19. The Double D Company has a cost of capital of 10 percent. It has just purchased two new machines, each with no salvage value. Machine A cost $20,000 and has a depreciable life of four years. Machine B cost $21,000 and has a depreciable life of six years.

     For both machines calculate the present value of depreciation charges assuming

  a. sum-of-the-years'-digits depreciation

  b. double-declining-balance depreciation (assume a switch to straight line after 2 years for A and after 3 years for B).

     Which depreciation methods should be used if

  c. different methods can be used for each machine

  d. the same method must be used for both machines?

  (Round calculations to the nearest dollar.)

20. (Adapted from a problem by David O. Green.) The Precisely-Made Company set up a capital budgeting committee to review investment proposals. The committee applies a cost of capital rate of 12 percent to after-tax cash flows in making its decisions. The production manager proposes a project that involves an initial outlay of $12,000 for a machine and that recovers $4,200 at the end of each of the next four years (cash inflows less cash outflows). The salvage value of the asset is zero. Precisely-

Made uses sum-of-the-years'-digits depreciation when accelerated depreciation is allowed.

Consider initiating this project from the point of view of the capital budgeting committee at four different times—1953, 1954, 1962, and 1964—when the tax laws were different from what they were during the other three years. The applicable tax laws were as follows:

1953. Straight-line depreciation was required.

1954. Accelerated depreciation was allowed.

1962. An investment tax credit of two-thirds of 7 percent of the cost of capital outlays with a depreciable life of between three and five years was granted. That is, at the time the four-year asset is purchased. an amount equal to two-thirds of 7 percent of its cost is subtracted from the income taxes payable at the time of purchase. Accelerated depreciation was allowed. The depreciable amount was the initial outlay less the amount of the investment tax credit.

1964. The same conditions as 1962 but depreciable cost is the full cost, unreduced by the amount of the investment tax credit.

a. For each of the four different times of initiating the project, determine the net present value of the production manager's proposal. Assume that a tax rate of 40 percent of taxable income is applicable and that the Precisely-Made Company generates more income from other projects than any loss computed for this particular project. Round calculations to the nearest dollar. Notice how the same project can appear more or less attractive as the tax laws change.

b. If the appropriate debt rate used by the capital budget committee is 7 percent, what is the largest annual lease payment, due in advance, that Precisely-Made is willing to pay, assuming four payments, rather than buy the machine outright? Ignore the investment tax credit.

*21. The Dopuch Company purchases a machine for $12,000 that has no salvage value at the end of its useful life. The machine is to be depreciated on a straight-line basis. If the depreciable life is chosen to be two years, then Dopuch Company will receive no investment tax credit (see Problem 20 above and assume the 1964 treatment) but if a three-year depreciable life is chosen, one-third of 7 percent of the cost of the machine, or $280, will be granted as a credit towards Dopuch Company's income tax bill at the time of purchase.

Calculate the present value of the tax savings for two- and three-year depreciable lives of the machine. Assume a 40-percent tax rate and a cost of capital of:

a. 16 percent compounded semiannually.

b. 20 percent compounded semiannually.

c. Which depreciable life should be chosen?

(Round calculations to the nearest dollar.)

22. The Eastern States Railroad (ESRR) is considering replacing its power jack tamper, used to maintain track and roadbed, with a new automatic-raising power tamper. The present power jack tamper cost $36,000 five years ago and was estimated to have a total life of twelve years. If it is kept, it will require an overhaul two years from now that is estimated to cost $10,000. It can be sold for $5,000 now; it will be worthless seven years from now.

The automatic-raising tamper costs $46,000 delivered and has an estimated life of twelve years. ESRR anticipates, however, that because of developments in maintenance machines, the new machine should be disposed of at the end of the seventh year for $10,000. Furthermore, the new machine will require an overhaul costing $14,000 at the end of the fourth year. The new equipment will eliminate the need for one machine operator, who costs $16,000 per year in wages and fringe benefits.

Track maintenance work is seasonal so the equipment is normally used only from May 1 through October 31 of each year. Track-maintenance employees are transferred to other work and receive the same rate of pay for the rest of the year.

The new machine will require $2,000 per year of maintenance, whereas the old machine requires $2,400 per year. Fuel consumption for the two machines is identical. ESRR's cost of capital is 12 percent per year and, because of operating losses, pays no income tax.

Should the new machine be purchased? (Round periodic calculations to the nearest hundred dollars.)

23. (This problem and the next are adapted from problems by David O. Green.) Brogan must buy a crane. He can buy a new one from the factory for $150,000. Cromwell, a competitor, bought an identical model last week for $150,000, finds that he needs a larger crane, and offers to sell his crane to Brogan. The factory's and Cromwell's cranes have five-year lives with no salvage value.

Brogan uses sum-of-the-years'-digits depreciation where it is allowed, but the regulations do not permit accelerated depreciation for used assets acquired.

Brogan's cost of capital is 10 percent, and his tax rate is 40 percent. Tax payments occur at the end of the first and subsequent years. What is the maximum price Brogan can pay Cromwell and be as well off as buying from the factory?

24. Cromwell can sell his crane to Brogan (see Problem 23) or can trade in his crane on the larger model which also has a five-year life with no salvage value. The cash price of the larger model is $300,000, and the factory will give Cromwell an allowance of $135,000 if the "old" crane is traded in. Recall from Chapter 14 that if an asset is traded in, there is no tax loss recognizable at the time of trade-in, and the depreciable cost of the new asset is the book value of the old plus any cash "boot" paid at the time the new asset is purchased. Cromwell uses sum-of-the-years'-digits depreciation, has a cost of capital of 10 percent, and is taxed at a rate of 40 percent. If Cromwell sells to Brogan, any capital loss is fully deductible from taxable income at the time of sale, that is, immediately.

a. What is the lowest price Cromwell can get from Brogan and be as well off as trading in?

b. (Note: This part requires that Problem 23 has been worked.) At what price will the two agree for Cromwell to sell to Brogan? (Round calculations to the nearest hundred dollars.)

25. Hekman Products Company is going to acquire a computer from Continental Business Machines (CBM). The computer will be worthless at the end of 4½ years because of obsolescence. CBM will sell the computer for $1,034,000 or will lease it for $132,000 per six months, paid in advance, with nine

payments altogether. Although the lease is noncancelable, CBM will allow Hekman, if it leases, to buy the computer at the end of any six-month period. Furthermore, CBM will reduce the purchase price as time passes. The purchase price at any time depends upon the amount of lease payments to that date. The purchase price will be reduced by 90 percent of the first two lease payments, 75 percent of the next two lease payments, and 50 percent of any lease payments after the fourth.

Hekman's debt rate is 8 percent compounded semiannually and its cost of capital is 12 percent compounded semiannually. Round calculations to the nearest hundred dollars.

  a. What is the lease-equivalent purchase price? If the computer must be purchased immediately or leased for 4½ years, what should Hekman do?

  b. Given CBM's policy of allowing lease with subsequent purchase at the end of any six-month period, what should Hekman do?

  c. Suppose CBM's policy were to reduce the purchase price by 80 percent of each lease payment. What should Hekman do?

26. Mr. Eichenfield offers to sell a mass spectrometer with a useful life of five years to David Scientific Systems, Inc. for $45,000 or to lease (non-cancelable) it for five years for $11,300 per year, payable in advance. After five years, the spectrometer will be obsolete and assumed to be worthless. David Scientific's cost of capital is 12 percent, its cost of debt is 8 percent, and it pays taxes at the rate of 40 percent.

  a. The lease-equivalent purchase price of the spectrometer is $48,726. Why? Present calculations.

    David Scientific Systems tentatively decides that purchasing is preferable to leasing since the purchase price is $3,726 less than the lease-equivalent purchase price. Mr. Eichenfield says the analysis is incorrect and supplies the following schedule to support his argument.

EICHENFIELD'S ANALYSIS

End of Year	Leasing Alternative			Purchase Alternative		
	Lease Payment	Taxes Saved	Present Value at 12% of Taxes Saved	D.D.B. Depreciation Expense	Taxes Saved	Present Value at 12% of Taxes Saved
	(1)	(2)	(3)	(4)	(5)	(6)
0	$11,300	$4,520	$ 4,520	—	—	—
1	11,300	4,520		$18,000	$7,200	$ 6,430
2	11,300	4,520	×	10,800	4,320	3,443
3	11,300	4,520		6,480	2,592	1,846
4	11,300	4,520	4.037	4,860	1,944	1,236
5	0			4,860	1,944	1,102
			$18,247			$14,057

(1) Given
(2) .40 × (1)
(3) Present value of annuity due at 12 percent

(4) Double-declining-balance is better than sum-of-the-years'-digits.
(5) .40 × (4)
(6) Present values at 12 percent × (5)

Mr. Eichenfield says that the present value of the tax savings from leasing is almost $4,200 larger than the present value of the tax savings from purchasing. Since the purchase price is only $3,726 less than the lease equivalent purchase price, leasing is superior when all factors are considered.

b. Respond to Mr. Eichenfield's argument. He is incorrect. Why?

Five

FINANCIAL
STATEMENTS
AND
THEIR
ANALYSIS

Chapter 25

Annual Reports to Stockholders

There are basically two types of financial statements: (1) those prepared primarily for managerial or internal use, and (2) those prepared for use by nonmanagerial or external groups—present and prospective investors, government agencies, employees, credit agencies, and others. This chapter is concerned primarily with statements directed toward external users of financial data.

Internal Reports

Most schedules and reports are prepared for management's use. They do not follow a standard pattern and are characterized by a high degree of detail. Management is, of course, interested in the major public statements—the income statement, balance sheet, and statement of changes in financial position. Those statements are usually prepared for management in considerably greater detail than those published in the annual report. Many other reports are prepared for management on a regular basis and not released outside of the enterprise. Some of them are explained below.

1. *Organizational unit operating statements.* A detailed schedule of operations may be prepared for the head of each production or sales department, division, plant or other appropriate organization unit. The actual performance figures frequently are compared with budgeted or standard-cost figures, as explained in Chapters 22 and 23.

2. *Analyses of selling costs.* These show results of distribution cost accounting. Selling costs may be analyzed by products, territories, salesmen, and so forth.

3. *Budgetary control statements.* Operations for the period are compared with benchmarks previously established such as budget projection, standard costs or ratios, and prior period results, as explained in Chapter 23.

4. *Cash flow schedule.* This schedule presents the cash flows with particular consideration given to how cash requirements were met, dividend decisions were implemented, and any cash generated by the business in excess of current requirements was used.

5. *Cash flow projection.* A budget is prepared which shows cash needs for the next period and how they are planned to be met.

6. *Special analyses.* Reports to the management on individual special topics are prepared as they are needed. These reports deal with decisions such as whether to make or buy, whether to lease or purchase, and whether to raise capital with equity or with debt financing.

External Reports

The statements prepared for those outside of the management proper are typically more condensed than those prepared for internal use. They include the following.

1. *Annual reports to stockholders.* The form and content of the annual report to stockholders are the primary concern of the discussion and illustrations in the rest of this chapter.

2. *Tax returns.* Special reports are required to accompany various tax payments. They vary in detail from a report of wage payments required for computing payroll taxes to a comparative balance sheet and an analysis of income and retained earnings in the federal corporation income tax return. Other tax returns are required for state income taxes, sales taxes, excise taxes, corporation franchise taxes, and, in some jurisdictions, personal property taxes.

3. *Stock exchange reports.* If the shares of stock of a corporation are listed on a stock exchange, regular statements must be filed with the officials of the exchange. These reports must be prepared in the forms prescribed by the exchange, but they are usually about the same as those prepared for stockholders.

4. *Reports to regulatory commissions.* Public utilities must file reports with governmental agencies such as the Interstate Commerce Commission, the Federal Power Commission, the Federal Communications Commission, or a state public service commission. These reports follow a prescribed form and usually include a balance sheet, an income statement, and a statement of changes in financial position as well as certain operating statistics.

5. *Reports to the Securities and Exchange Commission.* Almost all corporations, before offering a security issue to the public, must file financial statements with the SEC as part of the registration procedure required by the Securities Exchange Act of 1933. Corporations whose securities are listed on a national stock exchange, as well as many others meeting certain tests of size and ownership distribution, must file financial statements with the SEC as a part of the initial listing and subsequent annual reporting as required by the Securities Exchange Act of 1934.

6. *Reports to banks and credit rating agencies.* Specialized forms, designed to emphasize items significant for financial ratings of securities and granting of credit, are prepared for banks and credit rating agencies, such as Moody's, Standard and Poor's, as well as Dun and Bradstreet.

COMPONENTS OF ANNUAL REPORTS

Where the capital stock of the corporation is widely held and its affairs are of interest to the public in general, the annual reports become a matter of public relations. Experiments with more attractive and more readable forms have characterized many recent reports. Modern annual reports are often elaborate brochures containing a great deal of art work, photographs, charts, and even advertising for the firm's products.

The most comprehensive survey of published annual report practices is to be found in *Accounting Trends and Techniques*, mentioned in Chapter 1, published by the American Institute of Certified Public Accountants. This annual publication contains a cumulative survey of the practices followed in the annual reports of some 600 industrial and commercial corporations. Comparative tabulations show trends in various corporate reporting practices such as the types of statements presented, their form, content and terminology, and the accounting recognition, measurements, and presentations for transactions and items presented in the statements.

Illustrations selected from public reporting are interspersed throughout the chapter and show variations in reporting practices. Almost all of the financial statement data in the 1973 Annual Report to Stockholders of the General Electric Company are shown in Schedule 25.11. General Electric's annual reports are consistently among the best we see. GE provides copious explanations and discloses helpful items beyond those currently required. We think there is no better way to review your understanding of accounting than to attempt to understand all that appears in GE's statements.

Auditor's Report

An important section of the annual report to stockholders is the independent public accountant's opinion on the fairness of the covered financial statements, supporting schedules, and notes. The accountant's opinion is frequently described as the *accountant's report*, or sometimes merely as the *opinion*. It is often designated as being the report of the *auditor* or *certified public accountant*.

The auditor's report follows a standard format with variations to meet specific circumstances as appropriate. A recent report of the auditor for The Coca-Cola Company is presented in Figure 25.1. The report contains

Accountants' Report

**To the Board of Directors
The Coca-Cola Company
Wilmington, Delaware**

We have examined the consolidated balance sheet of The Coca-Cola Company and subsidiaries as of December 31, 1973, and December 31, 1972, and the related consolidated statements of profit and loss, earned surplus, and changes in financial position for the two years ended December 31, 1973. Our examinations were made in accordance with generally accepted auditing standards, and accordingly included such tests of the accounting records and such other auditing procedures as we considered necessary in the circumstances.

In our opinion, the accompanying statements, as identified above, present fairly the consolidated financial position of The Coca-Cola Company and subsidiaries at December 31, 1973, and December 31, 1972, and the consolidated results of their operations, changes in capital, and changes in financial position for the two years ended December 31, 1973, in conformity with generally accepted accounting principles applied on a consistent basis.

Ernst & Ernst

Atlanta, Georgia
February 28, 1974

Figure 25.1 From the Annual Report of The Coca-Cola Company

two paragraphs—*scope* paragraph and *opinion* paragraph. The scope paragraph indicates the financial presentations covered by the report and affirms that auditing standards and practices generally accepted by the accounting profession have been adhered to unless noted and described otherwise. Exceptions to the statement that the auditor's "examination was made in accordance with generally accepted standards" are rare in published annual reports. There are occasional references to the auditor's having relied on financial statements examined by other auditors, particularly for subsidiaries or for data from prior periods.

The opinion expressed by the auditor is at the heart of his or her report. The opinion may be *unqualified* or *qualified*. The great majority of opinions are unqualified; that is, the auditor does not have any exceptions or qualifications to his opinion that the statements "present fairly the financial position . . . of operations and the changes in financial position . . . in conformity with generally accepted accounting principles consistently applied."

Qualifications result primarily from material uncertainties of valuation or realization of assets, outstanding litigation or tax liability or from inconsistency between periods due to changes in application of accounting principles. A qualified opinion as to fairness is usually noted by the phrase *subject to*; a qualification as to consistency is usually noted by *except for*, with an indication of the auditor's approval of the change.

A qualification so material that the auditor feels he cannot express an opinion on the fairness of the financial statements as a whole must result in either a *disclaimer of opinion* or an *adverse opinion*. Adverse opinions and disclaimers of opinion are extremely rare.

A member of the American Institute of Certified Public Accountants (AICPA) is expected to adhere to the pronouncements of the body designated by the AICPA as the official source of generally accepted accounting principles.[1] A Certified Public Accountant may not, in general, attest that statements are in conformity with generally accepted accounting principles when the statements contain material departures from those principles. If, however, the CPA can demonstrate that, because of unusual circumstances, departures are required so that the statements are not misleading, then the CPA may attest to statements with material departures from generally accepted principles. The grounds for justifying departures are so stringent that such departures are rare in published financial statements.

Comparative Statements

With few exceptions, the primary financial statements are presented in comparative form, usually for the current and preceding year. Historical summaries usually present condensed statement information for five or ten years. It is generally recognized that comparative reports help to make clear the nature and trend of changes in operations, resources, and financing.

Summary of Significant Accounting Policies

A summarized statement of significant accounting policies is required as an integral part of the financial statement presentation.[2] The disclosure of accounting policies should identify and describe those accounting principles adopted by the reporting enterprise and the methods of applying the principles which substantially affect the determination of income, financial position, and changes in financial position. The summary statement may be either the first note to the financial statements or a separate statement preceding the statements. The General Electric Company, whose

---

[1] Until 1973, the Accounting Principles Board; since then, the Financial Accounting Standards Board.

[2] Opinion No. 22, Accounting Principles Board, AICPA, April, 1972.

report is shown at the end of this chapter in Schedule 25.11, provides much more detail than most other companies and intermixes the summary with other information in the annual report.

The following list indicates the areas of accounting principles and methods of application frequently presented in a summary statement of accounting principles:

> Basis of consolidation
> Foreign currency translation
> Method of recognizing profit on long-term construction-type contracts
> Method of recognizing revenue from franchising and leasing operations
> Inventory valuation basis
> Methods of accounting for:
>> Investments
>> Properties, depreciation and amortization
>> Research and development costs
>> Intangibles; Goodwill
>> Retirement and pension plans
>> Leases and rentals
>> Income taxes; Investment tax credits
>> Earnings per share

The annual report of the General Motors Corporation presents a summary called Significant Accounting Policies, shown in Figure 25.2, as the first note in its notes to financial statements.

THE BALANCE SHEET

Heading

The heading always gives the name of the company, the title of the statement, and the date. Although the title Balance Sheet is still the one used most frequently, a number of attempts have been made to find a less technical and more descriptive title. Statement of Financial Position and Statement of Financial Condition have been the two most frequently used substitutes in published reports. When the statement shows the combined position of a parent company and its subsidiary or subsidiaries, it is commonly titled consolidated balance sheet.

The date of the balance sheet in annual reports is the last day of the company's fiscal year. Most fiscal years coincide with the calendar year, but approximately one-third of the larger companies have adopted a "natural" business year which will bring year-end inventory taking, adjustments, audits, and tax-return preparation to the most convenient season of the year. For example, the fiscal year of Sears, Roebuck and Company ends on January 31, that of Stokely-Van Camp on May 31, that of American Motors Corporation on September 30, and that of International Harvester Company on October 31. Some companies have adopted a fiscal period of fifty-two weeks, thus having varying ending dates: Swift and Company

Notes to Financial Statements

Note 1. Significant Accounting Policies

Principles of Consolidation

The consolidated financial statements include the accounts of the Corporation and all domestic and foreign subsidiaries which are more than 50% owned and engaged principally in manufacturing or wholesale marketing of General Motors products. General Motors' share of earnings or losses of nonconsolidated subsidiaries and of associates in which at least 20% of the voting securities is owned is generally included in consolidated income under the equity method of accounting. Intercompany items and transactions between companies included in the consolidation are eliminated and unrealized intercompany profits on sales to nonconsolidated subsidiaries and to associates are deferred.

Translation of Foreign Currencies

Real estate, plants and equipment, accumulated depreciation and the provision for depreciation are translated into United States dollars at exchange rates in effect at the dates the related assets were acquired. Other assets, liabilities and deferred credits and reserves are translated at exchange rates in effect at the date of the balance sheet; other items of income and expense are translated at average exchange rates for the months in which the transactions occurred. Accumulated unrealized net loss from translation of foreign currency accounts of any foreign subsidiary is charged to income and accumulated unrealized net gain is deferred. Gains or losses on exchange contracts are included in costs and expenses when realized.

Income Taxes

Investment tax credits allowable under the income tax laws are deducted in determining taxes estimated to be payable currently and are deferred and amortized over the lives of the related assets. The tax effects of timing differences between pretax accounting income and taxable income (principally related to depreciation, benefit plans expense, sales and product allowances and undistributed earnings of subsidiaries and associates) are deferred, except that the tax effects of certain expenses charged to income prior to 1968 have not been deferred but are recognized in income taxes provided at the time such expenses become allowable deductions for tax purposes. Provisions are made for estimated United States and foreign taxes, less available tax credits and deductions, which may be incurred on remittance of the Corporation's share of subsidiaries' and associates' undistributed earnings included in the consolidated financial statements.

Inventories

Inventories are stated at the lower of cost or market. Cost is determined substantially by the first-in, first-out or the average cost method. Market value is current sales price less distribution cost for finished product and replacement cost for other inventories. Physical inventories are taken at all locations.

Common Stock Held for the Incentive Program

Common stock in treasury is held exclusively for payment of liabilities under the Incentive Program and is stated substantially at cost.

Property, Depreciation and Amortization

Property is stated at cost. Maintenance, repairs, rearrangement expenses and renewals and betterments which do not enhance the value or increase the basic productive capacity of the assets are charged to costs and expenses as incurred.

The annual group (composite) rates of depreciation are, with minor exceptions, as follows:

Classification of Property	Annual Group Rates
Land improvements	5%
Buildings	3½%
Machinery and equipment	8⅓% (Average)
Furniture and office equipment	6% (Average)

Depreciation is not provided in excess of 100% of the gross book amount of a given group as a whole. Depreciation on groups which are not 100% depreciated is, with minor exceptions, accrued at 150% and 100% of the applicable rate shown above for the first and second thirds, respectively, of estimated useful life and thereafter at 50% of such rate for the balance of time the assets remain in service. Use of this accelerated method accumulates depreciation of approximately two-thirds of the depreciable cost during the first half of the estimated lives of the property.

Expenditures for special tools are amortized, with the amortization applied directly to the asset account, over short periods of time because the utility value of the tools is radically affected by frequent changes in the design of the functional components and appearance of the product. Replacement of special tools for reasons other than changes in products is charged directly to cost of sales.

Goodwill

Goodwill relates to businesses acquired in 1943 and prior years and, beginning in 1970, is being amortized over a period of ten years at the rate of $6,344,246 per year, with the amortization applied directly to the asset account.

Incentive Program

A reserve is maintained for purposes of the Bonus Plan and Stock Option Plan to which may be credited each year an amount which the independent public accountants of the Corporation determine in accordance with the provisions of the Bonus Plan; however, for any year the Bonus and Salary Committee may direct that a lesser amount be credited. Bonus awards under the Bonus Plan, contingent credits under the Stock Option Plan and such other amounts arising out of the operation of the Incentive Program as the Committee may determine are charged to the reserve. As a result of tentative determinations of awards by the Committee, the amount provided is transferred to current liabilities, other liabilities and deferred credits at December 31.

If participants do not meet the preconditions entitling them to receive undelivered instalments of bonus awards and contingent credits, the amount of any such instalments is credited to income. Upon the exercise of stock options, the related contingent credits are proportionately reduced with the amount of the reduction credited to income.

Note 1. Significant Accounting Policies (concluded)

General Reserve Applicable to Foreign Operations

The general reserve applicable to foreign operations was established in 1954 and is available to absorb extraordinary losses, such as losses from discontinuing foreign operations in any locality, either voluntarily or because of conditions beyond the Corporation's control. There has been no change in this reserve since its establishment.

Pension Program

The Corporation and its subsidiaries have several pension plans covering substantially all employes. Generally, plans covering hourly-rate employes are noncontributory and those covering salaried employes are both contributory and noncontributory. Benefits under the plans are generally related to an employe's length of service, wages and salaries and contributions. The costs of these plans are determined on the basis of actuarial cost methods and include amortization of prior service cost over periods not exceeding 30 years. With the exception of certain overseas subsidiaries, pension costs accrued are funded.

Product Related Expenses

Expenditures for research and development and advertising and sales promotion are charged to costs and expenses when incurred; provisions for estimated costs related to product warranty are made at the time the products are sold.

Figure 25.2 From the Annual Report of General Motors Corporation

reported as of October 28, 1972, and October 27, 1973. Bausch and Lomb Incorporated reported on a fifty-two-week period in 1971 and 1973 and a fifty-three-week period in 1972.

Balance Sheet Form

Most published balance sheets follow the conventional procedure of presenting the items in two groups, one called Assets and the other appearing under a variety of titles. Liabilities and Stockholders' Equity is most common, as in the model balance sheet form shown for the Blackstone Manufacturing Company in Schedule 11.3. The account form with assets at the left and liabilities and stockholders' equity at the right is generally used unless the statement is sufficiently condensed to permit a vertical arrangement with assets being placed at the top. The balance sheets of Liggett & Myers Incorporated, Schedule 25.1, and of General Electric are examples of the conventional type presented in account form. Some corporations have adopted a variation of the balance sheet form where current liabilities are deducted from the current assets to arrive at the working capital; other assets are added to this figure and the long-term liabilities are deducted from the total, leaving a balance which is the total of the stockholders' equity. This figure is then analyzed to show the various stockholders' equity account balances. The balance sheet of the United States Steel Corporation, Schedule 25.2, is an example of this form.

Classifications within the asset, liability, and stockholders' equity sections vary widely in published reports except for the current asset and current liability categories. Balance sheets are increasingly presented as condensed statements with disclosures about accounting principles and methods as well as details of components included elsewhere in the report.

Assets. The model balance sheet form in Schedule 11.3 presents four categories of assets: current; investments; property, plant and equipment; and intangibles. Generally accepted accounting principles so clearly define current assets that the current asset items are quite uniform in published reports.[3] The following are included: cash; marketable securities or temporary investments; receivables; inventories; current prepayments.

There is considerable variation in the presentation of the noncurrent assets. Generally accepted accounting principles have not, as yet, officially defined classifications for noncurrent assets so that published reports include the following in various combinations: investments; property, plant and equipment; intangibles; deferred charges; other.

Liabilities. The model balance sheet form in Schedule 11.3 presents three categories of liabilities: current, long-term and indeterminate-term. Our presentation is consistent with the view that all items included in the balance sheet should be classified in accordance with the basic accounting

[3] *Accounting Research Bulletin* No. 43, Chapter 3.A (AICPA, June 1953).

equation as either assets, liabilities, or stockholders' equity. Reporting practice uniformly presents current liabilities in a section with its own subtotal. Presentation of the liabilities other than current liabilities is far less uniform. If there is long-term debt, it is usually shown in a separate category. Other noncurrent liabilities are frequently presented as separate items without further classification, except for the decreasing number of reports that show a classification, reserves—a practice which is discouraged by accounting principles.[4] The items not classified as liabilities or equities in published reports, but given separate recognition include: (1) deferred taxes, (2) minority interest in consolidated subsidiaries, (3) capitalized leases, (4) employee liabilities for deferred compensation, pension and retirement plans, and (5) estimated losses or expenses for items such as contingencies, foreign operations and discontinued operations. The undesirable heterogeneity of items included in the noncurrent liabilities section in published reports is further indicated by the frequent omission of totals for this "other" category and, sometimes, for total liabilities.

Stockholders' Equity. The model balance sheet form in Schedule 11.3 classifies the stockholders' equity into two categories: contributed capital and retained earnings. Contributed capital is classified into the amounts applicable to each class of shares. Current reporting practice generally classifies the stockholders' equity into three categories: capital stock (par or stated value), additional paid-in capital, and retained earnings. The statement or notes include detailed information for each class of shares, such as the number of shares authorized, issued, and held as treasury stock, the par or stated value per share, dividend rate and liquidation preference for preferred stocks, and other especially significant features.

The additional paid-in capital is usually presented in a single amount with a caption title such as Additional Paid-in Capital or Capital Contributed in Excess of Par (or Stated) Value. The terminology Capital Surplus and Paid-in Surplus persists even though the use of the term "surplus" is discouraged by accounting authority.[5] Changes in capital stock and additional paid-in capital are presented in notes to the financial statements or, increasingly, in a separate statement entitled Changes in Additional Capital, Changes in Stockholders' Equity, or Statement of Shareholders' Equity such as the one shown in Schedule 25.8 from the annual report of the W. R. Grace & Co.

The caption Retained Earnings has largely supplanted other terms such as Retained Income and the formerly predominate Earned Surplus. (The Coca-Cola Company still uses "earned surplus"; see its accountants' report in Figure 25.1.)

Frequently, bond indentures and other credit sources limit cash dividend payments and acquisition of treasury shares when retained earnings drop below a certain level. One way to recognize such restrictions

[4] *Accounting Research Bulletin* No. 43, Chapter 6 (AICPA, June 1953).
[5] *Accounting Research Bulletin* No. 43, Preface (AICPA, June 1953).

Consolidated Balance Sheet
as of December 31

Assets

Current Assets	1973	1972
Cash (Note 2)	$ 6,358,659	$ 12,214,048
Marketable securities—at cost which approximates quoted market value	3,197,182	35,534
Accounts receivable		
Customers (less allowances for discounts and doubtful accounts: 1973, $1,643,142; 1972, $1,353,660)	62,412,902	77,806,577
Others	6,414,186	5,889,256
Inventories (Note 1)		
Leaf tobacco	184,448,510	202,454,796
Bulk whiskeys and wines	34,751,388	29,421,512
Finished goods and work in process	37,494,267	40,512,115
Other materials and supplies	22,342,652	19,359,545
Total current assets	357,419,746	387,693,383
Investments		
Unconsolidated foreign subsidiaries and other companies—at equity in net assets (Note 1)	4,426,754	8,642,982
Other—at lower of cost or estimated market value	100,725	662,651
Total investments	4,527,479	9,305,633
Property, Plant, and Equipment—at cost (Notes 1 and 3)		
Land	7,541,192	7,635,578
Buildings	52,299,140	54,021,896
Machinery and equipment, etc.	101,756,318	100,830,592
Total	161,596,650	162,488,066
Less accumulated depreciation	58,685,828	62,680,760
Property, plant, and equipment—net	102,910,822	99,807,306
Franchises and Goodwill—at cost, less amortization (Note 1)	122,961,578	122,636,375
Deferred Charges and Prepaid Expenses	5,353,057	6,765,196
Total	$593,172,682	$626,207,893

See Notes to Financial Statements.

LIGGETT & MYERS INCORPORATED AND CONSOLIDATED SUBSIDIARIES

Liabilities

Current Liabilities	1973	1972
Commercial paper (Note 2)	$ 52,230,000	$ 70,187,842
Accounts payable	21,775,487	25,517,589
Dividends payable	200,552	201,427
Taxes payable and accrued	8,184,921	15,094,602
Current maturities of long-term liabilities	608,986	450,180
Estimated liabilities—discontinued operations (Note 4)	—	7,103,814
Other accrued liabilities	22,730,515	19,946,628
Total current liabilities	105,730,461	138,502,082
Long-Term Debt (Note 3)		
6% sinking fund debentures, due 1992	66,000,000	69,000,000
7.6% sinking fund debentures, due 1997	50,000,000	50,000,000
Other	6,431,096	11,529,586
Total long-term debt	122,431,096	130,529,586
Other Long-Term Liabilities	7,580,261	4,901,204
Minority Interest in Consolidated Subsidiaries (Note 1)	1,605,817	3,250,767

Stockholders' Equity

Capital stock (Notes 5 and 6)

	1973	1972
7% cumulative preferred stock, par value $100 per share—authorized and issued, 139,621 shares; in treasury, 1973, 25,020 shares, 1972, 24,520 shares	11,460,100	11,510,100
$5.25 cumulative convertible preference stock, par value $1 per share—authorized, 310,000 shares; issued, 1973, 119,403 shares, 1972, 132,875 shares (involuntary liquidation value, 1973, $11,940,300, 1972, $13,287,500)	119,403	132,875
Series preference stock, par value $1 per share—authorized, 1,000,000 shares; issued, none	—	—
Common stock, par value $1 per share—authorized, 12,000,000 shares; issued, 1973, 8,344,045 shares, 1972, 8,313,094 shares	8,344,045	8,313,094
Paid-in capital in excess of par values of capital stock	115,998,222	116,041,981
Retained earnings (Note 3)	225,846,540	218,548,754
Total	361,768,310	354,546,804
Less cost of common stock in treasury (1973, 160,934 shares, 1972, 147,177 shares)	5,943,263	5,522,550
Total stockholders' equity	355,825,047	349,024,254
Total	**$593,172,682**	**$626,207,893**

See Notes to Financial Statements.

Consolidated Statement of Financial Position

	Dec. 31, 1973	Dec. 31, 1972
CURRENT ASSETS		
Cash	$ 252,785,694	$ 213,511,153
Marketable securities, at cost (approximates market)	310,119,523	28,411,092
Receivables, less estimated bad debts	795,415,400	720,193,659
Inventories *(see page 22 and Note 4 on page 25)*	629,132,338	790,959,687
Total	1,987,452,955	1,753,075,591
Less		
CURRENT LIABILITIES		
Notes and accounts payable	573,031,368	437,322,277
Employment costs (except social security taxes)	449,564,891	425,373,328
Accrued taxes	340,490,998	299,400,400
Dividend payable	27,083,869	21,667,095
Long-term debt due within one year	14,407,995	12,873,954
Total	1,404,579,121	1,196,637,054
WORKING CAPITAL	582,873,834	556,438,537
Marketable securities, at cost (approximates market), set aside for plant and equipment additions and replacements	255,000,000	255,000,000
Investments in realty, leasing and finance operations	71,795,777	72,151,485
Long-term receivables and other investments, less estimated losses	261,510,077	209,448,296
Plant and equipment, less depreciation *(details on page 23)*	4,209,777,493	4,156,210,034
Operating parts and supplies	58,196,935	56,504,302
Costs applicable to future periods	74,801,414	67,619,422
TOTAL ASSETS LESS CURRENT LIABILITIES	5,513,955,530	5,373,372,076
Deduct		
Long-term debt, less unamortized discount (details on page 23)	1,420,312,767	1,515,566,095
Reserves *(details on page 22)*	100,276,769	100,276,769
Deferred taxes on income	182,210,627	180,046,388
EXCESS OF ASSETS OVER LIABILITIES AND RESERVES ...	$3,811,155,367	$3,577,482,824
OWNERSHIP EVIDENCED BY		
Common stock (authorized 90,000,000 shares; outstanding 54,169,462 shares)		
Par value $30 per share	$1,625,083,860	$1,625,083,860
Income reinvested in business	2,186,071,507	1,952,398,964
Total	$3,811,155,367	$3,577,482,824

W. R. Grace & Co. and Subsidiary Companies **Consolidated Statement of Income**

In Thousands (except amounts per share)	1973	1972*
Sales and operating revenues	$ 2,807,830	$ 2,343,429
Dividends and interest	15,909	12,634
Net gain on disposition of properties	2,753	2,320
Equity in earnings of less than majority owned companies (dividends received 1973—$6,150; 1972—$4,443)	6,548	4,420
	2,833,040	**2,362,803**
Cost of goods sold and operating expenses	1,996,467	1,658,110
Selling, general and administrative expenses	524,393	467,746
Depreciation and depletion	67,807	63,126
Research and development expenses	28,054	21,559
Interest expense	50,042	39,182
Income applicable to minority shareholders	3,785	2,653
	2,670,548	**2,252,376**
	162,492	**110,427**
U.S. and foreign income taxes:		
Current	66,869	47,171
Deferred	8,085	844
	74,954	**48,015**
Income before extraordinary items	**87,538**	**62,412**
Extraordinary items	**(2,902)**	**3,232**
Net income	$ **84,636**	$ **65,644**
Earnings per common and common equivalent share:		
Income before extraordinary items	**$2.96**	**$2.10**
Extraordinary items	**(.10)**	**.11**
Net income	**$2.86**	**$2.21**
Earnings per common share assuming full dilution:		
Income before extraordinary items	**$2.65**	**$1.94**
Extraordinary items	**(.08)**	**.09**
Net income	**$2.57**	**$2.03**

*Restated.

The Statement of Accounting Policies, page 29, and the Notes to Financial Statements, pages 34 to 38, are an integral part of this statement.

would be to appropriate retained earnings. In current reporting practice, such restrictions are usually included in the notes to the financial statements. Presentations of appropriated retained earnings, for whatever purpose, are rare in published reports.

THE INCOME STATEMENT

Heading

The heading of the income statement contains the name of the company, the title of the statement, the period covered, and, if appropriate, the term "Consolidated." Titles used in addition to the most common one, Income Statement, are Statement of Earnings and Statement of Operations. When a combined income statement and reconciliation of retained earnings is presented, the title indicates this combination. The statement of Dr Pepper Company shown in Schedule 25.4 is titled Consolidated Statements of Earnings and Retained Earnings.

Form and Content

The income statement follows one of two general formats: the single-step form or the multiple-step form. In the single-step form, all revenues and gains are listed and totaled, followed by a listing and total of all expenses and losses. The model income statement form in Schedule 11.3 illustrates the single-step form. A modified single-step form frequently adopted separates federal income taxes from all other expenses with an intermediate income amount being shown for income before federal income taxes and extraordinary items. The statement of W. R. Grace & Co. shown in Schedule 25.3 presents this intermediate income amount.

The multiple-step form results in various intermediate income subtotals such as gross margin, operating income, and income before federal taxes and extraordinary items. With the increased condensation of financial statements, use of the multiple-step form is decreasing in published reports. The statement of Dr Pepper Company shown in Schedule 25.4 follows the multiple-step form. The General Electric Company uses a modified form of the multiple-step income statement, showing only the intermediate classifications of "Operating margin" and "Income before taxes and minority interest" (Schedule 25.11, page 31).

Under either form, if there are extraordinary items, as described in Chapter 7, they are set forth separately below a subtotal titled Income before Extraordinary Items. The income statement of the W. R. Grace & Co. (Schedule 25.3) illustrates this presentation. It is worth noting that the extraordinary items shown there probably would not have been shown as an extraordinary item under the terms of APB Opinion No. 30 if these events had occurred after the effective date of the Opinion, September 30,

Dr Pepper Company and Subsidiaries

Consolidated statements of earnings and retained earnings

Years ended December 31, 1973 and 1972

	1973	1972
Net sales	$98,918,466	82,037,876
Cost of sales	50,791,111	38,859,902
Gross profit	48,127,355	43,177,974
Administrative, marketing and general expenses	31,262,480	28,343,000
Operating profit	16,864,875	14,834,974
Other income	1,502,848	847,108
Earnings before income taxes	18,367,723	15,682,082
Federal and state income taxes	8,632,223	7,492,841
Net earnings	9,735,500	8,189,241
Retained earnings at beginning of year	26,016,511	21,705,823
	35,752,011	29,895,064
Dividends paid — $.22¾ per share in 1973 and $.20⁴/₅ per share in 1972	4,299,399	3,878,553
Retained earnings at end of year	$31,452,612	26,016,511
Net earnings per share	$ .51	.43

See accompanying notes to consolidated financial statements.

1973. Instead, they will have been presented on a separate line in the expenses category.

Revenue

The revenue items included on the published income statement are presented under condensed captions such as net sales, interest, dividends, royalties, equity in earnings of unconsolidated subsidiaries and affiliates, and gains on disposition of assets or liquidation of liabilities. Detailed sources of sales revenue are frequently indicated elsewhere in the financial report, such as in statements showing line of business reporting. See, for example, the excerpt from the Liggett & Myers annual report shown in Schedule 25.10.

Expenses

The expenses shown in published income statements usually are presented in a highly condensed listing of four to six items called a *functional classification of expenses*, used by both W. R. Grace & Co. and by Dr Pepper in their income statements. The most frequent expense categories are: cost of goods sold; selling, general and administrative expenses; depreciation, depletion, and amortization; research and development; interest and debt expenses; employee stock option, retirement, and profit sharing plans; minority interest in income; income taxes.

Some firms use a *natural classification of expenses*, rather than a functional one. The natural classification groups items by the nature of the services used: purchases of materials, labor, other services, depreciation, taxes, and so on. A natural classification is used by the General Electric Company in its income statement. The SEC requires that if a natural classification of expenses is used, then the major items of a functional classification must be reported in footnotes to the financial statements. GE shows the amounts of items in a functional classification in the text of the left-hand column on page 34 of its annual report (Schedule 25.11).

Reports to the SEC must also disclose certain revenues and expenses that exceed one percent of total sales and revenues and that are not set out separately in the income statement. These items are: (1) maintenance and repairs; (2) depreciation, depletion and amortization of property, plant and equipment; (3) depreciation and amortization of intangible assets; (4) taxes, other than income taxes; (5) rents; (6) royalties; (7) advertising; and (8) research and development. Such detailed expense information, although not required in annual reports to stockholders, is increasingly shown in notes or other sections of the report.

General Electric discloses some of these items in the table "Supplemental Cost Details" shown in the left-hand column of page 34 in its report. (Note that according to the terminology used in this book, the word *cost* in that table should be *expense*. Costs are assets; gone assets are expenses.)

Extraordinary Items

Accounting principles drastically restrict those items which are to be included as extraordinary items in the income statement.[6] The criteria for items included in this classification are presented in Chapter 7. Recall that extraordinary items must be both "unusual in nature" and "infrequent in occurrence." In accord with the income tax allocation principle,[7] the income tax effect of a reported extraordinary item is recognized in the extraordinary item section of the income statement and excluded from the income tax expense category in the ordinary income section.

Earnings per Share

Earnings per share data must be shown in annual reports, right on the income statement. All the income statements illustrated in this chapter present the earnings per share data in the approved form. W. R. Grace & Co. presents data for primary earnings per share (earnings per common and common equivalent share) and fully diluted earnings per share in Schedule 25.3, as explained in Chapter 26.

Consolidated Income Statement Presentation

The basis of consolidation and the method of translating foreign currencies in consolidating foreign securities are usually noted in the summary of significant accounting principles or notes to the financial statements. The general practice is followed in the reports of General Electric and General Motors. The consolidated statements are presented after eliminating or adjusting for the impact of intercompany transactions, as explained in Chapter 18. The share of total income applicable to the minority interest in subsidiaries is deducted before determining consolidated net income. The W. R. Grace & Co. income statement presents the minority's share as "income applicable to minority shareholders." General Electric presents the minority's share of income as "minority interest in earnings of consolidated affiliates."

STATEMENT OF CHANGES IN FINANCIAL POSITION

A statement of changes in financial position is now required[8] as a basic financial statement for each period for which an income statement and balance sheet are presented. The statement is covered by the auditor's report. The form, content, and preparation of this statement are discussed in Chapter 19. The statement form focuses on changes in working capital: current assets minus current liabilities. The statement also discloses significant changes in financial position for the period even if they do not

[6] Opinion No. 30, Accounting Principles Board, AICPA, issued in June, 1973.
[7] Opinion No. 11, Accounting Principles Board, AICPA, issued in December, 1967.
[8] Opinion No. 19, Accounting Principles Board, AICPA, issued in March, 1971.

affect the working capital accounts. (For example, a security issued directly for land would be shown both as a source of funds, the proceeds of issue, and as a use of funds, the purchase of a long-term asset.) The net changes in each working capital account are presented, preferably, as a part of the statement of changes in financial position but occasionally as a separate footnote schedule. To show the analysis of changes in working capital separately, however, obscures the self-balancing nature of the statement.

Current reporting practice generally traces the flows of working capital, as in the reports of General Electric and United States Gypsum Company (Schedule 25.5). The conventional format starts with the amount of income before extraordinary items and adjustments thereto, resulting in a significant intermediate source component frequently entitled Working Capital (or Funds) Provided by Operations. A few companies have adopted a statement form that traces flows of cash and marketable securities, as illustrated in the statement of Zenith Radio Corporation in Schedule 25.6. Notice there the admirable treatment of the addbacks to funds produced by operations. Depreciation is not a source of funds, as Zenith makes clear.

OTHER ITEMS IN ANNUAL REPORTS

Reconciliation of Retained Earnings

Current reporting practice requires the reconciliation of beginning and ending retained earnings.[9] The reconciliation may be presented in a number of locations in the annual report: (1) as a separate statement of retained earnings as in the report of Lehigh Portland Cement Company, Schedule 25.7; (2) as the lower section of a combined statement of income and retained earnings as in the reports of Dr Pepper and General Electric; (3) in a statement of changes in stockholders' equity as in the report of W. R. Grace & Co. (Schedule 25.8); or (4) in the stockholders' equity section on the balance sheet.

Typical items appearing in the reconciliation of retained earnings are the following: beginning balance; net income of the period; dividends declared by class of shares whether in cash, in kind, or in stock; deductions arising from various transactions with stockholders; and the ending balance. Direct credits and charges to retained earnings arising out of unusual and infrequent transactions are rare. Restrictive criteria, explained in Chapter 7, are established for prior-period adjustments, which are excluded from the determination of periodic income and are to be presented as adjustments of the beginning retained earnings balance. The primary sources of such adjustments in published reports are settlements of litigation and income tax disputes. The Consolidated Statement of Shareholders' Equity of the W. R. Grace & Co. (Schedule 25.8) presents prior-period adjustments resulting from settlements of foreign expropriations of property and income tax disputes.

[9] Opinion No. 12, Accounting Principles Board, AICPA, issued in December, 1967.

consolidated statement of changes in financial position

For the years ended December 31
United States Gypsum Company

	IN THOUSANDS OF DOLLARS	
sources of funds	**1973**	**1972**
Net earnings	$ 51,090	$ 49,462
Provision for depreciation and depletion	22,727	19,966
Deferral of income taxes	3,000	2,700
(Income)/loss absorbed on real estate ventures	2,750	(230)
(Income)/loss absorbed on investments in other companies	224	(164)
Total funds from operations	79,791	71,734
Issuance of common stock for acquired companies	927	5,834
Current maturity of state and municipal securities	3,917	4,119
Decrease in investments in other companies (net)	65	—
Net book value of property, plant and equipment sold	2,353	5,000
Proceeds from exercise of stock option	—	30
Increase in long-term notes payable (net)	383	—
Other	—	172
Total funds provided	87,436	86,889

	1973	1972
disposition of funds		
Additions and improvements to property, plant and equipment	58,854	33,369
Additional investments in and advances to real estate ventures (net)	1,157	27,618
Additional investments in other companies (net)	—	441
Dividends	29,500	28,247
Purchase of common stock for treasury	—	11,262
Decrease in long-term notes payable (net)	—	4,218
Principal amount of debentures purchased for treasury	—	2,712
Other	7,983	—
Total funds expended	97,494	107,867
(Decrease) in working capital	$ (10,058)	$ (20,978)

	1973	1972
detail of change in working capital		
Cash	$ 2,663	$ 3,875
Marketable securities	3,245	1,030
Receivables	18,310	3,959
Inventories	25,156	8,050
Accounts payable and accrued expenses	(20,302)	(4,479)
Notes payable and commercial paper	(59,670)	(32,576)
Antitrust settlement	28,275	—
Taxes on income	(7,735)	(837)
(Decrease) in working capital, as above	$ (10,058)	$ (20,978)

The accounting policies and practices shown on pages 27 through 31 are an integral part of this statement.

consolidated statements of changes in financial position

in thousands of dollars

for the years ended December 31,	1973	and	1972
Source of funds:			
Net income	**$ 54,979**		$ 48,579
Add—Expenses which did not result in the use of funds—			
Depreciation	**14,386**		11,313
Deferred income taxes (Note 5)	**2,354**		1,047
Total funds provided from operations	**71,719**		60,939
Increase in accounts payable and accrued expenses	**50,885**		30,120
Collection of long-term receivables	**—**		9,790
Sale of stock under employees' stock purchase plans (Note 3)	**124**		549
Increase (decrease) in bank loans	**4,421**		(2,710)
All other, net	**3,987**		1,460
Total	**131,136**		100,148
Use of funds:			
Cash dividends paid	**28,186**		26,653
Expenditures for property, plant and equipment—			
Land and buildings	**20,032**		3,094
Machinery and equipment	**27,109**		12,003
Increase in receivables	**27,596**		33,212
Increase in inventories	**82,335**		9,002
Purchase of treasury stock	**8,963**		—
Increase in prepaid income taxes	**8,545**		8,039
Decrease (increase) in accrued income taxes	**18,904**		(10,458)
Total	**221,670**		81,545
Increase (decrease) in cash and marketable securities	**$ (90,534)**		$ 18,603

The accompanying notes to consolidated financial statements are an integral part of these statements.

Zenith Radio Corporation and subsidiaries

SCHEDULE 25.7 FROM THE ANNUAL REPORT OF LEHIGH PORTLAND CEMENT COMPANY

Consolidated statements of reinvested earnings

	Year Ended December 31,	
	1973	1972
Reinvested Earnings (Note 4)		
Beginning of year	$ 45,552,000	$ 38,380,000
Net Earnings	10,841,000	9,662,000
Dividends declared—80¢ per share (1972—60¢)	(2,836,000)	(2,490,000)
End of year	$ 53,557,000	$ 45,552,000

The notes are an integral part of the financial statements.

Adjustment of the beginning balance of retained earnings also arises out of reporting certain accounting changes. A business combination effected by the pooling of interests method usually results in a restatement of retained earnings. Other changes, that are reported on a retroactive basis and result in restatement of prior-period statements and adjustment of the opening balance of the current period, include the correction of accounting errors and certain specified changes of accounting principles. The W. R. Grace & Co. Consolidated Statement of Shareholders' Equity presents a prior-period adjustment for a change in an income tax accounting principle (Schedule 25.8).

Statement of Changes in Additional Capital

All changes in stockholders' equity items are disclosed, in accordance with accepted reporting practice.[10] Such changes are presented in several formats: (1) a statement of capital, as in the report of Westinghouse Electric Corporation (Schedule 25.9), (2) a statement of changes in stockholders' equity as in the report of W. R. Grace & Co. (Schedule 25.8), or (3) a schedule or disclosure in the notes to financial statements, as on page 40 of the General Electric annual report (Schedule 25.11). Transactions most frequently reported include: new financing by stock issues, conversions of stock or debt, business combinations, stock options and other employee benefit plans based on stock issues, as well as acquisitions or retirement of shares, including treasury shares.

[10] *Ibid.*

SCHEDULE 25.8   FROM THE ANNUAL REPORT OF W. R. GRACE & CO.

W. R. Grace & Co. and Subsidiary Companies   **Consolidated Statement of Shareholders' Equity**

In Thousands

Years ended December 31, **1972*** and **1973**

	Preferred Stocks	Common Stock	Paid in Capital	Retained Earnings	Total
Balance at January 1, 1972	**$ 11,139**	**$ 28,248**	**$213,346**	**$470,096**	**$722,829**
Cumulative effect of 1973 prior period adjustment for Peruvian investments	—	—	—	(11,512)	(11,512)
Cumulative effect of 1972 prior period adjustment for U.S. Federal income taxes	—	—	—	(12,000)	(12,000)
Cumulative effect of 1972 change in accounting principle for income taxes	—	—	—	(3,200)	(3,200)
Balance at January 1, 1972 as adjusted	**11,139**	**28,248**	**213,346**	**443,384**	**696,117**
Net income for the year 1972	—	—	—	65,644	65,644
Acquisition of businesses in purchase transactions	—	142	4,553	—	4,695
Prior years poolings of interests	—	475	(475)	—	—
Exercise of stock options	—	3	440	—	443
Purchase of preferred stocks	(1,094)	—	9	—	(1,085)
Other	—	75	623	—	698
Dividends paid:					
Preferred	—	—	—	(773)	(773)
Common ($1.50 per share)	—	—	—	(38,295)	(38,295)
Pooled companies—prior to combination with the Company	—	—	—	(77)	(77)
Balance at December 31, 1972	**10,045**	**28,943**	**218,496**	**469,883**	**727,367**
Net income for the year 1973	—	—	—	84,636	84,636
Acquisition of businesses in purchase transactions	—	135	2,609	—	2,744
Prior years poolings of interests	—	577	(577)	—	—
Exercise of stock options	—	3	378	—	381
Purchase of preferred stocks	(437)	—	29	—	(408)
Other	—	(526)	(63)	—	(589)
Dividends paid:					
Preferred	—	—	—	(728)	(728)
Common ($1.50 per share)	—	—	—	(41,886)	(41,886)
Pooled companies—prior to combination with the Company	—	—	—	(284)	(284)
Balance at December 31, 1973	**$ 9,608**	**$ 29,132**	**$220,872**	**$511,621**	**$771,233**

*Restated.

The Statement of Accounting Policies, page 29, and the Notes to Financial Statements, pages 34 to 38, are an integral part of this statement.

NOTES TO FINANCIAL STATEMENTS

To meet the requirements for adequate disclosure in financial statements, it is usually necessary to supplement the basic financial statements with additional information. Accordingly, current reporting practice presents a set of notes that are an integral part of the financial statements covered

SCHEDULE 25.9 FROM THE ANNUAL REPORT OF WESTINGHOUSE ELECTRIC
CORPORATION

Westinghouse

Consolidated Statement of Capital

	Cumulative Preferred Stock	Common Stock	Capital In Excess of Par Value	Treasury Stock At Cost	Total
Balance at January 1, 1972.........	$30,482,000	$272,642,000	$453,180,000	$ (8,378,000)	$747,926,000
Common stock issued: 842,046 shares under stock option, employe stock and savings and investment plans.................	—	2,631,000	27,194,000	—	29,825,000
377,109 shares for businesses acquired.......................	—	1,179,000	5,741,000	—	6,920,000
65,384 shares acquired for treasury..	—	—	—	(645,000)	(645,000)
4,470 treasury shares delivered for businesses acquired..........	—	—	85,000	143,000	228,000
Other – net...................	—	—	112,000	42,000	154,000
Balance at December 31, 1972......	30,482,000	276,452,000	486,312,000	(8,838,000)	784,408,000
Common stock issued: 210,118 shares under stock option, employe stock and savings and investment plans...................	—	656,000	6,863,000	—	7,519,000
1,047,537 shares acquired for treasury.......................	—	—	—	(36,296,000)	(36,296,000)
580,155 treasury shares delivered under stock option, employe stock and savings and investment plans ..	—	—	(1,575,000)	20,334,000	18,759,000
Other – net....................	—	—	256,000	577,000	833,000
Balance at December 31, 1973......	$30,482,000	$277,108,000	$491,856,000	$(24,223,000)	$775,223,000

Cumulative preferred stock, par value $100, 3.80 per cent Series B; authorized 374,846 shares at December 31, 1973 and 1972; 304,820 shares outstanding at December 31, 1973 and 1972.

Cumulative preference stock, without par value; 10,000,000 shares authorized; none issued.

Common stock, par value $3.125; authorized 120,000,000 shares at December 31, 1973 and 1972; issued 88,674,610 shares at December 31, 1973, and 88,464,492 shares at December 31, 1972.

Common stock held in treasury amounted to 798,453 shares at December 31, 1973, and 364,778 shares at December 31, 1972.

During 1973, a systematic plan for reacquisition of common stock of the Corporation was begun. All the shares will be used to supply the various plans under which common stock is distributed to employes.

by the auditor's report. The notes to financial statements of the General Electric Company present substantial additional data of significance to the reader of the annual report. As indicated above, a summary of significant accounting principles is included in the report as a separate section or in the notes section. As in the GE report, the notes frequently relate directly to many of the accounting principles used, providing specific additional description of transactions or detailed tabulations.

Historical Summary

Common reporting practice includes an historical summary in the annual report. The most common titles used are Summary or Review, prefaced by Historical, Financial, or Statistical. The comparative data usually cover five or ten years. The statements usually contain condensed information and excerpts from both the balance sheet and operating statements. These data are consistent with those in the current financial statements including any *pro forma* information. In order that the data be comparable, restatements of previously reported data are usually required for such events as business combinations effected by the pooling of interests method, other accounting changes, and changes in capital stock caused by stock dividends, splits, and recapitalizations. General Electric illustrates the types of information generally presented in an historical summary on pages 42 and 43 of its annual report.

Line of Business Reporting

The disclosure of supplemental information by line of business has been the subject of review by accounting authorities for several years. In 1970, the SEC expanded the requirements for reporting its annual report form (Form 10-K) to include information by line of business. The data to be reported for each line of business are its sales and its contribution, before income taxes and extraordinary items, to total corporate profit. Although line of business data are not required in annual reports to stockholders, the number of companies reporting such data is steadily increasing, and some such information appears in the majority of the reports of larger companies.

Line of business reporting in annual reports is described by a number of titles such as *diversified-company reporting*, *segmented reporting*, and *product-line reporting*. The information is classified by one or more of the following categories: by product line, by divisions or subsidiaries, by domestic and foreign operations, by private sector and government contract, and by geographical areas. Sales revenue amounts are usually presented. Information on income is presented less frequently and the treatment of allocated expenses to the different segments varies. Items which are frequently excluded in the calculation of product-line contribution to income include unallocated general corporate expense, interest, other income and expenses, income taxes, minority interest, and extraordinary items. The

SCHEDULE 25.10 FROM THE ANNUAL REPORT OF LIGGETT & MYERS
INCORPORATED

Operating Income and Revenues by Product Line (Dollars Expressed in Thousands)

for the nine years ended December 31, 1973

	1973	1972	1971	1970	1969	1968	1967	1966	1965
Operating Income									
Tobacco Products	$ 41,939	$ 29,822	$ 36,310	$ 37,716	$ 32,749	$ 36,284	$ 38,347	$ 37,323	$ 40,321
Spirits and Wines	29,435	31,452	30,568	26,149	24,757	23,279	19,113	13,858	2,143
Pet Foods	5,185	14,004	17,335	13,617	9,150	3,487	3,724	2,793	2,382
Other	3,860	4,125	6,694	4,928	3,307	1,038	303	(26)	—
Total	$ 80,419	$ 79,403	$ 90,907	$ 82,410	$ 69,963	$ 64,088	$ 61,487	$ 53,948	$ 44,846
Revenues (Excluding Excise Taxes)									
Tobacco Products	$247,371	$248,244	$250,036	$249,543	$240,356	$246,171	$259,145	$266,123	$265,371
Spirits and Wines	113,883	134,635	132,112	116,001	110,240	105,264	115,788	118,583	39,461
Pet Foods	163,720	153,608	143,727	129,642	110,192	65,121	47,647	35,028	23,794
Other	61,026	64,353	62,278	48,297	37,130	28,147	7,810	996	—
Total	$586,000	$600,840	$588,153	$543,483	$497,918	$444,703	$430,390	$420,730	$328,626
Revenues (Including Excise Taxes)									
Tobacco Products	$365,730	$373,297	$379,911	$385,202	$380,634	$399,137	$428,901	$447,188	$454,675
Spirits and Wines	138,447	164,993	168,919	147,118	140,080	131,291	151,984	153,489	54,892
Pet Foods	163,720	153,608	143,727	129,642	110,192	65,121	47,647	35,028	23,794
Other	61,026	64,353	62,278	48,297	37,130	28,147	7,810	996	—
Total	$728,923	$756,251	$754,835	$710,259	$668,036	$623,696	$636,342	$636,701	$533,361

Notes:

(1) Operating income represents income before interest, corporate expenses, other income and expenses, income taxes, minority interest, and extraordinary items.

(2) Revenues and results of operations of companies acquired by purchase during the period are included from dates of acquisition; companies acquired on a pooling of interests basis are included for the entire period; i.e., Austin, Nichols & Co., Incorporated and Mercury Mills, Inc.

(3) Revenues of spirits and wines in 1966 and 1967 include sales by Star Industries, Inc. and certain of its subsidiaries for the period that these companies were subsidiaries, May 26, 1966 to May 15, 1967 (excluding excise taxes: $45,191,345 for 1966 and $20,057,752 for 1967; including excise taxes: $49,141,555 for 1966 and $22,819,457 for 1967).

(4) Revenues of spirits and wines for the nine years shown above include sales of the wholesale liquor distribution business of Austin, Nichols & Co. until the closing of the last remaining Austin, Nichols' wholesale subsidiary in New York City on October 20, 1972. These sales, excluding excise taxes, were $34,839,010 in 1965 and $23,233,597 in 1972. Including excise taxes, these sales amounted to $40,212,386 in 1965 and $27,179,449 in 1972.

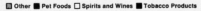

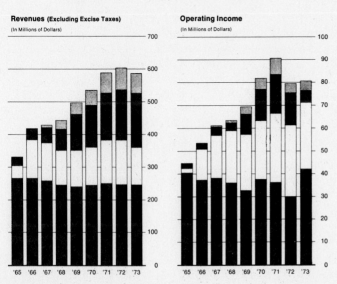

Revenues (Excluding Excise Taxes)
(In Millions of Dollars)

Operating Income
(In Millions of Dollars)

report of Liggett & Myers Incorporated in Schedule 25.10 illustrates reporting that presents the product-line contribution at the operating income level.

Graphic Presentation

Graphic presentations are frequently included in the annual report. The presentations, often in attractive formats, attempt to communicate quickly and forcefully certain internal relationships and trends more effectively than can be done with either text or tables. Many of the graphic presentations, as well as other sections of the report, make effective use of colors. The

Distribution of Sales Dollar, 1973 and 1972

1973 Net Sales
$1,064,427,000

1972 Net Sales
$870,532,000

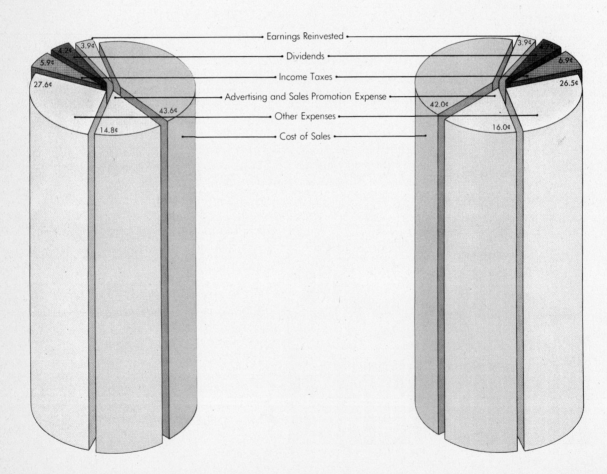

Figure 25.3 From the Annual Report of The Gillette Company

"pie chart" form is frequently used to indicate the disposition of the revenue dollar, as illustrated in Figure 25.3 in the report of The Gillette Company. Column, or "bar," charts are frequently used to indicate trends. The excerpt showing the product-line (or line of business) report of Liggett & Myers (Schedule 25.10) also illustrates this use of graphics in annual reports to stockholders.

COMPREHENSIVE FINANCIAL STATEMENT ILLUSTRATION

References to the annual report of the General Electric Company have been made throughout the chapter. The primary financial statements, related notes, auditor's report, statement of accounting policies, and financial highlights are shown in Schedule 25.11.

Audit and Finance Committee

The meetings held by this Committee during 1973 included two in which Committee members (no management personnel being present) met with the independent certified public accountants with respect to their audit of the accounts and records of the Company and their review and certification of the Company's financial statements. It also reviewed the internal accounting and auditing procedures of the Company to assure that the Company's system of financial controls is adequate and being operated effectively.

In furtherance of its function as a reviewing and recommending body to the Board and Company in financial matters, the Committee also reviews the financial position of the Company, its short- and long-term financing plans, specific financing proposals, major investment programs and opportunities, plans and programs involving the purchase or redemption of Company securities and dividend policy. We were gratified to be able to recommend to the full Board the dividend increase adopted in 1973.

John E. Lawrence, *Chairman*

1973 Financial Summary

This summary comments on significant items in the consolidated financial statements on pages 31, 32 and 33, generally in the same order as they appear in those statements.

The information contained in this summary, in the opinion of management, substantially conforms with or exceeds the information supplied in the annual financial statements constituting part of the report (commonly called the "10-K Report") submitted to the Securities and Exchange Commission. The few exceptions, considered non-substantive, are noted as appropriate in the following text. A reproduction of the following statements and summary is filed with that agency.

As an aid in evaluating the data in this Financial Summary, significant accounting and reporting principles and policies followed by General Electric are printed in blue.

Consolidated financial statements and accompanying schedules in this Report include a consolidation of the accounts of the Parent—General Electric Company— and those of all majority-owned affiliates (except finance affiliates since their operations are not similar to those of the consolidated group). All significant items relating to transactions between Parent and affiliated companies are eliminated from consolidated statements. Sales and net earnings attributable to each of the Company's major categories are summarized on page 3.

Except for fixed assets and accumulated depreciation, assets and liabilities of foreign affiliates are translated into U.S. dollars at year-end exchange rates, and income and expense items are translated at average rates prevailing during the year. Fixed assets and accumulated depreciation are translated at rates in effect at dates of acquisition of the assets. The net effect of translation gains and losses is included as other costs in current year operations. Translation losses for 1973 and 1972 were $3.5 million and $4.2 million respectively.

Net earnings include the net income of finance affiliates and the consolidated group's share of earnings of associated companies which are not consolidated but in which the group owns 20% or more of the voting stock.

During 1973, net earnings amounted to $585.1 million compared with prior year earnings of $530.0 million. Earnings per common share were $3.21 in 1973 compared with $2.91 in 1972. Fully diluted earnings per common share, which would result from the potential exercise or conversion of

(continued on page 34)

Statement of Current and Retained Earnings

General Electric Company and consolidated affiliates   (*In millions*)

For the year	1973	1972
Sales of products and services to customers . .	$11,575.3	$10,239.5
Operating costs		
Employee compensation, including benefits . . .	4,709.7	4,168.4
Materials, supplies, services and other costs . . .	5,690.5	4,973.1
Depreciation	334.0	314.3
Taxes, except those on income	113.5	116.3
Increase in inventories during the year	(227.2)	(147.3)
	10,620.5	9,424.8
Operating margin	954.8	814.7
Other income	183.7	189.2
Interest and other financial charges	(126.9)	(106.7)
Earnings before income taxes & minority interest .	1,011.6	897.2
Provision for income taxes	(418.7)	(364.1)
Minority interest in earnings of consolidated affiliates	(7.8)	(3.1)
Net earnings applicable to common stock . . .	585.1	530.0
Dividends declared	(272.9)	(254.8)
Amount added to retained earnings	312.2	275.2
Retained earnings at January 1	2,371.4	2,096.2
Retained earnings at December 31	$ 2,683.6	$ 2,371.4
Earnings per common share (*In dollars*)	$3.21	$2.91
Dividends declared per common share (*In dollars*)	$1.50	$1.40

The 1973 Financial Summary beginning on page 30 and ending on page 41 is an integral part of this statement.

Statement of Financial Position

General Electric Company and consolidated affiliates   *(In millions)*

December 31	1973	1972
Assets		
Cash	$ 296.8	$ 267.0
Marketable securities	25.3	27.3
Current receivables	2,177.1	1,926.0
Inventories	1,986.2	1,759.0
Current assets	4,485.4	3,979.3
Investments	869.7	754.9
Plant and equipment	2,360.5	2,136.6
Other assets	608.6	531.0
Total assets	$8,324.2	$7,401.8
Liabilities and equity		
Short-term borrowings	$ 665.2	$ 439.4
Accounts payable	673.5	558.1
Progress collections and price adjustments accrued	718.4	624.2
Dividends payable	72.7	63.7
Taxes accrued	310.0	308.6
Other costs and expenses accrued	1,052.6	875.7
Current liabilities	3,492.4	2,869.7
Long-term borrowings	917.2	947.3
Other liabilities	492.1	456.8
Total liabilities	4,901.7	4,273.8
Minority interest in equity of		
consolidated affiliates	50.1	43.4
Preferred stock	—	—
Common stock	463.8	463.1
Amounts received for stock in excess of par value	409.5	396.6
Retained earnings	2,683.6	2,371.4
	3,556.9	3,231.1
Deduct common stock held in treasury	(184.5)	(146.5)
Total share owners' equity	3,372.4	3,084.6
Total liabilities and equity	$8,324.2	$7,401.8

The 1973 Financial Summary beginning on page 30 and ending on page 41 is an integral part of this statement.

Statement of Changes in Financial Position

General Electric Company and consolidated affiliates (*In millions*)

For the year	1973	1972
Source of funds		
From operations:		
Net earnings	$ 585.1	$ 530.0
Depreciation	334.0	314.3
Income tax timing differences	—	(23.8)
Earnings of the Credit Corporation less		
dividends paid	(10.7)	(8.1)
	908.4	812.4
Major domestic long-term borrowings	—	125.0
Overseas Capital Corporation long-term borrowings	17.1	50.8
Increase in other long-term borrowings—net . . .	2.0	5.3
Newly-issued common stock	11.7	13.4
Total source of funds	939.2	1,006.9
Application of funds		
Plant and equipment additions	598.6	435.9
Dividends declared	272.9	254.8
Investments	114.8	40.6
Reduction in major domestic long-term borrowings	31.5	17.2
Reduction in Overseas Capital Corporation		
long-term borrowings	17.7	3.9
Other—net	20.3	(56.5)
Total application of funds	1,055.8	695.9
Net increase (decrease) in working capital . . .	$ (116.6)	$ 311.0
Analysis of changes in working capital		
Cash and marketable securities	$ 27.8	$ 8.3
Current receivables	251.1	184.7
Inventories	227.2	147.3
Short-term borrowings	(225.8)	130.4
Other payables	(396.9)	(159.7)
Net increase (decrease) in working capital . . .	$ (116.6)	$ 311.0

The 1973 Financial Summary beginning on page 30 and ending on page 41 is an integral part of this statement.

SCHEDULE 25.11 (*continued*)

(continued from page 30)

such items as stock options and convertible debt outstanding, were $3.18 in 1973 and $2.87 in 1972.

Sales of products and services to customers are reported in operating results only as title to products passes to the customer and as services are performed as contracted.

Sales in 1973 totaled $11,575.3 million, an increase of 13% over the 1972 level.

Costs are classified in the statement of current earnings according to the principal types of costs incurred. Operating costs, excluding interest and income taxes, classified as they will be reported to the Securities and Exchange Commission, were: cost of goods sold of $8,515.2 million in 1973 and $7,509.6 million in 1972; and selling, general and administrative expenses of $2,105.3 million in 1973 and $1,915.2 million in 1972. Supplemental details required by the SEC are shown in the table below.

Supplemental Cost Details		*(In millions)*
	1973	**1972**
Company funded research and development using National Science Foundation definitions	$330.7	$303.2
Maintenance and repairs	319.6	270.4
Social security taxes	225.8	167.5
Advertising and sales promotion	170.5	149.0
Rent	86.6	71.5

Employee compensation, including the cost of employee benefits, amounted to $4,709.7 million in 1973. During the year, agreements were reached with various labor unions as described earlier in this Report.

General Electric Company and its affiliates have a number of pension plans, the total cost of which was $135.5 million in 1973 and $107.6 million in 1972. The most significant of these plans is the General Electric Pension Plan in which substantially all employees in the United States who have completed one year of service with the Company are participating and the obligations of which are funded through the General Electric Pension Trust. Financial statements of the Trust appear at right.

Investments of the Pension Trust are carried at amortized cost plus a programmed portion of unrealized appreciation in the common stock portfolio. This accounting recognizes the long-term nature of pension obligations by stressing long-term market trends.

The funding program uses 6% as the estimated rate of future income which includes provision for the systematic

recognition of the unrealized appreciation in the common stock portfolio. This program has the objective of recognizing appreciation which, when added to cost, will result in a common stock book value approximating 80% of market value (consistent with Armed Services Procurement Regulations).

The actual earnings of the Trust, including the programmed recognition of appreciation, as a percentage of book value of the portfolio were 6.5% for 1973 and 6.6% for 1972.

Unfunded liabilities of the Trust are being amortized over a 20-year period and are estimated to be $474 million at December 31, 1973 based on book value of Trust assets compared with $323 million at the end of 1972. These amounts included unfunded vested liability of $377 million at December 31, 1973 and $239 million at December 31, 1972. The estimated market value exceeded book value of Trust assets by $309 million and $693 million at the end of 1973 and 1972 respectively.

Effective July 1, 1973, a supplementary pension plan was approved by the Company's Board of Directors, the purpose of which is to ensure that the pension benefits of long-service professional and managerial employees, when combined

General Electric Pension Trust		*(In millions)*
Operating statement	**1973**	**1972**
Total assets at January 1	$2,267.1	$2,071.8
Company contributions	125.9	102.2
Employee contributions	38.6	32.3
	164.5	134.5
Dividends, interest and sundry income	111.4	101.8
Common stock appreciation: Realized	34.2	44.8
Unrealized portion recognized	34.4	21.3
	68.6	66.1
Pensions paid	(115.6)	(107.1)
Total assets at December 31	$2,496.0	$2,267.1
Financial position—December 31		
Short-term investments	$ 51.3	$ 180.3
U.S. Government obligations and guarantees	56.0	60.1
Corporate bonds and notes	344.8	348.7
Real estate and mortgages	410.7	397.6
Common stocks & convertibles	1,530.6	1,211.1
Total investments	2,393.4	2,197.8
Other assets—net	102.6	69.3
Total assets	$2,496.0	$2,267.1
Funded liabilities: Liability to pensioners	$ 874.9	$ 799.9
Liability for pensions to participants not yet retired	1,621.1	1,467.2
Total funded liabilities	$2,496.0	$2,267.1

with their social security benefits, bear a reasonable relationship to their final average earnings. Obligations of this pension supplement are not funded. Current service costs and amortization of past service costs over a period of 20 years are being charged to operations currently. Cost for the partial year 1973 was $2.0 million.

Depreciation amounted to $334.0 million in 1973 and $314.3 million in 1972.

An accelerated depreciation method, based principally on a sum-of-the-years digits formula, is used to depreciate plant and equipment in the United States purchased in 1961 and subsequently. Assets purchased prior to 1961, and most assets outside the United States, are depreciated on a straight-line basis. Special depreciation is provided where equipment may be subject to abnormal economic conditions or obsolescence.

Taxes, except those on income, totaled $113.5 million in 1973 and $116.3 million in 1972. These taxes were mainly franchise and property taxes. They exclude social security taxes, which are included with employee benefits.

Other income amounted to $183.7 million in 1973, a decrease of $5.5 million from 1972. Significant items included in other income are shown below.

Other Income		(In millions)
	1973	**1972**
Net earnings of the Credit Corporation	$41.7	$41.1
Income from:		
Customer financing	32.4	26.8
Royalty and technical agreements	36.9	30.2
Marketable securities and bank deposits	17.7	19.1
Other investments	31.6	31.8
Sale of Honeywell stock	7.8	29.5
Other sundry income	15.6	10.7
	$183.7	$189.2

Net earnings of General Electric Credit Corporation were $41.7 million in 1973, about the same as in 1972. Condensed financial statements for the Credit Corporation appear on page 37.

In view of depressed stock market conditions during 1973, the Company sold only 168,000 shares of Honeywell common stock as compared with 370,000 shares sold during 1972. Capital gains (using average cost) from these sales were $7.8 million and $29.5 million respectively ($5.5 million and $20.7 million after taxes).

Interest and other financial charges increased to $126.9 million in 1973 from $106.7 million in 1972 primarily because of higher short-term borrowing rates. Amounts applicable to principal items of long-term borrowings were $58.3 million in 1973 and $52.5 million in 1972.

Provision for income taxes amounted to $418.7 million in 1973. Details of this amount are shown on page 36.

Provision for income taxes generally is computed using the comprehensive interperiod tax allocation method and is based on the income and costs included in the earnings statement shown on page 31.

Amounts of income taxes shown as payable are determined by applicable statutes and government regulations. Timing differences result from the fact that under applicable statutes and regulations some items of income and cost are not recognized in the same time period as good accounting practice requires them to be recorded. The cumulative net effect of such items is that earnings on which tax payments were required have been higher than earnings reported in the Company's Annual Reports. Accordingly, a deferred-tax asset has been established to record the reduction of future tax payments. Principal items applicable to U.S. Federal income taxes, and their effect on taxes payable are shown on page 36. Individual timing differences reflected in foreign income taxes were not significant.

Provision has been made for Federal income taxes to be paid on that portion of the undistributed earnings of affiliates expected to be remitted to the Parent. Undistributed earnings of affiliates intended to be reinvested indefinitely in the affiliates totaled $328 million at the end of 1973 and $252 million at the end of 1972.

U.S. Federal income tax returns of the Parent have been settled through 1964.

The Company follows the practice of amortizing the investment credit to income over the life of the underlying facilities rather than in the year in which facilities are placed in service. Investment credit amounted to $23.6 million in 1973 compared with $20.4 million in the prior year. In 1973 $10.6 million was added to net earnings compared with $8.3 million in 1972. At the end of 1973, the amount still deferred and to be included in net eanings in future years was $72.8 million. If the Company had "flowed through" the investment credit, this amount would have been included in earnings during 1973 and prior years.

Provision for income taxes amounted to 41.4% of income before taxes. Items accounting for the principal portion of the difference of 6.6 points between that rate and the 48.0%

Provision for income taxes		*(In millions)*
	1973	**1972**
U. S. Federal income taxes:		
Estimated amount payable	$321.2	$315.3
Effect of timing differences	0.4	(21.0)
Investment credit deferred—net	13.0	12.1
	334.6	306.4
Foreign income taxes:		
Estimated amount payable	71.4	48.1
Effect of timing differences	(0.4)	(2.8)
	71.0	45.3
Other (principally state and local income taxes)	13.1	12.4
	$418.7	$364.1

Effect of timing differences on U. S. Federal income taxes		*(In millions)*
Increase (decrease) in provision for income taxes		
	1973	**1972**
Tax over book depreciation	$ 12.1	$ 2.3
Undistributed earnings of affiliates	6.7	12.3
Margin on installment sales	1.1	(6.1)
Provision for:		
Warranties	(7.7)	(19.6)
Other costs and expenses	(2.4)	(5.9)
Other—net	(9.4)	(4.0)
	$ 0.4	$ (21.0)

U.S. Federal ordinary income tax rate were the effect of consolidated affiliates, 2.5 points; inclusion of the earnings of the Credit Corporation in before-tax income on an "after-tax" basis, 2.0 points; investment credit, 1.0 points; and lower taxes on capital gains, 0.3 points.

Minority interest in earnings of consolidated affiliates represents the interest which other share owners have in net earnings and losses of consolidated affiliates not wholly owned by the Company.

Cash and marketable securities totaled $322.1 million at the end of 1973, an increase of $27.8 million from the end of 1972. Time deposits and certificates of deposit aggregated $134.4 million at December 31, 1973 and $113.7 million at December 31, 1972. Deposits restricted as to usage and withdrawal or used as partial compensation for short-term borrowing arrangements were not material.

Marketable securities are carried at the lower of amortized cost or market value. Carrying value was substantially the same as market value.

Current receivables, less allowance for losses, totaled $2,177.1 million at December 31, 1973 as shown in the table below. The increase of $251.1 million, or 13% during the year, was due principally to the increase in sales in 1973. Other current receivables include the current portion of advances to suppliers and similar items not directly arising from sales of goods and services. Long-term receivables, less allowance for losses, are reported under other assets. Supplemental information on sources of charges and credits to allowance for losses is included in the Form 10-K Report.

Current receivables		*(In millions)*
December 31	**1973**	**1972**
Customers' accounts and notes	$1,996.4	$1,784.1
Nonconsolidated affiliates	0.5	0.6
Other	238.7	192.4
	2,235.6	1,977.1
Less allowance for losses	(58.5)	(51.1)
	$2,177.1	$1,926.0

Inventories are summarized below, and at the end of 1973 were $1,986.2 million compared with $1,759.0 million at December 31, 1972 and $1,611.7 million at January 1, 1972. About 84% of total inventories are in the United States and substantially all of these are valued on a last-in, first-out (LIFO) basis. Substantially all of those outside the United States are valued on a first-in, first-out (FIFO) basis. Such valuations are not in excess of market and are based on cost, exclusive of certain indirect manufacturing expenses and profits on sales between the Parent and affiliated companies. The LIFO basis values inventories conservatively during inflationary times, and on a FIFO basis the year-end 1973 inventories would have been $429.7 million in excess of this valuation. This excess increased $125.6 million during 1973 and $31.3 million during 1972.

Inventories		*(In millions)*
December 31	**1973**	**1972**
Raw materials and work in process	$1,276.1	$1,097.2
Finished goods	604.6	573.8
Unbilled shipments	105.5	88.0
	$1,986.2	$1,759.0

Working capital (current assets less current liabilities) totaled $993.0 million, a decrease of $116.6 million during

SCHEDULE 25.11 (*continued*)

1973. The statement on page 33 provides a summary of major sources and applications of funds as well as an analysis of changes in working capital.

Investments amounted to $869.7 million at the end of 1973 as shown below.

Investments		*(In millions)*
December 31	**1973**	**1972**
Nonconsolidated finance affiliates	$327.4	$277.6
Honeywell Inc. and Honeywell Information Systems Inc.	154.6	167.3
Associated companies	68.1	47.7
Miscellaneous investments	331.7	274.6
	881.8	767.2
Less allowance for losses	(12.1)	(12.3)
	$869.7	$754.9

Investments in nonconsolidated finance affiliates are carried at equity plus advances. Advances to these affiliates aggregated $0.7 million at the end of 1973 compared with a 1972 year-end balance of $15.8 million.

Investment in General Electric Credit Corporation, a wholly-owned nonconsolidated finance affiliate, amounted to $321.4 million at the end of 1973 and $275.8 million at the end of 1972. Condensed financial statements for the General Electric Credit Corporation and its consolidated affiliates are shown at right. Copies of their 1973 Annual Report may be obtained by writing to General Electric Credit Corporation, P.O. Box 8300, Stamford, Conn. 06904.

Investments in the common stock of Honeywell Inc. and Honeywell Information Systems Inc. (HIS), a subsidiary of Honeywell, are recorded at appraised fair value as of date of acquisition, October 1, 1970, when the information systems equipment business was transferred to HIS. The appraised fair value recognized such factors as the size of the holdings, the various requirements and restrictions on the timing of the sale or other disposition of the securities, as well as the uncertainty of future events.

At December 31, 1973, General Electric held 1,612,432 shares of Honeywell common stock compared with 1,780,-432 shares at December 31, 1972. Reflecting generally depressed market conditions, the shares on hand at the end of 1973 would have been valued at $113.1 million using the December 31 closing price. The market value of the shares on hand at year-end 1972 would have been $245.7 million. In addition, General Electric continued to hold an 18½% ownership in HIS.

As commented upon under Other Income, on page 35, General Electric sold 168,000 shares of Honeywell common stock in 1973 and 370,000 in 1972. Cumulative sales through the end of 1973 were 913,000 shares.

During 1975 through 1980, Honeywell has the option to purchase from General Electric, and General Electric has the option to require Honeywell to purchase, General Electric's interest in HIS. Payment would be in Honeywell common stock. General Electric has agreed that if the U.S. Attorney General so requests, it shall, prior to the end of 1980, exercise its option to require Honeywell to purchase General Electric's interest in HIS. General Electric has committed to the U.S. Department of Justice to dispose of current holdings of Honeywell common stock in stages by June 30, 1978, and all other shares of Honeywell common stock received for

General Electric Credit Corporation		*(In millions)*
Financial position		
December 31	**1973**	**1972**
Cash and marketable securities	$ 141.4	$ 120.9
Receivables	3,835.0	3,032.1
Deferred income	(396.7)	(313.8)
Allowance for losses	(76.7)	(70.0)
Net receivables	3,361.6	2,648.3
Other assets	27.0	20.3
Total assets	$3,530.0	$2,789.5
Notes payable:		
Due within one year	$1,756.2	$1,271.6
Long-term—senior	760.8	738.1
—subordinated	254.8	205.5
Other liabilities	437.5	314.3
Total liabilities	3,209.3	2,529.5
Capital stock	160.0	110.0
Retained earnings	160.7	150.0
Equity	320.7	260.0
Total liabilities and equity	$3,530.0	$2,789.5
Current and retained earnings		
For the year	**1973**	**1972**
Earned income	$ 406.4	$ 319.8
Expenses:		
Operating and administrative	117.0	102.0
Interest and discount	190.3	108.5
Provision for receivable losses	28.1	35.9
Provision for income taxes	29.3	32.3
	364.7	278.7
Net earnings	41.7	41.1
Deduct dividends	(31.0)	(33.0)
Retained earnings at January 1	150.0	141.9
Retained earnings at December 31	$ 160.7	$ 150.0

General Electric's interest in HIS by December 31, 1980.

A voting trust has been established in which General Electric must deposit all shares of Honeywell common stock received as part of these transactions.

Investments in associated companies which are not consolidated but in which the Company owns 20% or more of the voting stock are valued by the equity method.

Miscellaneous investments are valued at cost. On December 31, 1973, the estimated realizable value of these investments was approximately $405 million, an increase of $35 million during the year.

Plant and equipment represents the original cost of land, buildings and equipment less estimated cost consumed by wear and obsolescence. Plant additions were substantially greater in 1973 than in 1972 principally due to major additions to capacity in the Industrial Components and Systems category. Details of plant and equipment and accumulated depreciation are shown in the table below. Additions, dispositions, provisions for depreciation and other changes in plant and equipment, analyzed by major classes, are included in the 10-K Report. Expenditures for maintenance and repairs are charged to operations as incurred.

Plant and equipment		(In millions)
	1973	**1972**
Major classes at December 31:		
Land and improvements	$ 104.4	$ 103.0
Buildings, structures and related equipment	1,445.9	1,347.5
Machinery and equipment	3,138.5	2,828.2
Leasehold costs and plant under construction	231.0	170.5
	$4,919.8	$4,449.2
Cost at January 1	$4,449.2	$4,134.2
Additions	598.6	435.9
Dispositions	(128.0)	(120.9)
Cost at December 31	$4,919.8	$4,449.2
Accumulated depreciation		
Balance at January 1	$2,312.6	$2,108.5
Current year provision	334.0	314.3
Dispositions	(95.8)	(107.6)
Other changes	8.5	(2.6)
Balance at December 31	$2,559.3	$2,312.6
Plant and equipment less depreciation at December 31	$2,360.5	$2,136.6

Other assets, less allowance for losses of $15.1 million ($16.5 million at December 31, 1972), totaled $608.6 million at December 31, 1973. Principal items comprising these balances are shown below.

Deferred income taxes applicable to current assets and liabilities were $97.8 million and $94.1 million at the end of 1973 and 1972 respectively.

Research and development expenditures, except those specified as recoverable engineering costs on Government contracts, are charged to operations as incurred. Expenditures of Company funds for research and development are shown on page 34.

Licenses and other intangibles acquired after October 1970 are being amortized over appropriate periods of time.

Other assets		(In millions)
December 31	**1973**	**1972**
Long-term receivables	$173.4	$133.9
Customer financing	141.2	117.4
Deferred income taxes	131.0	130.5
Recoverable engineering costs on Government contracts	61.3	67.3
Deferred charges	32.4	23.5
Licenses and other intangibles—net	30.9	30.7
Other	38.4	27.7
	$608.6	$531.0

Short-term borrowings, those due within one year, totaled $665.2 million at the end of 1973, compared with $439.4 million at the end of the previous year. A summary of these borrowings at year-end 1973 and 1972, and the applicable average interest rate at December 31, 1973, is shown in the tabulation below.

The average balance of short-term borrowings, excluding the current portion of long-term debt, during 1973 was $594.7 million (calculated by averaging all month-end balances for the year). The maximum balance included in this calculation was $775.1 million at the end of November 1973. The aver-

Short-term borrowings		(In millions)
December 31	**1973**	**1972**
Banks		
Parent (average rate at 12/31/73—9.68%)	$ 99.0	$ 56.0
Consolidated affiliates (average rate at 12/31/73—11.87%)	158.7	115.6
Notes with Trust Departments (average rate at 12/31/73—7.93%)	215.8	215.9
Holders of commercial paper (average rate at 12/31/73—9.71%)	124.3	—
Other, including current portion of long-term debt	67.4	51.9
	$665.2	$439.4

age interest rate for the year 1973 was 9.9%, representing total short-term interest expense divided by the average balance outstanding.

Parent bank borrowings are principally from U.S. sources. Bank borrowings of affiliated companies, most of which are foreign, are primarily from sources outside the U.S.

Although the total unused credit available to the Company through banks and commercial credit markets is not readily quantifiable, informal credit lines in excess of $750 million had been extended by approximately 135 U.S. banks at year-end 1973.

Accounts payable at December 31, 1973 and 1972 are shown below.

Accounts payable		*(In millions)*
December 31	**1973**	**1972**
Trade	$583.4	$489.3
Collected for the account of others	67.0	60.1
Nonconsolidated affiliates	23.1	8.7
	$673.5	$558.1

Other costs and expenses accrued at the end of 1973 included compensation and benefit costs accrued of $385.6 million and interest expense accrued of $22.6 million. At the end of 1972, compensation and benefit costs accrued were $339.9 million and interest expense accrued was $19.5 million. The remaining costs and expenses accrued included liabilities for items such as replacements under guarantees and allowances to customers.

Long-term borrowings amounted to $917.2 million at December 31, 1973, compared with $947.3 million at the end of 1972 as summarized at upper right.

General Electric Company 6¼% Debentures are due in 1979.

General Electric Company 7½% Debentures are due in 1996. Sinking fund payments are required beginning in 1977.

General Electric Company 5.30% Debentures are due in 1992. In accordance with sinking fund requirements, debentures having a face value of $10.0 million, and reacquired at a cost of $8.1 million, were retired in 1973. Debentures outstanding at the end of 1973 amounted to $160.8 million after deduction of reacquired debentures with a face value of $29.2 million held in treasury for 1974 and future sinking fund requirements.

General Electric Company 5¾% Notes are due in 1991. At December 31, 1973, $106.2 million was classified as long-

Long-term borrowings		*(In millions)*
December 31	**1973**	**1972**
General Electric Company:		
6¼% Debentures	$125.0	$125.0
7½% Debentures	200.0	200.0
5.30% Debentures	160.8	171.9
5¾% Notes	106.2	112.5
3½% Debentures	84.3	98.4
General Electric Overseas Capital Corporation	181.4	182.0
Other	59.5	57.5
	$917.2	$947.3

term and $6.3 million was classified as short-term. Notes having a value of $6.3 million were retired during 1973 in accordance with prepayment provisions.

General Electric Company 3½% Debentures are due in 1976. Debentures having a face value of $16.1 million, and reacquired at a cost of $13.0 million, were retired during 1973 in accordance with sinking fund provisions. Debentures outstanding at the end of 1973 amounted to $84.3 million after deduction of reacquired debentures with a face value of $28.8 million held in treasury for future sinking fund requirements.

Borrowings of General Electric Overseas Capital Corporation (a wholly-owned consolidated affiliate) are unconditionally guaranteed by General Electric as to payment of principal, premium, if any, and interest. This Corporation primarily assists in financing capital requirements of foreign companies in which General Electric has equity interest. The borrowings include the Corporation's 4¼% Guaranteed Bonds due in 1985 in the aggregate principal amount of $50.0 million. The bonds are convertible through November 1975 into General Electric common stock at $65.50 a share. Sinking fund payments on any 1985 bonds not converted are required beginning in 1976. Also included are the Corporation's 4¼% Guaranteed Debentures due in 1987 in the amount of $50.0 million and convertible from June 15, 1973 to June 15, 1987 into Company common stock at $80.75 a share. During 1973, the Corporation issued 5½% Sterling/Dollar Guaranteed Loan Stock due in 1993 in the amount of £3.6 million ($8.3 million), convertible from October 1976 into General Electric common stock at $73.50 a share.

Other long-term borrowings were largely borrowings by foreign affiliates with various interest rates and maturities.

Long-term borrowing maturities during the next five years, including the portion classified as current, are $42.0 million in 1974, $43.7 million in 1975, $132.3 million in 1976, $33.4 million in 1977 and $31.3 million in 1978. These amounts are after deducting reacquired debentures held in the treasury for sinking fund requirements.

Additional miscellaneous details pertaining to long-term borrowings are available in the 10-K Report.

Other liabilities were $492.1 million at December 31, 1973 compared with $456.8 million at December 31, 1972 and included such items as the deferred investment tax credit, the noncurrent portion of the allowance for replacements under guarantees, deferred incentive compensation, and other miscellaneous employee plans costs. Supplemental information is included in the 10-K Report.

Preferred stock, $1.00 par value, up to a total of 2,000,000 shares has been authorized by the share owners. No preferred shares have been issued.

Common stock, $2.50 par value, up to a total of 210,000,000 shares has been authorized by the share owners. Shares issued and outstanding at the end of the last two years are shown below. The number of new shares issued varies between periods depending principally on the requirements of employee plans and the timing of deliveries of shares under the provisions of those plans.

Common stock issued and outstanding

	1973	1972
Shares issued at January 1	185,243,848	184,936,318
New shares issued:		
Stock option plans	274,409	296,002
Savings and Security Program	—	11,528
Shares issued at December 31	185,518,257	185,243,848
Deduct shares held in treasury	(3,370,759)	(2,895,999)
Shares outstanding at December 31	182,147,498	182,347,849

Common stock held in treasury for various corporate purposes totaled $184.5 million at the close of 1973. The comparable amount at the end of 1972 was $146.5 million. Purchases during 1973 totaled 1,698,126 shares including 344,826 at current market prices from employees who acquired them through employee plans other than stock option plans. Other purchases were primarily through regular transactions in the security markets.

Treasury stock dispositions are shown in the table at the upper right. During 1973, the General Electric Company delivered 105,000 shares in connection with the acquisition of Midwest Electric Products Inc.

Dispositions of treasury shares

	1973	1972
Employee savings plans	1,011,101	876,231
Incentive compensation plans	107,216	94,515
Business combinations	105,000	—
Conversion of Overseas Capital Corporation 1985 bonds	—	151
Other	49	28
	1,223,366	970,925

Included in common stock held in treasury for the deferred compensation provisions of incentive compensation plans were 1,222,422 shares at December 31, 1973 and 1,151,053 shares at December 31, 1972. These shares are recorded at market value at the time of allotment. The liability is recorded under other liabilities.

The remaining common stock held in treasury is carried at cost, $127.7 million at the end of 1973 and $96.1 million at the end of 1972. These shares are held for future corporate requirements including 1,500,931 shares for possible conversion of General Electric Overseas Capital Corporation convertible indebtedness described under long-term borrowings, for distributions under employee savings plans and for incentive compensation awards.

Amounts in excess of par value received for stock increased $12.9 million during 1973 which resulted from amounts received for newly-issued shares in excess of par value of $11.1 million, and net gains from treasury stock transactions of $1.8 million. During 1972, there was an increase of $27.8 million which resulted from amounts received for newly-issued shares in excess of par value of $12.6 million and net gains from treasury stock transactions of $15.2 million.

Incentive compensation plans provide incentive for outstanding performance to over 3,000 key employees. Allotments made in 1973 for services performed in 1972 aggregated $27.8 million. Allotments made in 1972 for services performed in 1971 totaled $24.0 million.

Retained earnings at year-end 1973 included approximately $169.6 million representing the excess of earnings of General Electric Credit Corporation over dividends received from this affiliate since its formation. In addition, retained earnings have been reduced by $0.6 million, which represents the change in equity in associated companies since acquisition. At the end of 1972, these amounts were $158.9 million and $1.5 million respectively.

The Stock Option and Stock Appreciation Rights Plan, approved by share owners in 1973 by 96.5% of the votes cast, as well as previous plans under which options remain outstanding, provided continuing incentive for more than 500 employees. Option price under these plans is the full market value of General Electric common stock on date of grant. Therefore, participants in the plans do not benefit unless the stock's market price rises, thus benefiting all share owners. Also, an employee can only exercise his option to the extent that annual installments have matured, normally, over a period of nine years. Thus the plans encourage managers and professional employees to have the long-term entrepreneurial interest that will benefit all share owners. Details of the 1973 Plan were included in the 1973 Proxy Statement.

A summary of stock option transactions during the last two years is shown below. At the end of 1973, there were 2,500,000 shares reserved for the 1973 Plan, and 2,123,266 shares covered by outstanding options granted under prior plans, for a total of 4,623,266 shares. Of this total amount, 803,209 shares were subject to exercisable options, 1,875,022 shares were under options not yet exercisable and 1,945,035 shares were available for granting options in the future. The number of shares available for granting options at the end of 1972 was 160,365; however, no options against these shares were granted and their availability was terminated May 1, 1973. Further details on stock options are available in the 10-K Report.

Stock Options	Shares subject to option	Average per share Option price	Market price
Balance at Dec. 31, 1971	2,388,931	$45.70	$62.62
Options granted	475,286	67.62	67.62
Options exercised	(297,244)	42.71	65.79
Options terminated	(90,062)	45.52	—
Balance at Dec. 31, 1972	2,476,911	50.27	72.88
Options granted	554,965	64.75	64.75
Options exercised	(273,569)	42.84	63.69
Options terminated	(80,076)	52.50	—
Balance at Dec. 31, 1973	2,678,231	53.96	63.00

Lease commitments and contingent liabilities, consisting of guarantees, pending litigation, taxes and other claims, in the opinion of management, are not considered to be material in relation to the financial position of the Company.

Report of Independent Certified Public Accountants

To the Share Owners and Board of Directors of General Electric Company

We have examined the statements of financial position of General Electric Company and consolidated affiliates as of December 31, 1973 and 1972, and the related statements of current and retained earnings and changes in financial position for the years then ended. Our examination was made in accordance with generally accepted auditing standards, and accordingly included such tests of the accounting records and such other auditing procedures as we considered necessary in the circumstances.

In our opinion, the aforementioned financial statements present fairly the financial position of General Electric Company and consolidated affiliates at December 31, 1973 and 1972, and the results of their operations and the changes in their financial position for the years then ended, in conformity with generally accepted accounting principles applied on a consistent basis.

Peat, Marwick, Mitchell & Co.

Peat, Marwick, Mitchell & Co.
345 Park Avenue, New York, N.Y. 10022
February 15, 1974

Ten year summary

On worldwide basis of consolidation	1973	1972	1971	1970
Sales of products and services	$11,575.3	$10,239.5	$9,425.3	$8,726.7
Employee compensation, materials and all other operating costs	10,620.5	9,424.8	8,688.3	8,177.8
Operating margin	954.8	814.7	737.0	548.9
Other income	183.7	189.2	152.0	106.8
Interest and other financial charges	(126.9)	(106.7)	(96.9)	(101.4)
Earnings before income taxes & minority interest	1,011.6	897.2	792.1	554.3
Provision for income taxes	(418.7)	(364.1)	(317.1)	(220.6)
Minority interest	(7.8)	(3.1)	(3.2)	(5.2)
Net earnings	585.1	530.0	471.8	328.5
Earnings per common share *(a)*	3.21	2.91	2.60	1.81
Dividends declared per common share *(a)*	1.50	1.40	1.38	1.30
Earnings as a percentage of sales	5.1%	5.2%	5.0%	3.8%
Earned on share owners' equity	18.1%	18.0%	17.6%	13.2%
Cash dividends declared	$ 272.9	$ 254.8	$ 249.7	$ 235.4
Shares outstanding—average *(In thousands) (a)*	182,051	182,112	181,684	181,114
Share owner accounts—average	537,000	536,000	523,000	529,000
Market price range per share *(a) (b)*	75⅞ -55	73-58¼	66½-46½	47¼-30⅛
Price/earnings ratio range	24-17	25-20	26-18	26-17
Current assets	$4,485.4	$3,979.3	$3,639.0	$3,334.8
Current liabilities	3,492.4	2,869.7	2,840.4	2,650.3
Total assets	8,324.2	7,401.8	6,887.8	6,198.5
Share owners' equity	3,372.4	3,084.6	2,801.8	2,553.6
Plant and equipment additions	$ 598.6	$ 435.9	$ 553.1	$ 581.4
Depreciation	334.0	314.3	273.6	334.7
Employees—average worldwide	388,000	369,000	363,000	397,000
—average U.S.	304,000	292,000	291,000	310,000

(Dollar amounts in millions; per-share amounts in dollars)

1969	1968	1967	1966	1965	1964
$8,448.0	$8,381.6	$7,741.2	$7,177.3	$6,213.6	$5,319.2
7,961.4	7,733.8	7,100.3	6,545.3	5,568.1	4,930.6
486.6	647.8	640.9	632.0	645.5	388.6
98.7	86.3	91.4	72.4	72.1	69.9
(78.1)	(70.5)	(62.9)	(39.9)	(27.4)	(21.2)
507.2	663.6	669.4	664.5	690.2	437.3
(231.5)	(312.3)	(320.5)	(347.4)	(352.2)	(233.8)
2.3	5.8	12.5	21.8	17.1	16.1
278.0	357.1	361.4	338.9	355.1	219.6
1.54	1.98	2.00	1.88	1.97	1.22
1.30	1.30	1.30	1.30	1.20	1.10
3.3%	4.3%	4.7%	4.7%	5.7%	4.1%
11.5%	15.4%	16.5%	16.2%	18.0%	11.7%
$ 235.2	$ 234.8	$ 234.2	$ 234.6	$ 216.7	$ 197.7
180,965	180,651	180,266	180,609	180,634	179,833
520,000	530,000	529,000	530,000	521,000	516,000
49⅛-37	50¼-40⅛	58-41¼	60-40	60⅛-45½	46¾-39⅜
32-24	25-20	29-21	32-21	31-23	39-32
$3,287.8	$3,311.1	$3,207.6	$3,013.0	$2,842.4	$2,543.8
2,366.7	2,104.3	1,977.4	1,883.2	1,566.8	1,338.9
5,894.0	5,652.5	5,250.3	4,768.1	4,241.5	3,788.2
2,426.5	2,402.1	2,245.3	2,128.1	2,048.1	1,896.4
$ 530.6	$ 514.7	$ 561.7	$ 484.9	$ 332.9	$ 237.7
351.3	300.1	280.4	233.6	188.4	170.3
410,000	396,000	385,000	376,000	333,000	308,000
318,000	305,000	296,000	291,000	258,000	243,000

Requests for Additional Information
Additional information, including financial statements of the General Electric Pension Trust and the Company's Form 10-K Report, are available to share owners upon request. Requests should be sent to:
Investor Relations,
General Electric Company,
570 Lexington Avenue,
New York, N.Y. 10022.

(a) Amounts have been adjusted for the two-for-one stock split in April 1971.

(b) Represents high and low market price on New York Stock Exchange for each year.

QUESTIONS AND PROBLEMS

1. What are some of the advantages of using the "natural" business year instead of the calendar year for accounting purposes?

2. What is the advantage of presenting current assets first in the asset classification?

3. Indicate where you would present the following account balances on a balance sheet:
   a. Treasury Stock (at cost of shares acquired)
   b. Discount on Bonds Payable
   c. U. S. Treasury Notes
   d. First Mortgage Bonds (portion due five months after date of the balance sheet)
   e. Reserve for Self-insurance
   f. Advances to Subsidiaries
   g. Advertising Costs.

4. Suggest better or alternative titles for the following balance sheet accounts:
   a. Reserve for Bad Debts
   b. Earned Surplus
   c. Reserve for Federal Income Taxes
   d. Accrued Interest on Notes Receivable
   e. Capital Surplus
   f. Reserve for Depreciation.

5. Explain briefly the nature of each of the following balance sheet items:
   a. Investment in subsidiaries not consolidated, $904,191.
   b. Unamortized long-term debt issuance costs, $352,759.
   c. Goodwill and other intangible assets, $1.
   d. Excess of cost of certain shares of stock of the Rowe Corporation over applicable portion of underlying net assets, $859,267.
   e. Prepaid expenses and deferred charges, $588,089.
   f. Marketable securities at amortized cost (market value, $4,683,497), $4,299,770.
   g. Property construction fund, $4,928,144.
   h. Accumulated depletion of timberlands, $11,573, 928.
   i. Unamortized cigar-machine licenses, leasehold improvements, and patent rights, $173,764.

6. What is the advantage in presenting the amount of accumulated depreciation as a deduction from plant assets on the balance sheet?

7. What facts regarding the capital stock of a corporation should appear on its published balance sheet?

8. Explain the differences, if any, between the items referred to by the following pairs of terms.
   a. Accountant's report and auditor's report
   b. Qualified opinion and unqualified opinion
   c. "Subject to" opinion and "except for" opinion
   d. Balance sheet and statement of financial position
   e. Extraordinary items and prior-period adjustments

    f. Income applicable to minority shareholders and minority interest

    g. Statement of changes in financial condition and funds statement

    h. Premium on bonds and premium on stock.

  9. Explain the nature of the following items in a statement of income and retained earnings:

    a. Cost of goods sold

    b. Contribution to employees' retirement plan

   *c. Provision for depreciation

    d. Minority interest in subsidiary company's earnings

    e. Dividends on common stock

    f. Interest and amortization of discount on bonds payable.

10. Why should special mention be made of depreciation in published income statements?

11. What is the advantage of presenting comparative statements in a corporation's annual report?

12. What is the purpose of presenting schedules of comparative statistics in the annual reports?

13. What are some of the limitations in the effectiveness of comparative statistics?

14. Accounting data, especially income statement data, are sometimes presented in the form of a pie chart. Describe this form of presentation. Why may this graphic form be less effective than using divisions of a rectangular bar?

15. Indicate the location of each of the following items in the financial statements of the Desmond Manufacturing Company. Use the following key (not all numbers will be used).

Balance Sheet	Statement of Income and Retained Earnings
(1) Current assets	(6) Revenue (major source)
(2) Noncurrent assets	(7) Cost of goods sold
(3) Current liabilities	(8) Selling expenses
(4) Long-term liabilities	(9) Administrative expenses
(5) Stockholders' equity	(10) Other revenues
	(11) Income distributions
	(12) Retained earnings adjustments
	(13) Retained earnings appropriations

    a. Accumulated Depreciation on Factory Equipment

    b. Bonus to Officers

    c. Delivery Equipment

    d. Finished Goods Inventory (ending)

    e. Gain on Sale of Plant Assets

    f. Paid-in Capital

    g. Patents

---

* Hints, key numbers, or (partial) answers appear in the back of the book between the Appendix Tables and the Glossary.

  h. Premium on Mortgage Bonds Payable
  i. Federal and State Income Taxes Payable
  j. Refund on Prior Year's Income Taxes
  k. Reserve for Expansion
  l. Expansion Fund
  m. Union Dues Withheld
  n. Work in Process Inventory (ending).

16. Indicate the location of each of the following accounts in the financial statements of Wydown Retail Stores, Inc. Use the key shown for Problem 15.
  a. Advances to Salesmen
  b. Cash Surrender Value of Life Insurance
  c. Credit Balances in Customers' Accounts
  d. Depreciation—Furniture and Fixtures
  e. Goodwill
  f. Interest Payable
  g. Interest Receivable
  h. Interest Revenue
  i. Marketable Securities
  j. Merchandise Inventory (ending)
  k. Notes Receivable Discounted
  l. Officers' Salaries
  m. Office Supplies Used
  n. Petty Cash Fund
  o. Profit on Sale of Machinery
  p. Purchases—Merchandise
  q. Rent Received in Advance
  r. Unexpired Insurance.

*17. Indicate the location of each of the following accounts in the financial statements of the Rod Manufacturing Company. Use the key shown for Problem 15. Suggest better titles for reserves, where such titles could be used.
  a. Bond Sinking Fund
  b. Discount on Bonds Payable
  c. Discount on Capital Stock
  d. Dividends Declared
  e. Dividends Payable
  f. Dividend Revenue
  g. Factory Superintendent's Salary
  h. Gain on Sale of Plant Assets
  i. Interest Revenue
  j. Office Labor Cost
  k. Overhead (Factory)
  l. Patents
  m. Raw Materials Used
  n. Reserve for Contingencies
  o. Reserve for Depreciation
  p. Reserve for Federal Income Taxes
  q. Reserve for Fire Insurance
  r. Reserve for Possible Decline in Inventory Value
  s. Reserve for Sales Discounts
  t. Reserve for Uncollectible Accounts

u. Sales

v. Trademarks, Copyrights, and Goodwill

w. Treasury Stock

x. U. S. Treasury Bills.

18. The 1976 annual report of the United States Auto Corporation contains the following detail concerning selected items appearing in its financial statements:

	Balance Dec. 31, 1975	Additions	Deductions	Balance Dec. 31, 1976
Plant and Equipment (at cost)				
Land	$ 80,764,894	$ 681,249	$ 235,473	$ 81,210,670
Plant, Mineral and Manufacturing	4,109,137,728	483,991,386	52,647,893	4,540,481,221
Transportation	578,362,527	30,205,352	4,781,463	603,786,416
Total	4,768,265,149	514,877,987	57,664,829	5,225,478,307
Less				
Depreciation and Depletion for Plant, Mineral and Manufacturing ..	2,592,306,787	261,741,684	52,163,549	2,801,884,922
Transportation	297,963,515	18,739,371	2,696,899	314,005,987
Total	2,890,270,302	280,481,055 a	54,860,448	3,115,890,909
Net	$1,877,994,847	$234,396,932	$ 2,804,381 b	$2,109,587,398

a Wear and exhaustion of $276,008,777 shown in the consolidated statement of income comprises depreciation and depletion of $280,481,055 (including amortization of emergency facilities of $115,811,742), less profit of $4,472,278 resulting from sales.

b Includes $7,276,659 proceeds from sales and salvage of plant and equipment, less profit of $4,472,278 resulting therefrom.

Assume the use of the following accounts:

Cash in Bank

Cash on Hand

Land

Plant, Mineral, and Manufacturing Equipment

Transportation Equipment

Accumulated Depreciation—Plant, Mineral, and Manufacturing Equipment

Accumulated Depreciation—Transportation Equipment

Profit or Loss from Sales and Salvage of Plant and Equipment

Wear and Exhaustion of Facilities

Present journal entries for the following:

a. recognition of total depreciation and depletion for the year.

b. recognition of retirement and sale of all facilities including any gain or loss on the disposition.

°19. Prepare the stockholders' equity section of the balance sheet of the Livingston Manufacturing Company using the following information:

Authorized capital stock:
6.6% Prior Preferred Stock, par value $50 per share, cumulative, 35,000 shares.
6.68% Convertible Preferred Stock, par value $50 per share, cumulative, 100,000 shares.
Common Stock, no-par, stated value of $5.00 per share, 2,000,000 shares.

Subscribed stock:
Subscription of 1,000 shares of 6.6% Prior Preferred Stock at $55 has a balance due of $22 per share.

Issued stock (only "fully paid" shares have been issued):
29,000 shares of 6.6% Prior Preferred Stock at $53 per share.
87,000 shares of 6.68% Convertible Preferred Stock at $51 per share.
1,500,000 shares of Common Stock at $7.50 per share.

Treasury stock:
5,775 shares of 6.68% Convertible Preferred Stock reacquired at a total outlay of $283,000.
Under the law of the state in which the company is incorporated, the acquisition of treasury shares requires a restriction of retained earnings by an amount equal to the outlay.

Unappropriated retained earnings:
Balance at balance sheet date, $3,200,000.

Retained earnings appropriation:
A reserve for possible future expansion has been established, $515,000.

20. Prepare the stockholders' equity section of the balance sheet of the Rochester Company from the following data:

Authorized capital stock:
8% Cumulative Preferred Stock, par value $100 per share, 1,000 shares.
5½% Convertible Preferred Stock, par value $10 per share, cumulative, 20,000 shares.
Common Stock, no-par, stated value of $2 per share, 250,000 shares.

Subscribed stock:
750 shares of 5½% Convertible Preferred Stock, subscribed at $12 per share; collection of $10 per share has been made.

Issued stock (only "fully paid" shares are issued):
8% Cumulative Preferred, 420 shares at $110 per share.
5½% Convertible Preferred, 13,000 shares at $11.50 per share.
Common, 225,000 shares at $4 per share.

Held in treasury:
8 shares of 8% Cumulative Preferred Stock acquired by an outlay of $900.
1,100 shares of 5½% Convertible Preferred Stock acquired by an outlay of $13,200.
(Under the law of the state in which the company is incorporated, the acquisition of treasury shares requires a restriction of retained earnings by an amount equal to the outlay.)

Retained Earnings items:
Retained earnings, $755,000.
Reserve for fire insurance, $65,000.
Reserve for sinking fund, $50,000.

21. The comparative balance sheets of the Montgomery Baking Company for the year ended December 31, 1975, are shown below. Comment upon any significant or unusual items or features.

PROBLEM 21

MONTGOMERY BAKING COMPANY
Balance Sheets
December 31, 1975 and December 31, 1974

Assets

	Dec. 31, 1975	Dec. 31, 1974
Current Assets		
Cash in Banks and on Hand	$ 5,145,023	$ 5,241,712
U. S. Government Securities, substantially at Cost ..	600,000	707,294
Accounts Receivable:		
Trade—less Reserve of $30,425	2,422,207	2,293,919
Other	56,166	169,215
Inventories, at Lower of Cost or Market:		
Raw Materials and Products	1,979,450	2,178,608
Wrappers, Fuel and Other Supplies	1,011,378	1,076,673
Total Current Assets	$11,214,224	$11,667,421
Investments		
Mortgages Receivable	$ 137,325	$ 143,850
The British Pie Company, Ltd. (90% of equity, at		
cost)	176,851	176,851
	$ 314,176	$ 320,701
Property and Plant at Cost		
Land	$ 2,418,225	$ 2,364,045
Buildings	15,737,278	15,424,490
Machinery and Equipment	16,424,856	15,808,364
Delivery Equipment	8,634,695	8,497,149
	$43,215,054	$42,094,048
Less: Reserves for Depreciation (including $9,653,063		
and $10,337,492 respectively, applicable to fully		
depreciated assets)	27,145,418	26,565,281
	$16,069,636	$15,528,767
Deferred and Prepaid Items		
Prepaid Insurance, Taxes, etc.	$ 225,307	$ 439,159
Deferred Charges (pans, trays, crates, etc.)	712,298	538,137
	$ 937,605	$ 977,296
Intangible Assets	$ 2	$ 2
	$28,535,643	$28,494,187

PROBLEM 21 (*continued*)

Liabilities and Capital

	Dec. 31, 1975	Dec. 31, 1974
Current Liabilities:		
Accounts Payable	$ 2,517,104	$ 2,463,648
Dividends Payable on Preferred Stock	76,235	77,940
Current Prepayment Due on Long-term Debt	250,000	250,000
Salesmen's Guarantee Deposits	159,968	161,847
Provisions for Federal Income Taxes—$980,123 at Dec. 31, 1975 and $1,169,432 at Dec. 31, 1974 less U. S. Treasury Notes of $900,000 and $1,048,000, respectively	80,123	121,432
Accrued General Taxes, Interest, etc.	383,851	399,142
Total Current Liabilities	$ 3,467,281	$ 3,474,009
Deferred Federal Income Taxes	$ 154,061	$ —
Long-term Debt (Excluding prepayment above):		
9% Note, due March 31, 1977 (minimum prepayment of $250,000 due annually)	$ 3,450,000	$ 3,700,000
Capital Stock and Surplus:		
Capital Stock:		
Preferred Stock, 5½% cumulative, $100 par value; redeemable at $105 per share and entitled to $100 per share on liquidation: Authorized, issued and outstanding—55,449 shares in 1975 and 56,659 shares in 1974 ...	$ 5,544,900	$ 5,665,900
Common Stock of $1 par value: Authorized—1,250,000 shares Issued and Outstanding (after deducting 18,051 shares in 1975 and 13,051 shares in 1974 in Treasury, at par value)—814,202 Shares in 1975 and 819,202 Shares in 1974	814,202	819,202
	$ 6,359,102	$ 6,485,102
Capital Surplus	5,887,624	5,937,199
Earned Surplus, since September 15, 1956 ($5,506,964 restricted as to payment of dividends on common stock as of December 31, 1975 under terms of 9% Note)	9,217,575	8,897,877
	$21,464,301	$21,320,178
	$28,535,643	$28,494,187

---

*22. (AICPA adapted.) The following statement of source and use of funds of The D. Sweeney Company as prepared by the corporation's accountants is shown below.

PROBLEM 22

THE D. SWEENEY CORPORATION
Statement of Source and Use of Funds
For the Year Ended December 31, 1975

Source of Funds

Net Income	$ 52,000
Depreciation and Depletion	59,000
Increase in Long-term Debt	178,000
Common Stock Issued under Employee Option Plan	5,000
Total Sources	$294,000

Use of Funds

Cash Dividends	$ 33,000
Expenditures for Plant	202,000
Investments and Other Uses	9,000
Total Uses	$244,000
Increase in Funds for Year	
Sources minus Uses	$ 50,000

Analysis of Changes in Funds

Increase in Cash	$ 53,000
Increase in Receivables and Inventories	5,000
Less: Increase in Current Liabilities	(8,000)
Increase in Funds for Year	$ 50,000

The following additional information is available on the D. Sweeney Corporation for the year ending December 31, 1975.

(1)
Depreciation Expense	$ 58,000
Depletion Expense	1,000
	$ 59,000

(2)
Increase in Long-term Debt	$600,000
Retirement of Debt	422,000
Net increase	$178,000

(3) The Corporation received $5,000 in cash from its employees on its employee stock option plans, and wage and salary expense attributable to the option plans was an additional $22,000.

(4)
Expenditures for Plant	$222,000
Proceeds from Retirement of Plant (book value $16,000)	20,000
Net Expenditures	$202,000

(5) A stock dividend of 10,000 shares of Sweeney Corporation common stock was distributed to common stockholders on April 1, 1975, when the per-share market price was $6 and par value was $1.

(6) On July 1, 1975, when its market price was $5 per share, 16,000 shares of Sweeney Corporation common stock were issued in exchange for 4,000 shares of preferred stock.

(7) The income statement for the year contains the following lines.
Extraordinary Items

Loss on Expropriation of Plant in South America ..	$10,000
Less: Applicable Taxes	4,000
Total Extraordinary Loss	$6,000

a. Identify the weaknesses in the form and format of the Sweeney Corporation's statement of source and use of funds.

b. For each of the seven items of additional information for the statement of source and use of funds, indicate the preferable treatment, if any, and explain why the suggested treatment is preferable.

°23. The trial balance of the Thomas Manufacturing Company at December 31, 1975, after closing the production cost accounts, is as follows:

Accounts Receivable	$ 262,000	
Accumulated Depreciation—Buildings		$ 24,000
Accumulated Depreciation—Machinery and Equipment		72,000
Allowance for Uncollectible Accounts		7,000
Administrative Expense Control	340,000	
Advances on Special Orders		6,900
Buildings	110,000	
Cash in Bank	13,500	
Common Stock		350,000
Cost of Sales	1,467,500	
Dividends from Stock in Subsidiary		4,000
Dividends on Common Stock	17,500	
Dividends on Preferred Stock	12,000	
Dividends Payable		14,750
Factory Supplies	2,800	
Federal Income Taxes	41,200	
Federal Income Taxes Payable		41,200
First Mortgage Bonds Payable (10%)		50,000
Finished Goods	91,000	
Interest Charges on Notes	1,680	
Interest Charges on Bonds	4,500	
Interest Earned on Notes		220
Interest Payable		2,600
Interest Receivable	100	
Investment in Subsidiary	60,000	
Land	24,000	
Machinery and Equipment	260,000	
Notes Payable		26,600
Notes Receivable	45,000	
Notes Receivable Discounted		26,000
Patents	25,000	

Payroll Taxes Payable		11,700
Petty Cash Fund	150	
Preferred Stock		200,000
Premium on First Mortgage Bonds		2,500
Raw Materials	84,000	
Reserve for Contingencies		32,000
Reserve for Sinking Fund		50,000
Retained Earnings		95,940
Royalties Earned on Patents		5,000
Sales		2,460,000
Sales Discounts	49,000	
Sales Returns and Allowances	35,000	
Selling Expense Control	480,000	
Sinking Fund	57,500	
Sinking Fund Revenue		1,700
Undeposited Cash	700	
Unexpired Insurance	1,400	
Vouchers Payable		91,000
Withheld Income Tax		15,420
Work in Process	105,000	
	$3,590,530	$3,590,530

At their last meeting of 1975 the board of directors authorized an increase of $5,000 in the reserve for contingencies and voted to increase the reserve for sinking fund to the amount of the sinking fund, both actions to be recorded as of December 31, 1975. The entries had not been recorded at the time of the preparation of the trial balance.

Preferred stock: 6-percent, cumulative, par $100 per share, authorized $500,000, callable at 110, preference in case of involuntary dissolution at $105 per share and accrued dividends.

Common stock: No-par authorized 50,000 shares, outstanding 35,000 shares.

a. Prepare a well-organized statement of income and retained earnings.

b. Prepare a well-organized balance sheet.

*24. The adjusted trial balance of the Interstate Sales Company at December 31, 1975, is as follows:

Accounts Payable		$ 75,000
Accounts Receivable	$ 73,750	
Accumulated Depreciation—Building		40,000
Accumulated Depreciation—Equipment		95,000
Administration Expense Control	178,600	
Advances by Customers		1,250
Allowance for Uncollectible Accounts		6,500
Building	90,000	
Cash in Bank	60,800	
Cash on Hand	1,200	
Common Stock		200,000
Cost of Goods Sold	984,000	
Dividends on Common Stock	20,000	
Dividends on Preferred Stock	6,000	
Equipment	240,000	
Federal Income Tax	31,420	
Federal Income Tax Payable		31,420

Interest Charges	4,200	
Interest and Dividends Receivable	1,250	
Interest Payable		300
Investment in Stock of Interstate Stores, Inc.	61,000	
Land	15,000	
Merchandise Inventory	135,000	
Notes Payable		30,000
Note Payable to Insurance Company (8%; due 1/1/78)		50,000
Notes Receivable	15,000	
Payroll Taxes Payable		660
Preferred Stock		100,000
Prepaid Rent	3,000	
Reserve for Contingencies		20,000
Retained Earnings		50,210
Revenue from Interest and Dividends		5,100
Sales		1,462,000
Selling and Delivery Expense Control	226,300	
Supplies on Hand	5,400	
Unexpired Insurance	2,100	
United States Government Bonds	18,000	
Wages Payable		3,600
Withheld Income Tax		980
	$2,172,020	$2,172,020

Additional data:

Preferred stock: 6-percent, cumulative, $100 par value, preference in involuntary liquidation of $110 per share, 1,000 shares authorized and issued.

Common stock: no-par, 30,000 shares authorized; 20,000 shares issued and outstanding.

The investment in the stock of Interstate Stores, Inc. is accounted for with the cost method.

a. Prepare a well-organized statement of income and retained earnings.

b. Prepare a well-organized balance sheet.

*25. The following data are taken from the adjusted trial balances of the Hickory Manufacturing Company as of December 31, 1974 and 1975. The brackets indicate amounts to be determined in the solution of the problem.

	December 31, 1974		December 31, 1975	
Accounts Payable		$ 97,320		$ 98,715
Accounts Receivable— Net	$ 580,335		$ 617,530	
Accrued Expenses and Withholdings Payable..		99,800		99,700
Administrative Expense Control	449,160		447,260	
Bonds Payable (6%) ...		300,000		300,000
Cash	114,080		149,485	
Common Stock		100,000		[ ]
Cost of Goods Sold	3,207,840		3,220,390	

	December 31, 1974		December 31, 1975	
Depreciation of Plant and Equipment	45,710		48,825	
Discount on Bonds	25,000		[ ]	
Dividends on Common Stock—Cash	50,000		[ ]	
Dividends on Preferred Stock—Cash	6,000		6,000	
Dividends Payable	—			[ ]
Federal and State Income Taxes	104,975		122,675	
Federal and State Income Taxes Payable		104,975		111,675
Gain on Sale of Plant ...	—			[ ]
Interest Charges on Notes	2,900		3,100	
Interest Charges on Bonds	20,000		[ ]	
Interest and Dividend Revenue		16,010		18,070
Inventories	616,120		633,690	
Investments in Subsidiaries	162,000		162,000	
Notes Payable		51,500		53,400
Notes Receivable	65,600		68,400	
Plant and Equipment— Net	391,880		[ ]	
Preferred Stock		100,000		100,000
Premium on Common Stock		700,000		[ ]
Prepaid Insurance	8,240		7,640	
Retained Earnings	[ ]			[ ]
Royalties Revenue		37,020		44,285
Sales		4,552,320		4,605,275
Selling Expense Control.	642,530		656,230	
	$6,492,370	$6,492,370	$6,662,860	$6,662,860

Additional data:

(1) Preferred stock: 6-percent, cumulative, $100 par value, 2,000 shares authorized.

(2) Common stock: $1 par value, 150,000 shares authorized.

(3) On January 10, 1975, a 10-percent stock dividend was declared on common stock, issuable in common stock. The dividend was capitalized at $10 per share.

(4) On March 31 and September 30, 1975, dividends of 25¢ per share were declared payable on April 20 and October 20, 1975, respectively. On December 31, 1975, an extra dividend of 12½¢ per share was declared payable on January 20, 1976.

(5) Plant and equipment items having a cost of $39,240 and accumulated depreciation of $32,570 were retired and sold for $15,000. Acquisitions during 1975 amounted to $71,500.

(6) The bonds were issued on June 30, 1957, and mature on June 30, 1987. There have been no retirements since issuance.

a. Prepare a well-organized comparative statement of income and retained earnings.

b. Prepare a well-organized comparative balance sheet.

c. Prepare a well-organized statement of changes in financial position.

26. The adjusted trial balance of the Winston Sales Company as of December 31, 1975, is as follows:

Accounts Payable		$ 135,000
Accounts Receivable	$ 283,000	
Accumulated Depreciation—Building		70,000
Accumulated Depreciation—Furniture and Fixtures		50,000
Allowance for Uncollectible Accounts		8,000
Bonds Payable (10%)		140,000
Building	190,000	
Cash	95,000	
Common Stock		300,000
Dividends on Common Stock	30,000	
Dividends on Investment in Common Stock		13,000
Dividends on Preferred Stock	12,000	
Federal Income Taxes	47,000	
Furniture and Fixtures	110,000	
General and Administrative Expenses	191,000	
Government Securities	20,000	
Income Taxes Payable		47,000
Interest Charges	14,000	
Interest Earned		6,000
Investment in Common Stock	130,000	
Land	10,000	
Merchandise Inventory	395,000	
Payroll Payable		12,000
Preferred Stock		200,000
Premium on Common Stock		100,000
Prepayments	15,000	
Purchase Discounts		32,000
Purchase Returns and Allowances		14,500
Purchases of Merchandise	1,731,500	
Reserve for Expansion		50,000
Retained Earnings		116,000
Sales		2,245,000
Sales Discounts	35,500	
Sales Returns and Allowances	32,500	
Selling Expenses	203,000	
Taxes Payable—Other than Income Taxes		6,000
	$3,544,500	$3,544,500

Additional data:

(1) The merchandise inventory at December 31, 1975, is $405,000.

(2) The preferred stock has a par value of $100 per share, is entitled to a 6-percent cumulative dividend, and has a priority in liquidation of $105 per share. There are 2,000 shares authorized and outstanding.

(3) The common stock has $10 par value; 50,000 shares are authorized; 30,000 shares have been issued and are outstanding.

(4) There were no issuances or retirements of capital stock during the year.

(5) The Reserve for Expansion account was increased by $10,000 during the year.

(6) The investment in common stock is accounted for with the cost method.

a. Prepare a well-organized statement of income and retained earnings.

b. Prepare a well-organized balance sheet.

27. The adjusted trial balance of the Carter Manufacturing Company as of December 31, 1975, is as follows:

Accounts Payable		$ 142,100
Accounts Receivable	$ 231,600	
Accumulated Depreciation—Buildings		129,000
Accumulated Depreciation—Machinery and Equipment		333,000
Allowance for Uncollectible Accounts		6,100
Bonds Payable (10%)—Par		300,000
Buildings	306,000	
Capital Contributed in Excess of Stated Value		250,000
Cash in Bank	26,450	
Common Stock		400,000
Cost of Goods Sold	1,907,500	
Discount on Bonds	6,000	
Dividends on Common Stock	40,000	
Dividends from Investment in Common Stock		20,000
Dividends on Preferred Stock	18,000	
Factory Supplies	19,700	
Federal Income Taxes	80,200	
Finished Goods	239,200	
General and Administrative Expenses	205,800	
Goodwill	20,000	
Imprest Fund	150	
Interest Charges on Bonds	30,600	
Interest Charges on Notes	3,600	
Interest Earned		3,800
Interest Payable		6,600
Interest Receivable	610	
Investment in Common Stocks	250,000	
Land	50,000	
Loss on Sale of Plant Assets	3,700	
Machinery and Equipment	774,000	
Marketable Securities	32,000	
Notes Payable		66,000
Notes Receivable	22,500	
Notes Receivable Discounted		11,800
Preferred Stock		300,000
Raw Materials	146,500	
Refund of Prior Year Income Taxes		6,200
Reserve for Expansion		50,000
Retained Earnings		182,080
Sales		2,531,100
Sales Discounts	36,700	
Sales Returns and Allowances	32,600	

Selling and Delivery Expenses	156,300	
Sinking Fund	75,000	
Sinking Fund Reserve		75,000
Taxes Payable		83,200
Undeposited Cash	520	
Unexpired Insurance	1,450	
Wages Payable		10,100
Work in Process	189,400	
	$4,906,080	$4,906,080

Additional data:

(1) Preferred stock: 6-percent, cumulative, $100 par value, preference in liquidation of $104 per share plus accrued dividends, 5,000 shares authorized, 3,000 shares issued and outstanding.

(2) Common stock: no-par, $10 stated value per share, 50,000 shares authorized, 40,000 shares issued and outstanding.

(3) There were no issues or retirements of capital stock during the year.

(4) The Sinking Fund Reserve and the Reserve for Expansion were increased during the year in the amount of $10,000 each.

(5) The investment in common stocks is accounted for with the cost method.

a. Prepare a statement of income and retained earnings.

b. Prepare a balance sheet.

28. The following data are taken from the records of the Cunningham Company.

	December 31	
	1975	1974
	Adjusted Trial Balance	Post-closing Trial Balance
Accounts Payable	$113,000	$114,000
Accounts Receivable	93,000	89,500
Accrued Liabilities	8,000	10,000
Accumulated Depreciation	190,000	160,000
Administrative Expenses	85,000	
Allowance for Uncollectibles	4,000	3,500
Cash	60,000	62,500
Common Stock ($25 par value)	210,000	210,000
Cost of Goods Sold	600,000	
Current Prepayments	15,500	13,500
Federal Income Tax	24,000	
Income Taxes Payable	24,000	25,000
Interest Charges	3,000	
Marketable Securities	20,500	16,000
Merchandise Inventory	120,000	123,000
Mortgage Payable	60,000	60,000
Organization Costs	8,000	8,000
Plant and Equipment	452,000	415,000
Preferred Stock (6%)	100,000	100,000
Premium on Common Stock	5,000	5,000
Reserve for Contingencies	10,000	5,000
Retained Earnings	22,000	45,000
Sales	800,000	
Selling Expenses	55,000	
Treasury Stock—Common (par value)	10,000	10,000

A 6-percent dividend was declared and paid on the preferred and common shares during the year.

Preferred stock: 6-percent, cumulative, $100 par value, entitled to preference of $103 in liquidation, 1,000 shares authorized, issued, and outstanding.

Common stock: $25 par value per share, 10,000 shares authorized, 8,400 shares issued.

a. Prepare a statement of income and retained earnings for 1975.

b. Prepare a comparative balance sheet.

c. Prepare a statement of changes in financial position for 1975.

29. The following data are taken from the records of the Barr Sales Company:

	December 31	
	1975	**1974**
	Adjusted Trial Balance	**Post-closing Trial Balance**
Accounts Payable—Merchandise	$ 8,400	$ 9,160
Accounts Receivable	25,100	25,900
Accumulated Depreciation	4,600	5,600
Allowance for Uncollectible Accounts	400	430
Cash	27,802	21,810
Common Stock ($10 par value)	55,000	50,000
Cost of Goods Sold	155,000	
Deposits by Customers	420	
Depreciation	1,000	
Dividends on Common Stock—Cash	5,375	
Dividends Payable	2,750	2,500
Federal Income Tax	3,600	
Federal Income Tax Payable	3,600	2,400
Furniture and Fixtures	21,000	20,000
Gain on Sale of Land	1,500	
Installment Contracts Payable	2,000	
Interest Charges on Mortgage	482	
Interest Earned on Investments	500	
Interest Payable on Mortgage	50	
Interest Receivable	50	30
Investments	14,000	15,000
Loss on Sale of Investments	300	
Merchandise	33,450	31,150
Mortgage Payable (5%)	10,000	10,000
Other Expenses	26,293	
Premium on Common Stock	4,500	4,000
Premium on Mortgage	122	140
Prepaid Rent	300	
Rent Expense	3,600	
Reserve for Contingencies		5,000
Retained Earnings	26,110	23,860
Sales	210,000	
Salesmen's Commissions	12,400	
Salesmen's Commissions Payable	600	800
Uncollectible Accounts Adjustment (Sales)..	800	

Additional information:

(1) During the year the company retired fully depreciated fixtures which

had cost $2,000. These were the only dispositions of furniture and fixtures.

(2) Furniture and fixtures acquired on May 10, 1975, were financed one-third down, one-third due May 10, 1976, and one-third due May 10, 1977.

(3) On December 9, 1975, the company sold a parcel of land which it had purchased on January 14, 1975, at a cost of $8,000.

(4) On June 15, 1975, the company purchased additional investments at a cost of $3,200. This was the only acquisition during the year. All investments are accounted for with the cost method.

(5) Merchandise was delivered during the year on customers' deposits in the amount of $1,200. All other deliveries were on account.

(6) On January 2, 1975, the board of directors declared a five-percent stock dividend. The dividend was capitalized at $11 per share.

(7) On June 20, 1975, and December 20, 1975, the board of directors declared the regular semiannual 5-percent cash dividends.

(8) On June 30, 1975, the company issued 250 shares of stock for cash.

a. Prepare a well-organized statement of income and retained earnings for 1975.

b. Prepare a well-organized comparative balance sheet.

c. Prepare a well-organized statement of changes in financial position for 1975.

Chapter 26

Analysis and Interpretation of Financial Statements

Financial statements alone do not always convey the real significance of a firm's operating results and financial position. To make these statements more meaningful, special calculations are often made in the form of ratios, percentages, or unit analyses which assist in the comprehension of important relationships and trends. A few statistics of this type are presented in published reports, but most are more commonly found in schedules of internal operations and in manuals or reports issued by organizations that supply investment and credit information to investors.

The following discussion presents some of the more significant computations and is intended merely to indicate some of the possibilities rather than to be a complete presentation of the subject. The analysis will be focused on three types of calculations: (1) those designed to show the profitability and efficiency of the business, (2) those that seek to indicate the current liquidity of the business, and (3) those designed to indicate its long-run solvency.

Financial Statement Ratios

Important financial relationships may be expressed in the form of ratios. The ratio may be in percentage, decimal, or common-fraction form. The percentage form is the most common presentation.

Some ratios refer only to balance sheet data; some, only to operating statement data; others, to both balance sheet and operating statement data. This latter type of ratio, which integrates balance sheet and operating statement data, requires particular attention if both the numerator and the denominator are to be representative of the same period. In order to be representative, balance sheet data are best calculated as weighted averages of the daily data of the period covered by the operating statement. Frequently, however, only the amounts as of the end of the period are used. In the presentation that follows, an average of the beginning and ending data, adjusted in some cases for substantial changes which would make the adjusted average more representative of the period, will be used in the calculations.

Rates of activity, such as a rate of earnings, are usually expressed as annual rates. Where operating data of a period less than a year are used in calculating the rate, the operating data are first annualized; for example, quarterly operating data are converted to an annual basis by multiplying by four, resulting in rates that should be labeled with some modifying expression such as "at an annual rate of 12 percent."

Illustrative Data

Data shown in Schedule 26.1 for the financial position and operations of the M. & M. Equipment Company from January 1, 1975, to December 31, 1975, will be used as a basis for most of the ratios illustrated.

MEASURES OF PROFITABILITY AND EFFICIENCY

Usually the most important questions asked about a business are: How profitable is it? How efficiently is it run? Most statement analysis is directed to various aspects of these questions. Some of the measures of profitability and efficiency relate earnings to resources or capital employed, other computations compare earnings and various expenses to sales, and a third group of calculations seeks to explain profitability by measuring the efficiency with which inventories, receivables, and plant assets are administered.

Rate of Return on Total Capital

The most important of the ratios is the one that shows the rate of return earned on the total capital or resources employed by the enterprise. This is sometimes described as an *all-capital earning rate*. The total capital employed is indicated by the total of either side of the balance sheet, the total assets, or the total equities. Since the earning rate during the year is being determined, an average that will reflect changes in the invested capital during the year should be used in the denominator. A crude but usually satisfactory figure for average invested capital can be obtained by adding the total assets at the beginning and end of the period and dividing by two.

In order to be consistent, the income figure to be compared with total capital must be the income before deducting any distributions to the furnishers of capital; that is, both the minority share of income (shown in consolidated income statements) and interest charges must be added back to the net income figure. Since interest is a payment to a source of capital, the amount of interest charges, net of income taxes, must be added back to net income to measure the return on capital. To make the adjustment for interest charges in the illustration, first compute the average tax rate paid by M. & M. Equipment Company on taxable income. That rate is 36.8 percent (= $700,000/$1,900,000). Net income to shareholders in the illustration is $1,200,000. To this must be added the $200,000 of interest expense less the $73,600 (= .368 × $200,000) of income tax savings already accounted for by its deduction, or $126,400 [more simply calculated as (1 − .368) × $200,000]. Thus, income before distributions to furnishers of capital is $1,326,400.

In the M. & M. Equipment Company illustration, the balance sheet totals at the beginning and end of the year were $15,500,000 and $16,-600,000, respectively. The average invested capital for the year would be computed as $16,050,000 = ($15,500,000 + $16,600,000)/2. The all-capital earning rate would be:

$$\frac{\$\ 1,326,400}{\$16,050,000} = .083 \text{ or } 8.3\%$$

This percentage is ordinarily the most important single fact that can be determined from the analysis of the operations of a business enterprise. All of the operations are summarized in the income figure before payments to suppliers of capital. Income for a period can be compared with past results and with the income of other enterprises, especially since income before payments to suppliers of capital is not affected by changes and variations in the plans of financing.

Rate of Return on Stockholders' Equity

A ratio of more immediate interest to stockholders, although of less general value, is the rate of return on stockholders' equity or investment. Again, since a rate of return during the year is sought, an average equity or investment figure is needed. The following calculation is based upon the data for the M. & M. Equipment Company:

Stockholders' Equity, Jan. 1, 1975	$ 9,200,000
Stockholders' Equity, Dec. 31, 1975	9,800,000
	$19,000,000
Average Stockholders' Equity	$ 9,500,000

The net income is divided by this average investment figure to obtain the rate of return on the investment of the stockholders:

$$\frac{\$1,200,000}{\$9,500,000} = .126 \text{ or } 12.6\%$$

SCHEDULE 26.1 ILLUSTRATIVE DATA FOR FINANCIAL STATEMENT ANALYSIS

M. & M. EQUIPMENT COMPANY
Comparative Balance Sheets
As of December 31

Assets

	($ in Thousands)	
Currents Assets	1975	1974
Cash	$ 1,300	$ 1,100
Marketable Securities	300	300
Accounts Receivable (Net)	2,600	2,500
Inventories	7,300	6,900
Total Current Assets	$11,500	$10,800
Noncurrent Assets		
Plant and Equipment	$ 5,200	$ 4,500
Less Accumulated Depreciation	1,300	1,000
Net Plant and Equipment	$ 3,900	$ 3,500
Land	1,200	1,200
Total Noncurrent Assets	$ 5,100	$ 4,700
Total Assets	$16,600	$15,500

Liabilities and Stockholders' Equity

	1975	1974
Current Liabilities		
Accounts Payable	$ 1,600	$ 1,700
Accrued Payables	800	900
Income Taxes Payable	300	200
Notes Payable	1,900	1,200
Total Current Liabilities	$ 4,600	$ 4,000
Long-term Liabilities		
Bonds Payable (8%)	$ 2,000	$ 2,100
Mortgage Payable	200	200
Total Long-term Liabilities	$ 2,200	$ 2,300
Total Liabilities	$ 6,800	$ 6,300
Stockholders' Equity		
Contributed Capital		
Preferred Stock (6%, $100 par)	$ 2,000	$ 2,000
Common Stock ($1 par)	500	500
Additional Paid-in Capital	2,500	2,500
Total Contributed Capital	$ 5,000	$ 5,000
Retained Earnings	4,800	4,200
Total Stockholders' Equity	$ 9,800	$ 9,200
Total Equities	$16,600	$15,500

SCHEDULE 26.1 (*continued*)

M. & M. EQUIPMENT COMPANY
Statement of Income and Retained Earnings
Year of 1975

		($ in Thousands)	Percent of Total Revenues
Revenues			
Sales		$26,500	101.5%
Less Sales Allowances, Returns, and			
Discounts		600	2.3
Net Sales		$25,900	99.2
Interest and Other Revenues		200	.8
Total Revenues		$26,100	100.0
Expenses			
Cost of Goods Sold		$20,500	78.5
Selling and Administrative Expenses:			
Selling Expenses	$2,200		8.4
Administrative Expenses	1,300		5.0
Total Selling and Administrative Expenses ...		3,500	13.4
Interest Expense		200	.8
Income Tax Expense		700	2.7
Total Expenses		$24,900	95.4
Net Income to Shareholders		$ 1,200	4.6
Dividends			
Dividends on Preferred Stock	$ 120		
Dividends on Common Stock	480		
Total Dividends		600	
Addition to Retained Earnings for Year		$ 600	
Retained Earnings, January 1, 1975		4,200	
Retained Earnings, December 31, 1975		$ 4,800	
Earnings Per Share of Common Stock,[a] $2.16			

---

[a] Explanation in text: ($1,200,000 — $120,000)/500,000 shares.

Ordinarily it is assumed that the change in retained earnings occurs uniformly throughout the period. The issuance of additional shares at other than the midpoint of the period would justify adjusting the average of the beginning and ending stockholders' equity to make it more representative of the investment during the period.

Rate of Return on Common-Stock Equity

The rate of return on the common-stock equity can be computed in the same manner. The net income assignable to the common-stock equity is the net income of $1,200,000 less the preferred-stock dividends of $120,000 (6 percent of $2,000,000) or $1,080,000. Assuming that the preferred stockholders have no claim against the retained earnings, the average investment of the common stockholders is $7,500,000 (the average $9,500,000 equity less the preferred stock's par value of $2,000,000). The rate of return on the common-stock equity is:

$$\frac{\$1,080,000}{\$7,500,000} = .144 \text{ or } 14.4\%$$

Needless to say, if there were no preferred stock outstanding, the rate of return on the common stock equity would be identical with the rate of return on the stockholders' equity. In the illustration, the rate of return on the common-stock equity is greater than the rate earned on the total stockholders' investment (12.6 percent) because only 6 percent must be paid on the preferred-stock equity. The rate of return on common-stock equity exceeds the all-capital earning rate (8.3 percent) by even more, because the current liabilities carry no explicit return and the bonds were issued at a rate of 8 percent.

Earnings per Share on Preferred Stock

A calculation, which indicates the degree of protection of preferred stockholders and the safety of their dividend, is often made in connection with preferred stock. The net income for the year is divided by the number of shares of preferred stock outstanding. Since the par value of the preferred stock in the illustration is $100, there are 20,000 shares of stock outstanding ($2,000,000/$100), and the earnings per share figure is:

$$\frac{\$1,200,000}{20,000} = \$60 \text{ per share}$$

This does not mean that the preferred stock is entitled to receive $60 per share or that preferred-stock equity has increased by that amount. It merely means that the annual dividend requirement is well protected. The relationship could perhaps be expressed more effectively in another form—the dividend has been earned ten times ($= \$60/\$6$).

Earnings per Share on Common Stock

Earnings per share is, in most cases, calculated by dividing the net income for the period, less preferred-stock dividends, by the average number of common shares outstanding during the period. The common stock of M. & M. Equipment Company has a par value of $1 per share, so there were 500,000 shares outstanding throughout 1975. The preferred dividend was $120,000 so the calculation of earnings per share would be

$$\frac{\$1,200,000 - \$120,000}{500,000} = \$2.16 \text{ per share}$$

If there had been an issue (or retirement) of stock during the period for cash or other assets, the weighted average of shares outstanding would be used in the denominator.

This calculation of earnings per share is satisfactory if the enterprise has a relatively simple capital structure with only preferred stock and common stock outstanding. A corporation may also have outstanding commitments to issue shares of common stock under certain circumstances. Examples are convertible bonds, convertible preferred stock (both of which may be exchanged for common stock at a predetermined rate), stock options, and warrants (both of which give their holders the right to buy common shares at a predetermined price). For convenience, we call these commitments to issue common stock *residual securities*.

These commitments to issue common stock came into greater use in the 1960s as a part of the business-combination movement of that period. There was no standardized procedure for indicating the effect of such securities on earnings per share until the Accounting Principles Board adopted Opinion No. 9 in 1966[1] and then amended it in Opinion No. 15 in 1969.[2]

Accounting Principles Board Opinion No. 15 recognizes that a company with convertible securities, options, and warrants outstanding has committed itself to issuing common shares at the discretion of the owner of these securities. It requires the enterprise to recognize the potential common stock nature of these securities in calculating earnings per share and in many cases requires the calculation and reporting of two separate amounts for earnings per share.

The two earnings-per-share calculations used by corporations with residual securities are called the *primary* earnings per share and the *fully diluted* earnings per share. Understanding those two calculations requires understanding the concepts of *common stock equivalents* and *dilution* of earnings per share. These two concepts and the mechanics of calculating the two earnings-per-share amounts are explained in Appendix 26.1 of this chapter.

The figure for earnings per share on common stock is highly significant both to present and prospective stockholders. Dividends are important, especially to investors who plan on dividends as a regular source of spendable funds, but a stockholder's investment increases in value as the corporation earns its net income, whether or not it is distributed. For the prospective investor in shares of common stock, the earnings per share provides a figure that can be compared with the market value of the stock

---

[1] Opinion No. 9, Accounting Principles Board, AICPA, issued in December, 1966.
[2] Opinion No. 15, Accounting Principles Board, AICPA, issued in May, 1969.

in order to determine the rate of return currently being earned on the investment. It is a starting point in the investor's estimates of the rate that may be earned in the future. For example, assuming that the common stock of the M. & M. Equipment Company is selling for $25 per share at the end of 1975, the earnings yield per share is 8.6 percent ($= \$2.16/\$25$). The *price-earnings ratio* is the reciprocal of the earnings yield: 11.6 to 1.

Percentages of Revenue

One method used to measure profitability and efficiency is to prepare an income statement with a column of percentages shown in addition to the basic figures. Each income statement item is expressed as a percentage of the total revenue figure. The statement of income and retained earnings for the M. & M. Equipment Company contains income data expressed as a percentage of total revenues (Schedule 26.1).

Certain of these percentages are watched closely by management. The *operating ratio*, the percentage of total operating expenses to net sales, is often considered an important basis for judging the general effectiveness of operations. (Operating expenses are usually viewed as all expenses other than interest and income taxes; net sales is usually used in the denominator rather than total revenues.) In the M. & M. Equipment Company illustration, the operating ratio is $24,000,000 divided by the net sales of $25,900,000 or

$$\frac{\$24,000,000}{\$25,900,000} = 92.7 \text{ percent}$$

Sometimes income tax and interest expenses are included in the numerator; in other cases nonsales revenues are included in the denominator. The individual items on detailed schedules of selling and administrative expenses are frequently expected to bear a certain relationship to sales volume. In making comparisons and interpretations, however, the fact that not all expenses vary in proportion to sales must be taken into account. For example, if sales increase, a relatively fixed expense such as real estate taxes should show a decline in percentage while a relatively variable expense such as delivery costs should remain at approximately the same percentage.

Analyses of the revenue dollar, as shown in the M. & M. Equipment Company statement of income and retained earnings, are frequently given to stockholders and used in general publicity, but such information is rarely useful to anyone outside of the management because of the difficulty of interpreting the figures. A net income equal to 6 percent of revenues may be extraordinarily high in some industries, but normal or low in others. Changes in this ratio over time may give some evidence of managerial effectiveness. The important factor, as far as nonmanagerial groups are concerned, is not the ratio of net income to sales but the ratio of net income to the capital employed.

Turnover of Asset Items

In an effort to judge the efficiency of management in special areas, the *turnover* of various asset items is calculated. The three asset items most frequently analyzed in this way are inventories, receivables, and plant and equipment.

Inventory Turnover. A significant indicator of the efficiency of the operations of many businesses is the inventory turnover, or the number of times the average inventory has been sold during the period. The calculation involves dividing the cost of goods sold by the average inventory. In the illustration the average inventory is $7,100,000 [= ($6,900,000 + $7,300,000)/2]. The inventory turnover is

$$\frac{\$20,500,000}{\$\ 7,100,000} = 2.89 \text{ times per year}$$

In many cases, like the illustration, only the beginning and ending inventory figures will be available for the calculation of the average inventory, but monthly figures should, if possible, be used, especially where there are significant seasonal fluctuations in the amount of the inventories.

The M. & M. Equipment Company is a manufacturing concern. In retail and wholesale operations, the merchandise turnover receives even greater attention, because it is frequently viewed as an important indicator of marketing success.

The interpretation of the turnover figure involves two opposing considerations. Management would like to sell as many goods as possible with a minimum of investment in inventories, but it must also be prepared to give good service to its customers, which may mean keeping a relatively high inventory on hand. An increase, then, in the rate of turnover seems to indicate a more profitable use of the investment in inventories, but it may instead mean poorer service to customers, which may eventually more than offset any advantage gained by decreased investment.

Merchandise turnover standards vary a good deal from one type of business to another. The turnover in food stores, for example, will be considerably higher than in furniture stores.

A variation of this calculation indicates the average number of days that the merchandise is kept on the shelves. The number of days in the period, 365 days for a year, is divided by the inventory turnover. In the case of the retailing and wholesaling concerns this ratio indicates the average number of days that salable merchandise is on the shelves before being sold. Expressing inventory turnover in terms of average days on hand is frequently considered to be a more useful form for appraising the liquidity of the inventory asset than expressing it simply in terms of turnover. The inventory of M. & M. Equipment Company was on hand an average of 126 days (= 365/2.89).

Analysis of Receivables. A turnover figure for receivables, similar to that obtained for merchandise, could be calculated. It would be

$$\frac{\text{Sales on account}}{\text{Average accounts receivable}}$$

Probably a more useful way of analyzing receivables, however, involves the calculation of the average collection period or the number of days' sales in the average amount of accounts receivable on the books during the period. There are two steps in the calculation: (1) divide the net sales on account by the number of days in the period to get the average day's sales, and (2) divide the average amount of accounts receivable by the average day's sales on account to get the number of days' sales in accounts receivable or the average collection period.

The average accounts receivable of the M. & M. Equipment Company is $2,550,000 [= ($2,500,000 + $2,600,000)/2]. Assuming that all sales were made on account, the calculation would be:

$$\frac{\$25,900,000}{365} = \$70,959 \text{ per day} \tag{1}$$

$$\frac{\$2,550,000}{\$70,959} = 35.9 \text{ days} \tag{2}$$

This calculation offers a rough indication of the degree to which the credit policy of a business is being enforced and gives a general impression of the condition of the accounts receivable. The interpretation of the figure depends upon the credit terms offered by the M. & M. Equipment Company. If the firm offered terms of "30 days EOM" (due in thirty days from the end of the month of sale), the results would indicate that the accounts receivable were being handled well. If the terms of "net 30 days" were offered, the results would indicate that collections were not being made in accordance with the stated terms. Such a condition would warrant a review of the credit and collection activity for an explanation and possibly for corrective action to be taken.

Turnover of Plant and Equipment. Another indication of efficiency is the amount of sales per dollar of investment in plant and equipment. In general, the higher the ratio the better, but some excess capacity may be desirable to make sure that peak loads can be handled effectively. In the calculation, the sales figure is divided by the average investment in land, buildings, and equipment. The result is sometimes called the *ratio of sales to plant and equipment*. This ratio for the M. & M. Equipment Company would be:

$$\frac{\$25,900,000}{.5(\$5,100,000 + \$4,700,000)} = \$5.30 \text{ of sales per dollar of plant}$$

A variation in this ratio is the substitution of the cost of goods manufactured for the net sales figure in the numerator. The ratio will vary a great deal from one industry to another; "heavy" industries have a large investment in plant and equipment assets and show a low rate of turnover, while the retail and service types of business would, in general, have a higher rate.

MEASURES OF CURRENT LIQUIDITY

The current ratio and the acid-test ratio are the two principal measures used to indicate current liquidity.

The Current Ratio

The current ratio is computed as follows:

$$\frac{\text{Total current assets}}{\text{Total current liabilities}}$$

It is commonly expressed as a ratio such as three to one or ten to one, meaning that the current assets are three times or ten times as large as the current liabilities. The current assets of the M. & M. Equipment Company at December 31, 1975, total $11,500,000; the current liabilities total $4,600,000. The ratio calculation is:

$$\frac{\$11,500,000}{\$\ 4,600,000} = 2.50,$$

or a ratio of 2.50 to 1.

This ratio is supposed to indicate the ability of the concern to meet its current obligations and is, therefore, of particular significance to short-term creditors. Although a generous excess of current assets is desirable, changes in the trend of the ratio may be difficult to interpret. For example, when the current ratio is larger than one to one, equal increases in both current assets and current liabilities result in a decline in the ratio, while equal decreases result in an increased current ratio. Assume, for example, first that each of the figures used in the preceding calculation has increased $2,000,000 and then that each amount has decreased $2,000,000. The resulting current ratios are as follows:

$$\frac{\$13,500,000}{\$\ 6,600,000} = 2.05 \text{ to } 1 \qquad \frac{\$9,500,000}{\$2,600,000} = 3.65 \text{ to } 1$$

If a corporation has a profitable year, the large current liability for income taxes may cause a decline in the current ratio. In a recession period, business is contracting, current liabilities are paid off, and even though the current assets may be at a low point, the ratio will often go to high levels. During a boom period, the reverse effect is shown. In other words, a very high ratio may reflect unsatisfactory business conditions while a falling ratio may accompany profitable operations.

The current ratio is also susceptible to "window dressing"; deliberate steps can be taken that will result in a financial statement that presents a better condition at the balance sheet date than the average or normal conditions would justify. For example, toward the close of a fiscal year normal purchases on account may be delayed, or advances to officers may be collected and the proceeds used to reduce the current liabilities so that the current ratio will appear as favorable as possible in the annual financial statements.

Thus, while the current ratio is probably the most common ratio presented in statement analysis, it has a limited value, its trends are difficult to interpret, and, if overemphasized, it can easily lead to undesirable business practices as well as misinterpretation of financial condition.

Acid-Test Ratio

A variation of the current ratio, usually known as the *acid-test* ratio or *quick* ratio, is computed by including in the numerator of the fraction only those current assets that could be converted into cash very quickly. The items usually included are cash, marketable securities, and receivables, but it would be better to make a study of the facts in each case before deciding whether or not to include receivables and to exclude inventories. In some businesses the inventory of merchandise might more easily be converted into cash than the receivables of another business. The receivables and inventory-turnover rates, which were considered earlier in the discussion, give some indication of the liquidity of these two asset groups.

In the calculation, the sum of the highly liquid assets is divided by the total of the current liabilities. A ratio of approximately one to one was formerly thought to be necessary in order for the ratio to be judged satisfactory. Recognizing the importance of good asset management, most analysts are now willing to accept lower acid-test ratios, down to say .6 or .7, as being satisfactory. As of December 31, 1975, the accounts of the M. & M. Equipment Company indicated cash of $1,300,000, marketable securities of $300,000, and net accounts receivable of $2,600,000. Current liabilities were $4,600,000. The previous analysis of the average collection period of 35.9 days might lead to a questioning of whether all of the receivables should be included in the calculation of the ratio. Assuming that all receivables were to be included, the calculation would be:

$$\frac{\$1,300,000 + \$300,000 + \$2,600,000}{\$4,600,000} = \frac{\$4,200,000}{\$4,600,000} = .91$$

MEASURES OF LONG-RUN SOLVENCY

The principal measures that are used to predict solvency over longer periods are the several variations of the equity ratio and a ratio usually described as "times interest earned." Both of these ratios are, however, subordinate to estimates of probable future profits as indicators of future solvency. To the extent that calculations of current profitability and efficiency, discussed in a preceding section, can be projected into the future, they also indicate long-run solvency.

Equity Ratios

There are several variations of the equity ratio, but the one that is probably the most meaningful relates the total of the stockholders' equity to total equities (or total assets) and expresses the result as a percentage. As of

December 31, 1975, the total equities or assets of the M. & M. Equipment Company amounted to $16,600,000, and the total of the stockholders' equity accounts amounted to $9,800,000. The calculation of the equity ratio is:

$$\frac{\text{Total stockholders' equity}}{\text{Total equities (or assets)}} = \frac{\$ \ 9,800,000}{\$16,600,000} = .590 \text{ or } 59.0\%$$

This percentage provides an indication of the nature of the financial plan used by the enterprise, that is, the policy followed in connection with financing with borrowed capital as compared with financing with stockholders' or owners' investment. Such a percentage can be compared with standards for the industry and with other points in the history of the concern.

In general, the higher the equity ratio, the less is the likelihood of financial reorganization or liquidation in the future. The periods of the 1930s and, to a lesser degree, of the early 1970s demonstrate the importance of a sound capital structure in maintaining solvency during lean periods. The problem for many businesses is to decide how much financial risk they can afford to assume by obtaining funds by the use of bonds, which have a relatively low interest cost but require fixed, periodic payments and a principal payment at maturity.

In appraising the adequacy of the equity ratio, it is customary to vary the standard inversely with the stability of the firm's earnings. The more stable the earnings of the business, the lower the equity ratio that would be considered acceptable or safe. Public utility equity ratios are customarily low, but the stability of their earnings makes the ratio acceptable to many investors.

The equity ratio is sometimes expressed in other ways. One variation relates total liabilities to total assets or equities. This is, of course, the complement of the proportion of total stockholders' equity to total equities. In the earlier example, since stockholders' equity was $9,800,000 or 59.0 percent of the total equities of $16,600,000, total liabilities must be $6,800,000 or 41.0 percent of total equities. Another form of the equity ratio measures stockholders' equity as a multiple of total liabilities. It is sometimes described as a worth-debt ratio. The word *worth* in this term refers to net worth, which is sometimes used as a substitute title for stockholders' equity. In the illustration, the worth-debt ratio would be $9,800,000/$6,800,000, or a ratio of 1.44 to 1. The reciprocal of this ratio, called the *debt-equity ratio*, is often used in the literature of financial analysts.

Times Interest Earned

A ratio which is of particular interest to bondholders and which gives some clue to long-run solvency is calculated by dividing the total net earnings by the interest charges for the period. It is described as "times interest earned" or "times fixed charges covered." The purpose of the calculation is to indicate the relative protection of the bondholders and noteholders and to assess the probability of the firm's being forced into receivership by a failure to meet required interest payments. If the interest charges are earned only once or twice, the position of the creditors is uncertain, but if they are earned ten or twenty times, their position is well protected.

There are two variations of this ratio: in one, the income figure used is net income plus interest and income tax expense; in the other variation, net income plus only interest expense is used. For example, using the data in the statement of income and retained earnings of the M. & M. Equipment Company, the two variations would be:

$$\frac{\$2,100,000}{\$200,000} = 10.5 \text{ times} \tag{1}$$

$$\frac{\$1,400,000}{\$200,000} = 7.0 \text{ times} \tag{2}$$

The first calculation (10.5 times) is a better index of earnings available for interest because the income tax rates are applied to the figure for income after the deduction of interest charges. The ratio is directly comparable with the computations for other periods because it is unaffected by changes in income tax rates. The second calculation (7.0 times) may present the absolute position of the creditors more accurately, however, because the income taxes have to be paid out of current funds and legally they occupy a position superior to that of unpaid interest.

OTHER CALCULATIONS

Book Value per Share of Stock

If there is only one class of stock outstanding, the book value of a share of stock is calculated by dividing the total stockholders' equity by the number of shares of stock outstanding (in the hands of the public). For example:

Capital Stock (at $10 Par)	$250,000
Capital Contributed in Excess of Par	25,000
Retained Earnings	133,500
Total	$408,500
Number of Shares Outstanding	25,000
Book Value per Share, $408,500/25,000	$16.34

If there is more than one type of stock, the total book value of each type must first be computed and then divided by the number of shares of that type outstanding. Book value for this purpose can be defined as the amount to be received in case of dissolution, assuming that present book values of all assets would be realized.

The book values of M. & M. Equipment Company's two classes of shares as of December 31, 1975, assuming that in case of dissolution the preferred shares were entitled to $110 per share plus any dividends in arrears, might be shown as follows:

Total Stockholders' Equity	$9,800,000
Less: Book Value of Preferred Stock (no dividends	
in arrears), 20,000 shares at $110 per share	2,200,000
Book Value of Common Stock	$7,600,000
Book Value per Share of Common Stock,	
$7,600,000/500,000 shares	$15.20

The computation of book value per share of capital stock is one of the more common figures prepared in the analysis of balance sheets, but it has a limited usefulness. It can best be employed in comparison with the market value per share. If, as is often true, the market value exceeds the book value, the presumption is either that the rate of return to a share of stock is relatively high and is expected to continue high for some time in the future, or that the assets are undervalued or not all disclosed on the balance sheet. Just the opposite conclusions can be drawn when the market value drops below book value. Book value is one of the factors on which market value is based, but it is not apt to be the dominant factor.

Additional Computations

Manufacturing costs are expressed in terms of "per unit" costs in order to compare different periods, to prepare budgets or bids, and, in general, to check plant efficiency. Truck operating costs are calculated on a "per mile" basis for similar reasons. Index numbers can be prepared by means of which the operating results of each year are expressed in terms of some base period. There is almost no limit to the number of special percentages, ratios, and unit-cost figures that can be computed to supplement and assist in interpreting and using the information obtained from the accounts.

SUMMARY OF RATIO DEFINITIONS

There are essentially two kinds of commonly used ratios:

1. Those that summarize some aspect of operations for a period, usually a year and
2. Those that summarize some aspect of financial position at a given moment—a moment for which a balance sheet has been prepared.

Table 26.1 lists the ratios, classified either as "period" or "moment" ratios, described in this chapter, and shows separately both the numerator and denominator used to calculate the ratio.

For all ratios that require an average balance during the period, the average is most often derived as one-half the sum of the beginning and ending balances. Sophisticated analysts recognize, however, that when companies use a fiscal year different from the calendar year this averaging of beginning and ending balances may be misleading. Consider, for example, the all-capital earning rate of Sears, Roebuck, and Company whose fiscal year ends on January 31. Sears chooses a January 31 closing date at least in part because inventories are at a low level and are therefore easy to count—Christmas merchandise has been sold and Easter merchandise has not yet all been received. Furthermore, by January 31 most Christmas purchases have been paid for, so receivables are not unusually large. Thus, at January 31 the amount of total assets is lower than at many other times during the year. Consequently, the denominator of the all-capital earning rate, total assets, for Sears is more likely to represent the *smallest* rather than the *average* amount of total assets on hand during the year. The all-capital earning rate for Sears and other companies that choose a fiscal year-end to coincide with low points in the inventory cycle is likely to be overstated: a denominator that is less than average implies a ratio that is too large.

TABLE 26.1 FINANCIAL RATIOS DEFINED

	Ratios Summarizing Operations of a Period	
Ratio	**Numerator**	**Denominator**
All Capital Earning Rate	Net Income + Minority Share of After-tax Income + Interest Charges Net of Tax Effects [a]	Average of Total Assets during the Period.
Rate of Return on Stockholders' Equity	Net Income	Average Stockholders' Equity during the Period
Rate of Return on Common-Stock Equity	Net Income — Preferred-Stock Dividends	Average Common Stockholders' Equity during the Period
Earnings per Share on Common Stock [b]	Net Income — Preferred-Stock Dividends	Average Number of Common Shares Outstanding during the Period
Operating Ratio	Operating Expenses (Ordinarily: Total Expenses — Interest and Tax Charges) [c]	Net Sales
Inventory Turnover	Cost of Goods Sold	Average Inventory during the Period
Days of Average Inventory on Hand	365	Inventory Turnover
Receivables Turnover	Net Sales on Account	Average Accounts Receivable during the Period
Average Collection Period of Receivables	365	Receivables Turnover
Turnover of Plant and Equipment	Net Sales	Average of Land, Buildings, and Equipment Accounts during the Period

TABLE 26.1 (*continued*)

Ratios Summarizing Financial Position at a Moment in Time		
Ratio	**Numerator**	**Denominator**
Times Interest Earned	Income before Interest and Tax Charges [d]	Interest Charges
Current Ratio	Total Current Assets	Total Current Liabilities
Acid-Test or Quick Ratio	Quick Assets (Ordinarily: Cash, Marketable Securities, and Receivables)	Total Current Liabilities
Equity Ratio	Total Stockholders' Equity	Total Equities (= Total Assets)
Worth-Debt Ratio [e]	Total Stockholders' Equity	Total Liabilities
Book Value per Share of Common Stock	Total Stockholders' Equity — Preferred Stock Equity	Number of Common Shares Outstanding
Price-Earnings Ratio	Market Price per Share of Common Stock	Earnings per Share of Common Stock for the Last Year

[a] Interest charges net of tax effects = $(1 - t) \times$ Interest charges where t is the average tax rate.
[b] See Appendix 26.1 for possible complications where there are convertible securities, options, or warrants outstanding.
[c] Sometimes, the numerator is total expenses including tax and interest charges, and the denominator is all revenues.
[d] May be merely income before interest charges.
[e] Debt-equity ratio is the reciprocal, or inverse, of the worth-debt ratio. We include minority interest in total liabilities.

LIMITATIONS OF STATEMENT ANALYSIS

These analytical computations have a number of limitations that must be kept in mind by anyone preparing or using them. The major limitation of ratio analysis is that the ratio data are drawn from financial statements. The amounts shown on the financial statements result from historical cost procedures and, thus, may depart substantially from current valuations. The conservative bias of most accounting conventions means that assets are likely to be understated and net income probably also understated, although current reported net income is influenced by the effect of conservative practices of many past years as well as of the current year.

The figures computed from a single set of statements seldom have any great significance by themselves. They must be compared with past results or with standards external to the particular business. The trend, rather than the figures for a particular period, is usually the important consideration. Furthermore, no notion of the size of significant differences is provided by the calculations. Is a change in earnings per share from $2.50 to $2.55 a significant one? The answers to such questions are beyond the scope of most studies done by financial analysts.

The figures for one business enterprise are rarely completely comparable with those of another. There are always many differences in method of operations, nature of the product or service, prices paid for plant and equipment, which, for instance, may give radically different depreciation costs for the same type of assets, maintenance policies, method of financing, and so on, which make comparisons of dubious validity. Some trade associations have promoted the use of uniform accounting systems and interpretations and have accumulated valuable comparative statistics, but the possibilities in this direction are limited.

The results of business operations are affected by general economic conditions, competitive conditions within an industry, and other such factors, as well as the decisions and policies of the management. Any statistics, then, must be interpreted in the light of such circumstances.

The analyst must be on the alert for important changes that may destroy the comparability of his calculations. For example, writing off goodwill, substituting no-par-value stock for par-value shares, and mergers or reorganizations will make many of the past figures incommensurate with present computations.

Not many results of statement analysis can be used as direct indicators of good or poor management. They merely indicate probabilities or matters which should be investigated. For example, a decrease in the turnover of raw material inventory, ordinarily considered to be an undesirable trend, may reflect the accumulation of quantities of scarce materials that will keep the plant operating at full capacity after competitors have been forced to restrict operations or close down. The statistics must be combined with an investigation of the facts before definite conclusions can be drawn.

EFFECT OF PRICE-LEVEL CHANGES

Accounting records are maintained in terms of dollars, but unfortunately, the value of the dollar itself is subject to change. During periods of major price movements, this instability gives rise to many operating and reporting problems for business. The problems extend to almost all aspects of accounting, but they are usually most keenly felt in connection with the income statement and balance sheet reporting related to plant assets and to inventories.

The relatively long life of most plant assets means that there is an opportunity for their present costs to depart substantially from recorded original costs. Depreciation charges based on original cost may thus also be inadequate measures of the current economic significance of plant assets used during the period.

In the period of rapid price-level change immediately following the end of World War II, some businesses adjusted their depreciation charges to reflect current costs of plant. (See the 1947 annual reports of the United States Steel Corporation and The Timken Roller Bearing Company.) Both the Committee on Accounting Procedure of the American Institute of Certified Public Accountants[3] and the Securities and Exchange Commis-

---

[3] Accounting Research Bulletin No. 33, *Depreciation and High Costs*, AICPA, December, 1947; restated in Accounting Research Bulletin No. 43, AICPA, June, 1953.

sion,[4] however, expressed the view that depreciation should be based on actual initial cost of plant, and the practice of charging depreciation based on current costs disappeared. It was succeeded in many firms by the use of accelerated depreciation methods.

Early postwar treatments of accelerated depreciation were quite varied among companies adopting the method. Further, accelerated depreciation was then not usually deductible in computing taxable income. Later, the Internal Revenue Code of 1954 recognized accelerated depreciation calculated on a systematic basis, specifically mentioning two methods, the double-declining-balance method and the sum-of-the-years'-digits method. In many cases, especially for growing firms, accelerated depreciation on historical costs may result in depreciation charges not too far different from straight-line depreciation on current costs. Although the effect of the accelerated methods is to charge more depreciation to the earlier years than to later years, the total depreciation over the lives of the assets is limited to the historical cost. Should the firm stop growing, the excess of accelerated depreciation over straight line would gradually disappear.

The LIFO inventory-flow assumption represents an effort to have the income statement reflect more current costs of raw materials and merchandise. In periods of rapidly rising prices, net income using LIFO may be substantially less than under FIFO, especially for firms with relatively slow inventory turnover.

All firms are faced by the very real operating problem of adjusting to price-level changes, but this problem is not always reflected in their financial statements. There is an increasing tendency for management to supplement the financial statements in an attempt to give the readers assistance in comprehending the nature of the problem as well as the effect of price-level changes upon the financial statements.

The Accounting Principles Board has suggested, but has not required, that firms issue supplemental *general price-level adjusted financial statements*. In such statements all monetary assets and liabilities, such as cash, notes receivable or payable, and bonds, are shown at their present or nominal value. All other asset and liability amounts are adjusted with a general price-level index, such as the Gross National Product (GNP) Deflator. For example, the cost of a plant asset acquired for $100,000 when the GNP Deflator index was 110 would be shown as $109,091 in general price-level adjustment statements issued at a time when the index was 120 ($109,091 = $100,000 \times 120/110$). Depreciation charges would be based on the $109,091 valuation rather than the $100,000 one. The construction of general price-level adjusted financial statements is a topic for advanced accounting courses.

Recent surveys reported in *Accounting Trends and Techniques* show that *none* of the approximately 600 large companies surveyed issue general price-level adjusted statements, even in supplemental form. We applaud the widespread nonacceptance of such statements for we think they are

---

[4] *Fifteenth Annual Report of the Securities and Exchange Commission* (1949), p. 179.

a feeble attempt to solve a real problem. Modern accounting has valuation problems that are independent of general price-level changes. These pressing problems are those of valuing, for example, fixed assets, marketable securities, and inventories. Their valuations should relate to the changing current costs of similar items rather than reflecting the movement in a general price-level index. When these specific valuation problems are solved, the solution will undoubtedly resolve most of the accounting problems created by general inflation.

The major weaknesses, in our opinion, of general price-level accounting are that:

1. It uses a general index to calculate costs for all items whereas costs of all items do not change proportionately.
2. It ignores the ability of lenders to anticipate inflation in setting interest rates for borrowers.[5]

APPENDIX 26.1: CALCULATION OF PRIMARY AND FULLY DILUTED EARNINGS PER SHARE

Accounting Principles Board Opinion No. 15 requires the calculation of both a primary earnings per share and a fully diluted earnings per share in some cases. Primary earnings per share is calculated with adjustments for dilutive common stock equivalents. Fully diluted earnings per share is calculated with adjustments for all dilutive residual securities. These terms and the calculations required are explained in the discussion that follows. It omits certain technical details and procedures used in more complicated circumstances.

Common Stock Equivalents

Residual securities that are judged to be nearly the same as common stock are called *common stock equivalents.*[6] Common stock equivalents are securities whose primary value arises from their ability to be exchanged for common shares rather than for their own cash yields. Whether or not a particular residual security is classified as a common stock equivalent is determined at the time that security is issued, and the classification is not changed thereafter.

1. *Convertible securities.* The holder of convertible securities is provided a yield either in the form of preferred dividends or bond interest

---

[5] The case for general price-level accounting is stated in Statement No. 3: Financial Statements Restated for General Price-Level Changes, Accounting Principles Board, AICPA, June, 1969. The case against general price-level accounting is persuasively presented by Clyde P. Stickney and David O. Green in "No Price Level Adjusted Statements, Please (Pleas)," *The CPA Journal,* 44, 1 (Jan. 1974), 25–31.

[6] In APB Opinion No. 9, *residual securities* were defined to be those items called *common stock equivalents* in Opinion No. 15. Opinion No. 15 uses *residual securities* to refer to items that affect both primary and fully diluted earnings per share.

payments. A test is used to determine whether the particular convertible security appears to be held for its own yield or whether it appears to be held for its conversion rights. The test operates on the assumption that, if the cash yield at the time of issue is substantially below the yield otherwise available to the investor, it was purchased in large part because of its conversion privilege. The test compares the cash yield to the buyer at time of issue (lowest interest or dividend receivable during any of the first five years of issue divided by the market price of the security at the time of issue) with *two-thirds of the bank prime rate* for loans at the time of issue. If the cash yield on the residual security is less than two-thirds of the bank prime rate, the security is classified as a common stock equivalent. Once a security is classified as a common stock equivalent, it will continue to be classified that way.

2. *Options and Warrants.* Some securities do not offer a cash yield to their holders. They are options or warrants. The only reason for holding them is the right to acquire common shares at a specified price. Options and warrants are always considered to be common stock equivalents.

Dilution

The earnings-per-share calculations recognize the potential decrease or *dilution* in the earnings per share that would occur if the residual securities were converted into common stock.

Convertible Securities. Convertible securities do not produce new proceeds to the corporation when they are converted from their original form, debt or preferred shares, into common shares. The number of common shares is increased, and the earnings formerly used for interest payments or for preferred dividends is now available for or "belongs to" common stock. The conversion of a convertible security increases both the denominator and the numerator in the earnings-per-share calculation. To ascertain whether or not a convertible security is dilutive with respect to a base earnings-per-share calculation, start with that earnings-per-share calculation. Add to the *numerator* the net (after-tax) amounts that would result from not having to pay preferred dividends or bond interest once the securities were converted into common stock. Increase the denominator by the number of common shares to be issued assuming conversion. Calculate a new earnings per share. If the resulting figure is less than the earnings per share used as the base, then the convertible security is *dilutive* with respect to that base. If larger, the convertible security is *antidilutive*. A separate test of dilution is made for each class of convertible security.

Options and Warrants. An increased number of common shares and additional cash proceeds to a corporation will be produced when options or warrants are exercised. There is no change in the numerator because options and warrants do not require periodic payments to their holders. To determine the effect on the earnings per share of exercised options and warrants, we must assume some use for the additional cash proceeds. The dilution test for *primary earnings per share* assumes that all proceeds are used to retire outstanding common shares at the average market price for the period. The dilution test for *fully diluted earnings per share* assumes that all proceeds are used to retire outstanding common shares at the larger of the weighted average price for the period or the price at the end of the period. If the number of shares that would be issued on exercise of the option or warrant is larger than the number of shares assumed to be retired with the proceeds received from exercise, then the option or warrant is *dilutive*. If the number of shares issued is smaller than the number assumed retired, the effect is *antidilutive*. A separate dilution test is performed for each class of options and warrants.

Antidilutive residual securities are not used to adjust the reported primary and fully diluted earnings per share because to include them would increase the reported figures.

Primary Earnings Per Share

The calculation of primary earnings per share includes adjustments only for dilutive common stock equivalents. Start with net income less preferred dividends as the numerator and the weighted-average number of outstanding shares as the denominator. For each class of common stock equivalents, ascertain if that class is dilutive. Adjust the numerator and denominator of the calculation for each class of common stock equivalent that is dilutive. Residual securities that are both common stock equivalents and dilutive are treated in the calculation of primary earnings per share as though their rights to common stock had been exercised (a) at the beginning of the period under consideration, but (b) at the average price for the entire period.

Fully Diluted Earnings Per Share

Fully diluted earnings per share includes adjustments for all dilutive residual securities. Assume that all dilutive options and warrants are exercised and that the proceeds are used to retire common stock at the larger of average price for the period or end-of-period price. Compute an earnings per share on that assumption. For every possible combination of potential conversion of convertible residual securities, compute an earnings per share. (If there are r classes of convertible residual securities, there will be 2^r such combinations and a calculation for each one.) That is, if there are two classes of convertible securities, A and B, compute an earnings per share assuming that:

1. Neither A nor B is converted
2. Only A is converted
3. Only B is converted
4. Both A and B are converted.

The smallest of these calculated earnings-per-share figures is fully diluted earnings per share.

Illustrations of Primary and Fully Diluted Earnings Per Share

If the above rules seem complicated, that is because they are. The Accounting Principles Board's original opinion specifying the calculations is over sixty pages long and a year after the opinion was issued, an unofficial interpretation of over one hundred pages was issued to explain and interpret the opinion itself. The following illustration is adapted from that unofficial interpretation.[7]

Assume the following data about the capital structure and earnings for the Layton Ball Corporation for the year 1975.

Number of Common Shares Outstanding during 1975 (weighted average)	2,500
Market Price per Common Share on December 31, 1975	$25
Weighted-Average Market Price per Common Share during 1975	$20
Options Outstanding during 1975:	
Number of Shares Issuable on Exercise of Options	1,000
Exercise Price	$15
Warrants Outstanding during 1975:	
Number of Shares Issuable on Exercise of Warrants	2,000
Exercise Price	$30
Convertible Preferred Stock Outstanding (March, 1966 issue):	
Number of Shares	1,500
Shares of Common Issuable on Conversion (per share)	1
Dividends per Share	$1
Market Price at Time of Issue	$20
Prime Rate at Time of Issue	6%
Convertible Bonds Outstanding (December, 1968 issue)	
Number	100
Shares of Common Issuable on Conversion (per bond)	10
Coupon Rate	4-1/6%
Proceeds per Bond at Issue (= par value)	$1,000
Prime Rate at Time of Issue	6¾%
Net income for 1975	$9,500
Tax rate for 1975	40%

Is the Convertible Preferred Stock a Common Stock Equivalent? Since the yield to buyers of the issue in 1966 was 5 percent (= $1/$20), and since 5 percent is larger than two-thirds of the bank prime rate (6 percent) at the time of issue, the convertible preferred stock is not a common-stock equivalent. (If the dividend rate dropped to $.50 per share in 1970, these shares would be classified as common-stock equivalents since the *lowest* return during the first five years is the numerator of the yield-test fraction.)

Are the Convertible Bonds Common Stock Equivalents? Since the yield to buyers at the time of issue in 1968 (4⅙ percent) is less than ⅔ the bank prime rate (6¾ percent) in 1968, the convertible bonds are

---

[7] "Computing Earnings Per Share: Unofficial Accounting Interpretations of APB Opinion No. 15," AICPA (July, 1970).

common-stock equivalents. The convertible bonds are each convertible into 10 shares of common so that the conversion of the entire issue would imply the issue of 1,000 new shares of common. Each share of stock issued would result from the conversion of one-tenth of a bond. The interest payments on such a fractional bond are $4\frac{1}{6}$ percent of par value per year. If the bonds were converted, those interest payments would be saved. Since interest expenses are deductions from revenues in the calculation of taxable income and the income tax rate is 40 percent, the after-tax increase in net income from conversion of bonds into stock is only $2.50 per share [= (1 − .40) × .041667 × $100]. That is, the conversion of one-tenth of a bond into one share of common will save about $4.17 of interest expense but only $2.50 of net income.

Are the Options Dilutive? Since each option can be exercised for $15 and the proceeds must be assumed to be used to retire stock at an average price of $20 per share, the options are dilutive for the primary earnings-per-share calculation. The number of shares outstanding would increase if the options were exercised. The proceeds of the exercise would be $15,000 (= $15 × 1,000) and would imply an increase of 1,000 shares. The proceeds would be used to retire stock at a price of $20 per share so that 750 shares (= $15,000/$20) would be retired. For primary earnings per share, the net increase in common shares outstanding resulting from exercise of options would be 250 (= 1,000 − 750). For fully diluted earnings per share, the proceeds are assumed to be used to retire common at the year-end price, $25 per share. The net increase in common shares for the fully diluted calculation is 400 shares (= 1,000 − $15,000/$25 = 1,000 − 600).

Are the Warrants Dilutive? Since each warrant exercised must be accompanied with a cash payment of $30, which is greater than both the average and year-end market prices of common, the warrants are not dilutive. Even though they are common-stock equivalents, they must be ignored in the subsequent calculations.

The analysis done so far can be summarized in Schedule 26.2.

The starting point of the calculation is based upon the amounts from the financial statements. It is net income less preferred dividends divided by the weighted-average number of common shares outstanding. This figure is calculated as:

$$\frac{\$9,500 - \$1,500}{2,500} = \$3.20 \text{ per share}$$

Primary Earnings Per Share. This figure is calculated as the minimum of two separate calculations:

1. earnings per share assuming exercise of only the dilutive options:

$$\frac{\$9,500 - \$1,500}{2,500 + 250} = \$2.91 \text{ per share}$$

2. earnings per share assuming exercise of dilutive options and conversion of bonds:

$$\frac{\$9,500 - \$1,500 + \$2,500}{2,500 + 250 + 1,000} = \$2.80 \text{ per share}$$

Since the result from the second calculation is smaller than from the first, the convertible bonds are dilutive and the primary earnings-per-share figure is $2.80. (A residual security will be dilutive for a given earnings per share when the "charge against net income per common share embodied in the residual security" is less than that earnings per share used as the base. Here, the $2.50 after-tax increase in net income per share is less than the base, $2.91 and, so, is dilutive.)

Fully Diluted Earnings Per Share. This figure is calculated as the minimum of four separate calculations. (Since there are two convertible residual securities, the number of combinations is $2^2 = 4$.) In these calculations, the dilutive options are taken into account but the antidilutive warrants are ignored. The number of common shares is assumed to increase by 400 as a result of options exercised at the year-end price.

1. Assume that neither convertible security is converted:

$$\frac{\$9,500 - \$1,500}{2,500 + 400} = \$2.76 \text{ per share}$$

SCHEDULE 26.2 LAYTON BALL CORPORATION

Effect of Capital Structure on Earnings Per Share (EPS)
of Common Stock for 1975

		Residual Security		
	Options	Warrants	Convertible Preferred	Convertible Bonds
Common-Stock Equivalent	yes	yes	no	yes
Net Increase (Decrease) in Common Shares on Exercise or Conversion:				
Primary EPS	250	(1,000) a	1,500	1,000
Fully Diluted EPS	400	(400) b	1,500	1,000
Dilutive:				
Primary EPS	yes	no	? c	?
Fully Diluted EPS	yes	no	?	?
Charge Against Net Income Per Common Share Embodied in Residual Security	0	0	$1	$2.50

a 2,000 — (2,000 × $30)/$20 shares.
b 2,000 — (2,000 × $30)/$25 shares.
c Whether or not the convertible securities are dilutive depends upon the earnings-per-share base used for an individual computation.

2. Assume that only the preferred stock is converted:

$$\frac{\$9,500}{2,500 + 400 + 1,500} = \$2.16 \text{ per share}$$

3. Assume that only the bonds are converted (adding $2.50 per share to net income):

$$\frac{\$9,500 - \$1,500 + \$2,500}{2,500 + 400 + 1,000} = \$2.69 \text{ per share}$$

4. Assume that both stock and bonds are converted:

$$\frac{\$9,500 + \$2,500}{2,500 + 400 + 1,500 + 1,000} = \$2.22 \text{ per share}$$

Fully diluted earnings per share would be reported as $2.16 per share, the minimum of these four calculations. Notice that the minimum of these four calculations did not occur when both classes of convertible securities are assumed converted. Once the preferred stock is assumed to be converted, the bonds are antidilutive since $2.50 (the "charge against net income per common share embodied in the residual security") is larger than $2.16.

The Layton Ball Corporation would report primary earnings per share of $2.80 and fully diluted earnings per share of $2.16. The effects of ordinary and extraordinary items of income are shown separately, according to generally acceptable accounting principles, within the primary and fully diluted earnings-per-share figures, preferably on the face of the income statement.

Of the income statements reproduced in Chapter 25, only that of the W. R. Grace & Co. (Schedule 25.3) shows both primary and fully diluted earnings per share figures. General Electric (Schedule 25.11) shows primary earnings per share in the income statement and fully diluted earnings per share in the footnotes on page 30. Fully diluted earnings per share need not be disclosed if, as is true for GE, it is more than 97 percent of primary earnings per share.

QUESTIONS AND PROBLEMS

1. The percentage of net income to sales for Companies A, B, and C is 5 percent, 4 percent, and 2 percent, respectively; however, Company C is much more successful than either of the others. Explain how this can be.

2. Under what circumstances will the rate of return on the common-stock equity be more than the return on total capital? Under what circumstances will it be less?

*3. "Net income is influenced by the effect of conservative practices of many

---

* Hints, key numbers, or (partial) answers appear in the back of the book between the Appendix Tables and the Glossary.

past years as well as of the current year." How?

4. Distinguish between a residual security and a common stock equivalent.

5. What is the difference between primary earings per share and fully diluted earnings per share?

6. Explain the difference between the treatment of convertible preferred stock and convertible bonds in calculating dilutive effects of those issues.

7. The following comparative percentages are obtained from the financial statements of Companies Y and Z:

	Co. Y	Co. Z
Net income to sales	3%	5%
Net income to stockholders' equity	12%	9%

Compute for both companies how many dollars of sales were made for each dollar of stockholders' equity.

8. On the basis of the data presented in Problem 7, which company would appear to be more successful?

9. The following data are taken from the 1975 annual reports of the Barr Company and the Stix Company:

	Barr Co.	Stix Co.
Sales	$1,000,000	$1,200,000
Net income of the enterprise	60,000	60,000
Average total assets during the year	750,000	500,000

a. Determine the percentage of income to sales for each company.
b. Determine the all-capital earning rate for each company.
c. Comment on the relative operating results of the two companies.

*10. The earnings of the Kansas Corporation have averaged $4.80 per share of common stock for the past five years. What would you be willing to pay for a share of the stock if you were to assume that the earnings record would continue and you wished to earn 12 percent on your investment?

11. At December 31, 1975, the book value per share of the common stock of the Westminster Corporation was $28. At the same time, the price of the shares on the market was quoted at $42. What reasons might there be for this difference?

*12. The total stockholders' equity of the Lucas Company at December 31, 1975, is $13,500,000. The 5-percent cumulative preferred stock outstanding has a par value of $1,000,000. In case of dissolution, the preferred stock is entitled to a premium of 5 percent plus any dividends in arrears. At December 31, 1975, the 1975 and 1974 dividends have not been paid. There are 950,000 shares of common stock outstanding. Determine the book value per share of common stock.

13. Indicate the effect (increase, decrease, no effect) upon the total book value of common stock (the common stockholders' equity) of the following:
a. the declaration of a cash dividend on the common stock

b. the issue of shares of common stock as a dividend to common stockholders

c. the sale of plant at less than its book value

d. the earning of net income

e. the issue of bonds at a premium

f. the acquisition of treasury stock (common) on the market

g. the issue of common stock at a discount

h. the retirement of preferred stock at less than its book value

i. the appropriation of a portion of retained earnings as a reserve for contingencies.

14. Indicate the effect (increase, decrease, no effect) of each of the following transactions upon the book value per share of the common stock of the Sharewood Company (the present book value is $55 per share):

a. The retirement of a fully depreciated asset from service.

b. An assessment of additional income taxes for a previous year.

c. The sale of marketable securities at less than book value.

d. The destruction of a building by a fire. The company is fully insured.

e. The issue of additional shares of common stock as a dividend to common stockholders.

f. The payment of a cash dividend to common stockholders.

g. The appropriation of a portion of retained earnings as an addition to the reserve for contingencies.

h. The retirement of bonds at more than book value.

i. The issue of preferred stock at a premium. The stock is entitled to par plus unpaid cumulative dividends in the event of dissolution.

j. The issue of additional shares of common stock at par value, $50 per share.

k. The reacquisition of 100 shares of common stock at $51 per share. The shares are canceled.

°15. The December 31, 1975, post-closing trial balance of the Pershing Products Company includes, among others, the following account balances:

5% Cumulative Preferred Stock, $100 par value	$ 4,800,000
Premium on Preferred Stock	240,000
Retained Earnings	32,500,000
Reserve for Contingencies	1,000,000
Reserve for Uncollectible Accounts	2,000,000
Reserve for Depreciation	3,200,000
Reserve for Bond Sinking Fund	2,500,000
Sinking Fund	2,500,000
Common Stock, $5 par value	15,000,000
Premium on Common Stock	3,000,000

The preferred-stock contract provides that, in event of dissolution, the preferred stockholders shall have a prior claim to $110 a share plus dividends in arrears.

a. Calculate the book value per share of common stock; assume that there are no dividends in arrears.

b. Calculate the book value per share of common stock. Assume that no dividends were declared on the preferred stock in 1974 or 1975.

16. If sales were to increase from $600,000 in 1975 to $700,000 in 1976, would you expect the percentage of administrative costs to sales to increase, decrease, or remain relatively constant? Explain.

*17. If the amount of sales were to increase 15 percent in a year primarily because of expansion into a new sales territory, indicate which of the following expenses you would expect to increase, decrease, or remain relatively constant, as a percentage of sales:
    a. cost of goods sold
    b. uncollectible accounts adjustment
    c. delivery expenses
    d. depreciation of warehouse.

18. In calculating the merchandise turnover, when might the use of the average of the beginning and ending inventories lead to an inaccurate result?

19. Does a decrease in the merchandise turnover necessarily indicate an unsatisfactory trend?

20. Why is the ratio of borrowed to total invested capital usually greater for public utilities than for industrial enterprises?

21. Indicate the advantages and disadvantages of a low equity ratio.

22. When is a current ratio too low? When might it be too high?

23. Might there be a decrease in the amount of working capital and at the same time an increase in the current ratio? Illustrate.

24. Assuming an excess of current assets over current liabilities, indicate the effect of the following upon the current ratio:
    a. collection of an account receivable
    b. payment of an account payable
    c. acquisition of merchandise on account
    d. acquisition of merchandise for cash
    e. acquisition of machinery on account
    f. acquisition of machinery for cash
    g. sale of marketable securities at less than book value
    h. sale of an investment at less than book value.

25. Assuming an excess of current assets over current liabilities, indicate the effect of the following upon the current ratio:
    a. The acquiring of government bonds for cash.
    b. The borrowing of funds from a bank on a noninterest-bearing note.
    c. The issuance of bonds for cash.
    d. The discounting of a note receivable at the bank. The proceeds equal the book value.
    e. The payment of a short-term note at the bank.
    f. The recording of accrued interest on a note receivable.
    g. The receipt of a noninterest-bearing, two-month note from a customer to apply on his account.
    h. The sale of machinery and equipment at less than book value.

26. Following is a schedule of the current assets and current liabilities of the Lewis Company:

	Dec. 31, 1975	Dec. 31, 1974
Current Assets		
Cash	$ 355,890	$ 212,790
Accounts Receivable	389,210	646,010
Inventories	799,100	1,118,200
Prepayments	21,600	30,000
Total Current Assets	$1,565,800	$2,007,000
Current Liabilities		
Accounts Payable	$ 152,760	$ 217,240
Accrued Payroll, Taxes, etc.	126,340	318,760
Notes Payable	69,500	330,000
Total Current Liabilities	$ 348,600	$ 866,000

The Lewis Company operated at a loss during 1975.

a. Calculate the current ratio for each date.

b. Explain how the improved current ratio is possible under the 1975 operating conditions.

°27. The following data are taken from the finanical statements of the Manno Company:

	Dec. 31, 1975	Dec. 31, 1974
Current assets	$210,000	$180,000
Noncurrent assets	275,000	255,000
Current liabilities	78,000	85,000
Long-term liabilities	75,000	30,000
Capital stock, 10,000 shares	300,000	300,000
Retained earnings	32,000	20,000

	1975 Operations
Revenues less operating expenses	$ 78,500
Interest charges	3,000
Income taxes	33,500
Dividends declared	30,000

Calculate the following ratios:

a. rate of return on total invested capital

b. rate of return on stockholders' equity

c. earnings per share of stock

d. current ratio (both dates)

e. times interest earned (two alternatives)

f. equity ratio (both dates).

28. The following are the stockholders' equity accounts appearing in the post-closing trial balance of the Beggs Company at December 31, 1975:

Common Stock, 100,000 shares	$1,800,000
Preferred Stock, 6%, 4,500 shares	450,000
Premium on Preferred Stock	10,000
Retained Earnings	173,000
Retained Earnings Appropriated for Contingencies	90,000

The preferred stock is entitled to par value plus accumulated dividends in case of liquidation. No stock was issued during 1975. There are no preferred-stock dividends in arrears.

The following data appear on the statement of income and retained earnings for 1975:

Income before Interest and Taxes	$460,000
Interest on Bonds	15,000
Income Taxes	225,000
Dividends	120,000
Appropriation of Retained Earnings for Contingencies	18,000

a. Prepare a partial statement of income and retained earnings beginning with the income before interest and taxes.
b. Calculate the following ratios:
 (1) rate of return on stockholders' equity
 (2) rate of return on common-stock equity
 (3) book value per share of common stock at 12/31/74 and 12/31/75
 (4) earnings per share of preferred stock
 (5) earnings per share of common stock
 (6) times interest earned (two alternatives).

*29. The Horrigan Company earned $240,000 during a year when there were 120,000 shares of common stock outstanding during the year. Also outstanding were 20,000 warrants each of which could be exercised to purchase one share of common for $30. The average price of common was $40 during the year.
a. Compute net income divided by the actual number of common shares outstanding.
b. If warrants are assumed to be exercised, what will the proceeds to the company be?
c. Assume that the proceeds are used to purchase common stock. How many shares would be retired?
d. What is the net increase in common shares outstanding if the warrants are assumed to be exercised and the proceeds used to retire common stock?
e. Compute primary and fully diluted earnings per share.

30. Feltham Company earned $37,500 for the year after paying taxes at the rate of 40 percent of taxable income. It had 10,000 shares outstanding during the year which sold for an average price of $40 per share. A 6-percent semiannual coupon convertible bond issue of $100,000 had been issued several years ago at a time when the prime interest rate was 8 percent. Each $1,000 of par value is convertible into 10 shares of common stock. In addition 4,000 warrants were outstanding during the year. Each warrant can be exercised to purchase one share of common for $25.
a. Compute net income divided by the actual number of common shares outstanding.
b. Are the bonds common stock equivalents? The warrants?
c. Compute earnings per share assuming conversion of the bonds but not exercise of warrants.

    d. Assuming exercise of warrants but not conversion of bonds, compute earnings per share.

    e. Assuming both exercise of warrants and conversion of bonds, compute earnings per share.

    f. What is primary earnings per share?

    g. What is fully diluted earnings per share?

31. The Jones and Gardiner Company has 4,000 common shares outstanding for the year as well as 2,000 shares of Class I convertible preferred stock and 3,000 shares of Class II convertible preferred stock. Both classes can be converted into common on a one-for-one basis. The Class I convertible preferred is a common stock equivalent and is paid a dividend of $1 per year. The Class II convertible preferred stock is not a common stock equivalent and is paid a dividend of $1 per year. Jones and Gardiner Company earned $20,000 for the year, before any dividend payments.

    Compute the following:

    a. net income divided by the actual number of common shares outstanding.

    b. earnings per share assuming conversion of Class I stock only

    c. earnings per share assuming conversion of Class II stock only

    d. earnings per share assuming conversion of both Class I and Class II stock

    e. primary earnings per share

    f. fully diluted earnings per share.

32. Suppose that the Class I convertible preferred of the Jones and Gardiner Company (see Problem 31) paid a dividend of $2.50 per year. Repeat the requirements of Problem 31.

°33. Refer to the data of General Products Company in Problem 25 in Chapter 18 and the additional information given below. Present the following calculations for the year 1974:

    a. rate of return on all capital

    b. rate of return on stockholders' equity

    c. rate of return on common stockholders' equity

    d. earnings per share of common stock

    e. operating ratio

    f. net income (to stockholders) to sales ratio

    g. turnover of inventory

    h. turnover of plant and equipment

    i. average collection period for receivables

    j. book value per share of common stock (use the average number of shares outstanding for year)

    k. times interest earned (two alternatives)

    l. working capital amount

    m. equity ratio

    n. current ratio

    o. acid-test ratio

    p. debt-equity ratio (include minority interest in total liabilities).

Additional information for General Products Company:

	(In Millions of $) December 31			
	1976	1975	1974	1973
Current Receivables	1,926.0	1,741.3	1,573.7	1,364.5
Current Liabilities	2,869.7	2,840.4	2,650.3	2,582.6
Inventories	1,759.0	1,611.7	1,555.3	1,495.2
Plant and Equipment	2,136.6	2,025.7	1,749.4	1,637.1
Cost of Goods Sold	7,509.6	6,962.1	6,423.6	6,346.1
Income Tax Expense	364.1	317.1	220.6	231.5
Interest and Other Financial Charges ..	106.7	96.9	101.4	78.1
Stockholders' Equity	3,084.6	2,801.8	2,553.6	2,426.5
Total Assets	7,401.8	6,887.8	6,198.5	5,894.0

	(In Thousands of Shares)		
Common Stock Shares Outstanding—			
Average for Year	182,112	181,684	181,114

34. Refer to Problem 33 above and repeat items (a) to (p) for the year 1975.

35. Refer to Problem 33 above and repeat items (a) to (p) for the year 1976.

36. Refer to the data of General Products Credit Corporation in Problem 25 in Chapter 18 and the additional information given below. Present the following calculations for the year 1974:
  a. rate of return on all capital
  b. rate of return on stockholders' equity
  c. rate of return on common stockholders' equity
  d. operating ratio, using total revenues in the numerator
  e. average collection period for receivables
  f. times interest earned (two alternatives)
  g. equity ratio.
Additional information for General Products Credit Corporation:

	(In Millions of $) December 31			
	1976	1975	1974	1973
Interest and Discount	108.5	99.8	116.7	105.6
Income Tax Expense	32.3	25.8	17.3	15.2
Stockholders' Equity	260.0	231.9	190.0	165.3
Total assets	2,789.5	2,358.7	2,157.0	2,035.6
Receivables (Net)	2,648.3	2,262.0	2,068.9	1,905.7

37. Refer to Problem 36 above and repeat items (a) to (g) for the year 1975.

38. Refer to Problem 36 above and repeat items (a) to (g) for the year 1976.

39. The information shown below is taken from the financial statements of the Southern Oil Company for the years ending December 31, 1975 and 1974. Present the following calculations for the year 1974:
  a. Earning rate on all capital. (Assume total assets as of December 31, 1973, to be $18,207,500,000.)

PROBLEMS 39 AND 40

SOUTHERN OIL COMPANY
Statement of Financial Position

Assets	1975	1974
	(In Millions of Dollars)	
Cash	$ 921.0	$ 866.1
Receivables	1,198.3	1,173.2
Inventories	1,676.0	1,566.0
Plant and Equipment	11,930.4	11,305.3
Other Long-term Assets	4,589.5	4,331.2
Total Assets	$20,315.2	$19,241.8

Liabilities and Stockholders' Equity

	1975	1974
Current Liabilities	$ 3,329.7	$ 3,240.1
Long-term Liabilities	5,392.6	5,051.0
Capital Stock (average shares outstanding in 1975: 224,100,000, in 1974: 221,000,000)	2,640.5	2,608.4
Retained Earnings	8,952.4	8,342.3
Total Equities	$20,315.2	$19,241.8

SOUTHERN OIL COMPANY
Statement of Income for the Years 1975 and 1974

Revenues	1975	1974
	(In Millions of Dollars)	
Sales	$20,461.7	$18,143.3
Other Revenue	701.4	553.4
Total Revenues	$21,163.1	$18,696.7
Expenses		
Crude Oil and Product Purchases	$ 6,283.8	$ 5,520.7
Other Expenses	11,194.0	10,199.4
Interest and Other Financial Charges	261.7	241.6
Income Taxes Expense	1,962.0	1,425.0
Total Expenses	$19,701.5	$17,386.7
Net Income to Stockholders	$ 1,461.6	$ 1,310.0

b. Rate of earnings on stockholders' equity. (Assume that stockholders' equity as of December 31, 1973, is $9,870,300,000.)

c. Rate of earnings on common stockholders' equity.

d. Earnings per share of common stock.

e. Operating ratio.

f. Net income (to stockholders) to sales ratio.

    g. Turnover of inventory. (Assume that the year-end inventory approximates an average of inventory during the year.)

    h. Turnover of plant and equipment. (Assume that the year-end plant and equipment inventory approximates an average of plant and equipment during the year.)

    i. Average collection period for receivables. (Assume the year-end receivables approximate an average of receivable during the year.)

    j. Book value per share of common stock (use average number of shares outstanding for year).

    k. Times interest earned (two alternatives).

    l. Working capital amount.

    m. Equity ratio.

    n. Current ratio.

    o. Acid-test ratio.

    p. Debt-equity ratio.

40. Refer to Problem 39 above and repeat items (a) to (p) for the year 1975.

41. Refer to the statement of income and retained earnings for the month of June and the balance sheet of the Wright Merchandise Company for June 30, 1975, in Chapter 11 of the text. (Schedules 11.1 and 11.4) Present the following calculations for June 30, 1975 (assume that the June 30 balance sheet account approximates an average of the account balances during the month).

    a. rate of return on all capital

    b. rate of return on stockholders' equity

    c. rate of return on common stockholders' equity

    d. earnings per share of common stock

    e. operating ratio

    f. net income (to stockholders) to sales ratio

    g. turnover of inventory

    h. turnover of property, plant and equipment

    i. average collection period for receivables

    j. book value per share of common stock

    k. working capital amount

    l. equity ratio

    m. current ratio

    n. acid-test ratio

    o. worth-debt ratio.

Appendix A

Compound Interest, Annuity, and Bond Tables

TABLE 1 FUTURE VALUE OF \$1

$$F_n = P(1 + r)^n$$

r = interest rate; n = number of periods until valuation

Periods n	1%	1½%	2%	3%	4%	5%	6%	7%	8%	10%	12%	20%
1	1.01000	1.01500	1.02000	1.03000	1.04000	1.05000	1.06000	1.07000	1.08000	1.10000	1.12000	1.20000
2	1.02010	1.03022	1.04040	1.06090	1.08160	1.10250	1.12360	1.14490	1.16640	1.21000	1.25440	1.44000
3	1.03030	1.04568	1.06121	1.09273	1.12486	1.15763	1.19102	1.22504	1.25971	1.33100	1.40493	1.72800
4	1.04060	1.06136	1.08243	1.12551	1.16986	1.21551	1.26248	1.31080	1.36049	1.46410	1.57352	2.07360
5	1.05101	1.07728	1.10408	1.15927	1.21665	1.27628	1.33823	1.40255	1.46933	1.61051	1.76234	2.48832
6	1.06152	1.09344	1.12616	1.19405	1.26532	1.34010	1.41852	1.50073	1.58687	1.77156	1.97382	2.98598
7	1.07214	1.10984	1.14869	1.22987	1.31593	1.40710	1.50363	1.60578	1.71382	1.94872	2.21068	3.58318
8	1.08286	1.12649	1.17166	1.26677	1.36857	1.47746	1.59385	1.71819	1.85093	2.14359	2.47596	4.29982
9	1.09369	1.14339	1.19509	1.30477	1.42331	1.55133	1.68948	1.83846	1.99900	2.35795	2.77308	5.15978
10	1.10462	1.16054	1.21899	1.34392	1.48024	1.62889	1.79085	1.96715	2.15892	2.59374	3.10585	6.19174
11	1.11567	1.17795	1.24337	1.38423	1.53945	1.71034	1.89830	2.10485	2.33164	2.85312	3.47855	7.43008
12	1.12683	1.19562	1.26824	1.42576	1.60103	1.79586	2.01220	2.25219	2.51817	3.13843	3.89598	8.91610
13	1.13809	1.21355	1.29361	1.46853	1.66507	1.88565	2.13293	2.40985	2.71962	3.45227	4.36349	10.69932
14	1.14947	1.23176	1.31948	1.51259	1.73168	1.97993	2.26090	2.57853	2.93719	3.79750	4.88711	12.83918
15	1.16097	1.25023	1.34587	1.55797	1.80094	2.07893	2.39656	2.75903	3.17217	4.17725	5.47357	15.40702
16	1.17258	1.26899	1.37279	1.60471	1.87298	2.18287	2.54035	2.95216	3.42594	4.59497	6.13039	18.48843
17	1.18430	1.28802	1.40024	1.65285	1.94790	2.29202	2.69277	3.15882	3.70002	5.05447	6.86604	22.18611
18	1.19615	1.30734	1.42825	1.70243	2.02582	2.40662	2.85434	3.37993	3.99602	5.55992	7.68997	26.62333
19	1.20811	1.32695	1.45681	1.75351	2.10685	2.52695	3.02560	3.61653	4.31570	6.11591	8.61276	31.94800
20	1.22019	1.34686	1.48595	1.80611	2.19112	2.65330	3.20714	3.86968	4.66096	6.72750	9.64629	38.33760
22	1.24472	1.38756	1.54598	1.91610	2.36992	2.92526	3.60354	4.43040	5.43654	8.14027	12.10031	55.20614
24	1.26973	1.42950	1.60844	2.03279	2.56330	3.22510	4.04893	5.07237	6.34118	9.84973	15.17863	79.49685
26	1.29526	1.47271	1.67342	2.15659	2.77247	3.55567	4.54938	5.80735	7.39635	11.91818	19.04007	114.4755
28	1.32129	1.51722	1.74102	2.28793	2.99870	3.92013	5.11169	6.64884	8.62711	14.42099	23.88387	164.8447
30	1.34785	1.56308	1.81136	2.42726	3.24340	4.32194	5.74349	7.61226	10.06266	17.44940	29.95992	237.3763
32	1.37494	1.61032	1.88454	2.57508	3.50806	4.76494	6.45339	8.71527	11.73708	21.11378	37.58173	341.8219
34	1.40258	1.65900	1.96068	2.73191	3.79432	5.25335	7.25103	9.97811	13.69013	25.54767	47.14252	492.2235
36	1.43077	1.70914	2.03989	2.89828	4.10393	5.79182	8.14725	11.42394	15.96817	30.91268	59.13557	708.8019
38	1.45953	1.76080	2.12230	3.07478	4.43881	6.38548	9.15425	13.07927	18.62528	37.40434	74.17966	1020.675
40	1.48886	1.81402	2.20804	3.26204	4.80102	7.03999	10.28572	14.97446	21.72452	45.25926	93.05097	1469.772
45	1.56481	1.95421	2.43785	3.78160	5.84118	8.98501	13.76461	21.00245	31.92045	72.89048	163.9876	3657.262
50	1.64463	2.10524	2.69159	4.38391	7.10668	11.46740	18.42015	29.45703	46.90161	117.3909	289.0022	9100.438
100	2.70481	4.43205	7.24465	19.21863	50.50495	131.5013	339.3021	867.7163	2199.761	13780.61	83522.27	828×10^5

TABLE 2 PRESENT VALUE OF $1

$$P = F_n (1 + r)^{-n}$$

r = discount rate; n = number of periods until payment

Periods = n	1%	1½%	2%	3%	4%	5%	6%	7%	8%	10%	12%	20%
1	.99010	.98522	.98039	.97087	.96154	.95238	.94340	.93458	.92593	.90909	.89286	.83333
2	.98030	.97066	.96117	.94260	.92456	.90703	.89000	.87344	.85734	.82645	.79719	.69444
3	.97059	.95632	.94232	.91514	.88900	.86384	.83962	.81630	.79383	.75131	.71178	.57870
4	.96098	.94218	.92385	.88849	.85480	.82270	.79209	.76290	.73503	.68301	.63552	.48225
5	.95147	.92826	.90573	.86261	.82193	.78353	.74726	.71299	.68058	.62092	.56743	.40188
6	.94205	.91454	.88797	.83748	.79031	.74622	.70496	.66634	.63017	.56447	.50663	.33490
7	.93272	.90103	.87056	.81309	.75992	.71068	.66506	.62275	.58349	.51316	.45235	.27908
8	.92348	.88771	.85349	.78941	.73069	.67684	.62741	.58201	.54027	.46651	.40388	.23257
9	.91434	.87459	.83676	.76642	.70259	.64461	.59190	.54393	.50025	.42410	.36061	.19381
10	.90529	.86167	.82035	.74409	.67556	.61391	.55839	.50835	.46319	.38554	.32197	.16151
11	.89632	.84893	.80426	.72242	.64958	.58468	.52679	.47509	.42888	.35049	.28748	.13459
12	.88745	.83639	.78849	.70138	.62460	.55684	.49697	.44401	.39711	.31863	.25668	.11216
13	.87866	.82403	.77303	.68095	.60057	.53032	.46884	.41496	.36770	.28966	.22917	.09346
14	.86996	.81185	.75788	.66112	.57748	.50507	.44230	.38782	.34046	.26333	.20462	.07789
15	.86135	.79985	.74301	.64186	.55526	.48102	.41727	.36245	.31524	.23939	.18270	.06491
16	.85282	.78803	.72845	.62317	.53391	.45811	.39365	.33873	.29189	.21763	.16312	.05409
17	.84438	.77639	.71416	.60502	.51337	.43630	.37136	.31657	.27027	.19784	.14564	.04507
18	.83602	.76491	.70016	.58739	.49363	.41552	.35034	.29586	.25025	.17986	.13004	.03756
19	.82774	.75361	.68643	.57029	.47464	.39573	.33051	.27651	.23171	.16351	.11611	.03130
20	.81954	.74247	.67297	.55368	.45639	.37689	.31180	.25842	.21455	.14864	.10367	.02608
22	.80340	.72069	.64684	.52189	.42196	.34185	.27751	.22571	.18394	.12285	.08264	.01811
24	.78757	.69954	.62172	.49193	.39012	.31007	.24698	.19715	.15770	.10153	.06588	.01258
26	.77205	.67902	.59758	.46369	.36069	.28124	.21981	.17220	.13520	.08391	.05252	.00874
28	.75684	.65910	.57437	.43708	.33348	.25509	.19563	.15040	.11591	.06934	.04187	.00607
30	.74192	.63976	.55207	.41199	.30832	.23138	.17411	.13137	.09938	.05731	.03338	.00421
32	.72730	.62099	.53063	.38834	.28506	.20987	.15496	.11474	.08520	.04736	.02661	.00293
34	.71297	.60277	.51003	.36604	.26355	.19035	.13791	.10022	.07305	.03914	.02121	.00203
36	.69892	.58509	.49022	.34503	.24367	.17266	.12274	.08754	.06262	.03235	.01691	.00141
38	.68515	.56792	.47119	.32523	.22529	.15661	.10924	.07646	.05369	.02673	.01348	.00098
40	.67165	.55126	.45289	.30656	.20829	.14205	.09722	.06678	.04603	.02209	.01075	.00068
45	.63905	.51171	.41020	.26444	.17120	.11130	.07265	.04761	.03133	.01372	.00610	.00027
50	.60804	.47500	.37153	.22811	.14071	.08720	.05429	.03395	.02132	.00852	.00346	.00011
100	.36971	.22563	.13803	.05203	.01980	.00760	.00295	.00115	.00045	.00007	.00001	.00000

TABLE 3 FUTURE VALUE OF AN ANNUITY OF $1 IN ARREARS

$$F = \frac{(1 + r)^n - 1}{r}$$

r = interest rate; n = number of payments

No. of Payments = n	1%	1½%	2%	3%	4%	5%	6%	7%	8%	10%	12%	20%
1	1.00000	1.00000	1.00000	1.00000	1.00000	1.00000	1.00000	1.00000	1.00000	1.00000	1.00000	1.00000
2	2.01000	2.01500	2.02000	2.03000	2.04000	2.05000	2.06000	2.07000	2.08000	2.10000	2.12000	2.20000
3	3.03010	3.04523	3.06040	3.09090	3.12160	3.15250	3.18360	3.21490	3.24640	3.31000	3.37440	3.64000
4	4.06040	4.09090	4.12161	4.18363	4.24646	4.31013	4.37462	4.43994	4.50611	4.64100	4.77933	5.36800
5	5.10101	5.15227	5.20404	5.30914	5.41632	5.52563	5.63709	5.75074	5.86660	6.10510	6.35285	7.44160
6	6.15202	6.22955	6.30812	6.46841	6.63298	6.80191	6.97532	7.15329	7.33593	7.71561	8.11519	9.92992
7	7.21354	7.32299	7.43428	7.66246	7.89829	8.14201	8.39384	8.65402	8.92280	9.48717	10.08901	12.91590
8	8.28567	8.43284	8.58297	8.89234	9.21423	9.54911	9.89747	10.25980	10.63663	11.43589	12.29969	16.49908
9	9.36853	9.55933	9.75463	10.15911	10.58280	11.02656	11.49132	11.97799	12.48756	13.57948	14.77566	20.79890
10	10.46221	10.70272	10.94972	11.46388	12.00611	12.57789	13.18079	13.81645	14.48656	15.93742	17.54874	25.95868
11	11.56683	11.86326	12.16872	12.80780	13.48635	14.20679	14.97164	15.78360	16.64549	18.53117	20.65458	32.15042
12	12.68250	13.04121	13.41209	14.19203	15.02581	15.91713	16.86994	17.88845	18.97713	21.38428	24.13313	39.58050
13	13.80933	14.23683	14.68033	15.61779	16.62684	17.71298	18.88214	20.14064	21.49530	24.52271	28.02911	48.49660
14	14.94742	15.45038	15.97394	17.08632	18.29191	19.59863	21.01507	22.55049	24.21492	27.97498	32.39260	59.19592
15	16.09690	16.68214	17.29342	18.59891	20.02359	21.57856	23.27597	25.12902	27.15211	31.77248	37.27971	72.03511
16	17.25786	17.93237	18.63929	20.15688	21.82453	23.65749	25.67253	27.88805	30.32428	35.94973	42.75328	87.44213
17	18.43044	19.20136	20.01207	21.76159	23.69751	25.84037	28.21288	30.84022	33.75023	40.54470	48.88367	105.9306
18	19.61475	20.48938	21.41231	23.41444	25.64541	28.13238	30.90565	33.99903	37.45024	45.59917	55.74971	128.1167
19	20.81090	21.79672	22.84056	25.11687	27.67123	30.53900	33.75999	37.37896	41.44626	51.15909	63.43968	154.7400
20	22.01900	23.12367	24.29737	26.87037	29.77808	33.06595	36.78559	40.99549	45.76196	57.27500	72.05244	186.6880
22	24.47159	25.83758	27.29898	30.53678	34.24797	38.50521	43.39229	49.00574	55.45676	71.40275	92.50258	271.0307
24	26.97346	28.63352	30.42186	34.42647	39.08260	44.50200	50.81558	58.17667	66.76476	88.49733	118.1552	392.4842
26	29.52563	31.51397	33.67091	38.55304	44.31174	51.11345	59.15638	68.67647	79.95442	109.1818	150.3339	567.3773
28	32.12910	34.48148	37.05121	42.93097	49.96758	58.40258	68.52811	80.69769	95.33883	134.2099	190.6989	819.2233
30	34.78489	37.53868	40.56808	47.57542	56.08494	66.43885	79.05819	94.46079	113.2832	164.4940	241.3327	1181.881
32	37.49407	40.68829	44.22703	52.50276	62.70147	75.29883	90.88978	110.2181	134.2135	201.1378	304.8477	1704.109
34	40.25770	43.93309	48.03380	57.73018	69.85791	85.06696	104.1838	128.2588	158.6267	245.4767	384.5210	2456.118
36	43.07688	47.27597	51.99437	63.27594	77.59831	95.83632	119.1209	148.9135	187.1022	299.1268	484.4631	3539.009
38	45.95272	50.71989	56.11494	69.15945	85.97034	107.7095	135.9042	172.5610	220.3159	364.0434	609.8305	5098.373
40	48.88637	54.26789	60.40198	75.40126	95.02552	120.7998	154.7620	199.6351	259.0565	442.5926	767.0914	7343.858
45	56.48107	63.61420	71.89271	92.71986	121.0294	159.7002	212.7435	285.7493	386.5056	718.9048	1358.230	18281.31
50	64.46318	73.68283	84.57940	112.7969	152.6671	209.3480	290.3359	406.5289	573.7702	1163.909	2400.018	45497.19
100	170.4814	228.8030	312.2323	607.2877	1237.624	2610.025	5638.368	12381.66	27484.52	137796.1	696010.5	414×10^6

Note: To convert this table to values of an annuity in advance, take one more period and subtract 1.00000.

TABLE 4 PRESENT VALUE OF AN ANNUITY OF $1 IN ARREARS

$$P_A = \frac{1 - (1 + r)^{-n}}{r}$$

r = discount rate; n = number of payments

No. of Payments = n	1%	1½%	2%	3%	4%	5%	6%	7%	8%	10%	12%	20%
1	.99010	.98522	.98039	.97087	.96154	.95238	.94340	.93458	.92593	.90909	.89286	.83333
2	1.97040	1.95588	1.94156	1.91347	1.88609	1.85941	1.83339	1.80802	1.78326	1.73554	1.69005	1.52778
3	2.94099	2.91220	2.88388	2.82861	2.77509	2.72325	2.67301	2.62432	2.57710	2.48685	2.40183	2.10648
4	3.90197	3.85438	3.80773	3.71710	3.62990	3.54595	3.46511	3.38721	3.31213	3.16987	3.03735	2.58873
5	4.85343	4.78264	4.71346	4.57971	4.45182	4.32948	4.21236	4.10020	3.99271	3.79079	3.60478	2.99061
6	5.79548	5.69719	5.60143	5.41719	5.24214	5.07569	4.91732	4.76654	4.62288	4.35526	4.11141	3.32551
7	6.72819	6.59821	6.47199	6.23028	6.00205	5.78637	5.58238	5.38929	5.20637	4.86842	4.56376	3.60459
8	7.65168	7.48593	7.32548	7.01969	6.73274	6.46321	6.20979	5.97130	5.74664	5.33493	4.96764	3.83716
9	8.56602	8.36052	8.16224	7.78611	7.43533	7.10782	6.80169	6.51523	6.24689	5.75902	5.32825	4.03097
10	9.47130	9.22218	8.98259	8.53020	8.11090	7.72173	7.36009	7.02358	6.71008	6.14457	5.65022	4.19247
11	10.36763	10.07112	9.78685	9.25262	8.76048	8.30641	7.88687	7.49867	7.13896	6.49506	5.93770	4.32706
12	11.25508	10.90751	10.57534	9.95400	9.38507	8.86325	8.38384	7.94269	7.53608	6.81369	6.19437	4.43922
13	12.13374	11.73153	11.34837	10.63496	9.98565	9.39357	8.85268	8.35765	7.90378	7.10336	6.42355	4.53268
14	13.00370	12.54338	12.10625	11.29607	10.56312	9.89864	9.29498	8.74547	8.24424	7.36669	6.62817	4.61057
15	13.86505	13.34323	12.84926	11.93794	11.11839	10.37966	9.71225	9.10791	8.55948	7.60608	6.81086	4.67547
16	14.71787	14.13126	13.57771	12.56110	11.65230	10.83777	10.10590	9.44665	8.85137	7.82371	6.97399	4.72956
17	15.56225	14.90765	14.29187	13.16612	12.16567	11.27407	10.47726	9.76322	9.12164	8.02155	7.11963	4.77463
18	16.39827	15.67256	14.99203	13.75351	12.65930	11.68959	10.82760	10.05909	9.37189	8.20141	7.24967	4.81219
19	17.22601	16.42617	15.67846	14.32380	13.13394	12.08532	11.15812	10.33560	9.60360	8.36492	7.36578	4.84350
20	18.04555	17.16864	16.35143	14.87747	13.59033	12.46221	11.46992	10.59401	9.81815	8.51356	7.46944	4.86958
22	19.66038	18.62082	17.65805	15.93692	14.45112	13.16300	12.04158	11.06124	10.20074	8.77154	7.64465	4.90943
24	21.24339	20.03041	18.91393	16.93554	15.24696	13.79864	12.55036	11.46933	10.52876	8.98474	7.78432	4.93710
26	22.79520	21.39863	20.12104	17.87684	15.98277	14.37519	13.00317	11.82578	10.80998	9.16095	7.89566	4.95632
28	24.31644	22.72672	21.28127	18.76411	16.66306	14.89813	13.40616	12.13711	11.05108	9.30657	7.98442	4.96967
30	25.80771	24.01584	22.39646	19.60044	17.29203	15.37245	13.76483	12.40904	11.25778	9.42691	8.05518	4.97894
32	27.26959	25.26714	23.46833	20.38877	17.87355	15.80268	14.08404	12.64656	11.43500	9.52638	8.11159	4.98537
34	28.70267	26.48173	24.49859	21.13184	18.41120	16.19290	14.36814	12.85401	11.58693	9.60857	8.15656	4.98984
36	30.10751	27.66068	25.48884	21.83225	18.90828	16.54685	14.62099	13.03521	11.71719	9.67651	8.19241	4.99295
38	31.48466	28.80505	26.44064	22.49246	19.36786	16.86789	14.84602	13.19347	11.82887	9.73265	8.22099	4.99510
40	32.83469	29.91585	27.35548	23.11477	19.79277	17.15909	15.04630	13.33171	11.92461	9.77905	8.24378	4.99660
45	36.09451	32.55234	29.49016	24.51871	20.72004	17.77407	15.45583	13.60552	12.10840	9.86281	8.28252	4.99863
50	39.19612	34.99969	31.42361	25.72976	21.48218	18.25593	15.76186	13.80075	12.23348	9.91481	8.30450	4.99945
100	63.02888	51.62470	43.09835	31.59891	24.50500	19.84791	16.61755	14.26925	12.49432	9.99927	8.33323	5.00000

Note: To convert this table to values of an annuity in advance, take one less period and add 1.00000.

TABLE 5 BOND VALUES IN PERCENT OF PAR: 6-PERCENT SEMIANNUAL COUPONS

Bond Value $= 6/r + (100 - 6/r)(1 + r/2)^{-2n}$

$r =$ yield to maturity; $n =$ years to maturity

Market Yield % Per Year Compounded Semiannually	½	5	10	15	19½	20	30	40
3.0	101.478	113.833	125.753	136.024	144.047	144.874	159.071	169.611
3.5	101.228	111.376	120.941	128.982	135.118	135.743	146.205	153.600
4.0	100.980	108.983	116.351	122.396	126.903	127.355	134.761	139.745
4.5	100.734	106.650	111.973	116.234	119.337	119.645	124.562	127.712
5.0	100.488	104.376	107.795	110.465	112.365	112.551	115.454	117.226
5.1	100.439	103.928	106.982	109.356	111.037	111.202	113.752	115.293
5.2	100.390	103.483	106.177	108.262	109.731	109.874	112.087	113.411
5.3	100.341	103.040	105.380	107.181	108.445	108.568	110.458	111.578
5.4	100.292	102.599	104.590	106.115	107.180	107.283	108.864	109.792
5.5	100.243	102.160	103.807	105.062	105.935	106.019	107.306	108.053
5.6	100.195	101.724	103.031	104.023	104.710	104.776	105.780	106.359
5.7	100.146	101.289	102.263	102.998	103.504	103.553	104.288	104.707
5.8	100.097	100.857	101.502	101.986	102.317	102.349	102.828	103.098
5.9	100.049	100.428	100.747	100.986	101.149	101.165	101.399	101.529
6.0	100	100	100	100	100	100	100	100
6.1	99.9515	99.5746	99.2595	99.0262	98.8685	98.8535	98.6309	98.5088
6.2	99.9030	99.1513	98.5259	98.0650	97.7549	97.7254	97.2907	97.0546
6.3	99.8546	98.7302	97.7990	97.1161	96.6587	96.6153	95.9787	95.6364
6.4	99.8062	98.3112	97.0787	96.1793	95.5796	95.5229	94.6942	94.2529
6.5	99.7579	97.8944	96.3651	95.2545	94.5174	94.4478	93.4365	92.9031
6.6	99.7096	97.4797	95.6580	94.3414	93.4717	93.3899	92.2050	91.5860
6.7	99.6613	97.0670	94.9574	93.4400	92.4423	92.3486	90.9989	90.3007
6.8	99.6132	96.6565	94.2632	92.5501	91.4288	91.3238	89.8178	89.0461
6.9	99.5650	96.2480	93.5753	91.6714	90.4310	90.3152	88.6608	87.8213
7.0	99.5169	95.8417	92.8938	90.8039	89.4487	89.3224	87.5276	86.6255
7.5	99.2771	93.8404	89.5779	86.6281	84.7588	84.5868	82.1966	81.0519
8.0	99.0385	91.8891	86.4097	82.7080	80.4155	80.2072	77.3765	76.0846
8.5	98.8010	89.9864	83.3820	79.0262	76.3899	76.1534	73.0090	71.6412
9.0	98.5646	88.1309	80.4881	75.5666	72.6555	72.3976	69.0430	67.6520

TABLE 6 BOND VALUES IN PERCENT OF PAR: 8-PERCENT SEMIANNUAL COUPONS

$$\text{Bond Value} = 8/r + (100 - 8/r)(1 + r/2)^{-2n}$$

r = yield to maturity; n = years to maturity

Market Yield % Per Year Compounded Semiannually	½	5	10	15	19½	20	30	40
5.0	101.463	113.128	123.384	131.396	137.096	137.654	146.363	151.678
5.5	101.217	110.800	119.034	125.312	129.675	130.098	136.528	140.266
6.0	100.971	108.530	114.877	119.600	122.808	123.115	127.676	130.201
6.5	100.726	106.317	110.905	114.236	116.448	116.656	119.690	121.291
7.0	100.483	104.158	107.106	109.196	110.551	110.678	112.472	113.374
7.1	100.435	103.733	106.367	108.225	109.424	109.536	111.113	111.898
7.2	100.386	103.310	105.634	107.266	108.314	108.411	109.780	110.455
7.3	100.338	102.889	104.908	106.318	107.220	107.303	108.473	109.044
7.4	100.289	102.470	104.188	105.382	106.142	106.212	107.191	107.665
7.5	100.241	102.053	103.474	104.457	105.080	105.138	105.934	106.316
7.6	100.193	101.638	102.767	103.544	104.034	104.079	104.702	104.997
7.7	100.144	101.226	102.066	102.642	103.003	103.036	103.492	103.706
7.8	100.096	100.815	101.371	101.750	101.987	102.009	102.306	102.444
7.9	100.048	100.407	100.683	100.870	100.986	100.997	101.142	101.209
8.0	100	100	100	100	100	100	100	100
8.1	99.9519	99.5955	99.3235	99.1406	99.0279	99.0177	98.8794	98.8170
8.2	99.9039	99.1929	98.6529	98.2916	98.0699	98.0498	97.7798	97.6589
8.3	99.8560	98.7924	97.9882	97.4528	97.1257	97.0962	96.7006	96.5253
8.4	99.8081	98.3938	97.3294	96.6240	96.1951	96.1566	95.6414	95.4152
8.5	99.7602	97.9973	96.6764	95.8052	95.2780	95.2307	94.6018	94.3282
8.6	99.7124	97.6027	96.0291	94.9962	94.3739	94.3183	93.5812	93.2636
8.7	99.6646	97.2100	95.3875	94.1969	93.4829	93.4191	92.5792	92.2208
8.8	99.6169	96.8193	94.7514	93.4071	92.6045	92.5331	91.5955	91.1992
8.9	99.5692	96.4305	94.1210	92.6266	91.7387	91.6598	90.6295	90.1982
9.0	99.5215	96.0436	93.4960	91.8555	90.8851	90.7992	89.6810	89.2173
9.5	99.2840	94.1378	90.4520	88.1347	86.7949	86.6777	85.1858	84.5961
10.0	99.0476	92.2783	87.5378	84.6275	82.9830	82.8409	81.0707	80.4035
10.5	98.8123	90.4639	84.7472	81.3201	79.4271	79.2656	77.2956	76.5876
11.0	98.5782	88.6935	82.0744	78.1994	76.1070	75.9308	73.8252	73.1036

Hints, Key Numbers, and Solutions to Questions and Problems

CHAPTER 1

1.1   Accounting is an information system which provides significant and meaningful financial information from which decisions regarding the allocation of a society's resources can be made.

1.10   Consult state law concerning these regulations. Dr. Wilton T. Anderson's "CPA Requirements of the States," *Collegiate News and Views*, Spring 1972, provides a convenient, if somewhat out-of-date, summary of the requirements.

1.15   If financial reports are conservative, then the firm may have greater "true" net income and net assets than the financial statements show. A current stockholder might infer from his annual report that the corporation was not doing so well as it "actually" is. Such a stockholder might sell his shares only to find later that he would have gained if he had held on to them. Even if the stock market is efficient, as we think it is, and sees through the accounting numbers to the "truth," an individual investor may, from conservative statements, think the firm is overpriced in the market and be persuaded to sell. Had the financial statements been less conservative, the individual might not have sold.

1.16   The company may pressure the auditor to relax his principles. If the auditor objects, the client can fire him and seek another less scrupulous. This makes it difficult to maintain standards higher than those observed by the marginal accountant. The solution? The

SEC has enunciated a policy requiring that corporations changing accounting firms must announce the reasons for the change, and the public accountant must give his side of the story as well. Or accountants might be subject to professional review by outside reviewing bodies composed of nonpracticing accountants. A more drastic step would be for the public, through taxes, to pay for audits of publicly held corporations. Then we would have the problem of assigning accountants to firms, but an open bidding procedure could solve that problem.

1.17 (a)   **PAYOFF TABLE**

		Weather	
Purchases	Cost	Rain	Clear
10,000	$3,000	$2,000	$2,000
20,000	$6,000	−$1,000	$4,000

(b) Buying 10,000 hot dogs always profits him $2,000. If he buys 20,000, he will make $4,000 half the time and lose $1,000 half the time for an expected profit of $1,500. Consequently, he will buy 10,000 for every game and make $2,000.

(c) He would buy 20,000 on clear days and 10,000 on rainy days. His expected profit is ($4,000 + $2,000)/2 = $3,000.

(d) He finds perfect information worth, on average, $3,000 − $2,000 = $1,000 per game.

CHAPTER 2

2.6 a, d, h

2.7 a, c, g, h

2.8 a. Investment in Government Bonds .... $ 7,500
     b. None
     c. Merchandise 245
     d. None (no evidence of legal transfer of title)
     e. Deposit on Machinery Contract 4,500

2.9 a. None
     b. None
     c. Unearned Subscriptions .... $ 10
     d. Advances on Equipment Contract 4,500
     e. Wages Payable 10,000
         Payroll Taxes Payable 800

2.10 a. 2   e. 2   i. 2
      b. 1   f. 1   j. 1
      c. 3   g. 2   k. 2
      d. 1   h. 1   l. 3

2.12 a. Liability. Prepayments or Advances to Suppliers
 b. Liability. Investment in Bonds
 c. Asset. Deposits or Customers' Balances
 d. Asset. Interest Payable
 e. Asset. Unearned Premiums
 f. Liability. Prepaid Rent

2.18

BAY CITY MANUFACTURING COMPANY
Balance Sheet
December 31, 1975

Assets

Current Assets

Cash	$ 12,015	
Notes Receivable	18,540	
Accounts Receivable	47,870	
Interest Receivable	360	
Raw Materials on Hand	19,120	
Goods in Process	24,365	
Finished Goods	41,010	
Factory Supplies	8,920	
Total Current Assets		$172,200

Noncurrent Assets

Land	$ 13,880	
Buildings	254,360	
Machinery and Equipment	427,500	
Organization Costs	7,500	
Total Noncurrent Assets		703,240
Total Assets		$875,440

Liabilities and Stockholders' Equity

Current Liabilities

Accounts Payable	$ 24,240	
Wages Payable	19,850	
Property Taxes Payable	13,435	
Withheld Income Taxes	8,195	
Total Current Liabilities		$ 65,720

Long-term Liabilities

Bonds Payable		150,000
Total Liabilities		$215,720

Stockholders' Equity

Capital Stock	$400,000	
Additional Paid-in Capital	40,520	
Retained Earnings	219,200	
Total Stockholders' Equity		659,720
Total Liabilities and Stockholders' Equity		$875,440

2.19

TRI-CITY LAUNDRY
Balance Sheet
September 30, 1975

Assets

Current Assets

Cash on Hand	$ 500	
Cash in Bank	1,000	
Accounts Receivable	1,500	
Supplies	500	
Unexpired Insurance	250	
Total Current Assets		$ 3,750

Noncurrent Assets

Cleaning Equipment	$15,000		
Less Accumulated Depreciation	7,500	$7,500	
Delivery Equipment	$ 4,000		
Less Accumulated Depreciation	1,500	2,500	
Total Noncurrent Assets			10,000
Total Assets			$13,750

Liabilities and Proprietorship

Current Liabilities

Accounts Payable	$ 700	
Wages Payable	400	
Taxes Payable	250	
Equipment Contract Payable	3,300	
Total Current Liabilities		$ 4,650

Proprietorship

Alan Hanson, Capital	$4,550	
Frank Howard, Capital	4,550	
Total Proprietorship		9,100
Total Liabilities and Proprietorship		$13,750

CHAPTER 3

3.7 (a) (3) Increase   Asset   Cash in Bank $33,000
              Decrease Asset   Cash on Hand   33,000
          (6) Increase   Asset   Office Equipment   625
              Decrease Asset   Cash in Bank   125
              Increase   Liability   Accounts Payable   500

   (b) (3) Debit   Cash in Bank $33,000
              Credit   Cash on Hand   33,000
          (6) Debit   Office Equipment   625
              Credit   Cash in Bank   125
              Credit   Accounts Payable   500

3.9 (a) (1) Investment in bonds, $10,500.
          (3) None.
          (5) Accounts receivable, $850.

3.10 (a) $7,500 profit; ⅔ to Allen, ⅓ to Pearl.

3.11 (a) Total current assets $41,765.
           Total assets $108,265.

   (b) (1) $75,400 — $67,500 = $7,900; Net income of $7,900.

3.13   (1) $153,200.

3.17 (b) (1) None.

          (3) Income taxes payable $4,800.

CHAPTER 4

4.6 (a) $800   (b) $800   (c) $800   (d) $800
     (e)   0   (f)   0   (g)   0   (h) 0

4.12 (1) Organization Costs or Accounting System, $780.
      (2) Marketable Securities, $4,590.
      (3) Land, $750.
      (4) Receivable from Insurance Company, $3,000.

4.14 (a.1) Dr. Revenue—Commercial Photography   18,090
             Dr. Revenue—Printing Service   4,680
                  Cr. Income Summary   22,770

4.23

PRIMA COMPANY
Income Statement, Year of 1975

Revenues:
Sales $212,000
Interest Earned   700

Total Revenue $212,700
Expenses:
Cost of Goods Sold $126,500
Property Taxes   1,700
Depreciation   2,000
Interest Charges   500
Other Expenses   56,800

Total Expenses   187,500

Net Income .... $ 25,200
Less: Dividends   2,000

Increase in Retained Earnings .... $ 23,200
Retained Earnings January 1, 1975   76,000

Retained Earnings December 31, 1975   .... $ 99,200

T-account methods for deriving the solution are shown below. Transactions (1)-(9) correspond to the numbered cash transactions. In transactions (10)-(21), "p" indicates figure was derived with "plug" and "c" indicates a closing entry. The final check is that the debit to close Income Summary in (21) matches the plug in Retained Earnings. All figures in thousands of dollars.

($ in 000's)

	Cash				Accounts Receivable		
	✓ 40.0	(4)	114.0		✓ 36.0	(1)	144.0
(1)	144.0	(5)	5.0	(10p)	149.0		✓ 41.0
(2)	63.0	(6)	0.5		185.0		185.0
(3)	1.0	(7)	57.5				
		(8)	1.2		✓ 41.0		
		(9)	2.0				
			✓ 67.8				
	248.0		248.0				
	✓ 67.8						

Merchandise—Inventory

	✓ 55.0	(15p)	126.5
(11)	121.0		✓ 49.5
	176.0		176.0
	✓ 49.5		

Accrued Interest Receivable

	✓ 1.0	(3)	1.0
(12p)	.7		✓ .7
	1.7		1.7
	✓ .7		

Prepaid Costs

	✓ 4.0	
(13p)	1.2	
	✓ 5.2	

Buildings, Machinery & Equipment

✓ 47.0	

Accounts Payable Miscellaneous

(7)	57.5		✓ 2.0
		(13)	1.2
	✓ 2.5	(14p)	56.8
	60.0		60.0
			✓ 2.5

Accounts Payable Merchandise

(4)	114.0		✓ 34.0
	✓ 41.0	(11p)	121.0
	155.0		155.0
			✓ 41.0

Accrued Property Taxes Payable

(8)	1.2		✓ 1.0
	✓ 1.5	(16p)	1.7
	2.7		2.7
			✓ 1.5

Accumulated Depreciation

		✓ 10.0
	(17p)	2.0
		✓ 12.0

Mortgage Payable

(5)	5.0	✓ 35.0
	✓ 30.0	
	35.0	35.0
		✓ 30.0

Capital Stock

	✓ 25.0

Retained Earnings

(9)	2.0		76.0
	✓ 99.2	(21p)	25.2
	101.2		101.2
			✓ 99.2

Sales

(19c)	212.0	(2)	63.0
		(10)	149.0
	212.0		212.0

Cost of Goods Sold

(15)	126.5	(18c)	126.5

Interest Expense

(6)	0.5	(20c)	0.5

Income Summary

(14)	56.8	(12)	0.7
(16)	1.7	(19)	212.0
(17)	2.0		
(18)	126.5		
(20)	0.5		
(21)	25.2		
	212.7		212.7

4.25

SECUNDA COMPANY
Cash Receipts and Disbursements Schedule
Year of 1975

Receipts:		
Collections from Customers		$85,000
Disbursements:		
Suppliers of Merchandise and Other Services	$81,000	
Mortgage	3,000	
Dividends*	10,000	
Interest	2,000	
Total Disbursements		96,000
Decrease in Cash		$11,000
Cash, January 1		20,000
Cash, December 31		$ 9,000

* Notice that the Retained Earnings balance decreased from the 1/1 post-closing amount to the 12/31 *preclosing* amount. The usual way the Retained Earnings balance can decrease during a period *before* the books are closed is through a distribution of Retained Earnings in the form of dividends.

CHAPTER 5

5.1   (1) Dr. Raw Material Used 360
           Cr. Raw Material 360
      (5) Dr. Raw Materials 4,800
           Cr. Accounts Payable—Consolidated Pipe Company.. 4,800
      (6) Dr. Accounts Payable—Consolidated Pipe Company 4,800
           Cr. Cash in Bank 4,704
           Cr. Raw Materials 96

5.12 (1) a   (2) b   (3) a   (4) a

5.15 Finished Product on Hand, August 31, 1975 .... $ 112,620
      Total Assets August 31, 1975 1,027,980

5.18	d.	Work in Process, October 31, 1975	$ 31,400
5.21	c.	Work in Process, July 31, 1975	$ 214,675
	f.	Retained Earnings, July 31, 1975	240,500
	g.	Total Assets, July 31, 1975	1,301,675
5.24		Total Assets, January 1, 1975	$ 108,400

CHAPTER 6

6.12 A complete record of all of the transactions of the period must be in the accounts at the end of the accounting period. If the posting period were longer, the information would not all be in the accounts. If the posting period were shorter, the data would be in the accounts as a result of the several postings. The end of one posting period must coincide with the end of the accounting period.

6.13 Each item relating to a subsidiary ledger account would have to be posted twice, once to the controlling account and once to the subsidiary ledger account.

6.17 1975 (Partial Answer)

Apr. 1	Cash on Hand	5,200	
	Accounts Receivable—J. A. Jones		5,200
7	Accounts Receivable—Ringling Sales Company	5,000	
	Sales		5,000
8	Factory Utilities	55	
	Office Utilities	15	
	Accounts Payable—Union Electric Company		70
10	Withheld Income Taxes	889	
	Cash in Bank		889
11	Office Supplies Used	44	
	Supplies on Hand		44

6.19 a. Cash Disbursements Journal: Accounts Payable, Dr.; Salaries, Dr.; Other Accounts, Dr.; Cash in Bank, Cr.; Cash on Hand, Cr.; Purchase Discounts, Cr.; Withheld Income Tax, Cr.; Payroll Taxes Payable, Cr.

Cash Receipts Journal: Cash on Hand, Dr.; Cash in Bank, Dr.; Cash on Hand, Cr. (Deposits); Accounts Receivable, Cr.; Sales Discounts, Dr.; Other Accounts, Cr.

Purchases Journal: Merchandise, Dr.; Other Accounts, Dr.; Accounts Payable, Cr.

Sales Journal: Accounts Receivable, Dr.; Sales, Cr.

General Journal: Other Accounts, Dr.; Other Accounts, Cr.

6.20

a. false	b. false	c. true	d. false	e. false
f. true	g. true	h. true	i. false	j. true
k. true	l. false	m. false	n. false	o. false
p. true	q. false	r. true	s. true	t. false
u. true	v. false	w. false	x. false	y. true
z. true				

6.21

			c.
a. Amount Columns in the Journal:		**b. Entries**	**Postings to Ledger**
Cash on Hand, Dr.	$26 + 90 =$	116	1
Cash on Hand, Cr.	$26 + 8 =$	34	1
Cash in Bank, Dr.	$26 =$	26	1
Cash in Bank, Cr.	$15 + 10 + 4 =$	29	1
Accounts Receivable, Dr.	$100 =$	100	1
Accounts Receivable, Cr.	$90 =$	90	1
Merchandise, Dr.	$20 =$	20	1
Accounts Payable, Dr.	$15 =$	15	1
Accounts Payable, Cr.	$20 =$	20	1
Sales, Cr.	$26 + 100 =$	126	1
Other Accounts, Dr. .	$4 + 10 + 8 + 4 + 2 + 1 =$	29	29
Other Accounts, Cr.	$4 + 2 + 1 =$	7	7
		612	46

Nonamount columns:

"Other Accounts": Account Titles

Ref.

Date

Explanation

Check Number

d. 612 postings.

6.22 Trial Balance Columns Total $2,330.

6.25d: 6.26d; 6.27c. Trial Balance Columns Total $33,270.

6.27 d. Net Income for October .... $6,700.

6.27 h. Trial Balance Columns Total $29,040.

CHAPTER 7

7.5 a., b., e., f., g.

7.7 (b) Yes, an extraordinary item; although if the property were located in an area experiencing frequent typhoons, the answer might be no.

7.19 a. (3)   b. (1)   c. (3)   d. (1)   e. (1)   f. (3)
    g. (1)   h. (2)   i. (1)   j. (1)   k. (3), possibly (1)   l. (3)

7.23 Under the completed sales method of recognizing revenue, no expenses are recognized, or matched to revenue, until the sale is completed and revenue is recognized. Under the percentage of completion method of recognizing revenue, the proportion of costs incurred for the period as a percentage of total costs to be incurred for the sale is used to quantify both the amount of revenue recognized for the period and the amount of cost recognized as expenses of that period. Under the cash collection, or installment, basis of recognizing revenue, cash receipts are the revenue for the period, and the proportion of cash receipts during the period as a percentage of total cash receipts is used to quantify the portion of total costs that are treated as expenses of producing that revenue for the period.

Partial answer for Period of January 1, 1976 through March 31, 1976.

Basis	Revenue	Expenses	Net Income
Production	$ 70,000	$ 60,000	$ 10,000
Sales	700,000	600,000	100,000
Cash Collection	161,000	138,000	23,000

7.26   Partial answer.

	a.i.		a.ii.
Date	Estimated Tax for Year (Tax Returns)	Quarter Ending on	Tax Expense for Quarter for Financial Statements
4/15/75	$713,500	3/31/75	$185,500
6/15/75	809,500	6/30/75	240,000
9/15/75	761,500	9/30/75	144,000
12/15/75	833,500	12/31/75	276,000

CHAPTER 8

8.6

| Petty Cash .... | 50 | |
| Cash in Bank .... | | 50 |

Postage	12	
Express	10	
Office Supplies	8	
Cash in Bank		30

8.9

| Driver's Change Fund .... | 40 | |
| Cash in Bank .... | | 40 |

Gasoline and Oil	6	
Sales Returns	14	
Cash on Hand	145	
Accounts Receivable		60
Sales		105

8.12   Solution assuming no check register is used with the payroll bank account:

a. (1) Payroll Bank Account 2,000
            Cash in Bank 2,000
    (2) Office Salaries (or Salaries Payable) 6,000
            Cash in Bank 5,170
            FICA Tax Payable 360
            Withheld Income Tax 470
    (3) No additional entry.

b. (1), (2): Check register.

Solution assuming payroll check register is used:

a.   (1)   Same as above.

     (2)   Payroll Bank Account 5,170

             Cash in Bank   5,170

     (3)   Office Salaries (or Salaries Payable) 6,000

             Payroll Bank Account   5,170

             FICA Tax Payable   360

             Withheld Income Tax   470

b.   (1), (2): Check register.

    (3): Payroll check register.

8.15   Adjusted book balance, April 30 .... $ 6,340

8.18 a. Adjusted book balance, May 31   4,096

8.21 a. Adjusted book balance, November 30 334,279

8.23 c. Adjusted book balance, March 31   6,210

CHAPTER 9

9.2   b.   The entry to record the sales discounts of the period is not made until the end of the period when all of the sales have been recorded, but the discounts taken on this period's sales have been debited to the Allowance account all during the period.

9.5   The costs that were incurred in making the sale, the costs of handling the return, and any reduction in value of the merchandise returned should not, logically, be charged against other completed sales. The best procedure would be to charge all such costs to an account called Cost of Returns.

    If the goods are returned in a later period, the revenues of the period of the sale are inflated and those of the period of return are understated. There is some tendency for these differences to cancel out, but the canceling effect is far from accurate.

9.6   This is due to the bracket arrangement of the tax rates and the practice sometimes followed of collecting from the merchant a certain percentage of his total taxable sales. For example, in some states the tax does not apply to small sales, say under 20¢, and if the tax is calculated as a percentage of total sales, merchants doing much of their business in articles selling for less than 20¢ will pay more taxes than they collect.

    At some brackets, the tax rate is higher than the average which is computed on the basis of the total sales. For example, if 3¢ is charged on a 50¢ sale, this is 6-percent tax, but when the merchant pays the tax, if the rate is 5 percent, he only pays 2.5¢ to the government. If many of his sales are of this sort, he may collect more tax than he pays.

9.9   If the Sales, Uncollectible Accounts Adjustment figure is derived at the end of the accounting period, but Accounts Receivable are written off during the period as information about bad debts becomes available, then the Allowance for Uncollectibles will have a debit balance whenever the amount of bad debts written off during the period exceeds the opening credit balance in the Allowance account. Since balance sheets are prepared only after adjusting and closing entries are made, both the Sales, Uncollectible Accounts Adjustment and the Allowance for Uncollectible accounts will ordinarily be made current with appropriate adjusting entries before the balance sheet is prepared. The answer applies to the Allowance for Sales Discounts question as well. In the sales discount context, the revenue contra, Sales Discounts, substitutes for the Sales, Uncollectible Accounts Adjustment in the other context.

9.19 Gross Margin on Cost = 39.31 percent
Gross Margin on Net Sales = 28.22 percent

9.21
a. (4)	b. (2)	c. (3)X	d. (2)X	e. (1)X
f. (2)	g. (2)X	h. (1)X	i. (4)	j. (4)
k. (4)X	l. (2)	m. (2)X	n. (1)	o. (1)X

9.25 c. Net Sales $1,790,893

9.28 d.

	a.	b.	c.
Accounts Payable	$9,712	$9,900	$9,900
Less: Allowance for Purchase Discounts . .	—	—	188
Net Payables	$9,712	$9,900	$9,712

CHAPTER 10

10.13 a.
1/1–3/31	Office Supplies Used	6,000	
	Accounts Payable		6,000
3/31	Office Supplies	300	
	Office Supplies Used		300

10.14 Hint: Total Depreciation charges are $1,526.

10.18 f. Retained Earnings overstated by $1,710.

10.20 f.
| December 31 | Office Supplies Expense . . . . | 10 | |
| | Office Supplies . . . . | | 10 |

10.21 Income tax expense is $838.

10.26 Bonus to manager is $752.

CHAPTER 11

11.8 a. False   b. False   c. True   d. False   e. False   f. False
g. True   h. True   i. True   j. True

11.20 a., e., f., h.

11.23   Merchandise Cost of Goods Sold $119,300

11.28   Net Income to Owner for April, 1975 .... $583

11.30   Net Income to Stockholders for Quarter $4,608

11.34   Retained Earnings December 31, 1975 .... $17,028

11.35   Retained Earnings December 31, 1975 .... $30,002

11.36   Retained Earnings on June 30, 1975 .... $12,525

CHAPTER 12

12.1   a. Cash 1,000
                Sales 1,000
           b. Cash 1,000
                Sales 1,000
                    Cost of Goods Sold 800
                    Merchandise 800

12.11   (2) None   (4) Overstated   (6) Understated
           (8) None   (10) None

12.13   a. Perpetual-inventory system

        (1) First-in, first-out method:
            Cost of withdrawals: 9,000 units $50,000
            Inventory, November 30: .... 2,000 units $12,000
        (2) Weighted-average method:
            Cost of withdrawals: 9,000 units $50,250
            Inventory, November 30: .... 2,000 units $11,750
        (3) Last-in, first-out method:
            Cost of withdrawals: 9,000 units $51,000
            Inventory, November 30: .... 2,000 units $11,000

        b. Periodic-inventory system:

        (1) Inventory, November 30: .... 2,000 units @ $6 $12,000
            Cost of withdrawals: .... 9,000 units   50,000
        (2) Inventory, November 30: .... 2,000 units @ $5.64 $11,280
            Cost of withdrawals: .... 9,000 units   50,720
        (3) Inventory, November 30: .... 2,000 units @ $5 $10,000
            Cost of withdrawals: .... 9,000 units   52,000

12.17   a. $250   b. $245   c. Same as (b)   d. $260
           e. $270   f. $252   g. $257.16 ($= 4 \times$ $64.29)

12.20   Inventory at Cost, July 31, 1975 .... $64,000

12.23   Inventory, July 4, 1975 .... $64,000

12.26   1. $27   2. $48   3. $16   4. $46

12.29

Gross Margin on Sales

	a	b
1974	$524,000	$510,000
1975	$462,000	$466,000

12.30 a. Perpetual inventory records are not used.
(1) First-in, first-out:

	Cost
Total Inventory	$3,800
Raw Material Used	$5,700

(2) Last-in, first-out:

Total Inventory	$3,300
Raw Material Used	$6,200

(3) Weighted-average:

Inventory, 6/30	$3,564

b. Perpetual inventory records used.
(1) First-in, first-out:

Raw Material Used	$5,700
Raw Material Inventory	$3,800

(2) Last-in, first-out:

Raw Material Used	$5,900
Raw Material Inventory, 6/30	$3,600

(3) Weighted average:

Raw Material Used	$5,770
Raw Material Inventory, 6/30	$3,730

12.38

	1972	**1973**	**1974**	**1975**
End-of-year LIFO inventory at original cost	$157,500	$179,674	$154,423	$212,116

CHAPTER 13

13.5 a. 12 percent per period; 5 periods

13.6 a. $122

13.7 a. $27

13.8 a. $1,424

13.9 a. $4,003

13.10 a. $16,984

13.11 a. $447

13.12 a. $1,700

13.13 a. $9,405

13.14 a. $27,900

13.15 a. $48,839

13.16   a. $13,425

13.17   a. $300,000/(10.637 × 1.08) = $26,114

13.18   a. $26,743

13.19   a. $15,000 × (4.212 × .890) = $56,230

13.20   a. $1,855

13.21 $396

13.22   a. $14,955   13.23   a. $53,000   13.24   a. $50,000

13.25   a. $6,000 × [1+ 1/((1.04)² − 1)] = $79,529

13.26   a. $25,000 × (1.08)⁻⁵ × [1 + 1/(1.08¹⁰ − 1)] = $31,696

13.33   b.   Fifty-five dollars per month in advance discounted at ½ percent per month is equivalent to $55 + $55/1.005 = $109.73 per two months, paid in advance; $3,400/$110 = 31 so that the purchase price is based upon the number of months required for the present value of an annuity of $1 paid in advance to be 31. Scanning the 1 percent column in Appendix Table 4, we see that an annuity *due for* 37 periods has a present value of $31.11. The purchase price is equivalent to about 74 months of rental payments. This computation is only approximate.

13.34   b.   **Total Present Value of Cost at 10 Percent**

Purchase	$1,000
Plan *A*	977
Plan *B*	932
Plan *C*	889 (preferred alternative)

13.35   See Figure 24.1 in Chapter 24; the line is not straight.

CHAPTER 14

14.3   Loss on Trade-In....... $600

14.7   Gain on Disposal of Equipment....... $60

14.8   Calculate the remaining life of the asset first.

14.10   The Loss on Disposal of Building in 1977 is, then, $3,750.

14.12

	1st Year	2nd Year
a.	$80,000	$72,000
b.	10,000	10,000
c.	80	70

14.14 b.

Year	Depreciation Charge
1	$18,000
2	9,000
3	4,500
4	4,500

14.22 The factory building account shows $424,848 of costs including, somewhat arbitrarily, all of items (11) and (14). Items (11) and (14) might be prorated in part to the office building. Item (8) is not included, but some companies are now capitalizing such costs, rather than expensing them.

14.26 b.

Year	Depreciation Charge for Year
1973	$12,000
1974	16,720
1975	14,512

14.28 a. Let B_t represent the book value at the start of year t. Then $B_t = 2/3 B_{t-1} + \$2,500$; set $B_t = B_{t-1}$ and solve for $B_t = \$7,500$

14.29 a.

Depreciation Method	Present Value of Total Depreciation Expense Discounted at 10 Percent Per Year
Straight Line	$5,065
Double-Declining Balance	5,238
Sum-of-the-Years'-Digits	5,130

CHAPTER 15

15.7 a.

	5/20/75	Notes Receivable	600.00	
		Interest Receivable	4.00	
		Accounts Receivable—S. McQueen		604.00
	6/30/75	Interest Receivable	5.33	
		Interest Earned		5.33
		Interest for 1⅓ months.		
	10/20/75	Cash on Hand	624.00	
		Notes Receivable		600.00
		Interest Receivable		9.33
		Interest Earned		14.67
b.	4/20/75	Accounts Payable—S. McQueen	600.00	
		Notes Payable		600.00
	6/30/75	Interest Charges on Notes	9.33	
		Interest Payable		9.33
	9/30/75	Interest Charges on Notes	12.00	
		Interest Payable		12.00
	10/20/75	Notes Payable	600.00	
		Interest Payable	21.33	
		Interest Charges on Notes	2.67	
		Cash in Bank		624.00

c.   4/20/75 Notes Receivable 600.00
                   Accounts Receivable—R. O'Neill 600.00
       5/20/75 Accounts Payable—McGraw Co. 604.00
                   Notes Receivable Discounted 600.00
                   Interest Earned 4.00
      10/20/75 Notes Receivable Discounted 600.00
                   Notes Receivable 600.00

15.8
       12/1/74 Cash 12,600
                   Notes Payable 12,600
      12/31/74 Interest Charges on Notes 105
                   Interest Payable 105
       2/28/75 Interest Charges on Notes 210
                   Interest Payable 210
       2/28/75 Notes Payable (original note) 12,600
                 Interest Payable 315
                   Notes Payable (new note) 12,600
                   Cash 315
       3/31/75 Notes Payable 12,600
                   Cash 12,600

      The following entry is optional at this time.
      Interest Charges on Notes 105
          Interest Payable 105

15.17

Period	Liability at Start of Period	Effective Interest 11%	Nominal Interest 10%	Discount Amortization	Unamortized Discount at End of Period	Net Liability at End of Period
0					$3,568	$156,432
1	$156,432	$17,208	$16,000	$1,208	2,360	117,640
2	117,640	12,940	12,000	940	1,420	78,580
3	78,580	8,644	8,000	644	776	39,224
4	39,224	4,314	4,000	314	462*	39,538

* Charge off remaining discount of $ 462 ⎫
                                              $39,538 ⎭   total = $40,000.

15.19   a. $80,490   b. $6,704 gain   c. $60,854

15.20   a., b., and c.
Present value of interest expenditure savings less net outlay to refund is $24,240.

15.22

Date	Total Payment	Interest Payment	Principal Payment	Balance
9/1/75				$24,000.00
10/1/75	$266.64	$240.00	$ 26.64	23,973.36
11/1/75	266.64	239.73	26.91	23,946.45
12/1/75	600.00	239.46	360.54	23,585.91
1/2/76	266.64	235.86	30.78	23,555.13

15.25   Hint: Treat the additional acquisition cost as if it were additional premium. The quarterly interest revenue is $12,500.

15.26 See hint for 15.25. The gain on sale of investment is $130,000.

15.29 (Partial answers)

	a. 12/1/75	b. 12/1/76	c. 12/1/89
Interest Charges	125,000	122,750	57,500
Interest Payable	125,000	122,750	57,500
Cash	250,000	245,500	115,000

15.30 Hint: The periodic payment that will grow to $1.00 in 10 periods at 5 percent per period is $1/12.57789 = $.0795; see Appendix Table 3. Interest revenue recorded on 12/31/91 is $48,893; on 6/30/92 is $75,187.

15.31

Issue *C* sells for	$ 935,812
Original discount	64,188
	$1,000,000

Credit to bond discount, effective interest method:

First payment	$240
Second payment	250
Third payment	261

Semiannual credit to bond discount using straight line: $1,070.

15.34 a. $5,545
b. The September 30 balance sheet shows liability for outstanding coupons of $6,630.

15.37

	a.	b.
Net Income	$422,767	$395,093
Credit to Deferred Tax Liability	10,329	23,153

CHAPTER 16

16.5 (1)

Common Stock Subscriptions Receivable	120,000	
Common Stock Subscribed		100,000
Premium on Common Stock		20,000

16.8 (1)

Assets	77,500	
K. S. Robin, Capital	3,750	
P. T. Vincent, Capital		81,250

(2)

Goodwill	15,000	
K. S. Robin, Capital		15,000
Assets (detailed)	100,000	
P. T. Vincent, Capital		100,000

(5)   **Condensed Balance Sheet for Treatment (2)**

Assets	(2)
Assets (Other than Goodwill)	$200,000
Goodwill	15,000
	$215,000

Liabilities & Capital

Liabilities	$ 15,000
K. S. Robin, Capital	100,000
P. T. Vincent, Capital	100,000
	$215,000

16.11 (5)
Land	100,000	
Option on Land		3,000
Cash		40,000
Capital Stock		50,000
Premium on Capital Stock		7,000

16.12 c.
Total Current Assets	$69,800
Total Current Liabilities	3,800
Total Capital	80,000

16.15 (1)
Cash	6,300	
Marketable Securities		6,000
Retained Earnings		300

16.16 a. (2)
Goodwill	15,000	
Stone, Capital		7,500
Baker, Capital		7,500
Cash on Hand	40,000	
Gould, Capital		40,000

b. (2)
Cash on Hand	40,000	
Stone, Capital		1,875
Baker, Capital		1,875
Gould, Capital		36,250

16.18 a. Morgan, $50,000. Remington, $40,000.

b. Morgan, $51,200. 1/3 of ($100,000 + $53,600).
Doyle, $61,200. $60,000 + 1/2 ($53,600 − $51,200).

16.20 a.
Cash on Hand	112,000	
Peterson, Capital		4,000
Munice, Capital		4,000
Haldman, Capital		104,000

e.
Peterson, Capital	33,333	
Munice, Capital	33,333	
Haldman, Capital		66,666

16.22 c.

Schedule of Partners' Capital Accounts

	Walter	Ron	Kelvin	Total
Capital, 1/1/75	$80,000	$36,000	$24,000	$140,000
Additional Investment	—	14,000	4,000	18,000
Share of Net Income	11,168	24,742	19,050	54,960
	$91,168	$74,742	$47,050	$212,960
Drawings	6,000	12,000	9,000	27,000
Capital, 12/31/75	$85,168	$62,742	$38,050	$185,960

16.24 b. The capital accounts of the Keswicks show the following:

A. K. Keswick, Capital				S. R. Keswick, Capital			
(1)	2,400		✓ 75,000	(1)	1,600		✓ 50,000
(2)	720	(3)	60	(2)	480	(3)	40
(5)	133	(4)	318	(5)	89	(4)	212

Total capital now is $120,208 ($72, 125) of A. K. Keswick plus $48,083 of S. R. Keswick). Jarman will have to contribute $60,104 to be a one-third partner.

   d. Total Current Assets $126,304
       Total Assets 195,534
       Total Current Liabilities 15,222
       Total Capital 180,312

16.26 b. Total Assets $152,000
           Total Liabilities 20,000
           Total Capital 132,000
       d. Total Current Assets $581,800
           Total Liabilities 445,400
           Total Stockholders' Equity 713,400

CHAPTER 17

17.3

Distribution of Net Income

	Durance	Sinn	Total
Salary Allowance	$10,000	$10,000	$20,000
Balance in Proportion to Average Capital ...	8,000	4,000	12,000
Total	$18,000	$14,000	$32,000

17.11 a. Balances on December 31, 1975: Gordon, $87,720; Ginn, $123,280

17.12 a. $ 6,000
       b. $21,600
       c. $ 1,667
       d. $13,267
       e. — $1,767
       f. $38,500
       g. $14,200

17.19 (1) Treasury Stock 500,000
                Cash in Bank 500,000
            Retained Earnings 500,000
                Retained Earnings Restricted by Acquisition of
                    Treasury Stock 500,000

17.20 (1) Retained Earnings 8,000
                Dividends Payable—Preferred Stock 8,000
            Dividend of $2.50 per share on 3,200 shares.

17.21   (1)   Cash 2,415,000

                Common Stock 2,300,000

                Additional Paid-in Capital 115,000

     (2)   Cash 492,000

          Discount on Bonds 8,000

                Bonds Payable 500,000

     (3)   Interest on Bonds 20,200

                Cash 20,000

                Discount on Bonds 200

     (9)   Bonds Payable 500,000

          Interest on Bonds 20,200

                Discount on Bonds 200

                Sinking Fund 500,000

                Cash 20,000

   (12)   Cash 770,000

                Common Stock 700,000

                Additional Paid-in Capital 70,000

17.22   Net Income for 1976 .... $80,000 (= $85,600 — $5,600)

17.23   a.   Cash 5,500,000

          Preferred Stock 5,500,000

      To record issuance of $7 convertible preferred
stock at $110 for 50,000 shares.

      Preferred Stock 5,500,000

          Common Stock 2,500,000

          Premium on Common Stock 3,000,000

      To record conversion of 50,000 shares of preferred
stock into 250,000 shares of common stock.

17.27   a.   The footnotes should disclose the conditions of the purchase warrants such as the number of shares and the price at which these warrants could be exercised. The reason is to indicate the amounts of potential dilution of common stockholders' equity. Without this information, shareholders might overestimate the potential growth in the market price of their stock and might make poorer investment/disinvestment decisions.

   b.   Yes, this constituted dilution of the equity, but it can be argued that such dilution already took place when the warrants were initially issued.

   c.   There are several alternative ways of measuring the cost of the warrants and, therefore, of the loan:

     (1) $50 — $30 = $20 is the cost of the warrants or the present value of the estimated effect on future earnings per share when the warrants are exercised.

     (2)   Start with the initial proceeds from the loan. Subtract the initial market price of the warrants. Recompute the effective yield on the debt.

     (3)   Estimate the interest rate that the company would have to pay to borrow without warrants and find the present value

of future payments at that rate. Difference from $5,000,000 is value to be assigned to the warrants.

Warrants do increase the consideration given to the lender and, hence, the cost of the loan.

17.28 a. (1)

Stock Subscriptions Receivable	792,000	
Preferred Stock Subscribed		600,000
Common Stock Subscribed		192,000

(4)

Cash	786,720	
Notes Receivable	5,280	
Stock Subscriptions Receivable		792,000

(8)

Preferred Stock Subscriptions Receivable	130,200	
Preferred Stock Subscribed		124,000
Premium on Preferred Stock		6,200

620 shares at $210.

(13)

Cash	225,000	
Common Stock Subscriptions Receivable		225,000

12,500 shares at $18.

Cash	138,200	
Common Stock Subscribed	160	
Premium on Common Stock	40	
Common Stock Subscriptions Receivable		138,400

6,910 shares at S20 collected, 10 subscriptions canceled.

(15)

Preferred Stock	3,000	
Premium on Preferred Stock	50	
Common Stock		2,400
Premium on Common Stock		650

15 shares of preferred exchanged for 150 shares of common.

b. Preferred Stock: 6% cumulative, par $200 per share, convertible into ten shares of common on or before (date). Authorized, 5,000 shares. Retired, 15 shares.

Unissued, 900 shares, of which 20 are subscribed.

Subscribed, 20 shares	$ 4,000
Issued and Outstanding, 4,085 shares	817,000
Premium on Preferred Stock	6,150
	$827,150

Common Stock: no-par value, $16 stated value. Authorized 100,000 shares.

Reserved for conversion, 40,850 shares.

Issued and Outstanding, 39,060 shares	$624,960
Premium on Common Stock	53,290
	$678,250

CHAPTER 18

18.6 The equity method shows on one line of the income statement revenues exactly equal to the extra income attributable to a subsidiary that would be shown on a consolidated income statement after the subtractions for "minority" interest in earnings of the subsidiary. The balance sheet totals for the equity method and consolidated statements differ, even though the reported income effects are the same. Proper accounting with the equity method involves the same kinds of eliminations and adjustments as are used in preparing consolidated statements.

18.12   a. $2,000   b. $7,500   c. $7,500 — ($10,000/40) = $7,250.

18.14

	b (in 000's)	e
Common Stock at Par	$150	$250
Premium on Common Stock	50	0
Retained Earnings	275	225
Total Stockholders' Equity	$475	$475

18.20   b.   Subsidiary's Current Balance Sheet (in $000's)

Current Assets	$145	Current Liabilities	$ 67
Plant	68	Capital Stock	100
		Retained Earnings	46
Total Assets	$213	Total Equities	$213

18.21   Partial answer.

Consolidated Balance Sheet
December 31, 1975

Assets		Equities	
Cash	$ 31,000	Accounts and Notes Payable	$ 63,800
Accounts and Notes Receivable	106,800	Dividend Payable	1,250
Inventories	345,000	Other Liabilities	154,000
Plant Assets	512,000	Minority Interest	33,450
Goodwill	11,400	Capital Stock	600,000
		Retained Earnings	153,700
Total Assets	$1,006,200	Total Equities	$1,006,200

18.25   a.   Advances to Credit Corporation   **(in Millions)**

December 31, 1974 .... $10.7

b. i.   Net Income from Credit Corporation
            Dividends $15.0
            Undistributed Earnings 4.9

            $19.9

c. i.   Under cost method only dividends of $15,000,000 would be shown.

d. i.   If consolidated:

	(in Millions)
Earned Income	$247.5
Less Operating Expenses	227.6
Revenues from Credit Corp.	$ 19.9

For December 31, 1974	b. ii	c. ii	d. ii
Assets Except Investments	$5,606.3	$5,567.6	$7,724.6
Investments	430.2	495.9	430.2
Liabilities	3,603.6	3,603.6	5,559.9
Retained Earnings	1,712.1	1,739.1	1,874.1

CHAPTER 19

19.5   c. Shown as offsetting source (other) and use (asset) of working
capital in amount equal to the fair market value of the site.

e. Loss included in net income from operations, but since the
loss did not use working capital, an addback for losses not
using working capital must be included.

f. Loss included in net income from operations. Since merchandise
inventory is a component of working capital, no addback is
required.

19.9   Proceeds = Book value plus gain on disposition
        = $830,000 − $190,000 + $52,750
        = $692,750

19.15

(Partial) Sources and Uses of Working Capital

17,810	

From Operations	
Income and Additions	Subtractions
Income 54,170	
Depreciation 109,760	
Loss on Sale of Plant and	
Equipment 7,780	

19.22

(Partial) Sources and Uses of Working Capital

1,345	

From Operations	
Income and Additions	Subtractions
Income 5,814	2,591 Earnings retained by Ellwood
Depreciation 234	Credit Corp.
Deferred Taxes 33	22 Gain on Sale of Plant and
Bond Discount Amortization 8	Equipment

19.25

QUINTUS COMPANY
Balance Sheet
for December 31, 1975

Assets

Current Assets

Cash	$ 11,376
Receivables	31,055
Inventories	46,492
Total Current Assets	$ 88,923

Noncurrent Assets

Land	$ 4,356
Plant and Equipment	158,603
Less Accumulated Depreciation	(59,538)
Investment in Quintus Credit Corp.	1,438
Patents	305
Goodwill	9,200
Total Noncurrent Assets	$114,364
Total Assets	$203,287

Liabilities and Stockholders' Equity

Current Liabilities

Accounts Payable	$ 31,613
Income Taxes Payable	6,897
Total Current Assets	$ 38,510

Long-term Liabilities

Bonds Payable	$ 51,550
Premium on Bonds Payable	107
Deferred Taxes	9,782
Total Long-term Liabilities	$ 61,439

Stockholders' Equity

Preferred Stock	$ 4,485
Common Stock	20,803
Premium on Common Stock	5,784
Retained Earnings	72,266
Total Stockholders' Equity	$103,338
Total Liabilities and Stockholders' Equity	$203,287

CHAPTER 20

20.1 a. Production overhead that is accumulated directly by production departments benefits those departments only and thus is directly attributable to them. An example is the foreman's salary. Production overhead that is accumulated in clearing accounts benefits several departments simultaneously and so must be allocated on some basis.

b. The principle is that activities which benefit from the incurring of costs should be charged with those costs. The principle fails in the case of true joint costs, when it is impossible to discern the degree to which several departments benefit from the incurring of a single cost.

20.4 Cost accounting figures are used for internal control. There is no need for consistency in practice among firms because there are no comparisons made of various firms on the basis of cost accounting data. Trade associations, however, often suggest methods that become widely adopted.

20.11 a. (1) Factory Supplies 1,500
             Accounts Payable 1,500

         (2) Raw Materials 15,000
             Accounts Payable 15,000

         (3) Wages and Salaries Payable 22,000
             Cash 17,820
             FICA Tax Payable 1,320
             Withheld Income Tax Payable 2,860

         (4) Superintendence 20,000
             Maintenance 12,000
             Nightwatchmen's Wages 2,000
             Wages and Salaries Payable 34,000

         (5) Payroll Taxes—Factory 3,500
             Federal Unemployment Insurance
                 Tax Payable 1,200
             State Unemployment Insurance
                 Tax Payable 1,000
             FICA Tax Payable 1,300

         (6) Depreciation of Machinery 6,000
             Accumulated Depreciation—Machinery 6,000
             Depreciation of Factory Building 5,500
             Accumulated Depreciation—
                 Factory Building 5,500

         (7) Work in Process (or Raw Materials Used)—
             Department 271 1,400
             Raw Materials 1,400

20.11 b. Overhead accounts are: Superintendence, Maintenance, Nightwatchmen's Wages, Depreciation of Machinery, and Depreciation of Factory Building. Payroll Taxes—Factory might be viewed as overhead but is better treated as an adjunct to labor cost and, hence, as a product cost.

20.14   Hint: Use these allocation ratios:

	Wholesale	Retail
Number of Calls	1/10	9/10
Number of Invoice Lines	1/7	6/7
Gross Sales	2/5	3/5

20.15   Hint: Use the information given in "Other Operating Data" as the allocation basis. Depreciation is allocated on the basis of floor space.

20.16   Hint:

	Total	Clothing	Accessories	Shoes
Direct Expenses	$230,000	$88,640	$83,920	$57,440
Indirect Expenses	91,680	37,368	36,087	18,225

20.17   a.   Cleaning: .435($50,000) + .343($60,000) = $42,330
             Mixing: .215($50,000) + .358($60,000) = $32,230
             Pouring: .350($50,000) + .299($60,000) = $35,440

        b.   Cleaning: .40($52,000) + .30($58,000) = $38,200
             Mixing: .40($52,000) + .20($58,000) = $32,400
             Pouring: .20($52,000) + .50($58,000) = $39,400

        c.   Cleaning: .45($55,000) + .35($64,000) = $47,150
             Mixing: .25($55,000) + .40($64,000) = $39,350
             Pouring: .30($55,000) + .25($64,000) = $32,500

20.19   By the time Quality Control costs are to be allocated, the amount to be allocated is $37,437.50 = $20,000.00 + $12,000.00 + $5,437.50.

20.20   a.   Allocate Personnel (P) $60,000

Department	Chargeable Hours	Fraction	Allocation
Computer	150	1/10	$ 6,000
Administration	150	1/10	6,000
Extruding	500	1/3	20,000
Slicing	250	1/6	10,000
Nozzles	450	3/10	18,000
	1,500	1.0	$60,000

Allocate Computer (C) $100,000 + $6,000 = $106,000

Department	Chargeable Hours	Fraction	Allocation
Administration	600	1/2	$ 53,000
Extruding	300	1/4	26,500
Slicing	200	1/6	17,667
Nozzles	100	1/12	8,833
	1,200	1.0	$106,000

Allocate Administration (A) \$50,000 + \$6,000 + \$53,000
= \$109,000

Department	Chargeable Hours	Fraction	Allocation
Extruding	200	1/3	\$ 36,333
Slicing	100	1/6	18,167
Nozzles	300	1/2	54,500
	600	1.0	\$109,000

b.

		Services Performed Here			
	Service Departments	**C**	**P**	**A**	
Services	Computer (C)	—	.10	.27	⎫
	Personnel (P)	.08	—	.18	⎬ S
	Administration (A) ..	.46	.10	.01 [a]	⎭
Used	**Production Departments**				
	Extruding (E)	.23	.33	.18	⎫
Here	Slicing (S)	.15	.17	.09	⎬ P
	Nozzles (N)	.08	.30	.27	⎭
		1.00	1.00	1.00	

Costs to be Allocated .. \$100,000 \$60,000 \$50,000

[a] To make column sum equal 1, .01 is allocated here.

c. 1. Let a_{SC} be the fraction of computer output allocable to slicing.
$$a_{SC} = P_{SC} + a_{SC}S_{CC} + a_{SA}S_{AC} + a_{SP}S_{PC}$$

  2. Let a_{NP} be the fraction of personnel output allocable to nozzles.
$$a_{NP} = P_{NP} + a_{NP}S_{PP} + a_{NA}S_{AP} + a_{NC}S_{CP}$$
Let a_{SP} be the fraction of personnel output allocable to slicing.
$$a_{SP} = P_{SP} + a_{SP}S_{PP} + a_{SA}S_{AP} + a_{SC}S_{CP}$$

  3. Let a_{EA} be the fraction of administration output allocable to extruding.
$$a_{EA} = P_{EA} + a_{EA}S_{AA} + a_{EP}S_{AP} + a_{EC}S_{AC}$$

d. $(I - S)^{-1} = \begin{bmatrix} 1.172 & .152 & .347 \\ .195 & 1.044 & .243 \\ .564 & .176 & 1.196 \end{bmatrix}$

$A = P(I - S)^{-1}$
$= \begin{bmatrix} .23 & .33 & .18 \\ .15 & .17 & .09 \\ .08 & .30 & .27 \end{bmatrix} \times \begin{bmatrix} 1.172 & .152 & .347 \\ .195 & 1.044 & .243 \\ .564 & .176 & 1.196 \end{bmatrix}$

	Production Departments	Services Performed Here		
		C	**P**	**A**
Service				
Costs	Extruding	.435	.411	.375
Allocated	Slicing	.260	.216	.201
Here	Nozzles	.305	.373	.424

e. Extruding: .435($100,000) + .411($60,000) + .375($50,000) = $ 86,910
    Slicing: .260($100,000) + .216($60,000) + .201($50,000) =   49,010
    Nozzles: .305($100,000) + .373($60,000) + .424($50,000) =   74,080
                                                                 $210,000

20.21 Use three simultaneous equations to calculate the variable cost of producing 500,000 kilowatt hours of electricity:

$$E = \$10,000 + .4S$$
$$S = \$20,000 + .7W$$
$$W = \$ 5,000 + 1E$$

Variable cost of electricity is 4.311¢ per kilowatt hour, which is more expensive than the outside price; electricity should be purchased.

CHAPTER 21

21.5   Cost per unit: $170.

21.11   a.   Total Cost: $15,400.
        b.   Gross Margin: $2,700.
        c.   Total Debits to Work in Process: $780,000.

21.17   a.   (1) $5 per unit.
              (2) $4.75 per unit.

21.22   a.

	(1) Labor cost basis	(2) Labor hr. basis
Cutting Dept.	60%	$3 per hr.
Assembling Dept.	100%	$4 per hr.
Painting Dept.	80%	$4 per hr.

        b.

Cutting Dept.	$3,000	$2,850
Assembling Dept.	$4,000	$3,600
Painting Dept.	$ 440	$ 432

21.26   a.

	Process X	Process Y
Total Process Costs	$217,653	$348,177

        b.

Process X Production	$0.435 per unit
Process Y Production	$0.725 per unit

21.28   a.   Hint: Prepare a table with three columns: Product, Net Realizable Value of Output, and Joint Costs Incurred up to Split-off. There are *two* split-off points.
        b.   Hint: Prepare a table with four columns: Product, Fraction of Total Units, Costs to be Allocated, Allocation. Remember that there are *two* split-off points.

21.29   a.   and b. see 21.28.
        d.   Assume that the squeezed petals are a by-product of process *B*. Then the Process *B* costs are reduced by $1,000.

CHAPTER 22

22.6   a.   Price Variance = Actual Costs — Budgeted Costs
                     = $9,525 — $9,375 = $150($U$)
           Standard Fixed Overhead Rate
           Per Unit of Base Activity = $9,375/2,500 units = $3.75 per unit
           Capacity Variance = [2,500 (standard production) — 2,000
                             (actual production)] × $3.75
                     = $1,875($U$)
           Quantity Variance = (2,500 — 2,500) × $3.75 = 0.

      b.   The quantity variance is caused by a deviation between actual
            units of base activity used for actual production and standard
            units of base activity for actual production. Output is the
            measure of base activity, so there can be no such deviation
            since the standard number of units of output per unit of output
            is equal to one. Whenever an output measure is used for the
            activity base, the quantity variance will be zero.

22.11   (a)   Materials 100,000
                Materials Price Variance 5,500
                    Accounts Payable 105,500

                Work in Process 97,810
                    Raw Material 96,940
                    Material Quantity Variance 870

                Work in Process 440,145
                Labor Quantity Variance 6,255
                    Labor Rate Variance 49,600
                    Wages Payable 396,800

        (b)   Material Price Variance = $5,500 U
               Material Quantity Variance = — $870 F
               Labor Rate Variance = — $49,600 F
               Labor Quantity Variance = $6,255 U

22.13   *Material A*
        (a)   Units Purchased = $210,000
        (b)   Standard Unit Price = $4.00/pound
        (c)   Total Standard Material Cost = $800,000

22.15   *April—Variable Overhead*
              price variance = $800 U
              quantity variance = $1,500 U
              Fixed Overhead
              price variance = — $2,700 F
              quantity variance = $2,200 U
              capacity variance = $2,200 U

22.20   Hint: During the first quarter the actual overhead rate is:
              $742,000/1,060,000 = $.70

22.22   Hint: Allocate first the variable costs and then the fixed costs of the service department. Accumulate unit costs for P_1 and P_2 in separate accounts, then combine for the total cost.

22.24   Hint: Compute the fixed overhead capacity variance first, $1,500U. Derive next the standard number of direct labor hours for actual production.

22.26   Hint: If there is no ending work in process inventory, then, using standard costs, input $+$ beginning balance $-$ output $=$ variance.

b. Material Quantity Variance—W .... $ 700 (F)
    Labor Quantity Variance—W .... 4,100 (U)
    Material Quantity Variance—C .... 1,175 (U)
    Labor Quantity Variance—C .... 1,125 (F)

22.27   Hint for green machines. Compute variances in this order: direct materials, fixed overhead, variable overhead, direct labor.

Hint for yellow machines. Compute tableau entries in the following order.

	Actual Costs Incurred	Price and Rate Variances	Raw Materials Inventories at Standard Cost		Actual Input at Standard Prices	Capacity Variance	Quantity Variance	Actual Output at Standard Prices
			Purchased	Used				
Direct Material	1	2	3	4	5		8	6, 7
Direct Labor	14	13a			15		13b	16
Variable Overhead					9, 13c		21	10, 13d
Fixed Overhead					11, 18	19	17	12, 20

13a through 13d are solved simultaneously for
    $w =$ variable overhead rate per direct labor hour
    $x =$ standard direct labor hour wage rate
    $y =$ direct labor hours worked during the month
    $z =$ standard direct labor hours per finished yellow machine

The solution is: $w =$ $.50 per direct labor hour,
$x =$ $4.00 per hour, $y =$ 11,250 hours, $z =$ 3 hours.

CHAPTER 23

23.6   (a)   25,000 units.   (b) $200,000.
       (c)   60,000 units.   (d) $400,000.
23.8   (a)   Income = $496,000;   (b) Sales = $3,000,000.

23.11 (a) Yes.
     (b) Income without government contract = $3,100,000.
         Income with government contract = $3,300,000.

23.14 (a) The offer should be accepted.
     (b) It would not be worthwhile to build an additional plant to increase sales to AMF.

23.17 (a) Operating income = $552,500.
     (b) $1.425 per unit.
     (c) $.8125 per unit.

23.19 (a) 300,000 cookies.
     (c) Semiautomatic.
     (e) 700,000 cookies.

23.23 Locomotive A should be put on stand-by.

23.26 Hint: Costs that have been, or will be, incurred regardless of the decision are irrelevant.

23.27 If a 10-percent decline in sales is 1 million cars, then sales decreased from 10 million cars in 1968 to 9 million in 1969.
Let F_{68} and F_{69} represent total fixed costs in 1968 and 1969.
Let C_{68} and C_{69} represent contribution per car in 1968 and 1969.
Then
1. $F_{69} = .8F_{68}$
2. $C_{69} = C_{68} - \$100$
3. $\$80,000,000 = -F_{69} + 1,400,000C_{69}$
4. $\$300,000,000 = -F_{68} + (.18 \times 10,000,000)C_{68}$
Solving, $F_{68} = \$600$ million, $F_{69} = \$480$ million, $C_{68} = \$500$, and $C_{69} = \$400$.

23.32 (b) Costs = $25,000 per month + $1.65 per unit produced.

CHAPTER 24

24.6 a. Present Value of after-tax cash savings from refunding = $43,800 − $28,000 = $15,800.

24.8 The query ignores the part of the statement that says the marginal investment of *average risk*. If the cash flows from all investments projects were as certain as debt payments, then the cost of capital would be the debt rate.

24.9 b. 10 percent

24.10 b. 7 years

24.12 b. 6.14 years

24.13 Project B: Internal Rate of Return = 10 percent.

Year	Depreciation for Year	Book Value End of Year
0	—	$10,000
1	$ 627	9,373
2	690	8,683
3	759	7,924
4	835	7,089
5	919	6,170
6	1,010	5,160
7	1,111	4,049
8	1,223	2,826
9	1,345	1,481
10	1,479	2
	9,998	

24.21   a.   At 8 percent per half-year

End of Year	Tax Savings .40 × $6,000	Present Value of Savings
1	$2,400	$2,057
2	2,400	1,764
		$3,821

c.   If the cost of capital is 8 percent per half-year, then use a three-year life; at 10 percent per half-year, use a two-year life. If the cost of capital is 18.14 percent per year, then either life gives the same present value of tax savings.

CHAPTER 25

25.9   (c)   The periodic amortization of plant assets' cost should be called depreciation expenses (or charges).

25.17   a. (2)   b. (4)   c. (5)   d. (11)   e. (3)   f. (10)
g.** (1)   h. (10)   i. (10)   j. (9)   k.** (1)   l. (2)
m.** (1)   n.* (5)   o. (2)   p. (3)   q.* (5)   r.* (5)
s. (1)   t. (1)   u. (6)   v. (2)   w. (5)   x. (1)
*n., q., r.: Usage is correct but poor; instead designate as appropriated returned earnings.
o.: Accumulated
p.: Payable
s., t.: Allowance
**Product costs, closed to various inventories.

25.19   Total Stockholders' Equity $20,711,000

25.22   b. (4)   The expenditure for plant acquisitions should not be reported net of the proceeds from plant retirements. Both the outlay for acquisitions and the proceeds from retirements should be reported. Furthermore, the $4,000 gain on disposition of plant should be subtracted from working capital produced by net income because without such a subtraction, that gain is double-counted. Since the statement balances in spite of this omission, an offsetting error must have occurred; see (7).

b. (7) The extraordinary loss, net of tax effects, should be shown separately from net income. That is, ordinary income should be shown as $46,000. Extraordinary items should show a net-of-tax loss of $6,000 with an addback of $10,000 to indicate a loss that used no working capital. Thus working capital from operations as reported must be increased by $4,000 for the extraordinary loss which used no working capital.

25.23 Net Income for Year $52,040

25.24 Net Income for Year $42,580

25.25 **Trial Balance Information**   **12/31/74**   **12/31/75**

Retained Earnings $333,425 $309,660
Dividends Payable   13,750

Straight-line amortization of bond discount is used.

CHAPTER 26

26.3 Consider advertising or research and development expenditures, for example. Conservative practice often expenses these items in the period of their occurrence rather than capitalizing them as assets. Obviously, to expense an item in the current period reduces this period's income. Notice, however, that if previous periods' expenditures had not been expensed then, they would now be assets requiring current amortization charges which would further reduce this period's income. The effect of the original expensing is to make this period reported income larger than it should be, to the extent that the previous period's expenditures benefit the current period. Of course, total income over the life of the firm is not changed.

26.10 $40.00.

26.12 Book value per share of common stock $13.

26.15 (a) $\dfrac{53,760,000}{3,000,000} = \$17.92$ per share.

26.17 (a) No change.   (b) No change.
      (c) No change or possibly some slight increase caused by additional mileage.   (d) Decrease.

26.27 (a) 9.78%
      (b) 12.88%
      (c) $4.20 per share
      (d) 1975: 2.69 to 1; 1974: 2.12 to 1

(e) Before income taxes = 26.17 times
After income taxes = 15 times
(f) 1975 = 68.45% 1974: 73.56%

26.29 (a) $2 per share (b) $600,000 (c) 15,000 shares
(d) 5,000 (e) $1.92 per share (both EPS figures)

26.33 (a) 6.5% (b) 13.2% (c) 13.2% (d) $1.81
(e) 93.7% (f) 3.8% (g) 4.2 times (h) 5.2 times
(i) 61.45 days (j) $14.10 (k) (i) 6.42 times, (ii) 4.24
times (l) $684,500,000 (m) 41.2%
(n) 1.26 to 1 (o) .671 to 1 (p) 1.43 to 1

Glossary

Abnormal Spoilage. Spoilage that should not occur if operations are normally efficient. Good practice treats this as an expense of the period, not a product cost. Contrast with normal spoilage.

Absorption Costing. The method of costing that assigns all manufacturing costs, whether fixed or variable, to units produced. Sometimes called full costing.

Accelerated Depreciation. Any method of calculating depreciation charges where the charges in the early periods are larger than those calculated under the straight-line method. Examples are double-declining-balance and sum-of-the-years'-digits methods.

Acceptance. A promise to pay which is equivalent to a promissory note.

Account. Any device for accumulating items relating to a single asset, liability, proprietorship, revenue, expense, etc.

Accountancy. The British word for accounting; in the United States, it is used to mean the theory and practice of accounting.

Accountant's Report. Auditor's report.

Accounting. An information system conveying information about a specific entity. The information is in financial terms and is restricted to information that can be made reasonably precise.

Accounting Entity. Any economic unit for which a system of accounts is maintained.

Accounting Equation. Assets = Equities = Liabilities + Proprietorship.

Accounting Event. Any occurrence that must be recorded in the accounting records.

Accounting Period. The time period for which operating statements, such as the income statement and the statement of changes in financial position, are prepared.

Accounting Principles. The principles that explain current accounting practices and guide in the selection among alternative treatments for reporting transactions.

Accounting Principles Board. See APB.

Accounting Rate of Return. Average income from a project divided by average investment in the project.

Account Payable. An amount owed to a creditor, usually arising from purchase of merchandise or materials and supplies; not necessarily due or past due.

Account Receivable. A claim against a debtor usually arising from sales; not necessarily due or past due.

Accretion. Increase in economic worth through physical change, usually said of a natural resource, such as an orchard, that increases in worth through natural growth. Contrast with appreciation.

Accrual. Recognition of an expense (or revenue) and the related liability (or asset) that is caused by an accounting event, frequently by the passage of time, and that is not signaled by an explicit cash transaction. For example, the recognition of interest expense or revenue for a period even though no explicit interest payments are made.

Accumulated Depreciation. A preferred title for the contra-asset account that shows the sum of depreciation charges on an asset since it was acquired. Other titles used are Allowance for Depreciation (acceptable term) or Reserve for Depreciation (poor term).

Acid-Test Ratio. Sum of (cash, marketable securities, and receivables) divided by current liabilities. Some receivables may be excluded from the numerator. Often called the quick ratio.

Additional Paid-in Capital. An alternative title for capital contributed in excess of par.

Adjunct Account. An account that accumulates additions to another account; for example, Premium on Bonds.

Adjusted Bank Balance. The balance shown on the statement from the bank plus or minus appropriate adjustments such as for outstanding checks or unrecorded deposits.

Adjusted Trial Balance. Trial balance taken after adjusting entries but before closing entries. Contrast with pre- and post-closing trial balances.

Adjusting Entry. An entry made at the end of an accounting period to record a transaction or other accounting event, which for some reason has not been recorded during the accounting period or has been improperly recorded.

Adjustment. A change in an account produced by an adjusting entry.

Administrative Expense. An expense incurred for the enterprise as a whole as contrasted to expenses incurred for more specific functions such as manufacturing or selling.

Advances from Customers. A preferred term for receipts of funds in advance of the rendering of the service that will cause revenue to be recognized. A liability account.

Aging Accounts Receivable. The process of classifying accounts receivable by the time elapsed since the debt came into existence for the purpose of estimating the amount of uncollectible accounts receivable.

AICPA. American Institute of Certified Public Accountants; see Chapter 1 for a description.

Allocate. To spread a cost from one account to several accounts or to several periods.

Allowance. A balance sheet contra account except when used in the context of a sales (or purchase) allowance.

Amortization. The general process of allocating acquisition cost of assets to the periods of benefit. Called depreciation for plant assets and depletion for wasting assets (natural resources).

Annual Report. A report for stockholders' and other interested parties prepared once a year including a balance sheet, an income statement, a statement of changes in financial position, the auditor's report, and perhaps comments from management about the year's events.

Annuity. A series of payments, usually at equally spaced time intervals.

Annuity Certain. An annuity payable for a definite number of periods; contrast with contingent annuity.

Annuity Due. An annuity where the first payment is made at the start of period one (or at the end of period zero).

Annuity in Advance. An annuity due.

Annuity in Arrears. An ordinary annuity where the first payment occurs at the end of period one.

Annuity Method of Depreciation. See compound interest depreciation.

APB. Accounting Principles Board of the AICPA. It set accounting principles from 1962 through 1973.

Appreciation. An increase in economic worth caused by rising market prices. Contrast with accretion.

Appropriation. An expenditure authorized for specified amount, purpose, and time. See Retained Earnings Appropriation for a different context.

Appropriation Account. Account set up to record specific authorizations to spend; it is credited with appropriations amounts and debited with expenditures and encumbrances.

Articulate. Said of the relationship between any operating statement (for example, income statement or statement of changes in financial position) and comparative balance sheets, where the operating statement explains the change in some major balance sheet category (for example, retained earnings or working capital).

Assess. To value property for the purpose of taxation; the assessment is determined by the taxing authority.

Asset. A future benefit or service potential.

At Par. Said of a bond or preferred stock selling at its face amount.

Attest. What the auditor does when he gives his opinion that the financial statements are fair.

Audit. Systematic inspection of accounting records involving analyses, tests, and confirmations.

Auditor's Report. The auditor's statement of the work he has done which gives his opinion. Opinions are usually unqualified but may be qualified, or the auditor may disclaim an opinion in his report. Often called the accountant's report.

Audit Program. The procedures followed by the auditor in carrying out the audit.

Bad Debt. An uncollectible account receivable; see Sales, Uncollectible Accounts Adjustment.

Bailout Period. In a capital budgeting context, the amount of time that must elapse before cash inflows from a project including potential scrap value of assets acquired equal or exceed the cash outflows. Contrast with payback period. Bailout is superior to payback because bailout takes into account, at least to some degree, the present value of the cash flows after the termination date being considered. The potential scrap value at any time includes some estimate of the cash flows that can occur after that time.

Balance. The difference between the sum of debit entries minus the sum of credit entries in an account. If positive, the difference is called a debit balance; if negative, a credit balance.

Balance Sheet. A statement of financial position which shows total assets = total liabilities + proprietorship.

Bank Balance. The amount of the balance in a checking account shown on the statement from the bank. Compare with adjusted bank balance.

Bank Prime Rate. See prime rate.

Big Eight Firms. The eight largest public accounting (CPA) partnerships; in alphabetical order: Arthur Andersen & Co.; Coopers & Lybrand; Ernst & Ernst; Haskins & Sells; Peat, Marwick, Mitchell & Co.; Price Waterhouse & Co.; Touche Ross & Co.; Arthur Young & Company.

Bond. A certificate to show evidence of debt. Coupon bonds have attached to them coupons which can be redeemed at stated dates for interest payments. The par value is the principal or face amount of the bond payable at maturity. The coupon rate is the amount of interest payable in one year divided by the principal amount.

Bond Discount. From the standpoint of the issuer of a bond, the excess of the face amount of a bond over the sum of [initial issue price plus the portion of discount already amortized]. From the standpoint of a bond buyer, the difference between face amount and selling price when the bond sells below par.

Bond Premium. Exactly parallel to bond discount except that the issue price (or current selling price) is higher than par value.

Book (verb). To record a transaction.

Book Inventory. An inventory that results, not from physical count, but from amount of initial inventory plus invoice amounts of purchases less invoice amounts of requisitions or withdrawals.

Book of Original Entry. A journal.

Book Value. The net amount of an asset or group of assets shown in the accounts which record the asset and reductions such as for amortization in its cost; of a firm, the excess of total assets over total liabilities.

Boot. The additional money paid or received along with a used item in a trade-in transaction for a new item.

Break-Even Point. The volume of sales required so that revenues and costs are equal. May be expressed in units (fixed costs/contribution per unit) or in dollars (selling price × fixed costs/contribution per unit).

Budget. A financial plan that is used to estimate the results of future operations. Frequently used to help control future operations.

Budgetary Accounts. In governmental accounting, the accounts that reflect estimated operations and financial condition, as affected by estimated revenues, appropriations, and encumbrances. Proprietary accounts show the actual transactions.

Budgetary Control. Management of governmental unit in accordance with an approved budget in order to keep total expenditures within authorized limits.

Burden. See overhead.

Business Combination. As defined by the APB, the bringing together into a single accounting entity two or more incorporated or unincorporated businesses.

Bylaws. The rules adopted by the stockholders of a corporation that specify the general methods for carrying out the functions of the corporation.

By-product. A joint product whose value is so small relative to the value of the other joint products that it does not receive normal accounting treatment. The costs assigned to by-products reduce the costs of the main products. By-products are allocated a share of joint costs so that the expected gain or loss upon their sale is zero. Often spelled as one word without a hyphen.

Callable Bond. A bond for which the issuer reserves the right to pay the obligation before maturity date. If the issuer agrees to pay more than the face amount of the bond when called, the excess of the payment over face amount is the call premium.

Call Premium. See callable bond.

Cancelable Lease. See lease.

Capacity. Stated in units of product, the normal amount that can be produced per unit of time.

Capital. Ownership equity in a business. Often used, equally correctly, to mean the total assets of a business. Sometimes used to mean capital assets.

Capital Asset. A tangible asset whose benefit is to be utilized over a long period of time rather than in the period of acquisition.

Capital Budget. Plan of proposed capital outlays and the means for financing them.

Capital Budgeting. The process of choosing investment projects for an enterprise by considering the present value of cash flows and deciding how to raise the funds required by the investment.

Capital Contributed in Excess of Par (or Stated) Value. A preferred title for the account that shows the amount received by the issuer for capital stock in excess of par (or stated) value.

Capital Expenditure (Outlay). An expenditure for capital assets.

Capital Gain. The excess of proceeds over cost from the sale of a capital asset.

Capitalize. To record an expenditure that will benefit a future period as an asset rather than to treat the expenditure as an expense of the period of its occurrence.

Capital Stock. The ownership shares of a corporation. Consists of common stock and preferred stock.

Cash. Currency and coins, negotiable checks, and balances in bank accounts.

Cash Basis. In contrast to the accrual basis, a system of accounting in which transactions are recorded if and only if cash is paid or received.

Cash Collection Basis. Installment method for recognizing revenue.

Cash Discount. A reduction in sales or purchase price allowed for prompt payment.

Cash Dividend. See dividend.

Cash Flow Statement. A statement similar to the statement of changes in financial position where the flows of cash, rather than working capital, are explained.

Certified Financial Statement. A financial statement attested to by an independent public auditor who is a CPA.

Certified Public Accountant (CPA). An accountant who has satisfied the statutory requirements of his jurisdiction to be registered or licensed as a public accountant. In addition to passing the Uniform CPA Examination administered by the AICPA, the CPA must meet certain educational and moral requirements that differ from jurisdiction to jurisdiction. The jurisdictions are the fifty states, the District of Columbia, Guam, Puerto Rico, and the Virgin Islands.

Chain Discount. A series of discount percentages; if a chain discount of 10 and 5 percent is quoted, then the actual price is the nominal price times .90 times .95.

Change Fund. Coins and currency issued to cashiers, delivery drivers, and so on.

Charge. A debit; as a verb, to debit.

Charge Off. To treat as a loss or expense an amount originally recorded as an asset.

Chart of Accounts. A list of names and numbers of accounts systematically organized.

Check Register. A journal to record checks issued.

Clearing Account. An account containing amounts to be transferred to another account before the end of the accounting period.

Close (verb). To transfer the balance of a temporary or contra or adjunct account to the main account to which it relates, for example, to transfer revenue and expense accounts directly, or through the income summary account, to a proprietorship account, or to transfer purchase discounts to purchases.

Closed Account. An account with equal debits and credits.

Closing Entries. The entries that accomplish the transfer of revenue and expense account balances to proprietorship.

CMA. Certificate in Management Accounting awarded by the Institute of Management Accounting of the National Association of Accountants to those who pass a set of examinations and meet a set of continuing education requirements.

Collectible. Capable of being converted into cash; now if due, later otherwise.

Commission. Remuneration, usually expressed as a percentage, of employees based upon an activity rate, such as sales.

Common Cost. Cost resulting from use of a facility (for example, plant or machines) or a service (for example, fire insurance) that benefits several products or departments and must be allocated to those products or departments. Many writers use common costs and joint costs synonymously. We feel that common costs are more easily allocable to the benefited products or departments than are joint costs. The difference is, however, one of degree, not of kind. See joint costs.

Common Stock. Stock representing the class of owners who have residual claim on the assets of a corporation after all debts and preferred stockholders' claims have been met.

Common-Stock Equivalent. A security whose primary value arises from its ability to be exchanged for common shares; includes stock options, warrants, and also convertible bonds or convertible preferred stock whose cash yield at any time within five years of issue is less than two-thirds the prime rate at the time of issue.

Completed Contract Method. Recognizing revenues and expenses for a job or order only when it is finished except when a loss on the job or order is expected.

Composite Depreciation. Group depreciation of dissimilar items.

Compounding Period. The time period at the end of which interest is calculated: the interest may be paid to the lender or added, or converted, to principal for the next interest-earning period.

Compound Interest. Interest calculated on principal plus undistributed interest previously earned.

Compound Interest Depreciation. A method designed to hold the rate of return on an asset constant. First find the internal rate of return on the cash flows from the asset. The periodic depreciation charge is the cash flow for the period less the internal rate of return multiplied by the asset's book value at the beginning of the period. When the cash flows from the asset are constant over time, the method is sometimes called the annuity method of depreciation.

Comptroller. Same meaning and pronunciation as controller.

Consignment. See on consignment.

Consistency. Treatment of like transactions in the same way in different periods so that financial statements will be more comparable than otherwise.

Consol. A bond that never matures; a perpetuity in the form of a bond.

Consolidated Financial Statements. Statements issued by legally separate companies that show financial position and income as they would appear if the companies were one legal entity.

Contingent Annuity. An annuity whose number of payments depends upon the outcome of an event whose timing is uncertain at the time the annuity is set up; for example, an annuity payable for the life of the annuitant.

Contingent Liability. A potential liability; if a certain event were to occur, such as losing a lawsuit, a liability would be recognized. Until the outcome is known, the contingency is merely disclosed in notes rather than in the accounts. A material contingency may lead to a qualified, "subject to" auditor's report.

Continuing Appropriation. A governmental appropriation automatically renewed without further legislative action until it is altered or perhaps revoked.

Contra Account. An account, such as accumulated depreciation, that accumulates subtractions from another account, such as machinery.

Contributed Capital. The sum of the balances in capital stock accounts plus capital contributed in excess of par (or stated) value accounts.

Contribution Margin. Contribution per unit.

Contribution Per Unit. Selling price less variable expenses per unit.

Control (Controlling) Account. An account that shows totals of entries and balances that appear in individual accounts in a subsidiary ledger. Accounts Receivable is a control account backed up with accounts for each customer.

Controllable Cost. A cost that can be influenced by the way in which operations are carried out.

Controlled Company. A company, a majority of whose voting stock is held by an individual or corporation.

Controller. The title often used for the chief accountant of an organization.

Conversion. The act of exchanging a convertible security for another security.

Conversion Period. Compounding period.

Convertible Bond. A bond that may be converted into a specified number of shares of common stock.

Convertible Preferred Stock. Preferred stock that may be converted into a specified number of shares of common stock.

Corporation. A legal entity authorized by a state to operate under the rules of the entity's charter.

Cost. An asset. Sometimes used informally to mean the acquisition price of goods or services.

Cost Center. A unit of activity for which expenditures and expenses are accumulated.

Cost Effective. Among alternatives, the one whose ratio of benefit to cost is highest. Sometimes said of an action whose expected benefits exceed expected costs whether or not there are other alternatives with larger or smaller benefit/cost ratios.

Costing. The process of determining the cost of activities, products, or services.

Cost Method. A way of accounting for an investment in another company in which the investment is shown at acquisition cost, and only dividends received are treated as revenue.

Cost of Goods Purchased. Purchase price of goods acquired plus costs of storage and delivery to the place where the items can be productively used.

Cost of Goods Sold. Inventoriable costs that are expensed because the units are sold.

Cost or Market, Whichever is Lower. A basis of inventory valuation where the cost is set at the lower of acquisition cost and current replacement cost.

Cost Sheet. Statement that shows all the elements comprising the total cost of an item.

Cost-Volume-Profit Chart. A graph that shows the relation between fixed costs, contribution per unit, break-even point, and sales.

CPA. Certified Public Accountant. The AICPA suggests no periods be shown in the abbreviations.

Cr. Abbreviation for **Credit (noun).** An entry on the right-hand side of an account. Also the ability or right to buy or borrow in return for a promise to pay later.

Credit (verb). To make an entry on the right-hand side of an account.

Cumulative Dividend. Preferred stock dividends that, if not paid, accrue as an obligation which must be paid before dividends to common stockholders can be declared.

Cumulative Preferred Stock. Preferred stock with cumulative dividend rights.

Current Asset. An asset whose future benefit will occur within a short time, usually one year. Current assets include cash, marketable securities, receivables, inventory, and current prepayments.

Current Fund. In governmental accounting, a synonym for general fund.

Current Funds. In governmental accounting, funds spent for operating purposes during the current period. Includes general, special revenue, debt service, and enterprise funds.

Current Liability. A debt that must be discharged within a short time, usually one year.

Current Ratio. Sum of current assets divided by sum of current liabilities.

Debenture. A bond not secured with collateral.

Debit (noun). An entry on the left-hand side of an account.

Debit (verb). To make an entry on the left-hand side of an account.

Debt Service Fund. In governmental accounting, a fund established to account for payment of interest and principal on all general obligation debt other than that payable from special assessments.

Debt Service Requirement. The amount of money required for payments of interest, current maturities of principal on outstanding debt, and payments to sinking funds (corporations) or to the debt service fund (governmental).

Declining-Balance Depreciation. The method of calculating the periodic depreciation charge by multiplying the book value at the start of the period by a constant percentage.

Defalcation. Embezzlement.

Default. Failure to pay interest or principal on a debt when due.

Deferred Charge. Expenditure not recognized as an expense of the period when made but carried forward to be written off in future periods.

Deferred Credit. Sometimes used to indicate advances from customers. Also sometimes used to describe the deferred income tax liability.

Deferred Income Tax. An indeterminate-term liability that arises when the pre-tax income shown on the tax return is less than what it would have been had the same treatment been used in tax returns as used for financial reporting. APB Opinion No. 11 requires that the firm debit income tax expense and credit deferred income tax with the amount of the taxes delayed by using different treatments in tax returns from those used in financial reports.

Deferred Revenue. Sometimes used to indicate advances from customers.

Deficit. A debit balance in the Retained Earnings account.

Demand Deposit. Checking account at a bank.

Depletion. Exhaustion or amortization of a wasting asset, or natural resource.

Depreciable Cost. That part of the cost of an asset, usually acquisition cost less salvage value, that is to be charged off over the life of the asset through the process of depreciation.

Depreciable Life. For an asset, the time period over which depreciable cost is to be allocated. For tax returns, depreciable life may be shorter than service life.

Depreciation. Amortization of plant assets; the process of allocating the cost of an asset to the periods of benefit.

Descartes' Rule of Signs. In a capital-budgeting context, the rule says that a series of cash flows will have a non-negative number of internal rates of return. The number is equal to the number of variations in the sign of the cash flow series or is less than that number by an even integer. (For example, the series —100, —100, +50, +175, —50, +100 has three variations in sign and must have one or three internal rates of return. In fact, it has only one, about 12 percent.)

Dilution. A potential reduction in earnings per share caused by the conversion of securities or by the exercise of warrants or options.

Dilutive. Said of a security that would reduce earnings per share if it were exchanged for common stock.

Direct Costing. The method of allocating costs that assigns only variable costs to product and treats fixed costs as period expenses. Sometimes called variable costing.

Direct Labor. Cost of labor applied directly to a product; contrast with indirect labor.

Discount. The difference between face or future value and present value of a payment. A reduction in price granted for prompt payment of a debt.

Discounted Payback Period. Amount of time that

must elapse before the discounted present value of cash inflows from a project equal the discounted present value of the cash outflows.

Discounted Bailout Period. In a capital budgeting context, the amount of time that must elapse before discounted cash flows from a project including potential scrap value of assets equal or exceed the present value of cash outflows. Contrast with discounted payback period.

Discount Factor. One plus the discount rate.

Discount Rate. Interest rate used to convert future payments to present values.

Discounts Lapsed (Lost). The sum of discounts offered for prompt payment that were not taken or allowed because of late payment.

Dividend. A distribution of earnings to owners of a corporation; it may be paid in cash (cash dividend) or with stock (stock dividend) or other securities.

Double-Declining-Balance Depreciation. Declining-balance depreciation where the constant percentage is $2/n$ where n is the depreciable life in periods, $n \geq 2$.

Double Entry. The system of recording transactions that maintains the accounting equation.

Double T-Account. T-account with an extra horizontal line showing a change in the account balance to be explained by the subsequent entries into the account, such as:

Trucks

42,000	

This account shows an increase in the asset account, Trucks, of $42,000 to be explained.

Dr. Abbreviation for **Debit**.

Drawings. Payments made to a sole proprietor or a partner during a period; charged to his or her capital account.

e. The base of natural logarithms; 2.71828182845-9045.... If interest is compounded continuously during a period at the stated rate of **r** per period, then the effective interest rate is equivalent to interest compounded once per period at the rate **i** where $i = e^r - 1$. Tables of e^r are widely available.

Earnings. Income, or sometimes profit.

Earnings per Share. Net income to common stockholders divided by number of common shares outstanding. See primary earnings per share and fully diluted earnings per share; see discussion in Chapter 26.

Effective Interest Method. A systematic amortization method for bond premium or discount that makes the interest expense for each period divided by the amount of the net liability (face amount less discount or plus premium) at the beginning of the period equal to the yield rate on the bond at the time of issue.

Efficiency Variance. A term sometimes used for the quantity variance.

Eliminations. Work sheet entries to prepare consolidated statements that substitute the subsidiary's assets for the parent's investment account and that remove from reported income any profits on intercompany transactions.

Encumbrance. An anticipated expenditure; funds restricted for anticipated expenditure. Expires either when paid or when a specific liability is incurred.

Enterprise. Any business organization.

Enterprise Fund. A fund established by a governmental unit to account for acquisition, operation, and maintenance of governmental services that are supposed to be self-supporting from user charges, such as for water or airports.

Entity. A person, partnership, corporation or other organization.

EPVI. Excess present value index.

Equities. Liabilities plus owners' equity.

Equity. A claim to assets; a source of capital.

Equity Method. A way of accounting for an investment in another company in which the proportionate share of the earnings of the other company is debited to the investment account and credited to a revenue account.

Equivalent Units. Used to translate nonhomogeneous units of work in process into a number of units of finished goods that would require the same costs.

Estimated Revenue. A term used in governmental accounting to designate revenue expected to accrue during a period whether or not it will be collected during the period.

Excess Present Value. Net present value of anticipated cash (inflows–outflows).

Excess Present Value Index. Net present value divided by initial cash outlay.

Except For. Qualification in auditor's report, usually caused by a change, approved of by the auditor, from one accounting principle to another.

Excise Tax. Tax on the manufacture, sale, or consumption of a commodity.

Ex-dividend. Said of a stock at the time when the regular dividend becomes payable to the owner on the record date.

Exercise. When the owner of an option purchases

the security that the option entitles him to purchase, he has exercised the option.

Expected Value. The mean or arithmetic average of a statistical distribution.

Expendable Fund. In governmental accounting, a fund whose resources, principal, and earnings may be spent.

Expenditure. Incurring a liability or paying cash to secure a good or service.

Expense (noun). A cost of producing revenue. A "gone" asset; an expired cost.

Expense (verb). To designate a past or current expenditure as a current expense.

Expense Account. An account to accumulate expenses; such accounts are closed at the end of the accounting period.

Extraordinary Item. An expense or revenue item characterized both by its unusual nature and infrequency of occurrence that is shown net of tax effects separately from ordinary income on the income statement.

Face Amount (Value). The nominal amount due at maturity from a bond or note. The amount of a stock certificate is best called the par or stated value, whichever is applicable.

Factory Cost. Manufacturing cost.

Factory Expense. Usually an item of manufacturing cost other than direct labor or direct materials.

Fair Market Price (Value). Price (value) determined at arm's length between a buyer and a seller, each acting rationally in his own self-interest. May be estimated by other means in the absence of a transaction.

FASB. Financial Accounting Standards Board. An independent board responsible for setting accounting principles since 1973.

Favorable Variance. An excess of standard cost over actual cost.

FICA. Federal Insurance Contributions Act. The law that sets Social Security taxes and benefits.

Fiduciary. Someone responsible for the custody or administration of property belonging to another.

FIFO. First-in, first-out; an inventory flow assumption by which inventory values are determined from most recent purchases and cost of goods sold is determined from oldest purchases.

Finance (verb). To supply with funds through the issue of stocks or bonds or through the retention of earnings.

Financial Accounting. The accounting for assets, equities, revenues, and expenses of a business.

Financial Accounting Standards Board. See FASB.

Financial Expense. An expense incurred in raising funds.

Financial Position (Condition). The assets and equities of a firm displayed on the balance sheet.

Financial Statements. The balance sheet, income statement, statement of retained earnings, and the statement of changes in financial position.

Financing Lease. A lease treated by the lessee as both the borrowing of funds and the acquisition of an asset to be amortized. Both the liability and the asset are recognized on the balance sheet. Expenses consist of interest on the debt and amortization of the asset. The lessor treats the lease as the sale of the asset in return for a series of receivables. Contrast with operating lease.

Finished Goods. Manufactured product ready for sale.

Firm. A partnership; informally, any business.

First-in, First-out. See FIFO.

Fiscal Year. Any accounting period of twelve consecutive months chosen as the reporting period by an enterprise.

Fixed Assets. Plant assets.

Fixed Cost (Expense). An expenditure or expense that does not vary with volume of activity, at least in the short run.

Fixed Liability. Long-term liability.

Flexible Budget. Budget that shows expenditures as a function of activity levels.

Float. Checks that have been credited to the depositors account at his bank but not yet debited to the drawer's account at his bank.

FOB. Free on Board some location; the invoice price includes delivery at seller's expense to that location.

Franchise. A privilege granted or sold.

Full Costing. Absorption costing.

Fully Diluted Earnings Per Share. Smallest earnings-per-share figure that can be obtained by computing an earnings per share for all possible combinations of assumed exercise or conversion of residual securities.

Function. In governmental accounting, said of a group of related activities for accomplishing a service or regulatory program for which the governmental unit is responsible. In mathematics, a rule for associating a number, called the dependent variable, with another number or numbers, called independent variables.

Functional Classification. Income statement reporting form in which expenses are reported by functions, that is, cost of goods sold, administrative expenses. Contrast with natural classification.

Fund. An asset or group of assets separated from others in the accounts.

Fund Balance. The excess of assets of a fund over

its liabilities and reserves; the not-for-profit equivalent of stockholders' equity.

Funded. Said of a pension plan or other obligation when funds have been set aside for meeting the obligation when it becomes due.

Funds. Net working capital; current assets less current liabilities.

Funds Statement. Until APB Opinion No. 19, a name often used for the statement of changes in financial position.

Gain. Excess of revenues over expenses from a specific transaction.

General Debt. Debt of a governmental unit legally payable from general revenues and backed by the full faith and credit of the governmental unit.

General Fixed Assets. Those long-term assets of a governmental unit not accounted for in enterprise, trust, or intragovernmental service funds.

General Fund. Assets and liabilities of a nonprofit entity not specifically earmarked for other purposes.

General Journal. The journal to record all transactions not recorded in specialized journals.

Generally Accepted Accounted Principles. As defined by the APB and FASB, the conventions, rules, and procedures necessary to define accepted accounting practice at a particular time; includes both broad guidelines and relatively detailed practices and procedures.

General Expenses. Selling and administrative expenses.

General Partner. Member of partnership liable for all debts of the partnership; contrast with limited partner.

Going Concern. A business assumed to remain in operation long enough for all current plans to be carried out.

Goods. Items of merchandise, raw materials, or finished goods. Sometimes extended to include all tangible items, as in goods and services.

Goodwill. The excess of cost paid for an acquired firm over the current value of net assets of the acquired.

Gross. Not reduced by deductions or subtractions.

Gross Margin. Sales minus cost of goods sold.

Gross Margin Percentage. $100 \times (1 - \text{cost of goods sold/sales})$.

Group Depreciation. A method of calculating depreciation charges where assets are considered together rather than separately. See Chapter 14.

Historical Cost. Cost of acquisition.

Holding Company. A business which confines its activities to owning stock in and supervising management of other companies.

I. Identity Matrix.

Ideal Standard Cost. Costs that would be incurred under the best possible conditions.

Identity Matrix. A square matrix with ones on the main diagonal and zeros elsewhere; a matrix I such that for any other matrix A, $IA = AI = A$. The matrix equivalent of the number one.

Imprest Fund. Petty cash fund.

Income. Excess of revenues over expenses for a period.

Income Accounts. Revenue and expense accounts.

Income Distribution Account. Temporary account debited when dividends are declared; closed to Retained Earnings.

Income Statement. The summary of revenues and expenses for the period ending with net income for the period. Earnings per share are usually shown on the income statement; the reconciliation of beginning and ending balances of retained earning may also be shown.

Income Summary. An account used in problem solving that serves as a surrogate for the income statement. All revenues are closed to the Income Summary as credits and all expenses, as debits. The balance in the account, after all other closing entries are made, is then closed to Retained Earnings or other proprietorship account.

Income Tax. An annual tax levied by the federal and many state governments on the income of an entity.

Incremental Cost. Costs that will be incurred (saved) if an activity is undertaken (stopped).

Indeterminate-term Liability. A liability lacking the criteria of being due at a definite time. This term is our own coinage to encompass deferred tax liability and minority interest.

Indirect Costs. Costs not easily associated with the production of specific goods and services; overhead costs.

Indirect Labor Cost. An indirect cost for labor.

Indirect Material Cost. An indirect cost for material.

Insolvency. Inability to pay debts when due.

Installment. Partial payment of a debt.

Installment Method. Recognizing revenue and expense in proportion to the fraction of the selling price collected during a period.

Insurance. A contract for reimbursement of specified losses; purchased with insurance premiums. Self-insurance is not insurance but merely the willingness to incur the loss while saving the premium.

Intangible Asset. Any nonphysical asset such as a patent, trademark, or goodwill.

Intercompany Elimination. See eliminations.

Interest. The charge or cost for using money; frequently expressed as a rate per period.

Interest Factor. One plus the interest rate.

Interfund Accounts. In governmental accounting, the accounts that show transactions between funds.

Interim Statements. Statements issued between the beginning and end of the fiscal year.

Internal Audit. An audit conducted by employees for managerial purposes to ascertain whether or not internal control procedures are working; as opposed to an external audit conducted by a CPA for financial reports.

Internal Control. The procedures carried out by management of a business to attempt to insure that operations are carried out or recorded as planned.

Internal Rate of Return. The discount rate that equates the net present value of a stream of cash flows to zero.

Interpolation. The estimation of an unknown number intermediate between two (or more) known numbers.

Inventory (noun). The balance in an asset account such as raw materials, work in process, and finished goods.

Inventory (verb). To calculate the cost of goods on hand at a given time.

Inventory Equation. Beginning inventory + additions − withdrawals = ending inventory.

Inventory Turnover. Number of times the average inventory has been sold during a period; cost of goods sold for a period divided by average inventory for the period.

Inverse. See matrix inverse.

Investment. An expenditure to acquire property or other asset; the asset so acquired; hence a current expenditure made in anticipation of future income.

Investment Tax Credit. A reduction in income tax liability granted by the federal government to firms that buy new equipment. The tax credit has been a given percentage of the purchase price of new capital assets purchased whose depreciable life is at least seven years. A smaller tax credit is granted for purchases of assets with shorter lives. The actual rules and rates have changed over the years; see Problems 20 and 21 of Chapter 24.

Invoice. A document showing the details of a sale.

Issue (verb). When a corporation exchanges its stock (or bonds) for cash or other assets, the corporation is said to issue that stock (or bonds).

Job Development Credit. The name used for the investment tax credit in the tax law of 1971.

Job-Order Costing. Accumulation of costs for a particular, identifiable item as it moves through production.

Joint Cost. Cost of simultaneously producing or otherwise acquiring two or more kinds of goods that must by the nature of the process be produced or acquired together, such as the cost of beef and hides of a cow. See common cost.

Joint Product. One of two or more outputs from a process that must be produced or acquired simultaneously.

Journal. The place where transactions are recorded as they occur.

Journal Entry. A recording in a journal, of equal debits and credits, with an explanation of the transaction if necessary to explain the transaction so recorded.

Journalize. To make an entry in a journal.

Lapse. To expire; said of, for example, an insurance policy or discounts available for prompt payment.

Last-in, First-out. See LIFO.

Lease. A contract calling for the lessee (user) to pay the lessor (owner) for the use of an asset. A cancelable lease is one the lessee can cancel when he chooses. A noncancelable lease requires payments from the lessee for the life of the lease and usually has many of the economic characteristics of debt. See financing lease and operating lease.

Least-and-Latest Rule. Pay the least amount of tax as late as possible within the law to minimize the present value of the tax liability for a given set of operations.

Ledger. A book of accounts.

Liability. Usually a legal obligation to pay a definite (or reasonably certain) amount at a definite (or reasonably certain) time in return for a current benefit. Some of the criteria are not met by items classified as liabilities where there are special circumstances. See Chapter 15.

Life Annuity. A contingent annuity in which payments cease at death of a specified person(s), usually the annuitant(s).

LIFO. An inventory flow assumption where the cost of goods sold is the cost of the most recently acquired units and the inventory cost is the sum of costs of the oldest units.

Limited Liability. Stockholders of corporations are not liable for debts of the company.

Limited Partner. Member of a partnership not liable for debts of the partnership; every partnership must have at least one general partner who is fully liable.

Liquid Assets. Cash, marketable securities, and receivables.

Liquidation. Payment of a debt; sale of assets in closing down a business.

Long-term. Due more than one year hence.

Loss. Excess of cost over selling price for a single transaction; negative income for a period.

Lower of Cost or Market. See cost or market, whichever is lower.

Maintenance. Expenditures incurred to preserve an asset's service potential.

Management. Executive authority that operates a business.

Management Accounting. Reporting designed to enhance the ability of management to do its job; contrast with financial accounting.

Manufacturing Cost. Costs of producing goods, usually in a factory.

Marginal Cost. Incremental cost.

Markdown. The reduction of a previously established retail price.

Market Price. See fair market price.

Marketable Securities. Stocks and bonds of other companies held that can be readily sold on stock exchanges or the over-the-counter markets and that the company plans to sell when funds are needed. Classified as a current asset.

Matching Principle. The concept of recognizing related expenses and revenues in the same accounting period.

Material (adjective). Relatively important.

Material (noun). Raw material.

Materiality. The concept that accounting should recognize only those events that are relatively important (no operable definition yet exists) for the business.

Matrix. A rectangular array of numbers or mathematical symbols.

Matrix Inverse. For a given square matrix, A, the square matrix inverse is the matrix, A^{-1}, such that $AA^{-1} = A^{-1}A = I$, the identity matrix. Not all square matrices have inverses. Those that do not are called singular; those that do are nonsingular.

Maturity. The date at which an obligation, such as a bond, becomes due.

Merchandise. Finished goods bought by a retailer for resale.

Merger. The joining of two or more unrelated businesses into a single legal entity.

Minority Interest. The stockholders' equity of a subsidiary company allocable to those owners who are not part of the controlling (majority) interest.

Mortality Table. Data on life expectancies or probabilities of death for people of specified ages.

Mortgage. A claim given by the borrower (mortgagor) to the lender (mortgagee) against the borrower's property in return for a loan.

Multiple-step. Said of an income statement where various classes of expenses are subtracted from revenues to show such intermediate items as gross profit and operating profit.

Natural Classification. Income statement reporting form in which expenses are classified by the nature of items used, that is, purchases of materials, labor expense, purchases of services, depreciation. Contrast with functional classification.

Net. Reduced by all relevant deductions.

Net Assets. Total assets minus total liabilities.

Net Current Assets. Working capital.

Net Income. The excess of all revenues for a period over all expenses of the period.

Net Present Value. Discounted or present value of all cash inflows and outflows of a project.

Net Realizable Value. Selling price of an item less reasonable costs to make the item ready for sale.

Net Worth. The owner's equity. Assets less liabilities.

Nonexpendable Fund. A governmental fund, whose principal, and sometimes earnings, may not be spent.

Nonprofit Corporation. An incorporated entity with no owners who share in earnings.

Normal Spoilage. Costs incurred because of ordinary amounts of spoilage; such costs should be prorated to units produced. Contrast with abnormal spoilage.

Normal Volume. The amount produced in units during a period if capacity is used as planned.

Note. An unconditional written promise by the maker (borrower) to pay a certain amount on demand or at a certain future time.

Note Receivable Discounted. A note sold or assigned by the holder to another. Usually the seller receives less than the face amount of the debt and, if sold with recourse, it is the contingent liability of the seller until the debt is paid.

Obsolescence. A decline in market value of an asset caused by improved alternatives becoming available that will provide more cost-effective benefits; the decline in market value is unrelated to physical changes in the asset itself.

On Account. Said of a purchase or sale when payment is expected sometime after delivery.

On Consignment. Said of goods delivered by the owner to another to be sold by the other person; the owner is entitled to the return of his property or payment of an amount agreed upon in advance.

Open Account. Any account with a nonzero debit or credit balance.

Operating Accounts. Revenue and expense accounts.

Operating Expenses. Expenses incurred in the course of ordinary activities of an entity.

Operating Lease. A lease accounted for by the lessee without balance sheet effects. Rentals are merely shown as expenses of the period or as product costs. The lessor keeps the asset on his books and shows the rental payments as revenues. Contrast with financing lease.

Opinion. The auditor's statement containing his attestation or lack thereof. The name given to pronouncements of the APB that make up much of generally accepted accounting principles; there are thirty-one Opinions issued from 1962–73.

Opportunity Cost. The present value of the income that could be earned from using (or selling) an asset in its best alternative use to the one being considered.

Option. The legal right to buy something during a specified period at a specified price. Employee stock options, discussed in Chapter 17, should not be confused with put and call options traded in various public markets.

Ordinary Annuity. An annuity in arrears.

Organization Costs. The costs incurred in planning and establishing an entity: example of an intangible asset. Often, since the amounts are not material, the costs are treated as expenses in the periods incurred even though the expenditures clearly provide future benefits.

Original Cost. Expenditure for an asset by its current owner. In public-utility accounting, the cost to the entity first devoting the asset to public use.

Original Entry. Entry in a journal.

Outlay. The amount of an expenditure.

Out-of-Pocket. Said of a variable cost, usually paid for with cash.

Output. Quantity of goods and services produced.

Outstanding. Unpaid or uncollected. When said of stock, the quantity of shares issued less treasury stock.

Overabsorption. Credit balance in an overhead account; occurs when more overhead costs are applied to product than are incurred.

Over-and-Short. Title for an expense account used to account for small differences between book balances of cash and actual cash in petty cash and change funds.

Overhead Costs. Any manufacturing cost not specifically associated with the production of identifiable goods and services.

Overhead Rate. Standard rate at which overhead costs are applied to product.

Owners' Equity. Proprietorship; assets minus liabilities.

Paid-in Capital. Sum of balances in capital stock and capital contributed in excess of par (or stated) value accounts. Same as contributed capital.

Parent Company. Company owning more than 50 percent of the shares of another company, called the subsidiary.

Partnership. Contractual arrangement between individuals to share resources and operations in a jointly run business. See general and limited partner.

Par Value. Face amount of a security.

Past Service Cost. Present value at a given time of a pension plan's unfunded benefits assigned to employees for their service before the inception of the plan. A part of prior service cost.

Patent. Exclusive rights granted by the government to an inventor for seventeen years to enjoy the fruits of an invention.

Payable. Unpaid but not necessarily due or past due.

Payback Period. Amount of time that must elapse before the cash inflows from a project equal the cash outflows.

Payroll Taxes. Taxes levied because salaries or wages are paid; for example, FICA and unemployment compensation insurance taxes. Typically, the employer pays a portion and deducts part of the employee's wages for the other portion.

Pension Fund. Fund, the assets of which are to be paid to retired ex-employees, usually as a life annuity.

Pension Plan. Details or provisions of employer's contract with employees for paying retirement annuities.

Percent. Any number, expressed as a decimal, multiplied by 100.

Percentage Depletion. Deductible expense allowed by the federal income tax regulations; computed as a percentage of gross income from a natural resource independent of the unamortized cost of the asset.

Percentage of Completion Method. Recognizing

revenues and expenses on a job or order in proportion to the costs incurred for the period divided by total costs expected to be incurred for the job or order.

Period. Accounting period.

Period Expense. Expenditure, usually based upon the passage of time, charged to operations of the accounting period rather than capitalized as an asset.

Periodic Inventory. A method of recording inventory that uses data on beginning inventory, additions to inventories, and ending inventory in order to find the cost of withdrawals from inventory.

Perpetual Inventory. Records on quantities and amounts of inventory that are changed or made current with each physical addition to or withdrawal from the stock of goods; an inventory so recorded.

Perpetuity. An annuity whose payments last forever.

Petty Cash Fund. Currency maintained for expenditures that are conveniently made with cash.

Plant. Plant assets.

Plant Assets. Buildings, machinery, and land.

Plug. In making a journal entry, often all debits are known, as are all but one of the credits (or vice versa). Since double-entry bookkeeping requires equal debits and credits, the unknown quantity can be solved for by subtracting the sum of the known credits from the sum of all the debits (or vice versa). This process is known as plugging. The unknown found is called the plug.

Pooling of Interests Method. Accounting for a merger by merely adding together the book value of the assets of the merged firms. Contrast with purchase method.

Post. To record entries in a ledger; usually the entries are copied from a journal.

Post-closing Trial Balance. Trial balance taken after all revenue and expense accounts have been closed.

Pre-closing Trial Balance. Trial balance taken at the end of the period before adjusting and closing entries.

Preferred Stock. Capital stock with a claim to assets after bondholders but before common stock. Dividends on preferred stock are income distributions, not expenses.

Premium. The excess of issue (or market) price over par value. For a different context, see insurance.

Premium on Capital Stock. Alternative title for capital contributed in excess of par.

Prepaid Expense. An expenditure that leads to a deferred charge; strictly speaking, a contradiction in terms for an expense is a gone asset.

Prepaid Income. See advances from customers.

Prepayments. Deferred charges.

Present Value. Value today of an amount or amounts to be received later discounted at some interest rate.

Price Index. A series of numbers, one for each period, that purport to represent some average of prices for a series of periods.

Price Level. The item from a price index for a period.

Price Variance. Rate variance for materials, labor and, sometimes, overhead costs.

Primary Earnings Per Share. (Net income to common stock plus interest, net of taxes, or dividends paid on common stock equivalents) divided by (common shares plus the number of common shares issuable if all common stock equivalents were converted into common shares).

Prime Cost. Sum of direct materials plus direct labor costs.

Prime Rate. The rate for loans charged by commercial banks to their most preferred risks. For the earnings-per-share purpose of deciding whether a security is or is not a common-stock equivalent, the corporation should use the rate in effect at the bank at which it does business or an average of such rates if the corporation does business with more than one bank. The *Federal Reserve Bulletin* is considered the authoritative source of information about historical prime rates.

Principal. An amount on which interest is charged or earned.

Principle. See generally accepted accounting principles.

Prior-Period Adjustment. A debit or credit directly to retained earnings (that does not affect income for the period) to correct retained earnings for such things as lawsuit settlements and changes in income tax returns of prior periods.

Prior Service Cost. Present value at a given time of a pension plan's unfunded benefits assigned to employees for their service before that given time. Includes past service cost.

Proceeds. Funds received from disposition of assets or from the issue of securities.

Process Costing. A method of cost accounting used by determining average costs from total cost divided by the equivalent units of work done in a period. Typically used for assembly lines or for products that are produced in a series of steps that are more continuous than discrete.

Product. Goods or services produced.

Product Cost. Any manufacturing cost that can be inventoried; that is, costs that are not period expenses.

Production Cost Account. Account for collecting product costs.

Production Method. Percentage of completion method for recognizing revenue.

Profit. Excess of revenues over expenses for a transaction; sometimes used synonymously with income.

Profit and Loss Sharing Ratio. The fraction of operating income or loss allocable to a partner in a partnership. Need not be the same fraction as the partner's share of capital.

Pro Forma Statements. Financial statements as they would appear if some event, such as a merger or increased production and sales, had occurred. Pro forma is sometimes spelled as one word.

Progressive Tax. Tax for which the rate increases as the taxed base, such as income, increases. Contrast with regressive tax.

Promissory Note. Note.

Proprietorship. Assets minus liabilities.

Prorate. To allocate in proportion to some base; for example, to allocate service department costs in proportion to hours of the service used.

Prospectus. Formal written document describing securities to be issued.

Provision. Allowance.

Proxy. Written authorization given by one person to another so that the second person can act for the first.

Purchase Method. Accounting for a merger by adding the acquired company's assets at the price paid for them to the acquiring company's assets. Contrast with pooling of interests method.

Purchase Order. Document authorizing a seller to deliver goods with payment to be made later.

Qualified Report. Auditor's report containing a statement that the auditor was unable to complete a satisfactory examination of all he thinks relevant or that he has doubts about some item reported in the financial statements.

Quick Ratio. Acid test ratio.

Rate of Return. Cash flows or income per period, divided by asset value at the beginning of the period or average asset value for entire period.

Raw Material. Goods purchased for use in manufacturing.

Reacquired Stock. Treasury stock.

Real Estate. Land and its improvements, such as landscaping.

Realize. To convert into funds.

Realizable Value. Net realizable value.

Receipt. Acquisition of funds.

Receivable. Any collectible whether or not it is currently due.

Recognize. To enter a transaction in the books.

Reconciliation. A calculation that shows how one balance or figure is derived systematically from another.

Record Date. Dividends are paid on payment date to those who own the stock on the record date.

Redemption. Retirement by the issuer, usually by a purchase, of stocks or bonds.

Register. Collection of consecutive entries in chronological order such as a check register. It may serve as a journal.

Registered Bond. Principal of such a bond and interest, if registered as to interest, paid to the owner listed on the books of the issuer. For a bearer bond, payments are made to the person who possesses the bond.

Regressive Tax. Tax for which the rate decreases as the taxed base, such as income, increases. Contrast with progressive tax.

Rent. Charge for the use of land, buildings or other assets.

Reorganization. A major change in the capital structure of a corporation that leads to changes in the rights, interests, and implied ownership of the various security owners. Usually results from a merger or agreement by senior security holders to take action to forestall bankruptcy.

Replacement Cost. For an asset, the current fair market price to purchase a similar asset.

Report. Financial statement; auditor's report.

Reserve. Properly used, a term referring to an account that earmarks or appropriates retained earnings. Appropriating retained earnings is itself a poor and slowly vanishing practice, so the word should seldom be used in good accounting. Used in the past also to indicate an asset contra or an estimated liability. In any case, reserve accounts have credit balances and are *not* pools of funds. In governmental accounting, an account recording a portion of fund balance that is segregated for some future use and is not available for other purposes.

Residual Security. Any security whose value is in major part determined by its right to be converted into or exchanged for common stock. Options warrants, convertible bonds, and convertible preferred stock.

Restricted Assets. Governmental resources restricted by legal or contractual requirements for specific purposes.

Restricted Retained Earnings. That part of retained earnings not legally available for dividends. Bond indentures and other loan contracts can curtail the ability of the corporation to pay dividends without formally requiring a retained earnings restriction. Use of retained earnings restrictions is declining.

Retail Inventory Method. Ascertaining inventory costs by using ratios of cost to selling price. That is, cost of sales = (1 — markup percentage) × sales; and closing inventory = (1 — markup percentage) × closing inventory at retail prices.

Retained Earnings. Net income over the life of a corporation less all income distributions; owners' equity less paid-in capital.

Retained Earnings Appropriation. An account set up by crediting it and debiting Retained Earnings. Used to indicate that retained earnings are not available for dividends. The practice of appropriating retained earnings is unsound unless all capital is earmarked with its use.

Revenue. The monetary value of a service rendered.

Reversal (Reversing) Entry. An entry in which all debits and credits are the credits and debits, respectively, of another entry, and in the same amounts. The rationale for such an entry is explained in Chapter 11.

Reverse Stock Split. A stock split in which the number of shares is decreased. See stock split.

Royalty. Compensation for the use of property, usually copyrighted material or natural resources, expressed as a percentage of receipts from using the property.

Ruling an Account. The process of summarizing a series of entries to an account by computing a new balance and drawing lines to indicate the information above the lines has been summarized in the new balance. The steps are as follows. (1) Compute the sum of all debit entries including opening debit balance, if any. (2) Compute the sum of all credit entries including opening credit balance, if any. (3) If the amount in (1) is larger than the amount in (2), then write the excess as a credit with a check mark. (4) Add both debit and credit columns, which should both now sum to the same amount and show that identical total at the foot of both columns. (5) Draw a double line under those numbers and write the excess of debits over credits as the new debit balance with a check mark. (6) If the amount in (2) is larger than the amount in (1), then write the excess

as a debit with a check mark. (7) Do steps (4) and (5) except that the excess becomes the new credit balance. (8) If the amount in (1) is equal to the amount in (2), then the balance is zero and only the totals with the double line beneath them need be shown.

Sale. A revenue transaction where goods or services are delivered to a customer.

Sales Allowance. A reduction in invoice price usually given because the goods received by the buyer are not exactly what was ordered.

Sales Discount. Reduction in sales price usually offered for prompt payment.

Sales, Uncollectible Accounts Adjustment. The preferred title for the contra-revenue account to recognize actual or estimated loss from accounts receivable that are not paid. Formerly, often called bad debt expense and treated as an expense, not an adjustment to revenue.

Salvage Value. Actual or anticipated selling price of a used plant asset to be sold.

Schedule. Supporting set of calculations which show how figures in a statement are derived.

Scrap Value. Salvage value.

Security. Document that indicates ownership or indebtedness.

Self-balancing. A set of records with equal debits and credits such as the ledger (but not individual accounts) or a fund in nonprofit accounting.

Self-insurance. See Insurance.

Selling and Administrative Expenses. Expenses not specifically identifiable with production.

Semifixed Cost. Costs that increase with activity as a step function.

Semivariable Cost. Costs that increase strictly linearly with activity but that are positive at zero activity level.

Serial Bonds. An issue of bonds that mature in part at one date, another part on another date, and so on; the various maturity dates usually are equally spaced.

Service Department. A department providing services to other departments, rather than work on salable product.

Service Life. Period of usefulness of an asset.

Services. Useful work done by a person, a machine, or an organization.

Share. A unit of stock.

Short-term. Current. Ordinarily, due within one year.

Simple Interest. Interest calculated on principal when interest earned during the period of the loan is neither added to the principal nor paid to the lender. Contrast with compound interest.

Single-step. Said of an income statement where the word income appears no more than once above extraordinary items; all ordinary expense items are shown before any are subtracted from revenues.

Sinking Fund. Assets and their earnings earmarked for the retirement of bonds.

Skeleton Account. T-account.

Sole Proprietorship. All owner's equity belongs to one person.

Special Assessment. A compulsory levy made by a governmental unit on property to pay the costs of a specific improvement or service presumed not to benefit the general public but only the owners of the property so assessed.

Special Revenue Debt. Debt of a governmental unit backed only by revenues from specific sources such as tolls from a bridge.

Split. Stock split.

Split-off Point. The point where all costs are no longer joint costs but can be identified, if not with individual products, then with a smaller number of joint products.

Standard Cost. Anticipated cost of producing a unit of output.

Standard Price (Rate). Anticipated price expected to be paid for materials or labor.

Stated Capital. Capital contributed by stockholders.

Stated Value. Term used for capital stock only if no par value is indicated. Stated value per share may be set by the directors (in which case, capital in excess of stated value may come into being) or may be calculated as stated capital divided by the number of shares issued.

Statement of Changes in Financial Position. As defined by APB Opinion No. 19, a statement which explains the changes in working capital for a period by showing sources and uses of working capital and the changes in the working capital accounts themselves.

Step Cost. Semifixed cost.

Step-down Method. The method for allocating service department costs that starts by allocating one service department's costs to production departments and to all other service departments. Then a second service department's costs, including costs allocated from the first, are allocated to production departments and to all other service departments except the first one. In this fashion, the costs of all service departments, including previous allocations, are allocated to production departments and to those service departments whose costs have not yet been allocated. This method gives the same answers as the more logical matrix method explained in Appendix 20.1 only

if there are no reciprocal service relations, either direct (A serves B and B serves A) or indirect (A serves B, B serves C, and C serves A).

Stock. Inventory. Capital stock.

Stock Dividend. A dividend that results in a debit to retained earnings and a credit to capital stock accounts. Contrast with a stock split, which requires no entry into capital stock accounts other than a notation that the par or stated value of the shares has been changed.

Stockholders' Equity. Proprietorship of a corporation.

Stock Option. The right to purchase a specified number of shares of stock for a specified price at specified times, usually granted to employees. Contrast with warrant.

Stock Split. Increase in the number of common shares outstanding resulting from the issuance of additional shares to existing stockholders without additional capital contribution by them. Does not increase the total par (or stated) value of common stock outstanding since par (or stated) value is reduced in inverse proportion. A three-for-one stock split reduces par or stated value to one-third of its former amount. Stock splits are usually limited to distributions of 20 percent or more. Compare with stock dividend.

Stores. Raw materials and supplies.

Straight-line Depreciation. If the depreciable life is n periods, then the periodic depreciation charge is $1/n$ of the depreciable cost.

Subject To. Qualifications in an auditor's report, usually caused by a material uncertainty in the valuation of an item such as future promised payments from a foreign government.

Subscription. Agreement to buy a security, or to purchase periodicals.

Subsidiary. Said of a company more than 50 percent of whose stock is held by another.

Subsidiary Ledger. The ledger that contains the detailed accounts whose totals are shown in a controlling account.

Sum-of-the-Years'-Digits Depreciation. An accelerated depreciation method where the charge in period i ($i = 1, \ldots, n$), where n is the depreciable life in periods, is the fraction $(n + 1 - i)/[n(n + 1)/2]$ of the depreciable cost.

Sunk Cost. Costs incurred in the past that are not affected by, and hence irrelevant for, current decisions.

Surplus. A word once used but now considered improper to use; prefaced by earned to mean retained earnings and prefaced by capital to mean capital contributed in excess of par.

Suspense Account. A temporary account showing

amounts of receipts or expenditures pending their specific identification and disposition. Such accounts do not appear in financial statements.

T-Account. Account form shaped like the letter T with the title above the horizontal line. Debits are shown to the left of the vertical line; credits, to the right.

Tangible. Having physical form.

Tax. Charge levied by a government.

Temporary Accounts. Revenue and expense accounts, their adjuncts and contras, production cost accounts, income distribution accounts, and purchases-related accounts (which are closed to the various inventories).

Time-Adjusted Rate of Return. Internal rate of return.

Time Deposit. Cash in a bank earning interest; contrast with demand deposit.

Times-interest Earned. Ratio of pre-tax income plus interest charges to interest charges.

Trade Discount. A discount from list price offered to all customers of a given type.

Trademark. A distinctive name, sign, or symbol. Exclusive rights to use a trademark are granted by the federal government for twenty-eight years and can be renewed for another twenty-eight years.

Trade Payable (Receivable). Payable or receivable arising in the ordinary course of business transactions. Most accounts payable (receivable) are of this kind.

Transaction. An exchange between the accounting entity and another party or parties that leads to an accounting entry.

Transfer Agent. Usually a bank or trust company designated by a corporation to make legal transfers of stock and, perhaps, to pay dividends.

Treasury Stock. Capital stock issued and then reacquired by the corporation. Such reacquisitions result in a reduction of stockholders' equity, and the amounts are usually shown on the balance sheet as a contra to all of stockholders equity. No gain nor loss is recognized in transactions involving treasury stock.

Trial Balance. A listing of account balances; all accounts with debit balances are totaled separately from accounts with credit balances. The two totals should be equal. See adjusted, pre-closing, post-closing trial balance.

Turnover. The number of times that assets, such as inventory or accounts receivable, are replaced during the period. Accounts receivable turnover, for example, is total sales on account for a period divided by average accounts receivable balance for the period.

Unadjusted Trial Balance. Pre-closing trial balance.

Unamortized Bond Discount (Premium). The balance in the bond discount (premium) account.

Underapplied (Underabsorbed) Overhead. An excess of overhead costs for a period over costs applied or charged to products produced for the period.

Underlying Document. The record, memorandum, voucher, or other signal to make an entry into a journal.

Underwriter. One who agrees to purchase an entire security issue for a specified price, usually for resale to others.

Unearned Income (Revenue). Advance from a customer; strictly speaking, a contradiction in terms.

Unencumbered Appropriation. Portion of an appropriation not yet spent or encumbered.

Unfavorable Variance. An excess of actual cost over standard cost.

Unissued Capital Stock. Stock authorized but not yet issued.

Useful Life. Service life.

Value. Monetary worth; the term is usually so subjective that it ought not to be used unless most people would agree on the amount; not to be confused with cost.

Variable Annuity. An annuity whose periodic payments depend upon some uncertain outcome such as stock market prices.

Variable Cost. Costs that change as activity levels change.

Variable Costing. Direct costing.

Variance. Difference between actual and standard costs. In accounting the word has a completely different meaning from its meaning in statistics.

Vested. Said of pension plan benefits that are not contingent on the employee continuing to work for the employer.

Voucher. A document that serves to authorize the disbursement of cash.

Warrant. A certificate entitling the owner to buy a specified amount of stock at a specified time for a specified price. Differs from a stock option only in that options are granted to employees and warrants are sold to the public.

Warranty. A promise by a seller to correct deficiencies in products sold.

Wasting Asset. A natural resource having a limited

useful life and, hence, subject to amortization called depletion.

Watered Stock. Stock issued for assets worth less than par or stated value.

Weighted Average. An average computed by counting each occurrence of an item, not merely the number of different items.

Withdrawals. Assets distributed to an owner.

Withholding. Deductions from salaries or wages, usually for income taxes, to be paid by the employer, in the employee's name, to the taxing authority.

Working Capital. Current assets minus current liabilities.

Work in Process. Partially completed product.

Worth. Value.

Write Off. Charge an asset to expense.

Write Up. To increase the recorded cost of an asset with no corresponding disbursement of funds.

Yield. Internal rate of return on a stream of cash flows; cash yield is cash flow divided by book value.

Index

(See also Glossary on pages 917–934.)